ENCYCLOPEDIA OF CONTEMPORARY AMERICAN CULTURE

ENCYCLOPEDIA OF CONTEMPORARY AMERICAN CULTURE

Edited by Gary W. McDonogh,
Robert Gregg, and Cindy H. Wong

London and New York

First published 2001
by Routledge
11 New Fetter Lane, London EC4P 4EE

Simultaneously published in the USA and Canada
by Routledge
29 West 35th Street, New York, NY 10001

Reprinted 2002

Routledge is an imprint of the Taylor & Francis Group

Typeset in Baskerville by Taylor and Francis Books Ltd
Printed and bound in Great Britain by TJ International, Padstow, Cornwall

British Library Cataloguing in Publication Data
A catalogue record for this book is available from the British Library

Library of Congress Cataloging in Publication Data
Encyclopedia of contemporary American culture / edited by Gary W.
McDonogh, Robert Gregg, and Cindy H. Wong.
p. cm.
Includes bibliographical references and index.
1. United States–Civilization–1970–Encyclopedias. 2. Popular culture–
United States–Encyclopedias. I. McDonogh, Gary W. II. Gregg, Robert,
1958– III.Wong, Cindy, H., 1961–

E169.12 .E49 2001
973.92'03–dc21
00-055326

ISBN 0–415–16161–4

Contents

Editorial team

General editors

Gary W. McDonogh
Bryn Mawr College, USA

Robert Gregg
Richard Stockton College, USA

Cindy H. Wong
College of Staten Island, City University of New York, USA

Consultant editors

David Bishai
The Johns Hopkins University, USA

David Gerstner
University of Otago, NZ

Sandra Gilchrist
New College of the University of South Florida, USA

Rick Halpern
University College London, UK

Gail Henson
Bellarmine University, USA

James Kraus
Lehman College, City University of New York, USA

Dewar MacLeod
Cronkite Productions, Inc., New York, USA

Edward Miller
College of Staten Island, City University of New York, USA

Randall Miller
St Joseph's University, USA

Enrique Sacerio-Gari
Bryn Mawr College, USA

List of contributors

Paula Adams
Kansas, USA

Jon Anderson
Catholic University of America

Robert Anderson
Denver, CO

Frank Anechiarico
Hamilton College, USA

Marc Balcer
Morgan Stanley Dean Witter

Alyson Bardsley
College of Staten Island, City University of New York

Mariaelena Bartesaghi
Annenberg School for Communication, University of Pennsylvania

Jim Baumohl
Graduate School of Social Work and Social Research, Bryn Mawr College

Linda-Susan Beard
Bryn Mawr College

Gabrielle Bendiner-Viani
New York City

Courtney Bennett
Annenberg School for Communication, University of Pennsylvania

David Bishai
The Johns Hopkins University

Kent Blaser
Wayne State College

A. Joseph Borrell
Richard Stockton College of New Jersey

Daniel Bosch
Preceptor in Expository Writing, Harvard University

Mark Brewin
Annenberg School for Communication, University of Pennsylvania

Will Brooker
University of Cardiff, Wales, UK

Juan Burciaga
Bryn Mawr College

Jennifer Campbell
Graduate School of Social Work and Social Research, Bryn Mawr College

Arati Clarry
Hilo, Hawai'i

Emily Clough
University of Minnesota

Demetrios J. Constantelos
Richard Stockton College of New Jersey

Laura L. Coogan
Jacksonville, FL

Alison Cook-Sather
Bryn Mawr College

James David
Boston, MA

James Devitt
Columbia University

Miguel Díaz-Barriga
Swarthmore College

Matthew Durington
Temple University

Robert Francis Engs
University of Pennsylvania

Carmen C. Esteves
Lehman College, City University of New York

Beryl Fernandes
Seattle, WA

Steve Ferzacca
Bryn Mawr College

Jessica Fishman
Annenberg School for Communication, University
of Pennsylvania

Stacilee Ford
University of Hong Kong, HK

Elizabeth A. Galewski
Annenberg School for Communication, University
of Pennsylvania

Kathleen Galligan
Bristol, Maine

David Gerstner
University of Otago, NZ

Sandra Gilchrist
New College of the University of South Florida

David Goldston
Washington, DC

Judith Goode
Temple University

Mireille Gouirand
Bryn Mawr College

Susan Marie Green
California State University – Chico

Robert Gregg
Richard Stockton College, USA

Charlotte Greig
Cardiff, Wales

Laura Grindstaff
University of California – Davis

Amy Hale
Institute of Cornish Studies, Truro, UK

James Heinzen
Rowan University

Pamela R. Hendrick
Richard Stockton College of New Jersey

Gail Henson
Bellarmine University

Sharon Ann Holt
Philadelphia, PA

Tracey E. Hucks
Haverford College

Susan Brin Hyatt
Temple University

Rodger Jackson
Richard Stockton College of New Jersey

Deborah Jermyn
University of Wales, Cardiff, Wales

Edward Johanningsmeier
New York University

Lenard W. Kaye
Graduate School of Social Work and Social
Research, Bryn Mawr College

Nicole Marie Keating
Annenberg School for Communication, University
of Pennsylvania

Kate M. Kenski
Annenberg School for Communication, University
of Pennsylvania

Sheila Kerr
Joint Services College, Bracknell, UK

Jeffrey R. Kerr-Ritchie
Binghampton University, NY

Jeannie J. Kim
Princeton University

Jinyoung Kim
College of Staten Island, City University of New
York

James Kraus
Lehman College, City University of New York

Isabel Kriegel
Boston, MA

Emma Lapsansky
Haverford College

Roger D. Launius
National Aeronautics and Space Administration

Brian Levin
California State University – San Bernadino

Paul Lyons
Richard Stockton College of New Jersey

Ramona Lyons
Cigna, Philadelphia, PA

Dewar MacLeod
Cronkite Productions, Inc., New York, NY

David McBride
Routledge, New York

Gary W. McDonogh
Bryn Mawr College, USA

Stephen Miles
New College of the University of South Florida

Edward Miller
College of Staten Island, City University of New York

Terry Monaghan
University College London, UK

Janice Newberry
Bryn Mawr College

Stephen D. Norton
University of Maryland

Anahid Ordjanian
Queen's University, Belfast, UK

Marc L. Ostfield
Fire Island Pines, NY

Max Page
Yale University

Julie Parr
University of Pennsylvania

David J. Phillips
University of Texas – Austin

Richard Porton
College of Staten Island, City University of New York

Susanna Prough
General Manager of the Philadelphia Classical Symphony

Aparna Rayaprol
Ahmedanad, India

Warren Riess
Bristol, ME

Jefferson I. Ritchie
Louisville, KY

Randy A. Rodriguez
University of Minnesota

Brad Rogers
Duke University

Charles Rutheiser
The Johns Hopkins University

Lisa Saltzman
Bryn Mawr College

Susan Schulten
Department of History, University of Denver

Melinda Schwenk
Doctoral Candidate, Annenberg School of Communication, University of Pennsylvania

Robert Schwenk
National Aeronautics and Space Administration

Susan Scotto
Mount Holyoke College

Sarah Shillinger
University of Wisconsin

Elliott Shore
Bryn Mawr College

Bianca T. Siegl
University of California, Los Angeles

Sarah Smith
New York City

Mary-Christine Sungaila, Esq.
Horvitz and Levy

Emiko Tajima
University of Washington

Hunter Ford Tura
Harvard University

Sharon Ullman
Bryn Mawr College

Lorelei Atalie Vargas
University of Michigan

Frazer Ward
Maryland Conservatory of Art

Jim Watkins
Black Mountain, NC

Colville Wemyss
London, UK

Thomas M. Wilson
Queen's University, Belfast, UK

David Witwer
Lycoming College

Morgen Witzel
London, UK

Cindy H. Wong
College of Staten Island, City University of New York

Julie Pritchard Wright
San Francisco, CA

Eric A. Zimmer
Jesuit Community, St. Joseph's University

Introduction

Assembling an *Encyclopedia of Contemporary American Culture* at the cusp of the twenty-first century raises many questions about the very terms in the title, as well as the methods by which we can approach such a massive, variegated and changing topic. As such, it is important to explain the choices we have made, as editors and writers, in preparing this volume as well as how we feel it can best be used. At the same time, having read and thought about the many issues which myriad authors discuss within this volume, it is also important to underscore repeated themes and questions that have arisen about American culture in the course of this project.

From the beginning, it has been evident that part of the definition of contemporary American identity and significance in the world has emerged within the very hegemony of this culture and its diffusion worldwide since the Second World War. Whether talking about **Hollywood** cinema, **suburbs**, **NATO** or a pervasive commodity like **Levi Strauss** blue jeans, American culture has provided both a worldwide image of a complex "modern" society and a template for reactions to that society and its power. Moreover, American projections abroad have been shaped by American **colonialism** and **war** as well as decontextualized images from **advertising**, news, political rhetoric and **mass media**. In order to guide users towards a basic understanding of the "Americanness" of products, practices and images, therefore, we recognize that articles on any topic need to be written bearing in mind readers' knowledge of American culture and of the transformations that culture has undergone in different milieux worldwide.

Yet, at the same time, American culture has changed in the past and is changing dynamically in the present through the very status of the United States as a meeting ground for world cultures, immigrant and transient. While globalism is a topic of intense current discussion, American culture has been global since the first encounters of European and **American Indian** (and the Africans and Asians who followed in due course). One cannot talk of contemporary American culture without recognizing **African American** music, Muslim **education**, **Hasidic** businessmen, Southeast-Asian temples, **Hispanic** urbanization, **Japanese** and **British** investments, European **fashions**, multiple varieties of Chinese **food**, and competing varieties of wine and whiskey as constitutive of a changing cultural landscape. Nor can one express these features without noting the conflicts erupting in diversity, the polarizations and contests, as well as the renewals of American culture this same diversity can facilitate. No encyclopedia can encompass the total experience and changes of the contemporary US; instead, our intent is to provide road signs for readers to suggest how they might become aware of this complexity and change, as well as its ramifications. We conceive of American culture as a process rather than as a finished object.

The sheer size of the United States, its regional differences and the plethora of peoples and places within its boundaries also make the compilation of an encyclopedia a formidable task. While other nations have witnessed growing diversity in the second half of the twentieth century, the ongoing process of **immigration** to the United States has brought to the country ethnic groups from all over the world. Further, for every major city in Spain or

Japan, there are five of equal size in the United States. Even for every film star in Britain, there may be myriad in **Hollywood** alone (some of whom may be **English**, **Chinese** or **French**). Criteria for selection, therefore, has been very difficult. Where one might find one short essay regarding a Japanese or German actor, architect or playwright in other references on contemporary national culture, in this volume, figures of equivalent stature must be situated in longer essays about **theater**, film **actors**, **architecture** and **literature**.

Yet this is not intended to be the final reference, so much as an intermediary guide. For much of the audience for whom we write, we also recognize that there are many other references available, ranging from specific handbooks including *The Encyclopedia of Southern Culture*, *The Dictionary of American Biography*, *The Encyclopedia of African American Women*, *The Encyclopedia of New York*, *The Encyclopedia of Rural America*, *The Encyclopedia of Multiculturalism*, Ephraim Katz's *Film Encyclopedia* or David Bianculli's *Dictionary of Teleliteracy* that offer more specialized overviews. There are also general reference works like the *Encyclopedia Americana*, Microsoft *Encarta World Book* and even the *Encyclopedia Britannica* that share some topics with this work, and cover others in greater depth. Finally, all of these topics have been the object of scholarly examinations and journalistic discussion in the United States and outside of it. Given the proliferation of such resources and the simultaneous limitations of access which many readers outside the US may have to them, we endeavor here to provide a clearing house on contemporary culture, to outline debates and resources while answering immediate questions (and suggesting the deeply American interest of debate over these answers).

Hence in order to make an encyclopedia, whose assumed authority might otherwise reify all that it describes, sufficiently sensitive to the rapidly changing dynamics of contemporary American culture and the multiple reactions already present to it worldwide, we aim both to provide concise, open information and to give multiple readings of the American enterprise. In short, the encyclopedia endeavors to look for America at the same time that it establishes its boundaries and crosses them.

In responding to our intended audiences, we endeavor to observe the United States both inside out, and outside in, avoiding any sense of "exceptionalism" or a unique and privileged history (though that, too, is part of American culture). In this regard, the primary and consultant editors and the contributors have offered divergent vantage points, perspectives and global connections that have facilitated such endeavors.

Before proceeding further, let us begin by clarifying the key terms of the title. The operational meaning of "American" here is the United States, broadly conceived to include **borders** and attempts to cross boundaries (whether border **cities**, illegal immigrants, **trade** or transnational corporations). It does not encompass other North American states – **Canada**, **Mexico**, Central America (see **Latin America**) and the **Caribbean** – although their images and relations are dealt with. The entries comment on US citizenry, products, politico-cultural connections, and involvements abroad as well (whether by the military as in the **Gulf War** or by **expatriates**). We do realize that the equation of "America" and the "United States of the North" has been a sensitive issue for Latin Americans; we beg the indulgence of readers in following vernacular usage in the US, while recognizing its limitations and connotations.

The meaning of "contemporary" is shaped in large part by the historical experience and definition of "American." Contemporary America requires a historical understanding of what many have called the "American Century," the period since the Second World War. While the world dominance that the United States gained after that war is now contested, much of modern American life emerged out of or in response to its new-found position in the world. In the historically focused longer entries and even in other smaller sections we seek to provide a sense of this background – e.g. **African American literature**, **dance** or **food**, among others.

This does not mean we homogenize the decades since 1945; rather we try to elucidate processes as well as points of change. At one point, for example, we discussed an article on "the 1960s" as an emblematic decade dividing an old and new America, including changes in civil and gender rights, foreign policy, lifestyle and the image of

Kennedy, **Johnson** and **Nixon** as **presidents**. Yet for both events and people of this decade, the groundwork for fundamental changes and involvement had been laid earlier. Moreover, the cultural imagery of the 1960s often fails to include one of the transformations which we have explored at length here – the re-emergence of immigration as a fundamental feature of American life. One may look for the 1960s, then, under Kennedy, **Vietnam War**, **Civil Rights movement**, **Stonewall Riot**, immigration, **cities** and many other topics to appreciate continuities and changes in contemporary life. Where possible, we have asked authors to suggest future potential developments and problems; these issues are also treated in further readings suggested in the articles.

Our use of "culture" focuses on beliefs, representation and praxis, from the anthropologist's perspective, and "everyday life," from the social historian's vantage point. For a society as variegated as the United States it has been essential for us to deal with a wide range of topics, from **economics** and aspects of mass consumption to **religion** and entertainment, while relating these to one another as much as possible. Chinese food in America, for example, was formed over the period of a century within a particular labor **migration** and construction of **race** and difference: the American story of *chop suey* as a **creolized** menu. Yet recent immigrations and successes of new urban and suburban **Chinatowns** have produced an elite and varied cuisine to rival any Chinese metropolis, serving an immigrant clientele, new American audiences (themselves of extraordinarily diverse backgrounds) and transient **tourists** and business people. To set this out in a clear and simple fashion requires a consistent set of linkages through which articles not only provide concise information, but also teach generative principles about the many conflicts within American society today.

We recognize, however, that there are expectations concerning "culture" that must also be met. Certainly, we have tried for a balanced vision of facets of "high culture," including the arts, sciences and academic studies, "mass culture," associated with **mass media** and consumption, and the more difficult question of "**popular culture**." In all these areas, we have been concerned to discuss not only the phenomena themselves, but questions of ideology and imagery. What do **museums**, **fashion** or **comics** mean in terms of their context of **class**, **race** and **gender**? What do the portrayals of issues or groups in mass media (especially films as an international medium) tell us about the construction of culture – and alternative viewpoints? Where are the contradictions and the ambiguities between envisioning the American dream and living it?

At the same time, we have been selective in mapping out broad topics rather than seeking to detail all possible examples and meanings. US higher **education**, for example, encompasses over 3,000 **colleges and universities**. To provide only 100 words on each would nearly fill the entire volume. Instead, we have provided synthetic articles within a clear general framework of education which will encompass basic structural divisions (colleges and universities, **community colleges**), differences exemplified in associations (**Ivy League**, **California** and **state systems**), social and cultural choices (traditionally **black colleges**) and features of the American collegiate experience that may differ from those of Europe, Asia, Latin America, Africa or Australia (the college **campus**, **commencement**, **NCAA** college **sports**, etc.). While individual entries have thus been limited to a few cases of high international saliency, these broader entries provide contexts (and references) for those considering an American higher education as it might also help other readers to make sense of the college settings which play their own roles in Ralph **Ellison**'s *The Invisible Man*, Spike **Lee**'s *School Daze*, or ongoing debates over **affirmative action** in the California state system.

In order to provide a coherent and yet manageable volume we have decided that diversity – **race**, **gender**, **class** and space – should constitute our organizing template throughout the volume. These underpin articles that employ interdisciplinary and comparative approaches. Rather than segregating or ghettoizing groups by providing each one with its own section, individual authors (where possible) have framed their essays around our organizing concepts. Hence, while there are specific entries on **Jews**, **homophobia**, **Vietnamese Americans** and **homelessness**, we have endeavored to ensure that these citizens and topics are addressed, where relevant, in articles ranging from cities to aspects of discrimination to the media. We have also allowed disagreements to remain between authors tackling different perspectives on these issues.

Certain central topics, in fact, *demand* multiple perspectives if they are to cross effectively the cultural and political boundaries evident in contemporary America. The Vietnam War, **abortion**, race, **censorship** and other topics remain divisive issues in American society. To understand the meaning of these issues requires that a reader appreciate the reasons why Americans divide. In general, then, the authors dealing with such topics have provided a reasoned statement of the divergent viewpoints – not necessarily a safe or homogenous one. At the same time, we have tried to provide linkages and alternative perspectives. When discussing the **body**, for example, we provide different perspectives on race and **privacy**, and recognize the ways in which media representations of the body reflect and change American attitudes in order to complement discussions of gender, **abortion**, stars and race among other issues. Other entries like **freedom**, privacy and class talk about shared albeit debated values. Again, rather than closing off the American century by defining it neatly and efficiently, we wish to address. it and interrogate it with our contributors and our readers with a view to revealing its complexity and dynamism, and thereby, perhaps, to change it for the future.

Acknowledgements

Over the course of the last five years, many people have helped us on this project and deserve our acknowledgement here. This certainly includes our consulting editors – both those who helped us in the initial phase of the project and those who became mainstays as the work reached its conclusion. An equal debt of gratitude goes to our contributors, who not only produced thoughtful essays, but also provided commentary on the project, our entry list and our own writings. This long conversation about what it is to be American, in fact, has drawn in students, friends and colleagues over the years from Bryn Mawr College, the University of Pennsylvania, Richard Stockton College of New Jersey, the College of Staten Island, University of Hong Kong, Princeton University and Haverford College, with results that permeate the finished and ongoing work of this volume. The list is too long to thank individually here, but we trust that they will know on looking at the finished work.

We have also worked with a cadre of supportive colleagues at Routledge, including Fiona Cairns, who first suggested this project to us and later brought it to its conclusion, and Denise Rea, who worked with us in its maturing years. Among those with whom we have worked there, we also want to acknowledge the assistance of Dominic Shryane, Colville Wemyss, Matthew Gale and Ruth Graham.

This project has, over the years, taken time from our families who have nonetheless encouraged, cajoled and pushed us onwards. Here we would certainly like to acknowledge once again the support they have always given us, whether in conversations, moral support, food or diversion, or calls to brothers to ask about hot rods. Madhavi Kale, Chit Leung, Yuen Wong and Allen McDonogh have all shared their America with us. With this in mind, we especially dedicate this volume to our next generations of Americans: Nikhil Kale Gregg, Nadia Gregg Kale and Larissa Jiit-Wai McDonogh-Wong.

How to use this book

Structure

As we noted earlier, we consider this a primary resource and guide to more extensive work on issues relating to contemporary American culture. Thus, all longer articles provide a Further Reading section with other reference sources, current works and diverse approaches which we hope will be accessible through research libraries in the US and abroad and through the Internet. We have also categorized articles by length and breadth, reflecting topical complexity as well as a rough gauge of their importance to an understanding of American culture.

Hence, 2,000-word articles are designed to provide comprehensive overviews of fundamental issues. These include basic analytic categories like **class**, **race and ethnicity**, and **gender and sexuality**. They also include fundamental spaces and issues of American culture – the **city**, **religion**, **food**, **colleges and universities**, **popular music** and **life cycles**. Some article clusters reach this length, although they have been broken into parts (**theater** as text and theater as performance). Finally, we include **New York and its boroughs** as a 2,000-word article because it is impossible to say less, given its role as a capital and crucible for contemporary culture on a global scale.

Articles of 1,000–1,500 words cover both issues in the study of America and primary topics. These include problem-oriented pieces like **popular culture**, **homelessness**, **masculinity**, or the **body**. These are intended to be open-ended and provocative, raising questions as well as answering them. Other articles – we hope equally provocative – deal with central institutions, issues and topics. These include regions like **New England**, **Ha-** wai'i or the **South**, institutions of government, **education** and culture, religions and discussions of more specific intersections of categories like **ethnicity** and **literature**, or minorities and **television**.

More than 200 articles between 500 and 1,000 words provide critical tools for the reader in making sense of events, processes, periods and personages of the American century. These detail many cities, regions, ethnic groups, sports, businesses, patterns of recognition and interaction, while people, laws and events are explained and evaluated. Although 500 words seems to leave little room for complexity, our authors have shown ingenuity and craft in synthesizing debates and extending them through further readings. We have also considered here some issues of American values like **individualism**, **community**, **ethnic slurs** and **small-town ideals**.

Taken as networks or clusters (cross-references are indicated by bold typeface), these articles also allow for multiple perspectives. **Children**, for example, as creators and objects of culture are explored through babyhood and childhood as cultural categories and through **children's literature**, **magazines**, **music**, **museums**, **education** and **television** (as well as appearing as subjects within other articles). While the idea and experience of childhood is complex, these allow readers to make sense of images exported (or read at home).

Articles of 500–1,000-word categories have also dealt with genres. While we cannot list every television **sitcom** of the past fifty years, we provide articles on this and other genres of television, literature, music and movies.

Finally, short pieces offer identification, providing basic biographical, historical and spatial information. Here, difficult choices have been made – retaining Jimmy **Stewart** as an American icon, while perhaps not yet being sure of including Leonardo DiCaprio or Jennifer Lopez who might well hold a similar position someday. Some of these identifications have arisen from our knowledge of the production of cultural difference in the US. **Milk**, **barbeque**, **suicide** and **reunions**, among others, are not unique to the US, yet their cultural meanings merit special attention here anyway. Some issues have been clarified because we needed to learn about them, in becoming American, or because others who were not American simply asked what they were – **tipping**, **racial profiling**, **hot rods** and **referenda** have all been added in this way.

This is, we understand, a necessarily incomplete portrait of a nation-state and its multifaceted culture. Yet this is also the experience of America we have studied and lived on a daily basis. Through intersections, cross-referencing and the index, and through our sense of the encyclopedia as a clearinghouse guiding readers towards more specialized works, we hope readers will appreciate this complexity and respond to it.

We have also brought to this task the complexity of many authors with a diverse range of perspectives. Our authors include both Americans and non-Americans living in the US and those living abroad, representing many experiences of race, class, gender, age and sexuality as well as politics and beliefs. Professionally, while they have academic affiliation and experiences, not all are professionals in academics – we think it important that business people, doctors, clergy, planners, workers, journalists, students, architects and poets have all contributed. At the same time, we have tried to balance expertise and witness: these are not pronouncements of what it is like to be something, but explorations of shared and divisive meaning.

Certainly, the readers of this work may have questions – why not this, rather than that? Is this the most important work or representation of that topic? Why is my favorite film, or moment, or hero not here? To these readers we repeat: America, at its best, is not a canon or museum or cemetery, but a living, debated, contested and changing culture in a global context. We offer guidance and information, but America remains a culture we are all creating.

The Encyclopedia has taken shape over five years. During that time many events have occurred and been noted: two presidential elections, each producing its own political discourses; major foreign policy initiatives, including military engagements and trade negotiations; the **impeachment** of a president, the further entrenchment of the **Internet** and related economic expansion; increasing violence in schools, with growing debates over **guns**; and thousands of films and television shows/events, both reproducing and reinventing American cultural landscapes. All of these events and trends represent America, and as many as possible have been incorporated into the Encyclopedia as entries. All have influenced and shaped its development.

This has been a time of personal milestones as well. Two of the editors became citizens of the US during this time. Our vision of what needs to be said has been shaped by interactions with students in Hong Kong and across the Eastern United States, research outside and inside the US and hours of discussions with colleagues, friends and students worldwide. Our perspectives on America, its meanings and events have changed through life passages, changes in our cities and schools, political and economic issues, etc. They will change again, as will those of our contributors, after this encyclopedia is published. That, too, is culture, American or otherwise.

General Editors

Thematic entry list

As stated in the introduction, the articles in this volume have been arranged to give both overviews and more specific information, from different perspectives, concerning major discourses and experiences of contemporary American culture. In many cases, a longer thematic article (1,000 or 2,000 words) provides an overview and comprehensive bibliography, noting cross-references to more concise articles. Some of these shorter pieces refer to people or places; others deal with institutions, values and practices. In articles longer than 500 words, a selection of further readings encompasses both bibliographic references and additional research sources for investigation. In general, we have selected sources readily available in English, although drawing on a global range of scholars and viewpoints.

In addition, readers may wish to look at thematic sections which provide multiple perspectives and examples of cultural phenomena and interpretations. These themes include the following (with major articles marked by an asterisk):

Age groups and generations

American Association of Retired Persons (AARP)
babies
baby boom/boomers
children
children and television
children's literature
children's museums
children's music
child stars
games
Generation X
*life cycles/rites of passage
middle age
old age
retirement
slackers
teenagers
teen fiction
toys
see also education

Architecture

*architecture
bathroom
bedroom
cities
Danish modern
dinette
engineering
family room
garages/parking
Gehry, Frank
Graves, Michael
historic preservation
home
home, outdoor spaces
Johnson, Philip
Pei, I.M.
postmodernism
public art
public housing
Saarinen, Eero
suburbs and edge cities
Venturi, Robert
Wright, Frank Lloyd

Business and consumption

*advertising
antiques/reproductions
Apple computer

Civil rights

Mass media and journalism

Performing arts

Ailey, Alvin
classical music
concerts
Copland, Aaron
Cunningham, Merce
dance
drama
exotic dancing/strip clubs
Graham, Martha
musical, Broadway
musical, Hollywood
opera
performance art
performing arts centers
theater
see also film; music; television

Politics and government

abortion
Agnew, Spiro
Albright, Madeleine Korbel
American Civil Liberties Union (ACLU)
anarchism
assassination
Attorney-General
Berlin
Bicentennial
Bill of Rights
Brown family
Buchanan, Patrick
Bush, George and family
Cabinet
capital punishment
Carter, Jimmy
Castro, Fidel
censorship
Central Intelligence Agency (CIA)
China
Chisholm, Shirley
city hall
Clinton, William Jefferson
Cold War
communism
Congress
consumer safety
conventions
Cuba and Cuban Americans

Cuomo, Mario
Daley family
Daschle, Tom
Democratic Party
Dinkins, David
Dixiecrats
Dole, Robert and Elizabeth
draft
Dukakis, Michael
Eisenhower, Dwight David
Federal Bureau of Investigation (FBI)
Federal Communications Commission (FCC)
Ferraro, Geraldine
First Ladies
Ford, Gerald
freedom
Fulbright, James William
gambling and lotteries
gender gap
Gingrich, Newt
Goldwater, Barry
Gore, Albert Jr
governors
Helms, Jesse
Hill, Anita
House Committee of Un-American Activities (HUAC)
Humphrey, Hubert Horatio
immigration
impeachment
independent counsel
information
Iran
Iran-Contra affair
Ireland
John Birch Society
Johnson, Lyndon Baines
judicial activism
judiciary
Kemp, Jack
Kennedy, John F.
Kennedy family
Kent State shootings
Kissinger, Henry
Latin America
Left, the
Limbaugh, Rush
lobbyists
Luce, Claire Booth

Production

Race and ethnicity

Regions and borders

Religion

Ritual, family and life cycles

Rural life

ranching
small-town ideals
parks, national and state
see also regions and borders; urbanism and suburbs

Science and technology

anti-technology
biology
Borlang, Norman
chemistry
computers
engineering
genetics/genetic engineering
geography
Human Genome Project
information
Internet
mathematics
Nobel Prize
nuclear age
Pauling, Linus
physics
psychology and psychiatry
Silicon Valley
science fiction, film
science fiction, literature
science fiction, television
Space
Tennessee Valley Authority (TVA)
unabomber
video cassette recorder (VCR)

Sports and leisure

Ali, Muhammad
Ashe, Arthur
astroturf
basketball
bowl games
bowling
boxing
Brundage, Avery
camping
celebrity
cheerleading
chess
clubs, city and country
computer/video games
couch potatoes
fairs

field hockey
figure skating
fishing, commercial and angling
football
frisbee
gambling and lotteries
golf
guns
halls of fame
Harlem Globetrotters
hockey, ice
horses
humor
hunting
in-line skating
Jordan, Michael
King, Billie Jean
lacrosse
Lee, Bruce
little-league baseball
Louganis, Greg
marching bands
martial arts
mascots
National Collegiate Atheletics Association (NCAA)
Nicklaus, Jack
Olympians
Olympic Games
physical fitness
Robinson, Jackie
rodeos
rowing (crew)
running
sailing
skateboarding
skiing and snowboarding
soccer
softball
sports and gender
sports and media
sports and race
sports stadiums
steroids
Superbowl (Sunday)
surfing
swimming
tennis
theme parks
Title IX

Values

Visual arts

Abbey, Edward

b. 1927; d. 1989

Writer and ecologist of the **Southwest**. Sometimes
called the "Thoreau of the Southwest," Abbey
combined a deep, lyrical love for the mountains
and deserts of his adopted region with radical
environmental proposals to preserve it. Among his
major works are *Fire on the Mountain* (1962), *Desert
Solitaire* (1968) and *The Monkey Wrench Gang* (1975).
His impact and following have continued to grow
even after his death.

GARY McDONOGH

Abernathy, Ralph

b. 1926

Associate of Martin Luther **King**, Jr. and fellow
pastor of a Montgomery congregation at the
beginning of the Montgomery Bus Boycott. Afterwards, he joined King in founding the Southern
Christian Leadership Coalition, becoming its
secretary-treasurer. He remained in this position
until King's **assassination** in 1968, when he took
over as president. Later that year, he led the Poor
People's Campaign in **Washington, DC**, building
Resurrection City, USA, a small encampment of
huts in the heart of the city. He then organized
Operation Breadbasket, designed to persuade
African Americans to buy only from companies
that did not discriminate against them.

ROBERT GREGG

abortion

In 1973 the US **Supreme Court** struck down
Texas criminal abortion legislation outlawing all
abortions except those necessary to save the
mother's life, declaring that the constitutionally
protected right of privacy was "broad enough to
encompass a woman's decision whether or not to
terminate her pregnancy." The Court's decision in
Roe* v. *Wade denounced as unconstitutional laws
restricting a woman's right to an abortion during
the first trimester of pregnancy, permitted states
limited regulatory rights in the second trimester
and allowed complete proscription of abortions in
the third trimester, after the fetus had "quickened"
or reached viability. This momentous and controversial decision single-handedly: (a) invalidated
existing abortion legislation in forty-nine states;
and (b) transformed abortion from a criminal act
into a legitimate medical procedure. On a more
tangible and immediate level, *Roe* meant that a
woman with an unwanted pregnancy need no
longer turn to questionable "back-alley" abortion-
ists or travel to a state where abortion was legal in
order to terminate her pregnancy.

Roe v. *Wade* represented a victory for the
contemporary women's movement, for whom
social control over women's reproductive capacity
had become a central concern. While abortion
rights had not been championed by nineteenth-
century feminists, by 1970 modern feminists had
made it a prominent issue. Framing the issue as one
of a woman's right to control her own body, feminists came to regard reproductive control as a pre-
requisite to personal and political empowerment.

They therefore advocated access to safe and legal abortion regardless of a woman's race or class.

Liberal feminists were the first to target abortion rights. At the organization's first national conference, the **National Organization for Women (NOW)** passed a controversial resolution supporting "[t]he right of women to control their own reproductive lives by removing from the penal code laws limiting access to contraceptive information and devices, and by repealing penal laws governing abortion."

Abortion was also the first major issue for radical feminists in the late 1960s. They took a somewhat different view of the issue from the liberal feminists, however. They did not seek, as the liberal feminists did, to invalidate abortion laws because of their interference with women's autonomy and privacy. Instead, they sought to invalidate abortion laws because they viewed society's control of women's reproductive role as the fundamental source of women's oppression.

While *Roe's* impact was immediate and far-reaching, the right it announced (the right of a woman to choose an abortion) came under equally immediate and enduring attack. By the 1980s, abortion had become a controversial and divisive social, political, moral and religious issue (see **Roman Catholics**). A political candidate's stance on abortion (whether "pro-life" or "pro-choice") became one of the premier litmus tests voters used to ascertain a candidate's ability and desirability to serve in office. Pro-life advocates picketed and protested abortion clinics, lobbied for legislation restricting abortion rights, and urged that *Roe* be overturned. During the 1980s and 1990s, pro-life advocacy at times erupted into violence, leading most notably to abortion clinic bombings and the murder of doctors known to perform the abortion procedure. Based in part on the success of pro-life advocates' lobbying efforts, legislatures enacted statutes further restricting the abortion right announced in *Roe*. As challenges to these statutes reached a more conservative Supreme Court, the basic right to choose became substantially stripped-down.

By 1998, the twenty-fifth anniversary of the *Roe* decision, the Court had affirmed the right to an abortion, but had nonetheless approved numerous limitations on that right. The Court upheld state and federal laws that: (a) prohibited abortions in public hospitals unless they were necessary to save the woman's life; (b) eliminated Medicaid funding for lower-income women seeking abortions; (c) required pregnant teenagers to obtain parental consent or judicial approval for the procedure; and (d) prohibited doctors practicing in federally funded family planning clinics from counseling their patients about abortion or referring them to abortion providers. The Court rejected such restrictions as spousal consent and mandatory hospitalization, however.

With advances in medical technology and the corresponding earlier onset of fetal viability, *Roe v. Wade's* trimester approach has come under increasing attack as well. Some have described the decision as being on a collision course with itself, opining that the decision may be further undercut in the future by the development of technology itself rather than by pro-life advocacy efforts.

Further reading

Luker, K. (1985) *Abortion and the Politics of Motherhood*, Berkeley: University of California Press.

Ross, S., Pinzler, I., Ellis, D. and Moss, K. (1993) *The Rights of Women*, 3rd edn, Carbondale: Southern Illinois University Press.

Weddington, S. (1993) *A Question of Choice*, New York City: Penguin.

Weisberg, D. Kelly (ed.) (1996) *Applications of Feminist Legal Theory to Women's Lives*, Philadelphia: Temple University Press.

MARY-CHRISTINE SUNGAILA, ESQ.

abstract expressionism

Coined as a critical term in relation to the work of Wassily Kandinsky, abstract expressionism generally refers to the artistic movement that emerged in New York City during the 1940s and 1950s, known more broadly as New York School Painting. Born of a confluence of European immigration and American regionalism, abstract expressionism, or, as the critic Harold Rosenberg dubbed it, "Action Painting," ranged from the intricately woven paint skeins of Jackson Pollock's "all-over" abstractions to the gestural violence of Willem de Kooning's figurative female portraits.

Originally celebrated as an unmitigated triumph of American cultural ascendancy, most resoundingly and enduringly in the contemporaneous criticism of Clement Greenberg, and retrospectively, in the art historical work of Irving Sandler, in the 1970s, revisionist social art historians explored the degree to which its success stemmed from the easy metaphoric affinity of the presumed individuality and **freedom** evinced in its surfaces with the rhetoric of **Cold War** political ideology.

More recent feminist scholarship has excavated and interrogated the ways in which gender and identity shaped both the production and reception of New York School Painting, as is powerfully emblematized in a juxtaposition of "Jack the Dripper," who "spread paint like seed," upon the prone canvas with the Color-Field painter Helen Frankenthaler, who "bled" upon the unprimed canvas with her painterly "stains" and "flows."

Further reading:

Leja, M. (1993) *Reframing Abstract Expressionism: Painting and Subjectivity in the 1940s*, New Haven: Yale.

LISA SALTZMAN

Academy Awards ("Oscars") *see* awards

acid rain

Formed when sulfur dioxide (SO_2) and nitrogen oxide (NO_x) emissions from the burning of fossil fuels (primarily from coal-burning utility plants, **automobiles** and **trucks**) mix with water vapor in the atmosphere. The acidified water then falls to the Earth as rain or snow, where it can damage trees at high altitudes, leach nutrients from soils, damage buildings and public sculptures and, most notably, acidify lakes, where, in sufficient concentrations, it can kill off all aquatic life. The Northeastern United States, particularly the Adirondack mountains in northern New York State, have suffered the greatest harm from acid rain.

Acid rain first became the focus of scientific and political attention in the 1980s, and the Clean Air Act Amendments of 1990 contained the first legislative attempt to deal with the problem. The law set a cap on sulfur dioxide emissions from power plants and reduced the amount of nitrogen oxides that could be emitted per unit of energy.

See also: environmentalism

DAVID GOLDSTON

action movies

Rock 'em, sock' em, he-man, brawling, sprawling, blood and guts masculine cinematic confections that have been a mainstay of **Hollywood** production and appeal to audiences for decades. Using scenarios drawn from Westerns, adventure, **war**, **superheroes** or even terrorism, these movies showcase a **masculinity** of bravado, blood and violence. Key stars over decades have ranged from the suave Douglas Fairbanks, Jr or Errol Flynn to grittier portrayals by Bruce Willis, Sylvester Stallone, Wesley Snipes or Arnold Schwarzenegger. Some women, including Sigourney Weaver (*Alien*) and Linda Hamilton (*Terminator*) have expanded the genre, while Hong Kong stars like Jackie Chan and Chow Yun-Fat have also shown box-office appeal and even gained cult status. Box office, rather than art, after all, is the appeal that these epics offer to young men with or without dates on a summer evening, negotiating masculinity by fantasy and imitation.

GARY McDONOGH
CINDY WONG

actors

Actors create the illusion of believable characters through imaginative dramatization. Throughout American history, actors have worked in a variety of venues, including **theater**, film and **television**. Since the Second World War, most prominent actors have been known primarily for their film work, although many of them also perform in theater, television and **advertising** (in descending degree of "legitimacy," if not remuneration).

Famous actors ("**stars**") have a powerful cultural influence since they reflect and structure our ideals, particularly with respect to aspects of social identity, including **race**, **class**, gender, sexuality, ethnicity and **religion**. Because these "ideals" are often manufactured according to Eurocentric values, many actors from marginalized groups have been excluded from this vision.

In the postwar period, acting in America has been greatly influenced by the theories of Konstantin Stanislavski (1863–1938), a Russian actor, producer and theorist. In 1948, Lee Strasberg started the Actors Studio in New York, basing his approach on Stanislavski's theories. This approach, known as "method acting," stresses emotional truth and internal transformation (i.e. "living the part"). Prior to Stanislavski's work, many actors were primarily concerned with external signs of characterization (gesture, expression, costuming, vocal tone, etc.). Stanislavski didn't discount the importance of these elements, but emphasized that most great acting can be linked to a "creative state of mind," which promotes organic and convincing performances. American acting teachers such as Lee Strasberg and Stella Adler have carried awareness of this "method acting" style throughout the United States.

One of the first American actors to become known for "method acting" was Marlon **Brando** in *On the Waterfront* (1954). Until this time, American acting had been characterized by a more mannered style, particularly during the silent film era defined by such stars as Mary Pickford, Lillian Gish, Charlie Chaplin, Buster Keaton and Louise Brooks. With the rise of "talkies" in 1927, acting styles became less histrionic, but still mannered in comparison with "method acting," which took hold in the postwar era. Notable stars in the 1930s and 1940s included Cary Grant, Katharine **Hepburn**, Spencer Tracy, Ingrid Bergman, James **Stewart**, Judy **Garland**, Clark Gable, Vivien Leigh, Orson **Welles**, Bette **Davis**, Gary **Cooper**, Hattie McDaniel, Henry Fonda, Joan **Crawford**, John **Wayne**, Carole Lombard, Humphrey **Bogart** and Lauren **Bacall**. After the emergence of method acting, acting styles in America generally became less formal and more

subtle – a shift often explained by the increasing prevalence of the cinema (associated with the close scrutiny of the camera) and the declining popularity of live theater. "Method acting" has remained popular into the twenty-first century, though each decade is characterized by varying styles and personalities.

After the Second World War, many of the actors working during the 1930s and early 1940s continued to be active in the **Hollywood** studio system, which dominated American film-making for most of the twentieth century. After 1945, however, there was a move towards realism in American film-making that dovetailed nicely with Stanislavski's emphasis on natural, organic acting styles. Until the 1950s, however, this new realism was mostly characterized by grittier themes (such as in film noir), as opposed to different acting styles. Actors like Rita Hayworth, Robert Mitchum, Lana Turner, Kirk **Douglas**, Barbara Stanwyck and Fred MacMurray (as well as a number of those mentioned above) became **stars**. By the 1950s, television began to absorb many of the audiences usually reserved for the movies, creating a new venue for aspiring actors, and encouraging **directors** to experiment artistically. At around this time, the "method acting" described by Stanislavski began to be incorporated into the Hollywood tradition more fully, although the light entertainment typical of the Hollywood tradition continued. New stars like James **Dean**, Grace **Kelly**, Montgomery Clift, Doris **Day**, Harry Belafonte, Rock **Hudson**, Elizabeth **Taylor**, Jack **Lemmon**, Sidney **Poitier**, Audrey **Hepburn** and Paul **Newman** began to appear, and comic actor Marilyn **Monroe** became famous as a blonde sex symbol and icon of an era.

By the 1960s and 1970s, Hollywood clearly felt the squeeze created by the new competition on the small screen. The volatile political climate at this time, characterized by the **Vietnam War**, the **Civil Rights movement** and the **women's liberation** movement, also influenced creative expression during this period, and "method acting" firmly took hold as increasing numbers of actors were offered challenging dramatic or comedic roles. A new generation of "serious actors" (or actor/comedians) emerged, including Jane Fonda, Peter Fonda, Dustin **Hoffman**,

Diane Keaton, Jack **Nicholson**, Robert **De Niro**, Anne Bancroft, Warren Beatty, Woody **Allen**, James Earl **Jones**, Mia Farrow, Jodie **Foster**, Michael Douglas, Susan **Sarandon**, Al Pacino, Clint **Eastwood**, Cicily Tyson, Jon Voight, Shirley **Maclaine** and Robert **Redford**.

In the late 1970s and 1980s, Hollywood started to move away from dramas towards **blockbus-ters**. In these films, the main stars were often the special effects, yet many actors of this generation took their craft quite seriously and studied "method acting" – sometimes for years before they began acting professionally. As the directors of this period became known as the "film school generation," the actors of this period might also be known as the "acting school generation." This generation in-cluded such actors as Meryl Streep, Jessica Lange, Richard Dreyfuss, Laurence Fishburne, Glenn Close, Jason Scott Lee, William Hurt, Angela Bassett, Tom **Hanks**, Denzel **Washington**, Kathy Bates, Kevin Kline and Morgan Freeman.

Nearing the 1990s, **independent films** began to emerge in opposition to the Hollywood scene. Bolstered by the Sundance Institute founded by Robert Redford and the Independent Feature Project in **New York**, the "Independents" chal-lenged the blockbuster ethic, which was increas-ingly prevalent in Hollywood. Actors such as Parker Posey, John Turtorro, Adrienne Shelley, Frances McDormand and Ed Burns strove to create offbeat characters imbued with a real sense of individuality.

Further reading

Cook, D.A. (1996) *A History of Narrative Film*, New York: W.W. Norton.

Daw, K. (1997) *Acting: Thought into Action*, Ports-mouth, NH: Heinemann.

NICOLE MARIE KEATING

ACT UP (AIDS Coalition to Unleash Power)

Founded by Larry Kramer, playwright, novelist and founder of the Gay Men's Health Crisis (GMHC), in March 1987 in New York City.

Kramer rallied a small group of gay activists to respond to the government's refusal to deal adequately with the burgeoning **AIDS** crisis – a crisis disproportionately affecting homosexual men. Through an effective blend of agitprop street theater, massive protests and demonstrations at federal institutions, creative and media-savvy dis-tribution of "safe-sex" information, and unified anger, ACT UP pushed the US government and the Food and Drug Administration into changing stringent and stagnant policies. ACT UP groups came into being across the country and eventually Paris and London also joined in. Without the activism of ACT UP, the US AIDS epidemic would have been even more devastating.

See also: gay and lesbian life and politics

DAVID GERSTNER

Adams, Ansel

b. 1902; d. 1984

Adam's dramatic black and white photographs shaped American visions of the **West** from the 1930s onwards. His landscape compositions relied on strong natural features, exquisite detail and the interplay of light and shadow. He produced breathtaking images of national parks like Yose-mite. He also helped establish **photography** as an academic discipline in the US. See *This is the American Earth* (1960) among other published collections.

GARY McDONOGH
CINDY WONG

addiction

Behavior associated with a dependence on either a substance or activity that is harmful when used to excess. When addicted, the user is either unable or unwilling to stop his or her behavior. In the compulsive need for and use of a drug, addiction can involve either a physical or a psychological need. When addicted, the user also experiences increased tolerance for a substance. When more broadly defined, addiction can also refer to the compulsive need for an activity, i.e. "addicted to TV," or "addicted to jogging."

Addiction is measured in the degree of harm that it causes the user. Thus, an addiction to **coffee** is not considered a serious addiction because science has not shown that coffee consumption produces significant health hazards. An addiction to heroin is considered extremely harmful because of the physical and social conditions commonly associated with heroin addiction: HIV, hepatitis, endocarditis, cellulitis, overdose and collapsed veins. In the early twenty-first century, addictions to activities such as sex, **gambling**, video games, the **Internet** and **pornography** are talked about frequently.

Some substances which are physically addictive and used illegally include opiates, stimulants, inhalants, depressants and barbiturates. New drugs of the 1980s and 1990s that appeal to young people in dance clubs are Ecstasy, an amphetamine/hallucinogen combination drug and ketamine (Special K), a depressant. The National Institute on Drug Abuse estimates that 1.5 million people in the US over the age of twelve were chronic cocaine users, and about 2.4 million people have used heroin at some point in their lives. The most widespread addictions in the United States, however, are tobacco and **alcohol**, both legal mind-altering substances. NIDA estimates that in 1996 there were 62 million smokers in the US, and an additional 6.8 million who used smokeless tobacco.

Treatment for addictions come in many different forms. For drugs which are clearly physically addictive, like heroin, substitution treatment is available. Methadone is most commonly substituted for heroin, and is strictly regulated by the federal government. Methadone programs are located mainly in large **cities**, so addicts who live in rural areas and small towns either do not have access to methadone treatment, or may have to travel many hours to get to an available clinic. New forms of heroin substitution, such as buprenorphine, are also available.

Abstinence-based programs often use a "12-step" approach which was developed by Alcoholics Anonymous, and has since been adopted by Narcotics Anonymous, Cocaine Anonymous, Gambling Anonymous, and other national projects that seek to support addicts who are "in recovery" from their addictions. The 12-step approach, since it is based on submitting to a higher power or religious figure, has some critics. Alternatives to 12-step programs have also arisen, which often center the addict as the controlling party in the process of recovery, rather than a higher authority.

During the 1990s a new philosophy of treating the harms associated with drug use emerged. Harm reduction calls for prevention and treatment programs which do not expect that abstinence is the only option for dealing with the consequences of drug use. Instead, harm reduction proponents advocate measures which will decrease the harms associated with illicit drug use, i.e. prevent HIV transmission, overdoses and other diseases associated with using dirty syringes. Needle exchange programs which prevent bloodborne diseases among injecting addicts are good examples of harm reduction programs, and are springing up in areas of the country where drug use and drug traffic are more common.

JULIE PARR

adoption

American parentage is culturally based on shared blood, and, more recently, on shared DNA. The basis for "real" parentage has produced ambivalent feelings towards adoption. While Americans have long adopted, early adoptions were typically within the extended family or were highly guarded secrets with all records sealed. These early adoptions were frequently the result of out-of-wedlock births, which were socially taboo. In recent years, closed adoption has become a hotly contested issue, with advocacy groups like Bastard Nation seeking to end closed records. The search for birth parents and for biological children is a frequent topic of television talk shows. Highly publicized cases in which adopted children have been returned to birth families have led to a mistrust of domestic adoptions for most Americans. Open adoption, in which the birth parents may remain a part of the child's life, provides a new, highly demanding option, but one limited in numbers.

Moreover, identity politics, combined with an emphasis on blood relationships, have made trans-racial adoptions very controversial within the US: the National Association of Black Social Workers has publicly condemned such adoptions. This controversy is combined with a rising national out-of-wedlock birth rate, as well as a declining rate of adoption to make the process more difficult. The ability to determine paternity through DNA testing has made the termination of biological parental rights more problematic. State governments and the social services establishment are less favorable to adoption, even while the American fosterparent system is coming under attack.

These obstacles, combined with the apparent rise in **infertility**, have forced more **middle-class** white couples to seek to adopt privately or internationally. Private adoptions are typically handled through **lawyers** and are quite expensive. Advertisements for healthy white infants, who are in high demand, appear in **college** newspapers across the county, illustrating the growing demand for these adoptions. Although international adoptions are not new, the search for infants has expanded from Korea (in the 1950s and 1960s) to **China**, **Russia**, Yugoslavia, as well as **Latin America** and other parts of Asia. Transnational adoption has also sparked the debate on the unequal power relationship between the first-world adopting parents and the third-world adoptees.

The cherished ideal of the nuclear **family** with two biological children has come under assault as single parents and gay parents turn to adoption as well. Like the blended families resulting from **divorce**, these new family forms do not corre-spond with popular views of what a real family is in America. Adoption is becoming one of the important elements in the redefinition of the American family. The "triad" of relationships resulting from adoption – the adoptive parents, the adoptees and the birth parents – represents new forms of American kinship informed both by the longstanding cultural logic of biological rela-tionships that define what constitutes the American family and the reality of new social relationships that produce something different.

Further reading

Schneider, D. (1968) *American Kinship*, Englewood Cliffs: Prentice-Hall.

STEVE FERZACCA

advertising

The development of a mass society based on mass consumption depends on introducing the consumers to the product; this is done most effectively through advertising. Mass advertising made possible the development of mass **newspapers** in the mid-nineteenth century. During the same time, advertis-ing agencies formed first to serve as brokers between the newspaper and the client, and later to help the client in devising ways of reaching the reader/consumer. This interaction also consolidated the position of the advertisers who became major players in all subsequent commercial media in America. In 1999, $17 billion was projected to be spent on advertising, something over $399.40 per person.

Some products advertised in America during the mid-nineteenth century remain dominant in the advertisement world today. Brand names, thus name recognition, became important through advertising. Consumers began to demand Camp-bell's soup (1869), **Levi Strauss**'s overalls (1873) and **Procter & Gamble**'s Ivory soap (1879). Another product, patent medicine, commanded half of advertising space in the late nineteenth century. In the 1990s, prescription drugs were once again allowed to be advertised, changing both pharmaceutical development and the etiology of disease. Patent medicine advertising was also important because it created a crisis with its exaggerated false claims, and brought in the government to regulate the truthfulness of adver-tisements, alongside self-regulation by the indus-tries themselves.

When **radio** came along in the early twentieth century, advertisers found a new venue to push their products. Because of the large revenue already visibly generated through advertising, Americans chose to adopt commercialism rather than other financial means, like tax collection, to support the broadcasting industries. By the early 1920s, many radio shows, like the **soap operas**, were sponsored by particular products. Advertising firms, such as Young and Rubicam, produced popular radio shows with Jack Benny for their clients. Early **television** shows also carried sponsors' names, for instance Milton Berle's *Texaco Star Theater.* Today, Procter & Gamble still own television soaps like *As The World Turns.*

Postwar Americans live in a world permeated by commercial images. Yet, while advertising does not guarantee more sales, it does promote name recognition: the absence of advertising is perceived as a detriment to sales. At the same time, advertising does not simply sell a product, it promotes consumerism and produces consumers. This has enabled **consumerism** to become the American way of life.

The industry also refined its tools in order to understand and reach the consumer, as well as to measure the effectiveness of their advertisements. George Gallup began polling of public opinion, while A.C. **Nielsen** sold indices of food and drug sales. Advertisers found out that women made most of the decisions about what to buy for the household, so many advertisements were created with a female audience in mind. While soap operas were major poles for women listeners and viewers in both radio and television, **Hollywood** has used its glamorous stars to sell particular images for women. By the 1940s, it used product placement to sell Bette **Davis**' transformed look in *Now Voyager* through press releases urging women to buy the cosmetics Bette used.

Advertising does not exist in an unconstrained marketplace, however. The Federal Trade Commission (FTC) and later the **FCC**, the Food and Drug Administration (FDA) and other government agencies have all regulated advertising in one form or another. **Consumer Reports**, consumers' union and other private groups examine whether advertising claims are truthful or not; Ralph **Nader** and other public interest researchers have also challenged corporate claims. The industry trade group, the American Association of Advertising Agencies, established in 1917, also has regulated its practice to protect the credibility of the industry. However, the government, in general, favors the advertising industries. While blatantly false claims are not tolerated, in the era of deregulation, the **Supreme Court** extended 1st

Amendment protection to advertisement (1976), and **Congress** removed the FTC's power to stop "unfair" advertising (1980). Furthermore, added financial incentives are given to advertisers where advertisement expenses are tax write-offs.

Advertising does not simply create brand names and sell products, but it also helps define culture. One of the most successful advertising icons is the Marlboro Man, the archetypal cowboy created in 1955 to change Marlboro from a woman's cigarette to a man's cigarette. The sales of Marlboro soared 3.241 percent within one year. The Marlboro man, though controversial, has become a global emblem of American **masculinity**, rugged, individualistic and tough. The Aunt Jemima icon, an 1893 image of an **African American** woman who served happily, was attacked in the 1950s for its portrayal of the black mammy stereotype. Yet it has not disappeared, but has undergone various modernization schemes to represent changing sensitivity towards race while maintaining brand identity. **Automobiles**, the quintessential American symbol, are the most advertised items in the country, urging Americans to have more than one car and new cars every few years.

In the 1990s, with ever more sophisticated rating systems, advertisers do not simply want to reach as many people as possible, but also want to target, through **niche marketing**, particular groups of people who are prone to spending more money. At the same time, since the **mass media** is totally dependent on advertising, media content has been affected by the changing input of advertisers. *Fortune*, for example, reported that *Forbes* magazine "systematically allows its advertising executives to see stories and command changes before they are run." In 1999, many major advertisers, like Procter & Gamble, General Motors, **IBM**, are once again providing financial support for the WB network to develop **family** friendly television shows. Other niche appeals to **teenagers** or minorities may define television or cinema products so as to exclude dialogue about shared/public values. In the early twenty-first century, the **Internet** has become an ever expanding medium for advertising.

Advertising not only sells products, but also sells the Government too. During the Second World War, the War Advertising Council was formed to promote voluntary advertisement campaigns. This unit was later renamed the Ad Council. It specializes in making advertisements for non-profit and social issues, which radio and television stations are required to play as public service requirements in their licensing.

Politicians and **lobbyists** also use advertising. In the wars on drugs of the 1980s, comprehensive advertisement campaigns were launched in different media to push for behavioral change accompanying legislation. In the 1990s, debates over **healthcare** have been fought through intensive advertising inside the Beltway, regardless of how effective messages or coverage may have been nationwide. Political campaigns are also big spenders for advertising. In 1999, George **Bush**, the favored candidate for the **Republican Party** for the 2000 presidential election, raised so much money for his campaign that he foreswore the federal money for the primaries which would restrict his spending. For others, this proves a final dilemma of product and image that advertising has fostered within American mass society.

Advertising, in fact, brings together the economic and political success of the American century with more troubling themes – massification (versus ideals of **individualism**), manipulation instead of **freedom**, image instead of truth. These contradictions, juxtaposed to the pervasive power of advertising not only in commerce but in politics, literature, education and healthcare, suggest dilemmas the nation has yet to resolve.

Further reading

Jones, J.P. (ed.) (1999) *The Advertising Business: Operations, Creativity, Media Planning, Integrated Communications*, Thousand Oaks: Sage Publications.
Rotzoll, K.B. and James, E.H. with Hall, S.R. (1996) *Advertising in Contemporary Society: Perspectives towards Understanding*, Urbana: University of Illinois Press.

CINDY WONG

advice columnists

Advice columnists have been a staple of American newspaper copy in the twentieth century, particu-larly in sections of the newspaper that cater to women's interests. Generally women themselves, advice columnists often respond to letters from their readers. These letters ask about some personal or **family** issue, such as possible marital infidelity or poor relations with in-laws. Some other advice columnists specialize in matters concerning housekeeping and household economics, or proper **etiquette**.

As with the notion of newspaper columnists more generally, the mixture of objective and interpretive reporting that characterized so much pre-twentieth century journalism generally makes it difficult to find a starting point for the institution in its present form. The initial impetus for the modern American advice column, however, probably came in the late 1800s with an influx of immigrant readers or other residents newly arrived to the city, who were often confused about how to act in the unfamiliar American urban environment. One of the first advice columnists was Marie Manning, who began writing a regular column for the romantically confused in 1898 under the pen name "Beatrix Fairfax." When she moved to William Randolf Hearst's *New York Journal*, her editor gave her a column of her own when queries concerning romantic entanglements threatened to overwhelm the writers on the "Letters to the Editor" desk. Another famous early advice columnist was "Emily Post," who dispensed etiquette advice. Two of the most famous and most widely syndicated American advice columnists in the postwar era have been sisters Ann Landers (Eppie Lederer) and Abigail van Buren ("Dear Abby").

Further reading

Buckley, C. (1995) "You got a problem?," *The New Yorker* 71(39): 80–5.
Olson, L. (1992) "Dear Beatrice Fairfax..." *American Heritage* 43(3): 90–7.

MARK BREWIN

affirmative action

First officially used in 1961 by President John **Kennedy**, who issued an executive order requiring employers who had contracts with the federal government to take "affirmative action" to ensure they did not discriminate against **African Americans**. Simultaneously with passage of the Civil Rights Act of 1964, which prohibited discrimination in employment, President Lyndon **Johnson**, by executive orders, extended affirmative action to other minorities and required federal contractors to actively recruit and set long-term goals to increase minority employment. By the late 1970s, the concept had expanded to cover women, and its scope embraced all levels of public employment, educational institutions and many private businesses.

Initially, it was widely accepted as a natural concomitant to the **Civil Rights movement** and the **War on Poverty**. It was viewed as an effective remedy to compensate for the accumulated impact of past discrimination as a means to apportion equitably government employment and publicly financed education, and as a method to endure racially, ethnically and multiculturally diverse student populations. It was also an instrument to insure that the racial and ethnic composition and life experiences of urban public employees, especially **police** officers and fire fighters, more closely mirrored the increasingly minority communities they served.

Affirmative action quickly became an extremely controversial national lightning rod for racial and social tensions. The conservative electorate responsible for the **Reagan** presidency, criticism spearheaded by a small group of **black conservatives** such as Clarence **Thomas** and increased competition for ever scarcer government employment and places at elite public universities coalesced in opposition. Affirmative action was labeled "reverse discrimination," "racial preference programs" and "discriminatory quota systems."

In upholding the general principle of affirmative action in *Bakke* v. *University of California* (1978), the **Supreme Court** ruled that race could be considered along with other factors in university admissions, but fixed racial quotas could not be utilized. In *Fullilove* v. *Klutnick* (1980), the Court upheld the requirement that ten percent of federal funds for public works be allotted to qualified minority contractors. But, in 1989, the Court outlawed the use of similar set-aside programs by states unless precise evidence of racial discrimina-

tion existed. Finally, in 1995, the **Rehnquist Court** limited federal set-aside programs to those justified by a "compelling government interest."

Anti-affirmative action sentiment solidified in successful referenda in **California** and **Washington**. Immediately, there were drastic declines in the number of African Americans and **Latinos** at the prestigious campuses of the California state system.

While many voluntary private sector employment and university admissions programs remain intact, affirmative action, a crucial factor in raising minority educational levels and middle-class membership, is rapidly becoming a victim of the changing social agenda of a conservative era.

Further Reading:

Carter, S.L. (1991) *Reflections of an Affirmative Action Baby*, New York: Basic Books.

Nieli, R. (ed.) (1991) *Racial Preference and Racial Justice*, Washington, DC: Ethics and Public Policy Center.

JAMES KRAUS

Africa

President Bill **Clinton**'s 1998 visit to Africa, while taken by some as a distraction from domestic scandals, marked a potential breakthrough in American relations with Africa. The US, without the colonial entanglements of Europe (except for Liberian resettlement schemes) had subsequently become involved in Africa through missionary work there by both whites and blacks.

After the Second World War, foreign aid and development projects, including the Peace Corps, increased US presence, as did political intervention, from boycotts of the apartheid regime in South Africa to disputes with individual regimes. This rarely involved the military exercise of **Somalia** or the bombing of Sudan, although Africa was a constant market for US arms, as well as a site for **CIA** activity motivated by imagined **Cold War** exigencies (as in the 1965 assassination of the Congo leader, Patrice LeMumba, followed by support for Mobutu).

Yet all this intervention has often been based on a continuing sense of distance tinged with superiority, even if African and Afrocentric studies, from ethnography to politics, have begun to bring home the rich history and cultures of a continent. Hence, while Bosnia received daily media attention, the horrors of Rwanda or Sierra Leone evoked no active intervention or adoption of refugees. These relations with Africa are complicated by millions of descendants of those torn from Africa by slavery, for whom the continent may be a distant albeit unfamiliar homeland. W.E.B. **Du Bois** chose to end his distinguished life in Ghana, and **Afrocentric** scholarships and cultural revivals have made often-generalized clothing and food more mainstream. African music has probably been the area of deepest crossover. Other **African Americans** have found that profound cultural, religious and social gaps make Africa a deeply unfamiliar place, in which they are outsiders or even considered "white."

Modern African **migration** to the US has been extremely small, with sub-Saharan immigrants accounting for only 2 percent of all immigrants in 1985, long after the watershed of **immigration** reforms. These were often students and professionals, a "brain drain" from African nations, as well as intellectual and political exiles like Wole Soyinka.

Illegal immigrants have become associated in the 1990s with peddling and ethnic resources. The documentary *In and Out of Africa* (1995) reveals the dialectic of African and American goals and attitudes in the arts trade, while the Amadou Diallo shooting in **New York** City, NY underscored the racial settings into which African migrants fit.

GARY McDONOGH

African Americans

The last half-century has witnessed a massive relocation of African Americans away from **farms**, plantations, towns and **cities** in the **South** towards a more national and urbanized existence associated with factories, assembly-lines, service jobs, professional work and unemployment all within the context of burgeoning globalization.

This structural shift has shaped the cultural experiences of African American people.

Mass **migration**, together with the **Civil Rights** and **Black Power** movements, and **affirmative action** policies, has wrought a unique degree of social differentiation among black Americans. One consequence has been the expansion of an African American **middle class**, with an estimated one-sixth of black families earning over $50,000 annually by the early 1990s. The influence of this new class is evident through the prominent placement of individuals like President **Clinton**'s former advisor Vernon Jordan, former Joint-Chief-of-Staff Colin **Powell** and **Supreme Court** Justice Clarence **Thomas**. It is also clear from the emergence of groups like the congressional Black Caucus and university academics whose political and intellectual influences are unprecedented. With this black middle class have come passionate arguments among black **intellectuals** about the manner in which to respond to the increasing social bifurcation of African American life. Struggles against slavery and second-class citizenship have historically united black people. Over the last generation, however, civic incorporation together with middle-classness has riven this traditional solidarity.

Meanwhile, poorer African Americans have been buffeted by global capitalism and by economic deprivation in inner cities. According to the 1991 federal census, over 30 percent of black families live below the poverty line. It has been estimated that more than 10 million African Americans are confined to fourteen cities with segregated black populations of at least 200,000, which denotes residential apartheid. For instance, there are fourteen job applicants for every available job in the fast-food industry in central **Harlem** because of the increasing globalization of the US economy. Perhaps the most striking feature of this postwar globalization is the degree to which the conditions of poor blacks resemble those of the poor world rather than those of the richest nation in history. Economist Amartya Sen points out that African Americans are richer than Chinese citizens and South Indian peasants, but have lower life expectancies than these people. The infant mortality rate in **Washington, DC** is 15 per 1000 babies born (1996) compared with 11 in Barbados,

10 in Jamaica and 7 in Cuba (1997). Rather than famine, poverty in the US causes poor **diets**, with higher rates of obesity and heart attacks. Perverse representations in the dominant culture can be found in fast-food advertisements and on cigarette billboards directly targeting poorer minorities, while healthier black bodies adorn magazine covers, radiate from television screens, and saturate the sporting arena.

Professional sports has served as one escape hatch from poverty and the **ghetto**, especially since Woody Strode and Jackie **Robinson** began the integration of modern sports in the late 1940s. It is unclear how many African Americans earned their living through sports during the era of the Negro Leagues from the 1920s to 1940s, but it is likely that there are far more blacks earning a living from professional sports today. In 1997, blacks accounted for 80 percent of 361 NBA players, 67 percent of 1,815 NFL players and 17 percent of 1,100 major league **baseball** players. Over the last two years, golfer Tiger **Woods** and **tennis** sisters Serena and Venus Williams have courted enormous prestige and earning power; while heavyweight boxer Mike Tyson earned $60 million in six years and **basketball** guard Michael **Jordan** earned $16 million alone in commercial endorsements in 1992. Indeed, "Air" Jordan assumed an unprecedented global commodification through slick sports shoes **advertising**. In the process, company stockholders made a fortune, while the global spotlight revealed the company's naked exploitation of factory workers in poor Asian nations.

Less remarked upon is the degree to which these poorly paid jobs are part of a process of globalization with devastating consequences for urban black life. The former exploitative commodity chain of slaves, sugar, cotton and popular consumption has been replaced by overseas cheap labor and shoddily manufactured goods advertised by African American sports stars, with youngsters fighting and killing other youngsters for sports shoes. Indeed, contemporary sport functions as terrible schooling for black youth. According to a 1995 *New York Times* survey of the top twenty college **football** teams, three-quarters of these teams had graduation rates for scholarship players below 60 percent. A 1997 survey revealed that 66 percent of black

youth aged thirteen through eighteen believed they would make a living through professional sports. It is true that sports can pave the way out of poverty for some; a late 1980s study revealed that five-sixths of blacks in Major League baseball born since 1940 had working-class backgrounds. Most black youth, however, never make it into professional sports, and those few who do are often ill-prepared for life after their careers in professional sports.

Most disturbing of all, the dominant culture continues to feed parasitically off black sporting prowess, oblivious to the social costs involved. The question modern sport raises for African American **popular culture** is: who pays the high price for "He Got Game"?

Much like sports, popular **music** serves an ambivalent role in African American culture. A rich and varied tradition of spirituals, work songs, **blues**, **gospel music** and **jazz** suggests that music "be the food" of African American life. Changing jazz styles – bebop (1940s), hard bop and cool jazz (1950s), modern jazz (1960s), jazz funk, and **fusion** (1970s) and the new jazz swing (1990s) – make it hard to generalize about jazz, yet it is clear that jazz is part of a movement culture which reflects a disembedded modern people. While relatively unappreciated by most Americans – public **television** and **radio** stations continue to define classical music as only a European genre – jazz is the US' classic music and is arguably the most serious musical contribution of the US to world culture.

In more recent decades, an assortment of other popular black musical genres have emerged, including: 1950s R&B, characterized by the group ballad and doo-wop style; 1960s **soul**, symbolizing a black aesthetic of pride, purpose and people-hood; and 1970s funk, **disco** and crossover. Currently, hip-hop, emerging from the fusion of rhythmic poetry and poverty-stricken city life has taken alternate directions with nationalist rappers like Public Enemy and Sister Souljah to blaxsploi-ters like Geto Boys and Snoop Doggy Dogg.

It is important to emphasize that many of these genres emerged from structural transformations in African American life. It is also significant to note the consistent globalization of African American popular music from jazz through hip-hop, with the latter currently being the fastest growing musical form in Europe. It should be added, however, that this European musical appreciation has exotic and imperialist undercurrents, while its exploitative features are particularly prominent. The wealth of black music contrasts with the relative poverty of blacks working in the music industry. Furthermore, real existing urban poverty, despair and discontent inform musical genres like **rap** and hip-hop, which then become consumer products and in turn reduce a complex African American class structure to one negative racial stereotype of under-classness. Meanwhile, the dominant culture feeds off these images, especially through record-buying, hipster jean-wearing, bored white suburban youth, while black youth on elite college **campuses** consume this music as a means to gain their "props" with the "real folk" outside academe's privileged and safe walls.

It might be argued that African Americans have progressed from being a talented tenth in the 1890s to a talented third in the 1990s. Apart from fostering a false set of values for unsuccessful blacks, this argument ignores the precarious position of the black middle class who increasingly find themselves under attack for enjoying "discriminatory" entitlement. It also ignores the broader context of a dominant national and global culture which has historically been quite comfortable with the exploitation of people of African descent.

Further reading

Gates, H. L. Jr and West, C. (1996) *The Future of the Race*, New York: Knopf.

Ruck, R. (1993) *Sandlot Seasons*, Urbana: University of Illinois Press.

Sen, A. (1999) *Development as Freedom*, New York: Knopf.

Woodward, K. (1999) *A Nation within a Nation*, Chapel Hill: University of North Carolina Press.

JEFFREY R. KERR-RITCHIE

African Methodists

Nearly 4 million African Methodists belong to two denominations: African Methodist Episcopal and AME Episcopal Zion. The denominations grew out of schisms occurring in white **Methodists'** churches in **Philadelphia** and **New York** City at the end of the eighteenth century, when black church-goers objected to the church's segregationist seating practices. Developing into national denominations in the first half of the nineteenth century, the AME and AME Zion churches grew in the wake of the emancipation of slaves into two of the largest denominations among **African Americans**. In the second half of the century the AME Church spread to **Haiti**, Liberia and South Africa.

After the 1920s, with the influx of large numbers of Southern Baptists into Northeastern cities, the denominations' influence began to decline. While churches generally lost influence to the rising black professionals, African Methodist denominations lost out to both elite churches catering to these professionals and the more charismatic churches from Baptist to Holiness, catering to poorer blacks.

The last thirty years have witnessed a dramatic reversal of fortunes for African Methodist churches. Although still outnumbered by the Baptists, African Methodists have taken on a leadership role in the Congress of National Black Churches (CNBC), an organization that was virtually created through the AME church's initiative (with the financial support of foundations who, in the 1970s, were looking for a more conservative alternative to **Black Power**).

This new strength comes, in part, from the denomination's highly centralized bureaucracies, allowing them to have more influence in the CNBC than the decentralized Baptist denomination. But, more importantly, it derives from the denomination's theology, which, by marrying together nationalist (African) and European (Methodist) traditions, speaks to the dual political and religious influences of many black suburbanites. Thus, the Ebenezer AME church, formerly located in **Washington, DC**, has revitalized itself by moving its congregation into a black Virginia suburb.

The renewed prominence of the African Methodist churches is apparent when we take into consideration their vocal support for Clarence **Thomas**, the fact that the first black community President **Clinton** visited after his inauguration was an AME Church, and the fact that

Christopher Darden, prosecuting attorney in the O.J. **Simpson** trial, has been a prominent member of the largest AME church in **Los Angeles, CA**.

African Methodists have not created an alternative theology or liturgy from that of white Methodists that would preclude reunification (though the flexibility of Methodism has allowed for different kinds of hymns, more gospel in nature, to gain widespread acceptance in these churches). Yet they have resisted reintegration with white Methodists throughout their history because they have felt that the United States discriminated against them and so they need their own autonomous churches.

Further reading

Lincoln, C.E. and Lawrence, H.M. (1990) *The Black Church in the African American Experience*, Durham: Duke University Press.

ROBERT GREGG

Afrocentrism

This is the reorientation of history and cultural studies to situate the origins of African American identity (and other cultural features) in Africa in opposition to "Eurocentrism." Although interest in Africa was apparent in earlier intellectuals like W.E.B. **Du Bois** and participants in the **Harlem** Renaissance, this was more clearly a revindicationist movement of black nationalism after **civil rights**. Among its major proponents are professors Molefi Kete Asante of Temple University, author of *The Afrocentric Idea* (1987) and Leonard Jeffries of CUNY. Another heated debate, suggested by Martin Bernal's *Black Athena* (1987), emerged over the claims of African origins for "Western" civilization. Historical revision, unfortunately, has sometimes been clouded by inter-ethnic debates, as well as by dubious scholarship, although discussion has gnawed away at the implicit and accepted centrality of northern European experiences and perspectives. See **literature, race and ethnicity**.

GARY McDONOGH
CINDY WONG

afterlife

The majority of Americans believe in some form of life after death. Often, this is shaped by Christian traditions of eternal reward for a moral life. Other religions also offer some form of enlightenment or reincarnation that has found followers outside of the faith community as well. Religious practices and beliefs, moreover, have intersected with scientific examinations of "out-of-body" experiences and attempts to communicate with the dead through spiritualism and mediums. This has been a goldmine for popular publications as well as theological speculation.

This topic has also been a rich area of speculation for American media. **Horror films**, for example, have long explored malign elements of evil and revenge associated with widespread concepts of hell and Satan; threats of Satanism have also flared in community witch-hunts across the country (sometimes focused on childcare). While these concepts are not as popular nor as well-defined as heaven, they nonetheless remain part of a substrate of American theology.

Meanwhile other, lighter films and television have focused on the activities of angels in everyday life, from Frank **Capra**'s classic postwar angelic alternative to noir, *It's a Wonderful Life* (1946), to several television series of the 1980s and 1990s (*Highway to Heaven*, 1984–91, *Touched by an Angel*, 1996–). Angels, drawing on European representations, have also become widely marketed jewelry items, sometimes divorced from any particular religious meaning.

Other versions of heaven also stand out for their differences in time and perspective. These would include all-black heavens as **Hollywood** minstrelsy (*Cabin in the Sky*, 1943), a spate of **yuppie** heavens, involving litigation (*Defending your Life*, 1991) and technicolor consumption (*What Dreams May Come*, 1999). Diane Keaton also created *Heaven* (1987), a talkative documentary with interviews and film clips. Reincarnation has also been used to tackle issues of gender stereotyping in *All of Me* (1984) and *Switch* (1991). While these are scarcely philosophical reflections, their use of normative expectations underscores the pervasiveness of the basic tenets of civic **religion** in the nation.

Further reading

Lewis, J. (1995) *Encyclopedia of Death and the Afterlife*, Detroit: Visible Ink.

GARY McDONOGH

CINDY WONG

Agent Orange

A herbicide and defoliant used by US forces in Vietnam to remove leaves from trees that provided cover for North Vietnamese and Vietcong forces. Named for the orange stripe on the fifty-five-gallon drums in which it was stored, Agent Orange included traces of a dioxin, known to cause a variety of health problems and congenital deformities. Prostate **cancer**, spina bifida, non-Hodgkin's lymphoma, Hodgkin's disease and respiratory cancers are a few of the diseases linked to the chemical put out by Monsanto Corporation (which covered up information about the dioxin contamination in the product). Several thousand Vietnam **veterans** exposed to Agent Orange receive treatment from the Veteran's Administration hospitals; the Vietnamese on whom the chemical was dropped have not received compensation of any kind.

ROBERT GREGG

agents (film)

Film agents are negotiators on behalf of actors, directors and others within **Hollywood** deal-making of the post-studio era. Typically portrayed in **mass media** as leeches because of their lack of creative roles and the high percentages they demand (10–15 percent of the deal), they increasingly represent important packagers of film and **television** productions and even gateways into the profession, a role that has spread into sports, arts and other arenas (see Tom Cruise in *Jerry Maguire*, 1996). Major talent agencies have included MCA and William Morris, while agents like Michael Ovitz have gained name recognition in their own right.

CINDY WONG

Agnew, Spiro

b. 1918; d. 1996

Thirty-ninth **vice-president** of the United States, under **Republican** President Richard **Nixon** (1969–73). A popular figure in the conservative political establishment, Agnew was forced to resign in 1973 amid allegations that he had accepted bribes and kickbacks as vice-president and while in office in Maryland years earlier. The scandal marked the beginning of an era in which Americans' instinctive mistrust of government reached unprecedented heights. Only a year after Agnew stepped down, President Nixon was forced from office as a result of the **Watergate** scandal.

SARAH SMITH

agriculture and agribusiness

While the reputation and power of the US as a high-tech industrial and post-industrial power permeates imagery and actions at home and abroad, the US economy has long had firm foundations in agricultural production for domestic and foreign sales. Agricultural exports totaled more than $60 billion annually in the late 1990s, while the export of knowledge and technology also reinforces the global status of American agribusiness. While agriculture is linked ideologically to the family **farm** and rural life or small-town values, since the Second World War, production has been dominated by corporations characterized by larger landholdings and supply networks, industrial and scientific management techniques, vertical integration, global ties and government support. In 1992, only 2.4 percent of American farms produced more than $500,000 in sales, but this accounted for 46 percent of all farm sales. Associated with these industrial farms and ranches are corporate suppliers, research institutions (commercial, government and state universities) and **lobbyists**.

Corporate agribusiness responsible to stockholders has created tight controls within American production in which a handful of businesses can control beef production or Cargill, Continental and Archer Daniels Midland control three-quarters of grain exchanged globally. These companies, in turn, become powerful voices in policy-making in the US, through lobbying and party contributions. The links of production and distribution in large conglomerates also limit markets and possibilities for independent farmers and, in turn, for consumers. Chicken production, for example, has been reshaped through assembly-line controls dominated by mega-companies that render chickens immobile while they are stuffed with special foods, supplements and even pink contact lenses (that help unstressed growth). In this context, free-range or organic chickens emerge as elite alternatives of production and taste.

Such huge and concentrated farming creates conditions for environmental problems beyond their reliance on chemical fertilizers, insecticides and, controversially, genetically engineered crops. More that two-thirds of all hogs, for example, come from farms of more than 1,000 heads. This concentration became disastrous as 1999 floods in North Carolina spilled their wastes into the state water system.

Agribusiness has been a source of debate concerning government subsidies and favoritism, environmental issues and, in the late 1990s, the long-term health effects of genetically engineered crops (which make producers dependent on companies each year for new seeds). Yet this industry also supplies the US and the world with abundance and choice at low prices that challenge simple questions of quality versus quantity or monopoly versus artesanal farm production. In both regards, agriculture and agribusiness, while constantly changing, promise to remain at the center of US economics, politics and lifestyles for generations to come.

Further reading:

Goreham, G. (ed.) (1997) *Encyclopedia of Rural America*, Santa Barbara: ABC-Clio.

GARY McDONOGH

AIDS

An acronym for Acquired Immune Deficiency Syndrome, AIDS describes an illness that attacks and weakens the body's immune system, making it difficult to fight off diseases. Thus, people with AIDS can become very ill with diseases that are rarely life-threatening for people with strong immune responses.

AIDS is caused by the Human Immunodeficiency Virus (HIV), along with probable other factors (e.g. **alcohol**, recreational drugs, other diseases or viruses) that lead to symptomatic illness and death. Although survival rates have increased, most HIV-positive individuals eventually develop AIDS. Individuals, however, may be infected for years without showing symptoms and may still be capable of transmitting HIV through unprotected sexual intercourse, blood-to-blood contact from sharing drug needles or blood transfusions, or from mother to child during pregnancy, labor and/or breastfeeding. HIV cannot be transmitted through casual contact such as hugging, shaking hands or sharing cups and utensils.

In 1981, physicians in **New York** City and **Los Angeles** noted they were treating gay men for previously rare infections, calling the illness GRID (Gay-Related Immune Deficiency). The name AIDS was created in 1982 as **public-health** officials realized that AIDS was linked to 1970s "junkie pneumonia" deaths reported in US urban areas and was, thus, a bloodborne illness that damaged the immune system and not simply a disease of gay men.

By the 1990s, AIDS was a leading cause of death in the US. Increasing numbers of people in the US are infected through male–female sexual activity; heterosexual transmission (from men to women *and* from women to men) already represents the overwhelming risk factor for HIV infection in most of the world. By 1998, more than half-a-million US citizens had been diagnosed with AIDS and about 50 percent of them had died. Almost 2 million Americans are already infected with HIV. In the year 2000, there are more than 200 million HIV-infected people worldwide.

Even though first identified in the US, the vast majority of the world's HIV-infected people live in the developing world. Studies indicate that more than 10,000 people worldwide are infected with the virus every single day. More cases of AIDS developed between 1998 and 2000 alone than the total number during the entire history of the epidemic to date. It is, therefore, clear: the decade to come will be significantly more difficult than the already difficult decade past.

The AIDS epidemic flourishes by exploiting existing societal inequalities and discrimination. Thus, the people hardest hit by the epidemic have frequently been already marginalized populations (e.g. gay men and IV drug users in the US; **migrant laborers**, sex workers and the poor worldwide). The epidemic's impact only exacerbates the discrimination and marginalization experienced.

Research throughout the 1990s indicates that a vaccine against HIV infection is a long way off. Even if a vaccine becomes available, it is doubtful whether it will be widely distributed in the developing world. Additionally, there remain significant questions of legal liability for any vaccine-related injury. *Prevention* strategies addressing behavior change are, therefore, absolutely imperative to stop the spread of the epidemic. In the US and worldwide, however, governments have been exceedingly slow to accept the importance of prevention to change risky sexual and drug-related behaviors. While a number of African countries, for example, have implemented government-supported condom marketing programs on radio and television, the US government and national mass media consistently reject any frank public discussion of condoms or sexual behavior.

Rock **Hudson**'s death from AIDS in 1985 brought the disease to the attention of the mainstream American public. Despite the ravages of the epidemic both in the US and globally, however, it was not until 1987 – more than six years after the disease was identified – that US President Ronald **Reagan** even uttered the word "AIDS" in public. Clearly, a disease that primarily affected stigmatized populations was not worthy of significant government attention – or funding. Earvin (Magic) Johnson's disclosure in 1992 that he was HIV-positive helped to increase popular awareness of the extent of the epidemic; political will, however, has yet to follow.

AIDS has been the galvanizing force behind a new generation of political and social activists. Building on the foundations of the women's movement and gay and lesbian activism, **ACT UP** (the AIDS Coalition to Unleash Power) used dramatic demonstrations and civil disobedience to call attention to the epidemic and force the government – and the medical and pharmaceutical establishments – to be more responsive to those with HIV and those at risk of infection. In the early 1990s, the US **Supreme Court** ruled that laws preventing discrimination based on disability include people with AIDS.

Despite political resistance, a lasting positive legacy of the epidemic may be increased societal openness in discussing sex, sexual decision-making, and **gay and lesbian life**. With the increased visibility of gay people, however, has come an increase in reported anti-gay **hate crimes**. The generation of young gay people **coming out** in the age of AIDS has the advantages that come with increased visibility and acceptance, coupled with a life-threatening illness and escalating rates of anti-gay violence.

Intense political and social debates continue around issues such as: mandatory testing for HIV; government reporting of names of HIV-infected individuals; contact tracing for partners of HIV-infected individuals; criminal punishment of HIV-positive individuals who engage in behavior that could transmit the virus; public and private insurance coverage for AIDS-related medications and illnesses; access to approved and experimental treatments; and the continued inadequacy of government funding for AIDS treatments and prevention. In the late 1990s, improved treatments became available which, for the first time, slowed the epidemic's death rate in the US. These treatments are, however, very expensive and often not within the reach of the poor in the US or worldwide.

Further reading

Burkett, E. (1995) *The Gravest Show On Earth: America in the Age of AIDS*, Boston: Houghton Mifflin Company.

Mann, J. and Tarantola, D. (eds) (1996) *AIDS in the World II: Global Dimensions, Social Roots, and Responses*, New York: Oxford University Press.

Shilts, R. (1985) *And the Band Played on*, New York: St. Martin's Press.

MARC L. OSTFIELD

Ailey, Alvin

b. 1931; d. 1989

Choreographer and dancer who brought a variety of **African American** expressions into American **dance**. With his **New York** City-based Alvin Ailey Dance Company, he created exciting works like "Revelations" (1960) and also became a symbol of multicultural American dance on tours abroad. Since his premature death, Judith Jamison has developed the company and his rich legacy.

GARY McDONOGH

AIM (American Indian Movement) *see* American Indians

air-conditioning

A machine to cool, dehumidify and circulate air was invented in 1902 by Willis Carrier of Brooklyn. Its impact expanded with compressors in the 1930s and window units in the 1950s. Yet while these technological advances slowly became global, their impact on American society remains crucial. After the Second World War, air conditioning facilitated life in humid regions like the **South** and **Southwest** for new immigrants and regularized production and services (the earliest uses of air-conditioning in the South were in industry). Beyond this nascent **Sunbelt**, year-round climate control also changed **architecture**, although risking the "sick building syndrome" in which diseases are re-circulated through an air system. It has also altered relations with the environment, especially as life has become encapsulated in air-conditioned homes (or rooms), cars and offices: **New Urbanism**, for example, re-establishes the porch and street interactions in opposition to this technological climate.

GARY McDONOGH

air force, US

Aerial military divisions that emerged under the aegis of the **army** in the early twentieth century and separated as a department in 1947. The army, navy and marines also have aviation divisions, responding to technological possibilities of air flight as well as changing warfare. The air force has become central to modern military action from **Vietnam** to the **Gulf War**; its pilots have a glamour among military personnel – President George **Bush** and Senator/Presidential candidate John McCain were both pilots, albeit for the **navy**. The Air Force academy, outside Colorado Springs, was founded in 1954. Personnel on active duty numbered 363,479 in 1998, 18 percent of whom were women. See **Pentagon**.

GARY McDONOGH

airlines *see* aviation, commercial

airports

While often the first experience of America for contemporary visitors and immigrants, airports provide ambivalent gateways to American **cities**. Sometimes monumental in **architecture**, like earlier railroad stations, they have struggled to keep pace with the ever-changing demands of technology and consumption, hence airports embody piecemeal constructions of old and new terminals. **Chicago**'s O'Hare, the nation's busiest airport, serves as many as 75 million passengers annually. Moreover, airports must provide industrial and commercial services and aviation maintenance, as well as passenger services within a competitive national market.

Aviation's rapid postwar development eclipsed models that had envisioned municipalities and neighborhoods with their own airports, combining speed with accessibility. **New York** City's state-of-the-art La Guardia Field, for example, opened in 1940, but reached near capacity in 1941. Hence, the city built Idlewild Airport (later JFK) on a site six times as large by 1947. Here, individual airline buildings by Eero Saarinen (TWA), Skidmore Owings Merrill and others created a congested "architectural zoo," with growing surface transportation problems. The port authority subsequently took over and expanded the 1929

Newark Airport, while smaller airports and heliports contributed to dense transportation webs.

Given corporate competition and complex flight linkages, for most people airports have become less sanctuaries of leisure travel and more calvaries of transfer and delay – notorious for travelers grounded by weather and strikes. Yet, terminals struggle with design identity, efficiency and service; hence, Helmut Jahn's recent United Terminal at O'Hare must function beyond its beauty. New airports have moved further out to function as inter-urban centers (**Dallas**-Fort Worth) or multi-service nodes, but complaints also faced **Denver**'s new airport, whose design echoes the Rockies, because of the expensive ride into town. Similarly, despite Saarinen's soaring Dulles terminal, outside **Washington** members of **Congress** continually expand the convenient National (Ronald **Reagan**) Airport.

Cities, airlines and consumers are all players in creating and changing these urban spaces. Connections, especially through hub airlines or markets opened by competing airlines, facilitate **tourism** and business; hence, governments compete with expensive concessions. Geography also plays a role – beside Chicago's centrality, **Los Angeles** International (LAX) and **San Francisco** International (SFI) have become Pacific gateways and New York offers multiple connections to Europe, as **Miami** does for Latin America. Intermediate hubs like Denver, **Atlanta**, **Minneapolis** and **Houston** have transformed location and corporate ties into power.

Despite their economic centrality, airports as public monuments are rarely seen from outside except at drop-off and pick-up points. Instead, scant expressions of local identity rely on interiors, constrained by needs of movement and security – a major concern exacerbated by terrorism since the 1980s. **Southwest** motifs may distinguish Albuquerque from the images of Independence Hall in **Philadelphia**, but many airports become "non-places," recalling the facelessness of **suburbs**. Interior services, such as stores, restaurants, etc., may emphasize the local, for example, sourdough in San Francisco, lobster in **Boston**, but **fast foods** also snare family travelers. In the 1990s, however, revisions of the **Pittsburgh** airport to include an active mall have sparked interest in the

airport as a destination that may transform the future.

Further reading

Kaplan, J. (1994) *The Airport*, New York: William Morrow.

GARY McDONOGH
CINDY WONG

air-traffic controllers' strike

Testing the limits of deregulation and a new presidency, 14,000 members of the Professional Air Traffic Controllers' Organization struck on August 3, 1981 for higher wages, despite provisos to federal employees forbidding such job actions. The ensuing traffic chaos intensified when President Ronald **Reagan** dramatically fired all air-traffic controllers – sending a definitive signal about **union** activism and management to the public and private sector. This also devastated those adapted to this highly stressful job; only in 1993 did President **Clinton** sign a bill allowing them to return to work.

GARY McDONOGH
CINDY WONG

Alaska

The 49th state, Alaska represents a vast, mythic territory for many Americans, embodying images of opportunities, of the last **frontier** and of the struggle of humans against **nature**. Since its purchase from Russia in 1867, it has been a place of extremes, epitomized in its initial label as "Seward's Folly" by those who found the wealth of **Cuba** much more appealing. In size, Alaska dwarfs all other states: its 615,230 square mile area surpasses the combined acreage of Washington, Oregon, **California**, Idaho, Nevada and Utah. Thirty-one thousand miles of coastal inlets dwarf the entire Eastern seaboard. Yet its population remains tiny – 615,900 – and only 160,000 acres have been cleared for development. Alaska's largest city, Anchorage, despite amassing nearly half of that population (257,780), barely tops the size of small **cities** in the lower 48. Nonetheless, the riches of the state, from nineteenth-century gold rushes to its fisheries to oil fields since the 1960s, also conjure visions of wealth and opportunity despite a high cost of living produced by sheer size and transportation costs.

Images of vast plains of snow, bays of glaciers and the nation's highest mountain also evoke a vivid and unyielding landscape torn by volcanoes and earthquakes (more than 1,000 a year above 3.5 on the Richter scale). Yet Alaska also encompasses ecological zones as distinct as its marshy interior, southern rainforests and arctic tundra.

Alaska's Aleutian islands constituted the original land bridge by which the earliest inhabitants crossed from Asia to North America. Various indigenous populations adapted thereafter to its climate and geography – most notably the Eskimos (**Inuit**) who live in northern Alaska and **Canada**. The gentler southern coasts, interior and lower panhandle were also home to Athabaskan tribes like the Tlingit and Haida, linked to populations of British Columbia and the Pacific Northwest. Aleuts still live in the southern islands that bear their name, which have also seen strong military development.

The panhandle area became the first point of contact between Native Americans and Europeans with Russian colonization in 1714; monuments of the Russian capital of Sitka still illustrate this heritage of 150 years of domination. The panhandle remained the center of the state's population into the twentieth century, as well as the site of the current capital, Juneau.

The potential of the northern reaches of the state, however, were explored by fishermen, trappers and miners, and especially by those lured to the state by gold strikes from 1848 onward. These spurred the development of Anchorage in the late nineteenth century, although the city really only took shape as a midpoint on the railroad from the ice-free port of Seward to the interior **mining** capital of Fairbanks, 200 miles south of the Arctic circle. By 1920 Anchorage still had only 1,865 people, growing significantly only after military and economic investment during and after the Second World War.

The opportunities of Alaska, incorporated as a US territory in 1912, also delayed its statehood by those who feared **taxes** or limitations on fisheries and free enterprise. Bills to admit the state were successfully thwarted for generations before responsibilities of citizens to pay for local government were clarified in the 1950s and the state admitted in 1959. This also opened the state to increasing private land ownership after nearly a century of domination by the US government; issues of public and private land, as well as Native American claims, have continued to shape development. Alaskan politicians tended to be **Republican** and often have defended development.

Alaskan state development thereafter was shaped by **oil and gas**, which now account for 85 percent of tax revenues, including a roughly $1,000 dividend returned to citizens each year under the Alaska Permanent Fund (established 1980). While petroleum has been extracted from various points, most now comes from fields on the North Slope, beginning with Prudhoe Bay in 1968, which had produced 9 billion barrels by 1996 with an estimated reserve of 3.1 billion in addition to natural gas resources. These reserves on the Arctic sea were connected to US markets by the trans-Alaska Pipeline, 800 miles in length, constructed by a consortium of oil companies between 1974 and 1977. The oil industry has also spurred concerns for **environmental protection** both in the pipelines' intrusion into wilderness and horrific spills like the Exxon Valdez disaster.

These spills also directly influence Alaska's second-largest industry, **tourism**. Over 1 million visit annually for cruises or explorations of the state's extensive **park** system and other resources. Prime attractions include Glacier Bay National Park, Katmai National Park and Denali National Park, as well as the 1,100 mile dog sled race on the Iditarod Trail, run since 1973. Tourism also stimulates a growing service and construction sector alongside traditional industries like **fishing** (Alaska supplies more than half the US catch) and **forestry**.

Tourists, moreover, reaffirm the image of Alaska reinforced by **television** (*Northern Exposure*'s 1990–5 portrayal of the cockeyed town of Cecily, CBS) or movies from Chaplin's *Gold Rush* (1925) to *The Edge* (1997) and *Limbo* (1999). These, like literary memoirs including Joe McGinnis' *Going to Extremes*

(1980) and Larry Kaniut's *Danger Stalks the Land* (1999) continually stress the agonistic elements of the **frontier** state, eclipsing the everyday struggles and creations of a special place and culture within America.

Further reading

Falk, M. (compiler) (1995) *Alaska*, Oxford, England: Clio.

(1996) *The Alaska Almanac*, Anchorage: Alaska Northwest.

Hunt, W. (1976) *Alaska: A Bicentennial History*, New York: W.W. Norton.

GARY McDONOGH

Albee, Edward

b. 1928

Powerful Pulitzer-Prize winning American playwright, known for such searing and revealing works as *Who's Afraid of Virginia Woolf?* (1962, movie 1966). While his works have been shaped by experimentation with absurdist visions and new theatrical techniques, he also grapples with American social issues and has produced notable explorations of women's reflections on American culture (Grandma in *American Dream*, 1960, or *Three Tall Women*, 1991). Other well-known works include *The Zoo Story* (1959), *The Death of Bessie Smith* (1960) and *Tiny Alice* (1964).

GARY McDONOGH
CINDY WONG

Albright, Madeleine Korbel

b. 1937

Appointed **Secretary of State** in 1997 under President **Clinton**, Albright was the first female to occupy the post and the highest-ranking woman ever to serve in the federal government. Before becoming Secretary of State, she was the US representative to the **United Nations** for four years. In both positions, Albright established a unique style. Blending a hawkish reliance on the threat of military force with personal warmth, she helped the US forge diplomatic inroads with longstanding enemies. Her political rise blazed a trail for women in the male-dominated realm of international affairs.

SARAH SMITH

alcohol

Rum, beer, whiskey and wine have flowed through American history from colonial trade and encounters with Native Americans to contemporary issues as diverse as health, criminality and connoisseurship. Cocktail parties, champagne dinners, smoky **bars** and the combination of sports, **television** and beer are all familiar contemporary American images in **Hollywood** or everyday conversation. Uses, meanings and marketing of these various forms of alcohol, moreover, have been strongly associated with the social construction of **gender** (especially **masculinity**), **class**, **race**, ethnicity, morality and even regional identity or urbanity. Yet, despite the complexities of "The Alcoholic Republic," the US has also witnessed strong sentiments for the control of alcohol consumption, based on religious and moral arguments. These sentiments have created bans at the local level and also led to the Constitution's 18th Amendment (1919) – Prohibition – which made the ban national (and also reified anti-German sentiment in the aftermath of the First World War). Controls on drinking for those under twenty-one, **taxes** on alcohol and limits on alcohol sales still remain features of national interests in American spirits.

The end of Prohibition with the 11th Amendment (1933) proved a watershed in American attitudes towards alcohol, if only in the collapse of any consensus or overall control. In fact, taxes on newly legalized spirits provided needed revenues in the Depression, while new jobs and production rapidly re-established liquor as part of American life, eclipsing ongoing temperance campaigns. Nonetheless, roughly 30 percent of Americans choose not to drink.

Who drinks what, where and to what extent has also varied throughout American history. Rum gained early prominence in the triangle trade, linking the colonies with the Caribbean and African slavery. Whiskeys of various sorts accompanied westward expansion, while Bourbon (from Kentucky) and the mint julep became emblematic of the **South**. Imported wines, liquors and liqueurs have been marketed as badges of sophistication, while most beers became "workingman's drinks" via local production and taverns.

While many local beer producers have disappeared, names of larger conglomerates – Anheuser-Busch, Coors, Pabst, Schlitz – memorialize the impact of Central European producers (even if American beer often seems a pale derivative of more robust, flavorful European varieties). Despite new premium brands and micro-breweries, beer faded as the country's most popular drink in the twentieth century in favor of distilled spirits.

Although the Founding Fathers brought in casks of Madeira and American grape stocks, which saved European production after phylloxera devastated vineyards in Europe, wine generally has been a secondary product in the US, associated with immigrants and Mediterranean climates like **California**. Other states, apart from the West Coast centers, now produce quality wines based on American grapes (and more idiosyncratic varietals based on local produce like oranges). American wine production and consumption have soared in the early twenty-first century, moving from ethnic niches to cosmopolitan middle-class tables, although the US still ranks in the second tier of wine consumption globally.

Historically, **Irish** and British Americans, **Italian Americans** and Latino/Caribbean Americans have been identified as heavy consumers of alcohol, although ethnic associations have decreased over time (stereotypes continue, however). **Religion**, too, plays a factor since many fundamentalist Protestant groups (as well as **Mormons**) ban alcohol, while Catholics and **Jews** prove more tolerant. This also extends to ceremonies. During Prohibition, wine for the Catholic Eucharist was a special category; in Protestant communions, however, one may find grape juice substituted for wine.

Alcohol is viewed as a special danger for vulnerable, innocent youth, leading to legal penalties for providing liquor to them. Nonetheless, the temptations of drinking are part of teenage culture at schools and in social life. Various sweeter, fruitier and lighter combinations – wine coolers, flavored wines, blush wines – even cater to younger drinkers (or appeal to perceptions of a feminine market).

Imagery and marketing complicate any analysis of consumption or establishment of a clear culture of consumption. **African American** neighborhood organizers, for example, complain of billboards and advertisements targeting young blacks with the glamour of cigarettes and specialized niche brands of malt liquor. Liquor stores, especially if owned by immigrant entrepreneurs, have become flashpoints of urban confrontation. Native Americans, too, have faced long and eviscerating struggles with alcoholism and related inherited conditions (Fetal Alcohol Syndrome) that mark the continuing impact of alcohol as a weapon settlers used to undermine the tribes. In these cases, and others across **class** and **gender** lines, while drinking itself may not be seen as a problem – and, indeed, may be seen as a part of conviviality and sophistication – loss of control is treated as a shameful condition. This affirms a general moral identification of alcohol with evil.

Media, sermons and other discourses may translate this judgment into images of adolescents open to risky sexual behavior, decaying winos (generally shown as male), abusive fathers or quiet, despairing housewives drinking behind closed doors. These negative portraits are the stuff of Hollywood depictions of excessive use from, for example, the *Lost Weekend* (1945) or *Days of Wine and Roses* (1962) to *Barfly* (1987) and *Leaving Las Vegas* (1995). Nonetheless, Hollywood has shown its own American schizophrenia as these searing portraits meet other images of sophistication or the sociability of bars and celebration. **Television**, where **advertising** is limited to beer and wine, has worked with the government to censor messages about alcohol and drugs (especially in teen-directed shows). Yet, as in cigarette propaganda, condemnation is undercut by talking frogs (Budweiser), sparkling images of wine and chit-chat, and off-screen intertexts of stars and parties. **Celebrities** checking into the Betty Ford clinic to "dry out" compete with images of good times, reinforcing America's conflicting attitudes.

Alcoholism in the United States is associated not only with health risks, but also with abusive behaviors and accidents, especially when alcohol and **automobiles** mix. This has spawned home-grown approaches to combating alcohol, like the **self-help** program of **Alcoholics Anonymous**. Mothers Against Drunk Driving (MADD) and other grassroots groups, meanwhile, have fought for more severe punishment of drunk drivers. These campaigns have become complicated by both the general acceptance of the presence of alcohol and debates over alcoholism as a disease or disability.

Outsiders in the US may be bewildered by the variety of controls on beverage sales. Grocery stores in **Florida** and California sell wine and beer, but in Pennsylvania one must go to separate state-licensed distributors. Other states provide patchworks of "wet" and "dry" counties, where the nearest distributor may be miles away. Many liquor stores, moreover, are closed on Sunday, and some states control alcohol sales in times that might be associated with church-going, late at night or on election days. Licenses for the sale of alcohol in public establishments also vary; restaurants without licenses may allow a BYOB ("bring your own bottle") accompaniment. In all, these rules embody the uneasy attitudes of morality, respectability, health and taste that American society embraces when the cork is pulled.

Further reading

Barr, A. (1999) *Drink: A Social History of America*, New York: Carroll & Graf.

Lender, M. and Martin, J.K. (1987) *Drinking in America*, New York: The Free Press.

Wilsnack, R. and S. (1997) *Gender and Alcohol*, New Brunswick, NJ: Rutgers Center of Alcohol Studies.

GARY McDONOGH
ROBERT GREGG
CINDY WONG

Alcoholics Anonymous

Self-help group to combat alcohol addiction through a twelve-step program to quit and stay dry. Founded by Bill Wilson and Doctor Bob Smith in 1935, it has become a worldwide fellowship and model for other programs.

See also: addiction; alcohol; self-help

GARY McDONOGH

Algiers Motel incident

An incident of police brutality occurring during the **Detroit, MI**, **race riots** of 1967, when a report of sniping led the Detroit **police** to invade the Algiers Motel. During interrogation of the occupants, ten **African American** men and two white women, three men were shot and killed, while many of the others were badly beaten. The riots themselves had been caused by reports of racially motivated police brutality during the raid on an after-hours club – motivation confirmed in the Algiers Motel incident and in the account of it published by John Hersey in 1968.

ROBERT GREGG

Ali, Muhammad

b. 1942

Charismatic first three-time heavyweight **boxing** champion who transcended sport as an icon of the **Black Power** and anti-**Vietnam War** movements. Born Cassius Marcellus Clay, Muhammad Ali was a light heavyweight gold medallist at the 1960 **Olympic Games**. A professional sensation for his speed with words as well as fists, his claims to be "the prettiest" and "the Greatest" were precursors to "Black is Beautiful." He won the championship in 1964, but was reviled for joining the **Nation of Islam**, friendship with **Malcolm X** and for changing his name. In 1967, boxing organizations stripped his title for refusing induction into the army because of religious beliefs. Unable to box again until 1970, Ali spoke out publicly against the war and on racial issues. His conviction for draft evasion was overturned by the **Supreme Court** in 1971, public opinion having swung against the war. Ali then became very popular, even among non-boxing fans, and cemented his fame in three epic matches with Joe Frazier: the first, in 1970, pitted two undefeated champions. Ali lost, won a rematch, regained the title by upsetting George Foreman in Zaire in 1974, and beat Frazier again in "'The Thrilla' in Manila'' in 1975.

Though afflicted with Parkinson's Syndrome, Ali lit the Olympic torch in 1996, and acts as a goodwill ambassador for orthodox **Islam**.

FRAZER WARD

Allen, Woody

b. 1935

Highly original American film-maker, born Allen Stewart Konigsberg in Brooklyn. Beginning as a stand-up comedian, he ultimately earned a world-wide reputation as an incredibly prolific and innovative writer, **director** and actor. He became famous for his hilarious portrayal of neurotic, intellectual Jewish New Yorkers (e.g. *Annie Hall*), but has experimented with many different film genres, including serious drama and offbeat musicals. In the summer of 1992, he gained additional public notoriety for his romantic relationship with Soon-Yi Previn, adopted daughter of his long-term romantic partner Mia Farrow.

See also: actors

NICOLE MARIE KEATING

alternative medicine

More commonly referred to as complementary medicine (also as additional medicine, integrative medicine, and natural health), this includes myriad medical practices and perceptions that have expert systems knowledge and technique and often require periods of training, whether formal or informal. The United States National Institute of Health defines alternative medicine "as those treatments and healthcare practices not taught widely in medical schools, not generally used in hospitals, and not usually reimbursed by medical insurance companies." In one way or another, alternative medicine is defined in opposition to what is referred to as the "dominant" system in the United States – biomedicine. Nonetheless, recent surveys in the United States show that Americans appear to be favoring "alternative" medicines in greater proportion to "biomedical" practitioners and healthcare.

Common complementary health choices include osteopathy, chiropractic, acupuncture, ayurveda, bio-feedback, homeopathy, naturopathy and traditional Chinese medicine. Many people also would see several massage techniques (body work, manual healing methods), herbal medicines, aromatherapy, spiritual healing, bio-electromagnetic application, **diet**/nutrition/lifestyle changes, various mind/ **body** interventions and perhaps all varieties of **folk medicine** as alternative medicines. The distinguishing feature of alternative medicine is a holistic conceptual framework that sees all aspects of the body (anatomy, nervous system, vascular systems, musculature, and so forth) as an integrated system or structure, itself interrelated with the body's physical, social and cultural environments, or in some cases with spiritual aspects of a person and of health.

Alternative health approaches are said to consider the "whole person," whereas biomedicine is a medical approach that seeks specific etiologies for specific diseases. Similarly, alternative health-care approaches are also thought to place an equal importance on the illness experience as well as the physical pathology of the disease. Biomedicine is said to be concerned only with abnormalities in the structure and function of body organs and systems, while alternative medicines include the lived experience of physical and physiological abnormalities when diagnosing disease and considering therapeutic interventions.

The coexistence of alternative healthcare with biomedicine illustrates a dynamic "medical pluralism" in the United States. This medical pluralism represents a desire on the part of the American public for approaches to healthcare other than biomedicine, efforts towards the professionalization of several complementary medicines, and the historical impact of the complex relations of healthcare provisions with social structure (**class**, **gender**, **race**). In spite of the dominance of biomedicine, medical pluralism is the norm, historically anchored in a milieu of healthcare fads, technological developments, social movements and changing opinion regarding the efficacy of biomedicine. The revitalization of **midwifery** and home births in recent decades is an example of the coming together of these various elements that inform a changing desire for alternative medicines. The professionalization of alternative medicines indexes a medical system in the United States organized within a capitalist economy and offered to the American public as "consumer medicine." With professionalization, alternative medicines become insurance options.

Social class, ethnic groups and the greater numbers of migrants and immigrant groups, and gender issues related to health and healthcare are all important factors in a dynamic medical pluralism in the United States. Finally, as with folk medicine, discontentment with modern life, dominated by technological advances, fragmented by alienation and the dissolution of community life, has encouraged some to seek alternative medicines because they are believed to be natural therapies that have descended from primordial traditions and practices.

Further reading

Baer, H. (1995) "Medical Pluralism in the United States: A Review," *Medical Anthropology Quarterly* 9(4): 493–502.

Frohock, F. (1992) *Healing Powers*, Chicago: University of Chicago.

Last, M. (1996) "The Professionalization of Indigenous Healers," C. Sargent and T. Johnson (eds) *Medical Anthropology*, Westport: Praeger, pp. 374–95.

National Institute of Health Office of Alternative Medicine (1994) *Alternative Medicine: Expanding Medical Horizons*, Pittsburgh: Government Printing Office.

STEVE FERZACCA

Altman, Robert

b. 1923

Brilliant, sarcastic **director** whose films have etched an acid vision of modern America at **war** (*M*A*S*H*, 1970), on crime sprees (*Thieves Like Us*, 1973), in **Sunbelt** aspirations (*Brewster McCloud*, 1971) or in a quest for fitness (*Health*, 1979). These films alternated with complicated lyrical works and smaller films linked closely to **theater**; Altman also faced some big-budget problems. After a lengthy hiatus, Altman's caustic wit reemerged with *The Player* (1992), satirizing **Hollywood** itself.

CINDY WONG

Alzheimer's disease

A degenerative brain disease resulting in memory loss, this disease affects approximately 4 million Americans. Symptoms include confusion, personality and behavior change, and impaired judgment. The disease usually begins by influencing short-term memory before affecting other sections of the brain. Although the disease can affect people in their thirties, most individuals diagnosed with the disease are over sixty-five years old according to the Alzheimer's Association, making this a particular concern – and image – of the elderly. There is no cure, although donepezil and tacrine are used to relieve some symptoms.

Further reading

The Alzheimer's Association: http://www.alz.org

KATE M. KENSKI

American (census category)

Census category first used in 1980 when census takers began to inquire about the ancestry of the US population. In previous years, questionnaires had asked merely for the respondent's birthplace. When **ethnicity** was asked for, however, the multicultural nature of the country and the intermarriage that had occurred between different ethnic groups over the years made it difficult for some to report their ancestry. Someone who was equally Scottish, German, Italian and Irish was inclined just to answer "American," explaining why this became the fastest growing "ethnic" group in the United States. The category "American" also fitted in with the prevailing white **backlash** against non-white Americans, since it clearly "whitened" the person designating him/herself in this way. Someone who had one-quarter of the same heritage noted above replaced by African or Chinese descent could be designated **African American** or **Asian American** respectively, although they might contest this classification.

ROBERT GREGG

American Association of Retired Persons (AARP)

Dr Ethel Andrus founded AARP in 1958. Now the nation's largest and oldest organization of older Americans, its membership is over 33 million. A non-profit, non-partisan organization, AARP is governed by an elected, twenty-one member volunteer Board of Directors. Its extensive volunteer network makes it one of America's most effective lobbying groups, both nationally and locally. AARP also co-chairs the Leadership Council of Aging Organizations, a coalition of non-profit organizations that represents the public-policy interests of older Americans. AARP members receive a variety of discounts, services and products, ranging from health insurance to prescription drugs.

See also: old age; retirement; Social Security

COURTNEY BENNETT

American Broadcasting Company (ABC network) *see* networks, television

American Civil Liberties Union (ACLU)

Headquartered in **New York**, the ACLU is the largest public-interest legal organization in the United States, with over 60 staff attorneys, 2,000 volunteer lawyers and 275,000 members. The ACLU was founded by Roger Baldwin in 1920 in the wake of America's Red Scare, when the **Supreme Court** upheld the criminal convictions of prominent American leftists who expressed unpopular political views. It is dedicated to the preservation of individual rights through litigation,

legislation and public education, and also fought the mistreatment of women, **gays and lesbians**, racial minorities, political dissidents and prisoners. The ACLU has opposed the death penalty, loyalty oaths for government employees, state restrictions on free expression and **abortion**, and government entanglement with **religion**. Despite its defense of extreme right groups as well, "card-carrying members of the ACLU" have become standard targets for conservative attacks.

BRIAN LEVIN

American dream *see* American images abroad; assimilation; immigration

American Express *see* credit and credit cards

American Film Institute

Non-profit foundation for film established in **Washington, DC** in 1967 under the aegis of President Lyndon **Johnson**'s support of the National Endowment for the Arts. Its mission is to preserve and advance film through restoration, cataloguing and training future film-makers (primarily at its **Los Angeles** campus). It offers achievement awards, lectures and honorary degrees, publishes the journal *American Film* and operates a showcase theater at **Disneyworld**. Despite its success at restoring and cataloguing historical films and raising consciousness about the loss of American film heritage, its goals and accomplishments sometimes have been clouded by controversy.

CINDY WONG

American images abroad

"For the European, even today, America represents something akin to exile, a phantasy of emigration, and therefore a form of interiorization of his or her own culture," wrote Jean Baudrillard in *America* (1988: 78). Americans abroad in the early twenty-first century face profoundly dichotomized, contradictory images in which they participate and through which they are interpreted as myths, nation and individual actors. One image is the *Ugly American* (from Eugene Burdick and William Lederer's influential 1958 novel), aggressive and destructive, whether through ignorance, malevolence, intervention or neglect. A second image is that of America and Americans as bearers of liberty, technology, progress and prosperity as broadcast over international airwaves by Voice of America. Most Americans prefer the latter, which underpins the rhetoric of business, missionaries, development aid, **mass media** and even **tourism**. While propagandistic, this ideology often imbues individual actors, including expatriate rebels, and ironically reaffirms an image of close-mindedness abroad. The first image is also polemic – thrown against the US by enemies, allies/competitors and leftist critics at home. While both images are transmitted through multiple media – **Hollywood**, news, music videos, **world fairs** – at home and abroad, both are also grounded in actions, policies and events intensified by American economic, political and military expansion in the early twenty-first century.

These images, of course, take shape in concrete local contexts. Arkush and Lee's *Land of Ghosts* splendidly analyzes and anthologizes changing Chinese readings of America since the nineteenth century. Unlike many of the European elite, for example, who characterized America as young and uncouth (albeit energetic and rich), Chinese leaders saw America as an example of modernity and its discontents. Chinese immigrants – like generations from every country on earth – dealt with the promise and disillusion of an American dream rent by **class** and racial discrimination. America has been read as a friend to democratic reformers and the nationalist regime it propped up after 1949, and bitter enemy to the communist regime it sought to isolate on the mainland. Renewed ties of trade and **immigration** with this mainland have produced deeply ambivalent relations in the 1980s and 1990s, including the polemic attacks of the *China that Can Say No*, as well as the Goddess of Liberty in Tienanmen Square. Moreover, friends and enemies have expressed perplexity at differences in **family**, **gender**, absence of hierarchy and **food**.

The postwar French, by contrast, soon found that liberating allies could be overbearing friends. The success of American mass culture (abetted by the Marshall plan) has pitted those who protect the purity of French language, culture, markets and difference against those who adopt **rock**, Coca-Cola, **film noir**, blue jeans and **Brando**. Meanwhile, in third-world nations, the image of a rich nation as a goal for emigration or emulation continually crashes against military intervention or exploitation in which American business and policy participate.

Commentators worldwide have underscored the contradictions between American public ideals and the realities of racism, poverty, crime, **guns**, social breakdown and unbalanced consumption that accompany world power. As racial tensions have boiled over in Europe since the 1980s, for example, more than one national analyst has exclaimed "This is not America!"

In these complex realms of imagery, one may try to distinguish the United States as a myth and a political and cultural agent from its citizens. The wealth and mass consumption of international travel and the globalization of business has opened an American presence beyond the wealthy **expatriate**, dedicated missionary and eccentric exile. Scholars, students, the military, tourists, artists, minorities, revolutionaries, **Peace Corps** workers, medical workers and evangelists can provide more varied experiences and attitudes to nuance stereotypes. Moreover, **immigration** reforms since the 1960s have created increasing transnational families and citizens who balance American and other identities. Nevertheless, many people *know* America through media before they meet a living American.

Yet, public discourses of individual freedom, democracy, hegemonic Western values and independence, coupled with economic and political power, have become global policies. Part of the tragedies of Hungary, **Vietnam**, Cuba, **Somalia**, **Iran** and Rwanda is not only American action (or inaction), but American justification in the name of "**freedom**," "democracy" and American interests. American mass media may explore this painful paradox, especially with regard to Vietnam, but it should be balanced with the recurrent scenario of ***Star Trek***, in which "galactic" rules of non-intervention invariably are broken to end racism, promote democracy, impose peace or facilitate trade. While a student, tourist or diplomat abroad may insist America "is not like that," actions and interpretations underscore the contradictions at the center of the nation's dilemmas in the twenty-first century.

Further reading

Baudrillard, J. (1988) *America*, New York: Verso.

Fischer, F. (1998) *Making Them Like Us*, Washington, DC: Smithsonian.

Kuisel, R. (1993) *Seducing the French*, Berkeley: University of California.

GARY McDONOGH
CINDY WONG

American Indian reservations

American Indian reservations comprise territories within the United States' borders that serve as the homelands for American Indian tribes. According to the 1990 United States census, approximately one-quarter of the 1,959,000 American Indians currently live on the 314 federally recognized reservations. American Indian reservations are concentrated in the western part of the United States, although there are reservations, containing nearly 44 million acres, in all parts of the country. They incorporate not only vast cultural differences, but distinctive experiences of **history** and context, ranging from the elaborate casinos of Connecticut to the problems of unemployment (up to 70 percent), substandard housing, **alcohol** and poverty plaguing reservations like Pine Ridge, South Dakota, which President **Clinton** highlighted in his 1999 visit.

The relationship between American Indian reservations and the United States federal government was shaped by an 1831 United States **Supreme Court** decision, which agreed with the Cherokee Indian nation that the state of Georgia had no jurisdiction over it since American Indian tribes were "domestic dependent nations." This definition has formed the basis for the current legal relationship between American Indian tribes and the federal government, and, in essence, a definition of American Indian tribes.

Cherokee Nation v. *Georgia* led to the creation of the legal concept of limited sovereignty. According to this concept, tribes are nations with rights to internal self-government on federally recognized reservations. Yet sovereignty has also been limited. For example, the United States adopted a policy of Indian Removal in the 1830s, moving American Indian tribes to distant areas until they could be assimilated into mainstream society. Eventually this policy placed all federally recognized Indian tribes on reservations.

While theoretically American Indian tribes are totally independent from any other government within the reservation boundaries, federal Indian policy also has emphasized **assimilation** and trusteeship over Indian interests and rights of later immigrants who have encroached on Indian lands by lease or illegal appropriation. The government has even intervened to divert growing wealth from cattle or **oil** to reservations (South Dakota, Oklahoma). An emphasis on the privatization of Indian lands and the disposal of "surplus," for example, reduced tribal lands from 119,373,930 acres in 1887 to 40,236,442 acres in 1911. Current acreage has grown since a 1933 low of 29,431,685 acres.

Reservation locations were determined in a number of ways. Some tribes, like the Cherokees of Georgia, were forcibly moved to Indian Territory, which eventually became the state of Oklahoma. A few tribes, like the Menominee of Wisconsin, were able to escape removal, gaining a reservation on marginal land in their original territory. Indians like the **Florida** Seminoles or **Southwestern** Navaho and Pueblo tribes also fought long to hold and regain their lands. Settlement over land claims has been a major political issue in the 1980s and 1990s in Maine, the **Midwest**, the Southwest and the **West**.

Tribal self-government first gained national attention during the war of 1812 when many United States citizens feared American Indian tribes might conspire with foreign enemies to threaten national security. Hence, under the doctrine of limited sovereignty, no tribe may establish independent relationships with foreign governments. Eventually the doctrine of limited sovereignty was refined to mean that although state and local laws do not apply on reservations, federal laws can be enforced.

Foreign-policy issues also led to a debate about the citizenship status of individual American Indians. An American Indian could become a US citizen only by renouncing his tribal citizenship. During the First World War, many volunteered even though, as non-citizens, they were not subject to the draft. After the war, a political movement arose to grant US citizenship to American Indians who served in the war. Some tribes opposed the idea of US citizenship for individuals, viewing this as an attempt to destroy the right of tribal self-governance. The American Indian Citizenship Act of 1924, a compromise bill, granted dual citizenship to American Indians, who became full citizens of the United States and the states where they resided while remaining citizens of their respective tribes.

The last component of the Supreme Court's definition of American Indian tribes was domestic. This means that the reservations are the direct responsibility of the United States federal government and are held in trust for tribes. This ensures that neither an individual tribal member nor tribal governments can endanger the tribe's land base by disposing of it. Even through their elected legislatures, tribes may not sell or lease reservation land without the federal government's permission. This regulatory authority is invested in the Bureau of Indian Affairs (BIA), a division of the Department of the Interior. However, the BIA has also been accused of mishandling Indian funds, while development has often led to disputes about ownership and rights in recreational lands and even subdivision projects which had been granted to tribes in early treaties. This has kindled animosity between reservations and their neighbors.

Gambling has also become an arena of competition and conflict. In the 1970s, gambling was regulated only at the state level. Because state laws do not apply on reservations, some tribes opened high-stakes bingo parlors and casinos on reservation land. Some states objected, arguing that the right to operate gambling establishments had become a privilege that some, but not all, of their citizens enjoyed. The states were also

concerned that gambling affected the entire state without access to accrued revenues. In response, **Congress** passed the Indian Gaming Regulatory Act of 1988 in an attempt to re-establish the balance between the needs of the state and those of the tribe. This law grants individual states some control over gambling on reservations, but prohibits state control over low-stakes traditional gambling between tribal members. This has also created divisions between those reservations able to make use of their metropolitan settings and those for whom underdevelopment has made reservations prisons, as depicted in *Thunderheart* (1992) and the documentary *Incident at Oglala* (1992).

Further reading

Anderson, T. (1995) *Sovereign Nations or Reservations?*, San Francisco: Pacific Research Institute for Public Policy.
Deloria, V. and Lytle, C. (1984) *The Nations Within*, New York: Pantheon.

SARAH SHILLINGER

American Indians

The term "American Indian" refers to the indigenous people of North America. Neither the term nor the concept existed before Columbus landed in the Americas. Before European contact, indigenous people living in the Americas thought of themselves not as members of one large group, but rather as members of separate and distinct political units. Both a member of the Iroquois League (in New York State) and a member of the Passamaguady (a **New England** group) would have been amused by the idea that they had a common culture. Their societies differed as much as German does from Italian society. European settlers coined this collective term because they did not recognize or understand the differences among the indigenous groups. As first the colonies – and later the United States – grew, the tendency to see American Indian groups as homogenous and interchangeable intensified.

The US government often constructed American Indian policy without regard for the distinctive needs of a specific American Indian group's history or culture. For example, in the middle to the late nineteenth century, federal policy was designed to force American Indians onto reservations. Although the policy was universally applied, each American Indian group responded differently to reservation life. The reservation experience was more disruptive to the nomadic Lakota (Sioux) groups of the Great Plains than it was to the sedentary Pueblos of the **Southwest**.

Despite the official lack of recognition of tribal distinctiveness, these differences and identities have survived among the nearly 2 million American Indians (1,959,000 according to the 1990 US census). Even today when American Indians from different reservations meet, the first question asked is usually: "What tribe are you from?" The answer is a specific tribe, and may include the more specific information of clan affiliation. Clans, the basic unit of American Indian tribes, are large interrelated familial and communal groups. This familial structure contrasts with the nuclear-family structure of mainstream American society. Some clans are patrilineal with membership descending through the father, while others are matrilineal with membership descending through the mother. Clan membership is determined at birth and only rarely altered through **adoption**. In traditional American Indian society a person's primary allegiance is to the clan, and this forms the basis of a communal, clan-based identity. Because traditional American Indians consider **marriage** within clans to be incest, one parent does not share clan members with his or her biological children. This system tends to strengthen extended patrilineal or matrilineal bonds, while weakening those of the nuclear **family**.

Most American Indians still retain tribal and clan identities today. The communal nature of this identity has often been in conflict with mainstream society and governmental policy. Official attempts to undermine the communal clan identity began in colonial New England with the establishment of Praying Towns. Missionaries designed and oversaw these villages where American Indians could live away from their tribes in a European family structure and ultimately assimilate into European culture. The missionaries believed that in order to convert American Indians to Christianity it was first necessary for them to abandon their clan

identities to develop an individual relationship with God.

Official attempts to weaken the communal nature of American Indian identity have continued into the twenty-first century. The goal of the federal government's policy of relocation in the 1950s was the destruction of the communal identity and the clan system. American Indian nuclear families were moved from reservations to major **cities** in order to assimilate them into mainstream society. To discourage them from returning to their reservations, the nuclear families were moved as far as possible from their tribes. Despite these precautions about one-third of relocated families returned to their reservations within a year.

Even among the two-thirds of American Indians who stayed in the cities, the urban experience did not eliminate the communal identity. The social conditions that American Indians faced in these cities reinforced their communal identity. Many of these urban immigrants found themselves unemployed or in low-paying jobs because their reservation-based skills were often useless in the urban job market. Their lack of marketable skills plus the racism they experienced forced them to congregate in crowded, poor **neighborhoods**. American Indian communities developed in relocation cities like **Chicago, IL** and **Minneapolis, MN**, where these neighborhoods became known as "Red Ghettos."

The American Indian Movement (AIM) was founded in one such neighborhood in Minneapolis. AIM taught that the tribes had survived because they were communal in nature. AIM's revitalization movement of the 1960s and 1970s created a renewed sense of pride in tribal culture. The current demand by many American Indian tribes for increased sovereignty has its roots in the revitalization movement fostered by AIM.

Demand for sovereignty manifests itself in different ways among different tribes. For example, many tribes are currently suing states for acknowledgement of off-reservation **hunting** and **fishing** rights. Many states held tribal members to local hunting and fishing laws despite treaties guaranteeing these rights. American Indian tribes in the state of Washington were the first tribes to challenge the state's jurisdiction over American Indian hunting and fishing. In 1974 federal District Court Judge

George Boldt ruled that tribes in Washington had retained the right to hunt, fish and gather on the lands they had previously owned. The crux of the fishing rights controversy was communal identity versus individual rights. The tribes argued that the fishing rights, guaranteed in the treaties, belonged communally to the tribe. These rights could not be sold, abrogated or exercised by individual tribal members, but only by the tribes as a whole. The Washington experience inspired other tribes to challenge state authority over them. The Ojibwa of Wisconsin have also insisted that off-reservation hunting and fishing rights are collectively held. Many tribes believe that the collective exercise of treaty rights and the maintenance of a communal identity are essential to their continued survival.

Further reading

Cohen, F.G. (1986) *Treaties on Trial*, Seattle: University of Washington Press.

Harmon, A. (1998) *Indians in the Making*, Berkeley: University of California Press.

Owens, L. (1994) *Other Destinies: Understanding the American Indian Novel*, Norman, OK: University of Oklahoma Press.

SARAH SHILLINGER

American League *see* baseball

American Medical Association

Its origins in nineteenth-century attempts to professionalize the practice of American medicine and bring it under the control of a single corporate organization, the American Medical Association became the dominant force shaping medical practice in the United States following the Second World War. During the 1980s and 1990s, however, as **lawyers** have chipped away at doctors' prestige, seeking redress for patients in cases of alleged malpractice, and as insurance companies increasingly pushed physicians to cut costs, the AMA has had to fight to maintain its dominant position.

Throughout its existence, the AMA has remained the main bastion of opposition to what it describes as "socialized medicine" – anything that might resemble a national health system. Frequently the AMA was able to stifle debate on this issue by drawing on widespread disdain for anything that might be associated with America's **Cold War** adversary, the Soviet Union. Post-Second World War prosperity has enabled many in the burgeoning **middle class** to afford private insurance. Many prefer a medically advanced, but unequal system to one that provides universal access, but which may involve more inferior medicine.

When the federal government endeavored to provide assistance for those who fell through the cracks in this system, generally the elderly and poor, the AMA did its best to oppose such efforts. The AMA campaigned against Medicare (healthcare for those over sixty-five years old), for example, because physicians believed it represented a step towards socialized medicine and would lead to the establishment of a "bureaucratic task force" that would invade "the privacy of the examination room." Both Medicaid and Medicare ended up being adopted in **Johnson**'s "Great Society" legislative package, but only after they were framed as extensions of the existing Social Security system. Doctors had been assured that they would be able charge their usual fees for elderly and poor patients.

Attempts were made to push for a national system of healthcare during the first **Clinton** administration. Hillary Clinton's healthcare plans were successfully undermined by a powerful alliance of the AMA and insurance companies, as well as by the First Lady's inability to build a consensus on the issue, but this was also just one, albeit premature, initiative and not necessarily the end of the story.

Pressure to change may lead the AMA to alter its position in the future. The so-called "Patient Bill of Rights" (while offered in different guises by **Democrats** and **Republicans**) represents an attempt by **Congress** to respond to considerable dissatisfaction among Americans with the current healthcare system. With so much disaffection evident, the issue of **healthcare reform** is likely to remain an important issue in future presidential and congressional campaigns. Added to this, the AMA continues to feel threatened by the power of both attorneys and insurance companies. Under a private system of healthcare the pressure to sue for malpractice is greater than under a nationalized system, partly because one physician is forced to advertise his or her services as superior to another's and also because the provision of healthcare is given a price tag (inevitably leading to the question of whether the patient has received value for money). As malpractice suits increase in number, doctors' own insurance fees escalate, and attorneys' ongoing investigations of doctors bring to light a growing body of information that further reduces the public's faith in the performance of medical practitioners. The AMA under such circumstances has tried to restrict such information and has even stated its opposition to reporting medical errors occurring at hospitals around the country. But if the Association pushes too hard in this direction it runs the risk of attracting further journalistic muckraking and of seeming to be akin to **tobacco** corporations (that withheld information about the dangers of smoking). The likely result would be ever-larger jury judgments in malpractice suits against physicians.

In addition, insurance companies, particularly the Health Maintenance Organizations (HMOs) have already begun to interfere with the sacred doctor–patient relationship once prized by physicians in the AMA, and which it was feared a socialized system might undermine. As the HMOs begin to give doctors and hospitals less reimbursement for the services they offer, and also endeavor to ration particular services (again as it was feared a socialized system would do), many hospitals have been going bankrupt. The result is that there is at present a problem rather similar to the high levels of competition that capitalists found inimical to their interests during the Progressive Era, and which led them in the direction of greater corporatism and increased government regulation. With the AMA currently feeling embattled, and with options open that were not there during years of rabid anti-communism, it is not out of the question that some form of national healthcare system will receive the support of America's physicians during the next decade.

Further reading

Starr, P. (1982) *The Social Transformation of American Medicine*, New York: Basic.

ROBERT GREGG

American studies

From its inception in the 1930s and 1940s, American studies scholars have debated the definition, purpose and methodology of the field. Early scholarship fomented international recognition of American art, literature, and music, whereas post-Second World War nationalism and **Cold War** anxieties kindled scholarship that focused on **history**, policy and the American character. Seeking to interpret the United States to its citizens and to the world, the "myth and symbol" model of American studies linked texts to larger symbolic meanings in US culture. In applying literary criticism and historical analysis, scholars discussed themes, social patterns and institutional configurations that made the United States unique or exceptional.

In the late 1960s and 1970s notions of American exceptionalism were challenged by the **Civil Rights movement**, **feminism** and the **Vietnam War**. American studies embraced and critiqued social science, **anthropology**, art history, **folklore**, local studies, **philosophy**, music and **psychology**. In the early twenty-first century, American studies competes with but is complementary to, other interdisciplinary programs in ethnic studies, women's studies, gender studies, gay studies, postcolonial studies and **cultural studies**. The definition of American studies now may include the study of **Canada** and **Latin America**, and the field considers their global presence in business, diplomacy and **popular culture**. These changes are reflected in *American Quarterly* and *American Studies*, two of several American studies publications that feature new scholarship, discuss methodology and pedagogy, and link academic study to social change. New technologies are enhancing teaching and research, and offer ways to enhance further the interdisciplinary and international focus of the field.

STACILEE FORD

Americans with Disabilities Act

As Robert Dole proclaimed in his 1996 campaign, the 1990 Americans with Disabilities Act identified rights of America's largest minority group: some 60 million with physical or mental conditions demanding accommodation in school, workplace and leisure. This act marked the triumph of a quiet **civil rights** revolution that has nonetheless changed the face of the US – from access ramps in buildings or transport to an inclusiveness of the disabled as agents as well as victims in mass media. This recognition entails a new concept of citizenship, whether confronting the "perfection" of **Hollywood** stars or athletes or challenging cultural stereotypes of incompleteness or inadequacy. Still, this revolution has faced criticism from those who fear the costs of accommodations, while some disabled have feared the loss of distinctive institutions and cultures as well as new inequalities.

Various categories of physical and mental difference have been identified and stigmatized in American life since their inception. Public institutions have been created at the state and local level to deal with those who are blind, deaf, mentally challenged or suffering with long-term conditions. Many were fearful and depressing places that forced those who could do so to opt for private facilities or family care. Few institutions provided any framework for a positive, collective identity, although Gallaudet University (founded in 1864 for those who are deaf) would later be the site of important 1988 student actions rejecting the perceived paternalism of a non-deaf president. Other institutions, however, forced minorities into erroneous or deficient treatments; the "deaf community," for example, has been divided for decades over rights to **American Sign Language (ASL)** versus assimilative oral techniques. While disabled heroes emerged – Hellen Keller, **veterans** of **war** and labor, and even Franklin **Roosevelt**, confined to his wheelchair by **polio** – many preferred to exclude them from mainstream American life, economics and politics, or to meet their needs with paternalistic service. Indeed, Hollywood stars claimed Oscars for "acting" blind, deaf, or disabled when those living with these conditions found no work on screen. Notable and powerful exceptions include double amputee/ veteran Harold Russell as a returning sailor in *Best Years of Our Lives* (Best Supporting Actor, 1946) and, decades later, deaf actor Marlee Matlin's Oscar for *Children of a Lesser God* (1986). It has taken even

longer for media, from advertisements to narrative programs and news, to incorporate the disabled without focusing the story on them.

Various issues and movements, apart from the civil-rights model, slowly changed attitudes in the postwar period. The National Federation for the Blind, founded in 1940, marked an initial effort for socio-economic advancement organized around a shared disability. The spread of polio and the successful campaign against it brought disabilities into families and communities, and at the same time offered the possibility of a solution through concerted action. De-institutionalization and mainstreaming in the 1960s and 1970s also introduced those who had been locked away into classrooms and other social milieus.

Yet these students, workers and citizens encountered difficulties in both prejudice and physical access to buildings and resources. Hence Ed Roberts, who founded the Center for Independent Living in 1972 after working to change Berkeley, drew explicit parallels between the disabled and challenges facing **African Americans**. Meanwhile, Judy Heumann, who founded Disabled in Action in 1970, adopted protest marches and **sit-ins** to draw attention to multiple discriminations.

These movements gained real impact with provisions of the 1973 Rehabilitation Act, which barred discrimination against the handicapped in federal programs, whether by design or prejudice. Still, accommodations were often slow and ill-conceived: wooden ramps attached to back doors were symbols of difference as well as adaptation. Moreover, while changing technologies might help some – in home-based communication for the immobilized, for example, or new extensions of materials adapted to other senses or limbs – they limited others. Those who are blind in America, for example, face 70 percent unemployment, which is exacerbated by visual dependencies in new technology like the computer screen.

Mental issues are among the most difficult categories of disability in terms of complexity and compensation. **Depression**, learning disabilities and syndromes like Attention Deficit Disorder, as well as classifications of **alcohol** and drug dependencies as disabilities have all sparked debate.

The **AIDS** epidemic also entailed another extension of the concept of disability in terrain fraught with moral issues for many. The recognition of new causes, syndromes and relations to genetics, environment and ergonomic patterns of work also make the category of "disabled" a perennial challenge for policy-makers.

The 1990 ADA, then, gave formal charter to a movement towards incorporative citizenship that goes beyond the publically and historically recognized categories of **race**, **class**, **gender** and **ethnicity**. In the early twenty-first century, policy and accommodations are still taking shape, turning to the **Supreme Court**, government offices and institutional experts, as well as members of increasingly organized disabled networks to understand conditions, experience and accommodations. Only through this process will the US constitute a new and inclusive equality, as well as recognize the unique potential of individuals and groups.

Further reading

Davis, L. (ed.) (1997) *The Disability Studies Reader*, New York: Routledge.

Lane, H. (1992) *The Mask of Benevolence*, New York: Knopf.

Pelka, F. (1997) *The ABC-CLIO Companion to the Disability Rights Movement*, Santa Barbara: ABC-CLIO.

Reynolds, C. and Fletcher-Janzen, E. (2000) *Encyclopedia of Special Education*, New York: John Wiley & Sons.

GARY McDONOGH
CINDY WONG

Amish

The Amish were named after Jacob Ammann, a seventeenth-century Swiss Mennonite Bishop, who inspired his followers to establish communities governed by strict rules of behavior and dress. The Amish moved from Europe to the Pennsylvania colony in the early eighteenth century, and currently live in many rural parts of the US, where they practice old-fashioned farming techniques and eschew the trappings of modern life, including electricity, **automobiles**, **television** and higher education. The Amish are notable for successfully perpetuating theocratic societies which exist largely outside the control of federal and state laws. The Amish figured prominently in the film *Witness* (1984).

MELINDA SCHWENK

Amos 'n Andy

Radio serial, relying on white minstrelsy, that came to early CBS **television** (1951–3) with **African American** actors Alvin Childress and Spencer Williams, before being driven from the air by **NAACP** protests. The show embodies problems of racial stereotypes that have continually plagued **mass media**, even in sympathetic portraits like the 1950s domestics of *Beulah* or the later black middle class of *Julia* and the *Cosby Show*. David Bianculli suggests it is not the content of the show itself that developed strong characters and broad slapstick, but the lack of a wider, varied context that made this singular representation so problematic. Issues of artistic ownership and control and audience also separate this world from African American humor of the 1990s.

Further reading

Bianculli, D. (1996) *Dictionary of Teleliteracy*, New York: Continuum.

GARY McDONOGH
CINDY WONG

amusement parks *see* Disneyland and Disneyworld; theme parks

anarchism

During the early **Cold War**, the anarchist tradition was kept alive by Dwight Macdonald's lively journal, *politics* (1944–9). Avoiding the era's Manichean politics, Macdonald published independent thinkers who rejected the platitudes of both Cold-War America and Soviet-style state socialism. By the 1960s, some of the New **Left**'s less dogmatic members rediscovered anarchist thought. Murray

Bookchin's "post-scarcity anarchism" served as a rejoinder to Marxist-Leninist sectarianism, while Noam **Chomsky**, the prolific linguist-activist, rekindled interest in anarcho-syndicalism.

More recently, younger "post-leftist" anarchists have questioned the anti-authoritarian credentials of Bookchin and Chomsky. This new tendency, distinguished by a militant opposition to technology, received considerable media attention during protests against corporate globalization during the 1999 **Seattle, WA** meeting of the World Trade Organization.

Further reading

Porton, R. (1999) *Film and the Anarchist Imagination*, New York: Verso.

RICHARD PORTON

androgyny

Conventional wisdom defines androgyny as a combination of traditionally feminine and masculine elements. While androgyny is conceived of most often in terms of clothing, it also may extend to include mannerisms and behavior. Mainstream America, in general, which tends towards biological determinism, understands androgyny in terms of fashion and does not recognize it as a legitimate gender identity. Conversely, many feminist and **queer** theorists who do not view **gender** as necessarily dichotomous give androgyny a place on the spectrum of gender possibilities.

Androgyny as a contemporary fashion grew out of the 1950s bohemian and working-class youth styles to become most notably embodied in the male hippie of the 1960s, who rebelliously grew out his hair in girlish locks. In the 1970s, lesbian feminists rejected established gender categories and adopted a "unisex" uniform, which consisted of short hair, slacks and an absence of make-up. In the 1980s, lesbian commentators, favoring a revival of gender categories, exposed the lesbian "androgyny" of the 1970s as an imitation of **working-class** men's attire.

As **fashion** codes gradually relaxed over the twentieth century, androgyny has become increasingly acceptable as a style for American women today. However, while conventional symbols of **masculinity**, such as suits, short hair and pants, have become fair game for women, men still risk persecution for wearing conventional signs of **femininity**, such as skirts, high heels and barrettes.

Further reading

Weston, K. (1993) "Do clothes make the woman?," *Genders* 17: 1–21.
Wilson, E. (1990) "Deviant dress," *Feminist Review* 35: 67–74.

ELIZABETH A. GALEWSKI

Angelou, Maya

b. 1928

Born Marguerite Johnson in segregated Arkansas, Maya Angelou is best known for her autobiographical novels, such as *I Know Why the Caged Bird Sings* (1969), her poetry, which she read at President **Clinton**'s inaugural celebration in 1993, and her **civil rights** activism. A northern coordinator for the **Southern Christian Leadership Conference**, appointed to the Bicentennial Commission by President **Ford**, and by **Carter** to the Observance of International Women's Year, Angelou is now arguably the most visible American poet. Her work deals with the intersection of **race** and **gender**, highlighting the impact of **segregation** and racism on **African American** communities and gender relations within them. *I Know Why* recounted the experience of being raped as a young girl, while her best-known poetry, *And Still I Rise* and *Phenomenal Woman* (1978), has, as the titles suggest, celebrated women and perseverance.

ROBERT GREGG

angels *see* afterlife; atheists

animal rights (movement whose goals range from environmental concerns to extension of individual and human rights to non-human species) *see* nature; pets

animals and the media

The construction of **nature**, wild and tame, speaks eloquently to changing beliefs throughout American history. **Folklore** abounds with animal helpmates like Paul Bunyan's giant blue ox babe or the subversive **African American** trickster tales of Br'er Rabbit outwitting his captors. Contemporary media build upon these images in popular shows where intelligent, benevolent and witty animals – dolphins, horses, dogs, a rare cat and overactive chimps – assist humans to develop their humanity. These overlap with more documentary depictions that may nonetheless denature the wild. Yet, lurking beyond these friendly figures is savage nature – unleashed, for example, in furious attacks in *Them!* (1954) by giant ants, *Jurassic Park* (1993) or *Wolf* (1994).

Rin Tin Tin (1916–32) and Lassie (a helpful female family collie played by a male dog with additional human actor sounds) provided gendered templates for domestic animals in movies (1923–31 and 1943–50, respectively). Lassie's television debut came in 1947 (ABC). He/she reappeared for the next three decades, including a cartoon version (1973–5). Dog companions also help delineate major characters in movies and shows, including comments on snobbery and affectation in the 1990s hit *Frazier*, or more heroic sidekick roles (*Benji*, 1974; *Turner and Hooch*, 1990). Cats, despite their popularity as **pets**, prove harder to work with, although they appear in **witchcraft** representations. Both cats and dogs are frequently used in **advertising**.

Other media play on curiosity about mammals "closer" to humans (Flipper the dolphin and various chimp shows and films). Some creatures, moreover, crossed the line through animation or tricks, like the wise-cracking, talking horse of CBS' sitcom *Mr Ed* (1961–6). In all, one sees valued traits of American relationships and citizenship read across species – loyalty, independence – and an interesting continuing irony about humans. **Disney**'s animated features, from *Mickey Mouse* to *Tarzan* (1999), have pushed this interlocutor/mimic role even further.

Animal documentary traditions have also blurred relations of nature and culture. Early television programs were especially linked to **zoos** and zookeepers creating bridges between the wild and the familiar, including interactions with talk-show hosts. *National Geographic*, America's premier explorer of the exotic, has also produced more scientific studies of animals ranging from whales to domestic cats. Meanwhile, Disney's live-action films and television (*Seal Island* (1948), *Jungle Cat* (1960), etc.) have created characters and life narratives in the wild.

This immediacy and humanity of nature reaffirms both the meaning in wilderness and its essential humanity, a charter for appropriation. Yet nature can also convey power and uncertainty, as **horror**, **sci-fi** and disaster media suggest, and *Cujo* (1983) replaces *Lassie*. In the 1990s, videos of fighting and killing by wild animals are even marketed alongside reality shows like "Cops." Hence, representations of animals and nature, like their manipulation in pets, **parks** and **food** production, provide multiple visions of American identity.

See also: nature

Further reading

Wilson, A. (1992) *The Culture of Nature*, Cambridge, MA: Blackwell.
McKibben, B. (1992) *The Age of Missing Information*, New York: Plume.

GARY McDONOGH
CINDY WONG

animation

The use of drawings and photographs of three-dimensional objects to tell stories preceded the technologies of film, television and computer with which they now coexist. Winsor McKay's pioneering *Little Nemo* (1908) and *Gertie, the Trained Dinosaur* (1909) and, later, New York-produced characters, such as Felix the Cat, excited both audiences and distributors. Yet, Walt **Disney**'s studio, style and sales have set the model for American animation. Through Disney studios, animation has become a specialty for children and families, relying on color and music, as well as personality and narrative. Many competitors, in fact, have emerged from divisions within the Disney studio rather than from alternative traditions. Technological innovations from the use of celluloid to live-action modeling to computer-assisted design have changed the production and quality of the medium itself, yet it remains within this general paradigm.

Disney set himself apart from early competitors by his awareness of the values of character, narrative, sound and color, as well as the possibilities of linking onscreen features to off-screen commercialism. With the introduction of sound in 1927, Disney characters like Mickey Mouse and Donald Duck, and works like *Silly Symphonies* commanded attention. In 1937, Disney gambled successfully on the lush musical feature *Snow White and the Seven Dwarfs*, which set the standard for the genre thereafter. By *Pinocchio* (1941) the level of animation multi-planing and thematics became even more complex, while *Fantasia*, a box-office failure at the time, wed classical music with creative animation.

Other studios competed with Disney in short films that accompanied theatrical features. In the 1940s, disgruntled Disney employees founded United Productions of America, whose style in cartoons like John Hubley's *Mr Magoo* offered a more "modern" feel that would have an international impact. *Tom and Jerry* was created by William Hanna and Joseph Barbera. Other competitors included Warner Brother's *Looney Tunes* stable of aggressive, even violent cartoons, including Bugs Bunny (Chuck Jones) or Tweety Pie and Sylvester (Fritz Freleng). These characters, and others, found new life on Saturday morning children's television.

American animation, even at Disney, declined in the 1960s and 1970s because of rising costs and other production decisions. Computer animation and new Disney initiatives sparked a 1980s renaissance with features like *The Little Mermaid* (1989), *Beauty and the Beast* (1991) and especially *The Lion King* (1994), which grossed over $300 million. These not only took on attributes of musicals – stories, songs, even "star voices" – but reappeared as live productions on **Broadway**. Other competitors for this reborn market include the Spielberg collaborators of Dreamworks, who produced *Prince of Egypt* (1998) and *The Road to El Dorado* (2000), and Warner Brothers', who produced *The Iron Giant* (1999). The combination of animation and live action (as in *Mary Poppins*, 1962) has again filled the screen since *Who Framed Roger Rabbit* (1988), including the synergy of sports celebrity and cartoons of *Space Jam* (1996). By the end of the decade, however, FOX closed its studios and Disney remained champion.

Both in creative features (using television showcases as well as theaters) and as components of live-action films, animation continues to provide an alternative imagination of reality, from *The Simpsons* or *South Park* to animated political cartooning. Ralph Bakshi's *Fritz the Cat* (1972), for example, raised issues of sexual adventure far from Disney. While the possibilities of animation continue to excite independent producers, the sheer marketing and cultural permeation of the Disney feature and its imitators continue to dominate the primary meanings and readings of this art form.

Animation techniques also continue to develop, especially through use of computer animation that has already created a new look in hits like *Toy Story* (1995) and *Toy Story II* (1999). These techniques can also be used to add vivid imagery to live-action movies like *Titanic* (1998) or *Gladiator* (2000). At the same time, live backgrounds have also been incorporated into animated features, as in Disney's *Dinosaur* (2000). These hybrid creations suggest changing boundaries of genre, as as well as reminding us that animation is not "just for kids."

Further reading

Thomas, B. (1991) *Disney's Art of Animation*, New York: World.

Thomas, F. and Johnston, O. (1984) *Disney Animation: The Illusion of Life*, New York: Abbeville.

GARY McDONOGH
CINDY WONG

anthropology

American anthropology studies the human condition across cultures in both the past and present, as well as considers the primate family in general. For most of the twentieth century this "holistic perspective" fostered a "four-field approach," including archaeological, physical, linguistic and cultural anthropology. What held the four fields together was the concept of "culture" – whether embodied in the material remains of past human activity, the physical attributes of Homo sapiens, or their relatives and ancestors, as a guide for human action or media of meaning and interpreting experience.

The four-field approach emerged from earlier natural histories that sought to catalogue in genealogical relationships all observable elements of nature, including humans. Anthropology concerned itself with non-western peoples, the "simple societies of the primitive world," while sociology became the study of "modern complex societies of the West." In America, the readily available non-western subjects were **American Indians**, while British and French anthropology examined social structure and meaning among colonized peoples.

In recent years the four-field approach has become the source of heated debate, with many academic departments abandoning it as an organizing principle. Increasing specialization and cross-disciplinary ties have contributed to this. Perhaps most significant to this fragmentation is a divide between those who embrace anthropology as a "science" and those who link it to a challenge to Eurocentric meta-narratives that include science itself as a subject of study.

Because of its cross-cultural, multi-temporal, relativist perspective, anthropologists have always considered all phenomena on their own terms, whether employing the comparative method or seeking universal or particular features. In the late 1960s and the 1970s other academic disciplines of study, particularly the humanities, began to look to anthropology for theoretical orientations that became pivotal in "de-centering" conventions of study that refracted unequal relations of power, Euro- and ethnocentric. Yet, the anthropological perspective did not play much of a role in the "**culture wars**" that followed (Rosaldo 1994).

American anthropology continues to reflect and shape social forms and practices in the study of the human condition. Once holding the contradictory position as a handmaiden of the European and American colonial enterprise while acting as advocate of non-western peoples in the face of imperialism, anthropology now is a contested site in the contemporary politics of identity. Local and global flows, displacements, and re-integrations of populations which have produced ethnic politics as a site of contestation, and a fragmented "social imaginary" (Appadurai 1996) are both the subjects of contemporary anthropology and the cause of some of its recent theoretical and practical reformations.

The face of American anthropology is increasingly female and increasingly "other" (see Behar and Gordon 1995). Post-colonial theorists from what once were the peripheries of the Euro-American core also have entered the anthropological enterprise. Anthropology as a "science," the notion of holism, the comparative method, the culture concept, relativism, fieldwork, analytical and interpretative frameworks, and forms of textual presentations have all come under attack as symptoms of an inequality in power relations between western and non-western peoples, places and spaces.

This critique of anthropology, often referred to as the "crisis of representation" (Marcus and Fischer 1986) has led to ill-feeling among anthropologists. Contemporary American anthropology is increasingly seen to be a cultural anthropology that often includes linguistic anthropology, with archaeology and physical anthropology aligned with each other or completely separated. Some archaeologists and physical anthropologists, meanwhile, believe that cultural anthropology has lost its subject – culture – to other disciplines, which has led to its demise as a subfield.

What relevance does anthropology have for contemporary American culture? More so than ever before anthropologists, particularly cultural anthropologists, are engaging in research here at "home." Medical anthropology, practice anthropology and its problem-solving orientation, urban ethnographies, film and media studies, a revitalized partnership with **folklore** and folk-life studies, and an interest on the part of the corporate world in anthropology have brought it closer to the surface of public culture.

Further reading

Appadurai, A. (1996) *Modernity at Large*, Minnesota: University of Minnesota.

Behar, R. and Gordon, D. (eds) (1995) *Women*

Writing Culture, California: University of California.

Harris, M. (1968) *The Rise of Anthropological Theory*, New York: Harper & Row.

Marcus, G. and Fischer, M. (1986) *Anthropology as Cultural Critique*, Chicago: University of Chicago.

Rosaldo, R. (1994) "Whose cultural studies?," *American Anthropologist* 96(3): 524–9.

STEVE FERZACCA
JANICE NEWBERRY

antiques/reproductions

American **middle** and **upper classes** live between ideologies of **mobility**, equality and opportunity and expressions of status valuing that which is old, inherited or unique. While elite collectors raided Europe over the past century (and eventually contributed to **museums** as rich store-houses of the global past), antiques as inherited and acquired goods have wider domestic meanings. While memories and **family** histories may be linked to humble objects from the past – quilts, furniture, books, paintings and photographs – more extensive antique sales have also drained Europe and, increasingly, the Third World in order to supply proof of connoisseurship, status and even ethnic heritage. For offices, **hotels** and other institutions as well, antiques (or quality reproductions) project status and sobriety. These evaluations, in turn, sustain an ever-hotter market among serious collectors and museums for the best specimens of both American and foreign production in the past.

This burgeoning market, ranging from flea markets, shops and decorators to elegant auction houses, nonetheless limits the accessibility of the past while opening the door to reproductions as cultural capital. Often sold through museum stores or high-end retailers, these may be direct reproductions of jewelry, artworks or furniture, but also entail reproduction of motifs – indicating knowledge as much as copying – transposed to ties, appointment books, children's **toys**, etc. **Gentrification** and home-ownership have also fostered markets for "antique" fixtures or adaptations of modern conveniences, while hotels and offices have affirmed these tastes. Reproduction posters, dolls and collectibles extend this marketing of the past into lower-end sales, generally without questioning the heritage reproduced or the divisions embodied in both "authentic" and "fake" appropriation.

GARY McDONOGH
CINDY WONG

anti-technology

The "American Century" has been built on high technology, whether in images of material progress, technological fixes for problems of the environment, health, technology itself or the volatility of tech **stocks** and e-commerce at the turn of the millennium. Nonetheless, technology has also met with resistance and rejection. Motivated by values of a simpler life, for example, groups as diverse as **hippies** and the **Amish** have publicly rejected some technologies; extreme **survivalists** have also sought to escape dependency on technology and its global connections. More often, resistance seems embodied in everyday ignorance of how technology works: standard American **humor** about people's inability to control a **computer**, **VCR** or electronic device. This is sometimes contrasted with the seemingly more comprehensible and remediable **automobiles** and machines of the 1950s, which evoked their own technological specters at the time. Resistance also pits images of high tech **fashion** and design against history and comfort, or highlights relations of **gender** and technology (where men are expected to be fixers) and differences of age, as generations raised on computers and video games replace skills valued by their elders.

GARY McDONOGH
CINDY WONG

Apartheid *see* Africa

Appalachia

The green hills and broad valleys of the Appalachian Mountains evoke profoundly dichotomous meanings in American life. The largest chain in the East, these mountains often have been portrayed as natural havens, escapes from coastal urbanization. At the same time, the region has been characterized by isolation and poverty that symbolize for policy-makers and media the failure of the American dream.

The Appalachian Mountains stretch across fourteen states, from Maine to Georgia; they include ranges known locally as the Berkshires, Taconics, Lehighs, Shenandoahs and Smokies. These relatively gentle slopes and broad valleys have influenced generations of painters and writers; the Berkshires in Massachusetts, for example, harbor artist colonies, while other ranges shelter elegant resorts and tourist development (especially the Smokies and Virginia's Shenandoahs). State and national **forests**, as well as federal parks like Great Smoky Mountain National Park in Tennessee and North Carolina now protect the beauty of the Appalachians. The 2,000 mile (3,200 km) Appalachian trail, first developed by volunteers in the 1920s, traverses much of the East Coast, a journey explored in Bill Bryson's (1998) *A Walk in the Woods.*

Yet Appalachia's natural beauty contrasts with another brutal image, which developed after the Civil War, that portrayed its Southern ranges as a region of extreme backwardness and poverty. In literature and film (476 movies between 1904 and 1929), local residents or "hillbillies" came to denote ignorance, isolation and internecine violence, even if they were occasionally championed as decadent heirs of an English yeoman tradition. The problem of Appalachia was tackled with the **Tennessee Valley Authority** and other development projects of the New Deal; in 1965, it became special target in the **War on Poverty**, defended by politicians from West Virginia, Kentucky and Tennessee. Yet, in 1999, Appalachia still figured in the itinerary when President Bill **Clinton** looked at American poverty.

Both images miss the complexity of Appalachian social ecology and history. The decline of farming and community, for example, was linked to large-scale outside acquisitions of the land and the dangers of the coal mines that made the region a constant source of emigration to the North. Moreover, Appalachian peoples have included **African Americans** and Native Americans, as well as diverse white populations – all of whom "hillbilly" images ignore (a point underscored in John Sayle's 1993 film *Matewan*).

Compelling voices, nonetheless, have spoken from and for Appalachia, from John Fox's romantic turn-of-the-century portraits to Harry Caudill's *Night Comes to the Cumberland* (1963). Barbara Kopple's compelling *Harlan County, USA* (1976) chronicles the travails of coal miners and **unions**. Generations of bluegrass and **country and western** musicians have conveyed the soul of Appalachia over local radio and through recordings. Appalshop, a grassroots media cooperative, has also fought stereotypes while preserving the complexity of local traditions and struggles.

See also: nature; rednecks; South

Further reading

Davis, D. (1999) *Where there are Mountains*, Athens: University of Georgia.
Turner, W. and Cabell, E. (eds) (1985) *Blacks in Appalachia*, Lexington: University Press of Kentucky.

GARY McDONOGH
CINDY WONG

Apple computer

The story of two men, Steve Jobs and Steve Wozniak, who founded Apple in a garage in the 1970s, and went on to challenge corporate behemoth **IBM** in the burgeoning personal computer market is in one sense a retelling of the singularly American story of the self-made person. Apple can also be seen as the next chapter of the 1960s counterculture, when a generation that once disdained corporate culture came to embrace and transform it into their own image. This aspect is emblematized by the informal, creative work environment which Jobs fostered, and by the philanthropic efforts to which Wozniak funneled his profits. The company's most famous product, the Macintosh, became popular in part as a symbol of the values that Apple embodied.

ROBERT ANDERSON

Arab Americans

Although "Arab" refers to members of a language group from the **Middle East** and North Africa, the term has been muddled in the US by historical shifts, global Islamic politics and widespread stereotypes of fanatic Muslim "others." In fact, many Arab Americans are Christians (90 percent of those who arrived before the Second World War) and long-term citizens. Yet the 2–3 million Americans of Arab descent face continual possibilities of discrimination, vividly depicted in the mass round-ups of the 1998 movie *The Siege*, which spurred vigorous Arab American protest. These representations belie Arabs' long presence in the States, their complexity and their integration into diverse settings.

Arab **immigration** began in the late nineteenth century with young males coming from Lebanon (then part of the Ottoman empire), pursuing wandering mercantile careers in North and South America; one is remembered as the "Persian" in the musical *Oklahoma*. This brought family and friends over before 1920's immigration curbs (perhaps a total of 100,000), and generally they became highly assimilated.

Immigration renewed after the Second World War with students and professionals from Arab states (primarily Muslim). Christians and Muslims from Lebanon, Palestine, Iraq, Egypt and other areas have also escaped traumatic local conditions, as well as pursuing economic security. Men and families have led immigration rather than single women – Arab American women have felt special strains between new social mores and their roles within families and a variety of Arab/Muslim gender roles.

Most Arab Americans are urban, concentrated in **New York** City, **Los Angeles, CA**, **Chicago** and **Detroit, MI** (200,000 citizens of Lebanese and Palestinian descent). They belong to diverse Orthodox and **Roman Catholic** traditions, as well as Protestant faiths established by missionaries, although most are now Muslim. Valuing education and labor, they have established themselves in politics – senators James Abourezk (South Dakota) and George Mitchell (Maine), and Clinton Health and Human Services Secretary Donna Shalala, Wisconsin. They have also succeeded in mass media (comedian/impresario Danny Thomas, actor F. Murray Abraham), although they are sometimes typecast as other "ethnics." Ralph **Nader**, consummate American crusader and presidential candidate, is also of Arab descent.

Yet divisions in the contemporary Middle East continually reinforce American prejudices. The Arab–Israeli war of 1967 became a watershed for Arab American identity, and the Association of Arab-American University Graduates, Inc. and the American-Arab Anti-Discrimination Committee, among others, emerged in this era. Nonetheless, in the 1990s, mass media caricatured Arabs as greedy merchants and oppressed, but sensual females in **Disney** and *Star Wars*, while denigrating Arab cultural and political claims as extremist in contrast with the moral values of Israeli lobbying. Universities often treat Arabic as a dead language despite 246 million speakers worldwide and 355,000 speakers in the US – more than Hindi, Russian or Yiddish. Thus, Arab Americans are resisted within the melting-pot despite strong claims of history and participation.

Further reading

McCarus, E. (ed.) (1983) *The Development of Arab-American Identity*, Ann Arbor: University of Michigan.

GARY McDONOGH

architecture

The International Style exhibition at the Museum of Modern Art in New York in 1932 is often cited as the beginning of **modernism** in America. Curated by Philip **Johnson** and Henry-Russell Hitchcock, the exhibition attempted to codify European trends alongside examples of the modern style in America. This International Style – characterized by white walls, flexible plans and a glass-and-steel industrial aesthetic – became the prevailing architectural style in the United States following the Second World War. Meanwhile, in prominent schools of architecture, European architects such as Ludwig **Mies van der Rohe**, Marcel Breuer and Walter Gropius transformed American architectural education into atelier-based institutions that embraced the tenets of the European modernist tradition.

In the 1950s, glass box modernism became the preferred style for American corporations, institutions and universities; examples include works by Eero Saarinen and I.M. Pei. At the same time, American architects embraced brutalism, based on the later Le Corbusier and the philosophical discourses of authenticity. This style is exemplified by Louis I. **Kahn**'s Yale University Art Gallery (1951) and Paul Rudolph's Art and Architecture building at Yale (1964).

The bombastic nature of Rudolph's building served as a point of rebellion for the student followers of architects such as Robert **Venturi**, who favored a more pluralistic approach, or what he called a "messy vitality," over the bland formalism of high modernist practice. With the publication of Robert Venturi's *Complexity and Contradiction in Architecture*, these sentiments were championed by colleagues like Robert A.M. Stern and Charles Moore.

Venturi's ideas were further elaborated in *Learning from Las Vegas* (1972), which celebrated the stylistic collision of the **Las Vegas** strip, and described the specific kitsch of the area as a form of American vernacular. This eclecticism became known as **postmodernism** in architecture, and rapidly took hold in both the academy and the corporate realm. The pervasive nature of postmodernism is evidenced by the erstwhile modernists who embraced this style, for instance Philip Johnson's AT&T building in Manhattan (1983) or Michael **Graves**' Portland Public Services building (1982).

At the same time as Venturi's historicist critique, **New York** intellectuals and academics reacted against what they derisively called modern "style" during the 1960s. Following global events of May 1968, a split emerged in the architectural profession between the academy and the corporate milieu in the United States. Under the teachings of British architectural historian Colin Rowe – whose reconceptualization of architectural history advocated a typological understanding of historical form – influential figures such as the New York Five (Peter Eisenman, Michael **Graves**, John Hejduk, Charles Gwathmey, Richard Meier) transformed the intellectual climate of American schools

of architecture. Because of their belief in autonomous architecture with its own series of generative rules, the teachings of the New York Five exacerbated the division between universities and the profession, creating a perceived split between architectural theory and practice. While corporate firms such as Skidmore, Owings, and Merrill were designing the John Hancock Tower of 1970, for example, Peter Eisenman was questioning notions of domesticity with a divided **bedroom** in his House VI in Connecticut.

Eisenman's efforts to question architectural norms through formal manipulation gradually became deconstructivism, which attempted to link architectural discourse and post-Derridean literary theory. The pinnacle of this movement – characterized by tipping walls and non-orthogonal geometric organizations – was exemplified by Peter Eisenman's Wexner Center (1994) in Columbus, Ohio. The hermeticism of this academic architecture suffered a crisis of legitimacy during the 1990s with increasing globalization and the pressure of market forces.

Another trend in American architecture that characterized the immediate postwar cultural context was the persistently American vernacular style that took hold, particularly in the **Midwest** and West Coast, as a form of regionalist architecture using traditional materials and methods of construction. The largely residential works of architects such as William Wurster and Bruce Goff, were dismissed in academic circles for their embrace of prefabricated materials and organicism. Frank Lloyd **Wright**, often regarded as the greatest American architect of the twentieth century, had by this time departed from his familiar prairie houses. He was designing more formally inspired buildings, as evidenced by his designs for the Guggenheim Museum in New York (1960) and his 1955 skyscraper at Bartlesville, Oklahoma. Wright's planning models, however, such as Broadacre City, influenced the development of the American **suburbs** in the postwar period and their dependence on the **automobile**. Emerging from this trend are figures such as Charles and Ray Eames, who pioneered an era of structural and visual experimentation through their furniture design and film. American regionalism has remained influential through the teachings of

Taliesin – founded by Frank Lloyd Wright – and through the work of late twentieth-century architects such as Paolo Soleri and Will Bruder.

While the often unbuilt architecture of the academy has continued on its autonomous trajectory, the architecture of the suburbs has followed a more conservative path. Following the Second World War, the domestic climate was characterized by projects such as **Levittown** in which entire **neighborhoods** were designed within strict guidelines that provided specific domestic amenities – attached garage, eat-in **kitchen**, **lawn**. The idealization of the nuclear **family** at **home** also produced competitive markets to embellish these prescribed desires; thus, the boom of the suburbs supported the car industry, lawn-care suppliers and appliance industries.

In the 1980s and 1990s, the reclamation of Main Street and small-town atmosphere has produced towns such as Celebration and Seaside, **Florida**, with similar aesthetic guidelines and master planning to control the perceived malaise of suburban sprawl and, ultimately, prescribe a suburban lifestyle. Led by architects such as Andres Duany and Elisabeth Plater-Zyberg, **New Urbanism** – through typological and stylistic guidelines – is slowly equalizing the suburban ideal through large-scale, planned communities. Other recent trends in American architecture have ranged from the expressionistic work of **Los Angeles, CA** architects such as Frank **Gehry**, Eric Owen Moss and Morphosis to the more reticent work of Tod Williams and Billie Tsien and Steven Holl.

Further reading

Architecture: the AIA Journal and *Progressive Architecture* (should be illuminating, as are studies of particular architects, works and contexts).

(1932) *The International Style*, New York: W.W. Norton.

Katz, P. (1994) *The New Urbanism*, New York: McGraw-Hill.

Kostof, S. (1987) *America by Design*, New York: Oxford.

Stern, R. (1977) *New Directions in American Architecture*, New York: G. Brazilier.

Venturi, R. (1996) *Complexity and Contradiction in Architecture*, New York: Museum of Modern Art.

Venturi, R. with Brown, D.S. and Izenour, S. (1972) *Learning from Las Vegas*, Cambridge, MA: MIT.

JEANNIE J. KIM
HUNTER FORD TURA

Armenian Americans

Armenians began arriving in the US in large numbers in the late nineteenth and early twentieth centuries, when they were driven out of historical homelands by the Ottoman Turks. The largest diasporan community is in the US, where there are over 1 million Americans of Armenian descent. The greatest concentration is in **California**, where in 1983 an Armenian American, George Deukmejian, was elected **governor**. Since the Second World War, Armenians have emigrated to the US from diasporan communities in Egypt, Romania, Bulgaria, Turkey, Lebanon, **Iran**, Iraq, Syria, the Soviet Union, as well as Armenia itself.

The earliest immigrants to the US organized themselves for mutual support, building a network of churches, schools, social clubs, political **parties** and philanthropic organizations. These still form the backbone of Armenian American community life. Each wave of Armenian immigrants has joined these institutions in search of fellowship and assistance. As a result they have been both sites of conflict between American-born and foreign-born Armenians, who differ due to decades of separation and culture change, and places where accommodation and innovation have been creating new forms of Armenian American culture. Perhaps the most influential institution has been the Armenian Apostolic (Orthodox) church, to which most Armenian Americans have ties if not direct affiliations.

Armenian Americans have joined the US mainstream. While they have been changed by it, they have also altered US society in significant ways. Influenced by the **white** "ethnic pride" movement of the 1960s, which led white Americans to rediscover their "roots," Armenian Americans established Armenian studies programs at such universities as Harvard, UCLA, Columbia and Michigan. The US diet has been affected by the production and marketing of foods favored by Armenians, such as yogurt, string cheese, raisins, figs and melons. Of the many Armenian Americans who have contributed to technology and industry, perhaps the most successful is Alex Manoogian, whose company developed the single-handled faucet. In the arts, literature and entertainment among those best known are actor/singer Cher (Cherilyn Sarkissian), painter Arshile Gorky, composer Alan Hovhaness, film director Rouben Mamoulian, journalist Ben Bagdikian and **Pulitzer Prize** winning author William Saroyan (*The Time of Your Life, The Human Comedy*).

Each year on April 24 Armenian Americans commemorate the "Armenian Genocide," marking events immediately preceding and during the First World War when between 800,000 and 2 million Armenians died in massacres and deportations at the hands of the Turks. The individual and collective tragedies of this period have taken on profound historical and political meaning for Armenian people everywhere, many of whom see this historical policy as one of genocide.

An independent Armenia was established in 1991 on the dissolution of the former Soviet Republic. This has been a source of joy and pride for Armenian Americans, whose moral and financial support for the new Republic of Armenia has been substantial.

Further reading

Bakalian, A. (1993) *Armenian-Americans*, New Brunswick: Transaction Publishers.

Mirak, R. (1983) *Torn Between Two Lands*, Cambridge, MA: Harvard University Press.

ANAHID ORDJANIAN

Armstrong, Louis "Satchmo"

b. 1901; d. 1971

Beloved **jazz** cornetist, singer and movie personality whose career spanned six decades. Born in poverty in **New Orleans**, Armstrong's talents led him to fame with swing bands in **Chicago** and **New York** City, NY, where his style moved from New Orleans Dixieland ensembles towards more innovative solos and scat singing (jazz improvisation without words). His unique gravelly voice also established American standards like "Hello Dolly!" and "What a Wonderful World," while he became known through concerts, movies and other appearances worldwide. His autobiography, *Satchmo*, appeared in 1956; he is also the subject of several documentaries.

GARY McDONOGH

army, US

Land and air military unit of the American military since the Revolutionary War; its undergraduate institution, the US Military Academy at West Point, New York, was opened in 1802. Despite worries about the obsolescence of ground **war**, the army has experienced continuing peacetime strength since the Second World War in weapons, budget and staff, and has seen action in **Korea**, **Vietnam** and the **Gulf War**. It also produced a postwar military president in Dwight **Eisenhower**. In addition to the standing army, its service pool includes the Army Reserves and the National Guards (state and federal). US army personnel in 1998 stood at 491,707, including 67,048 officers and over 65,000 women.

See also: Pentagon; war movies

GARY McDONOGH

art museums

Just as **Los Angeles** celebrated the completion of Richard Meier's lavish travertine marble Getty Center in 1997, an art compound generously endowed by the J. Paul Getty Trust, the Museum of Modern Art (MOMA) in **New York** City unveiled its plan to commission Yoshio Taniguchi for its own expansion and renovation. Emblematic of the late twentieth-century boom in museum planning and building, their insistently modernist design at once reveals its origins in **modernism** and modernization, and belies its place in, and reliance on, a resolutely **postmodern** present.

During the late nineteenth and early twentieth century, the transfer of cultural wealth from Europe to America, coupled with burgeoning industrial fortunes, allowed for the founding of America's own art museums in its major capital cities – from the Metropolitan Museum of Art in New York to the Museum of Fine Arts in **Boston, MA** to the **Philadelphia** Museum of Art.

During the course of the twentieth century, modernization and modernism saw their messianic destinies intertwined in the founding of such institutions as the MOMA in 1929. There, the fortunes of American capitalist enterprise, the clean lines of Bauhaus design and the secularized modernist teleology of Alfred J. Barr came together to form the premier institution of modern art in America. Yet these founding visions of modernist utopia quickly gave way to the forces of cultural ossification. In its pursuit of originality and the relentlessly new, in its avowedly progressive vision, the museum refused to acknowledge the degree to which it conferred upon the present the very mantle of tradition which that present had sought so desperately to escape.

The cutting edge issues and exhibits of museums in the **Northeast** and **California** are refracted in other smaller art museums across the country. Some, like the **Chicago** Institute of Art, **Baltimore**'s Walters Art Gallery, the Albright-Knox Collection in **Buffalo** and the Menil Museum in **Houston**, constitute important collections and buildings. Others recur in circuits of major travelling expositions – **Dallas**-Fort Worth, **Atlanta** or **Cincinnati**. Still others have revealed interesting facets of their city and collector – the idiosyncratic Barnes Collection, near Philadelphia, or **New Orleans** Museum of Arts' exploration of the links between Degas and his New Orleans relatives.

In the early twenty-first century we witness not the museum's ruins but, instead, its triumphantly vigorous presence. In an age of blockbuster exhibitions and expansion, the museum has become entrenched as a cherished cultural icon unto itself. In a postmodern present marked by the accelerated pace of planned obsolescence, the museum has emerged as that institution which might save society from the ravages of modernization, from the relentless pursuit of the new, its processes of ossification, of memorialization, coming to function as a potent antidote to the logic of late capitalist culture.

Further reading

Crimp, D. (1993) *On the Museum's Ruins*, Cambridge, MA and London: MIT Press.

Rogoff, I. and Sherman, D.J. (eds) (1994) *Museum Culture: Histories, Discourses, Spectacles*, Minneapolis: University of Minnesota Press.

LISA SALTZMAN

Ashe, Arthur

b. 1943; d. 1993

Eight years after being turned away from the Richmond City Tennis Tournament in 1955 because of his **race**, Ashe became the first **African American** on the US Davis Cup team, where he remained for fifteen years. His two Grand Slam triumphs included the 1968 US Open at Forest Hills and the 1975 Wimbledon tournament.

Ashe's dominance in **tennis** was limited by his commitment to social and political issues off the court. In 1973 Ashe was allowed into South Africa to play in its Open tournament, but received criticism from the African National Congress. Later, he became an outspoken critic of the South African government, and in 1985 was arrested at a protest rally against apartheid in **Washington, DC**. He was also arrested while protesting the **Bush** administration's treatment of Haitian refugees. Other public work included support for the NCAA's introduction of minimum requirements for college athletes (Proposition 48).

Ashe's playing career ended in 1979 because of heart problems. After by-pass surgery in 1983, he contracted **AIDS** from a blood transfusion. After his death, ironically, controversy arose as citizens and the city administration moved to place a memorial statue on Monument Row in Richmond, Virginia which had generally honored white Confederate heroes.

ROBERT GREGG

Asian Americans

Asian Americans represent the fastest growing ethnic groups in the United States. The 1990 census listed the population of Asians or Pacific Islanders as 7.2 million (2.9 percent of the American population). This figure nearly doubles the 1980 census figure of 3.7 million. A projected population for 2000 is 10.67 million. **Immigration** from Asia, by 1990, also represented nearly half (48 percent) of all legal entries to the US, compared with 5 percent in the years 1931–65. Since this group includes many recent immigrants, its relations with the many homelands are strong forces in forging **Pacific Rim** relationships.

Yet the category "Asian American" jumbles disparate peoples, languages, histories and experiences to fit "American" categories – even if Asian Americans themselves have found it useful in terms of political and cultural empowerment. "Asian American" generally includes people whose families originate in Asia and the Pacific Islands, but people from the Middle East, Central Asia and South Asia may be perceived as heirs of distinct cultural traditions, whatever their census or employment categorization. Culturally, the dominant image of an Asian American for most other Americans is a (recent) immigrant from East Asia who "looks Chinese"; heterogeneity is not widely acknowledged.

The first Asian Americans were Chinese and Japanese who came in the mid-nineteenth century under multiple restrictions. Filipinos and South Asians followed in the twentieth century. Koreans arrived primarily after the **Korean War**, just as **Southeast Asians** were linked to Vietnam. Overall, Asians had little American presence until the 1965 Immigration Act, which abolished racial and nationality quotas. In the ensuing twenty-five years, the Asian American population increased sevenfold.

In the twentieth century most Asians entered the US either as family members of naturalized citizens or as professionals. However, in the black/**white** racial polarization of America, Asian Americans have been even more invisible than **Hispanics**. In part, this reflects an "ease" of **assimilation**. The media have labeled Asian Americans as the "model minority" because of their socio-economic success, including their remarkable student representation in elite universities like Harvard, University of California-Berkeley and MIT (Massachusetts Institute of Technology, nicknamed Made In Taiwan). In fact, the labor of generations of Chinese, Japanese and Filipinos struggling to gain a stake has been eclipsed by an image of immigrant entrepreneurs and highly driven students. While some "Asian values" contribute to this, including strong **family** ties (often with Confucian overtones) and widespread cultural values of **education** and discipline, new immigration policies also favor family cohesion, education and capital. Meanwhile, an image of rapidly acquired wealth has antagonized local relations and hidden problems of the elderly, the culturally dislocated and those whose immigration experience is one of virtual servitude in sweatshops.

Moreover, Asian Americans are not seen as threatening: men have often been portrayed as smart but nerdy, preoccupied with math and science, while women are seen as the sexy Suzy Wong or subservient mail-order bride. This image of a successful, docile minority overshadows the diversity and the "Americanness" of Asians ranging from street **gangs** to Olympic skaters.

The most contentious issue facing Asian Americans is the difficulty defining Asian American. Often, Asian Americans come from countries that have fought each other for centuries. While their languages, foods, religions and clothes appear similar from a Euro-American perspective, differences in national and regional traditions are strongly marked among immigrants and their descendants – Vietnamese Chinese are not the same as Hmong or Viet, nor do early Cantonese immigrants share the language and experience of Taiwanese or Chinese from the mainland or the Chinese global diaspora. Asian Americans who have resided in the US for generations, suffering laws that divided families or interned them, have assimilated in different ways from those who have just arrived in the last few years or decades. However, this diversity is also a strength, which allows the group to act cohesively, with different voices against shared discrimination.

The notion of an Asian American identity, in fact, has been shaped by the success of the **Civil Rights movement** in the 1960s. Grassroots organizations, like the Asian American Legal Defense and Education Fund, serve all Asian Americans. In universities across the country, ethnic studies programs have incorporated sizeable Asian American sections, featuring Asian and Pacific American heritage week (or month) held every May. The label "Asian American" is more readily used by American-born generations than by immigrants, since the former have a shared experience of growing up in America as neither black nor white. Hence, "Asian American" can be both a self-selected term for political empowerment and an imposed category for the ethnic accounting.

While there are Asian Americans all over the United States, large communities are especially situated in metropolitan centers like **Los Angeles**, **San Francisco**, **New York**, **Chicago** and **Atlanta**. More Asian Americans are concentrated on the West Coast because of its relative geographic proximity to Asia and its diverse historical roots. While the original Chinatowns were **ethnic enclaves**, **middle-class** Asian American **suburbs** took shape in the 1980s. Yet many Asian Americans, especially those of the second or third generation, live in diverse communities all over the country. Friendships and intermarriage with whites (often class-based ties that eclipse marriage with **African Americans** and **Hispanics**, and with other Asian nationalities) are also producing new bi-racial and bi-cultural generations.

Older Asian Americans have been making headway in the political mainstream, including Senator Daniel Inouye and Representative Patsy Mink from **Hawai'i**, and Governor Gary Locke in Washington. However, in the 1990s fundraising scandals linked to overseas Chinese and a suspected Chinese espionage scandal have shown how Asian Americans are marked as different within the United States. Orientalist stereotypes of a shifty, unscrupulous Fu Manchu are alive and well, complicated by a widespread assumption that all Asians are born and have allegiances "somewhere else." Yet, the recent growth of the Asian American population as a result of the continual influx of immigrants has indeed made Asian Americans deeply transnational citizens, united by media, communication, travel and family ties to a global consciousness unusual within traditions of American isolation and assimilation. In fact, such transnational ties raise interesting questions about American identity itself. Is Shanghai-born I.M. **Pei**, whose career flourished in the US but who is also lionized in China, different from the Vietnamese American Maya Lin, or the European refugee Walter Gropius? Hong Kong film-makers Jackie Chan, John Woo and Ringo Lam work and live in the US; **tennis** star Michael Chang has fans across China. While the same issues of divided loyalties are raised with regard to **Irish American** supporters of the IRA or **Cuban American** exiles in **Miami**, Asian Americans as a whole seem to have been defined within a new global citizenship, wrapped in both suspicion and promise.

These issues also imbue media representation of Asian Americans as "others." In literature and film, however, many have countered this in a florescence of artistic creativity, especially since the 1960s. The seminal literary anthology *The Big Aiiieeeee!* (1974) reflects the frustrations many have felt as people marked as non-Americans despite their heritage, service and commitment (see **Asian Americans in cinema and television**).

Further reading

Amerasia (journal) Asian American Studies Center, UCLA.

Chan, J.F., Chin, L. Inada and Wong, S. (eds) (1991) *The Big Aiiieeeee!*, New York: Penguin.

Hing, B. (1993) *Making and Remaking Asian America through Immigration Policy 1850–1990*, Stanford: Stanford University Press.

Okihiro, G. (1994) *Margins and Mainstreams*, Seattle: University of Washington.

Takaki, R.(1998) *Strangers from a Different Shore*, Boston: Little Brown & Company.

CINDY WONG

Asian Americans in cinema and television

Not only did **Disney** turn to Asia for a global animated feature in 1998, but it chose a traditional Chinese tale of a woman who fought like a man to break stereotypes. Later, in a **television** broadcast, Olympic medalist Michelle Kwan interpreted the story on ice. Somehow, after all the spectacle, one could not still believe that American media had made a great leap forward in the understanding and incorporation of **Asian Americans** as subjects, creators and participants. But history, in fact, may guide that interpretation.

Early American cinema used stereotypes of Asians as foreign/exotic, servile, wise but enigmatic and often untrustworthy. Few actors of Asian origin made it in Hollywood – Sessue Hayakawa and Anna May Wong often played mysterious Oriental villains. Many Asian/Asian American roles were played by Anglos in series like Charlie Chan (Warner Oland) or Mr Moto (Peter Lorre), while Katharine Hepburn (!) became Mei Ling, a "tall" Chinese peasant, in *Dragon Seed* (1944). Furthermore, there has long been confusion of place and identity, between Asian American and imported Asian films and readings, which become lumped together.

American media have been slow in reflecting the burgeoning Asian American population since 1965. Breakthroughs in documentary and independent film led to *Joy Luck Club* (1993); however, it was still marked as an "Asian story." Images of urban **gangs** and drug connections have also overshadowed **Hollywood** films, especially as they interpret the gender roles of Asian American men as both strong enemies and weak, nerdish citizens.

One of the most vibrant areas of Asian American media is its independent voices, especially documentary. These voices of opposition, advocacy and cultural intimacy tackle issues marginal to the mainstream media, from the murder of a **Chinese American** in *Who Killed Vincent Chin* (1987) to a light-hearted detective story, Wayne Wang's *Chan is Missing* (1981).

Television inherited cultural stereotypes, while giving Asian Americans even fewer positions of independence from which to challenge them. Servants were long the predominant male role in the old western (*Bonanza*, 1959–73, NBC) or new West **prime-time soap operas** (*Falcon Crest*). Jack Soo as a policeman on *Barney Miller* (1975–82, ABC) opened wider visions of Asian citizenry. Females have been more scarce – *The Courtship of Eddies' Father* offered a subservient Japanese woman, while the 1980s sitcom *Night Court* introduced

a Vietnamese woman married to an **African American** court clerk over both families objections. Margaret Cho's Korean family **sitcom**, *All-American Girl* (1994–5) was a short-lived breakthrough. Connie Chung's brief career as television news anchor also made Asian Americans visible in non-narrative settings. But the most famous Asian Americans on TV have been Bruce **Lee** in the 1970s *Green Hornet* and George Takei (Mr Solo) in *Star Trek*. It may also be telling that satellite television, videos and paid retransmission make it possible for recent immigrants to watch Korean, Chinese and other shows rather than relying on American television. This experience may not suffice, however, for emergent American generations, nor does it reach beyond the language community.

One striking footnote points to the emergence of Asian Americans in a different way: **advertising**. Both multicultural commercials and faces/families promoting a wide range of products show Asian Americans gaining face and agency against stereotypes not yet overcome in other media.

Further reading

Leong, R. (ed.) (1991) *Moving the Image: Independent Asian Pacific American Media Arts*, Los Angeles: UCLA Asian American Studies Center.

Moy, J. (1993) *Marginal Sights: Staging the Chinese in America*, Ames: University of Iowa.

Xing, J. (1998) *Asian America through the Lens*, Walnut Creek: Altamira.

GARY McDONOGH
CINDY WONG

Asimov, Isaac

b. 1920; d. 1992

Russian-born biochemistry professor at Boston University, Asimov became better known for his **science fiction** and popularizations of science, especially for young people. An extraordinarily prolific writer (over 300 books), Asimov is remembered for his visionary *Foundation* trilogy (1951–3) whose images of a galactic empire in collapse certainly prefigure *Star Wars*. He returned to writing about this universe in the 1980s with new volumes, while continuing to write both scientific texts and popular mysteries.

GARY McDONOGH
CINDY WONG

ASL (American Sign Language)

Language primarily used by deaf Americans, based on hand shape, location, movement and expression augmented by finger spelling. Adapted from French models in the nineteenth century (and completely distinct from British signing), sign language was also repressed by institutions which denigrated it as broken communication and sought to force the deaf to read lips and vocalize. Since the 1980s, it has been increasingly recognized as a complex language, the structure and expressiveness of which differs from English. It has become a sign of community for the deaf; hearing speakers study it as a recognized foreign language in universities and **community** programs. Estimates of signers in the US vary widely, from several hundred thousand to 2 million.

GARY McDONOGH
CINDY WONG

assassination

Assassins (literally, "eaters of hashish") were an order of Muslim fanatics who specialized in killing Christian crusaders during the Middle Ages. In recent decades, "assassination" has come to refer almost exclusively to the murder of politically prominent persons. For example, whereas Mark David Chapman is the "murderer" of John Lennon, Lee Harvey Oswald was the "assassin" of John F. **Kennedy**.

The most shocking and controversial assassinations were the trio of killings in the 1960s, taking the lives of John and Robert **Kennedy** and Martin Luther **King**, Jr. The November 22, 1963 assassination of President Kennedy became one of those moments locked in Americans' memories; people who remember the assassination can recall exactly what they were doing and how they felt when they heard the news. All three deaths evoked massive outpourings of public grief. Following Dr King's death, riots broke out in several US cities because the assassination of the **Civil Rights movement**'s moral leader seemed to undermine any hope **African Americans** held for racial justice.

The official media and government response to the assassinations was to reassure the public that the assassins' bullets could not damage the operation of the nation's democratic institutions. The reassurance occasionally included positive actions, such as when President **Johnson** linked John Kennedy's martyrdom with the passage of the **Civil Rights Acts** of 1964 and 1965. Typically, many citizens have not been so easily reassured, and their doubts have led them to believe that, had President Kennedy lived, he would not have become deeply involved in the **Vietnam War**, or that Robert Kennedy would have won the 1968 presidential election and prevented much of the ensuing divisiveness in the nation's political culture.

In all three assassinations, a prime suspect was quickly identified, convicted in the court of public opinion, and marginalized as a lone fanatic, unconnected with any powerful groups that might have profited from the assassination. Moreover, in all three cases, the assassination investigations were hastily completed, leaving many alternative hypotheses untested. Furthermore, the importance of the **FBI** in conducting these investigations calls their findings into question because Bureau Director J. Edgar **Hoover** hated the Kennedys and King. In fact, the House Select Committee on Assassinations repudiated the key finding of the **Warren Commission** by asserting that Oswald did not act alone in killing President Kennedy, and was most likely carrying out the plans of organized crime leaders.

The controversy over these assassinations persists. Supporters of the official explanations find a platform in the media, whereas critics are given little access and are demeaningly called "conspiracy buffs." Controversies were fueled by Oliver **Stone**'s pro-conspiracy movie *JFK* (1991), and by the flurry of media stories arising from the King family's support of James Earl Ray's request for a trial in the year before his 1998 death.

Further reading

Scott, P.D. (1994) *Deep Politics and the Death of JFK*, Berkeley: University of California.

Summers, A. (1998) *Not in Your Lifetime*, New York: Marlowe & Co.

MELINDA SCHWENK

assimilation

As a "nation of immigrants," the United States has demanded that newcomers (and existing Native American populations) learn social and cultural citizenship, blending into the "melting-pot" in acceptable ways, whether in sports, military service or the preoccupations of life in the **suburbs**. Given public norms of **freedom** and democracy, however, negotiating acceptance and use of perceived values creates paradoxes.

Not all features are equal. For example, shared political economic goals of advancement within a liberal capitalist state have been primary, and those perceived as "outside political agitators" have met the limits of freedom, whether Scandinavian socialists or Latino Marxists. This entails patriotism as well: **Japanese American** males proved their loyalties in the Second World War by volunteering to fight while their families were interned in camps. The American dream is to make it, not to change it (when one's assimilation might be called into question). For early immigrants, postwar movement from **ethnic enclaves** into new suburbs provided a homogenous "Americanness." The stereotype of **Asian Americans** as a "model minority" because of their work, educational success and acquisition of middle-class goods reaffirms these goals.

Language also has been a primary but contested issue, especially with new immigrants who have used the discourse of **civil rights** and ethnic identity to maintain **language** and media. Most, like their nineteenth-century forebears, still learn English rapidly by the second generation: schools are a major force in teaching language and social mores. Yet tensions may arise between bilinguals and English monolinguals, threatened by prerequisites associated with bilingual status (see **English Only**). **Mass media**, since the turn of the century, have been seen as potent vehicles to teach immigrants language and customs. **Hollywood** studios, at the same time, often hid the ethnic origins of stars and producers in putting this American dream on screen.

Religion, by contrast, was a major assimilation issue in the nineteenth century when **Roman Catholic** and Jewish immigrants were perceived to threaten Protestant hegemony. This has faded over generations, but growing immigrant religions like **Buddhism**, **Islam** and Hinduism have "Americanized" some public activities to establish their status. Indeed, religion has become an "acceptable" form of diversity which immigrants might display – like **food**, **fashion** (on ritual or festive occasions), **parades**, **dance** and music. Often, these features can create a dual identity over generations as teenagers cast off everyday jeans and T-shirts (a global assimilation) and don unfamiliar costumes for school events celebrating multiculturalism. Transnational ties, in which beliefs and practices move between different worlds, further complicate the assimilation of some new immigrants.

Yet an ethos of potential assimilation and permissible diversity cannot mask the central historic dilemma of assimilation – one may vote, earn, talk, eat and dance like an "American," yet fail to "look" like one. This is especially true for **African Americans**, with centuries of participation in American society shaped by continual exclusion. Programs since the Civil Rights era have fostered, within limits, integration in schools, residences and workplaces. Yet middle-class blacks may complain that they cannot get a taxi, or face police harassment because of **race**, ignoring other American traits and commitments that constitute successful assimilation. The issue has also divided blacks from the debates of W.E.B. **Du Bois** and Booker T. Washington at the turn of the century, through the **Black Power** movement of the 1960s and its heirs. Assimilation here can be seen as giving up traits and values as well as taking on a shared culture, and must also confront the differences that remain after centuries of being in America and shaping American culture. Moreover, this is an internal debate as well: **middle-class** African Americans may be called "**whites**" or "Oreos" by other blacks (black on the outside, white on the inside, like "Bananas" for Asian Americans); "passing" – pretending to be white – is an extreme case that has nonetheless gained media and literary attention. Hence race remains the test – and failure – of the melting-pot.

GARY McDONOGH
CINDY WONG

Astaire, Fred (Fred Austerlitz)

b. 1899; d. 1987

Ballroom dancer, actor and singer (well, talker) who glided through decades of elegant **musicals** and movies with his sister Adele, long-time partner Ginger Rogers and Cyd Charisse, among others. His elegant continental styles balanced the earthier **masculinity** of Gene **Kelly**.

GARY McDONOGH

astroturf

Synthetic turf first used in **Houston**'s Astrodome, completed in 1965, to replace grass when it was learned that grass would not grow well in indoor stadiums. It was quickly brought into every indoor and many outdoor stadiums around the country, and was often used on porches and patios to give the appearance of perfect grass.

Thirty years later, astroturf is considered a very inadequate playing surface and is a cause of many major injuries, particularly in **football** since the surface itself provides only a thin padding over concrete. It has now fallen out of favor, like the multipurpose dome in which it "grew." Most **baseball** teams are now demanding more traditional-looking stadiums with real grass.

ROBERT GREGG

atheists

When the words "under God" were added to the **Pledge of Allegiance** in 1954, it highlighted a profound contradiction in the culture of America as a nation built on the separation of church and state. In a period of change, **religion** could nonetheless be added to civic duties rather than stripped from them in the name of democracy, science or modernity. The pluralism of religions in the US, despite controversies over doctrine, status and conversions, also creates a fundamental division between believers and non-believers. These general views were intensified in the **Cold War** by the identification of atheism with "godless **communism**." Even those rebelling against American civic religion often have turned to alternate spiritualities based in Asian religion, "**nature**," **feminism** or reinterpretations of a Judaeo-Christian deity in terms of science, cult personalities or imagery. This "prescriptive relationship between religion and the everyday lives of the populace" (see **religion**) fosters a widespread intolerance towards atheism. Meanwhile, atheists are forced to deny shared civic practice, political invocations of deity, social rituals at tables and **holidays** and constant minutiae of American piety on a daily basis.

Atheists, in general, have been silent non-believers, lacking the institutional support or public symbols adopted and even flaunted by American believers. Even dividing lines can be unclear. One may see the fish symbol labeling Christian cars mimicked and altered into a four-legged beast tagged Darwin, but this may indicate opposition to **scientific creationism** rather than a declaration of atheism. Moreover, Catholics, **Jews**, **Muslims** and Protestants have objected to Protestant pieties in schools or manipulative affirmations in sports and politics without denying religion per se. American flexibility within belief systems also makes atheism more difficult to delineate – are **Buddhists**, Taoists, **Unitarians** (not to mention polytheists) somewhere beyond the pale of American belief in a monotheistic god? Atheism may be presumed in discourses of science or social reform on the left (as more than one horror movie has said "but you are a man of science – surely you don't believe in all this superstitious mumbo-jumbo!"). Yet, even here, silence covers a range of beliefs and compromises without creating public declarations of alternatives. In political life, meanwhile, invoking some god and showing up at some ritual events are normative, whether or not politicians confess to any beliefs or responsibilities associated with them.

"Angels" are often normalized as jewelry and bric-a-brac without religious significance, except to those who would choose to actively object, which would seem to many to be petulance rather than belief.

Among the most vilified are those who have crusaded for constitutional guarantees, such as Madalyn Murray O'Hare who successfully argued for the removal of prayer from schools in the 1950s. Similarly, the **American Civil Liberties Union**, which deals with a range of constitutional issues, has been branded atheist for countering strategies of the **Christian Right** to introduce "prayerful silences" into schools.

Electronic communication has opened a new space of expression and communion among Internet infidels. Societies like the Rocky Mountain skeptics, the Philadelphia Association for Critical Thinking, the Skeptic Society (with its journal *Skeptic*) and the Freedom from Religion Foundation have flourished on the web. While the editor of *The Skeptical Review* argues for dramatic changes since the religious establishment can no longer control and "suppress" information, the pervasiveness of civic religion makes the future of atheism difficult to read.

ROBERT GREGG
GARY McDONOGH

Atlanta, GA

Atlanta has been a center for a "new" South in the post-Civil War era and the twentieth century. In both eras, this promise conveys civic hope and overlooks ongoing problems, especially those of **race**.

Incorporated as a city in 1847, Atlanta developed around the intersection of railroads linking the Atlantic and Gulf coasts with the Ohio Valley and the **Midwest**. Since the 1960s, a complex system of expressways and one of the world's busiest **airports** has made Atlanta one of the most dynamic regions in the country. By the late 1990s, the population of the twenty-county Atlanta metropolitan region soared to nearly 4 million (city population 425,000).

Nevertheless, Atlanta's growth has been very uneven, with most recent increases in employment and population taking place in a broad swath of suburban counties. Between 1970 and 1995, the central city experienced a steady decline in jobs and residents (modest growth reappeared in the late 1990s). As in many other US metropolitan areas, the urban/rural distinction partially corresponds to a racial divide. In 1960 two-thirds of the city's inhabitants were **white**; in 1980 an equivalent portion of the urban population was **African American**. In the 1990s, two-thirds of the suburban population was white, although African Americans, especially **middle-class** households, had increased markedly during the previous decade. Hence, African Americans dominate city government, while whites control the suburban political establishment, despite Atlanta's image as the "capital of the **Civil Rights movement**" and the presence of the Martin Luther **King**, Jr. Center.

For most of Atlanta's history, its social dynamics have largely been a matter of relations between native-born blacks and whites. Since the 1980s, however, the in-migration of transplants from other parts of the United States, as well as the arrival of several hundred thousand immigrants and **refugees** from **Latin America**, Eastern Europe, subSaharan Africa, the Middle East and South, East and Southeast Asia have changed the city. In the early 1990s, it was estimated that more than 60 percent of the metro area population was born outside of Georgia.

Atlanta's economy now includes **telecommunications**, finance, **conventions** and a wide range of business services. Its alluring business climate attracts billions of dollars each year in foreign, as well as domestic, investment. The presence of foreign capital, the expanded global reach of Atlanta-based companies, a global **television** network (**CNN**) and the 1996 **Olympics** reinforced boosters' claims that Atlanta is indeed "The World's Next Great International City."

Atlanta is also a regional center for higher education, especially for African Americans. It is home to five traditionally **black colleges** (Morehouse, Spellman, Clark, Atlanta, Morris Brown), as well as Emory University, Georgia Institute of Technology and Georgia State University. Professional sports teams also form an important component of Atlanta's identity as a major-league city, including the Braves (**baseball**), the Falcons (**football**), the Hawks (**basketball**) and the Thrashers (**hockey**).

See also: Africa

Further reading

Bayor, R. (1996) *Race and the Shaping of Twentieth Century Atlanta*, Chapel Hill: University of North Carolina.

Rutheiser, C. (1996) *Imagineering Atlanta*, London: Verso.

CHARLES RUTHEISER

Atlantic City, NJ

On Absecon Island, Atlantic City became a popular playground for the Victorian rich from nearby **New York** City, NY and **Philadelphia**. It was also famous in the early twentieth century for the boardwalk and amusement piers, and since 1921 has hosted the **Miss America pageant**. The city went into decline after the Second World War owing to the westward shift in population and growing access to air travel.

In part to stem this decline, the city turned to **gambling**. A year after the passage of the Casino Gambling Referendum in 1976, casinos modeled on those in **Las Vegas** opened along the **waterfront**. Debate continues about the value of this scheme. Some argue that the casinos have brought new employment and business to a declining city. Others maintain they have accelerated the displacement of poorer city residents, especially the long-established Northside **African American** community. This ambivalence is captured in the movie *Atlantic City* (1981), although without the racial dimensions.

In spite of opposition, casinos and gambling are firmly established. The leading casino owner, New York real-estate mogul Donald **Trump**, has persuaded the city to build a new highway tunnel to facilitate access to the newest of his four casinos. This will bring further displacement of residents and small businesses.

The city also hosted the 1964 **Democratic Party** Convention, at which the **Mississippi Freedom Democratic Party** tried unsuccess-

fully to force the party to seat the black delegates from Mississippi instead of the white-only delegates.

ROBERT GREGG

AT&T

Formerly American Telephone and Telegraph Company, AT&T was incorporated in March 1885 to take over the long-distance business of American Bell Telephone Company, founded by inventor Alexander Graham Bell and associates. As a monopoly, it was for years the sole American company for long-distance **telecommunications**. In December 1899, it became the parent company of the Bell System that provided local exchange. AT&T moved into **radio** in the 1910s, and after the First World War, it participated in the radio trust that set up RCA as a government-sanctioned monopoly. AT&T also owned the first station to accept advertising – WEAF. It was forced to divest itself of the Bell System in 1984. In 1995 AT&T split into three companies: a "new" AT&T for communication services; Lucent Technologies, for communications systems and technologies; and NCR Corp, for transaction-intensive computing.

EDWARD MILLER

atom bomb *see* nuclear age

Attica uprising

A riot which broke out at Attica prison, near Buffalo, New York, on September 9, 1971. The immediate cause was a rumor that inmates had been beaten, but the underlying unrest was caused by the horrendous conditions, including overcrowding, bad food and harsh punishments. The uprising was quashed by a brutal, indiscriminate **police** assault that killed forty-three men. Once order had been restored, prison officials set about systematic reprisals, for which the state was found liable in 2000 and forced to pay $8 million to the torture victims. The **governor**, Nelson A. **Rockefeller**, gained national attention and popularity from his decision to launch the assault at Attica, underpinning his appointment as President Gerald **Ford**'s **vice-president** in 1974.

ROBERT GREGG

Attorney-General

The prominent role of this position in contemporary American society was fashioned by A. Mitchell Palmer, a progressive Democratic Attorney General under Woodrow Wilson, who attempted to circumvent **Bill of Rights** freedoms to prosecute those who opposed American involvement in the First World War and later to purge the United States of communists and anarchists. These expanding powers, however, were constrained during the 1920s and early 1930s by the **Republican** Party's ascendancy and the growing visibility of J. Edgar **Hoover** at the nascent **FBI**. Many Republicans had opposed the war or Palmer's actions; they also made few demands on the Justice Department to bust trusts or other illegal economic combinations. Meanwhile, Hoover's very public campaign against crime elevated his own public image and deflected attention away from the Attorney-General.

President **Roosevelt**'s New Deal changed the role of federal officials dramatically. By transferring power from the states to the federal government, New Deal programs led to larger roles for federal officials. If states accepted aid from the federal government, then they would also have to accept some oversight in the allocation of funds and abide by federal laws outlawing discrimination (especially on the basis of race). Moreover, as government expenditure on defense increased, federal influence grew in both the **South** and the **West**.

The federal government was slow to use the new powers at its disposal, especially in the South, which remained a strong force within the Democratic Party. No Attorney-General intervened on behalf of victims of lynch mobs, but **civil rights** activists were quick to see the possibilities that came from the growing significance of the Justice Department. In the 1960s, James Foreman of **CORE** recognized that if **Supreme Court** decisions desegregating schools and interstate buses

were ever to be enforced, Attorney-General Robert **Kennedy** would have to be prodded into action. Activists' success in this endeavor, leading an Attorney-General who was skeptical about any political advantages for his brother in being outspoken in favor of civil rights to oppose the governors of several **states**, helped establish the position of the Attorney-General both positively and negatively in the consciousness of many Americans.

The Attorney-General is a presidential appointee, often closely identified with the sitting president – as were Robert Kennedy with his brother and Ed Meese with Ronald **Reagan**. Richard **Nixon**'s appointee, John Mitchell, previously a member of Nixon's law firm, became the head of the president's re-election committee, where he was responsible for organizing a break-in at Democratic headquarters. Resigning at the beginning of the **Watergate** scandal in 1972, he was subsequently convicted of conspiracy, obstruction of justice, and perjury, and served nineteen months in prison.

This tension concerning the Attorney-General has only intensified in recent years. The **backlash** against civil rights was motivated not only by a white racist reaction to **African American** and other minority advances in the last third of the twentieth century, but also by a sense of the growing intrusiveness of the federal government. The exaggeration of the role of the Justice Department in bringing about change in the South (recalling Reconstruction) has helped to cement some tightly knit, secretive hate groups and neo-Fascist organizations – the **Ku Klux Klan**, **survivalists** and militias. These focus their ire on the Justice Department and its agents in the FBI and Alcohol, Tobacco and Firearms [Agency].

Janet Reno, Bill **Clinton**'s Attorney-General and the first woman appointed to this position, found herself at the center of a continuing conflict between the Justice Department and organizations that believe the Founding Fathers would have opposed the kind of power wielded by federal authorities. Reno's first crisis came when the FBI confronted the Branch Davidians, a religious cult in Waco, Texas, whose siege turned into a bloodbath, although she was cleared by a congressional investigation.

On occasions, the position of Attorney-General in seeking American justice has placed the incumbent in the difficult position of overseeing the presidency itself. Meese needed to investigate the involvement of Reagan in the **Iran-Contra** scandal. Reno had to investigate allegations of misconduct in the Clinton administration, withstanding initial calls from the Republican Party, but later succumbing to pressure to investigate **Whitewater** allegations. She also expanded the purview of **Independent Counsel** Kenneth Starr to include many other issues, including those covered in the Linda Tripp tapes of Monica Lewinsky that led to the final **impeachment** process, an outcome that would have been less likely had Reno not initially given Starr his broad mandate.

ROBERT GREGG

Austin, TX

State capital and home of the University of Texas, Austin combines old Texas history and politics with a cosmopolitan and independent flavor. Austin's relaxed ambience has made it into a "hot" city for youth and music culture, as well as metropolitan expansion (the metropolitan area is predicted to soar from 999,936 to 1,656,298 by 2020). Growth restrictions and environmental issues have become major local concerns in the early twenty-first century.

GARY McDONOGH
CINDY WONG

automakers

The increasing automobility of Americans after the Second World War not only changed American geography and culture, but also benefited a set of key corporations that stood for American industrial power, and, later, its problems in global competition: "What's good for General Motors is good for the country." From its infancy in the early twentieth century, the automobile industry was characteristically entrepreneurial. Breakthroughs, such as the Five Dollar Day, which helped create a mass market, the assembly-line and parts standar-

dization are attributed to the industry's early years (1900–20). As it matured, consolidation put control into the hands of a few powerful automakers based in **Detroit**: General Motors, Ford and Chrysler became the "Big Three." Along with foreign competitors, these have constituted an oligopoly, which uses its market dominance to price vehicles for maximum profit.

In the 1960s, the US auto industry felt the threat of foreign imports. By this time, the US industry had become complacent, producing large, gas-guzzling hunks of steel targeted at the average American family. Furthermore, a strategy of planned obsolescence, wherein the Big Three produced technologically inferior cars in order to promote annual model changes, resulted in a perception that foreign cars were superior. Niches developed for outsiders in the **sports car**, **trucks** and, most significantly, the fuel-efficient segments of the market.

At first, European automakers like Volkswagen, Mercedes and Fiat made inroads in the US. By the 1970s, Japan's auto industry, protected domestically by governmental tariffs, brought its fuel-efficient, inexpensively produced car to the US market. Foreign imports, which averaged 22.2 miles per gallon versus just 13.2 for domestics, became an attractive alternative during US oil shortages in 1973 and 1979. Although US automakers responded with compact, efficient cars of their own (Ford Pinto, AMC Gemlin), Japanese automakers Honda, Toyota and Nissan gained significant market share in the US. As these foreign companies built assembly plants in North America and as the Big Three have acquired interests abroad in their own manufacturers and acquisitions like Ford's control of Aston Martin and Volvo, or the Chrysler–Daimler Benz merger, the limits of nation and globalism have become murkier.

In 1997, the Big Three accounted for 60.9 percent of US sales compared with 31.0 percent for Japanese automakers. Waning fears of energy shortages have led to a demand for "family trucks" – minivans and sports utility vehicles. American automakers have especially capitalized on the rising popularity of the new big car, producing 82 percent of trucks and **sports utility vehicles**.

The Big Three represent what many think of as big business – faceless corporations that stop at nothing to make a profit. **Union** strife, most recently at General Motors, has illustrated the classic battle between owners and workers. *Roger and Me* (1989) depicted the socio-economic devastation inflicted by plant closings in Flint, Michigan, a scene which has been repeated throughout the country. Auto workers are faced with the threat of lay-offs, **downsizing** and **bankruptcy** due to the mature nature of their industry.

Seven million Americans directly owe their livelihood to the automobile industry. By offering individual privacy and comfort, the automobile is both a status symbol and a necessity in modern American society. Its production and distribution as well are statements about American power and challenges in this century.

Further reading

James, F. (1993) *The Automobile Age*, Cambridge, MA: MIT Press.

MARC BALCER

automats

Horn and Hardart began operating self-service restaurants in the 1910s, with food behind small glass doors which were opened by inserting a coin (initially a nickel) into a slot. By the 1930s, such automats (restaurants without waiters) served a full range of lunch and dinner entrées; in the 1940s, more than fifty serviced **New York** City, NY alone. In their heyday, through the 1960s, automats provided inexpensive food in vast simple rooms that allowed customers to linger at tables – and fascinated tourists and children. Outpaced by fast-food restaurants, however, the last New York automat closed in 1991.

EDWARD MILLER

automobiles

Among the most pervasive "vehicles" of cultural change in twenty-first-century America is the gasoline-driven, individualized surface road transportation shell first mass-marketed by Henry Ford in 1908. While automobiles have become a global phenomenon, they intersected with an American nation growing in wealth, with space to expand, and valuing the **freedom**, **individualism** and equality that cars seem to embody. This proved especially true with a car-friendly government that has provided unlimited highways and limited fuel **taxes** while undercutting mass transit. Cars have altered the American landscape, changed social and family relations, and permeated popular culture from **road movies** to **drive-ins** to **soccer** moms. Since the Second World War, this pervasive presence has also faced critics decrying environmental costs, social changes and dehumanization associated with the centaurial symbiosis of person and car. Any rethinking of this dependency, however, faces its sheer normality in a nation where a driver's license is the most widespread national identity card and where cars are a necessity for all but the most urban (and marginal) of the nation's citizens.

Mass production (see **automakers**) rapidly made cars central to the American **family**. Registrations increased from 8,000 in 1900 to 8 million in 1920 (and 143 million by 1995). This demanded further changes, including improved roadways and services, urban regulations (and space for parking) and garages and other accommodations in residential areas. While some later critics have seen this as a period of villainous, conspiratorial destruction of mass transit alternatives and face-to-face community, cars also brought together outlying regions and isolated families and housewives on **farms** and **ranches**, allowing new explorations of the America glimpsed through mass media. Cars provided privacy for courtship and sex, which have remained important images in American life for decades. Movies, songs and literature celebrate America's love affair with the car in stories of adventure, glamour, crime and love. Yet, the ambivalence of dependence remains vivid in heart-rending images of impoverished Depression-era families, all their belongings piled into a car, seeking new opportunities in **California**.

While automobile production and travel were restricted by the Second World War mobilization, cars became fundamental elements of postwar suburban home-ownership, shopping and commuting to work. Here, the promise of automotive freedom faced the realities of longer commutes and multiple trips that have plagued sprawling metropolitan development ever since. Acres of parking surrounding shopping **malls**, churches, schools and other institutions placed competitive demands on urban centers, where garages and parking lots gouged holes in the fabric of urban life. Cars themselves, through the 1950s and 1960s, celebrated an exuberance of display in features including giant tail fins, bright and bi-colored paint jobs, larger motors and new handling. New comfort appeared – bucket seats, **air-conditioning**, sound and increased vision. In addition, the new car – traded in every year or every other year – was a symbol of American success.

While cars united America, they also divided it. Access to cars depended on money, which differentiated basic service vehicles and the luxurious Cadillacs, Lincolns and imported cars. In the twenty-first century, expensive **sports utility vehicles**, Lamborghini convertibles and third-hand junkers make statements about class (and, for some, about **masculinity**) every second on streets and highways. Cars also have provided a language of protest – the **hot-rod** of male **teenagers** in the 1950s, the multi-colored hippie vans of the 1960s, Cadillacs and other automotive status symbols in **African American** communities and the Chicano **low riders** of the 1980s and 1990s all have used mass-produced items to express individualism and difference.

In 1973–4 Arab states and other oil-producing countries cut back production and raised prices, which quadrupled gasoline prices at the pump and led to lines and restricted sales. This oil crisis underscored the vulnerability of American automobile dependence, challenged the nation's unbounded faith in cars and exploded markets for smaller, fuel-efficient and innovative foreign cars. Meanwhile, environmentalists were decrying hydrocarbons and other wastes that created dense clouds of smog over **Los Angeles, CA** and other cities and befouled waterways, while cars chewed up land for highways and associated development. In the US, motor vehicles are responsible for roughly 70 percent of all carbon monoxide emissions. Almost eclipsed in these concerns are 2 million disabling injuries and 40,000–50,000 deaths each year; cars are the single greatest killer of young people.

Federal regulations on fuel efficiency and emissions controls changed automotive styles, allowing the triumph of imported, more fuel-efficient smaller cars. Education, insurance and licensing restrictions, increased penalties (especially on drunk drivers) and collision features, including air bags and child restraints, have worked to make cars safer. Yet alternative mass transit or transit-oriented development faces generations for whom a car is a birthright and whose lives and homes are built around multiple, distant obligations and constant movement. In fact, as more women entered the workplace, juggling family obligations, their mileage quadrupled between 1983 and 1993.

Cars have become homes as well as symbols of the American family – for dating, sex, vacations and community participation (sports, school, church). Hence, in the 1980s and 1990s, many American cars have again become larger (with the popularization of mini-vans and sports utility vehicles), while adding residential comforts like telephones and VCRs. Continuing costly highway construction and raised speed limits have made more daily trips seem possible, if not desirable, creating trip-chains averaging six trips per household. The "carless," meanwhile, fall outside this family model. Some are trapped in **ghettos** far from jobs, while **old age** (post-driving) brings new dependency on mass transit and social networks.

The car remains central to American mass media. Radio, for example, while still part of home and office, has become a major medium of music and information for drivers (with competing tapes and CDs). Commercial **television** has been sustained by incessant **advertising** by automakers jockeying for name recognition and related services like gasoline, insurance and tires. Cars also underpin dramatic and **sitcom** narratives, including stereotypes of coming of age, **gender** (women as distracted drivers or nagging passengers) and problematic older drivers. Autos have even taken on character roles in the admittedly awful NBC sitcom *My Mother the Car* (1965–6), where a car was possessed by the spirit of the hero's mother or the slicker *Knight Rider* with its intelligent car. Police series like *Highway Patrol* (1955–9) and *Car 54 Where are You?* (NBC, 1961–3) put vehicular references in the title, while *Route 66* (CBS, 1960–4; NBC, 1993) made two guys in a '61 Corvette an American quest. Only westerns and science fiction seemed a respite, although the prehistoric *Flintstones* (ABC, 1960–6) and the futuristic *Jetsons* (ABC, 1962–3) adapted family cars to their universes.

Movies have also developed in symbiosis with the car – drawing patrons from ever further ranges and accommodating them with the drive-in in the 1950s and 1960s. Onscreen, cars may become monstrous – Stephen **King**'s *Christine* (1983) explored the passions of a 1953 Plymouth Fury possessed by the devil. Cars have more often become symbols of speed and freedom (*Rebel without a Cause*, 1955; *Thelma and Louise*, 1991), family (*National Lampoon's Vacation*, 1983), romance and sex (notably in *No Way Out*, 1987) and class. Whether the fantasy of the Batmobile, the child-like assistance of the Love Bug or dramas of races and chases, cars are ubiquitous.

Many urbanists and planners decry America's dependence on the automobile and attendant consumption, seeking ways to re-orient **cities**, families and individuals. Yet, despite public campaigns for new designs, mass transit, car-pooling and even reduced use, cars are built into the fabric of American social life and culture in ways that cannot be altered without fundamental changes. These need to work with rather than against the automobile.

Further reading

Dunn, J. (1998) *Driving Forces*, Washington, DC: Brookings Institution.

Kay, J. (1997) *Asphalt Nation*, New York: Crown.

Lewis, D. and Goldstein, L. (eds) (1983) *The Automobile and American Culture*, Ann Arbor: University of Michigan.

CHARLES RUTHEISER

aviation, commercial

From its invention through the **space** race, aviation continually invokes speed, progress and futurity. Yet American air travel has been shaped by longstanding patterns of government-fostered markets in public goods and competition among corporations and **cities** for consumers. Unlike other nations, the US government never established or controlled its own flagship carrier. Instead, Pan Am, TWA, American, Delta, Eastern, US Air, United, Northwest and others emerged through private entrepreneurship. Yet, as in **mass media**, governments have regulated safety, pricing, routing and traffic control while providing vital infrastructures. Moreover, military involvement in developing planes and technology (and training pilots) has underpinned constantly changing operations. Yet, while airlines have become mass transportation, with 500 million passengers annually, they also face complaints about responsiveness and complexity, erupting into a congressional Passenger's Bill of Rights in 1999.

America's first commercial flight connected St. Petersburg and Tampa in 1914. For the next decade, emergent airlines competed with minimal regulation. In 1927 the post office shifted airmail from military aircraft, systematizing routes and sustaining passenger flights (6,000 passengers flew in 1926). In 1934, however, the postmaster general and major domestic carriers American, Eastern, TWA and United faced collusion charges (Pan Am, meanwhile, was spreading American air power to Latin America and China). In 1938 the Civil Aeronautics Act established close regulation of airlines (on the earlier model of trains). Prices, routes and competition became tightly controlled; this system also prevented losses and fostered development instead of cost control.

Airline usage grew from 3 million passengers annually in 1940 to 19 million in 1950 and 58 million by 1960. Postwar four-engine aircraft and jets (1959) reduced flight time and increased seating, while other technologies improved safety. Yet, jumbo jets proved devastating expenses, outstripping demand and provoking a 1970s crisis despite 170 million passengers.

Deregulation in 1978 made the market cutthroat, swamping companies like Pan Am and Eastern despite growth on domestic and international routes. It also permitted new upstart companies – People's Express (later incorporated into Continental), Air West, Southwest, etc. – as nearly 300 million passengers flew annually by 1980. Discount fares broadened clientele but demanded cost-cutting that favored hub-and-spoke models, based around symbiosis of airlines and particular airports, covering more routes through interconnecting flights, but creating the sort of chain reaction delays which today still plague modern travelers.

Mass marketing has created cultural meanings of air travel as well. Early airline travel, domestic and international, was elegant, elite and, at times, dangerous. Even after the Second World War, the model traveler was a white male businessperson, served by young attractive female stewardesses, while a white male pilot flew – these themes were stressed in infamous, sexually slanted advertising campaigns. Discount fares, the corollary decline of competing systems (trains and buses) and family travel have made air travel more heterogeneous, although some remain excluded. Class differences can still be bought and marked both in general service and in access to charter or private planes. Brand loyalty in such a large, diverse market is sought through frequent-flyer mile programs, executive clubs and business privileges and up-grades, as well as special relations like Delta's links with **Disneyworld**.

In the early twenty-first century, airline connection prices, specials and reservations often seem a daunting morass: fares change and compete while passengers complain that food and service have deteriorated. The deregulated "democratic" market of American airlines makes travel a complex, sometimes frustrating bazaar as it connects and divides the nation and the world.

See also: airports; air force, US

Further reading

Morrison, S. and Winston, C. (1995) *The Evolution of the Airline Industry*, Washington, DC: Brookings.
Petzinger, T. (1995) *Hard Landing*, New York: Random House.

GARY McDONOGH
CINDY WONG

awards

Academy Awards set the tone, in terms of recognition, ceremony and glamour, for many media awards that now annually recognize both excellence and box-office receipts. These awards, especially as telecast internationally, reaffirm celebrity, glamour and values of American production despite questions about the nature of the selection process. They also eclipse many smaller local and festival awards around the country. These major awards and their spectacles reinforce economic success for studios, works and artists who position themselves through advertisements, gifts and screenings to "bring their works" to the attention of voters.

The Oscars, 13½ inch statuettes awarded by the Academy of Motion Picture Arts and Sciences, first appeared in 1927 when *Wings* captured Best Picture while German-born Emil Jannings won Best Actor. Oscar nominations are decided upon within specialist branches before the final vote of all academy members. As the ceremony has moved from a hotel auditorium to wider audiences, professional roles have been taken by comedian hosts (Bob **Hope**, Johnny Carson, Billy Crystal, Whoopi **Goldberg**), and sets and production numbers have become increasingly elaborate – as have jewelry, hair and costumes for stars. While moments of political intrusion are often remembered (Marlon **Brando**'s Native American substitute, George C. Scott's refusal, Richard Gere's pleas for Tibet), the Oscars tend to reaffirm the priority of **Hollywood** as the entertainment capital. Indeed, workers in technical fields and "lesser-interest" awards are relegated to earlier, less publicized ceremonies so that the narrative of the Oscars focuses on the final naming of the highest categories – Best Picture and Best Director. Foreign films were added as a category in 1947. In the 1990s, limited-voting awards like the New York Film Critics and Golden Globes gained increasing attention as forerunners for the Oscars.

The National Academy of Television Arts and Sciences held its first small ceremony for the Emmy in Hollywood on January 25, 1949. Its six categories remained broad, for example, Most Outstanding Television Personality (ventriloquist Shirley Dinsdale) and Most Popular Television Program (*Pantomime Quiz*; *KTLA*), reflecting the limited scale of a nascent industry that served only 1 million sets. In the second year, categories like Children's Television, Public Service and even

advertising were added; divisions of genre and gender became established in the 1950s. Regional awards also emerged in major markets somewhat later in the 1950s as performance and programming awards topped fifty by 1970. Like the Oscars, the awards became **television** events in themselves, including a separate daytime Emmy presentation. Emmys also have been torn between the recognition of changing definitions of quality or breakthrough achievements and popularity – how does one compare the investigative news of *60 Minutes* with **baseball** coverage, daytime **soaps** or musical variety? Nonetheless, this confluence promotes a sense of celebrity which increasingly crosses genres.

Other national media-award shows have emerged complementing these, like the televised spectacle of the Grammies (music) and Country Music Awards. **Broadway**'s Tony Awards (founded 1947) also have emerged to national television audiences and repackaging in Broadway advertisements that highlight the number of nominations (as well as debates over the constitution of each category).

Some awards also combine movies, television and other fields, for example music, while stressing popularity and pseudo-democracy (People's Choice), while others draw the attention of specific audiences – **MTV** awards have added younger-oriented categories like Best Kiss. Meanwhile, *Essence* magazine sponsors awards for African achievement and **ESPN** hands out the ESPYS. More serious retrospective awards, including Kennedy Center Honors and **American Film Institute** retrospectives, have also been packaged for wider audiences. **Cable television**, moreover, created new premiums such as the Cable Ace awards, which recognize the burgeoning power and diversity of these channels, even as they muscle into Emmys and Golden Globes.

Overall, awards as recognition may have vital meanings in terms of careers, box-office revenues, thematic trends and even corporate survivals. At the same time, as live televisual events, they bring the excitement of uncertain outcomes (as in sports events and **game shows**), individual triumphs and glamorous success to audiences in the US and worldwide.

GARY McDONOGH
CINDY WONG

B

babies

Any baby born in the US, regardless of the status of its parents, is automatically an American citizen. Nearly 4 million citizens were born annually in the 1990s, the birth rate having peaked above that threshold in 1990 with a birth rate of 16.7 per 1,000 and total live births of 4,158,000. Despite the rise in numbers, the birth rate is half of what it was in 1910, and has dropped from 23.7 per 1,000 in 1960. While there are many American babies, they are spread among more people whose cultural expectations of parenting, consumption, care and development Americanize babies in diverse ways.

Many babies born after the Second World War, for example in the **baby boom** and subsequent generations, experienced the movement from family **folklore** in pregnancy and childcare to more scientific medical models, mediated by physicians and authorities, especially Dr Benjamin **Spock**, whose attitudes on discipline and **freedom** changed childcare. As nuclear families have fewer children and fewer nearby relatives, in fact, patterns of information flow about babies have embraced books, neighbors, **mass media** and institutions, including parenting classes. Nevertheless, this apparent commitment to "better babies" has not overcome vast disparities in information and prenatal care, as well as problematic incidences of teenage pregnancy and infant mortality within the US.

Given widespread controls on natality and **family** size, the arrival of new babies generally evokes celebration within most American cultures. Showers before birth or adoption, religious ceremonies for the baby and parents (baptism or bris) and gifts, photos and exhibition all mark family and community participation in birth and babyhood as an event. Naming traditions vary from those who reinforce family continuity or cultural heritage to those who opt for names from **television** and pop culture. Yet, American news media also talk constantly of babies who are abandoned and abused as extreme cases that underscore a shared ideal of innocence and loving comfort.

As babies grow up, parenting includes a stress on **individualism** and freedom of movement and action. This leads to variations in discipline and personality across groups, which are sometimes mediated by shared daycare – one of the most expensive and difficult responsibilities of parenting in the US. Still, debates over issues like toilet training, corporal punishment and rules of behavior have also been part of discourses of baby and childcare since Dr Spock.

Babies are not only responsibilities and celebrations, they are also opportunities for marketing. As Paul Reiser writes in his wry *Babyhood* (1997: 42) "we watched other couples with babies and concluded that we not only had a lot of things to learn but a lot of things to go out and buy." Marketing includes advice books, **toys** and educational materials, **fashion**, healthcare paraphernalia as well as furniture. While all may be "for the baby," additional motivations (implicit in advertising) include making the baby smarter, prettier and more successful, flaunting care and wealth and protecting the baby against an uncertain world.

Depictions of babies provide celebratory moments to many mass media – whether long-running television shows or movies from D.W. Griffith's *Intolerance* to *Father of the Bride II* (1995). In 1992 the choice of fictional television newswoman Murphy Brown to have a child out of wedlock even entered American political debate as **Vice-President** Dan Quayle attacked her choice. The vulnerability of babies also suggests darker visions of America, whether in **crime** shows or on the news, asking how the responsibilities of the American dream are being met for a new generation.

GARY McDONOGH
CINDY WONG

baby boom/boomers

One generation above all others has felt it "owned" the American century. A legendary demographic blip that emerged with new suburban families after the Second World War has come to encompass those born between the mid-1940s and 1960. Boomers experienced and participated in **civil rights**, gendered and sexual revolutions, as well as the national traumas of **Vietnam** and **Watergate**. Later, they personified the **yuppie** successes/excesses of the 1980s, although many were left behind. At the end of the twentieth century, aging boomers focused more on childcare and health issues, ranging from hair loss and **Viagra** to **cancer**, heart disease and **AIDS**. They also threaten **Social Security** as the wave surfs into **old age** in 2010.

Despite the youthful **Kennedy** imagery that shaped their coming of age, boomers did not gain control of the White House until **Clinton**'s election. His presidency epitomized the uneasy changes of the generation, from gays to **war** to adultery. Still, as boomer taste and dollars have dominated **mass media**, subsequent generations were defined as children or alternatives (**Generation X**). In the 1990s, baby-boom culture was recycled (sometimes ironically) by mass media in **Hollywood**, popular music and **fashion**.

GARY McDONOGH
CINDY WONG

Bacall, Lauren (Betty Jean Perske)

b. 1924

"If you want anything, all you have to do is whistle" – this line from Bacall's 1944 **Hollywood** debut in *To Have and Have Not* – as a teenager – introduced a smart, beautiful and independent female who would also marry her co-star, Humphrey **Bogart**. Bacall's subsequent career with and without Bogart solidified this persona, despite problems with studios. Bacall earned a 1970 Tony on Broadway for *Applause*. "The Look," the astonishing voice, the image and the talent have made her a legend as she continues to select roles in her seventies.

GARY McDONOGH
CINDY WONG

backlash

Phenomenon associated with the political retrenchment following **civil rights**, women's and antiwar movements of the 1960s and 1970s. The backlash was first noted in the violent response of whites to **SCLC**'s 1966 march in **Chicago, MI**, followed by **Nixon**'s success drawing on the "Silent Majority," and the assault on **busing**. It is also seen as a reason for the failure of **ERA**, the growth of the anti-abortion movement and the rise of the "Moral Majority" during the **Reagan** era. Susan Faludi's *Backlash* (1991) has examined the reaction against **feminism**, and numerous studies have outlined the problems facing the **Democratic Party**, given the loss of much of its New Deal coalition.

The backlash has been captured in several television series: first in *All in the Family* (CBS, 1971–83) with Archie Bunker representing a not-so-"Silent Majority"; then in the 1980s series, *Family Ties* (NBC, 1982–9), which pitted Alex Keaton's political and social conservatism against his parents' 1960s idealism.

ROBERT GREGG

Baez, Joan

b. 1941

Folksinger and activist whose crystalline voice has rung out against abuses of power and on behalf of social equality worldwide. Baez mingled song and protest from the 1950s onwards, becoming a visible and vocal presence in the **Civil Rights movement** and anti-Vietnam campaigns. In 1979 she founded Humanitas Human Rights International, which she headed for thirteen years while maintaining an active concert and recording schedule and continuing to participate in protests. Her renditions of "We Shall Overcome" at the March on Washington and other songs have become anthems for a generation. Her memoirs include *And a Voice to Sing With* (1987).

GARY McDONOGH
CINDY WONG

Baldwin, James

b. 1924; d. 1987

A Pentecostal preacher during his teens in **New York** City, NY, loosely described in *Go Tell it on the Mountain* (1953), Baldwin left the church to become a novelist, playwright and essayist. Baldwin's other great novels, *Another Country* (1962) and *Tell Me How Long the Train's Been Gone* (1968), explore the intersection of **race** and sexuality, and the ways these have shaped American culture. His play *Blues for Mr Charlie* (1964) was based on the Emmett **Till** murder case. Baldwin rose to international fame with the publication of *The Fire Next Time* (1963), which, though conciliatory towards whites, considered the slowness of racial change in the United States, and warned of dire consequences if this continued – predictions seemingly fulfilled in ensuing **assassinations** and **race riots**. Sickened by the racial climate in the US, Baldwin lived in southern France.

ROBERT GREGG

Ball, Lucille

b. 1911; d.1989

After years as a minor movie actor, Ball and husband Desi Arnaz (1917–86) changed **television** comedy through their long-running hit **sitcom** *I Love Lucy* (1951–7) and further 1-hour shows. As a starring female comedian, Ball's rebellious streak and marvelous ingenuity for complicating the lives of her ensemble cast (including her pioneering onscreen pregnancy) delightfully controverted stereotypes of meek housewives. The couple also pioneered control of production and syndication through their Desilu Studios, which Ball took over after her divorce (1960). Desilu produced Lucy shows, as well as other hits like *The Untouchables*.

GARY McDONOGH
CINDY WONG

Baltimore, MD

The "Charm City" dominates Chesapeake Bay, and its **waterfront** recapitulates America's urban transformation. From a **Roman Catholic** colonial refuge, Baltimore became a mercantile port, guarded by Ft McHenry (where Francis Scott Key composed the "Star-Spangled Banner"). Industrial and commercial use took over in the nineteenth century, giving way in the late twentieth century to a new inner-harbor festival marketplace, **hotels**, cultural attractions and sports facilities, including the neo-traditional Camden Yards (home of **baseball**'s Orioles). Yet critics worry that this recreation zone, like splendid old suburbs, such as Roland Park, and the verdant campus of the Johns Hopkins University or its renowned Hospital and Medical School, does not reflect the problems of **race** and poverty that have plagued the modern city. Its population has dropped to 641,468 (2000 estimate), although the Baltimore-Washington metropolitan area, encompassing rural towns, **suburbs** and planned **communities** like Columbia, Maryland, has become the fourth largest in the country (7,285,846).

Despite a series of dynamic mayors, including Donald Schaefer and Kurt Schmoke, analyst David Rusk has used the city as a case study of the need for shared metropolitan taxation and planning. Half the city's neighborhoods are poor, incomes represent only 59 percent of suburban averages and the burdens of both poverty and an inadequate tax base fall hardest on a black urban majority (*Baltimore Unbound*, 1996).

Perhaps Baltimore's cultural reflections find a balance among past glories and contemporary dilemmas. John **Waters**, for example, has produced remarkably individualistic films that explore race, sex, aesthetics and neighborhood in the postwar city. Barry **Levinson** has also dealt with neighborhood and nostalgia in films like his Jewish family epic *Avalon* (1990), while observing the gritty reality of center city in the ABS series *Homicide* (1993–9).

Further reading

Rusk, D. (1996) *Baltimore Unbound*, Baltimore: The Johns Hopkins University.

GARY McDONOGH
CINDY WONG

Bambara, Toni Cade

b. 1939; d. 1995

Born and educated in **New York** City, NY, Bambara worked as an educator and social activist throughout her life. She began her literary career editing several anthologies of Black writers. She published her first short-story collection in 1972 and her first novel in 1980, winning the 1981 American Book Award. Her fiction usually revolved around her involvement in community activities and observations drawn from her students and her experiences in such places as **Cuba** and Vietnam. She also wrote screenplays, including an adaptation of her friend Toni **Morrison**'s *Tar Baby*, and worked on community documentaries.

JIM WATKINS

bankruptcy

A legal proceeding (commonly known as "Chapter 11") in which insolvent individuals or businesses are adjudged incapable of repaying debts, and their remaining assets are allocated for equitable distribution to creditors or reorganized for continued operation. Debtors are freed from most liabilities. The opportunity for a fresh start harmonizes with the American sense of fairness and compassion for those who have unwittingly fallen on hard times. Since the Constitution grants exclusive bankruptcy jurisdiction to **Congress**, it is subject to continuous, national political scrutiny from competing interest groups seeking, for example, to preserve protection for spendthrift consumers while limiting misuse by businesses and the wealthy. At the end of the century, bankruptcy proceedings are less socially stigmatized than ever before for both individuals and corporations who have encumbered debts within constant affluence and seeming opportunities of economic growth.

JAMES KRAUS

banks and banking

Banks traditionally are protectors and providers of money, intermediaries between those who have money and want it protected and those who need money to purchase **homes**, grow businesses or fund education. Banks take deposits and transfer this money to borrowers as loans, earning the spread between the low-interest borrowed funds and the higher-interest lent funds. The Federal Reserve, the industry's regulator, allows banks the special privilege of creating money by lending more than they receive in deposits. Hence, banking was and is a confidence business: the system works as long as depositors have confidence in a bank's solvency. Lost confidence results in depositors demanding their money back – an ominous event of the **Depression**. Deposit insurance, provided by the FDIC (Federal Deposit Insurance Corporation) and FSLIC (Federal Savings and Loan Insurance Corporation), was created as a New Deal reform to prevent bank runs. It protects up to

$100,000 of a depositor's money when a bank goes under.

Despite Depression fears, the banker has been a symbol of local tradition. Often a town's most prominent citizen, the banker was conservative, well-respected and often politically influential. Banking was once profoundly local, whether in small towns or major **cities**. Only locals, it was thought, could evaluate borrowers' ability to repay. "Banker's hours" – 09:00 to 15:00 – were a technical requirement. While adjusting the books each day was an exhaustive manual process, the staid, leisurely reputation of the banker persisted (as in *It's a Wonderful Life* (1946)).

American attitudes towards debt provided the impetus for the postwar growth of banking. European principles of thrift and avoidance of debt are ignored as Americans often prefer huge mortgages to tiny bank accounts. Home-equity loans even free up the value of one's house to allow current spending. US households have over $5.5 trillion in outstanding debt.

Technology also has profoundly altered the banks' and bankers' role as intermediary, smashed barriers to entry and prompted consolidation. Financial assets held by depository institutions have declined from 70 percent in 1932 to 40 percent in 1990. Much of this decline is explained by new institutions that provide savings and lending opportunities. The consumer credit industry, once a boon to banking, is now dominated by non-banking institutions. Credit cards provide a line of credit to individuals on which banks may earn healthy interest rates. By the mid-1980s, however, retailers (for example, Sears), phone companies (for example, **AT&T**) and manufacturers (for example, General Motors) had introduced **credit cards**, eliminating the bank as intermediary. These firms sold their receivables in a burgeoning money market where firms sold debt to mutual funds and institutions, again bypassing banks.

Mortgage securitization, wherein a firm buys a portfolio of mortgages and packages them into diversified, saleable investments, removed other lucrative servicing and pricing opportunities that banks held. Starting in the early 1980s, investment banks like Salomon Brothers securitized over 70 percent of all mortgages (Crawford and Sihler

1991: 138). Banks now require fewer deposits and can extract fewer fees for services because loans are sold after origination. Mutual funds have embraced securitized debt. Money Market Mutual fund assets total $1 trillion, reducing the traditional savings account and bank certificate of deposit customer base.

Today, insurance companies offer investments, automobile manufacturers offer credit and third-party providers offer payroll and processing services. The banking industry has traditionally been restricted from business diversification by the Glass-Steagal Act of 1933, but deregulation and changing conditions have forced re-evaluation. The consolidation of banking, supported by loosened restrictions on interstate operations, has been the main focus of this restructuring. Chartered banks in the US have fallen from 13,124 in 1979 to 9,143 in 1997. The FDIC estimates there will be fewer than 5,000 US banks by 2005. Behemoths Nationsbank, Chemical and Corestates have merged with Bank of America, Chase Manhattan and First Union to eliminate operational redundancies and become more competitive. Citibank, Chase Manhattan, Bank of America and First Union have nearly $1 trillion in deposits, and operate from **New England** to **California**.

This often raises the specter of problems in urban or neighborhood finances as national banks go for maximum profits. The community bank has difficulty providing the services of a larger bank because its expenses are spread over a smaller asset base. Legislation, including the Community Reinvestment Act, requires banks to lend in the communities in which they operate, but does not promote autonomous financial planning for these areas. Credit unions, which have acted as joint financial reserves for groups like teachers and government employees, have also been explored as a way to bring non-predatory financial services into low-income communities.

Banks now earn the majority of their income from fees, not the spread on deposits. Banking is also done through technology-intensive phones or 24-hour automated tellers, more than through branch offices, reducing the need for personal interaction and providing economies of scale to large, centralized banks.

Savings and Loans (S&Ls) once held a unique

place in the banking industry because they exclusively provided long-term, fixed-rate home mortgage loans. In the late 1970s, interest rates rose above 10 percent. S&Ls held portfolios of thirty-year mortgages earning as little as 5 percent, but had to pay double that to attract deposits. Additionally, banks offered savings accounts. Real-estate loans, provided in the early 1980s, imploded when land prices declined. Regulators were slow to respond to problems – five US senators were even accused of using their influence to deflect attention from crooked financier Charles Keating. Deposit insurance provided a crutch as S&Ls across the country shut their doors, yet healthy S&Ls came under pressure as individuals lost confidence in the entire industry. Ultimately, the Resolution Trust Corporation was set up to bail out the S&L industry and recover some of the massive losses. It is estimated the S&L bailout cost the country $1 trillion.

The banking industry faces numerous challenges. Confidence in banking has declined in recent decades. Banks must improve services at lower prices and still remain competitive with other service providers. In order to survive, banks and other financial institutions must continue to reinvent themselves.

Further reading

Mayer, M. (1997) *The Bankers*, New York: Truman Talley.

Crawford, R. and Sihler, W. (1991) *The Troubled Money Business*, HarperCollins.

MARC BALCER

Baraka, Imamu Amiri

b. 1934

One of the most original **African American** poets, playwrights and cultural critics to emerge from the 1960s, as well as a leading political advocate of black cultural nationalism. Under his birth name, LeRoi Jones, he gained notoriety in 1964 when four of his plays were produced off-Broadway in **New York** City, NY. His poems and plays constituted an eloquent assault on the racism

in mainstream American society. *Blues People* (1963), a volume of essays focusing on African American music, had a profound impact on Black Studies, helping transform analysis of black cultural traditions during and after slavery. Since 1967 he has published under his African name, been a leading force behind the 1972 National Black Political Convention in Gary, Indiana, and undertaken housing ventures in his hometown of **Newark, NJ**.

ROBERT GREGG

Barbara, Hanna *see* animation

barbeque (barbecue, Bar-B-Q)

Traditionally seen as originating in the Carolinas, and considered a cultural tradition throughout the **South**, a barbeque is an open-air feast of meat roasted in a red sauce over open coals, served with coleslaw, baked beans, potato salad and white bread. Factions argue the merits of beef, pork, chicken, mutton, goat and even sausages for the entrée, while devotees swear by certain types of wood (oak, hickory, citrus, etc.) for the right coals. The sauce has innumerable variations, but most consist of a tomato base with additives such as Worcestershire sauce, butter, lemon juice, molasses/honey, sugar, etc. – national cook-offs are generally judged according to the best secret sauce recipes. Regional variations are also highly contested. Although adapted to home grilling and commercial fast food, the mystique of the ultimate barbeque experience remains. Because the original chefs were mostly southern blacks, many believe the best barbeque is found in **African American** owned commercial establishments in out-of-the-way locations.

JIM WATKINS

Barber, Samuel

b. 1910; d. 1981

Lyrical composer who worked in various genres, winning **Pulitzer Prizes** for his **opera** *Vanessa*

(1958) as well as his "Second Piano Concerto" (1962). While his work is demanding and complex, it has also found favor with a wider public, especially his "Adagio."

GARY McDONOGH

Barbie

The Barbie doll is famous the world over as the leggy, blonde teenage model toy for girls. The doll was first released by the Mattel Corporation in the spring of 1959, ultimately becoming not merely a toy, but a cultural phenomenon. A clear departure from the baby-doll toys which were popular during that period, she was one of the first dolls to offer a window into an "adult lifestyle," replete with such fashion outfits as "Dinner at Eight," "Enchanted Evening" and "Picnic Set." She spawned the creation of her steady boyfriend Ken, along with countless additional product tie-ins, including the Barbie game, the Barbie van and numerous doll outfits, **fashion** accessories and doll sidekicks (younger sisters and **African American** and ethnic clones). As a powerful cultural icon, she helped shape the way generations of children conceptualize **gender**, **class**, **race** and **ethnicity** in contemporary society. Many feminists have argued that Barbie reinforces gender stereotypes, but **consumers** continue to support the pony-tailed doll wholeheartedly.

Although Barbie was in effect "born" in 1959, the Mattel Corporation was founded in 1945 in Southern **California** by art student Elliot Handler, his wife Ruth and their one-time foreman Harold Matson (hence the name "Mattel," formed by fusing the names Matson and Elliot – though Matson sold out in 1946). Barbie was essentially invented by a working woman – Mattel co-founder Ruth Handler. Both Barbie and Ken have real-life counterparts, since they are named after Ruth and Elliot's actual children. Although Barbie is in many ways synonymous with rigid, unrealistic, Euro-centric ideals of feminine beauty, it is important to note that Barbie was from the start a "career girl" (complete with requisite fashion accessories of course). Although she eventually found Ken, she has never been a wife or a mother – though she did have a bridal outfit.

Barbie is truly all-American, for she has roots in foreign lands. She was modeled after "Lilli," a plastic German sex toy for men (in turn modeled after "Lilli," a character in a popular comic strip in a German newspaper) that Ruth discovered while travelling in Europe. This may account for her impossible dimensions if projected life-size. Ruth's then teenaged daughter Barbara spotted the doll in a store and wanted one, and Ruth realized that this was the doll she had been imagining. While observing her daughter play games as a young girl in which she and her friends imagined their "grown-up" lives, Ruth knew that an adult woman doll for young girls would be a huge hit. Lilli's sultriness was toned down to make way for Barbie's Californian wholesomeness, and Barbie doll was born. Since that time, there have been numerous efforts to create ethnically diverse and global Barbie counterparts, but Barbie remains an enduring symbol of the deeply entrenched "tall, thin and blonde" ideal of female beauty in American culture.

Further reading

Lord, M.G. (1994) *Forever Barbie*, New York: Avon Books.

NICOLE MARIE KEATING

barns

Born as utilitarian farm structures to shelter livestock, cure **tobacco** and store hay, grain and machinery, barns have matured into coveted residential **architecture**. Classified stylistically as German, Dutch or English, they comprise innumerable shapes and have elaborate, timbered, post and beam framed internal spaces. As **suburbs** and edge cities engulfed farming areas and second recreational homes for urban residents proliferated, a passionate effort to preserve, restore and convert barns emerged. Barns, and their cousins, covered bridges, typify a romanticized nostalgia, partially nurtured by **folklore**, for the more civil values of the rural, small-town America of past centuries.

JAMES KRAUS

bars

Different from a French café or bar/tabac or an English pub, bars, even for the everyday visitor, are more of a retreat from the public sphere than an extension of it. Generally, the whole **family** does not go to the local bar.

Bars in America are often refuges, especially for smokers and drinkers, who are almost entirely pathologized. Similarly for homosexuals, gay bars are a hideaway, a place to mingle with other homosexuals without the intrusion of the law, although, until recently, **Stonewall** gay bars were often raided. Bars are the place of sexual possibility and hook-up; sometimes any single woman in a bar is seen as available (the novel/film *Looking for Mr Goodbar* (1977), for example, played out the "punishment" of such a single woman). In the 1970s, heterosexual single bars rivaled certain gay bars as spaces specifically designated for the playing out of mating rituals for the adult human.

Novelist Charles **Bukowski** sought out inspiration in such bars and found the inspired everyday poetry of the denizens of these darkened spaces. Bars also have been crucial places for the development of new forms of **popular music**, such as **jazz** (bebop) and new genres. Bars often host new talent before the performers either disappear or move into more traditional, official spaces with higher cover charges (patrons in bars are not charged unless there is live music or a live DJ).

In the 1990s, 1950s/1960s cocktails such as the martini and the Manhattan, as well as the new "Cosmopolitan" came back in style and demanded appropriate settings. These bars, either opened or redesigned with retro or contemporary styles, brought sophistication back. Live DJs replaced the **jukebox**, which allowed the user to set the tone. However, this "new" rendition does not entirely eclipse the bar's primary function as a space to drink, to mingle, to find someone new.

In some bars, the pool table is a crucial ingredient (as might be video and pinball machines, but slightly less dramatically). Leading pool players challenge one another and develop audiences as players drink and play in a game that involves skill and seemingly indicates sexual prowess. In other bars, pool is a playful pastime that fills up the hours among "regulars" who know one another and call the bartender by name.

The bartender plays a crucial role in the bar as a purveyor of **alcohol**, but also as a master of ceremonies who knows the ins and outs of the establishment. Friendly or curmudgeonly, the bartender sets the tone of the bar and introduces the new customer or initiate to its culture. The bartender serves the drinks to the customers (it's never a self-service situation) so that both power (and the rapidity of a buy back) places the bartender, structurally, in an esteemed position. This is particularly true in the early twenty-first century when the bar once more is a refuge from a restrained larger culture.

EDWARD MILLER

Barth, John

b. 1930

Barth was one of a group of influential American novelists and writers who became known in the 1960s for their turn to experimental fiction: his 1967 essay, "The Literature of Exhaustion," is often cited as a manifesto of sorts for American literary **postmodernism**. In novels such as *The Sot-Weed Factor* (1960), *Chimera* (1972) and *The Last Voyage of Somebody the Sailor* (1991), Barth sought to infuse traditional narratives and prose styles with late **modern** or postmodern themes and philosophical concerns. Barth spent most of his adult life in the academy, and is now a Professor Emeritus of Creative Writing at the Johns Hopkins University. Barth's love of storytelling – the figure of Sheherazade is a favorite motif – arguably has made his work more accessible than many other postmodern American writers.

MARK BREWIN

Barthelme, Donald

b. 1931; d: 1989

Barthelme became well known thanks to his innovative short stories, many of which appeared in *The New Yorker*. A literary postmodernist who argued that collage was the art form of the twentieth century, Barthelme was often linked to other experimental writers such as John **Hawkes**, William Gass, John **Barth** and Robert Coover. His stories featured surreal situations, outlandish characters and parodic takes on weighty intellectual issues such as the death of God and existential alienation. Behind Barthelme's playful style, however, was a more serious concern with how to respond to the moral and epistemological doubts of our age.

MARK BREWIN

baseball

The quintessential American sport, shoved aside by **football** in the 1960s and the popularity of **basketball** in the 1980s, is now enjoying a renaissance in the early twenty-first century. It is the stuff of American dreams, the sport of literature and of the pastoral life. Its birth is shrouded in conflicting claims, but popular myth and effective marketing have placed it before the Civil War, in Cooperstown, New York, a small village redolent of America's literary past and the **Main Street** ideal, on which the hallowed **Hall of Fame** recounts the sacred story. Football was largely associated with and still remains central to college life, not becoming a successful national professional sport until the advent of national broadcast television; neither did basketball, with urban roots that have remained its vital core. But baseball, the oldest of these three nineteenth-century inventions, developed by 1845 into a regular form, the "national pastime," was a profitable professional sport within the first generation of its appearance.

The major leagues, a term that effectively reduced its competitors to minor league and dependent status, trace their roots to 1875 when the National Association of Professional Baseball Players formed in 1871, and, controlled by the players, was replaced by the owner-dominated National League of Professional Baseball Clubs (NL). The second of the two major leagues, the American League (AL), emerged in 1900. From 1903 to 1953 both consisted of eight teams that played 154 games a year. A season-ending contest, the World Series, played continuously for ninety years until the owners canceled it during a labor dispute in 1994. **African Americans** and other players of color were excluded from the National League by the late 1880s. They formed their own Negro Leagues that flourished until just after the Second World War when Jackie **Robinson** broke the NL color line (1947).

These leagues built their teams in a belt of Eastern cities that would reach only as far west as **Pittsburgh**, **Chicago** and **St Louis**. Not until after the Second World War were the further **Midwest**, **West** and, much later, the **South** included in major league expansion. The move in 1958 of two of **New York**'s three teams, the Giants (NL) to **San Francisco** and especially the Brooklyn Dodgers (NL) to **Los Angeles**, signified and cemented the rise of the West and demise of the East in the American consciousness.

The names and performances of baseball players, divided between pitchers and all other players, and the statistical measures that allow decontextualized comparisons over a span of a century resound through the game's history as embodiments of its personality. There were the early pitching stars: Cy Young, who won the most games and after whom the award for the best pitcher is named; Christy Mathewson, the handsome gentleman of the New York Giants (NL); Grover Cleveland Alexander, the crusty left-handed competitor; Walter Johnson, the fire-balling stalwart of the largely losing team, the Washington Senators (Alabama); and Lefty Grove of the **Philadelphia** Athletics, the man who got stronger as the game went on. But it is the hitters who most captured the adulation of the public: Tyrus (Ty) Raymond Cobb, the battler of the **Detroit** Tigers (AL); Lou Gehrig, the iron man and "Joltin' Joe" DiMaggio, the elegant center fielder who married Marilyn Monroe (both of the New York Yankees); and Ted Williams, the "Splendid Splinter" of the **Boston** Red Sox whose prodigious talents have made him into the god of hitting. All are, however, dwarfed by the giant shadow of George Herman "Babe" Ruth, whose name has entered the language as an adjective for outsized. His accomplishments changed the game into one based on the home run or long ball, resulting in a sudden score with one swing of the bat, instead of a slower game. Yankee Stadium, opened in 1923 in the Bronx, New York, became known as the "house that Ruth built," the most venerable of baseball's venues.

In the 1950s, baseball entered a golden age, with powerful new hitters like the great center-fielders Mickey Mantle of the New York Yankees and Willie Mays of the New York/San Francisco Giants, who redefined the dichotomy of speed or power, leading the way for the modern superstar who combined both traits. The spread of the major leagues also led to a new kind of baseball stadium as an alternative to the ballpark, which was often outside the central city, surrounded by parking lots and not reachable by public transportation. Still, major-league baseball had purposely resisted innovations almost since the time of Babe Ruth. Segregated games were played only during the daytime into the mid-1930s (the technology for playing at night predated the First World War and was used to great effect in the Negro Leagues), shunning television broadcasts or convenient starting times, tying players to one team through the reserve clause system in a restraint of trade sanctioned by US congressional legislation, and its concomitant "farm" system of minor leagues, which, as the term implies, recreated a serf-like connection to one "organization." Add to that the resistance to the expansion of the two eight-team leagues in the face of large population growth. These were all more or less conscious attempts to keep the game "pure," and together helped to push the game into crisis by the early 1960s.

African American and **Latino** players, such as Roberto Clemente, helped to end the mindless control of tradition and revive flagging interest in baseball. Not all teams were integrated until 1958 and 1959 when Philadelphia and then Boston, two mediocre and rabidly racist organizations, finally and reluctantly accepted their first players of color. Curt Flood, of the St. Louis Cardinals, forced the end of the reserve clause system by filing suit to void his trade to the inhospitable Philadelphia

team, which helped lead to the skyrocketing of salaries through the ability to be released from unfair contracts. Teams like the **Cincinnati** Reds, "the Big Red Machine," the Oakland Athletics and the **Baltimore** Red Sox wrested the title from the traditional and perennial world-series champions, the New York Yankees, in the 1960s and 1970s. The number of teams expanded exponentially, almost doubling between 1960 and the end of the century, leading to the realignment of teams into divisions and the introduction of a playoff system. Increasing labor and management troubles have attended the growth in prosperity and renewed popularity of the game, with several work stoppages and a major strike in 1994–5. But further innovations, inter-league play and the explosion of home-run hitting in the late 1990s, led by Mark McGwire, Sammy Sosa and Ken Griffey Jr, have eclipsed some of the marks set by Babe Ruth and Hank Aaron, and restored baseball to its central role in the popular imagination.

Further reading

White, G. (1996) *Creating the National Pastime: Baseball Transforms Itself, 1903–1953*, Princeton: Princeton University.

(1996) *The Baseball Encyclopedia*, 10th edn, New York: MacMillan.

ELLIOTT SHORE

basketball

Basketball is a monumental presence in the shrinking global community of the early twenty-first century. On the strength of unprecedented commercial success in the 1980s and 1990s, basketball has become one of the most popular sports in the world. The game's social influence extends to spheres of **economics**, **race** and moral debate, while its sensational artistry has revolutionized the appeal of athletic competition as an outlet for fantasies of unfettered greatness and triumph over unthinkable odds.

James Naismith, a physical education instructor at a community youth center in Springfield, Massachusetts, invented basketball in 1891 as an indoor diversion for young male athletes during the

Northeast's cold winter months. (Women have participated in basketball since its inception, but accomplished female players have historically enjoyed fewer educational and professional opportunities than men.) Basketball caught on quickly at **high-school** and **college** levels after its invention. By the late 1930s, national intercollegiate tournaments that brought together teams from all over the country had begun to thrive.

A strong economy and the return of troops from abroad at the end of the Second World War opened new avenues for the growth of professional competition. Basketball achieved its first sustained success as a commercial enterprise during this period. The National Basketball Association (NBA) was formed through the merger of two struggling professional leagues in 1949. From its beginnings in remote outposts like Fort Wayne, Indiana, and TriCities, Washington, the NBA plotted a steady rise through the 1950s, showcasing pioneer superstars like George Mikan and Bob Cousy.

The NBA's introduction of a twenty-four-second shot clock in 1954 marked the beginning of an era of dynamic change for basketball. A faster, more competitive game began to take shape in the 1960s as an unprecedented influx of talent emerged at all levels of the game. A distinct basketball tradition that had taken root in **inner cities** was producing a growing number of **African American** players with unique skills. This urban tradition fostered individuality, a development that was at odds with basketball's legacy as a team sport. The rivalry between two African American NBA centers – Bill Russell and Wilt Chamberlain – embodied the struggle between these opposite impulses. Russell, a thoughtful and unselfish player, expanded the scope of defensive play with his prolific abilities as a shot blocker. Chamberlain was remarkable for his dazzling, but self-centered, offensive prowess. He remains the only player in the history of the NBA to score 100 points in a single game.

The advent of the American Basketball Association (ABA), an upstart rival to the NBA, in 1967 intensified the tug-of-war between finesse and teamwork. The ABA took its cues from inner-city playgrounds, where triumph depended as much on creativity as skill. ABA players expressed basketball's appeal as entertainment, developing a freewheeling ease that favored spectacular shots like the slam dunk. Julius Erving ("Dr J"), the ABA's marquee player, used his unusual mix of athleticism and grace during the 1970s to innovate the spectacular offensive moves that are standard fare in basketball competition today. Kareem Abdul-Jabaar, another outstanding player to emerge in the 1970s, stretched the bounds of the game further by combining an ethic of teamwork with a personalized style to become one of the most accomplished players in NBA history. Abdul-Jabaar, along with Chamberlain, remains one of the league's top three all-time scorers.

Despite the ABA's profound influence on the game, the market for basketball could not sustain two major professional leagues. A flagging ABA was folded into the NBA in 1977.

Due in part to a string of scandals about drug use among players, basketball's popularity began to decline after the merger. Some public criticism took on racial overtones, blaming the league's difficulties on the fact that the majority of its players were African American. Earvin "Magic" Johnson, an African American known for his energetic and flamboyant style, and Larry Bird, a soft-spoken, white player from the **Midwest** with a consummate technical command of the game, are widely credited with rescuing the NBA from its troubles. In addition to their extraordinary talent, Bird and Johnson revived a longstanding rivalry between their respective teams, the **Boston** Celtics and the **Los Angeles** Lakers.

In the 1980s, with a foundation built on the intensity and creativity of Johnson and Bird, basketball entered the most transformative era in its history. The timely interaction of a variety of social phenomena during this period fueled basketball's rise to untold heights of popularity and profitability. Michael **Jordan**, one of the most athletic and versatile players ever to compete in the NBA, is recognized as the most powerful catalyst for basketball's meteoric rise in the 1980s and 1990s. Jordan's spectacular talent and dramatic flair revolutionized the concept of basketball as entertainment.

Charming, handsome and well-spoken, Jordan's capital as a media figure today rivals his value as an athlete. While an active player, he drew sell-out crowds all over the country and boosted television ratings. Jordan has parlayed this appeal into multimillion dollar earnings from corporate endorsements. Although sports stars have historically lent their images to advertisers, Jordan's $2.5 million dollar contract with the athletic shoe company Nike in 1984 established product endorsements as a permanent part of the basketball landscape. In 1998 Jordan earned an estimated $70 million in endorsement and business deals – more than twice his annual salary from the Chicago Bulls.

Profound changes in the media industry during the 1990s also contributed to basketball's growth. Advances in technology and the emergence of media conglomerates created new markets all over the world. Basketball's expansion has extended new opportunities to female players, with the advent of a successful women's professional league in the mid-1990s.

Corporate America played a central role in basketball's prosperity in the late twentieth century. Companies sponsor exhibitions where aspiring high-school players showcase their abilities, universities are paid millions to use certain brands of athletic wear exclusively and shoe companies have even begun managing players' careers. Players' salaries have kept pace with basketball's progress, increasing from an annual average of $260,000 in 1984, the year Jordan entered the league, to an average of $2.4 million in 1998.

Despite their enormous earning potential, the social status of basketball celebrities remains ambiguous. As money replaces education as the premium offered to promising high-school talents, growing numbers of players forego athletic scholarships to enter the NBA. High schools, colleges and city playgrounds have turned into high-stakes proving grounds for young athletes aspiring to lucrative professional careers (as seen in the documentary *Hoop Dreams*, 1994). Missed educational opportunities and the rapid transition into fame and wealth appear to have contributed to the unruly and irresponsible behavior of some players both on and off the court. Violent outbursts by players have become regular occurrences during games. Similar tensions have escalated between coaches and players.

These trends have sparked public debate over NBA players' status as role models to millions of children. The skewed racial makeup of basketball seems to have complicated these dynamics. The NBA remains mostly white at the levels of management, ownership and, to a lesser degree, coaching, while the highly paid players are overwhelmingly African American.

Further reading

Ashe, A.R., Jr. (1988) *A Hard Road to Glory: Basketball: The African American Athlete and Basketball*, New York: Amistad.

Frey, D. (1994) *The Last Shot: City Streets, Basketball Dreams*, New York: Houghton Mifflin Co.

Sachare, A. (1998) *The Basketball Hall of Fame Hoop Facts and Stats*, New York: John Wiley & Sons, Inc.

SARAH SMITH

bathroom

The American bathroom is understandably associated with body waste and dirt, as well as privacy even in public space. Architecturally, bathrooms tend to be the most secluded spaces of the house; building codes do not require them to be naturally lit. Similarly, in many homes, the bathroom is the only room that can be locked. While bathrooms are often the home's smallest rooms, they are sites of many hours of daily bodily ritual, using a toilet, one or more sinks, bathtub and/or shower, mirrors, medicine cabinet and associated fittings (a bidet is seen as a marker of European influence). Because of the secretive nature of these practices, in the postwar context, the bathroom often seemed a forgotten space in visual culture. Nonetheless, *All in the Family* (CBS, 1971–) challenged contemporary values by prominently displaying a toilet in February, 1977. After breaking this social taboo, the domestic bathroom has become more visible in many cultural contexts, including mass media, advertising and home design.

Bathrooms are still private; hence, **middle-class** dwellings are expected to have multiple facilities, including utility washrooms and private bathrooms for master **bedroom** suites. Within the room, cabinets and closets often become hiding places of embarrassing paraphernalia, ranging from analgesic ointments to birth-control apparatus. **Privacy** is also linked to the gendering of public and private spaces: women are often associated with bathroom sociability (including childcare and conversations during waits), as well as extensive grooming in both private and public facilities. For men, the bathroom has been constructed as an isolated space, away from the **family** and certainly from male strangers, although this cultural invisibility has allowed public bathrooms to become known as gay rendezvous points ("tearooms"). The unisex public bathroom reflects the social changes of the 1960s, and is often associated with **college** dormitories, although it has figured as a prominent social space in television's *Ally McBeal* (FOX, 1997–).

"Bathroom humor" relies on bodily functions for response. Although considered unsophisticated, it pervades mass culture, including the comedy of George Carlin, Richard **Pryor** and Eddie **Murphy**, the cartoon *South Park* and teen-oriented films like *There's Something About Mary* (1998). Likewise, the bathroom is commonly the locus of illicit behavior ranging from benign teenage rebellion (*Smokin' in the Boy's Room* (1968), Brownsville Station) to sexual activity, particularly masturbation, the "quickie" and homoerotic practices (*Basketball Diaries* (1978) by Jim Carroll or the fiction of Henry Miller). Graffiti, whether humorous, racist or sexist, also appears in bathrooms. Cinematically, the bathroom also has been characterized as the site of violence (violation of privacy) in films such as Hitchcock's *Psycho* (1960).

In the 1990s, a luxurious domestic bathroom became an indicator of social status. Martha **Stewart** and Bob Vila invaded homes and cultivated a market for nostalgic tubs with claw feet and porcelain fixtures; other elite features include saunas, his-and-hers tubs and fireplaces. Advertising also markets bathroom products as sources of pleasure and well-deserved relaxation/escape. Hence, the domestic bathroom has gained status as a site of embellishment, and now shares with the **kitchen** a reputation as a coveted site of remodeling.

HUNTER FORD TURA
JEANNIE J. KIM

Batman

Created by Bob Kane and Bill Finger for Detective Comics in May 1939, Batman soon transcended the **comic** book to become an American icon, appearing in war bond promotion and an anti-Japanese film serial. The McCarthyite 1950s saw Batman and Robin accused of promoting homosexuality, while the 1966 television series, notorious for its camp humor, revived the character for the pop generation. Batman was dramatically reinvented in Frank Miller's "graphic novel" *The Dark Knight Returns* (1986), and again in Tim Burton's 1989 feature film. The **blockbuster** sequels which followed demonstrate the character's undiminished cultural potency in the early twenty-first century.

WILL BROOKER

Bay of Pigs

Following Fidel **Castro**'s efforts to nationalize American property in **Cuba**, President **Eisenhower** determined that he would have to be removed, and ordered the **CIA** to start training Cuban exiles in Honduras in preparation for an invasion. Before this plan could be carried out, Eisenhower's presidency ended and **Kennedy** was inaugurated. After being briefed by Eisenhower, Kennedy decided to move forward with the plan.

Backed by American air cover, the Cuban exiles were to land at the Bay of Pigs, and then quickly foment an uprising against Castro. However, Kennedy recalled the American aircraft at the last minute, leaving the invaders exposed, who, because the Bay of Pigs was a secluded section of the island away from major population centers, were either captured or killed without making any impact on the Cuban people.

The significance of the invasion was great. Embarrassed by its failure to act, the Kennedy administration forthwith felt that it could not afford any similar misfortunes in international affairs, leading to almost catastrophic results in the ensuing **Cuban missile crisis**, and setting the stage for the quagmire in **Vietnam**.

ROBERT GREGG

Beach Boys, the

Quintessential balladeers of surf, summer, sixties and **California**. Formed in 1961 by brothers Brian, Carl and Dennis Wilson, their cousin Mike Love and David Marks, they produced twenty albums by 1970, ranging from "California Girls" to the more complex concepts of *Pet Sounds* (1966, including "God Only Knows"), one of **rock 'n' roll**'s finest albums, or the classic "Good Vibrations" (1966). The band lost its way thereafter as a group and through personal stories of some members, including Brian's addictions and Dennis' 1983 drowning, while new British, California and **folk-music** sounds competed for the market. The band experienced a popular revival in the 1980s.

GARY McDONOGH

beat generation

Anticipating the counterculture of the 1960s, the beat generation rejected the life of the "**organization man**" and **suburban** culture. A generation weary of conventions, beat artists undertook a mystical search for salvation in **poetry**, **jazz**, sex and meditation. For them, suburban lifestyle restricted freedom and creativity, as did women and settling into marriage. Instead, beat artists strove to be down and out; vagrancy and mobility (often in a car, a symbol of suburban culture) were virtues. Allen Ginsberg's poem, "Howl" (1955) assailed the nation and its values, making heroes of drop-outs and drug users who had rejected families and jobs and taken time off from good behavior. The beats' bible, though, was Jack Kerouac's *On the Road* (1957), which describes Kerouac's four trips across America in the company of his friends, Neal Cassidy (perhaps the true moving spirit behind the beats), Ginsberg and William S. **Burroughs**. By the 1960s the term "beatnik" was widely used for anyone who took on the beat style, without the substance.

ROBERT GREGG

Beatles, the

English band from Liverpool that dominated the American music market from their appearance on the "Ed Sullivan Show" in February 1964 until their break up in 1970. Inspired by Elvis **Presley** and other **rock 'n' roll** musicians, the Beatles combined blues music with ballads popular among Motown's **girl groups** and the **Beach Boys** (both of whom suffered from the "invasion"). Although the group's popularity was threatened by John Lennon's comment that they were almost as big as Jesus, fundamentalist **backlash** consolidated the Beatles radical chic. This radicalism was further enhanced by comments opposing the **Vietnam War**, and by Lennon's protests with Yoko Ono on behalf of world peace.

Meanwhile, "Sergeant Pepper's Lonely Hearts Club Band" (1967) and the "White Album" (1968) helped alter the direction of **popular music**. The former, one of the first "concept" albums, was the last major collaboration of Lennon and Paul McCartney. Highlighting the band's move into more orchestrated melodies with influences ranging from English music-hall ballads to Indian music, the album seemed to represent the holistic, optimistic aspects of 1960s counterculture. The more anarchic "White Album," where each artist went off in his own direction, seemed to shatter all icons associated with "Sergeant Pepper's," a movement best summed up by McCartney's "Helter Skelter" (later connected to the Charles **Manson** slayings).

Following the break up, each member went on to varying degrees of success as solo artists. Lennon, the most politically vocal, became a resident of **New York** City, NY (with his own lengthy **FBI** file) until his murder in 1981 at the hands of a deranged fan who believed he had "sold out."

ROBERT GREGG

Beattie, Ann

b. 1947

Writer known for her mastery of both the **novel** and short story. Beattie combines comedy and insightful social observation in a deadpan style in her depictions of American life, focusing on **middle-class** and educated Northeasterners. *Chilly Scenes of Winter* (1976), her debut novel, was published in the same year as her first collection of short stories, *Distortions*. Her later works include the story collection *Park City* (1998), as well as novels *Picturing Will* (1989), *Another You* (1995) and *My Life, Starring Dara Falcon* (1997).

GARY McDONOGH

beauty pageants

While perhaps best known through national contests (**Miss America**, etc) or international pageants like Miss Universe, beauty pageants represent a much more complex system, defining femininity on the basis of body, face and personality (with occasional nods to talent or intellect). Pageants begin in babyhood – children and teen competitions have gained notoriety as exploitative arenas – and continue through Mrs America and events for older women. They may also represent localities and special events (as in the movie *Miss Firecracker*, 1989), ethnic groups (Miss Chinatown USA) or company sponsorship (Miss Rheingold was a famous brewery advertising device in **New York** City, NY). While touted as a step to stardom for some, they tend to be minor triumphs for most, often at great cost. While similar male events have emerged, they are eclipsed by more athletic or muscular competitions. "Drag" contests, however, do replicate and parody the female values of the pageants.

GARY McDONOGH
CINDY WONG

bedroom

Most American bedrooms, as typified by "bedroom packages" offered by furniture retailers and hotel rooms, include a bed, night table(s) and a dresser. Within this general framework, Murphy beds, futons, canopy beds and twin beds each ascribe different identities to their users. Bedrooms also differ in size, importance and meaning:

"master" bedrooms, usually larger spaces identified as the parents' room in nuclear **families**, may include adjacent dressing rooms or **bathrooms**, a king- or queen-size bed, picture windows and amenities such as walk-in closets and large mirrors. This bedroom is often a center for planning, control and entertainment, as well as sleeping, dressing and sex: hence, **televisions**, telephones and even **computers** are often treated as normal features. Yet, the bedroom is especially fraught with cultural associations as the main place for sexual activity. This has given rise to such slang as "bedroom eyes" (seductive) and "good in the bedroom" (sexually adept).

Historically, the bedroom has been considered among the most private realms of the **home**, associated with private behavior as well as seclusion. Hence, the parental bedroom has been represented in mass media as the locus of important and clear-headed decision-making. Some housing project rules require that it can be locked from the inside. In **suburbs**, especially middle-class suburbs, children expect their own bedrooms, equipment (phones) and rights to **privacy**. "Guest bedrooms" are also a feature of more affluent homes, although these may be multipurpose rooms equipped with a bed and minimal necessities. Servants' bedrooms are rare: even in pre-war homes and apartments these were often used for extra children's space, as offices or to accommodate additional family members (hence "mother-in-law apartment" for a bedroom located over a **garage**).

The number of bedrooms in a house or apartment is an expression of both wealth and status. In urban contexts, the studio apartment, in which the bedroom is undifferentiated from other domestic spaces, is considered appropriate for young adults and the lower classes, whereas, for example, Aaron Spelling's 123-room mansion represents his excessive wealth and opulence. Realtors cite the number of bedrooms as the first classification and selling point for homes.

In architectural discourse, the bedroom has been the locus of a critique on traditionally held mores about the American nuclear family. This critique is seen in the work of architects such as Peter Eisenman (House VI, Connecticut, 1972) and Philip **Johnson** (Johnson House, Connecticut, 1946).

An extension of this public/private split emerges in the idea of "bedroom communities" – suburbs around economic centers where domestic life is concentrated. Nonetheless, the division is not inviolate – the bedroom as the locus of voyeurism has been a theme in such films as *Sliver* (1993), and is exemplified in the rise of "web-cams." Bedrooms also figure prominently in displays of **celebrity** wealth in fashion and social **magazines**. Public bedrooms, however, may become sites of controversy: presidential bedrooms in the White House, particularly the Lincoln bedroom, have become a metaphorical site of political scandal and illicit sexual activity in the cases of Presidents **Kennedy** and **Clinton**.

See also: architecture

HUNTER FORD TURA
JEANNIE J. KIM

beer *see* alcohol

Bellow, Saul

b. 1915

Jewish American writer based at the **University of Chicago**, Bellow is considered a pathbreaker for a number of other Jewish writers, such as Bernard Malamud, Philip **Roth** and Cynthia Ozick. His first novel, *Dangling Man* was published in 1944, but his best-known works were written in the following three decades – *Adventures of Augie March* (1953), *Herzog* (1964) and *Humboddt's Gift* (1975), which earned him the Nobel Prize for Literature in 1976. These works explore themes of alienation and the modern predicament, the place of Jewish spiritual understanding in **cities** that seem to have lost their bearings and his own role and responsibility as a Jewish writer.

ROBERT GREGG

Bennett, William

b. 1943

A former **philosophy** professor and chairperson for the National Endowment for the Humanities, Bennett was an outspoken public servant through his four years of work as US Secretary of Education under President Ronald **Reagan**. Known for his directness, he supported a limited role for federal government in education and vouchers for disadvantaged children to attend private schools. Under President George **Bush**, Bennett in 1989 became director of the Office of National Drug Control Policy. He is also the author of several books that emphasize the importance of morals and values, as well as one of America's best-known cultural conservatives.

KATE M. KENSKI

Berlin

After the Second World War ended in Europe, Germany was divided into four zones controlled by the Soviet Union, Britain, France and the United States, as was its capital in the Soviet zone. Thereafter, Berlin became a symbol and proving ground of the **Cold War**. Hence in June 1948, when Soviets blockaded the city, the western Allies created an air-bridge or airlift which carried food, medicines and supplies to the city and built up a year's reserve to show determined support. Later, the destruction of the Berlin Wall, where John **Kennedy** had said "Ich bin ein Berliner," symbolized victory in the Cold War to many Americans.

KATE M. KENSKI

Bernstein, Leonard

b. 1918; d. 1990

An American composer and pianist, Leonard Bernstein also conducted the **Boston** Symphony and the **New York** Philharmonic Orchestras. A child prodigy, he was committed to bringing symphonic music to larger audiences, aided by his own **celebrity** status and **television**. Bernstein is perhaps best known for the rousing, modern music of *West Side Story* (1957), a re-staging of Romeo and Juliet among New York gangs; his *Candide* (1956) and *Chichester Psalms* have been performed in **opera** houses worldwide. A charismatic, passionate, politically involved and controversial individual, he reflected many of the social changes of the 1960s. Rumors about his personal and **family** life abounded during his life, and after his death his homosexual relationships were discussed in biographies.

EDWARD MILLER

Berry, Chuck

b. 1926

Rock 'n' roll pioneer known best for his flamboyant guitar playing, duck walk and run-ins with the law. His first single for Chess Records, "Maybellene," was released in 1955. The following year "Roll Over Beethoven" defined the spirit of rock 'n' roll, rising to the top of the charts. Mixing country music guitar picking with an **R&B** beat and incisive, humorous lyrics aimed at **teenagers**, Berry created an interracial music for an interracial audience in the 1950s. Still rocking in the early twenty-first century, he has been the single greatest influence on the subsequent development of **rock 'n' roll**.

DEWAR MACLEOD

Berryman, John

b. 1914; d. 1972

Berryman is America's master of homostrophy – our Yeats, except smarter, hornier and more drunk. (Yeats' smooth stanzas cure, Berryman's fracture; Yeats documents dissociation, while Berryman gives caesura psychological meaning.) Berryman's principle dramatic tool is an "interlocutor." His first, a strict form, led to Berryman's *Sonnets*

(1946–7.) Next came Anne Bradstreet, conjured in his great *Homage* (1956). In the 1960s Berryman, minstrelsy's "Mr Bones," and the best-dressed naked alter-ego in poetry, "Henry," sang *The Dream Songs*. Later, Berryman borrowed from group therapy to "confront" his life. Like his father, Berryman committed **suicide**.

DANIEL BOSCH

BET (Black Entertainment Television)

Cable network founded by Robert Johnson in 1979. Johnson artfully managed new forms of **television** distribution – sharing satellites and trading Time Warner stock for access – and advertisers targeting black audiences. Initial programming included older black films, music and some public service combined with many infomercials (often without black relevance). Series taken from other networks and new studio productions appeared in the 1990s. BET reaches 35 million subscribers; audiences tend to be young but predominantly non-**African American**. Hence, while an economic success story for blacks, it may not be providing the cultural leadership of films or music.

GARY McDONOGH
CINDY WONG

Bible belt

The Bible belt is a state of mind that begins at the edge of town and extends either side of a line from Virginia Beach to Tulsa, encompassing the **South**, **Texas** and much of the **Midwest**. It contains a subset of characteristically American religious figures – not **Quakers**, **Amish** or other **refugees**; not emigrant establishmentarians like Catholics or **Muslims**; not even Elmer Gantry; but home-grown Calvinists. Its roots are the "second great awakening" on the Western frontier that ushered in the nineteenth century and the fundamentalist movement at the turn of the twentieth century. Populating this state of mind are several generations of **white** and, more recently, **African American** southerners who use the Bible as a manual first for speech, then for thought and, ultimately, as a substitute for historical imagination.

It was this that H.L. Menken caricatured in the 1925 Scopes trial as America's Bible belt. When not actively derisory, the term has always registered port-city condescension towards the interior upland of the South and Midwest, and particularly towards the centrality of the Bible to the people whose rapid settlement of America's first West outran the educational and other institutions developed by the colonial bourgeoisie from **Boston** to **Savannah**. Unlike the religious utopianism that organized **New England** or the **Episcopalianism** of the tidewater, a religiosity of personal spirituality, Bible study and self-reliance carried early settlement beyond the colonial fringe. Such was the provincialism of Menken as to mis-recognize both its historical context and its social critique.

What arose as frontier religiosity developed as a critique of industrializing, Social Darwinist America. Mindful of community while profoundly skeptical about mass society, its underlying Calvinism fostered **individualism**, striving, personal rather than social perfection and rejection of intermediaries that also took anti-immigrant and anti-**intellectual** turns. Between the Scopes trial and the onset of desegregation, it became discredited on the left for social quietism and migrated to the political right, overcoming a century of suspicion of comfortable establishments and profound alienation from secular powers.

That transformation has accelerated with tensions over the modernization and increasing standardization of education since the Second World War. Turn-of-the-century battles over evolutionism have been rejoined over creationism, which is more **Sunbelt** than Bible belt in its embrace of the models and language of science. Political movements in Arkansas and Louisiana resulted in laws mandating "equal time" for teaching creationism alongside evolution in state-funded schools, which points to an underlying populism strong enough to overcome strong religious commitment to the separation of church and state. This migration to modernity, at least as technique, is nowhere more evident than in the refinement of televangelism by **Christian media** preachers such as Pat Robertson and Jerry Falwell, who both reach a national audience and founded alternative modern religiously based universities that bracket the historic Bible belt.

Further reading

Cash, W.J. (1941) *The Mind of the South*, New York: A.A. Knopf.

Greenhouse, C.J. (1986) *Praying for Justice: Faith, Order and Community in an American Town*, Ithaca: Cornell University Press.

Hill, S.S. (1980) *The South and the North in American Religion*, Athens: University of Georgia Press.

JON ANDERSON

Bible epics

Given the predominance of **religion** in American public discourse, film-makers often have looked to Judaeo-Christian narratives to inspire products for revival tents and **Hollywood** glory. Indeed, by the silent era, film-makers discovered that religious stories could cloak multiple and explicit sins – luxuriant orgies, scantily clad but sometimes repentant heroines and beefcake actors called to divine sacrifice. In the 1950s, the dialectic of sin and morality underpinned epics such as Cecil B. De Mille's second *Ten Commandments* (1956, after his silent 1923 version) that meshed lust, spectacle and barely clad hunks (Yul Brynner (Pharoah) and Charlton **Heston** (Moses)) with special-effect miracles and redemption. Other films also fleshed out the Old Testament "where needed," whether *Samson and Delilah* (1950) or *David and Bathsheeba* (1951).

Stories of Jesus and early Christianity received similar star treatment. The martyrs and revelation of *Quo Vadis* (1951), *The Silver Chalice* (1954), with Paul **Newman**'s debut, and *Ben-Hur* (1959), again with Heston, justified visions of delectable decadence and cinematic miracles in pagan Rome. The Christ narrative itself also reflects changing concerns over generations, from Jeffrey Hunter's blue-eyed Jesus in *King of Kings* (1961) to the 1973 hippie savior of *Godspell* and *Jesus Christ Superstar* to the tortured but still Anglo-Saxon Jesus of Martin

Scorsese's *Last Temptation of Christ* (1988), which drew protest from religious groups.

GARY McDONOGH

CINDY WONG

Bicentennial

The United States marks its creation to the day when colonial leaders signed the "Declaration of Independence," a document which outlined the reasons for the thirteen colonies to terminate formally their relationship with Great Britain. On July 4, 1776 the nation's founders affirmed the "inalienable rights" of the individual as "life, liberty and the pursuit of happiness." Although these rights were based on the assumption that "all people are created equal," the nation's founders, and its subsequent leaders, did not end race-based slavery until 1865 with the passage of the 13th Amendment to the US Constitution. Despite constitutional guarantees of equality, America's minorities were denied full equality of citizenship. The two decades prior to the 1976 US Bicentennial included citizens' most open questioning of the government's guarantees of liberty and equality. Not only did the nation's minority groups, including **African Americans**, **Latinos** and Native Americans, protest non-violently and violently for their rights, but many young people defied the government's authority to send them to Vietnam to fight a war they considered immoral.

National planning for the Bicentennial was further challenged by the **Nixon** administration's lack of credibility. The administration's planning committee was accused of being overly politicized and organized only to serve the political interests of Nixon. In August 1974, following two years of investigation into his administration's misdeeds, President Nixon resigned, leaving the US with its first non-elected president, Gerald R. **Ford**. While the US had officially ended its military involvement in the **Vietnam War** in 1973, the nation and the world were horrified by the images of the fall of Saigon in April and May 1975, when the US Embassy was overwhelmed by communist forces.

Created in 1974, the American Revolution Bicentennial Administration (ARBA) had the difficult task of organizing Bicentennial commemorative events within this vexing political environment. The ARBA, led by the former Secretary of the navy and future US Senator John W. Warner, was further challenged by a competing, private organization, the People's Bicentennial Commission, which attempted to turn the Bicentennial into a critique of the nation's institutional powers. Moreover, **civil-rights** leader Jesse **Jackson** called for blacks to boycott the official celebration. However, Betty Shabazz, the widow of **Malcolm X**, and Alex Haley served as active advisors on the ARBA. Other minority leaders requested a voice within the ARBA, which Warner granted. This group, the Bicentennial Ethnic Racial Coalition, sought to merge the Bicentennial efforts with urban renewal and recognition of America's cultural diversity. By 1976 the ARBA had created a national symbol for the Bicentennial and planned televised events in **Washington, DC**, **Philadelphia, PA** and **New York** City, NY. More importantly, the ARBA fostered local commemorations that were tied to people's personal histories and identities. Instead of focusing on national institutions of power such as the military or the **presidency**, the ARBA used the Bicentennial to forge a new image of America strengthened by its multicultural diversity.

Further reading

Bodnar, J. (1992) *Remaking America: Public Memory, Commemoration, and Patriotism in the Twentieth Century*, Princeton: Princeton University Press.

MELINDA SCHWENK

bicycles

When Lance Armstrong won the Tour de France with the US Postal Service team in 1999 and 2000, American media focused on the personal odds he had overcome in beating **cancer**. For most Americans, competitive bicycle racing remains a foreign sport, even though American Greg Lemond won the tour in 1986, 1988 and 1989 (overcoming his own hardships); such triumphs probably annoy Europeans more than they elate Americans. In *Breaking Away* (1979), in fact, the best

American cycling movie, the Midwestern hero pretends to be an Italian exchange student to explain his affiliation. The narrative of suffering also dominates **Olympic** bicycling coverage, where human interest stories deal with America's failure to win medals. Bikes, then, form part of American life rather than a specialized sport. As such they are both ubiquitous and, at times, dangerously invisible to drivers and policy-makers.

Automobiles ended the bicycle's turn of the twentieth century golden age as a primary vehicle. In the postwar period, though, bikes remain fundamental features of growing up, as well as of adult recreation. While sales peaked in 1973 at a postwar high of 15 million, they have remained steadily above 10 million per year. Tricycles, training wheels (and their removal) and multi-speed bikes track maturing independence for many American children. Schwinn's banana-seat Sting-Ray dominated suburban childhoods in the 1960s and 1970s, later giving way to the sportier MBX, with motocross features. Adult tricycles have also been promoted for exercise and independence in **old age**.

For **teenagers**, bikes compete with cars in enlarging social worlds or as a convenience on a college **campus**. For them, as for adults, increasingly expensive bicycles offer recreation alternatives and, occasionally, a commuter choice. This popularity has been shaped by innovations that include the rise of ten-speed touring bikes in the 1960s, followed by trail bikes with balloon tires and stronger frames (pioneered in Northern **California** in the late 1970s). Sophisticated multi-gear hybrid bikes dominate the market, along with mountain bikes, in the 1990s. Meanwhile, bicycles have entered professional worlds via bike messengers who specialize in artful movements through dense, congested **cities**; these messengers became the heroes of the 1995 sitcom, *Double Rush*.

For many years, these bicyclists would have ridden American bikes like Schwinn (founded 1895) and Huffy. While Americans design racing and innovative bicycles, production often concentrates overseas, sometimes with American assembly. Americans have also been innovators in recumbent bikes since the 1980s. Both cheap and prestigious foreign models absorb 30 percent of the American market.

In many areas, urban streets and suburban roads have been lobbied for bicycle lanes in an effort to decrease automobile congestion and pollution while protecting bicyclists from collisions. Meanwhile, many **parks** and beaches are transformed at weekends into cyclists' worlds, while off-trail areas may sustain serious damage from the growth of mountain biking. Workplaces, schools and homes also accommodate security concerns, while twenty magazines emerged between the 1970s and 1990s dealing with bike interests. Nonetheless, bikes account for only 10 percent of daily trips, in comparison with 30–40 percent in Europe.

Further reading

Perry, D. (1995) *Bike Cult*, New York: Four Walls Eight Windows.

GARY McDONOGH
CINDY WONG

BID (Business Improvement District) *see* neighborhoods; Times Square

bilingual education

Models of bilingual education range from those intended to retrain students from a first **language** to the sole use of English to those which support students' simultaneous development of two languages. In all models there is implicit or explicit tension between maintenance of cultural heritage and identity through language instruction on the one hand and **assimilation** and Americanization on the other.

Acceptance of bilingual education programs by the wider monolingual community can be correlated to the socio-economic status of those who attempt to develop them. Bilingual education was originally conceptualized and implemented by upper-status immigrant groups such as the Germans, who maintained bilingual German–English instruction in some schools in the United States for an uninterrupted period between 1840 and 1917. Beginning in the 1920s, immigration of lower-status peoples from Spanish-speaking and Asian countries prompted criticisms of bilingual education programs.

Legislation has been passed in support of bilingual education, including Title VII, which was added in 1968 to the Elementary and Secondary Educational Act of 1965 to provide financial assistance for local schools to design educational programs for children in whose households the primary language spoken was not English. However, interpretation and implementation of bilingual education varies, and it remains a controversial issue closely tied to socio-economic status. Some states maintain that well-conceptualized and implemented programs promote success among students (see **Texas**, for example), while other states reject the idea and incline towards **English-Only** laws and school policies (see **California**, for example).

See also: language

ALISON COOK-SATHER

Bill of Rights

The first ten amendments to the constitution, added by Congress as a block in 1789 and ratified by 1791, guarantee civil liberties to citizens and rights of the **states** and citizens. That this charter is often taken "as the Constitution" shows how important contemporary debates over its provisions, often decided by the **Supreme Court**, have been to changing fundamental American practices. As a living charter, however, one should be aware that the interpretation of these provisions also has shifted, especially from a focus on the engagement of public citizens with the limits of the state to a focus on individual rights within the state.

The 1st Amendment, for example, guarantees **freedom** of **religion**, speech, the press, assembly and petition, which have been worked out through a number of critical court cases in the postwar period, constraining **censorship**, separating church and state and defining political and public discourse. Much of this debate has involved the actions of liberal interest groups before judicial activist courts like those of the **Warren** era.

The 2nd Amendment, by contrast, deals with the right to bear arms, creating a focus for debates on **guns** and gun control. Here, constitutional defense has tended to be on the **Right**, while those on the **Left** have sought to limit applications of the amendment or even to repeal it.

After the 3rd Amendment, which prohibits forced quartering of soldiers in peacetime, the next five amendments deal with citizens' rights in criminal prosecution and punishment. Hence, the 4th Amendment prohibits unreasonable search and seizure, while the Fifth precludes double jeopardy or self-incrimination – often heard in the movie cliché "I refuse to answer on the grounds of the 5th Amendment self-incrimination."

The 6th Amendment guarantees **civil rights** in trials – a speedy process, the ability to confront witnesses and evidence, the rights to defense and to a jury. The 7th Amendment ensures rights to a jury in civil trials, and the Eighth precludes cruel and unusual punishment. Again, under the Warren court all five of these amendments became charters for rethinking the rights of the accused and the conduct of fair trials in the 1960s. Subsequent courts have sought to trim back these guarantees as they are sometimes seen as hindrances to effective police work or the conviction of criminals. The cruel and unusual punishment clause has appeared repeatedly in arguments about **capital punishment**.

The final two amendments limit government by reserving rights not delegated to the states and ultimately to the people. These have also provoked controversy as to whether interpretations of the federal Bill of Rights can be extended to state circumstances.

Further reading

Amar, A. (1998) *The Bill of Rights: Creation and Reconstruction*, New Haven: Yale University Press.
Bodenheimer, D. and Ely, J. (eds) (1993) *The Bill of Rights in Modern America*, Bloomington: Indiana University Press.

GARY McDONOGH
CINDY WONG

biodiversity

Biodiversity refers to the complexity of interactions among life forms and the environment, expanding conceptually on terms like ecosystem. The term has also taken on a strategic value as biologists and ecologists seek to influence policy by acting as spokespeople for nature and its values in planning and policy. This campaign, and the varying views of contemporary American scientists from Rachel **Carson** to E.O. **Wilson**, are collected and explored in David Takacs' *The Idea of Biodiversity.*

Further reading

Takacs, D. (1996) *The Idea of Biodiversity,* Baltimore: The Johns Hopkins University.

GARY McDONOGH

biology

There is a rich history of the study of life in all civilizations, though current methods stem primarily from Eurocentric roots. However, there is an increased attention to multicultural contributions to the understanding of biological processes. Biology is typically studied at two broad organizational levels – molecular/cellular and organismic/population. General inquiry is based on classical scientific methods which include development and testing of hypotheses, though feminists advocating interconnectedness of living systems have suggested that such approaches omit critical aspects of understanding complex entities. Inclusion of chemical, physical and mathematical techniques for examining complexities at different levels has become a defining trait of biological study since the mid-twentieth century.

Biology teaching has come under increasing scrutiny as technology provides alternatives to dissection and animal testing. Though some argue that substitution of computer programs for use of whole organisms creates an atmosphere of disrespect for the complexity of form and function, others contend that the destruction of living organisms for demonstration of simple principles shows equal disrespect for life. Curricular changes are beginning to incorporate ideas of bio-ethics alongside the creative discovery of scientific principles through active learning.

Popular discussions of biological problems such as population control (P. Ehrlich's *The Population Bomb,* 1968), pesticide hazards (R. Carson's *Silent Spring,* 1962), conservation and **biodiversity** (E.O. Wilson's *BioDiversity,* 1988) and genetic engineering (Suzuki and Knudsen's *Genethics,* 1989) have led to questions about science as social knowledge. Social Darwinism, the application of evolutionary concepts of resource allocation to humans, persists in current social programs. Use of IQ tests for providing access to **education** and other resources, as well as the influence of genetic testing on potential discrimination continue to emerge as controversial in popular literature.

Advances in biological technology have allowed the **genetic engineering** of food as well as medicines to become a part of everyday life. PCR (Polymerase Chain Reaction) has opened the door for sequencing DNA fragments, building comprehensive gene libraries (catalogues of known sequences), and constructing genetic hybrids. Public hysteria has been fanned over perceived problems of recombinant DNA techniques without widespread understanding of regulation, control and applications of recombinant organisms. For instance, microbial cocktails containing engineered organisms are found commonly in grease digesters of major fast food chains as well as at the frontlines of pollution eradication.

The fundamental question of defining life in a biological sense continues to be refined. As technology provides the ability to push the limits of life sustainability from the less than two pound premature baby to the continued body functioning of a brain-dead person, questions of what is life abound. Putative evidence of life on Mars, for example, was discovered from an extraterrestrial fragment recovered in Antarctica. Though no actual life forms were found, by-products of living organisms were taken from the fragment, stimulating speculation about what conditions might have allowed life to exist on this neighboring planet and what forces might have shaped its evolution.

Biology is also linked to cultural debates where research and theory intersect with policy and change. The mapping of the human genome and progress in gene therapy have raised questions of ownership as well as impact. The specter of "biopiracy" has also been raised as corporations seek to exploit resources that have been taken as common goods. Issues of the environment and human participation within complex ecological systems continue to keep biological knowledge and projections in the public eye.

Further reading

Bleier, R. (ed.) (1986) *Feminist Approaches to Science*, New York: Pergamon Press.

SANDRA GILCHRIST

birth

Almost 4 million **babies** are born in the United States each year. The infant mortality rate has dropped to about 7.6 deaths per 1,000 live births, although this remains higher than some other developed nations. Still, in the early twentieth century it was estimated that 35–40 percent of all American families experienced an early death. Today, fewer than 1 in 10,000 dies in childbirth. **Public health** concerns, nonetheless, focus on increasing prenatal care and nutrition in at-risk populations like **teen** pregnancies or mothers dealing with substance abuse.

Most births occur in hospitals, but expectant parents have a variety of options from which to choose. One-stop birthing rooms have replaced many of the multi-stage, multi-step labor, delivery and recovery units. These rooms create an environment that intends to make the birth experience more welcoming. Besides having all the technology and monitors of hospitals, other options include a jacuzzi or tub for those who want to be immersed while in labor and even delivery, as well as **kitchens** and subdued lighting for the room. These environments also bring the father/ partner and other **family** members into the birth process.

Techniques of birth vary in American culture. Mothers often prepare themselves – with the help of their spouse or a birthing partner – through systems of training, usually focused on relaxation and breathing techniques. Such techniques, often named after the individuals who developed them, include the Lamaze, Bradley, Odent, Kitzinger Psychosexual Approach and the Active Birth Method. Classes provide the instruction, support and education for the expectant parents.

Most Americans do not like to tolerate pain, so a variety of options exists to endure, avoid or manage the pain. For some, hypnosis, acupuncture, reflexology, aromatherapy, homeopathic remedies such as St. John's wort and Bach flower, or water provide the relief sought. For others, medications ease the various stages of labor and delivery. Narcotics such as Demerol and Stadol are common drugs provided, but they may affect the babies. Nitrous oxide or other inhalant anesthetics may be given during delivery. More common are local anesthetics, in particular the epidural, an anesthetic injected into the space outside of the spinal cord's outer membrane.

Home births with family members present and a doctor or a midwife attending as well as underwater births attract a number of pregnant Americans. Nevertheless, what American women demand are options in the birthing process.

The length a woman can stay in the hospital following a normal delivery, however, has been a subject of intense debate. Gone are the days when new mothers would spend a week in the hospital for a vaginal delivery and two weeks for a Cesarean. Insurance companies, in particular managed-care organizations, dictate the length of stay following most births. It took a federal act to allow new mothers a 48-hour stay.

Further reading

Diamond, S. (1996) *Hard Labor*, New York: Tom Doherty.

Kitzinger, S. (1996) *The Complete Book of Pregnancy and Childbirth*, New York: Alfred A. Knopf.

Selz, M. (1997) "Birth business," *Wall Street Journal* November 26.

GAIL HENSON

birth control *see* abortion; contraception

bisexuality

"Bisexual" is an adjective describing individuals who do not identify as only heterosexual or only homosexual. The prefix "bi-" indicates that these individuals are drawn to both sexes, although certain scientists have argued about the existence of more than two sexes.

"Bisexual" is perhaps best understood as an umbrella term that means different things to the people who use it to describe themselves. Some people who identify as "bisexual" experience their sexuality differently from other "bisexuals." For instance, certain individuals who identify themselves as bisexual are attracted to others regardless of biological sex, but only have sexual relations with one sex.

Bisexuality is nothing new. However, through media visibility, it has gained widespread recognition as a social category only in the latter part of the twentieth century. Before the term "bisexual" was coined in the 1890s, there were people who were attracted to others regardless of biological sex. However, they did not perceive themselves as "bisexual," because the group "bisexuals" could not have been said to exist.

Bisexuals traditionally have been and today still are widely regarded with suspicion by both heterosexual and homosexual individuals. One common stereotype states that bisexuals are sexually indecisive fence-sitters. The biphobic also see bisexuals as sexually promiscuous individuals. To counter these beliefs, the young bisexual community has fought for recognition as a legitimate sexual option, and has worked to discredit the myth of sexual excess.

See also: gender and sexuality

Further reading

Garber, M. (1995) *Vice Versa: Bisexuality and the Eroticism of Everyday Life*, New York: Simon & Schuster.

ELIZABETH A. GALEWSKI

Bishop, Elizabeth

b. 1911; d. 1979

Poet and translator of two places ("here" and "elsewhere") and two directions (south, at first – Key West, Brazil; then north – Nova Scotia, Harvard, Maine), Bishop inhabited each gratefully, without longing. Things ordinary (a typewriter,

four quarts of motor oil) and extraordinary (an enormous fish, a moose, a dog so closely shaved it's "pink") in her verse, prose poems and short fiction challenge fresh perceptions.

Distant friend (of poets Marianne Moore, Robert **Lowell** and Randall Jarrell), committed formalist and expatriate lesbian, Bishop's necessary correspondence distills the self her "one art" required her to lose.

DANIEL BOSCH

black *see* African Americans

black church and spirituality

For centuries black Christian churches have functioned as important religious, political and social institutions for **African Americans** in the United States. To date there are seven major black Christian denominations in the United States: African Methodist Episcopal (AME), African Methodist Episcopal Zion (AMEZ), Christian (formerly Colored) Methodist Episcopal (CME), National Baptist Convention, USA., Inc., National Baptist Convention of America, Progressive National Baptist Convention and the Church of God in Christ (COGIC). Historically, these churches functioned as safe havens from the social ills of slavery, political disenfranchisement, **segregation** and urban displacement. As some of the few autonomous black institutions in the United States, African American Christian churches served as mediators between an oppressed community's public struggles for full citizenship and its private efforts to maintain self-respect and self-determination.

Some scholars contend that the seeds of the modern black church were planted during the early period of enslavement. During this time, enslaved African Americans received their initial introduction to Christianity from Protestant missionary societies such as the Society for the Propagation of the Gospel in Foreign Parts (1701) and later from the evangelical activities of the Awakenings. Rather than embrace a Christian theology that justified their enslavement and legitimized their obedience, enslaved African Americans sought to create a theology reflecting their own interpretation of Christianity. Within this distinct understanding of Christianity, African Americans encompassed various forms of resistance. For enslaved communities, engaging in collective religious worship was in itself an act of resistance. African Americans gathered in densely forested areas or "hush harbors" for secret worship services. Secluded from the ears of their slave masters, they preached against the institution of slavery, worshipped in their own African-derived styles and prayed for their freedom. Within this "invisible institution," African Americans formulated a unique religiosity that would come to embody, in part, the spiritual substance of black churches.

As Christianity developed among enslaved and free blacks in the eighteenth and nineteenth centuries, debates in American culture focused on the efficacy of Christianity in creating communities of docile or rebellious African Americans. Slave rebellions closely connected to Christianity and black religious institutions began to surface in the first half of the nineteenth century. The potent combination of Christianity and resistance fueled the **Southern** insurrection plans of Gabriel Prosser in 1800, Denmark Vesey in 1822, and Nat Turner in 1831. Despite these prominent examples of religion and resistance, it remains largely inconclusive to what extent Christianity made African Americans more accommodative to or resistant against their oppressed social situations. What is conclusive, however, is that Christianity became a forum for exercising levels of autonomy and independence.

African Americans expressed their autonomy through the formation of independent black churches. Between 1773 and 1775 the earliest known separate black Christian church was established by an enslaved African American, George Liele, in Silver Bluff, South Carolina. Converted within this black Baptist community in Silver Bluff was another enslaved African American, Andrew Bryan, who later established the First African Church in Savannah in 1788. By 1830 this church housed some 2,417 free and enslaved black members. The eighteenth century also marked the rise of independent black Christian churches in the North. The independent church movement among free black Methodists in the North gave rise to the first separate African American Christian denomination in the United States. Although other historical churches such as the African Methodist Episcopal Zion Church (1801) and the Christian (formerly Colored) Methodist Episcopal Church (1870) helped to comprise the total body of black Methodists in the United States, the African Methodist Episcopal Church had by far the greatest appeal among African Americans. Established by an ex-slave, Richard Allen, in 1787 as an independent church in **Philadelphia, PA** and in 1816 as a separate black denomination, the African Methodist Episcopal Church quickly evolved into a network of black Methodist churches that extended into other states such as Maryland, Delaware and New Jersey. This new black denomination had as its collective mission abolitionism, racial unity, mutual aid and **education**. Several nineteenth-century colleges such as Wilberforce, Morris Brown, Allen, Paul Quinn and Shorter Junior College were, in fact, founded under the auspices of the AME church. As a direct result of its missionary endeavors in the South throughout the nineteenth century, the AME church was able to increase its pre-Civil War membership of 20,000 people to almost a half million in 1896. Its current membership stands at over 2 million of a total black Methodist membership of some 4 million, thus making black Methodists second in number only to the black Baptists (10 million) among black Christians in the United States. Within this context of black Christian membership, the rise of black Pentecostalism in the early twentieth century would eventually give birth to the third largest black Christian denomination in the United States, the Church of God in Christ (1907), with a current membership of over 3 million.

Although African American Baptists, **Methodists** and Pentecostals comprise a large majority of the black religious bodies in the United States, these Christian denominations by no means exhaust the historical diversity of black spirituality. Existing alongside these Christian denominations have always been alternative spiritual traditions that utilize African-derived rituals and folk beliefs as primary sources of power. During slavery, the hidden services of the "hush harbors" coexisted in enslaved communities with the presence of African conjure. The practices of conjure, often used interchangeably with "hoodoo," mirrored African rituals of divination, charm production and "root-work" or herbalism. Conjure and "hoodoo" created a space for the power of human agency within an elaborate spiritual world of spirits, ancestors, charms, divination and **folklore**. The coexistence of these two systems of religious thought are a direct reflection of the historical complexity of black religious identity. Historically, these alternative spiritual orientations were heavily concentrated throughout the southern US in places like **New Orleans**, Louisiana and the low country and sea islands of South Carolina and Georgia.

More recent expressions of African-derived spiritualities include traditional Congo, Akan and Yoruba-inspired traditions such as Santería (Ocha) and **Voudou**. Many of these recent traditions developed in the United States largely as a result of the efforts of African and African Caribbean immigrants, indigenous cultural and political nationalist movements in the 1960s and transatlantic travel to Africa on the part of African Americans. Although many of these recent traditions are not directly linked to the historical phenomenon of conjure/hoodoo in the US, they do possess a shared African orientation that remains significantly pronounced in black religiosity.

See also: religion; Nation of Islam/Black Muslims

Further reading

Lincoln, C.E. and Mamiya, L.H. (1990) *The Black Church in the African American Experience*, Durham: Duke University Press.
Raboteau, A. (1978) *Slave Religion*, New York: Oxford University Press.
Wilmore, G.S. (1984) *Black Religion and Black Radicalism*, New York: Orbis Books.

TRACEY E. HUCKS

black colleges and universities

Historically black **colleges** and universities number over one hundred institutions of higher learning. With a few exceptions, such as the Institute of Colored Youth, which became Pennsylvania's Cheyney State University, these institutions were established following the Civil War. Some, like the Hampton Institute of Virginia, were founded by missionary associations, while many were established by black denominations like the AME church to provide education for members and to train clergy.

The independent black educational institute became nationally renowned with the rise to prominence of Booker T. Washington at Tuskegee in Alabama. But the growth of the **NAACP** brought a challenge to the notion of racially segregated education, and support for such institutions began to wane significantly in the 1920s. Campus strikes and protests during that decade over the demands for increased black faculty placed continued pressure on college administrations and presaged the coming black militancy that would flower in the 1950s on many campuses around the **South**.

During the early years of the **Civil Rights movement**, students at black colleges like Fisk in **Nashville** and North Carolina A&T in Raleigh developed lunch-counter **sit-ins** in **five and dimes**, and became key participants in **freedom rides** and registration campaigns of **Freedom Summer** (see Ann Moody, *Coming of Age in Mississippi*, 1968). The radicalism/alienation of many of the students, out of step with conservative and elitist administrations, was captured in Ralph **Ellison**'s *Invisible Man* (1952).

The NAACP's achievement in persuading the Supreme Court to make its 1954 *Brown* v. *Board of Education* decision had a significant impact on black colleges. Integration resulted in the loss of many of the best black students and athletes to the leading white colleges and universities. Lincoln University, which had trained many prominent black lawyers and had a celebrated **football** program, now trained fewer **attorneys** and was forced to close down football in the early 1960s.

In the 1980s a financial revival began to occur at many of the colleges. Members of the black **middle class** felt that white-dominated institutions discriminated against them and so began to encourage their children to consider black colleges. This was matched by increased contributions to the

National Negro College Fund (with its successful advertising slogan, "a mind is a terrible thing to waste"), placing the institutions on a more secure footing. Connected to this change was the growing public image of the colleges fostered by the success of Bill **Cosby** and the *Cosby Show* (NBC, 1984–92). The Huxtables sent their eldest daughter to Princeton, but their second chose Hillman (loosely modeled on Spellman) and another went to Lincoln; Hillman became the setting for the spin-off *A Different World* (NBC, 1987–93). Cosby also supported these institutions: in 1986 he donated $1.3 million to Fisk and later gave the same amount to Central State, Howard, Florida A&M and Shaw. In 1988 he gave $1.5 million each to Meharry Medical College and Bethune Cookman College. His donation to Atlanta's Spellman, in 1989, was of a different order, amounting to $20 million. While such largesse has fostered the continued viability of black colleges, they continue to face financial difficulties and, owing to their perceived inferior status, problems retaining faculty and attracting students.

ROBERT GREGG

black conservatives

Until recently, African American **intellectuals** were assumed to be liberal and aligned with the **Democratic Party**. The 1980s witnessed the emergence of black intellectuals Thomas Sowell, Shelby Steele and Stephen Carter, among others, who questioned the value of what they described as the **civil rights** consensus. They were joined in this position by former activists, like ex-**Black Panther** Eldridge Cleaver, and **CORE** national director, Roy Innis, who shifted to the right. No longer dismissed as representatives of an outlandish strain of conservatism among a small minority of **African Americans**, these intellectuals are now an elite representing a **middle class** that has undergone a political shift to the right at least with regard to economic issues. Their success was embodied in the elevation of Clarence **Thomas** to the **Supreme Court**, and in the support found in the ranks of the **Republican Party** for black talk-show hosts Alan Keyes and Ken Hamblin.

Black conservatives contend that federal welfare programs have contributed to dependency among the poor, and that self-help programs reminiscent of Booker T. Washington are more appropriate remedies for urban deprivation. Further, in a return to the ideas of E. Franklin **Frazier** and the **Moynihan Report**, they have stressed the need to focus on the problems associated with African American men, arguing that the lack of male role models in families has created men unable to work for a living and prone to the influences of drugs and **crime**. Their appeal among African American feminist intellectuals has, not surprisingly, been weak. Further, while many of them object to Louis **Farrakhan**, many agreed with the underlying objectives of the Million Man March.

ROBERT GREGG

black English *see* language; linguistics

blacklisting

A general term for denying membership or employment, but used specifically with reference to Hollywood's collaboration with **Cold War** paranoia. Pressured by the House Un-American Activities Committee, the American Legion and **McCarthyism**, studios denied employment to those who had even vague associations with "communist-front" organizations. This dark era, spurred by House Un-American Activities Committee (HUAC) investigations in the later 1940s, produced both heroes and collaborators as actors confessed publicly and implicated colleagues. Meanwhile, the Hollywood Ten who refused to speak in 1948, including director Edward Dymytrk (who collaborated in a second investigation in 1951) and screenwriters Alvah Bessie, Ring Lardner, Jr. and Dalton Trumbo, were jailed for contempt of **Congress**. Later investigations ruined more **actors**, writers and **directors**; some, like Jules Dassin, were forced to move to Europe, others retired or fled, while some eked out a living writing covertly for others. While the blacklist faded by the end of the decade, scars lingered in individual lives and political divisions of Hollywood – decades later people protested a 1999 Academy Award recognition of Elia **Kazan**, who had "named names" before HUAC.

GARY McDONOGH

CINDY WONG

Black Panthers

The term "Black Panthers" was used first in Lowndes County, Alabama, during **SNCC**'s registration drives of 1963. Influenced by **Malcolm X** and SNCC's shift to **Black Power**, many former **civil-rights** activists began to move away from the non-violent message associated with Martin Luther **King**, Jr. In a society where, according to H. Rap **Brown** (1969), "Violence is as American as apple pie," non-violence seemed inappropriate. Instead, Huey Newton and Bobby Seale followed the admonition of Mao Tse Tung that "political power comes through the barrel of a gun." In many respects, these were rhetorical stances. In cities like Oakland and **Philadelphia** the Black Panthers were noted more for their community organizing (around demands for better jobs and housing, truly integrated schools and increased political power), than any actual use of military fire power. Law enforcement agencies, led by the **FBI**, endeavored to crush the movement leading to stand-offs and the arrest of many Black Panther leaders.

Debates about the impact of nationalist organizations like the Panthers continue. White liberals and some former civil-rights leaders tend to blame the Panthers and nationalism for destroying the civil-rights coalition. Those more sympathetic to the Panthers focus on the community organizing, and on the fact that the fear that the Panthers instilled in white Americans made the latter more willing to negotiate with civil-rights leaders.

Further reading

Brown, H. Rap (1969) *Die, Nigger, Die!*, New York: Dial Press.

ROBERT GREGG

Black Power

A slogan popularized, though not created, by Stokely **Carmichael** during the James Meredith march through Mississippi in 1966. Black Power became the dominant ideology of the black movement throughout the second half of the 1960s, promoted by **SNCC** under Carmichael and H. Rap **Brown**, as well as by the **Black Panthers**.

Black Power raised dread in the eyes of many whites, from southern reactionaries to liberal **civil-rights** activists, who saw it as the death knell of an interracial movement.

Its most visible symbol, the clenched right fist, is most often recalled in association with the Mexico **Olympics** of 1968, at which sprinters Tommie Smith and John Carlos made the salute in protest on the medal podium. It was also associated in the minds of many with **Malcolm X**'s *Autobiography* (1965), Muhammad **Ali**'s rhetorical flourishes and with phrases like "Black is beautiful" which had widespread currency through the early 1970s, especially in music.

ROBERT GREGG

blaxploitation films

Prior to the late 1960s, **African Americans** rarely had a voice in how they were represented in **Hollywood** films. With several years of declining box-office profits, along with the rise of the **Black Power** movement, Hollywood began to court black audiences with a series of inexpensive urban crime dramas, which "exploited" the audience's desire to see black heroes and heroines with nearly superhuman physical powers. White men were depicted as sniveling weaklings or corrupt businessmen. Black **directors** Melvin Van Peebles, Gordon Parks and Ossie Davis made, respectively, *Sweet Sweetback's Baadasssss Song* (1971), *Shaft* (1971) and *Gordon's War* (1973).

MELINDA SCHWENK

blockbusters

While the word may refer to any spectacular event, from an **automobile** sale to specialized **museum** exhibits (like the touring Cezanne retrospective of 1996) that draws crowds and media attention, it has come to be applied in a special sense to the production and marketing of movie packages in the late twentieth and early twenty-first century **Hollywood**. Blockbusters are expensive vehicles, generally based on both star power and special effects, that dominate multiple screens and box offices over weeks. Often released in summer to capture the leisure time of the youth market, these movies determine the release date and competing strategies of other films, generally in complementary genres (romance, more adult films, etc.) as well as recreating spectatorship. Moreover, they become tied to synergistic marketing through music, books, **toys**, promotional events and **fast food**, spending a sizable portion of the total original cost on promotions. In fact, the scale of promotions has become one of the defining features of the genre. As these definitional features suggest, they are also known more by their gross revenue than by themes or quality.

Blockbusters have become renowned for both their revenues in originals and sequels (*Jaws*, 1975–1987; *Jurassic Park*, 1993–2000; *Star Wars*, 1977–; *Independence Day*, 1997; *Men in Black*, 1999; *Titanic*, 1998); and for spectacular disappointments, *(Godzilla*, 1998; *Wild Wild West*, 1999). Such high-stakes gambles, however, have reshaped Hollywood, allowing different versions of the same product to be distributed through numerous media. Nonetheless, these films seldom garner respect as "quality" films, and few have won Oscars, except for the technical awards.

GARY McDONOGH
CINDY WONG

blockbusting

This urban strategy pits newly mobile **African American** families – as buyers – against entrenched white and often ethnic **neighborhoods**. These neighborhoods sometimes received new black families without incident, but realtors profited from both fear of **civil rights** and the need of blacks to escape urban ghettos, while mass media hyped the drama of destroying **community**. Blockbusting as a practice of purposely unsettling residents and exacerbating racial tensions was made illegal by the Fair Housing Act of 1968, although few enough ever admitted doing it. Osser's *Blockbusting in Baltimore* (UK Press 1995) provides a detailed study of one such movement.

GARY McDONOGH
CINDY WONG

blue collar *see* class; working class

blue jeans *see* Levi Strauss; fashion

blues

The blues is quintessential, twentieth-century American culture. Evolving from African chants and rhythms and the field shouts and gospel choruses of the nineteenth-century plantations of the **South**, with hints of ragtime, minstrelsy, vaudeville and other commercial sounds, the blues came to be performed usually by a sole singer with a guitar, picking out a riff in a twelve-bar, three-chord pattern, singing in a raw, throaty style of personal suffering and general hard times of the sorrows of love, work and life. Female vocalists such as Bessie Smith and Mamie Smith were popular on the "race records" of the 1920s, as were the solo bluesmen, many of them from the Mississippi Delta, such as Son House, Charley Patton and Robert Johnson.

Blues musicians began moving to **cities** along with the great **migration** of **African Americans** as the country began to prepare for the Second World War. With the war build-up came factory jobs and cash for leisure-time activities. In cities like **St. Louis**, **Los Angeles**, **Detroit** and, especially, **Chicago**, electric blues emerged as bluesmen plugged in their guitars and performed with small combos, often including a rhythm section, piano and harmonica. Guitarists like jazzman Charlie Christian, **Texas** transplant, Los

Angeleno T-Bone Walker and the first Sonny Boy Williamson pioneered the electric sound, combining the picking and riffing of acoustic blues with elements of **jazz** and **R&B**.

The guitarist Muddy **Waters** migrated to Chicago in 1943 and began playing an electrified version of the blues learned in the Mississippi Delta. By the 1950s he was playing regularly in clubs throughout the city and recording for Chess Records, a pioneering blues, R&B and **rock 'n' roll** label. Chess also recorded **Howlin' Wolf**, Sonny Boy Williamson, Jimmy Rogers, Chuck **Berry** and a host of other major blues talents, including Willie Dixon who often arranged and wrote for the label's acts.

Like all major postwar popular music forms, the blues mixed and matched from a wide range of styles, producing variations (often regional) such as the Louisiana swamp blues of Guitar Slim, the boogie blues of John Lee Hooker and the jump blues of Big Joe Turner. The mixing of the blues with other forms created the foundation for rock 'n' roll as performers like Chuck Berry and Bo Diddley added R&B, country and pop elements. While the emergence of rock 'n' roll in the mid-1950s cut into the popularity of the blues, it is universally acknowledged that electric blues forms the foundation of rock music.

While blues performances continued in clubs, the genre did not regain popularity until the British invasion of the mid-1960s. Rock bands from England like the Rolling Stones and the Yardbirds paid tribute to the blues, recording classic songs and touring with legends like Muddy Waters and Howlin' Wolf. Guitar-based rock, from Eric Clapton to Stevie Ray Vaughan, continues to rely heavily on the blues foundation for both its backbeat and lead guitar.

Further reading

Cohn, L. (1993) *Nothing But the Blues*, New York: Abbeville.
Palmer, R. (1981) *Deep Blues*, New York: Viking.

DEWAR MACLEOD

Bly, Robert
b. 1946

Bly's *Iron John* places him at the head of the recent "Men's Movement" and eclipses his prior eminence as poet, translator and theorist. In either mode, Bly insists that post-Enlightenment culture has gone awry, but that we may regain our spiritual and poetic bearings if we refuse to be like (his?) daddy. Editor of *The Fifties* (and *The Sixties* and *The Seventies*). He introduced many North American readers to the world's great poets (Neruda, Vallejo, Hernandez, Transtromer, even Rilke), yet Bly's exoticized, loose translations of highly formal poems served him in his local battle against academic formalism.

DANIEL BOSCH

boating *see* rivers; rowing (crew); sailing

boat people

A term labeling two **refugee** populations. After 1975, many Vietnamese braved pirates, storms and starvation in the South China Sea to reach refugee camps in Hong Kong and other areas from which they might seek haven in the US or other Western nations. In the Caribbean, overloaded rafts and small crafts from **Cuba** and **Haiti** sought to cross choppy, shark-infested waters to reach asylum in **Florida**. Here, coast-guard patrols were charged to intercept and turn back the refugees (or take them to the Guantanamo Naval Base in Cuba), leading to chilling televisual images of American forces denying the American dream to desperate families.

GARY McDONOGH
CINDY WONG

body

Is there an "American body"? Foreigners visiting the US often remark on the obesity of an affluent society, where one-quarter of children and one-fifth of adults are overweight. Parents of teenagers worry about skinny female **actors** and models who may force daughters into eating disorders, or the dangers of **steroids** or **violence** for their sons. **Medicine** and **Hollywood** stress fitness – the chiseled, toned bodies of both male and female **stars** in the 1990s make romantic leads of the 1950s look flabby to young audiences. Yet, are the bodies of **advertising**, film or *Playboy* "typical" or "real"? Is the body more like a machine (a common American trope in the twentieth century) or do we read it in more complex ways? Whatever body an American has and however he or she feels about it, the body remains a fundamental site of identity, pleasure, anxiety, representation, conflict and change. This article suggests linkages through the body with issues discussed at greater length elsewhere.

The body, after all, is where issues of **race** and **gender** are marked by appearance more than genetics (hence, issues of "passing" for **white** or cross-dressing and **transsexual** identities play upon the body). American phenotypic ascription of race is immediately read from the body, imposing **biology** on it. Gestures and **fashion** may distinguish racial and ethnic groups, at least in common stereotypes – Asians are "quiet," while **Italian Americans** "talk with their hands." **Race** and **ethnicity** are also demarcated by hair – whether "good" or "bad" hair among **African Americans** or the pervasive influence of a northern European blond coloring in **mass media** (although one faces contradictory images of "blondes having more fun" and "dumb blondes").

Gender is also affirmed by differences in fashion and ornamentation of the body, as well as appropriate "behavior" and activities in sports, **war** or other arenas. This is particularly true in clothing and exhibition of the body, although variations in costumes like swimwear illustrate vast differences in attitudes towards appropriate display, often with an underlying **puritanism** about revealing body parts associated with sex and desire. Nude beaches and skimpy beachwear are less common in the US than in Europe; the US has also continuing debates over the appropriateness of breastfeeding in public.

Gender also shapes American alterations and manipulations of the body, including widespread circumcision for American males, **body piercing** (especially ears for women), tattooing, with a faddish appeal in the 1990s, dyeing hair, depilation and various forms of plastic surgery now found among men and women, young and old. Cleanliness and avoidance of odor (except for appropriate perfumes), introduced in childhood as demands on girls more than rough-and-tumble boys, also form part of general body culture in contemporary US culture. These, too, are areas of anxiety in which advertising and media portray "the good body."

Gender and sexuality issues also have raised important questions of privacy and control of the body in the postwar period with regard to **contraception** and, above all, **abortion** – a point over which men and women have fought for decades about control of a woman's body and her right to make choices. **Feminism** has often argued the need for women to reclaim control of their bodies, as the title of a popular health manual – *Our Bodies, Ourselves* (1973) – evoked. Gay sexuality has also raised issues, cultural and legal, about rights to do with one's body as one chooses and where one may do this – the **bedroom**, the **bar**, the dance floor or the street. Other issues of body and privacy have emerged in terms of medical records and surveillance, especially in an **Internet/information** society.

Class is less clearly marked in the body in postwar America (although it converges with markings of race and ethnicity), although there are strong correlations of obesity and poverty. Images of class and clothing – "white collar" (**middle class**) versus "blue collar" (**working class**) or redneck – remind us of the complexities of these markers and divisions in American society.

These issues all converge in issues of activities by and on the body, especially violence. The body is part of sanctioned violent activities, especially for men in sports and war, where it endures the demands and sacrifice of citizenship. Women have made gains in participation in same-sex contact sports, although their roles in combat and other areas of bodily threat (**police**) may still be debated in any crisis in which a woman is hurt. Violence against women by men, whether domestic abuse or rape, has been a major issue for debate over the rights of the gendered body in the 1980s and 1990s.

The body is also a site of aging, leading to specific concerns in development and activities through the **life cycle**. The "rights of the fetus" have become part of the abortion debate as well as medical experimentation. **Babies** and children are closely monitored in terms of normal development, while teenage years are often characterized by a disjunction between bodily changes and social control. Bodies of children and teenagers, however, also demand particular protection in terms of potential exploitation in **pornography** and sex, themes constantly driven home by mass media.

With maturity, **diet**, fitness, cosmetics and **plastic surgery** become elements in a battle against aging that affirms the primacy of the youthful, trim body as an American ideal, especially since the rise of the baby boom (see *American Beauty*, 1999). While older models appear in advertisements and women past fifty have been featured in *Playboy*, they represent exceptions or appeals to particular audiences. In the US, **old age** is deeply associated with the failure of the body and with medical efforts to sustain its function.

Aging, gender and other representations and experiences mark the body as a site for medicalization – expert knowledge and rights to control actions. Here, interventions range from curing to manipulation to insistence on Cesarean births rather than "natural" childbirth to proscriptions on bodily activities like smoking in the name of general health. Medical research has also probed the frontiers of the body in genetic research, transplant/replacements and questions of reproductive technology, while staking claims via patents on "body parts." Emily Martin (1994) and others have highlighted these changing metaphors of the body and their wider implications.

Further reading

Bordo, S. (1993) *Unbearable weight*, Berkeley: University of California.

Boston Women's Health Collective (1998) *Our Bodies, Ourselves for the New Century*, New York: Simon & Schuster.

Jeffords, S. (1994) *Hard Bodies: Hollywood Masculinity in the Reagan Era*, New Brunswick: Rutgers.

Martin, E. (1994) *Flexible Bodies*, Boston: Beacon

McCracken, G. (1996) *Big Hair*, New York: Overlook.

Wakefield, W. (1997) *Playing to Win*, Albany: SUNY Press.

Weitz, R. (ed.) (1998) *The Politics of Women's Bodies*, New York: Oxford.

CINDY WONG

body piercing and tattoos

Body modification has existed around the world for centuries, but, in America, **body** piercing and tattooing rapidly shifted from a sign of subcultural membership to mainstream style. Although once associated with sailors, criminals and other supposedly "dubious" citizens, in the 1970s, body modification flourished among "modern primitives," who viewed the body as a site of expression and sexual freedom. The term "modern primitive" associates body modification with mystico-religious interpretations of *rites de passage*.

Early modification media (1970s to 1980s) included tattooing magazines and one piercing magazine, *The Piercing Fans International Quarterly*. Vale and Juno's *Modern Primitives* (1989) inspired a modification renaissance in the early 1990s, though piercing had already gained popularity with punks.

Piercing and tattooing became fashionable in the early 1990s. Body modification was featured everywhere: Gautier fashions, the Aerosmith video "Cryin," showing a girl getting tattooed and pierced, and Christy Turlington and Naomi Campbell, supermodels with pierced navels. Later, there was the piercing "rush" by adrenaline needle resuscitation of Uma Thurman's heroin overdose in *Pulp Fiction* (Tarantino 1994) and the *X-Files'* Agent Scully's brush with tattooing that left her with a poisonous, hallucinogenic urobouros at the base of her spine.

Marketed to **Generation X** as a way to complete a "look" of personal "difference," commodification of body piercing and tattooing peaked with rub-on tattoos and fake clip-on piercing jewelry. But, despite the hype, the meaning of body modification ranges from group affiliation, modern rite of passage and method of **teenage** rebellion to an expression of body aesthetics and reclamation.

Further reading

Sanders, C. (1989) *Customizing the Body*, Philadelphia: Temple University.

Vale, V. and Juno, A. (1989) *Modern Primitives*, San Francisco: Re/Search Publications.

RAMONA LYONS

Boesky, Ivan

b. 1937

Ivan Boesky's arrest signaled the end of the high-flying merger and buyout industry of the 1980s. As an arbitrageur, he sought to profit by speculating in the stock of takeover targets. As the author of a bestselling book, *Merger Mania* (1985), Boesky became a symbol of a booming industry. In 1985 he began accepting non-public, insider information which he used to make tremendous profits. Once caught, Boesky's cooperation with authorities led to the fall of junk-bond king Michael **Milken** and other prominent securities operators. The scandal left **Wall Street**'s reputation permanently scarred.

MARC BALCER

Bogart, Humphrey

b. 1899; d. 1957

Actor and symbol. Forty years after his death he is still identified as one of **Hollywood**'s greatest male **stars**. Where Gary Cooper was reluctant to be involved, and Jimmy **Stewart** shy, Bogart made Americans feel he might actually go bad – but was often redeemed. Scion of an upper **middle-class** family, he was typecast in juvenile roles on **Broadway** before his breakthrough as Duke Mantee in *The Petrified Forest* (play 1935, film 1936). Later, he defined an American anti-hero in *The Maltese Falcon* (1941), *Casablanca* (1943), *To Have and to Have Not* (1944), when he married co-star

Lauren **Bacall**, *Treasure of the Sierra Madre* (1948) and *The African Queen* (1951), for which he received an Oscar. In these films he was often paired with strong, interesting women. His films and even lines have become proverbs to generations of Americans rediscovering his brooding, lonely yet gentle masculinity, lovingly memorialized in Woody Allen's *Play it Again, Sam* (1972).

See also: actors

GARY McDONOGH

bomb shelters

Underground rooms of the **Cold War** which, at times of heightened paranoia like the **Cuban missile crisis**, families constructed and stocked to allow them to survive imminent nuclear holocaust, extending civil defense preparations for tornadoes or conventional weapons into a new age. Civic buildings also altered cellars and posted signs. Although many shelters never went beyond planning, they stimulated debates over inclusion and exclusion recalled in a 1962 song by comedian Shel Silverstein, "I'm Standing Outside of your Shelter Looking in." In subsequent decades these shelters faded into embarrassment and oblivion; a 1999 Hollywood comedy, *Blast from the Past*, ridiculed a Cold War family who spent decades hiding in one. Nonetheless, echoes of this bomb-shelter mentality recur in propaganda of **survivalists**, messianic Christians and even apocalyptic interpretations of Y2K.

GARY McDONOGH

Bookchin, Murray

b. 1921

Bookchin, an **anarchist** ecologist, worked through various leftist movements before finding the libertarian viewpoint most useful in critiquing American growth and proposing ecologically sensitive and just alternatives. The synthesis of anarchism and ecology which he has expounded since the 1950s has become known as social ecology; Bookchin founded and ran an institute of that name in Vermont. He argues that decentralization, community and absence of hierarchy are intrinsic to issues of energy management and environmental balance. Throughout his life, Bookchin also has been an activist in social movements and Green issues. Major works include *Post-Scarcity Anarchism* (1971), *The Ecology of Freedom* (1982), *From Urbanization to Cities* (1995) and *The Third Revolution* (1996).

GARY McDONOGH

borderlands

For nearly half its distance, the 1,947 kilometer US/Mexico border follows the Rio Grande river from Brownsville/Matamoros to El Paso/Ciudad Juárez, where it becomes a geometric line cutting across the Sonora and Mojave desert until it reaches San Diego/Tijuana. The region was sparsely populated until after the Second World War when development programs fostered the expansion of **agriculture and agribusiness**, **trade**, **tourism** and *maquiladoras* (assembly plants). Between 1930 and 1990, the population of El Paso increased from 102,421 residents to 515,342, while its "sister city" Ciudad Juárez grew from 19,669 to 789,522. During the same period **San Diego** went from 147,87 to 1,110,549 inhabitants, and Tijuana 8,384 to 698,752 inhabitants.

Because of this rapid growth, **immigration**, environmental and cultural issues have become a source of bi-national tension and concern. On a cultural level, the meaning of the border speaks directly to perceptions of US identity since many see it as a dividing line while others, including many **Chicanos/as**, emphasize the possibilities for cultural exchange and dialogue.

From 1521 to 1810, the settling of Northern Mexico – now the US **Southwest** – by Spanish soldiers, farmers and missionaries was sporadic because of violent confrontations with Native Americans and the region's arid climate. Attempts to settle the region, which included devising policies aimed at attracting Anglo settlers, continued after Mexico gained independence from Spain in 1810. US expansion led to the US/

Mexico War and the signing of the Treaty of Guadalupe Hidalgo (1848), which ceded Northern Mexico to the US. As Anglo settlers moved into the region, they dispossessed – through force, legal maneuvers and purchase – Mexicans of their land. In the US, racial segregation was the rule as Mexican Americans were seen and treated as a cheap labor force.

The introduction of new irrigation techniques and railroad lines in the 1900s led to the expansion of agribusiness and the wider use of Mexicans as **farm** labor. The "bracero" program, which was started in 1942 to provide US agribusiness with temporary Mexican field-hands, brought thousands of Mexican workers to the Southwest. When the program was ended in 1964, many workers settled in the border region and continued migrating to the US.

By the 1960s the border region was the site of a number of industries, including agriculture, defense, technology, petroleum, real estate and tourism. The economies of border **cities** have become tightly linked as goods, labor (both legal and illegal), tourists, shoppers and plant managers cross the border on a daily basis. On the Mexican side, the government promoted maquila (assembly-plant) manufacturing in cities such Tijuana, Piedras Negras, Ciudad Juárez and Nuevo Laredo. The Mexican Border Industrialization Program, which was started in 1965, sought to take advantage of the low-wages paid to and the high productivity of the Mexican workforce. The program allowed for the duty-free importation of machinery, equipment and materials under the condition that everything produced was exported. By 1975, 67,214 were employed in maquilas, by 1990, 460,293. The majority of these plants engaged in electronic and furniture assembly and textile production. Maquilas have generated controversy because of their low-wages, reliance on young women as employees, ecological impact and inability to provide jobs for the large number of migrants to the border region.

In order to control the entry of illegal immigrants the US has begun to militarize the border, including deploying marines for patrol duty. Militarization and **violence** on the border have led to concerns over the protection of human rights. Groups such as America's Watch have written reports critical of the Immigration and Naturalization Service's ability to guarantee the rights of legal and illegal immigrants. Attempts to limit illegal immigration – such as the 1986 Immigration Reform and Control Act which included employer sanctions for hiring undocumented workers – have had little impact on the migrant flow. Many of these issues of crossing and employment are depicted in the movie *El Norte* (1989). Most analysts agree that as long as there exists such a large disparity in Mexican and US wage rates – and a demand in the US for Mexican labor – illegal immigration will continue.

As a result of border industrialization, environmental problems have generated new legal issues and highlighted the need for greater bi-national cooperation. Problems such as cross-border flooding, sewage spills, the disposal of hazardous waste and air pollution have drawn the attention of environmental groups and policy-makers. Untreated waste from Tijuana has polluted beaches near San Diego and over half of the maquilas, most of which are owned by US and Japanese companies, have toxic-discharge problems. After 1990, with the signing of the North American Free Trade Agreement, both the US and Mexican governments began to voice concern over borderland environmental conditions. In 1992 US and Mexican environmental agencies devised the Integrated Border Environmental Plan, which focused mainly on educational programs and information sharing while paying little attention to enforcement. A number of US and Mexican non-governmental organizations have formed to pressure for improving environmental conditions.

For many who view US culture as being homogenous and bounded, the complexities and permeability of the border represent a diluting of US culture and ideals. Many Chicanos/as have challenged this view by emphasizing the porous and creative nature of identity and culture; cultural borderlands are not threatening exceptions, but rather regions of cultural exchange and dialogue. Indeed, this rethinking of US identity is needed for transforming perceptions of the US/Mexico border from a closed dividing line to a region where new forms of bi-national cooperation and cultural expression should be fostered and encouraged.

See also: Mexico, relations with

Further reading

America's Watch (1992) *Human Rights Abuses Along the US Border With Mexico*, USA: Human Rights' Watch.

Barry, T. (1994) *The Challenge of Cross-Border Environmentalism: The US–Mexico Case*, Albuquerque: Resource Center.

Herzog, L. (1990) *North Meets South: Cities, Space, and Politics on the US–Mexico Border*, Austin: University of Texas.

Vélez-Ibañez, C. (1996) *Border Visions: Mexican Cultures of the Southwest United States*, Tucson: University of Arizona.

MIGUEL DÍAZ-BARRIGA

Borlaug, Norman

b. 1914

Winner of the 1970 Nobel Peace Prize for his work in creating the Green Revolution in which limited acreage fed more and more people. Borlaug learned from his experiences of the **Midwest** Dustbowl and developed high-yield, low-pesticide dwarf wheat crops that proved effective in Mexico and then in South Asia in the 1960s. His later campaigns against famine in **Africa**, however, faced criticism for their impact on population growth and the crops' need for pesticides and irrigation.

GARY McDONOGH

Borscht Belt *see* Jews

Bosnia and Kosovo

During the second half of the 1980s, Yugoslavia's ethnically and religiously diverse republics – Slovenia, Croatia, Bosnia-Herzegovina and Macedonia – started to push for greater autonomy. In response, Yugoslav President Slobodan Milosevic, an avowed Serbian nationalist, endeavored to consolidate the position of Serbia in various ways. Slovenians and the

Croatians declared their independence. Forced to accept Slovenian independence, since almost no Serbs lived in that province, Milosevic went to war with the Croatians. The **Bush** administration remained onlookers (hoping that Yugoslavia would not break up into small provinces and not wanting involvement in another war so soon after the **Gulf War**) until news reports of "ethnic cleansing" prompted government officials to push for peace negotiations. The **Clinton** administration followed a more active policy favorable to the Muslims. Following accords between the disputing provinces, the United Nations sent in peacekeeping forces to Croatia.

The Serbs then turned their attention to Bosnia, with a multi-ethnic, generally harmonious population centered in the historically cosmopolitan capital, Sarajevo. Bosnia was now painted by Milosevic as a province marked by centuries of ethnic strife, with a Christian Serb minority at the mercy of the Muslims. Serbs bombarded Sarajevo, which had received no peacekeepers and which, with the international arms embargo on the region, was essentially defenseless. During this conflict (1992–5), the leader of the Bosnian Serbs, Radovan Karadzic, is alleged by the War Crimes Tribunal in The Hague to have established concentration camps and to have sanctioned torture, rape and massacres. As many as 200,000 Bosnian Muslims, Croats and Serbs may have been killed in this genocidal civil war.

The intervention of the United States, and the diplomacy of Richard Holbrooke, helped bring about the Dayton Agreement in November 1995, which partitioned Bosnia. The establishment of a NATO mission in the country brought peace, but the settlement's partition appeared to validate some of the Serbs' territorial demands and strengthened Milosevic's position in Yugoslavia, leading him to respond in a similar way to Kosovar nationalists as he had done to the Bosnians. Milosovic's refusal to recognize independence for Kosovo was followed by a Yugoslav onslaught on Albanian Kosovar forces in 1999, allegations of renewed genocidal activity and NATO military intervention (including the presence of US troops) that established greater independence for the province.

ROBERT GREGG

Boston, Massachusetts

History permeates contemporary Boston. While active as a **state** capital and financial center, the city's institutions, ethos and cultural diversity are all shaped by its colonial heritage and later cultural roles which encourage contemporary tourism, as well as shaping local landscapes, politics and divisions within a metropolitan area of 5 million inhabitants in New Hampshire and Eastern Massachusetts.

Founded in the 1630s by English Puritan settlers at the intersection of the Charles River and the Atlantic Ocean, Boston was the main settlement of the Massachusetts Bay Colony. Boston was a seat of revolutionary activity during the late eighteenth century, and is still closely associated with early American patriots Paul Revere, Samuel Adams and John Hancock, as well as the "Boston Tea Party" tax revolt of 1773. During the nineteenth century, Boston was considered "the Hub of the Universe" because of its geographic importance in terms of transportation, **economics** and culture. The nineteenth century also saw significant geographic expansions with the creation of bourgeois neighborhoods such as the Back Bay and the South End. **Immigration** from Italy and Ireland also helped create an ethnic blue-collar neighborhood culture, which defines such areas as the North End, South Boston and nearby Somerville and Charlestown to this day. Other cultural influences include **African Americans** (especially in Roxbury and the South End), Armenians (in Watertown), Portuguese and more recent immigrants from the Caribbean and Asia. Boston is still widely associated with white racism over such issues as **busing** and school integration. Loyalty towards the area's sports franchises (Celtics, Bruins, Red Sox, Patriots) has also defined the character of the city. Boston's ethnic neighborhood culture, well known for its distinctive accent, has been represented in such films as *Good Will Hunting* (1997) and **television** series such as *Cheers*.

Architecturally, the city is characterized by brick town houses in the older **neighborhoods** and the triple-decker type in the **suburbs**, although this was dramatically changed by urban renewal in the postwar era, including the creation of the Central Artery and the destruction of the West End in the

1950s, and the creation of a new Boston **City Hall** (designed by Kallmann, McKinnell and Knowles), completed in 1969. Recently, **gentrification** has attracted many young professionals back into the city, and Fanieul Hall is typical of urban festival marketplaces in historic locations.

Boston and its surrounding towns host over sixty colleges and universities, including Boston College, Boston University and Northeastern University. Cambridge, across the Charles River, is the site of both Harvard University and the Massachusetts Institute of Technology, and has long been considered a center of progressive politics and local nightlife. This large urban student population stimulated active underground music and art, producing such artists as Nan Goldin and rock bands as the Lemonheads, Juliana Hatfield and the Mighty Mighty Bosstones.

Further reading

Digby Baltzell, E. (1979) *Puritan Boston and Quaker Philadelphia*, New York: The Free Press.
O'Connor, T. (1993) *Building a New Boston*, Boston: Northeastern University.

HUNTER FORD TURA
JEANNIE J. KIM

Boston Pops

The **Boston** Pops began on July 11, 1885 when the Boston Symphony Orchestra inaugurated a *pop*ular concert; the Boston Pops Orchestra began to perform under its name in 1935. The typical Pops concert begins with an opening section of light classical music. The middle section features a classical or popular soloist, and the conclusion consists of music from Broadway show tunes, film music, hits from the big-band era or patriotic favorites like the marches of Sousa. The Pops often perform their rousing programs outdoors for free, for example, playing for the **Bicentennial** in front of 400,000 people – the largest audience ever for an orchestral performance. Its renowned conductors of the orchestra include Arthur Fiedler and

film composer John Williams. **Philadelphia**, **Los Angeles, CA** and other **cities** have similar series.

EDWARD MILLER

botánicas

During the late 1950s and early 1960s, the United States experienced a surge of **immigration** from Afro-Spanish Caribbean communities such as **Cuba** and **Puerto Rico**. Within these newly formed immigrant communities emerged a unique institution called the "botánica." Located throughout major urban **cities** in the United States, botánicas are small stores and shops devoted to the distribution of religious artifacts and supplies such as oils, candles, music, books, beads, powders, charms, amulets, statues, ceramic pots, baths and incense. The name "botánica" refers to the science of botany or plants. Hence, assorted herbs and plant life are some of the chief products sold there.

The items sold at botánicas are primarily used for the purposes of sacred ritual and spiritual healing. Much of the herbal pharmacopeia and spiritual supplies are related to the practice of various African-derived religious traditions such as Santería, Palo Mayombe, Espiritismo and Haitian **Voudou**. Practitioners of these traditions utilize local botánicas as sources for medicinal supplies, religious paraphernalia and spiritual consultation.

Further reading

Cregory, S. (1987) "Afro-Caribbean Religions in New York: The Case of Santeria," in C. Sutton and E. Chaney (eds) *Caribbean Life in New York*, New York: Center for Migration Studies of New York.
Murphy, J. (1988) *Santería: An African Religion in America*, Boston: Beacon Press.

TRACEY E. HUCKS

bowl games

The bowl games are the climax to the college **football** season. Begun with the Rose Bowl

(Pasadena), dating back to 1902, many bowl games were created by boosters in Southern **cities** wishing to attract tourists and investors. Once **television** networks began to purchase the rights to games for millions of dollars, they became very lucrative for the colleges represented. Each bowl committee (sugar, orange, sun, cotton, etc.) invites two teams to play according to their college conference records. Many sports analysts consider this an inadequate season finale as seldom do the two best teams have a showdown. The frequent cases of competing claims to the national championship have increased the clamor for a tournament, as in college **basketball**, that would produce a final four and an undisputed champion.

See also: Superbowl (Sunday)

ROBERT GREGG

bowling

Bowling became popular in the 1890s, quickly acquiring a beer-drinking and **working-class** image. However, the sport was open to both **genders** and, facilitated by the use of handicaps, which adjust for the differing abilities of players and teams, women began to compete early on. During the First World War, when many women entered the industrial workforce, the sport became a popular pastime for them, leading to the formation of the Women's National Bowling Association. After the Second World War, the image of the sport changed, becoming associated with **middle-class** housewives. Consequently, bowling alleys began to incorporate beauty salons and other shopping conveniences in close proximity to the lanes.

Bowling has advanced technologically with automatic pin-replacing and electronic scoring machines, new kinds of wooden surfaces, varnishes and balls, all of which have made the game easier for the recreational bowler, and more expensive for the serious bowler (each ball may cost as much as $200). Where once the alleys attracted teams formed around strong neighborhood or workplace associations, they are now increasingly becoming places where single families go for an afternoon's fun, and becoming another venue (along with

skating rinks, **zoos**, **YMCAs**) for birthday parties. Loud **disco** music and kids running around are the norm.

ROBERT GREGG

boxing

Boxing in its contemporary form is a sport in which men and increasingly, among professionals, women of closely matched weights fight with their fists in padded leather gloves. No bare description can account for the impact of boxing on American culture, or an appeal which persists despite, or perhaps because of, occasional ring deaths, and in the face of medical evidence that persistent blows to the head, even from gloved fists, can cause forms of brain damage. (The **American Medical Association** has frequently called for the sport to be banned.)

Ever since **African American** boxer Jack Johnson's championship reign (1908–15), boxing has been a crucible for issues of race and **masculinity**. Johnson's first championship victory, over Tommy Burns in Australia, provoked **race riots** in many American cities and gave rise to the racially charged search in the press and elsewhere for a "Great White Hope" (one of many boxing expressions that have entered common usage, including "double cross," "knockout," "up against the ropes" and "the real McCoy").

Boxers have traditionally come from economically oppressed minority communities, especially African American, **Italian American** or **Irish American**. Like other professional sports, boxing has been seen as a way to escape poverty, but success is rare, and boxers have frequently been financially exploited. Despite the successes of such great champions as Henry Armstrong, Sugar Ray Robinson and Joe Louis (whose knockout of the German Max Schmeling in 1938 was seen as a rebuff to Adolf Hitler's claim of Aryan racial superiority), black boxers' opportunities at the highest levels were restricted to the extent that white boxers could avoid them, until after the Second World War. Successful black boxers had to be very careful about their public image (Louis was instructed not to be photographed alongside white women). In the 1950s, however, this began to change with the combination of somewhat improved opportunities for black men following from their wartime service and, by the late 1950s, the advent of televised boxing and increased demand for talented fighters. African Americans have dominated the public face of the sport ever since, especially in the most visible heavyweight division, where the last undisputed white champion was Rocky Marciano, who retired in 1955. Many boxers in the lighter weight classes have been from Latin America and Asia, especially as boxing's market has expanded via global communications networks.

Since the 1960s, the three central figures in the public awareness of boxing have been the heavyweight champions Muhammad **Ali** and Mike Tyson, and the promoter Don King. Handsome, flamboyant and loquacious, Ali's public opposition to the **Vietnam War** and his claims to be "the prettiest" and "the Greatest," echoing the political slogan "Black is Beautiful," made him into a hero for many, and eventually one of the most famous men alive. Boxing was seen to fall into a lull after Ali's retirement in the early 1980s. By then the division of championships by separate sanctioning bodies meant that there were often multiple champions in each weight division, and without charismatic figures like Ali many fans lost interest.

Tyson's very different appeal sparked something of a popular revival. For Tyson, boxing was an escape from a much-publicized juvenile delinquent youth on the streets of Brooklyn, New York, and he became a protégé of the trainer Cus D'Amato. Viewed against Ali's speed and agility, Tyson was an explosive puncher who rose to prominence with a series of spectacular early round knockouts, and unified the title (won the title under each of the separate sanctioning organizations) in 1988. As champion, Tyson's malevolent, "gangster" rap image and his very public personal life were accompanied by rumors of continued delinquency and charges of sexual harassment. His marriage to actor Robin Givens collapsed, and, in a stunning upset, he was defeated by unheralded Buster Douglas in 1990. In 1992 Tyson was convicted in Indiana of the rape of a Miss Black America pageant contestant. His supporters claimed for him the same status as a legal martyr to racism that Ali

and before him Jack Johnson had attained. Paroled after three years, Tyson fought a series of inconsequential bouts that brought him a meaningless championship. However, he was unexpectedly and thoroughly beaten by Evander Holyfield in 1996 and again in 1997 when he was disqualified for twice biting Holyfield's ears.

The promoter Don King, his trademark upright hairstyle and motto, "Only in America," ubiquitous at major bouts, spans the championship reigns of Ali and Tyson. A former Cleveland numbers runner, once convicted of manslaughter, King secured the first $10 million purse for Ali's bout with George Foreman in Zaire in 1974, and the bloated prize-money, in tens of millions of dollars, for Tyson's comeback mismatches on pay-per-view television. Although he has avoided legal entanglements, his simultaneous promotional deals with opposing boxers have been associated with the perceived corruption of boxing.

FRAZER WARD

Bradbury, Ray

b. 1920

Bradbury, an explorer of the imagination, began his publishing career in the 1940s in pulp **magazines**. His later stories and novels combine **science-fiction** scenarios with deeply human twists of the imagination in search of meaning and identity and poetic imagery. He has also shown a cinematic awareness of American oddities and possibilities. Major works include the *Martian Chronicles* (1950), which reinvent an American narrative of discovery and adaptation, and *Something Wicked This Way Comes* (1962). His *Fahrenheit 451* was also made into a movie (1966).

GARY McDONOGH

Brando, Marlon

b. 1924

A powerful naturalistic actor who dominated the screen in the early 1950s with stunning performances in *A Streetcar Named Desire* (1951), where he gained stardom on Broadway, *Viva Zapata!* (1952), *Julius Caesar* (1953) and *On the Waterfront* (1954), for which he won an Oscar. In these roles, Brando, a method actor trained at Actors Studio, exuded rebellion, epitomized in images of his leather-clad motorcyclist in *The Wild One* that adorned dormitory walls for decades and in his adventurous off-screen life. After a slack period, Brando re-emerged to major stardom as Vito Corleone in *The Godfather* (1972) and in the tortured *Last Tango in Paris* (1972), although he took on limited roles through the 1990s. His characteristic speech, emblematic roles and expanding size made him a favorite target of imitators.

See also: actors

Further reading

McCann, G. (1993) *Rebel Males*, New Brunswick: Rutgers.

GARY McDONOGH
CINDY WONG

Brautigan, Richard

b. 1935; d. 1984

Brautigan was greatly influenced by the **beat generation** writers during the 1950s when he lived in **San Francisco**. He published **poetry** throughout his career as well as a collection of short stories, but was best known during the 1960s and 1970s as a novelist who achieved almost cult-like status in the counterculture through his absurdist plots, rebellious characters and wry, gentle sense of humor that obliquely poked fun at the Establishment. Brautigan dropped out of circulation during most of the 1970s, then reappeared in 1982 to publish a final book before apparently committing suicide in 1984.

JIM WATKINS

breakfast cereals

Developed in the nineteenth century as adult health foods, cereals became a multi-billion dollar American way of breakfast, especially for **children**, in the twentieth century. Toasted and stewed grains have given way to flavored, highly sweetened convenience foods served with milk. Commercials aggressively market their tigers, leprechauns and rabbits and other product tie-ins on or in the box. Concern with children's nutrition as well as adult health has widened the range of cereals to incorporate new grains and fruit/nut mixtures, while some advertising stresses associations with nature or sports (Wheaties, "Breakfast of Champions"). Still, it pays to read the label.

GARY McDONOGH

Broadway *see* drama and theater; musicals; New York and its boroughs; theater

Brodsky, Joseph

b. 1940; d. 1996

Russian-born Jewish poet who left the USSR in 1972 for exile after a life of protest and persecution. He became a US citizen in 1977 where he taught at Mount Holyoke College and also received a MacArthur Award. A bilingual writer, he published both poetry and essays. After winning the **Nobel Prize** for Literature in 1987, he also became American poet laureate from 1991 to 1992.

GARY McDONOGH
CINDY WONG

Bronx *see* New York and its boroughs

Brooklyn *see* New York and its boroughs

Brooks, Gwendolyn

b. 1917

Poet and novelist who became the first **African American** woman to win the **Pulitzer Prize** (1950). Her rich poetic career has explored the African American vernacular, where race shapes experience (*We Real Cool*, 1966). Her sometimes underrated novel, *Maud Martha* (1953), deals with the impact of prejudice within African American interactions, as well as conditions of the larger society. Other poems deal with racial issues of her home in **Chicago, IL**, including "Jump Bad" (1951).

GARY McDONOGH

Brown, H. Rap

b. 1943

Civil rights activist turned militant who succeeded Stokely **Carmichael** as the chairperson of SNCC in 1967. Brown continued to radicalize the organization, building on Carmichael's call for **Black Power** and rejecting non-violence as a viable method of protest. Claiming that "violence is as American as apple pie," he believed that the movement should respond in kind, and changed SNCC's name to the Student National Coordinating Committee. Charged with carrying firearms across state lines, he skipped bail and was captured after a gun battle with police in 1972. In prison Brown adopted the Muslim faith and the name Jamil Abdullah Al-Amin, and after parole from prison moved to Atlanta, where he later ran afoul of police.

ROBERT GREGG

Brown, James

b. 1928

Singer, songwriter, producer, musician, "Soul Brother No. 1" and "Mr Dynamite," James Brown emerged as a distinctive force in popular music in 1956 with "Please, Please, Please" backed by his Famous Flames. Born in South Carolina, Brown rose from rural poverty, a childhood as a shoeshine boy and convicted juvenile delinquent to fashion a unique form of gritty, gospel-influenced R&B. *The James Brown Show Live at the Apollo* (1963) is one of the great popular music albums of all time. Brown pioneered funk music and crossed over to white audiences with the hit "Papa's Got a Brand New Bag" (1965). Brown combined his grainy, deep-throated shrieking and shouting with pulsing polyrhythms, staccato horns and guitars, and an exhilarating stage show to earn the title of "the hardest working man in show business."

In the late 1960s, in the midst of the cultural and political turmoil in America, Brown became an ambiguous political figure, singing militant lyrics like "Say It Loud, I'm Black and I'm Proud" (1968) and touring Africa while entertaining American troops in Korea and Vietnam and encouraging black capitalism instead of ghetto rioting. Working with a new young band the JBs in the early 1970s, Brown recorded influential hit records – *Sex Machine* (1970), *Super Bad* (1970) and *Soul Power* (1971). Brown's influence on all black popular music from the 1950s through the 1990s was so powerful that he could rightly claim to be "the original **disco** man" and the original rapper.

DEWAR MACLEOD

Brown family

Californian **Democratic** political dynasty. Edmund G. "Pat" Brown (1905–) became a liberal Democratic **governor** (1959–67) and party power broker. His son, Jerry Edmund, Jr. (1938–), brought an edgier style to the governorship (1975–83), combining rigorous liberalism and celebrity status with Jesuitical overtones. These gained the national spotlight during repeated presidential bids (1976, 1980, 1992) and their aftermath as Brown dated stars and also worked with Mother Teresa in Calcutta. In the late 1990s, he re-emerged as a reformist mayor of racially divided Oakland. Sister Kathleen also ran for governor of California after a long career of public service.

GARY McDONOGH
CINDY WONG

Brown v. Board of Education of Topeka

In *Brown v. Board of Education of Topeka* and its companion cases the US **Supreme Court** unanimously held that the operation of separate public schools segregated on the basis of race was unconstitutional. The Court's 1954 decision found that separate schools for **African American** public school students was "inherently unequal," violating the 14th Amendment's guarantee of equal protection of the laws to all citizens. The Brown decision was the Court's first ruling to directly overturn the "separate but equal" doctrine articulated almost sixty years earlier in *Plessy* v. *Ferguson*, and laid the groundwork for ending legally imposed **segregation** in other public entities over the next decade. It is widely regarded by historians and legal scholars as one of the Supreme Court's most important decisions ever rendered.

BRIAN LEVIN

Brundage, Avery

b. 1887; d. 1975

Arguably the most powerful figure in the history of the modern **Olympic Games**. During his tenure as chairperson of the American Olympic Committee (1930–52), and vice-president (1945–52) and president of the International Olympic Committee (1952–72), Brundage proved a vigorous proponent of amateurism in Olympic sport. Although he regarded both professionalism and politics as inimical to the Olympic spirit, his application of these principles was often selective. Following the 1936 **Berlin** Games, his praise for Nazi Germany drew considerable criticism. Also, during the **Cold War**, he overlooked the conflict between amateurism and the state subsidy of communist-bloc athletes.

CHARLES RUTHEISER

Buchanan, Patrick

b. 1938

Political pundit and three-time candidate for US **president**, Buchanan has been a nationally recognized political figure since the 1970s, as well as a consistent and outspoken advocate of social conservatism and economic protectionism. In 1992 he challenged incumbent President **Bush** for the **Republican** nomination, and was widely blamed for aggravating tensions between the conservative and moderate wings of the party with his harsh "**family-values**" rhetoric. In 1996 Buchanan shifted his focus to economics. His attacks on corporate greed and the twin economic threats of unrestricted **trade** and **immigration** struck a resonant chord with **working-class** Americans. He declared his candidacy for the 2000 presidential election as a Reform Party candidate.

SARAH SMITH

Buck, Pearl (Pearl Sydenstreicker Walsh)

b. 1892; d. 1973

Buck grew up in China with her missionary parents, returning several times during her career and even teaching at Nanjing University. Her experiences of the small Chinese farming villages fueled a prolific writing career, including over 100 works. Her second novel, *The Good Earth*, highlighted a Chinese peasant family and earned her the Pulitzer Prize (1932), leading to the Nobel Prize for Literature (1938). Her novels also were frequently adapted to stage and screen with predominantly **white** casts: *The Good Earth* (1937), with Paul Muni and Luise Rainer, and *Dragon Seed* (1944), with Katharine **Hepburn** and Walter Huston. Buck created a foundation for international child assistance and Welcome House Social Services, an international **adoption** agency.

JIM WATKINS
CINDY WONG

Buckley, William *see* Right, the

Buddhists

The practice of Buddhism in the United States arrived with various Asian immigrant groups, from Chinese to Japanese and, later, Koreans and Thais, Cambodians and the various Burmese ethnic groups. Current congregations, or *sanghas*, tend to be located on the Pacific Coast, including metropolitan **Los Angeles** and the **San Francisco** Bay area, and some major cities in the East, such as **Boston** and **New York**. While the major groups practicing Buddhism in the US are Asian in descent, increasing numbers of non-Asian people find themselves attracted to the philosophical aspects of the religion and to meditation styles of Vipassana, Zen, etc. Buddhism's treatment of the concept of transience appeals to many people in the postmodern age. Many adherents find it useful as a means to grapple with the existential aspects of the times. Estimates of the number of adherents in the US range anywhere between 750,000 and 5 million people.

See also: Southeast Asians

ERIC A. ZIMMER

Buffalo, NY

Once a thriving multi-ethnic manufacturing and transportation center on Lake Erie, **suburban** flight and aging industries have reduced its population to 300,000 (metro 1,184,000) at the end of the century. Nearby Niagara Falls, a natural wonder shared with **Canada**, is a major tourist attraction especially associated with honeymoons. The Niagara also produces power for the region. While eclipsed by **Sunbelt** growth, Buffalo retains important sport teams (the Bills, **football**, and Sabers, **hockey**), the suburban campus of SUNY-Buffalo and the Albright-Knox Gallery. Mark Goldman's *High Hopes* analyzes the city's rise and decline.

Further reading

Goldman, M. (1983) *High Hopes*, Albany: SUNY.

GARY McDONOGH
CINDY WONG

Bukowski, Charles

b. 1920; d. 1994

German-born American and Californian fiction writer, prose poet and misanthrope, Bukowski published more than forty books, many with small presses. Chronicler of the seamy, his narrators define angry drunks (he wrote the movie *Barfly*), unapologetic macho men and beat geniuses too deeply invested in "real life" to be appreciated by critics. In Bukowski's monotonous poems, speakers celebrate booze, bad sex and bitterness as if they are being brutally honest, but Bukowski did not invite readers to join him in his America. His appraisal may be summed up as follows: "Fuck You. You couldn't take it."

DANIEL BOSCH

Bunche, Ralph Johnson

b. 1904; d. 1971

African American diplomat. Ralph Bunche developed an internationalist's vision during his undergraduate study at UCLA. A gifted intellectual, Bunche attended Harvard for graduate work in political science and prior to the Second World War taught at Howard University, made an extensive tour of Africa and provided vital input to Gunnar Myrdal's study of American **race** issues. The war propelled Bunche into international diplomatic service at the United Nations, where he won the Nobel Peace Prize in 1950 for brokering a Middle East peace agreement. At the UN Secretariat until 1971, Bunche sought to end colonialism and worked closely with all UN Secretary Generals, particularly Dag Hammarskjöld. President John F. **Kennedy** later awarded him the Presidential Medal of Freedom.

MELINDA SCHWENK

Burns, George (Nathan Birnbaum)

b. 1896; d. 1996

Part of a husband and wife (Gracie Allen, 1902–64) vaudeville team, originating in the 1920s, who made a successful transition to radio and then 1950s sitcom (CBS, 1950–8). Allen's effervescent naivete created wonderful language games as well as continual confusion; Burns, as a cigar-smoking straight man, constantly violated the fourth wall to address the audience (or watch sitcom events on television). After Allen's death, Burns tried other less successful series before returning to **Hollywood**, where he won an Oscar for *The Sunshine Boys* (1975). He played God in another series of the 1970s and 1980s. Indeed, he announced that he would play Las Vegas at 100; he did not quite keep that date.

GARY McDONOGH

Burroughs, William S., Jr.

b. 1914; d. 1997

Novelist and icon of gay and drug subcultures. Burroughs befriended Allen Ginsberg and Jack **Kerouac**, key members of the **beat generation**, in **New York** City, NY in the 1940s, became a heroin addict and accidentally shot his wife dead in Mexico (1951). Ginsberg was instrumental in the publication of *Junky* (1953), a pitiless account of addiction. Best remembered for the inventive, hallucinatory *Naked Lunch* (1959), which was subject to a legal battle in the United States after it was censored by the US Post Office, Customs Service and a state government. He also invented "cut-ups," a literary equivalent to collage.

FRAZER WARD

buses

In the *Chaneysville Incident* (1967), novelist David Bradley equated variations in mass transportation with **class** and **race** in America. Air travel was elite – important people (generally **white**) going to important places quickly whatever the expense. Train travel from great urban stations was **middle class** and mixed. Buses and bus stations, for Bradley as for much of America, occupied the bottom rung with its cheap but uncomfortable travel, relegated to marginal travelers without cars – poor, rural Americans, blacks, **Latinos** and the elderly. Two decades later, trains have declined and passengers complain that air comfort rivals that of buses. Yet buses remain icons of marginality.

Intercity bus travel initially expanded with interstate highways, competing effectively with trains in price and access to smaller towns. Rural bus stops could use existing crossroads, stores or restaurants (see *Bus Stop*, 1956). In cities, terminals became art deco monuments with tiles, glass and lighting that made train stations seem antiquated.

Greyhound Bus Lines, founded by Eric Wickman to transport Minnesota workers in 1914, became a major interstate carrier in the 1920s. Despite Depression struggles, Greyhound became the official transportation carrier of the 1933 Chicago World's Fair. Other smaller independent companies organized in 1936 as the Trailways system. Both were active in troop transport and development in the Second World War.

Greyhound's postwar slogan, "Go Greyhound, and Leave the Driving to Us," reveals its killing competitor – the private, family car. In the 1950s, interstate bus travel also became a site of protest in the civil-rights **South**, facing down **segregation**. As mass **aviation** expanded, bus travel became identified with the carless, and decaying stations evoked specters of dirt, crime and hustling (e.g. *Midnight Cowboy*, 1969). 1980s deregulation also challenged markets. By 1990 Greyhound faced **bankruptcy** reorganization.

At the end of the decade, Greyhound, Trailways and other lines have coordinated more effectively, with revenues exceeding $1 billion. Targeted consumers include students, senior citizens, leisure travelers, military personnel and rural dwellers (Greyhound serves 3,700 destinations with over 22 million passengers). Regional charter companies offer regional tours adapted to group schedules. Intensive routes – for example those connecting **New York** City, NY or **Philadelphia, PA** and casinos in **Atlantic City, NJ** – also have permitted renewed competition, even if subordinate to car travel.

Urban buses have echoed the travails of intercity buses. While offering advantages in terms of infrastructural investment and flexibility, buses have competed unsuccessfully with cars for the **suburban** commuters. In most cities, buses have become municipal responsibilities, integrated with other mass transportation options, rather than private corporations; some cities (notably in the **Sunbelt**) have effectively eliminated this service.

The 1994 thriller *Speed* contrasts **Los Angeles**' sleek, expensive new subway with the bus where the action takes place, which is occupied by minorities, the elderly and eccentrics. Minibuses have been proposed for special uses – transporting the disabled or elderly, for example. In addition, immigrants in densely populated areas like New York operate illegal systems to connect workers, jobs and shopping areas.

Public schools also operate extensive bus systems; their bright yellow buses evoke memories and caution in passing drivers. If public schools remain crucibles of democracy, so do these buses (which may also serve **private schools** and aftercare). Court-ordered **busing**, as a remedy for *de facto* segregation, however, also made these buses targets of hatred.

GARY McDONOGH
CINDY WONG

Bush, George and family

George Walker Herbert Bush (1924–), son of a senator and representative of the WASP elite, graduated from Yale University before serving as a navy fighter pilot in the Second World War. After the war, he followed the westward shift in American society, migrating to **Texas** and heading an oil-drilling firm. In 1966 he was elected to the first of two terms as a **Republican** member of **Congress**. He would later become ambassador to the United Nations (1971–3), chairperson of the Republican National Committee (1973–4) and director of the **CIA** (1976–7). After losing the 1980 Republican presidential nomination to Ronald **Reagan**, Bush served as his vice-president (1981–9).

In 1988 Bush and running-mate Dan Quayle defeated Michael Dukakis in the presidential election. Faced with escalating budget deficits, he abandoned his electoral pledge of "read my lips: no new taxes," and accepted a tax package that was designed to reduce the deficit but largely failed to do so as recession and an anemic recovery combined to produce the lowest growth rate since the Great Depression.

In foreign affairs, he ordered an invasion of **Panama** (1989) to depose Manuel Noriega, and in 1990 he committed the US to the reversal of Iraq's invasion of Kuwait, which was achieved (1991) in the Persian **Gulf War**. Bush also signed nuclear-disarmament agreements with the Soviet Union and Russia that called for substantial cuts in nuclear arms and the **North American Free Trade Agreement** with **Canada** and **Mexico**. In 1992 he was defeated by **Democrat** Bill **Clinton**.

Barbara Bush (1925–) was generally considered a mild-mannered, supportive **First Lady**, with the exception of her outburst against Geraldine Ferraro, Dukakis' running-mate. Her role as self-effacing "helpmate" redounded to her benefit when contrasted with the garish flamboyance of Nancy Reagan, who preceded her, and the more politically charged Hillary Clinton, who followed.

The Bush's eldest son, George Walker Bush (1946–), followed his father to Yale and also worked briefly in the oil industry (though with less success). As managing partner (1989–94) of the Texas Rangers **baseball** team, he gained public attention that would facilitate his election in 1994 as **Governor** of Texas, where he has set a record for the number of executions carried out. Capturing the Republican's 2000 presidential nomination, he set the early pace following his refusal to accept public money to finance his campaign, thus allowing him to get around limits placed on private donations. Widely considered a moderate in spite of his position on **capital punishment** (at least until the John McCain insurgency pushed him rightward politically), he initially reaped the benefit of the **backlash** against right-wing Republicans who led the protracted struggle to impeach President **Clinton**. Another son of the former president, Jeb, currently serves as Governor of **Florida**.

ROBERT GREGG

busing

The **Supreme Court**'s *Brown* decision in 1954 left unresolved the methods by which desegregation should be carried out. Schooling presented especially difficult problems. Since students have generally been assigned to the school nearest their homes, even if deliberate **segregation** is not practiced by school boards it may still reflect residential patterns. These patterns may be a legacy of segregation as black neighborhoods often clustered around black schools and white neighborhoods did likewise. But it could also follow from residential practices like **restrictive covenants**, common in northern **cities**, which kept **African Americans** out of certain neighborhoods and so, *de facto*, kept schools segregated. In a series of decisions (for example, *Swann* v. *Charlotte-Mecklenburg*, 1971, and *Keyes* v. *School District No. 1*, 1972), the Supreme Court determined that students needed to be moved from one school to another in order to desegregate them. Busing became the basis for accomplishing this goal.

The decision to bus children away from their local schools, not merely in the **South**, caused great anger and led to violent demonstrations, most notably in **Boston**. It became one of the key elements in the **backlash** against the **Civil Rights movement**, provoking the swing of the white ethnic urban vote to the **Republican Party** and **Nixon** (who appointed anti-integrationists to the Supreme Court). Often overlooked in discussions of busing is the pivotal case of *Milliken* v. *Bradley*, in which the Nixon appointees kept the process of desegregation from extending from the local district to the state level, refusing to acknowledge that suburbs had developed through "**white flight**" to establish *de facto* segregation of inner-city residents. Not including the suburbs in the process of integration, the federal courts left the poorest whites and blacks to fight over limited city resources. Busing failed and segregation haunts both urban and suburban public schools.

ROBERT GREGG

Byrne, David

b. 1952

Guitarist/lead singer of the pioneering band Talking Heads, which formed in 1975. Often miscategorized as **punk**, Talking Heads, clean-cut and preppy-looking, created a quirky, experimental sound that became indicative of **New York** rock. Their first hit, "Psycho-killer," contained lyrics in French about glory and words in English about a man upset by his lack of manners. In the 1980s, the band became increasingly involved in **African American** and world music, and, by the mid-decade, guest musicians joined them on records. Byrne has worked with theater artists Twyla Tharp and Robert **Wilson**, directed the "mockumentary" *True Stories* (1986) and shared an Oscar for the score for *The Last Emperor* (1987). Leaving the band in the late 1980s, he has collaborated with **Latin American** musicians and hosts a music show on **PBS**.

EDWARD MILLER

C

Cabinet

Advisors to the **president**, nominated by him and confirmed by the Senate, and executives for federal agencies. Although not strictly established in the Constitution, some Cabinet positions, including **Secretary of State**, **Attorney-General**, Secretary of Treasury, Secretary of War (later consolidated into Secretary of Defense), have existed since the George Washington administration. Others have been added subsequently to deal with issues of the interior, **agriculture**, commerce, labor, health and human services, housing and urban development, transportation, energy, **education** and **veterans** affairs. One original post, Postmaster-General, has been downgraded.

These officers may succeed to the presidency in order of seniority of their office, beginning with the Secretary of State, if they meet qualifications of age and birth. In addition, other officials hold Cabinet-level rank, recognizing their importance as presidential advisors. In the **Clinton** administration, these include the **CIA** Director, **EPA** Administrator, Director of the Office of Management and Budget, Director of the Office of National drug Control Policy, Ambassador to the **United Nations** and US **Trade** Representative.

Cabinet members tend to reflect their party and president: such positions may recognize excellence and add diversity to a **white** male executive structure, but also may reward political cronyism. Cabinet members have also become political targets, being investigated with increasing frequency over issues of influence peddling and political operations (allegations which have also proved true in some cases). Since the **Nixon** era, confirmation debates in **Congress** have also grown acrimonious as nominees have become lightning rods for many political issues beyond their qualifications. In general, they lack the power to oppose the president or survive changes in regime, unlike many European ministers. Some, like Elizabeth **Dole** and Dick Cheney, have sought higher office later.

GARY McDONOGH

cable television

Cable was first used in 1948 to send television signals through wire to remote mountainous parts of the United States. Over the decades, the cable **television** industry has changed from a delivery system for broadcast **networks** to one whose programming competes with broadcast television – by 1998, cable television attracted a larger monthly viewing audience than the combined broadcast networks. It is estimated that 68 percent of television households subscribe to cable television.

As a **telecommunications** industry, cable television is regulated by the **FCC**. Since cable companies have to use public land to lay cables, each cable company, usually owned by MSOs (Multiple Systems Operators), must negotiate a contract with the municipality which grants an operational monopoly in return for a licensing fee. While various proponents have envisioned competition among cable providers, this has only emerged in the largest cities. Satellites may, however, raise a potential challenge.

Given cable's relationship with communities, these also have demanded that systems provide local programming, as well as public access for citizens. Initially, the Telecommunications Act of 1984 required such access, leading to production facilities and channel space for delivery. Cable systems, however, have challenged these requirements, claiming that they violate their 1st Amendment rights.

Cable systems receive their revenue primarily through subscription fees that average around $30 per month in 1999. Many regulatory attempts have sought to control cable subscription fees; however, with the culture of deregulation in the 1990s, they became completely deregulated in 1999. As the industry grows, cable networks are increasingly deriving income from **advertising** revenues as well.

The cable industry has always claimed that it provides a diversity of choices to the consumer. The number of cable networks has indeed increased from 28 in 1980 to 174 in 1998; by 1998, over 57 percent of all subscribers received 54 channels or more. Home Box Office (HBO) became the nation's first pay-television network in 1972. The second major network is Ted Turner's Cable News Network (**CNN**), now a division of **Time Warner**. Other major cable networks include **MTV**, ESPN, TNN, C-Span, the **Weather** Channel and A&E. These networks televise **news**, music, sports, public affairs, **cooking**, children's television, **science fiction**, women's programming, etc. 24-hours a day to their subscribers. Cable includes niches for Spanish-language broadcasting (for example, Univisión) and other ethnic programming (for example, BET).

Cable claims to provide a great deal of family and children's programming to its subscribers, through educational and specialized channels (for example, Nickelodeon, **Disney**, the FOX Family channel). Providers also have attempted direct partnerships with schools, with programs like Cable High Speed Education Connection, which provide programming and cable Internet access to K-12 schools which allow them in.

Cable programming has wider impacts. A 24-hour cable news channel, highlighted during CNN's 1980 **Gulf War** coverage, has changed the landscape of news reporting. Broadcast network television news divisions are loosing viewership and money. News has become more immediate, although some blame the immediacy for a lack of in-depth reporting. ESPN and other sports media have not only offered more traditional sports, but have fostered growing audiences for **soccer**, women's sports and alternative sports/recreations (for example, **cheerleading**).

HBO, being a premium channel where subscribers pay extra to receive its signals, has showcased **Hollywood** and produced quality programming that has won frequent Emmy **Awards**. Cable television also gave birth to television home shopping with QVC and the Home Shopping Channel. These networks provide a friendly, homely environment onscreen, hawking all kinds of products to the audience/customers, who also call in and chat with hosts and celebrities.

This so-called diversity of choice is also a manifestation of niche marketing where products are targeted and produced, no longer for mass consumers, but for particular kinds of consumers. MTV, for example, promotes the importance of the teen and youth market, which is perceived to have a great deal of disposable income.

Cable networks like CNN and MTV are not simply American, but global. CNN can be watched in virtually all luxury hotels in the world, and MTV, with slight modifications, has global pop affiliates. While programming is adapted to world and regional audiences, an American story like the death of John F. **Kennedy**, Jr. dominated CNN worldwide.

In the late 1990s, the cable industry is also expanding into the **Internet**/online market. Cable can transmit data much faster than traditional phone lines. Hence, **AT&T** bought TCI and Media One in 1999, anticipating shifts in telecommunications wherever the technologies develop. Cable networks have also developed Internet sites, such as ESPN Sports Zone and CNN interactive.

The cable industry is not really in competition with other media outlets like broadcast television, **Hollywood**, the Internet or even newspapers. Media giants, like Time Warner, Disney, News Incorporated and AT&T, are not only vertically integrated, but simply own all media: cable is the medium, not the message.

Further reading

Waterman, D.H. and Andrew, A.W. (1997) *Vertical Integration in Cable Television*, Washington, DC: AEI Press.

http://www.neta.com

CINDY WONG

Caesar, Sid

b. 1922

Comedian best known for sketches that defined the humor of television's **golden age**. Creative, satirical and often truly bizarre, Caesar created memorable sketches for the NBC showcase *Your Show of Shows* (1954–7) in conjunction with Imogene Coca, Carl Reiner and Howard Morris (as well as the writing of Mel Brooks). Caesar appeared later in *Caesar's Hour* (1954–7), a few films and other appearances; his influence on television **comedy** continues to the present.

GARY McDONOGH

Cage, John

b. 1912; d. 1992

Philosopher, author and composer who forever changed notions of chance or indeterminacy in composition. One of his most famous works, "4'33"," consisted of the composer sitting at the piano for over four minutes without playing (allowing the audience to supply the sounds). Other works, which incorporated recorded music, radios and player pianos as instruments, showed not only musical genius but an unending inventiveness. He collaborated with other artists, particularly with his partner Merce **Cunningham**. This work, too, relied on chance meetings between sound and movement created separately, following distinct non-narrative trajectories. Cage's written work, especially *Silence* (1961), brought ideas from non-Western and avant-garde music and **philosophy** to new audiences.

EDWARD MILLER

Cajuns

Descendants of French settlers expelled by the British from **Canada** in the eighteenth century, these Acadians have developed a distinctive Creole society under subsequent regimes in southern Lousiana. Cajuns are especially characterized by close **family** and **community** ties, Catholicism, their French dialect and rural livelihoods along rivers and bayous that have fostered geographical isolation. While sometimes confused with **Creoles** of white or black French colonial ancestry, Cajuns became known in the twentieth century for spicy **food** (Paul Prudhomme, Emeril Lagosse), lively music with accordions, strings and vocals (Neville Brothers, Buckwheat Zydeco) and vivid media images as epitomized in films like *The Big Easy* (1986). This reviving cultural distinctiveness, nonetheless, has come under assault through the extension of **education**, media and government into the bayous.

GARY McDONOGH

California

Long a magnet for those pursuing the American dream, from the Gold Rush to the golden age of **Hollywood**, California grew explosively in the Second World War. Government spending for the war created thousands of jobs in a new defense industry, and millions migrated to such places as **Los Angeles** and Oakland. Unlike previous **immigration** into eastern cities, in California a new type of "centerless city" emerged, creating a new relationship between people and landscape. In the thirty years after the War, areas such as Orange County, south of Los Angeles, and Santa Clara County, south of **San Francisco**, went from rural to suburban to "post-suburban" in barely more than a generation. Orange groves and **ranches** were transformed into industrial parks, **malls**, subdivisions and the freeways and roads to connect them, first proposed by business leaders in 1942, and underwritten by the Interstate **Highway** Act of 1956. By 1962, California was the nation's most populous **state**.

The growth of California mirrored the general shift in population and power in the US from the **Northeast** and **Midwest** rustbelt to the **Southern** and Western **Sunbelt**. The shift paralleled the move from the old, industrial economy to the new **information**-based high-tech economy, fostered by defense spending throughout the **Cold War**, but also increasingly by the high-tech innovations which filtered into the consumer sphere, especially those from an area south of San Francisco named **Silicon Valley**.

The Cold War brought billions of dollars in government contracts – the money which created jobs. The jobs brought people, who created the need for new houses, schools, roads, sewers and social services. Most importantly, the people brought and bought cars, and the cars needed highways. Spreading outward, not upward as eastern cities had done earlier, with bulldozers razing orchards for more houses, offices, shopping **malls** and factories, these municipalities exacted enormous environmental costs.

Beginning in the immediate postwar period, both international capital and local political and business elites worked to fragment the environmental and social landscapes, most importantly through the proliferation of incorporated municipalities with separate, often separatist, "post-suburban" governmental units. **White**, **middle-class** residents in dozens of new outer polities sought, and discovered, methods for avoiding the burdens of urban citizenship (i.e. **taxes**), while shifting the costs of social services to the poor and people of color. The new, fragmented urbanism relied on growth and racial **segregation**, both of which would bring disastrous consequences.

The Watts rebellion of 1965 signaled that, despite the continued suburban ideal and the concomitant low-density housing, racial segregation in housing reflected and reinforced inequalities in power, leading to a breakdown of the social contract throughout California. Other developments in the 1960s highlighted major transformations in both the state and the nation. Berkeley's student-run Free Speech Movement provided the bridge between the Civil Rights movement and the antiwar movement. The founding of the **Black Panthers** in Oakland marked a shift from civil rights to Black Power. For the youth counterculture

of the 1960s, the Sunset Strip in Los Angeles and, especially, the Haight-Ashbury region of San Francisco stood as meccas of free love, hallucinogenic drugs and rock music performed at Be-ins and Love-ins by the Grateful Dead, Jefferson Airplane and others, culminating in the Summer of Love of 1967 and crashing to a halt with the violence at the Altamont concert in 1969.

Despite the 1960s rebellions, California was more often a force for political conservatism, home to the **John Birch Society** and two **Republican** presidents, Richard **Nixon** and Ronald **Reagan**. The reaction to the upheavals of the 1960s came with the "culture of narcissism" of the 1970s, when the personal liberation spirit turned into hedonism with a vogue for designer drugs, hot tubs and cultish, vaguely eastern religions. Any remnant of countercultural or progressive spirit was overturned as the taxpayer revolt of Proposition 13 enshrined a me-first politics, paving the way for the Reagan revolution of the 1980s. The home-owners' tax-revolt was hijacked by big business interests which engineered their own tax cuts, thus inaugurating slash-and-burn budget cuts to spending on social services such as schools.

The social and environmental impacts of postwar growth were felt continually by California residents. The folly of speculative post-suburban growth and the irresponsibility and unaccountability to the citizenry of post-suburban government was demonstrated by the bankruptcy of Orange County in the 1990s, the result of speculation in junk bonds.

Racial conflict, too, continued unabated. When, in 1992, four police officers, whom the whole world had seen on videotape savagely beating a traffic violation suspect, were acquitted, Los Angeles erupted in the largest single civil disturbance in American history. The fact that the police withdrew from the neighborhood once the violence began only underscores the Los Angeles Police Department's failure "to protect and to serve" areas populated by people of color. At the century's end, new revelations of widespread lying on the stand by police officers led to wholesale investigation into hundreds of convictions obtained by false testimony.

The environmental impact of unaccountable power in the hands of proponents of growth increasingly weighed on the minds and bodies of

Californians. While **edge cities** were supposed to counter the worst elements of urban pollution ("no dark, satanic mills spewing clouds of ash here"), **automobiles** filled the air with carbon monoxide and other toxins, semiconductor manufacturers filled the land with toxic waste, and drought, firestorms and mudslides in dizzying cyclical succession rearranged the landscape just as humans had before. Add to that the major earthquakes, which regularly shook parts of the state throughout the last decades of the twentieth century, and Californians were truly living in an "ecology of fear."

Further reading

Abbott, C. (1993) *The Metropolitan Frontier*, Tucson: University of Arizona Press.
Davis, M. (1992) *City of Quartz*, New York: Vintage.
Davis, M. (1998) *Ecology of Fear*, New York: Vintage.
Kling, R. *et al.* (eds) (1991) *Postsuburban California*, Berkeley: University of California Press.

DEWAR MACLEOD

California, University, System

Chartered in 1868, the University of California (UC) System eventually grew to nine campuses. For much of the twentieth century, the UC System, along with the twenty-three-campus California State University, provided affordable, quality undergraduate and graduate education for **California** residents. However, in the early 1990s, the UC System faced budget cuts, temporarily leading to overcrowding and significantly higher costs for students.

The UC System, which includes five medical schools and teaching hospitals as well as three law schools, has also been a cornerstone for top-notch research. Since 1939, the UC faculty has won thirty-two **Nobel Prizes**.

The UC System has often been at the forefront of political and social change. In the mid- to late-1960s, the Free Speech movement, a demonstration against the **Vietnam War** and racism, occurred on the Berkeley campus. In the 1970s, Allan Bakke, an engineer denied admission to the medical school at the Davis campus, sued the university, claiming he had been rejected only because he was white. In a decision that established parameters for affirmative-action programs, the Supreme Court ordered Bakke admitted, ruling that schools cannot use quotas to achieve racial diversity, but may consider race in the admissions process in order to reach this end. In July 1995, the UC system's governing board voted to end the admissions policy of preferences based on race and gender, while allowing **campuses** to give preference to applicants with disadvantaged backgrounds. The action effectively dismantled existing affirmative-action policies for campus admissions, but faced deep protests.

See also: state university system; affirmative-action

JAMES DEVITT

California sound

Distinctive "soft" rock music that emerged in the mid-1960s, embodied by bands like The Mamas and the Papas. Influenced by the new **folk music** of the 1950s and 1960s, their music was harmony-rich with complicated vocal arrangements that stood apart from hard rock, which features lead guitar and solo vocals. The sound, best heard in the song "California Dreaming," came to represent the more mellow, melodic sounds of the 1960s. Later, in the 1970s, with the Californian groups The Eagles and Fleetwood Mac – and vocalist Linda Ronstadt – the folk roots of the music gained a country influence.

EDWARD MILLER

Calley, William/My Lai

On March 16, 1968, Lieutenant William Calley, Jr., led twenty-five American soldiers into a small hamlet in South Vietnam on a routine search-and-destroy mission. There the platoon forced hundreds of Vietnamese villagers into a common ditch and shot them. The My Lai Massacre did not come to light until later, but, in March of 1971, all were acquitted except Calley, who was first sentenced to life, then to three year's house arrest. My Lai has come to symbolize the terrible brutality of the **Vietnam War** and the degree to which soldiers could be convinced that such an action was acceptable, even under the conditions of war.

SUSAN SCHULTEN

Cambodia bombing and protests

In January of 1969, Richard **Nixon** inherited a war that had humiliated his predecessor, and he immediately acted to restore American honor and win the war in Southeast Asia. By attacking North Vietnamese bases in neighboring Cambodia, Nixon hoped to convince the enemy to withdraw from Cambodia and sign a ceasefire agreement. Beginning on March 17, 1969, and continuing for fourteen months, Nixon sent American B-52s on 3,630 raids to Cambodia, dropping more than 100,000 tons of bombs.

The previous October, antiwar protests had involved more than 2 million Americans; therefore Nixon kept the bombings secret, and the White House informed the public that the B-52s were dropping their loads on South Vietnam. In November of 1969, Nixon announced that the nation would gradually withdraw its troops. But this decision created a problem for the flagging strength of the South Vietnamese forces, and so Nixon decided to authorize an invasion into Cambodia the following April. This failed to weaken the North Vietnamese, and only widened the war throughout Southeast Asia.

Responding to the incursion, as well as the recent discovery of the secret bombings, antiwar protests erupted across the country. Then, on May 4, Ohio National Guardsmen shot four student demonstrators at **Kent State** University. Hundreds of American universities reacted with protest, hundreds more closed to avoid further violence and, soon thereafter, 100,000 Americans marched on **Washington, DC** to oppose the war.

By June of 1970, the Senate terminated the **Gulf of Tonkin Resolution**, and began to limit Nixon's ability to prosecute a ground war in Southeast Asia. Nixon then intensified the bombing of Laos, renewed air strikes against North Vietnam

and, later, aided an ARVN invasion into Laos. But the disastrous outcome of the invasion only eroded American confidence in the war further.

At the same time, William **Calley** was found guilty of murder for his actions at My Lai, and 1,000 Vietnam veterans testified to their own war crimes, discarding their war medals on the steps of the Capitol building. Meanwhile, the *New York Times* began to publish secret Defense Department documents, which had been stolen by Daniel Ellsberg, a former **Pentagon** employee. The summer of 1971 thus symbolized a high point of disillusionment with the war, yet Nixon's plan to "Vietnamize" the war and gradually withdraw American troops eventually pacified domestic opposition.

In January of 1973, diplomatic talks in Paris produced a peace agreement. The United States accepted the demilitarized zone, and agreed to extricate its forces from the war. American troops were withdrawn by the end of March, but the North Vietnamese troops remained in South Vietnam, and the fighting continued. Then, after North Vietnam announced continuing support for the communist rebels in Cambodia, the American bombings of Cambodia resumed. For six months, 250,000 tons of bombs were dropped, targeting some of the country's most densely populated areas. **Congress** responded by banning the bombing of Cambodia and producing the War Powers Act, which directly limited the ability of future **presidents** to prosecute a war without a declaration from Congress.

Further reading

Isaacs, A.R. (1983) *Without Honor*, Baltimore: Johns Hopkins University Press.

Herring, G. (1979) *America's Longest War*, New York: Wiley.

SUSAN SCHULTEN

campaign finance reform *see* parties and elections; Political Action Committees

camping

The settling of the North American **frontier** led to a shift in the meaning of wilderness. While early accounts of the wilderness depicted it as dangerous and evil, the closing of the frontier led to a vision of the wilderness as an American Eden. Beginning after the Civil War, elite Americans began to make recreational visits to the wilderness, beginning at sites like Niagara Falls, the Catskills and the Adirondacks and moving west until Yellowstone was made the first true **national park** in 1872. The late nineteenth century saw the development of summer camps and wilderness vacations as a means to get in touch with particularly American values. The Boy Scouts, for example, with their emphasis on wilderness were designed to inculcate civic values and **individualism** through backwoods experience.

The American **automobile** industry allowed increased visits to the "wilderness," and, after the Second World War, many Americans took advantage of greater prosperity to tour America and camp in its campgrounds which developed in and around wilderness areas. Over time, camping developed as a way for urban, laboring Americans to get in touch with not only the values embodied in non-productive **nature**, but the peculiarly American nostalgia for the frontier. The association between camping and correct values has continued in outdoor programs, like Outward Bound, for troubled **teens**. While camping is often associated with the rustic experience of campfires, **cowboy** cooking and tents, more recently there has been a trend towards convenience. Recreational vehicles have replaced tents, and private campgrounds have developed alongside those operated by the National Park Service.

Summer camps focused on **children** and adolescents may also recall the wilderness in pseudo-Indian names, sports, crafts and facilities. In a prosperous and competitive market, however, these camps may also specialize in language learning, competitive sports, arts, computers and weight loss. These camps, whether day-oriented or distant from **cities**, also meet the needs of two-career families who cannot provide safe and organized home activities during school vacations.

Further reading

Cronon, W. (ed.) (1996) *Uncommon Ground: Rethinking* *the Human Place in Nature*, New York: W.W. Norton.

JANICE NEWBERRY

campus, college

One of the emblems of **college** life in America, whether in cinema or admissions literature, has been the tree-shaded campus on whose broad lawns social life, sports and commencement foster **community**. The conjunction of buildings and open space may take different forms depending on age, prestige or context. **Stanford University**, for example, developed a Mediterranean style, while the University of Virginia, with the famous influence of Thomas Jefferson, and the Johns Hopkins University favor federalist styles. Perhaps the most common model is collegiate gothic, imitating the halls and cloisters of Europe.

After the Second World War, colleges become architectural proving grounds in individual building (Louis **Kahn**'s work at Bryn Mawr and Yale, I.M. **Pei**'s campus for New College, etc.). Yet rapid growth, especially at public institutions like large, **state** schools, has often submerged early plans within a sea of vaguely **modern** and **postmodern** buildings and endless parking lots.

The urban campus adapts this pastoral ideal through enclosure and security when they have resources (University of Pennsylvania, UCLA, Columbia, Yale). Some special schools, like **medical schools** and other urban institutions, however, have integrated into the streetscapes around them (CUNY, Georgia State, etc). Yet even community colleges and business colleges may attempt to create this social space or take some distinction from historic preservation of older cityscapes. These campuses may also lack the sports facilities or residential buildings of wealthier or ex-urban universities.

The idea of the campus has strongly positive associations; even schools without cohesive development may favor it in promotional literature. The term also has been taken up by business and research consortia like those in **Silicon Valley**, although the "business campus" provides the form without the academic life or goals of the original.

GARY McDONOGH

Canada

Most popular histories of the relations between Canada and the United States sooner or later mention the fact that the two countries have shared the longest undefended border in the world for some 100 years. This is generally taken to evidence some sort of natural state of amity. A more reasonable explanation is that, with the two states differing so dramatically in military power, and Canada relying so heavily on the overwhelming economic and political might of its southern neighbor, the notion of military conflict would be redundant in the one instance and absurd in the other.

In earlier times, when Canada was still a British colony and the power relations between the two countries were more nearly equal, relations were not nearly as gentle. Less than thirty years after the American Revolution, Canada and the United States fought their first and only war, the War of 1812. This ended in a stalemate and seems to have suggested to both that any similar behavior in the future would be unproductive. Tensions over land disputes near the border would continue throughout the 1800s, but would never again result in armed engagement (Mahant and Mount 1984). In the early twenty-first century as well as the twentieth century, especially following the Second World War when American international dominance became general, formal relations between the two states have been quite close. Nonetheless, occasional disputes flare up. The **Johnson** administration disliked Canadian criticisms of US actions in **Vietnam**, and, since the early 1960s, Canada's relatively friendly relations with **Castro**'s **Cuba** have provoked some US opposition (Mahunt and Mount 1999). But the only true problem that Canada now presents to the American political elite is Quebec separatism and the instability it might bring. Even here, as the *separatistes* under Jacques Parizeau and Lucien Bouchard have developed ever friendlier relations with Washing-

ton, the issue has become less acute (Lamont 1994; Lemco 1994).

A general fear has existed within English Canada over American cultural influence almost since the beginning of its Confederation in 1867. In the past thirty years, this resulted in protectionist moves against American movies, **television**, **popular music** and **magazines**, which in turn provoked irritation in promoters of the US entertainment industry. Generally, though, popular culture manages to move back and forth across the border without much friction. If American culture is a massive influence on Canadian hearts and minds, individual Canadian artists – including Neil Young, Joni Mitchell, David Cronenberg, Atom Egoyan, Pamela Anderson and Mike Myers – insert themselves into American popular culture with relative ease. That there is little to distinguish these Canadians from their American counterparts has only tended to confirm the assumption among many in the US that the two countries now share essentially the same society, divided by a formal border and little else. This assumption, however, when articulated – and whatever its veridical status – infuriates Canadians.

Further reading

Lamont, L. (1994) *Breakup*, New York: Norton.

Lemco, J. (1994) *Turmoil in the Peaceable Kingdom*, Toronto: University of Toronto Press.

Mahant, E. and Mount, G. (1984) *An Introduction to Canadian–American relations*, Toronto: Methuen.

Mahant, E. and Mount, G. (1999) *Invisible and Inaudible in Washington*, Vancouver, BC: University of British Columbia.

MARK BREWIN

cancer

The word alone metonymically evokes fear. To many, cancer means pain, debilitating treatments, **body** mutilation, hair loss, the "silent killer" – the human body sabotaging itself; for many, a death-row sentence lived in hospital wards. Despite intensive research into causes and treatments, cancer remains a constant threat and topic for discussion for many Americans.

Cancer is the second leading cause of death in the US, killing over 1,500 people daily. Anyone is at risk, more so with age. Some segments of the population – such as women with a family history of breast cancer, smokers and individuals with inherited mutations – are at a higher relative risk. Over the years, work on identifying and controlling risk factors has been a primary thrust in cancer information – campaigns for breast cancer awareness have been taken up by many women's organizations and **mass media**, while **celebrities** have sparked conversation of prostate, lung and testicular cancer among men.

Treatment options have expanded from the conventionally medical, such as surgery, radiation and chemotherapy (an aggressive treatment to destroy cancer cells), to the alternative and holistic, like bodywork. The power of faith and human support during treatment has also drawn attention to the mind/body connection. Many movements have encouraged those with cancer to take charge of their own treatment through knowledge and choices among these alternatives. Recovery is declared if cancer patients are still alive five years after diagnosis, though not necessarily cancer-free.

While the vocabulary of medicine claims privileged access to the "true" description of the etiology and treatment of cancer, its intelligibility – or ability to speak to the ontology of the disease – is generated, constrained and supported within everyday language. As Sontag (1978) has argued, scientific discourse is both structured by and structuring of the metaphors of the "popular," themselves culturally and historically contingent. As with the once incurable tuberculosis and syphilis, cancer – still largely incurable – is identified with the deepest of social dreads (corruption, rebellion, decay), and is itself a metaphor used to impose horror on other things. **AIDS** was once described as a "cancer" of certain populations – the perfect example of the moral role of medical discourse in social condemnation. In the US, for example, cancer is metaphorically understood as a war: we speak of an "invasion," of mutant cells "colonizing" healthy organs and not of patients but of "survivors." The human body, as Douglas (1966) demonstrated, is the organizing metaphor for society; social ills are expressed in terms of infection and disease. "Cancer" is an aberration of the natural order, which the search for causes and for placing blame (as defiance of preventive behaviors) seeks to redress by force.

Further reading

Douglas, M. (1966) *Purity and Danger*, London: Routledge.
Sontag, S. (1978) *Illness as Metaphor*, New York: Farrar, Straus Giroux.

MARIAELENA BARTESAGHI

candy and gum

Sweets seemingly have a universal appeal. Yet societies worldwide have also developed styles and brands that set them apart – candied seeds in South Asia, designer chocolates in Europe or salty preserved fruits in China. The multicultural United States has imported all of these while adding its own twists to taffy, chocolates and gum. And, while generations of dentists have warned about cavities and generations have confiscated gum, the American sweet tooth sustains a multi-billion dollar industry. Halloween is a celebration of sugar as much as ghosts. Candies and companies also tell especially American stories.

Hershey, historically the number-one company, producing bars, "kisses" and peanut-butter cups, fostered the American democratization of chocolate, although its different taste is strange to European palates (Brenner 1999). By the turn of the century, its five-cent bars became widespread. Its rival, Mars, with $16 billion in sales worldwide, began in 1922. Still run by the Mars family, it is the nation's sixth-largest privately held company, with brands like M&M, Snickers and Milky Way. Cracker Jack, meanwhile, combined two American favorites – **popcorn** and sugar – with tiny prizes in every box. Its sailor logo has also changed over decades, situating the box in American nostalgia. Fanciful products like Victor Bonono's Turkish Taffy entered the market after the Second World War sugar rationing, only to disappear as a victim of later corporate consolidation. Upscale markets have been dominated by imported chocolates and hand-dipped or artisanal products.

Inventiveness and legends also incorporate candies into American **folklore**. Did you hear the story of a child star killed by pop rocks (small fizzy gum chips)? Marshmallow peeps – marshmallow shaped like chicks or rabbits, covered with colored sugar – have a web-site for fans, including scientific experiments to perform.

Candies are not only national, but also local and domestic. The candy store and penny candies evoke a lost emporium of **Main Street** in a world of multinationals and franchises that sometimes imitate older local stores. Nonetheless, family recipes for candies and cookies are brought out for parties and **holidays**, especially Christmas.

Gum also occupies a special niche in American dental records. The corporate giant is Wrigley's (as in Chicago's **baseball** field and tower). Founded in 1891 to distribute other products, Wrigley found the gum he gave away as a premium more successful than soap or baking powder. Juicy Fruit was introduced in 1893; Spearmint in 1894. Wrigley used **advertising** and premiums to compete and globalize his product. While servicemen came first in the Second World War (hence the image of GIs giving away gum), the company returned to US and world markets in the late 1940s. Eventually, sugar-free products and bubble-gum were added. Its Doublemint advertisements, with various twins and a catchy jingle, have also become part of American media folklore.

Gum has been touted as a release from stress, an alternative to smoking or food and a form of relaxation, although it is prohibited in schools, churches and other formal settings. With twenty companies and $2 billion in sales annually (300 sticks per person) candy marks a common break in the American day.

Further reading

Brenner, J. (1999) *The Emperors of Chocolate*, New York: Random House.

GARY McDONOGH

capital punishment

Capital punishment, or the death penalty, is the execution of an individual by the government, either federal or state, as punishment for a crime. Presently thirty-eight states, the federal government and the US military have death penalty statutes on their books. Since the **Supreme Court** ruled in 1977 (*Coker* v. *Georgia*) that the death penalty was a disproportionate punishment for rape, almost all capital crimes involve murder or the death of a victim that occurred in the course of another crime. The method of execution varies according to state, although lethal injection and electrocution are by far the most common.

All of the colonies had death-penalty statutes on their books and these policies remained largely unchanged after the American revolution. Although there were two periods of intense abolitionist activity in the nineteenth century, this largely ended by 1917. The entry of the US into the First World War, along with high-profile murders, such as the Leopold and Loeb case in the 1920s, led to a widespread resurgence of the death penalty. Throughout the 1930s and 1940s an average of 140 people were being executed each year. However, in the 1950s there began a rapid decline in this rate as popular support waned. This opposition was fueled in part by the controversial cases of Caryl Chessman and Barbara Graham, whose stories had been turned into highly successful books and films.

By the mid-1960s executions were down to less than twenty annually, and public-opinion polls showed opposition to the death penalty at an all-time high. In 1967 there began an unofficial moratorium that lasted ten years. Yet, in 1972, the US Supreme Court invalidated all existing capital punishment statutes. In a five to four decision (*Furman* v. *Georgia*) the court ruled that capital punishment violated the 8th and 14th Amendments because it was being imposed in an arbitrary and capricious fashion. There was an angry and swift reaction by many of the states, and several immediately implemented changes in their sentencing procedures in order to meet the Court's constitutional concerns. As a result of these modifications, the Court ruled in 1976 that states could re-institute the death penalty. A year later Utah executed Gary Gilmore by firing squad.

Since then, over 550 people have been put to death, with four states – **Texas**, Virginia, Missouri and **Florida** – accounting for 60 percent. The US has the largest death-row population in the world with close to 3,600 individuals currently awaiting execution: 46 percent are white, 43 percent **African American** and 8 percent **Hispanic**. Less than 1 percent are women or citizens of another country. Since 1970, eighty-two individuals have been released from death row after new scientific (genetic/DNA) evidence had established their innocence. Several polls conducted throughout the 1980s and 1990s saw a substantial growth in widespread public support for capital punishment, although it also saw the rise of numerous abolitionist organizations and a number of highly critical books and films (*Dead Man Walking*, 1997). Various local and state moratoria have emerged, although public support remains high.

Further reading

Berns, W. (1991) *For Capital Punishment*, Lanham: University Press of America.
Bedau, H.A. (1997) *The Death Penalty in America*, New York: Oxford.

RODGER JACKSON

Capote, Truman

b. 1924; d. 1984

Southern novelist, essayist and chronicler in elegant prose of American society. Capote's work represents a complex tapestry of American reflections, including his own homosexuality and regional memories, wars of class and culture in **New York** City, NY and a chilling portrait of contemporary violence in his non-fiction novel *In Cold Blood* (1966). Other important works include *Other Voices, Other Rooms* (1948) and *Breakfast at Tiffany's* (1958).

GARY McDONOGH

Capra, Frank

b. 1897; d. 1991

Sicilian-born **director** whose movies embody the **comedy** and pathos of the American dream. For a decade after the mid-1930s, Capra brought together character, comedy and sometimes dark shadings to stories of the triumph of small-town good and honesty over elites. Epitomized by *It's a Wonderful Life* (1947), which became a holiday staple, Capra's gaze also took in **gender** relations (*It Happened One Night*, Oscar 1924), politics (*Mr Smith Goes to Washington*, 1939) and a bitter view of **mass media** (*Meet John Doe*, 1941). During the Second World War, Capra devoted his energies to the *Why We Fight* documentaries. His vision, however, generally failed to capture audiences in the postwar world beyond nostalgic viewings.

GARY McDONOGH

Caribbean

The Caribbean region comprises not only the islands of the Greater and Lesser Antilles, but the nations that border the Caribbean Sea on the west and south. In the 1980s, this combination of mainland and insular territories was referred to by American policy-makers as the "Caribbean Basin." Whatever label is used, the history of US relations with the region has been characterized by an oscillation between benign neglect and all-too-active intervention.

The Caribbean region was a prime venue for US imperial ambition during the first third of the twentieth century. Between 1898 and 1933, the United States acquired **Puerto Rico** and the **Panama** Canal zone, and occupied **Cuba**, **Haiti**, the Dominican Republic and Nicaragua. From 1933 to the end of the Second World War, the US eschewed military intervention in favor of supporting a series of client-states amenable to the free play of US economic interests.

The **Cold War** marked the advent of a new era of interventionism. During the 1950s and 1960s, the US put down nationalist ferment in Puerto Rico, helped overthrow a popularly elected leftist government in Guatemala and struggled to cope with the socialist regime brought to power by the Cuban Revolution of 1959. Following the failure of covert military efforts to overthrow **Castro**'s regime, most notably at the **Bay of Pigs**, and the confrontation with the Soviet Union during the **Cuban missile crisis**, subsequent US policy aimed at the political and economic isolation of

Cuba and the containment of revolutionary tendencies in other Caribbean societies. The Alliance for Progress program distributed considerable economic assistance to the former British colonies of the Lesser Antilles. In 1965 the United States invaded the Dominican Republic to prevent "another Cuba in the Caribbean." A stabilized Caribbean emerged as a prime destination for North American tourists.

The United States' informal Caribbean empire began to unravel in the 1970s. The **Carter** administration negotiated a treaty that would eventually return the Panama Canal to Panamanian sovereignty by the end of the century. Leftist regimes emerged in Guyana, Jamaica, Trinidad, Panama and, towards the end of the decade, in Nicaragua and Grenada. Together with leftist insurgencies in El Salvador and Guatemala, the US viewed these developments as the result of external machinations rather than internal processes. During the 1980s, the **Reagan** and **Bush** administrations succeeded in overthrowing these regimes through military invasion (see **Grenada** and Panama) and by supporting internal rebels (the Nicaraguan *contras*), in addition to providing assistance to the Salvadoran and Guatemalan governments. Renewed military intervention was accompanied by the Caribbean Basin Initiative, which provided economic assistance in return for increased receptivity to investment by US-based corporations.

The end of the Cold War resulted in deep cuts in economic aid and a new era of benign neglect in US–Caribbean relations, save for an intensified economic embargo on Cuba. Even so, the Caribbean is more closely tied to the United States than ever before, as millions of immigrants from the Caribbean region now reside in the United States, where they add to the complex socio-cultural diversity of the contemporary American landscape.

Further reading

Langley, L. (1989) *The United States and the Caribbean in the Twentieth Century*, Athens: University of Georgia Press.

CHARLES RUTHEISER

Caribbean Americans

Caribbean nations long have endured the influence of the "colossus to the North." Yet, as ideas, styles and people have traveled north, they have established distinctive communities, complicating American minority politics and culture. Two million Caribbean immigrants have arrived since the 1960s (alongside **Puerto Rican** US citizens); large urban communities include Haitians in **New York** and **Miami, FL**, Cubans in Miami, Dominicans on the Eastern Seaboard, Jamaicans, Belizians and others. Some West Indian immigrant families come to embody the American dream – Colin **Powell**, former head of the Joint Chiefs of Staff and possible presidential contender, is the son of Jamaican immigrants, congresswoman Shirley **Chisholm** has roots in Barbados, singer Harry Belafonte in Jamaica and Martinique, actor Sidney **Poitier** in the Bahamas and writers Paule **Marshall** in Barbados and Edwige Danticat in **Haiti**. Others have been identified with problems of **race**, **class** and crime.

While the US has intervened in the Caribbean for centuries, it has not always been a one-way street. Cubans participated in the radicalization of the **Florida** cigar industry and Jamaican Marcus Garvey tested his models for pan-African unity in the US before being deported in 1927. Yet, except for elite or seasonal migrations, few West Indians went north: less than 500,000 had immigrated before the Second World War.

Political and economic movements, as much as new **immigration** rules, fostered subsequent migration. **Cuban Americans** fleeing **Castro** and Haitian **boat people** escaping Duvalier and crushing poverty gained particular **mass media** attention, while other West Indians tended to be conflated with existing black or emergent **Hispanic** populations. Some men gained citizenship by joining the military in the **Vietnam War**.

West Indian migrants often have proved more successful in business and education than existing **African American** populations: by the 1990s, their average income approached general norms and far surpassed that of other African Americans, while immigrants and their children gained responsibilities in politics, civil service, the military and business. Nonetheless, seasonal migrants like cane-cutters in South Florida and women leaving their families for domestic service underscore continuing exploitation. A Caribbean cultural presence may be more muted: fads for calypso, reggae and soca do not necessarily identify an American population so much as characterizing transnational styles. Caribbean **food** (especially Jamaican and Cuban) moved out of its ethnic communities in the 1990s.

West Indian success has exacerbated tensions between insiders and outsiders, especially as West Indians bring different cultures of color and class to the US – Afro-Cubans, for example, fall within multiple census categories, as do Caribbean Asians. Fair-skinned Creoles challenge the phenotypic classification of race in everyday life for both blacks and whites. Nor is theirs a simple story – Colin Powell, on the path to the White House, is balanced by Louis **Farrakhan** (with family origins in St. Kitts and Jamaica as well as **Boston**'s West Indian community), leading the **Nation of Islam**. Marshall, Danticat and others have explored ambiguous positions inside and outside of both American and Caribbean culture.

Moreover, political and economic issues in their nearby homelands influence both Caribbean communities and the image of West Indians in the US. This underpinned the problematic association of Haitian refugees with **AIDS** in the 1980s or the US invasion in the 1990s. Other difficulties face **Voudou** and **Santería**, which may include animal sacrifice, within American civic religion. West Indian immigrants also have been associated in the media with drugs, and brutalized by police and immigration authorities.

Further reading

Palmer, R. (1995) *Pilgrims from the Sun*, New York: Twayne.
Vickerman, M. (1999) *Crosscurrents*, New York: Oxford.

GARY McDONOGH

Carmichael, Stokely (Kwame Touré)

b. 1941; d. 1998

Stokely Carmichael was best known for his involvement in the **civil-rights** movement in the 1960s. In 1966 Carmichael was elected president of the **Student Non-violent Coordinating Committee** (SNCC), an organization developed in 1960 and a leading group in the new Civil Rights movement. Carmichael brought a new brand of leadership to SNCC, one that rejected integrationism, focused on the political and economic independence of the black community and turned attention towards the issue of black self-esteem. Though controversial for his views on violent resistance as well as his dismissal of women within SNCC, Carmichael was pivotal for his innovative and critical contributions to civil rights. After 1969, he lived in Guinea with his wife, folksinger Miriam Makeba. In 1978, he took the new name Kwame Touré, honoring Kwame Nkrumah and Sekou Touré.

SUSAN SCHULTEN

Carson, Johnny *see* late-night television

Carson, Rachel

b. 1907; d. 1964

Carson published *Silent Spring* in 1962. The book reoriented American environmental thinking away from conserving wild lands and toward the modern study of complex ecosystems. A professional biologist, Carson worked for many years in research and administration at the US Fish and Wildlife Service before writing her book. *Silent Spring* documented the impact of pesticides, especially the immensely popular DDT, on wildlife and public health. Carson was attacked by pesticide manufacturers as unpatriotic, unscientific and unfeminine, but her meticulous research persuaded President John **Kennedy** to order a federal investigation into pesticide use.

SHARON ANN HOLT

Carter, Jimmy

b. 1924

Jimmy Carter's **presidency** (1977–81) marks a transition between the challenges associated with the social movements of the 1960s and early 1970s and the conservative triumph of Ronald **Reagan** in 1980. Carter, a graduate of the US Naval Academy and a relatively unknown **governor** of Georgia, campaigned against the **Watergate** scandal. He was fortunate in running against the inept Gerald **Ford**, who was weakened both by his pardoning of Richard **Nixon** and by the mistrust he evoked in the increasingly dominant conservative wing of the **Republican** Party.

Carter's victory suggested a further weakening of the **Democratic** Party organization, a process already in motion with the **McGovern** reforms. The born-again Georgian entered office sustained only by his own campaign organization. His mastery of detail and his commitment to governmental efficiency rested on his belief that he could stand above politics – and politicians. As a result, his relations with **Congress** were poor. Carter faced a series of crises that finally brought down his presidency in a tidal wave of Republican conservatism.

On domestic issues, Carter was a social liberal and an economic conservative. His early legislation to deregulate natural gas, reform the tax code and introduce moderate **healthcare** reform antagonized the more liberal Ted **Kennedy** wing of the party. The shaky performance of the economy, wracked by stagflation, i.e. a lethal mixture of high unemployment and high inflation, was dealt a serious blow when **oil** prices soared in 1979 following the Iranian revolution. Carter appointed as Chairperson of the Federal Reserve System Paul A. Volcker, a conservative monetarist who proceeded to initiate deflationary, tight money practices which, in the short run, drove up unemployment without an immediate decline in inflation. As such, with the 1980 election pending, Carter presided over what appeared to be an economic debacle.

At the same time, Carter suffered from the energizing of the very evangelical Christians who had initially rallied to his candidacy. The accumulated impact of the cultural victories of the 1960s, especially the **Roe v. Wade** decision on abortion rights, but also liberalization regarding **pornography**, the elimination of **school prayer**, the rise of gay and lesbian rights contributed to attacks on the Carter administration at a disastrous conference on families, the religious right arguing that the **family** was exclusively nuclear.

Finally, Carter's foreign policy waffled between a human rights agenda articulated by his **Secretary of State**, Cyrus Vance, and the hard-line agenda of National Security Council head, Zbigniew Brzezinski. His success at Camp David in bringing Anwar Sadat and Menachem Begin together wilted before the following events: the criticisms of the **Panama Canal** treaty (1978), the Sandinista victory over Somoza in Nicaragua (1979), Cuban military efforts in Ethiopia and Angola in the late 1970s and, especially, the frustration over the Iranian holding of fifty-three Americans as hostages following the overthrow of the Shah (1979), the Soviet repression of Polish solidarity (1980) and the Soviet invasion of Afghanistan (1979). As a result, Carter, despite shifting to the Brzezinski position and sharply increasing military spending, was perceived as weak. Even his efforts to punish the Soviets by halting wheat deals and boycotting the Moscow **Olympics** backfired, as did the humiliating failure at rescuing the hostages.

In November 1980, the conservative Ronald Reagan decisively defeated a Jimmy Carter campaign torn by party discord, economic failure and international defeats. Since 1980, Jimmy Carter, perceived by most as a presidential failure, has seemed to many, through his humanitarian efforts, at home and abroad, to be one of the most successful former presidents.

Further reading

Carter, J. (1982) *Keeping Faith*, New York: Bantam Books.

Dionne, E.J., Jr. (1991) *Why Americans Hate Politics*, New York: Simon & Schuster.

Jones, C.O. (1988) *The Trusteeship Presidency*, Baton Rouge: Louisiana State University Press.

PAUL LYONS

Carver, Raymond

b. 1938; d. 1988

Postwar writer who fashioned stark portrayals of twentieth-century American life in pared-down, elegant prose. Although he also wrote poetry and essays, Carver – sometimes called the "American Chekov" – is best known for his short stories. These often featured characters bumping into the limits of their worlds in sudden, subtle epiphanies. An exemplary and much anthologized example of Carver's work is the story "Cathedral." Carver was often credited with influencing the growth of an informal school of writing – dubbed "**minimalism**" or "the new realism" – that became increasingly popular in the 1980s. In 1993 American film-maker Robert **Altman** directed *Short Cuts*, a movie based on Carver's stories.

MARK BREWIN

Cash, Johnny

b. 1932

Cash wrote songs, poems and stories after working with his parents growing cotton. As an adult, he became one of the most important American storytellers, expanding country music by adding a dark tone that went beyond love songs. His "Folsom Prison Blues" became a huge hit as his deep, resonant baritone voice, given to irony, took up the cause of the lonesome and dispossessed (echoed in his biggest hit, "I Walk the Line," 1956). **Prison** rights and Native American rights (Cash is one-quarter Cherokee) have long been primary concerns. Still active in music, **television**, film and **publishing**, his daughter June Carter has also become a popular singer.

EDWARD MILLER

casinos *see* gambling and lotteries; Las Vegas, NV; Atlantic City, NJ

Cassavetes, John

b. 1929; d. 1989

Multi-talented actor turned independent **director** in 1960. Dissatisfied with **Hollywood**, his films define a rugged style both cinematically and emotionally. His hand-held camera, long takes, improvisation, emotional themes often dealing with love and **marriage**, and personal vision permeate films like *A Woman under the Influence* (1974) and *Gloria* (1980), both starring his wife Gina Rowlands. Cassavetes became a pioneer for independent, personal film-making before its apotheosis in the 1990s. His son Nick (1959–) has followed him as a director.

GARY McDONOGH
CINDY WONG

Castañeda, Carlos

b. 1931; d. 1998

While a doctoral candidate in **anthropology** at the University of California, **Los Angeles, CA**, Casteneda published *The Teachings of Don Juan: A Yaqui Way of Knowledge* (1968), which recounted his spiritual and drug-induced apprenticeship with a Native American shaman. While other anthropologists soon questioned his data, the vivid adventures of this book and its bestselling sequels reverberated with both spiritual and pharmacological quests of the 1970s. As a mysterious pop cultural guru, he developed his shamanistic ideas into a spiritual program, "Tensegrity," which took on **New Age** and cultic overtones by the time of his death.

GARY McDONOGH

Castro, Fidel

b. 1927

Cuban president and perpetual thorn in the side of US administrations, Fidel Castro has outwitted the United States for over forty years, withstanding the **Bay of Pigs** invasion, **CIA** assassination attempts, blockades and other efforts to destabilize his regime.

Castro came to power in 1958 after over-throwing Fulgencio Batista, a corrupt and unpopular dictator whose own rise to power had been facilitated by President **Roosevelt**. Castro began as a **baseball**-loving Social Democrat, with considerable support from Americans initially, until he declined to accept American bank loans, believing that they had so many strings attached that they could not help bring development to Cuba. Instead, he began nationalizing US property, and, by the end of 1959, announced that he was going to join the communists and begin receiving aid from the Soviet Union.

After this declaration, the US began to prepare to overthrow Castro. He survived the **Bay of Pigs** invasion in 1961 and Robert **Kennedy**'s "Operation Mongoose." Castro then began to export his revolution, offering support to rebels and nations from Chile to **Grenada** in the western hemisphere, and aiding Angola in its efforts to fight the forces of apartheid in South Africa. The Cuban economy meanwhile collapsed, especially after the end of the **Cold War** with Soviet loans drying up, and, while the country managed to keep a social welfare system in place, opposition grew. Thus Castro met with growing repression, censoring the press, imprisoning many opponents of the regime and forcing others into exile in the US, where they joined exiles from the revolution in large Cuban communities in **Florida**.

Efforts to liberalize Cuba in the 1990s have led many to believe that Castro's rule may be nearing a close, but the final chapter has yet to be written.

ROBERT GREGG

catalogs

Sears Roebuck tells us one story. As this emporium, incorporated in 1893, spread outward from **Chicago, MI**, its illustrated catalogs became a mass medium of consumption in rural areas, outlying towns and among individual households of the **working** and lower-**middle classes**. By 1895 the catalog reached 532 pages, offering dry goods as well as hardware, appliances and even pre-fabricated housing. Sears, like J.C. Penney's and Montgomery Wards, overcame dislocations in space to unify America as a nation of consumers.

Yet, by the 1950s, sales by mail and through order centers competed with their own **department stores**, especially as they anchored **malls** supplying **suburban** home-owners. Later, these companies themselves, built on mass marketing and economies of scale, faced competition from warehouse and discount sales, leading to crises for all these retailers. Restructuring to define their consumption niches, Sears and Penney's let their catalogs die in the 1990s.

Meanwhile, another story of catalogs took shape around American mobility in the upper middle class. Department stores like **Dallas**' Neiman-Marcus and specialty entrepreneurs such as L.L. Bean and **Eddie Bauer** in outdoor clothing appealed to more sophisticated clients who were not outside American consumption, but dispersed through it. Book-of-the-Month clubs and spin-offs reinforced associations of culture and distribution of goods within imagined "communities." Through the 1970s and 1980s, this upscale marketing by mail exploded, combining glossy pictures and stylized captioning, ready telephone access, credit-card purchasing and targeted mailing. These catalogs responded to diverse upscale neighborhoods where aspirations differed from household to household. Moreover, they responded to new dislocations in time in two-career households where 24-hour accessibility from home facilitated consumption as an interstitial activity.

Thousands of catalogs today seem to reflect American diversity. Some transcend their connections with mall retailers. Neiman Marcus' Christmas extravaganza has become a regular news feature, while Victoria's Secret has become a part of American dialogues of heterosexual romance and sensuality, including a television spin-off, *Veronica's Closet* (1997–). Another catalog, based on the adventures of a fictional J. Peterman, became a regular feature of the long-running **sitcom** *Seinfeld*. Catalogs also transform geography: L.L. Bean has turned its Maine home-town into a mercantile center, and **museums** extend their recognition and support through sales of high cultural artifacts. Others create different imagined communities: **National Public Radio** offers culture with an attitude, from T-shirts to video collections. These catalogs nonetheless accumulate in mailboxes and on coffee tables with other catalogs that reinforce consumptive identities (Marlboro cigarette gear or a Mercedes-Benz owner's catalog), **ethnicity** or even **life cycles** – **birth** is greeted in middle-class zip codes by catalogs offering advice, products and status insecurity about the baby's "right start." Clothes, gifts, art and food all have been depicted, described and distributed in a booming industry that reminds Americans of what is missing in the midst of affluence.

Yet, through barriers of access and credit, these sales also reinforce divisions within American life – mailings by zip code and usage constantly divide potential customers from those outside specialized consumer worlds. **Television** sales networks prove more inclusive, while stressing the same features of visual imagery and descriptions that identify the consumer as well as the product: one is told who one will be as a consumer and how to show off products as well as use them. **Internet** sales and virtual catalogs also compete for the higher-end consumer, with an immediate responsiveness (to questions and targeting) that mail cannot offer, advancing some Americans from a world of **malls** into a world as a virtual mall in which potential products are always at hand; for example, historic Sears once again offers long-distance sales through its web-site. Through mass media and the Internet, moreover, this historically American pattern can be reinterpreted more easily on a global scale, threatening to leave the catalog as a final relic of the age of print.

GARY McDONOGH

CB radio (citizens' band radio)

CB radio is a set of forty audio channels set aside by the **Federal Communications Commission** so that individuals may broadcast short messages to listeners over a range of a few miles. No license is required to use CB radio. Though widely remembered as a fad, CB radio is still used to communicate information between drivers on US **highways**. CB channel 9 is designated for emergency services and is especially important in areas where regular telephone service is unavailable. CB radio enthusiasts contributed the phrase

"10–4" (the term signifies agreement with a speaker) to the American vocabulary.

A. JOSEPH BORRELL

celebrity

Since the 1950s, many cultural commentators have noted that society's heroes have been replaced by media celebrities. Jib Fowles (1992) believes celebrities fill a void in a contemporary, urban society where people feel anonymous or overwhelmed with options. Americans, shorn of the supports of **family** tradition, cultural heritage, **community** and church, turn to the appealing images of confident celebrities to build their personal identities. Indeed, by the 1920s, celebrities were also called "personalities." In place of a real community, the media offer a mechanism for the creation and maintenance of a "Star Village: a mythic community composed of the different types of people whom the American public wants to observe" (Fowles 1992: 67).

According to Fowles, this community usually comprises 100 people, or is about the size of the typical pre-twentieth century village in which most people used to live. **Hollywood** and non-actor celebrities constitute various social types – the athletic star, the *femme fatale*, the ingénue, the anti-hero, the mother, the captain-of-industry, the exotic lover. New types occasionally arise to fill new roles in the celebrity village. "The principle behind the creation of new types is that whatever is unresolved deep in the culture will eventually be projected upon the ranks of Star Village. New slots appear, displacing old ones, in response to something profoundly troubling to the spirit of the times" (ibid.: 71). Besides giving Americans a vicarious sense of belonging or a safe outlet for vicarious love and aggression, celebrities may also influence Americans to buy products or, for example, support the nation's war efforts by purchasing government bonds. Political candidates seek the endorsement of established celebrities whose consistent popularity with the public can reflect positively on the candidate.

Celebrities typically hire public-relations firms to handle the pressures of the media, whom the celebrities also court to promote their latest film or achievement. Because over 1,000 journalists cover entertainment, and with many more covering other celebrity fields, journalists feel the pressure to capture the star in a newsworthy comment or exploit. The cycle of celebrity creation and demise has quickened as media competition over celebrities has grown, with network **television** sponsoring several scandal and celebrity shows, including *Entertainment Tonight*, *Hard Copy* and *Access Hollywood*. The **cable** network "E!" is devoted to celebrity news, while magazines, like *People*, *US* and *Vanity Fair*, as well as talk shows, feed the public's desire to consume information about their favorite stars. Without satisfactory opportunities to know people, Americans rely upon the media to supply important information about human frailties and strengths, as told through coverage of celebrities. The media's urge to tear down the celebrity, usually over drug, monetary or sexual misdeeds, even before he or she has achieved star status enacts what Fowles calls Americans' "latent destructive urge" to find "gratification when an idol is rocked" (ibid.: 144). Nevertheless, the public also loves the "comeback story," where a celebrity re-invigorates a faltering career with new achievement. Not surprisingly, Hollywood has made many films about the joys and perils of celebrity, including *The Rose* (1979), *A Hard Day's Night* (1964), *A Star is Born* (1937, 1954, 1976) and Woody Allen's *Celebrity* (1999).

Further reading

Drucker, S. and Cathcart, R. (1994) *American Heroes in a Media Age*, Cresskill: Hampton.

Fowles, J. (1992) *Starstruck: Celebrity Performers and the American Public*, Washington, DC: Smithsonian Institution.

MELINDA SCHWENK

cemeteries and crematoria

While disposing of the dead concerns all societies, American cemeteries reflect special historical and experiential concerns. An avoidance of direct government responsibility (except in the general regulation of the marketplace) has promoted multiple, competing options for burial which are complicated by a sense of extensive land that has allowed the preservation of older cemeteries alongside new innovations. Racial, ethnic, religious and **class** differences also have multiplied the number and meanings of cemeteries nationwide.

American cemeteries fall into a few broad categories: family/community, church/religious, government and commercial. The last dominates late twentieth/early twenty-first century practice. In rural areas, family and church/congregation graveyards may still be central, and constitute places of pilgrimage and identity for widespread descendants. By contrast, metropolitan areas present a conflicting mapping of social change in their cemeteries and individual monuments to illustrious citizens.

The oldest **cities** include burial grounds no longer in use but maintained as historical memorials – **Savannah**'s colonial cemetery, or the African Burial Ground in **New York** City, NY whose discovery became a point of debate over place and presence. Nineteenth-century park cemeteries like Mt Auburn in Boston or Laurel Grove in **Philadelphia, PA** are also historic sites in their landscapes and "inhabitants," although they are also maintained and used by long-resident families (especially elites).

In addition to congregational burial grounds, **Jews** and **Catholics** have also established their own consecrated sites in many cities. In name and use these may also distinguish among different ethnic groupings as well – **Italians**, **Irish** and **Poles**, for example, have built different **Catholic** cemeteries in **Northeast** industrial cities.

In the **South**, divisions of **race** are common – either within cemeteries or in **segregated** clienteles. These differences are accentuated by the economics of caste which have made **white** cemeteries richer and better kept. **African American** cemeteries have faced inadequate endowments but have incorporated distinctive cultural traditions of burial and remembrance.

Government cemeteries include military burials, which are now straining available resources after the Second World War, **Korean War** and **Vietnam War** veterans for whom such burial is a less expensive option. Arlington National Cemetery, across the Potomac from **Washington, DC**, is reserved for special memorialization, for example, the Tomb of the Unknown Soldier and burial of President John F. **Kennedy**. Battlefield cemeteries are also maintained abroad.

Municipalities face responsibilities for burial of unclaimed or impoverished deceased. These may be contracted to commercial cemeteries or buried in a common potter's field.

Commercial cemeteries take on many of the solemnities of earlier community-based burials, but adapt these to a profit margin – using uniform in-ground markers to facilitate mowing, promoting special-interest sections or touting advance planning and purchase plans. These are by far the most expensive options, where funerals, burial plots, markers and care cost tens of thousands of dollars. As commercial enterprises, concerns about **bankruptcy** or mismanagement have frequently surfaced, leading to government restrictions on operation and even takeovers. Critics also target their vulgar excess: Evelyn Waugh's *The Loved One* (1948; movie, 1965) pilloried the famous Forest Lawn cemetery of **Los Angeles, CA**, decrying its commercialization of death and art.

In the late twentieth century, cremation became a more popular, cheaper option, overcoming religious and ethnic taboos. Ashes are stored in the home, religious shrines or commercial mausoleums or distributed in personally meaningful sites.

Burial has not been limited to humans alone. Pet cemeteries (and crematory facilities) complete the humanization of domestic **animals** amid extraordinary affluence that characterizes modern American relations with animals.

Further reading

Jackson, K. and Vergara, C. (1989) *Silent Cities*, New York: Princeton Architectural Press.
Meyer, R. (1993) *Ethnicity and the American Cemetery*, Bowling Green, OH: Bowling Green State University Popular Press.

GARY McDONOGH

censorship

Many Americans probably believe censorship is not only wrong, but also illegal under the **Bill of Rights**. Yet, in practice, many are also willing to accept government censorship in times of national crisis or military emergency. Jonathon Green, author of the *Encyclopedia of Censorship*, labels a

second, more controversial censorship as "castration" – the ability of some to determine what may be read or disseminated and who may see it. This may entail protection of "innocents," especially **children**, or avoid offending sensibilities of some groups (**New York** Mayor Rudolph Giuliani's claim that a 1999 exhibit of British art, "Sensations," offended **Catholics**). Censorship tends to focus less on political materials than sexual ones, although hate literature and **violence** have also become points of debate. The issue of censorship, however, has been highly politicized in government actions, court and legislative actions and citizen response.

Censorship for reasons of security, established in the World Wars, was institutionalized when President **Truman** allowed peacetime agencies to classify materials as "Top Secret," etc. While this system was subsequently modified, the Defense Department and other government bureaus control massive amounts of **information**, a position increasingly complicated by **computers** and **telecommunications** technology. The 1966 Freedom of Information Act allowed citizens to view much government information on themselves and, with restrictions, on other public figures. In other cases, though, like the 1971 **"Pentagon Papers"** case, a whistle-blower and news organization exposed secret information on American involvement in **Vietnam** as a form of civil disobedience that was ultimately upheld in the **Supreme Court**. Still, news media and citizens accepted restrictions on coverage during the **Grenada** invasion and the **Gulf War**.

Censorship with regard to taste and morality proves more divisive. The US lacks formal federal censorship for most domestic media, although federal laws have controlled distribution of obscene materials by mail (under the 1873 Comstock Act), importation of some materials and child **pornography**. These laws have faced test cases to determine obscenity versus free speech and art. These include the 1933 declaration that Joyce's *Ulysses* was art, not subject to the Tariff Act, and the 1957 Roth decision, which established a standard based on the interpretations of "average persons" (tested two year's later by Grove Press' distribution of *Lady Chatterley's Lover*).

Often, though, obscenity and censorship involve more local actions and standards – whether to display certain magazines, buy library books or locate sexually charged activities in areas against "community standards." Film censorship has also been the purview of states and cities: the phrase "banned in Boston" could be used to endorse a risqué film elsewhere. Censorship was even applied to newsreels before this was banned by court decisions.

Local schools and libraries have been especially sensitive areas. While sex is frequently an issue, battles over circulation and textbooks have ranged from protests against racial stereotypes to fundamentalist attacks on the wizardy of Harry Potter or evolution. The American Library Association's 1939 Bill of Rights challenged decades of local censorship of morality, taste and politics in local libraries, framing these institutions as open beacons of information and debate. Schools, however, have been subject to powerful **lobbying** by parents and organized groups in local institutions and statewide adoption of textbooks. Again, censorship arguments play on the special vulnerability of the child. Administrators also manipulate decisions and opportunities: censorship of high-school newspapers has grown since the 1988 Supreme Court decision in *Hazelwood School District* v. *Kuhlemeier.* Before Hazelwood, school-sponsored publications were permitted when "reasonably related to legitimate pedagogical concerns."

Despite these complex and contested structures of censorship and the Freedom of Speech issues debating both security and cultural claims, institutional self-censorship has also been prominent in American life. These include production codes for **Hollywood** and **comics**, media ratings of products and audiences – whether films, video games or music and control devices like the **V-chip** or various forms of parental control for sale to deal with informational issues of the **Internet**. Often, these entail debates on deeply divisive issues like sexuality and violence or their impacts.

Debates sometimes overlook subtler and yet troubling questions like those of ABC and **Disney**, where media conglomerates have created a climate in which **news** hostile to the corporate culture seldom is broadcast. **Political correctness** also evokes self-censorship. Omissions accepted so as not to offend (gay parents in elementary school books) or because of perceptions of audience (lack

of minority figures or interracial romance on network **television**) remind us that self-censorship has a deep toll when significant issues are never discussed This is epitomized in the dramatic **AIDS** slogan: "Silence = Death."

Further reading

Green, J. (1990) *Encyclopedia of Censorship*, New York: Facts on File.

GARY McDONOGH
CINDY WONG

Central Intelligence Agency (CIA)

Created by **Congress** in 1947, the Central Intelligence Agency (CIA) is the primary intelligence agency of the United States government. Its activities range from political and economic analysis to spying and covert operations. By law the CIA is limited to foreign operations; it is not supposed to undertake activities within the US – an operation left to the **Federal Bureau of Investigation** (FBI). In the mid-1990s, "the Agency," as the CIA is sometimes called, was estimated to have about 17,000 employees – the number is classified.

Public and media interest in the CIA has varied over time, but from its inception the CIA's very nature has raised perplexing questions about how a clandestine agency and a democracy can coexist. The secrecy that surrounds many CIA operations has also made it a favorite target of conspiracy theorists, a frequent inspiration for suspense novelists and a phobia for the pathologically paranoid.

The CIA came into existence at President Harry **Truman**'s urging with relatively little notice in the early days of the **Cold War**, its establishment being just one item in a massive law reorganizing the nation's defense operations. The CIA's forerunner was the Office of Strategic Services, which functioned during the Second World War, but the US had never had a permanent agency devoted exclusively to intelligence before the CIA was created.

Throughout the 1950s, the CIA engaged in numerous covert activities overseas that received little public notice and even less criticism. It helped overthrow the leftist prime minister of **Iran** in 1953, installing the Shah in his place. It also participated in a coup in Guatemala in 1954 to eliminate a reformist government there. Both actions were seen as part of an effort to stymie the **Soviet Union**.

One of the most successful CIA-sponsored efforts to spy on the Soviet Union itself – fly-overs by U-2 spy planes, which began in 1956 – ended up shattering the agency's sheltered existence when one of the planes was shot down and the pilot captured in 1960. To make matters worse, Soviet leaders were able to prove that President Dwight **Eisenhower** had initially lied to the American public about the operation – an early inkling of the credibility crises that were to plague Eisenhower's successors.

The U-2 affair was followed in 1961 by the far more disastrous **Bay of Pigs** invasion, an ill-fated CIA-sponsored attack on **Cuba** designed to overthrow Fidel Castro. The invasion was just the most public debacle in a series of CIA plans to get rid of Castro, which involved everything from fomenting unrest in Cuba to assassinating **Castro**.

Throughout the 1960s, the CIA was heavily involved in US operations in **Vietnam**, helping, for example, to overthrow the South Vietnamese government in 1963. But the CIA was also one of the most cautious federal agencies concerning Vietnam, its analyses frequently raising questions about the underlying assumptions of American policy.

In the end, the **Vietnam War** and the **Watergate** scandal (in which the CIA had abetted the cover-up) provoked the first detailed public and congressional scrutiny of the CIA. In 1975 special congressional investigations probed and publicized the darker side of CIA activities, including covert operations, **assassination** attempts and illegal spying on domestic dissidents. As a result, Congress set up permanent committees to oversee the CIA for the first time and put in place clear procedures to ensure that covert operations had presidential approval. In addition, President Gerald **Ford** issued an executive order prohibiting any federal employee from plotting or carrying out an assassination.

With its morale and prestige in tatters, the CIA limped through the remainder of the 1970s until President **Reagan** began strengthening the agency. But the CIA's involvement in the **Iran-Contra** affair led to another series of charges and investigations as the 1980s drew to a close.

The CIA began to remake itself yet again in the 1990s as the Cold War came to an end – an end that the CIA should have better foreseen, according to the agency's critics. But, while putting its house in order, the CIA discovered that it had been the home of several double agents, most notoriously Aldrich Ames, who had revealed to the Soviets the details of fifty-five clandestine operations and the names of thirty-four secret agents. Ames received a life sentence in 1994.

See also: espionage

Further reading

Powers, T. (1979) *The Man Who Kept the Secrets*, New York: Alfred A. Knopf.

Ranelagh, J. (1987) *The Agency: The Rise and Decline of the CIA*, rev. edn, New York: Simon and Schuster.

DAVID GOLDSTON

chain migration

Despite restrictive quotas, American **immigration** has also valued an American model of **family** and kinship. This allows those with legal residency to automatically sponsor spouses and **children**; citizens can also sponsor parents and facilitate entry of unmarried siblings. As these bring in further kin, a "chain" results which may underpin business and social cohesion. This process has become especially associated with networks in post-1965 immigration, although critics have charged abuses based on false marriages, fictive connections and the use of children born in the US to legitimate illegal immigrants.

CINDY WONG

Charleston, South Carolina

Downtown Charleston (population 80,414) preserves classic wood-frame houses, elegant churches and streetscapes that remind us of its colonial power in the coastal "Low Country," its connections to the West Indies and the antebellum divisions of master and slave. Continuing divisions between **black** and **white** underscore both conservatism and conflict in Southern society, although generally far away from **tourist** eyes. Charleston is also a military center, with multiple naval facilities as well as the Citadel, a military college forced to admit women in the 1990s.

GARY McDONOGH

Charlotte, North Carolina

Financial capital of the **Sunbelt** and, through aggressive **banking** mergers, for all US finance. The city was founded in colonial days; in the 1930s, nearby Gastonia became famous for violent **strikes** in the growing textile industry in the region. Yet, opportunities in banking and **service** have attracted people and investments in a spectacular transformation in the late twentieth century for both the cityscape and the society. While cultural facilities and government initiatives are grappling with growth, expansion sport franchises (Hornets in **basketball** and Panthers in **football**) have also laid claim to status as a "major-league" city. Yet despite 20 percent growth in the 1990s (expanding metropolitan population to 1,383,625), other North Carolina development in the Research Triangle (Raleigh-Durham/Chapel Hill, with both Duke and the University of North Carolina) has outstripped it and may well pass Charlotte by 2020. With strong growth in Greensboro, and resort development in the mountains and on the coast, this suggests fundamental re-orientations ahead in a **state** once defined by **white** conservative politics (see **Helms, Jesse**) and an older Southern heritage of **race**, **class**, **religion** and **regionalism**. Thomas Hanchett's *Sorting Out the New South City* (1998) provides a detailed analysis of Charlotte's development and insights into both the **South** and the Sunbelt.

Further reading

Hanchett, T. (1998) *Sorting Out the New South City*, Chapel Hill: University of North Carolina.

GARY McDONOGH

charter schools

The educational reforms of the 1990s allowed for community design within **public schools**. Parents, teachers and others (including corporate consultants) applied for special, independent but publicly funded charters to operate their institutions. Spreading especially through troubled urban school systems, this innovation allows for increased community commitment, program innovation and special needs of schools and neighborhoods, but also facilitates corporate involvement in planning and management.

GARY McDONOGH

Chavez, Cesar

b. 1927; d. 1993

Cesar Chavez grew up in a family that lost its small farm due to the Great Depression. In 1965 he founded the United Farm Workers of America, a **California**-based **union** for agricultural workers, which brought attention to the squalid conditions these workers endured and the low wages they earned for back-breaking labor. His call for a national boycott of table grapes eventually led to union agreements with several large growers. Chavez's work brought about improved wages and benefits for migratory agricultural workers throughout the **Southwest**; he also encouraged **Mexican Americans** to become more politically active.

A. JOSEPH BORRELL

Chavez, Denise

b. 1948

Award-winning **Chicana** author, activist, teacher, actor, Chavez is the author and editor of numerous novels and collections of **poetry**, short stories and **drama**. She received her Bachelor's degree in Theater from New Mexico State University in 1974, a Master's degree in Theater from Trinity University, and a Master's degree in Creative Writing from the University of New Mexico. In addition to writing, Chavez teaches, performs and organizes in southern New Mexico. Her emphasis on strong women and good storytelling appear in her best-known works *Face of an Angel* and *The Last of the Menu Girls*.

See also: theater

SUSAN MARIE GREEN

cheerleading

The Greek chorus of American athletic events, cheerleading developed at the end of the nineteenth century in the **Northeast** and **Midwest** as an extra-curricular school leadership activity to help motivate and inspire class loyalty and good citizenship. Primarily for males, after the First World War and the growth of co-educational institutes it became predominantly female, although in the 1960s and 1970s up to 40 percent of cheerleaders were male. Cheerleaders are usually selected for their social and leadership qualities, physical skills and popularity. Acolytes usually begin as mascots working with older cheerleaders.

In the last thirty years cheerleading – influenced by the popularity of gymnastics – has become more of an athletic event, developing under the auspices of several national associations which sponsor clinics, camps, workshops and nationally televised competitions since 1984. In 1999 there were an estimated 3,300,000 cheerleaders nationwide, half between the ages of twelve and seventeen (another 1.2 million under the age of twelve). The **South** and Midwest dominate, as they often do in competitions. In 1972 the **Dallas** Cowboys originated the first professional cheerleading squad.

Cheerleading is big business – supporting a star cheerleader can cost $5,000 per year, and supply companies reap millions. It is also big media – both the wholesome sensuality of students and more suggestive professional squads gain sports media attention, while stories of athlete–cheerleader romance, squad jealousies and even murderous mothers have been the stuff of teen movies for decades.

Further reading

Yellin, E. (1999) "School Spirit Inc.," *New York Times* July 17: C1.

JIM WATKINS

chemistry

Chemistry is vital for improving and sustaining the quality of human life, and the chemical process industries continue expanding to meet society's demands, producing over a million new chemicals a year worldwide. The US chemical industry alone employs over a million workers and is the largest segment of US manufacturing. The four main areas within chemistry are organic, inorganic, analytical and physical.

Organic chemistry studies carbon compounds and how to modify and combine them to synthesize new substances. Synthetics include dyes, perfumes, refrigerants used in **air-conditioners** and **plastics** such as Nylon, Plexiglass and Teflon – a polymer extensively used since the 1960s as a non-stick coating for pans. Compounds are also synthesized and screened for use as **drugs** or **agricultural** chemicals.

Inorganic chemistry treats all compounds, except for hydrocarbons and their derivatives. Advances in inorganic chemistry have yielded composite materials for constructing anything from better **tennis** rackets to more durable airplane wings. Semiconductors and high-temperature superconductors have also been produced, making possible faster **computers** and high-speed **trains**.

Analytical chemistry is concerned with determining the composition of substances. Advances since the 1950s involve increasingly sophisticated instrumentation and techniques, including ultracentrifuges, mass spectrometers and high-resolution chromatography. X-ray crystallography has also made it possible to analyze the structures of vitamin B_{12}, DNA and hemoglobin. Many techniques are employed to detect environmental pollutants and food contaminants.

Physical chemistry employs the instruments and methods of analytical chemistry to develop theories of chemical phenomena. Chemical thermodynamics measures variables like melting and boiling points, chemical kinetics studies reaction rates and electrochemistry examines chemical effects due to electric currents. Such information has facilitated research in and development of electronic components, alternatives for harmful chemicals and more.

Chemistry has increasingly fractured into various specializations. To mention a few: agricultural and food chemistry produce preservatives and flavorings, as well as fertilizers, pesticides and herbicides like 2,4-D, which led to rapid rises in crop yields after the Second World War. **Pharmaceutical** chemistry creates medicines and other drugs to treat **diseases** and extend and improve the quality of life. These include the antibiotics penicillin, tetracycline and aureomycin, as well as synthesis of **steroids** like progesterone, used for **contraception**, and hormones like insulin used in treating diabetes. Petrochemistry generates **petroleum**-based products such as gasoline, oil, waxes and plastics, as well as the raw material for most synthetic fibers.

The need to assess the benefits of chemicals versus their adverse consequences has always existed but been largely ignored by chemical manufacturers until the 1960s, creating the impression of an industry unconcerned with environmental pollution, health risks or product safety. Public concerns led to the creation of the **Environmental Protection Agency** in 1970 and passage of various laws thereafter to protect the **environment** and improve workplace safety. The US chemical industry has responded with programs, which include voluntary clean-ups, effluent reduction and safer disposal methods, and prioritizing employee health and safety issues, to regain public trust.

Further reading

Breslow, R. (1997) *Chemistry Today and Tomorrow: The Central, Useful, and Creative Science,* Washington, DC: American Chemical Society and Jones & Bartlett Publishers.

STEPHEN D. NORTON

chess

Often visible in the parks around major American **cities**, chess was nicely captured in the movie *Searching for Bobby Fischer* (1993). In 1972, at the height of the Cold War, chess caught the attention of the American public with the contest between American Bobby Fischer and Soviet Boris Spassky. The American prevailed, but, hating the limelight, Fischer became a recluse and refused to compete for the title again. With no American grandmasters of note to replace him, Americans had to satisfy themselves by watching different Russian champions compete, and trying to determine which Russian was "good" – a man with dissident leanings like Gary Kasparov, and which Russian was "bad" – a man who seemed to represent the Soviet system, for example Anatoly Karpov. A flourish of interest in the sport occurred with the brief re-emergence of Fischer, but otherwise the end of the Cold War has diminished attention paid to chess and relegated it to its former image as an elite, **intellectual** and, in high school, nerdy pastime. The emergence of computer chess has popularized the game in new venues.

ROBERT GREGG

Chicago, IL

Chicago, Illinois, located in the center of the Midwestern prairie on the banks of Lake Michigan, has always played a special role in the national imagination. Known as "The City of Neighborhoods," "The City of Broad Shoulders" (from a poem by Carl **Sandburg**) and "The City that Works," Chicago has been associated with an array of images, ranging from its reputation for political corruption to its fiercely "tribal" ethnic rivalries to its history of gangsters (particularly during the Prohibition era), to the violence that erupted during the Democratic National **Convention** of

1968, when the police and National Guard were unleashed by then-Mayor Richard J. **Daley** to quell anti-war demonstrations.

Chicago's cityscape bears the marks of its once unrivaled prominence as a center of industry though, like many of its companion rustbelt cities, manufacturing now employs only about one-fifth of workers (mostly in food processing). Chicago's once famous steelyards closed down in the early 1980s due to competition from cheaper steel produced abroad. Its location at the hub of the transcontinental **train** lines and its proximity to the cattle-raising farms of the **Midwest** had made it the center of the meat-packing industry at the turn of the nineteenth century, when the development of refrigerated train cars allowed freshly slaughtered meat to be safely shipped to markets in the East and elsewhere. The rise of **trucking** and the growth of the interstate **highway** system eventually obviated the need for a centralized location for meat-packing. Almost all the Chicago stockyards, whose appalling conditions had been immortalized by Upton Sinclair in his 1906 novel *The Jungle*, closed down between the 1930s and the 1960s.

Unlike many of the other rustbelt cities, however, Chicago has had the ability to reinvent itself, and, in the 1990s, it enjoyed an economic renaissance that seems to parallel its rebirth more than a century earlier after the famous fire of 1871. It remains the financial center of the Midwest and its main **airport**, O'Hare, is one of the busiest in the world. Old industrial areas which ring the central city (known as "the Loop" because of the pattern of elevated train tracks that surround the core) are now being redeveloped into loft apartments and condominiums, restaurants and artists' galleries; its natural setting on the banks of Lake Michigan is also being newly exploited. Lake Shore Drive, which runs along the lakefront from the city's northern tip to its southern tip, has been re-routed as it runs past the Loop so that institutions located on the Lake, including the Museum of Natural History, the Aquarium and the Planetarium, are now easily accessible on foot, as is the lakefront itself. Chicago sports teams include the Bears (**football**), the Bulls (**basketball**), whose most famous former player is Michael **Jordan** and two baseball teams, the Cubs and the White Sox. Wrigley Stadium, home of the Cubs, is one of the

few **baseball** parks still located in the middle of a city neighborhood, now known as "Wrigleyville." Chicago is also famous for its "Magnificent Mile" shopping district, on North Michigan Avenue, and the Art Institute.

Chicago hosts many **immigrant** communities, including East and West Europeans, **Mexicans** and **Asians**. Citizens of Japanese descent ended up in Chicago after being released from Midwestern internment camps following the Second World War. Its **African American** population increased rapidly in the Great Migration from the **South** between the World Wars and following the Second World War, so that they now make up about two-fifths of the city's residents. Overall, Chicago was demoted from second to third city in the US following the 1990 census, which the population of **Los Angeles, CA** surpassed.

In the 1980s, Chicago was roiled with political turmoil as its old **Democratic** Party "machine," which controlled the ward organizations and doled out patronage jobs and which had long been dominated by the city's "white ethnics," the **Irish** in particular, was overthrown with the election of the city's first African American **mayor**, Harold Washington. Despite the turmoil and racist invective that attended his first election in 1983, Washington proved a charismatic leader and was re-elected to office in 1987, although he died of a heart attack shortly thereafter. After an interim mayor, Richard M. Daley, son of the famous Richard J. Daley, was elected to office.

For social scientists, Chicago has always been associated with the Chicago School of **Sociology**, which flourished particularly during the 1920s and 1930s. These social scientists, based at the renowned **University of Chicago**, used the city as their laboratory. They conducted empirical research on particular neighborhoods and occupational groups, with a special interest in social problems caused by poverty. In the 1920s, a sociologist, Ernest W. Burgess, developed his theory that American **cities** were made up of "concentric zones," with an "administrative–business sector" at the center of the city, surrounded by a ring of slums and **ethnic enclaves**, which, in turn, was surrounded by a zone of slightly better-off immigrant neighborhoods, which was encircled by Zone 4, where the American-born **middle classes** resided. Zone 5 housed the **suburban** commuters. This model fostered the development of a human ecology perspective on the city, in which the urban environment was envisioned like a natural habitat made up of interconnected systems. Despite the fact that critics pointed out rather early on that the particular formation of Chicago and other cities was hardly "natural," but was the outcome of particular policies shaped by governmental and market interests, the "zonal development" model continued to be influential in urban studies.

Further reading

Cronon, W. (1991) *Nature's Metropolis: Chicago and the Great West*, New York: W.W. Norton.

Lindner, R. (1996) *The Reportage of Urban Culture: Robert Park and the Chicago School*, Cambridge, MA: Cambridge University Press.

Miller, D. (1996) *City of the Century*, New York: Simon and Schuster.

SUSAN BRIN HYATT

Chicago, University of

Founded by John D. Rockefeller in 1892 as an intellectual institution for the burgeoning metropolis, it has grown to be one of the most prestigious private, non-denominational universities in the world. The university has 12,000 students (75 percent graduate and professional) and more than 1,900 full-time faculty members on its Hyde Park campus, south of Chicago, designed by Frederick Law Olmsted. The university claims distinctions ranging from the birth of the nuclear age, with Enrico Fermi, to connections, especially in economics, with seventy-one **Nobel** laureates. It is also renowned for its innovative committees that move beyond disciplinary boundaries and a distinguished university press.

GARY McDONOGH

Chicanos/as

In common usage, the terms Chicano (male) and Chicana (female) refer to people of Mexican ancestry born and/or raised in the United States. They are roughly synonymous with the term Mexican American. Like the terms **Hispanic** or **Latino/Latina**, these are terms of political identity and personal choice. With a few exceptions, Chicanos and Chicanas are citizens of the United States and Chicano/Chicana cultures are American cultures.

Chicanos and Chicanas were legally created in the United States through the Treaty of Guadalupe-Hidalgo at the end of the Mexican American War in 1848. However, Chicanos and Chicanas' roots in the southwestern United States predate the arrival of the Spaniards in the late sixteenth century. In 1990 they remain geographically centered in the **Southwest**, although concentrations appear in every **state**.

Until the mid-1960s, the terms Chicano and Chicana were frequently used in derogatory, non-self-referential manners. In the 1960s, Mexican Americans, particularly on college **campuses**, began adopting and positively redefining the terms. By the late 1960s, clearly identifiable Chicano and Chicana movements existed, celebrating unique Mexican American experiences and demanding social equality.

The most often quoted definition of the term was penned in 1977 by Santos Martinez, Jr: "Chicano – a Mexican American involved in a socio-political struggle to create a relevant, contemporary and revolutionary consciousness as a means of accelerating social change and actualizing an autonomous cultural reality among other Americans of Mexican descent. To call oneself Chicano is an overt political act." This association with direct action has made "Chicano" and "Chicana" controversial terms of identity for some Mexican Americans.

Several theories about the origin of these terms exist. One of the most popular resonates with the indigenous interests and emphases of the Chicano and Chicana movements. It postulates that the terms originated from the ancient Aztec "Mexica" or "Mexicanos." Over time, the prefix disappeared and the soft "sh" sound of the letter "x" hardened into the "ch" sound used since the early 1900s.

Demographic figures vary widely, but, in 1990, the American population of Mexican descent, including Chicanos and Chicanas, was estimated at between 13 and 14 million. Throughout the last half of the twentieth century, the Chicano community has remained one of the fastest growing and most dynamic segments of American culture.

Further reading

Martinez, S. Jr (1977) *Dale Gas: Chicano Art of Texas*, Houston: Contemporary Arts Museum.

SUSAN MARIE GREEN

child abuse

Though child abuse has always existed, it was not until the 1960s that it became the subject of widespread public concern in the US. Drawing attention to the "Battered Child Syndrome," medical professionals documented deliberate, repeated physical abuse of **children** by their parents. Today, **newspaper** headlines and **television** broadcasts regularly expose cases of brutality that continue to evoke shock and horror. Over 3 million reports of suspected child abuse or neglect were made in 1996. Many cases are never even reported. Between 1990 and 1994, approximately 5,400 children died from abuse or neglect.

Early theories of child abuse were psychological, focusing exclusively on parental pathology. Present explanations are more complex, viewing child abuse as the product of multiple factors, including sociological elements, cultural norms and also characteristics of the parent, child and **family**. In a multicultural society, it is difficult to define child abuse; what some consider to be abuse, others see as acceptable discipline. Currently, for example, many debate whether corporal punishment is abuse.

Federal law defines child abuse broadly as "physical or mental injury, sexual abuse, negligent treatment, or maltreatment of any child under the age of eighteen" by a parent or caretaker. Broad definitions leave child welfare workers with considerable discretion and the difficult task of balancing the sometimes conflicting goals of protecting children and keeping families together.

Further reading:

Straus, M.A. and Gelles, R.J. (1990/1995) *Physical Violence in American Families*, New Brunswick: Transaction Publishers.

Daro, D. (1988) *Confronting Child Abuse*, New York: The Free Press.

EMIKO TAJIMA

childcare *see* babies; children; education and society; kindergarten and Head Start

children

Changes in **family** life and structure, along with fluctuations in wealth, shaped the context of children's experience after the Second World War. From 1945 to the early 1970s, American families grew steadily wealthier. The birth-control pill, introduced in the early 1960s, slowed the **birth** rate, so children grew up in smaller, richer families than ever before. Larger houses gave children more **privacy**, more wealth meant more toys, including **television**, more travel and, by the 1980s, more **computers** and other electronic devices. Meanwhile, a steadily rising **divorce** rate, followed towards the end of the century by more frequent remarriage, created a complex family structure with multiple residences, incomes and cultures. All these combined to increase the cultural and commercial significance of children and childhood.

Schooling reflected these changes. Attentiveness to children's individual personalities produced innovations in teaching techniques in the 1960s and 1970s, including open classrooms and **high-school** electives, though the 1980s and 1990s brought a resurgence of adult authority and a "return to basics." Parental involvement in schools eroded after the 1970s as demand for income encouraged adults to work longer hours and/or multiple jobs. Beginning in the 1980s, communications technologies lengthened the work day itself. Children's activities became more structured with playgroups, after-school care, organized sports and summer camp replacing the less-structured street play of earlier generations of children. New therapeutic approaches to troubled children emerged in the 1980s and 1990s, and therapists offered Ritalin and other prescription drugs to help these children "adjust" more readily.

Though the **Civil Rights movement** and new constitutional doctrines on equality improved social and economic opportunities for non-white citizens, non-white and recent immigrant groups stayed poorer than **whites**. **African American**, Asian and **Latino** children continued to play with their peers on public streets and in public playgrounds instead of in private rooms at home or in the supervised parks available to the more affluent. While prosperous minority families followed other **middle-class** families into the **suburbs**, the integration of professional sports provided African American and Hispanic children with new non-white role models of immense wealth and prestige to emulate. Beginning in the 1970s, growing racial disparities in wealth clashed with these children's heightened desires for both basic and glamorous goods, introducing new tensions into poor families and communities.

Gender expectations of children also changed as adults won increased educational, professional and recreational opportunities. Despite controversy, evidence of underachievement by girls led to new girl-centered initiatives, including girls-only math and science camps, magazines devoted to empowering girls and an increased sensitivity about schoolyard teasing.

Post-Second World War America has paradoxically both shortened and lengthened childhood. Children mature early as independent consumers, but remain dependent longer on more affluent parents. School days and years are longer, though pedagogy has become more respectful of children's individuality. Children receive more organized assistance with leisure, learning and emotional development, though working parents, underfunded public programs and the labor market often require even young children to shift largely for themselves.

Further reading

Nightingale, C. (1993) *On the Edge*, New York: Basic.

Zelizer, V. (1985) *Pricing the Priceless Child*, New York: Basic.

SHARON ANN HOLT

children and television

The domestic intrusion of **television** in postwar America included **children** in the television experience, often via anodyne programming entertaining anyone between the ages of three and eighty. Whether including a chimpanzee in morning television **news** or avoiding sexuality in prime time, television admitted children to "**family** viewing" even as it defined them as specific audiences. At the same time, non-children's television has been viewed with suspicion in terms of its impact on the innocent young whom it "pushes" towards crime, drugs or sex. Yet, apart from such general relationships between children and television, which continue to produce widespread outcry and inconclusive studies, programming, both local and national, also has specifically targeted children. Here, a profound duality of learning versus consumption has been contentious even while the spectrum of shows available on networks, public stations and **cable** channels like Nickelodeon or FOX Family has expanded continually. Together, both cultural issues and programming have influenced what children are in contemporary America.

Early children's shows on television used live **actors**, puppets and cartoons to capture their audience. Network shows included *Howdy Doody* (NBC, 1947–60), with fanciful, long-running characters and a child-filled peanut gallery, and *Captain Kangaroo* (CBS, 1955–84) and his familiar friends. Local shows featuring "T-Bar-V" ranch (in **Louisville**), "Mayor Art" (**San Francisco, CA**) or comedian Soupy Sales (**New York** City) showcased children as real participants as well; the ambience of these shows is captured ironically in Krusty the Clown in *The Simpsons*. Elements like warm, long-running characters in a home-like setting, multiple stories and forms of narrative and live children have continued in shows as diverse as *Peewee's Playhouse*, *Barney* and *Mr Roger's Neighborhood*.

Disney represents a special early and continuing chapter in children's television, from *Disneyland* (ABC, 1954–8) to *The Wonderful World of Disney* on the same network that it now owns at the end of the century. As David Bianculli observes, this essentially makes it not only the longest running weekly series in history, but also the longest running infomercial. The show has invariably highlighted Disney theme parks, trademark characters, mass-media products or some other aspect of corporate development. Here, the child is less consumer than pawn. In the 1960s, Disney's *Wonderful World of Color* pushed color television for NBC's parent company General Electric. In the 1990s, Disney also created its own premium channel as well as its merger/return to ABC.

Despite Disney's domination of **animation**, others also produced and packaged cartoon shows for children. Warner Brothers, for example, built anthologies around their theatrical, animated characters like Daffy Duck or Road Runner. William Hanna and Joseph Barbera produced *Huckleberry Hound* (1958–61) and *QuickDraw McGraw* (1950–61) which translated **sitcom** plots and movie scenarios like **westerns** into children's vaudeville, embodied in quick-talking bears (Yogi), plodding lawmen (Huckleberry Hound and Quick-draw McGraw) and less elaborate drawing. These cartoons roamed local stations for years in syndicated releases. Other animated shows appeared in evening hours, like the *Flintstones* (ABC, 1960–6), which aped the adult *Honeymooners*.

Saturday morning as a cartoon kingdom began to emerge in the 1960s as series by Hanna-Barbera, Sid and Marty Krofft and others glued children to the set between eight and noon. As Timothy and Kevin Burke (1999) note, Saturday morning became a magnet, drawing animated series out of prime time as well as fostering new opportunities for decades, ranging from talented animals to superheroes and varying in plot and quality of animation. The 1960s also spawned ironic fore-bears of later hip animated comedy like Jay Ward's *Rocky and His Friends* (ABC, 1959–61 and sequels) or *George of the Jungle*. While leavened with limp network educational series, Saturday morning also became a stronghold for targeted programming and **advertising** that provided product placements and vocabularies of life for **Generation X**. Shows and commercials sold millions of **toys** and boxes of **breakfast cereals**, while transmitting ideas ranging from victories of good and sharing over evil, or masculine domination where super-heroes were invariably white. While rules controlling such commercials were in place in the late 1960s, these were totally eliminated in 1983.

Because of commercialism as much as quality, Saturday morning galvanized attacks on consumer-ist television. Federal Communications Commissioner Newton Minow – famed for his description of television as a "vast wasteland" – and the later Action for Children's Television, begun in 1968, sought to control both content and relationships between advertising and programming (e.g. *Flintstones*' vitamins or other spin-offs). ACT's strategies, however, faced shifting regulation – while Jimmy **Carter** was interventionist to the point of considering a ban on advertisements, Ronald **Reagan** eliminated controls instead. Debate over the impact of violence also ensued, although network censors generally monitored content for children's shows.

In 1991 the Children's Television Act required broadcasters to certify educational content. Meanwhile, the **V-chip** promises home regulatory control over what children see (within the limits of what is offered). At the same time, alternative home programming has been cultivated with video sales and rentals.

Unlike these commercial offerings, educational television on **PBS** offered a vision of the child ready to learn. They attracted children not with dull lessons, but with the incredible invention of *Sesame Street* (PBS, 1969–) and spin-offs through Jane Cooney and the Children's Television Workshop. After thirty years, *Sesame Street* has become American folk culture as well as mass culture. It is also the most widely viewed children's television show worldwide. Other PBS landmarks include *Reading Rainbow, Where in the World is Carmen Sandiego?* (combining **game show** and geography), *Mr Roger's Neighborhood* (whose white neighborliness was satirized by Eddie **Murphy** on *Saturday Night Live*) and *Electric Company*. PBS later expanded its offerings to younger children with *Barney* – a giant dinosaur more annoying to many adults than the cynical *Muppets* – and the imported *Teletubbies*, targeting very young children.

The educational philosophy of PBS has been challenged by critics who decry the short attention span demanded by *Sesame Street* and the association of education and fun that may undercut expectations for school. More recently, concerns have been voiced that these learners are also being asked to consume. *Sesame Street, Arthur, Teletubbies, Barney* and other series offer games, toys, traveling shows and even theme parks that go beyond any formative/educational mission. While royalties replace government cutbacks in public media financing, these blur lines between learners and consumers.

In the 1990s, relations between children and television have intensified via multiple new options, including cable channels aimed at children (Disney, Nickelodeon) and/or inclusive of kids (FOX Family: *Nick at Night*). Video series allow home libraries and constant reviewing of treasured stories or episodes that change viewing patterns but also create new dependencies as children memorize scripts as well as characters. Television also crosses over into classrooms, especially preschool, where video screenings seem more acceptable. Commercial channels have also sought entry to the classroom as learning tools with paid advertisements to the alarm of parents and teachers.

Through this complicated history, conflicting images of children have emerged. Are they simply to be entertained passively (television as babysitter)? If educable, should the lessons be generally social (sharing is good), disciplinary (counting and spelling) or more complex (multiculturalism or Spanish on *Sesame Street*)? Are children innocent – to be spared complications of crime, family dysfunction, consumption or other problems facing them in the real world? Or should children's television talk about death and loss? These questions, writ large in children's exposure to adult television, prove complicated even within children's **self-help** programs like *Mr Roger's Neighborhood*.

Moreover, how can we conceive of children as active, even resistant viewers, skating on the ironic edge of cartoons like *Rocky and Bullwinkle* through *South Park* and *The Simpsons* (which some families will not let children watch)? M. Davis' *Fake, Fact and Fantasy* (1997) explores children's abilities to distinguish between television **violence** and real life as learning skills. As with other **mass media**, series and audiences are elements in the process of the formation of American culture rather than simple lessons or symbols.

See also: violence and media

Further reading

Bianculli, D. (1977) *Dictionary of Teleliteracy*, Syracuse: Syracuse University Press.

Burke, T. and Burke, K. (1999) *Saturday Morning Fever*, New York: St. Martin's.

Davis, M. (1997) *Fake, Fact and Fantasy*, Mahwah: L. Erlbaum.

Jordan, A. and Jameison, K. (eds) (1998) *Children and Television*, Thousand Oaks: Sage.

Minow, N. and LaMay, C. (1995) *Abandoned in the Wasteland*, New York: Hill and Wang.

GARY McDONOGH
CINDY WONG

children's literature

Children's literature generally refers to books and stories for readers from infancy through the ages of fourteen or fifteen. The American children's literature industry includes publishing houses, book weeks, specialty associations, conferences, storytelling associations and libraries; one Internet vendor in this prolific field lists 1 million titles, while the *New York Times Parents Guide* (1991) reviews over 1,700. American children's literature reflects concern for family, society and environment and increasingly seeks to deal with multiculturalism and social problems. The industry also has responded to new media ties as well as marketing associated with well-known characters.

Broad categories of children's literature respond to age, interests and skills, including picture books, read-aloud books, biography, **folklore** and legends, **history**, **religion**, series, ethnic narratives and poetry. Nursery rhymes, song books, coloring-in and alphabet books abound for young children; schools and media encourage parents to read to their children, while public **libraries**, schools and bookstores make books readily available for growing readers.

Picture books and read-aloud books are recognized annually in the Caldecott Awards for illustrated stories: Maurice Sendak, Eric Carle and Tomie de Paola are well-known author-illustrators. *Pat the Bunny* and *Good Night Moon* are babyhood classics, while other popular read-aloud books include *Millions of Cats*, *Madeline*, *The Little House* and *Make Way for Ducklings*. *Madeline* and *Curious George*, like the more recent *Arthur* series, also have media, toy and game tie-ins. The many works of *Dr Seuss* (Theodore Geisel) and Shel Silverstein's *A Light in the Attic* and *Where the Sidewalk Ends* provide comic verse, word play and catchy illustrations.

Series books introduce recurrent characters for older readers. Popular series of the **baby boom** include *Nancy Drew, Bobbsey Twins* and *The Hardy Boys*, which also demarcated gendered readers. By the 1990s, these had given way to the contemporary issues and social mixtures of *Sweet Valley Twins, The Baby-sitters Club* (aimed at girls) or the *Goosebump* horror tales. The British Harry Potter books have become **publishing** blockbusters.

Nonetheless, fairy tales and legends remain popular, reaching across time and space through lavishly illustrated editions, popular movie adaptations and accompanying books, CD-ROM games and board games. Some classic early American novels, such as *Little Women, Tom Sawyer, Huckleberry Finn* and *The Little House* (series), also retain their appeal for established readers. In the 1990s, for example, Frances Burnett's *A Little Princess* and *The Secret Garden*, both written before 1930, were revitalized by movies, stage plays, CD-ROM and newly illustrated editions.

Other books move children onward into new worlds. Here, the Newberry Awards recognize excellence in children's literature, including since the 1960s works that deal with issues of race, death and sexuality. **Science fiction** for children proliferated in the 1950s and 1960s, including Robert Heinlein's works and Madeline L'Engle's *A Wrinkle in Time*. Stories of aliens and anti-utopian societies, such as *The Giver*, maintain this tradition. The *Harry Potter* fantasy books captured the imagination of millions of young readers at the turn of the twenty-first century. Semi-documentary novels also inform and educate young readers: *My Brother Sam is Dead* treats the tragic disruption of a family during the Civil War, while *Number the Stars* depicts a child during the Holocaust. Non-fiction books dealing with environmental issues also reflect broader American concerns in the 1980s and 1990s.

Late twentieth century trends included works for the disadvantaged child, works written with limited vocabulary, and a new realism. Children's literature written by and about **African Americans**, **Asian Americans**, **Hispanics**, Native Americans, disabled citizens and children with illnesses all appear in books designed to spur reflection and conversation with parents and teachers.

See also: blockbusters

Further reading

Lee, L. (ed.) (1994) *The Elementary School Library Collection*, 19th edn, Williamsport: Brodart.

Jenson, J. and Roser, N. (1993) *Adventuring with Books*, 10th edn, Urbana: National Council of Teachers of English.

GAIL HENSON

children's magazines

Children's magazines abound, with an especially large number featuring health and science-related content. Children between the ages of two and fourteen and parents can choose from magazines of general interest, those featuring crafts, coloring pages and cut-out pages and others offering **history**, literature, sports, consumer news, **religion**, geography and entertainment. Generally, these contain sixty pages or fewer, and circulations range from 5,000 to 2.5 million. In the 1990s, these magazines increasingly used clever graphics, color and activities to extend the reading or educational experience for their audience. They also show links to consumerism and reproductions of **gender** and other divisions.

The most popular titles include the long-running, general interest *Highlights for Children*, with a circulation of 2.5 million and a stated mission of "fun with a purpose" for children aged between two and twelve. *Boy's Life*, the Boy Scouts of America publication, has a circulation of 1.3 million tied to its institutional framework. *National Geographic World*, a geography magazine for children between the ages of six and twelve, drawing on the popular adult magazine, has a circulation of 1.2 million.

As *Boy's Life* suggests, magazines for children recognize and reproduce gender differences. Girls magazines include *American Girl* (circulation 700,000), a spin-off of the popular American Girl books and dolls, and *New Moon: The Magazine for Girls and their Dreams* (circulation 28,000), which encourages pre-teen girls to become confident young women with dreams and positive role models from various ethnic communities. Teen-oriented *Girl's Life* includes traditional features such as pen pals, family advice, horoscopes and reviews of CDs.

Science and nature magazines include: *Chickadee* (ages three to nine); *Kids Discover* and *Odyssey*, for elementary school students; *Owl*; *Ranger Rick*, the National Wildlife Federation publication for elementary students; and *3–2–1 Contact*, the flashy and savvy science magazine for children aged eight to twelve, published by the Children's Television Workshop (CTV also has a preschool magazine, *Sesame Street*). Most have web-sites that extend children's experiences beyond the magazine.

The CTV and American Girl connections also suggest synergy in children's magazines and consumption. This permeates publications like *Crayola Kids*, *Disney Adventures*, a hundred-page, digest-sized publication covering **television**, sports, music and twenty-five pages of **comics**, and *Nickelodeon*, from the **cable** network.

Magazines with historical/cultural emphases include *Cobblestone*, *Calliope* and the anthropological *Faces* (for ages nine to fourteen). Meanwhile, *Cricket*, *Spider* and *Ladybug* provide stories, poems and games. *Stone Soup* provides a forum for writers and artists up to age thirteen. Other specialty magazines, whether *Zillions*, from consumer reports, or *Sports Illustrated for Kids* and *Soccer Jr.*, identify children as junior adults.

Further reading

Katz, B. and Katz, L. (eds) (1996) *Magazines for Libraries*, 9th edn, New Providence: R.R. Bowker.

GAIL HENSON

children's museums

Children's **museums** began in the United States with the Brooklyn Children's Museum (1899). The Association of Youth Museums has almost 400 members; of these, 200 museums are currently in operation and 100 are in the planning stages. Children's museums take many forms, from interactive centers for art, science and **nature** to hands-on discovery rooms in larger museums, not to mention museums entirely for children. They tailor exhibits to the developmental capabilities of **children**, complete with activities, language and displays appropriate for children of various ages, learning styles and developmental abilities.

When the Brooklyn Children's Museum was founded, John Dewey was teaching the then-radical notion that individuals learn powerfully through personal experience. Maria Montessori also influenced the early development of children's museums with her theories of teacher as facilitator and the value of children having independence and sharing activities and equipment. In 1901 the **Smithsonian** opened its first Children's Room with the theme "Knowledge begins in wonder."

In the 1960s, Jean Piaget's theories of child development affected educational institutions in powerful ways, particularly his assertion that to know an object is to act upon it. In 1961 Michael Spock, son of the famed pediatrician Benjamin **Spock**, took charge of the Boston, Massachusetts Children's Museum and revolutionized the museum world for children. He designed exhibits meant for interaction – the first being "What's Inside," showing the inner workings of everyday things such as toasters, water heaters, a car engine and a sewer system.

In keeping with Piaget's concepts of the stages of children's development, the staff developed spaces for children's needs. For example, for the sensory-motor stage (birth to age three), the staff developed a baby pit with mirrors, blankets and small climbing structures. A toddler area had small group activities like blocks, and older toddlers had arts and crafts materials available along with puzzles, play structures and activity tables.

Staff members became interpreters who were ready to answer questions and demonstrate components of exhibits. The Boston Children's Museum philosophy was that "the museum was for somebody rather than about something."

The hands-on science and technology center was born when Frank Oppenheimer opened **San Francisco, CA**'s Exploratorium in 1969. He believed "visitors should control and manipulate the elements of the exhibit and that staff or volunteer 'explainers' could help them understand what was happening" (Cleaver 1988: 10). His Exploratorium inspired the many science and technology participatory centers across the country.

Most children's museums strive to engage visitors in the experience of learning about the world they inhabit and encourage discovery, dealing with unknowns in a safe way, and making sense of new experiences. Exhibits created with an emphasis on the process of learning help visitors – whether children, **teenagers** or adults accompanying them – understand more about their own learning style and motivations for learning, whether visitors take a random or a linear or methodical approach to experiencing the museum.

Further reading

Cleaver, J. (1988) *Doing Children's Museums. A Guide to 225 Hands-On Museums*, Charlotte, VT: Williamson.

GAIL HENSON

children's music

In any culture, music contributes to the quality of children's early life experiences. Founding the first **kindergartens** in the nineteenth century, the United States adopted the theories, philosophies and methods of their German inventor, Froebel. Children's songs were an important instructional medium so Froebelian song materials were translated for America's teachers.

With the child-study movement in the early twentieth century, many researchers also studied **children**'s rhythmic and vocal development, again influencing publications about children's music. For example, early childhood songs in text were notated in the keys in which children can sing more comfortably.

However, children's music in educational settings seems to be losing emphasis since the mid-twentieth century. One reason is educational trends that focus more on math and science. Still, in early childhood education settings, such as preschool, music exists in a unique way. Children's musical experiences there include singing, moving to music, listening to music and playing or creating music with musical instruments. These activities tend to be limited by classroom teachers who are not necessarily musicians.

Regardless of educational or social trends, children's song remains important. American folk or traditional tunes such as "Twinkle Twinkle, Little Star" or "Old MacDonald" are children's popular songs, transmitted by word of mouth. There is also a wide variety of recorded lullabies and play songs, including songs from many cultures. Popular music such as **rock**, **jazz**, **New Age** and pop also form part of children's music. Many authors include tunes in children's books so children can sing through the words. Some musicians also have created songs for movement and rhythmic games.

Mass media is also an influential factor in children's music. **Television** programs for children, such as *Sesame Street* and *Barney*, are very popular among American children and they learn many songs from such programs.

Further reading

McDonald, D.T. and Simons, G.M. (1989) *Musical Growth and Development: Birth Through Six*, New York: Schirmer Books.

Choksy, L., Abramson, R.M., Gillespie, A.E. and Woods, D. (1986) *Teaching Music in the Twentieth Century*, New Jersey: Prentice-Hall, Inc.

JINYOUNG KIM

Childs, Julia *see* cookbooks and cooking media; food; PBS Public Broadcasting System

child stars

Since the pre-war glory days of Shirley Temple, **children** have emerged as some of the biggest stars in **Hollywood**. Most, like Macauley Culkin, who became a huge star due to the *Home Alone* films of the 1990s, embody an endearing cuteness that captured the heart of America – with the aid of much marketing. Common too, as many exposés have revealed, are the hardships many of these young stars endure. These include clashes with parents over money (Gary Coleman of the **sitcom** *Different Strokes*, as well as Caulkin), drug abuse as fame fades (David Cassidy, River Phoenix), **suicide** attempts and difficult adult lives. Elizabeth **Taylor** started her career as a child actor and went on to become one of the great sex symbols of the 1950s and 1960s, as well as one of Hollywood's constant tabloid stories.

Nonetheless, child stars may have family in the "business." For example, Hayley Mills was the daughter of English actor Sir John Mills. Drew Barrymore, who has grown up, gone into recovery and kept her stardom as a young adult, belongs to the Barrymore theatrical dynasty. Others raise the specter of the "stage mother" (*Gypsy*, 1962).

Other popular child stars who have managed to develop later careers include **director** Ron Howard, who started as a sincere young child, Opie, in *The Andy Griffith Show*. Marie and Donny Osmond, who emerged as **Mormon** pop singers in the late 1960s, have tried to resurrect their careers with a **talk show**. Jodie Foster and Cristina Ricci, meanwhile, broke the mold of child stars, presenting darker, more complicated versions of childhood (*Taxi Driver*, 1976; *Adam's Family Values*, 1993). Both have successful adult careers.

EDWARD MILLER

Chin, Frank

b. 1940

Chinese American author and activist. Chin's work has included **poetry**, **novels** (*Donald Duk*, 1991), plays (*Chickencoop Chinaman*, 1981) and essays on literature, voice and identity. As activist and co-editor of the groundbreaking anthology *Aiiieeeee!* (1974), Chin fought to find and preserve a variety of **Asian American** voices in literature and history, while combating racism and stereotypes. This has also led him to bitter debates with novelist Maxine Hong **Kingston** over authenticity and assimilation in the Asian American experience.

GARY McDONOGH
CINDY WONG

China

For the US, China has been a distant land that may be mysterious, enchanting or threatening. While the US, unlike Europe, occupied no protectorate in China during the late nineteenth and early twentieth century, China provided markets for both business people and missionaries. On the other hand, the Chinese have harbored strong suspicions about Americans, balancing admiration of some aspects of techno-modernity by concerns about social and cultural limits. Despite Chinese **immigration** to the US and growing American knowledge of China, suspicions as well as competitions often divide the nations.

The Second World War was a watershed in US–China relations. Fighting the Japanese as allies, the US recognized Chinese citizenship at home and, in Frank **Capra**'s *Battle of China*, touted the nation's commitment to democracy and peace. Yet, seeds of difference were already present that became climactic in the triumph of the Chinese Communist Party in 1949. This change reverberated in the **Cold War** US around claims about "who lost China" and opposition to Chinese communist intervention, played out in **Korea** (and, later, **Vietnam**). American commitments to nationalist forces who had fled to Taiwan nearly led to war in 1955 and 1958, and remain a source of conflict today. Moreover, American–Chinese relations have been triangulated by both states in terms of other ties and conflicts with the Soviet Union, **Japan** and India.

Nonetheless, an important shift in US policy came under Richard **Nixon**, who had baited the People's Republic of China for much of his career. Building on sporadic ongoing diplomatic talks and "ping-pong diplomacy," he sent **Secretary of State** Henry **Kissinger** to Beijing in 1971 for secret talks, followed by Nixon's dramatic state visit in 1972. Recognition of "the mainland," as many Americans refer to it, had repercussions for Taiwan/the People's Republic of China (then a totalitarian regime with strong lobbyists in Washington). Loss of its UN seat and wariness over American commitments and PRC intentions have complicated Taiwan, where America now practices a policy of "strategic ambiguity."

Sino-American contact grew in the 1970s and 1980s not only between people (journalists, scholars, tourists) and ideologies, but also between markets. Yet, in 1989, the US and China again reached point of decision when **television** broadcasted the brutal repression of students in Tiananmen Square, whose Goddess of Liberty recalled the American Statue of Liberty.

Ambivalence on the part of both the US and mainland China has marked subsequent relations.

Commercial ties have driven American corporate and political campaigns for "permanent normal trade relations" and entry into the World Tade Organization. Yet, human rights activists (including many concerned by **religion**), labor organizers and right-wing isolationists decry this rapprochement or demand concessions the Chinese are unwilling to give. This led to bitter confrontations (including those within the **Democratic Party**) before **Congress** approved PNTR status in May, 2000. Others asked why China should be given this status and Cuba embargoed. At the same time, Chinese courting of American support betrays a wariness of American morals as well as policies. Both misunderstanding and necessity will undoubtedly continue into the twenty-first century, despite increasing exchange and communication among their citizens.

Further reading

(1999) *Taiwan, the PRC, and the Taiwan Security Enhancement Act*, Washington, DC: US House of Representatives Committee on International Relations.

Chiang, A. (1988) *The United States and China*, Chicago: University of Chicago.

Christensen, T. (1996) *Useful Adversaries*, Princeton: Princeton University Press.

Vogel, E. (1999) *Living with China*, New York: W.W. Norton.

GARY McDONOGH
CINDY WONG

Chinatown *see* Chinese Americans; ethnic enclaves

Chinese Americans

The largest and longest-established **Asian American** community, Chinese numbers in America have also grown rapidly since 1965 through immigration from Taiwan, Hong Kong, overseas Chinese settlements and the People's Republic of **China**. Chinese Americans have become a so-called "model minority" in terms of success in education, business and even sports. Yet, as political scandals and espionage accusations made

clear in the 1990s, their "Americanness" was quickly called into question as a reflection of international relations as well as stereotypes of difference.

Like other immigrants in nineteenth-century America, Chinese American lives originally centered on involuntary **ethnic enclaves** ("Chinatowns"). Facing slurs, physical abuses and legal restrictions on **immigration** and citizenship, these **ghettos** became refuges for predominantly "bachelor" societies, where the male to female ratio reached 27:1 in 1890. Generally from Guangdong, in southern China, these Toisan/Cantonese laborers established complex "towns" with shops and living quarters. Many associations flourished, replacing the traditional familial support left behind in China. The only non-Chinese in Chinatowns were missionaries and police; for outsiders, these enclaves epitomized urban mystery and danger.

As Chinese immigration developed, Chinatowns were also transformed. Second-generation Chinese Americans became citizens and formed new organizations, such as the Chinese American Citizen Alliance, to express their voices. Chinatowns declined in numbers and vitality in the 1930s, while adapting to American **tourism** and tastes.

Abolition of the Chinese Exclusion Act (1943), the establishment of the People's Republic of China (1949) and the 1965 repeal of the 105 person quota imposed on China have all spurred growth of the Chinese American population in numbers and diversity. Chinatowns still provide familiar surroundings for those with little knowledge of American culture. Many low-skilled workers find jobs in ethnic restaurants and **sweatshops**; with scant knowledge of their rights, they face exploitation by employers. The importance of traditional groups has declined with integration and government social agencies like the Chinatown Planning Council in **New York** City, NY. Some Chinatowns also face **gang** activities (imputed to Vietnamese or Fukienese immigrants), aging populations and clashes with other encroaching urban groups.

At the same time, Chinese communities have left the inner city for outlying places like Flushing (Queens, New York), Greater **Los Angeles, CA** or **Sunbelt** cities. These new suburban enclaves incorporate diverse Chinese in landscapes dotted with Asian **malls** and restaurants. Other Chinese immigrants and their children have adapted quickly to suburban dispersion and rapid assimilation through education and business, sometimes alarming other ethnic groups.

In politics, Chinese Americans have built slowly on the citizenship allowed them after the Second World War and their new numbers. While **Democrat** Michael Woo ran unsuccessfully for **mayor** of Los Angeles, and conservative Matt Fong was defeated in his bid for the governorship of **California** in 1998, Democrat Gary Locke was elected governor of Washington state that same year. Yet the actions of Chinese outside of the US – a tense area of foreign policy – have had an impact on political citizenship. Under **Clinton**, fundraising scandals connected with the People's Republic and Taiwan tarred the civic image of American Chinese. China's access to American nuclear secrets, examined in the 1999 Cox report, seemed to question the actions and connections of all Chinese Americans.

The public face of Chinese as Americans suffers from decades of orientalization, from D.W. Griffith's 1919 *Broken Blossoms* to the 1960s Broadway **musical**/film *Flower Drum Song*. Since the 1960s, Chinese American film-makers, dramatists, novelists and academics have tackled these stereotypes in works by Wayne Wang, Frank **Chin**, Maxine Hong **Kingston**, Amy **Tan** and Gish Jen. Such authors explore the complexities of Chinese American history and intertwine them with other American ethnicities.

See also: Asian Americans; Asians Americans in cinema and television

Further reading

Chen, H. (1993) *Chinatown No More*, Ithaca: Cornell University Press.
Takaki, R. (1998) *Strangers from A Different Shore*, Boston: Little Brown.

CINDY WONG

Chisholm, Shirley

b. 1924

The first **African American** woman ever elected to US Congress, Shirley Chisholm became a member of the New York State Assembly in 1964 following a career working as an educational consultant for **New York** City day-care centers. In 1968 she was elected on the **Democratic** ticket to serve in **Congress**. After re-election in 1971, she lost in the New York presidential primary of 1972 – the first African American to run for this office.

ROBERT GREGG

chocolate

Americans love chocolate. They eat almost twelve pounds per person each year in products made using cocoa, baking chocolate, milk chocolate, and sweet and semi-sweet chocolate, ranking tenth among the world's consumers of chocolate. The first chocolate factory was established in **New England** in1765; names like Hershey and Mars are now synonymous with American chocolate, despite elite brands (Godiva) and local favorites. Chocolate played a role in nourishing American soldiers in the Second World War; US army D-rations still include three four-ounce chocolate bars.

Further reading

"The Story of Chocolate": http://www.candyusa.org

GAIL HENSON

Chomsky, Noam

b. 1928

Dissenting **intellectual** whose theory of linguistics revolutionized the study of **language**, but whose following (much of it European) comes from his radical political analyses. Working at the Massachusetts Institute of Technology in the 1950s, he dismantled behaviorism, the dominant school of thought in the social sciences. Through the study of linguistics, Chomsky showed that **children** did not merely respond to outside stimuli, but had innate capacity for language. The **Vietnam War** turned him towards political analysis, and, in a plethora of works like *American Power and the New Mandarins* (1969) and the essay, "**Cold War** and the university" (1997), he has dissected American imperialism abroad and the corporate capitalist culture at home.

See also: linguistics

ROBERT GREGG

Christian media

The mere title "Christian media" raises an awkward question – are there non-Christian or **atheist** media in the US? Certainly, statements about God and Christian values in the **news**, sports, contests, and **talk shows**, as well as assumptions about church as weekly activity in many series underscore a pervasive civic Christianity. **Jews** have had an ethnic presence in **radio** and **television** since the *Goldbergs* crossed over from radio to the golden age of television and have also had a lively press and literary output. Other religions make only exotic appearances in **mass media**, for example those of **Santería** and **Voudou** in *Miami Vice*, the *Hinduism* of the storeowner Apu in *The Simpsons*, or the mysterious "Chinese-flavored" religion of *Kung Fu*, despite their roles in ethnic media. Christian media, therefore, represent a self-identification within **publishing**, music, radio and television that often questions the morals or purity of other media. In this sense, Christian media start from widely shared knowledge and beliefs within the US and push them further, attacking enemies on the basis of issues and actions more than doctrines. On these foundations, a series of generally **white** male evangelical preachers have built empires that move beyond religion into **politics**, **education** and world affairs (see **Christian Right**). Yet, Christian media also incorporate science-fiction apocalypse, **children**'s games and toys, music videos and slogan-bearing T-shirts.

In some cases, these media have extended revivalist careers like that of Billy **Graham**, who relied on television specials rather than shows. The next step, however, was taken by televangelists like Pat Robertson, Jim and Tammy Faye Baker, Jack Van Impe, Jim Swaggart, Robert Schuyler, Jerry Falwell and others, who found their melodious preaching and fundamentalist answers attracted widespread audiences' support. The Bakers built their PTL (Praise the Lord) network into an empire, including a Christian Heritage **theme park** before it crashed on charges of embezzlement and improprieties. Robertson, with his 777 Club, used televangelism as a springboard for presidential politics, while Falwell has used Liberty College and his network to assert influence over issues from **abortion** to homosexuality. The media presence of such figures, however, does not equate to readership or support, as mass movements based in Christian media have discovered.

By contrast, **African Americans** have tended to become better known in local broadcasting, although Reverend "Ike" made a long career out of miracles, prayer-cloths and fundraising over national radio. Catholics, too, have generally had a quieter role in Christian media. Bishop Fulton J. Sheen showed a shrewd knowledge of television in the 1950s, but Catholic broadcasting has tended to be pious, local and focused on issues from the Eucharist to shut-ins. The Evangelical World Network, however, made a star out of the maternal nun Mother Angelica and raised the presence of conservative and evangelical Catholicism on **cable** nationwide.

In 1998 Lowell Paxson's PAX network launched a national network of Christian content – generally tame asexual series like reruns of *Touched by an Angel* or family game and variety shows rather than evangelists. In 1999 NBC acquired a substantial interest in PAX. Beyond radio and television, Christian media tend to synthesize old and new forms, which is apparent from venerable publishers like Zondervan or the Paulist Press. Christian bookstores, Christian music stations, concerts and church events all insist on Christian media and their message as alternatives to American corporate control even as these corporations themselves have invested in Christian media.

Further reading

Bruce, S. (1990) *Pray Television*, London: Routledge.

Kintz, L. and Lesage, J. (eds) (1998) *Media, Culture and the Religious Right*, Minneapolis: University of Minnesota.

Peck, J. (1994) *Gods of Televangelism*, Cresskill: Hampton.

GARY McDONOGH
CINDY WONG

Christian music

Accounting for a small fraction of American music sales, Christian music exists at the margins of the music business. For example, most religious albums are sold not at record stores but through religious bookstores. Many artists find tension between the view of their work as a religious ministry and the economic need to make profitable, popular music. Like the secular country music industry, the Christian music industry is based in **Nashville**, Tennessee, and is most popular in the Southern **Bible belt** states. Well-known Christian music artists include Amy Grant, the group DC Talk and Michael W. Smith.

A. JOSEPH BORRELL

Christian Right

Debates among **Republican** presidential hopefuls in the 2000 campaign again highlighted the presence of organized conservative Christians as both **lobbyists** and voters in American governance. The generally **white** male leadership of militant organizations like Ralph Reed, Jerry Falwell (founder of the Moral Majority), Pat Robertson (founder of the Christian Coalition) and Gary Bauer (founder of the Campaign for Working Families) have an impact not only through churches and followers, but also through **Christian media**, education and money; Robertson and Bauer have sought the presidential nomination in their own right. The popular base of these leaders and platforms, which have become contested votes in elections for decades, are more paradoxical. In a nation whose citizens generally define themselves as believers and whose everyday culture is permeated by Christian traditions, some also identify themselves as members of a beleaguered cultural minority, while others vary with regard to the public agenda of the Christian right.

As a political force, the Christian right has defined Christianity around sometimes exclusive beliefs and practices. While these groups may coincide with **Roman Catholics** on specific issues like **abortion**, for example, there are serious differences on other issues, including **capital punishment** and social welfare, as well as rhetoric that identifies the Christian right with Protestant fundamentalism. While women constitute primary agents in **family values** and the Christian household, spokespeople tend to be male and public positions often insist on a subservient helpmate and domestic femininity. And, while the traditions of **African American** churches are deeply rooted, social experiences and social agendas have also created a critical stance *vis-à-vis* the Christian right as a cultural and political movement among this and other minority populations.

Moreover, the political agenda of the Christian right focuses on key issues that define an interesting theological and political network within the broader possibilities of Christian belief and practice. In addition to protection of the **family** and the unborn, other recurrent themes include defending **marriage** against gay and **lesbian** claims, **school prayer**, **tax** reform, national defense, a moral and patriotic foreign policy and educational reform. The sexual scandals of the **Clinton** White House have provided vocal contrasts with regard to public morals and personal behavior, although critics in all these areas have harped upon the Christian need for tolerance and forgiveness and underscored the foibles of highly personalized leaders. While the focus of debate, moreover, often centers on national politics, grassroots organizations have had a strong impact at the local level (**school boards**) and in states of the **Bible belt**.

Conservative Christians themselves prove more varied. Some will embrace cultural issues but remain independent in areas of foreign policy or social welfare. Others adopt more culturally separatist positions, rejecting the messages of sexuality, consumption and the glamour of **mass media** – in extreme cases, they have created white supremacist/separatist factions. Still others separate religious beliefs and political action. Yet others seek to impose their beliefs, especially at a local level, through insertion of Christian teachings into school curricula, whether by posting the Ten Commandments in classrooms or by fighting against the teaching of evolution (see **scientific creationism**).

Attacks on the Christian right, from various political perspectives, respond to all these points – the actions and intolerance of individual leaders, the connections and contradictions among agenda issues (why protect the unborn and yet kill criminals?) and, especially, the place of sectarian values in a pluralistic society based on the separation of church and state. In an era where both Republican and **Democratic** presidential candidates are born-again Christians, this cross-cutting debate over religious culture, political strategy and "American values" proves both heated and divisive.

Further reading

Barkun, M. (1994) *Religion and the Racist Right*, Chapel Hill: University of North Carolina.

Kintz, L. and Lesage, J. (eds) (1998) *Media, Culture and the Religious Right*, Minneapolis: University of Minnesota.

Lienesch, M. (1993) *Redeeming America*, Chapel Hill: University of North Carolina.

Rozell, M. and Wilcox, C. (eds) (1995) *God at the Grass Roots*, Lanham: Rowman and Littlefield.

Wilcox, C. (1996) *Onward Christian Soldiers?*, Boulder: Westview.

GARY McDONOGH

Christian Scientists

American Christian denomination founded by Mary Baker Eddy (1821–1910). The Church of Christ, Scientist combines biblical devotion with faith in the healing powers of God through prayer. Expanding as the nation negotiated modernity at the turn of the twentieth century, its numbers peaked after the Second World War, with between 100,000 and 150,000 adherents worldwide. Known for imposing churches as well as many urban reading rooms, the church has also published the influential national **newspaper** *Christian Science Monitor* and made other forays into mass media.

See also: self-help; religion

GARY McDONOGH

cigars

In industrial America, the "stogie" became an emblem of masculine success, an appendage of political bosses and driving businessmen, or an invitation to adulthood in the private rooms of elites. Although some cigars are produced in the US and Central America, the post-Castro **Cuba** embargo devastated sales and yet taunted America for decades. In the 1990s, however, new generations revived the cigar as a marker of success and exclusivity in smoking clubs chronicled in celebrity magazines like *Cigar Aficionado*. Sales rose 50 percent between 1993 and 1997. In 1999 the Federal Trade Commission, concerned by smokers who considered cigars a safer alternative to cigarettes, requested mandatory health warnings.

GARY McDONOGH

Cimino, Michael

b. 1943

Michael Cimino's career exemplifies **Hollywood** hubris. Before age thirty, Cimino co-scripted the second "Dirty Harry" movie, *Magnum Force* (1973), starring Clint **Eastwood**, which examined the destructiveness of the Vietnam experience on four veteran cops. In 1978 Cimino directed and co-wrote the moody, Vietnam-themed *The Deer Hunter*, which won the Academy **Award** for Best Picture and gave Cimino the artistic and commercial freedom to direct his next project at the then-unheard of budget of $40 million. When *Heaven's Gate* (1980) flopped, the historic film studio United Artists went bankrupt and Cimino's promising career took a dive.

Further reading

Bach, S. (1985) *Final Cut: Dreams and Disaster in the*

Making of Heaven's Gate, New York: William Morrow.

MELINDA SCHWENK

Cincinnati, Ohio

Industrial and commercial center on the Ohio River, Cincinnati has long been characterized as a bastion of conservative **Republican** culture, with strong German, Irish and Catholic institutions, as well as a Protestant elite epitomized in the Republican Taft family. This conservatism, however, has been challenged by the city's universities and artists, including a famous debate over the obscenity of a 1989 Robert **Mapplethorpe** exhibit at the Contemporary Arts Center. Cincinnati also hosts strong professional sports traditions, including **football**'s Bengals and **baseball**'s Reds, whose owner, Marge Schott, was censored for racist remarks. Hence the city of 345,818 people (metro 1,948,264), despite its placid, home-town image, entails continual complexities and contradictions – indeed, shock **talk-show** host Jerry Springer was once its **mayor**.

GARY McDONOGH

circus

From its inception as entertainment during the Roman Empire, the circus has come to represent broadly any form of extravaganza that includes trained animal acts and human feats of strength and skill. Growing out of the decline of the sprawling, disreputable fairs of the eighteenth century, the modern circus' most common venue is the three-ring "Big Top," an enormous tent with temporary stadium seating that travels from town to town by rail or truck. Several different types of acts, such as trick horse riding, clowns and trapeze artists, may run simultaneously. Ringling Brothers, combined with Barnum & Bailey, has come to be the best-known traveling circus in the US. Circuses now face dilemmas from restrictions on animals to corporate control.

JIM WATKINS

Cisneros, Sandra

b. 1954

The daughter of a Mexican American mother and Mexican father, Sandra Cisneros grew up in poverty and spent much of her childhood moving back and forth between Mexico City and **Chicago, IL**. Her writing reflects this state of migrancy with its apparent longing for rootedness. Cisneros' award-winning works, the novel *House on Mango Street* (1983) and her book of poems, *My Wicked Wicked Ways* (1987), have made her a leading figure in **Chicana** literature.

ROBERT GREGG

cities

The United States is extremely urban: 80 percent of all people live in metropolitan areas, and over half of all citizens live in the forty metropolitan areas with a population of over 1 million. Cities have provided a "melting-pot" for the people, races, classes, genders and identities which constitute contemporary America. Nonetheless, American practices and values of urban living exist alongside centuries of anti-urban prejudice that identifies cities as hostile zones. These attitudes have been built into imagery as well as the political and economic structures of individual states and counties (which may control cities) and the nation as a whole – an ongoing encounter between utopian "cities on a hill" and *Bladerunner*.

American city-regions have been torn apart by political, social and economic changes met by contradictory efforts to reform and to escape. Post-Second World War decades have left a crippling legacy of urban decay alongside old and new monuments of urban power. Established industrial centers like **Philadelphia, PA** and **Detroit, MI** have hemorrhaged jobs, production and population, although **New York**, the largest American city, is expanding as a global metropolis, as is **Los Angeles, CA** as a **Pacific Rim** capital. Meanwhile, both **suburbs** and **Sunbelt** cities have exploded: in 1990 **Houston** overtook Philadelphia to become the nation's fourth-largest city. Yet new cities and metropolitan areas, like older ones, face racial and class polarizations, new transnational populations and shifting positions in world markets. Moreover, **white flight**, **crime**, drugs and poverty must balance creative urban expression in **rap**, centers for gay politics, strong ethnic voices and social movements from beatniks to **yuppies**.

History and process

Modern American urban strengths *and* dilemmas have taken shape through history. Despite the economic and cultural centrality of early cities, many saw them as dangerous reminders of European decadence in a nation of yeomen farmers and plantation households. By the industrial era, visions of cities as dank warrens for immigrant masses (for whom they nonetheless offered other dreams) or glittering domains of vice contrasted with traditional towns, fertile plains and open **frontiers**. Even reformers who sought to save the city often saw it primarily as a problem. The city was a place of paradox and conflict: while skyscrapers soared upwards in **Chicago, IL** and New York, other residents huddled in crowded tenements, fought in crowded streets or escaped via street cars, railroads and **automobiles**.

By the 1920s, cities held the majority of US citizens and formed nationwide webs of production, transportation and **information**, while providing **healthcare**, **education**, entertainment and **mass media**. As external **immigration** was curtailed, **African Americans** intensified their escape from southern farmlands, seeking work and equality in northern cities. Cities were associated with dreams and opportunities, whether in **Hollywood**, **Harlem**, or **Greenwich Village**. New urbanites used their opportunities both to join the mainstream and to explore difference – of race, gender, sexuality, politics, belief or lifestyle – an option that remains a subversive element of the city. The city thus seemed both tempting and dangerous to democratic society (and **white** hegemony).

The Second World War deepened rather than resolved the questions of previous decades. During the war, cities were magnets as production geared up after the Depression and incorporated women and blacks in newly autonomous roles. Returning **veterans**, however, re-envisioned an America based on domestic piety and opportunity, symbolized in the car and the suburb. Tract developments like **Levittown** became homes for new ex-urban generations, although linked by **family**, work and culture to nearby cities. Here many **baby boomers** grew up, placing demands on lands of **lawns** and **malls** while downtown became a place for Christmas displays, **zoos**, **museums** and ball games.

Crises and responses

Alongside new suburbanization, the historic congestion of cities provoked uneasiness. The "urban crises" of the 1960s, arising from shifts of production, population and resources, were often aggravated by the very plans to solve them like **urban renewal** and the **War on Poverty**. Attempts to open cities to all citizens in schools, jobs and politics, for example, led to confrontations among African Americans and Euro-Americans. This spurred some to flee the city while others became frustrated at the slow pace of reforms: riots scarred cities from Los Angeles to Detroit in the 1960s. Meanwhile, efforts to make the city attractive to suburbanites through pedestrian malls, highway accessibility and new public events and spaces cut through traditional **neighborhoods** and patterns of ethnic and **inner-city** life.

Some cities tried to escape politics, replacing **mayors** with city managers or professional planners, or consolidating city and county functions. Yet cities, suburbs and rural areas competed for state and federal funds. Programs like the **Model Cities** campaign raised high expectations but were only incompletely funded and caught in multiple bureaucracies. Nor could cheap and cosmetic reforms tackle the underlying problems of **deindustrialization**, shifting global production and disappearing jobs.

With riots, flight and decay in inner-city neighborhoods, American cities seemed to face dismal prospects in the 1980s, despite the nation's ever-increasing urbanization. This apparent paradox is explained by how Americans choose to live – *near* cities rather than in them. Cities remain centers for commerce, culture, sports, media and education. Yet, their populations risk polarization between the very poor and the rich, with **middle** classes in enclaves or suburbs. Hence, urban institutions realized the utility of branches outside their traditional venues – stores, multiplex cinemas, work **campuses** and new stadiums have become as much a part of the suburban landscape as of American downtowns. Second and third generation suburbanites might experience everyday life in **edge cities** or amidst clusters of malls, schools and work without ever going "to the city."

Yet other trends also balance this centripetal consolidation. First, urban growth continues to take new and creative forms as cities bring together new lifestyles and developments in transportation, tourism and services. Houston and **Dallas** have oil and computers, **Miami, FL** is a capital for Latin America, **Atlanta, GA** hosts strong media and commercial centers and **Seattle** offers aircraft and computers. The search for new opportunities also has renewed the potential of older cities, like New York's Silicon Alley or Philadelphia's attempt to concentrate sophisticated medical services.

Second, the changing needs of older cities have demanded new directions in urban use and value. Planners have created new urban public places and have re-thought urban life in more suburban terms with individualized homes and more green space. Downtowns, for example, may become specialized centers for culture, entertainment and meetings among metropolitan residents, the hub of many smaller urban complexes. Recycling historic buildings through preservation or even entire neighborhoods as urban service centers also has created new urban foci, like Inner Harbor of **Baltimore, MD**. Other cities have turned factories (Ghirardelli Square in **San Francisco, CA**), train stations (**Cincinnati**), post offices (**Washington, DC**), **markets** and other monuments of past urban life into new multipurpose attractions, although all stress consumption. Residentially, **gentrification** brings new people and investment into fixing up older urban neighborhoods, from Philadelphia's Society Hill to Nob Hill in San Francisco. These processes, again, have created conflicts with those dispossessed by rising property values or objecting to the destruction of living history in favor of a mythic/consumerist appropriation of the past. Still, conflict is neither new or avoidable in cities, even as people search for more just and incorporative development.

Finally, since the 1970s, old and new cities have grown from both young, transient American populations and new immigration from East and Southeast Asia, Latin America and other nations. Koreatowns, African markets and **Latino** barrios have grown or emerged anew in cities across the US. Twenty-somethings have created new spaces in **Boston**, Atlanta, GA and Los Angeles. Legal and illegal immigrants find safety and familiarity in numbers, shared customs and **language**, although exploitation has been evident within groups as well as in conflicts between them. Tensions between Koreans, blacks and **Hispanics**, for example, flared in the Los Angeles riots of 1992. Ethnic communities also have their own suburban flights, resulting in suburban Chinese cities around Los Angeles, California or New York City's new Chinatown in Flushing (Queens).

Other grassroots trajectories towards urban revitalization include new integration through public art and culture, including "alternative" facilities and sponsorship of artists like New York's **SoHo**. By contrast, the Castro Street area in San Francisco and New York's Greenwich Village have become centers of strongly self-conscious gay communities. In still other cases, squatters' movements have reclaimed abandoned housing and neighborhoods have turned the empty lands of urban renewal into community gardens.

In the new millennium, American cities evidently face problems as well as opportunities. As their infrastructures age, cities become more expensive to maintain than new suburban growth – despite the pollution, energy expenditures, social issues and time intrinsic to such diffuse housing. Dualization concerns critics because of its vivid inequalities as well as the expense this entails in education and **welfare** for a shrinking tax base. New cities and suburbs also risk the planning problems of suburban sprawl, economic concentration and overly rapid expansion that plagued their forebears. Neither these divisions, nor the ravages of drugs, urban epidemics of tuberculosis and **AIDS**, nor the growth of dependent welfare populations that challenge modern American cities, are products of cities in isolation, nor can they be resolved there. Those who have sorted themselves out into exclusive suburbs, paying less in the short run, are nevertheless still responsible as national citizens in an urban state.

In fact, are there any real competitors to take the place of the city? Suburbs often lack the sense of name, place and distinction that made New Yorkers proud enemies of Philadelphians, Chicagoans or Angelenos (the anti-Christ). Critics also argue that the class (and racial) division of suburbs also relinquishes the history of confrontation and learning from difference through which the city has created and renewed the US itself. The **Internet** also has been characterized as a new global city, complete with urban functions of market, forum and arcade, but again this may be premature. New technologies in the past raised similar concerns – telephones, movies and **television** were all seen as potential destroyers of American urban sociability and the destructive impact of automotive mobility posed a particular warning. Yet people often have shown flexibility in combining innovation and community: the Internet manages multiple tasks, opening up the city for sharing with friends and colleagues while having **coffee** and e-mail at an urban café. This information highway, however, does not incorporate everyone equally, nor does it resolve dilemmas of class, race and gender.

The diversity of American cities then, represents both the history and potential of an America of different cultures, people and opportunities, both conflicts and urban creations. To juxtapose the dark visions of *Batman* (1989) or *Who Killed Vincent Chin?* (1988) with the sunny suburban homes of *ET* (1982) or the peaceful rural retreats of *On Golden Pond* (1991) and some **children's literature** overstates both the values and divisions of contemporary American culture. Suburbs and even rural areas are no longer seen to be innocent of social and cultural problems, from domestic abuse to **gangs** to Walmart. Meanwhile, New Year's Eve in **Times Square**, presidential inaugurations and protest marches, using Washington, DC as their stage, and the **Olympic Games** of Atlanta and Los Angeles show how the urbanity of America is celebrated and built upon for the future. Its contradictions and complexities, in fact, are part of the character to be experienced individually in the cities that constitute the order of the pastoral nation.

Further reading

The American city has provoked elegies and polemics throughout its history. Among myriad texts in which these arguments might be pursued, consider:

Cisneros, H. (ed.) (1993) *Interwoven Destinies*, New York: W.W. Norton (the literature is vast but provides an interesting overview, balancing M. Sorkin's more critical 1992 collection).

Sorkin, M. (1992) *Variations on a Theme Park*, New York: Hill & Wang.

Jacobs, J. (1961) *The Death and Life of American Cities*, New York: Vintage (among classic studies of the modern city, it has had an enduring power).

Malcolm X (1965) *The Autobiography of Malcolm X*, New York: Grove (many urban works underscore problems, but as a personal choice this remains a compelling starting point).

GARY McDONOGH
CINDY WONG

city hall

"You can't fight city hall" is an American adage that expresses frustration with political power. Yet local government buildings also embody emblems and stories of the city. The movie *Philadelphia* (1993) opens with an aerial view of City Hall – a proud Second Empire-style building (1871–1901), replacing the older federalist one at Independence Hall. **Philadelphia, PA**'s costly project sought to be the tallest building in America, but fell into later disrepair with 1970s deindustrialization. Other edifices epitomize nineteenth-century industrial America or later Beaux-Arts urban reform (**St Louis, MO**, **San Francisco, CA**); **New York**'s 1803–11 miniature palace proves distinctly understated in a towering city. Fanciful revivals of Indian and Spanish motifs in the 1920s, the skyscraper **Los Angeles, CA** built to demarcate a new downtown (1926–8) and **Buffalo**'s art deco tower (1929–32) illustrate subsequent visions of modernity. A third wave of city halls emerged with 1960s **urban renewal** and increased federal presence, encompassing sculptural modernism in **Las Vegas** or **Dallas** (designed by I.M. **Pei**,

1965–78) and a federal local center for civic renewal in **Boston, MA**. Like the offices they shelter, all these city halls convey urban aspirations, memory, identity and power.

Further reading

Lebovich, W. (1984) *America's City Halls*, New York: Preservation Press.

GARY McDONOGH

City University of New York (CUNY)

Formed in 1961 from municipal institutions and serving almost 220,000 students, CUNY includes eleven urban colleges, six **community colleges**, law, medical and graduate programs. Descended from the Free Academy of 1847, CUNY remained free of tuition fees until 1973. Long the immigrants' springboard out of poverty, its student body has evolved from an earlier dominance of mostly Jewish, leftist **intellectuals** to its current diverse range of **African American**, **Arab American**, **Latino** and **Asian American** populations. As state and city funding have been slashed, however, CUNY faces increasing pressure to balance generally open admissions with "efficient results," a controversy polarizing university and city.

JAMES KRAUS

civic religion *see* religion

Civil Rights Acts

Following the **Supreme Court**'s *Brown v. Board of Education* decision, **Congress** began to enact legislation to protect the civil and voting rights of **African Americans**. The first piece of such legislation to be enacted since Reconstruction was the **Civil Rights Act** of 1957, which made it a federal crime to interfere with a citizen's right to vote. It also established the Civil Rights Commission to investigate any violations of the new law. In 1964 in the aftermath of the March on Washington

and the **assassination** of President **Kennedy**, **Johnson** passed a more far-reaching civil-rights bill designed to end discrimination in employment "based on race, color, religion, sex, or national origin." "Sex" was added by Southern opponents of the bill in the hopes of killing it, but to their chagrin it was passed anyway. The Equal Employment Opportunity Commission (EEOC) was established at this time to enforce the Act.

To bolster the 1957 law protecting voting rights the 24th Amendment was ratified in 1964, banning the levying of poll taxes in federal elections. Johnson followed this up with a Voting Rights Act in the next year, after Martin Luther **King**, Jr.'s march from Selma to Montgomery, Alabama, which had dramatized the voting issue. Banning poll taxes and literacy tests, the Act authorized the **Attorney-General** to send federal examiners to register black voters whenever necessary. Within a year a quarter of a million new black voters had been registered. The Voting Rights Act was re-adopted and strengthened in 1970, 1975 and 1982.

In 1991, in the face of several reverses and a weakening of the civil-rights laws at the hands of **Reagan** and **Bush** Supreme Court appointees, **Democrats** deemed it essential to enact another civil-rights bill, which would make the language relating to discrimination more explicit. More recently, gays and lesbians have been advocating for extension of civil-rights law to include sexual preference, while in 2000 laws protecting against age discrimination have been under assault.

ROBERT GREGG

Civil Rights movement

The Civil Rights movement spanned two decades (*c.*1948–68) in the historic battle for **African American** freedom in the United States. Its impacts were regional, nationwide and international. The movement was a unique partnership among local activists, national civil-rights organizations and the federal government, especially the federal courts. This partnership flourished most visibly between 1948 and 1965. During those seventeen years, the post-Reconstruction Southern system of race control was dismantled.

The movement is by far the largest interracial mass movement in American history. It changed the basic practice of race relations in the nation. The movement brought dignity, self-respect and national admiration to poor black people who had long been repressed and ignored, especially in the **South**. The movement also redefined the meaning of **freedom** in America. It established the right of the individual to protection from state or privately instituted discrimination. More importantly, it established the obligation of the federal government to serve as primary protector of individual rights.

The movement caused millions of Americans to embrace and celebrate the ideals expressed in the Declaration of Independence, the **Bill of Rights** and the "equal protection" clause of the 14th Amendment. For the first time in national history, a significant majority of the people believed the goals of freedom, justice and equality for all could be realized. While it would not fulfill the expectations of many, especially among African Americans, the movement still eradicated permanently the national acceptance of overt racist assumptions and practices.

Haphazard, erratic and disruptive throughout its course, its leadership often divided in conflict; nevertheless the movement managed to articulate certain commonly shared goals. Most central were the elimination of Jim Crow **segregation** and black disenfranchisement in the former Confederate States. These specific goals determined the origins, strategies and tactics of the movement during its most active phase.

The movement emerged in the aftermath of the Second World War because of changes in the African American population, in the Federal Government and in international affairs. Hundreds of thousands of black Americans had migrated to northern **cities** where they could vote, while enjoying lessened discrimination and better employment. Tens of thousands of black men had fought in the War and experienced the liberating influences of new, less racist environments. They and their families were no longer willing to suffer the institutionalized terror of Southern white racism. During this same era, the Depression and the War had increased the scope and size of the federal government. Most importantly, the national government had evolved an expanding role as protector of citizen rights, primarily in the economic arena up to 1945. With the coming of the **Cold War**, the United States claimed leadership of the "Free World," competing with the Soviet bloc for the allegiance of the underdeveloped, predominantly colored nations of the world. America's treatment of its own citizens of color was believed to be a potential determining factor in this international contest.

The convergence of these larger socio-political forces ignited the movement and a series of dramatic episodes ultimately resulting in landmark civil-rights legislation. The desegregation of the military in 1948 is less renowned than the later *Brown* decision of the **Supreme Court**, a case brought by the **NAACP**. Nonetheless, military desegregation incorporated all the forces that came to work in the movement for the next decades and, like them, had consequences far broader than anticipated. President **Truman**'s executive order integrating the armed services coincided with efforts by liberal Democrats to attract new black voters in northern cities. The Cold War necessitated a large, standing military. Black men were needed as career soldiers, but they would not submit to the racist treatment that had previously characterized the military. Much of the newly integrated force was stationed in the South, undermining the racial mores of the surrounding segregated communities. As veterans re-entered the civilian sector, many of the whites brought with them new acceptance of African Americans as co-workers, even supervisors, and many of the blacks developed new self-confidence and assertiveness in integrated settings.

The Montgomery Bus Boycott resulted in further evolution of the local black activist/federal government alliance and revealed the basic strategy of the movement. The targets for change would be southern segregation and voter discrimination. This strategy enabled movement activists to appeal to the majority of white Americans who lived outside the South. The movement's demands were presented simply as appeals to basic constitutional rights guaranteed to all. Participants in the movement also invoked the rhetoric of Christian salvation for this secular cause. Thus the movement incorporated two of the strongest impulses in the American character – belief in democratic principles and in Protestant Christianity.

The tactic of non-violent, direct action challenged Southern segregation and disenfranchisement as protesters refused to obey manifestly "unjust laws." Leaders (for example, Martin Luther **King**, Jr., Ralph **Abernathy**, James **Farmer** and Bayard **Rustin**) skillfully used the media, especially **television**, to contrast the dignity and righteousness of the abused demonstrators with the brutal and profane behavior of white **police** and citizenry. Through the boycott of city **buses** or **department stores**, local black activists utilized economic pressure to divide the white community while energizing and giving a sense of empowerment to their **working-class** supporters.

In the original bus boycott, victory resulted from a combination of the municipal surrender to black demands and the federal court decision outlawing segregated buses. **Sit-ins** and withholding of patronage led to gradual desegregation of some chain stores. The **Freedom Rides** of the early 1960s ultimately provoked the intervention of the federal courts and the Justice Department, even though they could not immediately end segregation in interstate transportation, and, throughout the 1950s, Southern **public schools** remained overwhelmingly segregated.

The high-water mark of the Civil Rights era – the March on Washington on August 28, 1963 – epitomized the movement's strengths and weaknesses. It was a magnificent spectacle. Two hundred thousand black and white Americans joined together peacefully professing shared social and religious visions and demanding specific reform that they believed would ennoble all Americans and provide a model to the rest of the world. There were, however, many discordant voices at the march. Many complained that the declared goals were too circumscribed, that African Americans needed protection from *de facto* discrimination and economic impoverishment in the North, as well as from *de jure* segregation in the South. Local leaders complained that the march had been co-opted by the nationally heralded leaders and white authorities.

No concrete change followed immediately from the march. In fact, some Southern opponents redoubled their efforts to defeat civil-rights reform. Nevertheless, the partnership embodied by the march prevailed. Within two years, the first significant civil-rights legislation since 1876 was enacted: the Civil Rights Act of 1964 and the Voting Rights Act of 1965.

After these legislative successes, the movement began to dissipate for several reasons. Most important was that many whites in the civil-rights partnership, including those in the federal government, believed that the principal goals of the movement had been achieved. Segregation in public accommodations was outlawed, the courts had been empowered to force school desegregation and the Justice Department could now intervene to guarantee fair elections throughout the South. Because of the movement's achievements, the demand for equality was taken up in northern black **ghettos**, among the poor, women, gays and lesbians and other national minorities. But opponents of change became better organized and effective, using the movement's techniques in their struggles, for example, to end **busing** or **abortion**. At the same time, white liberals redirected much of their energies to opposing the war in **Vietnam**. They also experienced confusion and anger at the rise of black cultural nationalism among African Americans despondent at the nation's failure to create a non-racist society.

Despite unfulfilled goals, the Civil Rights movement demonstrated the power of ordinary citizens to force permanent change when societal circumstances and the courage of both common people and their leaders converge to achieve an end. The movement transformed the meaning of freedom nationally and internationally. It established that governments are responsible for guaranteeing the rights of their citizens and that they may be legitimately resisted when they do not. Within the United States, the movement ended the right of white people to publicly humiliate black people. It invalidated claims to privilege based on color. It altered the basic practice of race relations, if not always the basic prejudices underneath. It has inspired freedom movements abroad from Eastern Europe to South Africa to **China**. The movement clearly sparked determined resistance to continued change by privileged elites in America. Nevertheless, the movement transformed and elevated Americans' expectations of themselves. That may be its most lasting consequence.

Further reading

Eagles, C. (ed.) (1986) *The Civil Rights Movement in America*, Oxford: University Press of Mississippi.

King, R. (1996) *Civil Rights and the Idea of Freedom*, Athens: University of Georgia Press.

Sitkoff, H. (1981) *The Struggle for Black Equality*, New York: Hill & Wang.

ROBERT FRANCIS ENGS

Clark, Dick *see* music, popular; television

class

Paul Fussell, in his wry analysis of class markers and behaviors, cites a woman who, asked by interviewers if she thought there were social classes in America, answered "It's the dirtiest thing I've ever heard of." Divisions by class, sometimes expressed in terms of **race** or **ethnicity**, pose fundamental problems for a nation based on premises of liberty, equality and justice for all. In fact, while such divisions clearly exist in the US, as in all industrial/post-industrial societies, the unique feature of American class is its consistent denial in public rhetoric. Narratives of upward **mobility** – the classic Horatio Alger story, after a nineteenth-century popular children's who specialized in rags to riches tales – are seen as proven in each generation by entrepreneurs, celebrities and even presidents, from Abraham Lincoln to Bill **Clinton**. When asked about their own class position, in turn, most Americans will identify themselves as **middle class**, whether they are poor or rich. In doing so, many Americans deny class as a system, and will find issues relating to sexuality, drugs, race and **religion** easier topics to address in news and social gatherings. However, this denial hides a deep status anxiety about falling out of the middle class or being overtaken and supplanted by rising social groups, which has often animated American politics.

When discussed, class is treated in the generally Weberian sense of status (or consumption), rather than in relation to a Marxist framework of political economics and power (for example, Vance Packard's (1959) *The Status Seekers*). Studies of class, in fact, have often been diffused by an ideological construction of a classless society, and have tended to use this construction as the basis for assuming that the "American experience" is "exceptional." For example, David Potter embodied such assumptions in a chapter title from the *People of Plenty* (1954), simply "Abundance, Mobility, and Status." These assumptions were widely held in the 1950s period of suburbanization and rapid economic growth, and still retain a strong hold in American political and cultural discourses.

Attacks on those who have concentrated and reproduced American social and economic power, from slave-owners to robber barons, often have centered on the violation of this classlessness rather than any sense of an ongoing struggle between classes (which might have been classified as communist during the **Cold War**). Studies that revealed the stratification of American society, like William Lloyd Warner's (1963) *Yankee City* or C. Wright Mills' (1951) *White Collar*, also focused on a wide range of features to define class, including housing, **education** and heritage. Moreover, such works did not pose an attack on the classes per se. Instead, as Warner's *Social Class in America* noted, they were intended as "corrective instruments," permitting "men and women better to evaluate their social situations and thereby better adapt themselves to social reality and fit their dreams and aspirations to what is possible" (1949: 5).

This sense of class means that political economic reform focuses on mediation rather than systemic analysis or conflict. That is, attacks on the rich stress obligations or deviations rather than structural polarizations, ignoring and ensuring the reproduction of class through economic and social capital. Reforms for the poor seek to bring them into the middle class rather than change a system that demands unemployment and low-wage work in order to survive. For those in between, adapting to class rather than changing it becomes the norm. The assumption is that Americans need to have "the hidden injuries of class" (see R. Sernett and J. Cobb's (1972) book with the same title) revealed to them; they are not self-evident and nor do they form the basis of strong class consciousness.

Even oppositional **intellectuals** have tended to diminish class in their analyses. The New **Left** intellectuals of the 1960s and 1970s discussed the emergence of corporate capitalism and showed how other elements in society, from the middle class "**organization man**" to working-class trade **unions**, were brought into the corporate consensus. The only opposition that could be hoped for, they argued, would be countercultural rather than anti-capitalist. Similarly, feminists in the same period described the American consensus in terms of patriarchy, and tended to underestimate the extent to which class (and **race**) differences would divide the feminist movement.

African American intellectuals, focusing on race, have also tended to ignore class on both sides of the racial divide. The **civil-rights** movement seemed to suggest that blacks could be integrated into a mainstream, which was often defined in a uniform, classless way. Black nationalists, meanwhile, talked in terms of a similarly uniform white society from which blacks needed to remain separate. Class divisions among African Americans have also been overlooked; the overriding tendency has been to define black communities in singular ways, characterized by the **ghetto** and the "Black Church." That African American communities have been sites of great divisions, has been evident since W.E.B. **Du Bois**' (1899) *The Philadelphia Negro*. Yet, where recognized, intra-racial antagonisms and stratification have also adopted a language of status (religion, color, gender and occupation) rather than that of class.

Similarly, calls for multiculturalism which recognize that society has moved beyond a strict bi-racial system have also deflected attention from class. While blacks may remain as a politically and economically constructed lower class, the sense of caste and status embodied in the term "ethnicity" has taken on ironic overtones as non-Asian Americans explain **Asian American** success. Clearly demarcated ethnic groups, while bringing different cultural practices to the fore from those of WASP (white, Anglo-Saxon Protestant) culture, will often be seen to be pushing for better status rather than highlighting potential social conflict. Moreover, in **gender** and class terms, what particular ethnic groups may project about themselves (for example, "strong" families and economically successful members of the community) may be very similar to those to whom they wish to be compared. Finally, in this area it is important to note that the commonly applied system of redressing past wrongs, namely **affirmative action**, is undertaken using the language of race and minorities rather than class.

Consumption patterns have also complicated class. While **fashion**, **automobiles**, housing, education, **language** and style all convey differences, many tokens of status are also taken to be accessible on the basis of money or work, especially in an age of affluence and global power. Hence, elitist associations with an **Ivy League** education are diminished somewhat by the belief that high grades and financial aid may make such opportunities available to the non-wealthy, while the same associations attached to clothes and style may be balanced by individual taste and discount shopping. Nevertheless, more complex differences indicate the perdurance of class formation. Those who vacation in Europe during college breaks or those who throw together Chanel and Prada to make their fashion statements lay claim to different class positions from those who have to "make do."

Mass media also mystify discussions of class. In the aftermath of the death of John F. **Kennedy**, Jr., for example, the news media were caught between a justification for devoting so much airtime to the accident because he was "like royalty" and their insistence that he was a "regular guy" or the nation's son. In the process, the facts that he was a grandson of one of the wealthiest men in the country and the stepson of one of the wealthiest men in the world, Aristotle Onassis, were lost. Discussing class origins and attributes (including the fact that he was flying his own private plane), would have seemed un-American in public discourse, which presumed the world would know about **celebrity** vacation spots like Martha's Vineyard.

Even where one might find class most noticeable, in the discussion of poverty, it may be explained away in terms of moral failure, a "culture of poverty" or a problematic **underclass**. The lower classes, it is argued, are where they are, not because of structural impediments brought about by capitalism, but simply because they are not working hard enough, focusing on sex or games, or the drinking class as a state of grace. One notes this in **Reagan** era debates over aid to the worthy poor that presumes everyone who wants to work can do so, which spawned the 1990s **welfare**

reform. This reform also underscores an insidious gendering of class in a society where women must work and also be responsible for childcare without support (explored by Katherine Newman (1999) in *Falling from Grace*).

As Richard Hofstadter pointed out in the 1950s, witnessing the rise of **McCarthyism**, American politics have been animated by deep-seated status anxiety, translating at times into paranoia. Populist anxieties about the emergence of a class-ridden society dominated by industrialists and peopled by immigrant masses carried over into fears associated with the communist menace and/or the advancement of African Americans. Kevin Phillips suggested that such sentiments formed the backbone of the emerging Republican majority and the conservative **backlash** witnessed with the election of **Nixon** and crystallized in the Reagan era. But such fears once again turned socio-economic differences into cultural differences. "Americanness" was attached to the notion of a "Silent Majority," and any vocal opposition was once again made to seem un-American. But this would not end altogether the politics of class, or "the politics of rich and poor" (as Phillips called it). In times of economic hardship, as American society becomes increasingly bifurcated between employees within high-tech industries and service workers eking out a poverty-level subsistence, the politics of class resurface. But, at the moment they make any impression, as with Bill **Clinton**'s first election when there seemed to be a mandate for "change," they are channeled, defused and denied.

In sum, Americans do recognize class difference, but express them in other terms, which may nonetheless have political and economic foundations. Some entail race – classifications and explanations on the basis of perceived skin color. Others are tied to **immigration** and recent arrival in the US. Yet, the ideological constructions used to explain away class must be measured against stark realities not only of division, but of increasing polarization embodied in dual cities and permanent marginality, as well as plutocratic elites whose fortunes run into the billions. Moreover, analysts decade by decade, from Warner to Packard to Fussell and Newman, have underscored the anxiety Americans have about maintaining and

losing status. Not talking about class will not make it go gently away.

See also: middle class; upper class; working class; "underclass"

Further reading

Fussell, P. (1983) *Class*, New York: Simon & Schuster.

Newman, K. (1999) *Falling from Grace*, Berkeley: University of California.

Packard, V. (1959) *The Status Seekers*, New York: D. McKay Co.

Phillips, K. (1990) *The Politics of Rich and Poor*, New York: Random House.

Potter, D. (1954) *People of Plenty*, Chicago: University of Chicago Press.

Sernett, R. and Cobb, J. (1972) *The Hidden Injuries of Class*. New York: Vintage Books.

Warner, W., Meeker, M. and Eells, K. (1949; repr. 1957) *Social Class in America*, Gloucester: Peter Smith.

GARY McDONOGH
ROBERT GREGG
CINDY WONG

classical music

As with all of the arts, one cannot summarize classical music in America since the Second World War with one word or phrase. Technology, new and old, musical ideologies, and quests for audience all have affected the production and presentation of music. The heritage of the classical canon as well as innovation have also created tensions for orchestras, audiences and "consumption" of music.

Postwar development of audio-tape recorders and long-playing records not only made performances accessible to a wider public, but also changed the ways in which music was created. The tape recorder gave composers greater control over the creation and manipulation of sound. Rather than being dependent on notation or the quality and interpretation of performers, composers recorded and arranged sound from materials of their own choosing. The next critical phase in technology was the arrival of the **computer** in the mid-1950s. Although originally too expensive for most composers, computers were used by academics to create calculated musical sequences.

Another major impact of technology in the twentieth century was the development of electronic music and the use of synthesized instruments. Electronic music involved recording environmental noises and electronically generated pitches and sounds, replayed in the music. The use of technology has redefined what music *is* for many composers. Hence, Edgard Varèse (1883–1965) called for "the liberation of sound...the right to make music with any and all sounds" (Kamien 1992: 531). This included electronic sounds, untraditional noises created from amplification, tapping, scraping, plucking and rubbing of traditional instruments, as well as the use of non-instruments, such as jackhammers, to create sound.

In style, the first postwar trend in American classical music was the abandonment of tonality for the twelve-tone system, first advocated by Arnold Schönberg (1874–1951) and then by his disciple Anton Webern (1883–1945). This method stimulated unconventional approaches to melody, harmony and form. In America, use of the twelve-tone composition, in its variations and transformations, became a means of re-affirming rather than repudiating the values of traditional tonal music. Even tonal composers such as Roger Sessions (1896–1985), with many of his works, starting with his violin sonata (1953), and Aaron **Copland** (1900–90) had either experimented with or been affected by the twelve-tone system, "I began to hear chords that I wouldn't have heard otherwise. Heretofore I had been thinking tonally, but this was a new way of moving tones about. It freshened up one's technique and one's approach" (Kamien 1992: 525).

A younger generation of composers adopted a revised version of the twelve-tone system, called serialism, in which groups of rhythmic values, dynamic levels or tone colors were organized into series, or an ordered group of musical elements. Composers like Milton Babbitt (b. 1916) used this method to compose mathematically. While this was a highly organized, controlled approach to music, in most cases the sound produced might seem random and chaotic.

A completely opposite contemporary movement was chance music, in which composers chose pitches, tone colors and rhythms by random methods, including coin tosses. The most famous American composer of this school was John **Cage** (1912–92). Cage's "Imaginary Landscape No. 4" (1951) for twelve radios gives directions for six performers to manipulate the wavelength and volume of the radios chosen by throwing dice.

In the mid-1960s, **minimalism** started to develop in reaction against the complexity of serialism and the randomness of chance music. Also influenced by non-Western music and *philosophy*, a new generation of composers, including Philip **Glass** (b. 1937), John Adams (b. 1947), Terry Riley (b. 1935) and Steve Reich (b. 1936), wrote seemingly hypnotic, repetitive music with a steady pulse and dynamic, clear tonality, and insistent repetition of short melodic phrases. The minimalist movement was accepted by the public during the 1970s and 1980s with Reich's "Music for 18 Musicians" (1976) and Glass and Adams' operas *Einstein on the Beach* (1976) and *Nixon in China* (1987).

Contemporary classical music is heavily influenced by **postmodern** theories of reusing the familiar, with the re-discovery of tonality. Many composers are returning to the roots of classical music, quoting music from the great masters. For example, in Ellen Taaffe's (b. 1939) "Zwilich's Concerto Grosso 1985," the composer quotes passages from a Handel sonata. The revisiting of preceding styles started in the 1960s with the works of Virgil Thomson (1896–1989), William Albright (1944–98) and William Bolcom (b. 1938) reviving earlier popular music, most notably ragtime. To the current composers, such as David Del Tredici (b. 1937), educated in the atonal, twelve-tone system, tonality is the "new" form.

The tercentenaries of J.S. Bach (1685–1750) and G.F. Handel (1685–1759) in the mid-1980s also contributed to a search for roots in classical music. More performing arts groups started to explore historically accurate performance practices, using reconstructed "period" instruments of the Baroque and Classical periods.

Classical music today must also relate to the changing American audiences. Traditionally, classical music had been supported by patrons, whether wealthy individuals or institutions. Fundamentally, this support structure has not changed –

composers and performing arts groups are funded mostly by their audiences, benefactors and institutions, such as **foundations** and government agencies. However, classical music activities have been shifting from the traditional centers like **New York**, **Boston, MA**, **Chicago, IL**, **Philadelphia, PA** and **Los Angeles, CA**, where there has been a great tradition of classical music for nearly over a century. Regional performing arts groups have sprung up with great success in the postwar era in cities like **Phoenix**, Raleigh, Omaha (Nebraska) and **Dallas**.

On the whole, classical music organizations have found that their income is consistently increasing more than their expenses. The total income of American orchestras was nearly $1,087 million in 1997–8, an increase of 8.2 percent ($82 million) from the previous year. Total expenses for the same year were $1,077 million, an increase of 6.5 percent ($66 million) over 1996–7. This was due mostly to increased ticket sales (up 7 percent between 1996–7 and 1997–8), individual giving (up 17 percent) and corporate and foundation grants (up 17 percent).

Recording technology has not only changed the way music is created, but also the way in which it is presented and appreciated. Long-playing records, **radio** and **television** allowed for the recording and broadcasts of historical performances. Audiences no longer had to travel to live performances. **Video**, **cable**, CD and DVD have added new dimensions to home enjoyment and potential support. Currently, performing arts organizations are embracing the **Internet**, with many in the process of setting up live "web-casts" of performances, as well as putting up audio files to promote new music and composers, and posting of educational materials for outreach projects. In these ways, American classical music has renewed its audience in the early twenty-first century.

Further reading

American Symphony Orchestra League (1999) *Up-To-Date Orchestra Facts*: http://www.symphony.org

Chase, G. (1987) *America's Music*, Urbana: University of Illinois Press.

Kamien, R. (1992) *Music: An Appreciation*, New York: McGraw-Hill.

Morgan, R.P. (ed.) (1993) *Modern Times*, Englewood Cliffs: Prentice Hall.

Salzman, E. (1974) *Twentieth Century Music*, Englewood Cliffs: Prentice Hall.

SUSANNA PROUGH

Cleveland, OH

When the Cuyahoga river caught fire and burned on June 22, 1969, it seemed a nadir for this industrial port on the Great Lakes. Yet Cleveland has also shown resilience in cleaning up its environment and rebuilding identities around downtown sports and cultural attractions, including the Rock and Roll **Hall of Fame**, while re-examining its complex ethnic heritages and relations to surrounding **suburbs**. Metropolitan population has grown again, to reach 2,911,683 in 1999. The *Drew Carey Show* (ABC, 1995–) has made it a weekly setting for a sitcom about work and neighborhoods that asserts Cleveland's identity as a working-class city.

GARY McDONOGH

Clift, Montgomery
b. 1920; d. 1966

Beautiful, sexually ambiguous and hungry, Clift embodied a troubled and introspective **masculinity** at odds with conventional representations of 1950s **family** and **gender** roles – a tension apparent as he plays off John **Wayne** in *Red River* (1948). In consummately American settings like this Western, the army (*From Here to Eternity*, 1953 and *The Young Lions*, 1958) or the inter-class drama of *A Place in the Sun* (1951), Clift haunts us with powerful acting and uncertain meaning. His last decade was overshadowed by a devastating **automobile** accident and consequent deterioration.

Further reading

McCann, G. (1993) *Rebel Males*, New Brunswick: Rutgers.

GARY McDONOGH

Clinton, William Jefferson

b. 1946

Bill Clinton, first **baby-boomer** US president (1993–2001) and three-time Arkansas governor, defeated incumbent George **Bush** and the eccentric Ross **Perot** in the 1992 campaign, despite controversies concerning extra-marital affairs (Gennifer Flowers), charges of financial corruption (**Whitewater**) and allegations about draft evasion. Clinton presented himself as "a different kind of **Democrat**," a New Democrat, more in line with the centrist Democratic Leadership Council, which he had headed.

Clinton's campaign mantra – "It's the economy, stupid" – embodies his administration's strengths and accomplishments as the United States' economy has adapted to globalization more successfully than its competitors in terms of economic growth, low inflation and low unemployment. Clinton's Secretary of the Treasury, Robert Rubin, succeeded in dominating domestic policy over more liberal voices like Robert Reich in implementing moderately progressive **tax** increases, significant cuts in the budget and, following the 1994 **Republican** congressional victories, the achievement of budget surpluses.

Clinton, a superlative politician with a seemingly infinite capacity to come to the brink of self-imposed disaster and then rebound and even flourish, began his first administration with impressive appointments to establish "a government which looks like America." Despite retreats on gays in the military and immigrant-bashing sections on **welfare reform**, Clinton has remained a cultural liberal, "mending but not ending" **affirmative action**, making moderate to progressive court appointments, initiating a **race** dialogue and passing a modest Family Leave Act.

As a "New" Democrat, he has sought to woo white, **middle-class**, **suburban** voters with tougher positions on crime, including subsidies for more **police**, targeted programs in **education** and protection of middle-class entitlements. In addition, in foreign policy, he has attempted to combine a human rights agenda – which led him to send US troops into **Haiti** – with military responses to Iraq's evasion of inspections and Serbia's ethnic cleansing in Kosovo. At the same time he remains haunted, as were his predecessors, by the **Vietnam War** legacy of an aversion to risking significant US lives in combat and, consequently, is subject to charges of inconsistency and ineffectiveness.

The 1994 congressional elections, which produced Republican majorities in both Houses and led to the speakership of Newt **Gingrich** and his "Contract With America," brought Clinton to his lowest point, as did in part a response to the defeat of his efforts to pass universal, or at least more comprehensive, **healthcare**. However, the Grand Old Party (GOP) threat of a government shutdown, skillfully manipulated by Clinton, revitalized his political fortunes, although at the cost of the passage of a welfare reform bill, which recklessly eliminated federal entitlements to the poor in devolving most decision-making to the states through block grants, caps on spending, more stringent work requirements and ceilings on eligibility.

Clinton's second term has been a rollercoaster driven by his **impeachment** following the revelation of an affair with Monica Lewinsky, a White House intern, his continuing popularity as the US economy's boom continues and a series of international crises, most notably in the former Yugoslavia. Clinton's "bridge to the twenty-first century" seemed to rest on a not always consistently framed, often opportunistic, blending of old New Deal and "Great Society" economic liberalism with modified, calibrated versions of identity politics, a determination to appear strong both domestically and internationally, a laser-like attention to the now majoritarian suburbs and a comfort with a multi-national, global, confident capitalism, tempered with not "big," but government nevertheless. His legacy remains problematic: a resilient, if not great, politician with a seriously flawed character.

Further reading

Dionne, E.J., Jr., (1996) *They Only Look Dead*, New York: Simon & Schuster.

Maraniss, D. (1995) *First in His Class*, New York: Simon & Schuster.

Drew, W. (1997) *Whatever It Takes*, New York: Penguin Books.

Greenberg, S. and Skocpol, T. (eds) (1997) *The New Majority*, New Haven: Yale University Press.

PAUL LYONS

clubs, city and country

Clubs emerged as elite meeting places in the nineteenth century along the male, upper-class and highly segregated lines of comparable British institutions. Some of these, ensconced in landmark buildings, continue to play a role in the social organization and business of cities like **New York** (Metropolitan Club), **Philadelphia, PA** (Union Club) and **San Francisco, CA** (Union Pacific Club). Other clubs also handle issues of elite reproduction, like debutante balls, although these declined after the 1960s; some specialized in athletic events like rowing, cricket and yachting. Professional associations (National Press Club or Army and Navy Club in **Washington, DC**) and alumni organizations represented similar prestige associations and edifices.

As **automobiles** moved people away from urban centers, country clubs emerged as complementary institutions, promoting social cohesion but adding on such features as more spacious clubhouses, golf, tennis and other recreational events, dining rooms and accommodations. In some cases, these clubs served to stimulate growth and define elite **suburban** districts. While these clubs tended to incorporate women and families (often around a male member or proprietor), they remained exclusive – not permitting **African Americans**, **Jews** or Catholic ethnics, depending on their locations. Some of these groups, in fact, organized alternative clubs delineating new suburban geographies.

After the Second World War and the Depression, many country clubs faced economic straits and pressures from development that engulfed them. This forced movements, consolidations, rebuilding and expanding membership to incorporate a broader **middle class**. Changing tastes in recreation meant crowding on **golf** courses and demands for pools, **tennis** and fitness facilities, as well as dining and dancing (while facilities were adapted for air-conditioned indoor spaces). Modernist clubhouses set the scene for many 1950s and 1960s depictions of suburban life and rites of passage such as **weddings** and anniversaries.

By the 1960s, social pressures also challenged exclusionary rules. Single women and businesswomen sued for access to both urban and country clubs, which they saw as locations for deal-making as well as recreation. Ethnic and racial barriers fell more slowly and bitterly – in 1990 the Professional Golf Association threatened Birmingham (Alabama)'s Shoals Country Club with loss of the PGA championship in order to open the club to blacks. Politicians also came under scrutiny for exclusive policies, forcing either changes in the clubs or loss of influential members.

While the economic expansion of the late twentieth century renewed many clubs, they remain exclusive because of entrance fees and annual payments as well as waiting lists for memberships. Hence, in many metropolitan areas, they still indicate gradations within the upper and middle classes based on heritage (old versus new money as well as lingering ethnic divisions).

Further reading

Mayo, J. (1998) *The American Country Club*, New Brunswick: Rutgers.

GARY McDONOGH

clubs/fraternal organizations

Americans, despite their **individualism**, are often described as a nation of "joiners." For many organizations, this produces a relatively passive pool of members who offer economic support in lobbying issues of the environment, ethnic heritage issues, or **community** organization. Others focus on service – volunteers in troubled areas or with special populations. Still others represent professional identities – doctors, **veterans**, or teachers – whose national assemblies may shape policy issues for the group and influence national policy. **College** alumni associations are important in fundraising and recruitment, while other educational institutions may also promote sociability and support. Still other clubs are more loosely defined civic or interest groups, which may, nonetheless, sponsor important initiatives. Some of these, as well as other groups, offer social and recreational spaces – whether **middle-class** country clubs or local ethnic and religious groups. Joining thus also divides Americans according to **race**, **class**, **gender**, **ethnicity** and locale, even as it may bring them together with cross-cutting identities.

Among the most widespread associations are those that offer broad civic and fraternal appeal. Of these, some are clearly offspring of older European Masonic movements or similar ritualized organizations – the 1950s sitcom *The Honeymooners* stressed the importance of lodge meetings, which was echoed in the later *Flintstones* and even *The Simpsons*. Ritual elements are also important in religiously affiliated associations like the Catholic Knights of Columbus and the Jewish Hadassah.

The Rotary Club, Kiwanis, Optimists and other groups foster civic involvement in schools, reform and international connections, while also offering regular social functions for urban movers. Many of these have been adult and male-dominated, although offering female auxiliaries and **high-school** affiliates; this division has been challenged since the 1960s.

Women's organizations, however, have also played important organizational roles. The League of Women Voters, for example, has been active in sponsoring political debates and voter information. Garden clubs – traditionally but not exclusively a woman's domain – have been involved in civic beautification. Book clubs, service clubs, and religious and charitable organizations have channeled generations of women's involvement in public life. In some cases, however, this has been marked by class exclusion based on history – Daughters of the American Revolution or Daughters of the Confederacy, for example.

Many of these clubs, female and male, have been organized around divisions of race and class. **African American** clubs, including Colored Women's Clubs, **fraternities** and sororities and religious associations also exercised strong parapolitical functions in eras of **segregation**, while they have delineated the associations of a distinctive black **middle class**. New immigrants have also formed new associations around religious and family organizations.

Such a list of American associations might stretch to include fan clubs, hobby and interest groups, pet owners, amateur athletics, motoring,

institutional support and a myriad of other reasons Americans find to come together and be different. In literature and **mass media**, moreover, these associations map out other meanings of class, sociability and interest – from the bored housewife to the person on the move in politics, reinforcing the complex geography of American identities.

GARY McDONOGH
CINDY WONG

CNN

International television news organization that broadcasts news and features worldwide through local **cable** television companies, satellite providers and the **Internet**. Founded by businessperson Ted **Turner** and headquartered in **Atlanta, GA**, CNN began continuous broadcasts of news stories to cable television subscribers on June 1, 1980. The network initially lost money and was dismissed as a farce by the three other American television networks. Live **Gulf War** coverage vaulted it into a more respected position, which was sustained by numerous local affiliates and advancements in satellite technology. Now owned by media conglomerate **Time Warner**, the network consists of various stations that broadcast on particular topics, such as sports and finance, to specific parts of the world. CNN currently has over 70 million subscribers in the United States alone.

BRIAN LEVIN

Coast Guard, US

Founded in 1790 as the Revenue Marine with the primary mission of protecting the United States from smugglers. The USCG acquired its current name in 1915 when the Revenue Cutter Service and the Life Saving Service merged into a single organization. The smallest of the armed services, it is controlled by the Department of Transportation during peacetime and by the Department of Defense during wartime. Individuals who join the USCG are subject to the Uniform Code of Military Justice and receive the same pay as members of the other armed services. Its primary missions include maritime search and rescue, maritime law enforcement, maintenance of aids to navigation, icebreaking, environmental protection, port security and military readiness. The USCG employs 38,000 active duty personnel and almost 43,000 reserve and auxiliary personnel. These "Coasties" (as members of the USCG are often called) operate over 1,000 vessels and over 200 aircraft.

People volunteer to join the Coast Guard for many reasons. In addition to the work, benefits, training and educational opportunities, many people feel that a job in the USCG offers the chance to work along the coast and an opportunity to protect the environment. On a typical day, the Coast Guard will seize illegal drugs, rescue people offshore and investigate marine accidents. All of this activity contributes to an atypical career that many Coasties enjoy throughout their work life.

LAURA L. COOGAN

Coca Cola *see* soda

Coen, Joel and Ethan

b. 1958 (both)

With Joel as the **director-screenwriter** and Ethan as the **producer**-screenwriter, the brothers have a uniquely skewed vision of ordinary life which permeates and complicates otherwise simple tales of murder, kidnapping and fraud with the human frailties of the characters themselves. As NYU trained independent film-makers, deeply critical of **Hollywood** legends in *Barton Fink* (1991), they have gained increasing budgets and acceptance, including a screenwriting Oscar for *Fargo* (1996), which also garnered a Best Actress Award for Joel's wife, Frances McDormand (b. 1958).

GARY McDONOGH
CINDY WONG

coffee

In **mass media** and everyday life, coffee has been part of the background of American life. Generally prepared in a weaker form than European expresso, this drink (with or without sugar and cream) can be consumed by the cupful during the work day, at social gatherings (as in the earnest conversations of television **soap operas**) and with dinner – during the meal as well as after. Many diners or **roadside** restaurants even place large pots of coffee on each table prior to customers ordering. Down from its height of popularity in the 1930s, coffee remains a very visible cultural landmark with the ongoing Starbucking of America and the development of designer coffees as well as new spaces for consumption.

Through the early twentieth century, leading coffee companies like Folger's, Hills Brothers, Maxwell House and A&P roasted coffee beans and supplied coffee in cans. Later, with the popularity of "instant" coffee, Folger's crystals were marketed as indistinguishable from the coffee "served in the finest restaurants," while Maxwell House "remained good to the last drop." Meanwhile, growing concerns at the beginning of the **physical fitness** fad that strong coffee might represent a health problem led to the popularity of (Sanka) decaffeinated instant coffee, followed by other brands.

During the 1950s, dissatisfied with coffee that didn't fit the advertised billing, William Black founded his own brand, Chock Ful 'o Nuts, in **New York**. Black was followed in Berkeley, **California**, by Alfred Peet, who dark-roasted quality beans at Peet's Coffee and Tea in Berkeley. As these better quality beans hit the market, new delivery systems – Mr Coffee and those of the German producers, Krups and Braun – became available, making the freshly brewed coffee more convenient than previous methods of percolation, and bringing lattes, expressos and cappuccinos out of the "finest" restaurants and into the **yuppie** home. Coffee-houses in New York, meanwhile, also offered more European expressos with beat poetry and smoky conversations.

These set the stage for three students in **Seattle** in the 1970s to establish Starbucks. When Starbucks' specialty brand went national it benefited from the increased demand for freshly brewed coffee made from quality beans at a time when the overall demand for coffee was declining. New chain stores began to push the smaller, local-owned cafés out of the market, while bookstores opened their own cafés for their customers.

FBI Agent Cooper (Kyle MacLachlan) seemed to represent the shift in American culture from quantity to quality in *Twin Peaks* (ABC, 1990–1), revealing his partiality for the Pacific Northwest town's "damn fine coffee." However, scandal revealed that some of the Starbucks' coffee had not been so fine – Robusta beans had surreptitiously been substituted for Arabica beans. Concerns over labor and environmental conditions have also shaped consumer preferences, perhaps giving some smaller cafés a new lease of life. Some believe their coffee purchases can help Haitians recover from economic turmoil, or express solidarity with **Cuba**; others see coffee growing as a way to save the rainforest.

Further reading

Pendergast, M. (1999) *Uncommon Grounds*, New York: Basic.

ROBERT GREGG

Cold War

From 1945 until 1989 the United States and the Soviet Union engaged in what came to be called a "Cold War." Although characterized as "cold" rather than "hot" because it involved little direct military engagement between the two parties, this conflict nevertheless proved enormously costly to not only the two primary countries involved, but also to the numerous surrogate nations who bore the struggle's most severe effects. This period of extreme tension had a monumental impact on both the international geopolitical scene and American domestic life and thought.

The Cold War dates from the collapse of the victorious Second World War alliance. Never particularly happy bedfellows, the United States and Western European allies had temporarily joined forces with the Soviet Union in order to defeat their common enemy, Germany. Having successfully repelled Germany from its soil, the Soviet army drove Hitler's troops back to **Berlin** and occupied the eastern half of Germany, including the capital. During their western sweep,

the Soviets also recaptured much of Eastern Europe, and proved reluctant to release their prizes. The Cold War emerged from this struggle to reshape the postwar political map.

Whatever sense of alliance America felt with the Soviet Union during the war rapidly disappeared after it ended. At the Yalta Conference of the major successful powers in February 1945, Joseph Stalin, the Soviet leader, had agreed in principle to hold free elections in the liberated countries as soon as possible. None happened, however, and within two years the Eastern European bloc – countries whose connection lay primarily in their shared political and economic allegiance to the Soviet Union – had solidified. The former British Prime Minister, Winston Churchill, coined the phrase "Iron Curtain" in 1946 to describe the Soviet Union's hold over Eastern Europe.

In 1947 President Harry **Truman** declared an American responsibility to respond to the yearnings of "free peoples" around the world. This "Truman Doctrine" was aimed specifically at countries with a perceived potential for "becoming" communist. In the same year, policy expert George Kennan wrote an article in the journal *Foreign Affairs*, which encouraged the United States to counter what it viewed as Soviet expansionism by engaging the Soviet Union in local conflicts. This policy, known as "containment," came to dominate American foreign policy for the next forty years. It called for American involvement in countries throughout the world if a threat of communism was identified. It was this policy of "containment" that most profoundly determined the "Cold War."

This policy was first played out on the Korean Peninsula from 1950 until 1953. The Cold War became "hot" as the Americans, Russians and Chinese engaged in the first of several "surrogate" conflicts that pitted the Americans against communist enemies – some real, some less so. Although a "surrogate" conflict, over 33,000 American soldiers died in Korea and a precedent for armed intervention was set.

America's containment imperative drove it to many other controversial policy decisions. For example, the **Eisenhower** administration toppled leaders in **Iran** and Guatemala with whose policies they disagreed. "Containment" also provided American leaders with the ideological justification to fund initially the French efforts to put down anti-colonial nationalists in Southeast Asia in the 1950s. Ultimately, America took over that war; between 1963 and 1975, 56,000 American soldiers died in the **Vietnam War**.

While the international geopolitical impact of this ideological competition became self-evident, its effect on domestic policy proved equally profound. American fear of communism produced an obsessive concern that communists living in America might somehow bring down the country's democratic institutions. Determined to resist such a fate, American leaders compulsively searched for anyone espousing views that they felt resembled ideas promoted by communism. Everything from discussions of economic disparity to concerns over racial prejudice came under the heading of suspect ideas. People speaking such thoughts became suspect themselves. Actual communists were arrested and many who held strong views on social justice, whether communist or not, found themselves under investigation as well. Although this assault on free speech is often credited to **Republican** Senator Joseph **McCarthy**, a particularly virulent anti-communist senator, anti-communist persecution was a bipartisan activity. Both **Democrats** and Republicans engaged in ferocious violations of civil liberties and human rights in their quest to "preserve" democratic institutions in America. The legacies of this Cold War in America included years of suspicion and thousands of ruined lives.

One can also trace the shattered remnants of civil society in the 1960s to a controversial foreign policy abroad. American youth began to resist the apparently endless struggle against a communist enemy who seemed to offer little direct threat. By the end of the 1960s, hundreds of thousands of protestors angrily voiced loud dissent at Cold War strategies. From the so-called "war at home" over Vietnam to the growing anti-nuclear movement, the "Cold War consensus" (the presumed domestic support for containment policies) began to unravel.

The official collapse of the Soviet Union as a dominant communist state provides the "date" for the end of the Cold War. Faced with a weakened economy and the forces of the international global marketplace, Mikhail Gorbachev, the Soviet premier, began a policy of "glasnost" (openness) in the mid-1980s. By 1989 it became clear that the Soviet Union under Gorbachev would no longer enforce iron discipline on its satellites. When the Berlin Wall (erected by the Soviets in 1961) began to come down in November 1989, the end was near. Within a few months, the Soviet "monolith" had collapsed – its authority undermined throughout the Eastern bloc and communism itself rejected within what soon came to be "Russia." Attitudes towards **Cuba**, nonetheless, reflect this lingering heritage.

The cultural meanings of the Cold War are legion as well – from the definitions of American **family**, home and values in media to the **blacklisting** of suspect communists in **Hollywood**. One also sees its schizophrenia at work in cultural works, exhibitions and ideologies projecting American values into global competition, whether directly or indirectly in Hollywood, and concerns at home with dire and subversive threats. These concerns, again, could be expressed directly (in mysteries, spy movies and related genres or films like *The Manchurian Candidate*, 1962), while also underpinning the unease of **science fiction** in the 1950s and 1960s. Cultural critics, including academics, media makers and activists, also attacked policies and mentalities of the Cold War in a range of resistance from Noam **Chomsky** to Stanley Kubrick's classic *Dr Strangelove* (1962). Indeed, the Cold War became intimately enmeshed with both high culture and everyday life for decades.

The Cold War dominated American foreign and domestic policy for over forty years. Its impacts are still being felt as the United States remains uncertain as to its role in the world if it is not engaged in an ideological battle with an overarching enemy.

SHARON ULLMAN

collectibles

Barbed wire, dolls, first editions, **baseball** cards and dinnerware have achieved a post-Marxist transmutation from use value to exchange value in becoming collectibles. The emphasis, however, is on acquisition and sales as much as appreciation and process – while collectors range from connoisseurs to middle people, the framework of collectionism in late twentieth-century America was that of the market rather than the Medicis.

The range of objects amassed, sorted, evaluated and disposed of maps out not only the commodities of American life, but also its history – **celebrities**, events from Civil War memorabilia to the *Titanic*, **antiques** and ephemera made rare by their use and disposability: Avon cosmetic bottles, advertisements, playing cards and beverage cans. They may be held and used within private circles, maintained in constant commercial motion or converted, in some cases, to the stuff of museums.

While stratification of culture and cash differentiates those who specialize in Monet from those concentrating on license plates, both follow a logic of reproduction and accumulation within industrial America, while they also reflect a nostalgia for a period of still local mass production – iron toys made in nineteenth-century factories speak of production and consumption on a scale very different from McDonald's daily output of toys worldwide. Collection implies uniqueness and limitation, although both are called into question as **catalogs** and home-shopping channels flog newly minted collectible items, from dolls to signed sports and *Star Trek* memorabilia. Often, past items are also taken as indices of economic growth – juxtaposing millions for De Kooning or Jasper Johns with the sale of an original **Barbie**, or the speculative market (via catalogs, **Internet** and classified ads) for Beanie Babies in the late 1990s. Production may, at least temporarily, collapse a collectible market; yet this in itself may yield a secondary nostalgia further down the line.

Yet, the meanings of collectionism transcend the market. Collections can shape social lives spent in weekend searches through antique stores, flea markets and other resources, as well as demands for home care and display. Collectibles also form the cores of social networks and collectivities – Trekkies as well as Picasso owners reinforce identities through dialogues and memories as well as objects. Americans can find who they are through what they own (and what ownership they display). Hence, Laurie Rozakis' *Complete Idiot's Guide to Buying and Selling Collectibles* (1997) notes that "Collecting something special, something that you have selected, allows you to express yourself. Your collection shows the world you are special." (1997: 9). To rethink the collections donated to the National Gallery or the Metropoli-

tan, as well as family room displays of beer cans raises intriguing questions about identity itself.

Further reading

Rozakis, L. (1997) *Complete Idiot's Guide to Buying and Selling Collectibles*, Indianapolis: MacMillan.

GARY McDONOGH
CINDY WONG

college *see* colleges and universities; black colleges and universities; campus, college; commencement/ graduation; community colleges/junior colleges; libraries, research; state university systems

colleges, Catholic

The 229 Roman Catholic **colleges and universities** in the US currently educate over 600,000 students. These institutions are affiliated with such religious institutes as the Jesuits and the Sisters of Mercy, or, in the case of Notre Dame, with the Congregation of Holy Cross. As of 1989, 44 percent (100) are comprehensive institutions and another 40 percent (91) are liberal-arts colleges, with the rest research institutions or junior colleges. Religious colleges tend to enroll higher numbers of women and part-time students than do non-religious institutions. They also tend to be located in the **Midwest** and the **Northeast** part of the country.

Historically, Catholics often felt unwelcome in many Protestant-dominated private and state colleges. Catholic colleges were established to create a religious environment for higher education and professional schools. These schools trained ever-increasing numbers of immigrant children and fostered inculturation in a Catholic milieu. They were highly effective at both tasks. Even in the late twentieth century, nearly 40 percent of these students were the first in their families to attend college.

After the Second World War, the **GI Bill** offered tuition funds to **veterans** and this influx of students caused many schools to expand greatly. The increase in the number of men with a college education fueled the postwar economy and propelled the percentage of college-educated Catholics upward. The children of these alumni often attended **parochial schools** and added to the expansion.

In the 1960s, the liberalizing effects of the Second Vatican Council were felt in the United States, and the increased numbers of wealthy and influential alumni contributed to a movement to make Catholic colleges more academically competitive. In the late 1960s, most institutions were turned over to boards of trustees, a majority of whom were lay people. At the same time, increasing openness to the new scientific methods shifted the focus of scholarship to a more scientific and a less specifically Catholic perspective. The percentages of priests and religious teaching in the colleges began to drop, with a concurrent hiring of lay people to respond to the increasing student population and the desire for increased professionalism. Ultimately, the debate over what it means to be a Catholic, or religious, college grew. A few institutions even disaffiliated themselves from the Catholic Church. Schools based their identity on the teaching of theology and the development of faith life revolving around campus ministry programs. Concerns persist that colleges are becoming less Catholic. Attempts by the **Roman Catholic** Church to address the issue of higher education in the United States have centered, since 1991, on the Apostolic Constitution *Ex Corde Ecclesiae* of Pope John Paul II, in which he defines the nature of a Catholic university. Feverish debate continues unabated on this question of Catholic identity.

Further reading

O'Brien, D.J. (1994) *From the Heart of the American Church*, Maryknoll, NY: Orbis.

Pope John Paul II (1991) "*Ex Corde Ecclesiae*," *Current Issues in Catholic Higher Education*, Winter: 31–42.

ERIC A. ZIMMER

colleges and universities

The United States hosts more than 3,000 institutions of higher education, serving 14 million highly varied students, learning/career plans and communities, as well as embodying national ideals of research and learning. While some institutions have existed for centuries, the 1944 **GI Bill of Rights** opened colleges as a social opportunity in a new way (college graduates tripled between 1930 and 1950). Subsequent social changes, including economic **mobility**, **civil rights** and the careers of the **baby boomers**, have elaborated on these changes: protests and explorations of the 1960s seemed a watershed in ideas and operations. Together, history and choice underpin widespread student aspirations for democratic opportunity and an ideal "fit" in terms of interests, personality, ability and finance. Colleges, in turn, may evoke multiple images of tree-lined **campuses**, **football**, **fraternities**, intellectual debate, **commencement** and careers, although experience sometimes controverts these stereotypes.

Higher education in the late twentieth and early twenty-first centuries has been shaped by deep divisions of **class** and opportunity, some of which have changed through **affirmative action**, social reform and curricular restructuring. The **Ivy League** is still not the same as a **community college** or part-time business program; variations in cost, program, reputation, history, tutelage and impact shade many meanings of the college experience for all participants. We look at these from the perspectives of student choices, institutional differences and operations, and representation.

The student perspective

American college admissions and education differ from traditions of many other systems worldwide. Students typically enter college after twelve years of schooling (rather than having an additional baccalaureate year); advanced students may enter earlier. There are no government-administered selection exams. Instead, privately administered **standardized testing** (SATs, ACTs) provide general standards to contextualize differences of schools, grades, activities, essays and references that constitute an admissions portfolio. Some students are guaranteed admissions to public universities by grades or examination scores.

By spring of 11th grade, **teenagers** and their families examine guidebooks and materials, prepare for entrance exams, talk with coaches and counselors, visit campuses and reflect on finances and grades. Family, teachers, recruiters and peers generally guide candidates towards an initial selection of colleges based on interests, location, ambience and possibilities. Colleges often have special procedures for foreign students and deal with physical and emotional disabilities, as well as with variations in background.

Selection criteria vary widely. Size, ranging from a few hundred to 80,000 at mega-state universities, is an important consideration. Programs may offer a wide selection, narrow pre-professional training, or a liberal arts education. Urban or rural settings within national and transnational choices are also a factor, although relative location may reflect students' needs/choices to live at home or in a place in which they are already settled or to move away. Activities are also important, since colleges and universities are social settings as well as academic institutions. Sports are intrinsic to many colleges as participant and spectator activities. Music, drama, social clubs, foreign study and **fraternities and sororities** also may be important extra-curricular features.

Costs figure prominently in selection as well. While there are still some free universities or programs that facilitate attendance at public institutions for minimal expense, the most expensive private colleges charge $30,000 or more for tuition, room and board. Although college, private and government support may be available, this remains a determinant and deterrent for many families and may extend the time that students need to complete their college career through part-time enrollments.

Students may apply to multiple institutions. Some colleges are extremely competitive: top schools accept only a fraction of those who apply, even after a student's pre-selection; others have relatively open admissions. Colleges, in turn, make selections and negotiations from within their applicant pool, leading to new negotiations.

College education for the student thereafter entails much more choice in classes, majors, relationships and even movement than have been found in systems in Europe or Asia. Many students change colleges during their career and may change their ideas of their primary interests and majors. For those away from home, college is a time of experimentation – sex, drugs, dress and bodily ornamentation. Some students are focused on long- and short-term goals; others constitute "**slackers**" for whom college lingers for years; still others must accommodate college along with work, family or other pressures – especially those who choose to complete their education after the "traditional age." Yet there are colleges to meet all these needs and situations.

Structure, variety and operations

Institutional variety and continuous change and expansion have created a complicated academic world in the US. Apart from community colleges and junior colleges (dealt with separately), the fundamental division is between colleges (focused on the first four years or undergraduate curriculum) and universities which incorporate post-baccalaureate academic research and professional programs. This also implies different possibilities of residential and curricular life, **research libraries** and laboratories, organization and impact, etc. Other divisions are based on funding and oversight, curriculum, location, clientele and prestige

Within both colleges and universities, the first four years are treated as general education with some pre-professional or disciplinary specialization, generally rewarded with a BA (Bachelor of Arts) or BS (Bachelor of Science), after which students may stop or pause in their education. Students who go on must reapply, often to different institutions in new admissions competition with new letters, exams, applications and interviews. This competition has intensified decade by decade, especially in medical, law, business and other schools seen as guarantees of economic security. Social work, theology, nursing, engineering and other fields also offer professional and research degrees at various levels. Professional schools demand students pay their own way; hence students may accumulate $100,000 in debt. Businesses may support some usable expertise; other options include military arrangements, trading tuition for later service.

Advanced programs in humanities, sciences and social sciences also may be highly competitive in prestige (all programs, even at prestige universities, are not equal) which, in turn, influences support from universities, government and, in the late nineteenth and twentieth centuries, corporate sponsorship. These graduate schools have offered teaching opportunities and fellowships for their best students.

Colleges and universities vary in their funding, including both public and private institutions. The primary public institutions are **state university systems**; although cities have also created colleges, many have been absorbed into the state because of rising costs. Even **City University of New York** relies heavily on state support. Private universities include religious colleges, which may receive denominational support. Other universities must strike a balance between endowment and tuition; some are operated for profit. Only military institutions are federally funded, although federal and **foundation** funds are important to many public and private colleges. Partnerships with industry and venture capital, especially in growth fields like biotechnology and computers, have changed university funding and research – to the distaste of some who see business setting agendas.

Differences of place and culture are also clear. **New England** is home to a strong liberal arts tradition and the prestige of the Ivy League – challenged by **Stanford University** and the University of Chicago among other prestige schools. While many universities have developed with **cities**, others were established in bucolic locations (the University of Virginia), stressing the pastoral ideal of reflective learning. The college town represents a particular symbiosis of the university as population (and employer) with surrounding communities that may result in special "town/gown" tensions. Religious colleges have followed denominational distribution to some extent – evangelical in the **South**, Catholic in urban areas of the **Northeast** and Midwest. Many traditionally **African American** colleges have been located in the South.

Some divisions, clear at the Second World War, nonetheless, have changed radically in subsequent decades. At that point, many American institutions were essentially **white** or black, except for immigrant/foreign students; quotas on Jews or Catholics were part of twentieth-century elite schools as well. The **civil-rights** movement in the 1950s challenged segregation of public institutions in the South and forced the issue of diversity

in other schools. Affirmative action, coupled with **immigration** and recognition of ethnicity, changed the face of American colleges in the 1970s and 1980s. Ironically, some prestigious colleges have become concerned about the disproportionate presence of Asians and **Asian Americans**, while qualified **Latinos** and blacks are hotly recruited. This has called into question the role of traditionally **black colleges and universities**.

Men's colleges through the postwar period included quite prestigious institutions like Harvard and Yale that co-educated in the 1960s and 1970s. Charges of discrimination later forced military academies and others to open up. Some women's colleges went co-ed at this time; others have continued to argue for distinctive education.

Programs also vary. Military institutions like West Point (**army**), Annapolis (**navy**) and the **air force** academy offer specialized programs with federal support through which nominated students can be trained for officer duty. Gallaudet College, by contrast, was founded for the American deaf and has emerged as a center for reconsideration of the meaning of disabilities. Berea College in Kentucky and other colleges specialize in work-study and regional development. The 1960s also saw the inauguration of experimental programs in larger institutions and in smaller schools favoring independent learning, sometimes without grades or with close mentoring – Bennington, Antioch, New College of the University of South Florida.

Class and prestige both among universities and among students reshape the social and cultural meanings of the institution. University prestige is based on being the best, hiring the best and reproducing the best. This status is generally granted to research universities with graduate programs (increasing their support), but is also claimed by intensive liberal arts.

Hence, in addition to students, colleges and universities select faculty through a winnowing process of scrutiny of their teaching and writing before granting them tenure, usually in their fifth to seventh year of an institutional appointment. Tenure was originally championed to protect **freedom** of speech in academic settings; it has come under fire as both a process favoring narrow criteria like publication and as a sinecure that no longer corresponds to the experience of other American workers and professionals.

Professors, in turn, may be both private and public **intellectuals**, focusing on classes and research or reaching out in publications and community events. Demands and rewards vary widely among colleges and universities. Facilities are also variable, including library and research support, laboratories and national and global connections.

Other staffing includes coaches (who may hold academic positions) and many non-academic positions. Here, demands in areas of advising, counseling for special students and groups, legal issues, fundraising and budgeting, as well as library, computer, clerical and other support staff have made non-faculty salaries and issues one of the dominant themes of university planning and student and faculty life (especially when labor organization in these areas influences the operation of the institution).

University administration also includes multiple levels of expertise associated with student life and issues, faculty, sports, alumni, finance and planning – generally under a president who must balance internal and external roles. Colleges and universities, private and public, also have boards of directors or trustees, elected and appointed, who may include distinguished alumni, major donors, prominent citizens and representatives from university constituencies.

Finally, alumni have strong roles in both public and private colleges as recruiters, supporters and even voices about current policy issues (antiwar campus activism in the 1960s, for example, often drew angry protests from alumni correspondents).

Yet the multiple meanings and possibilities of education always intersect with students and questions about the nature of education. Are universities to be composed of the "best" students academically? Those most able to pay? Those most likely to make money, to change the world, to represent diverse viewpoints and heritages, or to profit from special care? Should they be trained as specialized careerists or broad critical thinkers? With the end of the baby boom and the emergence of new technologies of knowledge and education (including distance learning and development of computer and/or video-based courses), colleges face rising costs, growing competition and real challenges.

Representation

Images and meanings of college have been reinforced by **mass media** for decades, including important early images in Frank Merriwell novels, Owen Johnson's *Stover at Yale* (1912) and Buster Keaton silent films. In the postwar period, teen audiences have made colleges a major subject for television and movies. Movies including *The Knute Rockne All American* (1940), *Tall Story* (1960), *The Group* (1967), tracing lives of graduates from a woman's college, *The Graduate* (1967), *Strawberry Statement* (1970), *National Lampoon's Animal House* (1978), *Slacker* (1991) and *Good Will Hunting* (1997), among many others, represent and explore differences, and often define college for a generation of students.

Similarly, colleges have figured as important settings on television (although they may entail very little classwork). *The Many Loves of Dobie Gillis* (CBS, 1958–63), for example, provided weekly meditations on sex, class and college. In the 1990s, Bill **Cosby** focused another **situation comedy**, *A Different World* (NBC, 1987–93), on the experience of traditionally African American colleges. Graduate and professional schools have also figured in mass media: law in the *Paper Chase* (1973), or medicine in countless television dramas. Academic literature (written by students and professors) also provides interesting insights into college life.

Further reading

Various guides aimed at prospective students explore and compare American colleges and universities according to criteria of ranking, size, special features and cost. General considerations of issues in late twentieth and early twenty-first century American higher education include:

Reuben, J. (1996) *The Making of the Modern University*, Chicago: University of Chicago.

Ehrenberg, J. (ed.) (1997) *The American University*, Cornell: Cornell University Press

Graham, H. and Diamond, N. (1997) *The Rise of the American Research University*, Baltimore: Johns Hopkins University.

Horowitz, H. (1987) *Campus Life*, New York: Alfred A. Knopf.

Levine, A. (ed.) (1993) *Higher Learning in America*, Baltimore: Johns Hopkins University.

GARY McDONOGH

ROBERT GREGG

CINDY WONG

college sports *see* National Collegiate Athletic Association

colonies and colonialism

Americans have been avid colonizers. Given the United States' history as a postcolonial nation, this statement may seem perplexing. But Americans have been deeply embroiled in colonial projects in establishing their place in the global order, whether in dominating **Latin America** and the **Caribbean** or annexing **Hawai'i** and the Philippines. This led to especially ambiguous politics in the aftermath of the Second World War, when the nation endeavored to come to grips with the break up of major empires and the increase of nationalism worldwide, while supporting its own interests of business and consumption.

Even thirteen colonies breaking away from British rule did not abandon the idea of controlling further land and even peoples. A century of expansionism on the American mainland followed, although technical niceties allowed Americans to claim they were never colonizers. The Louisiana Purchase, for example, opening up vast tracts of land to the United States, nonetheless transferred an area and its people from one colonial rule (French) to another (American). That this area was divided into territories later to be incorporated into the American federal system just made this colonialism one more akin to the French model than to the British model. The expansion of plantation slavery into the **Southwest**, wars against **American Indians** and **Mexico** and the purchase of **Alaska** all had colonial overtones. That these were wrapped up in the mystical language of "manifest destiny," suggesting that white Americans were destined to govern the whole North American mainland, should not distract from recognizing this colonizing mission.

Americans, as Walt Whitman pointed out as the nation's second century was opening, were forging their own "passage to India."

That second century would witness an immediate commitment to the expansionist impulse as the US competed with other major industrial nations. Wars with **Americans Indians** continued opening up new territories to largely European settlers. Then the US expanded to the Pacific, "opening the door" to Japan and acquiring Hawai'i and the Philippines (the latter in the Spanish-American War of 1898). In the Caribbean, meanwhile, the US took **Cuba** and **Puerto Rico** (also in the 1898 conflict), and established control over the **Panama** isthmus, while intervening regularly in other countries under its self-proclaimed rights under the Monroe doctrine.

The complex legacy of direct colonialism would also affect American relations around the world. Woodrow Wilson's support for self-determination applied only to European peoples, not those over whom they ruled in Africa and Asia (to the ire of W.E.B. **Du Bois**). Later, anti-**communism** translated into support for European masters against nationalists, who received moral and military support from the Soviet Union.

The Second World War brought a short-lived change in the American position on colonialism. Alliance with the Soviet Union weakened the negative association between communism and nationalism. Many Americans fighting against Nazism saw connections among fascism, colonialism and **segregation** at home. As the Japanese dislodged Europeans from much of East Asia, people questioned whether European colonialism had ended in the region; the British were beginning to lose their stranglehold on India, with Gandhi gaining a lot of support among Americans. Meanwhile, Americans appreciated nationalists and communists who, unlike their collaborating colonial masters, seemed willing to join them in the fight against Japan. Further, when the US lost the Philippines to the Japanese, American officials made strong promises about independence that would follow liberation from Japan. Nevertheless, while the US began to loosen its grip over Cuba and the Philippines, it made sure that the position of American businesses was secure, while **language**, culture and **tourism** continued to promote American hegemony.

While President **Roosevelt** had wondered about the advisability of allowing bankrupt European nations to re-establish control over their colonies, **Truman** decided that not supporting the French in Indo-China against America's erstwhile nationalist allies would run counter to the intentions of the **Marshall** Plan. Loss of **Vietnam**, Cambodia and Laos, his administration reasoned, would lead to a further French collapse in Algeria and then in France itself. Even when the French realized that the cost of retaining Southeast Asia was too great, they passed on the baton to the Americans who learned their lessons, not from the nationalists' victory at Dien-bien-phu, but from the bloody and successful British assaults on Malaysian nationalists.

Moreover, by this time, an anti-communist **Cold War** mentality had become firmly established in the United States. The "loss" of **China** to the communists had so shaken the American government that officials began to re-associate nationalism and communism. Once this took hold, the reaction to nationalist-inspired uprisings from Vietnam to **Iran** to Congo to Cuba to Guyana was to send in American forces (either military or **CIA** counter-insurgency) to oppose them. With the world divided neatly into those aligned with the Soviet Union and those loyal to the US, the latter had become a major neo-colonial power.

Defeat in **Vietnam** shook American anti-nationalist resolve for a few years, but **Reagan**'s destabilization of **Grenada** and continued tolerance of apartheid in South Africa showed that the connections were still largely in place. The collapse of the Soviet Union and the end of apartheid in South Africa, however, opened up new possibilities. Anti-communists like Marcos in the Philippines were no longer indispensable, while military bases could no longer be imposed on an independent country.

The language of neo-colonialism and imperialism shifted in the 1990s to a more value-free language of globalization. Yet, many legacies of colonialism and American support for other colonizers remain. Capital, largely in the form of **multinational** corporations, can now move more freely between nations, and those who profit from them are not exclusively Americans, but those who do the labor cannot move about so freely. Wealthier nations retain barriers to entry, ensuring that large exploitable pools of labor are available outside their borders to be used as **migrants** within the US when desirable, or as cheap laborers for a plant that has relocated outside the country. Profiting from cheap labor remains as important now as it was in the heyday of colonialism. As the "Made in USA" label has become a valuable asset for an article of clothing sold in America, it has become clear, however, that some of the best **department stores** are selling goods produced by the sweatshop labor of immigrants in the US, or by such laborers in places like **Guam**, **Saipan**, or other American territories.

The policies of US drug-enforcement agencies from Colombia to Panama and relations with **Castro**'s **Cuba** (for example, the Helms-Burton Act) provide a barometer of the level of American postcolonial policies. Anti-colonialism can still be a useful banner – as in American complaints about Chinese rule in Tibet – yet it represents a strategic interest to be balanced against others, as American silence on East Timorese bloodletting reaffirmed.

Finally, both media and business underpin a cultural hegemony that is read as a neo-colonial strategy by many who oppose the new American colossus and its values, even as their nations may acquire or emulate them. The processes and terms of colonialism have changed over time, but their silent and deadly entanglement with the American dream remains problematic and compelling.

Further reading

Kolko, G. (1988) *Confronting the Cold War*, New York: Pantheon.
Williams, W.A. (1980) *Empire as a Way of Life*, New York: Oxford.

ROBERT GREGG

Coltrane, John *see* jazz

Columbia Broadcasting System (CBS) *see* networks, television

columnists

Most journalists prior to the twentieth century did not distinguish as clearly as modern American journalists seem to between "fact" and "opinion."

Thus, Addison and Defoe in Britain or Benjamin Franklin in the United States wrote stories that modern readers would probably take for "columns." As the drive for objectivity became more important, however, a distinct sort of journalist began to appear in the pages of American newspapers. The origin of so-called newspaper columnists lies some time in the nineteenth century, when literary-inclined journalists began writing regular stories for newspapers. Some, like Ambrose Bierce, favored social or political satire; others, such as Lafcadio Hearn, produced humorous or colorful sketches of urban life. Although these writers were regularly featured in their papers, their writing was still not sharply distinguishable from the general news stories that surrounded them.

Columns developed a more important institutional role in the twentieth century as distinctions between "editorial" content – opinionated analysis of current events – and "news" – empirical descriptions – became more keenly drawn. Readers retained a desire for a more opinionated take on events: some guidance about not only what happened, but what the event in question *meant*. This resulted in more individual opinion columns.

Columnists' articles have generally appeared on the editorial pages, although they have expanded to sports and features. Gossip and trade news are special subgenres. Unlike editorials, columns are signed, meaning that they express the opinion only of the writer, not the newspaper as a whole. Columnists are often reporters of some standing and expertise or have had reputations in other fields, like Eleanor **Roosevelt** or Hillary Clinton. The writing in such columns is often more colorful and fiery than regular news, sometimes more analytical, but always more clearly subjective.

Famous newspaper columnists have included Walter Lippman, Walter Winchell, H.L. Mencken and Will Rogers. More recently, writers such as Molly Ivins and George Will have become popular enough among readers that their columns are syndicated. Some columnists develop reputations in one particular field. Dave Barry, for example, is known as a humor columnist; Red Smith was primarily a sports columnist.

Further reading

Riley, S.G. (1995) *Biographical Dictionary of American Newspaper Columnists*, Westport: Greenwood.
Mott, F. (1953) *American Journalism*, rev. edn, New York, MacMillan.

MARK BREWIN

comedy and comedians

Comedy resists definition. Some have argued that it is an adaptive strategy providing relief from the tragic or the mundane through laughter. To elicit this laughter, comedy assumes many forms. Types of comedy include slapstick, farce, black comedy, wordplay, burlesque, satire, vaudeville, **situation comedy** on **television**, stand-up comedy, clowning, mime, etc. However, some material considered "comedy" may not necessarily induce laughter. Comedy may simply refer to a presentation that focuses on the lighter side of life. In general, the term "comedy" has certain genre connotations, while the term "**humor**" refers to a comic quality causing amusement, such as dry humor, or buffoonery. Because of cultural assumptions regarding the nature and function of comedy, many members of marginalized groups (with respect to **race**, **class**, **ethnicity** or **religion**) have made their way into the entertainment industry through comedy, while the world of serious drama has been harder to penetrate. Women, however, have experienced more difficulty being taken "seriously" as comedians.

Since the end of the Second World War, one of the most important developments in American comedy has been the advent of the situation comedy on television. This form of comedy emerged from a long history of comedy in America – characterized by vaudeville, **film** comedy (including the silent film comedy of such luminaries as Charlie Chaplin, Buster Keaton and Harold Lloyd), **radio** comedy, stand-up comedy and variety television shows. Since the introduction of the VCR, **video** rentals, and **cable** television in the late 1970s, there has been much crossover between these various comedic venues. Many of the American comedians who started out with stand-up routines in comedy clubs and then moved on to film and/or television careers have become quite successful. (Consider the careers of Woody **Allen**, Bill **Cosby**, Ellen DeGeneres, Robin Williams, Whoopi **Goldberg** and Jerry Seinfeld – to name just a few.) Prior to this route, many American comedians started out in vaudeville (George **Burns** and Gracie Allen, for example, who went on to begin one of the first television situation comedies, *The George Burns and Gracie Allen Show*, which ran from 1950–8). Comedian Bob **Hope** also developed a genre of television specials based on his shows for American troops abroad, rebroadcast on holidays.

Still, there are comedians who are known primarily for certain types of comedy. Analysts have divided comedians into various types, including social commentators, politicos, observationalists, fringe players, wiseguys, etc. Other notable American comedians of the postwar era include (in addition to those mentioned above): Lily Tomlin, Eddie **Murphy**, Jackie Gleason, Jim Carrey, Chevy Chase, Gilda Radner, Walter Matthau, Margaret Cho, Jack Benny, Billy Crystal, Goldie Hawn, Jim Belushi, Jerry **Lewis**, Dean Martin, Johnny Carson, Jane Curtin, Richard **Pryor**, Lenny Bruce, Lucille **Ball**, Desi Arnaz, David Letterman, Sandra Bernhard, Flip Wilson, Jay Leno, Bill Murray, John Leguziamo, Mary Tyler **Moore**, Spalding Gray, Mel Brooks, Carl Reiner, Cheech and Chong, Roseanne, Steve Martin, Marilyn **Monroe**, Gene Wilder, Dan Ackroyd, Redd Foxx and Henny Youngman.

See also: humor; late-night television; sitcoms

Further reading

Museum of Television and Radio (1996) *Stand-Up Comedians on Television*, New York: Harry N. Abrams.

Marc, D. (1989) *Comic Visions: Television Comedy and American Culture*, Boston: Unwin Hyman.

NICOLE MARIE KEATING

comfort food

Comfort **food** evades precise definitions and descriptions. Described by one restaurant critic as "satisfying stick-to-your-ribs fare" that echoes "simpler times," and is "informal and ample;" others define it as food with lots of sugar, or more than fifty grams of fat. Some focus on comfort food's emotional and curative qualities, claiming that it evokes memories, eases emotional discomfort, alleviates boredom, or soothes upset stomachs. Definitely not for the calorie-conscious, comfort-food menus might include meatloaf, **fried chicken**, mashed potatoes, biscuits and gravy, rice pudding, milkshakes, tuna casserole, grilled cheese, or peanut butter and banana sandwiches on squishy white bread (or congee or miso soup for other ethnic food traditions).

COURTNEY BENNETT

comics

Comic strips as serially published, episodic stories with consistent characters appeared in the US newspapers in the late nineteenth century, drawing on European traditions of stories, caricature and publication. Comic books as separate publications with independent sales and narrative first drew on established strips. In the 1930s, they became a new genre with different audiences, themes and cultural issues. Despite overlapping form, content and readership, their histories have been differentiated in intriguing ways.

The first American comic strip, the *Yellow Kid*, appeared in William Randolph Hearst's *New York Journal* on October 18, 1996. Longer stories developed with strips like the *Katzenjammer Kids* and *Happy Hooligan*, often taking outsiders and tricksters as their long-running heroes. These comics often incorporated ethnic, racial and **class** stereotypes in slapstick situations that depended on the interplay of word and picture. Weekday comics followed in the 1900s, and Hearst added the full comics page to his **newspapers** in 1912, although the page included only four strips. The number of strips offered by competing newspapers grew over the next decades; distribution was soon controlled by syndicates like Hearst's King Features or the Newspaper Enterprise Association.

Comic strips appeal to a general audience. The *New York Times*, *Wall Street Journal* and *USA Today* carry none, although the *International Herald Tribune* makes a selection available to expatriates. In other newspapers, daily funnies and Sunday color sections have grown in pages to become **family** reading rituals.

The range of comics in contemporary newspapers still covers many themes worked out in early decades – domestic vignettes, adventures, humor with **children** and animals. Many strips treat family and office, like the long-running *Blondie*, *Dennis the Menace* or *Family Circus*. Smart **pets** and children also convey philosophical commentaries in decades of the remarkably creative ensemble of Charles Schulz's *Peanuts*; *Snoopy* earned global popularity. Later, Bill Watterson's *Calvin and Hobbes* evoked the imaginary world of a child and his tiger. *Prince Valiant* and the *Phantom* seek exotic adventure. *Beetle Bailey* offers **comedy** in an army that never fights, while *Dick Tracy* has battled generations of bizarre criminals. At the end of the twentieth century, some once-popular genres and strips have faded, including soap operas (*Mary Worth*) and adventure (Milt Caniff's *Steve Canyon*). Nonetheless, all these narratives convey the idea of material the whole family can read.

One of the areas of greatest change in the postwar era is replacement of ethnic, racial and gender stereotypes that constituted humor in early comics. Many comics still represent **white** worlds and heterosexual families. Yet Cathy explores the employment, family and dilemmas of a single working woman, while *Dilbert* has become a symbol of office politics, with clippings taped to cubicles across the nation. Even *Blondie*, icon of domesticity, took a job in the 1990s. Minority characters have appeared in *Peanuts* and other strips; in the 1990s, newspapers added focused **African American** stories in strips like *Jump Cut* and *Boondocks*.

Other timely specializations include political satire (*Al Capp* in Pogo, Garry Trudeau's **Doones-bury**, Berke Breathed's strips) and basic surrealism (Gary Larson). These cartoonists target issues and politicians (*Doonesbury* on gay weddings, media and **tobacco**, as well as the **presidency**) for educated, adult readers. Hence, some newspapers have censored strips or moved them to the editorial pages (see **editorial cartoons**).

Comic books

If comic strips began with children and immigrants, comic books began with **superheroes**. Booklets of reprinted comic strips had appeared at the turn of the nineteenth century, but separate stories emerged in the mid-1930s. *Detective Comics* offered single-theme issues in 1937. In June 1938, *Action Comics* introduced Superman; within three years, the Man of Steel was selling 1,250,000 copies per month and had crossed over to comic strips as well. The *Phantom*, *Captain Marvel*, *Batman*, *Captain America* and others followed, with comics booming during the Second World War at home and among GIs, as illustrated heroes fought Nazis and Japanese. These comics also established a format for a mass cultural myth of the dual-identity superhero in the golden age of comics.

Superheroes diminished in popularity after the war, replaced by crime and horror comics sold at drug stores, news-stands and other outlets to children and adolescents. These new consumers bought 180 million copies a year by 1941, alarming parents and educators who began a crusade against the lax morality, violence and other dangers of comics that would last for decades and foreshadow later debates over **music and television**, movies and video games. Alternatives were created including *Classic Comics/Classics Illustrated*, whose illustrated versions of world literature became crib sheets as well as portals to culture.

After Estes **Kefauver**'s Senate investigations and academic studies of deleterious impact, publishers themselves created the first substantive Comics Code in 1954. This created conditions for the revival of the sexless superhero and anodyne comics, including *Disney* and *Archie*. By the mid-1950s, nonetheless, superheroes old and new (including the Flash, Fantastic Four and others from *Marvel Comics*) offered the complex stories and aesthetic styles of comics' "second" golden age.

As Ariel Dorfman has pointed out, all of these texts tend to distill fundamental American myths into child-palatable forms. "Truth, justice and the American way" in *Superman* intersected with capitalism, derogatory stereotypes of foreigners and **intellectuals** and sexless ducks and mice in *Disney*. These messages, moreover, were consumed by children outside the US even while US parents discouraged comics.

The 1960s saw many changes in comic books, including increasing crossover to television and film. Contents also changed – inspired by social ferment around them, artists and writers incorporated drugs, war and racism into the comic world in the 1970s, although this phase proved short-lived. Instead, new relevance came from underground comics like those of Robert Crumb. Later, more adult stories, like *Darkman*, which offer narrative and visual experiments as well as sexual and violent plots, would underpin the serious comics of the end of the century. At the same time, collectors have sought the innocence of earlier comics as first editions of *Superman* and other relics of the golden age skyrocketed in price beyond the reach of children.

Comics no longer sell primarily to the child in the drugstore, but to older adolescent males or young adults. Moreover, these people are buying specialty store items, sometimes in plastic bags to preserve their **collectible** value or in brown paper to avert them from other eyes. In this development, while comic strips have reflected the changing **family**, comic books have followed the aging and concerns of the **baby boom**, while creating new experiences in Generation X. They also inspire movies like *Batman*, *Superman* and *X-Men* (2000).

Further reading

Barrier, M. and Williams, M. (1981) *The Smithsonian Book of Comic Book Comics*, Washington, DC: Smithsonian.

Blackbeard, M. and Williams, M. (1977) *The Smithsonian Book of Newspaper Comics*, Washington, DC: Smithsonian.

Dorfman, A. and Mattelart, A. (1975) *How to Read Donald Duck*, New York: International General.

Harvey, R. (1996) *The Art of the Comic Book*, Jackson: University of Mississippi.

Nyberg, A. (1998) *Seal of Approval*, Jackson: University of Mississippi.

GARY McDONOGH

coming of age

Adulthood is marked in American society, as in most cultures worldwide, by both rituals and responsibilities. Differences in individual and collective experience and values, however, make these passages of **teenage** years foci of anxiety as well as badges of maturity.

Judaism and many Christian traditions celebrate rituals around adult participation in the community (*Bar/Bat Mitzvah* confirmation, baptism in some evangelical traditions). American Catholics, nonetheless, have debated the meaning and timing of confirmation as a socially relevant life sacrament.

Other secular landmarks are reached – and responded to – in different ways throughout the teenage years. Obtaining a driver's license at sixteen (with some states permitting a learner's permit a year earlier) has become a major point of transition in an **automobile** culture. **Freedom**, responsibility and danger intertwine here in both mass culture and parental nightmares. Various **commencements/graduations** (especially **high school**), voting (at eighteen) and legal access to alcohol (at twenty-one) also indicate increasing responsibility as well as risk. These fixed ages also lead to attempts to anticipate or subvert the law, especially with regard to **alcohol** and **tobacco**.

Passages may be gendered in both religious and secular observations. Women, for example, are often still classified as adults in terms of sexuality and marriageability. In a small segment of immigrant families, female circumcision occurs as the girl reaches puberty, although avoidance of this tradition has also been used to claim refugee status in the US. The **quinceanos**, an often lavish celebration of a girl's fifteenth birthday, has become widespread in **Cuban American** and other **Latino** groups. This represents an adaptation of debutante parties held by the Cuban elite, augmented by the newfound affluence of many exiles: one father rented the Orange Bowl, **Miami**'s **football** stadium, for a party. Coming-out parties and debutante balls are generally considered upper class (and sometimes dated) formalities, but they have also served to reinforce **class** endogamy.

Meanwhile, at eighteen, men have been expected to register for the selective service. In the Vietnam era, this act became a boiling point of protest, as well as a commitment with potentially devastating consequences; while the **draft** was ended in the 1970s, registration remains an obligation. The US, with its longstanding tradition of a volunteer army, is unusual in the absence of compulsory military service as a male rite of passage – although it may be evoked in debates like the intergenerational conflict between Bob **Dole**, wounded in the Second World War, and Bill **Clinton**, who avoided service in Vietnam.

One of the crucial elements of coming of age, however, has even less ceremony: leaving home. American youths have often sought independence in living, whether moving away to **college**, taking an apartment with work-mates, joining a **commune** or defining a separate space in the home (basement or **garage** apartment). This can also be linked to entry into the job market and is hence dependent on cycles of employment opportunity. Since the 1980s, media have also focused on children who stay – or return – to the family home in their twenties or thirties as social dilemmas.

GARY McDONOGH

coming out

In the largely heterosexual context of American society, the process of revealing oneself as a homosexual or bisexual individual is termed "coming out of the closet." Coming out is, strictly speaking, a never-ending process, because there are always more people to tell. However, coming out is commonly understood as the period of time in which individuals first begin to tell people about their sexuality. Individuals generally make different decisions about which people in their lives they should tell about their sexuality, according to their personal situation.

ELIZABETH A. GALEWSKI

commencement/graduation

American graduations, from preschool through **Ivy League** doctorates, represent highly ceremonial public rites of passage. Typical features include academic robes (modeled on European ones), processions of faculty and students, music, prayers based in civic Christianity and speeches; graduations are also accompanied by rounds of parties and gifts. Friends and family attend these events even in early years, although young children may treat them as costumed play-acting. By **high school**, speakers, usually drawn from distinguished graduates or local celebrities, take on more importance, while the presence of **religion** has become a debate for many public institutions. High-school graduations also form part of a constellation of events, from the prom (a formal dance based on a romantic theme from movies or popular culture) to "socially accepted" disobedience (e.g. wearing inappropriate clothing to school). Graduation gifts and opportunities thereafter reveal stratification these communal rituals deny.

Colleges and universities expand graduation events, competing for well-known speakers via honorary degrees and/or fees up to thousands of dollars. More than 2,500 speakers are needed annually to please parents, contributors and media. Politicians may use such opportunities as campaign appearances; presidential candidates and their spouses receive particular media attention (with military academies especially visible sites for incumbents). Other coveted speakers include **intellectuals**, artists, journalists, social and ethnic leaders, and philanthropists/donors. Celebrities including Muppet Kermit the Frog, also prove entertaining alternatives.

Commencement talks range from autobiography to national and world affairs. Generally, however, these inspirational observations demand special responsibility from the group whose new maturity and citizenship the ceremony recognizes. Hence, the theme of beginnings (commencement) mingles with the ambivalent emotions of ending and leaving.

Large and highly established institutions foster distinctive programs, regalia and surrounding events. Some, for example, hold speeches on a separate day or break into component units to provide intimacy and individual recognition in conferring degrees (in English or, rarely, in Latin for the doctorate). Doctoral robes may have distinctive colors – crimson for Harvard, blue for Yale, etc. – although without the elaboration of many European institutions. Religious rituals may accompany these events too, whatever the affiliation of the institution.

The image of this rite of passage is prominent in literature and movies, whether *The Graduate* (1967), the prom chaos of *Carrie* (1976), or many **television** series (e.g. *Beverly Hills 90210*). It represents less a dedication to education within American life than a culture of recognition that democratizes many honors (even as institutions and individuals set themselves apart). Hence the prestigious model of university graduation has spread to younger age groups and to more limited programs (such as job-training programs or self-improvement courses). Even non-human settings like canine obedience schools may imitate this form, stressing the notions of individual achievement and group recognition as much as divisive special merit. The latter, none-theless, comes out in the distinctions among programs and rewards thereafter.

GARY McDONOGH

Commoner, Barry

b. 1917

Biologist whose initial concerns with cellular activity led him to become a public activist in postwar environmental issues, which he views as problems caused by human beings to be overcome by thoughtful intervention and changes. Commoner's work on the effects of radiation made him an outspoken opponent of nuclear weapons and testing. Over time, his concerns have encompassed production and consumption – pesticides, **auto-mobiles**, energy – as they affect a global ecological balance. Commoner founded the Center for the Biology of Natural Systems and the Citizens' Party, which ran him for **president**. His significant works include *The Closing Circle* (1971) and *Making Peace with the Planet* (1980).

SHARON ANN HOLT

communes

America has incorporated a long history of people choosing to embrace alternative communal socie-ties, from the initial vision of Pilgrims through later groups, including the Shakers, the Oneida com-munities, **Mormons** and socialists. This heritage was revitalized in the 1960s by youths using communal settings as support to escape commerci-alism and other American values. Some were

religious, with a special fascination with Eastern **religion**. Others, both ephemeral and longer-enduring, were defined by lifestyles, new values of **gender and sexuality**, "**nature**" and simplicity or vague countercultural ideologies.

Further reading

Hayden, D. (1976) *Seven American Utopias*, Cam-bridge, MA: MIT (gives a historical perspective).

GARY McDONOGH

communism

Communism has occupied quite diverse and conflicting positions in modern American culture. In the 1930s, during the years of the non-sectarian Popular Front against fascism in the world Com-munist movement, the Communist Party in the United States contributed to the development of powerful organizing campaigns in favor of Social Security, racial equality and industrial unionism. In the early years of the Great Depression, a number of prominent writers and **intellectuals**, including Theodore Dreiser, Langston Hughes, Richard **Wright**, John Dos Passos and Edmund **Wilson**, wrote favorably about communism, the American Communist movement and the Soviet Union. How-ever, the Communist Party itself remained commit-ted to a Leninist "militant-minority" methodology of social change, and usually adhered in public to the "line" of Soviet foreign policy. In the years just before the Second World War, the development of powerful moral critiques of Stalinism seriously began to complicate many intellectuals' interest in and enthusiasm for the "Soviet Experiment."

Partly as a consequence of its close association with Soviet communism, American communism has been both favored and abhorred by advocates of economic equality, the welfare state and labor unionism. Both the friends and enemies of **civil rights** and civil liberties have invoked anti-communism. Especially at the height of the **Cold War** in the 1950s, the American Communist Party was ritually denounced by members of the educa-tional, religious, political and cultural establish-ments, and communists or anyone associated with communism as an indigenous social movement were often persecuted or denied employment. However, few American elites believed that the American Communist Party was ever a real threat to the security of American institutions. Instead, communism and communists often came to represent the racial, ethnic and even gendered "other" in the midst of conflicts over what constituted "Americanism" in American political discourse.

Following the Second World War, conservative politicians were able to connect communism with New Deal liberalism in the popular imagination by exploiting populist undercurrents of resentment against state intervention and "social experimentation."

The conviction of Alger Hiss, a former mid-level official in the **Roosevelt** administration, for perjury in a spy case (1950) allowed **Republicans** to associate the New Deal with the disloyalty or incompetence of liberal policy elites. Following the conviction and subsequent executions of Ethel and Julius Rosenberg for atomic spying (1950–3), communism was linked more firmly than ever in the popular imagination with subversion, even though there is little evidence that either Hiss or the Rosenbergs seriously compromised American security. Large majorities of Americans came to believe that the Communist Party in the US should be outlawed and that communists should not be allowed to teach.

In the 1970s and 1980s, communism retained elements of its racial, **class**, ethnic and treasonous identifications for many Americans, and American politicians continued to more-or-less successfully portray world communism as America's most dangerous external enemy. Following the end of the Cold War and the fall of communist regimes in Eastern Europe and the Soviet Union, some astute critics even claimed to detect a loss of American national purpose.

Further reading

Denning, M. (1996) *The Cultural Front*, London: Verso.

Schrecker, E. (1998) *Many are the Crimes*, Boston: Little, Brown.

EDWARD JOHANNIGSMEIER

community

Community has a longstanding positive, albeit nebulous, value reiterated in American social sciences as well as political rhetoric. "Community groups," "community boards" and "faith community" all underscore civic virtues of cooperation, unity and citizenship in contrast to potentially divisive images of **clubs**, **neighborhoods**, or religious sects. Community service is an increasingly common requirement for **high-school** and **college** students in the late twentieth and early twenty-first centuries, while "community" appears in analyses and politics as an alternative to politics and government – a real America.

While community has thus entered the sacrosanct mythology of mom and apple pie for many Americans, these usages also betray certain negative aspects that demand attention. First, community may easily be used in an exclusionary fashion. Preserving "community," for example, sounds better than resisting integration or newcomers. Appeal to "community standards" also has a long career in **censorship** of American art and literature, from Joyce's *Ulysses* to the nudes of Robert **Mapplethorpe**.

Second, community can also be an imposition on others. To speak of the "black" or "**Asian American**" *community* (avoiding race) or "gay and lesbian" community implies a unity of action and experience, much less volition that does not reflect the lives or politics of individuals and groups that constitute these segments of American society. While Benedict Anderson's concept of an imagined community arising through shared media can provide insights into American nationhood as well as Southeast Asia, we must always watch who does the imagining.

Finally, community can be used in ways that are patently false. Sales brochures refer to **suburbs** and walled developments as residential or **gated communities**, despite the alienation that often characterizes them.

Nonetheless, the stress on building shared interests and dialogues – "community **video/ television**" or "community activism" – underscores the creative processes of American society and change, at times in opposition to inherited structures or government/corporate control. In the decline of government safety nets in health, education and welfare, "community service" also forces many Americans to confront the dualization of contemporary society and its consequences.

Further reading

Baltzell, E. (ed.) (1968) *The Search for Community in Modern America*, New York: Harper & Row.

GARY McDONOGH

community colleges/junior colleges

Two-year college programs, often focused on vocational goals, have grown rapidly since the Second World War to encompass more than 10 million students (about half part-time) in 1,100 institutions – about 44 percent of American undergraduates. Community colleges grant nearly half-a-million degrees annually, plus thousands of certificates. Programs are either terminal (AA/AS – Associate of Arts or Sciences) or preparatory for attendance at a four-year college. From **Philadelphia** Community College or East **Los Angeles** Community College to Native American institutions like Oglala Lakota College in South Dakota or New Mexico's Navajo-based Dine College, community colleges have created unique opportunities to democratize college and incorporate diverse students into its academic life.

While private junior colleges had emerged to fulfill these roles in the early twentieth century, "**community**" colleges were established after the Second World War as part of educational restructuring on the part of state universities to reach less-educated students, while not diluting their central **campuses** as research and teaching universities. They were intended to be located within commuting distance for high-school graduates as well, thus decentralizing state education, and to offer flexible schedules and cheaper classes (sometimes at the expense of professors). In the 1960s, these colleges became central to the planning of systems in **California**, Kentucky and **Midwestern** states and later expanding into the **Sunbelt**. Often envisioned for rural areas and small towns, they

were also incorporated into urban education, including the **CUNY** system in **New York**. They have also taken on responsibilities in professional retraining, adult education and **welfare**-to-work programs.

In 1996 California had more than 1.8 million students enrolled in 106 public community colleges; it was followed by Illinois, **Texas** and **Florida**. Of this total, roughly 137 colleges are private; technical institutes and private schools owned by families or corporations constitute a rather gray area in this educational branch. Some of these junior colleges, for example, specialize in women's education or the arts; Kilgore College in Texas has become known nationwide for its precision drill team, the Rangerettes.

While community colleges have proven immensely popular, they have also been easy targets for attack because of the non-academic nature of their vocational classes: the most popular programs tend to be in health services (registered nurse, dental hygiene, physical therapist), business, telecommunications and mechanical fields. The need for remedial programs in **language** and **math** that face many of the colleges also denigrates students and institutions as inferior rather than service-oriented (a frequent charge in New York City reforms). Community colleges are also involved in education and class, drawing poorer, minority immigrant and working students rather than the pool of elite liberal arts students or other four-year course students – 55 percent are **Hispanic** and Native American students. Their continuing success, on both an individual and a collective level, underscores both the opportunities and demands of American education in the early twenty-first century.

Further reading

Sutton, R. (1970) *Community College or Four Year Program?*, Lexington: University of Kentucky.
http://www.aacc.nche.edu (American Association of Community Colleges)

GARY McDONOGH
CINDY WONG

community organization

Community-based organizations have been a distinctive feature of American democratic life since the founding of the Republic, one that Alexis de Tocqueville praised as evidencing Americans' unique ability for what he called, "the art of association." Such organizations have been thought of as integral to American civic life, knitting together an ethnically diverse population through mediating between localities and **neighborhoods** and the more formal institutions of government. In contemporary usage, the term "community organizing" very often refers to a form of community-based action, which, like labor **union** movements, relies primarily on the use of confrontational tactics. Although collective action certainly existed in urban neighborhoods prior to the development of this model, community organizing in the US today remains most closely associated with the figure of Saul Alinsky (1909–72). Alinsky developed his model of direct action based on his experiences as a labor union organizer with the Council of Industrial Organizations (CIO). In contrast to community development work undertaken in many other national contexts, which usually relies primarily on governmental sources for funding and which tends to emphasize service delivery, Alinsky called for community organizations to raise their own funds and to remain politically autonomous.

His legacy lives on in many neighborhoods around the United States, although very few of the organizations existing today were actually founded by either Alinsky or his direct "heirs." The Industrial Areas Foundation (IAF), based in **New York** City, NY, continues to train organizers according to Alinsky's model. In any case, despite a variety of organizational structures and a multiplicity of different kinds of tactics and philosophies, Alinsky remains a seminal figure.

Over the past twenty years, there has been such an outpouring of works on the Citizen Action movement in the United States that it would be impossible to include mention of them all here. The best sources for an overview of the nature and role of both Alinsky-style neighborhood organizations and many other types of grassroots movements as well are books by H.C. Boyte. See: Boyte, H.C.

(1989) *CommonWealth: A Return to Citizen Politics*, New York: The Free Press; Boyte, H.C. (1984) *Community is Possible: Repairing America's Roots*, New York: Harper and Row; Boyte, H.C. (1980) *The Backyard Revolution: Understanding the New Citizen Movement*, Philadelphia: Temple University Press; Boyte, H.C. and Kari, N. (1996) *Building America*, Philadelphia: Temple University Press; and Evans, S. and Boyte, H.C. (1986) *Free Spaces: The Source of Democratic Change in America*, New York: Harper & Row.

Further reading

Bailey, R. (1972) *Radicals in Urban Politics: The Alinsky Approach*, Chicago: University of Chicago Press.
Silberman, C. (1964) *Crisis in Black and White*, New York: Vintage Books (includes a discussion of the work of the Temporary Woodlawn Organization (TWO), Alinsky's first project in an African American neighborhood (located on the south side of Chicago)).
Slayton, R.A. (1986) *Back of the Yards: The Making of a Local Democracy*, Chicago: University of Chicago Press.

SUSAN BRIN HYATT

commuting/mass transit

The sprawling of many postwar American **cities** has made the movement of massive numbers of people from home to work, school and other places an everyday planning nightmare, especially when done by car. Nevertheless, while mass commuting is constantly proposed as a solution to resultant dilemmas of cost, time and pollution, it is not an effective reality in most cities.

Some metropolitan areas, in fact, have inherited infrastructures of subways, **trains** and streetcars that, with **buses**, underpin extensive and viable systems in **New York** City, **Boston, MA**, **Chicago, IL** and **Philadelphia, PA** – although the latter is continually losing ridership. Other cities have invested in subway–bus combinations in the late twentieth and early twenty-first century, including **Atlanta, GA**, **San Francisco, CA**, **Washington, DC**, **Baltimore, MD** and **Los Angeles, CA**; some of these systems are only skeletal. Light-rail systems have also gained popularity as investments in **Miami, FL** and **Portland, OR**.

Yet, much of mass commuting in the end seeks to ameliorate the impact of the **automobile** through car-pooling, high-occupancy lanes on highways and incentives/disincentives for employers. Transportation-oriented development, in the longer run, may systematize connections to reduce automotive dependence, but American lifestyles and choices make effective mass commuting a tough sell politically and economically.

GARY McDONOGH

computers

The theoretical foundations of modern computing machines were laid in the early twentieth century when mathematical philosophers in Europe and the United States, spurred by the invention of internally consistent, non-Euclidean geometries, explored problems of rationality, provability and logic machines. These explorations culminated in the 1930s with the invention of idealized, hypothetical, general computing machines. The exigencies of the Second World War brought state funding to these mathematicians, and electronic calculating machines were built based on their theoretical designs. In Britain these machines were used to break German codes; in the US research was geared towards atomic-bomb production.

After the Second World War, British development of calculating machines languished, while in the US developers created private corporations and sought markets for their products. However, the secrecy of the previous research, the enormous government funding behind it and the narrow focus of their application had produced machines which were huge, complex, expensive and difficult to adapt or program. Markets for these machines were difficult to find and at first limited to government agencies, including the Department of Defense and the Census Bureau. In an attempt to create market consciousness, Remington Rand lent one of its machines, the UNIVAC, to CBS to assist in predicting the outcome of the 1952 presidential election. When it forecast the landslide

results more accurately than human experts, the computer entered popular consciousness as an omniscient "electronic brain."

Its use spread to large corporations in data-intensive industries such as banking and insurance. International Business Machines (**IBM**), renowned as the epitome of white, male, crew-cut, button-down efficiency, quickly became the dominant manufacturer of computing equipment. Payroll management became one of the earliest data-processing service industries. During this period, the instruction sets which guided the computer's operations, and the data on which the computer operated, were stored on "punch cards." These were pieces of cardboard, measuring about 2.5 inches by 6 inches, through which small rectangular holes were punched. The pattern of the holes represented a particular instruction or data point. They were fed into the computer by high-speed mechanical devices which frequently jammed. To prevent such jams, punch cards had to be handled carefully, and were often imprinted with the phrase "Do not fold, spindle, or mutilate." These cards became the mediator between millions of people and the world's largest and most powerful institutions. They became symbolic of computers themselves – vast storehouses of **information** – used by people who didn't really understand them to perform calculations of a complexity far beyond human capabilities, producing inscrutable and incontestable decisions. They were the embodiment of bureaucratic oppression. Bumper stickers and T-shirts proclaimed "I am a human being. Do not fold, spindle, or mutilate."

In the late 1960s and early 1970s, several technological and social changes occurred which altered the popular involvement with, and perceptions of, the computer. The first of these was the development of transistors, integrated circuits and microchips which permitted miniaturization, standardization and mass production of processors. The second was a development of a play, rather than work, culture around computers. This latter development proceeded, in part, from the increased availability of computers to college students on a time-share basis. As these students began to experiment with programming languages, human-machine interfaces and multiple-user machines, they developed very simple two-person games.

Hobbyists also began to buy computer kits publicized through popular magazines and to build machines, which, though rudimentary, had an adaptable design and public technical specifications. Thus computer use spread from corporate culture into the **middle-class**, college-educated, young male culture of the early 1970s.

In 1977 two of these men, Steve Jobs and Steve Wozniak, produced the Apple II in a **suburban** garage. At first marketed through hobbyist clubs, it became the first mass-market personal computer (PC). Originally useful only for word processing and game playing, it was not until the invention of business-oriented spreadsheet programs that the "PC revolution" started to take off. In 1984 Jobs and Wozniak introduced the **Apple** Macintosh, marketing it to both home and office users. Symbolically positioned against institutionalized, even totalitarian, bureaucratic power, the Macintosh was advertised as "the machine for the rest of us." This marketing approach was fabulously successful. Fortunes were made in computers, software and peripherals, and the new money was conspicuously young, male and west coast.

IBM, in a hurried attempt to extend their dominance from mainframe computing into the new realm of PCs, entered into non-exclusive license agreements with Intel (for microprocessors) and Microsoft (for operating-system software). IBM branding provided the assurance necessary to convince millions of users to make the substantial economic investment that a personal computer represented, and the Intel/Microsoft configuration became an industry standard, competing with Apple for the hearts and minds (and dollars) of US personal computer users. By the mid-1990s, IBM had lost its market share of PCs to other manufacturers, even though the technical standard was still referred to as "IBM-compatibility." Despite much of the hype surrounding the "PC revolution," the social diffusion of these machines in the early twenty-first century remains predominantly white, middle-class and male.

As PCs replaced mainframes in offices, internal networks linked individual machines to central data servers, reasserting centralized surveillance and control. Bill **Gates**, as the founder and principal stockholder of Microsoft, became the richest man in the US, his fortune rivaling those of Rockefeller,

Carnegie and the Vanderbilts. Thus PCs, originally imagined as machines for **freedom** and individuality, are again implicated in historically deep-seated reactions against big money and corporate power.

These tensions between centrality of power and diffusion, between freedom and domination, are exacerbated as processors are further miniaturized and incorporated into such amenities as cars and appliances, and as networking technologies and practices increasingly link these processors in various topologies of communication and control.

Further reading

Ceruzzi, P.E. (1998) *A History of Modern Computing*, Cambridge, MA: MIT.

Kling, R. (ed.) (1996) *Computerization and Controversy*, 2nd edn, San Diego: Academic Press.

Levy, S. (1984) *Hackers: Heroes of the Computer Revolution*, Garden City: Anchor/Doubleday.

DAVID J. PHILLIPS

computer/video games

Atari, an American company formed in 1972 by Nolan Bushnell, a University of California engineering graduate, became the first major company to dominate the computer and video-game market. Building on popular games like Pong, Asteroids and Breakout, Atari became the leading name in consoles for **televisions**, video-arcade games and personal **computers**. This lasted until 1984 when Atari unsuccessfully began to stress computer over console production at a time when the personal computer market was undergoing great change with considerable competition between the **Apple** Macintosh and **IBM** clones, partly because the console market itself had reached saturation point from over-production.

Into the vacuum moved Japanese companies like Nintendo, Sega and Sony who now dominate the American computer-game and arcade market. Nintendo markets popular games for its consoles and "game boys," while Sega's Genesis machine and Sony's PlayStation have grabbed a large share of the American market. Depicting street combat, **wrestling** or Kung Fu, the level of **violence** associated with these games has intensified, while the graphics have improved, sparking widespread fears that children are being desensitized to killing. The increased sophistication of personal computers, with the added possibility of downloading popular games like a new Pokémon craze, makes this a volatile marketplace, economically and culturally.

ROBERT GREGG

conceptual art

An international avant-garde visual arts movement that emerged in the mid- to late 1960s, conceptual art was concerned with the idea of art, and questioned the extent to which the production of objects was necessary. In this sense, it extended **minimalism**'s focus on the architectural conditions of aesthetic experience into an interrogation of broader institutional and linguistic conditions. Works that existed only as instructions or as photographic documentation of activities emphasized the idea of an artwork over its status as an object, and sought to explore conditions, such as viewers' expectations of institutional spaces like **museums**, or the relations between perception and the **language** used to describe it. Central figures included the British group Art & Language, Robert Barry, Mel Bochner, the Australian Ian Burn (also in collaboration with Mel Ramsden), the German Hanne Darboven, Douglas Huebler, Joseph Kosuth, Sol Le Witt, Adrian Piper and Lawrence Weiner. In a characteristically conceptual statement of October 12, 1969, Weiner wrote, "1. The artist may construct the work. 2. The work may be fabricated. 3. The work need not be built." Despite its critique of art as an elitist field, conceptual art met considerable resistance from popular audiences, but it has been a significant influence on subsequent developments in **contemporary (postmodern) art**.

Further reading

Meyer, U. (ed.) (1972) *Conceptual Art*, New York: E.P. Dutton.

FRAZER WARD

concerts

Concerts constitute a crucial part of American postwar cultural life; much be can learned from the choices of the viewer. In most larger American **cities**, there are distinct venues for **classical music**, **jazz** and **rock 'n' roll** music. Increasingly, touring artists who don't fit neatly into these categories have also ventured into these spaces. Ranging from individual performers or pianists playing just one night to a symphony doing a season, concert halls are a center for cultural activity (and social organization by **class**, age, **race** and **gender**). Unlike clubs, customers sit in assigned seating, with a traditional proscenium stage in a hall designed with acoustics in mind. It is a more formal way to hear music and hence, even in the casual twentieth century, people tended to dress up and make an appearance.

Many attempts have been made to reach out to non-traditional or younger audiences. One of the ways in which city agencies have done this is by sponsoring free out-of-door concerts in the summertime. In **New York**, for example, such luminaries as Luciano Pavarotti and Diana **Ross** have performed concerts outdoors, as have many other lesser-known singers and musicians. In smaller towns, churches and meeting halls are often used as spaces for concerts – for local performers as well as performers on tours. On **college campuses**, concert halls are an important part of campus life, as artistic directors try to bring in acts that will serve both the students and the local residents. Touring agencies and agents have helped to make this aspect of the music industry a large part of commerce that helps to sells albums.

See also: performing arts centers

EDWARD MILLER

Congress

The Congress of the United States is the legislative branch of the federal government, established by Article I of the Constitution. Congress comprises the 435-member House of Representatives and the 100-member Senate. Each House member represents a portion of a state, and all House districts include approximately the same number of people (pursuant to a 1962 **Supreme Court** decision). Each senator represents an entire state, and each state has two senators. The entire House is up for re-election every two years; senators serve six-year terms and one-third of the Senate seats are up for election in each election cycle. As a result of these structural distinctions, the House and Senate have significantly different rules and cultures and, frequently, different politics.

For most of the postwar period, Congress has been controlled by the **Democratic Party**. The Democrats controlled the House, without inter-ruption, from 1955 through 1994, often by wide margins, and they controlled the Senate during those years as well, except from 1981 through 1986. In the 1994 elections, in a stunning reversal, **Republicans** gained control of both bodies, and they held onto that majority, albeit by thinner and thinner margins, through 2000.

Ideological control of Congress followed a somewhat different pattern. Congress gradually became more liberal through the 1950s, but a conservative coalition of Southern Democrats (sometimes called **Dixiecrats**) and rural Repub-licans was often able to exercise a stranglehold over Congress into the early 1960s. Liberals gained control by the mid-1960s, swept in by Lyndon **Johnson**'s landslide victory in 1964 and replen-ished by the post-**Watergate** 1974 congressional elections. Conservatives gradually made a come-back through the 1980s before consolidating their power in the 1994 elections. In 1995 the keystone of the conservative majority was once again the **South**, now mostly represented by Republicans and exercising additional political muscle, thanks to the shift of population to the **Sunbelt**.

But, no matter who has been at the helm, the public attitude towards Congress throughout the postwar period has generally been one of scorn. From President Harry **Truman** running against the Republican "do-nothing" Congress in 1948 to member of Congress Newt **Gingrich** excoriating the Democratic Congress in 1994 to President Bill **Clinton** attacking the Gingrich-led Congress in 1996, Congress has been a reliable politi-cal whipping-boy, an object of public derision and dismay.

While its popularity has varied from year to year, Congress' approval ratings in polls since 1966 have been below 50 percent (after an unusual high point of more than 60 percent in 1965). Moreover, polling since 1960 has consistently found that the public has less confidence in Congress than in the other branches of the federal government, and often less confidence than in "big business" or the media. At a low point in 1991, fewer than 20 percent of those polled expressed a "great deal" or "quite a lot" of confidence in Congress.

Yet this contempt is not necessarily bred by familiarity. Polls have consistently found that while Americans disapprove of Congress as a whole, they like their individual representative. Asked how they would rate their individual Congress representa-tive, more than 50 percent of Americans – in many of the postwar years, considerably more – ex-pressed approval. That is one reason re-election rates for House and Senate incumbents have generally been higher than 80 percent – 94 percent for House incumbents between 1982 and 1992.

In addition, much of the public is unfamiliar with the basic workings of Congress. For example, a 1996 Harvard study found that 39 percent of those questioned could not say which party was in control of the House of Representatives – this at a time of repeated and very widely reported partisan clashes in the House.

The low opinion of Congress has endured, perhaps paradoxically, even though the institution has in many ways become more open, responsive and professional throughout the second half of the twentieth century. To start with a fundamental, the demographics of congressional membership have become more varied. The number of **African Americans** in Congress increased from two in 1947 to thirty-nine in 1999, the number of women increased from eight to sixty-seven in the same period, and the religious make-up broadened as well. House members, in particular, increasingly came from different walks of life; the percentage of seats held by **lawyers** dropped from about 60 percent in 1953 to about 40 percent in 1994, and people were more likely to be elected to Congress without having had previous political experience. In addition, while agitation for "term limits" on members of Congress increased through much of the 1990s, Congress had fewer long-time members, mostly because of a surge of retirements.

Each House and Senate member was also increasingly likely during the postwar period to vote his or her own district or state's interest rather than to be swayed by **party** leadership. (While party unity increased in the 1990s, this was generally due to the increased ideological consistency of party membership rather than to the increased power of party leadership.) This independence reflected, among other things, an increased use of polling, which gave members a sense that they knew better how their constituents stood on issues and changes in congressional rules, especially those initiated in the 1970s, which gave more junior members of Congress greater say over the drafting of legislation.

Throughout the postwar period, it also became easier for the public to follow congressional proceedings. Reforms in the 1970s made it easier for the public to get a complete view of committee proceedings. C-SPAN, a non-profit arm of the **cable**-television industry, was given permission to offer "gavel-to-gavel" coverage of the House in 1979 and the Senate in 1986. Furthermore, by the mid-1990s, many congressional documents were available over the **Internet**.

Groups outside of Congress also began to provide more information. Beginning with the liberal Americans for Democratic Action in 1948, interest groups issued annual "report cards" evaluating key congressional votes. By the 1980s more than seventy groups, across the political spectrum, were attempting to hold congressional feet to the fire in that manner. Public interaction with Congress, through mail, phone calls, visits and eventually e-mail, also increased throughout the postwar period, although an increasing amount of the mail consisted of form letters drafted by liberal and conservative interest groups.

All these changes led Congress to increase its institutional resources and to regulate its behavior differently. The size of congressional staffs exploded in the early 1970s and then stabilized. About 2,600 people worked for Congress in 1947; in 1991 the number was close to 19,000 (in both **Washington, DC** and local offices). Beginning in the 1970s, Congress began to do more to oversee the ethics of its members – although that hardly prevented recurrent scandals – and to crack down on the

most egregious junkets and other perquisites. **Lobbying** was subjected to more restrictions, and, perhaps most significantly, in 1974 campaign spending was made subject to enforceable restrictions and disclosure requirements for the first time.

None of this, however, stanched the growth of "interest-group" lobbying or the increasing flow of campaign funds into party coffers. With the federal government playing a growing role in American life and Americans' penchant for forming organizations (noted first by de Tocqueville in the early nineteenth century), more and more groups – business and labor, religious and secular, liberal and conservative – moved their headquarters to Washington, DC or hired burgeoning lobbying firms to ply the halls of Congress.

By the late 1990s, members of Congress were more likely than ever to accuse their foes of being in the pocket of some "special-interest" group – business, labor, environmentalists, trial lawyers, etc. The public's suspicion that Congress was controlled by "interests" that did not represent the "public interest," along with the inherently chaotic and combative nature of the congressional process, seemed likely to perpetuate the low esteem with which Americans of all stripe regarded Congress.

Further reading

Bacon, D., Davidson, R. and Keller, M. (eds) (1995) *The Encyclopedia of the US Congress*, 4 vols, New York: Simon & Schuster.

Dionne, E.J. (1991) *Why Americans Hate Politics*, New York: Simon & Schuster.

Dodd, L. and Oppenheimer, B. (eds) (1997) *Congress Reconsidered*, 6th edn, Washington, DC: Congressional Quarterly Press.

Rieselbach, L. (1994) *Congressional Reform: The Changing Modern Congress*, Washington, DC: Congressional Quarterly Press.

DAVID GOLDSTON

Congress of Racial Equality (CORE)

Civil-rights organization founded in 1942 by several white students at the **University of**

Chicago, along with black activists like James **Farmer**. CORE drew its inspiration from methods Gandhi employed in India, and developed the tactic of **sit-ins**, before their widespread adoption and success in 1960. Under Farmer's leadership, it organized the **freedom rides** in 1961, which succeeded (after **SNCC** intervened to continue them to their conclusion) in pushing the Interstate Commerce Commission to prohibit segregated facilities at bus terminals.

CORE's influence began to founder over the issue of the organization's interracialism (much of its membership had been white and many leadership positions were not held by **African Americans**). Exasperated by the sluggishness of reform in the **South**, many blacks in CORE began to promote black nationalism, a shift that became explicit with the election of Roy Innis to national director in 1968. Innis moved the organization away from civil rights altogether, and, after centralizing the organization under his control, began to promote self-segregation and black capitalism. Attempts by old leaders to regain control of the organization failed, and it has become a bastion of **black conservatism**.

ROBERT GREGG

Conroy, Pat

b. 1945

Born in **Atlanta, GA**, Conroy's autobiographical novels explore, often in glaring and confessional detail, his life in the **South**. Whether portraying an abusive, military father (*The Great Santini*, 1976), racist educational practices (*The Water Is Wide*, 1972), or the harsh discipline and racism of a military academy (*The Lords Of Discipline*, 1980), Conroy's poetic prose and evocative images have earned him broad critical recognition. Conroy has taken criticism for what is perceived as the "therapeutic" effusion of his work, but his characterizations of **families** in turmoil are almost surgical in their precision and depth. Several Conroy novels have been translated into powerful films.

JIM WATKINS

consumerism

While all societies consume, mass consumption has taken on intense and multiple meanings within American society since the nineteenth century when advances in mass production and a continental market demanded a new mass consumer. This new person was fostered by newspaper **advertising** and **department stores** that channeled new affluence. Later, **radio**, film, **television** and the **Internet** have all created commercial media in which sales, sponsorship, product placement and information become intertwined. Consumption, despite repeated anti-consumerist movements, is also deeply linked to identity and status – **class** is read as consumption rather than production.

Contemporary consumption is framed by its economic history of the Great Depression in the 1930s followed by postwar affluence. A Depression "mentality" and the experience of limited rationing in the Second World War directly influenced parents of **baby boomers**, as well as new generations themselves. Yet for many, products were our most important progress as new **automobiles**, appliances and materials created **suburbs** and recreated urban lifestyles. The postwar period, in particular, identified **children** and **teenagers** as consumers, shaping the intensive niche marketing that in later decades has driven **fashion**, media, music and other products. The **Reagan** era became a second spring for consumerism, from the borrowed designer dresses of the **First Lady** to the **yuppies** of **Wall Street**. Expanding **credit cards** (and debts) replaced savings as baby boomers and their offspring came into employment maturity at a time of apparently constant growth.

The postwar boom did not eliminate divisions in consumption even as it enshrined ideals of the marketplace. Among the struggles of the **civil-rights** movement were **African American** demands for equal consumption – access to previously segregated department stores or public accommodations. Women, as consumers for the home, dependent on a husband's salary, also learned to establish economic independence through consumption and credit histories. The poor were doubly exploited – unable to buy as readily, yet forced to consume cheaper or second-hand goods, or through plans like rental purchase or other financing agreements that doubled prices for inferior products. One might not buy a new automobile every year, for example, but one is forced either to find something to deal with increasingly diffuse metropolitan life, or become more marginal to an automotive culture.

Intellectual movements have spoken against this intensive consumption in various ways: the beatniks of the 1950s and **hippies** of the 1960s both represent anti-materialist movements – although their stress on handicrafts or imported goods betrays an alternative consumption as well. Religious groups have promoted spirituality rather than materialism, yet wealthy churches and consumer-based **religions**, exchanging miracles for donations, underscore a synthesis of God and mammon long criticized in American life. Environmentalists have also pointed out that another result of runaway consumerism is runaway waste, evident in overflowing landfills and polluted ecosystems nationwide, even while "green" products also sell. Political and economic analysts also warn of the dangers of dependent consumerism – whether in the oil crisis of the 1970s or the continuous trade imbalances of the 1990s. Yet, at the same time, American consumption is seen as a vital component of world economic revitalization, where a sneaker plant in Indonesia represents both exploitation and opportunity.

Indeed, after the 1990's extended growth and spending, consumerism is deeply ingrained in American society as an emblem of success, a source of individual satisfaction and a motor for American global power. At the same time, consumption is a discourse of division in a polarized society – where children may kill for expensive sneakers, while schools promote uniforms to "restrain" competition in the classroom. Indeed, extensions of consumerism into areas of public good challenge American dreams of equality and democracy. Should one have the right to buy media domination or political influence? Is the Internet a new agora or a new **mall**? Are education, healthcare and housing public rights or phenomena of the marketplace? Is freedom to consume, in fact, the pervasive yet hushed underpinning of the American dream, as well as the

engine of American nightmares at home and abroad?

GARY McDONOGH

consumer price index

Monthly statistic, computed by the United States Department of Labor, which measures the price changes of various goods and services, such as gasoline, **food**, or apartment rent, paid for by a typical American **family**. Large increases in the index indicate inflation, whereas small changes in the index, or even decreases, may suggest the economy is in recession. The prices of hundreds of everyday items, randomly collected across the country, are used to calculate the CPI, which is commonly used as a basis for calculating cost of living adjustments for workers and retirees.

A. JOSEPH BORRELL

Consumer Reports

Consumer research began in 1926 with F.J. Schlink after a series of articles in the *New Republic* underscored concerns with reliability and value. Schlink promoted scientific testing and published rankings for a wide range of products; his employees left after labor disputes in 1936 to found the Consumer's Union and the magazine *Consumer Reports*, published monthly for 4.5 million subscribers. *Consumer Reports* accepts no **advertising** and promises rigorous objective testing of **automobiles**, appliances and other products. Their dominance has been challenged since 1971 by J.D. Powers and Associates, a private firm that bases ranking on user surveys and also has closer ties with corporations who may buy their data for advertising. Issues of consumer safety as well as perceptions of unreliable manufacturing have made both sources important to educated consumers beyond everyday evaluations based on personal knowledge or brand name loyalty. This competition also suggests American cultural divisions between elite scientific observation and popular choice, as well as the complexities of a **consumerism** that promotes its own commercial self-evaluation.

Further reading

Noah, T. (1999) "People's Choice Awards," *New York Times Magazine* August 7: 42–5.

GARY McDONOGH

consumer safety

Ralph **Nader**'s *Unsafe at Any Speed* (1965) warned Americans that many "things" could kill as surely as people. Freedom to consume entails risks which have become hotly debated in the litigious ambience of the late twentieth and early twenty-first century, where not only faulty products – flammable children's pajamas, unsafe cars or faulty construction – but guns, tobacco and medicine have been subject to scrutiny in the courts and the media. While federal and state consumer product safety commissions, investigative journalism and lawsuits sometimes pin down clear dangers and culpable manufacturers or marketers, these class action lawsuits – representing claims of millions of smokers or thousands of women who received breast implants – have often faced more difficult questions of who is responsible in knowledgeable consumption and use, as well as what chains of causality must be established when billions of dollars in damages are at stake. Consumer-safety issues are frequent themes in both news, which duly publicizes weekly product recalls, and fictional media. Hence, Jonathan Harr's 1995 bestseller *A Civil Action*, which deals with the search for responsibility for cancer in a contaminated Massachusetts city, became a major 1999 film, followed by *The Insider*, which explores secrets of tobacco and **television**. In the end, it is unclear if the US is less careful in manufacturing or control, more litigious in its responses to product failure, or simply more embroiled in constant consumption where expectations and satisfactions do not coincide.

GARY McDONOGH

contemporary (postmodern) art

American art since the late 1970s has been characterized by both supporters and detractors as **postmodern**, but it is sometimes unclear whether the term refers to the contemporary social context of media-saturated global capitalism, or to new artistic styles. The question is complicated by the diversity of practices that the term has been used to identify. Some leading artists have elaborated or departed from aspects of **minimalism**, **pop art** and **conceptual art** to develop art that is critical of both specifically artistic and broader social institutions. This work, often in hybrid forms known as installation art, and sometimes site-specific (made for a particular space), characteristically employs **photography**, ready-made objects and materials, and texts. Key figures include Hans Haacke, Jenny Hoizer, Louise Lawler and Cindy Sherman. Other artists have taken the proliferating commodities of consumer culture (see **consumerism**) as their material; among them are Ashley Bickerton, Jeff Koons, Allan McCollum. Critical supporters of these kinds of postmodern art see it as theoretically sophisticated, while detractors see it as mere illustration of theory. Some of this work was influenced by **feminism**, which provided one of the models for work in the 1990s grounded in and meant both to express and complicate specific ethnic or sexual identities, by **African American** artists, including David Hammons and Fred Wilson, Native American artists, including Jimmie Durham, and gay artists, including Robert Gober. But the 1980s also saw a return to painting, characterized alternately by a pastiche of historical styles (David Salle), or a full-blown and sometimes overblown expressionism (Julian Schnabel).

FRAZER WARD

contraception

Birth control has long been a contentious issue in the US. Indeed, despite decades of battles by advocates like Margaret **Sanger** to disseminate information, only in *Griswold* v. *Connecticut* (1965) did the **Supreme Court** bar state laws censoring contraceptive advice. In the early twenty-first century, nonetheless, the issues surrounding contraception – sexual education, condom distribution, **abortion**, **religion** – remain volatile. Religious organizations, most notably the **Christian Right** and the **Roman Catholic** Church, represent the dominant conservative voices in the debate over contraception. Their fundamentalist opposition to premarital sex, abortion and contraception, in any form, promotes abstinence (no sex at all) as the only acceptable form of birth control. Anything else represents a moral transgression.

Though most people recognize that abstinence is, indeed, the best way to avoid pregnancy and STDs (sexually transmitted diseases), contraception has numerous advocates, like Planned Parenthood. In fact, many Americans believe that premarital sex has become an inevitable reality in our society. Accordingly, they have opted to work for the good of young people with the understanding that many of them have sex (often with more than one partner) prior to getting married. In this way, more liberal Americans accuse pro-abstinence contingents of being out of touch with the nation's youth. To minimize unplanned pregnancies and STDs they recommend far-reaching educational programs which inform young people about the dangers of unprotected sex. Some also support the distribution of free condoms in **public schools**.

Condoms are among the most widely used contraceptives, in part, because they also protect against sexually transmitted diseases (STDs). The birth-control pill is considered the most effective safeguard against pregnancy; moreover, it operates internally and does not interfere with the sexual act as the condom does. Its introduction in the 1960s, in fact, became a foundation for an American sexual revolution. Yet, the pill has potential side-effects and no effect on preventing the transmittal of STDs like **AIDS**. Alternatives like intra-uterine devices (IUDs) became controversial, with claims about devastating effects of the 1970s Dalkon shield, against which over 150,000 American women filed claims for $2.5 billion in damages (although critics accused the company and US agencies of dumping these IUDs into planning programs abroad). Diaphragms, on the whole, have been less common in the US than in other countries worldwide.

Purchasing condoms in stores is not only expensive, but also an embarrassing experience for many **teenagers** (and hence a staple of teenage movies). Distributing free condoms promotes safe sex and ensures that the contraceptives reach the people who need them most, ultimately reducing both births and abortions. Conservatives, however, contend that this encourages sexual activity among people whom, they believe, should not be having intercourse in the first place.

Most Americans, however, seem not to espouse beliefs as radical as these. While not everyone endorses the condom distribution plan, most appreciate the virtues of contraception. Condoms and pills are advertised on **television**, and doctors have prescribed the pill and other solutions to countless women.

JAMES DAVID

conventions

Downtown convention centers became late-twentieth century strategies for **cities** to promote **tourism** and **consumption**. Trade shows, business groups, religious associations and fraternal organizations are prime clients, but the plum is a national political party convention like those held in **Philadelphia, PA** (Republicans) and **Los Angeles, CA** (Democrats) in 2000. These events, held every four years before the elections, bring together thousands of party representatives in summer assemblies to formally choose presidential and vice-presidential candidates. Since the nineteenth century, these delegates have generally been chosen by primaries or caucuses at the state level, although elected officials and party bosses have also held power. The convention also establishes the party platform and national leadership.

Twentieth-century conventions have become battlegrounds at times; even after the Second World War the triumph of John F. **Kennedy** at the 1960 Democratic Convention and Ronald **Reagan**'s 1980 victory over Gerald **Ford** added drama to television coverage. These meetings have also been arenas for debates on critical issues like **civil rights**, **Vietnam**, **abortion** and the representation of women and minorities. These debates were especially divisive for Democrats in the 1960s and 1970s, before reforms in 1972 (that led to George McGovern's nomination; see **Mississippi Freedom Democratic Party**). Conventions also faced popular protest outside halls, like those that erupted at the 1968 Democratic Convention in **Chicago** and smaller protests at subsequent events.

Yet, with primary reform, conventions have become stages for propaganda and coronation of incumbents or victors decided months before, as is the case with Al **Gore** or George **Bush**, Jr. in 2000. Hence public interest has dropped with regard to spectacles and speeches, and networks no longer offer gavel-to-gavel coverage of political pep rallies/**infomercials**.

GARY McDONOGH

convict labor

Among the concerns of those demanding harsher punishments throughout American history has been the demand for labor as recompense or re-education for those imprisoned. Convict leasing, in the post-Civil War **South**, in which prisoners were passed to private bosses at minimal costs, often functioned as an extension of slavery before it ended in the 1930s. "Chain gangs," in which workers under public guards work on highways and other projects, have continued and are even cited as a deterrent because of the public humiliation involved. Within prisons, convicts have been employed in many day-to-day functions of the prison – laundry, food, etc.; in the 1990s, prisons also became areas for telephone services nationwide. Prisoners receive some or all of this money, although it may be taken from them for supplies or privileges within the system.

GARY McDONOGH

cookbooks and cooking media

Up to 1,000 cookbooks were published annually in the US in the late twentieth century. Such proliferation represents not only a diversity of audiences and tastes, but also a recognition of cooking as cultural capital (for the **middle class**), as well as a realm in which domestic knowledge has given way to outside mass-mediated expertise. Cookbooks, cooking television and other media, like **food** itself, thus embody critical changes in American society and culture.

This can be seen by successive editions of the classic *Joy of Cooking* (1931) created by Irma Rombauer. Unlike the equally popular *Better Homes and Garden Cookbook* (first published 1930; multiple re-editions), linked to a publishing empire, or the *Betty Crocker Cookbook* (1950; multiple re-editions) of food manufacturer General Mills, this was an individual effort, originally self-published. Early editions met the needs of a world where domestic service was disappearing. Collecting recipes from friends and additional information that now seems dated in its reliance on canned soups or overcooked pasta, Rombauer later adapted easily followed recipes to new conditions like wartime rationing. This tradition of change was continued by her daughter and her grandson, who produced the new 1997 edition. This last comprehensive volume – which ranges from beating eggs to comparing caviars – takes into account sophisticated palates and distinctions between newly available ingredients, global cuisines, health concerns and family dynamics that make **pizza** a meal category.

Joy of Cooking emerged in a relatively limited market. Postwar prosperity and nuclear **family** domesticity changed the needs and markets for cooking guidance. **Magazines** and the press also taught cooking (including published collections from food editors like the *New York Times*' Craig Clairborne). **Television** food shows also appeared with the earliest stations, incorporating cooking teachers like Dionne Lucas and showman cooks like James Beard, who linked his recipes to commercial endorsements as well as cookbooks. Julia Childs' inimitable **PBS** *French Chef* (1963–73), with sequels, set new standards in cookbooks and television for generations to come, re-establishing French cuisine as a goal, yet doing so with a love of food and an acceptance of kitchen mistakes that demystified haute cuisine. Her success was followed by other PBS shows and a **cable** food channel, again often linked to cookbook sales and celebrities.

Meanwhile, advertisers supplied recipes to enhance sales and create new uses for their products, from gelatin to cream cheese to soup. This onslaught for the food consumer increased with new machines – pressure cookers to microwaves to breadmakers – that altered the American **kitchen**. Some products, in fact, became identified with specific recipes: Nestle's chocolate chips and Toll House cookies or Chex cereals and snack mixes.

Other cookbooks have expanded with affluence and leisure, as well as exposure to new immigrants and travel. Prominent among cookbook categories and television shows are those that champion cuisines of Italy, France and Asia, as well as domestic regional/ethnic specializations like **Cajun**, **Southwestern** or soul food. Celebrity chefs become multimedia institutions with restaurants (chains), cookbooks, shows and guest appearances. Other writers incorporate the ethnography of food into their writings, like Paula Wolfert on the circum-Mediterranean or Marcella Hazan on Italy. Newspaper sections and magazines targeting affluent consumers – *Saveur, Food and Wine, Gourmet* – also combine narrative, pictorials and recipes. Often, these make demands on time and ingredients that set the process and results of cooking apart from everyday eating, reinforcing its cultural capital in the middle class. Other cookbooks meet specialized interests and needs, whether in preparation categories – basic, grilling, baking, speedy, etc. – or nutrition and diet, featuring light, low-fat and salt-free foods.

Clubs, schools, churches and other groups also elaborate **community** through cookbooks and cookbook sales. Folklorists and anthropologists have examined these food ways and contributed celebrations and collections patronized by institutions like the **Smithsonian**. Indeed, these complexities of community and change permeate media that permit cooking for status or raise questions of identity embodied in Jeff Smith's wry subtitle on his *The Frugal Gourmet on Our Immigrant Ancestors* (1990): "Recipes you should have gotten from your grandmother."

Further reading

Bower, A. (1997) *Recipes for Reading: Community Cookbooks, Stories, Histories*, Amherst: University of Massachusetts.

Mendelson, A. (1996) *Stand facing the Stove*, New York: Henry Holt.

Stern, J. and Stern, M. (1991) *American Gourmet*, New York: Harper.

GARY McDONOGH
CINDY WONG

Cooke, Sam

b. 1931; d. 1964

Classic **soul** singer of the 1950s and early 1960s, Sam Cooke mixed sensuality and sophistication with movie-idol looks and gospel-singer poise. His warm, confessional voice won him a devoted gospel following as lead singer for the Soul Stirrers and sent "You Send Me" to the top of the pop and R&B charts. It was the first of twenty-nine Top Forty hits for the Chicago-born singer, including "Chain Gang," "You Send Me," "Another Saturday Night" and "Twisting the Night Away," each proving the singer's versatility. Cooke was also a pioneering black entrepreneur who started his own music publishing company and record label. He died mysteriously in a shooting in 1964.

EDWARD MILLER

cool

In American youth and popular culture, "cool" is the desired pose. Cool is also a pervasive marketing tool. Coolness is in part about a confidence in appearance (in between trendy and nerdy), creating a visual style, but it is also a comment on an observable attitude – a mixture of nonchalance and self-absorption in attitude. Designer clothing comes in and out of style, for seemingly mysterious readings, making it cool to wear and, then, in a flash, "tacky." Places – discos, **neighborhoods**, cities – come into style and are cool. For example, recently South Beach in **Miami, FL** became cool – after the artists moved in, celebrities followed, but with the advent of too many tourists it became passé. Some bands are cool. These bands tend not to be the most highly regarded by the population at large, but a secret amongst those who consider themselves in the know. Those long considered to be the antithesis of cool – nerds and geeks – have become cool with the rise of hacker and now **Internet**-related culture. In time, they too will be passé.

Further reading

Frank, T. (1997) *The Conquest of Cool*, Chicago: University of Chicago Press.

EDWARD MILLER

Cooper, Gary

b. 1901; d. 1961

Whether stumbling into truth and love in **Capra** comedies (*Mr Deeds Goes to Town Goes to Town*, 1936; *Meet John Doe*, 1941), saving America reluctantly on the battlefield (*Sergeant York*, 1941, Oscar), or standing alone to define justice in the **West** (*High Noon*, 1952, Oscar), Cooper stood for American myths of masculine virtues – strong, silent, reluctant to become involved, yet ultimately committed to justice and truth. A star without appearing to want the trappings, Cooper's inter-texts made *Sergeant York* powerful propaganda for entry into the Second World War, perhaps also foreshadowing the apparent reluctance America overcame in global situations to follow.

GARY McDONOGH

Copland, Aaron

b. 1900; d. 1990

After study in **New York** City, NY and Paris (with Nadia Boulanger), Copland began a career of stylistic exploration ranging from abstract pieces to adaptations of American rhythms from **jazz** and **folk music**. He created classic anthems that recur in American public events, including themes from the ballets *Billy the Kid* (1938), *Rodeo* (1942) and *Appalachian Spring* (1944), which uses old Shaker hymns. His "Fanfare for the Common Man" (1942) has also become a standard. Copland also became known as a teacher, composer for movies and writer on music, as well as one of the US' most revered composers.

Further reading

Copland, A. (1960) *Copland on Music*, New York: Da Capo.

GARY McDONOGH

Coppola, Francis Ford

b. 1939

Director whose remarkable *Godfather* trilogy (1972, 1974 and 1990) defined an auteurial vision in American cinema through its sweeping mythic vision, lavish detail and extraordinary ensemble acting. Coppola directed and produced other singular films ranging from comedy (*Peggy Sue Got Married*, 1986) to the grim horror of **Vietnam** (*Apocalypse Now*, 1979). His career has also been plagued by numerous financial debacles that shuttered his independent studio, American Zoetrope in 1990. Coppola's vision has almost always focused on America – dreams as well as nightmares and failures – which permeated his intriguing biographical study *Tucker* (1988), as much as his own life.

GARY McDONOGH

Corvette *see* sports cars

Cosby, Bill

b. 1937

Born in **Philadelphia, PA**, Cosby was the first **African American** actor to star in a dramatic series on **television** (*I Spy*, NBC, 1965–8). Well-known for his **comedy** routines and stage act, often based on **children**'s stories and perspectives of the world, which were adapted for the cartoon series, *Fat Albert and the Cosby Kids* (CBS, 1972–7), he developed a less politically charged style than that of other black comedians like Dick **Gregory** and Richard **Pryor**. He parlayed his popularity into the top-rated family comedy, the *Cosby Show* (NBC, 1984–92), which anchored NBC's Thursday night programming and won several Emmys. The show presented the Huxtables, a black upper-middle-class **New York** City family steeped in "family values," who countered the black stereotypes then common on **television**. Cosby returned in 1996 with a similarly conceived family show, without achieving the same success.

See also: black colleges and universities

ROBERT GREGG

couch potatoes

Term denoting a person who merely watches rather than participates in sports, sits on the sofa surrounded by **pizza**, potato chips and beer, and phones in his or her bet to out-of-state **gambling** brokers. Often stereotyped as males between the ages of eighteen and fifty, advertisers target the couch potato constituency with commercials during *Monday Night Football*, Sunday afternoon **football** games, or during televised college **basketball** games. The commercials, often for beer, feature men sneaking off to watch sports (while wives complain bitterly).

ROBERT GREGG

country and western music

Country music emerged in the postwar period as one of the most popular forms of American music. Although its first fans and performers were **working-class** and rural whites of the **South**, it is now popular worldwide.

Country music's most recent influences are bluegrass music, **cowboy** music and western swing; its roots can be found in Scottish and English **folk music**, **Cajun** music and **African American** spirituals and **blues**. The music is renowned for plaintive songs about betrayed love, rendered in regional accents by voices often raw with emotion. The word "twang" has come to describe the vocal style of most country singers. The musical arrangements favor the steel guitar, the fiddle and the guitar, but the voice is always foreground. Concerts highlight singers and bands; the visual style of some of the performers – leather, lace and fringe – is also quite remarkable.

Most country performers remain white. Only two artists have challenged this norm: the black singer Charlie Pride, who was popular in the 1960s and 1970s, and the lesbian singer k.d. lang, who emerged in the 1980s and borrowed freely from country forms in order to create her own persona.

Since the war, country music can be divided into a few distinctive styles: honky tonk, the **Nashville** sound, outlaw country and urban cowboy music. In the 1940s and 1950s, the great Hank Williams, who sang of love and loss in robust, rough and ironic tones, epitomized the honky tonk style. Other popular honky tonk stylists were Lefty Frizzel and Kitty Wells. The Nashville sound was slicker, more produced and centered around the renowned Grand Ole Opry theater.

The silky smooth voices of Gentleman Jim Reeves and Eddy Arnold embodied this style in the 1950s and enlarged the fan base of country. Singers like Patsy Cline combined honky tonk with the Nashville sound and paved the way for other female singers like Loretta **Lynn**. Johnny **Cash**, Willie Nelson and Merle Haggard came to prominence in the late 1960s and established the style of outlaw country – a mixture of honky tonk with southern rock, which expressed a defiant blue collar perspective.

By the 1970s, country music began to go urban with Dolly Parton's crossover hit "9 to 5" and the success of Willie Nelson, Linda Ronstadt and others who mixed country with more mainstream pop. Following upon the pop-influenced new country of Reba McEntire and Randy Travis in the 1980s, Garth Brooks became in the 1990s a country-based crooner with mass sex appeal, bringing country music to its largest audience ever. Despite its great popularity at the century's end, country music has lost some of its emotive poetry, substituting polish for rougher tales of poverty and unfaithful lovers.

Further reading

Kingsbury, P. (ed.) (1996) *Encyclopedia of Country Music*, New York: Oxford.

EDWARD MILLER

courts *see* judiciary

cowboys

Whether John **Wayne** fighting the Indians or the Marlboro Man hawking **tobacco**, the cowboy has been a consummate symbol of American individualism and **freedom** worldwide. The legend was shaped by generations of penny novels, **western** movies and **television** shows (which contemporary cowboys have also watched). "Cowboy" conjures up a rugged **white** male on horseback, tanned by wind and work, drinking, smoking and fighting when he comes to town. Unfortunately, this imagery – and the slick boots, dance music and dude ranches that commercialize it – overlook the diversity and problems of past and present. "Cowboys" in the past included **African Americans** and **Latinos**, as well as white loners, in work that was often brutal, ill-rewarded and led not to ownership, but to continual labor and loneliness in a world especially hard on women and wives. As rail and trucks have replaced cattle drives and agro-business has favored fodder-fattened beef, being a cowboy remains an underpaid job and a demanding lifestyle, requiring organization, mechanical skills, endurance and knowledge of nature (horses, cows, weather). This way of life, even while changing, is celebrated in **rodeos**, the arts and **museums**. Meanwhile, students of the **West** allow us to understand how complicated cowboy life actually has been. The dilemmas of late twentieth-century cowboys have been poignantly chronicled in Jane Kramer's (1977) *The Last Cowboy* and novelist Larry McMurtry's *In a Narrow Grave* (1968).

Further reading

Kramer, J. (1977) *The Last Cowboy*, New York: Harper & Row.
McMurtry, L. (1968) *In a Narrow Grave*, Austin: Encino.

GARY McDONOGH

Crawford, Joan

b. 1904; d. 1977

Glamour, ambition and drive crystallized a star quality around Crawford that carried her through decades of success, although the off-screen cost of these qualities pervaded a muckraking biography (*Mommie Dearest*, 1978) and a highly stylized film biography in which Faye Dunaway portrayed her as a consummate monster (1981). Yet Crawford on screen often moved outside the comfort zone of **gender** stereotypes, whether in her wild roles in the 1920s or her working-girl personae of the 1930s. Crawford reinvented herself as the suffering mother in *Mildred Pierce* (1945) and later as a harridan opposite Bette Davis in *What Ever Happened to Baby Jane?* (1974). Her vivid image has lived beyond her both in the impact of her films as a chronicle of women and imagery and in the destruction of that star figure through *Mommie Dearest*.

GARY McDONOGH

creationism *see* scientific creationism

credit and credit cards

According to the Federal Reserve Board, outstanding consumer credit has soared from $6,577.8 million in January, 1943 to $1,370,880 million in October 1999. Much of this increase has come in revolving credit, a concept that appears in Federal Reserve statistics as of 1968, as major associations like Visa and Mastercard consolidated. By the late 1990s, over 2 billion credit cards circulated in the United States – roughly nine per person. Credit has facilitated consumerism (and debt) as hallmarks and dangers of the **middle class**; credit cards have become badges of identity as well as status. Yet, this global revolution has also excluded the poor in important ways.

Earlier credit arrangements incorporated divisions of wealth and **class**. **Department stores**, clubs and other services arranged billing or charge accounts for the bourgeoisie. American Express, founded in 1850, has carved out a niche based on travel, corporate money management and financial networking for an elite clientele, competing with Diner's Club and Carte Blanche. American Express charges a user's fee for this service and demands complete monthly payments; it also charges merchants more.

By contrast, those of limited means have depended on personalized arrangements which have sometimes kept them locked into debt with merchants or employers. Others have relied on lay-aways (planned pre-payment to gain necessary goods), as well as savings and denial. Through yet another scheme, rental-purchase, those without credit pay many times the value of goods as they use them before possessing them outright. In emergencies not covered by public assistance, the poor turn to families or fall into the hands of predatory loan sharks who compound high inter-ests on a weekly or monthly basis. Credit unions and similar community ventures have sought to establish more concrete savings and credit plans for workers and low-income groups.

Middle-class credit, by contrast, took shape in particular through consortia of banks that facili-tated payment through interconnecting branches in major cities. Franklin National Bank offered such a card in 1951, replacing experimental bank script. By 1966 the Interbank Card Association emerged, establishing global ties for what would become Mastercard within a few years. Visa emerged from the Bank of American Bankamer-icard (1958), consolidating national and interna-tional ties in the early 1970s and taking on its current name in 1976. Together, these cards now account for 75 percent of the American market; 50 percent for Visa, which issued 298 million cards in the US in 1998. They are also hotly marketed at people at the beginning of financial maturity: 70 percent of **college** undergraduates have at least one, while special offers (usually reduced initial financing) are mailed out weekly to target demo-graphics, and televised **advertising** underscores that "for everything else, there is Mastercard." Citizens, in turn, use these cards to establish credit ratings to validate future borrowing.

Since **banks** issuing one or both cards do not handle other cards, this Visa–Mastercard mono-poly has been attacked by American Express as well as by the smaller Discovery card, originally founded and backed by merchandiser Sears Roebuck. In fact, Visa and Mastercard have shown flexibility in organizing co-branding arrangements with airlines, vendors and even charities that account for 20,000 different kinds of credit cards available. The message of all, however, is the same: **consumerism** is part of American identity, and credit cards, like driver's licenses, are routinely solicited for identification as well as necessities for such practices as car rental.

Unlike American Express, Visa and Mastercard charge less and may have no user's fee; instead, 75 percent of their profits come from charges on balances left unpaid, which may reach 26 percent annually. The weight of this debt has contributed to growing bankruptcies and emphasized the alter-native of debit cards or check cards which draw money directly from accounts without exceeding available limits or charging interest. For those who have lost their credit rating, new markets for credit counseling, debt consolidation (often borrowing against house equity) and secured credit cards, which allow spending up to a fixed-deposit limit, all offer routes into American consumer debt.

Not all observers are sanguine about the ease or implications of this transformation of an American way of life. Critics have frequently raised questions about privacy and control of personal knowledge, especially as credit cards mesh with the ubiquities of e-commerce and increasingly smart cards are promoted. Yet, in this, it is also clear that the US is not alone: Visa has issued 800 million cards worldwide and touts itself as a universal currency, where the total expenses for 1998 products and services reached $1,400,000 million.

Further reading

Mandell, L. (1990) *The Credit Card Industry*, Boston: Twayne.

Ritzer, G. (1995) *Expressing America*, Thousand Oak: Pine Forge.

GARY McDONOGH
CINDY WONG

Creoles/creolization

Creolization refers to the development of new forms of **language** and expression from contact among diverse cultures. Black English vernacular, for example, represents a creolized linguistic form that has developed stable forms centuries after first contact, while Spanglish and Chinglish refer to contemporary transnational creoles. The recombination of various identities has made creolization a fundamentally American process from **Broadway** stage to **popular music** to **visual arts** to **food**.

Creole, however, is not used to categorize settlers in the US as it was in Latin America. As an ethnic term, it refers primarily to descendants of French creoles in Louisiana, whose dilemmas of ethnicity, **race** and **class** are detailed by Virginia Dominguez in *White by Definition* (1985).

GARY McDONOGH

crime *see* organized crime; police; prisons; violence

crime, television

America's fascination with crime permeates **mass media**. Indeed, critics frequently charge that media violence incites crime rather than reflecting it (evidence is murky). Still, as movie plots, fodder for **tabloid** news, investigative reports, local news hype or "reality" shows, criminal activity, investigation and prosecution permeate the everyday televisual world. These elements also have structured many long-running fictional genres, although, unlike film, the viewpoint of a criminal is rarely central. Hence, these series have created myths of good and evil for generations, while revealing changes and uncertainties about the nature of justice.

Jack Webb's *Dragnet* (NBC, 1952–9, 1967–70) altered radio models by its detailed focus on everyday police activity with a clear sense of authority (exaggerated in the revival that targeted countercultural elements). The show's "realism" was reinforced by the solemn warning "the story you are about to be told is true. Only the names have been changed to protect the innocent," as well as the retribution that closed each show. Ironically, Webb lionized the **Los Angeles** Police Department, whose racism and corruption would later spark major riots.

The hero cop continued for decades, including the noirish heritage and location shots of *Naked City*

(ABC, 1958–9, 1960–3), period violence in *The Untouchables* (ABC, 1959–63), intergenerational dynamics in *Streets of San Francisco* (ABC, 1972–7) and the idiosyncrasies of *Kojak* (CBS, 1973–89; ABC, 1989–90). Almost all these shows focus on detectives who unravel complex schemes amid increasing violence. Patrol cops faced tedium in Webb's spin-off *Adam-12* (NBC, 1968–75) and ridicule in *Car 54, where are you?* (NBC, 1961–3. Rural law met gentler humor in *The Andy Griffith Show* (CBS, 1960–8). Even the **FBI** had a hit show.

But were the police really friends and heroes? Even the **radio** heritage of the outsider private eye suggested police were not always just; others were there to cross the line, reopen the case and get the blonde an upright policeman, with whom she eventually could not be involved. Here, *Peter Gunn* (NBC, 1958–60, ABC 1960–1) was followed by *Mannix, Cannon, Tanner, Baretta*, etc. Aaron **Spelling**'s *Charlie's Angels* (ABC, 1976–81) showcased active albeit titillating females, while *Remington Steele* (NBC, 1982–6), *Moonlighting* (ABC, 1983–9) and others played up romance and detection. Angela Lansbury in *Murder, She Wrote* (CBS, 1984–98) provided a senior detective with **old-age** appeal. Minorities have been relatively absent, apart from Sammo Hung and Arsenio Hall in *Martial Law* (ABC, 1999–2000), a black partner in *Spenser: For Hire* (ABC, 1985–8) and Burt Reynold's Native American in *Hawk*.

Yet doubts and challenges also emerged within the police genre itself. The teen-marketed *Mod Squad* (ABC, 1968–73) turned a young woman and two angry youths, black and white, into police agents. *Barney Miller* (ABC, 1975–82) assembled diverse, jaded characters in a show where police work as comic relief. Lives, as well as process, became central to police drama.

This shift is frequently linked to *Cagney and Lacey* (CBS, 1982–8), which not only showcased female partnership, but also dealt with **family** issues, alcoholism and breast cancer. Ensemble complexity also permeates the creations of Steven Bochco and Thomas Milch, for example *Hill Street Blues* (NBC, 1981–7) and *NYPD Blue* (NBC, 1993–). Male and female, black and white, police on the beat, detectives and lawyers alike lie, fear, act heroically and wrongly and in one experiment – *Cop Rock* (ABC, 1990) – even sang. Barry Levinson created a gritty human ensemble set in **Balti-**

more, MD in *Homicide* (NBC, 1993–9), while enforcement and prosecution mesh in the 1990's *Law & Order* (NBC, 1990–), hewing close to current news. The raw police sexuality of *NYPD Blue* stands light years away, physically and emotionally, from *Dragnet*. Nor is justice easy or cases closed in a single episode.

Other action/crime genres also appeared sporadically on **television**. The 1960s saw secret agents enforcing justice worldwide in *I Spy* (NBC, 1965–8), where Bill **Cosby** pioneered black lead roles, *Mission Impossible* (CBS, 1966–73; ABC, 1988–90), enforcing a *"Dragnet"* morality against dictators worldwide, the Bondish *Man from U.N.C.L.E.* (NBC, 1964–8) and the wise-cracking *Get Smart* (NBC, 1965–9; CBS, 1969–70). This genre faded notably after the **Vietnam War** and **Watergate**. **Superheroes** also have shown up when police cannot help – especially in Saturday morning cartoons.

The year of 1989 also saw the debut of FOX's "Reality show," *Cops* (FOX, 1969), with cinéma vérité handheld videos and apparently unedited footage of police life and events on the street. Here, the "unvarnished truth" restates many of the concerns of **class** and **race** that fictional shows had first hidden and then, perhaps too readily, embraced.

In all these shows, fighting crime is not just fighting evil-doers. Police chafe against rules (echoing conservative debates about the **Supreme Court** decisions), criticize **lawyers** and judges, and sometimes pause to reflect on society gone wrong. In these themes and the human dramas they play out, these shows reflect and shape the discourse of crime and punishment in contemporary society.

See also: police; violence

GARY McDONOGH
CINDY WONG

crime fiction/mysteries

Crime and mystery writing as a genre have deep American roots, most notably with American Edgar Allen Poe's (1841) *Murders in the Rue Morgue*, considered the original detective story, and Anna Katharine Green's (1878) *The Leavenworth Case*, considered the first American detective novel. In the last decades of the century, American crime fiction has focused on realism, character development and psychological dimensions of action. Amateur and professional detectives, once urban males, have gained regional attributes and everyday problems, and increasingly include persons of color and women, as well as responses to social issues. They are also increasingly packaged as series, named by author, major characters or setting (Egyptian, **Hollywood**, etc.) in order to market to avid readers.

The most prominent category of American crime fiction and mystery is the murder mystery, but detective stories, courtroom sagas, spy novels and stories of theft and assault are also popular. Although British authors have been popular (Agatha Christie, Ruth Rendell, etc.), most popular authors are American. However, settings may vary widely over time and place. Mystery series are also popular in **children**'s and **teenage** fiction.

Police investigators appear in mysteries set around the United States. On the West Coast one may find John Ball's Virgil Tibbs, an **African American** detective from Pasadena or Susan Dunlap's Detective Jill Smith from Berkeley. On the East Coast one finds Lillian O'Dennel's Norah Mulcahany or Archer Mayor's Lieutenant Joe Gunther from Brattleboro, Vermont.

Private detectives and ex-cops, humorous amateurs and lawyers all make for popular lead characters in crime fiction. Erle Stanley Gardner's *Perry Mason* series has given way to bestsellers Scott Torow, John Grisham and Steve Martini, who have created legal thrillers that weave together law, courtroom scenes and intricate problem-solving that often rescues the featured lawyer/sleuth from danger. Private investigators – consummate antiheroes – include classic pre-war works by Dashiell Hammett and Raymond Chandler, as well as noirish series by Mickey Spillane and John T. MacDonald. Recent investigators also include journalists such as Sampson Dean, the African American reporter created by Mike Phillips.

Yet amateur sleuths, citizens caught up in events, are equally important in American crime fiction. Members of the clergy make detecting innocence and guilt take on special significance. These include Father Dowling, a Roman Catholic priest from the **Chicago, IL** area created by Ralph McInerny,

Rabbi David Small, a creation of Harry Kemelman, or Sister Mary Ursula of the Order of the Sisters of Martha of Bethany, **Los Angeles, CA** created by H.H. Holmes. Husband-and-wife teams such as the Orthodox Jewish housewife Rina Lazarus and Los Angeles Police Department Detective Peter Decker, created by Fay Kellerman, mingle professional and amateur investigation.

The stewpot of American culture is reflected in the increasing diversity of detective characters. Such diversity is reflected by women such as Sue Grafton's Kinsey Millhone, private investigator, Patricia Cornwell's Virginia coroner Kay Scarpetta or Jean Hager's Molly Bearpaw, an investigator for the Native American Advocacy League. Tony Hillerman has received an anthropological award for his depictions of Navaho and Hopi life and detection. Gay and lesbian figures move Joseph Hansen's Dave Brandsetter novels and Michael Nava's novels featuring Henry Rios.

Food plays a prominent role in detective fiction, as seen in Tamar Myers' *Too Many Cooks Spoil the Broth* (1994), Nancy Packard's *27 Ingredient Chili con Carne Murders* (1993) and the older, epicurean Nero Wolfe mysteries. **Pets** also appear in Lilian Jackson Braun's *The Cat Who...* series and Susan J. Conant's *The Dog Lover* series.

Other crime fiction subgenres include psychopathic killers, hospital settings, detective writers, academic settings and the underworld. Other authors of significance include Robert Campbell, Jane Langton and Mary Higgins Clark.

These bestselling books, generally seen as relaxation or beach reading, raise interesting questions about American attitudes towards crime and violence, worrisome in society and often attacked in **mass-media** representations. Mysteries have generally escaped this scrutiny to flourish as a major genre with strong **Hollywood** connections.

See also: crime, television; lawyers, television shows

further reading

Herald, D. (1995) *Genreflecting. A Guide to Reading Interests in Genre Fiction*, 4th edn, Englewood: Libraries Unlimited.

Lachman, M. (1993) *A Reader's Guide to the American Novel of Detection*, New York: G.K. Hall.

GAIL HENSON

Crosby, Bing

b. 1903; d. 1977

Crooner and actor, Bing Crosby, born Harry Lillis Crosby in Tacoma, **Washington, DC**, was first a successful popular singer in nightclubs and on **radio**. When he became a movie actor, he encompassed a genial humor that sold American Catholicism (*Going My Way*, 1944), adventure abroad (his road series with comedian Bob **Hope**) and even "White Christmas" (by Irving Berlin) as a bestselling anthem of family comfort for postwar America (from the **musical** *White Christmas*, 1954). Like other studio-packaged stars, Crosby's relaxed, fatherly persona was deconstructed by **family** biographers after his death.

GARY McDONOGH
CINDY WONG

C-SPAN (public affairs broadcast cable channel specializing in live and total broadcasts of major events and debates) *see* cable television

Cuba and Cuban Americans

In 2000 the case of six-year-old Elian Gonzalez galvanized issues and passions in American relations with **Castro**'s Cuba and the voices of Cuban Americans within US society and politics. Gonzalez, whose mother had died as they fled Cuba, was claimed by **Miami, FL** relatives as a **refugee** from a totalitarian regime. The US Justice Department, however, favored reuniting him with his father in Cuba. Taking Elian to **Disneyworld** and showering him with gifts, Cuban Americans also rallied in Miami and sought judicial and congressional recourse to keep the boy in the US, including a bill to grant him citizenship. Meanwhile, in Havana, others marched to claim the rights of a "kidnapped angel."

The Justice Department's dawn raid on the home of Elian's Miami relatives to return him to his father in Washington galvanized further Cuban American response, and even calls for an investigation of such "brutal action." Yet the lack of movement after this raid challenged Cuban American political clout. Even as Elian's fate dragged on in American courts for months, politicians began to speak of normalizing relations with Cuba (although not with the alacrity that was granted to China).

Such divisive feelings reflect the deep connections of people, places and interests that unite and separate the US and Cuba, especially since the revolution of 1959. These passions have been kindled by a long history of US intervention on the island, as well as by recent fears of its strategic role as a nearby foothold for communist organization and propaganda throughout **Latin America**. Yet, even more, these feelings reflect the special situation of first and second generation immigrants from Cuba, more than a million people (the third-largest **Hispanic** group), awaiting changes in the regime that will, in turn, change their lives. This suspended transnationalism becomes more complicated with decades of exile.

American relations with Cuba and the lives of Cubans in the United States have a long, complicated history. In the nineteenth century, Southern planters coveted Cuba as an enduring slave society. The island became a battleground for American expansion in the Spanish-American war. Since American occupation of Cuba during and after this war, the US has frequently intervened (under provisions of the 1901 Platt Amendment) in direct governance and indirect control of the island. It supported regimes like that of Fulgencio Batista, while investors created an American image of Cuba as a tropical escape – casinos and recreation rather than economic and social development. The US still maintains a naval base in Cuba – Guantanamo – after decades of a hostile regime.

Some Cubans found alternative meanings to this proximity through emigration to the US, establishing the cigar industry in Tampa, Florida's Ybor City and Key West, as well as **New York** City in the nineteenth century. Jose Martí also found refuge in the US to work for Cuban independence. Nonetheless, this population remained relatively small (under 50,000) until 1959, when Fidel Castro and his guerrillas claimed control of the island. As Castro's reforms and expropriations were seen to run against American interests, the US became embroiled in covert operations against the regime, including the ill-fated **Bay of Pigs** expedition. The 1962 **Cuban missile crisis** also pitted the **Kennedy** regime against the Soviet Union over the placement of strategic weapons in Cuba. The US came to impose sanctions, diplomatic isolation and embargo from the early 1960s onward. Castro found allies instead in the Soviet Union, and developed a Marxist regime that emphasized a new equality in economics, education and healthcare, while exporting revolution to the rest of the world – Che Guevara in Bolivia or more tragic interventions in Angola. The US remained obdurate despite gradually diminishing support from allies and human costs of the embargo in areas like medicine and **family** communication.

International relations, however bitter, were further complicated by Cuban **refugees** who fled the Castro regime. Over 150,000 refugees arrived in the early years of tense relations between the nascent Castro regime and the US. A highly urbane population, many settled in south **Florida**, where Miami's Calle Ocho/Little Havana emerged as a new Cuban metropolis. Arguing their case in fiercely anti-communist terms, Cubans gained rights to facilitated residence and citizenship, converting them eventually into a major voice in conservative politics.

This community grew later by special policies that permitted the airlift of Cuban nationals to the US between 1965 and 1973 (accounting for some 260,000 more people). The Mariel boatlifts in 1980 brought 125,000 new refugees to the US, including criminals released by Castro whose presence demanded complex investigations and incarcerations in camps across the US. Sponsorship of these refugees by churches and civic organizations spread Cubans – and the message of opposition to Castro – across the US and fortified the South Florida community.

In the years of Cuban economic crisis following the collapse of Soviet support and other problems, depiction of isolated rafts and dramatic escapes reminded the nation that Cuba was a place which people sought to flee from as well as return to. Here, however, the US government distinguished economic and political refugees and sought generally to return those escapees intercepted on the high seas. In the end, Cubans were allocated 20,000 entry visas annually, as well as other markers of special treatment in their **immigration** status, which set them apart. Meanwhile, President **Clinton**'s endorsement of the 1996 Helms-Burton Act strengthened the embargo and penalties for those who violate it, raising questions and opposition worldwide.

Yet Castro's regime did not fall, despite blockades and the economic collapse of its major ally. After four decades, then, the Cuban American community has faced new divisions as the second generation reaches maturity without any experience of the island itself. While many Cuban Americans have prospered in business, politics, culture and other sectors of the US economy, Cuban Americans are also divided by **class** and **race**. New generations have become Americanized as well: they do not see Spanish as their only formative **language**, nor do they feel the same intense Catholicism or nostalgia that binds together many in exile. Hence, responses to the Elian Gonzalez case become rituals of identity and community as well as demands for change and, ultimately, for return.

Among notable Cuban Americans are South Florida politicians, business people and cultural figures. Cuban Americans have made a mark in literature (Cristina García, Oscar Hijuelos), entertainment (Gloria **Estefan**), arts, dance and sports, especially **baseball**.

Further reading

Gonzalez-Prando, M. (1997) *The Cuban Americans*, Westport: Greenwood.

Perez-Firmat, G. (1994) *Life on the Hyphen*, Austin: University of Texas.

Perez, L. (1997) *Cuba and the US*, Athens, GA: University of Georgia.

US House of Representatives Hearings (1999) *US–Cuban Relations: Where are We and Where are We Heading?*, Washington, DC: Government Printing Office.

GARY McDONOGH

Cuban missile crisis

What was remarkable about the discoveries made by the U-2 plane flying over Cuba on October 14, 1962, was not the pictures of Soviet missiles being placed there, but rather the fact that Americans had previously been unaware of their existence. The missiles had traveled by sea to Cuba along with 42,000 troops and technicians to service and protect them.

The missiles were sent in part to cement the Soviet Union's alliance with **Castro**'s Cuba, and as part of Nikita Khrushchev's pledge to protect Cuba from US invasion, but, more importantly, as a response to the deployment of Jupiter missiles in Turkey. Having made an issue of the "missile gap" (the fabricated claim that the Soviet Union was ahead in the arms race) in his election campaign, and having been embarrassed the previous year by the **Bay of Pigs** fiasco, President **Kennedy** could not merely recognize the Soviet act for what it was and agree to remove the Jupiters. Instead, Kennedy heightened tensions immediately, demanding in a nationwide television address that the Soviets withdraw their missiles. He further warned that if a missile were fired from Cuba, Americans would respond by launching a missile attack on the Soviet Union. Acting in this way placed Khrushchev in a position from which he could not back down without considerable loss of political capital. For six days he refused to remove the missiles.

Kennedy's advisors were divided about whether to stick with the blockade they had established and wait out Khrushchev, or to bomb the missiles with the likelihood of killing numerous Russians. Letters were sent from Khrushchev to Kennedy, the first of which agreed to withdraw Soviet missiles in exchange for a no-invasion pledge from the US Government. This was immediately followed by another letter which demanded that Kennedy also remove the Jupiter missiles; the President would not agree to this demand. Fortunately, Robert Kennedy suggested that Americans should accept the first letter and ignore the second. Agreement was reached on October 27, but not before Americans came to the brink of bombing Cuba, triggering a missile attack on the US. Moreover, the fact that the Soviets were not fully in control of the missiles on the ground in Cuba created an extremely volatile situation. The agreement had both a public and private dimension. The public agreement fitted the terms of the first letter; but privately the Kennedy administration agreed to withdraw the Jupiter missiles, which had triggered the crisis in the first place.

Kennedy salvaged the prestige he had lost since the Bay of Pigs, but at great cost. People around the world were fully aware of their proximity to nuclear annihilation, and, while many Americans were happy that Kennedy had not blinked, others believed that he had overreacted. More significantly, Khrushchev, who had been pushing for reforms in the aftermath of Stalin's regime, lost much of his credibility as a result of the crisis and was later removed from power by Soviet hardliners led by Leonid Brezhnev. The **Cold War** would get colder still. The fears of annihilation that the crisis produced filtered into American culture in the ubiquitous private and public nuclear shelters, the bikini swimsuits (named after the atoll in which nuclear testing occurred), the movie *Dr. Strangelove* (1964) and in a growing fascination with horror movies.

ROBERT GREGG

cults

The United States has a long history of organizing religious sects, new **religions** and cults. The inherent **individualism** and right to self-determination that is fundamental to its culture makes it inevitable that many expressions of religion have emerged, many of them with cult-like characteristics. The term "cult" developed a negative stereotype as numerous cults arose in the 1970s. Current scholars prefer the term "new religion" or "alternative religion" to the term "cult." A recent publication cited over 1,000 cults, sects and new religions in the United States. The number continues to grow as mainstream Protestant denominations (**Presbyterians**, **Episcopalians**, Baptists and **Methodists**) lose their appeal, while immigrants from non-Christian, non-Protestant traditions continue to flourish in the country (Muslims, **Hindus** and **Buddhists**), **New Age** movements continue to proliferate and an increas-

ing number of individuals are alienated from religion altogether.

Major "new religions" or movements considered cults include the New Age movement, the Unification Church, the Way, the Hare Krishna movement, the WICA movement and other goddess religions, and the Church of Scientology. Other communities in the latter part of the twentieth century that enjoyed cult-like status but no longer exist, owing to mass suicides or conflicts with law-enforcement officials, included Jim Jones' People's Temple, MOVE, the Branch Davidians, and Heaven's Gate. **Mormons** and Christian Scientists, now generally considered "new religions," have also been considered cults, revealing the latter term's instability and its dependence on perspective.

Characteristics that distinguish alternative religions from mainstream religions have been variously identified – from any religion that departs from traditional interpretation to socially dangerous groups led by cynical leaders who exploit their members. Another list of categories for distinguishing new religions or cults from mainstream include: leadership (often lay or charismatic), organization (usually less bureaucratic), size (usually small), membership (usually requires conversion to a community that excludes the unworthy), worship (often fervent or spontaneous), dedication to duty (makes more demands on time and controls members' lives) and social status (often marginalized, uneducated or powerless) (Miller 1995: 3–4).

The New Age movement is considered the outgrowth of the 1960s counterculture. **Baby boomers**, former **hippies** and others suddenly seeking spiritual guidance may be drawn to New Age ideals as brought by David Spangler, a student of Alice Bailey, to America from the Findhorn Community in Scotland (described in *My Dinner with Andre*, 1981). These ideals are: 1. The possibility of personal transformation; 2. The coming of broad cultural/environmental transformation; 3. The transformation of occult arts and processes; and 4. The self as divine.

The Unification Church began in Korea in the 1950s with the Reverend Sun Myung Moon, but it came to the United States in 1971 when Moon went coast to coast speaking, defending **Nixon**, and proselytizing on college **campuses**. His followers believe that Moon has revealed a "new truth," as recorded in the 1973 Divine Principle, that he and Mrs Moon are the "true parents of humankind," that he is the messiah whose task is to establish the true family and that he has ushered in a "completed Testament Age." The true family begins with a "blessing," often found in mass weddings of thousands of couples at one time.

A former evangelical and Reformed Church of America minister, Victor Paul Wierville founded the Way in 1942. His teachings reject the Trinity and deny the divinity of Jesus. The Way grew explosively during the 1970s as part of the national Jesus People revival. Teachings are spread through Power for Abundant Living classes. This group has been the subject of numerous de-programming actions, as well as federal investigations for their training in deadly weapons.

The Hare Krishna movement – or the International Society for Krishna Consciousness – set American roots in the 1960s, when A.C. Bhaktivendanta Swami Prabhupada entered **New York** City's counterculture. It has aroused great hostility, particularly through aggressive solicitation at **airports** and public places.

The Church of Scientology is a distinctive American "new religion" founded by L. Ron Hubbard (1911–86). From his 1950 publication of *Dianetics: Modern Science of Mental Health*, his followers have asserted that humans can live without unwanted sensations and fears, that humans are essentially good and that thetans (humans as immortal spiritual beings) have lived many lifetimes before. This group has been the subject of numerous cult controversies, e.g. over **tax** evasion and health practices, and has a sizeable following among **actors** in **Hollywood**, including Tom Cruise, Nicole Kidman, Hilary Swank and John Travolta, who brought Hubbard's *Battlefield Earth* to the screen (2000), where it failed to become a summer blockbuster.

Further reading

Ellwood, R. and Partin, H.B. (1988) *Religious and Spiritual Groups in Modern America*, Englewood Cliffs: Prentice Hall.

Gallup, G., Jr. and Castelli, J. (1989) *The People's Religion*, New York: MacMillan Publishing Company.

Lewis, J.R. (1998) *Encyclopedia of Cults, Sects, and New Religions*, Amherst: Prometheus Books.

Miller, T. (ed.) (1995) *America's Alternative Religions*, Albany: State University of New York Press.

GAIL HENSON

cultural studies

The very attempt to define cultural studies would be seen by many of its practitioners as reductive and antithetical to the free-roaming spirit of a subject which, despite an extended and distinguished history, still prides itself on its ability to resist rigid disciplinary frameworks. During its evolution, cultural studies has incorporated a variety of approaches, yet has held them intact within itself rather than absorbing and conflating them. As such it should be seen less as a melting-pot than a cage of bees, where **feminism**, **anthropology**, **film criticism**, Marxism, postcolonialism, literary criticism, **postmodernism** and **queer** theory swarm in debate. As a consequence, it currently has no single established methodology.

Nevertheless, certain trends and patterns can be drawn from this seeming chaos, including a history which most would agree stretches back at least to Richard Hoggart's *The Uses of Literacy* (1957) and Raymond Williams' *Culture and Society* (1958). Cultural studies in Britain established a solid base through Hoggart's creation, with Stuart Hall, of the Birmingham Centre for Contemporary Cultural Studies in 1964. It would be inaccurate to draw any kind of "house style" from the debates within the Birmingham School, but we can identify an interest in "subcultural" **fashions** and behavior and in audience interpretation of popular texts, made more urgent through an engagement with feminism, with questions of "**race**" and identity, and with the Gramscian notion of "hegemony," as it applied to 1970s Britain.

These approaches to cultural studies were not exported directly across the Atlantic, but reached the United States through the filter of French theory – Bourdieu, Foucault and de Certeau – whose stress on a decentered micropolitics of society had increasing relevance to the complex and fragmented cultures of 1980s North America.

In practice, cultural studies in the USA has developed as a mutated anthropology: an investigation into the urban tribes of sunbathers, **mall** shoppers and **romance** readers which interrogates popular cultures and "subcultural" fan groups. As such, it brings the unseen – the trivial, the homemade, the "minority" reading – to light, and makes the familiar seem alien. Despite the shifts in content and focus, these studies invariably have in common with both their French and British counterparts a grounding in issues of cultural power and its relation to media representation. John Fiske's work on the quintessential landscapes and landmarks of the 1980s were highly influential here, although others have since questioned his optimism in the supposedly transformative power of audience readings.

If the North American academy gave cultural studies a boost in popularity and respectability, it also prompted a crisis: the expansion of the subject across universities and conferences meant that this "counter-discipline" had itself become an established and increasingly profitable media industry. Even as cultural studies becomes a truly international force, with important contributions from Australia, Italy, Hong Kong and even the virtual nation-states of the **Internet**, this paradox continues to hover over the subject and its practice.

Further Reading

Grossberg, L., Nelson, C. and Treichler, P. (eds) (1992) *Cultural Studies*, London: Routledge.

WILL BROOKER

culture wars *see* intellectuals/culture wars; multiculturalism

Cunningham, Merce

b. 1919

Dancer and choreographer who worked with Martha Graham. He presented his first solo concert in 1944, with music by John **Cage**, with whom he would maintain a lifelong relationship. He formed the Merce Cunningham Dance Company in the **Pacific Northwest** in 1953, and choreographed over 200 works thereafter for them and for ballet and **dance** companies worldwide. Cunningham has consistently focused on dance as an abstract art, where movement – even if determined by chance – is more important than narrative. In addition to collaboration with artists and composers, he has also experimented with film and video dance. His prodigious and creative work has earned him global accolades.

GARY McDONOGH

Cuomo, Mario

b. 1932

Democratic **governor** of New York (1983–94). An unapologetic liberal, Cuomo's fiery keynote speech at the 1984 Democratic convention earned him a national reputation as an eloquent critic of the **Reagan** administration. A skilled orator in an age when ideological battles were waged in **television** soundbites, he was a consistent voice of dissent against political trends such as **welfare** reform in the 1990s. He flirted with presidential runs in 1988 and 1992, but ultimately confined his political aspirations to New York, losing his bid for a fourth term to **Republican** George Pataki in 1994.

SARAH SMITH

curfew

Traditionally associated with war, civil disturbance and disaster, curfews have kept Americans in their houses during natural disasters and riots. In the 1990s, cities also used them to control **teenage** violence and victimization. **Chicago, IL** enacted a 10:30 weekday curfew for those under sixteen in 1955; most cities over 100,000 subsequently have added restrictions, including daytime curfews. Anchorage, **Alaska**, arrested on average 100 teens per month for violations of a 1996 rule requiring those under eighteen to be home by 23:00 unless permitted by parents or required by religion or work. Teenagers, however, have successfully sued these ordinances as violations of 1st Amendment rights.

GARY McDONOGH

D

Daley family

Richard Joseph Daley (1902–76) served as **mayor** of **Chicago, IL** from 1955 until his death. He was one of a generation of **Democratic** mayors of large **cities** known as "machine" politicians because of the large patronage networks they controlled. Daley's machine was widely credited with delivering a critical bloc of votes for John F. **Kennedy** in 1960.

The Daley family lived in the heavily Irish working-class **neighborhood** of Bridgeport, where fears of racial integration ran high. Because of his loyalty to similar communities, Daley resisted Martin Luther **King**'s efforts for neighborhood integration. Following a period of organizing and marches in Chicago, King remarked that northern racism was even more intransigent than that of the south. Daley's connections to **Washington, DC** attracted significant federal funding to Chicago in the 1950s and 1960s, much of which he used to construct large, high-rise public housing developments that concentrated Chicago's growing **African American** population. He was also credited with reviving Chicago's aging downtown infrastructure. Daley gained national publicity again in 1968, using heavy-handed tactics to subdue anti-war protesters at the Democratic National Convention.

In 1989 Daley's oldest son, Richard M. Daley, was elected mayor. In an effort to separate himself from his father's image, soon after beginning his first term, he moved out of Bridgeport into an integrated, gentrified new neighborhood just west of downtown.

Further reading

Biles, R. (1995) *Richard J. Daley: Politics, Race and the Governing of Chicago*, DeKalb: Northern Illinois University Press.

Cohen, A. and Taylor, E. (2000) *American Pharoah: Mayor Richard J. Daley: His Battle for Chicago and the Nation*, Boston: Little Brown.

Royko, M. (1971) *Boss*, New York: E.P. Dutton.

SUSAN BRIN HYATT

Dallas, TX

Formed by conjunctions of railroads, cattle, oil, finance and technology, the glassy spires of Dallas rise from the Central **Texas** plains, surrounded by highways and **suburban** sprawl. This wealthy city of 1,075,894 (1998 estimate) is also a center for art, **education** (Baylor, Southern Methodist and Dallas Universities), **medicine** and **religion**, especially massive evangelical churches. Neiman-Marcus **department store**, famed for its fabulous Christmas **catalog**, and **computer** maker Texas Instruments are also based there. Sports teams include the world champion Cowboys (**football**) and the Mavericks (**basketball**); **baseball**'s Texas Rangers play in adjacent Arlington. The city shares an **airport** with nearby Fort Worth in a metropolitan area of over 4 million, including fast-growing suburbs like Plano.

The **assassination** of President John F. **Kennedy** on November 22, 1963 and the televised events that followed inscribed Dallas on world consciousness; the sixth-floor museum in the Texas

Book Depository commemorates this tragedy. In the 1980s, the city's image was reshaped by the **prime-time** soap opera *Dallas*. The grittier realism of Errol Morris' documentary *Thin Blue Line* (1986) and other works recognize the **class** and racial diversity of the area and its problems.

GARY McDONOGH
CINDY WONG.

dance

The dynamic and innovative complexities of the populist and egalitarian aspirations of American dance in the twentieth century have also expressed the shift of the US from isolationism to the role of primary world power on the world stage plus internal racial problems concerning national identity. Contrasting perceptions of "what is American dance?" resulted, ranging from the external (that usually focus on the more popular multi-cultural forms) to fragmented internal visions (that depend on what sector of society is viewing what type of dance).

By the beginning of the twentieth century, America had produced two major "modernist" dance movements based on urban rhythms. Modern dance led by Louie Fuller and Isadore Duncan referenced back to early nineteenth-century salon dancing, but was forward in its use of day-to-day movement techniques. Authentic jazz dance (AJD) harnessed a unique American thrusting sense of rhythmic dynamics, which had first been worked out in minstrel shows, and which subsequently influenced most other American dance forms.

Modern dance began as a reaction against the decorative role of the female body in ballet and vaudeville, and asserted a creative 'high-art' status of the female form. Reflecting the burgeoning struggles for women's rights, it inevitably expressed the compromises the American suffragist movement made with racism. Early modern dance's "white" agenda overtly rejected "Negro influences" and acquired its original validation in Europe. The "Denishawn School" of Ruth St Denis and Ted Shawn, who overcame Duncan's free-form legacy, looked to Native American and South American dances for "folk" inspiration to formulate a systematic technique based on movement method. Images from Denishawn productions have a distinct, early **Hollywood** melodramatic look to them, but their highly gifted students have had a decisive impact on subsequent developments.

Authentic jazz dance developed through a series of push–pull impulses in conjunction with **jazz** music. New dance crazes led to demands for more bands, raising standards of musicianship and provoking further dance developments. World impacting social dance crazes like the cakewalk, one-step and Charleston defied a sustained campaign of racist moral outrage and were incredibly popular in **college** dances and Prohibition-defying drinking venues. A similar push–pull dynamic between stage and social versions of the same dance was at work which took the latest popular dance to new levels of technical complexity while ushering in its replacement. The segregated "jazz age" developed a complex network of black theatres around which these artists worked and from which they made occasional forays into **Broadway**. Hit shows like *Shuffle Along* (1921) and *Running Wild* (1923) brought the "carriage trade'" – upper-class **New York** – uptown where they were enthralled by an abundance of talent in clubs like the Cotton Club and Connie's Inn, largely run and owned by gangsters. Simultaneously, major **African American** stars emerged like Florence Mills, Josephine Baker and Bill "Bojangles" Robinson.

The 1929 Crash and the ensuing Depression struck hammer blows at this pattern of entertainment, and the dance forms that emerged afterwards were significantly different. **Segregation** was still in place, but **Roosevelt**'s New Deal engendered a new populist sense of American identity that shaped the ensuing dance developments. The lifting of the restrictions in 1934, which had almost wiped out the many forms of Native American dance, was complemented by a widespread enthusiasm for square dancing in the 1930s. The prejudicial element of early modern dance was overtaken by a new radicalism led by a third wave of young dancer/choreographers (the foremost being Martha Graham), who were christened "modern dancers." They looked to American cultural icons for inspiration. Black dancers struggling with the artistic straightjackets imposed on AJD acts or the associated intense exploitation began to establish a niche in modern dance that led to the emergence of artists of the caliber of Katherine Dunham and Pearl Primus.

Even the essentially foreign ballet residents in the US began to move in the same direction. The Ballet Russe de Monte Carlo had toured across the US for many years, and slowly created a demand for ballet. The realization of a distinct American identity had been held back in the pre-war years by Balanchine's feud with the management of the "Met." Balanchine's production *On Your Toes* (1936), set in a gangster idiom, was the first to tell an American tale. Lincoln Kirstein played a major role in promoting the concept of an American classic ballet style and wrote libretti for ballets which introduced American themes such as *Billy the Kid* (1938) and *Filling Station* (1938). The American Ballet Theatre, founded in 1939, out of which Jerome Robbins emerged, sustained a policy of featuring "stars" and classic works, although its turnover in choreographers often led to featuring new ones. Eventually, Kirstein and Balanchine's efforts resulted in the formation of the New York City Ballet.

Mocking high-art aspirations nevertheless remained highly popular in the **musical** dance comedy film of Fred **Astaire** and Ginger Rodgers and the slapstick of the Marx Brothers which, at the same time, accommodated to those selfsame values. The jazz tradition emerged from the wreckage of the Wall Street crash as "swing" to become the dominant popular influence in live entertainment. Included in this reincarnation were the social and stage dance forms created in the 1920s – lindy hop, rhythm, tap and various eccentric dance styles – to which the rapidly expanding swing bands gave a new lease of life. For one brief historical moment, when swing was the popular music of the day, the US achieved a kind of national cultural consensus that lasted until the outbreak of the Second World War.

The war eventually ushered in another major cultural re-adjustment as the US began to fulfill its role as a world power. AJD was considered to be socially inadequate to project the cultural image of the US to the world (although in practice this was exactly what was happening), while modern dancers were too divided among different schools to construct a unified picture. Instead, the US took the ballet road. Early in the war, before the swing identity was rejected, films made a case for American cultural diversity by adopting Latin/jazz themes which saw the emergence of the astounding Nicholas brothers as major stars in various dance-featured films directed by Nick Castle and Hermes Pan. The 1930s exploration of American themes bore fruit with Agnes De Mille's *Oklahoma!* (1943) on Broadway and Jerome Robbins' comedy ballet *Fancy Free* (1944). **Cowboys** and US sailors dancing ballet had replaced Russian peasants and, for a while, the Euro-American identity that the modern pioneers had searched for was actualized and popular, but based on ballet technique.

The new "musical" form, which used dance and song for narrative purposes, replaced the old Broadway revue that had ranged from the glories of Zeigfeld to the diverse skills of the all-black shows. Any hopes aroused by the musical film *Stormy Weather* (1943), which had merged AJD with black modern dance, were soon dashed by the lack of any sequels. *Oklahoma!* began a golden age of the musical which is generally thought to conclude with Jerome Robbins' *Fiddler On The Roof* (1964). A great deal of the new ballet and modern choreographic talent was diverted into a profusion of shows that alternated between the two technique forms. Michael Kidd was an outstanding ballet contributor with *Finian's Rainbow* (1947) and *Seven Brides for Seven Brothers* (1954), along with Robbins' *West Side Story* (1957). Helen Tamaris, another product of Denishawn, scored with her choreography for musicals like *Show Boat* (1946), which featured Pearl Primus, and *Annie Get Your Gun* (1946). Yet another Denishawn graduate, Jack Cole, was the major modernist in the background whose influence was often expressed via others. For instance, one of his former company dancers, Alex Romero, who worked at MGM as an assistant director, staged a Cole-influenced "Slaughter on 10th Avenue" scene for Gene **Kelly**, the *Jailhouse Rock* (1957) sequence for Elvis **Presley** and actually danced the "difficult" parts in the final *Fancy Free* ballet at the end of *On The Town* (1949) that Frank **Sinatra** couldn't handle. Bob Fosse's

Broadway breakthrough with *Damn Yankees* (1955), which featured the brilliant Louis Johnson's spectacular routine, was also strongly influenced by Cole.

After *Fiddler*, the Broadway musical appeared to be unsettled by the rapidly changing but dominating "youth culture." It found success in re-staging former hit shows, reversing the former progression by making stage hits out of hit film musicals or by striking lucky with the occasional hit musical that connected with contemporary rock/pop trends. Further respite was found in the old staple of shows about putting on shows, such as *A Chorus Line* (1975) and *Fame* (movie 1980, musical 1995), but they too faded.

Modern dancers had become "successful" in the postwar situation and were no longer driven by the anti-ballet ethos of their founders and 1930s political concerns. Downtown New York's artistic shift towards the abstract and minimalism pointed to new paths. Merce **Cunningham**, who was connected to avant-garde painting schools, became the best-known dancer to reject narrative in favor of chance, both in terms of composition and accompaniment. Paul Taylor, Trisha Brown and others adopted this rather peculiar definition of "**postmodernism**," which had more in common with better known examples of pre-war "modernism."

The evolving black modern dance companies were not willing to follow this lead. The expanding **civil-rights** struggles demanded commitment. Black dancers had made headway in the developing postwar dance scene and crossed between Broadway musicals and modern, but there was a continuing problem with "**race** casting" that frustrated major artists like Dunham and Primus. This led to a greater emphasis on setting up their own schools and conducting research in which they nurtured a new generation of brilliant young black dancers. Significant companies to facilitate the development of these new artists were Alvin **Ailey** in 1958 and Arthur Mitchell's Dance Theatre of **Harlem** in 1969. Interest in various forms of African dance grew in the 1970s as part of the black consciousness movement, which restored a great deal of the discarded dance vocabulary.

Twyla Tharp revised the American dance definition of postmodernism into a kind of historicism that re-worked many icons of American culture. In the 1970s, she was the first major white modern choreographer to use jazz music since the Second World War. Her American-sourced work in general surpassed her occasional lapses into classicism. Other choreographers have followed Tharp, and many of the former distinctions concerning "black dance" have been eroded. In the late 1990s, a greater willingness to work with jazz musicians was evident. However, the replacement of the essential "creative democracy" of AJD by the direction of the ballet master or choreographer has diminished the status of the dancer, despite some postmodernist token gestures towards dancers' creativity. Few, if any, of the major modern dance companies pay their dancers a living wage so they have to support themselves via part-time work. Ironically, the recognition that the founders of modern dance had set out to achieve in terms of its dancers has yet to be won.

Despite wartime successes, US ballet still needed help and the British Sadler Wells company's repeat tours fanned the flames. A major Ford Foundation grant helped establish the New York City Ballet in its purpose-built home in the Lincoln Center, as well as greatly to extend its ballet school. As the American musical lost its élan, new regional schools helped develop major regional ballet companies in **Miami, FL**, **Houston, TX**, **Atlanta, GA** and other cities. American ballet, like the musical, has tended to lose its former special sense of direction as it has become more established, but, unlike the musical, has had a greater legacy to fall back on.

Regarding developments in popular dance, the major jolt of wartime experience seemed to result in a postwar elder generation wanting excessively mellow dance music and a younger one demanding pronounced rhythms. The black community, which had turned in on itself in terms of **rhythm and blues**, found itself invaded by young whites, leading to a panic among those who believed that **rock 'n' roll** promoted excessive "African" bodily movements. Evidently, the "twist" temporarily resolved this problem while the English invasion, by repackaging rhythm and blues in a white form, solved it by selling it back to the US minus its intrinsic dance connection. Black creativity kept welling up in successive waves of 1960s **soul**, 1970s **disco** and 1980s hip hop. In some cases, the continuity was quite conscious. The tap maestro "Cholly" Atkins taught pop music vocal groups, like the Drifters and the Temptations, the old routines to improve the visual quality of their stage acts. In turn these movement patterns were imitated by new generations of young Americans and reproduced as the "new" dance styles of the 1970s. In other cases it was unconscious – as in the hip-hop breakdancers of the 1980s reworking Charleston footwork with a barely remembered but distinct throwback to the 1910s black American craze for Russian dance, which gave them many of their more spectacular sequences.

A strong American social dance identity, centered on the New York Harvest Moon Ball Dance contest, survived until 1974 when it too fell victim to the all-pervasive disco craze. American competition dancers have found it difficult to make much progress in the international ballroom world that adheres to the highly mannered English style, but they have been able to take control of the new "Theatre Arts" category, which essentially reprises classic "musical" sequences. A semi-hidden asset of American dance identity has been the two most "Americanized" of Latin dance forms – the mambo and **salsa** – which are still thriving in the city and preserve many core values. American dance has sustained the spirit of flamboyant rhythmic **individualism** that 1980s stars like Michael **Jackson**, **Madonna** and MC Hammer took to new heights, riding on the emergence of the globalized pop-video art form.

Recently New York has seen a significant enhancement of its American dance identity. Rhythm tap is back (led by the prodigy Savion Glover), lindy hop has swung out again onto the ballroom floor, the Fosse style is dominant once more on stage and formerly derelict 42nd Street theatres have been refurbished. Yet, American dance in New York, the self-proclaimed "world capital of dance," is threatened by soaring land values, which have eliminated adequate rehearsal rooms, and a general indecision as to the way forward. Radio City Music Hall and its legendary Rockettes are under a rumored emblematic ominous threat. Perhaps the legendary toughness of New York dancers will enable them to hang on and the future of American dance will not have to rest, for the most part, on whatever resources

American **colleges** can devote to preserving the nation's heritage.

TERRY MONAGHAN

Danish modern

In the 1960s, Scandinavian design evoked clean lines, simple elegance and bright colors as statements of modernity in walnut, steel and glass for American **suburban** homes and sleek new offices. This trend coincided for some with images of Scandinavia as consisting of progressive liberal societies, whether in politics or **pornography**. Decades later, this design fad underwent a nostalgic revival, while IKEA has appealed to **yuppie** consumers in major metropolitan centers with new generations of Swedish design.

GARY McDONOGH

Daschle, Tom

b. 1947

Born in South Dakota, Democrat Tom Daschle was first elected to the United States **Congress** in 1978 by only 139 votes. He served four terms in the House of Representatives before winning his current Senate seat in 1986. In the Senate, Daschle quickly got involved in the **Democratic Party** leadership, acting for six years as co-chair of the Democratic Policy Committee before assuming his leadership position in the 104th Congress. In the Senate's history, only Lyndon Baines **Johnson** had spent fewer years in the Senate before winning such a post. Daschle also serves on the Senate Agriculture Committee.

COURTNEY BENNETT

Dash, Julie

b. 1952

Independent African American **director-producer**, Dash has faced many problems in funding that have limited her output. Nonetheless, her lyrical vision, synthesizing poetry and music, underpins master works like *Four Women* (1978), while *Illusions* (1982) explores a black woman passing for white in 1940s **Hollywood**. *Daughters of the Dust* (1992), a stunning prelude to the **African American** great migration, set on the Gullah coast, was the first feature-length general release film by an African American woman. However, even after its critical success, Dash could not finance another feature; she has worked on musical shorts and a project on Zora Neale Hurston.

CINDY WONG

Davis, Bette

b. 1908; d. 1989

A grande dame of bitchiness, Davis brought intelligence and skill rather than beauty to her roles as a powerful woman whose goals conflict with social codes, whether in antebellum **New Orleans, LA** (*Jezebel*, 1938, Oscar) or twentieth-century **Boston, MA** (*Now Voyager*, 1942). While popular with female fans, Davis ran afoul of studios, suing Warner Brothers in 1936 for an unjust contract, which she lost. The studio, however, treated her with more respect, and put her in demanding roles. There were striking gaps in her career as she matured, despite her success as an older actor in *All About Eve* (1951) and her reinvention as an even older matriarch of horror (*What Ever Happened to Baby Jane*, 1962), as well as in Disney fantasies. Davis' unique voice, artful gestures (especially with a cigarette) and indomitable roles made many of her lines proverbial references among generations of American filmgoers, while her style created iconic status among gay commentators as well.

GARY McDONOGH
CINDY WONG

Davis, Miles

b. 1926; d. 1991

Jazz musician Miles Davis cut his musical chops on be-bop and nurtured his musicality in the **New York** City **jazz** lifestyle colored by American **race** relations. As a trumpet player, Miles was not known for a conventional virtuosity, but rather for the ways in which he used the trumpet with his raspy, muted sound (not unlike his own voice) to add color and nuance to his music. Davis' music was often the precursor of change and the avant-garde in jazz music. His recording, *Kind of Blue* (1959), remains one of the best examples of his unique musicianship. Davis politicized jazz music along racial lines and encouraged an ambivalent relationship with his audiences, particularly his white audience.

Further reading

Carner, G. (ed.) (1996) *The Miles Davis Companion: Four Decades of Commentary*, New York: Schirmer Books; London: Prentice Hall International.

Davis, M. (1989) *Miles, the Autobiography. Miles Davis with Quincy Troupe*, New York: Simon & Schuster.

Davis, M. (1959) *Kind of Blue* [sound recording], KCS 8163, S.l: Columbia Records.

STEVE FERZACCA

Day, Doris

b. 1924

If Bette **Davis** and Joan **Crawford** defined bitchiness on screen, Doris Day (born Doris Von Kappelhoff) came to epitomize virginal niceness for American society in the 1950s and 1960s – a non-sexual tease (ironically often paired with Rock **Hudson** in romantic comedies) whose independent career and sophistication melted at the altar. Her 1975 autobiography, *Doris Day: Her Own Story*, revealed that this charmed comedic life was as far from her own story as it was from that of many other struggling American women in those decades.

GARY McDONOGH

Day, Dorothy

b. 1897; d. 1980

Day, a **Roman Catholic** social activist, sought to

reconcile her early socialism with her 1927 conversion to Catholicism. She did this through the Catholic Worker's Movement, which offered hospitality to the homeless and hungry from the Depression onwards, and the newspaper *Catholic Worker* (founded 1933). Throughout her life, Day brought her deep faith and conscience to bear on issues of labor, **race** and pacifism. Since her death, some have sought to propose her as a fitting saint for the American century. Her autobiography, *The Long Loneliness*, appeared in 1952.

GARY McDONOGH

daycare *see* babies; children

Dean, James (Byron James)

b. 1931; d. 1955

Andy **Warhol** called him "the damaged but beautiful soul of our time" (McCann 1993: 125). Three starring roles – two in movies released after his **death** in a car crash – seared Dean in American and global consciousness as the consummate **teenage** rebel (*East of Eden*, 1955; *Rebel without a Cause*, 1955; *Giant*, 1955). Dean embodied the anxieties of teenagers in his life and screen presence, which have made him an enduring legend for subsequent generations and highlighted the dark side of **family values** and **Hollywood** success.

Further reading

McCann, G. (1993) *Rebel Males*, New Brunswick: Rutgers.

GARY McDONOGH

death

Repulsed and fascinated by death, Americans struggle to grasp its physical, psychological and social impact through both a medical understanding of bodily degenerative processes and philosophical and cathartic explorations of its meaning.

Americans avoid the signs of death, age and disease through their love of youth culture, "fitness" and **plastic surgery**. Biotechnical innovations, cryogenics, genome mapping and cloning have become a new **religion** that allows Americans to entertain fantasies of immortality.

Old age and death are profoundly medicalized; age is a medical "problem," death is a biotechnological failure to preserve life. The other sign of death, disease, is exemplified by the **AIDS** epidemic. Without cure, AIDS is death; the ultimate eros/thanatos combination where physical pleasures evoke necrophilia. But death is sometimes better than debilitation, a key debate when considering the euthanasia practices of "Dr Death," Jack Kevorkian.

Most Americans will die in hospitals or nursing homes; dying, grieving and disposing of the dead are hidden and institutionalized events, sanitized processes managed by specialized workers. Jessica Mitford's *The American Way of Death* (1963) pinpointed the exploitative practices of funeral professionals as they dispose of the dead at high costs to the bereaved. Mitford's work was revelatory, but American funerals are still cherished, expensive and necessary rituals.

Death anxiety is expressed in American media culture where mass deaths, at home or afar, are a spectacle. National news coverage and photos of the fiery death of David Koresh and Branch Davidian followers in **Waco**, Texas, are rivaled only by details and images of murders shown nightly on local **television** news. The extermination of populations in Cambodia, Rwanda and Yugoslavia, international airplane crashes and earthquake and flood disaster sites are common foci of American media interest, as the fascination with these images competes with discourses of prevention and aid.

Films like *Death Becomes Her* (1992) explore and parody dreams of youth and immortality alongside **tabloid** celebrations of serial murders and blockbusters advertising mass death and destruction. Death is evil and asocial, an offense to American sensibilities in Coppola's *Apocalypse Now* (1979) and Kubrick's *Full Metal Jacket* (1987), which display death for voyeurism, moralizing and catharsis within the "exotic" realm of war. The *Faces of Death* (1978–91) series and "real" underground images of death in "snuff films" emphasize the precarious pleasures of exploring death anxiety in a society often so intent on containing and obfuscating it.

Death images of Marilyn **Monroe**, John F. **Kennedy**, Elvis **Presley** and Princess Diana regularly circulate through tabloid news and **Internet** sites, the bizarre circumstances of their unexpected deaths meticulously reviewed. As public domain, celebrity deaths exacerbate American death anxiety.

In the end, despite its grotesque finery, death in contemporary America remains what it always has been – a primitive finality inseparable from rituals and representations designed to draw meaning from its summons. As each national holiday is marked by a ritualistic recitation of **highway** and **alcohol**-related death statistics, death is implicit to American life, an anxiety embedded deeply within the American psyche and cultural practices.

See also: cemeteries and crematoria

Further reading

Anderson, P. (ed.) (1996) *All of Us: Americans Talk About the Meaning of Death*, New York: Delacorte Press.

Nuland, S. (1994) *How We Die: Reflections on Life's Final Chapter*, New York: A.A. Knopf, distributed by Random House, Inc.

Mitford, J., (1963) *The American Way of Death*, New York: Simon & Schuster.

RAMONA LYONS

debts *see* banks and banking; bankruptcy; consumerism; credit and credit cards

deep ecology/Earth First!

Known for publicity-attracting acts of "eco-tage" or "monkey-wrenching," Earth First! takes direct action, under the credo "no compromise in defense of mother Earth!," against destructive environmental practices. Earth First! attracts not only **hippies**, who are drawn to its deep ecology message of biocentric equality and personal self-realization, but also western **rednecks** who wish to recapture **cowboy** mythology in the face of rapid western industrial development. Although most Americans disapprove of monkey-wrenching – especially when humans are injured – the radical positions of Earth First! make mainstream environmental groups appear very moderate and reasonable.

BRAD ROGERS

Dees, Morris S.

b. 1936

In 1967 Dees founded the Southern Poverty Law Center in Montgomery, Alabama, guiding it for years despite arson and death threats. Victories against **segregation** at the Montgomery YMCA (1969) and in the Alabama State Police led to nationwide work against **race** and gender discrimination and brutality in prisons, for fair housing, fair medical care, worker rights and safety, and just taxation. Since 1980, Dees and the Center have fought organized hate groups. An education program called "Teaching Tolerance" discourages the spread of hate, while legal victories, establishing that hate groups can be held collectively responsible for **hate crimes** committed by individual members, have bankrupted the Alabama **Ku Klux Klan** (1981) and the White Aryan Resistance Movement (1991).

SHARON ANN HOLT

defense *see* Pentagon; war, etc.

deindustrialization

Deindustrialization refers to the long-term economic and political shift whereby the United States has been steadily transformed from a manufacturing economy into a service economy. Where once manufacturing made up over a quarter of all employment in the nation, by the mid-1990s it made up just over 15 percent. In the place of these jobs, once the bedrock of a unionized, **middle-class** workforce, there has emerged a massive increase in the "**service sector**" (approximately three-quarters of the workforce today), whose jobs tend to be non-union, low-paid and unstable.

While deindustrialization has been almost wholly naturalized in the mainstream press and media, an inevitable product of an equally "natural" globalization, in fact it has been the product of political decisions as well as workings of economic markets. The resurgence of Europe and Asia – in part funded by the United States – after the Second World War ultimately created competitors to America's industrial dominance. Technology also made labor-intensive industries such as steel – a foundry of America's industrial might – more "efficient" with the use of automated machinery and **computers**. But this process has also been encouraged in recent years as politicians on both the **Left** and **Right** have embraced free trade as the answer to America's declining economic dominance. In the 1980s and 1990s, **NAFTA** – the North American Free Trade Agreement – galvanized both those who saw free trade as a way to spur American exports and those – led by the AFL-CIO (American Federation of Labor/Congress of Industrial Organization) – who saw the legislation as paving the way for further flight of industry to cheap-labor countries. While America remains the leading industrial power, jobs in traditional manufacturing bases continue to flee to Asia and to Central and South America.

The results of deindustrialization transformed the social and cultural landscape of urban America in the last quarter of the twentieth century. One could stand on Broad Street in the midst of North **Philadelphia, PA**, to take just one example, turn around 360 degrees, and see where 100,000 well-paid, and unionized, jobs had once been. Empty shells are all that remain. The economic power and associated political power have fled downtown to the financial and legal enterprises housed in skyscrapers and to the **suburbs** and exurbs, where those who could fled.

Artists and writers of all types have necessarily responded to a powerful new landscape. Where once the bustling factory complexes and unworldly machinery was a staple of American art – in, for example, the paintings of Ford's River Rouge plant in **Detroit, MI** by Charles Scheeler – now the empty factory and its declining **neighborhood** define the urban views of the late twentieth and early twenty-first centuries. The wonder at America's industrial might has been replaced by the more troubled views of urban America in a state of apparently steady decline. The works of writers such as Nelson Algren and Claude Brown, and later, John Edgar Wideman, to name just a few, take as their setting and theme the declining fate of the industrial American city. Perhaps the most powerful recent portrait of deindustrialization was Michael Moore's tragicomedy of the decline of Flint, Michigan, once a bastion of General Motors. *Roger and Me* (1989) portrays the social upheaval and physical collapse – from eviction to demolition of factories to the return of grass and trees – of a once-thriving industrial city.

Further reading

Bluestone, B. and Bennett, H. (1982) *The Deindustrialization of America*, New York: Basic Books.

Vergara, C. (1995) *The New American Ghetto*, New Brunswick: Rutgers University.

MAX PAGE

DeLillo, Don

b. 1936

Author of eleven novels, including *White Noise, The Names, Mao II, Underworld* and *Americana*, the title of which announced his gradually emerging project. DeLillo has patiently assembled individual and group portraits since the 1950s. He knows American quirks of character, especially quirks of **language**: no American writer alive has a better ear. Incomparably craft-conscious (humble before punctuation), DeLillo shames poets with his rhythmic, mouth-oriented prose and sometimes scares readers with his ability to access our internal modems, to appropriate and make art of our unspoken broken English. Other writers' narrators talk to themselves; his DeLilloquize.

DANIEL BOSCH

Democratic Party

The Democratic Party's origins are in the party created by Thomas Jefferson and James Madison in response to the pro-British, active government strategy of Alexander Hamilton's Federalists. It was later more fully democratized by Andrew Jackson in the 1820s and 1830s. This new democracy was a states' rights, pro-Southern coalition of **state** parties which maintained its identity through the crisis of the Civil War and Reconstruction at the cost of its predominance at the national level.

From 1861 to 1929, the Democrats were subordinate to the pro-business strategies of the **Republican Party** and suffered from contradictions between what, in the 1920s, became its "wet" and "dry" city and country wings. There was little cohesion in a party whose leadership had included Woodrow Wilson, William Jennings Bryan and Grover Cleveland. However, by 1928, the Democrats had fashioned a new, urban constituency made up of turn-of-the-century immigrants and their **children**, mostly Southern and Eastern Europeans, **Roman Catholics** and **Jews**, who rallied to the nation's first Catholic candidate for **president**, Al Smith from **New York**.

Smith's defeat, with the important intrusion of the Great Depression, spawned the New Deal coalition of Franklin D. **Roosevelt**, which dominated the nation until 1968. Under Franklin D. Roosevelt, Harry **Truman**, John F. **Kennedy** and Lyndon **Johnson**, the Democrats, building on the Progressive legacy, constructed a distinctively American version of the **welfare** state: **Social Security**, the rights of labor, regulation, moderate social planning, Keynesian economics, **healthcare**, unemployment, disability and modest welfare provisions. What the New Deal marginalized – **African Americans** and other minorities, and women – the Fair Deal, New Frontier and "Great Society" addressed.

The Democrats successfully claimed the mantle of "The Common Man," and excoriated the GOP as the party of **Hoover**, the Depression and "economic royalists" until the volcanic explosions of the 1960s subverted their mandate. Republican conservatives, sparked by the demagogic, populist appeal of George **Wallace**, which Richard **Nixon** parlayed into his "Silent Majority," were able to take advantage of the decade's dislocations (e.g. the **Vietnam War**, **race riots**, **campus** disorders and rising **crime** rates). The Democrats lost support among "ethnics," the descendants of turn-of-the-nineteenth-century immigrants and white Southerners.

Aside from the anomaly of the 1976 post-**Watergate** victory of Jimmy **Carter**, the Democrats floundered, holding on to their congressional domination, but losing, especially in the new **suburbs**, to more conservative Republicans. Between **Reagan**'s 1980 triumph and the Newt **Gingrich**-engineered congressional wins of 1994, the Democrats, perceived as a "tax and spend" and dovish party, seemed divided between a liberal wing, devoted to both New Deal and social movement-based policies (ranging from universal healthcare to gay rights), and a more conservative to moderate wing, organized by the Democratic Leadership Council, arguing for a more pro-defense, modified welfare state, pro-suburban strategy. Bill **Clinton** in both his 1992 and 1996 victories marked the seeming victory of the latter approach.

The Democratic Party remains the party of trade unionists, most minorities, liberal professionals and what critics called "identity politics," but under Clinton, who declared that "the era of Big Government is over," it sought to become a "new" Democratic Party committed to inclusion, modified racial policies, tougher approaches to crime and foreign policy. The federal government, albeit smaller and smarter, remained an article of faith and policy for the Democrats in the twentieth century.

Further reading

Edsall, T. and Edsall, M. (1991) *Chain Reaction*, New York: Norton.

Fraser, S. and Gerstle, G. (eds) (1989) *The Rise and Fall of the New Deal Order*, Princeton: Princeton University Press.

Brinkley, A. (1995) *The End of Reform*, New York: Alfred A. Knopf.

PAUL LYONS

De Niro, Robert

b. 1943

A consummate actor whose roles have often explored the meaning of urban ethnic (**Italian American**) life in America, especially in collaboration with directors Martin Scorsese and Francis Ford **Coppola**. Repeatedly nominated for Academy **Awards** in recognition of his finely engraved portraits of small-time hoods, dreamers and losers, De Niro won Oscars for his work in *The Godfather Part II* (1974) and *Raging Bull* (1980). He also created haunting, desperate characters in *Mean Streets* (1973), *Taxi Driver* (1976), *The Deer Hunter* (1978), *True Confessions* (1981), *King of Comedy* (1983) and *Cape Fear* (1991), while showing an ability to laugh at this image in *Analyze This* (1999). He also directed *A Bronx Tale* (1993).

GARY McDONOGH
CINDY WONG

Denver, CO

Denver (1998 metropolitan population estimate 2,365,345), capital of Colorado, emerged in the mid-nineteenth century as a center for gold, railroads, **ranching** and exchange for the plains and **Rocky Mountain** states. Remaining relatively small, it boomed after the Second World War as a federal center, including the Mint, multiple regional offices and military and aerospace interests. In the 1970s and 1980s, Denver underwent a further renaissance as a center for energy interests, including coal, **oil**, gas and oil shale, which transformed the skyline and underpinned the narrative of the night-time **soap opera** *Dynasty* (ABC, 1981–9). The city also emerged as a center for **Sunbelt** development of the mountainous West around winter sports, environmentalism and natural landscapes. The "Mile-High City" boasts professional franchises in **football** (Broncos), **basketball** (Nuggets) and **baseball** (Rockies), whose names evoke the history and images of the city, dramatically echoed in the peaks of it.

GARY McDONOGH

department stores

Macy's, Wanamaker's, Marshall Fields, Nieman-Marcus and other stores emerged in **cities** across the United States in the nineteenth and twentieth centuries as palaces of desire. They not only offered myriad goods, but also created a powerful sense of need within the household, especially for its ideal shopper – the **middle-class** housewife. Macy's filled nine stories with goods, becoming a mythic reference in movies (*Miracle on 34th Street*, 1947) and a **New York** City, NY institution through its Thanksgiving **parade**. It even offered its own bank.

Great stores and their owners became philanthropists and tastemakers. Marshall Fields was not only a store, but also a **Chicago, IL** philanthropist after whom the city's natural history museum is named. In smaller cities, families and stores proved just as central – Rich's in **Atlanta, GA**, Nieman-Marcus in **Dallas, TX**, Adler's in **Savannah, GA** – many reflecting the vision of pioneering Jewish merchants and their families. Less prestigious stores like J.C. Penney, Montgomery Ward and Sears Roebuck extended consumption outside the city through **catalogs** that offered clothes, tools, household goods and even prefabricated houses.

As **suburbs** expanded, department stores vaulted from downtown to **malls**. Suburban stores also had a new style – cleaner, more open and interwoven with other shops. In the 1960s, downtown department stores faced further challenges to urban life – stores in the **South** were boycotted to end **segregation** that had meant that an **African American** woman could not even try on a hat. In the 1970s, Sunday openings pitted the rhythms of downtown shopping against suburban weekends, forcing older stores to adapt amid recessions.

Many institutions have disappeared: Wanamaker's in **Philadelphia, PA**, I. Magnum, B. Altman's and others, sometimes consolidated into chains but no longer an emblem of urban triumph. Competition has also challenged the experience of shopping – service, comfort and overwhelming goods – which Rowland Macy and Joseph Wanamaker created.

Discount shopping represents a particularly interesting development. In the 1960s and 1970s, new chains offered less service and lower prices: K-Mart, Woolco, Walmart, Target, Zayres. Such stores had won crucial concessions on manufacturers' rights to control prices that challenged their more expensive competitors. Later, hangar-like warehouse stores like Sam's, BJs and Costco extended this discount mania, including higher-end goods. Manufacturers' outlets also offered bargains (seconds, discontinued and specially produced lines) for careful consumers, creating not only malls, but "regions" of outlet centers. Department stores have competed with outlets, even as they used them to dispose of post-sale goods in specialty outlets run by Sak's, Nieman's, Nordstrum's and Penney's among others.

Department stores also changed in the 1980s and 1990s. New York saw the construction of the extremely expensive new Barney's (later in receivership), while Japanese stores such as Takashimaya, Yaohan and Mizoguchi appeared in major urban centers. Nieman's and others expanded nationwide. Yet, other comprehensive chain stores gnawed into individual departments as well – Williams Sonoma for foodware, for example. Meanwhile, new catalogs offer alternatives for two-career families too busy to shop, while targeting specialist consumers rather than the general shoppers of the department store. **Internet** sales represent an emergent threat as well.

Hence, department stores, once monarchs of the city, are now competitors in a fragmented and sometimes placeless world of consumption. Some have tried out **cable**-shopping channels (or worked with established ones like HSC or QVC for special events). Others have highlighted their exclusiveness, historic charms, or convenience. Macy's legacy has adapted to both circumstances and imagination.

See also: consumerism

Further reading

Harris, L. (1979) *Merchant Princes*, New York: Harper & Row.
Leach, W. (1993) *Land of Desire*, New York: Pantheon.
Trachtenberg, J.A. (1996) *The Rain on Macy's Parade*, New York: Time Business.

GARY McDONOGH

depression

Often called "the common cold of mental health problems" – 10 percent of all Americans suffer from it, with one out of six experiencing a serious episode. Its causes are unclear. Its treatment (pharmacological and psychotherapeutic) costs the nation $43 billion a year, and its numbers are (inexplicably but surely) on the increase. Rates of clinical depression have increased in each succeeding generation after 1915. While it remains prevalent among the elderly, the age of diagnosis is gradually dropping. With the drug Prozac – arguably the panacea of the twentieth century – appearing on pediatricians' (as well as veterinarians') prescription pads amid a conspicuous arsenal of psychiatric pharmacopoeia, depression is still not being defeated.

So what exactly is it? An imbalance of neurotransmitters – the chemical messengers of the brain – is one answer. Hence the rebalancing by means of anti-depressant drugs, including SSRIs, MAO inhibitors and tricyclics, all but replacing electroconvulsive therapy. But why the imbalance? The answer to this is as comprehensive as whatever life may bring: family context, loss, poor self-esteem, womanhood, adolescence, drug abuse and possibly genetics.

While the ontology of depression belongs to medical discourse, depression exists within a discursive matrix of social relationships, themselves constrained by a variety of socialized and often tacit norms; for example: what behavior may be interpreted as depressed, how to talk and behave around a depressed person and the process of diagnosis. An understanding of depression cannot be divorced from the social and discursive processes in which it is embedded.

MARIAELENA BARTESAGHI

deregulation *see* mass media; aviation, commercial; cable television

Detroit, MI

The "Motor City" across the straits from **Canada** reached its apogee with Second World War production, when the automotive "Big Three" – Ford, General Motors and Chrysler – and related industries provided a solid industrial base, burgeoning employment and global clout. Five decades later, Detroit symbolizes the rustbelt – hemorrhaging people and jobs and deeply scarred by racial division. The estimated 1998 urban population plunged below 1 million (the metropolitan area exceeds 4 million). Where **Motown** music celebrated an exuberant city in the 1960s, the recurrent arson of "Devil's Night" – when abandoned property blazes on Halloween – provides an eerier emblem for the 1990s.

As Thomas Sugrue argues in *The Origins of the Urban Crisis: Race and Inequality in Postwar Detroit* (1998), Detroit's discrimination in employment and housing laid the foundations for later decline, foreshadowed in 1943 riots. While manufacturing drew diverse workers, neither owners nor the powerful United Auto Workers established equality. By the 1950s, automation cost jobs and the city lacked land for updated plants, which scattered around the US. The city's growing black population was slammed by **segregation** and diminishing opportunities. Bloody riots in 1967 increased **white flight** to Grosse Point, Oak Park, Dearborn Heights, etc., while the inner city languished. Capital and production shifts to cheaper assembly areas as well as the rise of foreign cars further drained the economy in the 1970s and 1980s, as an **African American mayor** Coleman Young tried to respond with urban patronage.

Detroit retains vestiges of its one-time wealth and power, from the Diego de Rivera murals in the Art Institute to its extensive library, Wayne State University and its successful sports teams – Tigers (**baseball**), Pistons (**basketball**) and Redwings (**hockey**). Yet continuing crises overshadow the city in Ze'ev Chafet's *Devil's Night* (1990) or the chilling future of *Robocop* (1987).

Further reading

Sugrue, T. (1998) *The Origins of the Urban Crisis: Race and Inequality in Postward Detroit*, Princeton: Princeton University Press.
Chafet, Z. (1990) *Devil's Night*, New York: Random.

GARY McDONOGH
CINDY WONG

diet

Diet refers to both the foods we normally eat and to special selections made for reasons of health or change in body weight. In a country where you can never be too rich or too thin, the term's cultural signification is tied to calorie cutting and weight loss. The combination of vast disposable income and variety of foods greater than any nation on Earth, with the equation of beauty and thinness, has contributed to Americans' schizophrenic approach to nutrition. Over half of the population has at one time or another attempted to control weight by controlling food intake. With the weight-control industry booming (miracle supplements, powders, "light" foods, prescription drugs, fitness clubs, tens of nationwide diet programs, such as Weight Watchers, and thousands of diet books and magazines), three-quarters of Americans are overweight. But regimens of near-starvation in order to be thin are also growing, especially among **teenagers**, where levels of eating disorders such as anorexia and bulimia are staggering.

The USDA (United States Department of Agriculture) recommends a variety of foods, low saturated fats, more consumption of fruits and vegetables and controlled carbohydrate intake. But the nation's quasi-obsession with fat has not yielded the desired results. The preponderance on the market of "low-fat," carbohydrate-rich snacks has coincided with high rates of obesity. While some may resort to fad diets (juice or cabbage soup anyone?), it is worth noting that the oldest, healthiest people alive today survived wartime food shortages and (gladly) ate steak. Food for thought.

MARIAELENA BARTESAGHI

dinette

Both the room or space set off from the kitchen and the furniture sets which have created an informal eating space for American families without servants, especially in the 1950s and 1960s. Dinette sets include tables and chairs of metal or Formica scaled down from the formal ostentation of the dining room. The dinette became a place of morning coffees (often seen in **soap operas**), **children**'s activities and other informal meals, as well as a background for more formal events. By the 1990s, the **kitchen** service-counter often replaced even this space for informal meals.

GARY McDONOGH

CINDY WONG

Dinkins, David

b. 1927

Mayor of **New York** City (1990–4). The first **African American** to lead New York City, Dinkins pledged to heal ethnic divisions in the nation's largest and most diverse metropolis. Dinkins' tenure was instead marred by racial violence – in particular, the 1991 Crown Heights riots that erupted over rifts between African Americans and Hasidic **Jews** in Brooklyn. Dinkins was plagued by allegations that he mishandled the crisis, criticism that subsequently contributed to his failed bid for a second term. He was defeated by former prosecutor Rudolph W. Giuliani, who had a strong law-and-order reputation.

SARAH SMITH

directors

As the person responsible for both the creative and technical form of a film, the director occupies a pivotal position in a collaborative art form involving people, talents and money. In the late twentieth and early twenty-first century, American directors have become integral to the packaging of movies, whether **Hollywood** or independents. Yet, this vision of director as the film's primary author belies his or her status under the studio system.

The earliest directors had wide-open opportunities: D.W. Griffith became a founding father of Hollywood. His own studio legacy, however, converted subsequent directors to workers *within* the system. While some became identified with distinctive styles and genres – e.g. Howard **Hawks** or John **Ford** with the **western** – others held control only through constant battle. Alfred **Hitchcock** manipulated the system; Orson **Welles** went into exile. Still others, though they produced masterpieces with materials and **stars** given them, rarely achieved "ownership" and faced arbitrary assignments. The well-established George Cukor (1899–1973), for example, was replaced after only ten days work on *Gone With the Wind* (1939).

Re-evaluation of the director's role came with the studios' collapse and the development of a film theory of "auteurship" based on European theory and practice of more autonomous control. In the 1960s and 1970s, older figures were re-evaluated, while new idiosyncratic visionaries arose, ranging from Sam **Peckinpah** to Woody **Allen**, Stanley Kubrick and Sylvester Stallone. Directorial ranks opened to film school graduates and the less prestigious realm of **television** directing.

In the new Hollywood, the director is a key player to be negotiated (along with stars) in a **producer**'s creation of a picture. Directors command power and prestige because of their vision (Tim Burton, Martin Scorsese) or their box office (James Cameron, Jonathan Demme). Steven **Spielberg** and George **Lucas** have become uniquely powerful through their own economic success. Others build directing on their acting (John **Cassavetes**, Barbra **Streisand**). Directorial centrality also pervades the formation and aspirations of independent cinema, despite anti-Hollywood trappings.

The budgets and operations of Hollywood, since the 1920s, also have attracted skilled directors from abroad. Ernst Lubitsch, Josef von Sternberg and Billy **Wilder** came from Central Europe; Czech Milos Forman made his US debut in 1971. In the 1980s and 1990s, Hollywood has drawn the Taiwanese Ang Lee and Hong Kong's John Woo.

Yet, even so, directing has remained a predominantly white male role for most of Hollywood's history. Despite pioneering work by Dorothy Aznar and Ida Lupino, women rarely have directed bigger-budget American movies; not one woman has been nominated for Best Director. Some early skilled **African American** directors like Oscar Micheaux (1884–1951) were able to produce and direct forty feature-length films within a segregated Black cinema, but integration was slow. Photographer-essayist Gordon Parks, for example, despite his sensitive *Learning Tree* (1969), found his career confined to **blaxploitation films**. Since the 1980s, Spike **Lee**, John Singleton and a few other black *males* have directed features; only Lee, however, has developed a substantive career. Recognition for black women remains minimal. Women, African Americans and other minorities – **Asian**, **Latino**, publicly gay people (after many closeted Hollywood directors) – have also directed independent and documentary cinema.

CINDY WONG

disaster movies

Generations of cutting-edge special effects have met scene-chewing acting (heroic sacrifice, cowardice, bonding) in **blockbuster** films about humans and catastrophes. The 1950s saw nuclear nightmares (monstrous animals and the scientists who loved them) like *Them* (1954). A 1970s renaissance included *Earthquake* (1974), *Meteor* (1979) and Irwin Allen shipwrecks and skyscraper fires (*Towering Inferno*, 1974). Both "nature" and human greed figure as causes. The genre also shares features with **science fiction**. Ensemble casts mingle current idols, caricaturish villains and glamorous couples, often with **children** at risk; **New York** City, NY, **Los Angeles, CA** and **Washington, DC** are frequent targets, reaffirming American images of superiority even in interplanetary crises. A vigorous 1990s cycle includes *Jurassic Park* (1993), *Twister* (1996) (tornadoes), *Volcano* (1997), *Godzilla* (1998) (transmuting Japanese nuclear nightmares), *Deep Impact* (1998) and *Armageddon* (1998) (meteors); *Titanic* (1997) shares features of the genre. This florescence reflected fears of the millennium, but it also pushed the frontiers of computer-generated effects and global box-office profits.

GARY McDONOGH

disco

Disco emerged in the early 1970s as the most important form of **dance** music in Euro-American markets – seen as affixed to a hedonistic, escapist and drug-drenched lifestyle – reaching its apex in New York's Studio 54. As a genre, the music featured syncopated rhythms placed forefront in the mix, with the use of many studio synthesizer effects from strings to percussion, as well as anonymous studio musicians. The tempo of disco songs was fast; the singers, mostly female and **African American**, decried their sufferings while insisting upon fortitude and resolve as in the disco anthem recorded by Gloria Gaynor "I Will Survive" (1977). Disco, by nature of the music and its outlets, furthered the careers both of singers and of record producers. Other disco stars include Donna Summer, Evelyn "Champagne" King, Cheryl Lynn, Grace Jones and the openly gay Sylvester (in fact, the Village People, another disco act that both mimicked and lampooned gay stereotyping, were not openly gay).

Although disco music was influenced by a pop predecessor, glam rock and its emphasis on the fantastic and theatrical, disco was often seen as opposite to heavy metal and album-oriented and arena rock that was also popular by the late 1970s and well instituted on the FM dial. In fact, by 1977, before **punk** spread, there was a "disco sucks" movement sponsored by radio stations that attracted **suburban** white youth, who insisted that disco was escapist, synthetic and overproduced. The music was biased in favor of the producer – as producers like Jacques Morali and Giorgio Moroder also became stars – but disco music attracted an urban audience of gays, blacks, **Hispanics** and **Italian Americans** clad in sparkles and prints who sang along with Alicia Bridges when she sang "I Love the Nightlife" (1979). It also fascinated film-makers again in the late 1990s.

EDWARD MILLER

discount stores *see* department stores

Disney, Walt
b. 1901; d. 1966

Walt Disney brought visions and values of small-town America to **mass media** and **theme parks**; his multimedia conglomerate continues to grow after his death. Disney characters, films, books, **toys** and places, aggressively marketed, have sold America as a magical kingdom to a global audience. Others have read the man and his legacy as an evil empire defined by exaltation of carefully controlled consumerism, with over 400 Disney stores around the world selling everything from lunch boxes to the Tarzan CD-ROM.

As an artist in Kansas City, Kansas in 1919, Disney became involved in the production of local **animation**/live-action shorts (Laugh-O-Grams). By 1923 he had moved to **Los Angeles, CA** and created his own creative team and formats for animation. By 1928, after business setbacks mediated by brother Roy, Disney produced *Steamboat Willie*, which united Mickey Mouse with sound (Walt did the voice). Over time, Disney's productions increased in quality (with music and color in the *Silly Symphonies* series), while merchandising of Mickey and other items built revenues.

In the 1930s, Disney Studios pushed the boundaries of animation, including the first animated feature film *Snow White* (1939) and the growing artistry and complexity of *Pinocchio* (1941) and *Fantasia* (1942), despite continuing financial concerns and sometimes problematic labor relations. After the Second World War, Disney's ability to control products and profits from re-releases, marketing tie-ins and new ventures provided a foundation to move into **television** and **Disneyland** (1955). The company also continued to control its labor force tightly, supporting **HUAC** investigations of Hollywood labor organizers.

From Disney's initial televisual outing, ABC's *Disneyland* (1954–8), which promoted the planned theme park on its first show, some form of Disney prime-time **children**'s television showcase continued for thirty years, although changing titles and networks (in addition to the child ensemble of the *Mickey Mouse Club*, ABC, 1955–9). Disney continued to seek creative development and public recognition through films like *Mary Poppins* (1964), plans for a larger, visionary Disneyworld and publicity suggesting him for a **Nobel** prize. At his death in 1966, primary ownership of the studio stayed with the family. Roy Disney finished the

Florida project before his death in 1971, by which time studio profits had reached $250 million.

Despite the creative heritage the Disney corporation controlled, the next decade saw diffuse initiatives in films and audiences. By the early 1980s, corporate Disney was vulnerable to takeover battles that attracted Ivan **Boesky** and Michael **Milken**. Finally, in 1984, the family reasserted control, bringing in Michael Eisner, Frank Wells and Jeffrey Katzenberg to revitalize the company. Their initiatives spurred Disney production in mature films (Touchstone, Hollywood Pictures, Buena Vista), distribution (Miramax), **radio**, television, **cable**, multimedia and, finally, the second golden age of Disney animation with *Who Framed Roger Rabbit?* (1987), *The Little Mermaid* (1989) and successors. Disney theme parks continued a global expansion in Tokyo (1983), a still-growing EuroDisney (1992) and Hong Kong (estimated opening 2005), augmented by the urban DisneyQuest concept and Caribbean cruises.

Disney's corporate growth was rocked by the Eisner/Katzenberg split (as well as problems with Michael Ovitz), and subsequent court cases dragged out details of finance and vituperation. In 1996, nonetheless, Disney moved to acquire the ABC network, creating a concentration of entertainment power that has generated worries about conflicting interests in journalism and creative competition. With Celebration, its new urbanist planned community near Disneyworld, the corporation has blurred the boundaries of theme park and idealized "real life."

The Disney saga revels in many themes of American ideology – making it through work, promoting freedom, supporting **family** and hometown. Darker shadows appear in heavy-handed control of labor, stereotypes of **gender**, **race** and place, and incessant selling, not of the last product but the next. Here, its expanse, power and ideologies remain themes of concern even as new generations of children worldwide delight in these products themselves.

Further reading

Eliot, M. (1993) *Walt Disney: Hollywood's Dark Prince*, New York: Carol.

Findlay, J. (1992) *Magic Lands*, Stanford: Stanford University Press.

Thomas, B. (1998) *Building a Company*, New York: Hyperion.

GARY McDONOGH
CINDY WONG

Disneyland and Disneyworld

In the 1950s, Walt **Disney**, founder and head of the immensely successful Disney Studios, came up with the idea for a new kind of amusement park, unlike existing boardwalks and midways. Disney's concept of a "theme park," in which all attractions were linked by unifying ideas such as the future, adventure, or fantasy, became reality in 1955 when Disneyland opened in Anaheim, **California**.

From its opening date, known internally as "Black Monday" because an unexpected crush of visitors filled the park to beyond its capacity, Disneyland proved enormously popular with **families**. Many **children** became familiar with "The Happiest Place On Earth" through Disney-produced children's **television** shows. In Disneyland visitors came face to face with characters they knew from Disney movies, such as Mickey Mouse, Snow White and Goofy. Many attractions at Disneyland also took their cue from Disney films. This unification of storytelling across media was both a creative breakthrough and a brilliant stroke of cross-marketing, spawning numerous imitators.

The concept also changed over time. The integration of Disney shows like "It's a Small World" reveals its sensitivity to changing cultural norms (although employees have been strictly controlled in look, attire and conduct). Disney also was frustrated by his inability to control the plethora of cheap motels and competing attractions that enjoyed a parasitic relationship with Disneyland. Hence, he bought up thousands of acres of undeveloped property in central **Florida**, just west of Orlando, for a second theme park, although he died before Disneyworld opened in 1971. While initially consisting of a replica of the west-coast park, Disneyworld grew to include EPCOT (Experimental Prototype Community of Tomorrow) Center, which Disney had envisioned as the ultimate product of his utopian ideal of a functioning city. In practice, EPCOT is merely another theme park, albeit one which uses technology, community and globalism as conceptual frameworks. In subsequent years, other attractions have been added and Disneyworld has supplanted Disneyland as the number-one tourist destination in the United States. Most recently, Disney's planned **community** concept became a reality when the new urbanistic town of Celebration, Florida began inviting residents to its locale within the Disney property. The corporation has also constructed Disneyland parks in **Japan** and France.

Disneyland and Disneyworld's most lasting achievement is their unprecedented pre-eminence as tourist attractions. One or the other has been the top US tourist destination for four decades. Overall, Disneyland and Disneyworld occupy a particular place in American culture as the ultimate embodiment of the American urge to escape reality and indulge in fantasy, and as a titan of an industry in which Americans have had particular success and are conspicuous consumers: dream-making.

Further reading

Bright, R. (1987) *Disneyland*, New York: H.N. Abrams.

Findlay, J. (1992) *Magic Lands*, Stanford: Stanford University Press

The Project on Disney (1995) *Inside the Mouse*, Durham: Duke.

ROBERT ANDERSON

divorce

Although the legal dissolution of **marriage** has existed throughout American history, divorce rates increased dramatically during the late twentieth century. This resulted from many factors, including the relaxation of legislation, secularization and heightened expectations for emotional satisfaction within marriage. Only two out of 1,000 American marriages ended in divorce in 1866 (the world's highest divorce rate at the time). By 1929 that increased to one out of six; by 1990 it was nearly one out of two. Even among cultural and religious traditions that proscribe divorce, it has become increasingly accepted.

For most of American history, adultery was the only acceptable justification for divorce. In the liberal social climate of the 1970s, the "no-fault" divorce became a critical innovation, allowing couples to divorce by citing "irreconcilable differences" or an "irretrievable breakdown of the marriage." The ease with which many people divorced caused some to argue that there has been an unprecedented breakdown in American **family** life – a "divorce epidemic" – which has led to harmful effects on the **children** involved and for American society as a whole. Others argue that the freedom to divorce is necessary because it reduces the stigma associated with ending what would otherwise be an unhappy or perhaps seriously abusive marriage. One might note that many conservative Republicans championing traditional values – Ronald **Reagan**, Bob **Dole** and Newt **Gingrich** – have been themselves divorced.

Though divorce may be less stigmatized than in former times, it still creates emotional and financial distress for those involved, especially for women (who tend to lose more economically) and offspring. Divorce has been cited as one of the highest causes of **stress** in American life, second only to the **death** of a loved one. As a result, there has been much debate about what to do – if anything – about this cultural pattern. For example, in an effort to reduce divorce rates, the Louisiana legislature passed the 1997 Covenant Marriage Act, which permits each couple marrying in Louisiana to limit the legal grounds of divorce in their case to adultery, abandonment, physical or sexual abuse, felony conviction, or separation of at least two years. Others, notably feminist leaders, have protested these trends as a regression to an era of stifled choices and oppressive living arrangements.

Divorce is also commonly presented in **mass media**, both in **television** and movie narratives, and celebrity lives reported in the press. Economic, social and cultural issues of divorce, in fact, provide a continuous thread in long-running **soap operas** and movies from *Adam's Rib* (1950) through *Kramer vs. Kramer* (1979) to the darkly comedic *War of the Roses* (1989) and beyond. In **Hollywood**, divorce can be seen as a happy ending – or a beginning.

Freedom and individuality are central to American culture, and, in some ways, the rising divorce rate reflects this emphasis on personal liberties. Predictions that rising divorce rates portend the end of marriage, however, seem greatly exaggerated.

Further reading

Newman, K. (1999) *Falling From Grace*, Berkeley: University of California.

Riley, G. (1991) *Divorce*, New York: Oxford University.

NICOLE MARIE KEATING

Dixiecrats

Democratic splinter party in the **South** during the 1948 elections. Disgruntled by President **Truman**'s **civil-rights** initiatives and fearing loss of local control, 6,000 Southerners met in Birmingham and nominated Strom **Thurmond** of South Carolina for **president** and Fielding Wright of Mississippi for **vice-president**. Less a visionary party than one of conservative **backlash**, the ticket captured 1.2 million votes and four states – Alabama, Mississippi, Louisiana and South Carolina. Yet, it was unable to throw elections in the House of Representatives or stop Truman. This movement foreshadowed the emergence of a conservative **Republican** South of the 1980s and 1990s.

GARY McDONOGH

Doctorow, E.L. (Edgar Laurence)
b. 1931

Novelist born and residing in **New York** City, known for mixing historical figures and fiction in novels like *The Book of Daniel* (1960), based on the Rosenberg case, *Ragtime* (1975), an adaptation of an eighteenth-century German historical narrative to the lives of New Yorkers at the beginning of the twentieth century (made into a **Broadway** musical in 1998), *Billy Bathgate* (1989), about Dutch Schultz's mob-dominated Bronx in the 1920s, and *Loon Lake* (1980), portraying American life during the Depression years of the 1930s. Doctorow has also been vocal politically as an editor-in-chief for *Dial Press* (where he worked with such writers as Norman **Mailer** and James **Baldwin**) and as a frequent contributor to left-leaning magazines like *The Nation*.

ROBERT GREGG

documentary

That film, **television** and video can record and transmit "real events" created their initial popularity. Despite the triumph of **Hollywood** and other narrative media, this realization also underpins a long history of American documentary production, criticism and distribution. Yet, documentary is hardly a simple or unchanging category. The "public" looks for "real" events in **news**, "reality television" and classroom movies, while documentarians debate more abstract truth in both form and criticism. A documentary is also a story, even if one claims a higher purpose: treating important social issues, forgotten, exotic or famous people, or great historical moments. Yet, documentarians manipulate all these while sharing technical and narrative frames and distribution with other media. Documentaries also have evolved with media technologies and institutional support.

Among the most important ancestors of American documentary are early ethnographic filmmakers like Edward S. Curtis, recording Native Americans, and Robert Flaherty (1884–1951), whose well-known *Nanook of the North* (1922) was complemented by more "American" films like *Louisiana Story* (1948). Both documentarians relied on "acted-out" sequences as they recorded "real life." Margaret Mead and others continued this ethnographic tradition, aimed primarily at academic markets. Documentarians could also draw on decades of social photography, including Jacob Riis, Walker Evans and WPA photographers, as well as wartime newsreels and propaganda.

Major changes came by the 1960s with readily portable cameras and synchronized sound recording. These gave the illusion of "real life" in action

(devices now imitated in fiction through moving cameras and jump cuts). This technology facilitated direct cinema, which stressed unmediated observation. Here, important documentarians include the Maysle brothers (Albert 1926–, David, 1932–87), D.A. Pennebaker (1926–) and Richard Leacock (1921–), while major works include Leacock's *Primary* (1960), Craig Golbert's *An American Family* (1972) and films by Frederick Wiseman (1930–), such as *Titticut Follies* (1967) and *High School* (1968). The intimacy and pervasiveness of the documentary eye and the use/reading of these films evoked questions about intrusion into private life: the Loud **family** responded angrily to their depiction on Public Television's *An American Family* (reprised in interesting ways with the 1999 **Public Broadcasting System** (PBS) serialization of an *American Love Story*), and *Titticut Follies* was barred from public showing for decades.

Television also changed documentary distribution and audiences. While documentaries (especially exotic or "nature" films) had occasionally played in theaters, their distribution more generally was limited to schools, **museums**, or other specialized settings. Television broadcasted documentaries to a large audience via PBS, including controversial films, such as Marlon Rigg's *Tongues Untied* (1989), which graphically treated gay sexuality across racial lines. Yet, in the 1990s, its independence faced pressure from government and conservative social lobbies; Ken Burns' *Civil War* (1990) exemplifies alternative public television documentaries with high production values, popular audiences, commercial tie-ins and a very safe subject. Commercial and **cable** networks also offer news, news magazines, star documentaries, biography (the title of a popular Arts & Entertainment channel series) and **MTV** shows like *Real Lives*. Commercial documentary, however, must sell to audiences and sponsors – hence it tends to avoid controversy as well as formal complexity. Nonetheless, classic television documentaries, especially via network broadcasting, have been in decline since the mid-1970s because of shrinking ratings. In the twentieth century, news magazines, **talk shows** and "reality" shows replaced earlier, more sober television documentaries. Cheap and fast to produce, they focus on emotional and sensational subject matters while concealing fundamental mediations.

With new distribution and materials, documentaries flourished as both a practice and a theoretical field in the 1980s and 1990s. Film schools teach through documentary exercises, while disciplines such as **anthropology**, **history** and sciences drew in documentaries. Industrial films, news television and political genres played with the form and implications of truth associated with documentary sobriety, while documentary makers and critics explored reflections on the claims and form of the genre, epitomized by Bill Nichols, Michael Renov, Trinh T. Min-Ha and others.

Documentaries today incorporate different genres, styles and relations to subjects and audiences. Bill Nichols, for example, elaborates four modes of documentary representation – expository, observational, interactive, reflexive. The expository mode teaches through direct address, exemplified in many educational products. Truth is obviously controlled by the film-maker, with heavy narration and silent subjects. Observational genres try to observe the subject without interference, seeking "unmediated" truth. As in direct cinema, film-makers sought to be "flies on the wall," presuming that the subject would become accustomed to the camera. Wiseman, however, reinterpreted objectivity by claiming his films are his visions, while asserting that what he saw actually did happen.

Interactive documentaries involve cooperation and questioning, even within the film; hence they may be linked to film-maker reflexivity as well. Theorist–film-maker Trinh T. Minh-Ha, for example, questions documentary practices, like sync-sound and real-time (as in long takes), that promote authenticity. Hence, in *Surname Viet Given Name Nam* (1989), Trinh took pains to reconstruct interviews that viewers could perceive as staged, complicating any reading of being Vietnamese in Vietnam and America.

Documentarians choose among these modes, depending on purpose, subject and audience – high-school films on butterflies or messages of environmental concern tend to be expository, while politicized explorations of identity seek radically reflexive tones.

Another recognition that emerged at the end of the twentieth century was that the subjects of documentaries have lives outside the film. Even in documentaries on distant historical subjects, people are connected to the subject by geography and shared national, ethnic, **gender** or **class** backgrounds. Subjects in documentaries and film-makers face consequences beyond the text. People of power generally control their images and can challenge unfavorable representations. For social documentaries (and news), subjects often occupy lower socio-economic positions. While this may record the forgotten and effect change, it may also categorize victims. Here, grassroots or **community** videography represents an alternative appropriation of truth by groups who affirm their own truth by their limited and highly contextual documentaries. While less significant in the market (or in academic criticism), these videos affirm the genre's flexibility amid demands made by claims of truth and power

Further reading

Nichols, B. (1991) *Representing Reality*, Bloomington: Indiana University Press.

Renov, M. (ed.) (1993) *Theorizing Documentary*, New York: Routledge.

Rosenthal, A. (ed.) (1988) *New Challenges for Documentary*, Berkeley: University of California Press.

CINDY WONG

Dole, Robert and Elizabeth

b. 1923 (Robert)

b. 1936 (Elizabeth)

Republican political couple and presidential candidates. "Bob" Dole, after Second World War injuries left him partially disabled, built a career in Kansas in national politics. As senator (1969–96), he twice served as majority leader (1985–7; 1995–6), but his skills in debate and deal-making did not carry him through national primaries against **Reagan** (1980) and **Bush** (1988), nor as Republican VP against Carter in 1976 or president against **Clinton** in 1996. He later became a spokesman for **Viagra**. His second wife, Elizabeth

(m. 1975), a Harvard-trained lawyer from North Carolina, held various offices in Republican administrations, including Secretary of Transportation (1983–7) and Secretary of Labor (1989–90), before taking over the American Red Cross. She left in 1999 for a highly scripted presidential campaign that involved many women, but ultimately lost to George **Bush**.

GARY McDONOGH

domestic violence

In the US, about one-third of women are victims of domestic violence – violence between intimate partners occurs regardless of **race**, ethnicity, socio-economic status, age, or sexual orientation – during their adult life. Annually, some 4 million women are victims of serious assault. In 1993, approximately 1,300 women were murdered by intimate partners.

Domestic violence stories appear daily in **newspapers**; they are recurring items in **television news** reports, and are common themes of crime dramas and movies. Hence, when O.J. **Simpson**, an ex-**football** star, stood accused of murdering his wife, the fully televised trial became a media spectacle, gripping the nation for nine months.

The battered women's movement of the 1970s raised public awareness; activists established hotlines, shelters, counseling groups for victims and treatment programs for batterers, and struggled to get police and courts to take domestic violence seriously.

"Why doesn't she just leave?" Victims feel shame and embarrassment and may hide the abuse or blame themselves. Batterers gain control through physical force, threats, manipulation and isolation; victims may eventually feel powerless to escape. In fact, leaving a batterer can be dangerous for victims – when batterers feel they have lost power and control, they may become desperate, violent, even homicidal. Lack of resources and social support poses additional barriers. Despite obstacles, most domestic violence victims ultimately escape abusive relationships, often driven by concern for their **children**.

Further reading

Schechter, S. (1982) *Women and Male Violence*, Boston: South End Press.
Walker, L.E. (1979) *The Battered Woman*, New York: Harper & Row.

EMIKO TAJIMA

Donohue, Phil *see* talk shows, television

Doonesbury

Started by Garry Trudeau, while a Yale undergraduate in the late 1960s, this **comic** strip gained wide syndication and notoriety in the early 1970s as a vehicle for political satire which was set in the lives of a group of college students. The **Watergate** scandal provided fodder for some of the strip's most outrageous and insightful segments – a handful of which prompted **newspapers** to either relocate the strip from the comics page to the editorial page or to remove it entirely. In 1975, Trudeau won the **Pulitzer Prize** for political cartooning, thus becoming the first four-panel comic-strip cartoonist to win the award.

ROBERT ANDERSON

door-to-door sales

Memory of a pre-**Internet** America, door-to-door sales of brushes (Fuller brush men), vacuum cleaners, encyclopedias and bibles were all part of the incorporation of rural and even **suburban** America into national consumption. As envoys of modernity, these sales representatives (generally male) also had dubious reputations: the traveling salesman and the farmer's daughter is a standard scenario of American dirty **humor**. Yet their era was fading by the time of Albert and David Maysles' documentary *Salesman* (1969). While females also participated in these areas, they were known for appointment/party sales of domestic goods and cosmetics – Avon and Tupperware.

See also: consumerism

GARY McDONOGH

Douglas, Kirk and Michael

b. 1916 (Kirk)

b. 1944 (Michael)

Father and son **stars**. Kirk (born Issur Danielovitch) broke into movies through physical egocentric male roles, epitomized in his Oscar nominations as a boxer in *The Champions* (1949) and as Vincent van Gogh in *Lust for Life* (1956). Awarded a Presidential Medal of Freedom in 1981, he continued his acting career in the 1990s, while engaging in public service and authoring novels and the memoir *The Ragman's Son* (1988). Michael starred as a **television** detective in *Streets of San Francisco* (ABC, 1972–7). On screen, he has come to personify the deep ambiguities and frustrations of the white **middle-class** male, whether entrepreneur (*Wall Street*, 1987, Oscar for Best Actor; *Disclosure*, 1994), husband (*Fatal Attraction*, 1987; *War of the Roses*, 1989), worker (*Falling Down*, 1993) or **president** (*The American President*, 1995).

GARY McDONOGH
CINDY WONG

Dove, Rita

b. 1952

First **African American** poet laureate of the United States, as well as the youngest, in 1993–5. Her published works include *Yellow House and Corner* (1980) and *Mother Love* (1995); *Thomas and Beulah* (1986), which explores the stories of her grandparents, won the **Pulitzer Prize**. She has also published a novel, *Through the Ivory Gate* (1992). Much of her work seeks to deal with ordinary life; she is also interested in communicating **poetry** to **children**.

GARY McDONOGH

Dow Chemical

Multinational chemical company merging in 1999 with chemical giant Union Carbide for total worldwide sales of $24 billion. Dow and its affiliates have been tarred with accusations of environmental damage and US disregard for human life worldwide – Dow's association with napalm in the **Vietnam** era made it a popular target for **campus** protestors. Dow Corning, a corporation created by Dow and Corning Glass in 1943 to develop silicon polymers, has also been savaged by suits and debates over the health risks of silicon gel breast implants.

See also: deep ecology/Earth First!

GARY McDONOGH

downsizing

A nicer way of saying "lay-offs," emphasizing corporate/stockholder health and competition rather than the human cost of lost jobs, even within an expanding economy. Downsizing has been touted as a way of producing leaner and meaner companies with higher profits; these lay-offs since the 1980s have undercut both **community** stability (with plant closure) and the security of **middle-class** executives and their families.

CINDY WONG

draft

Although males aged between eighteen and twenty-five are required to register for possible conscription in the US, there has been no compulsory military service since 1973. Even before that date, the ideal of a voluntary **army** and exemptions for those with families or other reasons not to fight had precluded the idea of universal service. Moreover, conscription has been a fierce battleground for issues of patriotism and independence, especially in the era of the **Vietnam War**.

Colonial practices of universal white male military readiness were replaced in the nineteenth century by a voluntary military, although wartime conscription was instituted by both the North and the **South** in the Civil War. The Selective Service Act of 1917 authorized wartime conscription, but lapsed thereafter. The first peacetime draft, in 1940, accompanied preparation for the Second World War, but also lapsed afterwards, in 1947. Reconstituted in 1948 as a response to dwindling interest in the military, however, the Selective Service was extended for **war** and peacetime needs in 1950, 1951, 1955, 1959, 1963 and 1967.

As protest erupted against the Vietnam War, the draft became a special focus of attention. On the one hand, skillful use of exemptions (especially for college) allowed middle- and upper-class white males to avoid service: Bill **Clinton** was later accused of dodging the draft while George **Bush**, Jr. served in the Texas National Guard. Other opponents of the war favored direct resistance: burning cards, storming induction centers or leaving the country. The burden of military service fell on poor and minority inductees, where the lottery ranking birthdates from 1 to 365/6 (for leap year) evoked the specter of Shirley **Jackson**.

Inductions ended in 1973 and registration ended a year later. Since 1980, males have been required to register, but military actions have been conducted by all-volunteer forces.

GARY McDONOGH

drag shows

Performances based on cross-dressing, elaborated by celebrity imitations, lip-synching and ironic touches. Both males and females participate (although women's representations of the other often underscore the limited ornaments and gestures of American **masculinity**). Such performances often raise questions about both **gender and sexuality**. They have become political statements in gay rights settings (e.g. the Gay Pride **Parade** of **San Francisco, CA**), but also attract mixed audiences. Indeed, they have become increasingly mainstream through events like Wigstock, celebrities like Ru Paul, performance pieces by Lily Tomlin and other actors and even cross-dressing vignettes by celebrities like **New York**

Mayor Rudy Giuliani or **basketball** star Dennis Rodman. Movie depictions range from the comic (*To Wong Foo, Thanks for Everything*, Julie Newmar, 1995) to documentary explorations of subcultures where **race**, **class** and sexuality are questioned *Paris is Burning*, 1990).

GARY McDONOGH
CINDY WONG

drama and theater

America's greatest contribution to world **theater** to date is indisputably the twentieth-century **musical**. The American musical entertains audiences from London to Tokyo. Americans who never patronize other live theater inevitably will attend at least one musical, be it a **Broadway** touring show or their daughter's high-school play. At the beginning of the twentieth century, musical theater was romantic **comedy** complemented by song and **dance** numbers not necessarily related to the plot. Long on spectacle and short on substance, such musical comedies as Cole Porter's *Anything Goes* entertained audiences across the nation. The first half of the twentieth century saw steady growth in the sophistication and the popularity of the genre, culminating in the heyday of the Broadway musical in the 1950s and 1960s. While plays continued to employ lavish spectacle, song and dance, the storylines (books) were becoming more complex, the characters more developed and themes tinged with serious social issues. In 1943 Richard Rogers and Oscar Hammerstein created *Oklahoma* with a fully developed plot and songs and dances that served to further the story. This advent of the integrated musical was followed by a flurry of blockbuster hits from Rogers and Hammerstein (*Carousel, South Pacific, The King and I*). Lerner and Lowe (*Brigadoon, My Fair Lady*), Leonard **Bernstein** (*On the Town, West Side Story*) and Frank Loesser (*Guys and Dolls*) are members of a long list of artists who contributed to the golden age of American musical theater. This uniquely American form naturally became a major cultural export, and, by the 1980s, British and French lyricists and composers (Andrew Lloyd Webber, Alain Boublil, Claude-Michel Schonberg) had developed their own hybrid forms of musical theater to be re-imported for long runs on Broadway.

By the middle of the twentieth century, American mainstream, non-musical drama had settled into two popular genres. Fourth-wall realism abounded in the form of romantic comedies and "kitchen sink" dramas (usually set in one room of a **home** and centered around the personal, often **family**, conflicts of the central characters). These plays often depicted the American dream gone awry. Tennessee **Williams** wrote about the displaced aristocracy or pseudo-aristocracy (exemplified by heroines like Blanche Dubois in *A Streetcar Named Desire*) of the new **South**. Arthur **Miller**, in *Death of a Salesman*, brought audiences a painfully honest portrayal of the common person as tragic hero. Lorraine Hansberry's 1959 hit, *A Raisin in the Sun*, is an **African American** variation on this theme. Set in an urban America caught in the growing pains of desegregation and centered around one family's encounter with racial discrimination in housing, it enjoyed a successful Broadway run (ironically to mostly segregated audiences), winning its author a **Pulitzer Prize**.

Realistic drama has survived through the century, manifested later in plays by such authors as August **Wilson**, who has chronicled the dreams and frustrations of African Americans in plays set in each decade of the century. While Wilson's plays are largely linear realism, they are unique in the use of rich poetic language.

Neil Simon is the most commercially successful contemporary creator of the romantic **comedy** version of dramatic realism. His comedies from the 1960s, such as *Barefoot in the Park* and *The Odd Couple*, have endured with regular performances at dinner and community theaters. His prolific and popular body of work also includes the autobiographical comic dramas *Brighton Beach Memoirs* and *Biloxi Blues*, both written in the 1980s, which look at life from the perspective of growing up Jewish in America. Several of Simon's plays, along with many other authors' plays in the realist genre, have been turned into films. It could be argued that they are just as, if not more, suited to that medium with its ability to create a sense in the audience of eavesdropping on a private world.

Since the expressionist movement at the start of the twentieth century, fourth-wall realism has shared the American stage with more self-referential, non-realistic forms. Many contemporary American playwrights turned away from linear plot structures (in which each event seems inevitably to trigger the next, building to a predestined climax) to a style that celebrates the live and immediate audience/performer relationship. These plays often purposely draw attention to the means of production, constantly reminding the audience that they are watching a play instead of reality.

Many of the authors who have embraced this presentational style (inspired by the groundbreaking work of German playwright Bertolt Brecht) find it more suitable for framing the political and social critiques inherent in their works. **Asian American** playwright David Henry Hwang's play, *M. Butterfly*, draws a parallel between the sexist attitudes of patriarchal culture and the racist attitudes of the Western world towards the "exotic" East. Hwang uses several devices that highlight the artificial nature of performance: the main character narrates the story, speaking directly to the audience; several of the actors play more than one role; the play leaps backwards and forwards in time rather than following a linear plot line. These devices serve to remind the audience that they are watching a performance, and, by de-emphasizing plot, the play steers the audience's attention to the social and political issues behind the dramatic events.

Some playwrights, such as Edward **Albee** and Sam **Shepard**, mix elements of realism with surreal and absurd events to create their own deliberate distortions of the American dream. Albee's works often focus on the behaviors of the East Coast privileged class, while Shepard de-romanticizes the frontier spirit of the West. Other theater artists, such as Robert **Wilson**, create works that stretch the boundaries of nearly every definition of "theatre" by staging works that might last up to 23 hours (*Ka Mountain*, 1973), dispense with storyline altogether and are as much visual art as text-based drama.

These departures from realism are, in part, reactions against the realism of film and **television**. Because the camera can establish verisimilitude so much more effectively, many contemporary playwrights have sought to create forms that integrate and embrace the uniquely live nature of the theater experience.

See also: theater

Further reading

Marranca, B. and Dasgupta, G. (1981) *American Playwrights*, New York: Drama Book Specialists.
Coven, B. (ed.) (1982) *American Women Dramatists of the Twentieth Century*, Metuchen: Scarecrow.
Hill, E. (ed.) (1980) *The Theatre of Black Americans*, Englewood Cliffs: Prentice-Hall.

PAMELA R. HENDRICK

drive-ins

American automotive culture created intense demands for car-oriented services. Drive-in movies mushroomed from 300 after the Second World War to thousands in the 1950s. Along with drive-in restaurants, these provided convenient outlets for **baby boomer** families as well as **teenagers** exploring independence in their social and sexual lives. Movies faded in the 1970s as **suburban** expansion swallowed their valuable properties. **Fast-food** chains and **banks**, however, have incorporated "drive-*through*" windows, without the parking and in-car services shown in *American Graffiti* (1973). Other experiments like drive-in churches have had limited novelty value, but all emphasize Americans' continual synthesis of **automobiles** and lifestyle.

GARY McDONOGH

Dr Seuss (Theodore Geisel) *see* children's literature

drug culture

A term often associated with the rebellion, lifestyles and attitudes formed around **marijuana** and psychedelic drugs in the 1960s. In fact, there have been many drug cultures in postwar America, including those deeply divided by **class** (cocaine for the rich and powerful, crack or heroin in the

ghetto) and in severity of punishment. Moreover, the widespread use of **alcohol**, **tobacco** and pharmaceuticals suggests that the term "drug culture" might effectively characterize much of the nation, as well as those people and practices identified as antithetical to American health and morality. As an official cultural construct, the ongoing **War on Drugs** since the 1980s represents a concerted effort to delegitimize any use of illegal drugs. Yet drugs still pour into poor areas in the cities and other sites without strong government commitment to halt the importation of drugs from abroad.

GARY McDONOGH
CINDY WONG

drug policy

Distinctions between medicinal and non-medicinal, legal and illegal substances, are the result of a long and continuing debate about the morality of consciousness alteration, the intrinsic dangers of particular substances and the costs and benefits of various regulatory schemes. Including colonial regulation of taverns and **alcohol** sales to Native Americans, America has had some form of drug policy for over 300 years. The tensions in American drug policy – and recent objections to its application abroad – derive from longstanding conflict about the wisdom of prohibitions.

The template for American drug control was established by the regulation of alcoholic beverages. Until the 1850s or so, Americans drank huge quantities of alcohol, mainly in the form of distilled spirits, beverages with very high alcohol content (usually 40 percent or more). Per capita consumption was much higher than it is today. Men drank far more than women, and there is ample evidence that women suffered greatly from the whisky- and rum-related aggression of men. Indeed, the nineteenth-century temperance movement, arguably the most successful mass movement in American history, did not begin as an alcohol-prohibition movement, but as an anti-spirits campaign. Rooted in Protestant anxieties about self-control and sexual expression, women's dread of male **violence**, and the personal discipline required for success in an emerging market regime, the temperance movement successfully stigmatized the consumption of alcohol, particularly in its highly concentrated forms and especially in misogynist settings like the old-time saloon (the "anti-home," as temperance enthusiasts called it). By the end of the nineteenth century, abstinence (or extreme moderation) was a hallmark of middle-class respectability in America and, even today, roughly one-third of Americans do not drink alcoholic beverages. They are disproportionately women and are concentrated in regions of the country with long traditions of Protestant temperance agitation (the so-called "**Bible belt**" of the **Midwest** and **South**).

The temperance movement turned resolutely towards a Prohibitionist (rather than suasionist) position after the Civil War (1861–5). Long before the Volstead Act created a national prohibition of the manufacture and sale of alcoholic beverages (effective in 1920), many local and state governments adopted similar measures or created selective prohibitions against sales to minors, Native Americans, slaves, or drunkards. With the repeal of national Prohibition in 1933, a few **states** and some jurisdictions within states remained "dry"; virtually all retained a selective prohibition against sales to minors and installed or revived systems to oversee the liquor industry and regulate drinking places (to prevent the return of the saloon). Today, a few states (notably Pennsylvania) still operate state monopolies of wholesale and/or retail distribution of alcohol. Wholesale monopoly protects state revenues from alcohol sales, whereas retail monopoly (more common) also addresses problems of public order and sales to minors and intoxicated persons. Most states, however, only regulate wholesalers, license premises for on-site or off-site sales and investigate complaints. Since the late 1980s, a national drinking age of twenty-one has been imposed for all alcoholic beverages; most states have tightened their drink-driving laws; some have passed "server liability" laws (which impose civil penalties on irresponsible hosts) or imposed cheap-drink ("happy hour") restrictions. This recent movement towards closer alcohol regulation has gone under the banner of "neo-temperance," although many of its critics, notably those in the

alcohol beverage industry, have referred to it (incorrectly) as "neo-Prohibitionist."

The nineteenth-century temperance movement's turn towards political prohibition profoundly influenced policy towards other consciousness-altering substances. Particularly as pharmacists and physicians discovered the extraordinary prevalence of morphine addiction during the last decades of the nineteenth century (much of it the result of medical treatment), many states moved to regulate the sale of opiates and cocaine by the mechanism of a doctor's prescription. In 1914 the Harrison Narcotic Act created a federal registration system for dispensers of opiates and cocaine that was used in conjunction with state legislation to prohibit effectively the non-medical use of these drugs and their furnishing to addicts by physicians. Although its crude distinctions among substances have been greatly elaborated by subsequent federal legislation, the regulatory scheme erected by the Harrison Act has remained fundamental to American drug policy. Most contemporary proposals for policy reform – whether concerning the medicinal use of cannabis or the prescribing of methadone or even heroin to opiate addicts – rely on the mechanism of an expert intermediary, usually a physician. Even more radical proposals – for the legalization of cannabis, for instance – retain the long-established selective prohibition against consumption by minors that is applied to alcohol and **tobacco**. Most also incorporate a commodity **tax** modeled on those applied to alcohol and tobacco.

Current American distinctions between legal and illegal drugs cannot be understood on pharmacological grounds. (For example, no experts doubt that alcohol and tobacco-delivered nicotine are far more addictive and intrinsically dangerous to health than cannabis.) Rather, the legal status of various consciousness-altering substances must be seen in the context of the country's experience with Prohibition, which was not a happy one. Although alcohol consumption and alcohol-related problems declined during the first few years of Prohibition, the gradual organization of illicit supply, and the unregulated nature of the illicit market, provided both ample (if often impure) liquor and tremendous opportunity for criminal entrepreneurs. Moreover, after decades of disreputability, hard drinking became a mark of sophistication and rebellion among young people of the 1920s in much the same way that the consumption of cannabis and hallucinogens signified cultural dissent during the 1960s and 1970s. Further, the loss of alcohol tax revenue was a major blow to government, particularly during the Great Depression. By the late 1920s, even many women's organizations thought of Prohibition as a failure and favored a return to the older principles of moderation and a suasionist form of temperance.

The lessons of Prohibition did not extend immediately to policy concerning consciousness-altering substances other than alcohol, however. Primarily, this had to do with alcohol's status as America's traditional intoxicant. (Even Harry Anslinger, iron-fisted Chief of the Federal Bureau of Narcotics from 1930–62, was quite fond of Jack Daniels, a Kentucky whisky.) Other substances were exotic, associated with suspect groups like Mexicans (cannabis) or the Chinese (smoking opium). Moreover, the temperance and medical crusade against morphine, a very widely used substance, changed the social locus of its use. Whereas the typical morphine addict of the late nineteenth century was a middle-aged, rural woman using the drug on a doctor's order, changing medical practices and cultural mores increasingly isolated the use of morphine (and later, heroin) in "sporting circles" and among nightlife afficianadoes. By the First World War, it had become a drug of young, lower-class men (mainly) and cultural fringe-dwellers – groups against which sumptuary legislation could easily be directed, especially in the name of moral upliftment. As a practical matter of enforcement, until the 1960s, relatively few Americans used substances other than alcohol. The movement for the decriminalization or outright legalization of cannabis could arise only when that substance became popular among **middle-class**, **white** young people.

After Repeal, then, American drug policy incorporated substances developed specifically for medical use into a prescription regime; legalized or kept legal such commonly used substances as alcohol and tobacco (subject to regulation, selective prohibition and taxation); and criminalized or left illegal exotic substances consumed for "non-medical" reasons by small minorities. During the postwar era, international treaties, cemented with financial aid and linked to anti-communist political objectives, internationalized the American model of Prohibition, though it was applied with variable enthusiasm and honesty.

In the twenty-first century, Americans may need to relearn the lessons of temperance history. In its suasionist form, the temperance movement had a lasting impact on what Americans drank, and how much they drank under what circumstances. In its Prohibitionist expression, the temperance movement supported unenforceable laws that undid many of its accomplishments by creating unregulated manufacture, sale and consumption, and by undermining respect for law and individual restraint. Disillusioned alcohol Prohibitionists recognized that America could not be made alcohol-free, and that responsible regulation was the only practical method for managing its presence in society. Many disillusioned drug Prohibitionists now promote a similar message: it is better to reduce the harm associated with the inevitable use of now-proscribed substances than to perpetuate what has become an international system of banditry and political oppression. The future shape of American drug policy remains to be seen, but the growing number of states that have passed "medical cannabis" laws, the growing interest of policy-makers in needle exchanges, physician prescription of methadone and even heroin, and the first discussion of safe-injection rooms – all increasingly common features of Central European drug policy – suggest that the American policy model is in decline.

See also: alcohol

Further reading

Musto, D. (1999) *The American Disease: Origins of Narcotic Control*, New York: Oxford University.

Reinarman, C. and Levine, H. (eds) (1997) *Crack in America*, Berkeley: University of California.

Courtwright, D. (1982) *Dark Paradise*, Cambridge, MA: Harvard University.

Rose, K. (1996) *American Women and the Repeal of Prohibition*, New York: New York University.

Acker, C. and Tracy, S. (eds) (2000) *Alcohol and Drugs*

in American History, Amherst: University of Massachusetts.

JIM BAUMOHL

dual cities

Emerging in the 1980s and 1990s, this term describes the socio-economic **segregation** of urban society, with special reference to **New York**. During the 1977–87 boom, the top 10 percent experienced a 20 percent gain in income (almost half of all gains), while the situation of lowest percentiles declined, and the numbers of poor and **homeless** increased. Essentially, this metaphor focused attention on a disappearing **middle** (mediating) **class**.

Further reading

Mollenkopf, J. and Castells, M. (1991) *Dual City: Restructuring New York*, New York: Russell Sage.

GARY McDONOGH

Du Bois, W.E.B.

b. 1868; d. 1963

Towering **intellectual** of the twentieth century, remembered mostly for his opposition to Booker T. Washington's polices of accommodation, and for his suggestion in *Souls of Black Folk* (1903) that "the problem of the Twentieth Century is the problem of the color line" (1969: 3). Generally overlooked in commemorations of Du Bois' life are his contributions to the disciplines of **sociology** and **history**, his role as editor of the largest circulating newspaper among **African Americans** (*The Crisis*), his pivotal role in founding Pan-Africanism, his conversion to Marxism in the 1930s, the persecution he faced during the **McCarthy** years and his death while in exile in Ghana on the eve of the March on Washington.

Further reading

Du Bois, W.E.B. (1903) *Souls of Black Folk*, Greenwich: Fawcett, 1969 reprint.

ROBERT GREGG

Dukakis, Michael

b. 1933

Nationally known for an unsuccessful 1988 bid for the **presidency**, Michael S. Dukakis had a varied political career that spanned thirty years. A **lawyer** by training, Dukakis graduated with honors from Harvard University's law school in 1960. In 1962 he won a seat in the Massachusetts state legislature. Other political posts he held ranged from Brooklyn, Massachusetts town meeting representative to governor of Massachusetts. As **governor**, he served three terms before winning the **Democratic** presidential nomination in 1988. A **Greek American**, born in Brooklyn, Dukakis and Andrew Jackson are the only two presidential nominees whose parents were both immigrants.

COURTNEY BENNETT

Dungeons and Dragons

The most popular of a series of "role-playing" **games** first released widely in the mid-1970s, Dungeons and Dragons is particularly appealing to **teenage** boys who seek an outlet for their creativity, as well as a means of escape from the travails of adolescence. Moderated by a "Dungeon Master" with access to the game's detailed rules and reference books, Dungeons and Dragons creates a portrayal of middle Earth populated by warriors and wizards, in which players play the parts of heroes of their own imaginings. The complexity of the game and its level of realism sometimes inspires players to act out their parts, and leads to accounts, some themselves more hysterical than authentic, of young people who have become entranced by the game.

ROBERT ANDERSON

Dylan, Bob

b. 1941

Singer/songwriter, née Robert Zimmerman. Arguably the most influential individual in the development of modern **rock** and **folk music**. Although his music sold modestly and received limited **radio** time, Dylan's blending of folk/ protest traditions with his own poetic, mystical, sometimes hallucinogenic style influenced virtually all later rock music. "The Times They Are A-Changin" (1964) is a classic of the 1960s counterculture. Other acclaimed work includes the "Highway 6l Revisited" (1965) and "Blonde on Blonde" (1966) albums. He has also produced albums like "Nashville Skyline" (1969), which exhibits influence from **country music**, and "Slow Train Coming" (1979), which shows his religious interest.

KENT BLASER

E

Earl, Harley

b. 1893; d. 1969

Industrial designer and head of styling at General Motors (1926–59), Earl was responsible for the general trends in American **automobile** styling from the 1920s to the end of the 1950s, most notably for the excesses of fins, chromium, curved glass and other styling details of post-Second World War American car design. Earl gave buyers a little **Hollywood** glamour and individuality at mass-production prices in designs that captured the optimistic, technological *zeitgeist*, appealing to the dreams and aspirations of the rapidly expanding, affluent **middle class**. Earl's department was also responsible for most GM designs, including **buses**, **trains** and home appliances.

Further reading

Gartman, D. (1994) *Auto Opium: A Social History of American Automobile Design*, London: Routledge.

COLVILLE WEMYSS

Earth Day

The first Earth Day, held on April 22, 1970, was a national day of rallies and teach-ins expressing support for environmental protection. Events were held in major **cities** as well as on most college **campuses**. In the end, some 20 million people took part, calling attention to the swelling support for environmentalism across the country. Later annual celebrations still revolve around this concept, with local clean-up efforts and political speeches. They have had limited results; yet, without being decisive in any specific issue, each Earth Day underscores the extent to which environmental issues have become a national priority.

See also: deep ecology/Earth First!

BRAD ROGERS

Eastern-European Americans

The first phase of Eastern-European **immigration** is generally accepted to have begun in the 1880s, although small numbers from the **Russian** and Austro-Hungarian empires had arrived before this time. This first wave lasted until 1914, by which time nearly 7 million Russians, Ukrainians, Lithuanians, Belorussians, Poles, Czechs, Slovaks, Hungarians, Serbs, Croats, Slovenes and Romanians had arrived in the US from Eastern Europe. Following the two world wars, there was a further smaller wave of immigrants, **refugees** from the postwar chaos, and more political refugees arrived in subsequent decades.

The immigrants of the first wave were motivated by both push factors and pull factors. Between 1880 and 1914, the Austro-Hungarian empire was in a state of economic turmoil as changes in land-ownership structure and collapsing agricultural prices, coupled with population increases, meant a surplus of population in rural areas in particular. Many young men were also anxious to be conscripted into the Austro-Hungarian army. Russia was embroiled in many of the same problems, and, additionally, a series of persecutions known as "pogroms" killed or drove out many thousands of **Jews**.

At least 90 percent of those who left Eastern Europe during this period went to the US. The pull factor here was the reputation of the US as a "promised land." Freedom to worship, for Jews, Doukhobors and other religious groups, was part of the appeal; there was also the idealized vision of America as a land of opportunity, where it was possible to rise "from rags to riches." This last was reinforced by the activities of recruiting agents, who were active in the Austro-Hungarian empire in particular, and who painted a glowing picture of opportunities in America.

Settlement patterns of Eastern-European immigrants varied. Many of the Jewish refugees settled in **New York** City, first on the Lower East Side and later in Brooklyn and other districts. Other groups, however, though they arrived initially in New York, moved on relatively quickly. Large numbers found their way to the rapidly growing industrial centers of the **Midwest**, where unskilled labor was urgently needed. Today, large proportions of the populations of states from Pennsylvania west to Ohio and Illinois are of Eastern-European descent.

Eastern-European immigrants have added much to the character of the US today. Individual immigrant communities, such as the Jews of New York and the Poles of **Chicago, IL**, remain culturally vibrant. More generally, the view of the US as a land of opportunity, where poor and oppressed peoples can find freedom and riches, has become part of America's general view of itself. The fact that many of the immigrants found the hard work, poverty and nativism little better than what they had left behind did not color this vision.

In the late twentieth century there has been a resurgence of interest in the cultural identities of many of these groups. In the wake of the success of the **Black Power** movement, many groups such as the Poles and Ukrainians began espousing a more heightened sense of identity. In this they are also following the example of the Eastern-European Jews, who, from their arrival, had a history of involvement in political movements, including socialism and Zionism.

MORGEN WITZEL

Eastman Kodak

Film and imaging company founded by George Eastman (1854–1932) in Rochester, New York. Eastman produced rollable film on transparent cellulose that made the camera an everyday **family** experience and fostered the growth of motion pictures and x-rays. The company, which became Eastman Kodak in 1892, pioneered color film, safety film and a range of home products from Brownie cameras to smaller instamatics in the 1960s, as well as home movie cameras and slide projectors. In the 1990s, Kodak remained a global corporation with sales of $13.4 billion in 1998 (down $1 billion from 1997), facing competition from innovative film and camera technologies abroad and digital media, where it has struggled to stay abreast.

GARY McDONOGH

Eastwood, Clint

b. 1930

Actor and director who has come to embody the lank, brooding, taciturn loner in the old **West** and contemporary **police** drama. Eastwood's career began with the long-running television **western** *Rawhide* (CBS, 1959–65), but took off after his 1960s trilogy of "Spaghetti westerns" with Sergio Leone (e.g. *A Fistful of Dollars*, 1964). In the 1970s, he alternated this **cowboy** persona with that of an edgy violent policeman in *Dirty Harry* (1971), whose tag line "Make my Day" was even taken up by President **Reagan**. Eastwood has subsequently established himself as a more serious actor and **director**, gaining dual Oscar **Awards** for his reinterpretation of the western in *Unforgiven* (1992). Off-screen, he has served as mayor of Carmel, **California** and has been the subject of a famous "palimony" suit.

See also: actors

GARY McDONOGH

Ebonics *see* language

ecofeminism

Ecofeminism is a variant of social ecology, combining the goals of the environmental movement with those of the women's movement. Ecofeminism posits a close connection between **nature** and women as categories and experiences. In post-structural critiques of dominant Western culture, eco-feminists such as Vandana Shiva and Carolyn Merchant suggest that women and nature have suffered equally from patriarchal oppression. Ecofeminism simultaneously acknowledges this twin oppression and embraces the positive connotations shared between women and nature. While ecofeminism is vulnerable to accusations of essentialism and biological reduction, the affinity between women and nature is said to be a model for environmental care.

Further reading

Merchant, C. (1992) *Radical Ecology: The Search for a Livable World*, New York: Routledge.
Mies, M. and Shiva, V. (1993) *Ecofeminism*, Atlantic Highlands: Zed Books.

JANICE NEWBERRY

economics

The theoretical foundation for how people and firms make decisions about consumption and production of goods and services. Alfred Marshall, a noted economist, referred to economics as the "study of mankind in the ordinary business of life (Buchholz 1996:4)".

The concept of scarcity, that one can't have everything, underlies economic thought. Scarcity combined with choice leads to the primary economic problem: the determination and interaction of supply and demand. All of these questions, in turn, are central to American business, government and thought. Hence economics has been a popular discipline for students and policy-makers, and Americans have dominated Nobel Prizes in the field since 1970, especially through strong departments at the **University of Chicago**, Harvard, MIT, Yale, Princeton and the University of **California** (economists are also found at major business schools like Harvard, **Stanford** and Wharton).

Within the field, microeconomics deals with the behavior of individual consumers and firms. Macroeconomics focuses on the larger picture; the total level of economic activity such as employment, national income and inflation. The primary value of both is in their predictive power in the real world. Unfortunately, most economic theory requires assumptions that cannot be replicated in life. The violation of "*ceteris paribus*" – the notion of "all other things constant" – makes extracting the effects of a single policy from all other noise factors nearly impossible. While economists have developed rigorous models through Econometrics and Chaos Theory, they rarely tell the entire story. For example, economics may be able to prove an association between interest rates and inflation, but it often cannot indicate which causes the other. The conservative nature of its proponents and the failure of economics to reflect reality accurately led Thomas Carlyle to refer to economics as "the dismal science." Economic theory is often better at explaining what has happened than what will happen.

At the same time, data mining – the concept that if you look at enough data, you'll eventually find something that proves your point – has supported some dubious economic arguments. For example, economics is often used to support political rhetoric. In the early 1980s, Ronald **Reagan** promoted a plan to cut **taxes** in order to increase tax revenue. The plan, now referred to as supply side economics, argued that reducing **taxes** can increase revenue by increasing general economic activity. Then **presidential** candidate (and future supply sider himself) George **Bush** referred to this plan as "**Voudou** economics." Politicians of every background use economic theories to justify their preferred policies.

The blending of disciplines has created new avenues for growth in economics. Urban economics, **gender** economics, environmental economics and many others have found their way into the curriculums of American universities. The sub-disciplines often seek to quantify that which is not easily observed or explained using more traditional methods. Increasing globalization also presents challenges for economics because assumptions may not be consistent across cultures and data are difficult to compare across borders. The definitions of utility, happiness and wealth, to name a few variables, are far from universally accepted, despite what economics may have one believe.

Further reading

Buchholz, T. (1996) *From Here to Economy*, New York: Plume.

MARC BALCER

Ecstasy *see* addiction

Eddie Bauer/L.L. Bean

Long-established companies from opposite ends of rugged America that define an outdoor "look" and **nature** as a fashion kingdom. Eddie Bauer founded his sport's store in Seattle, Washington, in 1920, later adding casual gear and women's apparel to the expedition resources it featured. Sold to General Mills in 1968 (and retailer Spiegel in 1988), the store has expanded globally to $1.7 billion in sales, with 600 stores and active catalog and e-commerce trade backed by unconditional guarantees. Its rival was founded in 1912 by Leon Leonwood Bean in Freeport, Maine, whose water-proof boots for hunting launched a line of 16,000 guaranteed products and $1 billion in sales, primarily **catalog** and online. The main retail store in Freeport, open all day, everyday, has become a tourist attraction in itself. Their clothing and lifestyle items have been copied by other brands and successfully exported as an American style.

GARY McDONOGH
CINDY WONG

edge cities *see* suburbs and edge cities

editorial cartoons

Editorial cartoons, evolving from the art of caricature, normally appear on the editorial or Op-Ed pages of American **newspapers**. Generally single-panel drawings with some text, they provide entertainment along with political commentary since the central characters usually caricature actual people and issues. Prominent modern editorial cartoonists include Patrick Oliphant, Signe Wilkinson and Garry Trudeau (famous for **Doonesbury**, a "political cartoon" in comic-strip format). The **Pulitzer Prize** for editorial cartooning has existed since 1922.

See also: comics

Further reading

Edwards, J.L. (1997) *Political Cartoons in the 1988 Presidential Campaign*, New York: Garland (studies the meaning and impact of editorial cartoons).

NICOLE MARIE KEATING

education and society

Educational models and opportunities in the United States reflect and embody national issues of socio-economic power and mobility, and are influenced as well by how the United States perceives itself in the international arena. When internal discord related to the diversity in American society comes to the forefront of national attention, the focus in education is on how best to manage that diversity. When the United States perceives itself in or on the verge of international threat or weakness, the focus in education shifts to how best to reposition the United States to re-establish its power.

While both these national and international frames of reference lead to the construction of educational models which facilitate and restrict educational opportunities, both responses to international threat and to national issues of socio-economic power and mobility are played out in relation to a fairly consistent socio-political hierarchy of power, privilege and access within which people are positioned. Where individuals are located in the hierarchy depends on who they are (defined by **race**, **class**, **gender**, etc.), what role they are playing (professor, parent, teacher, student, etc.) and in what context (university, **public school**, alternative school, etc.). Those at the top of the hierarchy, those who generally hold most of the positions of power in schools and constitute the hegemonic culture in society, tend to be professional, **white**, upper-middle class and male. As the group in power, those at the top of this hierarchy tend to embrace a model of education whose aim is the maintenance of the status quo through the standardization, de-culturalization, acculturation and stratification of a diverse population. Based on a conservative, deterministic, right-wing perspective held by current educational theorists such as E.D. Hirsch, the goal of this model is the maintenance of schooling in the United States in the image constructed by the culture of power, and Social Darwinism is its extreme. Most public schools and many mainstream **private schools** tend towards this model in more or less subtle attempts to keep the existing socio-political hierarchy intact.

In opposition to and in ongoing tension with the conservative model is a model of education committed to challenging the status quo through critical analysis of society and the striving for equity, social justice and the empowerment of all US citizens. Based on constructivism, which assumes that knowledge and understanding must be built between and among people and ideas in context and thus vary across people, times and places, this progressive, **left**-wing model has been advocated by educational theorists such as John Dewey, and cultural relativism is its extreme. Some public schools, some private schools and most alternative educational programs tend towards this model in an attempt to challenge the status quo and facilitate educational access and opportunity to a wider range of people in the socio-political hierarchy. Furthermore, measures such as **affirmative action** and the educational projects of special interest groups (see **education: values and beliefs**) are also attempts to work against socio-economic inequities which have become institutionalized.

At the height of the **Cold War**, education in the United States focused on standardization and the production of students who could compete in the global economy. The most significant world event following the Second World War that had a profound and lasting effect on education in the United States was the launching of Sputnik in 1957. This event prompted fears that the Soviet Union was surpassing the United States socially, economically and militarily, partially through better preparation of students in the sciences and **mathematics**. In response, education was catapulted onto the national agenda, and there was an increase in spending of federal monies on education. The National Defense Education Act loans (1958) were created to support pre-college curriculum revision and **college** attendance for a broadening **middle class**. The aim was to produce a more highly educated citizenry as a bulwark against **communism**, a residual from the **McCarthy** era in the early 1950s, and other international threats. Education during this time focused on traditional subjects and conservative approaches to teaching them, thus reflecting an educational model focused on developing a uniform and unified, goal-directed curriculum which would better prepare students in math and the sciences.

At times of greater internal conflict, issues of diversity and access within the country become foregrounded. So, for instance, with some of the social and political resistance and fragmentation of the 1960s – the **civil rights** and antiwar movements, widespread challenges to institutional authority, the free speech and **women's liberation** movements – calls for a more inclusive curriculum and a more critical perspective influenced the schools. At the same time, legislation such as the Elementary and Secondary Education Act (1965) provided money to school districts for curriculum materials and resources and buildings – money allocated based on enrollment levels and degree of need (towards urban and rural areas), with increasing support for poorer districts. Efforts to educate a wider band of the population also included open enrollment (1968–70) at **community colleges**.

The 1970s saw the rise of what was known as a back-to-basics movement. In 1983 publication of a report called *A Nation At Risk* again raised fears that the United States wasn't competing well enough with **Japan** and West Germany and its world standing and standard of living were in jeopardy. Concerns for educational reform became an increasing focus and national agenda item. In the mid-1980s, John Goodlad (*A Place Called School*, 1984) offered system-wide and structural critiques of schools and suggestions for reform, whereas Theodore Sizer (*Horace's School*, 1984) created a fictional character who epitomized what schooling should be and argued for more authentic, progressive, teacher-supported, participatory, active critical thinking, and the empowerment of teachers and students.

The tension between conservative models of education to maintain the status quo and progressive, critical models aimed at addressing diverse needs and offering greater access continued to inform the debates about education and society in the 1980s and 1990s. In these decades it became more explicit that educational models and opportunities reflect and embody national issues of socio-economic power and mobility. Although location of individuals in the socio-political hierarchy of power and access in the United States depends in part on who they are and their positions, the United States is a meritocracy and there is a rhetorical commitment to educational access and opportunity, which suggests that anyone who has the will and tenacity can improve his or her position in society. Like other versions of the American dream, public education is free and available to all, and therefore, according to the rhetoric, what one achieves is directly proportional to how hard one works.

Generally, ascension of the socio-political hierarchy requires the successful completion of time and coursework in, degrees conferred by and performances defined by legitimate educational institutions and the accompanying acquisition and appropriation of the values, knowledge, language and behaviors of the dominant culture. If one successfully negotiates this set of hurdles one may earn the right either to reinforce or to criticize and attempt to change existing educational structures and practices and, by extension, the socio-political status quo. However, critics suggest that there is only a surface commitment to equal opportunity, democracy and social justice, and they raise questions about whether this is really the American educational agenda. They ask who actually gets access and opportunity and support, and at what cost. These are questions most relevant to those who do not belong to the culture of power, who argue that there are costs associated both with remaining in their positions and with attempts to reposition themselves. Some, such as Richard **Rodriguez**, argue that to succeed in school and society, one has to conform to the status quo and adopt the values of the dominant culture and, in doing so, abandon one's **home** culture. Others such as Lisa Delpit (*Other People's Children*, 1985) suggest that one can maintain one's own cultural identity and appropriate the discourses and practices necessary for success in school and society.

In the 1990s, there have been, on the one hand, national attempts at standardization, such as the **Bush** administration's call for national standards (*Goals 2000*) – standards by which all students would be measured – and the **Clinton** administration's argument that all **children** have a right to quality education, but that education should look like and be tested according to conservative and **standardized testing**. On the other hand, there has been a proliferation of educational options both within and outside the public-school system, reflecting a growing dissatisfaction with any single, standardized model.

The various educational models and opportunities which exist in the United States, then, are emphasized or ignored in response to attitudes towards diverse peoples and their educational needs, particular interests within national boundaries and by perceptions of waxing and waning international threats. Individuals and groups must strive with greater or lesser degrees of support to negotiate the American educational system.

See also: elementary school

Further reading

Spring, J. (1994) *The American School: 1642–1993*, New York: McGraw-Hill, Inc.

ALISON COOK-SATHER

education: values and beliefs

Reflective of the diversity of values and beliefs about education, the wide range of formal and informal educational opportunities in the United States includes: mainstream educational models, such as most **public schools** and some **private schools**; **religious colleges**; ethnic school programs; schools set up by different special interest groups; and continuing post-secondary education.

Systems of public education are government-controlled and therefore must reflect and teach government-sanctioned materials and interests. As the mainstream educational institutions, public schools are premised on and dedicated to the transmission of the values and beliefs of the dominant culture – generally white, upper-middle class, Protestant males – and traditional school subjects, such as English, **history**, **mathematics** and science, are most often taught through the perspectives of that group. National, state, and local curricular standards to which public schools must adhere tend to reinforce these choices, unless a local governing body, such as a **school board** or teachers on their own initiative within the walls of their individual classrooms, elects to supplement the prescribed curriculum. There are some exceptions to the dominant model of public schools – including **Afro-centric** schools, **gay/lesbian/bisexual** schools (such as the Harvey **Milk** School) and charter schools with different foci, such as students with special learning needs – which make explicit their support of and focuses on these under-represented groups.

Premised on the claim that public education offers equal opportunity to all, there is a rhetoric of public education for democracy which says that all children have the right to free education and, in turn, have the responsibility to contribute to the welfare of the country – the majority from support, not leadership, positions. Efforts such as the 1960s **War on Poverty**, supported by passage of the Economic Opportunity Act of 1964 and the Elementary and Secondary Education Act of 1965, and programs such as **Head Start**, Upward Bound and The Job Corps were attempts to ensure the education of low-income **children** and **teen-agers**, but, critics argue, preparing them primarily for vocational positions.

Unrestricted by national and state standards, and created by and for the elite or particular interest groups, some private schools embrace and pursue the same values and goals as public schools. However, they bring to the endeavor from the institutional side greater resources, smaller class sizes and a greater variety of teachers (since teachers need not be state-certified to teach in a private school), and they draw on and cater to a population of students which more often than not belongs or aspires to the cultural elite.

Some private schools strive against the mainstream, however. Dissatisfied with some of the ways that mainstream schools address (or avoid) issues, such as evolution, sex education and non-traditional interpretations of historical events, some groups have established alternative forums within which to preserve and transmit their culture and values. One such educational option, religious colleges, emerged for a variety of reasons: **Roman Catholic** schools formed in reaction to Protestant evangelism and Protestant ethics and values, which insisted on a narrowly defined Americanism; white Christian academies were created as a reaction against racial integration and teachings they believe are not Christian, such as evolution; **Quaker** schools were created to pursue an ideal of education based on principles of non-violence, equity and social justice; and **Jewish** day schools proliferated as a result of a swelling of religious sentiment after the Holocaust and the establishment of Israel.

Other private schools based on a pedagogical approach also offer alternatives: Montessori schools, generally for preschool and kindergarten-aged children, emphasize providing a stimulating environment for children in which they can learn, at their own pace, the elementary aspects of what will later be emphasized in school; Waldorf schools, based on the work of Rudolf Steiner, are built on the principle that the child as a whole must be nurtured and developed – emotionally, physically, spiritually, academically – to produce a well-rounded and happy human being. Finally, military schools, particularly after the Second World War and the increased mechanization resulting from **war**, focus on discipline, obedience, literacy, comprehension of the need for a particular war and special technical skills as they embody the values of **patriotism** and national service.

Alternative models of education have also coexisted with public- and previously mentioned private-school options, created to serve constituencies outside the social and educational mainstream, such as religious, socio-economic and ethnic minority groups. After-school – afternoon, evening and weekend – programs supplement regular public or private school education and strive to maintain and pass on particular values and traditions; community centers, camps, **Sunday schools** and health organizations (such as the **YMCA** and **YWCA**) all see high enrollment and participation. Ethnic educational opportunities generally run more on the after-school, supplementary model and, like the various forms of part-time religious education, ethnic schools saw a proliferation with the influx of **immigrants** in the wake of the Second World War. Corporate education also blossomed after the Second World War and has continued to grow, as have proprietary schools.

A desire for self-improvement – ongoing or continuing education after or in addition to compulsory schooling and higher education – is also valued by some. Of those who wish to ascend the socio-economic hierarchy (see **education and society**), there are, in addition to public schools, adult-literacy classes for both native and non-native speakers. These classes are generally run by non-profit organizations, community organizations (such as churches), or through nationally and locally sponsored programs such as the Adult Literacy Project in **Philadelphia, PA**. Some members of the upper socio-economic classes see self-improvement as a virtue and either return to traditional school contexts to further their education or pursue alternative forms of education.

All of the educational options addressed here reflect the possibilities for education to preserve, transmit and/or challenge the values and beliefs both of groups – including religious, cultural, or social values – and of the United States as an entity – including democracy, **freedom** and meritocracy.

Further reading

Cremin, L. (1988) *American Education: The Metropo-*

litan Experience, 1876–1980, New York: Harper & Row

ALISON COOK-SATHER

Ehrlich, Paul

b. 1930

One of the great popularizers of **environmental** concerns during the 1960s and 1970s. His book, *The Population Bomb* (1968), co-authored by his wife, Anne, brought Malthusian concerns over population growth and the inevitability of resource scarcity into the political realm. This book also became the most widely read and discussed environmental book of the era, surpassing even Rachel **Carson**'s *Silent Spring* (1962) in sales. Although many of Ehrlich's dire predictions have not come true, they were responsible for bringing to light the notion that there may be genuine ecological limits to human growth.

See also: deep ecology/Earth First!

BRAD ROGERS

Einstein, Albert

b. 1879; d. 1955

Physicist whom *Time* magazine chose as "Man of the Millennium." **German**-born Einstein was most famous for his theory of relativity and related re-conceptualizations of physics in the early twentieth century, for which he received a **Nobel Prize** in 1921. When Hitler came into power, Einstein left for the United States, where he accepted a position at Princeton University. He had pointed out the possibility of an atomic bomb in the late 1930s, but was not involved in the actual building of the bomb. Instead, he became known as both a pacifist (although not with regard to Hitler) and a Zionist, interests on which he continued to work and speak out until his death.

CINDY WONG

Eisenhower, Dwight David

b. 1890; d. 1969

President between 1953 and 1961, following his success as commander of the Allied Armed forces during the Second World War. Eisenhower labeled himself a "dynamic conservative," fiscally conservative, but socially liberal. He generally accepted the New Deal as fact, and even went so far as to expand **Social Security** coverage, raise the minimum wage and extend unemployment insurance. With the creation of a new Department of Health, Education and Welfare to coordinate government social programs, the size and scope of the federal government continued to expand during the Eisenhower years. He also dispatched the 101st Airborne Division to **Little Rock, AR** in 1957 to protect the **African American** children integrating Central High School.

Eisenhower is often remembered for his commitment to expanding American **highways**, which radically altered the nation's social landscape through **suburbanization** and contributed to the increasing reliance on **automobiles** and the declining influence of railroad networks.

In his **foreign policy**, Eisenhower remained tied to containment of the **Soviet Union**, even while he proclaimed a "new look" designed to push back **communist** regimes around the world. His **Secretary of State**, John Foster Dulles, argued that the United States should make it official policy to want and expect liberation for these Communist-dominated nations. But, partly owing to his economic conservatism, Eisenhower also wanted to cut military expenditures. Liberation cost more than containment in both money and lives, and could not be carried out by someone who wanted to cut the budget. The "new look," then, came to mean greater reliance on the threat of **nuclear weapons**, which, though expensive, were cheaper than conventional forces. The policy developed into "massive retaliation," suggesting that any Soviet hostility might escalate into a nuclear war. Secretary of Defense, Charles E. Wilson, the former CEO of General Motors, observed that this new look provided "more bang for the buck."

The old-look foreign policy remained in place, however, in the US' actions in the East and Southeast Asia. Only a few years after terminating the conflict in **Korea**, Eisenhower began to commit large development and military resources to the Republic of South **Vietnam**, setting the stage for a long, costly military commitment for his successors.

In his farewell address, Eisenhower warned of a number of emerging problems: the communist "menace" and too much spending on both warfare and **welfare**. The speech is remembered for his final warning of the growing influence of what he termed "the military-industrial complex." As one of the architects of this complex, he knew whereof he spoke.

ROBERT GREGG

Eisenman, Peter *see* architecture

elections *see* parties and elections

elementary school

Elementary school refers to the institution that provides the first four to eight years of a child's formal education. The number of years of instruction varies from **community** to community, depending on the size of the school population. At the present time, most elementary schools enroll children of ages five to twelve, kindergarten through sixth grade. Some elementary schools include a preschool. The socio-economic status among elementary students in a school is usually similar, but political and social developments may lead to the planning of enrollments so that students from diverse backgrounds attend the same school. For instance, the mainstreaming of special-needs children into classroom settings was mandated by Public Law 94-142 in 1975.

Parents who have **children** of elementary school age are compelled to provide institutions for their children to be educated. Schooling is free in public elementary school. In other words, taxpayers pay for school buildings, teachers' salaries and school supplies and equipment. While their children attend school, however, parents spend more on buying books, field trips, photographs, lunches and so forth. These expenditures depend on the state or local school district.

The elementary school curriculum includes **language** arts, **mathematics**, social studies, science, music and art. Subjects such as mathematics, social studies and science encompass various content areas. For example, science programs are composed of materials from biological and physical areas, and mathematics includes work in geometry. Elementary school teachers, in contrast to secondary school teachers who are specialists in specific subjects, are expected to have and to be able to impart a broad knowledge covering each area of instruction.

The most common approach to teaching or instruction in elementary schools is currently a thematic approach in an integrative curriculum. This emphasizes thematic or problem-focused units of study, and the contents are blended through activities of a variety of discipline areas. For example, a unit called "animal" might include representative activities such as a survey regarding class members' favorite animals, making bar graphs, visiting **zoos**, and so forth.

American elementary schools are struggling for several reasons in their curriculum to satisfy the needs of students as well as society. Multicultural education is one of the important issues in the American elementary school curriculum. It is a trial to understand students from diverse backgrounds, which include not only ethnicity or socioeconomic status, but also different intelligence levels, learning styles, and so forth. To satisfy the needs of individual students from multicultural backgrounds, elementary school teachers and educators try to find appropriate teaching strategies. At the same time, American elementary schools deal with the issue of social efficiency, or the need to provide stability in the face of potentially radical social change. That mission took the form of enjoining curriculum-makers to devise programs of study that prepare individuals specifically and directly for the role they will play as adult members of the social order.

Further reading

Kliebard, H.M. (1995) *The Struggle for the American Curriculum*, 2nd edn, New York: Routledge.

Nielsen, M.E. (1989) "Integrative Learning for Young Children: A Thematic Approach," *Educational Horizons* 68(1): 18–24.

Petty, W.T. (1976) *Curriculum for the Modern Elementary School*, Chicago: Rand McNally College Publishing Company.

JINYOUNG KIM

Ellis, Bret Easton

b. 1964

Novelist of the literary brat pack of the 1980s, whose debut novel *Less than Zero* (1985) depicted an empty, **drug**- and sex-driven **Los Angeles, CA**. Ellis' fascination with the glamour and darkness of an urbane world of pop culture and affluence reached a crescendo in *American Psycho* (1991), the obsessive chronicle of an all-consuming **yuppie** murderer, which caused a flap when dropped by its original publisher, Simon & Schuster.

GARY McDONOGH

Ellison, Ralph

b. 1914; d. 1994

Novelist best known for his 1952 novel, *Invisible Man*. Set between 1930 and 1950, and covering some of the events in Ellison's own life, *Invisible Man* struck a chord with many **African Americans**, who felt that white America failed to see them, except only as **stereotyped** characters or figments of their own imaginations. Born in Oklahoma, Ellison had attended Tuskegee Institute before moving to **New York** City in 1936 to become a writer. After his first work was published in Richard **Wright**'s journal, Ellison worked with the New York Writer's Project. In 1999 Ellison's long-awaited unfinished novel, *Juneteenth*, drafts of which had previously been destroyed by fire, was edited for publication by John F. Callahan.

ROBERT GREGG

Ellroy, James

b. 1948

Novelist and memoirist, darker than noir. Ellroy has been the obsessive investigator and recreator of 1950s **Los Angeles, CA** – violent, verbal, dominated by sex and power, in novels like *The Black Dahlia* (1987) and *LA Confidential* (1987, film 1997). In soul-searching memoirs, he has explored the unsolved murder of his own mother and other intersections of his own life, crime and the city (see his *Crime Wave* (1995)). Weaving fragmented Hollywood fictions and realities and grittier racialized Los Angeles, Ellroy deconstructs the city's iconic meanings, dark sides to a city of the sun.

GARY McDONOGH

empowerment zones

Economic development strategy signed into law by **Clinton** in 1993 (appropriating earlier **Republican** ideas to revitalize **neighborhoods** through entrepreneurial zones with minimal government interference). Block grants of $100 million were given to cities like **Philadelphia, PA**/Camden and **Baltimore, MD**, as well as to rural areas to encourage industrial relocation into specific areas through tax grants, job training and placement and other assistance as well as general neighborhood programs administered under community boards. Doubts have been raised about the long-term success of these investments, which recall the **Model Cities** programs of the 1960s, despite a sharper economic focus.

GARY McDONOGH

Endangered Species Act

The Endangered Species Act was enacted in 1973 amid growing concern that species were becoming extinct at an accelerating rate due to the increased use of pesticides and other chemicals, the destruction of habitats to make way for **suburbs** and other development, and excessive **hunting** and **fishing**. Under the Act, the federal government lists an animal or plant species as "endangered" if it is in danger of extinction and as "threatened" if it is "likely to become an endangered species within the foreseeable future." Once listed, no one may "harass, harm, pursue, hunt, shoot, wound, kill, trap, capture or collect" a member of the species or damage its habitat. The Endangered Species Act is one of the strictest federal **environmental** laws and perhaps the most controversial. The Act's critics have charged that it has blocked needed economic development to protect "insignificant" species (such as the snail darter and kangaroo rat), and that it interferes with private property rights.

DAVID GOLDSTON

enemies

Foreign policy, domestic discourse and **mass media** have often coincided in the identification of "acceptable" external American enemies, both vilified and **stereotyped**, with potentially painful consequences for those who might be associated with these groups within the US. The culture of the select reviled enemy as global metaphor for American identity pervaded wartime propaganda of the twentieth century, which vilified the Spanish, Turks, Germans and Japanese. In the last case, racial features were cruelly caricatured even as the rights of resident **Japanese Americans** were trampled on by their confinement in concentration camps. In the **Cold War**, this sense of a powerful foe focused on **communism** – the "evil empire" of the **Soviet Union**, the nearby threat of **Cuba** and continuous concerns with Asian enemies – Chinese, Vietnamese and Korean.

With the collapse of many communist regimes, the question of "suitable" foreign enemies has become more ambiguous for politicians and media. *Lethal Weapon II* (1989), for example, turned to white South Africans; **Russian** mobsters have become frequent villains for movies and **television** (*The Saint*, 1997; NBC's *Law and Order*, 1990–). Saddam Hussein and Manuel Noriega have also been cast as arch-enemies, as were Slobodan Milosevic and the Serbs amidst ongoing Balkan conflicts (a sense of "enemyship" was parodied in the 1997 film *Wag the Dog*, which created a fictional engagement and heroic actions in Albania). The need for and manipulation of enemies remains fundamental to American politics, whether justifying military expenditures or actions abroad, or in defining the American dream against those denied some aspect of it. Yet these images continue to cause deep conflicts within a multicultural society. For example, 1999 congressional and FBI concerns about Chinese espionage in American nuclear research evoked a specter of an inscrutable Asian enemy and divided loyalties that deeply worried Americans of Asian descent, among others.

GARY McDONOGH
CINDY WONG

engineering

The practice of organizing the design, production and operation of devices, systems, or processes to meet recognized needs. The engineering profession is typically characterized as applied science. Though engineers do *apply* scientific knowledge when necessary, the technological artifacts they produce are not derived from science in any straight-forward manner. Engineering knowledge is autonomous and identifiably different from scientific knowledge. Consequently, engineering is not merely *applied* science.

Congruent with the "applied science" myth is the equally misguided belief that technical applications emerge naturally from basic research in the pure sciences. This has led to an emphasis on funding for basic research and an attendant failure to champion support for applications research. The gradual weakening of US industrial hegemony over the last fifty years and its shift from trade surpluses to chronic deficits is partly due to ineffective application of scientific knowledge.

The technological knowledge and artifacts produced by engineers affect virtually every aspect of society. Technological determinism embodies the widely held belief that such technology is the driving force behind social change. However, while the impact of airplanes, **automobiles**, **computers**, mega-**cities**, **telecommunications**, and more all bear witness to the social transformations made possible by engineering technology, techno-

logical determinism trades on a misrepresentation of engineering practice and its relationship to society.

Much of the force of technological determinism derives from histories of technology which focus explicitly on scientific and technical details. These "internal approaches" portray the emergence of technological systems as essentially value neutral. This purported neutrality insulates from criticism the social factors driving technological advances and masks the symbiotic relationship between engineering and society. The deficiencies of such analyses are nowhere more evident than when considering engineering design.

Since the Second World War, engineering design has increasingly been accepted as the defining characteristic of true engineering practice. It distinguishes the engineer, *qua* engineer, from the engineering technician or mechanic who merely produces or operates technological artifacts. The design process encompasses everything from initial conceptualization to production of artifacts. Various non-technical factors influence and constrain the design process, including engineering styles, social determination of engineering goals and the need to optimize designs.

Optimization is essential to engineering design. It seeks to adapt engineering artifacts to particular goals and values, maximizing intended benefits and minimizing undesirable consequences. Prior to the Second World War, optimization was often confused with efficiency – the maximization of output with respect to input – and treated as an inevitable consequence of proper application of the design process. Methods were developed and deployed for maximizing efficiency, but optimization was not treated explicitly. After the Second World War it became clear that optimal designs were not necessarily the most efficient, and engineers searched for mathematical methods to objectively establish optimal systems.

It was discovered that mathematical models of engineering systems could not ignore values. Engineering designs can be expressed as "criterion functions." These functions represent design parameters as variables multiplied by weighing coefficients. The coefficients provide quantitative measures of the value of each design parameter, thus revealing the extent to which engineering artifacts and systems are shaped by and explicitly incorporate human values.

Value judgments permeate every branch of engineering. Civil engineers design roads, bridges, dams, **airports** and more. Though concerned more with utility and efficiency than aesthetic or symbolic expression, civil-engineering designs are still imbued with social values. For instance, early waste-disposal systems were almost solely concerned with quick and efficient removal of refuse from population centers. In designing waste-disposal systems today civil engineers must consider **environmental** impacts. This is a clear reflection of society's growing anxieties over environmental pollution. The work of mechanical engineers, who design dynamic systems like machines and engines, has been similarly affected. With the increasing complexity of specialized machines and their integrated utilization in manufacturing processes, various physical and mental health problems have arisen for operating personnel. US Government health and safety standards respond to public concerns over such issues by, in effect, legislating incorporation of certain values into engineering designs. Nuclear engineering is likewise affected. US nuclear power plants are optimized with human and environmental safety considerations in mind. Such designs may not be the most efficient in terms of energy output, but they do reflect the importance society places on safety.

Awareness of the "value-ladenness" of engineering design is particularly evident in the impact women have had on the marketplace over the last few decades of the twentieth century. As women have acquired financial power, industry has been made to realize that designs optimized for males cannot be expected to serve best all consumers. As one of the major industrial forces in the US economy, automotive engineering illustrates this shift. Automobiles were traditionally designed for males. However, women tend to be shorter than men and thus had trouble reaching steering wheels and brake pedals and seeing over instrument control panels. Automobile designs have been altered to address these issues. Women are also more concerned with functional safety features such as delayed interior lighting, airbags and anti-lock brakes, and they have led the drive to make such features standard on all cars.

Nevertheless, US engineering remains dominated by a rigorous professionalism that emphasizes the purely technical. US engineers are trained and generally function as specialists who provide solutions to technological and commercial problems which emerge out of existing social systems. Though responding well to such challenges, US engineers are not trained to place society's needs in broader contexts. This serves to buttress fundamentally flawed systems. Despite curriculum reform efforts to raise awareness of their social responsibilities, young engineers remain ill-prepared to address the most pernicious problems facing contemporary American society, such as poverty, environmental degradation and the impact of **consumerism** on energy and environmental resources.

Further reading

National Academy of Engineering (1999) *Frontiers of Engineering*, Washington, DC: National Academy.

Paul T.D. (ed.) (1991) *Critical Perspectives on Nonacademic Science and Engineering*, Bethlehem: Lehigh University Press.

Sladovich, H. (ed.) (1991) *Engineering as a Social Enterprise*, Washington, DC: National Academy.

STEPHEN D. NORTON

English in America

Cricket and cucumber sandwiches in **Hollywood** come to mind, with an English actor like David Niven (in his autobiography, *The Moon's a Balloon*, 1972) left wondering why he is able to find work with not much talent to draw on besides a cute accent. Or the life, death, traveling exhibits and collectibles of Diana Windsor, part of a surrogate royal family for Americans, who, like the Peter Sellars character in *Being There* (1979), just like to watch.

But the English in America have not merely been aristocrats, and their country is more than fodder for public broadcasting, like ***Masterpiece Theater***, in which England is portrayed as fundamentally **white** with rather quaint and even charming ideas about **class** divisions. Americans often respond viscerally to such television fare.

Indeed, the **Republican Party**'s assault on public broadcasting has had some genealogical connection with the old mid-western populist and middle-American suspicion of things British.

The United States has had a love–hate relationship with the country from which it sprung in revolution and from which many claim descent, and the English in America have needed to learn the nature of this relationship as they endeavor to exploit the country to their full advantage. The hate part is clearly understood – revolution is a source of powerful animus indeed. Additionally, the largest immigrant groups in the United States were the descendants of Irish and Germans, the former linked to anti-colonial nationalism and the latter from a nation that contested European sovereignty. Later, immigrants from British colonies – **South Asia**, the **Caribbean**, Hong Kong – also have ambivalent feelings towards the English.

Love came from sharing constitutional ideas with the British, and from fighting alongside them in two world wars (though the first one saw Americans shedding their blood in defense of the British Empire in the most unpopular war ever fought by the US). Since the Second World War, and certainly since the Suez crisis, Britain has been a junior partner, a base for American planes and cruise missiles. Americans have felt fairly comfortable envisioning Britain as a former empire, seeing themselves as the inheritors of British global dominance. Hence Americans could buy London Bridge and rebuild it in the middle of a desert (even if it turned out to be the wrong bridge). And if a Margaret Thatcher was still a potent enough force to motivate a wimpy president to go to war with a tin-pot dictator, so much the better.

But wealthy English speculators, under the cloak of their irrelevance, also sneaked into the United States during the 1980s to buy up major parts of American real estate – **newspapers**, companies, **banks**. While Americans were anxiously eyeing the Japanese and Germans, the English undertook far larger transactions of their own. Indeed, Thatcher's virtually bankrupt Britain became a profitable haven for privateers who could play on the markets across the ocean.

But perhaps "the Brits" felt that this was merely payment for the debt the United States owed them in the realm of **popular music** and culture. Apart from highbrow television, the English invasion was most noticeable from the mid-1960s to the present in wave after wave of innovative music. Beginning with the **Beatles** and the Rolling Stones, following through the psychedelic bands like Pink Floyd and Yes, through singer/songwriters as diverse as David Bowie (who became closely involved with artists producing the **Philadelphia** sound), Elton John and Joan Armatrading, and continuing with a dissonant crash with the **punk** excesses of the Sex Pistols, the English contribution to American music has been profound, in many instances fitting within the process of co-opting and commercializing **African American** music. The success of Mike Myers' spoof on 1960s Britain in the "Austin Powers" movies pays tribute, in a rather warped way, to this legacy.

The excesses of Thatcher and **Reagan** have given way to the centrists Bill **Clinton** and Tony Blair. The old partnership of the 1950s has been revived, with Blair coming to the support of Clinton at every available opportunity, and Clinton returning the favor whenever this might be of use to the prime minister.

Moreover, the old 1890s liaison – the "cute accent" gets the "All-American girl" – has returned as a match too. The hugely successful *Four Weddings and a Funeral* (1994) established a template for the Anglo-American, all-white lovefest. This was then repeated in James Cameron's (1997) remake of "Love Boat", with a sinking feeling, followed by *The Parent Trap* remake (1998), in which it was shown that Americans and English truly were very rich twins divided at birth. The love affair has been reprised once again in the whitest *Notting Hill* (1999) ever captured on camera. Of course, this celebration of Anglo-American hegemony forgets one important fact: the Titanic hit an iceberg and sank.

ROBERT GREGG

English Only

Backlash campaign since the 1980s seeking to establish the "official" status of English as a state and federal **language** to the exclusion of multilingual materials or required bilingual competence in official settings (sometimes extended into business as well). By 1999 twenty-five states had passed some form of official English law. Active proponents have been organized by US English, founded by **California** Senator S. Hayakawa in 1983; opponents include organized ethnic groups, the **American Civil Liberties Union** and the National Education Association. This has become a contested issue in multicultural metropolises like **Miami, FL**, although some **immigrants** support its ideal of rapid assimilation.

GARY McDONOGH

environmentalism

In 1992 the Earth Summit in Rio de Janeiro joined together ideals of environmental movements with realities of politics in discussing five major headings of global concern: climate change, **biological diversity**, deforestation, Agenda 21 and Earth Charter. The summit underscored the diverse environmental interests of developed and developing countries. Though US organizations are often the most visible in world conferences, hundreds of governmental and non-governmental organizations (NGOs) concerned with the environment have been established in other countries. However, many criticized the summit as little more than a global, political attempt to risk-control and manage environmental challenges through science and technology without consideration of cultural and ecological consequences.

Critics of early environmentalism noted that issues generally concerned **middle-aged** people from upper-income levels who were mainly interested in the preservation and management of wilderness for future generations. Both the focus of environmentalism and the age group concerned shifted in the 1970s as young people, influenced by antiwar movements and the counterculture of the time, began to recognize that environmental degradation threatened the future of life on Earth. Nonetheless, there were still strong stratifications of the movement with voices of the poor and of minorities notably missing.

The current wave of environmental activities in the US can be traced to the 1960s and early 1970s when people like Murray **Bookchin** (*Our Synthetic*

Environment, 1962) and Rachel **Carson** (*Silent Spring*, 1962) began to question the rapid advancement of technological innovation without social and environmental constraint. In 1970 Americans celebrated the first **Earth Day**, focusing attention on human interactions with the Earth and laying groundwork for groups such as the Environmental Defense Fund and the Natural Resources Defense Council. Additionally, roots of the National Environmental Policy Act (1970) (creating the Environmental Protection Agency), Clean Air Act (1970), Clean Water Act (1972), Ocean Dumping Act (1972), **Endangered Species Act** (1973) and Safe Drinking Waters Act (1974) grew from this early interest. In 1978 **Love Canal** (Niagara Falls, New York) refocused national attention on the detrimental effects of hazardous waste on humans and their environment. Divergences also grew within environmentalists: The term "**deep ecology**" was coined by Naess in 1973 to champion self-realization and biocentric equality in contrast to the utilitarian treatment of nature by Western society. This has underpinned radical action in environmental protests as well.

Agriculture in the US and worldwide became a focus for modern environmentalism with soil erosion, aquifer depletions, desertification, saline incursion into irrigated soils, climate change from land clearing, deforestation, resistance of pests to pesticides and loss of **genetic** diversity in food crops as problems with global implications. Despite the Green Revolution, importing high-yield agricultural techniques to developing countries to increase food production, concerns grew about population growth and what constitutes "sustainable development." The notion that too many humans exist to allow coexistence with the rest of nature continued as deep ecologists suggested population reduction and a return to simpler ways of life. Early solutions for population control included zero population growth, the notion that reproduction should be for replacement or reduction in numbers only.

The 1980s brought more attention to the environment as implications of **acid rain** and heat pollution were recognized worldwide. Urban heat islands, created from high concentrations of concrete, human beings and combustion products from transportation, were identified as major contributors to build-ups of pollutants, especially particulates, around American **cities** and **suburbs**. Issues of urban pollution mobilized the **Environmental Justice** Movement to emerge from the shadows of mainstream environmentalism. It focused on racism and exposure to environmental hazards, noting the general lack of attention by mainstream, predominantly white, environmental organizations to problems concerning people of color. Out of this split grew the People of Color Environmental Leadership Summit in 1991 and many **neighborhood** projects, from **Los Angeles, CA** to the **Northeast**.

The 1980s and 1990s saw a strong **backlash** against environmentalism with environmental burdens placed on businesses and governments overwhelming available resources. The so-called "unholy trinity" of risk assessment, unfunded mandates and property rights emerged through the 1990s to threaten progress in environmental legislation. When the Exxon Valdez ran aground and dumped its oily cargo into one of the most pristine marine areas of the United States, there was a flurry of environmental activity from cleaning wildlife and shorelines to changing regulations for shipping such substances (see **oil spills**). However, as pictures of oil-soaked birds and marine mammals yielded to reports of clean-up fraud and environmental infighting, the event's impact evaporated. During the early 1990s, many environmental organizations showed dramatic decreases in membership and financial support, perhaps as legislation intruded further into the lifestyles of the **middle class**. However, during this same time period there was an increased interest in ideas of **ecofeminism** (a term coined by Francoise D'Eaubonne in 1974) as a part of the environmentalist movement, connecting the domination of women and the domination of **nature** as scientific and political issues.

Free-market environmentalism emerged as a part of the backlash from earlier intensive centralized regulation of environmental concerns. These environmentalists suggest that decentralized tools such as market-value user fees, environmentally responsible incentives (such as rewards for **recycling** and waste reduction) and free markets will solve more environmental challenges than increased regulation and governmental control.

However, many critics of such ideas point to the lack of development of environmental **economics** to incorporate valuation of things such as scenic beauty in contrast with shoreline development. Further, questions of how to privatize management of assets such as coral reefs and migratory herds on a broad scale have received little attention. Testing of free-market environmental ideas in real situations has been conducted on a limited basis with some success, although strong concerns about the broader applications of such an approach to environmental problems remain.

Further reading

Fowler, C. and Mooney, P. (1990) *Shattering. Food, Politics, and the Loss of Genetic Diversity*, Tucson: University of Arizona Press.

Sachs, W. (1993) *Global Ecology. A New Arena for Political Conflict*, London: Zed Books.

Wheale, P. and McNally, R. (1990) *The Bio-Revolution: Cornucopia or Pandora's Box?*, London: Pluto.

SANDRA GILCHRIST

Environmental Protection Agency

The Environmental Protection Agency (EPA) is the primary federal agency responsible for enforcing environmental laws, including those governing air and water quality and the disposal of hazardous wastes. Created by an executive order issued by President Richard M. **Nixon** in 1970, it consolidated disparate environmental programs previously distributed among several agencies. The EPA both issues the regulations to carry out the nation's environmental laws and, in conjunction with the states, enforces those regulations. The EPA has been a lightning rod for criticism from conservatives, who have charged that the agency's regulations are not based on science, are too expensive and stifle business. In 1995 one conservative member of **Congress** went so far as to compare the EPA with the Gestapo. Despite such attacks, the agency's programs have remained intact. For example, attempts by President Ronald

Reagan's EPA administrator to weaken the agency resulted in her resignation.

See also: deep ecology/Earth First!; environmentalism

DAVID GOLDSTON

environmental racism/justice

"Environmental racism" refers, generally, to environmental problems or decisions that have a disproportionate adverse effect on racial minorities. A classic example of "environmental racism" would be deciding to locate a hazardous waste dump in a minority **neighborhood** solely or largely on the basis of **race**.

The notion of "environmental racism" – and the environmental justice movement that sprang up to combat it – came of age in the 1980s. While isolated battles over environmental racism were fought earlier, the issue became a matter of broader concern to environmentalists, government officials and the general public in 1982 when rural **African Americans** in Warren County, NC bitterly protested the state's decision to locate a dump for soil contaminated with toxic chemicals in their area.

The protest led to a congressionally mandated study by the US General Accounting Office in 1983 that found that hazardous waste sites in the **South** tend to be located near African American neighborhoods. Other landmarks in the environmental justice movement include a study by the United Church of Christ in 1987 that expanded on the GAO study; the First National People of Color Environmental Leadership Summit, which was held in **Washington, DC** in 1991; a report by the *National Law Journal* in 1992 that found that under the **Superfund** program, the **Environmental Protection Agency** was likely to clean up toxic-waste sites in minority neighborhoods more slowly and to seek smaller penalties against polluters there; and Executive Order 12898, issued by President **Clinton** in 1994, which, for the first time, charged federal agencies with making environmental justice concerns a priority.

Until the advent of the environmental justice movement, the environmental movement tended to be seen as **white** and **middle class**, and increasingly dominated by large, national environmental organizations. The environmental justice movement, with its grassroots, poor minority appeal may change that.

The movement continues to bring up additional, more complex issues, such as the unexplained fact that poor blacks and **Latinos** have high rates of asthma and that those rates are rising.

As a movement that combines two politically charged issues – environmental protection and **civil rights** – the environmental justice movement has been enormously controversial. Its detractors charge, among other things, that it will make it more difficult to locate job-producing facilities in minority neighborhoods where the jobs are most needed. In addition, legal battles have arisen over how and whether Title VI of the **Civil Rights Act** of 1964 can be used to bring environmental justice claims.

See also: deep ecology/Earth First!; environmentalism

Further reading

Bullard, R. (ed.) (1994) *Unequal Protection: Environmental Justice and Communities of Color*, San Francisco: Sierra Club Books.

DAVID GOLDSTON

Episcopalians

Although not governed by the Anglican Church in Great Britain, the Protestant Episcopalian Church of the United States of America has remained in the Anglican communion, which has allowed the church to enjoy a richly **multicultural** outlook. More than half of all Anglicans are non-white, and the world church has worked to ordain local clergy, of whom **Nobel Peace Prize** winner Archbishop Desmond Tutu is a notable example.

In spite of their origins in the Church of England, Episcopalians had a rocky start on American shores. Most colonial settlements were started by the Puritans (Congregationalists), **Baptists** and **Quakers**, with Episcopalians settling primarily in Virginia and the coastal areas of South

Carolina and Georgia. The Church of England largely ignored the spiritual needs of its colonial members, refusing to permit an American bishop and the establishment of a colonial church organization. Over half of those who signed the Declaration of Independence were Episcopalians, but the church suffered during and after the Revolutionary War because many of the clergy were British loyalists.

During the nineteenth century, Episcopalians remained largely on the East Coast, unlike **Methodists** and Baptists who followed waves of settlers into the interior of the country. The Episcopal Church ordained women as deaconesses, starting in 1855, but did not officially sanction the ordination of women as priests and bishops until 1976. Both ordained men and women may be married. The Episcopal Church made few attempts to include minorities in integrated congregations or in the church's hierarchy, but in the 1950s **African American** men were enrolled in Episcopal seminaries. A black woman, Barbara Harris, was consecrated as the first female bishop in 1989. Although Episcopalians of all races now worship together, conservative members have resisted female clergy, and some Episcopalians have converted to the more traditionally patriarchal Eastern Orthodox and **Roman Catholic** faiths. Conversely, roughly half of all US Episcopalians were not raised in that faith. Controversy over the ordination of **homosexual** clergy and the marriage of **gay** parishioners has also caused internal turmoil for the church. While some congregations forbid openly gay clergy, others accept celibate gay clergy, while a few congregations welcome gay clergy who live in committed partnerships.

Three pillars sustain Episcopalianism: tradition, faith and reason. Sunday and weekday services link Episcopalianism to the beginnings of Christianity, despite the church's sixteenth-century break from Roman Catholicism and papal authority. Religious services, rites and doctrines are published in *The Book of Common Prayer*, which was updated in 1979. Episcopalians may develop new services, such as rites for healing, and incorporate rites from other Anglican communion prayer books. Some disagreements are solved by having two or more forms of services and prayers, from which individual parishes may choose. The Bible is not considered the literal word of God, and Episcopalians are encouraged to use reason in their interpretation of the Bible.

Despite its small numbers (only 2.5 million Americans consider themselves Episcopalian), the church has often taken on the responsibilities of a national church, as evidenced by the seventy-five-year effort to construct the National Cathedral in **Washington, DC**. Open to persons of all faiths, the cathedral was where Martin Luther **King**, Jr, preached his last Sunday sermon.

Further reading

Bernardin, J. (1994) *An Introduction to the Episcopal Church*, Harrisburg: Morehouse Publishing.
Prichard, R. (1991) *A History of the Episcopal Church*, Harrisburg: Morehouse Publishing.

MELINDA SCHWENK

equality *see* class

Equal Rights Amendment (ERA)

Proposed amendment to the United States Constitution that was designed to do away with all sexually discriminatory laws and practices. Approved by **Congress** in 1972, it was never ratified by the requisite number of states and went down to defeat on June 30, 1982 by a narrow margin. The text of the amendment passed by Congress in 1972 declared simply: "Equality of rights under the law shall not be denied or abridged by the United States or by any state on account of sex."

The amendment was first introduced in Congress in 1923 by a militant women's suffrage group, and reintroduced without success each year thereafter through the 1960s. As far back as the first women's rights convention at Seneca Falls, New York in 1848, **feminists** had recognized that much of the discrimination women faced was supported and nurtured by the legal system itself. In the 1970s, led by the then-fledgling women's advocacy group **NOW**, feminists revived the push for an equal rights amendment that would, in one fell swoop, eradicate these long-held discriminatory laws and practices. Labor **unions**, however, continued to oppose the measure on the grounds that it would nullify state laws designed to protect the health and safety of women workers. Only after federal courts had voided many of these protective labor laws under Title VII did organized labor drop its opposition to the ERA and provide critical support to NOW's efforts to urge its passage.

After an unprecedented nationwide feminist campaign, the ERA was finally approved by a landslide in both the House and Senate in 1972. Before it could be formally adopted as a constitutional amendment, however, the ERA had to clear one more hurdle: it had to be ratified by a minimum of thirty-eight of the fifty **states**. It was ratified by only thirty-five, despite the efforts of a powerful pro-ERA coalition. ERA opponents, consisting primarily of conservative religious and political organizations, had managed to convince just enough people that the measure would unduly jeopardize traditional lifestyles.

In the end, the ERA's defeat became largely symbolic. With the rise of feminism, many of the discriminatory laws the ERA was originally designed to eradicate had already been struck down, one by one, during the decade-long struggle for the amendment's ratification.

Further reading

Ross, S., Pinzler, I., Ellis, D. and Moss, K. (1993) *The Rights of Women*, 3rd edn, Carbondale: Southern Illinois University Press.

Schneir, M. (ed.) (1994) *Feminism in Our Time: The Essential Writings, The Second World War to the Present*, New York: Vintage.

MARY-CHRISTINE SUNGAILA, ESQ

Erdrich, Louise

b. 1954

Born of a Chippewa Indian mother and **German American** father, Erdrich grew up in North Dakota and earned a degree in **anthropology** from Dartmouth in 1976. Her first book, *Love Medicine* (1984), won the National Book Critics Circle Award. Subsequent novels have further developed the characters from her first book, drawing on both sides of her heritage to explore the interaction of **Native Americans** and their European American neighbors. Her use of multiple narrators and recurring characters has been likened to Faulkner. Most of her work has been a collaboration with her late husband, Michael Dorris, who committed suicide in 1995.

JIM WATKINS

espionage

Espionage is the practice of spying to secretly observe something or someone. This ancient, universal activity is summed up in the cliché "the second oldest profession." Contemporary American culture incorrectly associates espionage with the **Cold War** and the **CIA**'s creation in 1947; yet America has a rich history of espionage between Nathan Hale and the appointment of Rear Admiral Sidney Souers, the first director of the CIA.

Espionage studies may concern organizational development, composition, culture and ethics, domestic and foreign powers and functions, missions, methods, performance, management, reform and reorganization. American espionage is also influenced by its **enemies** and its allies. For example, America began covert operations in Europe in response to **Soviet** subversion. America's pre-eminent ally, Britain, played a decisive role in educating a generation of American intelligence officers during the Second World War; consequently, the Anglo-American intelligence alliance remains unique. The US also has espionage relationships with other states such as Israel, with alliance partners in **NATO**, coalition partners and the UN. Intelligence sharing is a key issue in America's post-Cold War security agenda. Spies may steal political, diplomatic, military, economic, scientific and technological secrets. Non-governmental organizations, such as corporations and multi-nationals, also conduct economic, commercial, scientific and technological espionage. Espionage and counter-espionage are also subject to US and international laws.

In fiction the spy, like the hunter, the scout and the detective, becomes an American icon, revealing American hopes and fears, and political, moral and cultural attitudes towards espionage. Espionage conspiracy theories reveal alienation, anxiety and a rejection of rationalism, symbolized by the popularity of *The X Files*. Spy fiction's glamour and thrills distort the spy world, whether the spy is a hero or villain. Reality is more ordinary. The spy's survival kit contains clandestine techniques, courage, political savvy, good luck and a sense of humor.

Espionage excites political and ethical debates because espionage requires secrecy and democracy requires openness. American democracy has been acutely sensitive to these issues since the mid-1970s. Consequently, the US pioneered democratic oversight of espionage and leads the field in historical declassification. Intelligence practitioners debate the relative merits of espionage and technical intelligence collection, and espionage and open-source information. Sherman Kent, America's leading theorist of strategic intelligence, doubted clandestine techniques and argued for open sources and social-science methods. During the Cold War, American espionage supported containment, a political, military, economic and psychological strategy designed to contain Soviet power and protect Western values, not least the right to self-determination and diversity. In the post-Cold War period, globalization, openness and the communications revolution revived the debate between open and secret sources, and human and technical means. All-source, real-time intelligence was the first line of defense in the new world disorder. Paradoxically, as American technology surged ahead, America faced difficult security challenges in **Somalia** and **Bosnia**, which flagged up the need for human intelligence. Espionage will remain part of American statecraft, continue to exercise America's conscience and engage America's allies and enemies.

Further reading

Bryan, G.S. (1943) *The Spy in America*, Philadelphia: Lippincott.

Felix, C. (1963) *A Short Course in the Secret War*, New York: E.P. Dutton.

Peterson, N.H. (1992) *American Intelligence, 1775–1990, A Bibliographic Guide*, Claremont: Regina Books.

SHEILA KERR

ESPN *see* sports media

Estefan, Gloria

b. 1957

Cuban American singer whose appeal and musical style cut across lingual boundaries and musical genre definitions. In 1975 she joined the group Miami Sound Machine, headed by her now husband, Emilio. As her popularity grew, the Sound Machine name was dropped. Today, the Estefan collaboration has resulted in over twenty albums and numerous pop hits. In 1990 she was severely injured in a bus crash in Pennsylvania and was temporarily paralyzed, but has since made a full recovery. Among her most popular songs are "Bad Boys" (1985), "Coming Out of the Dark" (1991) and "I See Your Smile" (1992).

A. JOSEPH BORRELL

ethnic enclaves

Immigrants to American cities were often confined to **ghettos** outside fashionable residential and commercial **neighborhoods**, through which they established cohesive albeit defensive communities. Since the nineteenth century, names of variable dignity from "Chinatown" or "Little Italy" to "Niggertown" have embodied the dual faces of American **assimilation** – being in America but not quite belonging. In other areas, more neutral names demarcate complex and dynamic areas – **Italian**, **Jewish** and **Latino** immigrants to **New York** City, NY's Lower East Side or the multiple populations of **Harlem**. Moreover, while these enclaves could be seen as havens and creative elements in the melting-pot, history cannot ignore the poor housing, exploitative labor, neglected services and outside rejection, including physical attacks, that kept immigrants in ghettos.

Suburban opportunities after the Second World War offered escapes for assimilated generations of white enclave residents, while the **civil-rights** movement and urban renewal in the 1960s sought to eradicate the worst abuses of **segregation** and the poverty associated with it. Yet, racism continued to block opportunities for some, while after 1965, new immigrants poured into cheap, available housing. The elderly, left behind by families and progress, have also posed special problems of security and services.

Some urban enclaves have found new life in the 1990s metropolises as service centers for dispersed populations and foci for ethnic-chic restaurants and shopping. New names, **food** and faces also reflect the presence of new immigrant populations making it in America – **Miami**'s Little Havana/ Calle Ocho, multi-ethnic Central American and African restaurants and residents of **Washington**'s Adams-Morgan, or "Little Saigon" in nearby northern Virginia. **Class** is a critical element in ethnic and racial development and attitudes – "Chinatowns" have become **tourist** sites in ways that inner-city black or **Hispanic** neighborhoods have not.

In **Sunbelt** cities, new enclaves have emerged along suburban **highways** rather than in older center cities, claiming an alternative locus of cheaper space for stores and residences. Near **Los Angeles, CA**, meanwhile, suburban cities like Monterey Park and Alhambra have become the first Chinese-majority cities in the nation. Even Chinatown in Manhattan, New York faces competition from new immigrants in outer boroughs like Queens and Brooklyn.

Ethnic enclaves have offered transitional spaces for newly arrived families, and maintain traditions, associations and monuments of the past for future generations. Legal and medical services, media (**newspapers** and videos), foodstuffs and restaurants, and religious centers all provide continuing linkages in **community** (within definitions of ethnicity acceptable to American diversity). Festivals, movies (whether *Godfather II* (1974) or *Joy Luck Club* (1993)), museums, web-sites and tourist-oriented services also convert former ghettos into images of American success, despite the popula-

tions that may still be packed into cramped apartments or sweatshops on upper floors.

See also: assimilation; class; immigration; suburbs and edge cities

Further reading

Gan, H. (1982) *The Urban Villagers*, New York: The Free Press.
Chen, H. (1989) *Chinatown No More*, Ithaca: Cornell.

GARY McDONOGH
CINDY WONG

ethnic food

While assimilationist pressures have told **immigrants** to learn English, support American economic and political culture and give up **leftist** politics, animal sacrifice and political allegiances abroad, other traits have been enshrined as "acceptable" markers of ethnic difference – costumes for school pageants, religious festivals and **parades** and, above all, **food**. Even on the universalist holiday of Thanksgiving, stuffings for the turkey and side dishes reflect regional and national heritages, which can also be celebrated at school and urban festivals. Some once-ethnic foods – hot dogs, **pizza**, tacos and kebabs, among others – have crossed over into a heterogeneous American cuisine. But family recipes, ethnic restaurants and **neighborhoods** and **cookbooks** also celebrate diversity and even cosmopolitan knowledge in the food-conscious late twentieth and early twenty-first centuries.

Ethnic cuisine, in fact, implies an American standard, usually defined on the basis of regional variations on Anglo staples of meat, bread and potatoes, salads and vegetables, etc. Some ethnic cuisines have gone far beyond their own groups in altering this standard. Italian foods like spaghetti and lasagna are staples of even Asian households. While **Mexicans** often face prejudice as immigrants, tacos are part of fast-food culture at home and in drive-ins.

Other cuisines have demanded ingredients, markets and restaurants that provide economic stakes for immigrant populations as well as opportunities for "crossover." While **Chinese** cuisines once adapted to American norms and palates, the growth of Asian populations after the 1960s supported more critical clienteles for specialties like dim sum, and other varieties of Chinese cuisine, as well as Korean, Vietnamese and Japanese food. Moreover, these restaurants and the markets that supply homes and businesses serve as places of employment, economic stakes and social centers for ethnic communities.

The price of ethnic food varies. Japanese food, for example, often demands high-end prices (given ingredients in sushi and sashimi). High-prestige foods move beyond the label of ethnicity – especially French and Northern Italian cuisine. Meanwhile, other cuisines, especially those of Africa, remain exotic.

Fashion also comes into play as Americans treat food as adventure as well as comfort. Fads have established Spanish, Thai, Mediterranean and, in the late 1990s, Latin American cuisine, as alternatives in trendy restaurants and cookbooks. In many cases, these claim an authenticity beyond the ethnic group established in the US.

The American melting-pot has also created fusion food. Some were produced outside of the US – Cuban Chinese immigrants, for example, pioneered fusion. French with Thai (and other Asian) cuisine, **Pacific Rim** cuisine and new American chefs have taken ethnic dishes as building blocks for culinary renovation shocking to ancestral countries.

Hence ethnicity in food, as in other areas of American life, is both a heritage and a starting point in shaping identities, interactions and markets.

Further reading

Smith, J. (1990) *The Frugal Gourmet on Our Immigrant Ancestors: Recipes You Should Have Gotten from Your Grandmother*, New York: William Morrow.

GARY McDONOGH
CINDY WONG

ethnicity *see* race and ethnicity

ethnic slurs

Underlying generations of ethnic and racial separation in America is a complex mixture of competition, envy and suspicion of the "other." Ethnic slurs have been and continue to be used to define and enforce cultural boundaries in the United States.

The number and variety of ethnic slurs and racial epithets in American culture indicate the extraordinary importance placed on group distinctions. The legacy of American slavery includes the use of labels to categorize and dehumanize **African Americans**, and the effect of other ethnic slurs is similar, though not as virulent. The message to the individual at whom a slur or epithet is directed is that whatever else you may think you are or have worked to become you are nothing more than a "wop" (**Italian American**) or a "nigger" (African American), and you will be treated as such.

Treatment runs the gamut from whispered slurs and subtle snubs to beatings and murder. These words, even when they are used in jest, change a person into an object and a target.

The use of ethnic slurs in American **comedy** became a complex and controversial topic in the late twentieth century. Comedians instinctively play on social animosities and fears, and few topics have the explosive charge of ethnic and racial identity. Godfrey Cambridge, Dick **Gregory** and Richard **Pryor** used racial epithets and stereotypes in their stand-up comedy routines, first to African American audiences in the 1960s and then, in modified form, to national audiences. Comedy including ethnic slurs, when performed by a member of the group that is usually targeted by the slur can have the effect of bolstering group identity and defusing the power of the slur. On the other hand, comedic or any other use of slurs that gets a wide audience has the side-effect of keeping slurs in circulation, and, it may be argued, giving them the acceptability of use by those who might be most offended. Nonetheless, the most heavily weighted ethnic slur in American culture was used as the title of Dick Gregory's 1964 autobiography and by the 1990s rap group "NWA – Niggaz With Attitude." At the same time, it became part of street language in cities between young African American men as a label and a greeting. Other ethnically oriented comedians also have played with slurs in their comedy routines – for example, Alan King and Jackie Mason among **Jewish** comedians and the Italian American comedian Pat Cooper.

As much as slurs have been burlesqued and defused, they retain their power. Among other kinds of slurs and insults, they are recognized in American constitutional law as "fighting words" immune from the free-speech protections of the 1st Amendment. In spite of their currency, slurs have been rejected by the educated **middle class**. After the **civil-rights** movement and the heightening of ethnic identification, it was considered impolite or "incorrect" to depersonalize a group or individual with a slur. A reaction against the norm of incorrectness began in the late 1980s, when conservative commentators included the ban against ethic slurs among other proscribed behaviors in their critique of **political correctness**.

Further reading

Esman, M.J. (1994) *Ethnic Politics*, Ithaca: Cornell University Press.
Gregory, D. (1994) *Nigger: An Autobiography*, New York: Dutton.

FRANK ANECHIARICO

ethnic studies *see* literature, race and ethnicity

etiquette

Class and status anxiety in an apparently egalitarian society have created ample opportunity for social advisors to judge correct behavior, especially with regard to formal ritual occasions like **weddings** and funerals. At the same time, etiquette as a social code of the elite was also identified with **assimilation** through **mass media**, permitting a series of published social arbiters to flourish from generation to generation. Emily Post's 1920s *Etiquette*, for example, drew on the cachet of old money to advise on problems dealing with servants, accents and travel, as well as special occasions. Amy Vanderbilt, with another

established name, took on a similar role for the postwar **middle class**.

While many **baby boomers** rejected such stylized behaviors as inauthentic in the 1960s, the uncertainties of multicultural lives as well as ongoing life crises have produced new figures for millennial behavior. These again cater to individuals without **family** guidance or education in such social traditions. Miss Manners (Judith Martin) in her columns and books adapts an ironic Victorian voice to current questions of shifting **gender**, family and ethnic conjunctions; Martha **Stewart**, while focused on style, conveys guidance in living for the leisured middle class. Etiquette has also been conveyed by mass media as part of the portrayals of class, as well as explorations of character, issues of **marriage**, bereavement, etc.

There are, of course, class and ethnic differences in behavior, ranging from expectations of participants in ritual events to issues of loudness, assertiveness or presentations of self in social situations that continuously divide multicultural and intergenerational gatherings. In such a setting, formality (derived from European models) may constitute a neutral ground or an additional layer of repression or exclusion.

Further reading

Martin, J. (1982) *Miss Manner's Guide to Excruciatingly Correct Behavior*, New York: Atheneum.
Post, E. (1997) *Etiquette*, 16th edn, New York: Funk & Wagnalls.
Vanderbilt, A. (1957) *Complete Guide to Etiquette*, Garden City: Doubleday.

GARY McDONOGH

Evangelical Christians *see* Christian Right; Methodists; religion; Southern Baptists

Everly Brothers

b. 1937 (I. Donald)

b. 1939 (Philip)

I. Donald and Philip Everly were born in Kentucky to parents who soon left the coal-mining region to work in **radio** stations. The brothers signed to Cadence Records in 1957 when they released their biggest hit, "Bye Bye Love" (1958). Appearing at **Nashville**'s **Grand Ol' Opry**, they brought rockabilly-influenced acoustic guitar rhythms and folk-like vocal harmonies to a **country** stage; they were the first act to perform there using drums. Also known for "Wake Up Little Susie" (1958) and "Cathy's Clown" (1958), the Everly Brothers influenced numerous popular performers and songwriters, including **Simon and Garfunkel**, the Mamas & the Papas, Crosby, Stills & Nash and the Byrds.

EDWARD MILLER

evolution *see* biology; scientific creationism

exercise *see* physical fitness

exotic dancing/strip clubs

American striptease, with its roots in nineteenth-century French striptease, came to prominence in the mid-1920s when burlesque **theater** began to feature it as a way to attract audiences.

By the 1930s, when both G-string-clad chorus girls and **police** raids on clubs where they performed were common, striptease artists would combine skits and musical performance with elaborate costumes in order to avoid prosecution. Great striptease artists of this period included Gyspy Rose Lee and Ann Corio. Later on, exotic dancers turned showgirls in **Las Vegas**' hotels and casinos had begun performing elaborately choreographed and costumed shows.

Dancers in many strip clubs perform stage shows (known colloquially as "air-dancing") as well as "table dances," in which the dancer performs on a small, more private stage for individual patrons. In the 1990s, clubs in many states began to offer "lap dances," in which a nude or semi-nude dancer performed gyrations while sitting on the lap of the fully clothed patron. Depending on the clubs where they dance, strippers may work exclusively for tips, receive a minimal "shift pay," or even be required to pay the club for time spent on stage. In the

1990s, dancers at **San Francisco**'s Lusty Lady became the first group of exotic dancers to form a **union**, and this movement to unionize is now growing throughout the country.

Several American movies have focused on strippers, including *Gypsy* (1962, 1993), based on the life of Gypsy Rose Lee, *Showgirls* (1995) and *Striptease* (1996), starring Demi Moore, who received a fee of $12 million for her role in the film. Striptease and burlesque have also served as inspiration for mainstream dancers and choreographers, most notably Bob Fosse, whose **jazz** choreography drew extensively on the burlesque tradition.

Exotic dancing came under renewed scrutiny in late 1990s **New York** City, where Mayor Rudolph Giuliani successfully lobbied for legislation to prevent strip clubs and other adult establishments from operating within 500 feet of residences, schools, day-care centers and places of worship. This trend has resulted in a return to shows more in the burlesque tradition, with both more substance and more clothing.

SUSAN SCOTTO

expatriates

While **immigration** has been a central theme of American life, some Americans also choose to emigrate, becoming Americans abroad or in exile. In the late twentieth and early twenty-first centuries, this expatriate population has increased and diversified. According to government statistics, approximately 1,590,000 US citizens lived abroad in 1959. Two-thirds of this group were members and dependents of the US armed forces. In 1997 the numbers had increased to approximately 3.3 million civilians, including only 200,000 military personnel. These figures, in fact, only represent expatriates who are officially registered at US embassies and consulates globally. It is estimated that an additional 1.5–2 million citizens live outside of the US.

The majority of US expatriates are employees and dependents of US companies or multi-national corporations with strong ties to North America. The expatriate population also includes teachers, students, research scholars, missionaries and writers. **Retirees**, either returning to their homelands or seeking cheaper living (which has created gated American colonies in Mexico), also become *de facto* expatriates. In the **Vietnam** era, **Canada** and Scandinavia were seen as havens for protestors or those avoiding the **draft**; the **Soviet Union**, **China** and **Cuba** have all appealed to small groups on ideological grounds. For protestors, and for some very wealthy citizens, renunciation of citizenship has been a part of this movement; others retain their ties whether or not they return to the US with any consistency.

Despite reductions in benefits packages during the past few decades, the expatriate life is in many respects a privileged existence. Housing and education allowances, **tax** exemptions, travel opportunities and the chance to learn about a different culture hold significant appeal for many. Despite global communication and transportation and a trend towards localization in hiring practices, American expatriates continue to be a significant presence in such places as London, Hong Kong, Mexico City, Tokyo, Paris and Toronto.

Literary and historical representations of expatriates are sparse, although they may figure more in movies set in foreign locales – either as hero/heroines or "interpreter" of local customs. Early expatriates such as Benjamin Franklin, Thomas Jefferson, Washington Irving and Nathaniel Hawthorne nonetheless recorded their experiences in Europe, and American students studied at European universities throughout the eighteenth and nineteenth centuries. Missionaries and merchants were the most common nineteenth-century expatriates living in Asia, Latin America and Africa.

The best-known American expatriates are the self-exiled artists and writers in Paris between the First World War and the Second World War. Ernest Hemingway, Gertrude Stein, Anais Nin, John Dos Passos, F. Scott Fitzgerald and Henry Miller wrote about the tensions inherent in the expatriate existence; Josephine Baker and James Baldwin saw Paris from a different racial perspective. Questions of identity, disillusionment with one's home environment and the search for an intellectual, spiritual and geographical home are recurrent themes in later quests further afield based on religious search (**South Asia**), racial identity (Africa as a "homeland" for **African Americans**) or identification with "nature" and the primitive.

Although these seekers seem to share little common ground with late twentieth century traders, language instructors, exchange students and consular employees, all share an experience of dislocation that has been examined in postcolonial and women's **history, sociology, anthropology** and human-resources management. By being outside the US, they test the limits and interpretations of American society – whether its global reach or the possibility of escaping it altogether.

See also: American images abroad

Further reading

Pizer, D. (1996) *American Expatriate Writing and the Paris Moment*, Baton Rouge: Louisiana State University.
Osland, J.S. (1995) *The Adventure of Working Abroad*, San Francisco: Jossey-Bass.

STACILEE FORD

F

fairs

Like their ancestral European celebrations, American fairs have combined leisure, commerce and politics. State fairs annually showcase **agriculture**, commerce, industry, natural resources, and domestic/folk skills alongside generous dosages of entertainment and Midway curiosities. This color and excitement has made them frequent settings for films and musicals. Other fairs may represent local/county celebrations, or bring together ethnic groups, streets or religious congregations. The image of the fair, in turn, has been extended to less celebratory settings like "job fairs" or "college admissions fairs."

See also: worlds' fairs

GARY McDONOGH

family

The concept of "family" is complex. Diverse experiences of family depend on age, gender, ethnicity, socio-economic status, sexual orientation and religious affiliation. Throughout American history, competing interest groups have tried to provide the definitive explanation of the concept of family and influence social policy.

The US Census Bureau defines family as two or more people living together, related by blood, marriage, or adoption. What this statistical concept fails to convey is the complex ways people join together to support each other through the raising of children, the division of economic resources, and the love and nurturing that are key to family life. Thus, both the structure and function of what constitutes a family are aspects of debate.

Politicians often invoke the concept of family to advance political agendas. A "**family-values**" platform is conservative, envisioning two parents with **children** – a nuclear family. The husband is the wage-earner and the wife a full-time homemaker. "Family values" often presuppose the **Christian Right** ideology and opposition to abortion. A more liberal perspective focuses on the affective ties between members, their commitment to each other, and planning parenthood. Either concept relies on an ideal type of family that rarely matches the reality of individual experience.

The US Census statistics indicate changes in family structure over time. Since 1970, delays in **marriage** and an increase in **divorce** rates have contributed to reducing the number of people living in family households. Divorce is common, with 50 percent of all marriages ending in divorce. The number of single women raising children has doubled. "Blended" families due to remarriage create complex step-parenting relationships. Women are also joining the workforce at an unprecedented rate.

The degree of autonomy families exercise in disciplining and educating their children is also changing. Stricter definitions of **child abuse** sometimes necessitate outside intervention. The surge of interest in home schooling represents a move away from outside influences.

Many options for affinity-based family relationships exist. Spouses or partners, despite raising children, may live apart due to job demands.

Others live in committed relationships without children and still consider themselves "family." Members of religious groups, especially within the **African American** culture, often refer to each other using familial terms such as "mother," "sister," or "brother" when no blood or marriage relationship exists, but where there is a supportive relationship.

"Are you family?" can be asked by a gay or lesbian person to inquire about sexual orientation. Homosexuals, when rejected by their family of origin, often turn to a chosen social network to act as family members. Efforts are under way in many states to recognize same-sex marriages. Some municipalities and businesses recognize partnership relationships through the provision of domestic-partner benefits. Religious organizations are divided about supporting such unions.

The concept of family is a complex, multi-layered construction. A person may hold different working definitions of the concept depending on the context.

See also: gender and sexuality

Further reading

Carter, B. and McGoldrick, M. (eds) (1989) *The Changing Family Life Cycle*, Cambridge, MA: Allyn & Bacon.

JENNIFER CAMPBELL

family restaurants

Categorized less by their **food** (generally bland mainstream American) than by their use. Family restaurants tolerate and promote the presence and activities of **children** with special treats, spaces, games and rewards, as well as budget prices. This normative image of **family** allows for some variation among chains (**McDonald's** and other fast-food restaurants with sit-down space) and restaurants with servers – Friendly's, Howard Johnsons (with motels for travelers), Chili's, diners, etc. **Neighborhood** and ethnic restaurants, however, also do strong family business – **pizza**, tacos, **barbeque** and dim sum have crossed over from

their **ethnic enclaves** to allow for large and creative familiar groupings.

GARY McDONOGH
CINDY WONG

family room

The living room, like the earlier parlor, often presents a **home**'s formal visage to visitors. Behind the **kitchen** or down the stairs, however, another space in the postwar American home has fostered informal domesticity, conveyed as well in names like "rumpus" or "recreation" room. In this family room, worn furniture, recreational equipment and the debris of **children** and **pets** have defined informality. Collective events from **television** and popcorn to **teenage** dances to adult parties with bars and pool tables have identified this space with flexibility, memorabilia and comfort, private yet central values for the family and home.

GARY McDONOGH

family values

Political rhetoric, a term especially but not (unfortunately) exclusively associated with conservatives. The term elevates models of the **middle-class**, two-parent monogamous heterosexual family as mores for all social issues, without recognizing the multiplicity of **family** forms, roles and challenges that constitute contemporary American society. Many conservatives have claimed that the lack of family values results in homosexuality, single-parent families, **teenage** pregnancy, drug abuse, sexual abuse and domestic violence. Still, given the emotional and ideological appeal of the family, it becomes a particularly divisive way of phrasing issues, especially when touted by white men with unstable marriages.

GARY McDONOGH
CINDY WONG

Farina, Richard

b. 1937; d. 1966

Poet, composer, folk-singer and novelist of Irish-Cuban heritage. His *Been Down so Long it Looks Like Up to Me* (1966) has been recognized as a classic of post-beat generational unease. With his wife Mimi (sister of Joan **Baez**), he explored folk music, ballads and political satire before his untimely death in a motorcycle accident.

GARY McDONOGH

Farmer, James

b. 1920; d. 1999

Alongside Martin Luther **King**, Jr., Ralph **Abernathy** and Bayard **Rustin**, Farmer is considered one of the principal leaders of the **civil-rights** movement. He helped found **CORE** in 1942 and became its director, leading **sit-ins** and the **freedom rides**. *Freedom When?* (1965) revealed his continuing commitment to non-violent resistance, though he began to support some tenets of **Black Power**, such as black self-determination and local control. He left CORE in 1968 and stood for Congress, losing to Shirley **Chisholm**, and was appointed assistant secretary of Health, Education and Welfare by **Nixon** in 1969, but resigned from this position after a year.

ROBERT GREGG

farms and farm life

Since the early days of the Republic, yeoman farmers and farm families have been seen as repositories of American values and traditions, as well as backbones of **economics** and politics. To foreign observers like De Toqueville or Crevecouer, or the philosopher-president Thomas Jefferson, such farmers epitomized American ideals of **freedom**, hard work and **individualism** in a new nation, 86 percent of whose inhabitants were rural. Generations of literature, art, political discourse and, in the twentieth century, movies have contrasted rural virtue and urban decay (even

though America's great "sin," slavery, was essentially rural). Contemporary "country style" decor and crafts and weekend farmers affirm this ideological presence even in an urbanizing nation in which farm life has declined radically in both economic value and numbers of citizens living on the **family** farm.

Government policies, technology, corporate expansion and globalization since the Second World War have vastly changed the function and meaning of the family farm. Hence a modern novel/movie like Jane Smiley's *1000 Acres* resituates *King Lear* as a tragedy of a farm family destroyed by ambitious expansion and modernization. FARM AID concerts, which began in 1985, have allowed artists like Willie Nelson, Bob **Dylan** and John Mellencamp to call attention to rural debt and loss of lands to agribusiness and urban sprawl. These concerts have distributed $14.5 million in direct aid and more in research on long-term solutions for family farms and communities.

Farms in the US are generally defined as lands that produce or are capable of producing $1,000 in sales. Most such farms are still family owned (90 percent), although these include family corporations that hire outside labor (for instance, migrant workers are the norm in **California**). Yet, their involvement in American economic and social life has also changed in important ways in the twentieth and early twenty-first centuries.

First, the diversified and self-sufficient farm, with notable exceptions like the **Amish**, is a relic of the past. Where in the 1950s, for example, the average dairy holding was 5.8 cows – suitable for family and local needs – by the 1990s it had risen to 61, reflecting a move towards more efficient specialized production. Farmers specialize in one crop oriented to national and global markets – grains like wheat and corn, meat, fruit, **tobacco**, even specialized truck or organic produce for urban markets. Agricultural sciences have dramatically increased productivity per farm laborer in all of these since the 1940s, making the US the precursor to a global green revolution.

Production is linked to wider networks of support and consumption. Since Franklin **Roosevelt**'s response to the collapse of the Dust Bowl, government policies have sought to control prices and a regular supply of food to consumers, while also supporting farmers – an incipient conflict met by conflicting regulations. Sometimes, for example, farmers were subsidized to retire land from production, leading to charges of huge subsidies for growing nothing. Since 1992, these policies have changed to even out and limit support without forcing land to be vacant.

Railroads and **trucking** have tied farmers as well to wide national markets for decades. Hence, fruit from California, Texas and Florida appears year-round in **New York** City and **Chicago, IL**, while production of beef, sugar and chicken has also been regionally concentrated. Transportation has allowed exports of American surplus in grains and other agricultural goods, but has also opened markets to agricultural goods from other nations that are competitive in terms of price, variety or quality. Again, the intertwining of family farms and global markets produces both expanded possibilities and new vulnerability.

In the twentieth century, farmers also increased cultural links to wider American populations as **automobiles**, **radios**, **televisions** and **computers** have ended enforced isolation that once deeply constrained women and families. Indeed, some farms are now linked to rural-suburban combinations ("ruburbs"), where big-box stores like Walmart, technology supplies and urbane conveniences have eclipsed small-town values once associated with, and reinforcing, farm life. New technologies of farming, whether fertilizers and insecticides, newly bred or engineered crops, or expanded production, also demand more expertise – state universities support large agricultural teaching and research establishments – and yet also create dependence on corporate supplies, capital flow and markets.

These changing connections and values of the family farm reached a crisis in the 1970s, when downward prices and the energy crisis hit many farms, especially those that had expanded under younger and more educated owners. While the family farm may continue as a cultural icon, in fact, numbers have decreased from 6 million in the 1940s to roughly 2 million in the 1990s, while the percentage of Americans living on farms slipped from 23 percent in 1940 to under 2 percent. The consolidation of larger corporate agribusiness, the increasing competition of foreign producers and

the spread of urban land uses also threaten both this image and reality of the American dream.

Further reading

Goreham, G. (ed.) (1997) *Encyclopedia of Rural America*, Santa Barbara: ABC-CLIO (a basic initial resource for any research on American farm life).

GARY McDONOGH
CINDY WONG

Farrakhan, Louis

b. 1933

Louis Walcott grew up in **Boston, MA** where he became an accomplished musician, playing in the city's nightclubs. In 1955 he was recruited by **Malcolm X** for the **Nation of Islam**, and became Louis X (referred to in Malcolm X's *Autobiography* (1965)). He was given the name Farrakhan by Elijah Muhammad about the same time that he replaced Malcolm as head of the Black Muslim Temple in **Harlem, New York** and as national spokesman for the organization. Three years after not being picked to succeed Elijah Muhammad on his death in 1975, Farrakhan broke with Wallace Muhammad and established his own Nation of Islam, which he said was the legitimate successor to the earlier organization. Unlike Muhammad, Farrakhan has engaged in politics extensively, supporting Jesse **Jackson** for president in 1984, taking positions in international affairs supporting Libya's Khadafi and making a series of widely reported anti-Semitic remarks. His influence extends beyond the Nation of Islam, as shown in his organization of the 1996 Million Man March in **Washington, DC**.

ROBERT GREGG

fashion

Fashion in America can be discussed from two different perspectives – as a general statement about American styles, based on generally casual conformity, or in terms of the growth of an art and industry of couture as artifice. In the latter realm,

American designers freed themselves during and after the Second World War from slavish imitation of European models to compete in a global market that ranges from Paris and Milan to Tokyo and Hong Kong. In either case, fashion tends to be a highly gendered, classed and racialized enterprise where commodities transform bodies, sexuality and identity.

An American style, in the broader sense, has been less defined by aesthetics than by comfort and mass consumption. In the twentieth century, Americans bought more than 9 billion items of clothing annually, but they do not necessarily stress individual panache in everyday dress. Workplaces tend to mean conventional clothes (uniforms or pseudo-uniforms, like dark suits and white shirts). **Teenage** conformity long has been epitomized by the dominance of blue jeans and T-shirts as basic wardrobes, but also reflects trends in apparel, accessories and style (see *Clueless*, 1989), as well as **race** relations. Hip hop baggy pants and baseball caps have different meanings on white suburban college students and black, inner-city youths; minorities also display designer labels as marks of status and identity.

Clothing needs are met by a variety of prices and qualities of merchandise, with competition for brand name recognition pitting **GAP**, J. Crew, Express, Limited, Delia and others against each other, for example, for the youth market. Other brands have established reputations for conservative clothes for the workplace – Brooks Brothers, Anne Klein, Talbot, etc. Names have also created wider markets by moving from clothes to perfumes, accessories and household goods. Many people buy clothes according to what they can afford, whether in boutiques, **department stores**, discount stores or thrift shops, or via **catalogs** and online commerce. Still, the appeal of vintage clothing or sales shopping allows consumers to extend budget and style.

While certain Americans may have gained global reputations for their individual senses of style – Wallis Simpson, Grace **Kelly**, Jackie Kennedy **Onassis** – other prominent women have been embraced for their "sensible" look – like **First Ladies** Mamie Eisenhower, Pat Nixon, Barbara **Bush** or even the power-suited Hillary Clinton. **Hollywood** stars are often taken as the epitome of male fashion, from Cary Grant to Denzel **Washington**. For men not directly involved in fashion or media of display, an interest in fashion is often taken as anomalous, or even a failing in **masculinity**. Despite the "Peacock Revolution" of the 1960s, which introduced **hippie** clothes, colors and extravagant styles, American male fashion in public realms remains conservative and unobtrusive.

Despite these consistencies in general choices and ideal types, the American fashion industry has offered more and more new choices and forms of consumption and display since the end of the Second World War rationing. It has also aggressively asserted an American ethos in fashion – and fashion production – in distinction to European couture. The pioneer designers of the 1960s included Halston, Mary McFadden and Anne Klein, who extended their influence through ready-to-wear clothes, many of which appealed to **middle-class** women entering the workforce, balancing jobs and style. The 1960s were also marked by more idiosyncratic fashions associated with hippies and imported Carnaby Street designs, as well as the rise of designer jeans.

Subsequent decades saw the rise and globalization of many important American designers. Donna Karan designed clothes for the professional woman, Ralph Lauren offered classic, "preppy clothes," while Calvin Klein, Perry Ellis and others established visible looks and trademarks. The 1980s, according to Silverman (1986), became an era to celebrate aristocratic clothes in design as well as exhibits – and in the presidential style of the **Reagan** White House.

Designers continued to emerge and change in the 1990s. Tommy Hilfiger has appealed to the youth market, while Vera Wang and others competed in specialty gowns. New designers debut at New York's Fashion Week or outside Bryant Park. Production of many of these labels, however, has moved offshore. Americans also continue to buy from European designers: elite shopping areas like **New York**'s Fifth Avenue, **Los Angeles**' Rodeo Drive or **Miami**'s Bal Harbour offer boutiques for Chanel, Prada, Fendi, Gucci, Armani, Zegna and other global fashion logos. Meanwhile, American designers have been hired to revitalize staid European lines.

Many of these designers, in fact, offer multiple divisions to reflect differential purchasing power. While Donna Karan's name marks her expensive line, for example, DKNY provides a pricey but mass market alternative; Calvin Klein and CK follow the same division, reinforcing a design empire through multiple products and sales, although also risking over-extension.

While these lines reinforce divisions of **class** and gender, fashion also raises important questions about age and **race**. High fashion often offers clothes that look good on the young, but often only the older rich can afford them. Certainly, female fashion models, who have emerged as celebrities in their own right, have tended to offer young, thin and sometimes exotic looks and bodies. This has led to complaints about the objectification of the female body and the negative impact on female self-images. Male fashion models only gained some celebrity recognition in the 1990s with brooding, lean and muscled bodies whose display remains linked to questions of sexuality and identity as well as clothes. In both groups, exotic racial mixtures have been highlighted without serious integration of the design establishment or couturier clients. Design remains dominated by white males.

Fashion is constantly tied to other media. Stars at the Academy **Awards** become advertisements for designers and "looks." Media events such as the phenomenal success of *Titanic* (1997), Clark Gable's appearance without an undershirt in *It Happened One Night* (1934), or the King Tut **blockbuster** exhibit at the Metropolitan Museum all had an impact on design and taste in subsequent seasons. Other tie-ins occur through celebrities and labels: Michael **Jordan** is linked to both Warner Brothers' character clothing and sneaker endorsements, while logos of sports teams are popular in male casual wear.

Some of these trends, of course, may be lamented by those who attend New York's Fashion Week or those who have pontificated on American fashion from the pages of major periodicals like *Vogue*, *Harper's Bazaar*, or the more trade-oriented *Women's Wear Daily*. Nor will they be preserved, perhaps, in museum collections devoted to fashion like that of New York's Metropolitan Museum. Nonetheless, they embody, rather literally, the complexity and creativity of American life.

Further reading

Hollander, A. (1994) *Sex and Suits*, New York: Alfred Knopf.
Laver, J. (1983) *Fashion*, New York: Oxford.
Silverman, D. (1986) *Selling Culture*, New York: Pantheon.

GARY McDONOGH
CINDY WONG

fast food

Food defined by speed of service, responding to the needs of a population on the go – by **automobile**, between errands, or in fragmented family visits. Food combinations stressing meat, carbohydrates and sugar provide rapid satisfaction (with attendant dangers of obesity and other health problems). Franchises mean **food** is also standardized, familiar and relatively cheap. **Toys** lure **children**, while **teenagers** (and the elderly) find part-time jobs in fast-food outlets. Whether offering hamburgers, **pizza**, tacos, French fries, sodas, ice-cream, or even salads, chains like **McDonald's**, Taco Bell, Kentucky **Fried Chicken** and many others have also become symbols – albeit incomplete – of American food and eating abroad.

GARY McDONOGH
CINDY WONG

Federal Bureau of Investigation (FBI)

For much of its history the FBI has been linked inextricably in the public mind with its first director, J. Edgar **Hoover**. Since the 1970s, critics have highlighted many of Hoover's excesses and introduced periodic reforms. But, with his passing, the agency reshaped its public image without examining some fundamental questions about the relationship between a police organization and a democratic society. Praising Hoover for creating a strong law-enforcement agency, the organization has been slow to eliminate all of his unconstitutional practices. Subsequently, it has used some of the same fears that created Hoover's organization to forestall change, calling it into question in cases like its assaults on **militias** and on the Branch Davidian compound in **Waco, TX**, as well as its responsiveness to outside oversight.

The FBI's roots were planted in the aftermath of the First World War, a period of widespread violation of constitutional rights in the name of national security. Anxieties engendered by the 1917 Russian Revolution, concerns about domestic radical organizations like the Industrial Workers of the World (IWW) and the association in the mind of many Americans of socialism and anarchism with immigrants, allowed **Attorney-General** A. Mitchell Palmer, and his assistant, Hoover, to undertake widespread arrests and deportations. The first "red scare," however, was insufficient to provide legitimacy for a large federal police organization. The fears of the early 1920s gave way to late 1920s complacency. During the early 1930s, therefore, the organization's director, Hoover, turned to another stereotype of **immigration**, the identification of immigrants with **organized crime**, for his bureau's meal ticket. In this process he was helped significantly by the efforts of **Hollywood** in the early 1930s, and particularly the movies of James Cagney (*Public Enemy*, 1931), Edward G. Robinson (*Little Caesar*, 1931) and George Raft (*Scarface*, 1932), depicting dangerous, larger-than-life gangsters. Lined up against these villains were Hoover's *G-Men* (1935). The FBI director undertook a massive public-relations campaign to create an image of the federal agent as fearless and incorruptible, presenting his agents as clean-cut, white and **middle-class** men. Events like the killing of Dillinger became public spectacles, virtual lynchings, with trophies from the shooting displayed on the director's desk. Just as lynching established particular social practices in the **South**, Hoover's publicly performed law-enforcement practices normalized the role of the FBI agency.

The Second World War brought a new role of locating the foreign agent on American soil, but the most significant modern developments for the growing FBI occurred in response to the emergent **civil-rights** movement. The movement arose in part out of a new relationship between the federal government and segregationist southern states, and this relationship required increased federal police

intervention. The FBI was very slow to fulfill this new role, notwithstanding movie portrayals as in *Mississippi Burning* (1988), which erroneously depicted the Bureau as a key force for change. Only when freedom riders refused to halt their journeys through the South, and when other civil-rights activists refused to stop their work registering rural blacks, forcing the **Kennedy** administration to protect them, did FBI agents act. Civil-rights activists themselves often believed that the FBI remained on the sidelines until after their beatings.

But the FBI once again used events to bolster its public image. The murders of three activists (two of them white) in Philadelphia, Mississippi in 1964, led to a very public investigation undertaken by the FBI, which eventually unearthed the bodies of the young men who had been killed with the collusion of local police authorities. This performance, reassuring as it was for many northern liberals, and played for all its worth to **television** audiences in the Hoover-endorsed *FBI* series (ABC, 1965–74), masked Hoover's other more sinister work during this period.

This work involved the wiretapping of Martin Luther **King**, Jr.'s home and office on the assumption that he was working with known communists. Endorsed by the Attorney-General Robert Kennedy (who worried about his brother's identification with civil-rights leaders), this wiretapping revealed no "reds" under beds, but did produce salacious material that Hoover could add to his files (which most likely also covered John Kennedy's philandering).

Hoover also turned to his counter-intelligence program (COINTELPRO) to infiltrate black militant organizations, the new left and the antiwar movement. The growing number of **race riots** in the mid-1960s led to the establishment of a "Ghetto Informant Program" in 1968, in which 3,250 agent provocateurs were employed to infiltrate organizations like the **Black Panthers**. Just as Hoover had helped create a "red scare" in the 1920s by sometimes creating organizations where there were none, so the FBI contributed to the exacerbation of racial tensions in black **ghettos**.

This work is now generally acknowledged as part of Hoover's excesses. What is less clearly recognized is the manner in which such actions contributed to the understanding of the direction in which the movement towards racial equality was moving, and the extent to which their legacy has scarred American society. Hoover's vision that the riots were the result of the work of **Black Power** advocates was in direct contrast to the arguments of the **Kerner Commission**, which recognized the social roots of discontent. While Hoover has been vilified for his work during this period, his understanding of the period has survived, contributing to the **backlash** that occurred against the Civil Rights movement.

During the **Watergate** years, many of the FBI and **CIA**'s illegal activities came to light. Reforms occurred to such an extent that many conservatives began to feel that the federal policing agencies had been eviscerated, leaving the nation vulnerable. Now the Bureau benignly advertises itself as an enforcement agency complementing other local and state police forces, providing a sophisticated laboratory (to which *Homicide*, (NBC, 1993–9) detectives could turn when necessary) for studying fingerprint, DNA and other forensic evidence. It also undertakes investigation of telemarketing fraud, security fraud, bombings and major art thefts – not to mention the paranormal, as seen on the *X-Files* (FOX, 1993–). Yet the feeling that there may have been some legitimacy to Hoover's methods has been rekindled among many Americans by events like the bombing of the federal building in Oklahoma City, Oklahoma, and fears associated with "foreign" (usually cast as Muslim, sometimes also immigrant) threats associated, once again, with increased involvement of American forces overseas. However, as in the case of the FBI's handling of the Waco confrontation with the Branch Davidians and the apparent cover-up of its agents' use of incendiary tear gas, such sentiments of legitimacy are quickly turned to excess.

Further reading

Bennett, C. (1948) *The F.B.I. The Basis of an American Police State*, Girard: Haldeman-Julius Publications.

Breuer, W.B. (1995) *J. Edgar Hoover and his G-men*, Westport: Praeger

Garrow, D.J. (1981) *The FBI and Martin Luther King, Jr*, New York: W.W. Norton.

Kessler, R. (1993) *The FBI*, New York: Pocket Books.

ROBERT GREGG

Federal Communications Commission (FCC)

Governmental unit that oversees the communications industry. Its chairperson and members are appointed by the **president**, subject to congressional approval. The Commission began with the Communications Act of 1934, which reorganized the previous Federal Radio Commission. Although the importance and activity of the FCC varies, its stance towards **telecommunications** and broadcasting industries has remained constant: it protects the ability of business to utilize public airwaves for profit. While its charter demands that it protect the public interest and access to its airwaves, in effect, the FCC has favored corporate conglomeration in allocating broadcasting licenses and decisions not to ensure a growing place on the broadcasting spectrum for public and educational broadcasting. Currently, the FCC, while fining disc jockeys like Howard Stern for obscenity, is also involved in trying to assert "decency" on the **Internet**. Such endeavors again might promote larger corporate interests.

EDWARD MILLER

femininity

There has been and continues to be a considerable amount of disagreement as to the precise nature of "femininity" in contemporary America. While there is a general consensus as to the stereotypical meaning of "femininity" (passive, emotional, delicate, irrational, mysterious, nurturing, maternal, submissive, heterosexual and strongly linked to nature – qualities that have been largely devalued in favor of their stereotypical masculine counterparts), the origin of this "femininity" is not as clear.

In general, the contemporary American mainstream believes that "femininity" is biologically determined. This ideology, which has dominated for centuries, conceives of "femininity" as a biological imperative inherently embedded in being "female." In other words, "femininity" is not socially constructed; it is hard-wired into female bodies. Certain feminists support this position, seeing traditionally feminine qualities as indicative of the power women may wield over men. This largely heterosexual model posits that women, with their mysterious sexuality and deep ties to the Earth mother, inherently control men, who crave the elusive emotionality and feminine eroticism that is missing from their own biologically determined **masculinity**.

On the other hand, most feminists agree that "femininity" and other gender categories are socially constructed. According to this position, "femininity" is a gender category that society has assigned to female individuals. In other words, gender corresponds to the social constructs "woman," "womanliness" and "femininity;" and to "man," "manliness" and "masculinity." Biology is reserved for sex, which is defined in terms of the biological categories "male" and "female."

Social constructivists counter the claims of biological determinists by stating that "femininity" cannot be biological because not all women are feminine. Indeed, some feminist theorists state that there is no such thing as a "woman," since there is no single, unified experience which brings all females together. "Women" are just *people*, these theorists assert, and gender categories have been imposed upon individuals as a means of social control. Feminists also point to the mutability of "femininity" in order to argue in favor of social constructivism.

In its current practical application, "femininity" has become increasingly difficult to pinpoint. With the gradual relaxation of dress codes for women since the beginning of the twentieth century, women's entrance en masse into the paid workforce in the 1960s, and the second mobilization of the feminist movement, traditional "femininity" has lost hold as a meaningful descriptor of modern womanhood. Today, an American woman may deviate from the conventional definition of femininity and still be considered a "feminine" woman. Unlike in the past, a "feminine" woman of the 1990s may wear pants and other traditionally "masculine" attire, have her own career and embrace an active sexuality.

However, the stereotypes of the past still persist. Across the United States, certain parts of traditional "femininity" are still upheld as the ideal standard for women. Mainstream America also continues to believe that females are inherently "feminine" due to their biology. The idea of a unified feminine essence still pervades our culture.

See also: gender and sexuality

Further reading

Butler, J. (1990) *Gender Trouble*, New York: Routledge.

ELIZABETH A. GALEWSKI

feminism

The term "feminism" first came into use in the 1910s to describe an emerging movement committed to mobilizing women as a distinct social group and eliminating social hierarchies between men and women. As contemporary feminist Naomi Wolf succinctly puts it: "Feminism can be defined as women's ability to think about their subjugated role in history, and then to do something about it." But feminism has had a fragile hold on women's consciousness in the twentieth and early twenty-first centuries, achieving great strides towards gender equality and then receding, only to re-emerge once the modest gains already achieved start to slip.

The leaders of the first wave of feminism in America were Elizabeth Cady Stanton and Susan B. Anthony, whose work eventually helped women gain the right to vote in 1920 with the enactment of the 19th Amendment to the Constitution. Feminism then disappeared from the American scene for several decades, giving way to a "post-feminist" period in which the earlier suffragists were decried as "man-haters" out of touch with the needs of contemporary women. But feminism re-emerged in the 1960s, more influential than ever. It is this second wave of feminism, roughly starting with the publication of Betty **Friedan**'s *The Feminine Mystique* in 1963 and ending with the defeat of the **Equal Rights Amendment** in 1982, which epitomizes modern American feminism.

Gloria **Steinem**, the founder of *Ms Magazine*, and Friedan, are widely viewed as the leaders and icons of this movement. With the **Civil Rights movement** providing an inspirational backdrop, Friedan's fledgling group, the **National Organization for Women (NOW)**, advocated for **abortion** and reproductive rights, equal opportunities in the workplace and at school, and passage of an Equal Rights Amendment to the US Constitution. Women got all but the latter. In 1973 the **Supreme Court** affirmed a woman's right to an abortion in *Roe v. Wade*. Under Title VII of the **Civil Rights Act** of 1964, it was declared unlawful for employers to discriminate on the basis of sex. By 1986 the US Supreme Court had interpreted this provision to include a claim for **sexual harassment** as well. In 1972 Congress passed **Title IX**, which prohibited discrimination on the basis of sex in any federally funded educational program or activity.

But, with the defeat of the Equal Rights Amendment, followed by Geraldine **Ferraro**'s failed vice-presidential bid in 1984, the golden age of American feminism came to an end. Feminism again lay dormant with the coming of another so-called "post-feminist" era. A *Time/CNN* poll found that only 33 percent of women were willing to call themselves "feminists," and only 16 percent of them were college-aged. College-age women in the 1980s (who had not participated in the **women's movement** of the 1960s and 1970s, but had nonetheless benefited from gains made during that time) forgot, or never knew, that the struggle for the vote took over seventy years, that abortions had not always been legal in America, or that in their mothers' lifetimes women could not obtain credit on their own. They wrongly believed that sex discrimination was a thing of the past. The repercussions for women were serious: without an active feminist movement, there was decreased access to abortions, abortion-clinic violence and limited funding and public support for rape-crisis centers, women's health facilities and battered women's shelters.

Then, in 1991, two events converged to revitalize the movement: the publication of **Pulitzer Prize**-winning journalist Susan Faludi's *Backlash: The Undeclared War Against American Women* (1991) and the confirmation hearing of future US

Supreme Court Justice Clarence **Thomas**, at which his former colleague Anita **Hill** testified that he had sexually harassed her at work. *Backlash* in particular, which documented a "powerful counter-assault on women's rights" and an intense societal resistance to the modest advances towards gender equality achieved by the women's movement, provided a clarion call to widespread action.

This wake-up call resulted in a "third wave" of feminism in the 1990s. This third wave did not reflect a single monolithic view of the appropriate path to gender equality. Instead, it encompassed many disparate strands of thought, such as liberal feminism, difference feminism, radical feminism and critical feminist theory. Feminism also blended with more traditional legal, political and film theories to provide a broad, multi-disciplinary perspective on women's status in society.

See also: women's liberation

Further reading

Faludi, S. (1991) *Backlash*, New York: Crown.
MacKinnon, C. (1987) *Feminism Unmodified*, Cambridge, MA: Harvard University Press.
Schneir, M. (ed.) (1994) *Feminism in Our Time*, New York: Vintage.
Rowbotham, S. (1997) *A Century of Women*, London: Penguin.

MARY-CHRISTINE SUNGAILA, ESQ.

Feminist Art

As the second wave of **feminism** awakened a generation of American women in the late 1960s, so too did it galvanize a community of women artists. Where such artistically matriarchal figures as Georgia **O'Keefe**, Helen Frankenthaler and Eva Hesse had ambivalently occupied their identities as women artists, producing work that while critically construed as "feminine" was never resolutely feminist, the post-1968 generation of female artists was proud and defiant in its assertion and celebration of female identity. Motivated by the very real conditions of discrimination and inequality, this first generation of feminist artists sought to redress the historical condition into which they were born.

Producing their most influential work during the 1970s, such artists as Eleanor Antin, Judy Chicago, Adrian Piper, Faith **Ringgold**, Carolee Schneemann and Miriam Schapiro returned to the historically objectified female body and reclaimed it as a subject. In such collaborative art projects as *Womanhouse* (1972) and *The Dinner Party* (1979), Chicago, Schapiro and their artistic sisters elevated women's experience and an iconography of the female body to the realm of high art.

While the activism of that first generation of feminist artists saw its continuation in the work and demonstrations of such political organizations as the Guerilla Girls and the Women's Action Coalition (WAC), by the 1980s a second generation of feminist artists had emerged, displaying markedly different aesthetic and political strategies. Renouncing the celebratory language and bodily imagery of their predecessors as deeply essentialist, such women as Jenny Holzer, Barbara Kruger, Martha Rosler and Cindy Sherman sought to deconstruct, rather than reconstruct, culturally normalized conceptions of gender and identity. Working primarily with **photography** and written text, these artists avoided the representational practices and corporeal iconography that so marked the work of their antecedents and sought instead to expose, explore and dismantle the rigid binary logic of sexual difference. At the same time, such deconstructive strategies opened up a space for a more expansive investigation of issues of **race**, as is exemplified in the work of Sandra Bernhard, Anna Deavere Smith, Lorraine O'Grady, Lorna Simpson, Kara Walker and Carrie Mae Weems.

From the vantage of the late 1990s, it is possible to celebrate the extraordinary gains achieved by women artists in little more than twenty-five years. Yet it is also worth considering whether the founding politics and ideals of feminism, rooted in the experiential difference of women, have been eroded, if not lost, to the theoretical forces of deconstruction and anti-essentialism that continue to shape and inform the production and reception of contemporary art.

Further reading

Broude, N. and Garrard, M. (1994) *The Power of Feminist Art*, New York: Henry N. Abrams, Inc.

Isaak, J. (1996) *Feminism and Contemporary Art*, London: Routledge.

LISA SALTZMAN

Ferraro, Geraldine

b. 1935

First female candidate for **vice-president** of the United States; former New York congressional representative and senatorial candidate. Her 1984 nomination to the **Democratic Party**'s ticket as candidate for vice-president signaled the emergence of the women's movement as a force in mainstream politics, highlighted the power of women voters and the significance of the **gender gap** and redefined the possibilities for American **women in politics**. Although she was ultimately defeated, Ferraro's presence on the ticket encouraged other aspiring female politicians to run for office and caused female voters to contribute more money than ever before to a candidate's campaign.

MARY-CHRISTINE SUNGAILA, ESQ.

field hockey

In the United States this is almost exclusively a women's sport that spread through women's colleges in the **Northeastern** and **Mid-Atlantic** states during the early twentieth century in spite of its vigorous aspects – believed inappropriate for young women. Since becoming an **Olympic** sport for women in 1980, it has spread beyond its "**Seven Sisters**" image. In the 1990s, heated debates also have erupted, especially in **high schools**, about boys playing field hockey on girls' teams. Such debates may intensify as immigrants arrive from areas such as **South Asia**, where field hockey has been popular among schoolboys and men.

ROBERT GREGG

figure skating

Sport popularized in the 1930s by the **Olympic** championships and performances in ice shows and films of Norwegian Sonja Henie, who deviated from the staid dress and mannered skating style of her predecessors. Tenley Albright became the first American Olympic gold medal winner in 1956; her achievement increased the popularity of the sport in the late 1950s and early 1960s. The first American skater to gain national attention (both in the rink and in the world of **advertising**), Dorothy Hamill, combined athletic prowess with the grace and musicality of a dancer. Hamill challenged assumptions about women's athleticism in her 1976 Olympic triumph and created the spin known as the "Hamill Camel" – now standard in women's competitions. But, while able to perform triple jumps in practice, Hamill was the last woman to win an Olympic gold medal without triple jumps.

Men's figure skating, marked until recently for its accentuation of athleticism over grace, has never matched the popularity of women's skating. In the 1980s, however, the ascendancy of Olympic medallists Scott Hamilton and Brian Boitano on a tide of patriotic fervor brought attention to the sport. Pairs figure skating and ice dancing have been dominated until recently by Russian skaters, and the best American skaters, perhaps lacking enthusiasm for the ballroom style of dancing, have steered clear.

The growth of commercialism in the sport has been very noticeable in the 1990s, with multi-million dollar advertising and professional contracts offered to those who win major amateur competitions. Quite strict divisions between amateurs and professionals remain in the sport (so that only the former are eligible to perform in the Olympics), while sports like **soccer**, **basketball** and **hockey** have eased up in this regard. Skaters generally, therefore, use the amateur competition as a stepping stone to riches to be gained from a professional contract, which includes traveling competitions as well as more thematic ice shows – **Disney** on Ice, Grease on Ice, Icecapades, etc. In 1991 and 1992, Kristi Yamaguchi won the World Championship and the Olympics and then turned professional, while the notorious assault on Nancy Kerrigan in 1994 was prompted by the desire of Tonya Harding's handlers to benefit from the possibility that she might win a medal at the upcoming Olympics. Michelle Kwan is one American skater who has held back from turning professional. Losing out on a gold medal at the Nagano Winter Olympics in 1998, she has waited for 2002. Meanwhile, Tara Lipinski, the fifteen-year-old star who surpassed Kwan, immediately turned professional.

ROBERT GREGG

Filipino Americans

Filipino Americans constitute the second-largest group of Americans of Asian descent; almost 60,000 Filipinos enter the US every year. Filipino **immigration** to the US prior to the annexation of the Philippines to the US in 1898 was negligible. By 1910, Filipinos could travel freely to the US, which started a slow trend that continued after Philippine independence in 1934 (when immigrants reached 100,000). Most immigrants were male farm workers. Military collaboration also facilitated naturalization and acceptance during and after the Second World War.

The 1965 Immigration Act, coupled with neo-colonial economic difficulties in the Philippines, increased the number of Filipino Americans from 200,000 in 1965 to over 1,400,000 by 1990. Women now predominate among the immigrants, some to join their husbands, but most because there are now more employment opportunities for women than men, especially as nurses. The largest Filipino American **communities** are found in **California** (52 percent) and **Hawai'i** (12 percent), but they have also spread out to the **Midwest** and the East Coast. Most reside in metropolitan areas, including, for example, Manila Town in **Los Angeles, CA** and middle-class enclaves like Daly City near **San Francisco, CA**.

Filipinos, despite their long presence in the US have a muted media exposure in comparison with other Asian groups. By contrast, the US has become a central locus of Filipino life and identity in the works of Filipino novelists such as N.V.M. Gonzalez and Jessica Hagedorn.

Further reading

(1986–7) "Filipinos in American Life," *Amerasia Journal* 13(1), Los Angeles: Asian American Studies Center, UCLA.

Hing, B.O. (1993) *Making and Remaking Asian American Through Immigration Policy, 1850–1990*, Stanford: Stanford University Press.

Root, M. (ed.) (1997) *Filipino Americans: Transformation and Identity*, Thousand Oaks: Sage.

CINDY WONG

film *see* Hollywood and various genres – documentary; independent films/videos; road movies, etc.

film criticism/theory

Before James Agee's tenure as film critic for *The Nation* and *Time* from 1941–8, American film criticism was rarely taken seriously. Agee's incisive reviews paved the way for the most significant journalistic critics of the postwar era – Manny Farber, Andrew Sarris and Pauline Kael.

While Agee's literary sensibility enlivened his work, the more idiosyncratic Farber brought a painter's eye and a superb command of the American vernacular to his quirky assessments of everything from neglected "B-movies" to the experimental films of Michael Snow. Active from the 1940s through the 1970s, Farber is probably best known for his distinction between "white elephant art" – prestigious, but empty and self-important films – and "termite art" – unpretentious movies redeemed by their low-key stylistic innovations.

Sarris and Kael were the dominant critical voices of the 1960s, and both writers attracted numerous disciples and imitators. Sarris' *The American Cinema* proposed an American version of the highly polemical auteurism of *Cahiers du Cinéma*. His elaborate rankings of American **directors**, which he only half-ironically labeled his pantheon, proved extremely controversial. Kael demolished Sarris' auteurism in a characteristically acerbic article entitled "Circles and Squares." Famously

hostile to theoretical generalities (her critique of Sarris included the assertion that "film aesthetics as a distinct, specialized field is a bad joke"), Kael favored intuitive, visceral evaluations of movies and was praised for her slangy, wise-cracking prose.

By the 1970s, academic theorists rejected the impressionistic, relatively apolitical criticism of Kael and Sarris. *Cineaste* and *Jump Cut*, leftist film journals radicalized by the antiwar movement and the **Civil Rights movement**, published translations of European theorists such as Adorno and Horkheimer, while devoting considerable space to third-world films and radical documentaries ignored by mainstream critics. While Kael boasted that she never saw a film more than once, American academics, under the sway of semioticians like Christian Metz, favored meticulous textual analysis.

The impact of the academic engagement with European theory was particularly profound in feminist circles, and a journal such as the Berkeley-based *Camera Obscura* synthesized post-structuralist analysis and second-wave feminism's critique of male ideology. *Camera Obscura* theorists deployed the work of Jacques Lacan and Louis Althusser (especially as filtered through the work of French film-theorist Raymond Bellour) to claim that most **Hollywood** narratives were animated by an oedipal impetus that reinforced patriarchal attitudes. Subsequent feminist theorists paid more attention to the role of the female spectator; Mary Ann Doane and Tania Modleski, for example, challenged the view that women were incapable of deriving some form of pleasure from the male-dominated commercial cinema.

The penchant for occasionally hermetic "grand theory," which reached its zenith during the 1970s, inspired an inevitable backlash. The 1980s marked a revival of historical criticism informed by empirical research – David Bordwell, Kristin Thompson and Janet Staiger's delineation of what they termed the "classical Hollywood cinema" is a paradigmatic example. Their emphasis on normative elements in prototypical Hollywood films, particularly an ingrained tendency to foreground characters as "causal agents," set the stage for publications advocating cognitive theory as an alternative to semiotics by Bordwell and his colleague Noel Carroll. Cognitivism aligned formalist analysis with an interest in the vicissitudes of human perception, but, as Robert Stam points out, the cognitivist agenda – despite its rhetoric – is not always antithetical to semiotics or psycho-analytic theory.

By the 1990s, burgeoning interests in **multi-culturalism**, postcolonial theory and **queer** theory infused new life into film studies. These disparate, although undeniably related theoretical strands, derived sustenance from broader tendencies in **cultural studies** that emphasized popular art instead of high culture. Multiculturalists and queer theorists nevertheless retained much of the skepticism concerning the "dominant culture" which inspired the New Left.

Multicultural film theory moved quickly from an earlier generation's preoccupation with "negative images" of **African Americans**, **Latinos** and **Asian Americans** to a more nuanced critique of how Eurocentric assumptions permeate popular culture, as well as a parallel exploration of how alternative cinematic practices can offer an anti-dote. Post-colonial theory was more concerned with the intersection of **race** and film in the "Diaspora" – the terrain where exiled Africans, Asians and Latin Americans created what was termed a "hybridized" cinema in the West. Post-colonial theory was unquestionably indebted to the radical assault on Eurocentrism outlined by Edward **Said** in *Orientalism* (1978). Yet Ella Shohat argued that postcolonial theorists, in their zeal to transcend the Third Worldism of the **Cold War**, ignored the fact that the ravages of colonialism have not disappeared.

Queer theory mirrors many of the tensions and contradictions that inform multicultural and post-colonial theory. Cinematic queer theorists, unlike an earlier generation of gays and lesbians, were equally disinclined to promote politically correct "positive images." Prominent queer theorists such as Alexander Doty championed the decidedly "incorrect" images that fueled the "New Queer Cinema" and dissected "queerness" in heterosexual entertainers like Jack Benny.

Although the chasm between popular film criticism and academic theory often seems un-bridgeable, a handful of film reviewers – Jonathan Rosenbaum, B. Ruby Rich and J. Hoberman –

encouraged a dialogue between film journalism and academic film theory during the 1990s.

Further reading

Cook, P. and Bernink, M. (eds) (1999) *The Cinema Book*, London: British Film Institute.
Farber, M. (1998) *Negative Space*, New York: Da Capo.
Hill, J. and Gibson, P. (eds) (1998) *The Oxford Guide to Film Studies*, Oxford: Oxford University.
Stam, R. (2000) *Film Theory*, Malden: Blackwell Publishers.

RICHARD PORTON

film festivals

The first US-based international film festival was launched in **San Francisco, CA** in 1956, twenty-four years after Mussolini endorsed the first of its kind in Venice. Today, more than 100 film festivals run from January to December every year, from Park City, Utah, to **Houston**, to **New York** City, to Sarasota. Some festivals, like Sundance and WorldFest Houston, attract a great deal of attention. Others specialize in formats such as **animation** and documentary, or films about Native Americans, gays and lesbians, **Asian Americans**, **Latinos**, **African Americans**, Underground issues, **children**, ethnography, women's issues and many other issues.

America lagged behind Europe in launching film festivals in the 1950s because of **Hollywood**. The all-powerful studios did not want to supply many films to European festivals, diminishing American exposure. Furthermore, film festivals have been showplaces for art films. Early Hollywood had no interest in mixing commerce with art, while many Europeans did not find Hollywood films worthy of their attention. Not until the breakdown of the studio system and the development of independent films would world film festivals start to value American products. At the same time, more and more festivals sprang up in the US to showcase the variety of American productions (including studios).

The second major US festival was launched in New York in 1963, when foreign film-going was in vogue as a highbrow cultural activity; it landed the unknown Roman Polanski on the cover of *Time*. By the early twenty-first century, the festival in New York, with its limited number (twenty-five) of films shown, is no longer as important; many of its films already have distributors lined up. Film festivals, in the latter part of the twentieth century, have been important outlets for **independent films**, making these films as well as their film-makers known to the critic and the public, and thus creating a marketplace.

In many ways, successful independent films and the film festivals that promote them benefit each other. *Sex, Lies, and Videotape*, with a $1 million budget, won the Audience Prize at Sundance in 1989. It was then picked up by Miramax and grossed $7 million. Since then, Sundance (founded in 1981 by Robert **Redford**) has become the premier film festival in the US for both "Hollywood types" and aspiring independent **producers/directors** who brave the cold in Park City, Utah. Sundance has promoted Native American film and has also established an Independent Film Archive at the University of Southern California. An alternative to Sundance, Slamdance, established in 1995, shows films rejected by Sundance.

Some cities use film festivals to attract visitors and to promote the image of the city, like the Nortel Palm Spring International Film Festival (started by the late Sonny Bono, a former entertainer and mayor of Palm Springs) or the French Film Festival in Sarasota, Florida. Other film festivals focus on distribution, like the American Film Market in Santa Monica, California, which screens over 600 films in nine days. This is a prime distribution event for English-language films, including such hits as *Silence of the Lambs*.

Yet film festivals can be small and less mainstream. Nextframe, for example, is a student film and video festival organized by Temple University in Philadelphia. The San Francisco International Gay and Lesbian Film Festival has just finished its twenty-three-year run, obviously focusing on **queer** cinema. Resfest Digital Film Festival is devoted to the exploration of digital form in film. The Chicago Underground Film Festival only accepts films with a budget below $1,000 per minute.

See also: film noir

CINDY WONG

film noir

Although French critics coined the epithet "black film," film noir represents a unique, indigenous American genre. Emerging after the Second World War, noir's images and plots swirled with moral ambiguity, skewed destinies and fractured relationships: inverting the American dream. Urban rather than suburban, sensual rather than domestic, driven by fate rather than any bright future, they spoke of postwar changes, nuclear threats and McCarthyite paranoia.

While underworld films had appeared in the 1930s, noir really erupted in the 1940s, drawing initially on hard-bitten mystery writers like Dashiell Hammett (*The Maltese Falcon*, 1941), Raymond Chandler and James M. Cain (screenplay and original novel for *Double Indemnity*, 1944). Noir was especially identified with RKO, although other companies like Paramount (*Double Indemnity*) and United Artists (*D.O.A.*, 1949) produced classic examples. As Senator **McCarthy** evoked the Red specter abroad and at home, production swelled in the 1950s, surviving the dismantling of the studio system. Production diminished rapidly with changing domestic and foreign concerns of the 1960s: *Manchurian Candidate* (1962) was withdrawn from circulation because of the dark shades it cast on the **Kennedy** assassination. Noir also lost to color and new marketing techniques as movies competed with the sunnier worlds of **television**.

The characteristic visual style of film noir relied on high contrasts in black and white, using night and shadows as primary elements. Camera angles were also less "neutral" than in Hollywood cinema: directing and yet disorienting the viewer. Frames were shattered by intervening objects, and characters were seen only in harsh light from the side or in shadows. Plots, driven by fate rather than logic, were morality plays rather than cogent narratives.

Film noir was also highly urban, underscoring the economic and moral tensions of the postwar city. Warehouses, **waterfronts**, nightclubs and dangerous streets set the stage, although **directors** also used monumental **architecture** like **train** stations, skyscrapers and bridges. **New York** City, NY, **Chicago, IL**, and **Los Angeles, CA** became key noir cities, while "sunny sites" like amusement parks (*Strangers on a Train*, 1951) or California beaches took on destructive meanings (*Kiss Me Deadly*, 1955).

Women evidenced new power in film noir. While often duplicitous or even villainous, they moved the action along at the expense of men who were lost, confused or ignorant (Barbara Stanwyck versus Fred MacMurray in *Double Indemnity*). The femme fatale's slinky costumes, posture and inevitable cigarette identified her as openly sexual – the antithesis of the bright, cheerful suburban housewife. Men, by contrast, were baggy-suited detectives, reporters, lawyers, insurance agents or policemen – trapped and destroyed rather than liberated.

Although film noir is identified with B-movies, Orson **Welles** produced one of the last great noir films in *Touch of Evil* (1958), while **Hitchcock** shared elements of noir style. Moreover, noir continues to fascinate audiences and film-makers as diverse as Godard, John Woo and Wim Wenders. Both the style and the moral ambiguity of noir are used in later American movies like *Chinatown* (1974), *Blade Runner* (1982) and *L.A. Confidential* (1997).

See also: Ellroy, James

Further reading

Kaplan, E. (ed.) (1980) *Women in Film Noir*, New York: Limelight (provides interesting gender perspectives).
Silver, A. and Ursini, J. (eds) (1996) *Film Noir Reader*, London: BFI.

GARY McDONOGH
CINDY WONG

financial aid

Intended to offer a greater range of students access to various educational options, financial aid to schools and students comes in several forms. **Private schools** are maintained primarily by high tuition rates, but many private schools have endowments which allow them to offer partial or complete financial support to some of their students.

Public school education from **kindergarten** through 12th grade is free to students, and funding sources include revenues generated from local property **taxes**, allocations from the state based on levels of poverty, and monies from the federal government, usually in the form of grants for special needs. The Elementary and Secondary Education Act of 1965 included titles aimed at enhancing educational opportunities for "under-privileged" **children**, including Title I, which provides funds for the improvement of educational programs for students identified as educationally "at risk."

While K-12 public education is free, post-secondary education is not, and there is a range of financial aid possibilities available to students wishing to attend both public and private institutions beyond the **high-school** level. Three major financial aid sources are **college** scholarship money, drawn from endowments; grants or aid, which are a variation of loans with low to no interest; and work-study money from the Department of Labor, including Pell grants and Stafford loans. Application for aid is made through the colleges, each of which receives a particular allocation of loan money, and colleges must adhere to various guidelines by which federal money is allocated and recipients selected.

ALISON COOK-SATHER

Fire Island

A barrier island, accessible only by boat, 2 hours east of **New York** City. With no roads, Fire Island's seventeen **communities** each have distinctive identities. Remoteness and isolation, notably, made Cherry Grove the world's earliest predominantly gay town from the 1930s onwards. Cherry Grove and neighboring Fire Island Pines are internationally famous summer destinations for gay and lesbian residents and visitors. In the 1960s, Fire Islanders helped create the Fire Island National Seashore **national park**, stopping developers who hoped to build a **highway**. This helped preserve the unique and remote seaside blend of natural resources and residential communities.

MARC L. OSTFIELD

First Amendment *see* Bill of Rights

First Ladies

The wife of the president occupies a central but largely undefined role beyond ceremonial duties and expectations of help in campaigning, outreach and family life. Each First Lady has imposed her own stamp upon the role. In the late twentieth century many, especially **Republicans**, appeared feminine, dutiful wives in their public persona. Others have brought more extensive questions and changes to the White House, evoking both admiration and rejection. Their iconic status is memorialized in a **Smithsonian Institution** exhibit of First Ladies in characteristic gowns.

Anna Eleanor **Roosevelt** (1884–1962), for example, proved an outspoken liberal during her husband's four terms and afterwards, when she remained active in the **Democratic Party** and international affairs. This evoked both devotion and hatred that often divided along political and social lines. Her successors, Democrat Elizabeth Virginia Wallace ("Bess") Truman (1885–1982) and Republican Mamie Geneva Dowd Eisenhower (1896–1979), took on more typically domestic roles in the 1950s, embodying small-town, **Midwestern** values; vice-presidential candidate wife Patricia Ryan Nixon (1912–93) also symbolized these values when her husband refuted influence-peddling charges by referring to her plain cloth coat. While Mrs Nixon would later become a protector in her husband's scandal-ridden administration, Jacqueline Lee Bouvier Kennedy **Onassis** (1929–94) brought youth (aged thirty-one), beauty, style and patrician charm to her husband's brief Democratic presidency and became a beloved symbol as widow and mother after his death. She also made the role of First Lady more publicly active in terms of restoration of the White House

and support for the Arts. Her cosmopolitan charm on a state visit to Paris led her husband to quip that he was the man who had accompanied Jackie to France.

After **Kennedy**'s assassination, Democrat Claudia Taylor "Lady Bird" Johnson (1912–) promoted local and national beautification. Similarly, after **Nixon**'s resignation, another Republican wife, Elizabeth Bloomer "Betty" Ford (1918–), restored light to White House life. She also became a mentor in discussing her battles with **cancer** and drug and **alcohol** dependency, which led to the formation of the Betty Ford Clinic.

In the 1970s, Democratic wife Rosalyn Smith Carter (1927–) established a more "hands-on" position in government, attending Cabinet meetings and touring internationally, which led to accusations of interference that also plagued her Republican successor, Nancy Davis Reagan (1923–). Reagan used her position to campaign against drugs ("Just Say No!"); her love of designer **clothes**, wealthy friends, astrology and her influence on her husband were all attacked by critics. Barbara Pierce **Bush** (1925–), although devoted to literacy campaigns, also restored domesticity to the White House.

The last First Lady of the millennium, Hillary Rodham Clinton, revived many of Eleanor Roosevelt's liberal public roles – and vicious criticisms. Her search for a balance between feminist independence and American expectations of wives and mothers has been evident in changes of style and presentations of self. With her intelligence, legal background and drive, she initially appeared as a "partner" in the administration, notably in **healthcare reform**, but galvanized hatred among conservatives for this and other policy and personal issues. Public sympathy for her grew during the **impeachment** procedures. In 2000 she moved out of the White House to pursue her senatorial bid in New York, an independent career no former First Lady has ever attempted within her political marriage. Whether she marks a new role model for the First Lady will be tested by future candidates and perhaps by the "first man" to shape this public/private role.

GARY McDONOGH

fishing, commercial and angling

Commercial fishing in the United States, as worldwide, has been affected by environmental degradation. The main source of this degradation since the 1970s has been over-fishing by fleets of vessels competing in a very lucrative market. According to the National Marine Fisheries Service, American fishing vessels caught 9.5 billion pounds of fish and shellfish in 1991, worth about $3.3 billion. This was double the amount of fish caught in 1970. Generally, American fishermen have caught Alaskan pollock, menhaden, salmon, crab and cod, with **Alaska** dominating the industry, followed by the **Texas**/Gulf and Chesapeake regions. American consumers' constant demand for shrimp, however, has led to a large fisheries trade deficit.

The reduced harvests that have resulted from the depletion of numerous fish species have only exacerbated the problem in the short term as increased prices for fish have made competition more intense. In the long term, livelihoods are threatened and whole fishing towns have been hit by widespread unemployment. In addition, the need both to reduce costs (sometimes in the area of safety procedures) and to locate harvests at a greater distance from the shore has made work – for those who are able to find it – more dangerous. In many instances, the vulnerability of old fishing populations has enabled new immigrants to establish their own fishing vessels, though the continued deterioration of the harvests makes this only a short-term replacement.

Attempts to control the amount harvested have had significant consequences in international relations and in relations among social groups within the United States. The Japanese have often resisted American attempts to limit the amount of their catches, leading to friction between the two nations. Within the United States, **American Indian** fishing rights have been established by treaties and so cannot be challenged or altered according to environmental exigencies. For example, whaling remains legal for **American Indian** tribes on the west coast, while for other fishermen there are strict prohibitions in place. However, the traditional whaling methods used by **American Indians** limit the number of whales that they can catch.

Meanwhile, angling is the second most popular recreation in the United States behind **swimming**. An estimated 50 million Americans participate in the sport, 69 percent of them men. The sport is controlled by the states, which set the rules and regulations and give licenses to anglers to fish. Thirty-four million such licenses were given in 1994. But, before assuming that widespread eradication of fishing populations is occurring in the streams and ponds of the United States, it should be remembered that it is estimated that 90 percent of the fish are caught by only 10 percent of the anglers. This suggests that most anglers have little clue about what they are doing, are quite possibly motivated by other things about the recreation besides the catch alone (a suntan and a snooze) and perhaps would not enjoy it much if they caught fish too frequently.

Environmental issues also affect fishing significantly. During much of the twentieth century, rivers around the country were so polluted as a result of untreated industrial waste flowing into them that they were almost completely bereft of fish. With the intervention of the **Environmental Protection Agency** and the growing concern over the environment as a political issue, many states have taken initiatives to clean up rivers and other waterways. Many such bodies of water are now seeing the reappearance of fish populations that have not been seen for decades.

In addition to pollution, global warming and long hot summers in many parts of the US have altered the conditions for anglers. In many ponds, streams and rivers dead fish have been found in the middle of each summer floating on top of algae. Dry weather and heat contribute to the growth of such algae, which then consume the oxygen in the water and cause the fish to suffocate. Where this is not the case, the warm water leads fish like carp and striped bass to head for cooler, fast-moving streams that are more difficult for the angler to master, or for deeper spots in lakes and streams where they are beyond the reach of the anglers' lures. In other words, the fish can adapt to the changing weather better than the anglers, who are increasingly left with little more than a cancerous sunburn on the embankment.

ROBERT GREGG

Fitzgerald, Ella

b. 1918; d. 1996

Dubbed "The First Lady of Song," Ella Fitzgerald's musical career spanned almost sixty years and extended to forays into movies and **television**. In 1934 she won an amateur contest at the Apollo that led to her 1935 recording debut with the Chick Webb orchestra. In 1938 a swinging adaptation of the old nursery rhyme, "A Tisket, A Tasket," was her first commercial success. In the late 1950s, she recorded with Louis **Armstrong** and Duke Ellington. The first black woman ever awarded a Grammy, Fitzgerald went on to win twelve more.

COURTNEY BENNETT

five and dimes

Typical **Main Street** emporia, offering cheap notions, cosmetics and gifts – the name referred to the initial prices. F.W. Woolworth (founded in Lancaster, Pennsylvania in 1879) later constructed a skyscraper in **New York** and claimed to be the largest retailer in the world, while Kresge, McCrory's and others were immortalized in songs and movies. In the 1950s, Southern "five-and-tens" became sites of **civil-rights** battles when blacks fought to integrate their lunch-counters. In the 1960s, these spun off discount retailers Woolco and K-Mart, which by the 1980s effectively overwhelmed their parents and eventually even replaced them on downtown avenues.

See also: consumerism

GARY McDONOGH

flea markets *see* yard sales/flea markets/ consignments

Florida

Mild climate and more than 1,200 miles of coastline have been the impetus of steady population growth for the Sunshine State since the Second World War. During the war, Florida thrived economically as a major military training area. Needed infrastructure supporting rapid postwar growth was thus in place. Exposure of servicemen to the area as well as the inviting climate made Florida a haven for retirees and winter residents, swelling sizes of some cities tremendously during the "season" (winter months in south Florida and during the fall in northern Florida). Year round nearly 20 percent of visitors are attracted by **Disneyworld** alone. Residents such as John and Mabel Ringling, Ernest **Hemingway**, Tennessee **Williams** and Jack **Kerouac** were among those lured to Florida for its climate and natural beauty. Migrant workers also increase local populations as they follow harvesting cycles. **Tourism**, citrus, cattle and phosphorus are currently at the base of Florida's economic development, though film is becoming important.

African Americans such as Mary McLeod Bethune played a significant role in shaping Florida's cultural and economic identity, as chronicled in the more than 141 sites listed for the Florida Black Heritage Trail. Native Americans are also prominent. **Cuban Americans** and **Haitian Americans** now constitute a significant proportion of the populations in major growth centers, contributing unique cultural influences to areas such as **Miami, FL** (Little Havana) and Tampa (Ybor City).

Florida is also well known for its unique natural beauty, which is well illustrated through writings of Marjorie Stoneman Douglas (*The River of Grass*), William Bartram (*Travels*; naturalist art also displayed in the British Museum) and Marjorie Rawlings (*The Yearling*), as well as Miccosukee and Seminole Indian art and numerous roadside **folk artists** such as E.B. Ott and Ruby Williams. Zora Neale Hurston (*Of Mules and Men*) described not only the rich environment of rural Florida, but also provided insight into the struggles of people to coexist in Florida's subtropical environment. Environment is also a strong feature in works of John MacDonald (Travis McGee series) and science-fiction writer Kate Wilhelm. Florida's Keys and sunsets are postcard symbols for the state.

In the 1950s and 1960s, Florida achieved prominence in the glory days of **NASA**. Climate played a role in the selection of Cape Canaveral as a primary US spaceport. Though hurricanes and lightning are common, the strategic location for tracking as well as the generally good weather have made the Cape the primary shuttle launch/ recovery site. The spaceport spurred economic growth and sparked an educational boom in Florida. Today, the extensive network of **community colleges**, private **colleges** state universities (ten with the newest opening its doors in 1997) leaves no Floridian more than an hour from access to higher education.

The Museum of Florida History, opened in 1977 in Tallahassee, provides a glimpse into the rich past and present of Florida.

See also: museums

Further reading

Downs, D. (1995) *Art of the Florida Seminole and Miccosukee Indians*, Gainesville: University Press of Florida.

Gannon, M. (ed.) (1996) *The New History of Florida*, Gainesville: University Press of Florida.

SANDRA GILCHRIST

flower power

Slogan of 1960s **hippie** changes, evoking color, peace and creativity as well as any reference to nature. Like other motifs and slogans of the period – "Summer of Love," "groovy," "psychedelic," etc. – it has become a period marker for nostalgic media. Nonetheless, the vivid image of flowers inserted into gun barrels of this period was recreated in 1999 protests against the World Trade Organization meetings in **Seattle, WA**.

GARY McDONOGH

folk art

Several distinctions should be made between folk art and the more familiar high art, the art of the masters and of most museums. In contrast to the materials, practices and intentions of high art, folk art makes use of common materials, cheap and readily available, such as those employed by Grandma Moses, who used house paint on Masonite to portray scenes of rural New York State. The creative act itself is usually self-taught, without the benefit of allegiance to or education in a particular school or movement. The intentions of folk art, rather than to express universal concepts or use broad, culturally recognizable imagery, are highly personal and generally concentrate on topics of regional interest. Folk art usually finds its voice through an intensely individual expression.

A further distinction should be made between folk art and the closely associated primitive art (the product of so-called "primitive" societies, such as the tribal cultures of sub-Saharan Africa and Australian Aborigines) and popular art (art produced for a mass audience). Though often lumped together, folk art is generally the product of the rural environment of an industrialized society, and, rather than being mass produced for a broad popular audience, it is often unique in production and values. These classifications are often lumped together under the general heading of "primitivism," denoting a naive expression on topics of limited appeal.

Folk art can be differentiated from folk craft in that the latter is the commercial production of a traditional form of hand manufacturing, such as quilting or basket weaving.

JIM WATKINS

folklore

The term "folklore" has somewhat different connotations in popular and professional usages. Most Americans generally understand folklore to refer to traditional narratives, beliefs or practices, often transmitted orally, which have no basis in truth, and "the folk" themselves are believed to be non- or preliterate; yet this is not the case. This notion has its roots in the antiquarian scholarship of the eighteenth and nineteenth century, influenced by theories of Romantic or cultural nationalism, where conceptions of "the folk" were equated with European peasant cultures, which scholars believed held the distinctive "folk souls" of each nation. Early American folklore research concentrated on marginalized groups within

American society. Thus, "folklore" was the preserve of **African Americans**, recent immigrant groups and Southern Appalachians, who were at that time perceived as the earliest "white indigenous" American peoples. Early American folklorists collected tales, beliefs and songs, often looking for "survivals" from the parent African or European culture. Later, with the rise of trade-union activism in the 1920s and 1930s, "the folk" expanded to include the working classes. "Folk music" was then not confined to Euro-originated ballads and African American musics, but also became more widely applicable to workers' music and, later, other protest music. **Folk art** was similarly a genre of preservation of memories (although it later became a hot commodity in more sophisticated urban galleries and auctions as well).

In the 1960s, the field of folklore in the United States shifted dramatically in terms of theory and subject matter. Richard Dorson was one of the first scholars to champion folklore as a modern academic discipline distinct from either literary studies or **anthropology**, with comparative ethnographic and archival methodologies at its heart. Folklorists then began to lessen the emphasis on survivals and to explore wider aspects of behavior, communication and the relationship of folklore and tradition to society within a more pluralistic paradigm. The result of this was not only an expansion of the subject matter that folklorists researched, but also a new conceptualization of that "the folk" actually were. Rather than only representing the more marginalized groups within a society, the folk became essentially any subgroup who demonstrated stylized, distinctive cultural forms, ranging from the **family** to the workplace. Thus, everyone is actually a member of a variety of folk groups. American folklorists also began researching urban cultures and exploring the role of technology and **mass media** on traditions and tradition formation. As a result, categories such as "Xerox lore" and "urban legend" have become fruitful areas of study. In the twentieth century, American folklorists engaged with a very wide range of material. Although "folklore" may imply to some an emphasis on narrative or belief, the field comprises a number of different artistic genres, including **dance**, **food**, speech narrative, festival, music, art, ritual, medicine and **religion**.

Folklorists also research occupational and business culture, **tourism** and all aspects of popular culture.

A new emphasis on multiculturalism and the shift of the model of American cultures from "melting-pot" to "mosaic" has resulted in an increased public interest in folklore in the 1990s. Since the 1930s when the federally funded Workers Education Administration hired folklorists to collect traditions from various cultural groups in the United States, there has been a close association between folklore, folklorists and public bodies. Many states have folklore commissions that hire folklorists to identify distinctive **communities** and individual artists, and then help to educate the public about their work. Folklorists often work with **museums**, festival organizers and, increasingly, with tourism officials to promote and raise awareness of various cultural traditions. Perhaps the most well-known example of public folklore display in the United States is the annual **Smithsonian** Festival of American Folklife, which each year showcases various traditions and practices of a particular state. In addition to public-sector and arts organizations, some folklorists also work in the private sector, assisting in inter-office communications and diversity training.

Further reading

Brunvand, J. (1996) *American Folklore*, New York: Garland.

Dorson, R. (1976) *Folklore and Fakelore*, Cambridge, MA: Harvard.

Zeitlin, S., Kotkin, A. and Baker, H. (1982) *A Celebration of American Family Folklore: Tales and Traditions from the Smithsonian Collection*, New York: Pantheon.

AMY HALE

folk medicine/herbalists

Folk medicine is usually defined as those medical beliefs and practices that come from "indigenous" cultures (for example, Native Americans), or treatments and therapies learned from parents and grandparents in the guise of home remedies. Herbalists offer plant medicines often thought to be milder and safer than chemical pharmaceuticals. The increasing interest in folk medicine and medicinal herbs and plants (phytopharmaceuticals) represents not only widespread displeasure with "biomedicine" in the United States, but also a heightened concern over the health consequences of life in a modern, technological society. Folk medicine and herbalists are seen as medical practices that reproduce healing processes found in nature.

See also: alternative medicine

Further reading

Hand, W.D. (1980) *Magical Medicine*, Berkeley: University of California.
Snow, L.F. (1993) *Walkin' over Medicine*, Boulder: Westview Press.
Risse, G.B., Numbers, R.L. and Leavitt, J.W. (eds) (1977) *Medicine Without Doctors*, New York: Science History Publications.
Tyler, V. (1993) *The Honest Herbal*, Binghamton: The Haworth Press.

STEVE FERZACCA

folk music

"Folk music" is a general, and often rather vague, term used to describe the oral musical traditions of rurally based **communities** in Europe and America. Since the 1960s, with the growth of the music industry, "folk" has also come to mean a genre within popular music: it usually designates a type of music which aspires to certain perceived virtues in the tradition, such as singers who can perform in communal situations without a great deal of technical equipment, songs with a social message, and so on. More recently, the term "roots music" has begun to replace "folk," reflecting the marketing of ethnic musics, which began in the 1980s, from around the world.

Broadly speaking, until the middle of the twentieth century, there were isolated farming communities in Europe and America that continued to sing and play a more or less fixed repertoire of ballads, songs and tunes handed down orally over generations. The advent of the Industrial Revolution in the eighteenth century fragmented these communities, first in Britain and later in the US. As agricultural workers migrated to the cities to find work in factories, other forms of entertainment, such as (in Britain) the music hall, superseded the old songs, stories and ritual celebrations of the countryside.

At the turn of the nineteenth century, enterprising scholars, musicologists and collectors like Cecil Sharp, Percy Grainger and Francis J. Child traveled to areas such as the Scottish highlands and the Appalachian mountains, where the old ways of life still persisted, writing down and recording the last remnants of this rich musical culture. However, the "revivalists," as they were called, tended to romanticize certain aspects of the culture, seeing it somewhat mystically as the collective art of the "folk," instead of what it was: a hybrid music, some of it brought in by gypsies from other parts of the world, some of it composed as early as the fifteenth century by hack writers and sold as broadside ballads (the equivalent of **tabloids**) in the streets and markets of cities and towns.

During the 1930s and 1940s, collectors like Alan Lomax traveled across America, visiting singers in Pentecostal churches, penitentiaries and cotton fields, and recording them for the **Library of Congress**. Some singers, such as Leadbelly, had a vast repertoire, and Lomax gradually pieced together a collection of core songs like "Barbara Allan" and "Lord Randall," together with hundreds of variants, which now form the basis of American folk music.

As the recording industry gathered momentum, promoters like John Hammond put out records of **blues** and Negro spirituals by early stars of the vaudeville circuit such as Bessie Smith. In the wake of the Depression, Woody Guthrie initiated a politically conscious form of folk music, singing at union meetings and labor camps around the country. His songs told of the hardship and poverty he encountered; "This Land is Your Land" became a rallying call for activists, and was regarded by many as America's "alternative" national anthem. Guthrie was joined by Pete Seeger and others in a group called the Almanac Singers, who performed at strikers' demonstrations. In 1948 Seeger was blacklisted by **McCarthy**'s un-American Activities Committee, but continued to sell out concerts abroad.

During the 1950s and 1960s, the **civil-rights** movement brought black singers such as Leadbelly to the attention of a white public for the first time. The movement also produced its own stars, the greatest being Bob **Dylan**, who infused the folk tradition with new vigor and passion, rediscovering old folk songs and writing new ones in the context of America's political struggle.

By the end of the 1960s, a new breed of popular singers was emerging. The popularity of artists like Paul **Simon** and Joni Mitchell meant that any singer-songwriter with an acoustic guitar and/or a social message was now dubbed a "folk singer," whether or not they had any connection with the folk tradition – a situation that persists to the present day.

Folk music as a commercial style has waxed and waned. The success of the Greenwich Village scene songwriters like Fred Neil and Tim Hardin was short-lived and the troubadour tradition appeared to die out in the 1970s and 1980s, kept alive only by the efforts of mostly Texan boho songwriters like Townes Van Zandt and Butch Hancock. In the 1990s, however, a new generation once more rejected the commercial mainstream of the music business and returned to neo-folk styles. In the US, Ani DiFranco and Dar Williams have followed pioneers like Michelle Shocked, while in Britain, Billy Bragg, Kate Rusby and Eliza Carthy continue to revive the folk tradition kept alive since the 1960s by folk artists like Martin Carthy, The Watersons and June Tabor.

Further reading

Cantwell, R. (1996) *When We Were Good, The Folk Revival*, Cambridge, MA: Harvard University Press.

Harry Smith (ed.) (1997) *Anthology of American Folk Music* [sound recording], Washington, DC: Smithsonian Folkways Recordings.

CHARLOTTE GREIG

Fonda family

Hollywood dynasty chronicling changing meanings of American life and **celebrity**. Henry Fonda

(1905–82) embodied the speech and values of middle America in dramatic and comic roles on screen and stage, from *Young Mr Lincoln* (1939) and *Grapes of Wrath* (1940) through the wartime reflections of *Mr Roberts* (1955) to the aging love of *On Golden Pond* (1981), for which he won an Oscar. Henry's daughter, Jane (1937–), underwent more volatile transformations – from the sexual protégé of husband Roger Vadim in *Barbarella* (1968) to an antiwar activist, married to Tom Hayden, to a **star/producer** of exercise videos in the 1980s, and finally to the wife of media titan Ted **Turner**. Her brother Peter (1939–) became identified with the **hippie** rebellion of *Easy Rider* (1969), which he produced and starred in, only regaining stardom in the 1990s. Peter's daughter, Bridget (1964–), has established herself as a forceful female lead actor.

See also: actors

GARY McDONOGH

food

American food, long denigrated as too bland and derivative, has nonetheless spread all over the world by the early twenty-first century. Contemporary trends, however, are contradictory. While long venerating convenience and technology, other trends celebrate diversity and playful innovation or, alternatively, ideologies that severely restrict dietary choice for physical and spiritual well-being. Food producing, processing and marketing corporations have both shaped and responded to these cultural demands with an outpouring of new commodities: processed foods, new and fashionable types of restaurants, **cookbooks**, media events and **diet** programs.

Historical processes

In the early **history** of the Republic, American eating was based on English food with indigenous supplements. Except for colonial trade items (molasses, sugar and rum), most food was produced and consumed locally. Diverse regional and ethnic cuisines proliferated as new populations immigrated and new ecological zones were settled in the nineteenth century, producing creolized systems such as those in the African-influenced plantation **Southeast**, the multicultural Mississippi delta and Spanish-dominated territories of the **Southwest**. Industrialization in the nineteenth century urbanized the nation. Work moved further from **home**, changing schedules of eating and leisure. Abbreviated work meals and new venues and occasions for recreational meals developed. The development of railroads changed the scale of food production and distribution as national markets for cattle and grain emerged.

A massive wave of labor **immigration** beginning in the 1850s and accelerating between 1880 and 1920 produced **ethnic enclaves** of food producers and purveyors. Occasions for public communal eating such as local fairs, community suppers and commercial eating venues (e.g. German beer gardens in the **Midwest** and Chinese restaurants serving California miners) transformed some ethnic foods into popular mainstream items, although taste and form were modified to please a mass audience. The iconic American hot dog and hamburger entered the mass diet through this process.

In the early twentieth century, there were institutional attempts to create a national cuisine based on Anglo conformity. This was partly a response to the perceived threat to unity posed by new migrants. While immigrant **communities** adapted their eating patterns to their new settings, social workers and dieticians attempted to suppress exotic immigrant diets as unhealthy.

A desire for a standard national cuisine also reflected commercial interests involved in the rapidly expanding mass production and marketing of food. New products engendered by industrialized canning and freezing and preserving packaged cereals and grains, along with refrigerated rail cars expanded food availability. The consolidation of mass food production into conglomerate national brands (e.g. General Foods and Standard Brands) and mass warehousing (e.g. Atlantic and Pacific (A & P)) created a mass market in which producers, distributors and **advertising** media (**radio**, homemaking **magazines**) were mutually interdependent.

The first national cookbooks popularized in the 1930s such as the *Fanny Farmer, Better Homes and Gardens*, and *Good Housekeeping* cookbooks were built around the Anglo-American cooking and baking of **Northeastern** states. Central to this cuisine were meals of meat (roasts, chops and steaks), potatoes and vegetables; bland, starched cream sauces and gravies were also prevalent. This cuisine avoided the use of garlic and other spices used in new ethnic foods. For example, as commercially produced spaghetti was encouraged by the wheat industry, the tomato sauce prescribed with it was not the slow-cooked reduction of meat, vegetables and spices of genuine *ragu*, but fast-cooked and bland. At the eve of the Second World War, **ethnic food** remained largely within enclaves except for a few anglicized items with wide acceptance and localized crossovers related to intermarriage, immigrant servants and communal events.

The postwar decades

Trends in food in the 1950s and 1960s celebrated modern technology. Wartime mass feeding led to improved industrial technologies for processing food into canned, dehydrated, boneless and skinless items far removed from their natural forms. At the same time, firms' processing and marketing of food consolidated into still larger conglomerates. The interests of corporate processors in mass marketing paralleled the optimistic desire for modernity of upwardly mobile suburbanizing households.

Many of the new products merely gave the illusion of dietary innovation. Novelty in processing (frozen and dehydrated versions of ordinary foods) and packaging masked a lack of variety in content as old products were served in different shapes (sweetened cereals) and flavors (varieties of Hamburger Helpers). Magazine recipes gleaned from processor-advertisers evoked "innovation" through mixing different products from the same conglomerate. The emblem of the age, the TV dinner, enshrined the Anglo-American platter – meat, vegetables and starch covered with sauce or gravy.

As more women entered the workforce, advertisers touted convenience but also extolled the virtues of homemaking. Homemade baked goods, made easy by new mixes and refrigerated dough, symbolized this role and supported the bake-sale as the foundation of suburban community fundraising. New categories of between-meal "snack" foods also were mass produced as eating on the run proliferated.

While most food was still prepared and consumed at home, work in corporate conglomerates significantly altered the daily schedules of consumers. Workers ate food prepared and consumed outside the home in efficient cafeterias. A major expansion of eating places with take-out facilities was launched to fit the needs of **families** squeezed for time. Family-owned Chinese restaurants and **pizza** parlors moved from Chinatowns and Little Italys to newly built **middle-class** communities. Here, they supported new schedules, presenting limited "made in America" menus reflecting mainstream customer preferences. Independent **drive-in** restaurants foreshadowed the **fast-food** chain. Howard Johnsons, an early restaurant and **motel** chain designed to fit the needs of the new **automobile** traveling culture, prided itself on its standardized, predictable menu.

This period saw little change in the traditional American restaurant, in which special occasions were celebrated with long, leisurely meals. Often decorated with historical American motifs, they were evaluated in terms of cleanliness rather than cuisine.

Late twentieth century shifts

In the 1970s, eating in America became a focus for reaction to the routinization of modern life. As a major form of recreation and leisure, eating "good" food became valued as a source of pleasure worthy of major time and resource investments. Three notions of "good" eating worked with and against each other in this process. Aesthetic knowledge and taste marked **class** distinction. Diversity in foods became a way to express one's own ethnic identity or to experience pleasure in "otherness." At the same time, belief systems related to biomedicine, Asian spirituality, ecological movements and an increasing focus on the body as the "fabricated self" defined "good" through restriction and self-discipline.

Except for brief moments (late nineteenth-century Gilded Age) and exceptional groups (academics), aesthetic style and high cuisine were never important as cultural capital in America.

This changed as new professional and corporate managerial classes began to use food as a marker of distinction. Men as well as women required gastronomic knowledge when entertaining at home or selecting the right chefs and restaurants. Formal French haute cuisine was the initial standard, marked by the extraordinary success in the 1960s of Julia **Childs**' *The French Chef*, on television as well as in the **kitchen**. Upscale food magazines (*Gourmet, Bon Appetit*) disseminated the code of "good" taste.

The new gastronomic code rejected many elements of America's mass-produced, processed diet. It extolled time-consuming, handmade dishes. Authenticity and closeness to nature were exemplified by peasant dishes and rediscovered food varieties such as organ meats, root crops and traditional varieties of greens (developed by Alice Waters in Berkeley, **California**).

Authenticity did not preclude playful innovative rule bending. In the 1980s and 1990s, fluency in traditional cuisines was required of chefs, but fashion demanded creative innovation, new taste combinations which fused and made references to different styles. Food critics and writers proliferated. As the demand for fashionable food expanded, celebrity chefs opened chain restaurants. Labor-intensive cooking as a leisure-time hobby spread to a large middle-class population through an explosion of cooking classes, celebrity TV chefs and, ultimately, a food **cable** station serving a mass audience. Cookbooks became one of the major domains of publishing. The market required the constant production and packaging of new commodities.

Ethnic and regional cuisine became elevated as an antidote to modern over-processing and refining. A succession of American regional cuisines such as **Cajun**, Creole and Southwestern rose in status. Their essential elements seemed to represent an authentic, timeless past. Strong flavors like garlic and chilies found favor, and fresh spices replaced the standardized canned Americanized curry and chili powders, herbs and spices. Specialized regional cuisines from China such as Szechuan and Mandarin displaced Americanized Cantonese food. As demand for new designer food grew, new categories of broadly defined cuisines such as pan-Mediterranean, pan-Asian and pan-Latino cuisines, as well as fusions like French-Asian were constructed.

Interest in ethnic cuisine was not limited to the upscale consumer. Since the war, US discourses about national unity have shifted away from Anglo conformity towards an emphasis on roots and heritage. This was partially a result of the **civil-rights** movement, followed by **Bicentennial** celebrations of ethnic heritage. The nation was seen as a mosaic or tapestry of ethnicities, each making contributions. Foodways (unlike "moral" values or **religion**) was an unthreatening cultural domain through which to display group contributions and experience "otherness." Churches, schools and communities produced ethnic fairs and festivals at which traditional foods were exchanged. The post-1965 new immigration bringing Asian and **Latino** populations into America increased the significance of and exposure to new cuisines for a broader population.

Countercultural reactions to modernity define "good" food through restrictive rules and self-discipline as a means to take control over life. Participants in movements that resist materialism or ecological degradation may restrict their diet to natural, organically grown, unrefined foods, or vegetarian foods. Others focus on the fitness or aesthetic of the body as "a temple," clearly a major aspect of self that could be perfected by following similar diets stemming from biomedical and Asian spiritual roots. For the uncommitted public, mass food processors responded with a series of sugar- and fat-free or "lite" products which deny the need for self-discipline.

In the past two decades, the amount of food prepared and eaten outside the home has risen to 60–75 percent of total consumption. The restaurant industry is critical in cities where **tourism** is a major industry. Upscale restaurants invest significantly in ambience to enhance the total experience of eating-out events.

In the more prosaic everyday realm of eating out, regional and ethnic food icons have been commodified as mass-produced, standardized items, marketed through national and multinational fast-food chains such as Kentucky Fried Chicken, Taco Bell, Subways, Pizza Hut and Manhattan Bagels. Items often lose their essential qualities in the interests of mass sales and profit.

For example, Subways uses a softer bread roll than the signature crusty Italian bread and McDonald's develops bagel sandwiches that violate Jewish food rules by using pork-based bacon, ham and sausage mixed with dairy (cheese).

Yet, it is this corporately produced popular American food culture which is spreading to a world which is eager to consume American culture. Contemporary fast-food chains and retro 1950s Johnny Rockets hamburger outlets are ubiquitous. Ten former American diners have been set up in Europe in the past two decades. Meanwhile, Americans navigate between technologically fabricated and artisan food; snacking/grazing and leisurely recreational meals; and restricted eating for well-being versus indulgence for pleasure to show their ambivalence about modern life. Yet it is these modern products that symbolize America to the rest of the world.

Further reading

Brown, L.K. and Mussell, K. (eds) (1984) *Ethnic and Regional Food Patterns in the United States*, Knoxville: University of Tennessee.
Gabaccia, D. (1998) *We Are What We Eat*, Cambridge, MA: Harvard University.
Levenstein, H. (1993) *Paradox of Plenty*, New York: Oxford University.
Mintz, S. (1997) *Tasting Food; Tasting Freedom*, Boston: Beacon.

JUDITH GOODE

Food and Drug Administration (FDA) *see* pharmaceuticals; thalidomide

football

The National Football League (NFL) is the most popular sports league in the United States, football surpassing **baseball** in the 1970s as America's favorite spectator sport. The organization has thirty franchised teams organized into the American and National Football Conferences. These teams are separately owned, but share about three-quarters of their revenues with each other, most significant of which is the money deriving from

1998 television contracts with CBS, FOX, ABC and ESPN to the tune of nearly $18 billion over eight years.

American football developed in the middle of the nineteenth century out of rugby. The American game developed new rules at the beginning of the twentieth century ostensibly to make it safer (too many college boys were getting injured and killed), but the long-term effect of these reforms was the establishment of a game with few rivals in terms of lethalness. Football is a veritable *Rollerball* (1975), in which part of the attraction is seeing an opposing team's player spearheaded and taken out of the game.

If baseball is the game that harks back to a pre-industrial age of artisans, football embodies industrial society. No other game has achieved the time-work discipline and intense division of labor as football. In football each person is given a few specified tasks to learn by rote. Only one player combines several functions on the field – the foreman quarterback. It is his job to ensure that each player gets his production schedule and performs his task properly. The linemen will hold the opposing line, blockers will block, wide receivers will run down field, turn their heads and bodies to make a catch, run five to ten more yards (if they are lucky), and be brought crashing to the ground by several defenders. The foreman will make adjustments in the huddle, management will call in a new play from the sideline and the workers will set off to perform their tasks once more. Such a division of labor also shapes the training required to play the sport. A linebacker's job is to lift weights and eat, bulking up with the ingestion of various body-building drugs. He needs to study film of his opposing linemen to learn their moves, and he needs to learn the play book. Like an industrial worker, he will suffer the hardest knocks and will have the shortest life expectancy. Kickers, meanwhile, will strengthen their kicking legs on an adjacent field.

Football has become the mainstay of sports **television**, dwarfing all other contenders. Indeed, it is the success of football in its relationship with TV that accounts for its hold on the public attention. As a game of downs, of precision plays performed with brief intervals for reorganization, football is a very easy sport to present. The camera technician seldom has to chase after a ball in a free-flowing game. Instead, just as players are returned to positions after every play, so every camera can be redirected to its pre-assigned position. Moreover, the time between downs means that each play can be presented several times with commentary covering every minute detail.

The National Football League came into existence in 1922 around a few East Coast and **Midwest** teams – the **Washington** Redskins, Green Bay Packers, **New York** Giants, **Philadelphia** Eagles and **Chicago** Bears. The league did not attract large crowds (like college games) until it became truly national, absorbing teams established in **San Francisco, CA** and **Los Angeles, CA** in 1950, and until the success of CBS and NBC's television coverage (see **sports media**).

In 1959 a competing professional league, the American Football League, was brought into existence as a result of the efforts (supported by the ABC network) of two young Texas multi-millionaires, Lamar Hunt and Bud Adams, whose bids for franchises for their hometowns of **Dallas, TX** and **Houston** had been rejected. Although many of the teams in the AFL were not profitable, the league managed to survive long enough to threaten the NFL, until an agreement was brought about that united the leagues in 1967, and created the season finale, **Superbowl Sunday**. Since then the NFL has been able to fight off any challenges, such as that of the United States Football League in the mid-1980s, using its congressional exemption from antitrust legislation to ensure its continued monopoly.

Racial practices in football have followed a pattern more akin to **basketball** than to baseball. There are many **African American** (but few **Asian American**) athletes in the sport (over 50 percent of the players), but they still face obstacles. Often blacks have been competitive or excellent quarterbacks at the university level, only to be put at wide receiver in the professional game. The unwritten rule against selecting black quarterbacks was broken to some extent when Doug Williams led the Redskins to victory in Superbowl XXII, but Williams was sidelined a season after winning the Superbowl, something that would have been unlikely in the case of a white quarterback. Other black quarterbacks have often faced hostile home crowds, and have been traded earlier than might have been the case with their white counterparts. Likewise, there have been few black coaches in football, and men like Ray Rhodes at the Philadelphia Eagles were not given the freedom to purchase players that might have been accorded a white coach.

Injury is almost inevitable in football, if not from the common playing surface of **astroturf**, then from the fact that players wear protective padding and helmets. Whereas in the game of rugby a tackler generally pulls an opposing player down to avoid injuring him or herself, in football the aim is to knock the player down. Padding makes this possible, and injuries to the knees, which cannot be protected, are one consequence. Since games are often determined by a quarterback's efforts, he receives much of the defense's attention. Many quarterbacks, like San Francisco 49'ers' Steve Young or Denver Broncos' John Elway, have been sidelined with concussions, while others, like Green Bay Packers' Brett Favre, have had to fight addiction to the painkillers that make playing possible. There are few quarterbacks like 49'ers Joe Montana, who, in the words of a Chicago Bears linebacker, could just "get up, spit out the blood and wink at you, and say that was a great hit." The plight of the average quarterback is nicely chronicled in *North Dallas Forty* (1979).

Violence is a common feature of football, one of its objectives being to knock an opposing player out of the game even when he may not have the ball. In recent years, this violence has spread to the bleachers, though it has not reached the proportions witnessed in soccer stadiums around the world. In cities where the fans are most notorious, city administrations have decided to open courts at the stadiums so that a judge can immediately punish any violent fans. Organizations tracking cases of domestic abuse have also made claims that the highest incidence of such violence occurs on Superbowl Sunday.

Further reading:

Kaye, I.N. (1973) *Good Clean Violence*, New York: J.B. Lippincott Company.

Oriard, M. (1993) *Reading Football*, Chapel Hill: The University of North Carolina Press.

ROBERT GREGG

Forbes family/magazine

Through three successive generations, the Forbes family has sustained a financial **publishing** enterprise around the popular *Forbes* magazine. Millionaire Malcolm S. Forbes Sr., known as much for his flamboyant lifestyle as for his publishing prowess, built the magazine his father had founded in 1917 into an enduring symbol of wealth and excess, with features such as the annual list of the world's richest people. The Forbes' influence has also extended to electoral politics. Malcolm Sr. was a New Jersey State senator and ran unsuccessfully for **governor**. Malcolm (Steve) Jr. made a failed bid for the 1996 **Republican** presidential nomination, building his candidacy around demands for tax reform. He was an unsuccessful candidate again in the 2000 primaries, despite notable spending.

SARAH SMITH

Ford *see* automakers; Detroit, MI; foundations; sports utility vehicles

Ford, Gerald R.

b. 1913

Thirty-eighth **president** of the United States, the first to become so without being elected either to that office or the **vice-presidency**. A highly regarded moderate **Republican** from Michigan, he served in **Congress** for twenty-five years, first elected in 1948, and as House Minority Leader from 1965 to 1973. He was chosen by Richard **Nixon** under the terms of the 25th Amendment to replace Spiro **Agnew** (who had resigned after pleading no contest to a charge of tax evasion), and, within a year, after the **Watergate** scandal had led to Nixon's resignation, he took the oath of office as president (August 9, 1974). As president he endeavored to deal with inflation and recession, the energy crisis and a general post-Vietnam and Watergate malaise. After limited success in dealing with the economy and in negotiations on nuclear weapons with the Soviet Union, Ford lost the 1976 election to Jimmy **Carter**.

His wife, Betty (1918–), was a well-respected **First Lady**. A vocal supporter of the **Equal Rights Amendment**, she also suffered a diagnosis of breast **cancer** while in the White House and used this as a chance to educate Americans about this disease. Then, after recovering from **alcohol** dependency in 1978, she founded the Betty Ford Center in 1982, which is now considered the leading treatment facility for alcoholism and drug **addiction** (and so is frequently mentioned in the tabloid coverage of athletes, movie stars and other celebrities).

ROBERT GREGG

Ford, John

b. 1894; d. 1973

Known as the foremost director of **westerns** in **Hollywood** history, none of Ford's six Academy **Awards** for direction were for westerns. Renowned worldwide as one of America's finest cinematic storytellers, principally because of his blending of characterization, action, dialogue and landscape, Ford, who directed 125 films from 1917 to 1966, was born John Martin Feeney in Maine, and moved to Hollywood in 1914. Both lauded and criticized for his patriotism, sentimentality, pride in being **Irish American**, political conservatism, irascibility, and loyalty to friends, many of whom, like John **Wayne** and James **Stewart**, were part of his acting "family," Ford remains one of the undisputed geniuses of American narrative cinema.

THOMAS M. WILSON

foreign/art films

Hollywood has created the foreign film in the US. While European nations may bemoan the fact that 70 percent or more of films that dominate their marquees have American origins and Hollywood **blockbusters** top the charts from Hong Kong to Buenos Aires, roughly 98 percent of the films shown in the US are domestic. The remainder, then, are marked as different and specialized – in terms of content, audience and even venue. Yet audiences have developed clear expectations of classical Hollywood formulae, recognizable characters – if not **stars** – and movies in English that continually constrain the market; art films, by contrast, are subtitled rather than dubbed for mass distribution. Moreover, Hollywood has appropriated international stars and settings within its own production – whether borrowing (as in Chow Yun Fat in 1999–2000's *Anna and the King*) or remaking (*Three Men and a Baby*, 1987, remaking a 1985 French hit).

Certainly some non-American films achieve mass distribution. British films in particular share language and stars with Hollywood, have been popular for decades and are even marked with a certain epic cachet. Canadian films have been hard pressed to compete with American resources; hence, **directors** like Atom Egoyan often occupy a liminal status. In the 1980s, Hong Kong films also gained wider markets through the international stardom of Jackie Chan, although directors like John Woo and Ringo Lam have also succumbed to the budgets of Hollywood in producing American versions of style and stories – a path followed in earlier generations by directors like Josef von Sternberg, Fritz Lang and Alfred **Hitchcock**.

There are important exceptions too. Roberto Benigni's *Life is Beautiful* (1998) also received a wide distribution (as well as Oscar accolades) in both dubbed and subtitled versions. The Oscar for best foreign film (inaugurated in 1947) has recognized many major directors. Despite repeated recognition of Japanese films in the 1950s, and a few co-productions thereafter, it has also tended to reaffirm European films as art. Only one **Latin American** film has won the accolade.

The audience for "foreign films," then, is presumed to approach film with critical expertise, dedication and a seriousness that tends to preclude importation of popular romances and comedies (although **pornography** has been an importable category). For decades, this also entailed specialized publicity and venues. In fact, the art cinema has been marked by cramped quarters, alternative high culture accoutrements (expresso bars, bookshops) and an erudite dedication to film that might mix current releases with retrospectives on directors like Bergman, Kiorastami, Fellini or Kurosawa. Other films have been screened in cinema clubs, especially on college **campuses** or in major metropolitan centers. Smaller cities might have one cinema that survives on a mixture of artistic and semi-popular films. **Film festivals** also have screened works that no national distributor would risk – films that are not necessarily anti-American but are, at least, unfamiliar to the American spectator.

Some foreign films are also linked to ethnic populations in the United States. International politics – as in films from **China** or the former Soviet Union – may also support distribution. In the early twentieth century, certain populations were able to support independent theaters – like those of major Chinatowns or **Hispanic** neighborhoods; others rented halls for special showings. In an era of mass **video** and satellite **television**, this taste has been satisfied by videos available in specialty shops, grocers and other sites, as well as direct retransmission of external broadcasts. While these tend to offer more popular foreign-language films (rather than "art" films), their audiences are circumscribed. Nonetheless, Chinese theaters profited from the boom in Hong Kong films.

Meanwhile, cinema classes and critics have created an international canon of "serious" films that constitute high film culture even without box-office clout. Here, the impact of auteurs has been important in both availability and acceptance – people will watch a film by Truffaut, Saura, Wenders or Ray rather than identifying the product with a particular national origin. Overall, the equation of "foreign" and "art" excludes many popular films outside the US as it shapes the stylistic and intellectual demands imposed on American independent/artistic productions.

See also: film criticism/theory

GARY McDONOGH
CINDY WONG

foreign investment

By 1990 the market value of US direct investment abroad measured $714.1 billion compared with $530.4 billion for foreign investment in the US (Graham and Krugman 1991: 17). Instead of making products domestically and exporting them, corporations have become multinational, acquiring foreign assets with which to produce goods for sale in local markets. The United States has long been at the forefront of this movement: Coca-Cola, Nike and General Motors have contributed to the Americanization of the world by investing directly in local distribution networks. Subsidiaries, once the vehicle for tight control over foreign operations, have become more independent as firms realize the value of the cultural knowledge and skills of its foreign employees.

US firms have long sought foreign markets as growth opportunities. For example, the Big Three automakers have produced cars in Europe for decades, forcing smaller, local manufacturers to consolidate operations. Such investment has caused a backlash that includes sanctions, tariffs and public outcry against foreign "invasion" of products and ideas.

The fear of foreign cultural and even physical invasion did not hit American shores until the 1980s. While the United Kingdom and the Netherlands have long held significant US investments, it was not until a weakened dollar allowed foreign firms to acquire US assets at "fire-sale" prices that Americans took notice of the phenomenon of foreign investment and multinational corporations. Anecdotal evidence, such as Japanese purchases of cultural icons such as the Rockefeller Center by Mitsubishi and Columbia Pictures by Sony, led to fears that the US was losing its leadership role in the global economy. Ironically, the Rockefeller Center was ultimately sold at a massive loss to Mitsubishi just six years later. While Japanese companies gobbled up $57 billion in US real estate from 1987 to 1990, American firms invested more than that in other countries. Regardless, globalization is creating a reality in which Japanese firms Toyota and Honda produce identical cars whether they come off a Tokyo or **Cleveland, OH** production plant.

The fear of capital flight long led countries to place restrictions on inflows and outflows of investment and currency. Restrictions on direct foreign ownership of institutions and land, as well as limits on currency conversion are common examples. With the onslaught of technology and free-trade reforms in the late twentieth and early twenty-first centuries, most countries have accepted globalization. The General Agreement on Tariffs and Trade (GATT) provides for neutrality with respect to foreign-investment ownership. Without capital controls, domestic fiscal and monetary policies approach futility. For example, increasing domestic interest rates to combat inflation attracts foreign investment, which may fuel further inflation. The 1990s environment of "hot money" (institutions ready to divert assets at a moment's notice) requires refocused attention on capital flows. Developing countries such as India, Malaysia and **China** maintain strict controls with varying success.

Investors worldwide are realizing the need to invest globally. Americans and non-Americans alike are investing as much as 25 percent of their portfolios in foreign assets. International mutual-fund assets have mushroomed to over $400 billion. Foreign corporations, it is realized, have no specific allegiance to their country of origin, but are primarily focused on creating profits for their shareholders. This fact further dispels the fear that foreign investment will create any serious national security threats.

Further reading

Graham, E. and Krugman, P. (1991) *Foreign Direct Investment in the United States*, Washington, DC: Institute for International Economics.

MARC BALCER

foreign policy *see* thematic entry list

forests and forestry

Vast woodlands and towering trees have impressed successive generations of American explorers and pioneers, and have also provided resources for building and fuel for these settlers as they cleared forest lands for agriculture and settlement. Nevertheless, the United States remains surprisingly wooded – roughly one-third of the nation's total land surface. This entails extensive coverage in both the urban Northeast (**New England** and the **Mid-Atlantic**) and the **Pacific Northwest**, while the Great Plains have relatively minimal tree coverage. Western forests tend to be dominated by evergreens, including pines, firs, spruces and the gigantic redwoods of the Pacific Coast. Eastern forests tend to be hardwoods or mixtures of types, including the panoramas of oak, maple, beech and other trees that make autumnal leaves an event throughout New England each year.

America's diverse forests have shaped historical narratives of humans and nature, whether tales of Native Americans or heroic woodsmen like Paul Bunyan or Daniel Boone. They have also shaped American representations of landscape and are fundamental to **mass media** as diverse as *Trail of the Lonesome Pine* (1936), *Sometimes a Great Notion* (1971) and **Disney**'s *Pocahontas* (1996). They have been recognized and preserved as important components of urban **parks** and local identities, as well as beloved and highly visited **national parks** and forests from the Smoky Mountains to Yellowstone and Yosemite. Forests, for many people, *are* "nature."

In the twenty-first century, trees and forests represent not only a renewable resource, but also an expanding one. Yet, that resource is also the source of bitter fights over management and ownership of forests and parklands. These controversies often reflect differences between economic perspectives, environmental perspectives and sentimental-ideological construction of the forest. Ownership of forest lands is divided between government proprietorship, which dominates the **West** and **Alaska**, and private management. While much of this private ownership does not involve logging *per se*, large corporate owners have developed extensive single-species, regularly planted tree farms that worry environmentalists because of their lack of diversity and flexibility.

Federal forests have become controversial because of their openness to leased commercial cutting, which has meant the loss of old growth forests as wood is sold to Asian markets. As in private "tree farms," this logging can destroy

unique environments, which has pitted environmentalists and measures like the **Endangered
Species Act** against loggers and their families as
well as corporate interests, producing violent
confrontations on both sides. Various strategies of
ecological management, however, have emerged in
the Pacific Northwest to reach a compromise
between employment and environment.

Further reading

Davis, R. (1983) *Encyclopedia of American Forests and
Conservation History*, New York: MacMillan.
Bunting, R. (1997) *The Pacific Raincoast*, Lawrence:
University Press of Kansas.

GARY McDONOGH

Foster, Jodie

b. 1962

Actor and director who has brought intelligence
and disturbing psychological depth to extremely
varied roles. A child actor for **Disney**, Foster made
a startling breakthrough in 1976 as the edgy addict
in *Taxi Driver* and as a 1920s nightclub star in Alan
Parker's *Bugsy Malone*. Foster won Oscars for her
gritty portrayal of a working-class, gang-rape
victim in *The Accused* (1988) and again for her *pas
de deux* with Anthony Hopkins in *Silence of the Lambs*
(1992); she has also worked in French cinema and
with Woody **Allen**. Her directorial debut was the
1991 *Little Man Tate*, focused on the situation of a
child prodigy.

See also: directors

GARY McDONOGH

foster care

State-run system to place **children** from abusive or
otherwise damaging homes in temporary substitute
care, usually through licensed families. The foster-
care system, once seen as a partial substitute for
adoption as well as a means of protecting children,
has been accused of neglect in regulation and
reliance on financial incentives to foster parents,

resulting in cases of crowding, insecurity and sometimes abuse from foster parents which turns already
troubled children into potential drop-outs, homeless
children, runaways or criminals. Nonetheless,
roughly 500,000 children pass some time in foster
care each year while reforms move slowly ahead.

See also: home; family

GARY McDONOGH

foundations

Non-governmental and non-profit funds, usually
from a single source and administered by trustees for
various social and cultural purposes, represent a vital
feature of American postwar society. Foundations
control hundreds of billions of dollars in funds and
administer grants of more than $2 billion annually to
augment and shape programs in social welfare,
universities, **museums**, health, **education** and
other areas. The origins of these foundations can be
found in religious or charitable trusts that have
existed worldwide for millennia. They also participated in the early American nation, although few
major trusts today antedate those established by
turn-of-the-century robber barons. Their enduring
authority can be seen in new moguls of the
information age: a $5 billion gift by Bill and Melinda
Gates to their foundation in 2000 made it the largest
in the US, with assets of over $21 billion. In 1999,
there were roughly 50,000 active grant organizations
of this type; the largest 10,000 controlled $304 billion
(92.3 percent of total assets) and awarded $14.3
billion (90 percent).

In the classic pattern, rich corporations, people or
families constitute independent foundations (the
dominant structure) as a return to society or to
enhance the family and corporate image. Some of
the largest private American foundations thus bear
names associated with big businesses like Ford,
Rockefeller, Gates, Mellon, Packard, Hewlett,
Lilly, and Pew. Apart from the Gates Foundation, the
other largest foundations by assets include the Lilly
Endowment ($11.5 billion), the Ford Foundation
($9.5 billion) and the David and Lucille Packard
Foundation ($8.9 billion). Ford has been the largest
grantor, at $400 million annually, followed by the
W.K. Kellogg Foundation and Lilly; Gates and his

wife distributed $16 billion in 1999, again setting new standards. This philanthropic route was also developed in the 1990s by George Soros, Ted **Turner**, Jim Clark of Netscape and others.

Other types of foundations, including many corporate foundations, rely on continuing donations rather than endowments. Operating foundations focus on special programs, while community foundations may draw from many sources to deal with the issues of a particular locality.

These non-profit enterprises facilitate the development of social, economic, political, artistic, scientific, medical and other projects. Some foundations are general in scope while others develop special initiatives – the Spencer Foundation in Education, the John and Catherine T. MacArthur Foundation in peace, the Annenberg foundation in communication/education, etc. Education is a favorite field, directly and through institutions as well as funding academic research. Health, social and international issues are also prominent causes. Yet, foundations are not simply philanthropic. They also move the nation's cultural and social policies. Foundations, in many ways, react to certain national issues, like global warming, civic journalism, campaign finance reforms and national cultural policies, while they are also forerunners, trying to support studies to provide certain knowledge about issues and shifting national policies. Conservative foundations like the Heritage Foundation, however, promote very different agendas.

Concerns about non-profit independence demand government regulation of boards and policies. Worries range from their relations to corporations and taxes to continuing concerns about the involvement of non-profit groups with political parties.

The US government has also used the independent foundation model to promote research and the arts. The National Science Foundation, for example, was established during the **Cold War** (1950) to promote intersecting interests of scientific and technological development, science education and defense. It focuses especially on physical sciences, life sciences and engineering. It has also funded social science work, occasionally amid controversies about the implications of government funding like the scandals that highlighted misuse of anthropological data during the **Vietnam War**.

In 1965, following President **Kennedy**'s stress on American Arts, **Congress** created the National Foundation for the Arts and Humanities as another para-foundational independent agency. One section, the National Endowment for the Arts, has promoted creation of and access to art in America. Yet it has also proved a catalyst for conservatives attacking its support for controversial **performance artists** or those like Robert **Mapplethorpe** who challenged generalized norms of sexuality and **religion**. While the NEA has an independent board and head, controls on funding allow censorship and punishment to creep in. Another wing, the National Endowment for the Humanities, funds research and projects in academic arenas and museums as well as outreach programs. It has also been criticized for supposed leftism as well as academic irrelevance of projects, although it remains a major resource for scholars in its summer and long-term grants. The NFAH also includes a foundation devoted to museum services.

Further reading

Falkenstein, J. and Jacobs, D. (1999) *The Foundation Directory*, New York: The Foundation Center.

GARY McDONOGH
CINDY WONG

FOX *see* networks, television; cable television

franchises

Often taken as the demise of American identity, local and regional, franchises also represent an economic negotiation of individual aspirations and cultural expectations. Behind **McDonald's**, Holiday Inn **motel** rooms, many gas stations, camera stores, florists and weight-loss centers there is both a tested plan and an individual entrepreneur striving for success while meeting the franchiser's (and customers') demands for uniformity. Franchises offer dreams of independence and wealth, although they also may lock owners and families into work as self-exploitative and struggling **mom-and-pop stores**.

Franchising involves a "parent" company which negotiates an agreement with an individual owner to market products and services, as well as reputation. This entails both an initial fee (and establishment costs) and an ongoing relationship through royalties. Franchising also entails negotiation not only of appropriate buyers, but also of sites, localizations and business relations, which may include more direct co-ownership.

Early franchise arrangements in place by the 1920s included **automobile** dealerships, soft-drink bottlers and service stations, which accounted for 75 percent of franchise income in the 1990s. These include franchise empires of chains within chains. In the postwar period, new opportunities in **fast food** and motels, responding to new lives built around cars, **highways** and suburbia, spurred renewed interest in franchises. Franchises soon turned to cities, smaller towns and increasing diversity within shopping centers and **malls**, while Century 21, founded in 1972, has revolutionized **real-estate** sales through interconnected offices nationwide.

Franchise sales in 1999 reached $1,000 billion, and franchises employed 8 million people – as many as the automobile industry. Despite the commitments under which owners operate, however, their failure rate is significantly lower than the failure rate for independent businesses (8 percent for franchises in their first five years as opposed to 77 percent for independent businesses).

Among the most common franchises encountered by Americans are many fast-food services, convenience stores, home-care stores, motels, real estate, clothing, athletic wear, **computers** and travel. Franchises cater to varying **class** demands, although issues of racial opportunity in ownership as well as service have erupted as public issues, most notably with the food chain Denny's. This model has also allowed for both the extension of American forms and products abroad and imitation by other chains in Europe, Asia and **Latin America**.

Further reading

Ludden, L. (1999) *Franchise Opportunities Handbook*, Indianapolis: JIST.

Luxenberg, S. (1985) *Roadside Empires*, New York: Penguin.

GARY McDONOGH

Francis, Connie

b. 1938

Born Concetta Rosa Maria Franconero, this dark-haired, upbeat singer became a favorite among early 1960s youth. Her hits "Who's Sorry Now?" (1958) and "Where the Boys Are" (1960) revealed a desirous but bubbly **femininity**. She became a film **star** with the rise of 1960s **teenage**/beach films, and appeared in *Where the Boys Are* (1960), *Follow the Boys* (1963) and *Looking for Love* (1965). She won a $3 million suit in 1974 against a **motel** in one of whose rooms she had been raped; the highly publicized episode left her emotionally scarred and she put aside her career until 1993.

EDWARD MILLER

Franklin, Aretha

b. 1942

Born in Memphis, Tennessee, and raised in **Detroit, MI**, Aretha Franklin is considered the "Queen of **Soul**." Trained throughout her youth in gospel singing in church, her vocal range and abilities transcend those of most singers in the music business. She was signed to Columbia Records in 1960, but did not have her first hit until 1967. In that same year she recorded "Respect" which reached number one on the **popular music** charts, and quickly became a virtual anthem for both **Civil Rights** and **women's movements**.

Further reading

Greig, C. (1999) *Icons of Black Music*, San Diego: Thunder Bay Press.

ROBERT GREGG

fraternities and sororities

National fraternal organizations deeply associated with American college life and imagery. The first, Phi Beta Kappa, was founded in 1776 at William and Mary College in Virginia; it is now a national academic honor society. Social fraternities began in the 1820s; sororities followed in the 1850s, expanding with women's educational opportunities. **African American** fraternities and sororities began in 1906, while Latino organizations took shape in the 1970s. Over fifty national fraternities and sororities have 4 million members at US **colleges and universities**.

Fraternities and sororities function as units of socialization and **community** on the local college (chapter) level. During "rush" week, incoming students are selected and pledged; initiation rites range from humorous events to brutal hazings involving physical pain that have drawn negative publicity and university intervention. The selection process has also led to charges of elitism and discrimination.

Some fraternities and sororities offer university housing; others exist as social and service organizations charging only operating/membership fees. While the organizations argue that they are a stabilizing influence for academics and service, critics have viewed their parties as centers of alcohol and sexual excess. Hence, some colleges have banned these organizations; nevertheless, in **Ivy League** schools and state university systems, "Greek life" (from the traditional three Greek letter names of these groups) and the Pan-Hellenic Council are central to student life and organization.

Similar organizations are associated with professional career choices and academic honors within these fields, like Tau Beta Pi for engineering (founded 1885). "Greek" associations have been especially strong in the formation of the African American **middle class**; black fraternities and sororities include roughly 1 million members.

Colorful albeit exaggerated images of fraternity and sorority life – parties, camaraderie, competition – abound in teen-oriented media, including *National Lampoon's Animal House* (1978). The realities of fraternity and sorority life, however, are both more ordinary and more complex.

Further reading

Ross, L. (2000) *The Divine Nine*, New York: Kensington.

GARY McDONOGH

Frazier, E. Franklin

b. 1894; d. 1962

African American sociologist who made important contributions to understanding black experience. Frazier generally used an **assimilation** model, arguing that Africans had been stripped of their culture during the process of enslavement in Africa, the middle passage, and slavery in the Americas, and tended to see black culture negatively. *The Negro Church* (1962) was becoming more like its white counterpart, while the *Black Bourgeoisie* (1957) was characterized by people who had "escaped into a world of make-believe." Frazier's ideas were picked up by people like Daniel Patrick **Moynihan**, whose arguments about the black **family** being a "tangle of pathology" were based on *The Negro Family* (1939). Though these ideas were largely discredited as "blaming the victim" in the 1970s, they have found their way back into mainstream political discourse, especially in arguments about the **underclass** and the need for **welfare reform**.

ROBERT GREGG

freedom

Freedom, according to the philosopher Isaiah Berlin, can be thought of in a negative and a positive sense. The former, which can be traced back to the classical liberal philosophy of Bentham and Mill, is the absence of obstacles and barriers that would prevent individuals from realizing their various goals and aspirations. Here, promoting liberty is primarily a matter of removing, or at least minimizing, the constraints on what a person is allowed to do. Positive liberty, on the other hand, is a broader sense of the term, and arises from a view of the individual as having a potential that requires active assistance in order to be realized. Fostering positive liberty entails providing individuals with the goods and services that they would require in order to achieve their aspirations.

Since the Second World War, there has been a fierce ongoing debate about the proper role of institutions, both public and private, for furthering these different senses of freedom. In large part the debate has been centered on questions of negative liberty, especially with regard to the following topics: recreational drugs, **abortion**, **guns**, **gambling** and **pornography**. These issues have divided people into those who believe that the government should remove its restraints with regard to one of these issues and those who feel that, at least with regard to this particular subject, the government must impose some restriction on individual behavior in order to promote the public good. There has been a general trend towards increasing individual liberty with regard to these topics, but this has not been constant. For example, while many drug laws were liberalized in the 1970s, there was a backlash against this in the 1980s and 1990s with a large increase in federal and state penalties for drug-related activities.

The debate about positive liberty has been less prominent, but it regularly crops up. With regard to this the most significant period is clearly Lyndon **Johnson**'s "Great Society" (1963–7). This was the largest attempt, since **Roosevelt**'s New Deal, to create an active role for the state. The goal was to provide its citizens with freedom from sickness, poverty, hunger and ignorance so that they might achieve their greatest potential. Medicare, Medicaid, Head Start, public broadcasting, food stamps and many other programs were either instituted or initiated during this period. Much of the political and social momentum since then has been against this approach, although the prominence of the debate over nationalizing **healthcare** in the 1990s demonstrated that the issues are far from settled.

While the distinction between negative and positive liberty is useful, it can also be misleading as it may imply a sharp division between the two. However, what began as a struggle to achieve a greater level of negative freedom may later turn into a battle for more extensive positive freedom. For example, perhaps the most important struggle for freedom in the postwar United States was the **civil-rights** crusade. In the 1950s and 1960s, it

was initially concerned with removing the institutional barriers that had restricted minorities from voting and had radically constrained where they could live, eat, work, or attend school. Eventually, many of these obstacles against **African Americans** were eliminated through **Supreme Court** decisions, like *Brown v. Board of Education*, and federal legislation such as the **Civil Rights Act** of 1964 and the Voting Act of 1965. As these barriers were removed, however, there were others who felt that their removal alone would not be adequate in promoting genuine freedom for African Americans. They argued for a more activist role for institutions through such programs as **affirmative action** and economic opportunity zones in poorer **neighborhoods**.

RODGER JACKSON

freedom rides

First organized by **CORE** in 1961, integrated groups would travel on Greyhound **buses** from **Washington, DC** down through Alabama and Mississippi, and would refuse to conform to the segregationist practices in the bus stations regarding washroom facilities. Such practices had been outlawed for terminal accommodations associated with interstate travel by the **Supreme Court** in the 1960 decision of *Boynton v. Virginia*.

After one bus was fire bombed in Anniston, and another was attacked in Birmingham, students fresh from the lunch-counter **sit-ins** joined the rides and insisted that they continue, against the opposition of **Attorney-General** Robert **Kennedy**. Kennedy agreed to protect the riders with National Guardsmen, but many were arrested on arrival in Jackson, Mississippi.

See also: segregation

ROBERT GREGG

Freedom Summer

Led by Bob Moses of **SNCC** through the Council of Federated Projects (COFO), an umbrella group uniting Mississippi **civil-rights** organizations, the

1964 Freedom Summer was designed to send white and black students from around the country into the state to register **African Americans**. Whites responded by expanding their police forces and organizing **Ku Klux Klan** and other white supremacist organizations to meet them. Within a few days of Freedom Summer's start, three volunteers – two white people (Andrew Goodman and Micheal Schwerner) and one black person (James Chaney) – disappeared. The **FBI** discovered their bodies six weeks later buried in an earthen dam. The disappearance, discovery and revelations about Klan involvement increased media interest in COFO's work in Mississippi. This increased tensions between white and black activists, the latter having witnessed many blacks disappear previously without media attention. Registration of blacks in the state was limited, although the **Mississippi Freedom Democratic Party** grew out of the Freedom Summer.

ROBERT GREGG

Freemen

Freemen, also known as Constitutionalists, believe that white Christian males are sovereign citizens beyond the jurisdiction of governmental authority. Freemen have established their own renegade judicial system, known as common-law courts, autonomous townships and their own monetary system, which makes use of fraudulent financial instruments. They derive their beliefs from segments of the Bible, the Magna Carta, Articles of Confederation and the US Constitution. Freemen have been implicated in a variety of offenses ranging from fraud to armed robbery. In 1996 a group of Freemen and their followers were engaged in an eighty-one-day stand-off with the **FBI** in Brussett, Montana. In June 1996 the Freemen peacefully surrendered to the FBI.

BRIAN LEVIN

free speech *see* Bill of Rights; California, University, System; censorship

French Canadians *see* French in America

French in America

Although more than 10 million Americans claim French ancestry (more than Poles or Native Americans), this pales beside the claims of German and Irish ethnics. Franco-Americans are also divided by their historical experiences of coming to the US, directly or through other colonial possessions. Yet, relations of international history, culture and **class** tend to separate these immigrants from general American principles of ethnicity. Perhaps no other European group is so closely identified with its homeland rather than with an American ethnic identity.

France has a strong historical image in the US as a historic co-revolutionary ally, from Lafayette and the American Revolution to shared struggles in the World Wars. The Statue of Liberty, consummate symbol of the US is, after all, a centennial gift from France. France has also been a model of elegance for **fashion**, **architecture** and style, and an image of sensuality from Bernhardt to Bardot. While hordes of American tourists and expatriates, and mass cultural marketing – movies and **McDonald's** – may alarm French cultural critics (see **American images abroad**), the two countries maintain a close, continuing relationship on many levels which seems to overshadow the immigrant experience.

Direct migration from France to the US was also early and especially evident in the formative periods of the American Republic, when France provided leadership and service in American Catholicism and important commentaries on the American dream through De Tocqueville and Crevecouer. This migration was swamped by larger waves from other parts of Europe and later global **immigration**. French migrants (or claims to "Frenchness") are often associated with positions of education, art, fashion or other high cultural realms; this might be exemplified in Jacqueline *Bouvier* Kennedy as a public citizen of French descent. Between 1941 and 1990, however, French immigration actually surpassed legal Irish immigration.

French-American citizenship has also been constituted through secondary migrations and expansion. Early Huguenots settled in South Carolina, for example, were joined by French West

Indian planters escaping unrest in Hispaniola. **Cajuns** and **Creoles** in Louisiana, meanwhile, were incorporated into the United States through acquisition of this former French colony.

French Canadians, an ancestry claimed by 2–5 million Americans, represent a special secondary migration in many **New England** areas where families sought industrial opportunities in periods of underdevelopment in contiguous Quebec. These immigrants built strong settlements around churches and families. Other French Canadians have created more temporary "colonies" in the US around winter homes and retirement complexes in **Florida** and the **Sunbelt**.

In the late twentieth and early twenty-first centuries, France has actively promoted a pan-French identity of language and culture that often is represented through high cultural and language activities – art shows, university programs, **film festivals** or the Alliance Francaise. Yet despite this external support – or perhaps because of it – French Americans lack the cohesive identity one associates with Germans, Irish or Italians. One interesting test point for this identity, in fact, will be seen in the growth of Caribbean (Haitian) and African Francophones as American ethnics.

See also: Caribbean Americans; German Americans; Irish Americans; Italian Americans; Onassis, Jacqueline Bouvier Kennedy

Further reading

Louder, D. and Waddell, E. (1983) *French America*, Louisiana State: Baton Rouge.

GARY McDONOGH

Friedan, Betty

b. 1921

In 1963 Betty Friedan published *The Feminine Mystique*. Interviewing hundreds of American housewives and mothers, Friedan found deep dissatisfaction among many. An instant bestseller, the book sparked the modern feminist movement, premised on the notion that women are equal, socially and politically, with men. This movement spawned the **National Organization for Wo-**

men (NOW) in 1966, with Friedan as its first president, which aimed to eliminate barriers to full gender equality. Though criticized by many as appealing only to middle-class white professional women, Friedan's *Feminine Mystique* and NOW were pivotal challenges to a society premised on gender inequality.

See also: feminism; gender and sexuality

SUSAN SCHULTEN

fried chicken

Staple of the **Southern** Sunday dinner table for both blacks and whites which is served with corn bread, potatoes, gravy, boiled greens with fatback, iced tea and followed by rich pies. Recipes vary between regions and families, often incorporating differences in coating (flour, breadcrumbs, batter) and seasoning (cinnamon, red pepper, etc.). While attacked for unhealthy fat (and dehumanizing processing) and denatured in **fast-food** chains worldwide, fried chicken remains a symbol and delight of the South.

GARY McDONOGH

frisbee

A craze believed by many to have originated when Yale students began to throw upside-down **pizza** pans borrowed from a New Haven restaurant. The first plastic disks were developed by Fred Morrison and Warren Fancioni in the late 1940s. Frisbees were then mass produced in the late 1950s by the company Wham-O. As the craze grew in the 1960s, a new non-contact sport developed called "Ultimate," in which the objective is to get the frisbee into the opposing team's end zone. Ultimate is popular at the club level on most US college **campuses**.

ROBERT GREGG

frontier

Throughout the late eighteenth and nineteenth centuries the American frontier – the mobile line of settlement – moved from the Eastern Seaboard to the West Coast. In 1890 the US Census Department declared the frontier closed, but, in 1893, historian Frederick Jackson Turner argued that it continued to shape American identity. Current scholarship in Western history and American studies complicates Turner's thesis, arguing that in addition to being a site of white conquest, the frontier was a space of intercultural contact between diverse Native American groups and Europeans, Africans and Asians. The frontier has functioned powerfully as a contemporary metaphor for social and technological innovation, recalled in John F. **Kennedy**'s claims for a "new frontier," and as a mediascape in genres like the **western** and **science fiction**.

STACILEE FORD

Frost, Robert

b. 1874; d. 1963

Poet. Frost's poems of **New England**, **nature**, rural life and ordinary people constitute a beloved legacy for many Americans who memorize lyrics from "Stopping By Woods on a Snowy Evening" or "Fences" in school or remember him as a patriarchal public figure. Critics and fellow poets have underscored the complexity of these apparently effortless lines and their content, including glimpses of underlying terror which those quoting his familiar lyricism often overlook.

GARY McDONOGH

Fulbright, James William

b. 1905; d. 1995

Educator and statesman, Fulbright was president of the University of Arkansas before being elected to the Senate in 1945. He soon established the government-funded international program for the exchange of students and professors that bears his name. For three decades, Fulbright, who headed the Senate Foreign Relations Committee, was also a beacon for globalism and critical thinking in foreign affairs. In the 1950s, he opposed **McCarthyism** and, in the 1960s, also came to oppose the war in Vietnam. Among his thought-provoking writings are *The Arrogance of Power* (1967) and *The Pentagon Propaganda Machine* (1970).

GARY McDONOGH

Fuller, Richard Buckminster

b. 1885; d. 1983

Inventor, engineer and mathematician whose optimism about technology and growth made him a scientific guru of the postwar era. Nimble in combining structures and dynamics (and labeling his projects with catchy names like his Dymaxion corporation), Fuller as inventor was best known for the geodesic dome (patented 1947), which distributes stress artfully and efficiently and which was used in the striking US Pavilion for Montreal's Expo '67. He also worked with general systems theory and the applications of science and technology to world peace. *Operating Manual for Spaceship Earth* (1969) provides a strong sense of the relations of science, philosophy and global vision in his work.

GARY McDONOGH

fusion

The history of this multiplex musical category tracks an advent in American music, as well as the entanglements of a global **mass media** with local musics. Fusion as an experiment in musical aesthetics and as a marketable category of music begins as an era in the history of **jazz**. In the late 1960s, jazz musicians, pioneered by Miles **Davis** (for example his recording "Bitches Brew," 1970), combined "traditional" jazz musical forms with those from **rock** music to form jazz fusion. Rock guitarist Jimi **Hendrix** and the **R&B** funk-rock of Sly and the Family Stone had particular influence on jazz music. Throughout the 1970s, many jazz musicians continued to experiment with combinations of acoustic and electric instrumentations, or left behind the acoustic sound altogether for an amplified, electronic one. Rock rhythms and percussion styles replaced the bebop, swing styles common to jazz music and were used more frequently as compositional features. Rock musicians as well embraced fusion as a small number of rock bands featured jazz ensemble arrangements with solo improvisation.

Fusion of the 1960s and 1970s heralded not only a blurring of the boundaries between rock and jazz music, but also the emergence of a global sound. Jazz music had a history of incorporating other musical styles, mostly from Africa and from Latin American countries, and jazz fusion continued with this inclusive worldview. Fusion in the 1980s and 1990s, however, represented the blending together of sounds, instruments, rhythms and composition styles into a "polyphonic" genre of music referred to as world music, world beat, global fusion, world fusion, or just fusion music that loosely encompasses recordings of local musics from around the world to create the polyphonic forms produced for consumption on a world market. The "fusion" of local traditional musics with "Western" music is said to celebrate the recognition of other musical forms and instrumentations, while at the same time symbolizing musical expression in a global world. Paul **Simon**'s Grammy-winning "Graceland" (1986) recording, a blend of American pop music with the music of black South African musicians, is held up as an exemplar of contemporary fusion (although not without controversy). In the late 1990s and early twenty-first century, fusion represents what sometimes appears to be a hodge-podge of musical productions that can include the coming together of so-called "traditional" musics from Africa, Asia, South America, and so forth with what has been referred to as a "universal pop aesthetic," that is "Western" (Taylor, 1997). Fusion can also include "new and old world music," "ancient future world fusion" and "folk fusion music" that can bring together the music of the Andes with Appalachian music, for example.

While fusion grew from experimentation in musical aesthetics, it also was the product of changing musical tastes and a record business increasingly oriented towards a world market. Fusion's "hybridity" marks a fluidity of economic and aesthetic relationships between the music traditions of local worlds and the modern, often Western, tastes of a global culture. Although some would argue that hybridity has always been a feature of music and fusion should only be applied to the American jazz and rock fusion music.

Further reading

Berendt, J.E. (1991) *The Jazz Book: From Ragtime to Fusion and Beyond*, Brooklyn: Lawrence Hill Books.

Frith, S. (ed.) (1989) *World Music, Politics, and Social Change*, New York: Manchester University Press.

Taylor, T.D. (1997) *Global Pop: World Music, World Markets*, New York: Routledge.

STEVE FERZACCA

G

gambling and lotteries

The legal gambling industry has experienced almost unparalleled growth in the past twenty-five years. In 1976 Americans bet $17.3 billion legally, by 1996 they bet $586.5 billion. According to a 1999 Gallup Poll, 70 percent of adults and 26 percent of teens have taken part in some form of legal gambling, with lotteries being the favorite form of betting for most Americans. Fifty-seven percent of Americans have purchased a lottery ticket within the last year, while 31 percent have gambled in a casino. But these figures represent a fraction of the gambling that occurs in the United States, since much sports gambling is still illegal.

Until 1988 (leaving aside gambling on Wall Street), legal gambling included state-controlled lotteries, casinos in and around **Las Vegas, NV** (since 1931) and in **Atlantic City**, betting at horse- and dog-racing tracks (legal in thirty-six states) and all sports betting in Montana, Nevada, North Dakota and Oregon. In that year, Congress passed the Indian Gambling Regulatory Act, allowing Native Americans to operate casinos on their land, and this was followed by other **communities** endeavoring to cash in on expected gambling revenues. In 1989 Iowa became the first of several states to legalize riverboat gambling, and by the end of the 1990s there were over 170 casinos in twenty-five states.

State lotteries began in New Hampshire in 1964, followed by New York State in 1967 and New Jersey in 1970. Within a year, lottery sales had surpassed the $100 million mark, and they were quickly adopted by numerous states, spreading by 1999 to thirty-seven states and the District of Columbia. In 1988 the Multi-State Lottery Association began combining lottery efforts in several states, leading ten years later to the world-record jackpot of $295.7 million for its "Powerball" game. States have used their lottery revenues for many things, initially largely for funding education and support for older citizens, but more recently for building new **sports stadiums**. While gambling has benefited some communities, others have suffered – from the displacement of residents occurring in Atlantic City to the **organized-crime** involvement in the Las Vegas industry to the problems associated with **addiction**.

Illegal sports gambling has become mainstream from colleges to **television** sports shows, 90 percent of it focused on team sports (mainly **football**, followed by **basketball** and **baseball**). There are now more than 700 phone services offering advice and gambling tips, generating revenue in millions of dollars annually. In the mid-1980s, Pete Axthelm gave point-spread picks on NBC's pre-game NFL show, while CBS countered with Jimmy "the Greek" Snyder (until he was fired for making racist comments). All **newspapers** now offer betting lines, including point spreads, and many provide columns with betting tips and advice. **ESPN** for a short time even presented *Sportsline* from Caesar's Palace in Las Vegas, providing lines and pre-game information on upcoming games. Growth of this illegal industry is likely to continue as **Internet** betting increases in popularity.

Sports gambling has been associated with many of the major sports scandals – from the beginnings of baseball in the nineteenth century, through the 1919 "Black Sox" scandal, to the seven college basketball point-shaving incidents from 1947 to 1950, down to more recent scandals at Tulane and Boston College. Pete Rose was banned from baseball for betting on games while he was coaching the **Cincinnati** Reds, and even Michael **Jordan** was forced to admit to a gambling problem that threatened his position in basketball.

Further reading

Abt, V., Smith, J.F. and Christiansen, E.M. (1985) *The Business of Risk*, Lawrence: University Press of Kansas.

O'Brien, T.L. (1998) *Bad Bet*, New York: Times Business.

ROBERT GREGG

games

Games for **children** reflect the culture, everyday life, social mores and technology of society. Some games are spontaneous, requiring only imagination, and easily passed on through generations. Others involve technological literacy and virtual reality. Games are part of the $22.6 billion toy industry in the United States; video games constitute another $5.5 billion. Some games also continue through adult life.

Psychologists view playing games as a useful enterprise for developing imagination and vocabulary and learning rules and interpersonal skills. General categories for games include card and tile, board, word and picture, target, war and fantasy, and electronic (video and **computer**) games. Educational and religious games also use the same formats. Yet some popular children's games that do not fit into these categories include hide and seek, steal the bacon and duck duck goose. These games require no special equipment and provide safe but stimulating entertainment for young children.

Popular card games for children include old maid, crazy eights and Uno. Other card games like rummy, pinochle, poker and bridge may be acquired as children age, and are frequently played among adults as well as in families or gendered social gatherings. Related tile games include dominoes,

scrabble and mah-jong, with the last popular among both **Chinese Americans** and some **Jews** as an adult game. Scrabble and dominoes also attract adult and tournament players.

Board games have existed since the 1700s, but their popularity has grown at the end of the century, in part because of their lasting play value and character. They also do not require batteries or many mechanical parts and have simple goals: to win a race or achieve a certain number of points. Some are games of luck, while others require considerable decision making. Popular first board games include Candyland and Chutes and Ladders. Parcheesi, Monopoly, Clue, Battleship, Careers and Risk attract older children while introducing them to the worlds of **real estate**, work, war and crime. Milton Bradley is one of the foremost American producers of such games; its Monopoly, in fact, used the streets of **Atlantic City** to constitute its original board. Children of all ages love checkers and **chess**, primarily games of skill which become more serious pursuits for older adults, in tournaments and at play in city parks.

Word and picture games engage the imagination and verbal skills of the child. Twenty questions and hangman are popular informal children's games of this category; Pictionary, Trivial Pursuit and Boggle again bridge to more adult play. Jigsaw puzzles are also popular among many age groups.

War games and fantasy games have almost cult-like followings. War games may be played on boards or through simulations that are very accurate. **Dungeons and Dragons** has enjoyed immense popularity among adolescents. While fantasy games die out among adults, war re-enactments have a large following.

Target games include pin the tail on the donkey and attempting to break a piñata, both often associated with birthday parties. Darts and horseshoes survive as adult games, often among men.

Video games and online computer games have changed the concept of children's games and also have influenced adult purchases and play. Children have a huge smorgasbord of computerized and video fare from which to choose. They can enjoy puzzle games and matching games appropriate for toddlers on up, as well as trivia games or contests in which the player is pitted against the computer, as in Chessmaster or Solitaire. They can kill humans or aliens in the privacy of their own computer station or interact with other players at **home** or in other sites. As war games did in the past, these have alarmed parents and politicians because of their violence and addictive appeal, although the evidence of direct impact is not clear.

As noted, adolescent and adult games tend to emerge from the formats of these basic categories. They may be matured by wagers (see **gambling and lotteries**), drinking or sexual activity, or by complexities of rules, strategy and knowledge. Yet they still tend to recreate **family** and **community** in rather similar ways.

See also: toys

Further reading

Leisure Products, Standard and Poor's Industry Surveys, March 12, 1998.

GAIL HENSON

game shows

A staple of American media whose format has extended to classrooms and social events. **Mass media** contests with **celebrities**, average citizens, or both, have offered rewards ranging from charity donations to $1 million. Drawing on **radio**, **television** games as **prime-time** events reached their apogee in the 1950s. Since then, they have been daytime staples and syndicated products that fill out local schedules. These games are distinguishable on the basis of contest rules, participation and vulgarity, as well as rewards.

Early quiz shows like The $64,000 Question (1955–9), Twenty-One (NBC, 1956–8) or Tic Tac Dough (NBC, 1957–8) were immensely popular weekly evening shows, turning "ordinary" citizens with extraordinary knowledge into **stars**. Questions could be complex, but the visible struggle suited American beliefs and hopes. This popularity waned when congressional hearings revealed that contestants, including Columbia instructor Charles Van Doren, had been coached in their answers (as depicted in Quiz Show, 1994). As Steven Spark notes, this collapse opened evenings to other series

and drew lines between news and entertainment for decades.

Yet these big-stakes shows were not the only option of the 1950s. Other prime-time shows included long-running celebrity matches created by Mike Goodson and Bill Todman, who dominated the genre for decades. Their What's My Line? (CBS, 1950–67) highlighted repartee among **actors** and **columnists** guessing the occupations of ordinary and star contestants. I've Got a Secret (CBS, 1952–67), To Tell the Truth (CBS, 1956–67), The Price is Right (NBC, 1956–63; ABC, 1963–5) and Beat the Clock (CBS, 1950–8; later ABC and syndication) also focused on distinguishing the truth – whether stumping celebrities or demonstrating physical and economic acuity. Meanwhile, these shows emphasized the jovial, male, white announcer who might have other serious roles: newsman Hugh Downs hosted Concentration (NBC, 1958–73); Walter Cronkite led Its News to Me (CBS, 1951–4). Comedian, Groucho Marx's You Bet Your Life (NBC, 1950–61) displayed Groucho's wit more than contestants' prowess.

These shows and their successors found additional lives as board and party **games**. Indeed, television enshrined live competition as deeply American – in television sports, show business (Ted Mack's Original Amateur Hour, various networks, 1948–70; Star Search, syndicated, 1983–97), **beauty pageants** or media **awards**. This model extended to College Bowl (NBC, 1953–70) (pitting university teams against erudite questions) and high-school imitators nationwide. Even Sesame Street (PBS, 1969–) invented the unctuous Guy Smiley to host educational games.

Goodson and Todman's hegemony ended in the 1970s with Family Feud (ABC and syndication, 1976–94) and the New Price is Right (various networks, 1957–, with a total run of roughly four decades. A subsequent entrepreneur, Chuck Barris, created hits like Dating Game (ABC, 1965–73; syndication) and Newlywed Game (ABC, 1966–74; syndication), more notable for vulgarity in their sexually loaded questions and answers. Barris also created the Gong Show (NBC, 1976–78; syndication) – a talentless talent show that effectively ridiculed hapless contestants.

In the 1990s, game shows found new life through syndication. Merv Griffin, a 1960s **talk-**

show host, produced global game shows like *Wheel of Fortune* (NBC and syndicated, 1975–) and *Jeopardy* (ABC and syndication, 1990–) (the latter famed for knowledge rather than luck). A European import of 1999, *Do You Want to Be a Millionaire?*, has also raised stakes and moved towards prime-time, spawning a succession of new titles like *Greed* (FOX, 1999–), *Twenty-One* (NBC, 1999–) (again!) and survival contests based on European hits. Meanwhile, **cable**'s game-show channel reruns earlier (post-scandal) shows, while other channels have created contests about music, state history and sports. Kid's game shows also mix education and **family values** with physical competition and green slime.

Obviously, Americans share game-show elements with other nations. Yet these remain American in their sense of individual heroism, the production of instant celebrities and a belief in the equality of luck that underpins lotteries as well as politics.

See also: education: values and beliefs

Further reading

Marc, D. and Thompson, R. (1992) *Prime Time, Prime Movers*, Syracuse: Syracuse University Press.

Stark, S. (1997) *Glued to the Set*, New York: Simon & Schuster.

GARY McDONOGH

gangs

Despite a long history of immigrant successes, accusations of gang formation often challenge new groups in American society. These stereotypes emphasize different lifestyles or opportunities, but may also control **community** organization or justify exclusion because of culture, **race**, **class** or generation. These charges have denigrated **African Americans**, **Irish Americans**, **Chinese Americans** and **Cuban Americans** in turn. Meanwhile, the specter of clandestine **organized crime** – whether *tongs* among Chinese, or the Mafia among Italians – has justified **police** surveillance, **mass media** sensationalism, missionary reform and policies ranging from vague

urban renewal to **gated community** withdrawal.

Those defined by such negative views have been more diverse. Criminal behavior emerges from many social forces, including realistic socialization in urban life. In many cases, however, the **neighborhood** or ethnic group smeared by the acts of a few has been deeply divided by these same actions. This is evident in African American community campaigns against contemporary black-on-black violence. Gang accusations, moreover, often show groups embodying fundamental American beliefs. Virtue, for example, is defined in loyalty to groups and localities, although gangs have promoted strong **individualism** as well. Gangs also gender crime – they have been strongly associated with males, while females, although likely to belong to associations, are depicted as isolated criminals or fallen women. Finally, gangs have come to symbolize negative traits of urban disorder versus rural tranquility or the safety of the small town and the protected **suburb**.

The twentieth-century history of gangs has been more complex. In the 1920s and 1930s, as urban wars winnowed crime families, new youth gangs continued to spring up in changing environments. The transformations of American society after the Second World War, however, changed the ideological landscape of crime and fear. As suburban havens welcomed the **middle class**, the city could be perceived as a "realm of hoodlums". Nonetheless, hot rodders (with anti-social "traits") turned hallmarks of suburbia – cars and nurtured **teenagers** – into problems evident in Marlon **Brando**'s *The Wild One* (1954).

Study and policy *vis-à-vis* gangs also have been shaped by politics and representation. Hence, in the 1960s, researchers sought integrative solutions as their authors detailed portraits of young men in gang nations such as Vice Lords of **Chicago, IL** or the street-corner networks of **New York** City and **Washington, DC**. Blacks, and later, **Hispanics**, figured prominently among depictions of urban problems: Leonard **Bernstein**'s *West Side Story* (1961) recast *Romeo and Juliet* as a conflict between **Puerto Rican** and "American" **teenage** gangs. Nonetheless, some gangs were incorporated into urban renovation and neighborhood/racial pride.

As urban residents demanded equality, however, new questions surfaced. Riots, shifting family patterns and urban decay in the 1960s emphasized the social problems facing new generations. By the 1970s, statistics on gangs and organized opposition increased. Meanwhile, drug trafficking and new weaponry, which linked organized crime and local gangs, heightened urban violence. As consumerist values in the media bombarded those with less access to resources, drugs and crime proved tempting, despite consequences. When new immigrants formed associations to facilitate **assimilation**, they were also tainted by reference to gangs. Thus, established Chinese American communities complain about the violent incursions of Fukienese and **Southeast Asians**.

The 1980s and 1990s witnessed new extensions of crime and association. Women have increasingly public roles in all levels. In 1992 riots in **Los Angeles, CA**, the notorious gang nations of the city, Crips and Bloods, emerged as potential peacemakers, which the Los Angeles Police Department could not be. Meanwhile, **news** and policy-makers continue to focus on drugs, corruption and drive-by violence.

Mass media have long contributed to a sense of gangs as a pervasive urban problem. Gangsters have been a movie staple from James Cagney in *Public Enemy* (1931) to modern depictions such as *The Godfather Trilogy* (1972; 1974; 1990), *New Jack City* (1991) and *Pulp Fiction* (1994), as well as documentaries like A. Mishan's *Bui Doi* (1994).

Quite apart from the real and violent nature of many other aspects of American society, crime, gangs and other associations around illegal activities have multiple meanings and interpretations, encompassing assimilation, protest and solidarity, as well as mere gain or pleasure. Gangs develop from strength as well as weakness, solidarities and alliances as well as divisions. As such, they entail neither simple problems nor simple solutions.

Further reading

Barker, G. (1950) *Pachuco*, Tucson: University of Arizona.

Campbell, A. (1991) *The Girls in the Gang*, Cambridge, MA: Basil Blackwell.

Cummings, S. and Monti, D. (1993) *Gangs*, Albany: SUNY.

Whyte, W. (1955) *Street-Corner Society*, Chicago: University of Chicago.

GARY McDONOGH

GAP

Ubiquitous chain that began as a music and jeans store in **San Francisco, CA** in 1969. GAP took on a more designer look with Mickey Drexler in 1983, when it also purchased Banana Republic. While it targets **baby boomer** infants and **children** with simple designs and interchangeable components, its primary market remains **teenagers** and twenty-somethings looking for cool clothes and even the transition to adulthood with GAP ties and coats. This appeal has made the company notable for well-designed (and globally copied) advertising campaigns featuring celebrities and ordinary teenagers launching **fashion** trends like khakis and vests.

See also: advertising

GARY McDONOGH

garages/parking

American's fascination with **automobiles** has altered homes and public spaces. For houses, these range from suburban extensions of the roof to ward off weather – the carport – to separate structures that may include additional spaces for storage or work. These are especially associated with male activities or escape in **mass media** representations of the **home**. Suburban sprawl and status have created a demand for two- and three-car garages even in subdivisions. Garages are also part of the **family** life cycle: garage apartments (upstairs) may provide rental income or may be used for older **children** or relatives; garages may also be converted into living spaces for growing families.

In cities, garage space may be premium **real estate** for apartment and house dwellers, creating a labyrinth of garage privileges and street regulations. Public garages (and the asphalt scars of parking lots) have become frequent postwar urban projects for urban commuter populations. In contrast to private garages, these spaces are often seen as dangerous, especially for women, while they become the scenes of countless car chases and crime shows in **mass media**. Meanwhile, in suburbs, public parking for **malls**, business **campuses**, schools and **motels** eats up new acres across the US daily.

GARY McDONOGH

gardens

The private garden has long been part of the American domestic ideal. Implicit in the "American dream" of a **home** with a white picket fence is the green **lawn** inside that fence. Individual gardens come in all shapes and sizes, from subsistence food production to flower-cutting gardens to manicured topiaries. The centerpiece of the stereotypical garden is the lawn. More varied elements include flowering plants and trees, water features and vegetables. Gardens are both ornamental and functional, often serving as extended living areas complete with outdoor furniture. Rural yards in the **South**, where weather permits outdoor activity year-round, become outdoor rooms where cooking, washing and social activities take place.

The trends of contemporary **architecture** have generally been slow to influence gardens and landscape architecture. In the 1980s and 1990s, there was a shift towards relaxed planting styles, inspired by regional natural settings and a yearning for the wild, historic American landscape. Shrinking property sizes are another major factor in changing garden design. Container gardens have sprouted in cities, on corporate plazas, small yards, roofs and window boxes. Busy lifestyles that preclude a weekend of lawn mowing, and rising water costs have also led to lower-maintenance gardens.

Plantings and garden styles change drastically from one region to another according to climate. **Southwestern** gardeners often plant succulents which thrive in arid climates, a water-efficient practice called xeriscaping, though they also grow water-dependent lawns, an imitation of the tradi-

tional temperate climate's yard. The southeast supports more lush, tropical species, and the northern states grow a variety of smaller annual and perennial plant life.

Community gardening in America tends to flourish in times of economic hardship or war. The First World War had Liberty Gardens, the Great Depression necessitated **community** gardening and, during the Second World War, the Victory Garden program contributed to national vegetable production. Such gardens were not generally popular again until the 1970s, when they were promoted with **urban-renewal** efforts as a way to heal urban blight.

In many cities, community gardens have been developed in vacant lots where buildings have been torn down and not replaced. Some start as squatters' gardens, without approval from municipal authorities; others are started by city agencies or special interest groups with community support. They utilize raised planting beds, which conserve water and space, and are often divided into small plots tended by a single individual or **family**. Community gardens are often hard to preserve on a long-term basis because of **real-estate** pressure, and their creation and preservation has been a catalyst for and product of community activism as people work to maintain valuable **neighborhood** resources. Some municipalities have sponsored work-training programs in community gardens for disadvantaged youth. Such gardens reinforce community ideals, preserve a neighborhood's green open space and, when well tended, can yield substantial quantities of produce.

Further reading

Fogle, D. (1988) *Clues to American Garden Styles*, Washington, DC: Starhill.

Ottesen, C. (1987) *The New American Garden*, New York: MacMillan.

BIANCA T. SIEGL

Garland, Judy
b. 1922; d. 1969

Singer and actor. Garland became a "child"

sensation with *The Wizard of Oz* (1939) and her Andy Hardy movies with Mickey Rooney. Her vibrant, expressive voice outlasted her movie career (with notable exceptions like her Oscar-nominated role in *A Star is Born*, 1954), but her off-screen suffering, including failed marriages and struggles with **alcohol** and drugs, haunted her life and image. Nonetheless, she made comebacks in the 1950s and 1960s before her death from drugs. She also became a gay icon; hence "Judy Garland" park may designate a gay encounter area.

GARY McDONOGH

gated communities

These often walled residential areas, concentrated in **suburban** America but also found in urban centers, have restricted access and complex social meanings. The main intention of gated communities is to provide security to residents who dwell within them. An array of security devices segregate residents and non-residents, including armed guards, intercom systems, video surveillance cameras and gates controlled by codes or electronic identification cards. Gated communities are also symbols of **class** ascension and privilege, and usually contain amenities such as private golf courses, country clubs, lakes and parks closed to the public (work and shopping still lie outside the gates). It is estimated that 3 million or more American households have moved to gated communities in the last two decades (Blakely and Snyder 1997).

Gated communities supposedly represent ideal **communities** sold by **real-estate** and land developers as safe havens from the ills of urbanization. This duplicates the historical selling point of suburban development and represents a paradox for the creation of gated communities. If the suburbs are safer, why are gated communities necessary? In this sense, gated communities are symbolic of a "fortress" mentality that has seized many urban residents in recent years due to rising crime (Davis 1990). Ironically, there are no proven trends to show that "gatehoods" are relatively safer than "neighborhoods."

Further reading

Blakely, E. and Snyder, M. (1997) *Fortress America: Gated Communities in the United States*, Washington, DC: Brookings Institution.
Davis, M. (1990) *City of Quartz*, New York: Vintage Books.

MATTHEW DURINGTON

Gates, Bill/Microsoft

b. 1955

Born in **Seattle** to a prominent family, Gates attended Harvard University with the intention of becoming a lawyer like his father, although at age thirteen he was already working on his first computer program. An awkward adolescent who rarely went to parties, Gates has become Harvard's most famous and wealthy drop-out as the brains behind the world's largest software company, Microsoft.

The myth of Microsoft's origin goes like this: one day in December 1974, Gates contacted the manufacturer of the Altair 8800 (a do-it-yourself computer) to inform them that he could provide software. To fill the contract Gates and his friend Paul Allen (who worked at Honeywell) formed "Microsoft." The company struggled until IBM asked Gates to provide an operating system for its first PC. Gates bought the QDOS system from another company, renamed it MS-DOS and licensed it to IBM. Owing to Gates' successful maneuvering, the success of the PC became inextricably linked to the rise of Microsoft.

At first Microsoft focused on the software market; its word-processing program Microsoft Word rivaled WordPerfect and other programs. Meanwhile, at thirty-one, Gates became a billionaire when his company went public. The company changed focus in 1987 with the introduction of Windows, the operating system now on virtually every PC, although it is not universally endorsed. Even within the ranks of non-Macintosh users, some prefer the Unix and Linux operating systems, criticizing Windows for being "buggy" and flawed.

In 1995 the company changed focus again, this

time turning towards the **Internet** and pushing its browser, Internet Explorer, tied to the functioning of the computer's desktop. The bundling of software (which didn't include IE's rival Netscape) has come under scrutiny from the Justice Department, whose preliminary decision stated that Microsoft had engaged in monopolistic practices, thus continuing a series of antitrust investigations. Regardless, Microsoft is now a major player in Internet-related and entertainment businesses and has entered into alliances with NBS and with the **cable** station and web-site MSNBC.

In 1998, the Justice Department began court actions against Microsoft for antitrust violations, especially with regard to bundling Internet software with its PC operating system and maintaining a monopoly for that system. After a preliminary finding of fact in November, 1999, on April 3, 2000, Judge Thomas Jackson ruled that Microsoft had in fact violated the Sherman Anti-trust Act and soon recommended divisions in the operation of the company. Public reaction as well as stock-market interest has been intense.

Nonetheless, Gates remains one of the world's richest men; he has recently begun to involve himself in philanthropy with the Bill and Melinda Gates **foundation**, and has talked about the need to return to creative outlets. His lifestyle, meanwhile, combines elements of the American **middle class** and its success stories with the opulence of a 40,000 square foot mansion. His company, both loved and hated, has become one of the foundations of the century ahead.

EDWARD MILLER

Gates, Henry Louis, Jr.

b. 1950

Widely considered, since publication of *The Signifying Monkey* (1988), the dean of letters among **African American intellectuals**, reinforced by his regular contributions to journals like *The New Yorker*. Also noted for his impact on black studies with the establishment, first at Duke and then at Harvard, of strong liberally inclined African American studies departments, carving out a middle ground between the more Afrocentric

programs of Molefi Kete Asante and Leonard Jeffries, and the Marxist orientations of **intellectuals** like Manning Marable and Robin D.G. Kelley. Gates has also promoted the study of gender in edited work on black women writers (for example *Reading Black, Reading Feminist*, 1990). His memoir, *Colored People*, was published in 1994.

ROBERT GREGG

gay and lesbian life and politics

After the 1969 **Stonewall** riots, the call for an active gay and lesbian political agenda became paramount. Through often spirited activism and persistent grassroots politics, a gay and lesbian movement cavalierly came into being. As this coalition gained momentum, important social changes occurred not only at state level, but in areas such as **psychology**, **education**, **religion** and media representation. At its best, the gay and lesbian movement has forged a powerful visibility in the political arena. At its worst and most banal, the movement has served to create a new demographic for commercial **advertising**. In any case, these changes were not always agreed upon by either the popular heterosexual culture or gay and lesbian activists themselves.

As the gay and lesbian movement quickly learned, the constituency of any radical movement is unequivocally diverse. The difficulty inherent to any coalition-building is the sometimes obstreperous struggle to proactively engage these differences for a unified cause. What became apparent to many post-Stonewall gay and lesbian activists was that the "lifestyle" did not simply occupy a univocal position. While there was much political agreement that "liberation" was a good and important thing to have, the very definition of liberation took on multiple and complex meanings.

At the outset, the very terms used to describe the movement began to fragment. Was a drag queen a gay man? Did the S&M leather dyke share the same political desire as the lesbian who thrived on a life in the country? Should bisexuals be included in the gay and lesbian political caucus? Can there be such a thing as a gay Republican? Where does the transgender (pre-operative, post-operative, non-operative) fit into the "gay and lesbian" schema? How "out" is out? Does one only tell one's friends? family? co-workers? fellow students? Needless to say, there has been much contention within the movement. It is no wonder that as diversity superseded the original intention of gay and lesbian organizations the question was asked: how can a gay and lesbian movement continually expand its cultural base in order to encapsulate the vicissitudes of sexual identity? Sensitivity to difference among many gays and lesbians has led to an ever-evolving nomenclature that takes into consideration the variance of social categories. One need only peruse, for example, the pages of the *Gayellow Pages* whose objective in 1973 was to "[inform] the lesbian, gay, and bisexual community." In 1998 the new sexual identities that struggle for cultural position were laundry-listed on the front page of the phone book. Inclusion serves in the marketing of difference. Hence, the *Gayellow Pages* now informs a consumer that is referred to as the "gay, lesbian, bisexual, *and* transgender community." There will, of course, be additions.

Indeed, gay and lesbian (bisexual, transgender, etc.) life is besotted with consumer goods that purportedly support our irreducible needs, wants and pleasures. Books, movies, **television** programs, clothing manufacturers, furniture stores, realtors, restaurants and other traditional commercial establishments rigorously vie for gay and lesbian customers. Even non-traditional commercial venues such as sex-toy shops, leather bars and sex clubs, and their exotic wares, have strategized effective advertising campaigns that appeal to their niche audiences.

Political organizations such as the Gay and Lesbian Alliance Against Defamation (GLAAD) and the National Gay and Lesbian Task Force (NGLTF) have kept their names, but have over the years changed their mission statements to embrace and include transgender people, as well as other progressive sexual and non-sexual movements. The pendular side of these politics is the Washington-based lobbyists such as the Human Rights Campaign (HRC) and the Republican Log Cabins who seek to diversify gay and lesbian initiatives through beltway politics. While HRC seeks to negotiate the political terrain of both the **Demo-**cratic Party** and the **Republican Party**, the Log Cabins ideologically place all their stock in the Republican agenda. Most recently, both groups have been accused of conservative initiatives that are perceived as being out of political step with many gays, lesbians and transgenders.

Marriage, **AIDS**, **homophobia**, public sex, **abortion** and racism continue to be (as the movement itself) some of the highly debatable issues that homosexuals wrangle over. The stakes are certainly high in the ongoing adjustments of the political landscape. The dynamics of power in the now historical movement rapidly shift between gay white stock brokers and radical activists. What is striking, however, is also the rapidity with which these glaring differences can *and* do unify. Whether it has been at an AIDS demonstration or a memorial march for Matthew Shepard (a twenty-one-year-old Wyoming student who was a victim of deadly homophobia in 1998), gays, lesbians, transgenders, queers, dykes on bikes, stockbrokers, students, poets, painters, theorists, historians and clerics have rallied together to flag the insidiousness of heterosexism and homophobia.

In the twenty-first century, the arguments over difference in what was once known as the "gay and lesbian movement" will undoubtedly continue. In fact, the debate will probably become more contentious as more people identify themselves as *not* heterosexual. Not only are there more voices added to the cacophony of sexual politics, but the geographical dispersion of this population is growing larger. While the urban gay "**ghetto**" of the Stonewall era has clearly thrived, many homosexuals have chosen to find permanent dwellings on rural farms, in small towns and in the suburbs. The political and cultural implications of these population shifts remain to be seen. Add to these demographic changes the "gay and lesbian" workers who constitute an economy of many different ethnicities, moralities and financial strata, and one will find that the sexuality of everyday life in America is certain to trigger a politically raucous twenty-first century.

See also: Fire Island; gender and sexuality; queer

DAVID GERSTNER

gay and lesbian press

It is arguable that the "gay and lesbian" press began with the dramatic moment when Oscar Wilde was seen carrying an issue of *The Yellow Book* on his way into prison for acts of "gross indecency." Although gay and lesbian "issues" covertly (or not so covertly) emerged during the early part of the twentieth century in **theater** and arts journals like *Broadway Brevities* and the avant-garde journal *View*, it was not until 1953 that gay and lesbian political concerns came to the fore in the publication *One* (under the auspices of the Mattachine Society) and in the Daughters of Bilitis' **newspaper** *The Ladder*. Since **Stonewall** (1969), the proliferation of the gay and lesbian press has been tremendous if not (in some cases) troublesomely banal (*Out*, for instance).

DAVID GERSTNER

Gaye, Marvin

b. 1939; d. 1984

Marvin Gaye helped to shape the "Motown sound" that moved **soul** music into mainstream American popular culture. He became Hitsville's leading man when matched with Mary Wells in duets in 1964. After numerous hits, Gaye's greatest moment came with the *What's Going On* album (1971), when he turned from soul ballads to problems of the **inner-city** and Vietnam; this became the first soul-concept album. Gaye made a comeback with "Sexual Healing" (1981), which featured the return of his sweet, plaintive tones in one of pop music's most sensual songs, rivaling his previous "Let's Get it On" (1981). His personal life, however, had become increasingly difficult; his father shot him in an argument in 1984.

EDWARD MILLER

Gehry, Frank

b. 1929

Winner of the Pritzker Architecture Prize (1989), Canadian-born Gehry is known for the sculptural elements in his designs, as well as his ability to relate buildings to a human scale. Gehry's work reached **celebrity** status with the spectacular Guggenheim Museum in Bilbao, Spain (1997). The titanium-clad building consists of multitudinous curves designed with the help of the most advanced computer-design programs. Gehry's work has prompted the question: what comes after **postmodernism**? In addition to the Guggenheim, Gehry has designed two lines of furniture and continues to design at his firm based in **Los Angeles, CA**.

ISABEL KRIEGEL

gender and sexuality

Americans in the last half of the twentieth century often felt as if they had become suddenly inundated with an obsessive fascination with gender and sexuality. The most commonly evoked cause – the movement for equal rights for women that emerged out of the 1960s ferment (known to historians as **feminism**'s second wave) – has propelled fundamental alterations in women's legal and personal status in many areas of the world. Yet, the very name – the "second wave" – suggests that what appears to be a "modern" issue carries significantly deeper roots.

When we discuss gender, we mean the assumptions made about and the social roles occupied by individuals with specific physical characteristics that we denote as "male" and "female." Although we tend to assume two sexes (male and female) as "natural," scholars have pointed out that other societies have had different ideas. Some believed that there was only one physical **body** (for example, that women were men turned inside out); other societies believed that there were three or even more sexes. The particular social assumption about how many sexes even exist is often more a reflection of gender beliefs than any empirical knowledge. For example, the fact that a small, but significant, number of infants are born every year with the physical characteristics of both a male and a female (known as "intersexed" in medical terminology) has only recently received extended public discussion. Many individuals argue that they are transgendered – belonging to neither "official" category of current gender identification.

Since such basic gender identifications can be so fluid, it is not surprising that gendered ideas about what people should wear or the work they should do are also subject to dramatic change over time. In America, there have been ongoing historical struggles over the roles men and women should occupy – particularly in the public arena – since the country's inception. The most famous battle – the movement for women's right to vote – began officially in 1848 and took over seventy years of continuous activity until passage of the 19th Amendment to the Constitution in 1920.

Dramatic changes in gender relations did accelerate in response to the Industrial Revolution. As more people moved into urban environments and as factory employment needs increased, it became less clear who was "supposed" to work in what locales and who was not. Simultaneously, the rules for public activity proved less enforceable. Who was really there to tell the factory-shop girl she should not venture out to an evening's entertainment? In a relatively short time, rigid assumptions about "acceptable" behavior for both men and women began to collapse under the pressure of real-life circumstances. By the 1920s, following feminism's "First Wave," American women both had the vote and had received more PhDs than they would for another sixty years.

As the last fact reveals, gender assumptions are often the playthings of economic developments. Despite significant advances early in the twentieth century, much progress for women seemed to disappear in the face of the economic and political crises of the 1930s and 1940s. More traditional notions of gender roles reasserted themselves despite evidence of very real needs and possibilities to the contrary.

The growing dichotomy between supposed gender roles and actual gender behavior helped fuel the gender controversies in the last fifty years. The very fact that women successfully staffed defense-industry plants in large numbers during the Second World War – despite being told they were biologically unfit for such activity and fired once the war concluded – helped pave the way for important subsequent gender re-evaluation. While imagery in the 1950s presented a simple domestic

life in which women stayed **home**, in fact women constituted the fastest-growing group entering the labor market during this period. White women working in the 1950s proved essential to creating the highly prized growing **middle class**. As the economy of the 1950s and 1960s expanded, career doors opened. Women refused to be limited by simple prejudice about "appropriate" work, and the movement for access to all employment categories gathered steam. It is this ongoing insistence that has vexed so many in the last quarter century.

If gender assumptions are often shaped by economic circumstances, in America they are also determined by racial ideologies. Claims about proper "women's" work often applied only to certain white women. Those arguing against women working outside the home rarely worried that a significant proportion of **African American** women always did just that. Indeed, without the highly circumscribed categories of domestic and menial labor enforced upon African Americans, both male and female, it is unlikely that so many white Americans could have so successfully entered that desirable middle class in the post-Second World War era.

While gender questions are often assumed to be "only" about women, the nature of **masculinity** also changed profoundly in the same period. In an age of increasing bureaucratization and technology, physical strength and aggression – often hallmarks of behavior marked as "male" – became more liabilities than assets. Men have also had to adapt to women's refusal to limit their activities to home and child rearing. Although the most apparent "beneficiaries" of the gender struggles are women, men have also been changed almost as dramatically.

If shifts in gender roles and even in gender itself have hardly occurred quietly, debates over sexuality have raged even more loudly. The topics of gender and sexuality are natural cousins because they often impact on each other. This linkage is nothing new. Those studying sexuality in the late nineteenth century – a group of scientists known as sexologists – believed that they could determine "deviant" sexual practices based upon observed "improper" gender behavior. Thus, a quiet man who liked to cook was probably a homosexual; a woman with short hair who liked sports most likely a lesbian. As these examples indicate, stereotypes about sexuality remain even more obstinate over 100 years than do those about gender.

All societies have engaged in a wide variety of sexual practices. All societies have depicted or written about sexuality. Americans are no different in this regard. The seemingly accelerated pace of public sexual controversy in the late twentieth and early twenty-first centuries is a reflection of particular historical trends – some specific to the American context, some more reflective of broader changes.

The Industrial Revolution impacted sexual practice with the same force that it disrupted gender relations (and everything else). A stunning decline in average childbirth rates from eight children per family in 1800 to approximately three in 1900 trumpets the fact that heterosexuals made informed reproductive choices. On the **farm**, **children** were unpaid essential laborers. In the new post-industrial world order they became economic liabilities – mouths to be fed and impediments to capital accumulation. Men and women chose not to have children. They did not choose to stop having sex. In these raw demographic numbers lie the roots for much of what we call "modern sexuality." Men and women needed to discuss their decision; they needed to negotiate; they needed to have access to contraceptive devices. Ultimately, what they needed most was to find another way to understand and talk about the now primarily non-reproductive sexual practices they enjoyed with each other.

They did so in an increasingly urban environment that provided expanded anonymity and freedom from social restraints. The effects of modernization itself with developing leisure cultures, visual technologies, **mass media** and increasing mobility contributed to an expanded universe of sexual possibility and public presentation. All this was set in place in America by the 1920s. People wrote sex manuals for married couples; millions of dollars poured into sex education in the schools; Freud's ideas became enormously popular and homosexual subcultures flourished in numerous cities around the country. The very controversies that would so inflame the

second half of the century appeared well underway during the first.

As the twentieth century closed however, debates over both the proper place of sexuality and what sexuality is occupied the thoughts of many. Although the roots of these issues are apparent earlier, the claims made by the women's movement in the 1960s and 1970s that women owned their own bodies and held the sole rights to reproductive authority produced the fundamental conflict within the heterosexual **community**. The development of the pill in 1960 provided strong medical support for women's position. Completely divorced from reproduction, sexuality now demanded its own vocabulary. The early twentieth-century debates over female sexual satisfaction escalated into endless public discussions over how best to achieve sexual pleasure. Most importantly, the battle for reproductive autonomy was truly joined with the 1973 **Supreme Court** decision *Roe* **v.** *Wade*, which legalized **abortion**. This highly contested ruling formed the basis for years of struggle at whose core sat the question of women's sexual choices.

The women's movement set into motion a series of questions about sex, the answers to which seemed to call for greater sexual possibilities. Gays and lesbians, men and women who had already begun struggling for social acceptance in the 1950s, expanded that call into a demand for gay liberation in the 1970s and 1980s. The debate over homosexuality has been as ferocious as the argument over abortion. As homosexual-rights activists press their claims for equal rights and full acceptance with greater success, those opposed grow increasingly insistent and point to what they argue is a general decline in moral values. They look to the increased presence of children born to those not married, the large number of heterosexuals who choose to live together without marrying and the widespread popularity of sexual themes in popular culture as examples of unacceptable sexual chaos. The Defense of Marriage Act, passed by Congress in 1996, which prohibited the federal government from legally recognizing a "homosexual marriage" (should a state permit such a union), reinforced the perception of many that heterosexual marriage – perhaps heterosexuality itself – had become an institution in jeopardy at the end of the twentieth century.

From the emergence of sexually explicit magazines in the 1950s and 1960s, like ***Playboy*** and *Penthouse*, which catered to private male sexual fantasy, to the late twentieth-century expansion of **pornography** into the sexually integrated home through **video**, **cable** and the **Internet**, millions of Americans have responded eagerly to the much decried sexual culture. This continued discrepancy between values proclaimed and activities practiced has animated significant public discussion and numerous scholarly debates. Propelled also in large part by the women's movement, scholars began to look at the history of sexuality and gender roles in society. French philosopher Michel Foucault provided the central impetus with his influential introduction to the *History of Sexuality*, Volume I, published initially in 1976. Foucault outlined the socially constructed nature of sexuality (a point long illustrated by anthropologists) and laid out key analytic techniques for those who might follow. Many did. Among the numerous texts produced by this next generation of scholars, several of the most important include: *Sexual Meanings: The Cultural Construction of Gender and Sexuality*, Sherry Ortner and Harriet Whitehead (eds) (1981); *Gender and the Politics of History*, Joan Scott (1988); *Epistemology of the Closet*, Eve Kesofsky Sedgewick (1990); and *Gender Trouble* by Judith Butler (1996). Theoretically challenging, late twentieth-century scholars provided new methods and languages for discussing gender. Although some critics claimed that such work remained isolated in an "ivory tower," the development of this innovative scholarship clearly reflected the fact that the very real, day-to-day world of gender relations and sexuality surrounding everyone has been fundamentally transformed.

SHARON ULLMAN

gender gap

Term coined in the 1980s to refer to the emergence of a significant women's vote on specific issues and candidates. The 1980 election marked the first time that more women than men favored **Democratic** over **Republican** candidates, and it was also the first time in which a substantial feminist vote surfaced. The gender gap widened as the decade progressed and, correspondingly, women's power to sway elections grew. The women who made up this voting bloc largely supported, and fostered in candidates, a feminist agenda of progressive social policies, including pay equity, social equality, passage of an **Equal Rights Amendment** and reproductive rights.

MARY-CHRISTINE SUNGAILA, ESQ.

General Electric

"GE," founded in 1892, focused for decades on appliances and electrical products, from refrigerators to jet turbines, that ushered in modernity with slogans like "Progress is Our Most Important Product" and "We Bring Good Things to Life." The company, which employs 276,000 people worldwide in the 1990s after **downsizing**, has diversified to include the NBC **television** network and financial services.

GARY McDONOGH

General Motors *see* automakers; advertising; Detroit, MI; sports cars

Generation X

Widely known to be a term coined by Douglas Copeland's 1991 book *Generation X*, the term carries cultural meanings and targets a market. Generation X generally refers to people who grew up after the **Civil Rights Movement** and up to the early 1980s, after (and offspring of) the **baby boomers**. More importantly, Generation X is a state of mind – cynical, ironic and sarcastic – the slacker type. As a marketing ploy, Generation X aims for a mostly white **middle class** with a pretty carefree lifestyle.

CINDY WONG

genetics/genetic engineering

Genetics has played an important role in the development of civilizations through artificial selection of plant and animal features. This type of genetic manipulation is called classical in reference to observations made by Gregor Mendel. Genetic engineering, often discussed in the context of molecular genetics, is a science involving the manipulation of genes either within the original organism (host) or between organisms (transgenic). Both branches of genetic study are based on an understanding that the genetic code for cells is contained in DNA (deoxyribonucleic acid) and that this material is the blueprint for all proteins made by cells. The code is generally universal, nearly identical in all living cells, allowing transfer of material between organisms.

Hybrid plants and animals created from both classical and molecular means form the base of much of the world's foods today, and genetic resources have become important commodities in world markets. Though concerns have been raised about the efficacy of germ plasm manipulation in non-human organisms, world attention has focused on the science more intensely as humans have become the center of genetic research. Within the shadow of attempted national eugenics programs during the Second World War, questions of ethics as well as law are intertwined with scientific advances brought about through the Human Genome Project, a worldwide collaboration to locate the more than 100,000 human genes by 2005, and the patenting of genetically engineered higher life forms. Indeed, this project moved ahead far faster than imagined, raising both profound ethical and "business" questions about the ownership of the mapped genome.

Though fictional films like *Jurassic Park* (1993; novel by Michael Crichton) depict a level of genetic engineering beyond current capabilities, the advent of Dolly, the sheep cloned from her mother's cells, focuses attention on implications of current research. Popular notions of cloning that suggest a recreation of physical, mental and personality traits have given way to the reality that environment plays a large role in shaping the identity of an organism. The film *Boys from Brazil* (1978; novel by Ira Levin) illustrates the consequences of varying factors shaping personality.

Gene therapy and the production of medicines through genetic engineering have revolutionized modern medical practice. Gene therapy on humans began in 1990 and today nearly every **medical school** in the United States has at least one department working on gene-transfer research. Promising therapies for certain types of **cancers** and tumors, some forms of cystic fibrosis and diabetes, rheumatoid arthritis and hypercholesterolemia have spurred major pharmaceutical companies and the US government to invest billions of dollars into genetic research.

Such research is not without its downside. Population genetics is the study of the distribution of gene types within populations. With the advent of widespread and available genetic testing, the fear of genetic discrimination has increased. Such screening may lead to the documentation of genetic variations occurring without the presentation of symptoms. Such variations could be used to deny insurance or jobs based on the potential future manifestations of symptoms in individuals or offspring.

Further reading

Kevles, D. and Hood, L. (eds) (1992) *The Code of Codes: Scientific and Social Issues in the Human Genome Project*, Cambridge, MA: Harvard University Press.

SANDRA GILCHRIST

gentrification

Term originally popularized in Britain in the mid-1960s and 1970s, when working-class **neighborhoods** in London began to be renovated to provide new sources of housing for middle and upper-class residents, thereby displacing or threatening to displace long-term, lower-income households. As property values in particularly thriving urban centers like London, **New York** City, NY, **Los Angeles, CA** and **Boston, MA** continue to rise, gentrification has become more common as **inner-city** neighborhoods are reclaimed for higher-income occupants. The term and phenomenon it denotes became particularly pronounced in the 1980s and 1990s in the US and in Europe, as strategies to revitalize aging urban centers were implemented in cities now characterized by post-industrial economies based on a burgeoning **service sector** and geared towards attracting suburban and out-of-town tourists. Increasingly, industrial buildings and older types of housing are being rehabilitated to appeal primarily to young, urban professionals, forcing **working-class** and poor families out of neighborhoods that have become newly desirable due to their housing stock or their proximity to downtown. In *Upscaling Downtown: Stalled Gentrification in Washington, D.C.* (1988), anthropologist Brett Williams provides an ethnographic perspective on neighborhood change; Neil Smith's *The New Urban Frontier: Gentrification and the Revanchist City* (1996) discusses gentrification as an integral feature of late capitalism and the turn towards neoliberal social policies. Gentrification has also spawned a number of urban social movements in which residents have banded together to attempt to resist being displaced from their communities.

Further reading

Smith, N. (1996) *The New Urban Frontier: Gentrification and the Revanchist City*, London and New York: Routledge.

Williams, B. (1988) *Upscaling Downtown: Stalled Gentrification in Washington, D.C.*, Cornell: Cornell University Press.

SUSAN BRIN HYATT

geography

The social and historical study of humans in space received much less support in the United States than it did in Europe and Asia. Even the name "National Geographic Society" refers more to a magazine and project (supporting expeditions and photography) than to a professional association. Still, work on the American landscape coincided with other questions of the construction of national identity in important works by pioneering geogra-

phers Carl Sauer (see *Land and Life*, 1967) and J.B. Jackson (*Landscape in Sight: Looking at America*, 1997).

As with other social sciences, American geography later moved towards positivism and quantitative methods. Exemplified by the work of Brian Berry, this approach embraced putatively value-free methods from demography and economics in the modeling and mapping of spatial systems (see *The Changing Shape of Metropolitan America* (1977).

Since the 1970s, however, the impact of European scholars like David Harvey and Neil Smith, as well as the work of American geographers in Marxist traditions, has made an impact across the social sciences and some humanities. Important departments have included Harvey's position at Johns Hopkins, the University of California-Berkeley and the University of Southern California (with Jennifer Wolch, Michael Dear and Edward Soja in Planning). American-based geographers have discussed issues of postmodernity (for example, Soja's *Thirdspace*, 1996), identity (Yi-Fu Tuan's *Cosmos and Hearth*, 1996) and social justice/social change (Wolch and Dears' *Landscapes of Despair*, 1987; Smith's *The New Urban Frontier*,, 1996). Their awareness of the impact of space and place on society and culture, in turn, has contributed in methods and theory to other fields as diverse as **anthropology**, **sociology**, **history** and **cultural studies**.

GARY McDONOGH

German Americans

Immigration from Germany to America began in the seventeenth century as radical religious groups such as the Mennonites and Anabaptists fled from religious persecution at home to the relative tolerance of the American colonies. By 1776 Benjamin Franklin estimated that 150,000 German speakers lived in America. Many of them settled in the rural farming districts of Maryland, New York and Pennsylvania, while others went west to the then **frontier** district in Ohio. In the nineteenth century, war, political problems and economic problems in Germany and the Austro-Hungarian empire led to a peak period of German

immigration between 1815 and 1870; nearly 4 million German speakers came to the US during this period. Thereafter German immigration declined somewhat, to be replaced by large migrant flows from Eastern Europe. There was another wave of immigration following the First World War, and another following the Second World War and the partition of Germany; 150,000 Germans came to the US in 1950 alone. This latter group was a mixture of displaced persons, **refugees** from East Germany and war brides of American soldiers.

Unlike the later Eastern European arrivals, who sought work and wages, most of the German immigrants were interested in acquiring land. In the early nineteenth century they settled in the **Midwest**, particularly in Ohio, in and around cities such as **Cincinnati, OH** and **Milwaukee, WI** (today, nearly half the population of these cities is of German descent). These German communities remained highly homogeneous; during the American Civil War, regiments raised from among the "Dutch" (as they were known) often had to have staff interpreters as neither officers nor men could speak English. Even today, many of the Ohio communities are bilingual in German and English. Later arrivals moved further west, homesteading in Kansas, Nebraska, Wisconsin and the Dakotas. It has been estimated that by 1900, one-quarter of all German immigrants were engaged in farming.

German Americans have a long history of association and political involvement. Before the First World War, the German American Central Alliance focused mainly on domestic issues concerning German speakers, but it also pressed for US neutrality in the war. Earlier, German Americans such as Emma Goldman had also been active in socialist and anarchist movements. Between the wars, other strong German cultural movements emerged, some of which were suspected of supporting the Hitler regime in Germany. In fact, though, almost all German Americans supported the war effort and German American men served overseas in large numbers.

Today, some 55 million Americans claim German descent, more than any other ethnic group. German Americans have been prominent in every walk of life. German contributions to American culture have been immense, even if they are no longer recognized as distinctly German. Great German American figures include Albert **Einstein** and Samuel Pulitzer; more controversial ones include Werner von Braun, the rocket scientist who was spirited out of Germany at the end of the war to mastermind the US **space** program, having previously built rockets for the Nazis. On another level, the American brewing industry was founded by German immigrants (mostly from the Austro-Hungarian empire). All across America in the summertime, people gather at picnics and barbeques to drink beer and eat hamburgers and hot dogs made with frankfurters, implicitly acknowledging how German culture has become embedded in that of America.

MORGEN WITZEL

ghettos

The term "ghetto," originating in the Jewish urban enclaves of Europe, was adapted to the urban ethnic communities in the US at the beginning of the twentieth century. It found its most lasting association with the residentially segregated inner-city **African American** neighborhoods. Such **neighborhoods** first developed in northeastern cities, primarily in the 1920s, following the mass **migration** of blacks from the **South**. In the twentieth century, the "ghetto" referred almost automatically in speech and media to the most depressed and dangerous elements of black urban life.

These areas have changed themselves over time. Initially, new residents in these areas came full of expectations that they would secure industrial employment. Such jobs were not forthcoming, however, except in the period during and immediately after the Second World War. In the 1940s and 1950s, access to these jobs dried up as industries closed or moved out to the **suburbs**. In addition, whites moved out to these areas, leaving **inner-city** communities economically blighted.

In the 1960s, with urban **race riots**, a strong sense of nostalgia developed in relation to the old ghetto. New neighborhoods were seen as one-dimensional in their poverty, having once been viable, vibrant communities – sites of black churches, fraternal orders and other associations.

The growing literature on ghettos and ghettoization, therefore, tends to describe a point at which the areas began to develop supposedly dysfunctional characteristics, such as weak families, high levels of poverty, violence, prostitution and drugs. The riots themselves damaged the remnants of **community** that had survived.

Ghettoization was also described as a form of internal colonialism. In conjunction with the **Black Power** movement, many assumed that these areas needed to be decolonized and that blacks had to gain some self-determination before improvements would occur. Any potential for this to happen, tied to the **War on Poverty**, was lost with the economic downturn brought on by the **Vietnam War** and the OPEC crisis.

A recent tendency has been to accentuate the "culture of poverty" of people in these communities, suggesting, as Nicholas Lemann did in *The Promised Land* (1991), that such people brought a "sharecropping culture" with them from the rural South. This has tied in with the short-sharp-shock approach to **welfare reform**, which suggests that it is no longer advisable to give support to members of these ghettoized communities, especially single mothers vilified as "welfare queens." They must be removed from these environments and the mindsets fostered by the culture there by being forced to work. Such theories have been countered by scholars like Robin D.G. Kelley, Michael Katz and Adolph Reed.

Further reading

Kelley, R.D.G. (1997) *Yo' Mama's Dysfunctional*, Boston: Beacon Press.
Lemann, N. (1991) *The Promised Land*, New York: A.A. Knopf.
Osofsky, G. (1966) *Harlem: The Making of a Ghetto*, New York: Harper & Row.

ROBERT GREGG

GI Bill of Rights

Signed into law in June 1944, the Servicemen's Readjustment Act, better known as the GI Bill of Rights, offered education and home-loan benefits to Second World War **veterans**. The program helped to triple college graduates from 1939 to 1950 and kept returning soldiers and sailors out of the labor force longer, allowing the economy slowly to absorb job-seeking veterans. Similar programs were implemented for **Korean War** and **Vietnam War** veterans as well as reservists. Since 1944, more than 20 million veterans and dependents have participated in education programs and 14 million home loans have been guaranteed.

See also: colleges and universities; education and society

JAMES DEVITT

Gingrich, Newt

b. 1943

Newt Gingrich was elected Speaker of the US House of Representatives in 1995. His election capped a dramatic shift in American politics in which the **Republican Party** regained control of Congress for the first time in a generation. Gingrich is largely credited with formulating the "Contract with America," a platform for conservative ideas such as support for **welfare reform** and cutting **taxes**, which became a Republican mantra.

Though named *Time* magazine's 1995 Man of the Year, Gingrich found difficult the transition from opposition party member of Congress to congressional leader. Lacking the charisma of other politicians, Gingrich suffered from low ratings in national opinion polls. Weakened by a large fine for violations of ethics rules, he was almost removed from his leadership position in 1997, and then resigned a year later after the Republican Party's poor showing in mid-term elections.

First elected to the Congress in 1978, Gingrich previously taught **history** at West Georgia College after receiving his PhD from Tulane University. In his years before winning the Speakership, Gingrich was known for his effective use of **television** to reach Republican activists and rebuke the **Democratic Party**. His fierce partisanship earned him regular challengers to his seat in Congress from suburban **Atlanta, GA**. Gingrich's enthusiasm for technological solutions to complex human problems earned him derision – for example his recommendation for giving poor people laptop computers as a way to improve their conditions. He is the author of four books, including *To Renew America* (1995) which lays out his political vision.

A. JOSEPH BORRELL

girl groups

Between 1960 and 1964, a new trend developed within the nascent US popular music industry: groups of girls, some as young as thirteen, singing together in a vocal harmonic style that had its roots in the black gospel churches and in the popular doo-wop style of the **ghetto** street corner. The girl groups' songs were composed by a new wave of young, mostly Jewish songwriters who were influenced by **rock 'n' roll**, and who brought a fresh, **teenage** sensibility to the stale pop formulae of the light entertainment industry.

The first girl group to hit the national charts was the Chantels in 1958 with "Maybe." Arlene Smith, the lead singer, was a convent schoolgirl who had formed the group with her classmates. Smith herself had composed the song, but it was credited to her producer; the record sold well but the girls themselves made virtually no money. This pattern, in which the artists were exploited both artistically and financially, was to be repeated continually throughout the girl-group era.

In 1960 the Shirelles hit number one with the single "Will You Still Love Me Tomorrow?". Lead singer Shirley Alston had a plaintive, sweet, almost off-key vocal style that charmed a generation, and the song, written by teenage sweethearts Carole King and Gerry Goffin, seemed to sum up the innocence and sincerity of a young woman on the brink of her first sexual experience. The single kicked off a craze for girl groups, as new groups like the Crystals, the Ronettes and the Shangri Las rushed to repeat the Shirelles' success.

In the early 1960s, the pop songwriting industry (known as Tin Pan Alley) was centered around New York's Brill Building, where a number of new labels, producers, songwriters and artists set up stall to service the teenage market. It was a creative time for pop music: a song could be composed, hawked around the building, recorded, pressed and distributed in a matter of days. Three songwriting teams emerged as the major players in the girl-group explosion: King and Goffin, Cynthia Weil and Barry Mann, and Ellie Greenwich and Jeff Barry (who also wrote with producer Phil Spector). Between them, these songwriters wrote nearly all the classic songs of the period, from "Chapel of Love" to "Leader of the Pack," from "Da Doo Ron Ron" to "Be My Baby."

Meanwhile, in Detroit, Barry Gordy's newly established Motown label was grooming a girl group for stardom: the **Supremes**. However, the Supremes were slow to get a hit, while other girl groups like the Marvelettes, who scored the label's first number one with "Please Mr Postman," and Martha and the Vandellas found popularity. Finally, in 1964, the Supremes began their staggering run of hits, which established them as Motown's most successful act. Remarkably, the group's success coincided with that of the male British beat groups, such as the **Beatles** and the Rolling Stones, who were widely viewed as having destroyed the US pop industry. Even more remarkably, after the break up of the group Diana Ross managed to forge a brilliant solo career for herself, emerging as the first black female superstar in show business.

The girl-group phenomenon was largely ignored in the late 1960s and 1970s by rock critics who saw the music as "bubblegum" schlock, yet girl groups such as the Three Degrees, Sister Sledge, the Emotions and Labelle continued to attract a mostly female public. In the 1980s, groups like Salt 'n Pepa, En Vogue, SWV and TLC fused elements of hip hop with the "girl-talk" aesthetic of girl groups to create a new, more sexually explicit music directed at young women. More recently, the Spice Girls, a UK band with the message of "girl power," appealed to an ever younger generation of female pop fans.

Further reading

Greig, C. (1989) *Will You Still Love Me Tomorrow?*, London: Virago.

CHARLOTTE GREIG

Giuliani, Rudolph *see* Italian Americans; New York and its boroughs

Glass, Philip

b. 1937

Composer. Grandson of **Russian** Jewish immigrants, trained in **New York** City, NY (Julliard) and Paris while also influenced by **South Asian** and Arab music. Glass combines a certain minimalism with mysticism in musical events like his opera *Einstein on the Beach* (1976, with Robert **Wilson**). His music became familiar to a wide audience from the intense repeated score of the ecological polemic *Koyaanisqatsi* (1982).

GARY McDONOGH

Goldberg, Whoopi

b. 1949

Female actor and comedian who often has tackled issues of **race** and **class**. She gained screen prominence for her debut as the suffering Celie in *The Color Purple* (1985), although she won an Academy Award for *Ghost* (1990), the first black woman so honored since Hattie McDaniel (1939). She also served for several years as an acerbic and politicized emcee for the Academy Awards and developed a short-lived television **talk show**.

See also: actors

GARY McDONOGH
CINDY WONG

golden age of television

Epithet applied to the innovative (often live) developmental period of network **television** from 1948 to 1960. Among the shows taken as high points of this period are dramas like *Studio One*, *Playhouse 90*, *Kraft Television Theater* and other sponsored **theater** shows in **prime time**. Certainly, this produced many fine pieces in writing, acting and directing, including Paddy Chayefsky's *Marty*, which later won an Oscar as a cinematic

production. Many viewers and critics also fondly recall early comedy – both **variety shows** with Milton Berle or Sid Caesar and **sitcoms** like *I Love Lucy*, *The Honeymooners*, etc. Finally, this period was also taken as a high point for **news**, with the towering figure of Edward R. **Murrow**. In all these choices (which omit the hours of dross over the decade), one also sees standards set by **New York** urbane sensibilities that were challenged by **television**'s growing ties with **Hollywood** as well as its national expansion and appeal to new audiences. Robert Thompson, in *Television's Second Golden Age* (1996), argues that the 1980s produced more complex and broader medical, **crime**, **law** and other dramas that better merit such accolades.

Further reading

Thompson, R. (1996) *Television's Second Golden Age*, New York: Continuum.

GARY McDONOGH

Goldwater, Barry

b. 1909; d. 1998

A long-time **Republican Party** US senator from Arizona (1952–64; 1968–86) and failed presidential candidate, Goldwater is widely considered the founder – and certainly the galvanizer and emblem – of the postwar conservative political movement in the United States.

Although Goldwater had few legislative accomplishments as a senator and suffered a landslide defeat in the 1964 presidential election against Lyndon B. **Johnson**, his outspoken and unabashed conservative views were a kernel around which the conservative movement was rebuilt, beginning in the 1950s, in the wake of the New Deal and against the current of the postwar liberal consensus. Goldwater gave the conservative movement one of its rallying cries in his speech to the 1964 Republican convention in **San Francisco, CA**, stating "Extremism in the defense of liberty is no vice" and "moderation in the pursuit of justice is no virtue."

Goldwater's campaign brought many conservatives into the political arena, including Ronald

Reagan, whose victory in 1980 is often considered the flowering of ideological seeds that were planted in the 1964 campaign. Goldwater's philosophy came down to two core principles: a fundamentally libertarian opposition to the growth of federal programs at home and an adamant and aggressive opposition to **Russia** abroad. Both principles led his opponents to brand him "extreme," particularly during the 1964 campaign in which Goldwater suggested making Social Security voluntary and using low-level nuclear blasts to defoliate Vietnam. As a senator, Goldwater voted against the 1964 **Civil Rights Act**. These positions led to Goldwater's 1964 defeat – in which he received less than 40 percent of the popular vote and won only in Arizona and five Southern states – and his acolytes, while sharing his principles, moved away from his specific positions.

At the end of his career, Goldwater's libertarian attitudes sometimes put him at odds with the conservative movement, as he felt uncomfortable with the religious right and supported homosexual rights.

DAVID GOLDSTON

golf

In the period since the Second World War, golf in the United States has gained in popularity both as a spectator and participatory sport. In the late 1940s and 1950s, golf began to gain appeal as a status sport associated with the wealthy and with business. The obsession of President **Eisenhower** with the game – he played over 800 rounds while in office – symbolized a sport which was viewed as a pastime of the elite.

Just as golf was beginning to become a staple of televised sports, the arrival in the early 1960s of a new breed of professional golfers – young, athletic and charismatic – fed a new fascination with the game. No player symbolized the new feeling associated with golf more than Arnold Palmer. Palmer was blessed with both an excellent game and an easy-going charm which together won him a devoted following known as "Arnie's Army." Palmer, from Western Pennsylvania, rose from humble beginnings, encouraging others to reassess

the view that golf was just a game for the well-off. At the same time, a younger golfer named Jack **Nicklaus** emerged as a foil for the more popular Palmer. In time, Nicklaus would eclipse Palmer and become the most accomplished American golfer of all time.

As a result of the professional game's increased visibility, public and resort golf-course construction became a growth industry in the 1970s and 1980s as the **middle class** clamored for a place to play the game at a price within their reach. This period saw the continued rise in the profile of the professional game, and a host of new stars, including Tom Watson, Ben Crenshaw and Curtis Strange.

The 1990s, while still a boom time for the men's circuit, saw the rise of a second tour, the Senior Tour for men fifty years and older, as well as a somewhat more vitalized women's tour. Women constituted the largest group of new golfers in the 1990s. However, exclusionary practices still exist to bar women from some of the more prominent private clubs. Moreover, public courses sometimes discourage women's play, with the result that women also constitute the largest percentage of golfers who give up the game. The practice of minority exclusion continues as well, although the subject has become more hotly debated in the last few years. In 1991 the Professional Golfers' Association threatened to move its championship tournament from the Shoal Creek Golf Club because of the club's practice of exclusion, and a number of other clubs have been dropped from the professional tour for failing to recruit **African Americans** to their membership. Most recently, a young star named Tiger Woods has emerged who claims both African and Asian ancestry. His prominence may spur further re-examination of the membership practices at private clubs across the nation, and may encourage more minority youths to take up what has until now remained a sport played mostly by whites.

Further reading

Feinstein, J. (1999) *The Majors*, New York: Little Brown and Co.

ROBERT ANDERSON

Good Neighbor Policy *see* Latin America; Roosevelt, Franklin Delano

Gordy, Barry *see* music, popular; Motown

Gore, Albert, Jr.

b. 1948

Son of the distinguished **Democratic Party** senator from Tennessee, Gore grew up between **Washington, DC** and Carthage, Tennessee before attending Harvard and enlisting for service in Vietnam. He later worked as a journalist and attended Vanderbilty Divinity and Law Schools before joining Congress in 1977 and becoming a senator in 1984. He ran unsuccessfully in a crowded Democratic primary field in 1988, but became Bill **Clinton**'s running-mate in 1992, serving two terms as vice-president. Gore has claimed special commitment to and expertise in environmental issues (*Earth in the Balance*, 1992) and **telecommunications**. Heir to Clinton, in his 2000 presidential campaign Gore was both tainted by administrative scandals and unable to project the charisma that had carried Clinton through. His sober, wooden delivery and gaffes became the stuff of political satire. His performance at the Democratic **Conventions**, however, forced a tighter race with George **Bush**.

GARY McDONOGH

gospel music

While this may refer to traditions of white hymnody (which intersect with **country music**), "gospel" is more often identified with a black genre that emerged from spirituals after the turn of the nineteenth century, alongside ragtime, **blues** and **jazz**. This free-form singing, with emotive solos, antiphonal responses of repeated spiritual messages, instrumental back-up (piano and tambourine) and rhythmic choral support, was also associated with the rise of charismatic and spiritual churches. In fact, mainline black Protestant denominations avoided it for decades. Among its guiding spirits was Thomas Dorsey, who turned from blues to the composition of classic gospel

hymns like "Precious Lord, Take my Hand" (1932). Gospel influenced – and was influenced by – **rhythm and blues** and **soul**; artists Sam **Cooke** and Aretha **Franklin** embody this intersection in their work.

GARY MCDONOGH

gourmet food

Since the 1960s, "gourmet" (sometimes "continental") food has been associated with vague derivatives of classical French cuisine, using cream or wine sauces, expensive ingredients outside the northern European palate (olives, snails, pâté, wines) and elaborate presentations. As Jane and Michael Stern discuss this evolution in *American Gourmet* (1991), this cuisine, as American as chop suey, established itself in hotels and **kitchens** across the country, and often constitutes a separate section in supermarkets and **cookbooks**. Yet it is also a style many view with suspicion because of its "upper-class" associations.

Further reading

Stern, J. and M. (1991) *American Gourmet*, New York: HarperCollins.

GARY McDONOGH
CINDY WONG

governors

The governor is the head of the executive branch of **state government**. He or she is popularly elected, serving in most cases for a term of four years. The timing of governors' elections varies; some are elected in the same year as presidential elections, while others are elected in the mid-term elections that take place halfway through a presidential term of office.

Although the original intent in establishing state governments was that governors should enjoy powers within their states broadly analogous to that of the president, in fact there are substantial restrictions on governors' powers. Many aspects of governance for which they are nominally responsible, including **education**, public health and **welfare**, are also supervised by federal agencies that can override the governors' powers. Governors, like **presidents**, are also answerable to their state Senates and Houses of Representatives. In some cases, governors of states that have large urban centers with powerful **mayors** find their writ is limited with regard to the latter; the governor of **New York**, for example, is arguably less powerful than the mayor of New York City, who is nominally subordinate to him. The early practice of locating state capitals in relatively minor towns (such as Albany in New York, Harrisburg in Pennsylvania, or Sacramento in **California**) can also serve to increase governors' isolation from the main currents of affairs in their states.

Despite this, many governors do have significant impact on their states. Michael **Dukakis**' term as governor of Massachusetts saw important reforms affecting legal and social issues, while in **Texas** George W. **Bush**'s program of "caring conservatism" has claimed a similar impact.

Until comparatively recently, most presidents of the United States came from the ranks of the **Washington, DC** elite, with most having served previously as senators, members of Congress or **vice-presidents**; this was the case with, for example, John F. **Kennedy** and Richard **Nixon**. More recently, however, successful governors have increasingly used their position as a platform for presidential ambitions. Gerald Ford and George Bush are the only recent presidents not to have been governors. Meanwhile, Jimmy **Carter** (Georgia), Ronald **Reagan** (California), and Bill **Clinton** (Arkansas) all came from state rather than national politics. Michael **Dukakis**, Bush's unsuccessful Democratic opponent in 1988, was also Governor of Massachusetts. The majority of candidates seeking their party's nomination for the presidency in the last two decades have also been governors or former governors; other powerful governors such as Mario **Cuomo** have been pressed to stand, but have refused. George W. Bush (son of the former president) parlayed the weak governorship of Texas into a platform from which he became **Republican** presidential nominee in 1999. Among those discussed to balance the ticket was yet another governor, Tom Ridge of Pennsylvania.

Governors of wealthy, high-population states such as California, Texas, Massachusetts and New Jersey are often influential figures on the national scene, but many of those in the smaller states in the **Midwest** and **West** are all but unknown outside their own state. The election of a former professional wrestler, Jesse Ventura, as governor of Minnesota was one of the few events in state politics to make national headlines in 1998.

MORGEN WITZEL

graffiti

While painting and writing on buildings has a millennial history, graffiti in late twentieth-century America faced two contradictory evaluations. An explosion of extensive stylized words and pictures in vivid colors associated with particular artists on New York subways in the 1970s focused debate on graffiti as **popular art**, associated with hip-hop culture and urban vitality. Generally, these paintings are not seen in terms of political issues, although **race** and **ethnicity** underpin graffiti wars. Yet, while **museums**, art galleries and universities have championed this viewpoint, urban officials have identified graffiti with vandalism, danger, **gangs** and quality-of-life issues. Hence, cities have adopted zero-tolerance policies to remove graffiti immediately (especially in downtown areas), or to prevent it through design or alternatives like active public mural programs (**Philadelphia, PA**, for example, has covered nearly 2,000 walls in this fashion).

GARY McDONOGH
CINDY WONG

Graham, Bill

Rock promoter Bill Graham turned the concert hall, the Fillmore, into a legendary site for **San Francisco, CA** rock and one of the key meeting places for the counterculture that proliferated in the late 1960s in the Bay area. Graham started out as manager for the avant-gardist San Francisco Mime Troupe; when the troupe got into legal trouble for performing its risqué art publicly, he organized a fundraiser at the Fillmore with the Jefferson Airplane and The Fugs. Graham took over the hall and became renowned for promoting eclectic combinations of artists in a night's bill and introducing audiences to performers outside the mainstream. Graham died in a helicopter accident in 1991; the Fillmore continues today under separate management.

See also: rock 'n' roll

EDWARD MILLER

Graham, Billy

b. 1918

Preacher William Franklin Graham, Jr brought evangelical **religion** to the global stage via mass revivals and **mass media**. After his childhood in the Depression **South**, Graham turned to the fundamentalist ministry, founding his Evangelical Association in 1950. His primary vehicle was the mass crusade in urban centers from **New York** City to **Los Angeles, CA** (and eventually from London to Moscow), rebroadcast for multiple nights over **television** worldwide. Graham also became a conservative Christian confidant to US **presidents** from **Eisenhower** to **Clinton**, including the awkward Vietnam and **Nixon** years. His autobiography, *Just as I am*, appeared in 1997.

GARY McDONOGH

Graham, Martha

b. 1894; d. 1991

Dramatic doyenne of American modern **dance**. As both dancer and choreographer, Graham incorporated American cultural themes and classical dramas into her repertoire, translated into strong bodily expression and vivid movements. She also worked with major American composers like Aaron **Copland** and Samuel **Barber.**

GARY McDONOGH

Grand Ol' Opry *see* country and western music; Nashville and Memphis, Tennessee

Grateful Dead

They emerged from mid-1960s **San Francisco, CA** counterculture, adding a country accent to psychedelic music. Starting out at the Fillmore (see **Graham, Bill**), they came to be one of the hardest touring bands in rock history – in 1969 the band played 152 shows. Their shows were long, filled with improvisatory solos, with audiences of "deadheads" given to ingesting hallucinogens and dancing. Deadheads often followed the band around the country, recognizable in their tie-dyed attire and band insignia. A skull became "the Dead" logo and the band members – especially singer/guitarist Jerry Garcia, but also Bob Weir, Pig Pen and Mickey Hart – became legendary. The band ended when Garcia passed away in 1995 after a long struggle with drugs. Over 25,000 people paid their respects in San Francisco's Memorial Park.

See also: rock 'n' roll

EDWARD MILLER

Graves, Michael

b. 1934

Postmodern architect and theorist. Identified as one of the New York Five (with Peter Eisenman, Richard Meier, John Hejduk and Charles Gwathney), Graves has become known for his interweaving of colors, classical and figurative references and natural themes. Among his best-known works are the Portland Building and the Humana Headquarters (**Louisville, KY**). Graves, based at Princeton, has also extended his design in the classroom and through association with major corporations like **Disney** and Target, for whom he designed a housewares line.

See also: architecture

GARY McDONOGH

Great Lakes

Lakes Superior, Michigan, Huron, Erie and Ontario, five interconnected freshwater lakes, make up one of the largest surface freshwater reservoirs on Earth. (The polar ice caps and Russia's Lake Balaika are larger.) The 10,900 mile coastline touches eight US states (Minnesota, Wisconsin, Illinois, Indiana, Michigan, Ohio, Pennsylvania and New York) and two Canadian provinces, Ontario and Quebec. The 295,000 square mile Great Lakes watershed, including five rivers linking the lakes to each other and to the Atlantic Ocean, provides 95 percent of the United States' fresh-water supply

Unsurpassed water transportation routes and the region's seemingly limitless supply of lumber, iron and other metallic ores sustained the Great Lakes area from the 1820s to 1960 as the United States' premier center of industrial production. Well-paid **union** labor, making wood products, steel and later railroad equipment and cars, built the ethnically diverse industrial cities of **Chicago, IL, Detroit, MI** and **Cleveland, OH**. **Milwaukee** grew famous brewing beer from Great Lakes' water, while rivals Green Bay, Wisconsin and Kalamazoo, Michigan tapped the waters for their paper industries. **Buffalo, New York** prospered first by moving cargo around Niagara Falls and later as the headquarters of massive hydroelectric power systems utilizing Niagara itself.

The general decline of heavy industry in the urban **Northeast** after 1960 impoverished the region, which has tried to encourage **tourism**, leisure and summer-home development to replace good jobs lost in industry and shipping. Leisure had long contributed a share to the regional economy, especially at Mackinac Island in Michigan, Door County in Wisconsin and the area around Niagara Falls. Since 1960, **fishing**, boating, cruising and sightseeing have grown in proportionate importance as industry has declined. Sport-fishing mushroomed in Lake Michigan after the introduction of Coho salmon to the lake in the early 1960s. Old industrial **waterfronts** in Chicago, Detroit, Cleveland and elsewhere were reclaimed in the 1970s for leisure use. Since the 1980s, shipwreck-hunting cruises, restored historic lighthouse facilities and collections of Great Lakes shipping history

and lore have fed new tourist interest in the more romantic aspects of the region's industrial past.

The continuing importance of the Great Lakes' water both for consumption and leisure has generated numerous interstate and international cooperative efforts to control water quality, detoxify sediments, clean beaches and rebuild the damaged ecology of the whole region. Modern **environmentalism** has even given surviving Native American tribes new voices in regional deliberations, almost 180 years after they were defeated in the international scramble for control of the Great Lakes. Though its troubles are compounded by unexpected economic decline, the Great Lakes area really continues to struggle with the same age-old problem of balancing the claims of competing jurisdictions and contradictory uses for the region's great natural assets.

Further reading

Bastow, T. (1986) *This Vast Pollution*, Washington, DC: Green Fields.

Lloyd, T. and Mullen, P. (eds) (1990) *Lake Erie Fishermen*, Urbana: University of Illinois.

Wille, L. (1991) *Forever Open, Clear, and Free: the Struggle for Chicago's Lakefront*, Chicago: University of Chicago.

http://www.epa.gov.glnpo

SHARON ANN HOLT

Great Society *see* Johnson, Lyndon Baines; War on Poverty

Greek Americans

The first wave of Greek immigrants arrived in the United States in the 1890s, settling mainly in cities along the east coast. There are no exact statistics, but it has been estimated that between 1890 and 1930 some 450,000 Greeks had emigrated to the United States; more than 200,000 of them returned to Greece, however, either as volunteers during the First World War or because of the Great Depression in the States, and many more because they felt that they were not welcome in the United States.

The second phase of Greek **immigration** was between 1946 and 1960, following the end of the Second World War and the civil war, that left Greece in ruins. Most of the new immigrants came to the States for economic reasons and some as displaced persons. The third and final phase began in 1966 when the immigration laws were liberalized. It has been estimated that between 1945 and 1980 some 250,000 Greeks emigrated to the United States.

No accurate statistics exist, but, according to the 1990 census, in addition to those of immigrant status there are 1,110,373 Americans of Greek ancestry and there are nearly 400,000 whose mother tongue is Greek. All in all there may be close to 2 million Americans with Greek roots, most of them living in major cities throughout the United States.

While the early immigrants engaged in small business, including restaurants, newspaper parlors, dry-goods stores, shoemakers, tailor shops, grocery stores and bakeries, their descendants have turned to **education**, the sciences and professions. Thus today there are some 5,000 educators, **college and university** professors, including administrators of major universities, many physicians and lawyers, and many more in finance and business administration, including chief executives who served or serve major corporations such as **Dow Chemical**, Mobil Oil, Merck Pharmaceuticals, Thermo Electron, American Standard, Conoco, Boston Scientific, International Paper and Giant Foods – to mention just a few ranked by *Forbes* magazine.

Another major trend among Greek Americans of the second and third generation is interest in politics and civil service. In the last quarter of the twentieth century, Americans have seen a vice-president (Spiro Agnew), presidential candidates (Michael Dukakis and Paul Tsongas), members of a president's Cabinet (Peter Peterson) and advisers (George Stephanopoulos), several senators and members of Congress (Brademas, Sarbanes, Tsongas, Olympia Snow, Yatron, Gikas, Billirakis, Pappas, Galifianakis) of Greek origin. Even though Greek names are easily recognizable, there are many Greek Americans who have shortened or changed their names for business or professional reasons (Anagnostopoulos = Agnew; Petropoulos

= Peterson; Kyriazdis = Kress; Makris = Long; Papanikolaou = Paps). Today, one finds Greek Americans in every profession, including **radio**, **television**, **publishing**, athletics and more.

In addition to local and state Greek American organizations such as the Pan-Macedonian, Cretan, Peloponnesian and Thessalian societies, Greek American concerns are voiced through several national organizations such as the American Hellenic Institute, the World Council of Hellenes Abroad and the American Hellenic Educational Progressive Association (AHEPA).

Over the course of seventy-five years, the Greek American **community** has gone through transitions, adaptations and acculturations. Nevertheless, they maintain a strong consciousness of the contributions and value of their historic heritage. Recent sociological studies indicate that Greek Americans "statistically possess the highest degree of academic achievement, i.e., education and degrees, of any ethnic group in the United States."

See also: Greek Orthodox

Further reading

Moskos, C.C. (1989) *Greek Americans*, New Brunswick: Transaction Publishers.

Psomiades, H. III and Scourby, A. (eds) (1982) *The Greek American Community in Transition*, New York: Pella Publishing Company.

DEMETRIOS J. CONSTANTELOS

Greek Orthodox

The Greek Orthodox Christian Church in the United States is under the spiritual and administrative jurisdiction of the Ecumenical Patriarchate with headquarters in old Byzantion, Constantinople, present-day Istanbul, Turkey. The term "Greek," used to describe the church, is applied in a cultural and historical sense. Even though early Christianity was born in Hellenistic Judaism, it was nurtured by and blossomed through the Greek language, the thought-world and missionary activity of the Greek-speaking people under Roman rule for at least the first four centuries of our era. Today, Greek Orthodox is synonymous with

Eastern Orthodox, and is used by several churches of different ethnic and cultural backgrounds.

Doctrinally, the Greek Orthodox Church subscribes to the faith of early Christianity as it developed on the basis of the holy scriptures, and the understanding and interpretation by important church elders, local councils and ecumenical synods, and the living experience of the church in history. Maintaining continuity with the past, without remaining static in its interpretation, is a major concern of the Greek Orthodox Church.

The earliest Greek Orthodox **community** in the United States was founded in 1864 in **New Orleans, LA**. It served the needs of Orthodox Christians of various ethnic and cultural backgrounds. Between 1864 and 1900, there were but a few thousand Greek Orthodox Christians. By 1922 there were 139 Greek Orthodox communities throughout the United States, but there was no administrative unity – no coordinating head – and they resembled Greek city-states in the American continent.

The real history of the Greek Orthodox Church in the United States starts in 1922 when the Greek Orthodox archdiocese was chartered and began to bring under its aegis all Greek Orthodox communities in the Americas. There are no official statistics about the number of active members in the church. At the end of 1997, there were 525 organized church communities served by 586 pastors, 35 priests with lay professions and several retired clergymen. The archdiocese is under one archbishop, five metropolitans and three auxiliary bishops.

Most of the church's members between the early 1900s and 1945 were immigrants who came either from Greece or as **refugees** from Asia Minor, present-day Turkey, Egypt and other Near-Eastern countries and Eastern Europe. A new wave of Greek immigrants in the 1960s contributed to the establishment of new communities and educational institutions. At present, the archdiocese supports a liberal arts college, a theological school, an institution for the training of Greek language teachers and church workers, several homes for the aged, a mission center, several day and many afternoon Greek language and culture schools.

The Greek Orthodox Church in the United States is presently going through a transition. While for many years the leadership of the church was in the hands of immigrant parents and grandparents, today it has passed to second- and third-generation **Greek Americans**. Furthermore, Greek, as the official liturgical language of the church, is slowly but steadily yielding to the use of English, especially in communities of **Midwestern** and Pacific states. The transition has not been conducted without some tension between the founders and the inheritors of the churches. But no schisms or conflicts have impeded the growth and influence of the church, whose membership today includes many who have joined it either through intermarriage or through personal spiritual quest.

The Greek Orthodox Church in the United States views their faith (doctrine, ethos and liturgical life) as old wine put into new wineskins (cf. Matthew 9.17).

Further reading

Constantelos, D.J. (1998) *Understanding the Greek Orthodox Church*, Brookline: Hellenic College Press.

Papaioannou, G. (1976) *From Mars Hill to Manhattan*, Minneapolis: Light and Life Publishing Company.

DEMETRIOS J. CONSTANTELOS

Greenwich Village

South Manhattan area approximately bounded by Houston, Broadway, Hudson and 14th Street, identified with alternative lifestyles and cultures. A pre-war haven for artists and political activists, Greenwich Village became identified in the 1950s with the beat generation and coffee-houses and, in the 1960s, with the **Stonewall Riot** and gay lifestyles. The *Village Voice* champions such political and cultural positions, as a **neighborhood** newspaper with national impact. Yet the village also represents attractive commercial and residential **real estate**, forces of **gentrification** that have challenged its alternative qualities in the 1990s even while tourists come to seek them.

GARY McDONOGH
CINDY WONG

Gregory, Dick

b. 1932

Gregory's acid racial observations made an early crossover breakthrough in American **comedy** in 1961 via the **Playboy** Club and **late-night television**. Yet his **celebrity** converged with his growing commitments to the **civil-rights** struggle, as an entertainer and colleague of Dr. Martin Luther **King**, Jr. Adopting King's non-violence, Gregory extended his protests to include fasts against the **Vietnam War** and support for Native Americans. Since the 1970s, he has also been occupied with problems of hunger in America and the world. His 1964 autobiography, *Nigger*, remains an intriguing memoir of maturing in a racist America.

GARY McDONOGH

Grenada

Part of a long-term effort to dislodge communists from the Western Hemisphere, President **Reagan**'s 1984 invasion of Grenada was ostensibly undertaken to rescue American medical students studying on the **Caribbean** island following the overthrow of Maurice Bishop's government. The major concern, however, was the building of the Point Salines airport by Cubans. Instability came to the island following a coup by General Hudson Austin, one consequence of the US blockade that had weakened the Bishop government, and forced him to turn increasingly to **Castro** for aid. The invasion was a diplomatically difficult mission as Grenada was a former British colony and the assault was condemned by the United Nations. But it proved an easy operation even for the **Pentagon** at that time; the US Army quickly deposed Austin and established a new government. It also established new limits on media coverage which would create problems for the flow of information in the **Gulf War**. The medical students were saved, too.

ROBERT GREGG

Greyhound *see* buses

Grisham, John

b. 1955

One of the most popular and bestselling authors of the late twentieth and early twenty-first centuries, Grisham has mastered the intricate legal maneuvering that drives all of his plots. His main character is usually a brilliant if somewhat maverick attorney confronting the shortcomings of his profession as he schemes to correct or take advantage of the system to his or his client's benefit. Grisham has addressed several modern social ailments, such as the death penalty (*The Chamber*, 1994) or **homelessness** (*The Street Lawyer*, 1998). He has been a permanent fixture on the bestseller lists since 1990, and six of his ten novels have been made into movies.

JIM WATKINS

Groening, Matt *see Simpsons, The*

grunge

When Nirvana's *Nevermind* knocked Michael **Jackson**'s *Dangerous* off the top of the charts in 1991, **rock**, after years of taking second place to dance music, re-emerged. Grunge became the title that the recording industry and media gave to the sound of the **Seattle, WA** music scene, which was subsequently plundered for all available talent. Grunge signified a style – long hair, flannel shirts and torn jeans laid over a **slacker** ideology – as much as a sound – roughly a **punk**-metal fusion, with Nirvana at the pop/punk end, Pearl Jam in the hard rock middle and Soundgarden at the metal/punk end.

DEWAR MACLEOD

Guam

Located in the Pacific, far from the US mainland, Guam occupies an ambiguous position within

American politics, society and culture. This largest island in the Marianas chain, ceded by Spain in 1898, has been a primary American outpost ever since, including Japanese occupation (1941–4) and a hard-fought reconquest. Guam is an unincorporated, organized territory of the US, with a population of 133,152, whose people have been citizens since 1950. While they elect a **governor**, they do not vote in national elections, although they often figure colorfully in political conventions.

The Chamorros, Guam's primary Micronesian inhabitants and language group, have mixed culturally and socially with waves of successive colonizers and immigrants from nearby nations (Filipinos constitute 25 percent of the population). Both military goals and development geared to contemporary Asian tourism (the economic bases of modern Guam) have threatened this heritage, as well as the island's unique ecosystem.

GARY McDONOGH

CINDY WONG

Gulf of Tonkin Resolution

On August 1, 1964, North Vietnamese torpedo boats attacked an American destroyer as it conducted espionage in the Gulf of Tonkin off North Vietnam. Two nights later, two vessels reported another attack. Though no firm evidence of an attack by North Vietnam surfaced, President Lyndon **Johnson** used the reports to justify a retaliation against the North Vietnamese for repeated acts of violence. Johnson requested and received from Congress blanket authorization to respond as he chose to any future aggression by the North Vietnamese. The Gulf of Tonkin Resolution became the legislative foundation for the **Vietnam War**, as the United States never actually declared war upon North Vietnam.

SUSAN SCHULTEN

Gulf War

In August 1990, President George **Bush** undertook the biggest US military commitment overseas since Vietnam, deploying more than 500,000

troops in the Persian Gulf to defend Saudi Arabia following Iraqi President Saddam Hussein's occupation of Kuwait. Bush's firm response to Iraq's invasion came as a surprise to the Iraqi president. US Ambassador April Glaspie had informed Hussein eight days before the invasion that the American government held "no opinion on Arab–Arab conflicts," saying "the Kuwait issue is not associated with America." The Iraqis long had claims on territory in Kuwait and complaints that the Kuwaitis were bringing down the price of oil through over-production.

Hussein's smiles following this meeting were erased by British Prime Minister Margaret Thatcher's resolve to ensure that Bush did not "go wobbly" and allow the invasion to stand. While General Colin **Powell**, Chairperson of the Joint Chiefs, wanted to give an embargo and sanctions imposed on Iraq time to work, Thatcher and Bush decided by January that Hussein would not withdraw. Bush went to war against Iraq, launching a bombing and missile assault that left Hussein's forces crippled and unable to withstand the land assault which came over a month later.

Bush and his military chiefs received criticism for stopping the "Desert Storm" land invasion after only five days, before Hussein's Republican Guard was destroyed. This made possible Hussein's subsequent intransigence and resulted in a number of follow-up operations during **Clinton**'s administration. Constant engagement between American and British fighter planes and Iraqi air defense systems has continued since Desert Storm. Saddam Hussein remains in power and is extremely wealthy due to black-market deals in Iraqi oil. The citizens of Iraq have been suffering in large numbers, many dying as a result of malnutrition exacerbated by the world embargo.

In the United States, the war was especially noteworthy for the fact that, even though it was considered a triumph for Bush, this did not translate into electoral success in the next presidential election. It has also lingered as a source of disaffection for many veterans who suffered from what was called **Gulf War Syndrome**, and who had their claims of injury rejected by the **Pentagon**.

The war has already made it into American movie history, thanks to *Courage under Fire* (1996) and *Three Kings* (1999).

ROBERT GREGG

Gulf War Syndrome

Following the **Gulf War** in 1991, many **veterans** experienced unexplained neurological conditions. Initially, veterans and their advocates in the media and Congress claimed this "syndrome" was caused by chemical warfare by Saddam Hussein, by widespread oil fires, or by radiation from US weapons. A number of "blue-ribbon panels" set up by the US Government each came back with reports that contradicted most of the veterans' claims. The most controversial of these, the Presidential Advisory Committee, suggested that stress was the most likely cause, thereby linking complaints to the older wartime "shell shock." Nevertheless, the **Pentagon** has developed an anthrax vaccine for all military personnel, suggesting that fears about biochemical warfare have been heightened by this activism. Ironically, many National Guard personnel and Reservists have opted not to take the vaccine, citing distrust of the Pentagon's handling of claims about the Gulf War.

ROBERT GREGG

guns

In the early twenty-first century, one-third of American homes have guns (pistols, revolvers, shotguns or rifles), representing approximately 200 million firearms. In the late 1990s, the number of deaths from bullets declined, but still averaged eighty-seven deaths per day in America.

Firearms were introduced to America by the first European explorers, traders and settlers to hunt and fight. Most colonial towns required able-bodied males to own a musket and train with the local militia. Their skill and prudent use of guns to hunt, protect the **family** and town, and project the **community**'s power affected men's social and political prestige; this attitude is still held by many Americans. After the Revolution, Americans, surrounded by monarchies and wary of despots who might rise from among their own ranks, guaranteed the personal ownership of guns to allow the people to retain control of their new Republic. The 2nd Amendment to the Constitution (see **Bill of Rights**) became the backbone of gun-rights legislation for two centuries.

In the nineteenth century, the western **frontier** required continued gun ownership and skills until each area became settled. Post-emancipation blacks used firearms to protect their families, and rural Americans continued to hunt with firearms. As industrialization and urbanization progressed, the new city dwellers had less need for guns. A small percentage of men and women owned them for protection, crime, sports and collecting. By the end of the twentieth century, 80 percent of the American population lived in **cities**.

At the same time, Americans' spectrum of attitudes towards guns became a divisive force as a strong movement grew to limit, if not eliminate, the private ownership of firearms. It was fueled by an increase in the misuse of guns, especially by younger Americans, the use of more deadly 9mm handguns, children caught in the crossfires of **inner-city** drug wars, the crippling of President **Reagan**'s Press Secretary, James Brady, and school massacres. **Lobbyists**, like Handgun Control, fought for more laws to restrict the number of privately owned guns through registration and prohibition. By the end of the century, they were successful in passing federal laws to eliminate the sale of many military-style rifles and to require a check and waiting period for would-be handgun owners. Some cities and states enacted more restrictive gun laws or even sued gun manufacturers. Other groups sought to diminish gun violence in the media.

The opposition, generally led by the **National Rifle Association**, sometimes joined by the **American Civil Liberties Union**, has been powerful. Stressing personal defense, sports and the 2nd Amendment, they have fought many successful legal actions on local, state and federal levels. While many people oppose further gun regulation because they see it as a first step in the government confiscation of all firearms, they have pushed for tougher legal prosecution and sentences for people who use guns in crimes.

Further reading

Roleff, T. (1997) *Gun Control*, San Diego: Green-haven.

Weir, W. (1997) *A Well Regulated Militia*, New Haven: Archon.

KATHLEEN GALLIGAN
WARREN RIESS

gypsies

Roughly 1 million gypsies live in the US. Although present since colonial days, **immigration** is difficult to follow because many arrived under other national quotas; gypsies only became an "officially" recognized minority in the 1960s. Many concentrate in urban centers of the **North-east**, **Midwest** and **West**, but have expanded into urban areas in search of interstitial economic positions in commerce, repairs and entertainment. Gypsies generally maintain strong social and cultural boundaries with outsiders, making them an object of mystery and suspicion, depicted in media as foreign rather than ethnic.

Further reading

Sway, M. (1988) *Familiar Strangers*, Urbana: University of Illinois.

GARY McDONOGH

Haiti

One of the great "silences" in US **history**. Haiti sent volunteers to fight in the American Revolution, while the slaves' defeat of Napoleon's forces there allowed the United States to purchase the massive Louisiana territory. During the twentieth century, this small Caribbean nation became more dependent on the US, including military occupation from 1915 to 1934. The US later kept a watchful eye, provided aid and purchased most exports (largely **coffee**). The strongly anti-communist Duvalier regimes were kept in place by American government support.

Once the **Cold War** ended, possibilities opened up for democratic change. Opposition to the Duvaliers formed around Father Jean-Bertrand Aristide, and the Americans began to discourage attempts by the Tonton Macoute (Duvalier's secret police) to put down protests. In September 1994, after Aristide's election and almost immediate overthrow, President **Clinton** ordered American troops to invade Haiti again in "Operation Restore Democracy." Nonetheless, Haiti remains an impoverished nation and many Haitians seek to enter the United States as **refugees** (boat people) and immigrants.

ROBERT GREGG

Haitian Americans

Haitians represent the largest nationality group among black **Caribbean** immigrants, numbering approximately 500,000 in the United States, 70,000 in the Greater Miami area alone. The first group of Haitians to arrive by boat on South Florida shores landed at Pompano Beach on December 12, 1965. These political refugees and the other early immigrants seeking political asylum in the United States generally came from the upper-class families who had opposed the Duvalier regime in **Haiti**. They settled in a section of downtown **Miami, FL** which has come to be known as "Little Haiti." As was the case for anti-Castro Cubans, these first immigrants were followed by a wave of poorer immigrants, creating significant class tensions within the immigrant **community**.

American support for the Duvaliers, and for the democratic governments that followed it, has meant that Haitians have not been considered "legitimate" political refugees. In contrast to Cubans, whose island nation Washington considers a communist-pariah state, Haitians have never been given preferential treatment by immigration laws. The resentment that Haitians feel about this has become evident *vis-à-vis* immigration laws that have allowed Cubans who make it to the US to stay in the country.

Haitian refugees tend to be semi-skilled, have some education and have lived in urban areas in Haiti. But Haiti is generally undeveloped compared to the United States, and so, in addition to **language** difficulties as French speakers, Haitian immigrants have sometimes had more obstacles to overcome than their Caribbean neighbors. They have also remained separate and distinct from **African American** communities, divided by cultural, religious and language differences. In the late 1980s, widespread assumptions that immigrants from Haiti were bringing the **AIDS** virus into the United States also led to ostracism. The **New York** City, NY case of Abner Louima, a security guard arrested and tortured by members of the NYPD, has become a rallying cry for Haitians wanting to confront the bigotry against them.

Predominantly Catholic, Haitians have tended to worship within the parish church where they reside. Frequently, they hold services in Creole, separate from other Catholics, and adapt the liturgy to reflect styles of worship in Haiti. The growth of the Haitian community has also led to increasing interest in **Voudou** and African-based religions.

See also: immigration

ROBERT GREGG

halls of fame

Museums often linked to foundational myths about a particular game or pastime. **Baseball**'s hall of fame is in Cooperstown, New York, where the game was not in fact invented; **basketball**'s hall is in Springfield, Massachusetts, where that game was indeed created. Other halls of fame have been established at a particular location as a result of one city offering the most enticing deal. **Cleveland, OH** outbid **Philadelphia, PA**, for example, to become the site for the Rock & Roll Hall of Fame, in spite of the latter's claim to its own "sound" and to Dick Clark's *American Bandstand*. The museums include artifacts and memorabilia from individuals who have achieved greatness in a particular sport or music genre (**gospel**, **jazz**, rockabilly, polka), inductees being voted on a yearly basis. An International Association of Sports Museums and Halls of Fame was created in 1971 and now assists 130 member organizations worldwide.

ROBERT GREGG

Hamer, Fannie Lou

b. 1917; d. 1977

Born a sharecropper in Mississippi, Fannie Lou Hamer became involved in the **Civil Rights movement** when she volunteered to attempt registering to vote in 1962 as part of the **Black Panther** party registration drive organized by **SNCC**. Despite losing her job and being brutally beaten, she continued in the movement, helping to organize the **Mississippi Freedom Democratic Party**, which transformed the 1964 **Democratic Party** convention in **Atlantic City**. Best known for her slogans, such as "I am sick and tired of being sick and tired," Hamer later became involved in the National Council of Negro Women and the National Women's Political Caucus during the 1970s.

ROBERT GREGG

Hanks, Tom

b. 1956

Actor/**director**: Gary **Cooper** for the 1990s. Hanks' often childlike comedic persona in the 1980s (*Big*, 1988) gave way to a "man-next-door" "Americanness" in 1990s movies about **baseball**, romance, social change, **AIDS**, space and war. This is not facile – his portrait of a gay lawyer dying of AIDS in *Philadelphia* (Oscar, 1993) grew powerfully from this everyman association, as well as his acting skills. Meanwhile, *Forrest Gump* (again, best-actor Oscar, 1994), while immensely popular, evoked an unnervingly passive observation of the American century. It remains intriguing to see how this major box-office **star**'s choices intertwine with changing concepts of American life itself. Most recently, his focus has been manifest in the Oscar-winning *Saving Private Ryan* (1998) and Second World War commemorations.

See also: actors

GARY McDONOGH
CINDY WONG

hardware store

Specialists in materials, tools and advice for the home-owner interested in small do-it-yourself projects. Everything from nails to hand tools can be purchased, as well as lumber, paint and many other items. An outgrowth of the small-town general store of the nineteenth century, hardware stores have been an integral part of rural areas, providing mail-order services for seed, fertilizer and livestock. Recently, hardware stores have taken on an almost boutique status among young professionals. Individually owned hardware stores have decreased in the last twenty years due to the growth of retail chain mega-stores offering high-volume sales of numerous items.

JIM WATKINS

Harlem, New York City

Area of northern Manhattan to the Harlem River, variously defined – depending on the shifting racial and ethnic composition, and the resulting perception of desirability – as having boundaries of 110th Street or 96th Street, 5th Avenue or the East River on the east, and Morningside Drive or the Hudson River on the west. Although home to early Dutch settlers in the seventeenth century, Irish squatters in the nineteenth, and Jewish and Italian migrants from the Lower East Side in the early twentieth, Harlem has been most powerfully identified as the heart of **New York** City's African American **community**. It is best known as the center of the renaissance of **African American** culture and politics in the 1920s and 1930s, to which it gave its name. In the postwar period, Harlem became firmly entrenched as a predominantly poor African American **neighborhood**, which has nonetheless produced important political figures such as Representative Adam Clayton **Powell**, Jr., **Malcolm X** and David **Dinkins**, the first African American **mayor** of New York City. East or Spanish Harlem has also become a **Latino** center of culture and political power.

Further reading

Lewis, D. (1981) *When Harlem Was in Vogue*, New York: Knopf.

MAX PAGE

Harlem Globetrotters

African American basketball team formed by Jewish American Abe Sapperstein in 1927. The Globetrotters began as a serious team but gradually moved into the entertainment business, touring with an "opposition" team, but actually showcasing moves, which included, for example, Marques Haynes' dribbling and Meadowlark Lemon's half-court hook, seldom seen in the National Basketball Association. Wider audience interest grew following a 1951 film about the team's early days, and a 1970s cartoon show. Now over seventy years old, under African American ownership, and with a completely new roster of players and opponents, the Globetrotters bring their unique style of **basketball** to all parts of the world.

ROBERT GREGG

harm reduction *see* addiction

Harvard University *see* Ivy League

Hasidim

American Hasidim (literally, "pious ones") represent highly orthodox, socially conservative followers of mystical leaders who revolutionized Central European Judaism in the late eighteenth century. Hasidim arrived in the US in the 1940s, fleeing Nazi destruction and shattered communities after the war. Many chose the US over Israel because of the latter's secularism: the US seemed to offer a better context for their highly structured religious **community**.

Hasidim have settled by the thousands in the Williamsburg area of **New York** City and a few other urban centers. Hasidic men, highly visible with their black hats, beards, hair, dark coats and hats, have created specialized economic niches in photography and diamonds. They are set apart by their commitment to community and religious practice under the guidance of a rebbe, a charismatic spiritual leader. Differences in beliefs nonetheless divide Hasidim into sometimes conflicting courts. New York may have 25 to 30 such courts, with between 100 and 500 families; the Lubavitcher court includes 12,000–15,000 people. Nonetheless, many Hasidim share a commitment to traditional patriarchy, religious education (and avoidance of secular colleges) and communal support.

As exclusive Hasidim enclaves have grown, conflicts have emerged with neighbors. Tensions between Hasidim and **African Americans** in Crown Heights flared in 1981 after a traffic accident in which a young Hasid killed a Guyanese boy. The suburban Kiryas Joel district also sued its school district to prevent women bus drivers from transporting male students, pitting religious belief against gender equality (and losing). Hasidim have also posed dilemmas for other Jews, whom they sometimes approach as missionaries. Others, however, have sought to incorporate American marital and psychological counseling into their traditional frameworks. In all these ways, Hasidim grapple with the tensions of religious community and American identities.

Further reading

Mintz, J. (1992) *Hasidic People*, Cambridge, MA: Harvard.

GARY McDONOGH

hate crimes

Criminal offenses committed by someone because of the actual or perceived group characteristics of another person such as **race** or **ethnicity**. Over the past two decades, these crimes of discrimination have become the focus of increased media, legislative and law-enforcement attention in the US. Over forty **states** and the federal government have some form of hate-crime law. The most frequently protected categories (in descending order) are race, **religion**, **ethnicity**, gender, sexual orientation and disability.

Many state hate-crime laws have penalties that are too light or coverage that is incomplete. For instance, most states leave gays and lesbians outside of their protections. The application of federal **civil-rights** law to hate crime is also substantially limited by very narrow enumerated requirements. Attempts in 1997 and 1998 to broaden federal law failed in congressional committees.

Hate crimes may also go unreported and are often misclassified by law enforcement when reported. Only a small fraction of hate crimes are actually prosecuted under hate-crime statutes. There are two main types of hate-crime statutes – stand-alone civil-rights statutes and penalty-enhancement statutes. Stand-alone civil-rights laws generally punish discriminatory crimes that violate a victim's civil rights on the basis of a protected-status category like race. Penalty-enhancement laws increase the punishment for an underlying crime, such as an assault, when it is committed by an offender with a discriminatory motivation against a protected group category.

The United States **Supreme Court** unanimously upheld the constitutionality of hate-crime penalty-enhancement statutes in the 1993 case of *Wisconsin* v. *Mitchell*. In a case the previous year, *RAV* v. *St. Paul*, however, the Supreme Court invalidated a poorly drafted municipal ordinance that punished the use of threatening symbols based on the ideology conveyed. Cross burning and other types of threats could be criminalized, the court held, but the law must not target the offender's underlying belief. That court decision also had the effect of invalidating "hate-speech" codes at public **colleges** that punished students for expressing bigoted ideas about others.

The FBI, which has been keeping statistics since 1991, reported 8,734 hate-crime incidents in 1996. Race accounted for 61.6 percent of attacks, followed by religious-based attacks (15.9 percent), sexual-orientation-based attacks (11.6 percent) and ethnicity-based attacks (10.7 percent). **African Americans** were targeted for 42 percent of all hate crimes, while **Jews** were also targeted (13 percent). Some cities and states, particularly in rural or southern areas, did not meaningfully participate in the FBI's data-collection effort.

Over 90 percent of hate crimes are not committed by hate-group members or hard-core hate mongers; about half are committed by young people under the age of twenty-one. Many who commit these crimes do so for excitement as part of a group activity with friends. Offenders usually rely on false or exaggerated stereotypes of a victim's group to justify the attack.

Unlike crimes in general, hate crimes are disproportionately directed against individuals as opposed to property. These victimizations are much more likely to involve injury, serial attacks, groups of offenders and subsequent civil disorder than non-hate crimes.

Further reading

Levin, J. and McDevitt, J. (1993) *Hate Crimes: The Rising Tide of Bigotry and Bloodshed*, New York: Plenum.

Levin, B. (1999) *Hate and Justice in America*, New York: Aspen.

BRIAN LEVIN

Hawai'ian archipelago

Commonly distilled into images of an island paradise of sun, surf and hula, the Hawai'ian archipelago in fact consists of 132 islands, atolls and reefs (6,470 square miles), which constitute, according to many travel magazines, the world's favorite tropical-island destination. Only seven of its largest islands provide residence to the 50th state's 1.2 million citizens, agriculture, industry and tourists. This geologic system represents a complexity and diversity that is only challenged by the unique culture that inhabits it.

This "authentic" Hawai'ian culture was first established by the ancient Hawai'ians – "people of old" – and developed through the cultural contributions of each successive ethnic group to acculturate in Hawai'i. Nonetheless, it is often eclipsed by the manufactured cultural images that are advertised and subsequently produced in order to maintain the 6 million plus tourists who visit annually.

It is important that the "authentic" culture actually includes multiple components. The first is the native Hawai'ian cultural component and an indigenous population originating in AD400–500 from the islands of Marquesas and Tahiti. Later components arise from the cultural amalgam developed from immigrants of many ethnic origins that date from the late eighteenth century onwards. Although these components differ significantly in their relative ages, their contemporary interactions are virtually inseparable due to the cultural fusion developed through the past 220 years of intense acculturation. Hence, some argue that since there is no single dominant group, all Hawai'ians are minorities. This ideology permeates the state's cultural atmosphere.

The first settlers arrived in Hawai'i around AD 400 from Marquesas. Instigated by unknown factors, these early Polynesians followed the land-faring birds they saw flying far from their own shores in the hopes of finding a suitable new home. Five hundred to six hundred years later, mass migration from Tahiti brought complicated religious and class systems into Hawai'i's cultural realm. These settlers used a stellar navigational system focused on the North Star, or *Hokulea*, to transport people, animals and plants between Tahiti and *Havaiki* – the mythical homeland of the gods that later became Hawai'i. To bring order to a newly developing society, these Hawai'ians instituted the rigid *kapu* system that dictated behavior in each facet of life. This system was guided by a complex hierarchy of gods, ancestral spirits, *kahuna* (priests), and *ah'i* (chiefs). Their culture was rich with *me/e* (song), *oh* (chant) and hula. (In ancient times, the hula had spiritual significance and was danced only by men – a far cry from its current tourist sensuality.)

At the time of Captain Cook's "discovery" of Hawai'i in 1778, the Hawai'ian population had grown to 300,000 or more. Within the next seventy years, previously unknown diseases (smallpox, venereal diseases, measles, etc.) brought by sailors decreased the Hawai'ian population to only 50,000. During the same period, the foreign population increased, causing foreign governments to assert their influence in matters pertaining to land and political power. First, the British influenced the establishment of a monarchy. Then,

Russians and French tried to influence the developing political structure to support their expansionist tendencies. Finally, the Americans, primarily through early missionary efforts, influenced the course of Hawai'ian history that led to the overthrow of the monarchy and annexation.

By the 1870s, the sugar industry grew to dominate the economy. Its ever-increasing labor demand caused the importation of labor from around the world. These laborers came as indentured servants or in similar bonded conditions. They came mostly from the East (Japan, Okinawa, China, The Philippines), but also from European countries, including Germany, Norway, Spain and Portugal (Azores and Madeira Islands). Their absorption into mainstream society varied according to differing cultural practices regarding intermarriage and the strength of community ties with their countries of origin. However, as the laborers became aware of the hardships of contract labor and the possibilities off the plantation, many sought to leave the industry once their contracts were fulfilled. In response to the growing discontent among these laborers, the Republic of Hawai'i in 1890 passed legislation under which Asians, particularly Chinese, who left agricultural work had to return to their country of origin. While some did so voluntarily, most preferred to continue reaping the relatively higher economic benefits in Hawai'i. Hence, this stipulation froze the contract laborers' situation and led to increased intermarriage or the importation of spouses, mainly brides, from "home."

The Hawai'ian monarchy, which started with Kamehameha I in the eighteenth century, constituted Hawai'i's government until its illegal overthrow in 1893. This government developed through the ancient governance of ali'i and Kamehameha I's forceful consolidation of the chiefdoms of Kauai and Ni'ihau, Maui' Hawai'i, Oahu, Molokai and Lanai. However, with the increase in the number of "outsiders," conflicting beliefs regarding cultural practices were introduced. Such practices were adamantly denounced by the influential missionary presence and countered by cultural revitalists such as Lunalilo (Hawai'i's last king). In 1900 Hawai'i became a US territory.

In the twentieth century, early migrants were joined by immigrants from Korea, Vietnam, Puerto Rico and other Polynesian communities, as well as by more Caucasians (by boat) from the US mainland.

On December 7, 1941, the Japanese attack on Pearl Harbor brought the US into the Second World War. The war led to an increased Caucasian American population due to the expanding military presence on Oahu. This, in turn, became a watershed for tourist and **Sunbelt** development, a Hawai'ian dream for both mainlanders and foreigners (especially Japanese) who visit every year. With the increasing speed and availability of air travel, Hawai'i was ever more incorporated into the US, becoming a state in 1959.

Tourism has far surpassed the declining agricultural foundations of an older island, yet has raised conflicts about land use, respect for traditions, environmental planning – Hawai'i's volcanoes, valleys and waters are important resources in themselves and shelter countless unique species – and authenticity. Guided by active state recruitment, which, since the 1980s, has looked beyond the main island to development of Maui and other destinations, tourism has prompted mainland and foreign investment but has also made the island vulnerable to economic downturns like the Asian economic crisis.

Hawai'i's contemporary culture is thus complicated by **mass-media** renditions of "tourist island," whether Betty Grable's *Song of the Island* (1942), Elvis **Presley**'s *Blue Hawaii* (1961), the long-running **television** series *Hawaii Five-0* (CBS, 1968–80), or the incessant commodification of tourist promotions. The conflict of imagery and local complexity proves especially visible in urban centers like Honolulu (365,272) or tourist clusters such as Kailua-Kona. Nonetheless, the cultural contributions of multiple ethnic groups, accumulated during the past 220 years, continue to define distinctive histories, religions, arts, foods, clothing, etc. – a mix that comprises contemporary Hawai'ian culture and perhaps a vision of a more truly global and multicultural US.

Further reading

Daws, G. (1968) *Shoal of Time*, Toronto: MacMillan.

Trask, H. (1999) *From A Native Daughter*, Honolulu: University of Hawai'i Press.

ARATI CLARRY

Hawkes, John

b. 1925; d. 1998

Ironic and erudite, Hawkes' elaborate writings attempt to radically re-fashion fictional structures. A restrained writing style, combined with an interest in the erotic and violent spaces of the modern landscape, produce an eerie, often Gothic, atmosphere in his work. Although generally much admired by writers and critics who support the experimental conceits of avant-garde or **postmodern** literature, unsympathetic readers find his novels and short stories dry and often overly formal. A hint of his style and concerns can be gleaned from a provocative 1965 statement that plot, character, setting and theme were the true enemies of fiction. Hawkes' novel *The Blood Oranges* (1971) was the basis for a 1997 film of the same name.

MARK BREWIN

Hawks, Howard

b. 1896; d. 1977

Director, producer, script writer and storyteller. Beginning with silent films, Hawks developed a lengthy, varied and successful career marked by strong vision and relationships that complicate our expectations of many genres. An understated auteur, Hawk's movies are often milestones in retrospect, as recognized in a 1974 cumulative achievement Oscar. His works often develop American values of camaraderie, patriotism and male heroism as well as complicated male/female relationships (and their sexual overtones), showcasing **Hollywood** stars like Katharine **Hepburn** (*Bringing up Baby*, 1938), Humphrey **Bogart** (*To Have and To Have Not*, 1944), Marilyn **Monroe** (*Gentlemen Prefer Blondes*, 1953) and John **Wayne** (*Rio Bravo*, 1959). Hawks showed facility across genres – gangster films, comedy, melodrama, **westerns**

and even **science fiction** (*The Thing*, 1951) – creating an enduring and beloved cinematic legacy.

CINDY WONG

Head Start *see* kindergarten and Head Start; War on Poverty

health and disease

The American twentieth century began with a sense of optimism in health, as in other aspects of life. Epidemics and pandemics like the 1916 **polio** epidemic or the 1918 flu pandemic reminded Americans of the uncertainty of life, but became domestic war zones where applied bio-science waged battle against microbes, viruses, bacteria and other pathogenic enemies. Through hygiene, vaccination, drugs and improved **healthcare**, a whole host of infectious diseases disappeared. Medical advances during the Second World War – like the spreading use of penicillin – the ongoing professionalization of hospitals and medical care and the spread of health insurance pointed to the possibilities of a richer, healthier, productive nation. In the postwar period, Americans seemed well-fed (especially by comparison with war-ravaged areas), less threatened by disease and oriented to the new and supposedly healthier settings of **suburbia**.

Ideas of health and disease were also related to healthcare. In the first half of the twentieth century, physicians appeared as both healthcare givers and practicing scientists. "The Flexner Report on Medical Education" (1910) provided the standards for medical training in the United States that shaped the professionalization of American medicine, but also aided in the coloring of the profession as white and the gendering of the profession as male. With the establishment of the **American Medical Association** and the increasing role insurance companies played in the definitions of wellness, a capitalistic logic and "Fordist" image of health produced a poetics of health and wellness defined in terms of work, labor and productivity. These images, activities and associations were to have significant consequences on American healthcare provisions, practices and perceptions.

By the early twenty-first century, however, health and disease remain constant issues for discussions. Ironically, success on the battlefield against infectious diseases resulted in the transition to a disease profile of chronic degenerative diseases. Infant mortality at birth, often due to infectious diseases, decreased, while life expectancy increased. Life expectancy at birth for Americans climbed from 53.6 years for males and 54.3 years for females in 1920 to 66.6 years for males and 73.1 years for females in 1960. For those born in 1990, it has reached 73.5 years for males and 78.9 years for females. These changes in the American demographic profile, coupled with declining fertility rates, have re-shaped the age profile of American society. Greater numbers of older people living longer lives place this group at risk for many degenerative diseases. Changes in lifestyle and health behavior have been associated with leading causes of **death** among older Americans, which include metabolic and cardiovascular disorders, **cancer** and strokes.

The increasing prevalence of chronic degenerative diseases and the inability of American medicine to combat these health problems in the manner of the heroic battles against infectious diseases have led to new definitions of wellness and health that often target the behaviors and health habits of the afflicted. "Blaming the victim" has become a moral discourse on disease and wellness that shifts the responsibility of healthcare from the physician to the patient. Individuals have become dangerous to their own health by not controlling their behavior or avoiding "risks" of illness and disease. An emphasis on fitness, healthy **food** and lifestyles (avoiding **alcohol** and tobacco) and mental well-being have become important concerns for a wealthy, but aging, baby boomer **middle class**. At the same time, ideology and practice diverge in a wealthy society – while highly toned bodies may appear in **advertising** and **mass media**, obesity is a widespread problem starting in childhood. **Stress** and other mental and emotional conditions of "modern" life are also taken as both staples and problems.

The clear and present danger of the increasing rates of chronic diseases, along with the increasing cost and expense of healthcare, have re-shaped the provisioning of healthcare in the early twenty-first century, and have revitalized debates focused on cost and access to healthcare in the absence of systematic universal coverage. Large bureaucratic institutions and the emergence of managed healthcare have led to a disillusionment among Americans in the competency of healthcare. The inability of the physician as practicing scientist forever employing improved therapeutic technologies to "cure" the major health problems faced by Americans, in concert with the rise of psycho-social diagnoses, has created a mistrust of medicine. With the need to understand healthcare and the increased availability of knowledge, expertise and medicine for the lay person in the popular sector of health, a vibrant medical pluralism, which includes the dominant paradigm of biomedicine, but also "complementary," "additional" alternatives, shapes the landscape of early twenty-first-century health in the United States.

Moreover, the health transition presumed to accompany progress and modernity from a disease profile of infectious to chronic disease has created new concerns. Technological improvements in medicine, for example, the development of antibiotic medicines, in turn, have created "super germs" resistant to treatment. Emerging and re-emerging infectious diseases index global connections among peoples and environments. "Outbreaks" of cholera, for example, once again have appeared in American **cities**. Newly transported conditions or even reports from abroad, such as the discovery of Ebola fever, are projected as threats in mass media. HIV/**AIDS**, perhaps the most publicized of all infectious diseases for Americans and all other world populations, remains a complicated social and cultural condition, as well as a prominent medical syndrome that has defied any easy vaccination or cure.

It is also clear that health conditions and access to healthcare do not apply to all people equally. The arrival of Europeans in North America would start a devastating chain of disease and mortality for indigenous populations, especially those in areas of initial contact. Diseases were spread through other kinds of exchanges, and, at times, deliberately through infected trade goods. The institution of slavery was itself built upon human biology and health. Malaria-resistant West-African populations, which possessed the genetic trait sickle cells, were able to work in malaria-ridden colonies on plantations where native Indians had perished, mostly due to disease.

With nineteenth-century industrialization, factories also became sites of illness and accidents, while crowded tenements and incomplete infrastructures created havens for epidemics. This division of **class** and health (linked to other divisions of **race** and space) has continued to the present. In 1995 black infant mortality was almost three times that of white infants (15.1 per 1,000 versus 6.3 per 1,000). Poverty, lack of education and lack of services also contribute to early and continuing problems often concentrated in impoverished inner-city **neighborhoods**. Life expectancy, patterns of obesity, hypertension and various forms of psychopathology also illustrate the social production of illness and disease. For example, depression has been found to be more common in the United States in women and lower socioeconomic classes, and higher rates of depression are found in urban areas as well. This also suggests an important gendering of health in the US, where conditions associated with women have not necessarily been treated as seriously or even taken into account in terms of difference in dosage and side effects.

Several factors are significant in the social production of wellness and disease. First, there are the ways in which social relations themselves produce forms and distributions of wellness and disease in American society along racial, class, age and gender differences. For example, gender relations, of age, class and ethnicity, in association with social values in America placed on the attainment of certain kinds and images of bodies – thin, youthful bodies – in this century has led to alarming increases in the prevalence of anorexia nervosa and bulimia. These health conditions related to eating disorders, and obsessive and compulsive behaviors have for the most part plagued young, white, middle-class women, and represent the nexus of a cultural aesthetic that associates thinness, success, sexuality and control with social forms – gender relations – and practices – eating, diet, exercise and other bodily functions.

Second, differential access to both regular proactive care and special interventions, which may cost hundreds of thousands of dollars, depends on many factors, especially insurance, for which social structure matters. While **homeless** people in the United States may experience the same health problems that other Americans do, they lack support from a variety of networks. Hence, limited access to medical provisions only works to exacerbate sickness episodes. Medical pluralism in the United States is historically the product of differential access to healthcare due to class, race, gender and age differences.

A third factor, the role that the American healthcare system plays in the production of wellness and disease had, until recently, nearly always been considered in light of the former. Iatrogenic illness and disease caused by the health practitioner and a system of healthcare, whether lead poisoning due to the use of traditional medicines in the case of the use of azarcón or *greta* to treat empacho in **Latino** communities in the United States, or the appropriation of human birth as a health problem dealt with in hospital settings by physicians, has become a central feature in the increasing medicalization of American life. Perhaps nowhere else has this social process been more evident than in the area of mental health. From alcoholism to depression, from premenstrual syndrome to attention deficit disorder, the psychological history of human life has received close scrutiny in research and in therapy.

The popular sector of health has grown exponentially, and is easily that matrix of information – personal, mediated, expert, lay – where most people experience disease and wellness, make healthcare decisions and evaluate those decisions before making others. Schools have played a strong role in conveying health knowledge and regulation. In the late 1990s, both **newspapers** and **television** news devote regular space to health issues – local television, for example, has made medical reporters and features a norm. Magazines, both general and specialized (e.g. *Men's Health*), also promote this dialogue. Fictional depictions of disease have been staples of melodrama for centuries, and remain the stuff of **Hollywood** as well as television. More complex worlds of cause and cure, as well, have underpinned ongoing doctor shows, from *Dr Kildare* and *Marcus Welby, MD* to *ER*, where procedures, diseases and healthcare issues are brought to wider attention.

Electronic information and consultation via the **Internet** have also begun to have an impact on knowledge about conditions and treatments. Health also remains a staple of everyday conversation, as in many other societies around the world.

The US constantly boasts of the most advanced healthcare system in the world, pointing to flagship hospitals, research breakthroughs and striking contrasts in a century of development. In a sense, this reflects the American sense of inventing the national body by boasting about its care. While these advances are important, continuing and emergent conditions – sometimes related to the very sources of American wealth and power – as well as divisions in health, disease and wellness underscore the complexity of these themes in contemporary American culture.

Further reading

Baer, H.A., Singer, M. and Susser, I. (1997) *Medical Anthropology and the World System: A Critical Perspective*, Westport: Bergin & Garvey.

Barrett, R.C., Kuzawa, T., McDade and Armelagos, G. (1998) "Emerging and Re-emerging Infectious Diseases: The Third Epidemiological Transition," *Annual Review of Anthropology* 27: 247–71.

Brown, K.M. (1991) *Mama Lola: A Voudou Priestess in Brooklyn*, Berkeley: University of California Press.

Cassell, E.J. *The Nature of Suffering and the Goals of Medicine*, New York; Oxford: Oxford University Press.

Crawford, R. (1984) "A Cultural Account of Health: Control, Release, and the Social Body," in J. McKinlay (ed.) *Issues in the Political Economy of Healthcare*, London: Tavistock Publishers, pp. 60–103.

Fuchs, V. (1986) *The Health Economy*, Cambridge, MA: Harvard.

Hahn, R.A. (1995) *Sickness and Healing: An Anthropological Perspective*, New Haven; London: Yale University Press.

Henderson, G.E., King, N.M., Strauss, R.P., Estroff, S.E. and Churchill, L.R. (eds) (1997) *The Social Medicine Reader*, Durham; London: Duke University Press.

Illich, I. (1976) *Medical Nemesis*, New York: Bantam.

National Association for Public Health Statistics and Information Systems: http://www.naphsis.org

Navarro, V. (1993) *Dangerous to Your Health: Capitalism in Healthcare*, New York: Monthly Review Press.

Ryan, W. (1976) *Blaming the Victim*, New York: Vintage.

Snow, L.F. (1993) *Walkin' Over Medicine*, Boulder: Westview Press.

Starr, P. (1982) *The Social Transformation of American Medicine*, New York: Basic Books.

Waitzkin, H. (1991) *The Politics of Medical Encounters*, New Haven: Yale University.

STEVE FERZACCA
GARY MCDONOGH
CINDY WONG

healthcare and reform

Healthcare in America is organized around a medical triad comprised by: (1) patients; (2) providers; and (3) payers. Each of these elements and their system of relationships have evolved in a complex interaction of culture with a changing epidemiological environment. America is split over the roles and responsibility of the collective versus those of the individual. "We are all in this together" clashes with "He/she should have known better." As Americans have built systems to cope with health adversity the European communitarian ideal clashes with the ideal of the **frontier** household fending for itself in all things.

Over the last century, **tobacco**, **alcohol** and lack of exercise have taken the place of tuberculosis, measles and whooping cough as major health threats. In a society that often seeks to place blame, a biological shift in potential culpability has accentuated the schism between communitarian and individualistic responses to healthcare. As we search for an answer as to why Americans remain unable to reform the widely recognized failures in their health system, the interplay between the new epidemiology, responsibility and the medical triad loom large.

The US healthcare system relies on private insurance companies serving large groups assembled by the workplace. When insurance firms must assemble individual applicants into groups for health insurance, the result is much more costly both administratively and actuarially. Workplace-based insurance offers predictable gaps in any effort to cover the whole population. Not everyone is employed and not everyone is employed in a firm large enough to access low premiums and stable rates. The most glaring exclusions from employment-based insurance have been the poor and the elderly. Medicaid (for the poor) and Medicare (for the elderly) were piecemeal solutions that have staved off wholesale abandonment of the market-based approach. The remaining uninsured are primarily employed in small firms, earning wages high enough to disqualify them from Medicaid, but low enough so that payment of the substantially higher premiums (roughly 25 percent of the earnings of a minimum-wage worker) is not an option. The uninsured continue to number 10–15 percent of the population.

Uninsured patients have great difficulty in obtaining regular healthcare from private-practice doctors for chronic conditions. For acute care needs of the uninsured, hospitals (but not private-practice doctors) are required by law to offer services to all regardless of the ability to pay. Uninsured patients still receive bills from hospitals that they simply have no way of paying. Most US hospitals have adjusted to an environment that requires writing off a certain amount of services as charity care.

Healthcare costs have been another primary source of dissatisfaction with the US healthcare system. Even controlled for an aging population, US healthcare costs rise faster than inflation. Although, at 14 percent of GNP, US healthcare costs are higher than those of any other nation, stable high levels of costs would not be as much of a problem for the economy as the destabilizing effects of rising costs relative to all other goods. For employees whose rising productivity merits them increases in compensation the problem comes home in the typical corporate letter that reads "Congratulations on your five percent raise in compensation; however, because the premium for your health insurance has risen by twenty percent, your take-home pay will only rise by one percent." For governments committed to funding healthcare entitlements the problem is that tax revenue goes up only as fast as growth plus inflation, but healthcare costs rise faster. Govern-ments must either raise revenues or control healthcare costs.

There is now consensus among health econo-mists that the ultimate cause of rising healthcare costs is the steadily increasing volume and intensity of services due to technology. America is littered with cost-control efforts that have succeeded in achieving one-time reductions in healthcare costs. But the rise in costs always resumes.

No obstacle impedes the introduction of new and costly technology to healthcare, provided the technology is safe. Although some technologies have the potential to lower costs, many do not. The quintessential high-cost technology remains organ transplantation, which can cost $500,000 per quality adjusted life year. Americans' insistence on fighting **death**, disease and suffering at every turn frequently leaves no medical options spared as long as there is any hope of success. Health insurers have found themselves powerless in their recurrent efforts to restrain costly medical treatments re-commended by doctors. Although some customers might agree to forego coverage for costly life-saving technologies in exchange for lower premiums, American society is reluctant to enforce such contracts. American courts have not yet been able to say to the disgruntled dying, "you chose to spend your money on something other than extensive medical protection, now that you need expensive procedures you must bear the consequences."

By its nature, reform threatens those whose livelihood depends on the status quo. To explain the perpetual failure of healthcare reform in the US it is necessary to invoke more than the power of opponents to reform. America's failure to provide better access to care stems from the inability of the working uninsured to attract society's consensus that their hardship merits a social solution. For now, manifest opinion appears to be to withhold the safety net from the uninsured until there is proof that neither their health woes nor their lack of insurance can be solved through personal responsibility. For rising healthcare costs, stabiliza-tion will eventually come. One cannot live by healthcare spending alone. The point at which stability comes will speak volumes about just how much money Americans are willing to part with in order to maintain the battle against the onslaughts of nature.

Further reading

Butler, P. (1988) *Too Poor to Be Sick*, Washington, DC: American Public Health Association.
Ginzberg, E. (1990) *The Medical Triangle*, Cambridge, MA: Harvard.

DAVID BISHAI

health/organic food

The idea that certain foods – organic, unprocessed, raw and often vegetarian – are more "fit" to eat than others and the promise of overall good health through diet are interwoven in the fabric of three cultural meaning systems: holistic medicine, **hippie** counterculture and **environmentalism**. Together, these discourses critically address the dominant institutional social structure and encourage an alternative natural way of life.

With its rejection of the classic medical model and its focus on multiple aspects of physical condition, "alternative" medicine has moved the body from physicians' control of physicians into the realm of personal responsibility. Food becomes an important component of healthy lifestyle choices, alongside exercise and emotional well-being. Environmentalism's decoding of social problems likewise speaks to individual accountability in the salvaging of an endangered natural equilibrium. It encourages all but abandonment of agricultural pesticides and large-scale, inhumane animal rearing in favor of organic farming and a meatless diet. Foods like tofu, meatless burgers and nuts are the dietetic signifiers of nutritional and political coherence. Finally, the hippie and, more recently, **New Age** movements equate the natural with spirituality and peace, privileging the cruelty free choice of a vegetarian diet.

The disparaging adjective "junk" associated with food that is salty, starchy or, like **McDonald's**, fatty, fast and cheap, coupled with a growing multimillion nutritional supplement and animal protein substitutes industry suggests health food is here to stay.

MARIAELENA BARTESAGHI

Hell's Angels *see* motorcycles

Helms, Jesse

b. 1921

Republican senior senator of North Carolina, Helms was elected to the US Senate in 1972. A staunch fiscal and social conservative who is considered an extremist by his opponents, Helms opposes **abortion**, **affirmative action** and homosexuality, but supports school-sponsored prayer. Chairperson of the Foreign Relations Committee, Helms supports efforts to streamline the number of government foreign-policy agencies. Concerned with human-rights abuses, he called for the revocation of China's most-favored-nation status. He serves on the Senate Agriculture, Nutrition and Forestry and Rules and Administration committees. His seat is up for re-election in 2002.

KATE M. KENSKI

Hemingway, Ernest Miller

b. 1899; d. 1961

Nobel and **Pulitzer-Prize**-winning novelist, correspondent and essayist whose laconic prose with its subsumed emotions emphasizes a virile **masculinity** of struggle that also permeated the author's life. Hemingway participated in – and created lasting fictional works about – lives of men in war and its aftermath (*A Farewell to Arms*, 1929; *For Whom the Bell Tolls*, 1940), the lost generation abroad (*The Sun Also Rises*, 1926), bullfighting (*Death in the Afternoon*, 1932), hunting ("Snows of Kilimanjaro," 1952) and deep-sea fishing (*The Old Man and the Sea*, 1952). Often on the move, Hemingway spent long periods in Paris, civil-war Spain and **Cuba**, as well as Key West, **Florida**. His dramatic death, presumably suicide, raised questions about the masculinity he represented and his adjustments.

GARY McDONOGH

Hendrix, Jimi

b. 1942; d. 1970

Born in **Seattle, WA**, Hendrix developed his unique left-handed technique (on a right-handed guitar) while playing back-up on tour for R&B artists like Sam **Cooke** and Little Richard. After a short period living in **New York** City, NY, he moved to London and became a big influence in the emerging music scene in England (particularly with guitarists like Syd Barrett of Pink Floyd, and John McLaughlin). His band, the Jimi Hendrix Experience, recorded several hits, including "Purple Haze" and Bob **Dylan**'s "All Along the Watchtower," and soon his popularity spread back in the United States. Hendrix's performance of "The Star-Spangled Banner," at the **Woodstock** Festival in 1969, turned the anthem into suitable accompaniment for pictures of the dropping of Napalm in Vietnam, and revealed the subversive political potential of **rock music**. He died after a bout of mixing **alcohol** and drugs.

Further reading

Greig, C. (1999) *Icons of Black Music*, San Diego: Thunder Bay Press.

ROBERT GREGG

Henson, Jim

b. 1936; d. 1990

Master puppeteer and creator of the unmistakable Muppets. Henson broke into **television** via early morning local **children**'s television (1955–61), where he and his wife Jane Nebel worked with hand and stick puppets. Stardom came with *Sesame Street* (1969–), for which he created lively and enduring characters Kermit the Frog, Big Bird, Oscar the Grouch, Bert and Ernie, and others who have been companions for and teachers to generations of children worldwide. Not only are these characters colorful and cuddly – as later marketing has shown – but they also attract us by their humanity – fears and questions, selfishness (Miss Piggy, created by collaborator Frank Oz, has become a satiric icon for the "me"-generation) and

dealing with difference. Henson continued to experiment in other venues like *Saturday Night Live* (1975–6), but needed English support to produce his variety format *Muppet Shows* (1976–81), with guest stars from Milton Berle to Steve Martin, and movies like the *Muppet Movie* (1979). Henson's London studios, The Creature Shop, run by the family and with associations with **Disney**, have changed the way animals and fantasy creatures appear in movies like *Dark Crystal* (1983) and *Babe* (1997).

Further reading

Bacon, M. (1997) *No Strings Attached*, New York: MacMillan.

GARY McDONOGH

Hepburn, Audrey

b. 1929; d. 1993

Female actor. Surviving Nazi occupation in Holland to become a dancer and model, Hepburn brought both ethereal beauty and European style to American movies from her **Hollywood** debut in *Roman Holiday* (1953) onwards. Hepburn moved easily between casual humor and graceful elegance in films like *Funny Face* (1957) or *Breakfast at Tiffany's* (1961). Nominated for five Academy **Awards**, she essentially retired from the screen after *Wait Until Dark* (1967). Before her death, she became a UNICEF ambassador; in the 1990s she continued to be revered as a **fashion** icon.

See also: actors

GARY McDONOGH

Hepburn, Katharine

b. 1907

Female actor. A patrician presence of **New England** heritage on stage and screen. From *A Bill of Divorcement* (1932) onwards, Hepburn's intellectual style and range won her four Oscars, as well as eight other nominations. Several of her roles shaped views of the upper class and professional women – in *Philadelphia Story* (1940) or five movies with her lover Spencer Tracy, whose gender balancing and sparkling dialogue set high standards. As she aged, Hepburn explored a variety of new personae in *The African Queen* (1951), with Humphrey **Bogart**, the **western** *Rooster Cogburn* (1976) and the autumnal *On Golden Pond* (1981).

See also: actors

GARY McDONOGH

Heston, Charlton

b. 1923

Male actor. Heston's career became identified with larger-than-life heroes/hunks, especially Moses in the *Ten Commandments* (1954) and *Ben-Hur* (Oscar, 1959). He also took this he-man persona into less likely ethnic castings as a Mexican policeman in *Touch of Evil* (1958), or the Spanish *El Cid* (1961) and to science-fiction apocalypses like *Planet of the Apes* (1968) and *Soylent Green* (1973). This image also has intersected with his conservative politics, including his role as active spokesperson for the **National Rifle Association**, of which he became president in 1998.

See also: actors

GARY McDONOGH

heterosexuality

Normative sexual practice in the United States, entailing sexual and other relations between those gendered as male and those gendered as female, usually in dyadic couples. Reinforced by media images of love and romance, by legal and religious covenants of **marriage** and by social interactions, this norm is generally only called into question by recognition of alternative practice or calls to avoid implicit prejudices (heterosexist speech, for example) in politically sensitive settings. Given the widespread acceptance of the way "things are," questions about heterosexuality – whether as a general practice or in reference to a specific figure

like a celebrity – also evoke intense responses and defenses.

GARY McDONOGH
CINDY WONG

high school

Secondary education generally constituted by 9th, 10th, 11th and 12th grades (corresponding roughly to ages 14–17). It is separated from elementary education by an intermediate stage of middle school (grades 5–8) or junior high (grades 7 and 8), often housed in separate buildings. High school represents a crucial and difficult period of transition both academically and socially. Academically, it entails specialization, differentiation and competition – a transition to **college** for many, although some will only complete the education legally required of them (leaving when grade level or age permits). Socially and psychologically, moreover, this is a time of changing sexuality, independence, experimentation and peer relations which produces a strong group culture among **teenagers**, as well as sometimes highly charged relations with parents and educators. Hence, concerns with **education** and growth intersect with fears about violence, security, sexuality, drugs and adjustment in American images of high school.

In 1965, 11,610,000 students in grades nine to twelve were enrolled in public schools in the US, with an additional 1,400,000 in **private schools**. By 2000, numbers in public schools had risen to 13,357,000, a rise projected to continue, while those in private schools remained constant. In 1960, 41.4 percent of Americans completed four years of high school, while in 1997 this had risen to 82.1 percent (dropouts constitute roughly 5 percent of the high-school population). These numerical changes are only part of the changing meaning of high schools. High schools were primary sites for integration and racial conflicts from the 1950s onwards, for example. They also have been caught in the decline of **inner cities** (with aging "problem" schools), the rise of **suburbs** with a new consumer ethos, **class** and racial divisions and demands for huge student parking lots.

High schools must respond to these multiple changing demands, extremely diverse populations and contradictory needs while also constrained, in the case of public schools, by limited finances. Academic programs, for example, have become more costly in terms of computers and equipment required for sciences, libraries and research materials and changing demands for first- and second-language learning. Given the juxtaposition of students from different class and ethnic/racial backgrounds at the same school, moreover, school systems face the choice of dividing programs (tracking by strata of tested intelligence or career goals) or constructing an academic "middle ground" that will frustrate special students. Magnet schools, specializing in sciences, arts or other fields, represent an alternative for larger school systems (see *Fame*, 1980). At the same time, schools may be forced to cut teacher-intensive programs like art or drama to balance their budgets, or rely on **television** and large classes to deal with mass education. Private and parochial schools control selection of students more closely and raise funds for specific activities, but they, too, strain to compete and balance the needs of mass projects against individual changes and demands.

Counseling has also become increasingly necessary and complex, dealing with issues ranging from home life to learning disabilities to multicultural issues. Concern with **gender** stereotyping (male athletes versus cheerleaders) and sexuality, including gay issues, have also become prominent. In many areas, from sexual education and driver's education to civic involvement, the high school must take over roles previously managed by the **family**.

Other services in high school include food, basic healthcare and, increasingly, security. Lunch and breakfast may entail a form of **welfare** or a competition for privilege to escape campus.

In addition, high schools incorporate expanding extra-curricular activities, including sometimes massive sports programs, journalism (**newspapers**, yearbooks, literary magazines), travel, bands and orchestras, drama, volunteer and community service, pre-professional formation (Future Farmers of America, Future Teachers) and other interests, generally under faculty supervision. These promote both interests and leadership among students,

training for citizenship outside the classroom (or filling résumés for college applications and scholarship competitions). They may also become sites for intense competition among students for internal and external recognition. Such activities may also raise questions of **freedom** and censorship, for example, in the case of school newspapers, or the rights of students as citizens, in the case of drug tests for participation in activities.

American high schools, moreover, are **community** institutions, especially in the case of consolidated public institutions with several thousand students. Through social reproduction of community and parental involvement, programs in sports may become community surrogates. High-school events, whether crises or celebrations (school plays, **commencement**, conflict), are rallying points for a wide range of views and participation. At the same time, high schools reflect divisions of **race** and **class** within their catchment pools, and have proved vulnerable to violence, censorship, political debate and social crises, from integration in the 1950s to **guns** and school shootings in the 1990s. American news media, for example, have often explored perceived high school in terms of threats of drugs, **alcohol**, **tobacco** and sexuality. In the **Cold War** period, the impact of anti-American ideologies through teachers and materials was also prominent, although this has given way to concerns with covert agendas of culture and sexuality.

The intensity of concern with high school is magnified by its role as a shared experience in American society and by the consumer power of high-school students, who are primary targets for **advertising** and consumption in **fashion**, music, **Hollywood** and **fast food**. This creates a **mall** culture as a spatial displacement of high school itself (as soda shops figured as a hang-out in postwar generations). Hence, depictions of high school pervade American literature and **mass media**, although they illustrate distinctive paradigms. One is the celebratory/nostalgic vision of movies like *American Graffiti* (1973) or *Grease* (1978) and long-running **television** series like *Happy Days* (ABC, 1974–84) or *The Wonder Years* (ABC, 1988–93), which build on postwar generations of "innocent" high-school films (**teenage** werewolves, beach movies, etc. in the 1950s/1960s). Nostalgic issues are also sorted out in "high-school reunions," like *Peggy Sue Got Married* (1986) and/or episodes of television **sitcoms**.

Others have seen high school from the point of view of outsiders created by a conformist peer culture – J.D. Salinger's controversial classic *Catcher in the Rye* (1951), Jim Carroll's *Basketball Diaries* (film, 1995, linked by mass media to the Columbine High School massacre) or the television series *Freaks and Geeks* (1999–). These sometimes coincide with media representations of high schools as places of serious social malaise (*Asphalt Jungle*, 1950; *Dangerous Minds*, 1998).

Other popular genres have combined celebration and **soap-opera** sexuality (the long-running *Beverly Hills 90210* (FOX, 1990–2000), *Dawson's Creek* (WB, 1998–) or the movie *Can't Hardly Wait*, 1999). Still others show teenage difference and experience (*Breakfast Club*, 1985; *Pretty in Pink*, 1986) or provide social commentary (*Heathers*, 1989; *Clueless*, 1995; *Election*, 1999). High-school depictions, however, rarely deal with complex academic issues. As both a complex formative experience and one whose participants seek knowledge, guidance and shared experience, depictions of high school, whether insightful or commercial, promise to be a staple of mass media for generations to come.

See also: music, popular

Further reading

Angus, D. and Mirel, J. (1999) *The Failed Promise of the American High School, 1890–1995*, New York: Teacher's College.

McQuillan, P. (1998) *Educational Opportunity in an Urban American High School*, Albany: SUNY.

Phelan, P., Davidson, A. and Hanh, C. (1998) *Adolescent's Worlds*, New York: Teacher's College.

Wood, G. (1998) *A Time to Learn*, New York: Dutton.

GARY McDONOGH
CINDY WONG

high-school sports

High-school sports command enormous attention in American society. In many cases, school athletics dictate the morale of an entire community. With the public's mounting distrust of major professional and **college** sports, high schools are, to many, the last bastion of the unadulterated competitive spirit.

Several probing cultural studies, nonetheless, illuminate the world of high-school athletics. The documentary *Hoop Dreams* (1994) follows two promising young **basketball** players and their NBA aspirations. For some **inner-city** African American males, basketball seems to represent the road out of poverty. But, as the film poignantly illustrates, those who are talented and lucky enough to receive scholarships to college are few. The number able to *make a living* playing the sport they love is minuscule.

H.G. Bissinger's *Friday Night Lights* (1991), by contrast, chronicles the 1988 **football** season of the Permian High School Panthers in Odessa, **Texas**, where every Friday night **community** members cheer the team with religious zeal. Bissinger's study shows how the outcome of each game has an impact seemingly disproportionate to its importance: coaches face "For Sale" signs placed on their lawns following a loss against a rival. This devotion was only exacerbated, Bissinger suggests, by the 1980s collapse of the oil industry in Texas. A similar view pervades *All the Right Moves* (1983), which spotlighted a fictional Pennsylvania high-school football program. Here, a heartbreaking loss to a rival also spawns unreasonable, disturbing reactions from fans, players and coaches. Clearly, enormous external pressure weighs on certain high-school athletes.

But not all high-school athletes receive this attention. Until recently, the opposite was true for girls. This trend is slowly changing, due to legal requirements of **Title IX** at the college level and the popularity of college and professional leagues, including women's **soccer**, vitalized by the 1998 World Cup. Other programs – gymnastics, martial arts, even wrestling – are eclipsed by the major sports – football, basketball and **baseball**.

Some alternatives are nonetheless associated with affluence. **Golf** and certain racquet sports have a long tradition of upper-class participation; such games require expensive equipment and/or unusual venues, and **private (or prep) schools** have more resources. Nevertheless, some teams are also found at public schools. Lacrosse, squash and crew (**rowing**) are associated with white upper-middle class institutions. Swimming has also emerged at schools with special facilities.

Regardless of class, students who participate in high-school athletics are often characterized as "jocks," a largely negative term suggesting limited intelligence (in spite of presidential candidate Bill Bradley's coining of "intellectual jock" to describe himself). The attention paid to the student athletes often makes them popular and may give them what some see as excessive power over the lives of others in the school. This, in turn, has led to resentment, painfully evident in Colorado's Columbine High School shootings, where student killers targeted several athletic stars. For all its faults, though, high-school sport is one of America's most cherished institutions, and participation in athletic programs continues to be encouraged by parents and administrators alike.

JAMES DAVID

highways

One of the most ubiquitous and generic features of the contemporary American landscape, highways are also key symbols of contemporary American culture and a social institution in their own right. Together with cheap fuel and mass ownership of **automobiles**, highways facilitated the transformation of dense, central **cities** into sprawling metropolitan regions and allowed for decentralization of residential, commercial and industrial functions amongst a diffuse network of **suburbs and edge cities**.

Although imagined in Europe, the idea of paved, grade-separated, limited-access thoroughfare for the exclusive, high-speed use of **trucks** and automobiles was first realized in the United States during the early decades of the twentieth century. Prior to the 1920s, the network of paved inter-urban thoroughfares was virtually non-existent. By the Second World War, the United States was linked by an extensive network of "national roads," financed by an excise tax on gasoline. Highway construction received even greater support after the war. State and federal governments subsidized the construction of multi-lane highways to relieve urban traffic congestion and to link the

growing suburban frontier with central cities. In 1956 under President Dwight Eisenhower the Interstate Highway Act committed the federal government to paying 90 percent of the cost for the construction of 42,000 miles of high-speed multi-lane highways linking major urban centers. Of greater scale and capacity than their pre-war predecessors, these thoroughfares became known as "expressways."

Expressways radically restructured the built environment. In virtually every major American city, these new highways ran through and/or completely demolished poor minority **neighborhoods**. Together with **urban renewal**, highway construction displaced millions of Americans in the late 1950s and 1960s, and helped spur disinvestment in urban **real estate**. Although designed to facilitate the commutating of suburban residents to urban centers during the 1970s and 1980s, highways helped to siphon off factories, shopping **malls** and office space to the suburban fringes of metropolitan areas. By the late 1980s, the perimeter or beltway highways that had been originally designed to redirect through traffic around central cities had emerged as America's new **Main Street**. Yet, despite the continual augmentation of highway capacity, traffic volume and congestion expanded to fill, and exceed, the available space.

The energy crisis of the 1970s did little to reduce highway use. Indeed, in the twenty-five years following the oil embargo of 1973–4, highway congestion, suburban sprawl and pollution reached new levels. Despite various control devices, auto emissions remained the nation's leading cause of air pollution. Environmental legislation such as the Clean Air Act would seemingly require alternatives to the unlimited low-density vision of growth of the previous six decades, yet little consensus emerged on how to wean the United States from its unwholesome addiction to automobile use and highway construction. Instead, they are part of American culture – from James Dean to *Bladerunner* – as well as a threat to American life.

See also: road movies

Further reading

Lackey, K. (1997) *Roadframes: The American Highway Narrative*, Lincoln: University of Nebraska.

Rose, M. (1990) *Interstate: Express Highway Politics, 1939–1989*, Knoxville: University of Tennessee.

CHARLES RUTHEISER

Hill, Anita

b. 1956

Law professor. In 1991 Hill sparked a national debate on **sexual harassment** in the workplace when she leveled harassment charges against then-**Supreme Court** nominee Clarence **Thomas** at his Senate confirmation hearing. Hill testified that Thomas, previously her boss at the Equal Employment Opportunity Commission, sexually harassed her on the job. Thomas denied the charges. Hill's testimony, televised nationwide, transformed the confirmation process into a national educational program on sexual harassment and reinvigorated American **feminism**. The all-male Senate committee's questioning of Hill and confirmation of Thomas raised questions about their sensitivity to women's concerns and helped elect more women to public office.

MARY-CHRISTINE SUNGAILA, ESQ.

hillbilly *see* rednecks

Hindus

Hinduism first emerged in India as a complex constellation of religious systems. There is a long and checkered history of the spread of Hinduism outside India centuries before the emergence of the political nation as we know it today. In 1893 Swami Vivekananda delivered a lecture about Hinduism at the first World Parliament of Religions in **Chicago, IL**. In more modern times, the growth of the Indian diaspora around the world led to a simultaneous spread of Hinduism outside India, most visibly as a set of cultural practices.

In the new millenium, one can conceivably study most of the world's major **religions** in any of the metropolitan centers of the United States. The number of Asian Indians, a majority of them

Hindus, in the United States has grown steadily since the Immigration and Naturalization Act of 1965, and stands at about 1 million today. Hindu immigrants and their religious institutions struggled against considerable racial prejudice and discrimination before they began to be accepted as an integral part of American society.

Outside its land of origin, Hinduism has undergone several transformations unique to the diasporic condition of its practitioners, both in terms of ritual practices as well as in the role it plays in fostering and reinforcing community solidarity. As Raymond Brady Williams suggests, emigration involves a "crisis of epistemology" that focuses people's attention on their traditions or narrative in order to establish a "known world" (Williams 1988). One way in which Hindu immigrant groups in different parts of the world attempt to resolve this crisis is by building temples and maintaining indigenous social and cultural activities in the new society. Hundreds of Hindu temples and religious centers now dot the American landscape, enriching its multicultural milieu.

Many Indian immigrants indicate that they are more religiously active in the United States than in India. As distinctive identity markers religions, in particular, are mobilized and re-energized in the process of negotiating their identities in the new cultural environment. Hinduism, which was not an organized religion until the late nineteenth century in India, was considered to be more a philosophy and a way of life. Practice of Hinduism did not require visiting temples on a regular basis; rather, worshipping at home shrines was more important. However, in the United States, Hinduism quickly assumed a formal structure as fairly affluent, professional Indian immigrants, concerned about the socialization of their American Indian **children**, started establishing temples. Hindu temples in the United States are not only places of worship, but also serve as broader cultural centers that function as surrogate extended families to the community. Large Hindu temples like the ones in **Pittsburgh, PA**, **Houston, TX** and Chicago, IL are traditional in their architectural style and aim to replicate rituals in as "authentic" a manner as possible. As in its country of origin, Hinduism in the US takes various ethnic and sectarian forms, displaying enormous diversity in its iconographic representations and ritual practices. Apart from temples, there are quasi-religious groups that congregate to propagate the teachings of various gurus and religious leaders. Newsletters, brochures and other ethnic **mass media**, along with rapidly proliferating web-sites on the **Internet**, aid in promoting horizontal communication among the believers.

While religion, in general, has helped community solidarity in a positive way, since the early 1980s Hinduism in the diaspora, as in the home country, has become increasingly politicized. The World Hindu Council (Vishwa Hindu Parishad) has established branches all over the world and supports religious nationalist forces in India. They hold summer camps in various parts of the US to socialize second-generation **American Indians** from a very young age, and the Hindu Students' Councils attempt to further that process on college **campuses**. Many progressive Indians in the diaspora have organized themselves to challenge this pernicious process to destroy the secular ethos of the modern Indian nation. The struggle between these forces within the diasporic community represents an intense contestation over issues of identity.

Further reading

Rayaprol, A. (1997) *Negotiating Identities: Women in the Indian Diaspora*, Delhi: Oxford University Press.

Williams, R.B. (1988) *Religions of Immigrants from India and Pakistan: New Threads in the American Tapestry*, Cambridge, MA: Cambridge University Press.

APARNA RAYAPROL

hippies

Countercultural visionaries who have become consummate symbols of the 1960s. Abjuring business and **suburban** conformity, hippies envisioned alternatives that included **freedom**, shared possessions, experimentation in drugs, sexuality and lifestyles and a return to **nature**. While some have maintained this commitment, for others – and for media representations of the 1960s – hippies have been reduced to flowing

colorful clothes, psychedelia and exotic symbolism and memories of a drug culture, undercutting the ideas of political and economic reform that also underpinned "tuning in, turning on and dropping out."

GARY McDONOGH

Hispanics

Term used for people with ancestry in Spain or **Latin America**. Sometimes used (as in the census) to avoid classifications of race or ethnicity, although clarifications of these issues or national origin may be appended. A similar category is Hispanic surname, which avoids all these issues in a singular category (evoking problems in mixed marriages as well as for Asians, Italians, Germans and others who have come through **Latin America** to the US).

See also: Latinos; Chicanos/as; Puerto Ricans

GARY McDONOGH

Hiss, Alger *see* McCarthyism; Nixon, Richard M.

historic preservation

The movement to save historic structures is commonly dated as beginning in 1966, with the passing of the National Historic Preservation Act, which gave new powers to the National Park Service to administer and encourage preservation programs in every state. The political impetus for this act was the 1963 demolition of one of **New York** City's finest works of **architecture**, Pennsylvania Station, as well as more generally from a rejection of **urban-renewal** policies of the post-Second World War era.

In fact, the practice of preserving historic buildings and landscapes, as well as art and artifacts, dates back to the mid-nineteenth century at least, with the fight to save Mount Vernon, and encompasses activities far beyond the purview of the federal government. While the National Trust for Historic Preservation, chartered in 1949, remains the primary national advocacy organization (though as of 1998, without federal financial support), preservation is a predominantly local movement. It is based around private local efforts to save and rehabilitate historic structures, encourage private rehabilitation and promote public interpretation of historic resources.

Preservation, due largely to its traditional constituency of local, mainly female, well-off reformers, remains an elite undertaking (as in **Rockefeller's** stewardship of colonial Williamsburg). As such, the scope of preservationists' efforts remains narrow: architectural distinction as opposed to social or cultural significance continues to be the prime criteria for "listing" structures on local historic resources lists and the National Register of Historic Places. Nonetheless, as new groups have gained political and social influence, what is considered worth saving has broadened tremendously. State preservation offices, small-town historical societies and historical **museums** now routinely seek – at least in limited ways – to preserve and interpret the physical places of **African Americans**, women and other minority groups.

Further reading

Hosmer, C. (1981) *Preservation Comes of Age*, Charlottesville, VA: University Press of Virginia.

Lee, A. (ed.) (1992) *Past Meets Future*, Washington, DC: Preservation Press.

MAX PAGE

history

The history profession in America has changed dramatically in the past half century. The **GI Bill** after the Second World War brought about rapid growth in American higher education, including history programs. In the 1950s, the dominant interpretation of American history was the consensus school, which emphasized the homogeneity and lack of conflict in American culture and history, at least partly in reaction to the previous Progressive historians, who portrayed **class**, political and regional conflict as the motivating force in American history. Daniel Boorstin, Louis Hartz

and Richard Hofstadter were among the best-known and most influential historians working in the consensus tradition.

The 1960s saw the beginnings of a profound historiographical upheaval that is still underway today. This revolutionary "paradigm shift" had several components. Perhaps the most visible and controversial development was the emergence of a New Left school of history. Influenced by a growing sense of the problems and inequalities of American society, particularly in reaction to the **Vietnam War** and the **Civil Rights movement**, New Left historians criticized the consensus school for an overly complacent and congratulatory view of America's past, and instead emphasized the elements of exploitation, imperialism and racism in America's past. New Left history produced revisionist accounts of the **Cold War**, slavery and abolitionism, emphasized the pervasiveness of radical events and individuals in America's past, and often tried to write "history from the bottom up," focusing on lower-class or previously "inarticulate" elements of society. William Appleman Williams and Eugene Genovese were among the most influential New Left historians.

Related to New Left history was a profound and long-lasting development, the emergence of a "new social history." The most important accomplishment of social historians was to expand the focus of the discipline beyond an emphasis on **white**, middle-/**upper-class** males to a more inclusive perspective. The growth of women's and **African American** history was just the tip of the iceberg. Social historians examined an almost endless array of previously ignored subgroups of American society, including Native Americans, **Asian Americans**, **Hispanic Americans**, European ethnic groups, workers, the poor, the elderly, **children**, adolescents, gays and bisexuals, and so on. Following the example of the influential French Annales school of historiography, American historians also focused more attention on private behavior and everyday life, producing studies of topics from **marriage** and **family** life to the climate and environment, and nearly everything in between.

American historians have been caught up in "culture-wars" controversies between the left and right in recent years, including a bitter conflict over a planned 1995 Hiroshima memorial exhibition at the **Smithsonian Institution**. Historians have pondered the significance of **postmodern** theory for their discipline, and worried about growing specialization and loss of coherence. A chronically depressed and depressing job market has marred an otherwise unprecedentedly vibrant, challenging, innovative era in American historiography.

Further reading

Foner, E. (ed.) (1990) *The New American History*, Philadelphia: Temple University.

Kammen, M. (ed.) (1980) *The Past Before Us*, Ithaca: Cornell University.

Novick, P. (1988) *That Noble Dream*, New York: Cambridge University.

KENT BLASER

Hitchcock, Alfred

b. 1899; d. 1980

British-born director whose fifty-three films successfully straddled the worlds of art house and box-office yield. His first **Hollywood** production, *Rebecca* (1940), won the 1940 Academy Award for Best Picture. Hitchcock is famed for the control he exercised over all aspects of the film-making process, his amazing visual acumen and the haunting pervasiveness of his images in the collective unconscious. *Rear Window* (1954), *Psycho* (1960), *Vertigo* (1958) and *The Birds* (1963) indelibly altered American experiences of neighbors, showering and household pets, filling everyday America with shadows and ambiguity. His characters, similarly, are perpetually poised between the mendacity of order and the truth of chaos, where guilt and innocence, obsession and deliverance, nightmare and vision are forever flip sides of the same human coin.

MARIAELENA BARTESAGHI

Hmong *see* Southeast Asians

HMOs (Health Maintenance Organizations)

Managed-care programs, entailing the integration of insurance and care providers with fixed rates for services (and sometimes pharmaceuticals) as well as health incentives (**physical fitness** programs, etc.) came to dominate American **healthcare** in the late twentieth century. While praised for controlling costs and sometimes rationalizing care, they have also been criticized for their drive to keep expenses at a minimum and their corporate remodeling of the relationship and autonomy of doctors, **nurses** and patients.

GARY McDONOGH

hockey, ice

Sport developed in **Canada** during the nineteenth century. The name of its most prestigious prize, the Stanley Cup, derives from the governor-general who donated the bowl to the hockey league. Hockey spread below the border in the early twentieth century; the National Hockey League, built primarily around Canadian teams, was formed in 1917. Interest in the United States grew with the bringing of franchises to **Boston, MA**, **New York** City, **Chicago, IL**, **Detroit** and **Pittsburgh**, and then in the 1970s to **Philadelphia, PA** and Hartford among other cities.

Since 1980, the sport's base has shifted to the United States, a development symbolized in the trading of Wayne Gretzky, "the Great One," from the Edmonton Oilers to the **Los Angeles, CA** Kings in 1988. Two years later the NHL created its first expansion team in **Florida**. Once dominated by Canadian teams, at the end of the 1996–7 season the NHL had twenty-six teams, only six of which were in Canada.

Part of this growth in the US has been owing to the sport's profitability (until recent fears that it may have overextended itself). As in other sports, hockey teams are owned by corporate giants such as **Disney** and by major **mass media** and cable companies. These teams hold cities to ransom, bargaining for new leases on their arenas or for more funding from taxpayer dollars, threatening to move if their demands are not met. They are able to do so because city **mayors** and **governors** are constantly battling to win expansion teams or attract a team willing to relocate. Hockey, associated with white suburbanites who flock to the city for every game, brings in revenue. The game has never attempted to appeal to **inner-city** populations. There have been almost no **African Americans** in the league, and there are very few black and minority fans in the bleachers.

Another significant development of recent years has been the internationalization of NHL players. The game had long been an **Olympic** sport and northern European teams did very well (the Olympics were one reason for hockey's hold in colleges, since until the 1990s American Olympians were generally drawn from college ranks). Some of these athletes, beginning with the Swedes in the 1970s, came to the United States drawn by the high salaries. With the end of the **Cold War**, a large number of Russians and Czechs made use of their new freedom to emigrate. During the 1995–6 season, of the 640 players in the league, 389 were Canadian, only 108 were American, while there were 42 Russians, 34 Swedes and 26 Czechs.

This has resulted in a change in the way the game is played. The Canadian game was noted for its extremely physical aspect, Gretzky's agility and grace being the exception. Players wear padding and helmets, not only to protect themselves from the inevitable contact (particularly since the game is played with a stick, and the hard rubber puck can travel at high speeds), but also because the game is marked by brawling, believed to stimulate fan interest. The joke: "I went to a boxing bout and a hockey game broke out," is often repeated as nightly sportscasts feature fist fights between players which are calmly observed by referees who have no power to intervene. When the Philadelphia Flyers' Broad Street Bullies won in 1974 and 1975, led by Bobby Clarke and Bernie Parent, many assumed that physical play would always win championships.

However, European players have tended to be quicker skaters and more skillful with the stick, able to embarrass teams that rely on the body check. This has happened to Bobby Clarke's handpicked Flyers' "Legion of Doom," led by Eric Lindros, which has failed to win a Stanley Cup and has consistently been outperformed by playoff opponents.

Women have begun to play the game in larger numbers, in part inspired by the success of the US hockey team in the new-medal sport in the 1998 Winter Olympics. The women's game emphasizes skill over brute force (stricter penalties are given for infringements), though the intense rivalry between the Canadian and American women led to an Olympic showdown noted for the frequency of its body checking.

The spread of the game around the United States has been facilitated by the development of **in-line skating**, enabling people to play a version of hockey on parking lots and playgrounds around the country. This in turn has led to the emergence of a new semi-professional league of roller hockey, fast growing among the nation's children, serving the dual function of a sport to train youngsters who want to make their way towards NHL, and as a new commercial sport in its own right.

Hockey has been used in **mass media** – both news and fiction – to explore male destructiveness (*Slap Shot*, 1977). The growing appeal (and changing image) of hockey in the 1990s can be seen in its Disneyfication in *Mighty Ducks* (1992) and its sequel, as well as **Disney**'s acquisition of an Anaheim franchise with the same name.

Further reading

Fischler, S. and Fischler, S. (1996) *Great Book of Hockey*, Lincolnwood: Publications International.

ROBERT GREGG

Hoffa, Jimmy

b. 1913; d. 1975?

Controversial president of the **Teamsters Union** from 1957 to 1971. Hoffa represented to many observers the danger inherent in the growing power of **unions** in the 1950s. Beloved by his union members, he negotiated contracts that granted truckers generous wages and fringe benefits, making them the envy of other workers. While openly acknowledging his friendly relations with notorious **organized-crime** figures, he vigorously defended his honesty as a union leader. Jailed for jury tampering and mail fraud, his attempt to regain the union's presidency after his release ended with his apparent abduction and death in 1975, allegedly at the hands of the Mafia. His son, Jimmy Hoffa, later became leader of the Teamsters.

DAVID WITWER

Hoffman, Abbie

b. 1936; d. 1989

Visionary and surrealist politician. After work with **SNCC**, Hoffman founded the Youth International Party (yippies) in 1966, which sought to replace "Amerika" or the "Pig Empire" with a mixture of **anarchism**, Marxist revindications of **class** and **race**, drugs and political theater. His activism led to his famous arrest and conviction as one of the Chicago Eight for disrupting the 1968 Democratic National Convention. Hoffman went underground from 1974 to 1980, but re-emerged to political activity before his suicide. Works like *Woodstock Nation* and *Steal this Book* – a manual to living free – convey a vivid sense of personality and politics in the 1960s.

GARY McDONOGH

Hoffman, Dustin

b. 1937

Stage and film actor, Hoffman played in off-Broadway theaters in the 1960s. In 1967 Mike Nichols noticed his talent. With Hoffman's small stature, Nichols had him play a naive twenty year old in *The Graduate* (1967), for which he received a Best Actor Oscar nomination. In 1979 he won his first Best Actor Oscar for his role in *Kramer vs Kramer*. His role in *Rain Man* earned him a second Oscar in 1988. Hoffman is also a director and **producer** of stage, **television** and film productions.

KATE M. KENSKI

holidays

Holidays embody multiple calendars, memories and agendas within contemporary American society. Many formal national holidays tend to reinforce shared civic and historic values, yet they also have become foci of protest, illustrated in the anti-Vietnam book and movie *Born on the Fourth of July* (1989). Other celebrations are divided by **religion**, ethnicity, region and political meanings. Moreover, holidays vary in scope and seriousness. Thanksgiving produces national respite (and the heaviest travel of the year as families re-unite), while President's Day (combining Washington's and Lincoln's birthdays) is generally marked only by **department-store** sales, school lessons and post office closings.

An annual cycle of patriotic festivities has emerged since the founding of the nation, celebrated on Independence Day (July 4), usually outdoors with picnics, political rallies and fireworks. Other holidays remember the war dead (Memorial Day, last Monday in May) and workers (Labor Day, first Monday of September). These also delineate the summer/vacation season, underscored by the 1971 movement of Independence Day and Memorial Day, among other holidays, to Monday to create three-day weekends.

Thanksgiving, chartered by stories of pilgrims and Indians celebrating their friendship and survival at Plymouth Rock with a meal of turkey, squash and potatoes, was proclaimed a national holiday by George Washington in 1789. It was fixed on the fourth Thursday in November by Lincoln; Franklin Roosevelt moved it a week earlier to promote shopping. Here, diverse family traditions of food and fellowship blend with charity (meals at soup kitchens), commercial events (parades mark the beginning of holiday **consumerism**) and sports. While Thanksgiving evokes criticism by Native Americans, it remains the most widely celebrated expression of united national identity.

Other national public holidays include Columbus Day (October 12 or the second Monday in October), Veteran's Day (November 11) and presidential birthdays. A holiday honoring Dr. Martin Luther King, Jr. (third Monday in January) was added to national and state calendars amid intense polemics in the 1980s.

Special national commemorations have included massive celebrations of the American **Bicentennial** in 1976, and similar anniversaries of wars and battles, sometimes with re-enactments or political opportunities/speeches. The presidential inauguration celebrated on January 20 every four years has also taken on trappings of a national festival. In addition, whole months (Black History Month (January), Women's History (February), etc.) and days for specific causes and celebrities are recognized at the national, state and local level.

New Year's Eve, while not a patriotic holiday, inscribes the nation through shared media coverage of the crystal ball dropping in New York's **Times Square**, as well as urban festivals like First Night and many private parties. January 1 has become the day for parades and **football** bowl games deciding the rankings of the college season. **African American** communities have also celebrated January 1 as Emancipation Day.

In addition to civic celebration, holidays of Christian origin are widely shared and secularized. Halloween (October 31) has been transformed from a feast of the dead to a night celebrating **children** and **neighborhoods**, as costumed kids roam from door to door asking for candy. In some **inner cities** it has also become an excuse for arson and mayhem. Christmas (December 25) once dominated rhythms of school and work, but judicial decisions since the 1960s have tended to dis-establish its presence in public forums. Nonetheless, its general coincidence with Hanukah and the more recently invented Kwanzaa, which celebrates African American values, defines a winter holiday season for public life and commercial intensification.

Easter by contrast remains a more Christian holiday (with separate dates for Western and Orthodox traditions), but also proves less obtrusive since Sunday normally functions as a weekly public and business holiday. The proximity of Easter and Passover also reaffirms the centrality of Judaism and Christianity to American civic religion.

Hence, other religious ceremonies tend to be regarded as minoritarian, although they may demand special recognition, such as barring exams during Ramadan. Meanwhile, these holidays can take on the form of other American holidays, stressing family reunions and parties (as in the adaptation of Dimwali among South Asians), gifts or invitations to public awareness.

Religious and national festivals, celebrated in parades, rituals, picnics and fairs, also transform and delineate **ethnic enclaves**. These include St. Patrick's Day (March 17) for urban Irish, Columbus Day for Italians and the Virgin of Guadalupe (December 12) and Cinco de Mayo (May 5) for Mexicans. These are also popular events for politicians seeking ethnic votes. Firecrackers, dragon dances and restaurant specials announce Chinese New Year for tourists as well as Chinese Americans; other Southeast Asian spring festivals have also blossomed in new immigrant communities.

Localized communities also celebrate special founders or events. Confederate Memorial days were widespread in the **South**, although their celebration has waned with integration and immigration from the North. Abolition Day (March 22) (Puerto Rico), Pioneer Day (July 24) (Utah) and Huey P. Long Day (August 30) (Louisiana) all teach and celebrate local events. Emergent communities make use of the same American model to publicize their identity – Gay Pride Week and its parades have become major celebrations in **New York** City and **San Francisco, CA**.

Life-cycle holidays tend to reflect individual rhythms – birthdays, quinceañeros (fifteenth-year parties, especially among **Cuban Americans**), weddings, retirements, etc. However, **commencement**/graduation season, in the spring, produces rounds of parties among school-related networks.

Ultimately, many US holidays combine sentiment and commercialism. Mother's Day (second Sunday in May since 1912), for example, has become a major celebration of "**family values**," although long-distance telephone congestion, pre-printed cards and flowers by wire underscore the spatial divisions of modern **families**. Father's Day (second Sunday in June) was a later addition, followed by derivative recognitions like Grandparent's Day (first Sunday after Labor Day) or Secretary's Day (April 23). Paula Jones cited failure to recognize Secretary's Day as evidence of her mistreatment by Bill Clinton.

Most major festivals share "American features," including a stress on family/community, **food** (both public and private) and opportunities for both internal rituals and outward celebration in parades, speeches and parties. Whether one-time events like the Bicentennial or annual celebrations with multiple interpretations like Thanksgiving, they define shared memories and points of challenge within the national cultural project.

GARY McDONOGH
CINDY WONG

Holly, Buddy

b. 1936; d. 1959

Born Charles Hardin Holley in Lubbock, **Texas**, **rock-'n'-roll** pioneer Holly became a teen idol with hits such as "That'll be the Day" and "Peggy Sue." Featured on *The Ed Sullivan Show* and Dick Clark's *American Bandstand*, Holly was a singer, instrumentalist and songwriter who performed with the Crickets and as a soloist. Killed along with the Big Bopper and Ritchie Valens in a plane crash in Iowa, Holly's career and life-story inspired both a motion picture and a stage musical.

KATE M. KENSKI

Hollywood

The Hollywood film industry has dominated global film production, both in terms of style and sheer volume, for much of the twentieth century. To understand properly the phenomenon of Hollywood cinema, it must be examined both as a changing industrial system and as a distinctive stylistic approach to narrative film, since both of these make it much more than simply the geographical center of the American film industry.

Situated eight miles from **Los Angeles, CA**, Hollywood first began to attract attention as a base for film production in the early 1900s. Its ideal climate and location, close both to a big city and to the open countryside, made it a popular choice. Throughout the silent-film era, Hollywood developed steadily towards the cherished status of its so-

called "**golden age**," the era of production from 1930–48 and the period during which it consolidated its "classical" style. Its international success was achieved through a rigorous approach to film production, built around the oligopoly of the studio system.

The studio system consisted of eight key players. The "Big Five," namely Warner Bros, RKO, Twentieth Century FOX, Paramount and MGM, had all been active in taking over cinemas and expanding production throughout the 1920s. All five were self-sufficient in the areas of production, distribution and exhibition, and this "vertical integration" was crucial to their success. Beneath them in the hierarchy lay the "Little Three": Universal, Columbia and United Artists. While not vertically integrated, they were notable because they held agreements allowing them to show their films in the prestigious cinemas owned by the Big Five.

By 1930 these eight companies had carved up the American industry between themselves into a community of interests which allowed very little access to outsiders or independents. The key organizing principles of the studios involved the specialized division of labor, mass production along assembly-line methods, and the **star** system where careers were carefully masterminded and managed. Genre production led to certain studios gaining specialist reputations and developing an attendant "studio look," for example in the gritty gangster movies of Warner Bros. While highly successful, this process has since been criticized as an example of the industry's mass standardization during this period.

In 1948 the **Supreme Court** reached a decision in the Paramount Decree that vertical integration was in fact unlawful. The studios were forced to sell off their cinemas, thus ending their monopoly. At the same time, a number of additional cultural and demographic changes heralded a new age for Hollywood. The rise of **television** meant a new arena of competition. Furthermore, the return of GIs after the war led to a **baby boom**, with a surge of interest in domestic leisure and the development of new **suburbs** away from the city locations of prestige cinemas. Cinema audiences dropped dramatically. Hollywood fought back bravely in the 1950s with new innovations such as **drive-ins**, 3-D and a range of wide-screen formats, but the golden age had ended.

Though the end of vertical integration should have meant a far more accessible industry, the major studios ultimately remained dominant by retaining their control in the area of distribution. Nevertheless, some forty years later the independents of the 1990s arguably hold more influence and a bigger share of the audience than ever before. Most of the major studios are still active, but their survival has only been possible through a series of shifts in ownership since the 1960s so that most are currently owned by multinationals and conglomerates. The business interests of these companies are broad and often mutually supportive so that, for example, merchandising, television and video can be used both to promote interest in a film and ensure a long-term profit.

The studios of the golden age have acquired a mixed reputation over the years. They have often been rather pejoratively compared to factories, where a capitalist business ethic and concern with profits means that artistic concerns are low on the list of priorities. But the factory analogy, while apposite in some ways, does not always do the studios justice. Not only did this era produce some of cinema's most feted "auteurs," such as Howard **Hawks** and John **Ford**, it also established the "classical Hollywood" style, still evident in mainstream cinemas worldwide, that remains one of Hollywood's lasting legacies.

The keynote of classical style is continuity editing, an aesthetic of "transparency" which disguises the construction of the film-making process. Bordwell, Staiger and Thompson's seminal analysis of classical style (1985) identifies additional features such as the construction of a believable world, the centrality of clearly motivated characters, a cause–effect logic, linear narrative progression and a momentum directed at overcoming initial disruption with a strong sense of resolution and closure. However, stylistic variations since the 1970s – the so-called "New Hollywood" period – have demonstrated that these conventions are not immutable.

Reservations about the quality of Hollywood cinema are often indicative of the enduring cultural debate over whether the aims of "entertainment" and "art" are somehow intrinsically incompatible, raising fundamental issues as to what constitutes "art." The conglomerates and multinationals controlling the studios now are still accused of producing mindless, predictable **blockbusters**, and the classical Hollywood style, though resilient, is not without its critics. Left-wing critiques of Hollywood and its adherence to verisimilitude maintain that it was, and largely remains, a "dream-factory" churning out escapist fantasies for the masses. While contemporary Hollywood undeniably enjoys more freedom to negotiate the boundaries of classical style, such critiques suggest that Hollywood has an ideological agenda where naturalization and the emphasis on closure continue to distract the audience from the more irresolute nature of real-life conflicts.

See also: Hollywood, New

Further reading

Bordwell, D., Staiger, J. and Thompson, K. (1985) *The Classical Hollywood Cinema*, London: Routledge.

Bordwell, D. and Thompson, K. (1993) *Film Art*, New York: McGraw-Hill.

Cook, P. (1985) *The Cinema Book*, London: BFI.

DEBORAH JERMYN

Hollywood, New

Post-studio, end-of-the-millenium Hollywood since the 1970s belongs to a new industrial structure. Film is not the only product; the new Hollywood has become home to expanded mass entertainment entities, including **television**, **cable**, satellite, **publishing**, **newspapers**, music, merchandising, theme parks and other entertainment venues. The industries, now owned by multi-national conglomerates, like **Disney** or News Incorporated, are vertically integrated while they have expanded horizontally. Aggressively entering other world markets, they often control production, distribution and exhibition of transnational entertainment products, whether international film financing of non-American films, distribution of Hong Kong kung fu films, or ownership of multiplexes in Europe.

CINDY WONG

Holocaust museum

The United States Holocaust Memorial Museum in **Washington, DC** houses exhibits on the Holocaust, the systematic effort of the Nazis between 1933 and 1945 to exterminate the **Jews** of Europe and members of other groups the Nazis considered "undesirable." The **museum** also runs a variety of education programs and is a center for Holocaust scholarship. The bill creating the museum was approved by **Congress** unanimously in 1980, and the museum opened in 1993. The money to build the museum was provided exclusively through private donations, but the federal government pays for the museum's operational expenses. The museum draws far more visitors than originally anticipated and since the museum's opening, several states and cities have opened their own Holocaust museums and memorials. Congress' decision to charter the museum was in some ways a break with past practices as the museum does not focus on an event in American history, although its exhibits do deal with the US reaction to the Holocaust and its aftermath.

DAVID GOLDSTON

home

Not only America's **middle** and **upper classes**, but also its **working classes** have constituted a nation of home-owners for generations. Whether suburban ranch houses, urban row houses or, more recently, lofts, condominia and co-ops, home-ownership has been the mark of solid citizenship. Moreover, the generally detached home and yard enshrines principles of individuality, **family**, **freedom** and responsibility. In the 1990s, 70 percent of new immigrants acquired a home within twenty years of arrival; mortgages and government support, including tax breaks, reaffirm this centrality for old and new citizens. Apartments, primarily rental, denote the freedom of young adulthood or

the post-familial conditions of old age – high density residential hotels, as Paul Groth (1994) notes, imply failure rather than alternative housing. Economic crises are measured, in turn, by downturns in home construction and the problems of first-time buyers.

The ideal of home-ownership was ingrained in American culture in the early Republic. By the Victorian period, in **Philadelphia, PA**, for example, many workers acquired their own row houses while more elaborate cottages were built in streetcar and railroad suburbs. After the Second World War, **Levittowns** and other developments promised new **suburban** houses to expanding families of the **baby boom**. While mortgages represent imposing debts (an appropriate mortgage is calculated at four times annual family income), payments on interest are tax deductible, facilitating purchase. For many families since the 1970s, homes have become their primary investment, seemingly gaining in value every year. Losses have been terrifying signs of **neighborhood** decay (**blockbusting**, deindustrialization) or wider recession.

The ideal house also codifies basic elements of the American family, including individual space, casual living (including outdoor areas) and display. **Kitchens** as well as recreation rooms encourage "family time." **Bedrooms** for each family member and even individual **bathrooms** foster privacy. Gender roles have been emphasized in women's control of private spaces (**kitchens** and **bedrooms**) and display areas, while men are associated especially with dens/recreational rooms, **garages**/workshops and outdoor areas. Garages, additional rooms, architectural flourishes like cathedral ceilings, elaborate staircases and outdoor facilities also mark differences in status. These may be incorporated into building codes that require multi-acre lots or stylistic conformity. Competition fosters continual home improvement (also a title of a popular 1990s **sitcom** satirizing do-it-yourself efforts), which can draw on accrued equity. Relations with neighbors and local institutions (schools are generally supported by property taxes) sustain the ideological centrality of the house for citizenship.

As housing follows inflation, issues of affordability and **homelessness** have underscored the resources necessary to sustain the American dream. **Mobile homes**, rental properties and transient housing offer alternatives without undercutting the centrality of "home" to individual and family identity. Co-housing and specialized retirement or dependent planning have challenged the spatial meanings of home, as have feminist critiques (Wright, Hayden). Yet, the identity of America and home is underscored by **mass media** that treat both the attainment of home-ownership and the violation of the home as central dramas of American life.

See also: home; gardens; lawn/yard

Further reading

Groth, P. (1994) *Living Downtown*, Berkeley: University of California.

Hayden, D. (1984) *Redesigning the American Dream*, New York: W.W. Norton.

Wright, G. (1981) *Building the Dream*, New York: Pantheon. (The above three present interesting historical and social perspectives).

GARY McDONOGH

home, outdoor spaces

Pastoral ideals embodied in the stately mansions of Jefferson and Washington created a baronial relationship to the landscape difficult to replicate in mass housing. Yet the cultural ideal of the private, detached home, its domestic and public spaces, scarcely ends at the door. A well-tended grass front **lawn**, for example, became the ornament of American homes after the Civil War. Its setback from the streets shapes a characteristic American urban residential geography: lawns, sweeping or minute, landscaped with trees, bushes, ornaments and fences but often left to flow as a green sward along the street. This green sea reached its acme in **suburban** developments demanding one- to five-acre lots. Lawns are simultaneously private and public display spaces with their own technologies and investments, ranging from the lawn mower – pushed, powered or ridden – to chemicals and irrigation that create grass in deserts, at the cost of ecology and energy.

In cities, especially in working-class **neighborhoods**, this lawn abuts on places of semi-private sociability engaging windows, porches, stoops and alleyways that mesh street and home (as in Spike **Lee**'s 1989 *Do the Right Thing*). As suburbs sprawled, these front areas became engulfed and isolated by the gaping lawn – vestigial spaces for guests, vendors and other callers.

"Back" spaces are rather different. Urban homes may have sheltered gardens, service porches or multipurpose yards (with **kitchens** or **bathrooms**). In postwar suburbia, backyards grew in size, physical features and equipment to integrate them into the **home** and to extend domestic life into the healthy outdoors. Concrete or flagstone patios and wooden decks, connected to living areas by glass doors, epitomized a "California" style (associated with Richard Neutra), copied even in less welcoming climates. **Barbeques**, redwood, wicker, wrought-iron or plastic lawn furniture and **children**'s play sets convert the yard into an entertainment area for summer holidays, while flower and vegetable gardens provide hobbies and occasional resources. After the war, even swimming pools came within the reach of the middle-class home, especially in the **Sunbelt**.

These outdoor yet domestic areas have become common backdrops for family comedies on **television** and in movies (especially when male characters take over the gendered tasks of outdoor cooking). Landscaping and fences ensure familial boundaries and privacy as well as security for children, invited guests and pets. While some backyards are connected from house to house, shared outdoor spaces are more likely to be found in parks, around schools and at country clubs.

Apartment houses, motels, office parks and even urban housing complexes have came to provide similar outdoor spaces: balconies, tiny patios and **community**-access gardens allow some negotiated privacy. Yet, these developments also create public/private outdoor spaces for a casual American community, whether poolside conversations or structured neighborhood events. Nonetheless, such outdoor spaces (sometimes indoors) often generate noise and conflict.

Since the 1980s, **New Urbanism** has championed the porch and yard as spaces of sociability. Urbanists have also played with attaching abandoned urban-spaces to nearby homes and institutions to create a fabric of domesticated nature in the city. Yet the dialectic of public and private, individual ownership and community, are continually played out in complicated ways in these interstices of home and nature.

GARY McDONOGH

homelessness

For at least 150 years, Americans have used the adjective "homeless" to describe those without a domicile and to indicate an absence of ties to family or to a place and the people settled there. Understood in this broad sense of uprootedness, homelessness has been a recurrent (if not defining) feature of American life, particularly as the coincidence of livelihood, **family** and place declined with the rise of the market, the extension of the **frontier** and relentless urbanization. Indeed, by the 1870s, intermittent **migration** and precarious housing circumstances were such common hardships of working-class life that they warranted scarce comment. But note, too, an exotic, romantic strain in the understanding of homelessness in the tramp, at once a figure of menace and colorful resistance to industrial discipline, or legendary folk heroes who were homeless men like the Maine logger Paul Bunyan or the southwestern **cowboy** Pecos Bill. The term could encompass even the unmarried women who moved to the city for work in increasing numbers after the Civil War, or, during the Great Depression, families who, though housed, failed to meet state settlement (residency) requirements for public aid and thus were conveniently made federal charges. "Homeless" covered a big territory, including routine hardship, defiance, adventure and even bureaucratic expedience

This diffuse understanding of the term persists in popular culture; it is traced easily enough in the annals of labor, American bohemia, or the survivalist right. It is used now more than ever to define a bureaucratic category. During the 1980s, with a renaissance of shelterless poverty unlike any seen since the 1930s, the word was given a technical cast by scholars and policy-makers

needing to bound survey samples and target eligibility for special services and housing benefits. They constructed a narrow, operational definition that counted as homeless only people living in shelters, out of doors, or in places not meant for human habitation. Whatever injustice it does to history, however it scants the subtle cultural work of ambiguous words, this definition has the stamp of authority.

Numbers

Estimates of the size of America's homeless population came to be based on this literal notion of houselessness. These estimates, some as low as 250,000, rapidly became controversial because they were based on one-night surveys and seemed to many to minimize the extent of homelessness, even when narrowly defined. However, by the early 1990s, the development of computerized data systems in some US jurisdictions made it possible to amass unduplicated counts of shelter users over stretches of time, thus providing a dynamic enumeration of this population. Data from big cities like **New York** City and **Philadelphia, PA** and smaller cities and counties in **New England**, the **Midwest** and **California** showed that between 4.4 percent and 13 percent of the local poor made use of public shelter annually during the late 1980s and early 1990s. A national telephone survey found that between 2.4 percent and 3.1 percent of the adult population – that is, between 4.4 million and 5.7 million adults – had been homeless at some time between 1985 and 1990. There is no longer any reasonable doubt that homelessness grew rapidly during the 1980s and had assumed massive proportions by 1990. No evidence suggests that the situation has changed in subsequent years. As in previous generations, periodic displacement and resort to a public bed has become a common feature of life for poor Americans.

Causes

The homelessness that became so visible in the early 1980s resulted, at bottom, from the increasing numbers of individuals and families who could no longer afford to purchase housing. In large part, this was a consequence of a precipitous decline after 1974 in real wages, work opportunities and employment levels for a growing pool of **baby-boom**-generation workers, particularly poorly educated people of minority status. Similarly, the real value of most income maintenance benefits plummeted after 1974. In the 1980s many **states** or local jurisdictions dramatically curtailed or eliminated altogether General Assistance, the only welfare program available to able, non-elderly single men and women or couples without **children** in their custody – hence their disproportionate presence in shelters. After the mid-1970s, then, the poor became more numerous and they got poorer. Not only could fewer poor people establish and maintain independent households, but also friends and kin could not so readily afford to take them in for extended periods. Thus, time-honored traditions of mutual aid began to buckle, particularly in **African American** communities.

At the same time, the nation's supply of low-cost rental housing was shrinking as the result of changes in the federal tax structure, rising interest rates and faltering federal commitment to the production and maintenance of public housing. While ample growth occurred in the national housing stock throughout the 1980s, the number of low-end units fell dramatically and the vacancy rate in that sector of the market became increasingly small. By 1989 there was a 5 million unit shortfall in housing affordable to poor people.

Part of the "affordable housing gap" consisted of a dearth of "marginal housing," mainly the single-room occupancy **hotels** that had for generations provided regular shelter for the alcoholics, substance abusers and mentally ill persons who had always comprised some portion of the desperately poor. Such disreputable structures were systematically destroyed by **urban-renewal** projects and private **gentrification**. This has had an important impact on the characteristics of today's homeless population, of which perhaps 30 to 40 percent suffer from a current major mental disorder or a substance use disorder. The erosion of marginal urban habitats coincided with laws passed in most states in the 1970s which made it difficult for persons with a mental illness to be committed to a psychiatric hospital or to be retained there for more than a few days. Similar laws eliminated the commitment of alcoholics and

addicts and jail sentences for public drunkenness. This process of "deinstitutionalization" – a *de facto* change in housing policy – was intended to be accompanied by readily available residential care in local areas. Yet, after twenty years (longer in states like **California** and New York), **community** care remains an unfulfilled promise.

Further reading

Baumohl, J. (ed.) (1996) *Homelessness in America*, Phoenix: Oryx.

Hopper, K. and Baumohl, J. (1994) "Held in Abeyance: Rethinking Homelessness and Advocacy," *American Behavioral Scientist* 37(4): 522–52.

JIM BAUMOHL

homophobia

If capitalism necessarily operates on a cultural logic of difference (i.e. masculine competition), the homosexual/heterosexual binaries serve as capitalism's *de jure* oppositional categories of *sexual* difference. The late nineteenth century's rapid and urgent framing of the normative from the non-normative required a rhetoric (medical, juridical, popular) that imbued the latter as an object of fear and disdain. Along with any number of cultural "non-normatives" of this period, the homosexual was marked as a disgusting anathema to the bourgeois sanctity of the heterosexual **family**. Moreover, because the homosexual body was scientifically and popularly presented as an "invert" (a woman trapped in a man's body or vice-versa), the feminized male body (in particular) threatened the foundation of American **masculinity**. Thus, one might consider homophobia not so much a fear of the homosexual *as such*. More precisely, homophobia may be more fruitfully considered as a response to the particular nineteenth-century concept of what a homosexual was, i.e. the "effeminized" male.

Historians as diverse as George Chauncey in *Gay New York: Gender, Urban Culture, and the Making of the Gay Male World, 1890–1940* (1994) and Edmund Morris in *The Rise of Theodore Roosevelt* (1979) have demonstrated the castrating effect that the effeminized male body had on American notions of hetero-masculinity. If the body of the homosexual was generated as a site of perversity, the body of the normative masculine heterosexual American male was manufactured with similar gusto. Theodore Roosevelt's radical shift from dilettantish statesmen to rugged **cowboys** is one of America's more brilliant accounts of masculine heterosexual "invert" anxiety.

Even with the contemporary rethinking of the political, scientific and popular place of the homosexual in the twentieth century, the masculinized hatred towards homosexuals (often played out in crippling and deadly acts of violence) continued to occur. In the late 1990s, in so-called "post-gay" culture and complacent assimilation of/ by the "homosexual lifestyle" in "mainstream" society, homosexuals have signed a Faustian pact. In order to dispel homophobia, sexual difference has been veiled. Homosexuals, in other words, must necessarily present themselves as "normal" so as to avoid the violence that accompanies homophobia. In contemporary parlance, he or she is insisted upon to act "straight." One can be "out" as long as one does not act *too* gay. With difference effectively erased and the masculine/feminine order of things perforce in place, homophobia curiously repeats its nineteenth-century beginnings. It is clear that the louder and more egregiously one speaks the love that dare not speak its name, the stronger the challenge to hetero-normative culture's purported acceptance of homosexuality.

Further reading

George Chauncey, G. (1994) *Gay New York: Gender, Urban Culture, and the Making of the Gay Male World, 1890–1940*, New York: Basic.

Morris, E. (1979) *The Rise of Theodore Roosevelt*, New York: Ballantine.

DAVID GERSTNER

homosexual *see* gay and lesbian life and politics

hooks, bell

b. 1952

"Black feminist" **intellectual**, noted for such works as *Ain't I a Woman* (1981), *Talking Back* (1981) and *Outlaw Culture* (1994), in which she synthesizes **race**, **class** and gender to examine **African American** culture, which she locates in a society shaped by "**white** supremacist capitalist patriarchy." In her writings she outlines the limits of feminist solidarity, divided along the lines of race and class, as well as the corresponding limits of racial and class solidarity. Born Gloria Watkins, she writes under the name of her great-grandmother; the use of lower-case letters in her name deflects attention from her identity onto her ideas.

ROBERT GREGG

Hoover, J. Edgar

b. 1895; d. 1972

Director of the **FBI** from its creation as the Bureau of Investigation in 1924 until his death in 1972. Hoover was responsible for placing the FBI at the heart of American government by undertaking a rigorous process of professionalization, bureaucratization and highly publicized investigations of communists, gangsters and alleged spies. Following the war, Hoover extended his range and power beyond these areas into more controversial definitions of anti-Americanism, orchestrating a smear campaign against Martin Luther **King**, Jr. and using undercover agents to infiltrate the **Black Panthers**. It is also widely believed that he had gathered damaging information on most of the postwar **presidents**, which inclined them to keep him on at the Bureau. After his death, more questions arose about the power he had amassed at the FBI and his personal life, including his cross-dressing proclivities (in stark contrast to the image of the straight-laced G-man).

ROBERT GREGG

Hope, Bob

b. 1903

Although English-born, Hope amused Americans for decades with sharp one-liners on the stage, screen, television and the golf course. In movies, he was known for his partnership with Bing **Crosby** in comic "road" pictures in exotic locales; he also hosted the Academy Awards. Many knew him through television specials, including decades of entertaining American troops abroad with caustic but ultimately patriotic wit. Hope was also awarded the Presidential Medal of Freedom.

GARY McDONOGH

horror films

While rooted in European myths and classic cinema (*Cabinet of Dr Caligari*, *Nosferatu*), the horror genre reveals dark recesses of American culture – so much so that other nations have tried to ban these **Hollywood** products from the 1930s onwards. To read these as reflections of American society (and even as causes of changes) is tempting, yet this relationship of image and society is constantly complicated by powerful artists, technological innovations, marketing and intertextual relations with other media. Moreover, horror also speaks to continuing "positive" themes of American culture – a nation committed publicly to heaven (sometimes on Earth) also believes in hell.

American horror were already set high standards by the 1930s, when actor Lon Chaney, Sr and **director** Tod Browning had established careers. Studies of physical deformity and the supernatural skirted the edges of the "respectable" production code, which tinkered with lines or images but avoided these often primal figures. The year of 1931 alone saw archetypal figures in Tod Browning's *Dracula* (with Bela Lugosi), James Whale's *Frankenstein* (with Boris Karloff) and *Dr Jekyll and Mr Hyde*. Even Tod Browning's 1932 *Freaks*, mingling human deformity with vengeance mutilation, played (with cuts) – while European nations, closer to the horrors of the First World War, objected to the onslaught.

Horror film production continued through the Second World War (with occasional attempts to read distorted violence as European). It gained a new life with the Cold War when it intersected with **science-fiction films** exploring new technologies. Creatures distorted by nuclear holocaust swarmed the screen after *Godzilla* (1954) arrived

from Japan – giant tarantulas, shrews, ants, etc. Other menaces came from space – not only UFOs but mind-controlling Martians. Still other dangers lurked within the hearts of people embodied by compelling **actors**, such as Vincent Price and Christopher Lee, aided by new technologies like 3-D and Percepto (which supplied electric shocks to the audience at a crucial moment in *The Tingler*, 1959). Films like *I was a Teenage Werewolf* (1957) courted the **baby boom**; David Skal cites a California physician in that era who felt horror movies were "self administered psychiatric therapy for America's adolescents" (1993: 256). Serving this "need," American International Pictures emerged, with director Roger Corman, as the home of rapid and cheap B-movies based on blood rather than character or technology. At the same time, **television** and magazines helped keep alive classic older traditions.

In subsequent decades, monsters became more invasive and devastating. In 1968 *Rosemary's Baby* introduced demonized middle-class **children** who would disturb movies like the *Exorcist* (1973) or the *Omen* (1976). Women's roles have become stronger than brides or victims of the 1930s and 1950s, but horror still tends to be a man's game as demon or slayer – the *Alien* series (1979–) is an exception.

Increasing violence again made those outside America queasy. Explicit violence, present since the late 1950s, grew over decades in slasher movies as well as mainstream cinema. Physical distortions based on foam latex and digitalization also expanded the genre. Horror films, moreover, intertwined with works by authors like Stephen **King** or Anne Rice. King, in Brian De Palma's vision of *Carrie* (1976) created horror from an erstwhile center of American everyday life – **high school**. Both King and Rice root evil in American places and traditions in streams of novels that echoed the growing serialization of horror films, where *Halloween* (1978–) uses a shared American children's holiday as its ongoing framework. Meanwhile, in the 1970s, **blaxploitation** flicks like *Blacula* (1972) and *Abby* (1974) provided separate but equal demonics. At the same time, horror has been seen as an attractive lure for the increasingly important **teenage** market.

The 1990s, by contrast, saw a resurgence of quality horrors (instead of B-movies), reflecting and mining traditions. The Vietnam generation (for whom *Jacob's Ladder* (1990) provides an especially chilling memorial) grew up to an Oscar-sweeping *Silence of the Lambs* (1991), found humor in the *The Addams Family* (1991) and style in **Coppola**'s *Dracula* (1992) or the reflective *Gods and Monsters* (1998). New special effects have buoyed remakes like *The Mummy* (1999) and *Godzilla* (1998), while extreme violence and distortion were serialized in *Hellraiser* (1987) and the teen-oriented *I Know What You Did Last Summer* (1998). One might read these 1990s productions as apocalyptic, but for every Hannibal Lecter there is another romance or Disney flick. Horror is part but not all of American psyche – the temptation of the forbidden, but also a desensitized experience of the modern, mapped out in the American everyday.

Further reading

Skal, D. (1993) *The Monster Show*, New York: W.W. Norton.

GARY McDONOGH
CINDY WONG

horses

A century ago horses were common in work and sport throughout urban and rural America. In transportation and myriad occupations, they filled streets, linked farms and towns and extended human labor. Moreover, an infrastructure of trading, care and shelter formed part of human settlement, as it has for millennia. Yet, within decades, the **automobile** turned the horse into a rarer animal of leisure. Although the horse figures prominently in **Hollywood** and **television** through the popularity of the western and historical pieces, it has disappeared from everyday life. The **Amish** maintain it as a primary work/transport animal. Mounted police, carriage tours and similar roles remain in some cities. Yet, even on **ranches**, the ease of a pick-up **truck** means a horse is sometimes carried rather than carrier. Meanwhile, maintaining a horse has become an expensive, specialized occupation, especially in urban areas.

Riding is still popular among many Americans, especially those who live in open areas and the West. Stables and trails are also maintained in great city parks like Philadelphia's Fairmount Park. Ranches may maintain horses for recreation and work; dude ranches specialize in this union of man and nature.

Horse shows showcase precision horsemanship in equitation and more complex riding skills in dressage, jumping, reining and related events. Major official shows, sanctioned by the American Horse Show Association, include the National in **New York** City, the Devon Horse Show, near **Philadelphia, PA** and the American Quarter Horse Congress in Oklahoma. Specialized breeding groups and riding associations appear in pageants like the Rose Bowl **parade**.

Racing also remains a primary area in which humans meet the contemporary horse. Both harness and flat racing are popular in the US, the latter having been established since the seventeenth century. In some states, only on-track betting is permitted; New York and other areas allow people to bet at state centers as well. Racing usually takes place on a one-mile oval dirt track, although races themselves vary in distance and prizes. Among the most important horse races in the US are those of the Triple Crown: the Kentucky Derby (Churchill Downs, **Louisville**), the Preakness (Pimlico, **Baltimore**) and the Belmont Stakes at Belmont Park, New York. Other race-tracks in Florida and California take advantage of warm winter weather. Famous horses of the postwar period include Man o' War, Secretariat and Northern Dancer, while Eddie Arcaro and Willie Shoemaker became well-known jockeys.

Winning horses prove profitable after their racing careers through breeding fees. Thoroughbred sales occur annually in Kentucky and at Saratoga Springs (New York); breeding is controlled through the Jockey Club and the American Stud Book. Breeding and training require knowledge, investments and commitment.

American horse breeding has contributed to the development of several important strains of horses, including the American Quarter Horse, Appaloosa, Standardbred, American Saddlebred, Morgan and Mustang. Wild horses are found still on western ranges and on islands off the Atlantic coast.

There are also problems associated with horses. Policies regarding over-breeding of horses for sport, over-use of public lands by wild horses and horses used in the pharmaceutical industry (i.e. for production of the drug Premarin) continue to be controversial. Americans have strong prejudices against eating horseflesh, although it is used in dog food. Some horses live out their days on retirement farms, but many also face industrial disposal.

GARY McDONOGH

hotels

In a mobile nation, hotels and **motels** have become way-stations, luxurious homes and markers of despair. While public lodging is not unique to America, the range of its meanings nonetheless deserves scrutiny as keys to a changing landscape

Hotels once invited travelers to any town that claimed a train stop and a future. Luxurious accommodations and **celebrities** have been associated with metropolitan hotels of global prestige since the nineteenth century – the Plaza and Waldorf-Astoria in Manhattan, the Willard in **Washington, DC**, Palmer House in **Chicago, IL**, the St. Francis in **San Francisco, CA** and the Beverly Hills Hotel in **Los Angeles**, among others. Downtown hotels originally catered to businessmen, although wives and families were reunited at exurban resorts like the Breakers in Palm Beach and the Greenbriar in West Virginia which offered elegant accommodations, fine meals and select company. Divisions of gender and **class** in both hotels and ever-expanding resorts have changed along with the workforce and family travel since the Second World War. Elite hotels have also figured as settings for novels, plays and movies, with the Plaza a favorite for **children** (*Eloise*, Kay Thompson, 1955; *Home Alone*, 1990), and adults' (playwright Neil Simon's *Plaza Suite*, movie 1971); the St. Francis was a model for television's 1980s series *Hotel*.

Hotels have *created* the landscape of resort cities like **Las Vegas** and **Miami** Beach. In smaller cities, historic luxury, once perhaps subsidized by local governments seeking prestige, has become part of downtown revitalization, while new hotels nationwide compete for architectural renown and business. Hence, John Portman's **Atlanta** Peachtree Plaza became associated with atrium hotels, while the Bonaventure in Los Angeles became the type specimen for **postmodernism** to Fredric **Jameson**. Specialized boutique hotels and family-run bed and breakfasts are perceived to provide a more European ambience.

Hotel chains have played a major role in this commerce. Major chains linked ownership and management of urban prestige hotels by the 1920s, although most operated under independent names. Conrad Hilton expanded between the wars from a Texas base to buy the Waldorf-Astoria in New York and other prestige hotels while extending his scientific management through leases and management contracts worldwide in the postwar period; many hotels carried the Hilton name. Other major American-based chains include the Sheraton ITT and luxury specializations like the Omni, Westin and the global Ritz-Carlton. Hotel and motel properties have also been targets for foreign investment, as well as 1990s incursions of upscale chains like Nikko and Swissotel.

Hotels also have reflected divisions in American society – luxury is available for a price that distinguishes a suite in the Beverly Wilshire from a night's accommodation at the **YMCA**. Hotels also were segregated in many major American cities – small Southern towns might have no public accommodations for blacks at all until the Interstate Accommodations Act of 1965. Despite their urban fame, Americans have also been prejudiced against hotels as places to "live," whose residents seemingly reject the domestic **home** and its duties. Residential hotels were discouraged in most cities by the turn of the nineteenth century. Later, SRO (single room occupancy) and welfare hotels became known as urban blights. Literature, films (*Midnight Cowboy*, 1969; *Barton Fink*, 1991; *LA Confidential*, 1994) and crime television have used a range of hotels to map out social diversity, division and trajectories in the city.

Further reading

Groth, P. (1994) *Living Downtown*, Berkeley: University of California.

GARY McDONOGH

hot rods

Taking standard production model cars and making them faster as well as more distinctive produced its own look, culture, magazines and music, especially among **teenagers**, from the 1950s onwards. These were displayed in "shows" among peers and in drag races (racing over short distances from a fixed start, illegal when conducted on public streets). This culture permeates contemporary films like *Rebel without a Cause* (1955) and the later, nostalgic *Grease* (1978).

GARY McDONOGH

House Committee on Un-American Activities (HUAC)

Immediately following the Second World War, the federal government fought what it considered to be a growing communist menace within the United States. In part as a reaction to President Harry **Truman**'s strong anti-communist rhetoric, Congress developed its own program to fight internal subversion, stepping up the hearings and investigations of the existing House Committee on Un-American Activities (HUAC). The hearings gave Richard **Nixon** his first taste of national recognition, when Whittaker Chambers accused Alger Hiss, a long-time Democrat and close aide to **Roosevelt** during the New Deal and the War, of passing classified documents to the Soviets in the late 1930s.

SUSAN SCHULTEN

House of Representatives *see* Congress

Houston, Texas

The Port of Houston (1998 population estimate 1,630,864) dominates oil and gas shipping on Texas' Gulf of Mexico coast and has underpinned the modern growth of this **Sunbelt** metropolis. Houston began in 1836 as speculative real-estate venture; today, the city sprawls across **highways**, far-flung **suburbs**, **edge cities** and **malls** (metropolitan population nearly 4 million).

Houston proves more cosmopolitan than many other Sunbelt cities, with an important historic black population and many **Latinos** (old Tejano families, recent Mexican immigrants and Central American refugees), as well as global **migrations** of Asians and Africans. Citizens also include Sunbelt white-collar migrations, national and international, associated with shipping, oil and other activities. Houston boasts major medical centers and universities (Rice, University of Houston), as well as the Menil Museum.

Houston's enclosed stadium, the Astrodome, hosted professional baseball (the Astros); it figured in Robert Altman's *Brewster McCloud* (1970), but is now obsolete. The city also has **football** (the Oilers), **basketball** (the Rockets), **hockey** and a major **rodeo**. The **National Aviation and Space Administration** (**NASA**) stands closeby. Houston hosted the 1992 **Republican** presidential convention and is one of the homes of the presidential **Bush** family.

GARY McDONOGH

Howlin' Wolf (Chester Burnett)

b. 1910; d. 1976

A country **blues** artist with a deep, dark, guttural voice, Howlin' Wolf worked the farms and juke joints of Arkansas and Mississippi from the 1920s through the 1940s. Influenced by Jimmie Rodgers and Charley Patton, Wolf moved to West Memphis, Arkansas, after the Second World War where he formed his own band and became a popular DJ on KWEM. In 1952 he moved to **Chicago, IL** where he recorded for Chess Records and became a key figure in the electric blues scene, inspiring 1960s rock bands like the Grateful Dead and Rolling Stones.

DEWAR MACLEOD

Hudson, Rock (Schere, Roy, Jr.)

b. 1925; d. 1985

As the independent movie *Rock Hudson's Home Movies* (1992) argues, Hudson's career represents a telling lie embedded within American culture. Tall, hand-some Hudson romanced Doris **Day** in **sitcoms** writ large, while other romantic roles made him a popular male actor in film and **television**. At the same time, his secret identity was known to many gays, but was shielded from his general fan audience until his death from **AIDS**. The split between his public and private personae adds eerie intertexts to his film romances like *All that Heaven Allows* (1955) and *Man's Favorite Sport* (1964).

See also: actors

GARY McDONOGH
CINDY WONG

Human Genome Project

Attempt to locate and map more than 100,000 human genes and their 3,000,000 nucleotide bases by 2005. The global project began formally in 1990, supported in the US by the National Institutes of Health and the Department of Energy – the latter showing earlier antecedents in studies of radiation and genetic impact. The project has increased genetic knowledge and also has identified specific contributors to hereditary diseases like cystic fibrosis and colon cancer. Five percent of the budget has been set aside to consider ethical, legal and social issues (ELSI) that will arise. Many are concerned with the alteration of genes as well as the meaning of the identification of defective genes in a given population that would make them susceptible to discrimination. Annual US costs rose from $27.9 million (1988) to $303.2 million (1998) as the project accelerated completion to June 2000.

GARY McDONOGH
CINDY WONG

humor

Americans take their humor seriously. Although vaudeville, film and **radio** had embraced comedy as a sure-fire way to attract an audience, the post-Second World War comedian often takes on the role of the cultural commentator. The audience expects comics to "pattern their comic material

close to everyday reality, making obvious beha-vioral patterns explicit and tacit operating knowl-edge and other insights about American society objects of conscious reflection" (Koziski 1984: 57). In humor, the audience seeks both an explanation of and a rebellion against the incongruities of the social order.

In the politically repressive 1950s, stand-up comedian Mort Sahl and cartoonists Walt Kelly and Herb Block obliquely commented on the terror generated by Senator **McCarthy**'s witch-hunts for communists. After a blustering politician commands Kelly's swamp animals to look for communists, the opossum "Pogo" famously de-clared, "We have met the enemy and they is Us." In the late 1950s and early 1960s, stand-up comic Lenny Bruce crashed through society's norms on discourse and taste, while Mike Nichols and Elaine May, in a more sophisticated fashion, eviscerated conventional manners. Mathematics professor Tom Lehrer joked in his satirical songs about the nation's fear of atomic annihilation, sentiments which presaged the film *Dr Strangelove* (1962) in their attack on the absurd logic of nuclear warfare. Starting in 1952, *MAD* **magazine** mocked social conventions, as well as spoofing the decade's **Cold War** mentality in the cartoon feature *Spy versus Spy*. In 1958 Paul Krassner, who had worked for *MAD* and for Lenny Bruce, began the magazine *The Realist*, which became the progenitor of media satire for the next several decades. *The Realist* influenced *National Lampoon* and *Spy* magazines, the comic strip ***Doonesbury*** and the **television** series *Laugh-In* (Boskin 1997: 73).

Starting in 1960, comedian and political activist Dick **Gregory** became the first black stand-up comedian to address **race** issues with predomi-nantly white audiences. Unlike black political activists, black humorists, like Gregory, Nipsey Russell, Bill **Cosby**, Godfrey Cambridge and Flip Wilson, were welcomed into mainstream media venues, including television. Traditionally, humor on television has been tamer than humor on the comedy club circuit. From the 1950s through the 1970s, **prime-time** television had to be accep-table for the youngest, most impressionable audiences. Humor often pushes social boundaries, and, in the late 1960s, *Laugh-In* and *The Smothers Brothers* provided the prime-time audience with irreverent, sexy skits and jokes. In 1970, however, network executives canceled *The Smothers Brothers* because the show's jibes against tobacco advertisers and the Vietnam War irritated conservatives and the **Nixon** administration (Boskin 1997: 103).

In the confusing 1970s, Steve Martin engaged in anarchic behaviors which mocked people's self-absorbed seriousness. Like other successful comedians, Martin's humor translated to other media, including records, television and film. Joan Rivers, Bob Newhart, Richard **Pryor**, Chevy Chase, Roseanne, Jerry **Seinfeld**, Ray Romano, Bill **Cosby** and a host of other comedians moved from successful stand-up careers into other entertainment fields. Since 1975, NBC's *Saturday Night Live*, which airs after prime-time hours, has often used a dark-humored skit comedy to address social issues. The program has also offered a showcase for young comedians, like Bill Murray, Eddie **Murphy**, Chris Rock and Julia Louis-Dreyfus. Ironically, comedy clubs, the traditional breeding ground for new comics, have suffered in recent years because of the success of television programs devoted to showing stand-up routines.

Although American standup comedy, films and television programs have gingerly and unevenly approached political humor in the past, in 1996 Comedy Central successfully launched a satiric news show, *The Daily Show*, which humorously covered politics, the media and **religion**. Unlike *The Smothers Brothers*, *The Daily Show* and late-night **talk-show** hosts, Jay Leno and David Letterman have not faced censure or **censorship** for their increasingly pointed remarks on the **president** and other authority figures. Indeed, the boundaries of appropriate commentary on public figures have been stretched most vigorously by radio talk-show hosts like Rush **Limbaugh**, who leavens his bombastic political views with satires targeting liberals, women and democratic political figures. "Shock jocks" like Don Imus and Howard Stern have used their radio shows to push the limits of humorous free speech in their jokes about people and institutions. In turn, candidates for political office have sought the power of the witty riposte in response to political attacks. Candidate John **Kennedy** diffused the public's concerns about his wealth by reading aloud to audiences a fake telegram from his powerful father declaring that the senior Kennedy "will not buy one more vote

for Jack than is necessary to win the election." In 1968 candidate Richard **Nixon** tried to improve his public image by appearing on *Laugh-In*, where he uncomfortably recited one of the show's signature joke lines, "Sock it to Me."

Throughout the past five decades, Americans created jokes about the incongruities inherent in a democratic system. Minorities point out their struggles to achieve full American citizenship while members of the white majority somewhat nervously poke fun at their seeming imperfections, particularly those of new immigrants. As women gain more political and social power, comedians like Andrew Dice Clay build careers on denigrating them. Although America promises **freedom**, progress and equality, the social system invariably fails to create this promised world. Disasters, like the Exxon Valdez collision and the **NASA** space ship Challenger explosion, and bizarre criminal behavior, such as the murders by Jeffrey Dahmer and the marital problems of Lorena and John Wayne Bobbitt, quickly become fodder for jokes. Interestingly, the seemingly bland, family-oriented 1950s spawned a series of sick "dead-baby" jokes. Humor in various ages, therefore, "frequently serves as a warning system of emerging social issues. Society is vastly informed and enlivened by [humor's] prodding presence, spontaneous refraction of events and issues, criss-crossing within and between classes and ethnic groups and its notable resilience" (Boskin 1997: 204).

Further reading

Boskin, J. (1997) *Rebellious Laughter: People's Humor in American Culture*, Syracuse: Syracuse University Press.

Koziski, S. (1984) "The standup comedian as Anthropologist," *Journal of Popular Culture* Fall.

Veron, E. (ed.) (1976) *Humor in America: An Anthology*, New York: Harcourt Brace Jovanovich.

MELINDA SCHWENK

Humphrey, Hubert Horatio

b. 1911; d. 1978

As a US senator from Minnesota (1948–65 and

1970–8), Humphrey was a key supporter of the **Civil Rights Act** of 1964. While serving as **vice-president** under Lyndon B. **Johnson** (1965–9), he won a bitter fight for the 1968 **Democratic** presidential nomination that saw the party sharply divided over US involvement in the **Vietnam War**. Against a backdrop of violent clashes between antiwar protesters and police in the streets, Humphrey was steadfast in his support for the Johnson administration's Vietnam policy, earning him a lasting reputation for loyalty to the establishment.

SARAH SMITH

Hungarian Americans

Several hundred thousand Hungarians migrated to the US during the years 1880–1914, mostly landless young men seeking work. A substantial number, possibly as many as one-half, later returned to Europe. Of the remainder, many, especially those of Jewish origin, settled in **New York** City's Lower East Side; most of the others found their way to the industrial centers of the Midwest where work was plentiful. Like other Eastern European ethnic groups, the Hungarians encountered low wages, discrimination and poverty. Today, the majority of Americans of Hungarian origin are to be found in the upper Midwest, especially Illinois and Ohio. Several thousand Hungarian refugees also came to the US after the failed revolution of 1956.

MORGEN WITZEL

hunting

Hunting has been widely supported as both a pastime and a way of life in the United States. A requirement in some of the **frontier** regions of the country and tied to the policy of extinguishing the basis for **American Indians**' livelihoods, hunting remained a common practice throughout the nineteenth century. With the threat to a number of species as a result of uncontrolled hunting, protections were put in place to limit the carnage. Under President Theodore Roosevelt, **national** **parks** were established to protect large tracts of government land, particularly in the western sections of the country, and the scientific management of the resources in these areas included the control of hunting. Such approaches were reinforced by the Endangered Species Act of 1973, which provided mechanisms for the conservation of ecosystems on which endangered species depend.

Hunting has remained entrenched in American culture and society even while the population has become increasingly urban, and those seeking wild game to hunt sometimes need to travel great distances. Part of this continued support for hunting lies in the attachment of many to gun culture, promoted by the **NRA**, making hunting a **middle-class** pastime as opposed to one of the landed gentry as in many other countries. An upper-class fox hunting tradition was never visible enough to become a lightning rod for a vocal opposition to hunting in general. The movie *The Deerhunter* (1978) highlighted the pervasiveness of gun and hunting culture in rural areas of the US, contrasting the life of a Pennsylvania resident who hunted deer for sport with his experiences in Vietnam to accentuate the insanity of the latter.

Paradoxically, given the image of the hunter as the rugged individualist, hunting has become central to the scientific management of the environment. Since the 1930s, the Malthusian notion that habitats are able to support only a certain number of a species has been applied to the management of different species. But, instead of assigning professionals to crop the herds, federal and state authorities have assigned this task to private sportsmen and women. In each state, therefore, hunting seasons have been established (sometimes of varied duration for different species), federal and state regulations dictating the methods of killing, the number that can be killed in one day and therefore also the amount of game that may be in the hunter's possession. While such state control has helped to entrench hunting as part of game management, the system has faced growing opposition recently. In the 1990s, animal rights activists, who claimed that animals suffer under the system, carried out protests of various kinds and lobbied **Congress** to bring about a complete ban on hunting.

Hunters most often use rifles and shotguns to kill their game. Frequently, hunters use semi-automatic weapons, leaving carcasses riddled with lead. Reacting to this situation and claiming that less sophisticated weapons make the hunt more challenging anyway, many hunters are now return-ing to the use of bows and arrows or muzzle-loading rifles. Such developments towards clearer distinctions between weapons used for hunting and those used for "self-protection" may become more evident as the gun culture itself faces growing scrutiny in the wake of a slew of shootings at schools across the country.

ROBERT GREGG

Huston, John

b. 1906; d. 1987

Although he began as an actor and screenwriter, Huston's legendary presence as a director of films about loners and dark struggles overshadows these achievements (and a series of cinematic failures as well). His first picture, *The Maltese Falcon* (1941) captured the ambience of the American anti-hero, which he developed in subsequent films with Humphrey **Bogart**, including *Treasure of the Sierra Madre* (1948, Oscar for Best Director and Best Screenplay), *Key Largo* (1948) and *The African Queen* (1951). His opposition to **HUAC** activities in **Hollywood** eventually led him to live in Ireland, whose culture he explored in his last movie, *The Dead* (1988). Other landmarks include *the Asphalt Jungle* (1950), *Wise Blood* (1979), where he also turns in a haunting performance and *Prizzi's Honor* (1987). Huston also belonged to an American film dynasty: his father Walter (1884–1950) won an Oscar for his work in *Treasure of the Sierra Madre*; daughter Anjelica (1952–) won an Academy Award for *Prizzi's Honor* and sons Tony and Danny have also been involved with film.

See also: actors

GARY McDONOGH
CINDY WONG

I

IBM

The International Business Machine corporation (also known as "Big Blue" in Richard Delamarter's 1986 exposé), founded by Thomas J. Watson, long dominated the **computer** industry in the US. Watson had come up through National Cash Register, where he was jailed with other executives in 1912 for antitrust violations. Joining and taking over the CTR corporation, he expanded from calculating machines to massive computers and peripheral attachments that made IBM the most profitable company in the world in the postwar period. At the same time, the company became known for its crushing of competitors and regulation of workers (down to their white shirts). IBM faced its own lengthy antitrust suit from 1969 to 1982. IBM stumbled as personal computers hit the market, although it recovered with an industry standard in the 1980s. Nonetheless, it no longer provided the secure employment or national symbol that it once was despite continuing power. Its history and style are often opposed to the West Coast **Apple** and **Silicon Valley** entrepreneurs; parallels, however, may also be telling.

Further reading

Delamarter, R. (1986) *Big Blue*, New York: Dodd, Mead and Company.

GARY McDONOGH

ice cream

While not an American invention, this popular dessert has stimulated American ingenuity as well as consumption. The US claims invention of ice-cream sodas (1879, **Detroit, MI**), sundaes (Evanston, Illinois, late nineteenth century), cones (1904, **St. Louis, MO**), packaged treats like Eskimo Pies and Popsicles (1920s) and soft ice cream (1939). Off-setting summer overproduction in the dairy industry, ice cream has also been the victim of postwar corporate conglomeration. This has created room for boutique brands like Haagen-Das and Ben & Jerry's, whose inventive flavors evoke the **Grateful Dead** and other 1960s themes. Home ice-cream making, from hand-turned churns to electric machines, also has become a **family** summer ritual.

GARY McDONOGH

identity politics (contests in which individual and group identities become key factors in debate and decisions) *see* abortion; Clinton, William Jefferson

illegal immigrants *see* immigration

immigration

The United States is traditionally defined as a nation of immigrants. Images of poor, huddled masses welcomed by the Statue of Liberty just prior to disembarkation at Ellis Island and visions of a "melting-pot" assimilating new arrivals dominate public symbolism of this past. These characterizations, however, hide other histories of the country's immigrant past, including the discriminatory use of quotas to exclude certain groups and the potent forces of nativism that made many feel unwelcome after arrival. The benevolent image of immigration veils yet another history of the forced immigration of **African Americans** from Africa into slavery.

Indeed, there have been many immigration experiences and narratives. Fluctuating rhythms and patterns of movement have meant that experiences between and within groups have differed greatly over time. Many factors have influenced American acceptance of immigrants, including:

- Changing immigration laws. Early on, these varied from state to state before becoming tightly controlled by federal legislation. This first encouraged immigration, then cut it off in the 1920s. Doors reopened in the 1960s, widening in the 1980s, and spurred ongoing debates and divided legal and illegal populations.
- Fluctuations in the American economy as it went through periods of growth and recession. At times, this provided industrial work with "family wages," at other times high unemployment and only low-paid, low-skilled jobs.
- Regional differences and experiences for immigrants. Some arrived at ports in the industrialized **Northeast**, others in the developing **West**. Some, like the Chinese, found work as indentured laborers on the railroads, while others were able to establish themselves on **farm** land in the **Midwest**.
- Prevailing assumptions about particular immigrant groups according to shifting racial mythologies and hierarchies. The Irish and Italians were initially classified as non-white by many native-born white Americans, and the Chinese and Japanese became "a yellow peril," facilitating exclusion and **segregation**. Sometimes, perceived threats and responses have intensified in riots and civil actions. Catholics in the nineteenth century were suspected of papist

sympathies, while wealthy and poor **Jews** faced anti-Semitism. German cultural traditions were banned during the First World War, and West Coast Japanese were interned in the Second World War. In the 1990s, **Arab Americans** have been blamed for acts of terrorism, Haitians linked to **AIDS** and **Hispanics** labeled a threat to social services.
- The growth during the twentieth century of urban black communities, in some ways making it easier for European "ethnics" to "whiten" themselves, especially once they took advantage of government housing benefits after the Second World War and escaped their **ethnic enclaves**.

Other features complicate any discussion of immigrants themselves:

- The widely divergent conditions that many immigrants left. Some chose to leave their places of origin to improve their conditions at home. Others were forced to do so following rural displacement, famine, war or pogroms.
- The gender composition of immigrant groups. Early Italian and Chinese sojourners were mostly men, while Russian **Jews** fled pogroms in family groups.
- The intra-class, regional and religious differences dividing particular groups. Differences surfaced between first-wave migrants who established communities and second-wave immigrants who came as professionals to minister and to profit from them. Other antagonisms have divided Protestants and Catholics among the Irish, or Hong-Kong Chinese and mainlanders.

We might add to these the experiences of those who were absorbed as part of the US' imperial expansion, peoples residing in **American Indian** reservations, **Hawai'i**, **Mexico**, the Philippines, **Cuba** and **Puerto Rico**. Many would become potential citizens, albeit with ambivalent loyalties. Others allied themselves with the United States in wars (hot and cold) following the Second World War, from Greece to China and Korea to Vietnam, and became **refugees**, seeking aid from a sometimes less than grateful American people.

All these differences are discussed in individual articles on immigrant groups, settings and citizens.

Here, we focus on unifying themes of policy, analysis and contemporary questions that have shaped the meaning of immigration in America, especially since 1965.

History and policy

Prior to the Second World War, the primary ethnic composition of the country included descendants of northern Europeans and African Americans (the earliest immigrants) in their second, third or later generations. In addition, large numbers of so-called "new" immigrants, Russian and Polish Jews, Slavs, Italians and Japanese, had entered the country between 1880 and the 1920s, constituting first- and second-generation populations. The Chinese, coming in substantial numbers after the 1849 California gold rush, but excluded after 1881, constituted a large but dwindling population.

Immigration had peaked in the years preceding the First World War, after which controls were imposed. The Johnson–Reed Immigration Act of 1924 limited the overall number of immigrants and established quotas for each nationality based upon its proportion of the American population in the year 1880, prior to the influx of the "new" immigrants from southern and eastern Europe. This and other contemporary laws clearly favored northern Europeans.

The Second World War brought new refugees. The 1952 McCarran–Walter Act removed racial bars to immigration, although it imposed new ideological checks. Only the Simpson–Mazzoli Immigration Act of 1965 reopened mass immigration (without national quotas, but limited to 170,000 for the Eastern Hemisphere and 120,000 for the Western Hemisphere). This bill, a product of changing attitudes brought on by both the **Civil Rights movement** and American postwar internationalism, opened the door to new immigrant groups. Images of a racially divided society of whites and blacks, noted in the 1968 **Kerner Commission** report, were increasingly destabilized in the 1970s by the arrival of large numbers of Hispanics from Central America and the **Caribbean** and new **Asian Americans**.

Overall ceilings rose sharply in 1986 and 1990, with attention increasingly focused on controlling selection and illegal immigration. However, a commission headed by former member of Congress Barbara Jordan recommended lower ceilings on legal immigration as well. Debates have also surfaced about services (Social Security and Medicaid) for legally resident non-citizens as a complex category.

Understanding immigration

Competing images have prevailed among postwar scholars of immigration. Those working in the 1950s, clearly influenced by the **migration** out of cities into the suburbs and their endorsement of ideas associated with modernization theory, considered the immigrants to be, in Oscar Handlin's words, "uprooted" from their "old world" traditions, and re-forged by their experiences in the United States into "Americans." The "melting-pot" (title of a 1907 play by Israel Zangwill) was often invoked to describe this process. Indeed, by the 1950s, decades of restrictive quotas had disconnected many immigrants from their origins. Ethnicity became submerged as school children were asked where their grandparents were from rather than questioned about their own origins, second languages were erased through public schooling and many cultural organizations were "Americanized."

The "uprooted" narrative, however, downplayed the actions of the immigrants themselves. In effect, it made them look like victims. Authors sometimes even invoked imagery from African American experience to describe the travails of immigrants crossing the Atlantic. Some studies also betrayed nostalgia for worlds that had been "lost."

The 1960s renewed celebration of ethnic, immigrant culture. This was partly a result of the countercultural revolt against bland **suburban** culture, and partly a by-product of the Civil Rights movement's celebration of African American culture, which influenced "ethnic" Americans. It also showed the effect of new immigrants who would revive certain dormant cultural practices and lent renewed credence to the notion that the United States is a multicultural society.

For many scholars since the 1960s, then, the story of immigration is one more of "transplantation," in which immigrants have used their cultural traditions to help them adjust to modern industrial

America. Immigrants stayed together, using **chain migration** to help them establish close-knit ethnic **neighborhoods** (or "urban villages") within impersonal cities. They remained closely tied to their churches, synagogues and clubs, developed their own financial institutions, groceries and **radio** stations and used ethnic ties to keep their unions strong.

In describing this "transplantation," however, whole new "ethnic myths" were created, with traditions invented and patterns of continuity imagined. Moreover, different ethnicities and nationalities tended to be flattened (negative aspects of migration histories central to the uprooted story fell out of the picture) so that they only revealed one celebratory migration narrative. This simplification is clear in studies of gender, which played a critical part in the process of adapting to life in the United States. Many societies from which immigrants came were sharply patriarchal, and the process of "uprooting" involved in immigration often forced the male head of a household to rely on the work of his wife and children on arrival in the United States. Moreover, women in the workforce or among other women in their neighborhoods found that they had strong inducements to be independent. This led to uncertainty and strife in the lives of immigrants, often not sufficiently addressed in the scholarly studies of the subject. Yet it is a staple in the literature by daughters of immigrant families, whether Anzia Yezierska's stories about Jewish families in **New York** City, Paule **Marshall**'s descriptions of West Indians in Brooklyn or Maxine Hong **Kingston**'s stories of Chinese immigrants.

Another problem arising out of the transplanted story is its relationship to African American history. Post-1880 immigration occurred in the aftermath of emancipation, and African Americans became crucial, albeit negative, referents for the establishment of ethnic group identity and determining the "success" of a particular group. Looking for ethnic continuities, ironically inspired in part by the work of African Americanists delineating African survivals among slaves, ended up being a way of rewriting immigration histories. These could be stripped of the pathologies and dysfunctional characteristics (like violence and prostitution) that social theorists still attribute to ghettoized black communities. Here, the conjuncture of Daniel P. Moynihan's contributions to *Beyond the Melting Pot* (1963), a work that began the process of redefining ethnic histories, and the **Moynihan Report** on the "problem" of the black family is instructive. In short, the success of immigrants in escaping the **ghetto**, largely a product of the **GI Bill** giving affordable housing to white Americans, was attributed instead to their cultural baggage. African Americans, who did not receive this leg up from the government, were slowly moved from the category of "last of the immigrants" who would succeed in the future to a population group mired in a "culture of poverty." This story is encompassed in the Statue of Liberty itself. An offering from French Republicans to the United States to celebrate the emancipation of slaves, its origin was erased, and Ronald **Reagan** would celebrate it as a monument to white immigration at the statue's centenary in 1986.

In the late 1990s, immigration debates have focused once again on control. A primary target for both policy-makers and analysts has been the question of illegal immigration, estimated at 300,000 annually with perhaps 5 million resident in the US. The 1986 Immigration Reform and Control Act offered a complicated amnesty to those who had resided continually in the US for four years, while sanctioning employers who hired illegal labor. Often, this illegality was associated with the Mexican border, although other communities of Europeans and Asians emerged from "overstaying" tourist visas. The narratives of control have stressed how these illegal immigrants use up scarce resources; hence, California's 1994 Proposition 187 cut off all health and social services to illegal immigrants (actions held up by the court and politics). This debate, as well as federal restrictions on welfare for illegal and legal citizens in 1996, has also questioned **children** of illegal immigrants born in the US who have been considered citizens by birth. This question, while targeting a specific vision of clandestine border crossings, could mean a fundamental change in American citizenship.

Meanwhile, **mass media** tend to focus on ethnic nostalgia and **assimilation** (Coppola's *Godfather* trilogy) or success (Amy **Tan**'s *Joy Luck Club*). Nevertheless, the centrality of more complex questions is apparent in other recent films made in the US (for example, *Alien Nation*, 1988) and those that cross its borders (Gregory Nava's *El Norte*, 1984; Ang Lee's *The Wedding Banquet*, 1993; or Barbash and Taylor's documentary *In and Out of Africa*, 1993). In all, experiences, policies and narratives about immigration, varying among individuals, families and groups, are debates about America itself.

Further reading

Bodnar, J. (1985) *The Transplanted*, Bloomington: Indiana University.

Handlin, O. (1951) *The Uprooted*, New York: Little, Brown & Co.

Lowe, L. (1996) *Immigrant Acts*, Durham, Duke University.

Steinberg, S. (1981) *The Ethnic Myth*, Boston: Beacon.

Takaki, R. (1998) *Strangers From a Different Shore*, Boston: Little, Brown & Co.

GARY McDONOGH
ROBERT GREGG
CINDY WONG

impeachment

Impeachment is the ultimate power that **Congress** has over those in the federal judiciary and executive branch whom members of Congress believe are abusing their offices. Although it was a key element in the Constitution's balance of powers, **Congress** has only moved to impeach seventeen men (no women yet), seldom removing them from office. The process begins in the Judiciary Committee in the House of Representatives, which holds hearings on each particular case. If a majority of the committee believes there is enough evidence to go forward, it takes the case to the House for debate and a vote. Then, if a majority of representatives in the House agree, which constitutes the impeachment, the House managers present the case before the Senate. The senators (presided over by the chief justice of the **Supreme Court**) act as jurors in the case – a two-thirds majority being required for conviction.

Only two **presidents** have been impeached, Andrew Johnson in 1868 and Bill **Clinton** in 1999, though a vote of the congressional committee to impeach Richard **Nixon**, because he "prevented, obstructed, and impeded the administration of justice" in relation to **Watergate**, led to his resignation in 1974. In the Johnson and Clinton cases, the charges were brought by politicians who fundamentally disagreed with the presidents over major political and social issues. In the earlier instance, radical **Republicans** wanted a more vigorous assault on racial injustices in the **South**, while in the recent case the family-values right wing of a vastly different Republican Party endeavored to turn Clinton's sexual philandering into the sort of "crimes and misdemeanors" required to remove a president.

But impeachment proceedings in American history have almost always been about struggle over competing values. Like elections, most congressional impeachment proceedings have been stridently political affairs, arising not randomly throughout American history, but at critical junctures when ideological struggle has been especially intense. While such proceedings concentrate attention on the actions of particular individuals, they have arisen at moments of uncertainty and transition in American culture. Personality and politics have been deeply entwined throughout American history. This was the case in 1868 amidst the struggle over the aims of Reconstruction; in the early 1970s, at a time of intense struggle over the **Vietnam War** and domestic policies; and again in the late 1990s. In each case, impeachment proceedings had serious implications for political **party** realignment.

In their aftermath, the most important impeachment proceedings in American history have directly affected the balance of ideological groups within major political parties. In the recent case, the Republican Party, at every turn in Clinton's impeachment proceedings, sided with its most determined conservative wing. Beyond the issue of Clinton's conduct, this group had engaged in a crusade against both Clintons for several years. While the **mass media** often focused on the personal attacks, basic differences on public policies undergirded the conservative crusade. The House managers gambled that more media attention would turn public opinion against Clinton, and that, if Monica Lewinsky testified about her affair with Clinton, they would be able to reveal the president's alleged untruths. This gamble did not pay off; public opinion remained steadfastly in favor of bringing the "embarrassment" to a speedy end. The salaciousness of the information revealed in the hearings and trial turned the public against the messengers rather than the accused. Some of the tensions arising out of this failure carried over into the struggle over the Republican presidential nomination and the campaign for the 2000 election. While the more moderate wing of the party wished to turn attention away from the role it played in the impeachment process and has quickly aligned itself behind George W. **Bush** (making his primary campaign coffers among the largest ever), the radicals, led by men like Patrick **Buchanan** and Gary Bauer, continued to focus on Clinton (Buchanan going so far as to suggest that were he to be elected president the first thing he would do is read Clinton his rights).

In the aftermath of earlier impeachment efforts, political movements to alter the political landscape gained ground, feeding off disaffection in the country. Other factors were important in each movement, but disillusionment with the state of American politics was significant in each case. Recently, disillusionment with the state of politics has intensified. The Jesse Ventura election in Minnesota is an interesting manifestation of such sentiment, and perhaps suggests that one consequence of the impeachment process may be the growing success of a third-party movement.

The role of the media in covering the House and Senate proceedings was also intriguing. As a result of its impeachment coverage, **CNN** emerged into a prominence on domestic coverage equal to its leadership in covering the **Gulf War**. Assumptions that ratings would be low led to surprisingly modest coverage by most **networks**. CNN's closest rival was **National Public Radio**, the former providing the most detailed coverage and the latter providing extensive commentary. FOX and MSNBC decidedly tilted to the right during the proceedings. The web-site adjuncts to these outlets (and the major search engines) offered the public a new phenomenon: the ability to catch up

and explore aspects of the process in varying levels of detail via the **Internet**.

Further reading

http://www.stockton.edu/~gilmorew/0colhis/im-peach.htm

WILLIAM J. GILMORE-LEHNE
ROBERT GREGG

independent counsel

Archibald Cox, appointed special prosecutor in 1973 by Richard **Nixon**'s **Attorney-General** to investigate White House involvement in the **Watergate** break-in, ordered the president to turn over Oval Office tapes and was fired for refusing to back down. After Nixon's resignation, therefore, Congress passed the Independent Counsel Act to safeguard the investigative powers of the special prosecutor. Since 1973, twenty-three independent counsels have been appointed to investigate alleged abuses of power by **presidents** and other government officials. The most significant of these was Ken Starr, appointed by Attorney-General Janet **Reno** to investigate Bill **Clinton** and **Whitewater**. Starr's subsequent focus on the president's affair with White House intern, Monica Lewinsky, resulting in **impeachment** proceedings, led many to believe that the position had been tainted by the special prosecutor's partisan politics. After this investigation, the law was allowed to lapse.

ROBERT GREGG

independent films/videos

It is hard to define independent films/videos – "indies" – in late twentieth-century America. Indies can include training tapes made by a drug-rehab center, orientation films for new employees, Todd Hayes' *Poison* (1985) or the Oscar-winning big-budget *Dances with Wolves* (1990). Broadly speaking, independent films/videos are those not made by major studios which are vertically integrated with their own production and distribution arms. Film remains the primary medium for theatrical release, while videos gain audiences through broadcasting. Industrials are shown within an organization, while independent documentaries and lower-budget and shorter features seek exposure in **film festivals**, **museums** or on **television**. While Oscar winners like *Platoon* (1986) and *Silence of the Lambs* (1991) are considered independent films, directors like Woody **Allen**, Spike **Lee**, Oliver **Stone** and Quentin **Tarantino** blur the sense of independent as divorced from big money and big distribution. This entry concentrates on films not made by **Hollywood** stars and packagers.

The US offers little government subsidy for the promotion of independent works. Limited funds come from both private and public **foundations**, like Ford, MacArthur and the Corporation for Public Broadcasting, which runs programs like ITVS (Independent Television Service), and NAATA (National Asian American Telecommunications Association). Independent film/video-makers also rely on private donors as well as personal funds, including **credit cards**, to make their projects.

Once the indie is made, the film-maker needs to find a distributor. Some send their works to the film-festival circuits, others will try to approach distributors directly. Public or **cable**-access channels and the educational market are less remunerative; some products simply are not shown much.

Many indies flaunt lower production values as badges of authenticity, but some can have budgets of up to millions. However, there is also a tendency for independent works to challenge the formal styles of more mainstream works. Experimental and avant-garde works range from works by Maya Duran or the video art by Bill Viola to shorter essays and animation. Independent films have been strong showcases for minority and political issues, especially through documentaries, which always find more space in the indie's world. Examples include Marlon Rigg's *Tongue Untied* (1989) on gay issues in the **African American** community, *Finding Christa* (1991) on motherhood and adoption and *The Women Outside* (1995) on Korean women who "serviced" American soldiers in Korea.

On the other hand, other independent works starting at a very low budget eventually acquire national distribution, acting as a stairway to Hollywood for **directors** like Richard Rodriguez, whose *El Mariachi* (1992) cost only $7,000 to make. *The Blair Witch Project* (1999), made with a budget of $67,000, grossed more than $40 million in its first four weeks of release. These, however, are the exceptions.

Besides film festivals, indies rely on distribution companies, like Third World Newsreel, Latino Consortium and National Black Programming Consortium, for the non-theatrical markets as well as for-profit distribution companies that cater primarily to the education market, from Facet Videos to Churchill Films. Small associations like AIVF (Association of Independent Video and Filmmakers) and New Days Film provide relevant information and support to independent film/video-makers, as does the Sundance Institute, which began an Independents Archive in 1997.

See also: documentary

Further reading

Pierson, J. (1997) *Spike, Mike, Slackers & Dykes*, New York: Miramax.

CINDY WONG

Indianapolis, IN

State capital and **Midwestern** commercial center, known for conservative **Republican** politics and top-flight **basketball** (**high school**, **college** tournaments and the professional Pacers). While the 1990 population was 741,950, the city has grown through a notable downtown revitalization as well as its strong foundations in agriculture, pharmaceuticals and services; the metropolitan population for 2020 is projected at 1,770,525. In addition to many **museums** and cultural institutions, it also hosts one of America's most famous **automobile** races – the Indianapolis 500.

GARY McDONOGH

individualism

The concept of individualism is a relatively recent addition to political and social philosophy. Thomas Hobbes, John Locke and Jean Jacques Rousseau in the seventeenth and eighteenth century proposed influential interpretations of the role of the individual in the social context. Out of such appraisals came two major concepts that were to drive the evolution of Western society and help define the nature of individuals over the next 300 years. The Enlightenment focused on reason as the hard-and-fast guiding principal promoting such developing institutions as science and democratic politics as the mechanism of individual nourishment and progress. Romanticism, an almost instinctive refutation of reason as the sole moderator of human conduct, dwelt instead on the passions, emotions and internally derived principals of individuals coming to grips with their temperament and position in nature as the divining force in humanity. These two perspectives established and defined the core of the sometimes complementary, sometimes contradictory nature of American culture.

The American Revolution, driven by the enlightened principles of the "founding fathers" such as Jefferson, Franklin and Madison, drew from rationally derived ideals of political and social equality for all citizens with minimal governmental obstruction of individual expression. This grand experiment left plenty of room for the popular, "romantic" notion of cultural individuality (and for social differentiation). Beginning with the founding fathers, and continuing through a litany of sometimes dubious **folklore** – Johnny Appleseed, Daniel Boone, Davy Crockett, Wyatt Earp, George Custer, etc. – and outright myths such as Paul Bunyan, the westward expansion of European culture in North America was accompanied and often driven by the poeticization of the individual.

Despite the enlightened social perspectives of twenty-first-century America, the dichotomy of the role of the American individual still commands the cultural stage, often to conflicting messages. Political campaigns are marked by candidates striving to distinguish themselves from their opponents as individuals and reformers, while being financed by the largest, wealthiest and most homogeneous political system in history. Sports and mass-media **celebrities** constitute the bulk of modern cultural heroes and role models, whose claim on the American psyche derives from their fame and wealth, and whose conduct often refutes systemic ideals of behavior. American competitiveness now marks the political and sports industries to such a degree that victory at all costs, demonizing the adversary to the point of exclusionary differentiation, and total defeat and humiliation of the opponent are acceptable strategies. Meanwhile, the environmental movement has elevated the argument that the discerning individual, in opposition to lumbering bureaucracies and malignant industry, will elaborate the new role of humanity and be the last best defense against self-destruction, while free-market **consumerism** converges on the conceit of the individual to peddle mass-produced goods, essentially promoting objects as markers of cultural acceptability and superiority.

In the middle of the greatest economic upturn in history, such incongruities are prime elements of modern domestic terrorism, fostering reactionary and combustible individualism in the order of the **unabomber**, the Columbine **high-school** massacre in Colorado and the **Oklahoma City** bombing.

JIM WATKINS

infertility

From a purely medical perspective, infertility is "the inability to conceive after a year of unprotected intercourse or the inability to carry a pregnancy to term" (INCID 1997). Infertility, however, has also become a symbol of the lifestyle and social values adopted by white **baby boomers**. While some theories suggest that the documented increase in infertility may result from environmental toxins affecting both men and women, infertility is often viewed popularly as the cost to women of choosing career over **family**. By postponing childbirth until thirty-five years and older, women are placed at a statistically higher risk of infertility. The difficulty and expense of adopting white infants has increased the demand for infertility treatment.

An array of fertility services such as infertility clinics, donor egg and surrogacy services, legal services, sperm banks, newsgroups and support organizations, as well as drug treatments, surgical procedures and assisted reproduction technologies (ART) have emerged to satisfy the growing demand for **babies** from the affluent **middle class**. This constellation of services and technologies embodies the modern paradox created by the desire for a scientific, technological fix to satisfy what appear to be traditional American family values. But this technological fix also touches upon the deeply felt dilemma that advances in science pose as infertility treatments, procedures and ARTs appear to be meddling with "**nature**" and "God's work."

Further reading

Franklin, S. (1997) *Embodied Progress: A Cultural Account of Assisted Conception*, London: Routledge.

Holmes, H. (ed.) (1992) *Issues in Reproductive Technology I: An Anthology*, New York: Garland.

INCID (The InterNational Council on Infertility Information Dissemination) (1997) *Glossary of Terms*: http://www.inciid.org

Michie, H. and Cahn, N.R. (1997) *Confinements: Fertility and Infertility in Contemporary Culture*. New Brunswick: Rutgers University Press.

Stanworth, M. (1987) *Reproductive Technologies: Gender, Motherhood, and Medicine*, Minneapolis: University of Minnesota Press.

STEVE FERZACCA

infomercials

Extended (30-minute) **advertising** that often masquerades in the more neutral formats of a **talk show** or **news** program. Celebrity endorsements as well as testimonies from "ordinary people" sell kitchen equipment, body-care products and self-help/get-rich programs, especially on late night **cable** channels.

CINDY WONG

information

Popular accounts heralded the close of the twentieth century as the dawn of an "information age." In some utopian visions, technical and economic infrastructures of communication and data exchange, such as the **Internet**, promise a society of empowered, mobile and resourceful individuals. At the same time, information industries, such as hardware and software manufacturers, data collectors and managers, communication service providers and producers of cultural commodities, are increasingly global, integrated and concentrated. Thus information practice is at the nexus of contradictory trends towards **individualism** and corporate power, and the ideals and promises of the information age must be understood within current structures of information production and use.

The genesis of the information revolution may be located in the dawn of the industrial age, when processes of production, distribution and consumption became increasingly complex and geographically far-flung. Management and control of these industrial processes required methodization of data creation, information management and decision making. This methodization took the form of increasingly refined bureaucratic practice. Bureaucracy consists essentially of two processes. The first is rationality, in which activities, entities and decision processes are abstracted and formalized into information systems. Information production is largely the representation and formalization of phenomena. That is, phenomena are examined and evaluated according to their role in a particular rational process. Some ontological model is applied to the phenomenon to articulate it into constituent parts. Decisions are made regarding which parts are important enough to note and record, and what formal relations hold among those parts. This involves judgments that are informed not only by explicit, goal-oriented criteria, but also by deeply held and unexamined cultural beliefs. The second essential structure of bureaucracy is specialization, in which decision-making power is assigned to particular organizational nodes, and communication flow is channeled and restricted to those nodes. These three facets of information – its administrative purpose, its inherent valuation and representation of subjects, and its unequal distribution – make information production and processing a focus of struggles over representation and power.

The use of information technologies such as wireless phones, hand-held computers and remote access to databases and services via the World Wide Web has made it possible for many workers and consumers to free themselves from the geographic bounds of the office and the shopping **mall**. However, as those technologies transgress geographic bounds, they extend administrative bounds. Workers and consumers alike become subject to oversight as their location and activities are tracked through their media use. This information then becomes the property of the overseer, and may be used to rationalize the production and consumption processes in ways which benefit capital. In the case of the management/labor relationship, the information may be used to extract from workers their knowledge of how to do things, and formalize that knowledge into automated "expert systems," thus transferring to capital the embodied assets of labor. Similar processes occur when consumer data is collected, evaluated and manipulated into demographics and patterns of consumption. In each case, management has greater access to knowledge about a population than that population itself has. In addition to the modeling of the activities of a subject population, information and surveillance are used to act upon individuals in that population – to control the flow of work to individuals, to trigger fraud control processes in credit-card systems, to offer (or to choose not to offer) discounts on purchases, etc. In these ways, information is used both to model human behaviors and to impose that model on human populations.

Similarly, informational practices are used to convert communal resources to private resources as cultural practices are captured, recorded, commodified and sold back in the form of popular cultural products.

Finally, information is a structuring element of markets themselves. Markets are in part defined by the ability of the participants to interact with one another and to understand current market conditions. Imbalanced access to information resources (including networks and databases) produces im-

balanced market power. For example, corporate capital, able to access data and communicate globally, acts in a global labor market, while laborers themselves are often able to access only local resources, and so operate only in a local market. Thus information resources give corporate capital the power to negotiate the global labor market as a set of local markets, while labor is able to negotiate only their own local market.

Information products, such as databases, software, network services, video games and entertainment, enter the market economy as inputs to the production process, as vehicles of distribution, and as consumer items in themselves. However, information products offer special problems in this process of commodification, and significant social, economic and technical resources are being spent in order to alleviate these problems. For example, it is notoriously difficult to restrict the use of information to those who have paid for that use. This difficulty is compounded by the increasing immateriality of information – rather than purchasing a medium such as a book or compact disc containing certain, more or less permanent, information, users are increasingly likely to access information via electronic networks in the form of a recordable, reproducible and malleable electronic pattern. Organizations in advanced information economies are responding to these problems of commodification by developing encryption technologies capable of metering the use of information services, or limiting their use to certain people. Other responses include the propagation of copyright and database protection laws and treaties which ensure that corporate gatherers of information have legal recourse to establish and defend property rights in their information holdings.

Further reading

Gandy, O. (1993) *The Panoptic Sort*, Boulder: Westview.

Lyon, D. (1994) *The Electronic Eye*, Minneapolis: University of Minnesota.

Mosco, V. and Wasko, J. (eds) (1988) *The Political Economy of Information*, Madison: University of Wisconsin.

Poster, M. (1990) *The Mode of Information*, Chicago: University of Chicago.

DAVID J. PHILLIPS

in-line skating

Commonly referred to as rollerblading after the company created in 1980 by two **hockey** players in Minnesota who, wanting to train in the off-season, converted an in-line skate to meet their needs. With refinements like a braking device and new materials to make the boot lighter, they created a skate that could be used by professional athletes and recreational skaters alike. By the late 1990s more than thirty manufacturers created skates for a worldwide market; in the United States alone, there are more than 29 million skaters and roughly a quarter of all households own in-line skates, making this the fastest growing sport of the 1990s. In-line skating also spawned its own professional sport, roller hockey.

ROBERT GREGG

inner city

Under various designations, American urban cores long have been centers of interaction, consumption and power. Since the 1960s, the positive "downtown" has overlapped with the problematic inner city, divorced from affluent outward expansion. Other related terms (Central Business District, or specific usages like the Loop, Center City, Midtown, etc.) have taken on varied political and social meanings.

Since colonial times, the city has been a place where people of diverse social and cultural backgrounds have come together. Despite differences in status and wealth, neat separations often proved impossible until innovations in transportation allowed cities to expand in the nineteenth century, re-mapping wealth, culture and race. By the 1920s, social scientists of the Chicago School recognized different urban functional zones. Park and Burgess' studies, for example, identified a central business district containing political, economic and cultural services for the city (although limited residence).

Around this stood factories and working-class immigrant homes in a transitional zone of abandoned wealthy residences. This model suggested that the inner city was constantly renewed by new immigrants, while those who assimilated moved outward.

Relations between groups living and working at the urban core were not always friendly. As groups moved out, tensions could erupt between those who shared neither heritage, language, nor skin color. In other cases, the mingling at the urban center alarmed those who governed the city. Hence **Los Angeles**' downtown, where **Asian Americans**, **African Americans** and **Latino/as** met, was dismantled over time, separating **ethnic enclaves** and precluding joint political action.

Many aspects of the "inner city" as a problem were exacerbated by **urban renewal** and upheavals of social movements of the 1960s. Here, government and private interventions often worked at cross-purposes. **Highways** as routes to communicate between central areas and suburbs, for example, often dissected vibrant areas around the business district. Destruction of decaying houses and factories in the core also created open scars in the tightly knit fabric of the city. In this chaos, riots broke out from Los Angeles to **Washington, DC**, often laying waste to whole sections and driving out businesses, employers and residents.

In the 1970s and 1980s, **gentrification** brought predominantly white suburbanites in to restore the older homes at the center which previous generations had abandoned. Unfortunately, this often forced the eviction of other ethnic populations who found no housing near the center nor opportunities to move further out. Still, "success stories" like **Philadelphia, PA**'s Society Hill or **Savannah, GA**'s Historic District enriched the "inner city" alongside corporate towers and public buildings.

Modern theorists increasingly argue that post-industrial cities, defined by services and information rather than heavy production, no longer require the same spatial concentrations of the past. Government offices, corporate headquarters and even sports teams have left behind aging infrastructures in order to be closer to a larger group of **suburban** consumers in suburbs and **edge cities**. Downtowns may be defined in terms of "special" places like **museums**, cinemas, restaurants and markets. Yet the inner city has become associated with danger, poverty and **homelessness** for those who avoid it, and with waste and with rage for those who inhabit it.

As a human center where diverse Americans have met and established their claims, the inner city has been the cradle of a multicultural experience. Yet, as **television** and cinematic representations from the **Detroit, MI** of *Robocop* (1987) and the Los Angeles of *Blade Runner* (1982) suggest, these areas can also be identified with the ex-urbanites' worst nightmares.

See also: Main Street; urban planning

GARY McDONOGH

insurance *see* American Medical Association; automobiles; banks and banking; healthcare

integration *see* Civil Rights movement; segregation

intellectuals/culture wars

The culture wars at the beginning of the twenty-first century have their roots in earlier conflicts within the intellectual elite. These, in turn, are framed by a wider tradition of populist anti-intellectualism, whose advocates associated the intellectual elite with a European, "un-American" culture.

Within the intellectual elite at the turn of the twentieth century – men like John Dewey, Randolph Bourne, Thorstein Veblen, Herbert Croly and W.E.B. **Du Bois** (all of whom drew on ideas from either Germany or Britain) – divisions arose about the extent to which an intellectual tradition should be forged that was more responsive to the experiences of Americans living in a society shaped by large influxes of immigrants and the presence of **African Americans** amidst a majority European population. For the first half of the twentieth century, **New York** City remained the bastion of intellectuals with satellites in Harvard, Yale and the other **Ivy League** colleges.

Both the progressive era and the New Deal witnessed the collaboration between government and intellectuals, and the rise of government and **foundation**-supported **think tanks** for developing public policy. The late 1930s witnessed the coming to the US of many European intellectuals escaping the Nazis, many of whom were Jewish, as well as some Marxists. The intellectual milieu was shaped also by the arrival of leftist thinkers like C.L.R. James and other African and **Caribbean** immigrants who saw the United States as reinvigorated by the Popular Front and by its potential as a worldwide anti-colonial power. These intellectuals had significant influence, especially in universities and colleges, but this would be more than matched in American culture by the anti-intellectualism embodied by the emerging **McCarthyism** in the 1940s.

During the early years of the **Cold War**, many left-leaning intellectuals like Max Eastman, Sidney Hook, Lionel Trilling and Edmund **Wilson** veered away from Marxism and socialism, endorsing purges of communists and Popular Front leftists. Into the vacuum rushed resurgent liberal optimism, embodied in modernization theory. One of the standard bearers of this theory was W.W. Rostow, whose "non-communist manifesto" (*Stages of Economic Growth*, 1960) was endorsed within the **Kennedy** administration and by the foundation-supported development agencies. Other sociologists, like E. Franklin **Frazier** and Daniel Patrick **Moynihan**, and urban analysts like Lewis **Mumford**, who developed modernization-inflected social theories, also proved very influential among policy-makers.

The 1960s saw the beginnings of the culture wars with significant fragmentation occurring within the intellectual elite. First came the rise of the New Left critique (for example, Herbert **Marcuse** and Noam **Chomsky**) of the military-industrial complex, the countercultural, beat-inspired critiques of **suburbia** and the "**organization man**," along with the SDS-led assault on the university as a tool of the establishment. Then African American intellectuals (for example, James **Baldwin**, Amiri **Baraka** and Ralph **Ellison**) began to receive more widespread attention in tandem with the growing **Black Power** impulse and the campaigns for black-studies programs on college **campuses** around the country. Feminist intellectuals, likewise, emerged out of the women's movement, invigorated by Betty **Friedan**'s *Feminine Mystique* (1963), but also reacting to the misogyny they witnessed within the New Left. Robin Morgan's 1970 anthology of the **women's liberation** movement, *Sisterhood is Powerful*, pointed towards a radical feminism that gained strength during the 1970s.

Simultaneously, conservative intellectuals began to coalesce around the **John Birch Society** and William F. Buckley, Jr.'s *National Review*, infusing the **Republican Party** with new energy, especially the presidential campaign of Barry **Goldwater** and the **California** gubernatorial campaigns of Ronald **Reagan**. These new Republicans, seeing themselves as part of a "silent" or "moral" majority, drew strength from **backlash** against the **Civil Rights movement**, **busing**, legalization of **abortion** and what they saw as the lack of **patriotism** of the left, spawning neo-conservatives within the women's movement, like Phyllis **Schlafly**, and **black conservatives**, like Thomas Sowell.

Further shifts away from class to identity politics occurred in the 1980s with the demise of the Soviet Union. Francis Fukayama announced, prematurely, "the end of history" and the triumph of capitalism, the proof of which ought to have been found in the success of Harvard economists in bringing **Russia** into the world economy. At the same time, cultural politics continued, animated by **Afrocentrism**, and the emergence of new immigrant populations, **Asian Americans** and **Hispanics**, who began to organize politically to combat discrimination and exclusion. Calls were made for the development of ethnic and multicultural studies, along with new **Latino/a** and Asian American studies programs matching the firmly established African American studies programs.

In the 1990s, new layers were added to these cultural wars. Divisions began to emerge between advocates of traditional methodologies and disciplines (such as Arthur Schlesinger, Joyce Appleby, etc.) and those taking the Foucauldian turn to poststructuralism and **postmodernism** (for example, Edward **Said**, Gayatri Spivak and Homi Bhabha). The political positions taken by intellectuals on either side of this divide have varied from the conservative to the class-based intellectuals of the more traditional school, and from the politically quiescent and academy-focused to the left leaning and politically engaged among postmodernists.

During the 1990s, also, the term "public intellectual" gained widespread currency. With its echoes of the Gramscian organic intellectual this has been an attractive concept for American intellectuals, who, since the progressive era, have been more politically engaged than their European counterparts. Unlike the largely white sociologists of the 1950s, however, many of the new public intellectuals have emerged within the ethnic and African American studies programs, and have been very visible in centrist magazines from the *New Republic* to *Vanity Fair*. Some public intellectuals have received withering criticism for being celebrity intellectuals, pulling down salaries sometimes more than double those of their peers, and for helping to establish a veritable free-agency system within universities that are prepared to negotiate huge contracts to secure the latest talent.

While the complaints have been widespread, they have been most bitter in response to the newfound prominence of African American intellectuals, who, until the 1950s, had been largely excluded from the leading universities in the country. But the success of Henry Louis **Gates**, Jr., bell **hooks** and Cornel **West** has not been greeted with approval even from all African Americans. In the *Village Voice*, for example, Adolph Reed (also a black public intellectual) has accused such intellectuals of being the progeny of Booker T. Washington. But, with the publication of his similarly conceived assault on W.E.B. Du Bois (1997), Washington's main political opponent, Reed has left the *fin-de-siècle* intellectual with that old dilemma: what is to be done?

ROBERT GREGG

Internet

The Internet is presented by the highest government authority as "a global matrix of interconnected computer networks using the Internet Protocol (IP) to communicate with each other" that "encompass[es] all such data networks and hundreds of applications" (Clinton and Gore 1997). Its model of a decentralized network, open to all and to all sorts of information, with "smart" receivers (**computers**) that interact with each other has captured popular as well as technocratic imaginations as the "information super-highway" for a post-industrial service economy. By the late 1990s, some foresaw it absorbing all other forms of communication into a new model, alternative both to the telephone system and to **mass media**. Others saw it as a new world of capitalism, domain of e-commerce and volatile .com stocks.

The Internet originated in the workaday world of engineers, who conceived and built technologies for sharing scarce and distant computer resources in the 1960s. Beginning with remote access and transfer of electronically stored data, successive additions of electronic mail (1972) and electronic bulletin boards, known as Usenet (1980), spread computer networking from research labs throughout universities, while increases in capacity made it available for less technical, even avocational uses. Non-engineers began creating databases that could be accessed over the Internet from anywhere in the world, and creation of the "user-friendly" World Wide Web in 1990 finally made it accessible to the public. From four computers linked in a demonstration of the software (TCP/IP) that enabled the Internet in 1977 to 200 in 1983, the number of computers linked on the Internet grew to over 6 million in 1995 and continued increasing at 16 percent per month. In 1991 the National Science Foundation that had sponsored the Internet project lifted restrictions on commercial use, which surpassed **education** and research uses by 1993. Business uses and stock investments based on such usages dominated discussion of the Internet by the end of the decade.

Users soon noticed that the Internet obliterates geography and puts potentially peripheral places on a par with what have been centers. Scandinavian and provincial land-grant universities were enthusiastic adopters, and USENET, the software for open discussion of thousands of topics, was invented in Australia, a leader in online libraries. Visions of "virtual" libraries in cyberspace, and thus of a newly leveled playing field, accessible instantly anywhere in the world, motivated such efforts. At the same time, minor technologies for video conferencing, chat and what amounts to telephone calls via the Internet accelerate pressures to deregulate telephone monopolies and restructure **telecommunications** around functions (such as delivering a signal or providing content) rather than around end-uses, such as watching **television**, talking on the phone or transmitting data.

Convergence is not uniformly welcomed. If it's illegal, it's on the Internet: **pornography** and political oppositions found controversial outlets, followed by copyright infringement and mail fraud. What had been contained is freed by the Internet principle that all communication and information is equal, and boundaries everywhere are threatened. The US Congress passed a Communications Decency Act in 1995 that the **Supreme Court** ruled to be an unconstitutional infringement of 1st Amendment rights to free speech in 1997. Threats of piracy and politics spread worldwide: Singapore employs censors, and China declared that the Internet will be "just for business" in that country, while the government newspaper of Iraq denounced the Internet as an "American means to enter every house in the world" and "the end of civilizations, cultures, interests, and ethics" (Associated Press, February 17, 1997).

Such anxieties mark shifting boundaries and fragmentation of authority in the **postmodern** world. Generally, fears of electronic surveillance have given way to boosterism, led by US government promotion of a national information infrastructure. Nonetheless, liberal humanists tied to older means of communication share concerns over information free-for-all with parents at home and with authoritarian regimes overseas. Consumer advocates fear false marketing as well as well-targeted ploys; **children** and women are often portrayed as particular victims of Internet predators.

What the Internet fosters is a broad creolization and emergence of intermediate communities and mixed discourses that both increase alternatives and make them more public. In this respect, the Internet resembles less the **mass media**, with which it is often compared, than the print capitalism that brought ethno-linguistic communities into the early modern period. It favors horizontal or what enthusiasts call "virtual" communities of special interests that can be worldwide and almost instantaneously accessible. This is probably a more important impact of the Internet than visions of tele-commuting, cyber-selves or wired democracy.

It is easy to overlook how the Internet itself is a cultural product and socially organized, just as anxieties overlook how much it changes in going public. The Internet is actually a collection of technologies that began as work-arounds and embody work habits and values of engineers. E-mail, discussion groups and the World Wide Web fit into an overall communications ecology and enhance the relative power or ability of users to reach others, to form a public, to bypass conventional gate-keepers and, in some cases, establish new publics. Increasingly, expectations that it may be the leading edge of economic development, whether or not of a "third wave" or "information age," are the Internet's license. This has under-pinned competition for control of access providers, as well as competition among businesses on and off the net. New Internet giants like Yahoo, Amazon.com and others are surrounded by service providers, "navigators" and other commercial sites. These are advertising heavily in print and televisual media, producing a continual crossover as well as concerns about changes in local business (and the tax structures based on them).

The Internet's social structure has evolved from an engineering experiment into government-by-steering committee, while its culture has long since expanded beyond engineering values to those of the marketplace in a larger context set by deregulation and capitalist triumphalism. These values and structures are, in turn, further modified by, say, sinicization or similar domestication else-where as, for instance, exemplified in the over-whelming focus on the self that dominated thinking about the Internet in our society. In all, the Internet has become a lightning rod and laboratory for the linkage of **community** to communication in the post-industrial society.

Further reading

Clinton, W. and Gore, A. (1997) *A Framework for Global Electronic Commerce*, Washington, DC: US Department of Commerce: http://www.iitf.nist.-gov/eleccomm/ecomm.htm.

Hafner, K. and Lyon, M. (1996) *Where Wizards Stay Up Late*, New York: Simon & Schuster.
Leiner, B. *et al.* (1997) *A Brief History of the Internet, Version 3.1*, The Internet Society: http://www.i-soc.org/internet-history/

JON ANDERSON

Inuits and Aleuts (Eskimos)

Northern Aboriginal peoples whose homelands stretched from Greenland to Siberia. In 1990, nearly 55,000 lived in Alaska, with others settled in the continental US. Their traditional social and cultural life, although varied within this geographic scope, had adapted to nomadic hunting and **fishing** in an often inhospitable climate, relying on a strong nuclear family. This has been radically changed by Christian missionaries, government intervention and new economic opportunities generated by **tourism** and **oil**. These changes are often epitomized in the shift from dogsleds to snowmobiles, but they have also entailed cultural and linguistic dilemmas similar to those facing **American Indians**. In addition, environmental problems have also been concerns for Inuits. Despite these changes, the image of the traditional "Eskimo" remains stereotyped in American mass media, especially **advertising**.

GARY McDONOGH

Iran

US relations with Iran were dictated in the years following the Second World War by the desire for access to **oil**. The Shah granted British Petroleum access to Iranian oil fields and, in return for development aid, remained committed to the western nations. With the election of Mohammed Mossadeq as the new prime minister and the Shah's exile in 1951, however, this changed as the country's oil wells and refineries were immediately nationalized. President **Eisenhower**, claiming that the new leader was a puppet of the communists, decided to intervene and sent in **CIA** operatives to foment demonstrations against Mossadeq, leading to his resignation in 1953.

The Shah returned and, quickly making Iran the largest recipient of American aid outside NATO, he bolstered his secret police and armed forces. All this left a legacy of strong anti-American sentiment, which, following the Iranian revolution of 1979 and the rise of Ayatollah Khomeini, resulted in the invasion of the US Embassy in Teheran and the taking of sixty American hostages. President **Carter**'s failure to gain the hostages' release, coupled with the media demonization of Iranian Islamic fundamentalism, was chronicled every evening on ABC's *Nightline*, and became a key reason for his loss to Ronald **Reagan** in the 1980 elections.

The fact that the hostages were released to coincide with Reagan's inauguration led to the suggestion that a deal had been made between **Republican Party** leaders and the Khomeini government. Such connections were then further developed in the **Iran-Contra affair**, in which **Attorney-General** Edwin Meese revealed that arms had been sold to Iran in exchange for the release of hostages in Lebanon and that profits from these sales had been sent to contra rebels in Nicaragua in violation of congressional legislation forbidding such aid. This scandal, breaking in 1986, was the most serious of the Reagan presidency, undermining the US foreign policy of refusing to negotiate with terrorists, though, as Oliver **North** took the fall, it did not come close to dislodging the "teflon president."

Relations with Iran have been normalized with the emergence of Iraq, Iran's enemy throughout the 1980s, as the main threat to stability in the region.

ROBERT GREGG

Iran-Contra affair

The most serious scandal in the administration of President Ronald **Reagan**, the affair involved two linked, arguably illegal, covert US government operations that became public knowledge in November 1986. In the first operation, the government sold arms to Iran in an effort to secure the release of seven hostages who had been held in Lebanon since 1984 by terrorists allied with Iran. The arms sales contradicted the stated government policy of refusing to negotiate with terrorists, and of isolating Iran, and at least some of the sales may have violated federal law. In the second operation, the government used the proceeds from the arms sales to supply arms to a group of rebels, known as the contras, who were trying to overthrow the left-wing government in Nicaragua, known as the Sandinistas. The operation violated a federal law that had banned US aid to the contras. The scandal led to investigations by both **Congress** and an **independent special counsel**, but only a few relatively minor figures were convicted of any crimes, and in 1992 President George **Bush** pardoned all those charged or convicted because of the scandal.

DAVID GOLDSTON

Ireland

The American people and government have enjoyed amicable and supportive relations with the Republic of Ireland, an independent nation-state, and the smaller Northern Ireland, an integral part of the United Kingdom, since Ireland's division in 1920. However, relations were strained during the Second World War when the Irish state, then known as Éire, remained neutral. Northern Ireland, on the other hand, was the site of bases for US forces staging for the invasion of western Europe. Since the war, US–Irish relations improved greatly during the **Kennedy** administration, while US–Northern Irish relations were muted after the return of "the Troubles" in 1969 due to British insistence that they were strictly an internal affair. Since that time, however, the US, through the International Fund for Ireland, has provided capital for economic development in Northern Ireland, and the **Clinton** administration has played an important role in the peace initiatives of the late 1990s.

The US continues to welcome Irish immigrants, in what is part of the special relationship between the two lands, while **Irish Americans**, the second-largest group of European ancestry in the US, sustain wide social and cultural ties with families and friends in the "old country." Today Ireland, North and South, has become a favorite location for American corporations (particularly in the fields of services, software and communications) that want access to the European Union, which both Irelands joined in 1973.

THOMAS M. WILSON

Irish Americans

Immigrants from Ireland and their descendants. The Irish who came to America from the seventeenth to the early nineteenth centuries were Presbyterian Scotch-Irish from Ulster, the northern province of Northern Ireland, who later wished to be distinguished from the mostly Catholic, rural and poor immigrants who, because of the great famines in Ireland in the late 1840s, began the first wave of mass **immigration** to the US. In the hundred years after 1820, almost 5 million Irish entered America. In the 1840s, the Irish made up 45 percent of immigrants to America. While the numbers of new arrivals have declined since, they have continued to be an important thread in the American tapestry. Some estimates have 40 million Americans claiming Irish ancestry.

While the majority of Scotch-Irish settled in the Middle Atlantic states, the Irish Americans who hailed from the southern parts of Ireland settled throughout the US in both rural and urban communities. Initially discriminated against in the nineteenth century because of their **religion** and culture, in an era where many employers displayed signs of "No Irish Need Apply," by the twentieth century the Irish had assimilated into the American mainstream. In the cities many Irishmen found employment in the construction trade and in the civil service, principally in the **police** and fire departments, where their literacy and fluency in English gave them an advantage over other immigrant groups, while many Irish women worked as servants and seamstresses for the growing urban **middle class**. Found in every American **community**, the Irish have become particularly associated with the politics, culture, religion and economy of **New York** City, **Chicago, IL**, **Boston, MA**, **Philadelphia, PA** and **San Francisco, CA**, which along with most major American cities have sported at least one "Irishtown." These cities continue to hold parades on St. Patrick's Day (March 17) to celebrate Irish American accomplishments and identity.

Irish Americans are mostly followers of the Roman Catholic faith, and they have helped to sustain that church in America since their arrival. Patronage systems among the Irish in politics had an impact on party organizations in every major city, where many of the Irish working class supported the **Democratic Party**. The Irish have made remarkable contributions to all forms of elite and popular American culture. In contemporary America, the Irish have made great achievements in politics (the **Kennedys**, Tip **O'Neill**, Paul O'Dwyer, Richard J. **Daley**, Eugene **McCarthy**), cinema (John **Ford**, James Cagney, Grace **Kelly**, Spencer Tracy), religion (Francis Cardinal Spellman, John Cardinal O'Connor), drama (Eugene O'Neill, winner of the Nobel prize), literature (F. Scott Fitzgerald, Mary McCarthy, James T. Farrell) and journalism (Jimmy Breslin, Pete Hamill). Since the 1980s there has been a resurgence in immigration from Ireland, inspiring a revival in interest in traditional Irish culture, best represented in the success of the staged musical *Riverdance*.

Further reading

McCaffrey, L.J. (1992) *Textures of Irish America*, Syracuse: Syracuse University Press.
Thernstrom, S. (1980) *Harvard Encyclopedia of American Ethnic Groups*, Cambridge, MA: Harvard University Press.

THOMAS M. WILSON

IRS (Internal Revenue Service) *see* taxes

Irving, John

b. 1942

Autobiographical novelist, whose first works, *Setting Free the Bears* (1968), *The Water Method Man* (1972) and *The 158-Pound Marriage* (1974), developed themes that reached fruition in *The World According to Garp* (1978) and *Hotel New Hampshire* (1981). *Garp*, in particular, brought Irving considerable public attention, with its irreverence, its blending of absurdity and realism and its engagement with issues of sex and violence, which the author suggested were the embodiment of American culture. More recent works include *A Prayer for Owen Meany* (1989) and *The Son of the Circus* (1994), in which an aging, Indian-born Garp works among film stars, dwarfs and a murderer in Bombay.

ROBERT GREGG

Islam

Muslims came to America as slaves in the early days of the Republic; later immigrants from the Middle East established permanent communities by the late nineteenth century. Yet claims to an Islamic citizenship have been controverted by the continual dominance of a Judaeo-Christian civil tradition and the orientalist identification of Islam with distant and savage others, especially in the global political climate of the late twentieth and early twenty-first centuries. Moreover, the separatist claims of the **Nation of Islam**, promoting **African American** nationalism on the basis of a non-orthodox racial reinterpretation of Islam, have made the **religion** seem anti-American to many in the cauldron of the **Civil Rights movement**. Nonetheless, flourishing Muslim communities have sprung up throughout the US, bringing together established African and **Arab Americans** with diverse immigrants from South Asia, Africa, the Middle East and Albania. Like other immigrants, these Muslims confront the dilemmas of maintaining the rituals and practices of their religion in a diverse society as well as the intersection of very different interpretations and cultures of Islam. Still, 4–5 million Muslims live in the United States, but mosques remain unfamiliar and suspect landmarks. Islam is read more often as a symbol of fanaticism than as part of a religious dialogue within a polyglot discussion. Moreover, Islam lacks the **Hollywood** conversion cachet of Buddhism: **mass media** have tended to separate rather than integrate Islamic practice and "Americanism."

Arab Americans established the first US mosques, especially in Midwestern cities, in the late nineteenth and early twentieth centuries. Communities generally remained small, incorporating

Sunni, Shia, Alawis and Druze; the Federation of Islamic Associations acted as an umbrella group. An influx of Arab, Iranian and South Asian students and professionals after the Second World War expanded this **community** as a transnational faith.

Meanwhile, the Nation of Islam had claimed titles and symbols of Muslim orthodoxy (mosques, naming, etc.) since its foundation in the 1930s, although its messages and practices diverged from global traditions, as **Malcolm X** observed in his *Autobiography* (1965). This division shifted radically in 1975 when Warith Dean Muhammed, son of black Muslim leader Elijah Mohammed, pushed his group towards Sunni Islam and doubled the Muslim community in the US. The intersection of "Orthodox" Islam and Muslims coming out of African American traditions remains extremely complex, even if these groups are conflated in American imagery.

New **immigration** laws also facilitated even more diversity with the arrival of Muslims from Africa, Southeast Asia, China, the West Indies and other areas. These shifts have separated "Arab" (which also includes Christians) and "Muslim" as communities, although many Americans again confuse the two. In the early twenty-first century, American Muslims, with over 1,000 mosques, are united by Islam, but divided by interpretations of Islam, language, origins, **class**, **race**, **ethnicity** and gender.

These diverse Muslims have confronted rejection as outsiders, as well as pressures towards **assimilation** and adaptation in the formation of American Islam. Limitations in observing Islamic law have been imposed by the small communities (absence of halal meat). Work and school settings and rules have failed to recognize ritual needs, although these have been changed through court action as well as increasing social recognition that, for example, limits academic exigencies during Ramadan. Even here, these questions are decided within American institutions (courts, agencies dealing with discrimination, universities, etc.) rather than Islamic forums.

Women have been seen as a particular crucible for Muslim identity in terms of both observance of rules and transmission of the faith to **children**, especially in the frequent absence of schools. Diversity complicates gender roles – some Muslim women may come from cultures or classes that have not experienced veiling (pre-revolutionary Iranians and contemporary North Africans), yet these same Muslims may be shocked by the lack of Koranic knowledge, behavior (smoking) or assimilation of other Muslims, including taking Christmas as a national **holiday**. Identification of Muslim women abroad as oppressed also makes it difficult for American Muslims to defend their freedom of life choices, much less present Islamic feminism as an alternative. In other cases, women have also taken on leadership roles in mosques and Muslim organizations beyond those they would occupy in other Islamic societies worldwide.

American Islam, despite its strengthened foundations and participation in American life, is profoundly affected by the transnational connections of geo-politics, immigrant ties and **mass-media** imagery. Arab–Israeli conflicts, the Iranian Revolution, which cut off large communities of immigrants in areas like **Los Angeles**, the **Gulf War**, fundamentalist revivals and the specter of terrorism have identified Muslims to many Americans as enemies rather than potential or actual fellow citizens. Whether in theological dialogues, orientalist visions from **Hollywood** (*Raiders of the Lost Ark*, 1981; *The Siege*, 1999; *The Mummy*, 1999) or in everyday interactions among neighbors and colleagues, this distance imposes special burdens on those for whom Muslim and American are central identities.

Further reading

Haddad, Y. and Smith, J. (eds) (1994) *Muslim Communities in North America*, Albany: SUNY.

Wormser, R. (1994) *American Islam*, New York: Walker and Company.

Naficy, H. (1993) *The Making of Exile Cultures*, Minneapolis: University of Minnesota Press.

GARY McDONOGH
CINDY WONG

Italian Americans

The notion of an Italian American **immigration** is to some extent anachronistic. When immigration began from southern Europe in the 1880s, Italy was only newly formed into a single republic, and the regionally and linguistically diverse population making their way to the United States identified themselves according to the town or village from which they came. This tendency was accentuated by the fact that many of the early immigrants were seasonal migrants, returning to their home-towns frequently, moving back and forth between their homes and the United States and Argentina. Once Italians began to settle down in the United States and confronted the high degree of nativism among native-born Americans, this local identification began to change.

By 1972, 8.8 million Americans claimed Italian origin, while a further 14 million had Italian heritage. Most came in waves between 1880 and the First World War, and from 1919 until the terminating of large-scale immigration in the 1920s. They concentrated in areas where there were jobs, primarily **Northeastern** cities, though a few rural communities of Italians were established like Tontitown, Arkansas, Asti, California (where a number of winegrowers from Italy established themselves), and Roseto, Pennsylvania. As the formerly cyclical migrants began to settle, marrying in the United States, or more commonly bringing their families from Italy, Italian enclaves (commonly referred to as "Little Italy") emerged in **Boston, MA**, New Haven, **New York** City, NY, **Philadelphia, PA** in the northeast, **Chicago, IL** and **Pittsburgh, PA** in the **Midwest** and **San Francisco, CA**, **Los Angeles, CA** and San José in **California**.

Italians arrived in the US at a time when the Irish already controlled local politics through machines like Tammany Hall, and had established themselves through patronage networks on police forces. Stereotypes quickly emerged of the Irish cop and the Italian mobster, which were common in 1930s movies down to *Once Upon a Time in America* (1984). Italians have endeavored to combat this stereotype, focusing on the success of police commissioners like Frank Rizzo in Philadelphia and noting other ethnic groups' connections with **organized crime**, but the task has been made difficult by the fact that the best-known novel by an Italian American is Mario **Puzo**'s *The Godfather* (1969) and by Frank **Sinatra**'s well-known connections with the underworld.

Italians witnessed considerable upward mobility after the Second World War, like other European ethnic groups using the **GI Bill** to finance their moves out of **cities** and into expanding **suburbs**. Italian **neighborhoods** survived in cities, however, often tied to the Catholic parishes which remained in place, when Protestant churches had sold out to incoming **African American** migrants. Considerable animosity was noted between Italians and blacks in cities, partly because they were in close proximity on the social hierarchy, but also because Italian Catholics were more reluctant to leave their congregations than were **Jews** and Protestants.

Politically, Italian Americans voted **Democrat** like other Catholic immigrants. Fiorella La Guardia was the first Italian to rise through this party to be elected to Congress in 1916, before becoming **mayor** of New York City, and John Pastore became the first Italian to be elected a **governor** (of Rhode Island). By 1950 all three candidates in the mayoral election for New York City were of Italian origin. Mario Cuomo, governor of New York between 1983 and 1995, was for many years the best known Italian American politician.

The 1970s economic downswing brought a period of turmoil for many Italian Americans. This was captured in the popular 1977 **disco** movie, *Saturday Night Fever,* and more recently by Spike **Lee** in *Summer of Sam* (1999). During the 1970s, Italian Americans moved towards the **Republican Party**, part of **Nixon**'s "Silent Majority," remaining economically liberal but becoming increasingly socially conservative in the wake of the sexual revolution and **abortion**. Italian immigrants had been noted for being more restrictive towards women than other immigrant groups, and with the continuation of strong communities and allegiance to the Catholic church, these became the foundation of more conservative voting patterns. Following the **Reagan** era, the best known Italian American in politics may be the Republican mayor of New York, Rudolph Giuliani.

Further reading

Lopreato, J. (1970) *Italian Americans,* New York: Random House.

Agnelli, F.G. (1980) *The Italian-Americans,* Torino: The Foundation.

ROBERT GREGG

Ivy League

Seven Eastern universities – Harvard (Cambridge, Massachusetts), Yale (New Haven, Connecticut), Princeton (Princeton, New Jersey), Dartmouth (Hanover, New Hampshire), Brown (Providence, Rhode Island), Cornell (Ithaca, New York), Columbia (New York City) and the University of Pennsylvania (Philadelphia) – constitute America's oldest and most prestigious **college** association. Harvard, with an endowment of $13 billion, was founded in 1636, with Yale following in 1702, both with religious support. The University of Pennsylvania, was founded later by Benjamin Franklin. Mainly male until the 1960s, all are now co-educational.

The name evokes an elite style of academic life, with ivy-covered halls and gentlemen scholars, embodied in a **football** association that grouped these schools together in 1898. Although athletics continues to be a unifying feature, the schools are more likely to be characterized today by their wealth as private institutions (Cornell also includes some state programs). The renown of their faculties and the selectivity of their student body within the US and the world matches the importance of their libraries and laboratories as national resource centers.

All these schools include both undergraduate programs and well-known graduate and professional schools which have produced recent American leaders like John F. **Kennedy** (Harvard), Al **Gore** (Harvard), George **Bush** (Yale) and Bill and Hillary **Clinton** (Yale Law), as well as world figures like Benazir Bhutto (Harvard) and stars like Brooke Shields (Princeton) and Jodie Foster (Yale). All these schools have organized and active alumni networks.

In general, despite a widening student body since the 1960s, they appear in popular culture as shorthand for a social and economic elite (for example, "preppie" or Ivy League clothes in the 1950s and 1960s).

GARY McDONOGH

J

Jackson, Rev. Jesse

b. 1941

Born in Greenville, South Carolina, Jackson became a member of Martin Luther **King**, Jr.'s inner-circle of advisers just prior to the latter's **assassination** in 1968. Taking on the mantle of the **Civil Rights movement** and shifting it towards the economic and urban issues King had begun to embrace, he became executive director of Operation Breadbasket (1996–71), and then founder and national president of People United to Save Humanity (PUSH) from 1971–83. Popularizing the phrase "rainbow coalition" to describe his multi-ethnic and racial supporters, he ran for the **Democratic** presidential nomination in 1984, and then more successfully against Michael Dukakis in 1988, gaining significant influence at the Democratic Convention. During the **Clinton** presidency he was a key supporter of the administration during the **impeachment** crisis, was involved in diplomatic missions and has been one of the District of Columbia's elected but non-voting "shadow" senators.

ROBERT GREGG

Jackson, Michael

b. 1958

After leading the Jackson 5 to many successful singles as a child, music videos (**MTV**) recreated Jackson's tremendous solo career by showcasing his incredible talent for dance. "Thriller," "Beat It" and "Billy Jean," among other videos, gained effusive critical and popular acclaim. Later, though, Jackson ignited controversy over dramatic changes in his physical appearance, suggesting excessive plastic surgery. He also was accused of molesting one or more of the **children** who regularly came to visit his home. While the alleged misconduct – and many reclusive traits – made Jackson fodder for media jokes and gossip, he remains the "King of Pop."

JAMES DAVID

Jackson, Shirley

b. 1919; d. 1965

Haunted explorer of the dark recesses of American life, Jackson discovered horrific dimensions of **family**, **marriage** and **community** in novels like *We Have Always Lived in the Castle* (1953). She provides a chilling rearrangement of American values of individual responsibility, collective identity and **freedom** in her classic story, "The Lottery" (1949), read by generations of American students. Personal reminiscence and a selection of her unpublished stories were made available under the editorship of her children, L. Hyman and S. Stewart, in the 1995 collection *Just an Ordinary Day.*

GARY McDONOGH

Jameson, Fredric

b. 1934

One of America's most prominent leftist **intellectuals** and cultural critics. Most widely cited for his 1991 book *Postmodernism, or, The Cultural Logic of Late Capitalism*, which situated him as the leading theorist on **postmodernism** as a cultural condition and an aesthetic style undertaken by visual artists and writers. The term that Jameson used as being indicative of postmodernism was "pastiche." Jameson teaches at Duke University and is an editor of the controversial journal *Social Text*. He has written fourteen influential books in literary, film and cultural studies.

EDWARD MILLER

Japan, relations with

Japanese–American relations are often described through starkest conflict or cooperation. Prior to and during the Second World War, hostility prevailed. Yet, after the defeat of Japan, the relationship was envisioned by the US in terms of the cooperation needed to ensure Japan as a bulwark against Communist expansion in East Asia. Nonetheless, once the Japanese economy recovered from the war, a growing sense of competition returned, with many Americans feeling threatened by Japanese economic ascendancy, even while believing that emulation of Japanese business methods and strategies was crucial. The 1990s recession, devastating economies like that of Japan and the Asian "tigers," reduced many tensions between the US and Japan, although struggles over market access and control continue. However, Japanese–American relations have been more complex than these depictions suggest.

In the years leading up to 1941, Americans did not necessarily believe that the modernizing Japanese threatened their interests. Theodore Roosevelt even promoted Japanese interests in the region in 1907, supporting them in negotiations against Russia, and secretly agreeing to allow Japan control of Korea in exchange for limiting Japanese **immigration** to the US. Woodrow Wilson gave Japan the Chinese territory of Shantung (formerly controlled by Germany) in 1919, but refused to insert Japanese language supporting racial equality into his League of Nations Covenant. In addition, the two nations' economies were intertwined, with Japan relying on exports to the United States (where the "Made in Japan" label was becoming common. The Depression in America, thus helped eradicate Japan's export market, hastening the collapse of its liberal government, and the turn to military expansionism). And, in the war, Americans vilified and punished both Japanese and **Japanese Americans**.

Following the nuclear destruction of Hiroshima and Nagasaki in 1945 and the American agreement to allow the Emperor Hirohito to remain in place (though with altered powers), American regional interests, confronted by growing nationalist and communist insurgencies, seemed to warrant the rebuilding of Japan under US occupation (1945–52). The US retained military bases like Okinawa as staging posts for operations in Korea and as escapes for Vietnam "R&R" ("Rest and Recreation"). With America's strict limiting of Japan's military, the Japanese were able to develop their export economy, gaining ascendancy in global auto production and electronics, while seemingly limiting American imports to **baseball**. Harmony between the two nations was sometimes strained as American military expansion became increasingly reliant on a nuclear arsenal. Since the Japanese had experienced the real effects of "mutually assured destruction," they often have been outspoken in opposition to the use of nuclear arms (potentially stimulating American guilt about using these weapons).

With the slowdown of the American economy in the 1970s, the collapse of the American auto industry in the face of more fuel-efficient cars from Japan (2 million cars were imported in 1981) and the related growth of the US trade deficit with Japan ($16 billion in 1981), antagonism grew between the two governments. The **Reagan** administration pushed the Japanese to pay a larger share of its defense costs, trim car exports to the US and reduce barriers to the importation of American agricultural commodities. But the impact of these initiatives, continued during the **Clinton** presidency (though with less urgency), was limited owing to the generally recognized superiority of

Japanese manufactured goods throughout the 1980s.

Some racism inflects US responses to the Japanese; Japan sometimes virtually becomes "The Yellow Peril," though with some modification over older images. The fear that the Japanese were buying up many American companies, for example, was exaggerated (especially given larger purchases made by the English). Americans quickly provided cultural reasons to explain Japanese economic supremacy: lack of corruption or Japanese educational methods. Such talk disappeared during the 1990s, however. Competition with the European Community increased, thereby diminishing concern about Japan. When the **Pacific Rim** nation hit a severe economic crisis, this exposed high levels of corruption and inability to respond to new loci of competition like **China**. But, if trade disputes are lessening, other disputes grow. Japan shows signs of wanting greater military independence, including growing hostility to the presence of US naval bases, exacerbated by the rape of a Japanese woman by an American sailor in Okinawa.

Images of the Japanese in American media reflect this history and complexity. While Frank Capra's *Battle of China* (1945) used racist stereotypes, postwar films like *Teahouse of the August Moon* (1956) and *Sayonara* (1957) promoted intercultural understanding. Japanese business in the US has received comic sympathy in *Gung Ho* (1986), although racist/Orientalist overtones haunted the American-made *Black Rain* (1989; to be distinguished from the 1990 Japanese film on Hiroshima) and *Rising Sun* (1993). These attitudes also subtly shape many news reports on Japan.

ROBERT GREGG

Japanese Americans

Although among the earliest immigrants from Asia, Japanese Americans have not experienced significant growth since 1960s **immigration** reforms. Instead, the Japanese American experience is divided between an older citizenry (shaped by the Second World War persecution) and modern sojourners who intend to return to Japan at some point in their lives. It is especially striking that the rhythm of these connections is shaped as much by Japanese outward orientations as by American policy.

The first Japanese came as laborers around the 1880s, escaping poor areas of Japan for Hawai'i and the West Coast. By the 1920s–30s, many became small-business owners and agriculturalists, and were able, unlike the Chinese, to import their families. Yet, with the rise of Japanese militarism and Japan's 1941 attack on Pearl Harbor, anti-Japanese sentiment grew. One hundred and twenty thousand Japanese Americans on the West Coast (40 percent of the total population) had property confiscated and were interned in remote camps scattered around the country. Those in Hawai'i and the East were not interned, nor were citizens of German or Italian descent. After the war, when the camps closed, many returned to the West Coast, although they had lost homes, businesses and communities. Nonetheless, some Japanese Second World War **veterans**, mostly American-born, were able to reap the benefits of the **GI Bill**, and eventually entered the professional class. Daniel Inouye, the first senator of Japanese descent (from Hawai'i), was a decorated veteran. For others, the struggle for compensation and even recognition and apology for a racist wrong lasted for decades before redress bills were passed and signed in 1988. Many Japanese Americans have examined this experience in literature and film, forcing mainstream America to look at their history. Steven Okazaki won an Academy Award for *Day of Waiting* in 1991. Kayo Hatta's *Picture Bride* (1994), which focuses on the travails of earlier immigrants, gained studio funding and national distribution.

According to Bill Ong Hing (see **Asian Americans**), three factors have made America less attractive to Japanese immigrants since the Second World War. First, unlike the Chinese who were initially barred from bringing in families and then post-1965 established chain migrations, few Japanese people need to reunite with relations abroad. Second, the strong economy and low birth rate in Japan (especially since the postwar recovery) present no incentive to leave Japan. Third, the internment proved to the Japanese that Americans would not welcome them in times of crisis, a negativity fanned by anti-Japanese sentiments whipped up around manufacturing and trade issues since the 1970s. Today, many Japanese, however, enter the US not as immigrants, but as tourists and sojourners, including students, professionals and business people. Many stay in the US for a few years, orienting **community** reproduction towards their homeland through schools, grocery stores, bookstores and Japanese **cable** stations like those found in metropolitan **New York** City. Boutiques and **department stores** like Takashimaya also define a cutting-edge urban style.

Meanwhile, today's third- and fourth-generation Japanese Americans generally lack discernible residential patterns or linguistic differences. Japan towns in **San Francisco, CA** and **Los Angeles, CA** are now commercial centers and tourist attractions, rather than residential **ethnic enclaves**.

Further reading

Nakano, M. (1990) *Japanese American Women*, Berkeley: Mina.

Niiya, B. (ed.) (1993) *Japanese American History*, New York: Facts On File.

CINDY WONG

jazz

Style of **African American** music that started in the South, particularly in New Orleans, around the end of the nineteenth century. Syncopated and polyrhythmic, jazz's early influences can be found in nineteenth-century vernacular forms: ragtime, spirituals, stringbands, Dixieland. Jazz bands used European symphonic instruments, but emphasized the brass sections. Bands often had more than one trumpet or saxophone player as well as a string section, piano and rhythm sections. As jazz spread throughout the country and into Europe by the 1920s, bandleaders and composers such as Louis Armstrong became prominent. Bands became larger in the 1930s, and the complex music became simplified by white big bands such as those led by Glenn Miller and Jimmy Dorsey.

In the 1940s, swing music ended and bop emerged as the predominant form, originating from jazz clubs of **New York** City, NY. A new generation of musicians emerged such as Charlie Parker (saxophone), Dizzy Gillespie (trumpet) and Thelonious **Monk** (piano) who left the big bands to start their own smaller, more experimental ensembles. The great jazz vocalists of the era – Ella Fitzgerald, Sarah Vaughn, Betty Carter – took bop's vigorous rhythms and harmonic changes into singing styles and took up what came to be called scat singing: improvisations based on – but not necessarily loyal to – a recurring melody that mimicked instruments in their phrasing.

In the 1950s, jazz splintered off into a few styles. On the West Coast, a "cool" school emerged with practitioners such as Dave Brubeck, Gerry Mulligan and Chet Baker. In the late 1950s, a fusion between jazz and **classical music** emerged, exemplified by the Modern Jazz Quartet. Hard bop or soul jazz also emerged as a style that used **blues** themes in the music – this was performed by Art Blakey's Jazz Messengers. Also in the 1950s, an avant-garde developed that was less concerned with improvisations built around the melody and harmonic structure, but were investigating sound textures. These innovators were Miles Davis on the trumpet, Ornette Coleman on the saxophone, trumpet and violin and John Coltrane on the saxophone.

In the 1960s, jazz music was influenced by the rise of protest in the **African American** community. Saxophonist Charlie Shepp, for example, played angry, plaintive music that rejected the standard theme-improvisational solos-theme format of small ensembles. This music, however, never developed great commercial appeal. Instead, fusion music of the 1970s that moved to the more standard rhythms of **rock 'n' roll** and utilized electronic instruments reached a mass audience.

By the end of the century, neo-classicist virtuosos such as Wynton Marsalis emerged as key players in the world of jazz, bringing back the melody-centered musics of the 1920s and 1930s. Marsalis is currently artistic director of the jazz program at Lincoln Center of Performing Arts in **New York** City, signaling that jazz is now considered an officially recognized form of music, alongside European-based classical music in its rigor and history.

Further reading

Feather, L. and Gitler, I. (1999) *The Biographical Encyclopedia of Jazz*, New York: Oxford University Press.

Kernfield, B. (ed.) (1994) *The New Grove Dictionary of Jazz*, New York: Grove.

EDWARD MILLER

jeans *see* fashion; Levi Strauss

Jews

Jews account for about 2 percent of the population of the United States – a figure that has been relatively steady throughout most of the post-Second World War period, declining from a high of about 3.5 percent in 1940. Throughout the postwar period, the majority of that population has been native-born, mostly descended from the waves of poor Eastern European immigrants from the 1880s through the early 1920s, with smaller numbers descended from the wealthy German immigrants of the 1840s and from Holocaust refugees.

The Jewish population is concentrated in a few states, particularly in the Northeast – Jews accounted for about 9 percent of **New York** State's population in 1998 – and **Florida** and **California**. The population is, however, far more geographically diffuse than it was in 1945 when New York City was the epicenter of Jewish life to a far greater extent – as it was for American life as a whole. The population also has shifted from being predominantly urban to being predominantly **suburban** – again paralleling national trends.

But, throughout the postwar period, the very questions of who is a Jew – censuses tend to rely on self-identification – and what it means to be a Jew in the US have become increasingly complex. **Assimilation** has been the hallmark of Jewish life in the United States since 1945 as anti-Semitism has declined and most barriers to full Jewish participation in American life have fallen. The revival of ethnic identification in the US since the late 1960s and the interest in "**multicultural-**

ism" have in some ways made Jews (as a group) more visible, but have not altered the general tendency towards **assimilation**.

To take one key indicator, intermarriage has steadily increased throughout the period. In the mid-1960s, the Jewish intermarriage rate was only about 7 percent; by the end of the 1990s, the rate was about 50 percent; and in about one-third of US households with Jewish adults, one marriage partner was not Jewish.

As a result, intermarriage, which once was likely to lead to permanent rifts between parents and their intermarried children, is now more often accepted (however grudgingly) as a fact of life. While many rabbis will not perform intermarriages, many synagogues (particularly in the more liberal movements of Judaism) have shifted from inveighing against intermarriage to creating programs to encourage parents to give the children of interfaith marriages a Jewish education.

Assimilation – and a concomitant sense of having a secure place in American life – has sometimes made Jews (as a group) less visible to the general population and sometimes more so. For example, for decades following President Woodrow Wilson's appointment of Louis Brandeis to the **Supreme Court** in 1916, there was a general political understanding that there was a "Jewish seat" in the Court. (Wilson had been attacked for nominating a Jew to the high court.) Yet when President Richard **Nixon** chose in 1969 not to replace Justice Abe Fortas with another Jewish jurist, allowing the Jewish seat to lapse, only minimal controversy resulted – the general feeling being that Jews were such an active part of the legal and political scene that the "Jewish seat" was an anachronism. By the time President Bill **Clinton** appointed Ruth Bader Ginsberg and Steven Breyer to the Supreme Court, the fact that both were Jewish was generally not deemed significant enough for public comment.

On the other hand, media attention and public discussion of the "Jewish vote" has increased throughout the postwar period. This is in part due to a greater focus in both academia and the media on ethnic voting patterns and "interest groups." Jews, who have higher turnout rates than do other ethnic groups, can provide the deciding votes in several large states.

But the greater focus also reflects the tendency of an ever-more secure and financially healthy Jewish populace (and Jewish organizations) to take an active and visible role in the electoral process. While during the Second World War, Jews and Jewish organizations had generally limited their public efforts to raise concerns about the Nazi slaughter of European Jewry for fear of a backlash, during the postwar period Jews have not hesitated to push for US support for Israel, particularly in the wake of the Six Day War in 1967.

Jewish involvement in politics has also garnered attention because Jews have remained a stalwart, liberal **Democratic Party** constituency even as most white ethnic groups have shifted further to the right. Jews were the only white group that did not cast a majority of their votes for Ronald **Reagan** in 1984, for instance, although Reagan did win over a greater percentage of Jewish voters than had any previous **Republican** in the postwar period.

Still, the Jewish vote has become less reliably liberal over time. This in part reflects a shift in relations between Jews and **African Americans** – two key and often-linked constituencies from the days of Franklin **Roosevelt** through John F. **Kennedy** – which have become more tense and complicated. Many Jews and Jewish organizations played leading roles in the **Civil Rights movement**, but black–Jewish relations slowly soured with, among other things: the rise of black separatism; the **race riots** of the late 1960s (which often wiped out stores owned by Jews in **neighborhoods** which had become predominantly black as Jews moved to the suburbs); the efforts by blacks in the late 1960s to play a greater role in the New York City schools, which were dominated by Jewish teachers and principals; increasingly vocal anti-Semitism on the part of some black leaders, most notably Louis **Farrakhan** in the 1990s; and the rise of **affirmative action**, which particularly threatened jobs held by Jews in academia, where Jews were over-represented after having fought for decades to remove anti-Jewish quotas.

In culture, as in politics, **assimilation** has paradoxically sometimes increased the visibility of Jews. Throughout the postwar period, Jews have been prominent playwrights, **directors**, novelists, critics and academics, and, at least from the late 1950s on, have been more likely to deal with explicitly Jewish characters, issues and themes. Such authors as Phillip **Roth**, Saul **Bellow** and Bernard **Malamud** became lions of the literary establishment in the 1960s with their recognizably Jewish novels and short stories, while slightly older Jewish writers, such as the playwright Arthur **Miller**, did not highlight the Jewish background in their works.

The same trend was clear in popular culture. Although Jews had founded and run most of **Hollywood**'s major movie studios, films with recognizably Jewish characters and issues were a rarity until the postwar period. (*The Jazz Singer*, the first sound motion picture, produced in 1929, was a notable exception.) When the movie *Gentleman's Agreement* (1947), an examination of anti-Semitism, was released in 1947 (eventually winning an Academy Award), its Jewish subject-matter created a stir and many Jewish leaders feared a backlash. In the 1990s, when the **director** Woody **Allen** dealt with Jewish themes and characters, barely anyone batted an eye.

Characters identified as Jewish have become much more prevalent on **television** – another medium in which Jewish corporate leaders first had shied away from explicit Jewish themes. Comedians – another field long dominated by Jewish entertainers and writers – are much more likely to deal directly with Jewish subjects before general audiences, while in the early postwar period such material was generally presented solely to Jewish audiences at predominantly Jewish locations, such as the hotels of the so-called "Borscht Belt" in the Catskill Mountains north of New York City.

Jewish religious life has also become more visible to the general population even as fewer Jews belong to synagogues or practice their faith at home. The building boom of large, visible, suburban synagogues, which began in the 1950s and crested over the following decade, made Jewish houses of worship a much more noticeable physical presence in many communities. Moreover, beginning in the 1950s, the notion became widespread that the US had three major religious groups – **Protestants**, Catholics and Jews – equally deserving of respect, as did the idea that the nation was based on "Judeo-Christian" (as opposed to simply "Christian") values. Judaism was increasingly being referenced and in a way that made it seem part of the American mainstream.

At the same time, more Jews were moving away from orthodox approaches to Judaism into less traditional and fundamentalist branches, particularly Conservative Judaism, which sought to bridge the gap between orthodoxy and the more liberal Reform movement. After the 1950s, Jews on the whole were moving away from a focus on the practices and scholarship that emphasized the more unique aspects of the **religion**.

This has perhaps become most apparent in the transformation of Hanukkah – a quite minor **holiday** on the traditional Jewish calendar – into a major event, widely noted outside the Jewish **community** and very publicly celebrated as a kind of Jewish equivalent of Christmas, which occurs at about the same time. Ironically, Hanukkah commemorates a victory in ancient Israel over both enforced and voluntary assimilation.

Beginning in the late 1960s and continuing through the early twenty-first century, there have been small, but significant contrary trends towards increasing observance. A Jewish renewal movement began to reinvigorate Jewish traditions and to encourage a spirituality that some felt had been smothered by mainline synagogues. The number of Jewish **parochial schools**, known as day schools, began to rise and more of them were linked to the more liberal branches of Judaism. In 1999 Reform rabbis issued a statement encouraging Reform congregations to return to more traditional practices.

At the same time, Jewish congregations have had to grapple with new issues posed by changes in larger American society. While many leading feminists, such as Betty **Friedan**, were Jewish, traditional Judaism delineated clear and highly circumscribed roles for women. In the 1970s, some of the barriers to full female participation began to crumble, first in the Reform and later in the Conservative movements. The Reform movement ordained its first female rabbi in 1972, and the Conservative movement followed in 1985. In addition, a vibrant feminist Jewish scholarship developed to reinterpret traditional texts, uncover lost history and create new liturgy.

Still, by the late 1990s, Jews were more likely to define their "Jewishness" in ethnic or cultural terms than in religious ones, and to focus more on

an emotional link to Israel or the Holocaust as touchstones of their Jewishness than on synagogue or other organizational activities. As the immigrant generations pass away, debate in the Jewish community has increased about what it will mean to be Jewish in the US in the future. Al Gore's selection of Orthodox Jewish Senator Joseph Lieberman as his Democratic **vice-presidential** running mate in 2000 has stimulated discussion about Jewish identity and participation in American life, as well as resistance to this participation.

Further reading

Hertzberg, A. (1989) *The Jews in America*, New York: Simon & Schuster.

Sachar, H. (1992) *A History of the Jews in America*, New York: Random House.

Shapiro, E. (1992) *A Time for Healing*, Baltimore: The Johns Hopkins University Press.

DAVID GOLDSTON

Jim Crow   *see* segregation

John Birch Society

A small group of Americans organized the John Birch Society in 1958 to fight what they considered to be the growing influence of **communism** in the American government. Thought too radical by many, the society went as far as to accuse President Dwight **Eisenhower** of being an agent of the "communist conspiracy." Its growth in the 1950s and 1960s paralleled that of the political **right** in America generally. This new political right became a vocal critic of the **Democratic Party**, as well as of the liberal consensus that had dominated American policy since the New Deal. The society continues to agitate for economic and moral issues.

SUSAN SCHULTEN

Johns, Jasper *see* abstract expressionism

Johnson, Lyndon Baines

b. 1908; d. 1973

Elected vice-president in 1960, Lyndon Baines Johnson became president when John F. **Kennedy** was assassinated in **Dallas, TX** on November 22, 1963. Combining his legislative experience with public sympathy for the slain Kennedy, Johnson successfully guided many of Kennedy's legislative programs through **Congress** in 1964 and 1965, such as tax cuts for both individuals and corporations. Legislation passed during this period also marked the beginning of Johnson's "Great Society" programs. Early legislation included the **Civil Rights Act** of 1964, anti-discrimination legislation introduced by the Kennedy administration, and the **Voting Rights Act** of 1965.

Paralleling Johnson's accomplishments with domestic legislation was the United States' growing involvement in Vietnam. North Vietnamese torpedo boats attacked a US destroyer in the Gulf of Tonkin in early August 1964 and, Johnson believed, launched another assault two days later. While the attack was never confirmed, Johnson asked Congress for the authority to take military action against North Vietnam. Congress approved these powers in the **Gulf of Tonkin Resolution**, which provided the legal foundation for American involvement in the **Vietnam War**.

With Minnesota Senator Hubert **Humphrey** as his running-mate, Johnson won the 1964 presidential election in a landslide, getting over 61 percent of the vote against **Republican** nominee and Arizona Senator Barry **Goldwater**. In 1965 and 1966, Johnson continued to pass "Great Society" programs. These included Medicare and Medicaid, which provided **healthcare** for the country's senior citizens and for the poor. Two others, the Higher Education Act and the Elementary and Secondary Act of 1965, gave aid to schools. Johnson labeled these programs the **War on Poverty**.

As Johnson's domestic legislative successes increased, so did US engagement in the Vietnam War. In 1965 Johnson ordered American combat troops to South Vietnam. By 1968 there were over 500,000 US troops in South Vietnam, up from the approximately 16,000 military advisers there when Johnson became president.

From 1966 to 1968, Johnson continued his pro-civil-rights agenda. He appointed Thurgood **Marshall** to the **Supreme Court**, making Marshall the first **African American** to serve on the high court. However, Johnson faced heightened conflict at home as well as abroad. Opposition to the Vietnam War and racial unrest culminated in urban riots in slum areas of many American cities. To determine the causes of the riots, Johnson appointed a special commission, which issued its conclusions in the **Kerner Commission** Report. The report contended that the United States was moving towards two societies: black and white, separate and unequal.

The **Tet Offensive** in January 1968 revealed that an end to the Vietnam War was not imminent, and Minnesota Senator Eugene **McCarthy**'s strong finish against Johnson in the New Hampshire **Democratic** presidential primary showed the president's political weakness. Johnson surprisingly withdrew from the race in a televised address on March 31, 1968. On November 1, 1968, Johnson halted bombing on North Vietnam, temporarily spurring peace talks.

Further reading

Beschloss, M. (1997) *Taking Charge*, New York: Simon & Schuster.
Dallek, R. (1998) *Flawed Giant*, New York: Oxford University Press.

JAMES DEVITT

Johnson, Magic *see* basketball

Johnson, Philip

b. 1906

A major figure in the American art and **architecture** communities in the twentieth century, Johnson studied with German Walter Gropius at Harvard, was instrumental in promoting modern architecture in the United States and is credited with inventing the term "International Style." Still practicing at his ninetieth birthday, Johnson has been called an architectural "chameleon," as his projects have shifted from International Style modernism to neo-classicism, **postmodernism**, even expressionism. Among Johnson's more notable buildings are his Glass House in New Canaan, Connecticut, and Lincoln Center, the AT&T Building and the pink-glazed "lipstick building" in New York.

BIANCA T. SIEGL

Jones, James Earl

b. 1931

Distinguished stage and film actor, Jones made his Broadway debut in *The Blacks* in 1957 and his film debut in *Dr Strangelove* in 1964. Born in Mississippi and raised in Michigan, Jones majored in drama at the University of Michigan. In 1969 he became nationally known for his portrayal of heavyweight boxer Joe Jackson in *The Great White Hope*. Known for his deep voice, Jones has narrated many productions and is the voice of Darth Vader in the *Star Wars* trilogy. Jones' **awards** for his contributions include a Grammy, a Golden Globe, two Emmys and two Tony Awards.

See also: actors

KATE M. KENSKI

Jones, Quincy

b. 1933

One of the leading music and television **producers** of the 1980s and 1990s, as well as one of America's leading black entrepreneurs. Jones studied **jazz** as a trumpeter and began arranging some of the jazz greats in the 1950s. Known as Q, he began his foray into film with the soundtrack for *The Pawnbroker* (1965), the same year he won his first Grammy for Count Basie's "I Can't Stop Loving You." He owns Qwest Records and a **television** production company, while also producing in **Hollywood**. At the same time, he continues to be influential in the music industry, advancing the career of numerous rap artists, including Ice T and Big Daddy Kane.

EDWARD MILLER

journalism *see* newspapers; news, television; Pulitzer Prize

Joyner, Florence *see* track and field

Jordan, Michael

b. 1963

Widely acknowledged to be the greatest **basketball** player ever and, with his ability to soar over players, certainly the most exciting. Jordan was the beneficiary of NBA decisions to showcase individual talent at the end of the 1970s, leading to the rise of marquee players like Julius Erving, Magic Johnson, Larry Bird, and Isaiah Thomas, all of whom he eclipsed. Signed by the Chicago Bulls in 1984, Jordan almost single-handedly pulled the franchise up from the basement of the NBA to six championships between 1991 and 1998, an unbroken run interrupted only by his year-long retirement and attempt to break into major league **baseball** in 1993. Jordan's contribution to marketing has been as significant as his contribution to basketball. Earning more money from product sponsorship (especially Nike) than from basketball, he was one of the best known Americans around the world throughout the 1990s, his number 23 Chicago Bulls shirt seen on the backs of kids from Latin America and Europe to the Philippines.

ROBERT GREGG

judicial activism

Judicial activism connotes the extent to which judges substitute their interpretations of constitutional provisions for those of other branches of government and their willingness to impose affirmative duties upon governmental bodies. Although applicable to judges of all federal and state courts, it is most often used in reference to the justices of the **Supreme Court**. The term is ordinarily used in an accusatory manner to ascribe to justices, whose decisions one opposes, an inclination to make law through policy-oriented judicial decisions rather than following the literal language of the constitution and showing deference to the constitutional interpretations underlying legislative enactments.

Judicial activism is inevitably contrasted with judicial restraint. While activism is usually attributed to courts labeled "liberal," most notably the **Warren Court**, it has also been an instrument of conservative courts. The **Rehnquist Court** is seen as pursuing a conservative political agenda through a result-oriented decision-making process that disregards precedents and diverges from clear constitutional language. Both courts are viewed as having moved from a judicial ideal of reaching decisions by attempting to discern the original intent of the framers of the Constitution, determined largely through historical sources and narrow readings of precedents, to a process that has expanded the power of judicial review and emphasizes the spirit of the Constitution, often in terms of contemporary social needs. This practice opens justices to the accusation that they have reached out to accept groundbreaking cases that they then decide in a partisan manner by arriving at conclusions imbued with political preference.

Judicial activism is predominantly a post-Second World War phenomenon. The Court shifted its focus from narrow economic issues to questions of **civil-rights** and liberties, the protection of criminal defendants and the application for the provisions of almost all of the **Bill of Rights** to the states through the process of incorporating them in the Due Process clause of the 14th Amendment. This is not solely a constitutional trend. Judicial decisions have also broadly extended tort law, especially products liability, as precedents holding gun and tobacco manufacturers liable for their products illustrate.

It is hardly surprising that the judicial activism debate flourishes; Americans feel no constraints in second-guessing judges. Numerous provisions of the Bill of Rights and the 14th Amendment, which form the very foundations for constitutional protections of civil liberties, were intentionally written in open-ended language. Terms such as "due process" and "equal protection" invite varying interpretations and subjective, value-laden readings from both judges and lay persons which underpin both activism and criticism of it.

Further reading

Ely, J.H. (1980) *Democracy and Distrust*, Cambridge, MA: Harvard.

Neely, R. (1981) *How Courts Govern America*, New Haven: Yale.

Sunderland, L. (1996) *Popular Government and the Supreme Court*, Lawrence: University Press of Kansas.

US Congress (1997) *Judicial Activism: Defining the Problem and its Impact*, Washington, DC: US GPO.

JAMES KRAUS

judiciary

The American common law system contains a complex array of federal, state and local courts with exclusive and overlapping jurisdictional powers. Each state has a separate, comprehensive judiciary organized in a trial and appellate court hierarchy that parallels the structure of the federal courts.

In the process of interpreting and applying the law's generalities to decide specific cases, judges exercise a major responsibility for shaping public policies. Common-law jurisprudence enables judges to create law. The breadth of this power is demonstrated by the different constitutional approaches, especially in matters of individual rights and federalism, of the **Supreme Court** under Earl **Warren**, in a period of progressive **judicial activism**, and under William **Rehnquist**. **State** judges influence society equally, for example, by expanding legal theories of tort and products liability to encompass the heath risks of **tobacco**.

Administrative duties also emphasize judicial autonomy. Renowned federal judges and chief judges of the states' highest courts are powerful voices for court reform. The Supreme Court, subject to congressional approval, prescribes rules for procedures and practice for the federal courts, generating changes followed by many state courts. The ethical conduct and performance of judges is highly self-regulating; questions are resolved by judicial panels. Public confidence in the soundness of the rule of law is strengthened by political separation and independence of the judiciary from other government branches. Judicial insulation from short-term political repercussions tempts politically vulnerable executive and legislative bodies to leave resolution of compelling and contentious cases to receptive judges.

The litigious nature of American society pressures the judiciary. In the past twenty years, despite the growth of alternative forms of dispute resolution, federal cases have increased by 60 percent, and approximately 100 million state court cases are filed each year. This crowds dockets, delays trials, fosters rudeness and escalates controversies involving the election and appointment of judges.

Federal judges are nominated by the president and confirmed by a majority of the Senate. Supreme Court choices can have the most lasting impact of any presidential action: appointments are made for life and justices have served for over thirty years. State and local judges are elected or appointed. Election campaigns for the highest courts in large states require millions of dollars, exposing winners to accusations that their rulings are influenced by the large campaign contributions of **lawyers**, powerful law firms and business groups. State judicial appointments are usually made by elected officials on a partisan basis, constrained somewhat by the recommendations of local bar associations that evaluate aspirants' qualifications.

Most of the public gleans its knowledge and understanding of the judiciary from trials regularly televised on **cable** stations and though extensive **mass-media** coverage of **celebrity** cases. Popular "judge" shows, with mock trials of consenting parties, also shape perceptions. Still, the judiciary, especially the Supreme Court, remains America's most highly respected and trusted profession.

Further reading

Abraham, H. (1998) *The Judicial Process*, New York: Oxford.

O'Brien, D. (ed.) *Judges on Judging*, New Jersey: Chatham.

JAMES KRAUS

jukeboxes

Coin-operated machines that allow the user to select and play recorded music. Offshoots of nineteenth-century coin-operated player pianos, jukeboxes appeared in the 1930s, although sales took off after the war. People became mesmerized by styling details, including animated bubble tubes, revolving color columns and a revealed record-changing mechanism that enticed customers to play their favorites on the Wurlitzer or Rockola. Jukeboxes became ubiquitous in **bars** and malt shops from the 1940s to the 1960s; they remain symbols of those eras. They have reappeared in recent years due to nostalgia, although they now play CDs instead of 78s and 45s.

EDWARD MILLER

junior colleges *see* community colleges/junior colleges

junk food

Potato chips, **candy**, **popcorn** and other snacks are recognized by most Americans as high-calorie foods based on fat, salt and sugar. Yet obsessive snacking is part of American daily mobility. Use of food as individual escape as well as at parties, in sporting events and movies or on the street contributes to widespread problems of obesity and associated diseases. Manufacturers and marketers nonetheless make sales alluring through market placement and **advertising**; concessions are also important money-makers at cinemas and sporting events. Junk food, like **comfort food**, can be taken as a guilty secret, yet its costs are both obvious and dangerous.

GARY McDONOGH
CINDY WONG

K

Kahn, Louis

b. 1901; d. 1974

Architect most controversial for breaking away from the international style in his designs of the 1950s. Born in the Russian Empire, Kahn designed workers' housing and private residences in the 1930s and 1940s in the form of the international style. His mature works, including the Richards Medical Research Building (1960–5) in **Philadelphia, PA** and the **Salk** Institute for Biological Studies (1959–65) in La Jolla, California, attempted to look to history without reviving it in the creation of distinct "servant" and "served" spaces. This design technique made reference to both classical and medieval **architecture**, creating laboratories of architectural note for the first time.

ISABEL KRIEGEL

Kazan, Elia

b. 1909

Greek American **director** whose career was darkened by his willingness to testify before the **House Committee on Un-American Activities**. This sparked protests even when he was awarded a lifetime achievement **award** at the 1999 Oscars. Kazan, a co-founder of Actor's Studio and "method acting," drew superb performances from Marlon **Brando** (*A Streetcar Named Desire*, 1951; *Viva Zapata!*, 1952; and their master-work, the tense, naturalistic *On the Waterfront*, 1954), James **Dean** (*East of Eden*, 1955) and others. While his films pioneered adult representations of sexuality; his "social-message" dramas (e.g. *Gentlemen's Agreement*, 1947 on anti-Semitism) have not aged as well. Kazan also worked extensively in **theater** before devoting himself to writing and more personal films.

GARY McDONOGH

Kefauver, Estes

b. 1903; d. 1963

Crusading Tennessee Democratic senator and unsuccessful vice-presidential candidate (with Adlai **Stevenson**) in 1956. In the Senate, Kefauver conducted important investigations on many social issues, including his 1951 televised attacks on organized crime that brought government to a mass audience and won him an Emmy. Later, the generally liberal Kefauver showed equal zeal in pursuing relations between **mass media** (**television**, **radio**, **comics**) and juvenile **violence**, antitrust violations and **pharmaceuticals**. His presidential aspirations were overshadowed by images of the **South** in national politics, but his popularity and integrity paved the way for later southern presidents.

GARY McDONOGH

Keillor, Garrison/*Prairie Home Companion*

Initially a writer who gained some prominence for his contributions to literary magazines, Garrison Keillor gained wider notice during the 1980s for the homespun view of Midwestern **farm** life he presented in his weekly public radio show, *A Prairie Home Companion*. First broadcast in Minneapolis and later relocated to **New York** City, NY, the variety show's assortment of American music acts and **comedy** sketches is built around Keillor's centerpiece monologue, "The News from Lake Wobegon." Keillor's portrayal of this fictional Minnesota farming town draws from remembrances of his own childhood, and draws listeners by its loving depiction and gentle tweaking of **Scandinavian American** values and folk ways.

ROBERT ANDERSON

Kelly, Gene

b. 1912; d. 1996

Leaving Broadway for **Hollywood** in the 1940s, Kelly's dancing, choreography and directing revolutionized the Hollywood **musical**. He countered Fred **Astaire**'s ballroom rhythms with a more athletic and masculine, free-flowing style (and gravelly singing). He also incorporated symphonic jazz and ballet into movies such as the classic *Singin' in the Rain* (MGM, 1952), which he in the latter co-directed and co-choreographed. His own title number is an artful synthesis of **dance** and the camera using long takes to create magic. Although Kelly never received an Oscar, his lifetime achievements were recognized by the Kennedy Center and the American Film Institute in the 1980s.

GARY McDONOGH

Kelly, Grace

b. 1928; d. 1982

American princess. Kelly, born into a wealthy Irish Catholic Philadelphia family, passed through a striking albeit brief screen career (1951–6) into legend. Her roles sometimes played off her model's beauty and patrician heritage (*Rear Window*, 1954; *High Society*, 1956), although her Academy Award came for going against the grain in *The Country Girl* (1954). In 1956 Kelly abandoned films to marry Monaco's Prince Rainier, whom she met while filming with **Hitchcock**. After this "fairy-tale ending," she assumed new roles as mother, monarch and elegant cosmopolitan icon until her death in an **automobile** accident.

GARY McDONOGH

Kemp, Jack

b. 1935

Republican vice-presidential running-mate to Bob **Dole** in 1996, Kemp has a long career in public service. Emphasizing the need for tax-cuts to stimulate economic growth, Kemp served as US Representative for New York for nine terms from 1971 to 1989, and then served for four years as Secretary of Housing and Urban Development. Kemp was a professional **football** quarterback for thirteen years playing for the San Diego Chargers and Buffalo Bills. He is currently on the Board of Directors of Empower America, a public policy and advocacy group founded in 1993.

KATE M. KENSKI

Kennedy, John F.

b. 1917; d. 1963

John Fitzgerald Kennedy was the first "celebrity **president**" (1961–3). After an undistinguished career in the House of Representatives and the Senate, Kennedy campaigned for president as a generational critic of the **Eisenhower** years, which he linked with economic recession, educational mediocrity, a missile gap and international humiliations (for example the U-2 spy plane, **Castro** in **Cuba**, "Yankee Go Home" riots). He anticipated being a foreign-policy leader, with Keynesian techniques sufficing to revive and maintain economic growth.

Kennedy brought more than a touch of glamour to the White House; he was America's first president born in the twentieth century, movie-star handsome, married to the exquisite Jacqueline, and with a Harvard brain trust of "the best and the brightest." The Thousand Days of what would be called Camelot seemed to integrate the worlds of **Washington**, **Hollywood**, **Broadway** and Cambridge: Frank **Sinatra**, Robert **Frost** and the Bundys.

Kennedy's foreign policy was driven by a critique of Eisenhower's strategy of "massive retaliation," a budget-tight reliance on nuclear deterrence, air power and **CIA** machinations. Kennedy offered "flexible response," a more ambitious call for the ability to contain the Soviets along the East–West axis, but also to rise to the challenge of national wars of liberation with "counter-insurgency." As such, Kennedy inspired liberal idealists to take seriously the emergence of the Third World through both the Green Berets and the **Peace Corps**.

Domestically, Kennedy discovered that the **civil rights** revolution – the **sit-ins** and the **freedom rides** of 1960 and 1961 – forced his administration to respond to the call for racial justice. Partly in response to the ways in which **segregation** harmed US interests among people of color in the Third World, partly reacting to the pressures generated by events in the **South**, Kennedy reluctantly moved by 1963 to embrace legislative proposals to eliminate segregation.

On other domestic issues, the Kennedy administration had difficulties in achieving legislative victories in seeking modestly to expand **welfare** state programs; he is credited with stimulating the economy with a tax cut and upholding the public interest in forcing US Steel to rescind price increases. For the most part, he was a corporate liberal, committed to technocratic solutions within a pro-business, welfare state format.

Kennedy faced his most crucial tests abroad, initially during the Berlin Crisis, which led to the construction of the Berlin Wall and following the abortive **Bay of Pigs** invasion of Castro's Cuba. Kennedy's ad hoc style of leadership, which paid insufficient attention to issues of Castro's strengths, matters of terrain and the role of air support, contributed to the debacle.

Following this defeat, Kennedy continued to seek the subversion of the Castro Revolution through the CIA's Operation Mongoose. When intelligence discovered Soviet missile silos being constructed in Cuba, Kennedy responded with a dramatic, televised challenge of a naval blockade to Khrushchev, which brought the world closer to nuclear war than at any previous moment – or any since. Khrushchev adhered to the blockade, allowing time for compromises to be made – Soviet missiles removed, a US pledge not to invade Cuba and a secret agreement by the US to remove its Jupiter missiles from Turkey.

Kennedy increased US military personnel in South Vietnam from 600 to over 17,000 in response to the military successes of the National Liberation Front. Domestic opposition finally deposed Ngo Dinh Diem in a military coup and assassination in November 1963. Historians grapple with the "what if" regarding Kennedy and Vietnam. The weight of evidence suggests that Kennedy was likely to increase the Americanization of the war in the face of an impending communist victory. At the same time, there were signs of some moderation of Kennedy's **Cold War** militancy (for example the Test-ban Treaty and the Washington–Moscow Hot-line).

The legacy of this first **Roman Catholic** president remains as controversial as the **Warren Commission** Report's conclusions about his assassination on November 22, 1963. He inspired many Americans, particularly among youth, to ask "what they could do for their country." In that sense, Kennedy's New Frontier – astronauts, Green Berets, Peace Corps and VISTA volunteers – served as a contradictory catalyst to the social challenges associated with the 1960s.

Further reading

Beschloss, M. (1991) *The Crisis Years*, New York: Burlingame.

Parmet, H. (1981) *JFK*, New York: Dial Press.

Reeves, T. (1991) *A Question of Character*, New York: The Free Press.

Wills, G. (1982) *The Kennedy Imprisonment*, Boston: Little Brown.

PAUL LYONS

Kennedy family

Joseph Kennedy (1888–1969), a self-made man who had accumulated one of the largest fortunes in the United States from **Wall Street** and **Hollywood** movies, became the American Ambassador to Britain in 1938. Descended from Irish Catholic immigrants, Kennedy's success embodied the rags-to-riches myth of American **immigration** and **assimilation**. His appointment to the Court of St. James, which owed much to his friendship with President **Roosevelt**, was only a step in the Kennedy's dramatic rise to the status of American royalty and tragic mythology.

Nonetheless, Kennedy's isolationism and anti-Semitism during the Second World War meant the architect of Camelot was unable to gain the presidency and instead turned to his nine children by Rose Fitzgerald Kennedy. The eldest, Joe Jr., the father's first choice for president, died on a flying mission during the War. After the second son, John Fitzgerald (1917–63), survived his ordeal as commander of a torpedo boat *PT 109* in the Pacific, his father orchestrated his attempt to run for the House of Representatives for **Boston, MA**, using his wartime heroism and the family's Boston connections to sell him in an unfamiliar constituency. In 1946 Kennedy entered **Congress** as one of the few successful **Democrats** in a year of **Republican** dominance and the head of a new generation of Democrats. In 1952 when Republican **Eisenhower** trounced Adlai Stevenson in the presidential race, Kennedy defeated Henry Cabot Lodge in Massachusetts' Senate race, and soon thereafter married Jacqueline Bouvier, an elegant young journalist with intellectual and social credentials as well as her own features of the Kennedy legend.

Meanwhile, John's younger brother, Robert (1925–68), made a name for himself as an assistant to Joseph **McCarthy** in the attempt to purge communists from all branches of the government. Robert's connection with McCarthy would later seem anomalous in light of his much-touted radical credentials. Yet his father had tended to see Roosevelt's internationalism though the prism of communist or Jewish conspiracy.

After a less than distinguished period in the Senate, John Kennedy ran for the presidency in 1960, where the Kennedy machine defeated consummate parliamentarian and **Texas** Senator Lyndon B. **Johnson** for the nomination and barely defeated Richard **Nixon** in the general **elections**. With help from friends, John Kennedy also had become the celebrated author of *Profiles in Courage* (1954), for which he earned a **Pulitzer Prize**. At the same time, Robert matched Nixon in campaign strategy, including helping to get Rev. Martin Luther **King**, Jr. released from jail in the week before the election, swinging many **African American** votes to Kennedy (with a poor civil-rights record) and providing the slim margin of victory.

JFK created a special moment for the Kennedy myth, epitomized in the epithet "Camelot," linking his regime to the mythical age of King Arthur. The president's reliance on his **family**, especially his father's advice, and his younger brother continued with Robert as an activist **Attorney-General** in **civil rights** and a key role in Cuban interventions. Following JFK's assassination – again a defining moment for the nation – Robert continued serving Lyndon Johnson, although his contempt for the Texan made this short-lived, and he seized the opportunity of a vacant New York Senate seat.

In 1968, following Eugene McCarthy's strong showing against Johnson in the New Hampshire primary, "Bobby" Kennedy joined the race for the presidency. After winning the **California** primary in June, however, he was assassinated by Sirhan Sirhan.

This left Edward Moore "Ted" Kennedy as the remaining son (the daughters had public but less political and sometimes tragic lives). "Inheriting" the Massachusetts Senate seat, he had developed a strong reputation as a good legislator without the charisma of John or the political savvy of Robert. Nevertheless, the Kennedy mystique might have gained him the White House but for a July 1969 incident at Chappaquiddick, in which Edward drove off a bridge, drowning Mary Jo Kopechne. Kennedy's failure to report the accident immediately to police led to the widespread suspicion that he had been drunk. When he later tried to wrest the **Democratic Party** nomination from Jimmy **Carter** in 1980, the incident and other rumors haunted him. As the third most senior senator,

Edward has remained a powerful liberal voice in the Democratic Party.

In the next generation, while Kennedy "cousins" – including member of Congress Joseph P. Kennedy II (Massachusetts), Patrick Kennedy (Rhode Island) and Maryland Lieutenant-Governor Kathleen Kennedy Townsend – have been visible in politics and media, John F. Kennedy, Jr., became the focus of the family mystique. Since his birth to the charismatic first family and the photograph of him saluting his father's cortege in 1963, he has been treated by media and the public as a prince whose time on the throne would come. His legal career and political **magazine** *George* were followed in detail, as were his dating with and marriage to Carolyn Bessette. When, in July 1999, he crashed his single-engine plane at Martha's Vineyard en route to a Kennedy clan wedding in Hyannisport (although he was not qualified for the flight), the incident was treated as a national tragedy by media and government – and a tragic myth of the rise and fall of royalty brought full circle.

Further reading

Colier, P. and Horowitz, D. (1984) *The Kennedys*, New York: Summit.

Wills, G. (1982) *The Kennedy Imprisonment*, Boston: Little, Brown & Co.

ROBERT GREGG

Kent State shootings

In 1970 the US National Guard opened fire on student antiwar protesters at Kent State University in Ohio, killing four and wounding eleven others. The incident shocked the nation and galvanized student-led opposition to US military aggression in Vietnam and Cambodia. A wave of demonstrations erupted around the country in response, wreaking havoc on college **campuses** and increasing pressure on President **Nixon** to soften his stance on US intervention in Southeast Asia. The incident was one of many during the politically turbulent 1960s and 1970s that contributed to young people's alienation from the political process.

SARAH SMITH

Kerner Commission

Special Commission appointed by President Lyndon **Johnson** in July, 1967, to investigate **race riots** of the preceding two years. The final report of the National Advisory Commission on Civil Disorders, released in March 1968, detailed patterns of inequality and racism embedded in urban life. It also issued a warning: "What white Americans have never fully understood – but what the Negro can never forget – is that white society is deeply implicated in the **ghetto**. White institutions created it, white institutions maintain it, and white society condones it. Our nation is moving towards two societies, one black, one white – separate and unequal."

The Kerner Commission's report was characteristic of a time before the full impact of renewed **immigration** was felt. Race was one division in American society, but others were becoming increasingly apparent. Nevertheless, American society would become increasingly divided between those who benefited from the perquisites of **suburban** culture and those confined to **inner cities** as a growing **underclass**.

ROBERT GREGG

Kerouac, Jack

b. 1922; d. 1969

Poet and chronicler of the **beat generation**, a term whose meaning he defined. Best known for *On the Road* (1957), a beat pilgrimage across America, he later wrote *The Dharma Bums* (1958), appealing to Zen **Buddhism**, and *Big Sur* (1962). He remains an iconic figure for later generations.

GARY McDONOGH

kindergarten and Head Start

Influenced by the work of early nineteenth-century Swiss theorist Pestalozzi, who emphasized moral education, humane pedagogical methods, different processes for different stages of learning, and connecting learning to the real world, the word *kindergarten* – "child garden" – was coined by German educator Freidrich Froebel. Froebel believed that **children** needed to unite their spirits and their reason and be guided by an entity other than the **family** towards goodness.

Kindergartens arrived in America between 1848 and 1860, were incorporated into the school system in St. Louis by 1876, and subsequently emerged as the formal context in which children make the transition from **home** to school. This transition can be particularly difficult for children whose backgrounds, values and practices differ from the **middle-class**, Anglican values and practices which inform schools. In an attempt to ease this transition, Head Start was created under Title II of the Economic Opportunity Act of 1964. A program of child development for four- and five-year-olds from low-income homes, it targets children in what some educational psychologists call the critical period in human development, and it focuses on mental and physical health, **welfare**, recreation and remediation, as well as on intellectual development. Starting in 1965, Head Start has had high enrollment, and research indicates that the program succeeds in acculturating children to the culture of schooling.

The development of kindergartens has been characterized by a combination of attempting to structure children's entry into formal schooling and striving to address social inequities. In the late 1960s, the work of Swiss psychologist Piaget and Italian physician and educator Montessori influenced the development of kindergartens as places for children to discover and learn at their own pace. The conflict between behaviorist models and more child-centered approaches to education has yielded various models of kindergartens, but they are generally conceptualized, and often mandated, as necessary to the initiation of children into formal schooling.

See also: children's music

Further reading

Beatty, B. (1995) *Preschool Education in America*, New Haven: Yale University Press.
Shapiro, M. (1983) *Child's Garden*, State College: The Pennsylvania State University Press.

ALISON COOK-SATHER

King, Billie Jean

b. 1943

Born Billie Jean Moffit, in Long Beach, **California**, King won six Wimbledon championships, four US Open titles, was ranked the no. 1 women's **tennis** player in the world for five years and, through her struggle for gender equality, transformed women's sports. Her 1973 match against the fifty-five-year-old Bobby Riggs, the so-called "Battle of the Sexes," brought widespread attention to women athletes. King's straight set trouncing at the **Houston** Astrodome, in circus-like conditions, drew an estimated television audience of 50 million. An inspiration to players like Martina Navratilova, King led in the formation of the Virginia Slims professional tennis tour, started a **magazine** (*WomenSports*) and established a women's sports **foundation**.

ROBERT GREGG

King, Don *see* boxing

King, Martin Luther, Jr.

b. 1929; d. 1968

Martin Luther King, Jr. was the most charismatic and influential leader in the US **civil rights** struggle, 1954–68. His philosophy of non-violent direct action in resistance to unjust laws was founded upon the teachings of Jesus Christ and Mahatma Gandhi and refined through his own study of **religion** and **philosophy** at Morehouse College and Boston University. A middle-class, educated son of a southern black Baptist minister, King was representative of the new generation of southern **African Americans** after the Second World War who refused to submit to continued white oppression in the South. His beliefs in non-violence and the moral necessity for equality became the strategy of the entire movement.

King first emerged as a leader of the Movement in the Montgomery Bus Boycott in 1955–6. His primary base of operation was always the **South**. He was less successful in attempting to apply his beliefs and tactics to the problems of African American **ghettos** in the North. His philosophy galvanized white as well as black Americans, incorporating both in his vision of a "beloved **community**" in which there was justice for all. His beliefs, courage in the advocacy of them and his achievements in the face of violent resistance by Southern white authority brought him vilification from conservatives at home, but international acclaim abroad. While the FBI conducted investigations to discredit King, the international Nobel Committee presented King with its Peace Prize in 1964.

King's crowning moment was his "I Have A Dream" speech at the March on Washington in August, 1963. His greatest victories were passage of the Civil Rights Act of 1964 and the **Voting Rights Act** of 1965. King's opposition to injustice, however, was not confined by **region**, **race** or **class**. He reluctantly sacrificed much of his credibility among many black as well as white followers and much of his influence in national political circles by continuing to protest against poverty within the US and the unjust war in Southeast Asia during the 1960s. The official disfavor such actions brought from the highest levels of government and civil society made King more vulnerable to the forces of reaction. He was assassinated in April 1968 by a white gunman in Memphis, TN while participating in a garbage workers' strike.

Martin Luther King, Jr.'s articulation and advocacy of the ethical principles of his faith and the political ideals upon which the United States was founded inspired the nation. His murder for those same beliefs so shamed its people, black and white, that a majority coalesced to create a national **holiday** in his honor. In 1986 the federal government established January 15 as Martin Luther King, Jr. Day, the only national holiday to honor a non-office-holding US civilian. King's legacy, however, transcends such institutionalization. His moral philosophy and his advocacy of justice and equality for all people regardless of race, class or gender continue to inspire suffering peoples throughout the world.

Further reading

Lewis, D.L. (1970) *King, a Critical Biography*, New York: Praeger.

King, M.L., Jr. (1994) *Letter from a Birmingham Jail*, San Francisco: Harper.

ROBERT FRANCIS ENGS

King, Rodney

b. 1966

Victim of a savage beating by four white Los Angeles **police** officers who were caught on video by a bystander. The tape, frequently shown on network **news** shows, created widespread consensus about the officers' guilt. The **California** jury's May 1992 acquittal of the officers shocked many. It was explained by the jury's selection from the politically conservative suburbs of **Los Angeles, CA** and the fact that it included no **African Americans**, as well as artful defense strategies. Anger in South Central LA led to the most violent **race riot** in American **history**, during which fifty-four people were killed, thousands injured and property damaged in excess of $1 billion. Federal **civil-rights** charges were later brought against the officers and they were found guilty. King eventually disappeared from public view.

ROBERT GREGG

King, Stephen

b. 1947

Master of the American macabre in bestselling novels and chilling films. Born and resident in Maine, which provides apparently innocent settings for some stories, King specializes in nearly annual excursions to the horror beneath the normal, beginning with his revisit to high-school proms laced with telekenisis in *Carrie* (1973). If you cannot trust the prom queen, can you trust your **family**? No: *The Shining* (1976). Your car? No: *Christine* (1983). The dog? No: *Cujo* (1981). Your fans? No: *Misery* (1987). King seemed entrapped in his fictional universe when a driver severely injured him as he walked beside the road in 1999. In 2000, he became a pioneer in e-publication.

GARY McDONOGH

Kingston, Maxine Hong

b. 1940

Novelist. Kingston's vision of the struggles of **Chinese American** women of her **family**, seen through the prism of stories drawing on Chinese mythology in *The Woman Warrior* (1976), became a breakthrough in wider American acceptance of **Asian American** literature. Indeed, it became a widely used textbook in **high schools** and **colleges**. The sequel, *China Men* (1980), raised more political issues about historical discrimination against Chinese. In the 1980s, Kingston became involved in a bitter debate with Frank **Chin** over issues of authenticity and **assimilation** in **Asian American** literature. Her essay on fiction and identity, *Tripmaster Monkey* (1989), was less successful than her earlier works.

CINDY WONG

Kissinger, Henry

b. 1923

National security advisor and **Secretary of State** during the **Nixon** administration. Born in Germany, he fled Nazi persecution of the Jews in 1938, and, after the war, became a foreign policy and defense studies expert at Harvard University. Kissinger made a name for himself as a hawk, advocating a hard line towards the Soviet Union and other communist nations. During the **Vietnam War**, he pushed for the bombing of Cambodia, but also led the negotiations with the North Vietnamese – for which he would receive the **Nobel Peace Prize**. In the year prior to his appointment as Secretary of State in 1973, he advocated a policy of détente, and continued on this path until Gerald Ford's defeat in 1976 terminated his diplomatic career.

ROBERT GREGG

kitchen

In the typical American house, the kitchen is centrally located with direct relationships with both living and dining areas, which allows for ease of service for both daily life and occasional entertaining. This centrality has led to recent characterizations of the kitchen – particularly the kitchen table – as the new hearth of the American **home**. This phenomenon is reinforced by representations of the American **family** on **television**, including generations of **sitcoms** and **soap operas** in which many important family issues are debated and resolved at the kitchen table.

In this construction of the traditional family, the kitchen is largely associated with female domesticity, especially in the postwar **suburban** context. The role of **advertising** as well as the publication of **cookbooks** and **mass media** helped to define a mythic image of American women surrounded by stove, oven and refrigerator – perhaps with a pantry, laundry or storage nearby – which is still invoked by cultural conservatives. Servants, however, were already treated as unusual – the woman ran her own appliances, budget and household regime. This image also generated periodicals, such as *Redbook*, *Family Circle*, *Ladies' Home Journal* and *Better Homes & Gardens*, targeted at women and their kitchens. Industry-related publications, such as *Bath & Kitchen* or *Metropolitan Home*, have also successfully marketed clean, bright kitchens as indicators of a healthy home life and as coveted status symbols.

Kitchen spaces have also changed in the last five decades. The rise of the "island" in kitchen design is associated with greater flexibility and changing habits in food production and consumption. The late-twentieth-century phenomenon of single-parent homes or families in which both parents work has also contributed to a shift in kitchen design towards layouts that accommodate shorter meals, faster preparation and spaces used primarily for entertaining. In urban settings, the restaurant kitchen may replace the cultural associations of the domestic one, as indicated by an increase in exposed kitchens and **comfort food** on menus.

The competitive appliance market also has been crafted to determine preferences and ascribe status to the niche industry of kitchen remodeling. Basic stoves can be replaced with elaborate grills; refrigerators with Sub-Zeros or additional freezers; and dishwashers, trash compactors, disposals and other appliances converted to necessities. Often undertaken as a substitute for a complete home renovation, upgrades in appliances or changes in color schemes are generally seen as indicators of recent affluence or a change in the dynamic of the family. In lieu of traditional architects and designers, the aestheticization of the kitchen is being realized by home centers, spec-kitchen showrooms and cultural figures such as Martha **Stewart**. This emphasis on the kitchen as the epitome of the home has also generated a cultural counterpoint of more illicit behavior in the kitchen, as represented by films such as *Fatal Attraction* (1987) or *9½ Weeks* (1986).

JEANNIE J. KIM
HUNTER FORD TURA

Korean Americans

There was little **immigration** from Korea before the **Korean War** (1950–3), but numbers increased with the arrival of military wives and adopted orphans. Between new immigration laws in 1965 and 1990, however, the Korean American population increased from 45,000 to 800,000, becoming the third-largest **Asian American** immigrant group, after the **Chinese Americans** and the Filipinos. Moreover, by 1980, 81.9 percent of the **community** was foreign-born, many having fled the unstable economic and political climate in South Korea in the 1960s and 1970s.

While there are large Korean settlements in **Los Angeles, CA**, Queens (**New York** City, NY) and **Philadelphia, PA**, Korean Americans are scattered in many major cities across the country, including southern states, like **Texas** and Virginia.

Many are highly educated, including nurses, scientists and professionals.

Korean Americans are most visible to mainstream Americans as small-business owners in small grocers, liquor stores or laundries from Manhattan to South Central Los Angeles. With limited capital from pooled resources, many immigrants took over stores in economically depressed areas. Their recent immigration and lack of **neighborhood** ties coupled with an image of exclusionary success fueled widely publicized conflicts between **African Americans** and Korean Americans in the media, especially following the 1992 Los Angeles riots where many Korean-owned stores were destroyed. Films like *Do the Right Thing* (1989) and *Falling Down* (1993) have perpetuated stereotypes of hard-working, yet selfish Korean store-owners. Both Koreans and African Americans are now trying to solve these issues.

Korean Americans are the most Christian of the Asian Americans, even prior to immigration, with over 50 percent of the national population Christian. Korean American churches can be found throughout the US, linking them to American civic culture in ways that are different from Chinese Americans and Japanese Americans. Indeed, Korean Americans in economics, education and participation embody the American dream, which has exacerbated the tensions with those native-born Americans who have seen its promises crumbling.

See also: Asian Americans in cinema and television

Further reading

Light, I. and Bonacich, E. (1988) *Immigrant Entrepreneurs: Koreans in Los Angeles 1965–1982*, Berkeley: University of California Press.
Kim, E. and Yu, E.-Y. (1996) *East to America: Korean American Life Stories*, New York: New Press.

CINDY WONG

Korean War

Often considered the forgotten war in American **history**, the Korean War arose amidst fears of the spread of **communism** and the loss of **China**. It was called a "police action," undertaken under the auspices of the United Nations, without a formal declaration of war. As such it was a prototype of the kinds of wars later engaged in by the United States and/or **NATO** against Iraq and Yugoslavia, though with considerably less success.

At the end of the Second World War, Korea had been divided across the middle at the 38th parallel, with the Soviet Union controlling the North, and the United States controlling the South. The conflict began on June 24, 1950, when North Korea surprised Americans by invading the South. Although the **Truman** administration had recognized Syngman Rhee's nationalist regime in the South, it had only made public its intention to defend the Philippines and Japan, thereby seeming to indicate that South Korea would be left to fend for itself. But when the invasion occurred, Truman quickly responded by sending the Seventh Fleet to the region and ordering General Douglas **MacArthur** to prepare his forces for combat. Truman sought and received international support from the western European states (many of whom were hoping for American funding to aid rebuilding their economies), the British Commonwealth and both the Philippines and Thailand. With the Soviet Union boycotting the United Nations in support of China, the world body passed a resolution committing troops to repel the North Koreans.

In September, after the fall of Seoul, General MacArthur began his counteroffensive, landing troops at Inchon and cutting off communist forces in South Korea. The American strategy was an unqualified success and within a month the North Korean army was all but destroyed, leaving UN forces in possession of the entire region south of the 38th parallel.

Now convinced he was infallible, MacArthur decided to reunite Korea by continuing northwards. Truman and the State Department hesitated to support this, knowing that the Chinese had promised to intervene if the Americans moved beyond the 38th parallel, but McArthur assured them that the Chinese would not be able to cross the Yalu River. The wave of 200,000 Chinese soldiers quickly proved him wrong and drove his UN forces back into South Korea.

At this point, the Soviets proposed a truce to a receptive Truman, but MacArthur wanted to escalate the conflict to blockade Chinese ports and bomb military installations across the Yalu River. Determined to force the issue, MacArthur was publicly insubordinate to his commander-in-chief, threatening to destroy China if it did not concede defeat. For this he was relieved of command on April 12, 1951, returning to the United States to a hero's welcome of ticker-tape parades. Truman's action incensed his foes and further contributed to the anti-communist hysteria, with senators like Richard **Nixon** and Joseph **McCarthy** claiming that the State Department was in the hands of communists.

In 1952 an armistice was signed, but the fighting continued. While negotiations bogged down over the issue of prisoner exchange and the territorial integrity of North Korea, a new president, Dwight D. **Eisenhower**, pushed for the war to be won, or at least for peace with honor. The new **vice-president**, Nixon, advocated the use of the nuclear option, and nuclear brinkmanship became part of American strategy to keep the Soviet Union out of the conflict and to force Koreans to the bargaining table on American terms. Not until July 1953 was a final settlement reached, ending with the lines that had been drawn prior to the beginning of the conflict.

The impact of the war on American society and culture was considerable. The increase in tensions between the two major superpowers contributed to the rise of McCarthyism, exacerbating fears of communism already heightened by the "loss" of China and the Soviet Union's development of an atomic bomb. In addition, the fact that North Korea had been under the control of the Soviet Union prior to its invasion of South Korea, and that it was China who came to its defense once MacArthur moved north of the 38th parallel, cemented the idea of an indivisible communist bloc. This image of communism as a single political entity would stymie American foreign policy long after the tensions between the Soviet Union and communist China, which were becoming manifest during the Korean conflict itself, were evident, with particularly tragic consequences in Vietnam.

The failure in Korea also led to new foreign policy initiatives. Tainted by his inability to bring about a victory in Korea, leading John F. **Kennedy** to paint him as someone who was tied to the "containment" strategy, Eisenhower began actively to encourage nations to combat communism around the world. The "Eisenhower doctrine" offering support to countries in the Middle East was one part of this approach, as was his employment of the **CIA** in **Iran** and Guatemala. Moreover, the attempt to dislodge **Castro** in **Cuba**, which would come to be known as the **Bay of Pigs**, was begun under Eisenhower, though it was left to Kennedy to engineer the debacle.

The stalemate in Korea, however, limited American commitment to such cavalier initiatives (even during the Kennedy administration's celebration of counter-insurgency) and increased the nation's reliance on what John Foster called a "new-look" policy contained in the threat of nuclear weapons and "massive retaliation." The war in Korea had accelerated work on the hydrogen bomb, and its completion facilitated a shift from costly conventional forces to the relatively cheap nuclear stockpile.

The war also had a considerable impact on the domestic front. Over 5½ million Americans served in the war (for the first time in integrated units). Many returned after experiencing North Korean POW camps, and 103,284 came back wounded. The deaths of nearly 37,000 Americans were also devastating for all families losing relations. Yet, unlike in the case of the Vietnam War in the next decade, the war did not create vocal, widespread opposition. In part this was because of the anti-communist hysteria brought on by Truman's **Cold War** policies and by Senator Joe McCarthy's campaign. In addition, the economy, fuelled by the war expenditures, was booming. What Eisenhower would call the "military-industrial complex" was established during the Korean War. The need for armaments and military installations acted in a way similar to deficit spending in the Keynesian model. With GIs and defense-industry workers securing good wages and having plenty to spend them on, such as new housing development and **automobiles**, the economy could expand without the problem of inflation.

As "a forgotten war," the Korean conflict received little of the kind of attention from movies and **television** that other wars received. No major Korean War monument was built comparable to the **Vietnam Memorial** in **Washington, DC**. *Pork Chop Hill* (1959) was one of the rare movies made soon after the conflict, while *The Manchurian Candidate* (1962), which began with the conflict, was not shown for many years owing to its association with **assassination**. *M*A*S*H*, the popular movie (1970) and television series (CBS, 1972–83), which focused on a doctors' unit during the war, was shaped in part by a sensibility derived from the Vietnam War, though the sense of futility involved in a war marked by stalemate and diplomatic stumbling was also a constant feature of the Korean conflict.

Further reading

Hastings, M. (1987) *The Korean War*, New York: Simon & Schuster.

Giangreco, D.M. (1990) *War in Korea*, Novato: Presidio.

Paschall, R. (1995) *Witness to War, Korea*, New York: The Berkley Publishing Group.

ROBERT GREGG

Ku Klux Klan

The Ku Klux Klan is America's oldest terrorist hate group. It was founded in December 1865 in Pulaski, Tennessee by several well-educated ex-Confederate soldiers. The group took its name from the Greek word *kukios* meaning circle. The organization started as an adult **fraternity** devoted to performing weird rituals and practical jokes. It quickly evolved into a secretive regional terrorist and political organization countering new civil-rights laws and the federal military occupation of the post-Civil War **South**.

Led by ex-Confederate general and slaveholder, Nathan Bedford Forrest, the group gained over half-a-million members throughout the South. Hooded nightriders terrorized and killed **African American** activists and their sympathizers in addition to transplanted Northerners, while groups, such as the Louisiana-based Knights of the White Camilla, undertook similar activities. With increased public outcry and the threat of congressional hearings and legislation looming, Forrest disbanded the group in 1869. Not all factions followed his order. The Klan withered during the 1870s after a series of high-profile prosecutions and changes in the political landscape. When northern troops withdrew, the need for terrorism against blacks became less pressing as **Jim Crow** laws restricting the social, economic and political activities of Southern blacks were passed.

The second incarnation of the Klan took place in 1915, spurred by the racist pro-Klan motion picture, *Birth of a Nation* (1915), and resurrected by a roving preacher-salesman, William Simmons. The new Klan under Simmons barely stood out from the variety of conservative organizations of the day. In 1920 two Atlanta publicists signed on and changed its tone to be much more vitriolic against "immoral whites" and minorities, particularly Catholics. By the mid-1920s, the Klan had 4.5 million members and exercised considerable political influence, particularly in Indiana. After 1925, the Klan was plagued by more internal power struggles, a loss of political influence and bad publicity over horrendous crimes.

During the **Civil Rights movement**, the Klan emerged anew, leading to numerous murders, assaults, arsons and bombings in the 1950s and 1960s. While never regaining their former membership or political power, these white-hooded bands remain visible symbols of hate which have appeared sporadically in the 1980's and 1990's northern cities and suburban rallies, as well as outbursts against ongoing changes in the South. Using publicity as much as terror, they have sometimes claimed rights of free speech to legitimize their presence and voice their beliefs.

BRIAN LEVIN

L

labor *see* Left, the; strikes; unions; working class

lacrosse

Field sport that resembles both **soccer** and **hockey**, with a ball being moved towards the goal through the air using nets attached to sticks. Lacrosse's origins are found in the **American Indian** sport known as Baggataway, but it owes its spread in the US to elite prep schools and **colleges**. **NCAA** tournaments have been held since 1971 to establish national champions for both women and men's colleges, with the **Ivy League** universities initially dominant, but much less so thirty years later. Wooden sticks have been replaced by ones with plastic heads and aluminum shafts, which have made the stick lighter so that players are able to develop much better stick skill. The women's stick is of a slightly different design that requires greater finesse, possible in the women's game because less physical contact is permitted. For the men's game, though, protective gear, especially around the head, is required. The game is opening the doors to commercialization as indoor semi-professional leagues have been started, taking advantage of the diversity of sports coverage made possible by **cable** television, and as equipment makers sponsor exhibitions around the country and abroad to spread the sport.

ROBERT GREGG

language

While the United States is an English-speaking nation, no official government pronouncement confirmed this – at least until the **English-Only** campaigns of the 1980s forced this upon state legislatures. Nonetheless, generations of those absorbed by American expansion and immigrants have acceded to the domination of English in education, public life, media and everyday life just as the nation's projection abroad has gone through English channels. Older inhabitants – including **American Indians**, **Hispanic** and French residents and Hawai'ians – as well as generations of immigrants, have held onto their own languages for literary, ceremonial and **family** uses, despite transgenerational pressures to assimilate. Newer immigrants, while adding the variegated presence of more than 300 languages (and variable government support) to an American melting-pot, show similar patterns of change over time. Hence, in the 1990 census, 80 percent of the population spoke only English, while half of the remainder spoke English as well as another language. After more than two centuries, American English – distinguished from its British mother tongue and other colonial developments – represents a unifying feature of American national identity, discourse and media.

The unification of this distinctive language, however, has also recognized diversity and challenges as well as changes over time. By the early nineteenth century, works such as *Webster's Dictionary* and the *McGuffey Reader* distinguished American English from British counterparts. Distinctions have included forms and usages (often informal) and a rich vocabulary constantly supplemented by encounters with other speakers – Native American place names, diverse food names and basic vocabulary derived from multiple languages, including "buckaroo" (Spanish *vaquero* "cowboy"), "kibitz" (Yiddish and German words for being a busybody), "moccasin" (used by Virginians from 1612, from the Powhatan or Micmac), "shanty" (from the Irish *sean tig* "old house" or the French *chantier* "log hut"), "boss" (Dutch *baas*), "gung ho" (Chinese *kung ho*) and "juke" (Wolof *dzug*).

In the twentieth century, while **assimilation** to English with some bilingualism remained the norm, **mass media** like the Spanish-language **television** Telemundo and Univision underscored new transnational support for other languages with large communities of speakers in the US – with 20 million Spanish speakers, for example, the United States ranks sixth among world nations in this language. Yiddish, although limited in speakers (200,000+), survived as a medium of expression in the US after Hitler's devastation of Central European Jewry. Other important bilingual competencies in the US include French, German, Italian, various forms of Chinese, Tagalog, Polish and Korean, although many others have contributed to the expressiveness and vocabulary of American English. Meanwhile, Native American languages have been revived as expressions of national identity, just as Hawai'ian and Hawai'ian pidgin have claimed renewed emphasis. **ASL** (American Sign Language) has also received recognition as a distinct ("foreign") language.

Perhaps the most controversial language variant of the United States is Black English ("Ebonics"). African slaves, forcibly imported into the United States, combined the vocabularies, structures and rhythms of African languages and speech of the slave trade with English. In isolation, these became strongly marked dialects like Gullah of the **Southern coast**. In other cases, Black English occupies a post-creole continuum, in which distinctive forms of tense and pronoun use, dual negatives and other features may be used in certain circumstances, but "corrected" in others, especially by speakers who

switch fluently to Standard English. The role of Black English as a separate language has been debated by educators and linguists. Moreover, language structure shades over into distinctive styles of rhetoric, expressivity, wordplay and music that also define an African American tradition of English used by public figures like Martin Luther **King**, Jr. or authors like James **Baldwin** and Ntozake Shange.

Other variations in American English reflect historical differences of region, **immigration**, **class** and **education**. American accents may be identified with cities (Brooklyn, **New York** City, NY, Chicago, etc.), although **migration** also means that newer areas may lack any identifiable accent – one rarely speaks of a **Phoenix** or **Seattle** accent. **Sunbelt** development, however, has intersected with a strong regional accent – the Southern "drawl," involving lengthened vowels, weaker final consonants and melodious intonation. A distinctive New England accent includes a highly rounded "o" and back "a," as well as an extended final "r" – "Hahhvahhd" (for Harvard). The Brooklyn accent, by contrast, reflects the impact of immigrant Irish, German and Yiddish speakers in the shift from "th" to "d," or other marked traits. The normative accent of the US, reaffirmed by mass-media announcers, tends to be the flatter and nasal English of the **Midwest** and **West**. Regional accents, in turn, tend to reflect associations of regional culture – identification of a New England accent with powerful history and Yankee harshness, or of a Southern accent with ease but a lack of development. Ironically, the latter remained important in presidential politics for Johnson, Carter, Clinton, Gore and George Bush, Jr. (versus his father's **Northeastern** speech).

Accents also refer to class, though not as markedly as in the British system. Class, moreover, is mediated by region and, above all, by education – correctness of speech and vocabulary are taken as primary indicators. William Labov, in his studies of New York City speech, showed that speakers of various class backgrounds try to correct towards what they perceive as an educated norm in careful speech (indeed, he identified **middle-class** speakers who showed a tendency to overcorrect with linguistic insecurity). Etiquette books also warn about proper phrases and topics as well as usages to be avoided. Class is also read into "foreign accents": British and French accents in the US are taken generally to be indicators of higher status, while Asian and Hispanic accents suggest recent arrival or lower-class status.

Yet, all these indicators of class are challenged by language as a site of creativity and rebellion. Slang and jargons associated with particular groups have been vital parts of the reinvention of English from generation to generation. Some inventions have endured – from the ubiquitous "OK," which may have African roots, to more recent ephemera. Professional jargons circulate rapidly through **mass media**, despite those critics who decry their obfuscation or lack of creativity. Slang, as a creation of those outside the mainstream, occupies an even more confusing position as the slang of youth becomes the home language of new generations. One notes shifts, for example, not only in individual words but in the vocabularies of profanity and sexuality that **baby boomers** use fluently in contrast to their parents (and perhaps to **children** who are ingrained in proper speech as they develop their own rebellions).

Language is also about style and American values of **individualism**, "popular culture" and **consumerism**. Again, culturally constructed divisions like the fluidity of black preaching, the supposedly hard-nosed criticism of big-city speech or the politeness of women represent both ideological constructs and language practices. Multiple media represent and participate in a continual recreation of American language and language practices. Hence, the phrase "Make my day" (from Clint **Eastwood**'s hard-edged cop in *Dirty Harry*) was recycled by Ronald **Reagan** as president, while the advertising slogan "Where's the beef?" also appeared in political debates. Indeed, the ubiquity of English among 250 million speakers (as well as those who speak or "listen to" American products in other countries) has sustained music, literature, **advertising**, **television** and films as channels in which American English is continually reinvented and shared.

Further reading

Chapman, R. (1986) *New Dictionary of American Slang*, New York: Holt & Rinehart.

Dictionary of American Regional English (1985–) Cambridge, MA: Harvard.

Flexner, S. (1976) *I Hear America Talking*, New York: Simon & Schuster.

Labov, W. (1972) *Sociolinguistic Patterns*, Philadelphia: University of Pennsylvania.

Mencken, H.L. (1936) *The American Language*, New York: Alfred A. Knopf.

Rickford, J. (1999) *African-American Vernacular English*, Malden: Blackwell.

GARY McDONOGH

Las Vegas, NV

Soaring in neon exuberance over the hostile **Southwestern** desert, Las Vegas represents a fantasy of **gambling**, glamour and license to more than 30 million tourists annually. Jobs created by this fantasy, in turn, have made it one of America's fastest growing cities, reaching an estimated population of 404,288 in 1998, a 56 percent increase over 1990. The spectacle city of the Strip, **Elvis**, slot machines, cheap buffets and **wedding** chapels faces new demands for civic identity.

Las Vegas emerged from obscurity through water (artesian wells), power (Hoover Dam, 1928) and gambling, which Nevada legalized in 1931. By 1940 this 10,000-citizen resort had a Western flavor; northern Reno, the state capital, was more famous for gambling and **divorce**. Vegas' creation myth (recrafted in the 1991 movie *Bugsy*) cites mobster Bugsy Siegel as the genius who synthesized Los Angeles **modernism** and motels in the rebuilt Flamingo before his "untimely" death in 1947. Underworld connections, a continual concern of the Nevada gaming commission, were largely purged by the 1960s.

Las Vegas' subsequent development has challenged boundaries of neon, **architecture**, spectacle and taste. In the 1960s, Howard Hughes shaped the city as both owner-developer and reclusive billionaire. In 1966 Caesar's Palace established theme-park models, later followed by MGM Grand, Excalibur (medieval), Luxor (Ancient Egypt), Bellagio (artistic Italian) and Caesar's own archeological invention, complete with talking statues. In Circus Circus, another 1960s creation, high-wire acts flew over slot machines, prefiguring a shift to "**family**" entertainment in the 1990s. The late 1960s also saw the beginning of corporate Las Vegas, with ever-larger and more complicated casino-resorts, traded as joint-stock corporations by entrepreneurs like Steve Wynn and William Bennett.

Alongside neon cascades, erupting volcanoes and pirate battles, Las Vegas also meant show business. Frank **Sinatra** and his "rat pack," Elvis **Presley**, **Liberace** (who left his museum behind) and Barbra **Streisand** are identified with the city, as are bejeweled and befeathered chorus lines, lounge singers, magicians, call girls and animal trainers. Celebrities, in turn, use the city as a backdrop for films, **television**, **marriages** and **divorces**.

Beyond the glitter, Las Vegas faces the complexities of other American cities, including 1992 riots (after Rodney **King**) that underscored the dilemmas of its **African American** population. A significant **Mormon** population and growing families place demands on schools and other resources. New civic buildings, including a library/performing-arts center by Michael **Graves** and the University of Nevada, have created a city beyond the Strip. Even casinos are adding "reality" – Wynn's touted collection of European art – to glitter.

Yet for millions who know the city through media and visits, Las Vegas remains a city of dreams (Elvis' *Viva Las Vegas*, 1966; the James Bond thriller *Diamonds are Forever*, 1969; *Sister Act*, 1981) and nightmares (*Show Girl*, 1996; *Leaving Las Vegas*, 1997).

Further reading

Puzo, M. (1977) *Inside Las Vegas*, New York: Grosset & Dunlap.
Anderton, F. and Chase, J. (1997) *Las Vegas*, London: Ellipsis.

GARY McDONOGH
CINDY WONG

late-night television

For nearly fifty years, the time slot between the 23:00 local **news** and station sign-off has been dominated by one format – the live **talk show** – and one show – NBC's *Tonight Show* – under a succession of hosts. Other local stations generally fought back with movies and syndicated programming. CBS' *Tonight Show* offshoot, *Late Night with David Letterman*, ABC's *Nightline* and the syndicated *Arsenio Hall Show*, among others, have created viable alternatives, yet still within a conversational format.

Noting other experiments in late-night programming, NBC developed the *Tonight Show* from a local program hosted by Steve Allen, a witty, urbane New York comedian and pianist. Between 1954 and 1957, Allen created the formula for the ninety-minute show – a living-room ambience, complete with **family** (announcer and band) and varied **celebrity** guests, from sex symbols to poet Carl **Sandburg**. Comic features, music and excursions into the live audience and onto the street framed and paced the talk, incorporating a democracy of celebrity into late-night relaxation. This era also established union scale as guest payment (while growing commercial revenues poured into NBC coffers for generations). Celebrities, nonetheless, have used this teleforum to sell their movies, songs and **television** shows, careers, athletic achievements and humanity (including political candidates).

NBC revived *the Tonight Show* under Jack Paar (1957–62), who hosted John F. **Kennedy** and Richard **Nixon**, as well as show business celebrities. Paar also began taping shows in advance, although still with a live audience. Edgy, personal and combative, Paar walked off the show – on air – in 1960 after a fight with censors.

In 1962 Johnny Carson took over for three decades. Carson did not change his predecessors' formats, but overlaid them with a casual style that suited the Manhattan show's move to **California** in 1972. He made the monologue more topical, while his approval legitimated newcomers in stand-up **comedy**, music and film for decades. Both star guests and the sheer repetition of formulaic jokes, sketches and banter with announcer Ed MacMahon, made Carson a constant fixture in American life and language.

Carson's 1992 retirement created a battle between a frequent replacement host, stand-up comedian Jay Leno, and David Letterman. Letterman already had developed his sometimes surreal humor, more Allen than Carson, on NBC's *Late Night* (1982–92). Here, he took over a new 00:30–01:30 slot pioneered by Tom Snyder's intimate, discursive *Tomorrow* (1973–82). The "wars" ended with Letterman getting millions from CBS, creating competition in style, features and location (Letterman's **Times Square** versus Leno's California), although guests migrate between these shows and the younger-oriented talk shows that follow.

Meanwhile, in 1979, ABC began nightly broadcasts on the **Iran** hostage crisis. A few months later, this became the half-hour *Nightline*, hosted by Ted Koppel. *Nightline* provides analysis, contentious interviews and debates on hot news, and longer investigative, town meeting and location reports confronting American dilemmas of riots, prison, racism, presidential scandal and challenges abroad. With its sobriety and immediacy, *Nightline* has, at times, eclipsed variety-show rivals.

While various other syndicated talk shows and hosts have failed in the 1980s and 1990s, the *Arsenio Hall Show* (1989–94) was both a racial breakthrough for its **African American** host and a generational one, in contrast to the aging Carson. Hall, however, mixed super-hip with seriousness, including frank discussions of **AIDS** with Magic Johnson and poignant coverage/appeals for calm during the 1992 **Los Angeles** riots. A 1990s newcomer, Bill Maher's *Politically Incorrect* (ABC), throws together celebrities, politicians and "average" citizens in pointed discussions of politics and culture, especially during **Clinton**'s unfolding scandals, while PBS' Charlie Rose promotes erudite one-on-one exchanges.

Morning television provides information and family chatter to begin the day. Late-night has permitted adult talk to chronicle, comment on and sometimes create fifty years of American life, media, politics and change, whether packaged as **humor** and gossip or serious debate. These shows have emerged as significant sources of political information and opinion for viewers. In the 1990s, viewers also can escape to multiple **cable** options – movies, reruns, cooking and sports – or simply go to bed.

Further reading

Bianculli, D. (1996) *Dictionary of Teleliteracy*, New York: Continuum.

Carter, B. (1994) *The Late Shift: Letterman, Leno and the Network Battle for the Night*, New York: Hyperion.

GARY McDONOGH

Latin America

While the US has often portrayed itself as the champion of democracy and **freedom** in the Western Hemisphere, protector against outsiders and even a partner in Pan-American development, its neighbors have not always shared this image. Instead, the "Colossus of the North" has, in their eyes, made unilateral declarations of policy, intervened to protect murky interests and acted as a domineering patriarch. These images, and the experiences and actions that underpin them, often have made US relations with its American neighbors conflictive, even though goods, citizens and ideas cross borders. Moreover, experiences have varied among nations: while **Mexico**, the **Caribbean** and Central America have been constant foci of American activity, nations to the south have sometimes negotiated alternate ties with each other and with Europe.

US values have been embodied in statements that betray perceptions of Latin American weakness. The 1823 Monroe Doctrine of President James Monroe warned Europeans (without any ratification) not to intervene further in the Western Hemisphere. This vision later gained more force when used to justify US appropriation of territory in the west and claims of hemispheric interests. President Theodore Roosevelt's 1904 corollary, allowing the US to intervene in problem nations of the hemisphere, turned protector into policeman. While Franklin **Roosevelt**'s Good Neighbor policy (1935–45) sought a new appearance of partnership, including concessions to Latin American sovereignty, relations of power scarcely changed. US concerns expanded even more as the **Cold War** raised the specter of **communism** in Latin America.

Twentieth century US actions have betrayed deep ambivalence. Intervention to restructure debt or establish order, for example, also meant the US dictated terms by which **Haiti**, **Cuba**, **Panama** or Nicaragua might regain their autonomy. During the Cold War, professed ideals of freedom were sacrificed for stability of US political and economic interests. Bloody dictators were supported and popular movements suppressed with massive US aid, military support and **CIA** assistance. Leftist movements were destabilized by diplomacy and covert operations. Cuba, Mexico and Nicaragua, perhaps, best illustrate this pattern of intimate conflict, but the scenario extended as far south as the Allende regime in Chile.

US individuals and corporations have also made investments in Latin America (again, especially in nearby states), and have encouraged trade and "development." Loans and foreign aid have facilitated development programs, but have also insisted on neo-colonial dependencies and have created crushing debts. Medical, religious, scientific, agricultural, academic and even revolutionary assistance from the north each have created solutions and problems. Controlling disease or bolstering production, for example, raises new dilemmas if the US prevents population control or land reform.

Many US citizens, meanwhile, view Latin America through ignorance or stereotypes of laziness, instability or carefree abandon – combining **Disney**'s *Three Caballeros* (1945), noir nostalgia (*Gilda*, 1946; *Havana*, 1990), Carmen Miranda and news of seemingly endless war and poverty. Despite serious Latin American voices in scholarship, the arts and media (Univision, Telemundo), stereotypes remain strong.

Perhaps the most tragic dimension of this misunderstanding and pain has been the experiences and interests that the United States and Latin America actually *share* – their creation within patterns of global migration and exchange in the early modern period, their experiences as post-colonial republics, links to Europe, Africa and Asia, pre-contact American cultures and ongoing hybridization, even their landscapes. Latin Americans have watched **Hollywood** movies (including condescending stereotypes); visited, immigrated and even sought refuge in the US; competed in resources, production and sports; shared art, food and literature; and faced common problems of environmental degradation, the growth and distribution of drugs or the spread of **AIDS**.

Exchanges among Latin Americans and debates over the rainforest, efficient development or preferred media products provide alternative discourses the US often fails to hear. Through all this, the powerfully ambivalent US position as insistent leader has often betrayed the very freedom the US proclaims. The cry "Yankee go home," from decade to decade, nation to nation, reminds us that despite interventions that may resolve problems locally, for many intervention *itself* – and the presumption of a right to do so – remains the problem.

Further reading

Black, G. (1988) *The Good Neighbor*, New York: Pantheon.

Bonilla, F. (ed.) (1998) *Borderless Borders*, Philadelphia: Temple.

Coever, D. and Hall, L. (1999) *Tangled Destinies*, Albuquerque: University of New Mexico.

Falcoff, M. (1998) *A Culture of its Own: Taking Latin America Seriously*, New Brunswick: Transaction.

GARY McDONOGH
CINDY WONG

Latino/as

The term "Latino" was introduced to differentiate from the label "**Hispanic**," which is used in the United States to refer to individuals whose heritage is primarily from one or more Spanish-speaking countries. According to the US Census Bureau, a person is Hispanic if their ancestry is Mexican, Mexican American, **Chicano**, **Puerto Rican**, Dominican, or from other Spanish-speaking countries of the **Caribbean**, Central or South America or Spain. Political and social groups have long criticized the term Hispanic, claiming that it does not account for the varied socio-cultural experiences, as well as political, economic and social histories of the groups that compose this population.

The term Latino is the newest in a 160-year-old conflict of terminology. The term Latino is a condensed version of Latin America, which can be traced back to 1856. The phrase "Latin America" was used to refer to what was known as Spanish

America in an effort to ignore the region's connection to Spain, as well as its indigenous and African heritages. Ironically, today the term Latino is used to embody all of the legacies it was first used to disregard. While Latinos still includes the groups identified by the Census Bureau, it also embraces individuals from all Latin American nationalities, in addition to second- and third-generation English dominant American citizens and various non-Spanish speaking indigenous groups.

Latinos in the United States are a diverse sociocultural and demographic population. Most Latinos in the United States are either immigrants or the **children** of immigrants, with the exception of Puerto Ricans, who are the only group guaranteed US citizenship from birth through the Jones Act of 1917. While Latinos reside all over the United States, the majority live in **California**, **Texas**, **New York** and **Florida**, with a disproportionately high number living in urban areas. With the fastest population growth, it is estimated that by the year 2000 Latinos will be the largest minority in the United States. In the United States alone Latinos represent 11 percent of the population, an estimated 31 million, including 3.5 million in **Puerto Rico**. Of all the groups, Mexicans (64 percent) account for the largest number of Latinos in the United States, while Central and South Americans (22 percent), Puerto Ricans (12 percent) and Cubans (5 percent) compose the remaining Latino population.

Despite their divergent political, economic and social histories, Latinos found a way to converge in the late 1960s and early 1970s through participation in such social-activist groups like the Young Lords Party and the Brown Berets. Latinos fought against the economic and social injustice in their communities. With the Latino agenda being much more extensive today, Latinos are a growing force in the formal political arena, representing their communities at the local, state and federal levels to earn respect for their people, culture and tongue.

Further reading

Fox, G. (1996) *Hispanic Nation*, Tucson: The University of Arizona Press.

Oboler, S. (1995) *Ethnic Labels Latino Lives*, Minneapolis: University of Minnesota Press.

LORELEI ATALIE VARGAS

Latinos, as represented in media

Representations of **Latinos** in media vary significantly depending on whether they are self-generated or created by non-Latinos. Latinos began representing themselves positively and complexly in Spanish language **newspapers** in the mid-nineteenth century, to be joined in the early twentieth century by Spanish-language **radio** and literature. By the mid-1960s, self-generated Latino images appeared in **film**, **television** and **Broadway**.

More frequently during this time frame, non-Latinos represented these same experiences through commonly recognized stereotypes. Male and female images of the dark-skinned bandit, revolutionary, peasant, Latin lover and the seemingly less offensive Spanish aristocrat carried over from written to visual media at the beginning of the twentieth century. In the mid-twentieth century, to these enduring stereotypes were added the buffoon, the boxer, the gang member and the illegal alien.

Scholarly debates about the accuracy and impact of such images has continued since the 1970s. A 1994 study by the National Council of La Raza indicated **mass media** continually underrepresented and misrepresented Latinos despite modest gains made by other ethnic American groups after the **Civil Rights movement**. According to the same study, as Latinos and other Americans receive most of their information through mass media, the control and generation of Latino images remains of paramount importance.

Further reading

Pettit, A. (1980) *Images of the Mexican American in Fiction and Film*, College Station, TX: A and M U University.
Rodriguez, C. (ed.) (1997) *Latin Looks: Images of*

Latinas and Latinos in the US Media, Boulder: Westview Press.

SUSAN MARIE GREEN

Latter Day Saints, Church of the *see* Mormons

law and order *see* crime, television; Nixon, Richard M.; Reagan, Ronald; violence

lawn/yard

A patch of well-tended and mown grass in front of the house became the ornament of American homes after the Civil War – present even in **cities**, but reaching new dimensions in **suburban** development. While they might evoke manor houses and their meadows, lawns tend to be smaller, providing a setback from the street that shapes a characteristic American urban geography. Lawns may be landscaped with trees, bushes and ornaments, but are often left connected (in front) as a green plain along the street. Backyards have been more private recreational and work areas, although they may interconnect in suburban developments. The lawn has also demanded technological responses ranging from lawnmowers – push, powered and riding – to chemicals and irrigation which permit lawns in deserts and seashore areas, although at the expense of environmental degradation.

Further reading

Jenkins, V.S. (1994) *The Lawn: A History of An American Obsession*, Washington, DC: Smithsonian.

GARY McDONOGH
CINDY WONG

lawyers

Professionals educated in graduate programs and licensed by state bar associations to prepare and plead cases in lower courts and appeals courts, as well as to provide legal counsel to clients. The adversarial nature of the American common-law system provides lawyers a broad and flexible role.

This includes investigating facts, gathering evidence, trying cases, negotiating settlements, formulating business transactions, drafting legislation and urging courts to create new legal precedents. Competition, globalization and the impossibility of thoroughly mastering multiple areas of the law have lead to specialization, and have rewarded the combining of legal specialists into ever-larger law firms. Despite being authorized to perform a broader range of functions than colleagues in most European systems, lawyers are professionally constrained by only a loose construct of ethical standards, enforced by a largely self-regulating system administered by state bar associations and judicial tribunals.

Lawyers saturate US society. The **California** State Bar alone has close to 170,000 members. Although declining, the number of annual applications to law schools is 70,000. Roughly 40,000 enroll each year as first-year students at American Bar Association approved law schools. Many of these view a legal education as a tool, a method of critical thinking and problem-solving, and never practice law after becoming licensed attorneys.

Lawyers are despised, scorned and vilified for their adversarial role and simultaneously respected for their wealth, skill and power. More than 60 percent of the delegates at the Constitutional Convention in 1787 which drafted the United States Constitution were lawyers. At the beginning of the twenty-first century, lawyers account for 43 percent of the members of **Congress** and 16 percent of state legislators. Lawyers, such as Thurgood **Marshall**, were responsible for every watershed legal ruling of the **Civil Rights movement**. The legal profession's best face is represented by the **American Civil Liberties Union**'s protection of civil liberties and the thousands of hours of *pro bono* service lawyers provide the poor.

Lawyer television shows and films maintain enduring popularity despite having moved in the past twenty years from largely favorable portrayals to current characterizations, especially in films, of lawyers as cut-throat, often incompetent, predators. These same **television** shows and films also fail to reflect the reality of the profession's lack of racial and ethnic diversity. While the number of women attorneys at large firms has increased to 30 percent, only 7 percent of lawyers in the United States are from minority groups. Three percent are **African Amer-icans**, 2 percent are **Latinos** and less than 1 per-cent are **Asian Americans** or Native Americans, a problem that the decline in public affirmative-action admission programs will exacerbate.

The litigious nature of American society and the necessity of legal assistance in making many crucial life decisions assure the continued number and power of lawyers, despite the persistent public lack of confidence in the profession.

See also: affirmative action

Further reading

Abel, R. (1989) *American Lawyers*, New York: Oxford University Press.
Glendon, M. (1994) *A Nation under Lawyers*, New York: Farrar, Straus & Giroux.

JAMES KRAUS

lawyers, television shows

America in the late twentieth and early twenty-first centuries is known as an increasingly litigious society, in which trials and verdicts are covered in news and gossip and via books by the participants, guilty or innocent. This coverage enshrines the **lawyer** celebrity, who, while present in films, has been a particular staple of **television** drama.

If *Dragnet* is the type specimen for **police** shows, *Perry Mason* (CBS, 1957–66) is the type specimen for lawyers. Raymond Burr, who had appeared as a burly killer in **Hitchcock**'s *Rear Window* (1954), became an invincible lawyer whose clients, perse-cuted by the police, were invariably innocent. In a weekly morality play that has survived decades more in reruns, Perry, his sidekick private eye and love-struck secretary skated on the edges of the law in order to find the truth, while others confessed to adultery, fraud, greed and ultimately, the murder. Prosecutors lost although justice was served.

Mason's heroics questioned the efficiency if not the motives of police (although Burr later played a wheelchair-bound cop in *Ironside*), setting the stage for important dramas discussing major issues like *The*

Defenders (CBS, 1961–5) and many lesser shows. Yet, if these could tap into 1960s suspicion of police and government, lawyers, too, were found to be more human and more diverse than the white male heroes who created the genre. *L.A. Law* (NBC, 1986–94), a widely watched ensemble show of the 1980s, for example, jumbled office politics, courtrooms and bedrooms. In the 1990s, David Kelley's *The Practice* (ABC, 1997–) makes ethical issues central to a sometimes shady firm and beleaguered District Attorney's office, while *Ally McBeal* (FOX, 1997–) – the first hit show named after a female lawyer – treats law as a career/lifestyle rather than a crusade for justice. Again, human vulnerability and moral ambiguity are seen as essences of the law rather than as external hindrances: justice is one goal among many. *Law and Order* (NBC, 1990–) offers perhaps the most clear-cut moral universe, with its concentration on prosecutors making deals and losing cases).

The fictional narratives of crime and punish-ment of the 1990s, however, intersect with other media realities equally vulnerable and ambiguous. Extensive coverage of the O.J. Simpson trial and presidential scandals, as well as wider access to C-Span and Court TV, have made the uncertainties of real justice part of everyday life. "Courttain-ment" in which "real" judges (Judge Wappner, former New York City **mayor** Ed Koch, Judge "Judy") decide real civil cases with **sitcom** spiels also blurring the structures of authority and truth that seemed so clear decades before.

Just as crime and punishment have been crucibles of social change and cultural meanings, whether on-screen or off-screen, the integration of women and minorities as major characters in police and law dramas (judges, lawyers and detectives, as well as criminals), the growing violence of stories and depictions, and the huma-nization of lawyers have all reflected changing attitudes and prepared these changes.

GARY McDONOGH
CINDY WONG

Lear, Norman

b. 1922

Liberal **television** writer and producer and

political activist. Lear's shows, sometimes adapted from British models, raised questions of **race**, **class** and gender in ways that transformed not only the **sitcom**, but American conversations that responded to these hit shows. His first hit, *All in the Family* (CBS, 1971–9), put Carroll O'Connor's Archie Bunker, a working-class bigot from Queens, squarely at the center yet surrounded by direct challenges from his leftist daughter and son-in-law (played by Rob Reiner), naive questions from his wife Edith and increasingly diverse neighbors. Spin-offs followed, such as *Maude* (CBS, 1972–8), which introduced controversial discussions of **feminism** and **abortion**, although at times undercutting the strident liberalism of its title character, and spun off its own depiction of a black family in the projects, *Good Times* (CBS, 1972–9). *The Jeffersons* (CBS, 1975–85) followed Bunker's bigoted black neighbor (and critical wife) to a Manhattan penthouse, forcing other issues of class, race and interracial relationships. In *Sanford and Son* (NBC, 1972–6), Lear adapted the British *Steptoe and Son* to showcase legendary black comedian Redd Foxx as a crotchety, conniving junk dealer, transmuting some of the stereotypes and tricks that had condemned *Amos 'n Andy* decades earlier. While Lear's successes seem to capture the American dialogues emerging from the 1960s, by the 1980s he devoted more time to political opposition with his People for the American Way. He has had less success with return bids for television, although his characters and plots live on through constant reruns and mass-mediated "folklore."

GARY McDONOGH
CINDY WONG

Leary, Timothy

b. 1920; d. 1996

Psychologist and apostle of the hallucinogen LSD (d-Lysergic Acid Diethylamide). As a Harvard professor, influenced by Aldous Huxley, Leary tested LSD and psilocybin among criminals, seminarians and other volunteers. Expelled from Harvard, he explored altered consciousness and new social visions, becoming a 1960s guru to artists and **hippies**. After his 1967 drug arrest, the

Black Panthers helped him flee to Algeria and Afghanistan; he later served prison time. An amalgam of prophet and comedian, Leary epitomized an **intellectual** drug culture crushed by conservative **Republican** dominance. He died of **cancer**, after debating his **suicide** on the **Internet**.

GARY McDONOGH

Lebanon, troops in

The United States has sent troops into Lebanon on two occasions. **Eisenhower**'s plan to resist any communist aggression in the Middle East (known as the "Eisenhower Doctrine"), led to the sending of 14,000 troops there at the request of the Lebanese government, even though the threat came not from communists but from internal opposition. During **Reagan**'s administration, following conflict in Lebanon between Israel and the Palestinian Liberation Organization backed by Syria, **Secretary of State** George Schultz brought about a peace agreement, which stipulated that the US would commit 1,500 troops as part of a multinational peacekeeping force. In late 1983, however, a Muslim terrorist drove a truck full of explosives into the unprotected US Army barracks, killing 241 soldiers. Reagan at first kept the US force in Lebanon, not wanting to surrender to terrorism, but because of the unpopularity of this decision changed his mind. Eisenhower's involvement in Lebanon highlighted one aspect of the **Cold War** – the way in which the mask of anticommunism embroiled Americans in conflicts of a nationalist nature. The more recent case shaped later engagements of troops, especially as peace keepers, requiring that the US role be clearly defined, that peace actually be established and that American forces be sufficiently well-protected.

ROBERT GREGG

Lee, Bruce (Lee Yuen Kam)

b. 1940; d. 1973

Growing up in Hong Kong, Lee returned in 1959

to his birthplace, **San Francisco**'s Chinatown, and established the Jun Fan Kung-Fu Institute, teaching **martial arts** to people of any race (most Asian Martial Arts schools generally taught people of their own nationality or race). Lee then began to develop Jeet Kune Do, a syncretic art that includes techniques from all types of fighting – **boxing**, Thai kick-boxing, Japanese karate, etc. After playing the part of Kato in *The Green Hornet* (ABC, 1966–7), Batman and a Lone Ranger clone, Lee was enticed to make several movies in Hong Kong that became extremely popular in the United States. Lee died just prior to the release of *Enter the Dragon* (1973), which cemented his reputation and mystique.

ROBERT GREGG

Lee, Spike

b. 1957

Forerunner of a new generation of film-school trained black **directors**, Lee has expanded his films about **race**, **class** and gender into a more complex and enduring career with surprising tenderness as well as compelling questions both whites and blacks might prefer to forget. His films have spurred controversy and dislike from feminist critics of his debut, *She's Gotta Have It* (1986), to uneasy white and ethnic readings of *Do the Right Thing* (1989) or *Summer of Sam* (1999), which portray a divided **New York** City. Controversy has also plagued his relations with and criticism of **Hollywood**; although *Malcolm X* (1992) took on many of the trappings of a Hollywood production, **award** nominations that have eluded him most.

CINDY WONG

Left, the

In the early twenty-first century, there are a number of different American "Lefts" that are united primarily by their commitment to achieving more social and economic equality in American society. Although these Lefts remain quite fragmented and marginal in an organizational sense,

each one has produced vehement and incisive critiques of capitalism, liberal individualism and the commodification of social relations. They have, for the most part, abandoned or deeply problematized the Marxist and "scientific-socialist" approach of the pre-Second World War American "old" Left, and abhor the Bolshevik or Leninist model of revolution and social transformation. It is only in these senses that it is possible to speak of the American Left in the singular.

The modern American Left can trace much of its origins to the so-called New Left that emerged in the 1960s. This New Left was primarily university based, and, at least in its beginnings, abandoned what C. Wright Mills called Marx's "labor metaphysic" (which considered the working class to be the primary vehicle for revolutionary consciousness). For the New Left, alienation did not result primarily from an individual's relation to the means of production, but was instead created by a lack of democratic participation in the central institutions of American culture: primarily universities, the state, corporations and the military. The New Left was deeply influenced by the **civil rights** revolution and the feminist awakening of the 1960s and 1970s. These movements asserted that the traditional Left was unable to offer convincing explanations of racism and the continued subordination of women.

Broadly speaking, it is possible to trace two primary intellectual formations that emerged out of the successes and failures of the New Left. What may be called a social-democratic Left maintains that continuing problems of poverty and racism can begin to be addressed primarily through statist economic reforms, political mobilization within the existing framework of the American **party system** and the revival of an energetic labor-union movement. This social-democratic Left recognizes the importance of **class** in political and historical analysis, but is wedded to more-or-less traditional majoritarian and "realist" methods to achieve incremental change.

The other, so-called "cultural Left" is a quite complex phenomenon. It has been nurtured by several powerful philosophical critiques of modernism and Enlightenment rationality that were first articulated in Europe during and following the Second World War. For these critics and philosophers, including such diverse figures as Horkheimer, Adorno, Foucault, Irigary and Kristeva, the rise of totalitarianism in the twentieth century was the end result of a rationalist inner-logic of Western culture that first gained cultural hegemony in the West in the seventeenth century. The "cultural Left" critical formation scorns all forms of foundational metaphysics, Enlightenment universalism and economic determinism. The cultural Left celebrates the autonomy of dissident cultures of **race**, gender and **ethnicity**, and relentlessly historicizes routine assumptions about hierarchy and order. It is heterodox, particularist and perspectivist in orientation. It has been unjustly criticized as mere "identity" politics that has little to say to the "majority of Americans," and, while it shares many of the objectives of the social democratic Left, its analysis and methodology are obviously quite different.

In an era in which capitalism is more powerful than ever in world politics, it remains to be seen whether the different American "lefts" can create a compelling vision of an alternative social order.

ED JOHANNINGSMEIER

Lemmon, Jack

b. 1925

Comic actor in the best sense of both worlds – who else could convey the naivete of *Mr Roberts* (Academy Award, 1955), the drag humor of *Some Like it Hot* (1959), the burnt-out businessperson of *Save the Tiger* (Academy Award, 1973), the confused patriotism of *Missing* (Best Actor, Cannes, 1982) and so many other roles with such personality and mastery? Lemmon often plays an American everyman, decent and confounded by a twisted world, whether in comedy or tragedy, yet his versatility and craftsmanship set him apart and earned him American Film Institute Accolades in 1988. After four decades and multiple **awards**, he continues to delight audiences and won a Golden Globe for his **television** performance in *Inherit the Wind* (1999).

See also: actors

GARY McDONOGH
CINDY WONG

Leno, Jay *see* late-night television

lesbians *see* gay and lesbian life and politics

Letterman, David *see* late-night television

Levertov, Denise

b. 1923; d. 1997

Anglo-Californian poet and activist, raised in Essex, Levertov's early verse is "free" and relatively abstract; later poems are more concrete, yet continue to abjure regularities of line, stanza and margin. American influences include Black Mountain poets and Pound, though Levertov's speakers do not ventriloquize. Her feminist, antiwar teachings (as with Rukeyser's) come from lived experience (Hanoi, Berkeley's People's Park); her deep-image fables, elegies, travel transcripts and activist tracts pioneer an American poem authentically rooted in a specific self. That Levertov's consistent moral rigor coincides with formal laxity tests the position that right convictions lead to right poems.

DANIEL BOSCH

Levi Strauss

Founded as a dry-goods company in **San Francisco, CA** (1853) by the German Jewish immigrant Levi Strauss, this company was transformed by a new process in 1873 that used metal rivets at stress points in denim work clothes. In the twentieth century, these blue jeans escaped rough work – and playgrounds – to become uniforms for a casual lifestyle. Although **baby boomers** associated jeans with rebellions against established codes of dress, by the end of the century a vast variety of denims – in which Levi Strauss is only one competing brand – have become ubiquitous among all ages, classes and settings of the US as well as abroad. Levi Strauss, meanwhile, remains one of the largest privately held family corporations in the United States – a brief fling at public trading in 1971 ended with a 1985 buy back. Its worldwide sales stood at $6 billion in 1998 (slipping markedly from the year before), produced in thirty-two factories worldwide, with eleven in North America slated to close in 1999. Indeed, Levis, although a symbol of America, are more likely to be made worldwide in the region where they are purchased.

GARY McDONOGH

Levittowns

Preplanned, post-Second World War **communities** of low-cost, tract, mass-manufactured, single-family homes built by Levitt and Sons, Incorporated, which became worldwide construction models for **suburbs** and edge cities. The first Long Island Levittown had 17,447 houses. Their purchase, largely by **veterans** using federally insured mortgages, marked the beginning of **white flight** from **New York** City. **Restrictive racial covenants** and discriminatory sales practices barred **African Americans**. For purchasers, Levitt homes fulfilled lifelong dreams. Social critics viewed Levittowns as harbingers of the quintessential suburban lifestyle, places of monotony, conformity, social isolation and bigotry, the epitome of Malvina Reynold's "Little Boxes."

JAMES KRAUS

Lewis, Carl *see* track and field

Lewis, Jerry (Joseph Levitch)

b. 1928

Comedian who combines slapstick and sentimentality. Lewis became famous partnering stylish crooner Dean Martin (1917–95) in films like *At War with the Army* (1951) or *The Caddy* (1953). Later films like *The Delicate Delinquent* (1957) and *The Nutty Professor* (1961) solidified his boisterous solo comic persona; he later took on more reflective roles (e.g. *The King of Comedy*, 1983). Lewis' style has divided American audiences and critics, and he has often gained greater accolades abroad, especially in France. He has also been extremely active in work

with Muscular Dystrophy, although his sentimentalism has come under criticism there as well.

GARY McDONOGH

Lewis, Jerry Lee

b. 1935

Playing piano in seeming reckless abandon, Lewis, along with Chuck Berry, Little Richard and Elvis **Presley**, is one of the creators of **rock 'n' roll**. Known by his family and friends (including televangelist cousin Jimmy Swaggart) as "The Killer" for his performance technique, Lewis hit Memphis after reading of Presley's success as a white R&R singer and recorded "Whole Lot of Shaking Goin' On" (1957). He followed this huge hit with "Great Balls of Fire" (1957). During a tour of England, the press revealed he had married his thirteen-year-old second cousin; his career suffered until the late 1960s when he made a minor comeback.

EDWARD MILLER

Liberace

b. 1919; d. 1987

Favorite of the "blue-haired" set, this flamboyant pianist was better known for his on-stage theatrics than his music, mostly romantic period music and popular standards in an upbeat manner. Bejeweled in flowing sequined robes with his trademark candelabra atop his grand piano, he bantered with his audience and won their love. **Television** made him famous and **Las Vegas** kept him in the public eye. Although he was so outrageous, discussion of his personal or sexual life never seemed to enter the public fray; he once sued a reporter for stating that he was gay and won. His death from **AIDS**, which he tried to conceal, helped publicize the disease.

EDWARD MILLER

libraries, public

Creations of cities and states rather than the federal government, public libraries have been beacons of knowledge and refuges for generations of Americans, from **children** to the elderly, immigrants and the homeless. Libraries also have been sites of struggle over materials – **censorship** remains a constant threat – and social division, as segregated libraries scarred cities of the **South**. Some, like those of **New York** City, NY, **Philadelphia, PA**, **Chicago, IL** and **Los Angeles, CA**, have become international resource centers and architectural monuments to a vision of the city, as well as important public spaces. Others serve towns or small **neighborhoods** with books, meeting places, educational and career guidance and, increasingly, **Internet** access. Public libraries have earned the deep love of many Americans who treat them as a right to knowledge even as demands of service, finances and use challenge many systems to maintain their integrity.

Libraries vary in origins and extensions. The oldest circulating library in the US, the Library Company of Philadelphia, for example, was founded by the Junto Society and Benjamin Franklin in 1731; a public free library was chartered by the city 160 years later (1891). New York's Astor Library, founded by a merchant philanthropist, merged with others to constitute the New York Public Library in 1895. **New Orleans** assembled a public library with the help of nineteenth-century commercial lenders, while **San Francisco, CA**'s Board of Supervisors appropriated $24,000 for 6,000 books the public might read (but not borrow) in 1878–9.

Other libraries grew out of state initiatives: Vermont provided $100 to towns that would provide a matching $25 in 1896, and the Georgia Public Library there grew up in stores and homes of a small capitalist town.

Philanthropist Andrew Carnegie (1835–1919) patronized the construction of more than 2,500 library buildings – solid marble palaces with memorials to Western sages constitute an enduring image of "the library." These buildings housed children's facilities, reference services and government documents, as well as public spaces. Their growth has been linked in turn to the ongoing professionalization of librarians and definitions of knowledge within an American **community**; libraries created a symbolic **Bill of Rights** against censorship in 1939. Many have faced constant flare-ups about materials on **race**, sex and gender that may be found on children's and adults' shelves.

By the 1990s, libraries number over 8,000 nationwide and offer electronic services, audiovisual materials and reference assistance. This does not mean all are served well. While some older suburbs have strong systems, others have developed beyond existing rural facilities and do not find increasing state or local support. In the past, bookmobiles served outlying communities but now students may rely on schools rather than community spaces. Urban libraries face constant threats to budgets for staff as well as books; hours were severely curtailed in the New York system during the city's financial crisis.

Libraries also must respond to multiple constituencies in terms of language and interests: romance readers, civic advocates and high schoolers all have different demands that may entail scores of items checked out to each client. Books for the blind and foreign-language collections speak to other visions of citizenship. Electronic resources constitute a major issue in planning for the future, as they do in **college** and research libraries. More debates over censorship have been ignited by potential **Internet** access to objectionable sites.

Further reading

Toth, S. and Coughlan, J. (1991) *Reading Rooms*, New York: Pocket Books, (a marvelous anthology showing the enduring/endearing place of the library in the American imagination).

GARY McDONOGH

libraries, research (university and college)

Like the institutions of which they are a part, university and college libraries have embodied in their sense of grandeur the loftiest of American educational ideals. As neoclassical secular temples, gothic cathedrals, Norman castles, Victorian pa-laces or outsized utilitarian buildings, **campus** libraries have served as the rhetorical center of their institutions' educational program. Organized around a grand reading room with vaulted ceilings, the library functions as the place at the college where quiet reflection should yield lofty thoughts. Usually funded at 5 percent of the educational institution's overall budget, and named either for the most prominent private donors who have provided the building funds, or for the institution's founders or presidents, the library is that part of the institution that is least controversial.

At least since the turn of the nineteenth to the twentieth century (and especially after the Second World War), the numbers of volumes and the miles of shelving have been prominent markers of the relative ranking of the various university and private/public research libraries. Since the Second World War, even the biggest buildings have proven insufficient for storing the entire collection. Many university and some college libraries, even after numerous building additions and the installation of compact moveable shelving, have resorted to building or sharing large warehouses off site.

The older East Coast universities, Harvard and Yale, and the two eastern research libraries, the Library of Congress and the New York Public Library, have claimed the honors as the premier institutions of their kind. The Library of Congress is the largest of the world's libraries; Harvard the largest university library collection. These institu-tions, as well as their smaller private counterparts in the East and Stanford, the University of California and the University of Chicago, also amassed large collections of rare books and manuscripts from Europe, especially after the First World War, when the economic conditions of postwar life induced the wholesale transfer of cultural capital from the old world to the new.

The shift of the center of the university and college library world to the **Midwest** has accel-erated after the Second World War. The American Library Association, the leading national organiza-tion of librarians, is in **Chicago, IL**, as is the Center for Research Libraries, a shared repository for special materials from libraries around the country. The three great libraries at the Univer-sities of Illinois, Michigan and Indiana have been lavishly supported by their legislatures as a marker of state pride, rivaling their Eastern counterparts in size of collections. Michigan and Illinois house the country's premier library schools, having assumed that mantle from the private institutions, the **University of Chicago**, which closed its library school in the mid-1980s as did Columbia Uni-versity in the mid-1990s.

But it is not just the massive buildings, the great size of collections, measured for more than one hundred libraries in the millions of units – they are members of a group of large libraries known as the Association of Research Libraries, which maintains statistics on relative size of collections, budgets and staffs – that distinguishes American university and college libraries. Unlike the European models from which they have sprung, the campus libraries developed a service component that, when success-ful, merges the ideals of the institution with the practice of learning. Professional librarians, trained by the country's library schools, have made it a practice to humanize the huge scale of libraries and the information they contain for the students, faculty and researchers who use them. The relationship between the individual librarians and their patrons, facilitated by bibliographic instruc-tion, the creation of step-by-step guides to the use of the collections and services and the cataloging of materials into subject-specific open-shelf systems has distinguished American library practice for at least a century. Using rubrics developed by Melville Dewey – the Dewey Decimal System – and the Library of Congress' Classification and subject-headings systems, the physical organization of materials by subject has been the hallmark of the American library.

Electronic information technology came later to the university and college library than it did to the general US economy, but it has profoundly affected research libraries. Sharing cataloging information was the first step: the United States was the first place where a standardized record format, the MARC (Machine-readable cataloging record) for-mat, developed by the Library of Congress in the 1960s, took hold. This prepared the university and college library community to take advantage of the **Internet**, through the shared bibliographic utili-ties of OCLC (Online [first Ohio] Cataloging Library Center), the largest of its type in the world, and RLIN (the Research Libraries Information Network). The technological revolution of the 1990s permitted educational institutions to extend their walls outward through off-site access to research and undergraduate collections. This change has been felt most profoundly at the public universities, which have reached out to new populations through distance-learning programs, made possible by electronic full-text library collections. The librarians at the private and public institutions of higher learning have been at the forefront of making the World Wide Web useable and useful to students throughout the country, still applying the same principles of service and cataloging, large collections and ease of access.

Further reading

Wiegand, W. and Davis, D., Jr. (eds) (1994) *Encyclopedia of Library History*, New York: Garland.

ELLIOTT SHORE

Library of Congress *see* libraries, research (university and college); colleges and universities

life cycles/rites of passage

Biological events and changes of human life are given social meanings through both private reflection and public actions in American culture. From rituals welcoming the **birth** of a child through the fears surrounding **death**, these transitions are celebrated, acknowledged as points of crisis and stress, and incorporated into **family**, work and **community**. In so far as there is a typical or "model" American life cycle, these transitions tend to reflect the order of Judaeo-Christian traditions, codified and expanded by the state and glossed by **consumerism** and marketing. Questions arise, however, when Americans differ in their recognition and response to life cycles or are unable to recognize them because of economic insecurity. Moreover, rituals and meanings sometimes seem to fail to respond to changing conditions, like the increasing complexities of the transition to adulthood or the meanings of an extended period of mature adulthood, from the fifties into the eighties.

The birth of a child has social, psychological and religious significance for the family and the community into which the child is born. Rituals and medicine converge in the pregnancy and birth process, where technology has radically changed issues of **infertility** and control of births since the Second World War. Americans belonging to different religious and ethnic groups mark this in different ways: through ancestral or generational names, religious consecration, community celebrations and exchanges of gifts. High **teenage** and single-birth rates challenge these social celebrations, although the new child may provide important meanings for the mother, father and network. Public recognition of adoptions also has been adapted to these formats.

Birthdays, thereafter, remain important individual holidays, although they change over time. While children expect gifts, parties (and costly entertainment in **suburban**, **middle-class** homes), adults may play down these events. Special concern is attached to those that mark thresholds of a new decade – thirty, forty, fifty, etc. Hence, **sitcoms** joke about women who celebrate their twenty-ninth birthday repeatedly, while banter and pranks may alleviate the watershed of reaching the big "five-O."

Coming of age demarcates a second major stage, although there are many variations on how and when this is marked. Adolescence constitutes an extended component of the American life cycle where changes are social as well as biological. If adolescence is a time of multiple recognitions of change, adulthood proves much vaguer in its passages. American **advertising** and marketing strategies, for example, define distinct demographic categories of eighteen to twenty-four, twenty-five to thirty-four and thirty-four to fifty; in popular speech, "twenty-somethings" or young adults or "middle-age" also imply differences without any clear-cut transition.

Adulthood, in fact, implies a stabilization of social relationships, where the dominant culture model remains a family. Despite advertisers' insistence on the importance of attracting people of the opposite sex, dating and courtship in America do not follow any single pattern; they are segmented by region, culture, ethnicity, **class**, gender and **religion** as well as individual dynamics. Nor do they produce any single out-come. Nonetheless, roughly 70 percent of the population chooses to live in some form of a family, whose definitions continue to change on the basis of **divorce** and remarriage, as well as recognition of many kinds of commitment.

Weddings place civil and, in many cases, religious approval on the union of two persons. From the 1950s to the 1990s, the average age of the bride and groom at their first **marriage** has risen to the middle twenties. Weddings are notable occasions to display status and wealth. Yet, at this time, approximately 22 percent of the US popula-tion has never married.

Family, in turn, has been associated with an independent **home**, especially since suburban expansion opened new opportunities for the separation of nuclear families from parents and community. Many families also choose to have **children**, who may assure the continuity of family names, traditions and more. The sitcom model of a detached home, two photogenic kids, a dog and a station wagon (or **SUV** in the 1990s) masks many variations in real life. Above all, families have decreased in size – in 1994 the average family consisted of 3.19 members – and nearly half of all marriages end in divorce.

Family stages are also shaped by work, whether postponed, precluded or adapted to the increasing demands of families in which all parents work outside the home. Work itself provides a life cycle network for many adults, whether in baby showers or office romances. Work also produces adult crises, especially amidst the economic divisions and changes of the postwar period, in which dramatic expansions have been met with recessions and lay-offs as well as exclusions.

American media have not treated the aging process kindly or with dignity, although most of the country's discretionary income rests with indivi-duals fifty-five and over, who, in the early twenty-first century, may have decades of life ahead of them. As **baby boomers** have reached "**middle age**," they have found themselves caught between the youth culture they affirmed and negative images of **old age**. Some cultural historians have identified late middle age, usually in the forties and fifties, as a second adolescence, a time of significant transition, loss of one's identity and re-establishment of self as

one considers the inevitability of aging and one's own death. Since this may reflect diverse intersec-tions of marriage, work and family (shaped by **race**, gender and **class**), such transitions are not clearly demarcated socially. Instead of celebrating, in fact, many Americans talk about "midlife" crises, which may draw upon social and cultural features (especially "youthful" actions and changed appear-ance) as well as biology (menopause).

Advertising and marketing divide mature adult-hood into two stages – fifty to sixty-four and sixty-five and over – reflecting traditions of the work-place as much as biological or social changes. **Social Security** has affirmed retirement at sixty-five as a widespread milestone. Aging changes the family and household (the "empty nest" as children depart for **college** and independent life; disposal of a home and relocation). Other critical issues in these years may include loss of a spouse, adjust-ments to fixed and reduced incomes, and **health-care** issues. Family roles may be celebrated as rites of passage: the new role of grandparent may provide opportunities for nurturing, while **news-papers** and community and religious groups will join in the celebration of anniversaries, especially silver (twenty-five years) and golden (fifty years). Yet loneliness and burdens also arise. Caring for a spouse during this time may give purpose and direction, for example, but, despite medical assistance, it may exhaust the family's life savings. With individuals living longer, economic, health, educational, religious, media and marketing stra-tegies continue to seek and map out the demo-graphic trends that now extend into categories of the "old old" (those beyond their eighties), a rapidly expanding group.

Choosing how to manage this cycle of life, whether passively or aggressively, often determines the approach to the final stage, dying and death. The American way of dying is a multibillion-dollar industry, building on widespread beliefs in a life beyond human death. Nevertheless, it is the ultimate passage, irrevocably disrupting family and community, whether it comes at the end of a long and rich life or severs childhood, youth or young adulthood (taken as unnatural by most contemporary Americans, raised without local war or epidemics). Grief and mourning may be acknowledged through funeral rituals; the family and bereaved are encouraged to rely on the support of their friends, but to get on with life, or the family may divide over the will and disposition of the estate. A wide variety of public and private memorials – from commemorative monuments and cemeteries to more personal expressions and souvenirs – negotiate the finality of this passage.

In most of these experiences and interpretations, Americans scarcely differ from other global societies who endeavor to make sense of regular and intrusive changes in the lives of the men and women who compose them. Nonetheless, the diversity of peoples, expressions and interpretations evoked by these passages and the divergences between experience and established recognition underscore the complexity and changes of American culture.

Growth, transitions and rituals in American life have been investigated by social scientists, pondered by humanists and described in countless works of fiction and **mass media**.

Further reading

Sheehy, G. (1976) *Passages*, New York: Dutton. (Gives some interesting insights on changing experiences and meanings, especially in combination with her 1995 follow-up, which underscores emergent changes in cycles of adulthood and old age).
Sheehy, G. (1995) *New Passages*, New York: Random House.

GAIL HENSON

Limbaugh, Rush

b. 1951

Conservative political commentator. A nationally syndicated **television** and radio **talk-show** host, Limbaugh's gruff tirades against **taxes**, big government and **feminism** won him an enthusiastic public following in the 1990s. Scandals surrounding President **Clinton**, particularly those related to Clinton's alleged sexual indiscretions, were favorite targets for Limbaugh's barbs. Limbaugh's emergence as a national personality was part of an explosion in the influence of media that resulted in the blurring of distinctions between politics and entertainment.

SARAH SMITH

linguistics

Although many Americans consider this an abstract field, the study of **language** and meaning has, in fact, become a center for interdisciplinary interests and discussion. Its reach includes fields of communication and information processing linked to artificial intelligence and **computers**, questions of cognition and development from psychology and education, questions of meaning and truth from philosophy, issues of style and voice in literature and questions of society and culture. In all these, American scholars and thinkers have made important contributions to our understanding of language in general, as well as of its roles within American culture.

Indeed, from the early days of the American nation, scholars confronted questions of what language and identity meant, even if only to establish American standards for lexicon (Noah Webster) or education. Descriptive linguists later confronted the unique linguistic heritage of Native Indian tribes, documenting them in some cases as they disappeared. Anthropologists Edward Sapir and Benjamin Whorf also drew important contrasts between the worldviews embodied in these languages and those of Western Europe. Other approaches stressed function and relation among parts of language, while American linguistics learned from European structural linguistics in the 1930s and 1940s.

Noam **Chomsky** fostered a revolution in American linguistics in the 1950s and 1960s with transformational-generative grammar, which has thrived as both tool and theoretical arena. His stresses on individual effort, mechanisms of production, and grammaticality as accepted speech all evoke themes of American **individualism** and **community**. Some critics have argued that his concerns with free will and truth also intersect with his political activism.

Since the 1970s, linguists have also explored relations of language, society, meaning and change.

William Labov used sociological methods to document social divisions and changes in language; he also worked with black English formations as variations or alternatives to Standard English, a theme that has drawn conflicting attention from scholars, educators and families (see Rickford 1999). John Gumperz examined the strategic construction of conversations. Others have focused on the politics and ideologies of language, the nature and changes of bilingual communities, and critical relations of language, gender and power. The last has reached a wide popular audience in **self-help** books and works by Deboran Tannen, as well as feminist and gay critics. Recent work can be reviewed in central journals of the field, including *Language* and *Language in Society.*

Further reading

Chomsky, N. (1975) *Reflections on Language*, New York: Pantheon.

Gumperz, J. (1982) *Discourse Strategies*, New York: Cambridge.

Labov, W. (1972) *Sociolinguistic Patterns*, Philadelphia: University of Pennsylvania.

Newmeyer, F. (1980) *Linguistic Theory in America*, New York: Academic.

Rickford, J. (1999) *African American Vernacular English*, Malden: Blackwell.

Tannen, D. (1994) *Gender and Discourse*, New York: Oxford.

GARY McDONOGH

Lippman, Walter *see* columnists

literature, African American

African American literatures encompass a wide geographic territory which includes the United States, the **Caribbean** and Central and South America. The time frame also extends from the emigration and dispersal of peoples of African descent throughout the diaspora. In his comparative studies of international as well as trans-Atlantic slavery, sociologist and historian Orlando Patterson, in *Slavery and Social Death* (1982), dates the contact of Africans with the Atlantic world,

beginning in the late Middle Ages with the slave trade in the Atlantic islands of Madeira and the Canary Islands. Traditionally, African American literature was associated with the imaginative cultural products of US bondsmen and bondswomen, including those manumitted by law or by escape, and the freeborn. The almost exclusive focus of those literary studies was the written word. The genre preferences, moreover, were poetry, fiction and drama with the understanding that songs, folktales, sermons, essays and life stories were outside the realm of *belles lettres*.

The preoccupation with the written word also excluded the voices and cultural legacies of at least 4 million Southern slaves in the early 1800s who had no access to literacy as a result of violent repression, proscriptive legislation or the lack of opportunity. Leroi Jones (Amiri Baraka) offered a significant caution to scholars whose foundation for constructing an African American literary tradition depended almost entirely on written texts. In *Blues People: Negro Music in White America* (1963) Jones/Baraka insisted that tracing the line linking the spirituals to **blues** and **jazz** would help provide a more comprehensive understanding of African American historical and literary traditions, in part, because it would necessarily include practitioners and commentators from several economic classes, social communities and mentalities.

Since the critical and theoretical reconceptualizations of the 1960s regarding what constitutes the "literary" or what qualifies as "text," African American literatures are now recognized as embracing a continuum stretching from ancient African oral tradition to contemporary avatars of hip hop. The elements of that oral culture (praise-songs, epics, proverbs, riddles, folktales, etc.) serve as underpinnings for traditions transported, transmitted and reinvented for the specific locales of seventeenth through nineteenth century **Cuba**, Brazil, Surinam, Barbados, Richmond or **Boston**. The arbitrary distinctions between "literature" and the bio-mythographies known as autobiography have also faded. Slave narratives, the earliest of which appear in the 1750s, are no longer case histories as much as carefully crafted verbal portraits which share, with so-called fictive texts, as historian Hayden White affirmed, a concern with plotting, voice, narration, point of view and more. In Paule **Marshall**'s *Praisesong for the Widow* (1983) Avey Johnson, an upper-middle-class Westchester matron who has undergone a kind of cultural amnesia is reminded by her deceased Great Aunt Cuney, in the middle of a Caribbean cruise aboard the *Bianca Pride*, of the importance of telling and transmitting the stories of the ancestors to successive generations. In undergoing an allegorical Vodoun initiation, Avey returns to her given name, Avatara, and accepts responsibility for singing the ancient praisesongs of the would-be slaves who chose to walk home to Africa after their middle-passage transport to a place now known as Ibo Landing. She also rejects the experiential divides, dramatically alluded to in the Versailles Room which serves as the cruise ship's formal dining room, that reinforce apartheid notions of disciplinary, generic and cultural boundaries. That border crossing, a thematic and methodological pivot of African American literatures, surfaces powerfully in representative works that defy genre categorization: Jean Toomer's *Cane* (1923), Toni **Morrison**'s oeuvre and Toni Cade **Bambara**'s *Mama Day* (1993).

Contemporary scholars such as Henry Louis Gates, Jr., building on the Harlem Renaissance-era work of earlier folklorist-narrators, such as Zora Neale Hurston, trace lineage lines which connect, for example, West African insult poetry to tales such as "The Signifying Monkey" or the verbal duels of Caribbean calypso. There is an even shorter distance, moreover, between that cultural amalgam and the African American insult contests known as "playing the dozens."

In African American literatures, the word is a powerful tool of creation, destruction and transformation. Fiction-writer Toni Cade Bambara, among others, attests to a preoccupation with the potency of logos (word/language) as a key characteristic of an oral and written literature created by the muted and the unlettered. When that word is written, the cultural legacy of African American literatures usually begins with Lucy Terry's 1746 poem, "Bars Fight," or with the 1773 publication of Phillis Wheatley's *Poems on Various Subjects*. In that volume, a young **teenage** and sickly Boston slave creates verbal portraits, which are praisesongs in their own right, celebrating English and American aristocrats. Writing in

the poetic meter with much of the classic allusions of Dryden and Pope, Wheatley suffered for more than two centuries from the calumny that she had not used her privileged status or education as a slave-poet to combat slavery directly. In the last quarter century, however, there has been a revival of interest in the, perhaps, too subtle code by which Wheatley offers a stinging condemnation of slavery by assuring General Washington that the eyes of the world are fixed on its newest democratic experiment. Her self-deprecation in the midst of a poetic address to the students of what we now know as Harvard University is part of a pattern of a deliberate use of code to render opaque to masters and mistresses the subversion that hides behind the grin and the smile. Wheatley helps to establish a tradition of writing with invisible ink as a way of offering a scathing critique and parody of institutions that are and were incongruous in a new democratic Republic which uses "freedom" as a way of describing and defining its charisma. The immediate legatees of her consciously crafted dissimulation include writers such as William Wells Brown (*Clotel*, 1853), Charles Chesnutt (*Marrow of Tradition*, 1901), Pauline Hopkins (*Contending Forces*, 1900), Ralph Ellison (*Invisible Man*, 1947) and Charles R. Johnson (*Middle Passage*, 1990).

This use of double voicing functions simultaneously as a defensive and offensive weapon and as a re-appropriation of the dual consciousness W.E.B. **Du Bois** named in *Souls of Black Folk* (1903) as the albatross of African American experience. Nobel prize-winning novelist, Toni Morrison, a beneficiary of both oral and written traditions, also refers to such duality in her collection of 1990 Massey Lectures in the history of American civilization compiled in a volume entitled *Playing in the Dark: Whiteness and the Literary Imagination* (1992). Morrison asserts that the canon of American literature has its roots in the construction of blackness as a foil against which to define whiteness. She insists that American literature is inconceivable without the omnipresence of this largely invisible other who helps provide a sense of national identity and cohesion.

LINDA-SUSAN BEARD

literature, race and ethnicity

The decisions about whether and how to generalize about the study of minority literature are complex because of the history of minorities in the US and the academic study of their literatures and cultures. **African American** contributions to the literature and culture of the US are older than the Republic; however, academic institutionalization of their study came more recently, emerging with the **Civil Rights movement** in the 1960s. Interest in and study of the cultural production of other people of color followed, but whether and how they are analogous remains a topic of debate. Do we define minority cultures by country of origin, as in **Chicano** studies? By language, as in **Hispanic** literature? By broader area of origin, as in **Asian American** or **Caribbean**? Further, is it useful or true to focus on similarities among the experiences of ethnic minorities within and immigrants to the US – a shared history of diaspora, oppression, adaptation, contribution and resistance? Or is it more important to note the differences within these histories – slavery for African Americans, centuries of intertwined history for Chicanos/Latinos, no **immigration** tale to tell for **American Indians**? Further, how do we talk about and account for the influence of "home" cultures: the difference between, say, Japanese and Filipino culture and history that makes the idea of "Asian American" so hard to generalize? What difference does it make that many immigrant groups now, in the age of cheaper global travel, have a transnational identity, retaining personal and cultural ties to home countries rather than largely severing or transforming them upon immigration? Does a similarity of approach to minority cultures in any way repeat one of the errors of racism by defining these diverse literatures in terms of their difference from the presumed center, that is, mainstream white culture? Finally, at what point, if ever, does the importance of minority contributions to literature and literary study lead us to redefine American culture so completely that to define minority literature separately stops making sense?

While the movement to abolish slavery saw the publication of slave narratives and other important cultural documents that form the nineteenth-century canon of African Americans (the Harlem Renaissance and Black Arts movement are other crucial periods in an ongoing literary culture), it was the **Civil Rights movement** that established African Americans' crucial academic presence and the "recovery" of many. The existence of programs and departments in Black Studies, Africana Studies and African American literature and culture attests to the historical emergence of a diversity of approaches since the 1960s. Fueled by the Civil Rights movement in the 1960s and Aztlán in **California** in the 1970s, Chicano/**Latino** culture also entered the academy – as did the study of Native American literature and cultures. **Asian American** Studies also largely began as a West Coast, indeed a Pacific, phenomenon. By now, minority literature has become increasingly important among both academic and mainstream readers, students and critics of American literature in general.

The study of minority literature and cultures has grown, stimulating and stimulated by broader political events and by the poststructuralist literary theories that refused to see literary artifacts as aesthetic objects separable from the historical and political context in which they emerged. Minority critics and theorists noted how putatively "pure" aesthetic standards had been used by a white-male-dominated literary mainstream, consciously or unconsciously, to enforce or explain the devaluation and exclusion of the work of non-white authors' politically committed texts and non-traditional forms. Alternative literary theories emerged to account for the ways in which minority voices and the literary forms they used shaped, were shaped by, and provided insight into the strains of exclusion and oppression by mainstream culture, demonstrating that literary differences were not defects but occasions of and for reflection.

Emerging in the 1970s, Ethnic Studies marks an alliance and shared approach among minority scholars. The idea of Ethnic Studies is a commitment to seeing minority literature in cultural, historical and political context, and maintaining a sense of the cultural specificity of different traditions such as Native American or Asian Pacific Islander, while having a common ground for critiquing mainstream culture from the point of view of the excluded or forgotten margin.

While an awareness of the richness of minority discourse has reshaped the study of American literature and culture, many scholars affirm the continuing need for their separate study. This reflects both an affirmation of the literary and theoretical contributions they will make, and an insistence that social justice for minorities is far from having been achieved, either inside or outside the academy.

Writers of all ethnicities have enjoyed increased success and recognition, in genre fiction as well as in serious fiction and poetry. The emerging canons of especially well-known, popular and widely taught authors grow and change constantly. Dominating the last years of the twentieth century have been African American novelists Toni **Morrison** (a **Nobel** laureate), Alice **Walker** and Gloria **Naylor**. Among Latino writers and Chicano novelists and poets are the likes of Sandra **Cisneros**, Rudolfo Anaya and Cherrie Moraga, while such writers as Cristina García (from **Cuba**) and Julia Alvarez (from the Dominican Republic) also enjoy a high readership. Asian American writers abound: among them are **Chinese American** novelist Maxine Hong **Kingston**, and her antagonist Frank **Chin**, as well as the popular Amy **Tan** and Fae Ng. The late **Korean American** Theresa Kak Kyung Cha, writer and performance artist, is revered by poststructuralist critics, while, more recently, novelist Chang-Rae Lee has had wide critical success. Among **Filipino American** writers, Jessica Hagedorn is probably best known. There are also many Native American writers, though Louise **Erdrich**, Michael Dorris, MacArthur prize-winner Leslie Marmon **Silko** and Sherman Alexie probably stand out.

Organizations exist to foster the study of each tradition. Further, there are important umbrella organizations, for example the MELUS (multi-ethnic literatures of the United States) journal, established 1974, and annual conference established in 1986. As indicated earlier, no consensus exists about approaches to minority experience and literature. If, for example, Werner Sollors is associated with a traditional liberal view of **immigration** and **assimilation**, Ron Takaki's popular approach emphasizes, in contrast, the maintaining of cultural difference. Within each group are many well-established scholars. A constellation of high-profile African American scholars representing different points of view and emphases includes, for example, Henry Louis **Gates**, Jr., bell **hooks**, Barbara Christian and Houston Baker. Well-known Asian American scholars include Elaine Kim, Sau-ling Wong and Lisa Lowe; Chicano/Latino critics include Norma Alarcón, Alfred Arteaga and Gloria Anzaldúa.

ALYSON BARDSLEY

literature and gender

A variety of approaches to the topic of women and literature has emerged in the last thirty years as Women's Studies has solidified and expanded as an academic field, building on the earlier work of women writers and philosophers. While the rise of academic **feminism** in the US coincides to some degree with the **women's liberation** movement of the late 1960s and early 1970s, its history both extends back further in time and is also largely yet to be written.

Much feminist literary criticism and women-and-literature courses take writing by women as their object of analysis, noting that women have borne witness to their lives and assumed artistic authority despite patriarchal culture's prohibitions, its denigration of female minds and imaginations, and the material difficulties historically facing women writers, including the demands of wife- and motherhood and the limitations of women's education and property rights. But within feminist criticism emphases vary. Some readers and critics simply affirm the value of women's texts by according them attention equal to or greater than men's texts, looking to balance the historic dominance of the masculine point of view. Others attempt to identify a female tradition of writing – women writers consciously examining the status of their sex in their place and time and building upon the work of literary foremothers in the context of women's relative silence. Biographically informed approaches, using paraliterary documents and information in order to take account of the effect of social pressures and expectations on women's creative lives and expression, is held by some to be more effectively feminist than the more traditional approach of taking the literary object out of its context. Further, in a gesture critical of aesthetic hierarchies and cognizant of women's exclusion from their formation, literary importance and critical attention are accorded to non-traditional and unpublished writing genres like diaries and letters in this approach. Deriving alternative criteria from the form and content of women's writing – criteria that dissent from and criticize the existing literary canon – is a similar project of feminist criticism. This often results in the revaluation of popular, sentimental and politically or socially engaged writing: writing that manifests other interests and seeks out different audiences than does the high literary culture historically dominated by men. As a consequence of these approaches, much of literary history is in the process of being rewritten.

Feminist criticism is not limited to women's writing. Working on the assumption that gender roles are not a given but that gender is a social construct and gender ideology is propounded and reinforced through literature as through other social institutions, gender critics read literary texts from the masculine mainstream using gender as a lens. They explore these texts' unacknowledged gender biases and note their dependence on gender stereotypes, on the flattening and simplification of women characters and of relations between men and women. Further, they uncover these texts' regulation of gender roles through encouraging identification with normative gender behavior and punishment of gender deviance. Thus feminist critics extend their project to the examination and critique of masculine roles, deeming those roles no less constructed, and constricting, than the feminine; they further note the tacit enforcement of heterosexuality in much mainstream literature.

Beyond feminist approaches to literary works and literary history is the domain of feminist theory, in which writers work to limn the historical, political, psychological and linguistic means by which gender ideology has been formed and reproduced over time. Further, increasingly, the work of women writers and critics of color, third-world critics, **lesbians** and **working-class** writers has functioned to extend and critique earlier feminist criticism. These critics argue, from their various positions, that Anglo-European fem-

inism has historically been unselfconsciously white, **middle class** and heterosexual in its approach and focus, and has merely extended masculine individualist notions of the self to white women. Further, they argue that Western women were and have remained complicit with such forces as colonialism, racism and classism. While working to include the literature and history of such doubly excluded women, these critics further break down the category of "women" and attest to the multiplicity of women's lives and roles. Rather than claiming multiple victimization and exclusion based upon both gender and other categories of identity, they work to identify alternative histories and literatures, including the previously unrecognized traditions, notions of selfhood, and forms of power and **community**, among, for example, ethnic-minority, **queer**, or disabled women.

Gilbert and Gubar's work in the 1970s was an epoch-making look at an alternative set of women writers' practices and traditions. Elaine Showalter and Catherine Stimpson's early work is also from this period, while Carol Gilligan's work on "women's voices" as unique continues to have influence among those interested in identifying "women's ways of knowing." European psychoanalytic and poststructuralist criticism by Helene Cixous, Julia Kristeva and the Lacanian critic Luce Iragaray enjoyed a strong vogue in the 1980s. American critics doing their own work involving psychoanalysis and gender included Jane Gallop and Shoshana Felman. In the late 1980s and early to mid-1990s, Donna Harraway pioneered arguments from a postmodern, post-gender position, while Judith Butler incorporated poststructuralist philosophy in her work to emphasize that gender is performed rather than essential. These theoretical positions have influenced how women's work is read, de-emphasizing the idea of an alternative tradition and focusing instead on the constitutive and critical incoherences of "the subject" – i.e. the self-conscious individual – constituted under patriarchy and through its language. Alternatively, critics like Janice Radway, departing from an emphasis on academic expertise, have sought to learn and acknowledge what women readers of various class and educational backgrounds understand about their own cultural practices as readers. Among the various theorists pointing out the limitations of white feminism's approaches, some-times utilizing, sometimes criticizing its focus on the incoherence or non-existence of the subject, have been African American critics like bell hooks, Chicanas/Latinas like Gloria Anzaldúa and post-colonial thinkers like Gayatri Chakravorty Spivak.

The reading and teaching of literature by women is now the norm rather than the exception. Besides the existence of Women's Studies classes and programs, mainstream anthologies (like those from Norton, Longmans, and Heath) now incor-porate work by women side-by-side with that of men as a matter of course, and the anthologies have grown correspondingly. Further, both women-centered presses (like England's Virago, the Feminist Press of the City University of New York, or Kitchen Table) and mainstream publishers have joined in the process of publishing new women's texts and recovering and reprinting earlier ones. Mary Shelley's *Frankenstein* and Maxine Hong **Kingston**'s *Woman Warrior* (1976) are among the most-read books in **high schools** and **college** freshman courses throughout the US. The incor-poration of feminist approaches into the academic mainstream does not lessen the importance of feminist academic and para-academic institutions like the journals *Signs* (established 1975), *Women's Studies* (established 1972), *Women's Review of Books* (1984) and *Genders* (1988). These institutions and others continue to testify to the notion that from women's history and literature springs a fount of criticism of the mainstream and a celebration of the many other forms of seeing and being that exist.

ALYSON BARDSLEY

little-league baseball

Founded in Williamsport, Pennsylvania, in 1939, little-league **baseball** expanded rapidly into many **suburban** communities during the 1950s. With more than 5,000 leagues in the US and Canada, by 1960 baseball was easily the leading participant sport in the country. Leagues are divided into different age groups up to the age of twelve (fifteen in the senior leagues); play is colored by baseball rituals including a little-league pledge. Its world

series in Williamsport, televised on ABC's *Wide World of Sport*, recently featured teams from **Japan** and **Latin America**.

While little-league has sponsored clinics in Latin American countries like the Dominican Republic (noted for producing major-league players), it has not sponsored them in the **inner cities** of the United States. Only 15 percent of major leaguers are now **African American**, whereas in **basketball** the figure is closer to 78 percent.

In the 1990s, little-league is losing out to **soccer**; it has not attracted the large numbers of girls engaging in sport since the 1970s.

ROBERT GREGG

Little Rock Central High School

One of the leading cities of the New **South**, noted for its moderation on racial issues, Little Rock seemed likely to desegregate after the **Supreme Court**'s *Brown* decision. In 1957, however, Governor Orval Faubus, previously considered a moderate, who was facing a difficult bid for a third term, used the race card to help win re-election. In a televised address, Faubus announced that integration at Central High School could not proceed because it would precipitate violence and sent in the national guard to enforce this decision. The insistence of the **children**, in the face of virtual lynch mobs, forced the issue, leading President **Eisenhower** to federalize the Arkansas National Guard and send in the 101st Airborne Division.

ROBERT GREGG

lobbyists

The term "lobbyist" refers to any person or group that attempts to sway the actions of a political representative through a sustained effort at persua-sion. In the British Parliament of the seventeenth century, lobbyists would try to influence members personally as they walked through the lobby of the legislature to cast their votes, hence the origin of the term. In more recent times, lobbying is often accomplished through informal meetings between lobbyists (or their clients) and politicians, financial contributions, or, more publicly, through media campaigns and other forms of organized publicity. Although all political pressure groups try to "lobby" politicians in most modern liberal democracies, the word "lobbyist" is generally restricted to those whose professional livelihoods depend on their skill in directly influencing public policy on behalf of interested parties – such as trade unions, private companies, or industry organizations – who pay them to do so.

Lobbyists have been a part of America's public life for some time, and probably have always affected political decisions to some extent. In the 1800s they were often referred to as "lobbiers," and were already under attack. The American poet Walt Whitman called them "lousy combings and born freedom sellers of the Earth." Then, as now, critics feared the representative political process – whereby legislators try to consider and reflect primarily the interests of the people who elected them – was being subverted through the influence of paid "insiders" like professional lobbyists. In more recent years, opponents have accused powerful and rich lobbies, such as that of the **National Rifle Association**, of protecting the interests of their clients to the detriment of society. Such worries have only escalated in recent years as numerous high-placed political figures – men such as Michael Deaver, the former chief of staff for President Ronald **Reagan**, or former Secretary of the Treasury Lloyd Bentsen – left their formal political posts and moved directly into the more lucrative sphere of the private lobbying industry, such actions seemingly dissolving fully the barrier between private interest and public good. In 1998 journalists credited lobbyists working for the **tobacco** industry with sabotaging anti-tobacco legislation that most of the American public supported.

Despite criticisms of professional lobbyists and of insider lobbying, however, attempts to reform the political system so as to restrict their influence have been largely unsuccessful. In the 1990s, politicians of all ideological stripes found it worthwhile to decry the nefarious influence of money in politics, but little practical progress was made in solving the problem. Constitutionally, it is difficult to align any

restriction on political lobbying with the commitment to freedom of speech. It is also not clear that all lobbying is necessarily destructive of the democratic process; much lobbying, for example, is undertaken by public interest groups of all ideological stripes. More practically, any restriction that might pass constitutional muster would have to be voted upon by the very politicians who now profit so handsomely from the largesse of lobbyists and their clients. In the summer of 1997, a Senate investigation of lobbyists' influence in the federal political process provoked relatively little public interest. This had changed by the spring of 2000. The decision of Republican Senator John McCain of Arizona to put campaign finance reform at the center of his appeal during the spring's presidential primaries sparked national concern over the influence of big money in politics.

Further reading

Deakin, J. (1966) *The Lobbyists*, Washington, DC: Public Affairs Press.

Safire, W.F. (1978) *Safire's Political Dictionary*, 3rd edn, New York: Ballantine Books.

MARK BREWIN

Loewy, Raymond Fernand

b. 1893; d. 1986

French-born industrial designer of America's modern style, emphasizing streamlined flow and legibility, Thomas Hine characterized him as an engineer "of the emotions, making the connection between people and machines" (1986: 62). His classic designs include American icons such as the Coca-Cola bottle and the Greyhound bus, yet his work ranged from **fashion**, cookware and copy machines to automotive innovations for Studebaker and the American **space** program. Apart from his influence from the 1930s onwards in shaping the present and future, he was also a precursor to conglomerates through which architects (Michael **Graves**), fashion designers (Ralph Lauren) and **home** advisors (Martha **Stewart**) have created packaged styles for living as mass-market consumer goods.

Further reading

Loewy, R.F. (1979) *Industrial Design*, New York: Overlook.

Hine, T. (1986) *Populuxe*, New York: MJ.

GARY McDONOGH

Lorde, Audre

b. 1934; d. 1992

Outspoken **African American** lesbian feminist poet, memoirist and activist. Her published poetry includes *The First Cities* (1968), *Coal* (1976) and *Our Dead Behind Us* (1986). Among her other works, *Cancer Journals* (1980) depicts her experiences with breast **cancer**, while *Zami: A New Spelling of My Name* (1982) is constructed as a biomythography. Among political speeches, she was also the author of *Apartheid USA* (1986).

GARY McDONOGH

Los Angeles, CA

No other city, except perhaps **New York City, NY**, captures and reflects American imagination like Los Angeles. What began as an unpopulated, ecologically rich, mountainous and coastal land straddling numerous tectonic plates, evolved into one of the most densely populated, ethnically diverse and technologically developed cities in the world. In between these two extremes, Los Angeles was a gathering place for several indigenous groups, a Spanish colonial outpost and a northern Mexican **frontier**. LA remains a Promised Land for immigrants, an Anglo-American mecca and a global dreamscape.

At the heart of Los Angeles lies El Pueblo de Nuestra Señora Reina de Los Angeles de Porciuncula, founded by the Spaniards in 1781. In 1998, beyond the city (estimated population 3,597,536) and county bearing the name, Los Angeles extends over approximately 33,000 square miles in five counties with over 15 million inhabitants. The original indigenous and Spanish inhabitants, and subsequent Anglo- and **African American** settlers from the eastern United States, have been joined by large numbers of immigrants from every continent seeking a better life. In 1990 major local immigrant groups (populations over 100,000) included Armenians, Chinese, **Filipinos**, Guatemalans, Japanese, Koreans, Mexicans, Salvadorans and Vietnamese, a diversity that has accelerated since 1960s changes in US **immigration** law.

Yet, economic and demographic development of Los Angeles has been uneven. Local legislation in the early twentieth century favored **race** and **class** divisions, reinforced by social attitudes. The result was a highly segregated city where wealthy white suburbs bordered significantly poorer ethnic **neighborhoods**. A massive freeway system has fostered both **segregation** and metropolitan expansion, and added to the unique commuter character of Los Angeles' growth pattern. Between 1970 and 1990, the population rose 45 percent, while developed land surface area increased at almost ten times this rate. LA styles in **architecture** (with flowing interiors open to outdoor living), **fashion** and **food** reflect this suburban wealth. Sports teams like Anaheim's Mighty Ducks in **hockey** and amusements like **Disneyland** reflect centripetal growth as well (other major LA teams include the Lakers in **basketball**, Dodgers (moved from Brooklyn) in **baseball** and **football**'s Rams). Downtown development, including the Museum of Contemporary Art and surrounding office and residential towers, also has emphasized social and racial divisions.

These same divisions caused or exacerbated a number of major events in the city's contemporary history. In August 1965, after a decade of **urbanrenewal** programs destroyed African American neighborhoods and reduced already scarce employment opportunities and affordable housing, residents of the Watts **community** rebelled. Fourteen thousand National Guard troops were deployed and a state of martial law was declared. Thirty-five died and property damage totaled over $200 million. The **Kerner Commission** formed after the riots cited white-on-black racism as a major cause.

Five years after the Watts Rebellion, the peaceful August 29 **Chicano** moratorium against the **Vietnam War** turned into another riotous racial incident. In response to a minor theft of soda by **teenagers** at a local liquor store, Los Angeles

police and sheriffs rushed to nearby Laguna Park where 30,000 adults and **children** had gathered. Among the casualties was *Los Angeles Times* reporter Rubén Salazar, who was killed by a tear-gas projectile fired by police into a crowded bar.

On April 29, 1992 what became known broadly as the 1992 Los Angeles riots began. An acquittal of four white Los Angeles Police Department officers accused of using excessive force on African American motorist Rodney **King** sparked immediate protests that escalated into days of violence and rebellion. African American protesters were joined by **Latinos** who vented decades of oppression and frustration on targets in their own communities: local business owners and landlords. Korean immigrants in the affected areas were hit particularly hard. Arrests, deportations and other reprisals were severe but suspiciously slow, allowing the destruction of entire ethnic communities and furthering racial tensions. It was the largest American civil disturbance in the twentieth century with over $1 billion in damage and 13,000 arrests. The riots sparked uprisings in other urban areas nationwide.

Masking these serious socio-economic and political issues, however, are the glamorous and dangerous stereotypes of Los Angeles: **Hollywood**, mansions, movie stars, the fabulous Getty museum, earthquakes, wildfires and freeway shootings. In fact, whole books deal with the representation of the city, especially in film, which has both made Los Angeles a constant setting and transformed it into anywhere in the universe via Hollywood sets. In 1981 former Hollywood studio-system actor, California governor and US President Ronald **Reagan** said: "Film is forever. It is the motion picture that shows all of us not only how we look and sound but – more important – how we feel." Los Angeles has taken on a powerful public persona of its own, that of the decadent Hollywood star, extreme and highly visible in everything.

Separating the facts from the myths about Los Angeles' history is difficult, but therein lies its future. Numerous scholars in the late 1990s dubbed Los Angeles the third-world capital of the United States and suggested that it is a microcosm of both national and global socio-economic development. Global restructuring has caused a decline in the Los Angeles economy. Coupled with people of white, European ancestry becoming the new "minorities" in Los Angeles and around the world, nativist politics have increased. Policies such as California's Propositions 187 and 209, restricting immigrant and ethnic rights, are examples of this trend. Los Angeles' struggle for the future will be not just one of politics and economics, but ultimately one of definition of American identity.

Los Angeles has been highly documented, often by researchers affiliated with major local institutions like the University of California, Los Angeles, the University of Southern California or the Claremont Colleges.

Further reading

Acufia, R. (1996) *Anything but Mexican: Chicanos in Contemporary Los Angeles*, London: Verso.

Davis, M. (1990) *City of Quartz*, New York: Vintage.

Davis, M. (1997) *Ecology of Fear*, New York: Henry Holt.

Caughey, J. and Caughey, L. (1976) *Los Angeles: Biography of a City*, Berkeley: University of California.

Scott, A. and Soja, E. (1996) *The City: Los Angeles and Urban Theory at the End of the Twentieth Century*, Los Angeles: University of California.

Waldinger, R. and Bozorgmehr, M. (eds) (1996) *Ethnic Los Angeles*, New York: Russell Sage.

SUSAN MARIE GREEN

lotteries *see* gambling and lotteries; draft

Louganis, Greg

b. 1960

Best-known for his diving feats at the 1988 **Olympic Games** in Seoul, when he continued to compete after hitting his head against the board during the preliminary rounds. After being stitched up, Louganis came back to win the gold medals for both platform and springboard, as he had at the 1988 **Los Angeles, CA** games.

At Seoul, Louganis was already HIV-positive, taking AZT to enable him to compete. A year later he announced his retirement and became a stage actor. Two of his roles were as gay men; in 1994 he publicly acknowledged his sexuality at Gay Games IV in **New York** City. His autobiography, *Breaking the Surface* (1995), describes the experiences of a gay athlete.

ROBERT GREGG

Louisville and Lexington, KY

Founded in 1778 at the falls of the Ohio River, Louisville (population 255,511; metro 999,267) blends northern industrial urbanism and southern culture. A transport center, it also has produced cigarettes, bourbon, heavy appliances and **automobiles**. It is home to the Kentucky Derby at Churchill Downs racetrack on the first Saturday in May, the University of Louisville and broad-based local traditions in **basketball**, and Actor's **Theater**'s regional festival of New American plays. Rapidly growing Lexington (population 249,139), 100 miles away, is a center for Bluegrass **horse** farms and the University of Kentucky.

GARY McDONOGH
CINDY WONG

Love Canal

In 1978 news stories exploded about environmental disaster in a working-class **neighborhood** in Niagara Falls, New York. Love Canal – an 1879 project to market energy from the Niagara River – was used in 1942–52 to dump chemical wastes from Hooker Chemicals (later absorbed by Occidental Petroleum). The city subsequently acquired the site for a school, knowing its past, and also permitted homes. Odors and residues forced **EPA** investigations by 1976; most residents fled over the next three years. Yet, their battles for compensation clarified the need for **community organization** to fight for environmental protection and against problems of regulations and responsibilities in corporate environmental damage. Final suits were settled by 1998, with Occidental paying $400

million to federal and state agencies; some went to clean-up and some to residents who complained of transgenerational impacts. The contemporary study of A. Levine's (1982) *Love Canal* has been updated in L. Gibb's (1998) *Love Canal*. An iconic environmental disaster, its impact permeates movies and readings in cases like the Worcester, Massachusetts pollution central to the 1995 book *A Civil Action* and the 1999 movie that followed.

Further reading

Gibb, L. (1998) *Love Canal*, New York: New Society.
Harr, J. (1995) *A Civil Action*, New York: Random House.
Levine, A. (1982) *Love Canal*, New York: Lexington.

GARY McDONOGH
CINDY WONG

Lowell, Robert

b. 1917; d. 1977

He would not be a proper scion (such good **New England** stock!). He would not be a Harvard man (rather a "fugitive" at Kenyon College). He would not fight in the First World War (366 days in prison). He would not write Auden's English (*Lord Weary's Castle*). He would not abandon a precarious sanity (McLean's Hospital). He would not disown the America he'd inherited and he would "not scare" (*Life Studies*, 1959). He would not translate properly (*Imitations*, 1961). He would not divorce poetry from personality (*Notebooks*, *1967–8*, *The Dolphin*, *Day by Day*). He would be our greatest poet.

DANIEL BOSCH

low riders

American sedans retooled to hug the ground (or "dance" through manipulation of their hydraulic system), especially popular among Mexican Americans in the western **borderlands**. Since the late 1970s, low riders have become assertive "vehicles of display," boasting elaborate paint jobs, murals and interior additions. They have increasingly been recognized in the 1990s as ethnic symbols, while gaining visibility in car shows and *Low Rider* magazine (founded 1978). The disjunction of **automobile** and culture they imply becomes visible in *Bulworth* (1998) when the white hero finds his borrowed car rocking hysterically as he tries to drive it.

See also: Chicanos/as

GARY McDONOGH

Lucas, George and *Star Wars*

b. 1944

Film-maker George Lucas envisioned his film series as both a return to the Saturday morning movie serials he had loved as a youth and as a retelling of myths which had taken root long before he was born. As movies, *Star Wars* (1977), *The Empire Strikes Back* (1980) and *The Return of the Jedi* (1983) set new standards in special-effects production. They were especially popular with an audience segment which in the trilogy's wake would become the film studios' primary target: the youth market. In 1999 *The Phantom Menace* became the first installment of three prequels for the original *Star Wars*, with even more extensive merchandizing and licensing.

ROBERT ANDERSON

Luce, Clare Booth

b. 1903; d. 1987

Pathbreaking writer and public servant. Although born near poverty, she worked her way up through *Vogue* and *Vanity Fair* to marry *Time* magnate Henry Luce before producing her wonderfully catty play, *The Women* (1936), about gender and society. In the 1940s, she became a congresswoman from Connecticut. Later, she became the first woman ambassador to a major European country, serving in Italy between 1953 and 1957, perhaps as a nod to her highly publicized 1946 conversion to Catholicism. Luce continued to serve as advisor to **Republican** presidents for decades.

GARY McDONOGH

Lutherans

The 8.3 million Lutherans in the United States trace their origin primarily to immigrants from Germany and the countries of Scandinavia. Originally organized along national and language lines, American Lutherans now find themselves in eleven separate bodies, the largest of which is the Evangelical Lutheran Church in America (ELCA) with over 5 million members and almost 11,000 churches. The second-largest body is the Lutheran Church – Missouri Synod, with a little over 2,600,000 members in almost 6,100 congregations. The other Lutheran bodies, much smaller and regionally and ethnically diverse, include the Evangelical Lutheran Synod, the American Association of Lutheran Churches, the Apostolic Lutheran Church of America, the Church of Lutheran Brethren of America, the Church of the Lutheran Confession, the Conservative Lutheran Association, the Estonian Evangelical Lutheran Church, the Latvian Evangelical Lutheran Church in America and the Wisconsin Evangelical Lutheran Synod.

The ECLA is the fifth-largest Christian body in the United States. Its predecessor bodies date to the mid-eighteenth century. The Augsburg Confession provides the doctrinal standards of the church. It operates eight seminaries and twenty-eight **colleges and universities**.

The Lutheran Church – Missouri Synod, founded in 1847, has 6,000 congregations in the United States. It operates the largest Protestant elementary- and secondary-school system in the United States, with 13,795 students enrolled. Its **publishing** arm, Concordia Publishing House, is the third-largest Protestant publisher. The Arch Books' **children**'s series alone has sold more than 55 million copies. Two ministries reach out to blind and deaf people. One thousand volunteers in fifty work centers make Braille publications available for the blind. Of the eighty-five congregations for deaf people in the United States, fifty-nine are Missouri Synod Lutheran congregations.

Doctrinal disputes have marked Lutherans in America as they did the founder of the Lutheran branch of Christianity, Martin Luther. In the 1970s, for example, Missouri Synod Lutherans felt that their main seminary, Concordia Theological

Seminary, was not teaching the belief that the Bible was without error in its original manuscripts. Tensions rose to the point that when three-quarters of the students boycotted classes, the president was removed. Many faculty and students then established what became known as "Seminex," the Concordia Seminary in Exile.

On the other hand, a spirit of ecumenism has been blowing through the largest Lutheran denomination, the ELCA. It has entered into dialogue with the Roman Catholic Church over the basic theological issue of the Reformation, the doctrine of justification by faith. Lutherans and Catholics have come much closer to a mutual understanding on this issue as a result. Within the Protestant family, the Evangelical Lutheran Church in America has joined with the **Presbyterian Church** (USA), the United Church of Christ and the Reformed Church in America to recognize the validity of the ordination of each other's pastors.

Further reading

Ellwood, R. and Partin, H.B. (1988) *Religious and Spiritual Groups in Modern America*, Inglewood Cliffs: Prentice Hall.

Gallup, G., Jr. and Castelli, J. (1989) *The People's Religion*, New York: MacMillan Publishing Company.

Lindner, E.W. (ed.) (1998) *Yearbook of American & Canadian Churches 1998*, Nashville: Abingdon Press.

Melton, J.G. (1977) *Encyclopedia of American Religions*, Gale: Detroit.

GAIL HENSON
JEFFERSON I. RITCHIE

Lyme disease

Bacterial infection transmitted by ticks that live on deer or mice. Marked by a bull's-eye rash, malaise, fatigue and muscle aches, it is often misdiagnosed, although it will respond readily to antibiotics. If left untreated, it can become disabling. First noted in suburban Lyme, Connecticut, in 1975, by the early 1990s more than 10,000 cases were reported annually, chiefly in the **Northeast**, **Midwest**

and **California**. In these areas, it has challenged outdoor life patterns as people cover up and spray insecticides to avoid ticks, or abandon wooded areas altogether. Its suburban demographics may also have encouraged rapid development of a vaccine, which became available in 1997.

GARY McDONOGH

lynching

"Strange fruit hanging from the poplar trees," sang Billie Holliday in 1939 about the hanging and torture of **African American** males (generally) by mob violence, often in the **South**. As many as 4,000 people died in this way between 1889 and 1940. Lynching turned the racial divisions of American society into blood spectacle, especially in times of social crisis. Campaigns against this horror began at the beginning of the twentieth century; by the 1940s, it had generally disappeared (although federal legislation against it was never passed). It remains a horrifying occurrence (see Emmett **Till**) in postwar America, as well as an emotional reference in metaphors like "high-tech lynching" (see Clarence **Thomas**). Moreover, the brutal killing of gay student Matthew Shepherd in Wyoming and other **hate crimes** show that lynching may not be so far away from contemporary American life as most citizens would like to believe.

ROBERT GREGG
GARY McDONOGH

Lynn, Loretta

b. 1935

Trailblazing female singer/songwriter in **country music**, born in Butcher Hollow, Kentucky. At thirteen she became pregnant and left home to be with her husband Mooney. She taught herself to play guitar and won a talent contest soon after her eighteenth birthday. In 1960 she played at the Grand Ole Opry and thereafter moved her family to Nashville. In the 1970s, she released her biggest hit, "Coal Miner's Daughter" (1970), a loving anthem to her poor but proud rural background. In 1976 she became the first country artist to hit number one on the *New York Times* bestseller list with her autobiography, which Hollywood released as *Coal Miner's Daughter* (1980).

EDWARD MILLER

M

MacArthur, Douglas

b. 1880; d. 1964

Scion of an Army family, with experience of East Asia, General MacArthur made his name in the assault on the Philippines during the Second World War. After losing the islands in an ignominious defeat in 1942, he returned triumphant in 1944, staging his own arrival on the island of Leyte for assembled journalists.

Later, in July 1950, MacArthur was named commander of the United Nations' multinational force to aid South Korea. MacArthur orchestrated an amphibious landing at Inchon, surprising the North Koreans, who then began their retreat back across the 38th parallel. The general persuaded President Harry **Truman** to continue the assault to reunify the country, inciting the Chinese government to intervene. After MacArthur's forces had recovered from the onslaught of 300,000 Chinese, he still urged Truman to continue, but the president decided against this. Owing to Mac-Arthur's public pronouncements on the issue, Truman found it necessary to relieve MacArthur of his command in April 1951. Returning home, the general was met with a hero's welcome, including ticker-tape parades and an address to **Congress**. But the military establishment supported Truman, so MacArthur would go the way of the old soldier in the Army ballad he recited for Congress: he would "just fade away."

ROBERT GREGG

Maclaine, Shirley

b. 1934

A dancer from childhood onwards, Maclaine has also received acclaim as a female comedian and serious actor in four decades of Broadway and in movies. Her roles have ranged from hookers to First Ladies, sensual but vulnerable ingénues to formidable Southern matrons. After several nominations since the 1950s, she won an Oscar in 1983 for *Terms of Endearment*. A political activist in the 1960s, Maclaine has also become deeply associated with **New Age** mysticism and has written extensively on reincarnation.

See also: actors

GARY McDONOGH

MADD (Mothers Against Drunk Driving) *see* alcohol

Madison Avenue

Madison Avenue is a 5.5-mile stretch that bisects Manhattan Island, **New York** City. Madison Avenue boasts glamorous **hotels** (Biltmore, Ritz-Carlton), fashionable shops and upscale residences in the blocks just east of Central Park. It has an international reputation as an **advertising** and public-relations hotspot. Ironically, only a handful of agencies (Young and Rubicam and BBDO) have headquarters here. Regardless, New York City agencies boast $38 billion in annual advertising billings. The name was also linked to the American satirical magazine *MAD*, as well as many films.

MARC BALCER

Madonna

b. 1958

Twenty-four-year-old **Detroit, MI** native, Madonna Louise Veronica Ciccone (aka Madonna) burst onto the music scene in a **New York** City dance club in 1982. Soon after, her second album earned her first no. 1 hit and gold single, and the nicknames "Material Girl" and "Boy Toy." All of her first eleven albums reached the top 15, selling over a million copies each. Visible in many media, Madonna's acting credits include a **Broadway** play, and the films *Desperately Seeking Susan* (1985), *Evita* (1996) and *The Next Best Thing* (1999). **MTV** plays her music videos more than any other artist's. An astute businesswoman, she created Maverick Entertainment, her own multimedia empire.

COURTNEY BENNETT

magazines

Americans have a love affair with magazines, creating thousands of periodical publications serving every taste and interest. Magazines communicate ideas, convey popular tastes and persuade the people to think, vote, behave and appear in specific ways. The average American reads almost ten different magazine issues each month. Sixty percent of these readers are married and almost 80 percent live in a metropolitan area – with income and tastes advertisers and publishers want to reach.

Magazines have a lively tradition in the United States of exposing corruption and individual's vices, chronicling American history, as well as informing, entertaining and persuading their readers. The power of the visual wedded to the printed word could persuade Americans that Kennedy-Camelot years were perfect, while the faces of famine in Africa aroused sympathy and paternal-ism. Magazines, however, like other **mass media**, are also businesses, selling themselves and **advertising** goods and services to targeted readers. With the merger climate of the 1990s, the most widely circulated American magazines were owned by a few conglomerates, like **Time Warner** (TW), Hearst and News Corporations (NC).

The top five US magazines in advertising revenue at the end of the century were *People Weekly* (TW), *Sports Illustrated* (TW), *Time* (TW), *TV Guide* (NC) and *Newsweek* (Washington Post Co.). In terms of circulation per issue, the top five include *Modern Maturity* (for all **American Association of Retired Persons** members), *Reader's Digest*, *TV Guide*, *National Geographic* and *Better Homes and Gardens* (all associated with older readers). Time Warner thus owns the three most profitable magazines in the country. Moreover, these are linked to its other media interests: TW ran a thirty-two-page advertising insert to celebrate the fiftieth birthday of Warner Brothers' Bugs Bunny in its *Time, Life, People, Fortune* and *Entertainment Weekly*, reaching over 80 million readers.

Magazines have changed greatly over time. The first American magazines appeared in 1741 – Andrew Bradford's *The American Magazine* and Benjamin Franklin's *The General Magazine and Historical Chronicle*. Most early magazines lasted less than three years. They lacked a large, literate population, cheap paper, technology for mass printings, means for easy distribution and a solid financial base. In the early 1800s, education, transportation, population and printing technology changed rapidly, and magazines became instrumental in educating and entertaining the growing American Republic. Cheap postal rates and the ability to deliver across a greater area increased circulation. Magazines contained novels in serial form, social and political debate, fashion, advice for the home, religious and philosophical advice and travel accounts. Major titles included *The Literary Digest, Ladies Home Journal, Saturday Evening Post, Harper's Weekly* and *Scribner's Monthly*.

Until the end of the First World War, magazines also took an aggressive role in social reform. Investigative reporters (muckrakers) exposed corruption in politics and industry and took on causes such as birth control, child labor, sanitation and the meat-packing industry. Their dogged pursuit of records, interviews and the truth changed the way journalists investigated tough issues.

With postwar development, collegiate readers sought H.L. Mencken's *American Mercury* and George Jean Nathan's *Smart Set* during the Roaring Twenties. During the 1930s, photo-filled magazines such as *Look* and *Life* were born, providing a pictorial chronicle of American culture. Along with *The Saturday Evening Post*, these large-circulation reviews dominated the national market until the advent of **television** affected the numbers of readers and advertisers. General-interest magazines that have maintained their popularity through the decades include *Reader's Digest*, *National Geographic* and the postwar *TV Guide*; in 1947 *Reader's Digest* became the first magazine to have a circulation of more than 9 million. News magazines such as *Time*, *Newsweek* and *U.S. News and World Report* have also had large circulation figures, but must compete with other information sources.

Magazines in the new millenium succeed when they attract the market niche for which they are positioned. In addition to general consumer magazines and news, the largest categories of magazines (with examples) are trade journals reflecting specific economic niches; sponsored publications (*American Legion*, college alumni magazines); sports; sex (*Playboy*, *Penthouse*); intellectual/opinion (*Commentary*, *The National Review*, *The Nation*); humor (*National Lampoon*, *MAD*); business (*Forbes*, *Business Week*); religion (*Christian Century*, *Focus on the Family*); teens; and city publications (*New York*, *Philadelphia*). Large markets are also gendered into "women's" interest (*Good Housekeeping*, *McCall's*) and men's interest (*Gentleman's Quarterly*, *Argosy*), as well as gay and lesbian interest. Magazines targeting blacks and **Hispanics** suggest the normative readers of other magazines. *The Gale Directory of Publications and Broadcast Media* (1998) includes 7,141 trade/technical/professional publications, 2,591 magazines of general circulation, 459 religious, 391 agricultural, 208 college, 177 women's, 154 foreign language, 61 fraternal, 56 Hispanic, 38 Jewish and 29 black publications. There are also roughly 10,000 company and technical publications.

Various milestones in postwar American magazine publishing reflect changing market demands and consumer trends. The satirical *MAD*, targeting advertising and media, was founded in 1952. ***Playboy*** appeared in 1953 with Marilyn **Monroe** as its first centerfold. *People* magazine – sold in **newspaper** checkout lines – appeared in 1974 with glitzy pictures in the *Life* tradition, but more **celebrity** gossip. *Cosmopolitan* and ***Ms*** also challenged "women's" publications in the 1970s. Meanwhile, *Life*, *Look* and *Saturday Evening Post* disappeared, victims of television and more media choices. By contrast, *Vanity Fair*, a magazine that had enjoyed decades of popularity before dying in 1936, was revived in 1983; it continues to set trends for an affluent society.

Other milestones refer to business. Advertising constitutes almost half of the economic basis for most magazines. Key sources of advertisement revenue include **automobiles**, cosmetics, direct response, business, **food**, **pharmaceuticals**, **fashion**, **tourism**, **computers**, **alcohol** and **tobacco**. The Audit Bureau of Circulation provides circulation information to advertisers, stockholders and the magazine industry itself.

Circulation and subscriptions account for the other half. The prices of magazines have skyrocketed with increasing costs of printing, paper, delivery services and salaries. However, the cost of actually producing the magazine has fallen with the advent of desktop publishing methods and some other technological advancements.

Since the 1980s, niche marketing of magazines has sought to deliver the demographic and psychographic audience publishers and advertisers want. Demographic information such as age, educational and income level, geographic location and sex helps advertisers and editorial directors plan content for readers. Information about readers' values and lifestyles (VALS and VALS 2) also helps deliver the audience to writers and advertisers. Publications failing to respond to market demand cease, despite generations of tradition like *The Saturday Evening Post*, whose Norman **Rockwell** covers once epitomized small-town nostalgia. Magazines also target audiences and geographic regions through special editions. Advertisements for local and regional clients as well as articles appropriate for a target audience (e.g. **Latinos**) or region (e.g. tobacco farmers in the **South**) attempt to increase circulation and revenues.

In the 1990s, electronic magazines began to appear. This development has increased access to information and editorial content in **colleges**, **libraries** and among those with electronic access. They also stretch form and expression within writing and illustration, as well as intersecting with emergent commercialism on the Web.

Further reading

DeFleur, M. and Dennis, E. (1996) *Understanding Mass Communication*, Boston: Houghton Mifflin.

Fisher, C. (ed.) (1998) *Gale Directory of Publications and Broadcast Media*, 131st edn, Detroit: Gale.

GAIL HENSON

Mailer, Norman

b. 1923

Rugged author, journalist, film-maker and critic whose work is marked by macho bravado as well as liberal politics. Mailer came to fame with the passion and violence of *The Naked and the Dead* (1948), based on his Second World War service. He returned to the spotlight with *The American Dream* (1965) and *Why are We in Vietnam?* (1967), as well as his vivid, personalized journalistic accounts of peace marches (the Pulitzer and NBA honoree *Armies of the Night*, 1969) and the 1968 conventions (*Miami and the Siege of Chicago*, 1968). He also explored this non-fiction approach in *The Executioner Song* (1979). Mailer continues to act, talk and write, including the 1995 *Oswald's Tale*, about John F. **Kennedy**'s assassin.

GARY McDONOGH

Main Street

Center for commercial, communal, civic and ceremonial space in nineteenth and early twentieth-century small-town America. Although Sinclair Lewis' unflattering depiction of Gopher Prairie, Minnesota in his 1930 novel *Main Street* exposed negativity and restlessness there, Main Street's decline resulted from the popularity of the **automobile** and **suburban** expansion. **Disney** nonetheless championed it in the 1950s. Recent movements to re-establish Main Street as a commercial and communal center include **New Urbanism** and **historic preservation**. New Urbanist projects focus on the pedestrian in designing new Main Streets, while historically preserved Main Streets attempt to restructure the economy along shuttered, dilapidated corridors.

ISABEL KRIEGEL

Malamud, Bernard

b. 1914; d. 1986

Pulitzer-prize winning novelist and short-story author, born in Brooklyn, whose works chronicle many facets of the Jewish experience in America, as well as themes of memory, justice, **race** and **class** relations and **baseball** (*The Natural*, 1942). Powerfully written in elegant prose with poignant characters and encounters, these seminal works also include *The Fixer* (1966), *The Tenant* (1971), *Dubin's Lives* (1979) and *God's Grace* (1982). His complete collected stories were published in 1983.

GARY McDONOGH

Malcolm X

b. 1925; d. 1965

Often seen as the counterpart to Martin Luther **King**, Jr., Malcolm X became the inspiration for militant activists during the later stages of the **Civil Rights movement**, as it moved away from non-violent protest to advocacy of **Black Power**.

Born Malcolm Little in Omaha, Nebraska, and brought up largely in a detention home in Mason, Michigan, Malcolm X became a street hustler in **Boston, MA** and **New York** City, NY before converting in 1947 to the **Nation of Islam** while in prison. Largely self-educated and very intelligent, able to see through the hypocrisy of the way in which liberal white Americans responded to the Civil Rights movement, he quickly became national spokesman of the Black Muslims.

In opposition to King, Malcolm X proclaimed that the way for **African Americans** to advance was through force, not by seeking aid from white America. Preaching "an eye for an eye" and calling for fights against racism "by any means necessary," he underscored the paramilitary strength of the Black Muslims as the response to racial oppression and stressed self-help through black businesses.

Some commentators have argued that Malcolm X understood American society better than civil-rights leaders who believed they could move it towards racial equality and harmony. He refused to accept the common notion of an "American Dilemma," a tension between American ideals and the problems of caste and color. In this formulation, Americans merely needed to be persuaded to live according to their highest ideals. For Malcolm X, instead, American history was a record of **violence** against slaves, against **American Indians** and others; the great revolutionary documents had been formulated deliberately to exclude African Americans. As such, the United States was fundamentally violent; since power was the national obsession, African Americans needed to pursue power. Such ideas found adherents among student militants, like H. Rap **Brown** and Stokely **Carmichael**.

In the eyes of some supporters, Malcolm X was widely misunderstood at the time. Partly, this was because he had a penchant for shocking white America, and did so very effectively. Following President **Kennedy**'s **assassination**, he announced that the event was an instance of "chickens coming home to roost." He was accused by his detractors of preaching hate and being a racist in reverse. But, according to James **Baldwin**, he was concerned less with whites than with building self-esteem among blacks and "decolonizing" the black mind. Nevertheless, he did acknowledge later that he had been wearing "a racist straight-jacket" while with the Black Muslims.

King and Malcolm X may have been opposites in a way, but King depended upon Malcolm X for some of his success. While in the Birmingham Jail, King argued that white Americans needed to heed the call of moderate blacks like himself, lest they face more radical and violent elements. In their famous meeting in 1965, the two commented that in spite of obvious differences they both depended on each other.

Malcolm X broke with the Black Muslims in April 1964, following their reprimand for his Kennedy assassination comments. A pilgrimage to Mecca caused him to question much of Elijah Muhammad's preaching. He returned to the United States as El-Hajj Malik El-Shabbazz with the plan of building a more inclusive and internationalist organization to oppose racial oppression (the Organization for Afro-American Unity). He was assassinated in the Audubon Ballroom in **Harlem, NY** on February 21, 1965. Debates continue over whether the assassins were under the direction of the leadership of the Nation of Islam.

Malcolm X's influence arguably increased after his death with the posthumous *Autobiography of Malcolm X* (1965). In 1992 Spike **Lee** produced a film relying heavily on the *Autobiography*, after many scripts by black intellectuals had gone unmade, debates continuing about the manner in which his life and politics should be portrayed.

ROBERT GREGG

malls/shopping centers

Perhaps no other urbanist innovation of American society in the twentieth century has gained such global interest – and critical opprobrium – as the "mall," where the **automobile**, suburbanization and affluent **consumerism** converge. Yet, America's variegated shopping complexes have now been replicated globally, even in American (and other) urban centers. Malls, in addition, have become shapers of American **life cycles**. Yet they remain simulacra – "Americas" in which the "other," like bad **weather**, can be excluded and **consumerism** exalted.

Shopping centers emerged nationwide in the 1920s, via planned developments near **Baltimore, MD**, **Cleveland, OH**, and Kansas City and **Northeastern** train-based centers that also facilitated parking. Many were service-oriented, offering food stores, pharmacies, banks and perhaps a cinema or restaurant. This has remained the primary role of many "**neighborhood**" shopping centers, large and small, mushrooming at major intersections for drive-by errands. Yet, suburban consumers also attracted larger businesses, especially **department stores**, which established branches in automotive centers as well. Soon, these subsidiaries competed with downtowns, offering longer hours, convenience and **class** segregation of clienteles.

As suburbia grew, so did shopping centers. Victor Gruen Associates constructed the first enclosed two-story pedestrian malls at Southdale, near **Minneapolis, MN**, in 1955. Malls later became differentiated in terms of their draw – local, regional and mega-regional (Greater **Philadelphia, PA**'s mammoth King of Prussia has eight magnet stores in multiple buildings). As they grew, malls added attractions and services – food courts (with franchised food), movie cineplexes, office parks, theme parks, civic services and even **hotels**.

By the 1960s, downtowns not only competed with but imitated malls, as in **Detroit, MI**'s Renaissance Center or **Chicago, IL**'s multi-story Water Tower Place. Cities later found they could sell history or culture in festival marketplaces like Baltimore's Inner Harbor or add malls to train stations and **airports**. Less conscious "malling" expanded in the 1980s as franchised stores and styles transformed older urban neighborhoods like **SoHo**, where **Eddie Bauer**, Prada and Pottery Barn occupy historic storefronts. The latest urban innovations include multi-story amusement malls like **Disney** Quest and high-tech centers by Sony and Nike.

Suburban shopping has also diversified. Giant outlet malls – anchored by manufacturers, discount sales and department store remainders – compete with both downtowns and upscale malls for a range of consumers. New immigrants, Asian and **Latino**, have constructed ethnic shopping centers/malls, especially in the **Sunbelt**. Yet conspicuous omissions include the long-term absence of new shopping complexes in **Harlem, NY** and South Central **Los Angeles, CA**.

Meanwhile, malls have reshaped American behavior. For many, they offer one-stop anytime family outings, escaping bad weather outside. Malls cater to **children** with stores and holiday events – showcasing Santa Claus (once the domain of downtown department stores), and, in the 1990s, "safe" Halloween. In American **mass media**, mall life and **teenagers** are inseparable. Where 1950s movies featured teens at drive-in movies and restaurants, by the 1990s cars would be parked (or kids dropped off) outside malls. Sales of music, clothes, **food** and entertainment have recast suburban social life and dilemmas like teen shoplifting. For elderly consumers, malls offer social outings and secure exercise space (mallwalks).

Urbanist and media analyses of malls often prove harsh (Sorkin 1992; *Clueless*, 1995), belying the consumption that sustains ever more centers. Yet malls are not vital new public spaces either; their managements limit free speech, political actions and entry, supported by federal courts. Malls also create problematic built environments in their reliance on **automobiles** and **highways** (with mega-malls so large one can drive "within" them), especially when, in local or national recession, one must ask what to do with a dead mall. Ultimately, the most serious problems arise when the mall, as a shrine to **consumerism**, becomes a metaphor for education, belief, politics or identity. Yet this is not intrinsic to the mall itself, but to the society that finds its pleasures and reflections there.

Further reading

Sorkin, M. (ed.) (1992) *Variations on a Theme Park*, New York: Noonday.

Rowe, P. (1991) *Making a Middle Landscape*, Cambridge, MA: MIT.

GARY McDONOGH

malpractice *see* American Medical Association

Manson, Charles

Charles Manson was convicted in 1971 of masterminding 1969 murders at the home of actor Sharon Tate (with **coffee** heiress Abigail Folger among those murdered), and the butchery of Leno and Rosemary LaBianca. These murders were ritualistic acts, inviting numerous theories about their purpose and Manson's **cult** family. The most popular theory is that the murders were inspired by Manson's interpretation of the **Beatles**, including his belief that the song "Helter Skelter" referred to a coming race war which the murders were intended to provoke. The **Internet** still features a plethora of sites protesting Manson's innocence and those adamantly proclaiming that justice was served. Still in prison, with no likelihood of parole, Manson now preaches and sings over the Web about ecology and the environment. One of his followers was also convicted of trying to assassinate President Gerald **Ford**.

ROBERT GREGG

Mapplethorpe, Robert

b. 1946; d. 1984

Photographer. A master of neo-classical black-and-white composition, Mapplethorpe challenged the art world and American society with his subject matter. Alongside stunning flowers and male nudes that recreated visions of light and form, he created equally stunning gay and sado-masochistic tableaux that sparked firestorms of controversy over exhibitions, **censorship** and federal funding for the arts. Cancellations and arrests sometimes overshadowed the sheer power of his art, although his photographs now hang in major **museums** worldwide.

GARY McDONOGH
CINDY WONG

marching bands

While military music, uniforms and flourishes mark pageantry from Barcelona to Beijing, two Americanizations of the marching band deserve notice. First is the repertoire and impact of American composer John Philip Sousa ("Stars and Stripes Forever," etc.) on millions of parades to follow. Second, bands extend beyond the military and **police** to become major activities of **high schools** and **colleges**. Sports, civic events and pep rallies showcase them, and band members raise money to appear in nationally televised events like Macy's Thanksgiving Day Parade or Bowl parades. The elaboration of the band (incorporating male and female students), includes drum

majors and majorettes, flag teams and others to dazzle crowds.

GARY McDONOGH

Marcuse, Herbert

b. 1898; d. 1979

Philosopher and radical social critic, German-born Marcuse was one of the younger members of the neo-Marxist "Frankfurt" or "critical-theory" school. Forced out of Germany by the Nazis, he emigrated to the US in 1934, and remained in the US as a professor at the University of California, San Diego, when other members of the school returned to Germany after the Second World War. Marcuse's writings, especially *Eros and Civilization* (1955) and *One Dimensional Man* (1964), were among the most important foundations for New **Left** and counterculture radicalism in the 1960s.

KENT BLASER

marijuana

Psychoactive drug derived from cannabis sativa that has become a symbol of freedom or decay, depending on audience, regulators and use. Federal surveys of the 1990s noted that 69 million Americans over the age of twelve have smoked pot, including 10 million who had done so in the previous month. Nonetheless, 500,000 are also arrested annually as legislators, medical establishments and law enforcement crusade against the drug and its ramifications.

Established as a countercultural narcotic in the 1930s, marijuana also became a symbol of the vulnerability of (white) American youth in exploitation films such as *Reefer Madness* (1936), later seen as a camp classic. Here, marijuana was portrayed as the addictive first step on the road to dissolution, hard drugs and depravity.

This image was challenged by the 1960s, when pot became a more mainstream form of countercultural relaxation, from cultivation in large fields to small artesian plantings, distinguishing forms of selection and processing (sensimilla, hashish, hash oil) and colorfully named varieties like "Maui Wowie." Paraphernalia for processing and smoking became accoutrements of alternative lifestyles, available in headshops alongside tie-dyed clothes and ethnic items. Hence, presidential candidate Bill **Clinton** could carefully identify himself with a generation by admitting that he had smoked – but not inhaled – pot in his college days.

Marijuana, nonetheless, became a special target of later wars against drug use, including propaganda about effects ranging from decreased brain function to risky sexual and school behavior to schizophrenia. This led to destruction of domestic supplies and prosecution/vilification of users. This new criminialization not only changed patterns of "acceptable" public use, but decreased supplies and raised costs, even while more addictive drugs remained accessible.

There remains a continuing lobby for legalization, including NORML (the National Organization for Reform of Marijuana Laws). In the 1990s, these sometimes worked with those promoting marijuana for medical use (dealing with the effects of chemotherapy, glaucoma, **AIDS**, etc.). A 1999 Gallup poll showed that 73 percent of Americans favor legalization of medical marijuana; some western states have exempted patients from prosecution. These ballot initiatives, however, have been challenged by federal policies and enforcement. Marijuana, then, remains a divisive issue for **baby boomers** despite a more tolerant and experimental past.

GARY McDONOGH
CINDY WONG

Marines (United States Marine Corps)

Ground and air force established in 1775 under the aegis of the Department of the Navy (although not the navy itself), marines are known for rugged shock-troop action and rapid deployment to combat zones "from the Halls of Montezuma to the shores of Tripoli" as their battle hymn proclaims. In mass media, marines are often emblematic of **patriotism**, **masculinity** and traditions embodied in their motto *Semper Fidelis*

(always faithful), adopted after the Civil War. Their training and character have also been the grist of many movies. Nonetheless, the **sitcom** *Gomer Pyle, USMC* (CBS, 1964–70) offered a more comic view of the corps. In 1998, the US had 172,632 marines on active duty; less than 6 percent were women (compared with the air force's 18 percent).

GARY McDONOGH

markets

The geographic and cultural diversity of the United States, coupled with comprehensive transportation and refrigeration, insured a cornucopia of **foods** distributed through central markets to both **neighborhood** stores and daily buyers from the nineteenth century onwards. Yet **suburban** sprawl and **automobiles** favored multi-service megastores (supermarkets) connected by corporate chains like A & P or Acme, surrounded by acres of parking, where groceries, household goods, **pharmaceuticals** and other needs may be met for the week (or months in the case of bulk-sales warehouses). Meanwhile, neighborhood stores have adapted or disappeared, while urban markets themselves have altered drastically.

In the 1960s, **urban renewal** often saw city markets as antiquated, unhygienic, congested and ugly. Lands were cleared for center city developments and distribution processes to aseptic warehouses accessible to **trucking** and **highways**. In hindsight, however, many cities realized the character of these markets and their value for **tourism**. Hence, Lexington Market in **Baltimore, MD**, the Italian Market and Reading Terminal Market in **Philadelphia, PA** and other centers have been modernized with a retail orientation – adding cafes, souvenirs and prepared foods, for example. Moreover, regional growers and craftspeople learned to transform buildings (including movie theaters, banks and storefronts), public squares and parking lots into "farmer's markets" offering fresh produce and prepared goods to middle-class consumers. Such suppliers still presume the existence of supermarkets for basic sundries. Here, specialty stands within supermarkets often mirror market stands and shops, especially with regard to prepared foods.

Squeezed in this consumer evolution have been smaller stores – butchers, greengrocers, etc. – unless they serve the needs of poor communities where national supermarket chains have refused to move to "risky" neighborhoods. Some have also become expensive boutiques delivering to or catering for upper-class neighborhoods. Ethnic specialty shops also survive, although the consolidation of **Asian American** and **Latino** supermarkets has become noticeable in suburban enclaves where space is available and cars allow mega-stores to serve more dispersed and varied populations. Organic and health-food stores also have carved out specialty niches. Convenience stores, open 24-hours, offer emergency items, **junk foods** and, depending on local codes and setting, **alcohol**, tobacco and gasoline.

Time as well as taste continues to shape food buying in the early twenty-first century. **Internet** shopping and **television** purchases have been discussed as alternatives for the two-career family. Most striking is the quantity of "prepared" foods, beyond the canned food of the 1950s and the frozen specialties of the 1960s, which promise fresh gourmet treats.

All these markets have cultural meanings, ranging from nostalgia to alienation, within American cultural representations. Traditional urban markets convey a sense of ethnic time and place in movies like *Godfather II* (1974). The supermarkets, as hallmarks of suburban domesticity and anonymity, also become public social spaces (urban markets may, in fact, sponsor singles' nights). The **mom-and-pop store** often surfaces in urban crime stories. Spike **Lee**'s *Do the Right Thing* (1989) showcases not only an Italian family pizzeria at odds with a black neighborhood, but also a Korean greengrocer, an immigrant specialization that has become widespread in **New York** City and other cities. The transition from smaller local stores to convenience stores is also apparent in crime and **road movies**, in which the latter have tended to replace the former as sites of dramatic action.

GARY McDONOGH

marriage

Marriage is a fundamental yet dynamic institution within American culture, shaped by the relationship between larger historical processes and internal marital dynamics. There is no single story of marriage in America because this story is characterized by diversity, and the constant tension between prevailing ideals and actual experiences.

In the early twentieth century, the so-called "companionate marriage," characterized by emotional intimacy yet defined by highly structured roles for "husband" and "wife" was the prevailing cultural model. Following the Second World War, the institution of marriage in mainstream American life was greatly affected by the large numbers of American women who joined the workforce during the War to replace the thousands of men who had joined the military. Less economically privileged women had long been working outside of the **home**, of course (particularly in **African American** and immigrant communities), but until this time it had generally been viewed as a last resort rather than as a possibly desirable option. A more "egalitarian" model began to emerge, in which roles for "husband" and "wife" were less differentiated.

The 1950s, generally considered a socially conservative era, was actually a period during which increasing numbers of women in all communities began to work outside of the home. In the 1960s and 1970s this exploded into a radical shift with the **women's liberation** movement; undercurrents of change have led many to predict the "end of marriage." However, marriage continues to thrive, though these changes have entailed reconsideration of work issues, responsibilities, sexuality and legal ramifications from naming spouses and **children** to ownership of resources. Clinical counseling often focuses on maintaining and developing the marriage bond. At the same time, both **divorce** and remarriage have become more prevalent and acceptable.

For many, marriage represents the opportunity to express and reinforce a life-long commitment to a loved one. In contemporary America, the marital bond is often characterized by romantic love and emotional intimacy, although many marriages do not conform to this model. For some people, marriage constitutes a practical necessity for child-rearing and economic survival. In the late twentieth and early twenty-first centuries, such developments as blended **families**, gay relationships, single-parent families, multiple remarriages and new reproductive technologies have challenged rigid conceptions of married life, while often reaffirming the importance of its social and economic support.

Marriages in all forms (good and bad) have been the focus of television **sitcoms** and **Hollywood** products. In the former, companionate heterosexual forms dominated for decades, gradually giving way to broken and blended families as dramatic devices; **soap operas** have developed even more complex relations over decades. Hollywood, too, enshrined traditional models (despite intertexts of **celebrity** scandal), but has also explored issues of interracial, inter-class and gay unions as well as the breakdown of marriage and family.

Further reading

Kellogg, S. and Mintz, S. (1988) *Domestic Revolutions: A Social History of American Family Life*, New York: The Free Press.

NICOLE MARIE KEATING

Marshall, George

b. 1880; d. 1959

General of the Army and statesman. After a long military career, including service in the First World War, the Philippines and **China**, Marshall became Army Chief of Staff in 1939, guiding preparations for the Second World War. Command of the European invasion went to **Eisenhower**, while Marshall became a close policy advisor to **Roosevelt** and, later, special ambassador to feuding Chinese factions for **Truman**. As **Secretary of State** (1947–9), he fostered the Marshall Plan for rebuilding Europe with North American aid; he later served as Secretary of Defense. He received the **Nobel** Peace Prize in 1953.

GARY McDONOGH

Marshall, Paule

b. 1929

African American novelist of **Caribbean** (Barbadian) ancestry, who emerged onto the literary scene with her autobiographical novel *Brown Girl, Brownstones* (1959). Much of Marshall's writing deals with themes of estrangement of contemporary **African Americans** from their cultural roots and the need to journey back and deal with the ancestors and heritage to find renewal, questions that reverberate with the works of Gloria **Naylor**, Toni **Morrison** and others. Among her major works are *The Chosen Place, The Timeless People* (1969), *Praisesong for the Widow* (1983) and *Daughters* (1991).

GARY McDONOGH

Marshall, Thurgood

b. 1908; d. 1993

Civil-rights leader and **Supreme Court** justice. During his distinguished career directing the NAACP Legal Defense and Education Fund (1939–61), Marshall argued many landmark decisions in civil rights and the fight against **segregation** and other forms of discrimination, capped by the ***Brown* v. *Board of Education of Topeka*** decision of 1954. President **Kennedy** appointed him to the Second Circuit Court of Appeals in 1961; in 1965 Marshall became solicitor-general. Appointed to the Supreme Court by President **Johnson** in 1967 as the first African American justice, Marshall served until 1991. A liberal voice amidst a predominantly conservative court, his opposition to decisions of an increasingly conservative court with regard to the death penalty, which he opposed, as well as his civil-rights interests led to his nickname "the great dissenter."

KATE M. KENSKI

martial arts

The story of martial arts in the United States is closely connected with the post-Second World War history of the United States' connections with Asia.

Aikido, Judo and Karate, originating in **Japan**, were learned by American servicemen during the occupation of that country following its defeat in 1945. An Armed Forces Judo Association was established and this martial art was incorporated into air-force training in the 1950s. When Tokyo hosted the **Olympic Games** in 1964, Japan used this opportunity to establish Judo as an Olympic sport, and now as many as 400,000 Americans engage in Judo. Karate, meanwhile, was introduced to the United States in 1954 by Tsutomu Ohshima, who immigrated in 1954 and established the Southern California Karate Association, which grew into the nationwide organization, Shotokan Karate of America.

Tae Kwon Do, which was recognized as an official Olympic Sport at the 2000 Olympic Games in Sydney, Australia, was brought to the United States from Korea in the mid-1970s by Grandmaster Hyuk Kun Shim, who opened Shim's Martial Arts Academy in Elizabeth, New Jersey in 1976.

Kung Fu and Tai Chi, originating in China, have been affected by the United States' multiple connections with this nation, in terms of migration, political alliance and hostility, and economic trade, as well as the powerful impact of culture emanating from Hong Kong. Kung Fu was popularized in the United States through the career of San Francisco-born Bruce **Lee**. It then achieved crossover appeal in white and black communities with the television **western** series *Kung-Fu* (ABC, 1972–5), starring the martial-arts novice David Carradine, in a role for which Lee was turned down, and with the acting successes of Chuck Norris (Lee's adversary in *Return of the Dragon*, 1972), Jeanne-Claude Van Damme, Steven Seagal and Jackie Chan. The status of martial arts in American culture has been further enhanced by very popular and violent **video** and **computer** games.

ROBERT GREGG

Marx Brothers

Groucho (Julius, 1890–1977), Harpo (Adolf, 1888–1964), Chico (Loenard, 1886–1961), Gummo (Milton, 1893–1977) and Zeppo (Hebert, 1901–

77). Vaudevillians who brought unforgettable repartee and strongly defined comic characters to films like *Animal Crackers* (1930) and *A Night at the Opera* (1935). While individual lines and scenes have permanently enriched American **humor** and speech, the primary trio also conveyed interesting critical perspectives on class (Groucho's constant sarcastic romancing of the rich dowager), sexuality (the aspirations of Harpo's child-like mute) and immigration (Chico's Italian persona). While their comedies have continued to entrance audiences, only Groucho developed a strong television personality and career in the 1950s.

GARY McDONOGH

Marxism *see* class; communism; history; Left, the; working class

mascots

American sports teams, professional, **college**, **high-school** and **children**'s leagues have often adopted animals, mythic humans, or other symbols as emblems and animators for their activities. Many of these names are relatively unmarked culturally, except for images of strength, unity and locality – the **Denver** Broncos, **San Francisco, CA** 49-ers, or **Boston** Red Sox, among professional teams, or the Harvard Crimson, University of Southern California Trojans, or Nebraska Cornhuskers among colleges. One strongly embedded cultural tradition, however, of using Native American names or representations – Redskins, Chiefs, **Florida** Seminoles, or **Atlanta** Braves (and their "tomahawk chop") came under increasing attack in the 1990s for the derogatory mythologizations they impose upon a living Native American population. While some supporters argue that such names honor Native Americans and more suggest that they have nothing to do with living peoples (precisely the problem), pressure has grown to drop these names and attendant representations. The **Los Angeles, CA** school system adopted this policy in 1997, as have other institutions like **Stanford**. Recent expansion franchises in major-league sports have also carefully chosen animals or other phenomena – Ravens, Jazz, Saints, Kixx (**soccer**), etc. – and often rely on more fanciful figures like the **San Diego** Chicken or Philly Phanatic (Philadelphia Phillies) to raise fans' spirits.

GARY McDONOGH

masculinity

Many scholars, such as Gail Bederman and Michael Davitt Bell, have noted the ideological, aesthetic and performative variations and inconsistencies underscoring the cultural terms that define American manhood. At the same time, these and many other scholars (including George Chauncey, E. Anthony Rotundo, Michael S. Kimmel) recognize a persistent historical anxiety that drives the vigorous activity of the masculine enterprise. As these scholars see it, the anxiety-producing agent that enables the historical concepts of masculinity is the perceived threat of cultural *effeminization* (see **homophobia**). The rise of the new woman at the turn of the nineteenth century and her entry into the industrial-age workforce triggered a considerable cause for worry. The rapid development of industrial capitalism spawned paradoxical response since, on the one hand, the industrial age promised a virile and efficient world. On the other hand, the very same notions of progress ushered in quite a few unmanly and thereby undesirable social elements. One might suggest that the hyper-virile antics of American men at this time (weightlifting, sport) served as an activity to contain cultural excess, i.e. the feminine. Thus, the discourse of cultural conditions was often framed along gender lines: "effeminacy" was the sweeping generalization assigned to the cause of any ill-effect attending modern society. Sloth, "neurasthenia," homosexuality and other purported weaknesses observed in/on the male body were paradigmatic dysfunctions directly related to the "effeminizing" of American culture.

American artists, statesmen and religious individuals took to the cause of mastering the cultural parameters of masculinity that were apparently put at risk by cultural *and* corporeal effeminization. Ironically, the rigor with which men engaged the physical and emotional reconfiguration of manhood was often demonstrated with comical if not cartoon-like effect. "Sandow the Strongman" in Edison's film shorts (*c.* 1896) or the steel-like men that dominated the 1930s paintings of Thomas Hart Benton highlight the hyperbolic work involved with the presentation of virile American manhood.

Arguably, movies have been most instrumental in the shaping of an American consciousness of a masculine ideal during the twentieth century. Hollywood masculinity, however, is as varied as the cultural conditions that manufacture masculine identity. Shifting between the likes of Sandow and Clark Gable, Errol Flynn and Fred **Astaire**, Sylvester Stallone and Arnold Schwarzenegger, Bruce Willis and Leonardo DiCaprio, **Hollywood**'s representation of masculinity allows multiple, conflictive readings.

One thing remains certain: if the terms of masculinity are varied and are established relative to the contemporary (and mobile) discourse of "femininity," the *bête noir* of culture is an uncontained effeminacy of masculinity that announces itself as homosexual. It is no surprise, then, that some American men have practically made a career out of defending their perceived *un*masculine dispositions as differential masculinity. Politician Theodore Roosevelt's aristocratic upbringing ushered in charges of *dilletanti* politics by not a few New York State assemblymen in 1882, who calculatingly called him an "Oscar Wilde"; dancer/choreographer Gene **Kelly** produced a **television** program in 1958 entitled *Dancing, A Man's Game* to prove that ballet and **baseball** were really carved out of the same manly tradition; actor Kevin Spacey told the world that he intends to have children in hopes of refuting *Esquire Magazine's* claims that he is gay.

The inability to define a true American masculinity cuts across issues of **race** as well (although the terms that define American manhood usually find themselves organized around white man's Judaeo-Christian principles). Black men in particular have been viewed as threats and temptations by whites, while their masculinity has been shaped by economic, political and social repression. A contemporary example of the intersection of these themes is the emergence of the Christian Conservative Men's Movement, "The Promise Keepers." Established in 1990, the group proudly embraces (and is embraced by) **Asian American**, **African American**, **WASP** and **Latino** men who bond under the auspices of Christian (masculine) brotherhood. Multiculturalism is paradoxically useful in the conservative rhetoric that seeks to homogenize cultural identity. More importantly, masculinity is defined here as a sacred promise that defends **family** and women. Writers such as Eve Sedgwick-Kosofsky and Donna Minkowitz have pointed out the perfidy (i.e. misogyny and homophobia) that underlies the sentiment of this sort of "kinder, gentler" masculinity (see http://www.promisekeepers.org/fact.htm and http://www.promisekeepers.org/265e.htm).

The contemporary American political arena has also witnessed discomfiting shifts in the ways that masculinity is approached and discussed in relationship to family and homosexuality. In the 2000 **Republican** presidential primary, candidate John McCain found himself awkwardly defending his utterance regarding his "gaydar" that effectively allowed him to detect homosexuals in the military during the **Vietnam War**. Both the conservative right and gay **lobbyists** raised issue with McCain's provocative remarks. In the White House, Bill **Clinton**'s sexual escapades certainly made him a prime candidate for the Promise Keeper's "Reconciliation" program of prayer and devotion to family and wife. In the Monica Lewinsky affair, Clinton's masculinity presented not the dangers of effeminate manhood as much as he demonstrated *too much* masculinity; too much **heterosexuality**. Balancing gender is a central goal of an ideal masculinity.

The fluctuating yet certainly tightly managed social dicta that seeks balance and defines the cultural "effeminate" (woman, homosexual) as the cultural obverse of the masculine also functions to maintain the necessary binary structures, like heterosexual **marriage**, so central to a capitalist economy. But the ever-changing terms of the "masculine" (which perforce define the "feminine") put women, in particular, in the most impossible of positions. If one is *too* feminine (according to a strain of masculine tradition), one embodies the debilitating characteristics of the atrophying state. If one is *too* masculine, one is suspect of non-normative sexual desire. Yet Judith Butler, Leslie Feinberg and Riki Anne Wilchins have troubled the calm of these masculine waters that seek to keep sexuality and gender under such bifurcated logic. Films such as *Boys Don't Cry* (1999) have brought the uncertain state of masculinity (and its often violent resolution) into popular consciousness. American masculinity, like much of American culture, is one of the contradictory discourses that simultaneously appears concrete and indefinable.

DAVID GERSTNER

Mason, Bobbie Ann

b. 1940

Born in Kentucky, Mason worked as a journalist in New York before receiving a PhD in English from the University of Connecticut in 1972. Her first story collection, *Shiloh and Other Stories* (1982), describes the lives of rural people of her native state, and won the Ernest Hemingway Award in 1983. Mason's most famous novel, *In Country* (1985), recounts the efforts of a young Kentucky woman to come to grips with her father's **death** in Vietnam before she was born, and how her search for meaning helps others deal with the impact the war has had, and continues to have, on lives.

JIM WATKINS

mass media

While journalism, **television**, movies, music and informational mass media are all treated extensively in multiple articles, they also share several important characteristics as American mass media that set them apart from the structure and experience of other world media. These include the near absence of government ownership and regulations, their structures of corporate consolidation and their global presence combined with national insularity.

Newspapers and **publishing** established independence in 1791 before the American century on the basis of **Bill of Rights**' provisos for Freedom of the Press. The 1st Amendment, guaranteeing the freedom of speech, has allowed American media to be free generally from the handicap of official government **censorship** and control (except in certain emergencies), and has patterned the landscape of later media. However, the 1st Amendment also guarantees freedom of money. In the early twenty-first century, while everybody can express views freely, only those with deep pockets can easily reach the masses. Newspapers, television and other media pay attention to advertisers, political war chests and markets.

Even though airwaves are generally seen as public goods, the government has not owned and rarely censored them. Instead, government regulation has ensured an unquestioned culture of commercial broadcasting based loosely on the concept of the free markets in which **radio** and television **networks** are primarily funded through **advertising**. Another strongly held American belief in this realm is that competition benefits the consumer because it leads to "higher-quality" works, at least in a technical sense. This, however, prevents people with limited resources from producing and distributing works or reaching a wide audience trained to expect certain standards of "production values." While electronic media have taken shape as a free-for-all field, they have increasingly been viewed as commodities in the marketplace. Many **Internet** browsers rely increasingly on their advertising revenues.

Though relatively free, American broadcasting companies are under the supervision of the Federal Communication Commission (FCC). All media companies have to apply for a license from the FCC: to broadcast is a privilege, not a right. During the 1960s, for example, the FCC imposed rules for mandatory hours for educational and **children**'s television, and the fairness doctrine that guaranteed the airing of opposing views. However, with bills culminating in the Telecommunications Act of 1996, **Congress** clearly favored deregulation. These changes range from the national percentage of television stations a company can own (from 25 percent to 35 percent), to longer intervals between license renewal, to complete deregulation of **cable** rates. The FCC

has effectively allowed broadcasters unlimited power to *own* the media.

Still, media are not unchecked. Concerns over violence and sexuality generate grassroots responses that government has capitalized on so that media industries adopt self-censorship, from the **Hollywood** Production Code (1930s to 1960s) to film and television **rating** systems, to the proposed V-Chip. The mass-media industries polish their public image as responsible broadcasters even as they respond to less civic-minded markets.

While the government created public broadcasting channels in both radio (NPR) and television (CPB) in the 1960s, both have operated as independent corporations. There was initial debate on whether they should be funded by **taxes** or by allocation from Congress. It was decided that taxing broadcasting involved too much government intervention. Therefore, federal and other public funding (including corporate sponsorship) has become a hotbed for politics. In 1999, for example, Governor Jesse Ventura eliminated public funding for Minnesota Public Broadcasting, leaving them to rely on corporate underwritings and members' support. Reliance on public funding and corporate sponsorship has restricted the public broadcasting corporations' ability to be independent, once again, making it harder for minority viewpoints to air. Direct government-owned media have been limited to propaganda channels (Voice of America) and military media.

Freedom, hence, has not produced democratic media. Instead, corporations have centralized mass media – whether newspaper publishers, radio chains, television networks, music producers, cable suppliers or toll booths on the information highway. Since the 1980s, in fact, critics have noted the dramatic vertical integration of multiple media, coupled with the idea of synergy, in huge conglomerates like AOL/**Time Warner** or ABC/**Disney**. With mass media in the hands of a few unregulated big companies, which have ties with other non-mass-media companies, like GE, an over-riding commercialism can shape culture and politics. There is a further fear that the news departments in many of these companies will adopt self-censorship measures for self-preservation. While alternatives exist – public access on cable, **independent film**, grassroots **video**, micro-radio – they are peripheral to the audience and revenues of these mega-corporations.

Nor is the impact of these mass media limited to the US. Many major media conglomerates are global, like Rupert Murdoch's News Incorporated. They are, however, American based. American productions like **Hollywood** films and television are distributed all over the world. Hollywood **blockbusters** and television series outdraw even the most popular local works, except in a few markets (India, Hong Kong and Iran, for example). Meanwhile, Hollywood's huge national market is rarely disturbed by foreign films that make it beyond art-house distribution. Popular music, infused by an **African American** beat, has reshaped global traditions while absorbing new sounds and artists from Great Britain and, more recently, from Africa, the **Caribbean** and Latin America. While television faces cultural differences and tight government controls abroad, American productions of night-time **soaps**, dramas and even highly American **sitcoms** alarm foreign purists with their popularity (and become bargaining chips for regional and private networks). MTV, as both producer and distributor, reaches sixty-four countries with relatively transnational, yet homogenous products. In cable news, CNN is transmitted to 210 countries and territories worldwide. With the Internet as well, American corporate and technological domination seems to be evolving from this pattern within a new mass medium.

Further reading

Hazen, D. and Winokur, J. (eds) (1998) *We the Media*, New York: New Press.

CINDY WONG

mass transit *see* aviation, commercial; buses; commuting; trains

Mastercard *see* credit and credit cards

Masterpiece Theatre

English television shows imported by **PBS**, beginning in the 1970s. The first show, *Upstairs, Down-stairs* was a serial imported for many seasons, depicting the trials and tribulations of the Bellamy family and their many servants, set in Edwardian England. With this production, the tone of the series was set; it brought "highbrow" **television** made abroad to a seemingly well-educated American public, dissatisfied with American fare. Always introduced by a literary or thespian **celebrity** (initially the intensely Mid-Atlantic Alistair Cooke), the series has gone on to other adaptations of English novels, notably *Jewel in the Crown* and the soon-to-be camp classic *I Claudius*.

EDWARD MILLER

mathematics

Mathematics comprises both a set of pragmatic procedures (applied mathematics) and a set of rigorous deductive systems (pure mathematics). Pure mathematics derives its ultimate inspiration from practical problems, but its domain is purely mental. Beginning with axioms, which are rules for manipulating undefined terms, mathematicians proceed through the purely mental process of deductive inference to derive new mental constructs called theorems. While this abstractness seems to make pure mathematics utterly remote from experience, it does facilitate the application of these constructs to new areas. Also, through abstraction, pure mathematics strives to achieve absolute certainty. Alas, such certainty has proved elusive. Gödel's Theorem (1931) established that no formal system rich enough to include the natural numbers could be both consistent and complete. Either deductive reasoning cannot yield all that is true in mathematics, or it will yield contradictory results. Since pure mathematics is a mental construct, such a conclusion raises fascinating questions about the nature of the human mind.

Applied mathematics has been wildly successful in describing the natural world and in proving its usefulness in nearly every area of human endeavor. Since the time of Sir Isaac Newton (1642–1727), the physical sciences (especially **physics**) have sought mathematical description rather than ultimate causes. The effectiveness of a mathematical procedure as applied to science is typically evaluated not by the rigor of its justification, but by its ability to make predictions about the outcomes of experiments.

While the mathematization of the underlying laws of the life and social sciences has met with spotty success, there can be no doubt that the branch of mathematics called "statistics" forms the basis of nearly all research. Any study that is based on more than anecdotal evidence relies on statistical design and analysis. It follows that a rudimentary understanding of statistics is essential for anyone making decisions based on the results of research, including, for example, decisions about the efficacy and safety of new medications.

Computers have naturally had an enormous influence on mathematics. To begin with, by removing the computational burden from humans, **computers** affect the way we think about math education. Americans have always had difficulty deciding whether the goal of math education should be the mastery of procedures or the understanding of abstract concepts. The ubiquity of computers and calculators at the very least diminishes the need for arithmetical proficiency, while increasing the need to understand algorithms and numerical accuracy.

Computers have also opened the doors to fascinating new areas of mathematics, including chaos theory. The self-similarity of some fractal images (based on chaotic systems) suggests links between the visual arts and designs seen in nature. Chaos theory also links the qualitative and quantitative descriptions of phenomena with wide application to domains previously beyond mathematical analysis.

Further reading

Guillen, M. (1983) *Bridges to Infinity*, Los Angeles: Jeremy P. Tarcher.
Kline, M. (1980) *Mathematics: The Loss of Certainty*, New York: Oxford University.

ROBERT SCHWENK

Mayfield, Curtis

b. 1942; d. 1999

African American singer and composer. Draw-

ing on gospel roots, his smooth **Chicago, IL** sound and social vision produced anthems of **civil rights** and social change in the 1960s, including "Keep on Pushing," "People get Ready" and "This is My Country." Mayfield's work with the Impressions and as a solo artist also included romantic hits ("Gypsy Woman") and the score for the movie *Superfly* (1972). After a career slowdown and a crippling accident in 1990, Mayfield was recognized nationally and globally for his powerful vision and impact in the 1990s.

GARY McDONOGH

mayors

Cities are units of taxation, representation, service and identity. All these demand governance, which, since the American Revolution, has been vested in locally elected officials at City Hall. Over the centuries, patricians have given way to immigrant bosses, reformers, politicians and outsiders. In the early twenty-first century, a mayor, city council or city manager must manage conflicting factions and guide a city, while shaping regional, national and international images. Hence, mayors have included charismatic and controversial figures on the frontline of politics – LaGuardia and Giuliani in **New York** City, NY, Alioto and Feinstein in **San Francisco, CA**, the **Daleys** in **Chicago, IL**, etc. Only two American mayors, however (Grover Cleveland and Calvin Coolidge), have become president.

City governments vary widely in their constitution and powers, set by states (or the federal government for **Washington, DC**). Urban administration generally must appoint officers, set agendas and budgets (on the basis of local revenues and, in the postwar era, increasing federal intervention) and manage services including parks, security, education and ceremonial visits. Strong mayors control – or delegate to department heads and managers – most functions of government; others, however, share functions with their elected city councils, which may represent **neighborhoods** or interest groups. Depending on the city charter (itself often dependent on the state), **police** chiefs, Boards of Education, and somewhat autonomous institutions dealing with water, housing, transportation and health may further divide responsibility. Moreover, the complexities of urban laws and records mean that even small cities have bureaucracies that endure long after any mayor leaves office. Finally, city government must balance interests of state and federal government, competing regional interests and divided citizens. This becomes critical as development and welfare programs have become areas of shared responsibility or in emergent policy questions – environment or **immigration** – in which the city cannot control policies, although it must deal with consequences. The need for coordination also underscores the impact of **suburbs** on city administrations: cities are swamped by, yet cut off from, metropolitan growth. The era of annexation ended well before the Second World War, although few real consolidated planning and governance structures have emerged in expanding metropolitan areas. Suburbanites, in turn, may be more likely to identify a charismatic urban leader than the bureaucrats generally charged with the planning and politics of sprawl. Hence, mayors negotiate constantly – with other governments, unions, businesses and citizens.

Traditional mayors tend to be found in large American cities, older cities and the **Northeast**. Such mayors are intensely political, often within a highly partisan framework (although socialists dominated **Milwaukee** and reform candidates have beaten the system elsewhere). For most of the twentieth century, mayors were identified with political machines that organized, coerced and bought votes – with money or patronage – in order to promote party interests; Chicago's Richard Daley was such a kingpin. Local organization, from ward politics and political clubs through urban patronage, can play a strong role in state and national elections as well. The urban dead, according to folklore, have voted many times in Chicago and **Philadelphia, PA**. Civil-service reforms and other watchdogs have been used to control such party bosses.

Yet the immediacy and intensity of city government has made it an area of breakthroughs for those outside the system, including minorities and women. In the turn-of-the-nineteenth-century **South**, for example, Jewish mayors were elected as reformers from **Savannah, GA** to **New Orleans, LA**. Irish and Italian ethnics also made mayoralties stepping stones to urban recognition. Later, in the 1970s, **African American** mayors spoke to changing majorities optimistically or defensively; **Hispanic** mayors in **San Antonio, TX** and **Miami, FL** also have marked changes in urban demographics. Women have most readily gained urban power in small cities, but San Francisco, Chicago and Washington, DC all have elected women mayors.

Yet one must not over-emphasize macro-politics. In fact, most American cities have only figurehead mayors, eschewing personality and corruption for a professional city manager. This format, in which city councilors contract an administrator, was first adopted in Dayton, Ohio in 1913. It remains most common in the **West** and in cities of under 100,000, although these have become **Sunbelt** metropoles. City managers are apolitical, without the **community** roots mayors rely on; nor can they set policy independently.

Strong or weak, the mayor often shapes the image of the city in significant ways. In the 1960s, liberal **Republican** John Lindsay was stylish for New York, while Ed Koch proved down to earth and David Dinkins, as an African American, recognized the new minority mosaic in the city. Mayor Rudolph Giuliani focused on creating a "civil" city, sometimes crossing the line between quality of life and denying those who mar the clean city. By contrast, Mayor Marion Barry's arrest for crack possession seemed to epitomize the decay of Washington. Symbolism and power converge in the effectiveness of decisions, actions and planning.

Mass media are also critical. City government gains constant attention – political, economic and personal – in local **newspapers** and **television**. Mayors become spokespersons and lightning rods in crises: Tom Bradley addressed both fellow citizens and national media to calm a rioting **Los Angeles, CA**. Fictional media seem rather unsympathetic: movies and literature have concentrated on corruption and bossism from the 1930s onwards. Later cinematic mayors face crime or disaster until the "real" hero arrives – a *Batman* scenario. In television's *Spin City* (ABC, 1996–), in fact, a bumbling New York City mayor is completely managed by the administrators around him.

Further reading

Morgan, D. and England, R. (1999) *Managing Urban America*, New York: Chatham House.

Bissinger, B. (1997) *A Prayer for the City*, New York: Random House (an analytic chronicle of the Rendell administration in 1990s Philadelphia).

GARY McDONOGH

McCarthy, Eugene

b. 1916

Minnesota member of Congress who launched a quixotic antiwar challenge to President Lyndon **Johnson** in the 1968 **Democratic** primaries that galvanized youthful anti-Vietnam movements. While Johnson eventually chose not to seek the nomination, McCarthy was defeated by Hubert Humphrey's nomination by a deeply divided party lacerated by the assassination of Robert **Kennedy** as well as Chicago convention protests. McCarthy subsequently became better known as a commentator and poet, although his campaign buttons and bumper stickers remained liberal keepsakes for decades.

Further reading

McCarthy, E. (1987) *Up 'Til Now: A Memoir of the Decline of the Democratic Party*, San Diego: Harcourt Brace Jovanovich.

GARY McDONOGH

McCarthyism

The anti-communist movement associated with Joseph McCarthy was underway well before his election to the Senate in 1946. Though the American government had long worked to obstruct the presence of communists and socialists in American politics, this campaign took on unprecedented urgency after the Second World War.

The search for internal subversion was carried out by **Congress** through its **House Committee on Un-American Activities (HUAC)**, organized in 1938 and not abolished until 1975. Though relatively ineffective during the New Deal, after the war the committee stepped up its work, in part a response to President Harry **Truman**'s own increasingly strident anti-communist rhetoric and new internal security program. In fact, many scholars have argued that McCarthyism owed as much energy to the rivalry between the **Democratic** and **Republican** parties as it did to any "real" threat of communist influence over governmental policy.

Nationwide attention was given to HUAC in 1948 when, in front of a committee chaired by freshman **California** member of Congress Richard **Nixon**, Whittaker Chambers, a journalist and former member of the Communist Party, accused Alger Hiss of passing classified documents to the Soviets during the 1930s. Hiss, a highly respected Democrat who held influential positions in the federal government during the New Deal, and who accompanied President **Roosevelt** to the Yalta conference in 1945, could not be tried for subversion; the statute of limitations had expired. But Hiss was convicted of lying to **Congress**, and to many the possibility of his guilt legitimated the search for subversives within the government. To those who doubted his guilt, however, the hearings resembled a witch-hunt devoid of any hard evidence linking Hiss to the accusations.

The search for communists was not limited to the federal government, but also included the entertainment industry, higher education and the nation's literary community. Other targets of investigation and intimidation were American homosexuals, considered by some to be a poisonous presence by virtue of their sexual identity, just as communists were suspect for their political identity. In all, hundreds of lives were ruined by the careless and savage attacks made by a few overzealous men wielding substantial power.

The anti-communist crusade was linked to Joseph McCarthy in early 1950, after he claimed in a speech given in Wheeling, West Virginia, to have a list of 205 known communists working in the federal government. Though the number of "communists" McCarthy claimed to have identified changed over the next few years, what proved relevant for most Americans was the accusations themselves rather than their validity.

McCarthy's influence ended suddenly in 1954 when he made the mistake of investigating the presence of communists in the United States Army. A more absurd accusation could not have been made. The fact that a Republican was now in the White House signaled to many Republicans that McCarthy was now more of a liability than an asset to their party. Televised hearings revealed McCarthy to be a vulgar and disrespectful man, and his basis of support quickly evaporated. Censured by the Senate in 1954, McCarthy receded into obscurity and died an alcoholic in 1957.

See also: Cold War; Truman, Harry S.; gay and lesbian life and politics

Further reading

Fried, R. (1990) *Nightmare in Red*, New York: Oxford.
Oshinsky, D. (1983) *A Conspiracy so Immense*, New York: The Free Press.

SUSAN SCHULTEN

McCullers, Carson

b. 1917; d. 1967

Born in Georgia, and later a close friend of Tennessee **Williams**, McCullers is considered an heir to the Southern Gothic tradition of William Faulkner. An essayist and poet, she is primarily known for her allegorical fiction, which explores the feminine aspects of spiritual isolation in the **South** of the mid-twentieth century. She published *The Heart is a Lonely Hunter* (1940) at age twenty-three, following that with several well-received novels and a successful stage adaptation of her novel *The Member of the Wedding* (1946). McCullers battled a series of strokes and serious illnesses as well as personal tragedies throughout her adult life.

JIM WATKINS

McDonald's

Who hasn't tasted one of the "Billions and Billions served?" The McDonald Brothers, who had founded a burger and **barbeque** joint, complete with carhops, in the 1930s, revamped their system in 1948 to promote speedy service and cheaper **food** (and incidentally attract a **family** clientele). After lackluster franchise results, their project was acquired by salesman Ray Kroc in 1955 who went on to create a global empire. He redesigned the service, ambience and food itself to fit changing mores and new locations at home and abroad, while families, leisure and travel adapted in turn to the emblematic golden arches. This process is analyzed in John Love's (1986) *McDonald's: Behind the Golden Arches*, while Watson (1997) and others consider the interactions of McDonald's and Asia in *Golden Arches East*. Other major competitors in the hamburger and family-meal market include Burger King and Wendy's (with a folksy image), as well as regional chains like Carl, Jrs, Jack-in-the-Box (hit by food-poisoning scares) and Hardee's.

Further reading

Love, J. (1986) *McDonald's: Behind the Golden Arches*, Toronto: Bantam Books.
Watson, W. (ed.) (1997) *Golden Arches East*, Stanford: Stanford University Press.

GARY McDONOGH

McInerney, Jay

b. 1955

Bright Lights, Big City (1984) identified the Tennessee author with **New York** City, NY's literary brat pack, including Bret Easton **Ellis** and Tama Janowitz, and their **Generation-X** depictions of empty, **yuppie** lives in the big city. After becoming, in his own words, an overexposed literary **celebrity** as a twenty-something, McInerney has sought more serious themes and style, sometimes reflecting F. Scott Fitzgerald, in later novels like *Brightness Falls* (1992) and *The Last of the Savages* (1996).

GARY McDONOGH

McMurtry, Larry

b. 1936

Born in Archer City, **Texas**, McMurtry has chronicled the changing fortunes of modern – and sometimes disappearing – Texas with **humor** and insight. Unforgettable characters populate his small towns and **cowboy** society; he has also addressed the foibles of contemporary **Houston** (*Terms of Endearment*, 1975, film 1983) and **Las Vegas, NV** (*Desert Rose*, 1983). His popular works have also translated into major motion pictures (*The Last Picture Show*, 1966, film 1971) as well as landmark **television** miniseries and sequels based on the Pulitzer-prize-winning *Lonesome Dove* (1986), which richly recreates the tales of an 1870s cattle drive (**miniseries** 1989; sequels 1993 and 1995).

GARY McDONOGH

Means, Russell

b. 1939

American Indian activist. Means, an Oglala born on the Pine Ridge Reservation, founded and became national director of the American Indian Movement (AIM), which sought to both advocate for particular Indians and causes and to point out the racist assumptions in historical interpretations of treaties and events (like Columbus' arrival in the New World). While remaining active with AIM, since the 1990s he has broadened his interests to include film, music and memoirs.

GARY McDONOGH

Meany, George

b. 1894; d. 1980

President of the AFL-CIO from 1955 to 1979, George Meany was the most powerful labor leader at a time when labor **unions** had considerable influence in American politics. Born in **New York** City, Meany rose through union ranks to become the president of the New York State Federation of Labor and then head of the American Federation

of Labor in 1952. With the strength of the CIO compromised by the purges of communists, Meany was able to merge the two labor organizations, becoming the new federation's first president. Generally conservative in inclination (he refused to endorse the March on Washington), Meany was angered by **Democratic Party** reforms in 1972. He refused to support George McGovern for US president, the first time a labor leader had not supported Democrats since the New Deal. Meany renewed his support for the Democrats in 1976, but later denounced Jimmy **Carter**'s stagflationary economic policies. Having indirectly aided Richard **Nixon**, he did the same for Ronald **Reagan**, whose policies after Meany's death would significantly diminish the power of unions.

ROBERT GREGG

medical shows, television

The 1990s ratings dominance of *ER* (NBC, 1994–) grew from a long tradition of telling stories of life and **death** through the heroic figure of the doctor. Its roots lie in movies like *Young Dr. Kildare* (1938) and *Now Voyager* (1942) as much as the transformation of the American physician him/herself. Like *ER*, many shows have balanced disease and trauma, of which they may in fact provide public information, and the human character of the medical staff confronting them.

Early medical shows, from the 1950s *Medic* (NBC, 1954–6) onwards, made these issues primarily male, although nurses and female patients might provide emotional interests. Richard Chamberlain was **television**'s brash young Dr Kildare (NBC, 1961–6), before he became king of the **miniseries**. Vince Edwards defined a similar role in the rougher-hewn *Ben Casey* (ABC, 1961–6), with its solemn opening invocation of "Man/Woman/Birth/Death/Infinity." Both were based in hospitals, which also provided storylines for generations of medical shows as well as daytime **soap operas** like *General Hospital* (ABC, 1963–).

Early shows also tended to be white unless a specific point about integration was to be made. Later, the black **middle class** would appear in *Julia* (NBC, 1968–71), showcasing an **African**

American nurse, as well as the long-running *Cosby Show* (NBC, 1984–92). Bill **Cosby**'s character of the wise, warm Dr Clifford Huxtable, however, drew on another tradition of medical representation – the kindly family practitioner epitomized by Robert Young in the long-running *Marcus Welby, M.D.*, (ABC, 1969–76). Young was already known to many viewers as the **sitcom** father in *Father Knows Best* (CBS, NBS, ABC, 1954–63); working with a younger sidekick and **Hispanic** nurse, he covered not only a catalog of American diseases, but also topics such as sex-change operations. Like his precursors, he rarely lost a patient or faced existential or political crises.

The medical format has also been adapted to different contexts and programming stressing youth, age, gender (a few nursing shows as well as the doctor hunk) and intersecting with other formats. *Quincy, M.E.* (NBC, 1976–83) and *Diagnosis Murder* (CBA, 1993–) blended doctor and crime stories, while *Dr Quinn, Medicine Woman* (CBS, 1993–9) brought the respectable female physician to the Old **West**.

The ensemble cast of *St. Elsewhere* (NBC, 1982–8), with its fallible physicians, provided a precursor to both the action-driven *ER* (where hunk male doctors still outnumber females) and its sometimes more surreal rival *Chicago Hope* (CBS, 1994–). Together, these shows have broached medical issues ranging from **AIDS** to healthcare cutbacks, interwoven with **yuppie** personal dilemmas of job versus work, gender and racial discrimination and dealing with older parents. Malfeasance and malpractice became issues as well in all these shows.

Medical comedies have been less compelling overall. Yet *M*A*S*H* used bloody medical **humor** to examine the premises of war (albeit a distant Korea) and to become one of America's most-watched series. Bob Newhart also brought clinical **psychology** into a sitcom.

Doctor/medical shows intersect with changing attitudes and issues in American health, although almost all have taken for granted the social transformation of American medicine, in which the doctor has become wealthy, glamorous and powerful in association with his/her control of life and death. Moreover, these roles are reinforced by medical reporting on television, especially in local reports and information shows, and by the apparent roles of physicians in television advertising over decades. While these shows may educate audiences about disease, the need to entertain, resolve and attract transforms the image of the physician healer and expectations for medicine itself.

Further reading

Stark, S. (1997) *Glued to the Set*, New York: The Free Press.
Starr, P. (1982) *The Social Transformation of American Medicine*, New York: Basic.

GARY McDONOGH
CINDY WONG

medicine *see* American Medical Association; alternative medicine; body; folk medicine/herbalists; healthcare; medicine/medical schools

medicine/medical schools

Medicine is a profession that continues to attract entrants of exceptional talent with offers of status, meaningful service and comfortable compensation. Competition by **college** undergraduates for acceptance into medical school remains formidable. Entry into the medical profession requires completion of a baccalaureate degree followed by four years of medical school in order to qualify for a position in a postgraduate training program or "residency." Postgraduate training in a hospital setting has become an essential part of the qualifications for medical practice and can last from three to seven additional years.

Medical schools are responsible for not only imparting a knowledge base to students, but also inculcating a professional identity complete with professional norms and values. There is a natural asymmetry in power stemming from the asymmetry in knowledge between physician and patient that mirrors the asymmetry between teacher and student. Professional norms play a big role in limiting abuses of power. Because patients have limited ability to monitor whether the medical recommendations they receive are in their best interest, they entrust their very lives to physicians. These concerns are particularly acute in the US healthcare system, where physician compensation is related to the volume and nature of medical services. Fees for service physicians are rewarded for additional volume, whereas many managed-care organizations create financial incentives to limit the volume of medical services.

Under the stresses of a distorting payment system, the success of the doctor–patient relationship depends on the maintenance of professional norms to protect the interests of patients. These norms are maintained by: (1) selecting applicants for medical school who can signal the presence of altruistic concern; (2) early co-option of students as junior colleagues in the profession; (3) tying professional prestige to personal responsibility for patient outcomes; and (4) informal and formal censure for physicians whose treatment decisions show signs of pecuniary motivation.

All professions, medicine included, have suffered some erosion in trust and confidence. Always a nation of do-it-yourselfers, the **self-help** movement has left America less awed by doctors and more inclined to try to address health problems on their own. In working out their own solutions to health problems, Americans are increasingly likely to consult the **Internet**, reference books and alternative health practitioners for constructive input.

In addressing its shortcomings, the medical profession is handicapped by long delays between the time educational reforms are started and the time the students who benefit from these reforms enter practice. The long pipeline of medical training is part of the inherent conservatism of medical practice. The latest adaptation to wend its way through medical schools has been a move in practice style away from authoritarian paternalism towards cooperative teamwork in the doctor–patient relationship. Trainees who have learned to listen for constructive input from patients and to share medical advice as suggestions along with the reasoning behind them have been in the making for over a generation. However, only recently have the numbers of these new physicians begun to reach a critical mass in communities throughout America.

The next generation of physicians is being trained in an environment that is thoroughly infiltrated by economic concerns. Insurance-company policies and constraints are just as likely to be discussed in daily rounds as the latest vital signs and urine output. Hospitals and insurance companies both deploy cadres of "case managers" to question the financial impact of each medical decision. Although older generations of physicians see the presence of **economics** at the bedside as intrusive and unnatural, how a generation that has grown up in this system will adapt to the continued presence of an activist payment system is an open question.

The stress of medical training stems from a variety of sources. Perhaps foremost is the need for students to adapt to their continual exposure to the harsh realities of **death** and human suffering. The professional norm of "detached concern" for the suffering of individual patients does not come naturally to idealistic students selected on the basis of a high degree of empathy. Finding a way to be effectively present for the suffering of patients while maintaining the ability to objectively assess clinical situations is a difficult task to be negotiated during the process of professionalization. Errors of cynicism, inappropriate **humor** and depersonalization are common in this process. In the end there is a great deal of variation in how successful each physician becomes at merging detachment with concern. Overall, medicine tends to focus on physical processes rather than their meaning for whole persons. American society generally gives little space to suffering, preferring to deny its presence or attack its validity. Physicians as products of society mirror this attitude and often address suffering as an objective problem to be solved rather than a fact of life requiring adaptation.

Additional stresses for medical trainees come from long hours both in medical school and postgraduate training. Coupled with long hours is hierarchy. A chain of responsibility extends from the attending physician supervising residents who supervise interns who supervise medical students. Medical problems occur around the clock and the system must be able to respond at all hours. It has been challenging to find ways to couple the dual goals of 24-hour availability and continuity so that the same physicians and students maintain responsibility for a medical problem until it is resolved. To lower the demands on trainee hours, continuity of individual physicians has been replaced by continuity of physician teams in some medical schools. This permits the introduction of shift work into medical training and a concern that the norm of personal responsibility may be replaced by a watch-the-clock mentality.

Further reading

Becker, H.S., Geer, B., Hughes, E.C. and Strauss, A.L. (1961) *Boys in White: Student Culture in Medical School*, Chicago: University of Chicago Press.

Foster, G.M. and Anderson, B.G. (eds) (1978) *Medical Anthropology*, New York: Wiley.

Hahn, R.A. and Gaines, A.D. (1985) *Physicians of Western Medicine*, Boston: Reidel Publishing.

Mechanic, D. (1994) *Inescapable Decisions: the Imperatives of Health Reform*, New Brunswick: Transaction Publishers.

DAVID BISHAI

menopause

Postwar women can expect to live as much as one-third of their lives after menopause – a longevity that has stimulated reconceptualizations of "the change." Once a source of shame, the menstrual cycle from beginning to end has become both a medically treatable condition and a source of female dignity and empowerment.

Medical research linked the declining estrogen levels incident to menopause with osteoporosis, reproductive-organ **cancers** and heart disease in older women. Hence, physicians advocated hysterectomy to shorten menopause, relieve pain and pre-empt cancer. Doctors also prescribed artificial estrogen to prevent osteoporosis and to moderate hot flashes, headaches, irregular bleeding and declining libido, considered the most distressing symptoms of menopause.

Feminists, patients and some doctors resisted this model of menopause as a "disease," viewing rising rates of elective hysterectomy as evidence of doctors' continuing disrespect for women's bodies. Linkages between artificial estrogen and cancer spurred women to inform and treat themselves,

increasingly sharing information through the **Internet**. Though, for many women, surgery remained a welcome option, better hormone replacements and herbal supplements, exercise and nutritional therapies gained in popularity.

Women also affirm menopause as a positive liberation from the physical and social requirements of fertility. Aging **baby-boom** women and their daughters offer a large market for these new ideas. Representations of menopausal women now range from images of vital, sexually active independence to re-affirmations of ancient wise women and powerful crones.

Further reading

Laudau, C., Cyr, M. and Monet, A. (1995) *The Complete Book of Menopause*, New York City: Perigee.

http://www.menopauseonline.com;
http://www.menopause.org

SHARON ANN HOLT

mental health *see* addiction; depression; psychology and psychiatry; self-help/self-esteem; stress

Merchant Marine

The Merchant Marine encompasses the commercial uses of vessels and the people who operate them. Ships carry more than 90 percent of all goods imported to or exported from the United States. Although the vast majority of these are not operated by US citizens or the government, the international maritime community plays a significant role in American commerce. The Merchant Marine is not a branch of the military, but historically there have been close ties because of the key role supplies play during wartime.

Vessels that are operated commercially include tankers (which carry petroleum at all stages of the refining process and other liquid cargoes), container carriers (including dry, liquid and refrigerated containers), dry bulk carriers (for grains and ores), roll-on/roll-off ships, also called "ro-ro" (for **automobiles** and other rolling equipment), cruise ships (passenger ships), harbor craft (tug boats and spill-response vessels) and specialty ships (cable-laying vessels, research vessels, etc.). While cruise ships may have hundreds of seamen on their crews to meet the needs of the passengers, most of the cargo ships operate with less than thirty people (even on long international voyages), and harbor tugs can operate with a crew of only two or three.

Most Americans are not aware of the significant role the Merchant Marine plays as the carrier of the world's trade. Large commercial ships can only enter a limited number of ports, often located out of sight in industrialized areas of coastal cities. The rise of commercial air travel in the twentieth century also reduced awareness.

LAURA L. COOGAN

Meredith, James

b. 1933

In 1962 Meredith enrolled at the University of Mississippi, having had his application turned down the previous year. Governor Ross Barnett, however, defied federal courts and barred his entry to the college, triggering riots. President John **Kennedy** intervened, dispatching Army troops and federalizing the National Guard, forcing Barnett to back down. Four years later Meredith undertook a march from Memphis to Jackson to persuade **African Americans** to register to vote. On the second day of the march he was ambushed and wounded by a **white** man. The major **civil-rights** organizations, **SCLC**, **CORE**, **NAACP** and **SNCC** determined to continue the march. On this march, Stokely **Carmichael**, newly appointed head of SNCC, turned the rhetoric towards **Black Power**.

ROBERT GREGG

Merton, Thomas

b. 1915; d. 1968

Prolific American poet, essayist and author of *The Seven-Storey Mountain* (1948), his memoir of modern spiritual discovery. Born in Prades, France, but educated in the United States and England,

Merton converted to Catholicism in the late 1930s. In 1941 he entered the Abbey of Gethsemani in rural Kentucky. As a Trappist, the pull between inward experience and the outside world continued in Merton's life. He became increasingly attracted to Eastern mysticism in the 1960s, all the while involving himself in the Anti-**Vietnam War** movement and other left-wing political causes. Merton died in an accident while at a religious conference in Thailand.

MARK BREWIN

Methadone *see* addiction

Method Acting *see* actors; Brando, Marlon

Methodists

Evangelical Christian denomination, founded from within the Anglican Church by John Wesley and George Whitefield in the mid-eighteenth century, whose largest group of adherents, **white** and **African American**, live in the United States. Methodist denominations, while low church in ritual, are centralized and organized under the direction of bishops who supervise their own regions. This has allowed the denomination to be expansive, sending missionaries into new territories and countries previously unprovided for; it has also made it prone to schism and internal division.

The issue of **race** has been one of the major forces of tension among American Methodists. Both the African Methodist Episcopal (AME) Church in **Philadelphia, PA** and the AME Zion Church in **New York** City, NY were established in the nineteenth century by black men and women who could no longer abide the discriminatory seating practices in Methodist Churches. This division between white and black Methodists has remained, African Methodists now comprising as many as 4 million separate congregants in the United States.

Race caused another fundamental split in the mid-nineteenth century, when Southerners resisted the eradication of slavery, breaking away in 1844 to establish their own denomination, the Methodist

Episcopal Church, South. After the end of slavery, the MEC, South formed segregated churches for their "colored" brethren, which became, in 1870, the Colored Methodist Episcopal Church (later called Christian ME).

By the twentieth century, with pressure coming from other denominations that were growing more quickly – the more elite churches like **Episcopalians** and **Presbyterians** attracting wealthier Americans, the Baptists and Spiritualist churches appealing to poorer Protestants, and the Catholic church growing among immigrants – many Methodists felt the need for consolidation. In 1939, therefore, the MEC and MEC, South reunited, and then in 1968 the United Methodist Church (UMC) came into existence by combining the Methodists and other liturgically similar Protestant denominations. In the early 1990s, the UMC alone had a worldwide membership of about 50 million, 11 million of whom resided in the United States. Overall, Methodism was the third-largest affiliated Christian denomination in America with 13 million members and over 52,000 churches.

Besides a church organization conducive to expansion, Methodism has also increased its appeal by avoiding extremes, at least theologically. Once political issues that divide Methodists diminish in importance, then other differences can be smoothed over. The racial divide, however, is not one that Methodists can easily overcome.

Further reading

Norwood, F.A. (1974) *The Story of American Methodism*, Nashville: Abingdon.

ROBERT GREGG

Mexico, relations with

Mexico's relationship with the United States began with the settlement of Anglo-Americans in northern Mexico in the 1820s. Hostilities between the two governments and groups of citizens, particularly in what is now the southwestern United States, escalated into the Mexican American War of 1846–8. The Treaty of Guadalupe Hidalgo officially ended the war between the two nations, although portions of the treaty remain in dispute

over 150 years after its signing. Relations between Mexico and the United States and its citizens have fluctuated from cordial to violent.

On the macroscopic level, the relationship of the United States with Mexico in the last fifty years is a neo-colonial one. Mexico's material and human resources are continually utilized by the United States, on both sides of the border. This unequal status and exploitation began in 1848, and violent eruptions, such as the Mexican Revolution of 1910, have resulted. The Border Industrialization Program in the 1960s, and the North American Free Trade Agreement in the 1990s, have further eroded the Mexican economy and government and created domestic instability. At the beginning of the twenty-first century, issues such as the United States' militarization of the border in "wars" on drugs and undocumented **immigration** continue the legacy of distrust between the two nations.

At the microscopic level, the 1848 treaty awarded the northern half of Mexico to the United States, and, with it, the people on those lands. Personal and political ties remained between Mexicans living on both sides of the border and distinct cultural variations emerged. Mexicans and Mexican culture (and United States citizens and their culture) continue to move back and forth across the Rio Grande, suggesting the border between the two countries is more political than social. Despite at times hostile relations between the two governments, personal and **community** relations continue to thrive. Mujer a Mujer, a binational network of female workers discussing shared labor concerns, demonstrates the strength and utility of such ties.

One area which transcends both nations is the ecosystem they share. Since the 1960s, devastating water, air and soil pollution has affected all living organisms in both countries. The Coalition for Justice in the Maquiladoras is one example of a simultaneously grassroots and transnational organization formed to address shared concerns, such as the environment. This type of relationship between the United States and Mexico will necessarily increase as the number of Mexicans rises, both south and north of the border. The **Chicano/Chicana** population is one of the fastest growing in the United States. They have made **Los Angeles, CA** the second-largest

Mexican city, suggesting the complexity of United States–Mexican relations in the future.

See also: borderlands

Further reading

Griswold del Castillo, R. (1990) *The Treaty of Guadalupe Hidalgo: A Legacy of Conflict*, Norman, OK: University of Oklahoma.

Meyer, M. and Sherman, W. (1995) *The Course of Mexican History*, New York: Oxford University.

Pastor, R. and Castaneda, J. (1988) *Limits to Friendship: The United States and Mexico*, New York: Vintage Books.

SUSAN MARIE GREEN

Miami, FL

While **Florida** has marketed sun and beaches for generations, no other area has distilled this into the jazzy cosmopolitan styles of Miami, Miami Beach, Fort Lauderdale and other nearby communities constituting a metropolitan population of 3.5 million. These cities' many roles and images as capitals of the new Caribbean, trendsetters for youth, retirement havens for the elderly and glamorous **celebrity** resorts have nevertheless clashed with ethnic and racial divisions as well as the fragility of the Everglades ecosystem, which development continually threatens.

Miami's 1920s boom was crushed by a hurricane and the Depression, but the city rebounded after the Second World War as a resort for the urban **Northeast**. Among the diverse communities which expanded its Southern **African American** and **white** populations were **Jews** from **New York** City, NY and underworld figures with links to Cuba. In the winter season, entertainers as well as poorer "sun-birds" enlivened the beaches and palm-lined streets of the city, while elite enclaves took shape on exclusive islands and northwards in Palm Beach.

Castro's triumph in Cuba transformed Miami with the arrival of large numbers of **Cuban Americans** in the 1960s and again in the 1980s. These Cubans and their descendants have richly contributed to culture, music and politics while galvanizing other Latin American communities. Haitians also arrived in great numbers, complicating the racial panorama that trapped many native **African Americans** in **ghettos** and dead-end jobs beside the booming service-sector city.

Miami style – combining the art-deco buildings of South Miami Beach, the luxuriant foliage and tropical colors of **homes** and the cultural diversity of old and new populations – was distilled in movies like *Scarface* (1983), **television**'s *Miami Vice* (1984–9) and crime fiction from John D. McDonald to Carl Hiassen. Despite an emphasis on problems of drugs, crime and ethnic tension, the fast-paced, transnational style these showcased underscored Miami's continuing attractions for celebrities, tourists and new migrants. With the popularity of Fort Lauderdale for **college** vacations and the continuing elite renovation of areas like Palm Beach, Lake Worth and Miami's Coral Gables, this maps social and cultural complexity onto the still straining ecology of South Florida development.

Further reading

Moore, D. (1994) *To the Golden Cities: Pursuing the American Jewish Dream in Miami and Los Angeles*, New York: The Free Press.

Portes, A. and Stepich, A. (1993) *City on the Edge: The Transformation of Miami*, Berkeley: University of California.

GARY McDONOGH
CINDY WONG

Michener, James A.

b. 1907; d. 1997

Novelist whose first book, *Tales of the South Pacific* (1946), earned him a **Pulitzer Prize** in 1948 at age forty. *Tales* drew on Michener's experience during the Second World War as a naval officer posted to the region. In 1949 the work was converted into the Rogers and Hammerstein Broadway **musical**, *South Pacific*, and ran for 1,925 performances. After this first publication, Michener covered much of the world with his stories – *Hawaii* (1959), *Iberia* (1967), *Chesapeake*

(1978), *Alaska* (1985) and *Caribbean* (1989) – and even reached the final frontier, *Space* (1982). Part of Michener's appeal lies in the way he combines fact and fiction to condense complex and sometimes unsettling histories into singular and monumental narratives.

ROBERT GREGG

Mid-Atlantic region

This term includes at least part of New York, New Jersey, Pennsylvania, Delaware, Maryland and the District of Columbia. Generally, this encompasses the coastal subregion, the Delaware and Susquehanna River watersheds and Chesapeake Bay. While it is clear that the Mid-Atlantic includes the northeast corridor of cities that Interstate 95 links from **Washington, DC** to **New York** City, inland boundaries are more diffuse and vague: the **Appalachians** often seem to mark graded differentiation westward.

The Mid-Atlantic historically has been the center of economic and social power within the US. Apart from its claims as colonial cradle to many seminal events of American history, from the Revolution onwards, the region also contains a great many shared American cultural symbols: civic monuments in Washington, **Philadelphia, PA**, **Baltimore, MD** and **New York** City, NY; world-class **museums**, major universities and research centers in these and other cities; and the cultured landscapes of city, town and village. These are reflected in literature and **mass media** from colonial days to the early twenty-first century, when rock music, art and movies continue to depict and explore the region (*Philadelphia*, 1995; *Twelve Monkeys*, 1995; Barry **Levinson** and John **Waters**' films on Baltimore, Bruce Springsteen and many New York producers).

This cultural heritage reflects a long economic prosperity: until the mid-twentieth century, the Mid-Atlantic states were hubs for the production and shipping of goods to the nation and the world, made in and shipped from New York, Philadelphia, Trenton, New Jersey, Delaware, Wilmington and Baltimore. This combination of industrialization and urbanization, fed by European **immigration** and the great migration of Southern **African Americans**, allowed the Mid-Atlantic to distinguish itself from new England ("quaint and isolated") or the Southeast ("rural and backward"). This also gave the region political clout. Although the last Mid-Atlantic-born president was Franklin Delano **Roosevelt**, advisors, money and votes are consolidated *and* close to Washington.

As US manufacturing has moved overseas since the 1960s, there is a sense that the Mid-Atlantic's hegemony is being eclipsed by others. In a post-industrial economy, the region is now commonly associated with crumbling cities desperately attempting to revive themselves, sprawling **suburbs** connected by aging **highways** and railroads, and ever-present problems of pollution, drugs, crimes and poverty. **Tourism** still brings in revenues, but urban populations plummet each year as citizens have opted for new **Sunbelt** and **Pacific Northwest** opportunities.

Despite these changes, the Mid-Atlantic continues to offer promise to citizens and visitors alike. Its history and cultural diversity has been renewed by migration from Europe, Asia, Latin America and the **Caribbean** and Africa. Its landscapes include a wide range of cityscapes, small towns and rural landscapes shaped by centuries of care, as well as the rivers and bays of the coast. While **Southwestern** and **California** cuisine have been fashionable, Mid-Atlantic cities claim the best cuisine among European and other ethnic restaurants, while local specialties reflect the natural and cultivated resources of the area, whether Maryland crabs, **Amish** pastries or urban street **food**. In all, the region embodies the promises and dilemmas of America in the global century.

BRAD ROGERS

middle age

Middle age is a relative concept. Although the term literally means a mid-point between **birth** and **death**, most Americans consider it to fall in the years between forty and sixty. During these years, health problems or a parent's death remind us that life is finite. Balancing the needs of **children** and aging parents, while assessing career goals, creates a convergence of life events that is accompanied by a re-evaluation of the life lived, with adjustments of expectations for the future.

People experience becoming middle aged at different points, depending on life experiences. The early onset of chronic illness can evoke these feelings in the thirties. Likewise, good health and an active lifestyle may postpone the perception of middle age until the sixties or even seventies. For those starting families in their forties, the feeling of middle age may occur later in life. During the 1960s, the youth culture motto was "Never trust anyone over thirty." As those who chanted that slogan now enter middle age, they are reassessing their lives and redefining aging.

American culture is intensely youth oriented, thus middle age is rarely greeted with enthusiasm. The **baby boomer** population has embraced the anti-aging industry with gusto. Researchers are exploring options for delaying the aging process. **Plastic surgery**, hair transplants, **physical fitness**, **New Age** cures and vitamin and hormonal supplements may be sought to offset the effects of aging. Many of these remedies are expensive and only available to the more affluent.

Middle age is marked by health-related changes that will continue into **old age**, although there is no clear dividing line between the two stages. Physical signs can occur simultaneously with the development of chronic health problems. Loss of flexibility and stamina are common. Hormones change, signaling the onset of **menopause** for women. Male menopause – andropause – refers to the lethargy and depression that may accompany middle age.

Midlife crises can occur and may involve upheavals in relationships and careers. Some will recognize that the endless possibilities of youth are no longer available. Aware that life is half over, they may rebel against day-to-day routines. A teacher supporting a **family** may realize he or she will not become a famous screenwriter as he or she once dreamed. Others may suddenly regret a choice of partner and yearn for carefree youth. Men may marry younger women, cynically called "trophy wives," and start a new family. Women may pursue **education** or a career that was postponed due to child rearing.

Although many find midlife to be a stressful time of transition and re-evaluation, others find em-

powerment. New freedoms and opportunities become available as responsibilities to children and aging parents are fulfilled. Careers and finances may be more stable. Some will emerge from middle age feeling satisfied with their choices and excited about their life ahead.

Further reading

Porcino, J. (1991) *Growing Older, Getting Better: A Handbook for Women in the Second Half of Life*, New York: Crossroad.

Sheehy, G. (1999) *Understanding Men's Passages: Discovering the New Map of Men's Lives*, New York: Ballantine.

JENNIFER CAMPBELL

middle class

In his 2000 campaign, George W. **Bush** vowed to "tear down the tollbooths to the middle class" and "let everyone get a piece of the American dream." The middle class represents the unmarked, "unbounded" **class** in postwar American society, as earlier success stories have expanded with new **mobility**, **migration** away from markers of class history like urban **neighborhoods** and ethnicities and an economy of consumption in which workers, bourgeoisie and elites may share commodities and institutions. Nonetheless, this class remains ambiguous, divided in gender, **race** and interests and uncertain of its status and future – "fear" and "anxiety" prove surprisingly common words in contemporary reports on the middle class.

Boundaries and definitions underscore ambiguous concepts and uses of class as well. *Forbes* magazine, for example, labels $15,000–30,000 per annum lower middle class, puts middle class into the $35,000–75,000 income bracket and starts upper-middle class between $75,000 and $150,000 (D'Souza 1999), with concomitant differences in accumulated assets. Yet the same article notes that even the new **millionaires** assume "middle-class" behaviors, and the article omits a **working class** entirely (below $15,000 is considered poor).

Other divisions in American society also complicate the discussion. While the **white** middle class lies vaguely between the very wealthy and the working class, the African American middle class historically has incorporated workers with steady employment, not always skilled, because of the many blacks either under-employed or living below the poverty line. Similarly, women of the "middle class" have questioned their definition by domesticity in entering the job market and defining the two-career family as a norm. Katherine Newman (1999), however, has found that middle-class women face more anxiety and loss in **divorce** than do working-class women.

As noted in the overview article on class, these categories are defined by social and cultural characteristics as well. The middle class is strongly associated with business ownership and executive status, professional and some intellectual work and higher ranks of government service – "white-collar jobs." Income is complicated by the role of dual-income families, accumulated investments in homes, stocks and retirement funds and indebtedness. Class is also demarcated by **education**, social capital, culture and consumption. Middle-class choices in art, **fashion**, **tourism**, home and connections distinguish the middle class from stereotypes of the working class, on the one hand, while, on the other hand, resembling and confusing consumption patterns of the **upper class**. Here, differences often appear in class reproduction: going to Harvard, the **opera**, or **museums** are highbrow behaviors open to middle and working classes; having a part of the institution named after your family represents a different status. Ambiguities of mobility and class permeate the image of 1990s high-tech millionaires from middle-class backgrounds.

The middle class is paradoxically characterized as a shared goal (even upper-class scions identify with the middle class in public rhetoric, as George Bush and Steve Forbes have shown), and uncomfortable situations. After the immense prosperity of the 1950s, sections of the middle class often have seen themselves threatened in economic and personal security (recessions, **crime**, health, **downsizing**). They have wondered how to keep their status and transmit it to future generations – who, in the 1960s at least, sometimes claimed not to want this inheritance. This leads to political divisions between middle-class liberals, who support at least limited social reform, environmental

protection and multicultural recognition, and conservatives, concerned with shoring up their position by tax cuts, **family** support, mortgage deductions, etc. Hence, politicians as different as Ronald **Reagan** and Bill **Clinton** have appealed to the middle-class vote.

Mass-media imagery of the middle class takes many of the perquisites of social class for granted, unless the plot calls them into question as an individual or relationship crisis (e.g. *Falling Down*, 1993; *American Beauty*, 1999). At the same time, **Hollywood** glamour and stereotypes of gender, race and beauty may reaffirm middle-class anxiety – is the wedding in *Father of the Bride* (1950 and 1991) really what our daughter needs? Are out houses as neat and ordered as those of many **sitcoms** or Martha **Stewart**? Can our clothes compare with the fashions of *You've Got Mail* (1999) or our lives with the leisure and **New York** City apartments of **television**'s *Friends* (NBC, 1994–)?

The development of the African American middle class during and after the 1950s provides an important counterpoint. Mobility became possible in part through changes in the United States job market in a number of employment areas: government civil service, the armed forces, industrial labor and universities. Local and federal administrations were forced, either through political pressure from minority communities or **civil-rights** legislation, to begin combating discrimination in hiring and recruitment. Between 1960 and 1965 alone, 380,000 **African Americans** acquired white-collar employment, enlarging the black middle class to about 4 million, or one-fifth of the total African American population. Later retrenchment in **affirmative action** as well as downsizing and deregulation have affected this growth. The size of the black middle class continued to increase during the 1980s – as many as a third of all black families now earn between $25,000 and $50,000. Yet, the manner in which this increase occurred has not been very promising. In many instances, it has reflected both adults in a family moving into the lower-income levels of the middle class.

Members of the black middle class also face the problem of a polarizing American economy. In this, they have not been alone: the overall proportion of the workforce earning poverty-level wages rose from 25.7 percent to 31.5 percent during the 1980s, while the proportion earning three or more times poverty level actually fell, from 14.2 percent to 12.7 percent. The emergence of other immigrant middle classes – **Asian American** and **Latino** – has introduced new elements of competition for blacks and whites.

Ironically, media attention to the black middle class has grown as its position becomes more tenuous. Like other groups facing external pressures, threats have made members of this class more vocal and self-conscious about their politics, accentuating a trend, already detectable, towards black nationalism. The establishment of a more clearly defined class also increased the visibility of institutions representing it, from the black churches, **colleges** and clubs to the **NAACP**, as well as segregated **suburbs** and other spaces. Meanwhile, black middle-class conservatives have questioned both long-time connections of African Americans to the **Democratic Party** and policies associated with the welfare state. Nonetheless, continuing discrimination and harassment based on "guilt by association" fuel continuing rage.

Further reading

Bartlett, D. and Steele, J. (1996) *America: Who Stole the Dream?*, Kansas City: Andrews and McMeel.

Dent, D. (2000) *In Search of Black America*, New York: Simon & Schuster.

D'Souza, D. (1999) "The Billionaires Next Door," *Forbes*, October 11.

Ehrenreich, B. (1989) *Fear of Falling*, New York: Pantheon.

Frazier, E. (1966) *Black Bourgeoisie*, New York: The Free Press.

Fusell, P. (1992) *Class*, New York: Simon & Schuster.

Newman, K. (1999) *Falling from Grace*, Berkeley: University of California.

Rubin, J (1992) *The Making of Middle/brow Culture*, Chapel Hill: University of North Carolina.

GARY McDONOGH
ROBERT GREGG
CINDY WONG

Middle East

American foreign and domestic policy are often tied to two primary issues of this turbulent region: **religion** and **oil**. Religious ties have focused on the status of Israel (and Palestine) as a Holy Land for Christianity, Judaism and **Islam**, with special questions about Jerusalem. Since the birth of Israel as a state, the US has often acted as a guarantor of its sovereignty through military aid and diplomatic support. While this affiliation has rested on various ideological foundations, it also incorporates strong linkages between **Jews** in the United States and the Zionist commitment to Israel. This does not imply a monolithic Jewish lobby: there have been both tremendous economic, spiritual and political support for Israel among American Jews and severe criticism. Yet it means that issues of Israel must be addressed in local politics, especially in areas like **New York** City, NY.

Christian attitudes range from those who regard Jerusalem, Bethlehem and other centers as holy monuments divorced from their local/political history to those who would hasten the Apocalypse there. Some **Arab Americans** also see this area as both religious center and homeland, especially in the case of Americans of Palestinian descent, Christians and Muslims.

These linkages have led to intense American involvement in fostering regional peace with guarantees for Israel's security. American involvement in Lebanon grew out of these ongoing conflicts, while Presidents **Carter** and **Clinton** have hosted lengthy summits at Camp David in search of peace.

At the same time, the Middle East holds oil, often in Arab states towards which the US once adopted neo-colonial relationships. Here, alliance with Israel has been read as opposition to Arab claims. Ongoing difficulties with **Iran**, Iraq and Libya, as well as complex alliances with the conservative Islamic regimes of Saudi Arabia and Kuwait, have complicated American foreign policy while ensuring – even by war – the supply of relatively cheap fuel. The **Gulf War** underscored the complexity of power and dependency that binds the US to the past and future of this region.

GARY McDONOGH

Midwest

The Midwest is the most ambiguous and least well-defined of major American regions. In contrast to the **South**, the **West**, or **New England**, the Midwest has neither a sharp, clear historical identity nor a strong presence in contemporary popular culture. There are no music or movie genres called "midwesterns" and no traditions of Midwest literature or history comparable to that of the South or West. Even the geographic referent is uncertain. For some, the Midwest refers to the "Old Northwest," the states north of the Ohio River, between the Allegheny Mountains and the Mississippi River. But for others the heart of the Midwest lies in the plains states of Kansas and Nebraska, well to the west of the Mississippi. While an inclusive twelve-state definition centered on the Upper Mississippi–Missouri watershed – Ohio, Michigan, Indiana, Illinois, Wisconsin, Minnesota, Iowa, Missouri, Kansas, Nebraska and the two Dakotas – is becoming somewhat standard, there is no real consensus even on this most basic issue.

Another way of envisioning the Midwest is as the hinterland of **Chicago, IL**. The Midwest is encompassed by a large semi-circle or arc of economic influence stretching for some 500 miles around the great metropolis of the central US. But the strongest and most common identifying characteristic of the Midwest is **agriculture**. The Midwest is rural and agrarian, in contrast with the urban and industrial coasts. Because of this identification of farming and region, the encroachment of urbanization and industrialization from the east and the growth of cities like **Detroit, MI** and **Cleveland, OH** have gradually shifted perceptions of the region more to the west. Michigan and Ohio have lost some of their credentials as Midwestern states, and are more associated with the industrial northeast. Iowa, Kansas and Nebraska are now the most typical Midwest states.

Farming and pastoralism identify the Midwest with one of the abiding positive themes of American culture, going back to Thomas Jefferson and Abraham Lincoln. Thus, the Midwest is often seen as the best and most typical part of America, still resembling a small town and rural "golden age," before "America grew up and moved to the city," bringing all of the problems that have beset the urbanized nation. Americans think of the Midwest as the safest, most honest, hard-working, friendly, middle-class, egalitarian center of American culture. The Midwest is Lawrence **Welk**, Harry **Truman** and Dwight **Eisenhower**, Dorothy and Auntie Em and Toto in *The Wizard of Oz*, and **Main Street** in **Disneyland** (made to resemble Walt Disney's childhood hometown of Marcelline, Missouri). Above all it is farmers and small towns – to test wide acceptability, one asks "How does it play in Peoria?" Hence, commentator George Will opined that if God were an American, he would surely be a Midwesterner.

Nonetheless, the 1920s and 1930s were the apogee of Midwest pride and self-confidence. Since the Second World War, the Midwest's image has been somewhat tarnished. It has seemed to many an increasingly old-fashioned and out of touch backwater in a cosmopolitan, modernizing and multicultural society. Isolationism before the Second World War and **McCarthyism** afterwards hurt the region's reputation, in spite of **Truman** and **Eisenhower**'s political roles as native sons. Subsequent Midwesterners have led majority and minority parties in **Congress**, but Robert **Dole** lost to a Southern incumbent in 1996.

A prolonged farming crisis and economic problems in the 1970s and 1980s precipitated a drastic decline in the number of farms and farmers; disasters like floods, tornadoes and droughts recur as themes in news and fictional media. Many Midwest states began to lose population. People fled south and west in droves, leaving behind pejorative labels like **rustbelt** and snowbelt. A famous albeit controversial proposal envisioned returning much of the Great Plains to its early nineteenth-century state as a "Buffalo Commons." Some thought a notorious error in which the state of North Dakota was left out of the 1989 Rand McNally atlas was symbolic of the region's status. Economic hard times helped foster violent, terrorist individuals and organizations such as the *posse commitatus* and various "freemen" **militias**.

But there has also been a more positive side to the picture. Much of this has to do with things rural or "country." *Midwest Living* became a commercial success, touting the region's "clean air, genuine friendships, appreciation for the land, and **family** oriented values," in contrast to urban blight and decay. The *Mary Tyler Moore Show* (CBS, 1970–7), a long-running newsroom **sitcom** set in **Minneapolis**, and Garrison **Keillor**'s fictional Lake Woebegone, where "all the women are strong, all the men are good-looking and all the children are above average," reinforced more positive images of the region. The farming crisis of the 1980s elicited sympathetic literary and cinematic portrayals of the Midwest. While fictional accounts of the region, from Truman Capote's *In Cold Blood* to Jane Smiley's Pulitzer-Prize-winning *A Thousand Acres*, Robert **Waller**'s phenomenally popular *Bridges of Madison County*, or the **Coen** brother's quirky movie *Fargo*, have not ignored the darker side of the contemporary Midwest, elements of idealism and admiration are also evident in these works.

In short, despite vicissitudes, the Midwest seems likely to remain an important and evolving region, image and concept in contemporary American culture. An influx of **Asian Americans** and **Hispanic Americans** is altering the once homogeneously European population. Industrialization and urbanization are on the increase. But the Midwest also retains much of its earlier character. One indication is the increasing tendency of both Midwesterners and outsiders to refer to the region with an openly adulatory and congratulatory label as the nation's "heartland." Indeed, it sometimes seems possible that "heartland" may replace the more traditional but problematic "Midwest" as the primary label for this large and vital interior section of the nation. It is hard not to feel optimistic about any region that considers itself and is considered by others to be the "heartland" of a nation.

Further reading

Madison, J.H. (ed.) (1988) *Heartland: Comparative Histories of the Midwestern States*, Bloomington: Indiana University.

Shortridge, J.R. (1989) *The Middle West: Its Meaning in American Culture*, Lawrence: University of Kansas.

KENT BLASER

midwifery

Long-established practices of **birth** assistance by knowledgeable females, reinforced in the nineteenth century by immigrant cultures, were effectively challenged in the early twentieth century by medical professionalization and concerns about health and hygiene. Midwife-attended births fell from 40 percent in 1915 to 10.7 percent in 1935 – the latter generally non-white. The Frontier Nursing Service and other programs focused on the disadvantaged sparked a new professionalization of midwifery in conjunction with nursing in the 1930s. This foundation expanded after the 1970s, when midwives came to be perceived as less intrusive, "natural," home-based and even feminist alternatives to male-dominated obstetrics. More than 5,000 certified nurse-midwives, and other direct-entry practitioners (without nursing training) assist in prenatal and post-natal care for 150,000 births annually, roughly 7 percent of all births in 1998. While serving rural and other areas where physicians are inaccessible, midwives tend to operate in hospitals and birthing centers rather than in homes, with limited responsibility in difficult cases.

CINDY WONG

Mies Van Der Rohe, Ludwig
b. 1886; d. 1969

His phrase "Less is More" epitomized the International Style. His buildings expressed twentieth-century industrial society through skin-and-bones construction. Before emigrating to the US, he worked for Peter Behrens, then Germany's leading architect, and became associated with the Deutscher Werkbund and director of the Bauhaus from 1930 until it closed in 1933. He was appointed director of the School of Architecture at the Illinois Institute of Technology in 1937. Among his most famous works are the German Pavilion for the 1929 Barcelona Exposition and the Seagram Building in **New York** City (1958), designed with Philip **Johnson**. His style influenced the American skyscraper throughout the twentieth century.

See also: architecture

ISABEL KRIEGEL

migrant labor

Generally, migrant laborers are brought to the United States by employers who employ their services for a short time or for a specific job and then send them home until they are needed again. Often cyclical in nature, therefore, such **migration** creates a pool of cheap labor whose workers receive no benefits or protection offered to American citizens. The cost of reproducing the labor force is also borne by the laborers themselves whose families reside, like reserves of labor in virtual bantustans, in another country.

In many respects, migrant labor developed as a means to get around the problems associated with the emancipation of slaves. Southern planters' attempts to hire **Chinese Americans** and South Asian laborers during Reconstruction, for example, were thwarted by northern **Republicans** who, for a brief period at least, wanted to protect the freed people of the **South**. Required to employ **African American** laborers, Southerners instead used **violence**, prison labor, debt peonage and **segregation** to re-establish their cheap labor system. Elsewhere in the country there were fewer restraints placed on the use of migrant laborers. Chinese, Japanese, Mexican Americans and **Caribbean** citizens were all used. In the northeast, Italian **immigration** began as a cyclical, migrant labor system, with large numbers of Italians working in construction trades (often going to Argentina when production slackened in the winter) and sending money home to their families. While others have changed their status, laborers from Central America and the Caribbean are now a major part of this large pool of migrant labor in the United States.

Not surprisingly, migrant labor is often associated with **agriculture**. On **farms** the intensity of the productive system varies during the year, with planting and harvesting seasons demanding the most labor. Many farmers supply cheap housing (often merely dormitories) for workers. During intensive periods, farmers will supplement their migrant labor force with a "day-haul operation," choosing among laborers assembled at designated pick-up points. While almost all farms rely on some migrant labor, **Texas** has the largest population of migrant workers, mainly employed in the growing and picking of vegetables and citrus fruits. Others pick winter fruits in **Florida**. Many of these same farmers will move north to the **Great Lakes** region, Pennsylvania and Connecticut during the summer.

The nature of the labor (and conditions of migration) are such that it is difficult for migrant laborers to organize for higher pay and better working and living conditions. Consequently, most earn incomes well below the official poverty level. Early attempts by Cesar **Chavez** to organize **California** farm workers in the 1960s and 1970s, like **union** attempts to organize a strike among mushroom pickers in Eastern Pennsylvania during the early 1990s, met with limited success. Yet most migrant laborers remain vulnerable in the face of opposition and hostility from many in American society.

Over the past century, opposition to migrant labor has represented a strange mixture of humanitarian concern for the laborers combined with nativism (the desire to protect native-born laborers from competition with cheaper labor) and outright racism. A recent manifestation of hostility to such migrants can be found in California's Proposition 187, which attempted to deny illegal immigrants and their families school, healthcare and other welfare. Such opposition, however, has been constrained by the farming bloc which persuades **Congress** to safeguard the system, and by the desire of American consumers for the cheap commodities that such labor brings.

Predicting the future for migrant labor is difficult. Farming constituencies are declining in power nationally, but retain their strength at the **state** level. As such, particular states become more embattled in the face of a federal government that is committed to establishing **trade agreements**, like NAFTA, with countries in the Western hemisphere, which ultimately should reduce the discrepancy between the price of labor in the United States and elsewhere and diminish the attractiveness of such transient labor.

ROBERT GREGG

migration/mobility

Migration in the United States since the Second World War has often been associated with "the American dream" of upward mobility. Such identification is often mistaken, and assumes that migrants make rational choices, are always seeking better opportunities and generally experience such mobility. Although it is true that the growth of **suburbs** gave the appearance of great upward mobility, the myth of the American dream ignores the experiences of the large numbers of **refugees** who have no choice but to come to the United States, and of others who are forced to move within the country owing to some form of displacement (losing jobs, losing land, and so forth). In addition, migration is often not linked to either upward mobility or to displacement, but is rather a question of **life cycle** changes fundamental to maintaining status within the **middle class**. Middle-class Americans move frequently from the time the young adult goes off to **college or university** until he or she moves into a retirement colony.

The origins of belief in an American dream are longstanding. Nineteenth-century Republican ideology was founded on the notion that Americans could improve their social condition by moving away from a place of oppression to one where opportunities were more abundant. The popular Horatio Alger stories cemented the rags-to-riches story in the popular consciousness. Although social historians since the 1960s have brought into question the veracity of this myth (showing in many instances that few Americans who were born laborers really did make their way out of the **working class**), nevertheless the myth has remained powerful, and has helped inspire many migrations, both among immigrants arriving at US ports and among native-born Americans within the country. Even **African American** migration into northeastern cities, which began prior to the First World War and continued through the Second World War, and which radically altered such cities, is often spoken of in terms of an "exodus" out of the segregated **South** to the "promised land." Such characterizations gained hold in spite of the fact that the later years of this migration coincided with the **deindus-**trialization** of many cities and resulted in economic plight for many of the migrants.

The dangers of assumptions about the "American dream" lie most clearly in the fact that migrations (and perceptions about them) are often closely connected. The "success" of one set of migrants or immigrants is seen in contrast to the experience of others, and is often mobilized in political discourse through notions of "model minorities" or peoples marked by a "tangle of pathology." As such, these assumptions fit neatly into or even frame beliefs about **race** and **ethnicity** that become mobilized in public-policy debates. This is especially clear in the case of the migration of whites out of cities to the "crabgrass frontier" following the Second World War. Often labeled **white flight**, since the migration occurred partly in response to this influx of African Americans, many white city dwellers began to move to **suburbs**. Spurred on by the easy availability of mortgages for GIs returning from service in the Second World War (which African Americans have sometimes characterized as a "white ethnic handout," since benefits were often withheld from black **veterans**) and by the construction of networks of **highways** promoting **automobile** culture rather than public transportation, large numbers of the children of immigrants moved away from urban **neighborhoods** to live in the newly developed suburban tracts. While such whites reaped the perquisites of suburban lifestyle, the marker of their success, most African Americans remained trapped in **ghettos** characterized by limited opportunities. What the **Kerner Commission** would see as the emergence of "two societies" was a product of the emergence of a racial divide that was not just spatial (suburban/urban), but was also one framed by migration narratives (those who assimilated/those who could not do so because of an assumed "culture of poverty").

Other migrations of great significance to post-Second World War American society occurred as a result of the rapid development of the western United States, spurred by military expansion and the growth of the **oil** industry. In the aftermath of the restrictions on immigration passed between the 1880s and 1920s, very few migrants entering states like **California**, **Texas**, New Mexico and Arizona were first- and second-generation immigrants from Europe and China, the origins of many earlier migrants. Instead, many were of Mexican origin (exceptions to restrictions being made for immigrants coming from within the Western Hemisphere) for whom the region had long been familiar and marked by strong family and **community** ties crossing the boundaries of the nation state (many such "migrants" even questioned the legitimacy of those boundaries). In addition, migrants began leaving the "dust bowl" of Oklahoma to work as fruit pickers in **California**'s farming and wine industries (as in *The Grapes of Wrath*, 1939), and these were followed after the war by the kinds of migrants depicted in *The Lucy Show* (CBS, 1962–74), northeastern urbanites leaving their homes and making their way to the "land of opportunity." The movie industry too had established itself in **Hollywood** earlier in the century with the migration of prominent Jewish movie moguls west from **New York** City, and, focused on their own westward migration rather than the northern and earlier eastward migrations, the movie industry tended to promote images of Californian prosperity and opportunity. Such westward migrations diminished with the end of the **Cold War** and the decline of federal funding for the defense industry.

The easing of quotas in 1965 returned immigration to levels witnessed in the years before the First World War. Along with refugees flooding into the country following American involvement in the **Vietnam War** and support for regimes that were overthrown (Nicaragua and **Iran**), these immigrants have radically altered the demographic character of the country. Prior to the 1960s, Americans were largely of European and African American origin, with Chinese, Japanese, **Latinos** and **American Indians** represented by regional concentrations. Now, throughout the US, **South Asian**, Asian and Hispanic communities are growing rapidly, with the proportion of Europeans and African Americans declining.

Seeking cheaper land and labor, along with reduced **taxes**, corporations have moved steadily into the **Southern** and **Southwestern** regions, now often labeled the **Sunbelt**, and they have been followed by many northeastern and **Midwestern** workers seeking jobs. The economic revival and a perceived end to the racial turmoil

that had been associated with these regions have made them more attractive to outsiders.

Finally, older Americans have continued to migrate, sometimes into a nearby retirement home, but frequently also to areas of the country, like **Florida**, that have large post-retirement populations. Attractive to older Americans, especially during the winter months, Florida's identification with retirement-age Americans is seen in both movies, (e.g. *Cocoon*, 1985) and **sitcoms** (*Golden Girls*, NBC, 1985–92).

Further reading

Hart, J.M. (1998) *Border Crossings*, Wilmington: Scholarly Resources.

Jackson, K.T. (1985) *Crabgrass Frontier*, New York: Oxford University Press.

Lemann, N. (1991) *The Promised Land*, New York: A.A. Knopf.

Pedraza, S. and Rumbaut, R.G. (1996) *Origins and Destinies*, Belmont: Wadsworth.

ROBERT GREGG

Military Industrial Complex *see* army, US; Eisenhower, Dwight David; Korean War; Pentagon; war

militias

Sanctioned – theoretically – by the 2nd Amendment of the **Bill of Rights**, the militia movement in the late twentieth and early twenty-first centuries has primarily attracted die-hard, right-wing patriots. They support the right to bear arms and have a strong distrust of government; militias are especially strong in the **West**. Many advocate a white nation, excluding people of color, **Jews** and homosexuals. The militia movement has manipulated the media successfully in incidents like Ruby Ridge, where federal agents killed the wife of a militia activist. They have also used small media, including **video** and the **Internet** to further their mission and recruitment, from bomb-making manuals to political statements.

CINDY WONG

milk

Cow's milk, subject to strict government gradation and price controls, is an obsessive element of American diets, touted as the "perfect food." It also provides a national imagery of dairy farms and chores that typifies wholesome American life. The Dairy Council has produced years of effective advertisements supporting consumption, including a famous series showing celebrities from Spike **Lee** to Health and Human Services' Donna Shalala with a milk moustache. Nonetheless, it is no longer recommended for children under the age of one and Americans not of Northern European descent may be lactose-intolerant as adults.

GARY McDONOGH

Milk, Harvey

b. 1930; d. 1978

Gay rights advocate and representative of **San Francisco, CA**'s Fifth District on the Board of Supervisors. After being discharged from the military, Milk eventually migrated to San Francisco where he set up a business in the Castro district and organized the Castro Valley Association. After multiple campaigns, he became the city's first openly gay individual to gain high public office in 1977. Milk helped pass a city ordinance forbidding discrimination against gays and lesbians, but was assassinated at City Hall in November 1978 by a former supervisor named Daniel White, who shot Milk five times after killing then-Mayor George Moscone. After his death, nonetheless, Milk continued to be a symbol of both gay pride and the toll of homophobia in political actions in San Francisco and the nation. *The Times of Harvey Milk* (1984) provides a compelling visual record of the man, his context and impact.

KATE M. KENSKI

Milken, Michael

b. 1946

Michael Milken helped forge the corporate junk-bond concept that fueled explosive profit earnings for **Wall Street** securities traders in the 1980s. After amassing a personal fortune in the hundreds of millions of dollars, Milken was arrested for his involvement in an illegal, insider-trading scheme with Ivan **Boesky**. He pleaded guilty to securities fraud in 1990 and served two years in federal prison, in addition to paying millions in government fines and civil damages. The Boesky–Milken scandal raised public awareness of the growing threat of **white-collar** crime. Since his release from jail, Milken has endeavored to establish a Consortium for Prostate **Cancer** Research.

SARAH SMITH

Miller, Arthur

b. 1915

A leading American playwright since the success of *All My Sons* (1947) and *Death of a Salesman* (1949), the latter earning him a **Pulitzer Prize**. His dramas are often familial in setting, but engage with political concerns. The early plays dealt with issues arising out of the postwar prosperity, suggesting that this often brought with it unacceptable moral compromises, the 1947 play describing a man who had profited at the expense of the lives of American soldiers, *Death* focusing on the emotionally sterile life of a salesman in **New York** City (Miller's birthplace). In *The Crucible* (1953) Miller wrote about the Salem witch-trials, implying a parallel with the intolerance of the ongoing **McCarthy** trials, while *A View from the Bridge* (1955) questioned US **immigration** laws. Remembered also for a short-lived marriage to Marilyn **Monroe**, Miller has continued to be a prolific writer and outspoken political and cultural critic.

ROBERT GREGG

millionaires/billionaires

One million dollars has long seemed the threshold of American plutocracy, even if John D. **Rockefeller** passed the billion dollar mark in 1913. Yet *Forbes* magazine noted that in 1996 more than

110,000 families reported incomes of over 1 million, while the number of millionaire families topped 5 million at the end of the century and is expected to quadruple by 2010. Reflecting both prosperity and inflation, this benchmark now regularly figures in multimillion dollar contracts for sports figures, **Hollywood** stars, executives and the "young self-made millionaire" entrepreneurs of **Silicon Valley**. Yet it is also portrayed as an accessible goal for a typical American person in coverage of **lotteries** as well as **television** programs that promise wealth through **game shows** or televised marriage. Meanwhile, *Forbes* also noted that their list of billionaires had skyrocketed from 13 in 1982 to 267 Americans in 1999, led by Bill **Gates** (roughly $100 billion), whose personal charitable foundation alone has assets of over $21 billion. While affirming the American myth of rags to riches, these plateaus also raise questions about equality, **class** and opportunity for many Americans.

See also: upper class

Further reading

D'Souza, D. (1999) "The Billionaire Next Door," *Forbes* October 11, 1999.

GARY McDONOGH

Milwaukee, WI

With port access to Lake Michigan, Milwaukee developed in the nineteenth century as a major **Midwestern** producer of metals, machinery, capital goods and beer (Miller, Pabst). German **immigration** in the mid-1800s, followed by Poles and Italians in the late 1800s, provided labor for emerging industries. Milwaukee was a hotbed for unionism, including many **strikes**. City government was dominated by socialist reformers from the turn of the nineteenth century until 1960.

A strong philanthropic spirit supports performing arts, summer festivals and **museums**. Recreation includes professional sports (**baseball** (Brewers), **basketball** (Bucks)) and lakefront activities. Milwaukee was the setting of popular **television** comedies *Happy Days* (1974–84) and *Laverne and Shirley* (1976–83). The 1998 population estimate was 571,364.

MARC BALCER

minimalism

Avant-garde visual arts movement that emerged in the early 1960s, characterized best by three-dimensional objects in simple geometric shapes. Central figures included Carl Andre, Dan Flavin, Donald Judd and Robert Morris. These artists drew on early twentieth-century avant-garde art by Marcel Duchamp and Soviet artists to develop an art of serial repetition of units, made of common industrial materials, including plywood, steel, Plexiglass, fluorescent light tubes and bricks. These artworks were often fabricated in commercial workshops. This was in part a critical response to the dominance of abstract expressionist styles that emphasized the private experience of the artist, and the gesture of the artist's hand. As against modernist critical dicta, which held that the field of art was the exploration of its specific media, minimalism implied that art was equivalent to other, industrial forms of labor. The minimalists were theoretically sophisticated and wrote about their work in art journals, and some were concerned that their work should draw attention to the architectural conditions of the experience of art. By the 1970s, when minimalism was established as a style, in the hands of some artists it degenerated into corporate lobby decoration.

See also: architecture

FRAZER WARD

mining

Among American resources, those lying underground – **oil** and gas as well as minerals and water – have been critical elements in the economic and social transformation of the landscape. While mining may first evoke gold strikes that spurred settlement of **California** in 1849, longer-term development has also been associated with exploitation of lead, zinc, iron and coal. This exploitation, however, has gone beyond minerals themselves to include the men and women who worked them and the environment left behind. Hence, mining often has been a symbol of the promise and failure of organized labor in the US (as it has been worldwide).

Mines brought together immigrants from many races and backgrounds. Whites and blacks worked together in the **South**. Women, while not active in the mines as workers until the 1970s, sustained mining families and provided vital support for worker solidarity. Towns from Leadville, Colorado to Anthracite, Pennsylvania were organized around the mine, the company, the church and school – and little else.

Coal mining was associated with the **Appalachians**, especially as trains and roads opened access to Southern coal fields. Here, communities lived and died by the mines – through both fluctuating prices and fatal disasters. These communities also suffered from mechanization in the 1940s, which laid off many workers, and from later drives towards cleaner fuels. At the same time, working conditions decimated miners with black lung and other medical conditions. Meanwhile, strip mining, which took off top layers in order to gouge out useful coal, despoiled the landscape and waterways of the region.

The United Mine Workers of America united coal miners in 1890; it later split from the AFL in the 1930s under John L. Lewis (rejoining in 1989). Labor organization faced continuing problems, nonetheless, of racial division and owner opposition erupting into violence. Moreover, the union itself has faced charges of corruption and mismanagement – most notably in the 1970s when president Tony Boyle was implicated in the murder of reformist opponent Joseph Yablonski.

Television generally has portrayed mining only in news items about unions or environmental degradation. Mines have provided rich movie themes, however, generally viewed from the **Left**. These include Barbara Koppel's *Harlan County, USA* (1976), a **documentary** about a 1972 strike, and John Sayle's *Matewan* (1987), which recreated issues of 1920s West Virginia unrest.

See also: environmentalism

GARY McDONOGH

miniseries

Popular **television** format since the 1970s, involving 4–15 hours of narrative, somewhere between one-time specials and regular series. Miniseries offer flexible responses to market trends (including news items, historical reflections and popular novels) and may target audiences during **ratings** "sweeps." They also allow more character and plot development and lush use of exotic locales; they have attracted major cinematic **stars**, reinforcing their cachet. Sometimes linked to **PBS Masterpiece Theatre**, miniseries tend to be relentlessly middle-brow – evident from one of the earliest, Irwin Shaw's *Rich Man, Poor Man* (ABC, 1976) or *Upstairs, Downstairs* (PBS, 1975–80).

Roots (ABC, 1977) remains the watershed (if not the first) – the highest rated miniseries ever and among the most watched television programs. Beginning January 23, ABC broadcast this 12-hour dramatization of Alex Haley's family history for eight successive nights. Vivid images of capture, slavery, punishment, separation and love sparked conversations in families, schools and offices even if *Roots* did not evoke the racial catharsis some contemporary commentators predicted. Nor did the popular sequel *Roots: The Next Generation* (1979) or *Queen* (1993) change the overall problems of **African Americans** in television.

Other thematic clusters in miniseries include the Second World War (NBC's *Holocaust*, 1978, or *The Winds of War*, 1983, and ABC's *War and Remembrance*, 1988–9, based on novels by Herman Wouk), the West (especially work by Larry McMurtry like *Lonesome Dove*, 1989), crime (CBS' *Helter Skelter*, 1976) and exotic historical locales (feudal Japan in *Shogun*, 1980, and Australia in *The Thorn Birds*, 1983). The immense popularity of the last two earned star Richard Chamberlain the nickname "King of the Miniseries."

The miniseries continued as a programming tool in the 1980s and 1990s without its initial fanfare. Religious and fantasy themes have cropped up beside lengthy romances, historical recreations and other genres. One might also ask how these intersect with popular PBS **documentary** series by Ken Burns like *The Civil War* (1990) and *Baseball* (1994).

GARY McDONOGH

Minneapolis and St. Paul, MN

Twin cities at the head of the Mississippi River (combined metropolitan population (1998) of 2,831,234). Founded in the early nineteenth century, they have become centers for progressive arts, music and **education** as well as **economics** and politics in the upper Plains. St. Paul, an industrial/commercial center, is the state capital. Minneapolis is known for the University of Minnesota, progressive politics and its extensive urban lakes and **parks**. Active professional sports include **football** (the Minnesota Vikings), **baseball** (Twins) and **basketball** (Timberwolves), as well as winter activities. Nearby, in Bloomington rises the Mall of America, projected to expand to 10 million square feet.

GARY McDONOGH

miscegenation

The mixing of races, especially the **marriage** or cohabitation between a white person and a member of another race. Miscegenation has been susceptible to changing meanings insofar as racial categories have altered over time (see **race and ethnicity**). By the early twentieth century, as racial difference came to revolve around categories of **white**, black and Asian, and **American Indian**, notions of miscegenation balanced culturally constructed temptations. Certainly until the **Civil Rights movement**, black and white liaisons remained illegal and disturbing for many Americans, closely connected to the institution of lynching. In the aftermath of civil rights and changing **immigration** quotas in 1965, a revaluation of notions of color and race has occurred, with the result that miscegenation no longer carries the same weight as it once did.

ROBERT GREGG

Miss America pageant

The Miss America pageant is an annual beauty contest, taking place each September in **Atlantic City, NJ**, and broadcast on **television**. Beauty-contest champions from each **state** throughout the United States travel to Atlantic City to compete against each other for the "Miss America" title and accompanying prizes. The first official Miss America pageant took place in Atlantic City on September 7, 1921.

Further reading

Riverol, A.R. (1992) *Live from Atlantic City: The History of the Miss America Pageant Before, After and in Spite of Television*, Bowling Green: Bowling Green State University Popular Press.

NICOLE MARIE KEATING

Mississippi Freedom Democratic Party (MFDP)

An outgrowth of the **Freedom Summer** of 1964, the MFDP was formed when leaders of the umbrella **civil-rights** organization in Mississippi, the Council of Federated Organizations (COFO), realized that it could not register sufficient **African Americans** for the state's **Democratic** primaries to make any difference to the system of racial **segregation** and discrimination. Instead, COFO enrolled disenfranchised blacks in the MFDP, affiliated the new organization to the Democratic National Committee and sent delegates to **Atlantic City** for the 1964 Democratic Party convention. Debate at the **convention** about whether to recognize the MFDP delegates instead of those of the Mississippi Democratic Party was quashed by President **Johnson**, who feared white southerners would stampede to the **Republican Party**. While Fannie Lou **Hamer** argued passionately for the rights of MFDP delegates, Johnson argued that blacks needed to show him gratitude for passing the **Civil Rights Act**. The black convention movement was one of the legacies of the work of the MFDP.

ROBERT GREGG

mobile homes and trailer parks

The mobile home (trailer or recreational vehicle) would seem successfully to synthesize two great American twentieth-century obsessions: **freedom/mobility** and **automobiles**. Certainly, the emergence of automotive campers and trailers before the Second World War as well as accommodations for these compact homesteads offered this promise. Yet, during wartime shortages and their aftermath, a second vision came to dominate the industry – that of mobile homes as pre-manufactured alternative housing. By the 1980s, 90 percent of mobile homes remained stationary after their initial move; moreover, they represented one out of every three new single-family homes sold. Rather than mobility, ironically, they are identified with the lack of it, socially as well as literally, in retirement complexes, marginal housing or, at best, temporary or secondary dwellings. "Trailer parks," communities built to accommodate these homes, have gained especially negative imagery, reinforced by urban restrictions and limitations on financing.

The American origins of these homes preceded automobiles – in the covered wagons of westward migrations (commemorated in a 1929 commercial trailer), in elite train cars or even **gypsies** (the "motorized Gypsy van" was another prototype name). Generally, early mobile homes were individual modifications on existing transportation. Commercial production expanded in the 1930s, including the classic Airstream with sleek modern lines. Interiors were cramped, although aerodynamic fittings provided basic house services in ingenious ways. Some were residential but others roamed expanding **highways** and tourist sites – the 1939 New York World's Fair offered 1,200 trailer spaces in the Bronx.

The Second World War restricted gas and travel. Yet population displacements for industry and military meant new uses for the trailer home as "temporary housing." Truly temporary usage continued through the 1990s on construction sites, film locations, dorms and classrooms. Yet permanence also changed production and use. From the 1950s onwards, production moved towards larger units with private rooms and more extensive facilities. These included expandable structures and homes based on multiple sections. Once moved by trucks to a site they became permanent – sunk into the ground, built onto (carports, additional rooms) and landscaped. By the late 1990s, this manufactured housing cost from $10,000 to more than $100,000; even the latter remains "affordable" compared to new home construction.

In the 1990s, nearly half of all mobile homes resided in 24,000 "parks" scattered from expanding **Sunbelt** and metropolitan fringes to **New York** City (Staten Island). Parks have grown from 40–60 lots in the postwar era to an average of 200 sites. These developments often show concern with fostering **community** through decoration, streetscapes or recreational facilities. Half of mobile homes occupy private lots, including second homes for resorts or retirement.

Settlements have not eliminated movement, although these faced further setbacks with the fuel crisis of the 1970s. Compact recreational vehicles like the Winnebago, campers and modified of pick-up trucks have restated the mobile-home ideal in terms of access to the outdoors through automotive freedom.

Yet the social and media connotations of these homes remain clear – although they foster privacy and domesticity, they are non-standard, cheaper, impersonal and associated with transience. News coverage emphasizes weather damage and frailty (the **American Association of Retired Persons**, in 1999, said 75 percent of owners had complaints). Fictional media use them as settings for immigrants, the poor or outcasts; the epithet "trailer trash" conveys a sneer that might not be voiced politely in ethnic or class terms.

Further reading

Wallis, A. (1991) *Wheel Estate: The Rise and Decline of Mobile Homes*, Baltimore: The Johns Hopkins University.

GARY McDONOGH

Model Cities

Instituted by President **Johnson** in 1966 as an urban campaign within the **War on Poverty**, the Model-Cities program sought to coordinate federal, state and local authorities in social reform of slum-housing, poverty, disease, dependency and crime. Model Ccities soon faced challenges to its scale within cities and about how many cities could claim its scarce funds. By 1974 a more anti-urban **Nixon** presidency could point to its lack of accomplishments and shift funding to block grants. Nonetheless, individual programs and **community** leaders arising from them attest to the ideal, if not the realization of this program.

GARY McDONOGH

"model minority" *see* Asian Americans; immigration; race and ethnicity

modernism

To understand postwar American modernism one needs to consider the dynamic field of cultural production that preceded the postwar global hegemony of American culture. In fact, the postwar activity and dissemination of this modernism was arguably a cumulative endpoint of several decades of enthusiastic and creative energy around a particular brand of modernism. As Ann Douglas points out in *Terrible Honesty*, "[the] modern world as we know it today, all the phenomena that to our minds spell the contemporary... arrive on the scene [in the 1920s], and although these phenomena have been extended and vastly empowered in the decades since, they have not fundamentally altered" (1995: 192).

The opening of the Museum of Modern Art in 1929 signaled America's commitment to modernist tendencies in the creative arts of the twentieth century. But the term, modern, is a highly contentious one. If it is an impossible task to define and date precisely international "modernism," it may be possible, however, to trace the discursive terrain that manufactured *American* modernism. In other words, late nineteenth and early twentieth-century ideas of the modern (and, thus, modern*ism*) in America can be sketched as a complicated discourse that brings together a hyper force of creativity with vast amounts of capital, a fascination with **nature** and machine, an uncertainty of the use of **rural** and urban spaces, the failures and successes of efficient mechanical reproduction and assembly-line production and a dream of a recognizable American art. This amalgamation of disparate cultural activity played itself out in the creative forms of **poetry**, novels, painting, **photography**, film-making, **dance** and **architecture**.

The most influential voice for American modernism was that of the nineteenth-century poet Walt Whitman (1819–92). His elegiac poetry and prose fused the tropes of machine and **nature** in order to present his vision of an ideal America. In his *Democratic Vistas* (1870), Whitman eschewed the tradition of Europe as the driving force behind America's own creative enterprise. America, he claimed, needed to find its own unique national voice. Stripped bare of what he saw as the *dilettanti* art of Europe, Whitman proposed a creative sensibility that was manly in virtue and neither effeminate nor decadent in form and content. American art, in other words, should combine the heartiness of nature with the precision and function of a machine. Whitman's call did not go unheard.

American artists such as photographers/film-makers Paul Strand and Pare Lorentz, and photographers Lewis Hine and Alfred Stieglitz, painters Robert Henri, Georgia **O'Keefe** and Charles Sheeler, and architect Frank Lloyd **Wright** acknowledged Whitman as an important creative force in their work. These artists forged a modernist sensibility that sought to represent the American work of art as an intermingling of **Midwest** ruggedness with the promise of modern-age machinery. American artists, especially after the First World War, succeeded in producing an image that streamlined nature and machine while, more strikingly, it masculinized the parameters of American creativity.

"The general opinion is," wrote critic Henry McBride in 1922, "that [the new American artists] are to be as lusty as those that Walt Whitman prophesied for us." Lusty, but strong, virile, efficient and undeniably American, one need only look at the collaborative film project based on a Whitman poem ("Man(a)hatta," 1920) between Strand and Sheeler to see the poet's dream of a sublime American modern art come to fruition.

This lusty and virile American modernism wended its way through the twentieth century where it found its apogee in the work of abstract expressionist painter, Jackson **Pollock** (1912–56). Trained by the hand of regionalist painter, Thomas Hart Benton (1889–1975), Pollock (along with art critic Clement Greenberg in the late 1940s and early 1950s) championed an American art that, like Whitman, refused the "effeminate" European tradition and sensibility of art. Garbed in jean jacket, T-shirt and **cowboy** boots, Pollock exhibited both himself and his work as the pure American masculine ideal of artist and art. As Pollock saw it, he and his work were the profound (American) conjunction of man, nature and art. In 1944 he told painter Hans Hofmann, with perfect Whitmanesque sublimeness, "I am Nature."

To this day, the encomiums continue to be sung for this apparent modernist tradition extant between Pollock and Whitman. Carter Ratcliff, for example, states that Pollock's work "[evokes] a sense of the limitless possibility, the best of his canvases gave us – for the first time – a pictorial equivalent to the American infinite that spreads through Walt Whitman's Leaves of Grass" (1996: 3).

With Pollock, America had hoped to find its "pure" national voice, while it hegemonically positioned his work as *the* international representation of Modern Art. As Serge Guilbaut argues, Pollock's paintings emerged precisely at the moment when post-Second World War American culture began to saturate the world. Pollock's paintings now sell for millions of dollars and hang in many major international corporate centers and **museums**.

To be sure, the tension underscoring the notion of American modernism is riddled with complicated conflict. But the masculinist (and arguably misogynist and homophobic) influence of Whitman as it is reworked by twentieth-century artists cannot be underestimated. But there were interesting cracks in this earnest version of American art. While admiring the work of Whitman, artists such as poet Charles Henri Ford resisted the hetero-masculinizing of American art by championing a convergence of multiple strains of creative practice. His art journal, *View* (1940–7), co-edited with Parker Tyler, explored the perverse strains of surrealism, magic realism, the analytic art of Marcel Duchamp and the pleasures of the **Holly-**wood film. Painter Paul Cadmus and photographer George Platt-Lynes also embraced a non-American modern aesthetic.

Carl Van Vechten (photographer/impresario) along with painter Florine Stettheimer carried the exotic visions of Sergei Diaghilev's Ballet Russe to America. Van Vechten was also instrumental in launching the careers of several young writers (Langston Hughes, for example) who would later become associated with the **Harlem** Renaissance. Along with Hughes, Zora Neale Hurston and Countee Cullen penned a new literature and poetry that evoked the creative energies of life in 1920s Harlem. During the 1950s, film-makers/ artists Kenneth Anger and Joseph Cornell compiled the waste from culture industry production and adorned their films and *objets d'art* with it. Be-bop and swing **jazz**, modern dance, **advertising**, movies and egregious camp aesthetics were other vital forces of American modernism. Painters Robert **Rauschenberg** and Jasper **Johns** also turned away from the "pure" notions of abstract expressionism in order to present America to itself as a well-worn tradition of symbols and junk.

After Pollock's death, the 1960s witnessed a reinvestment and interest in European art movements such as Futurism and Surrealism – Andy **Warhol** and pop being, of course, the most visible transgression of the "pure" American art movement. Warhol's ability to play with representation within the quick and ever-(r)evolving universe of technology and media loosened the old-guard terms for American modernism. Many have argued that the 1960s can be marked as the historical break between modernism and **postmodernism**. Like modernism, postmodern is yet another term burdened with varying definitions of ideological weight.

Further reading

Douglas, A. (1995) *Terrible Honesty: Mongrel Manhattan in the 1920s*, New York: Farrar, Straus & Giroux.

Guilbert, S. (1983) *How New York Stole the Idea of Modern Art*, Chicago.

McBride, H. (1922) "American Art is Looking Up," *New York Herald* October 15.

Ratcliff, C. (1996) *The Fate of a Gesture: Jackson Pollock and Postwar American Art*, New York: Farrar, Straus & Giroux.

DAVID GERSTNER

mom-and-pop stores

Small retail establishments serving urban **neighborhoods**, these "corner" stores offer groceries and sundries, services and sociability, as well as occasional credit, for those beyond downtown commercialism. The nickname underscores the convergence of **family** and business in ownership, residence and self-exploitation, as spouses and children work long hours for limited profits. Nonetheless, these have been a respected step in economic mobility (as in *Dobie Gillis*, CBS, 1958–63).

As **white flight** altered urban neighborhoods, these establishments were trapped. Those who did not close sometimes found themselves isolated by **race** or language. While new neighbors saw their higher prices as indications of exploitation rather than commercial marginalization, aging owners worried about **crime** and hatred. This tension has remained when new immigrants buy out these family stakeholds (e.g. Korean shopkeepers and **African Americans** in **Los Angeles, CA**). Spike **Lee** portrays both the old and new stores in *Do the Right Thing* (1989).

GARY McDONOGH

Mondale, Walter Frederick ("Fritz")

b. 1928

Liberal **Democratic** senator of Norwegian American descent from Minnesota who became **vice-president** under Jimmy Carter (1977–81). After Carter's defeat, Mondale gained the 1984 presidential nomination, but he and running-mate Geraldine **Ferraro** were trounced by Ronald **Reagan**. Under Bill **Clinton**, Mondale returned to national public service as ambassador to **Japan** (1993–7) and special envoy to Indonesia.

GARY McDONOGH

Monk, Thelonious Sphere

b. 1917; d. 1982

Visionary composer and pianist who was part of the select group of musicians who created the postwar **jazz** genre of bebop, and whose influence continued into the post-bebop era. Moving to **Harlem** at the age of five, he studied with the great pianist Mary Lou Williams and started performing in 1934. Although his compositions and performance styles were valued by his peers, Monk was under-appreciated by jazz fans and critics during his early career. He was quirky, unorthodox and sparse as a composer, improvising at times from the melodic line and not the chordal structure. He employed abrupt tempo changes and melodic twists to invigorate his unorthodox playing – his signature stylings served to inspire other mavericks.

EDWARD MILLER

Monroe, Marilyn

b. 1926; d. 1962

Vulnerable, funny, alluring but not threatening, this platinum blonde with pouty lips and breathy voice remains the ultimate sex symbol of the postwar era decades after her mysterious suicide. Born Norma Jean Mortenson, she suffered through a horrendous childhood of abuse before escaping into **marriage**, modeling and film, where she debuted in 1948. Stardom came in the 1950s along with marriages to American **baseball** icon Joe Di Maggio and the playwright Arthur **Miller**. Along the way, Marilyn produced movies, characters and even scenes that live vividly in the American imagination – production numbers from *Gentleman Prefer Blondes* (1953), a blowing skirt from *The Seven Year Itch* (1955), the naive Sugar from *Some Like it Hot* (1959). Psychological problems and drugs marred her last years before her death from an overdose. This has been linked subsequently to her involvement with President John **Kennedy**, to whom she had offered a famous birthday tribute ("Happy Birthday, Mr President") before the lives of two icons of the 1960s were cut short. We do not forget either.

GARY McDONOGH

CINDY WONG

Moore, Mary Tyler

b. 1936

Female actor, dancer and comedian; her long-running **sitcom** roles personified changing images of American females. As Laurie Petrie, suburban wife and mother on the *Dick Van Dyke Show* (1961–6), Moore projected innocence and enthusiasm. These qualities were tempered as she portrayed a single woman in a **television** newsroom in the *Mary Tyler Moore Show* (1970–7); Moore won multiple Emmys in both roles. Her joint production company, with husband Grant Tinker, also contributed television milestones like *Hill Street Blues* (NBC, 1981–7). Her later career has seen expansion to dramatic roles in film (Oscar nomination for *Ordinary People*, 1980) and stage, alongside deep personal tragedies.

GARY McDONOGH

CINDY WONG

moral majority *see* Nixon, Richard

Mormons

The Church of Jesus Christ of Latter-day Saints, widely known as the Mormon Church, or the LDS Church, has over 10 million members. Mormons are found in 155 countries and territories throughout the world in more than 22,000 congregations and there are currently over 50,000 missionaries preaching worldwide. Over half of the members live outside of the United States. The largest non-US Mormon populations are in South America and **Mexico**, followed by Asia, Europe, Central America, the South Pacific, Canada, Africa and the **Caribbean**. The church has a male lay priesthood and, except for an extremely small number of general authorities, no paid clergy. Church members, both men and women, assist in the administration and spiritual sustenance of the congregations. Members are voluntarily tithed at 10 percent of their income. Participation in congregations, community service and missionary work extend well beyond Sabbath worship.

Joseph Smith, Jr., founder and first prophet, organized the church in 1830 at Fayette, New York. Persecution drove the Mormons from New York to Ohio, Missouri and Illinois where Smith and his brother Hyrum were martyred in 1844. Following his death, Smith's successor, Brigham Young, led the main body of the church west in the Mormon pioneer exodus that ended in the building of the Mormon Zion in Utah. Large numbers of European converts migrated west. Mormons were important colonizers of the western United States and, despite disputes over the economic structuring of Mormon society (strongly communitarian) and the practice of plural marriage among some church members (discontinued in 1890), Utah was granted statehood in 1896. Despite difficulties with the federal government and anti-Mormon sentiment nationally, the Mormon Church exemplified nineteenth-century American idealism. Mormonism can be seen as the embodiment of manifest destiny and the American dream.

In the post-Second World War period, the LDS Church has experienced a period of rapid growth, organizational consolidation and financial security. Currently it is undergoing the transition from an American to a global **religion**. Doctrinally, the church relies on the Bible and *The Book of Mormon: Another Testament of Jesus Christ*, as well as two smaller volumes, *The Doctrine and Covenants* and *The Pearl of Great Price*. Latter-day Saints believe the book is a record of God's dealings with his children in the Western Hemisphere from 600 BC to AD 421, culminating in the visitation and ministry of Jesus Christ in the Americas after his crucifixion.

The doctrine of continuing revelation (on an individual basis for all members of the church and through the president, sustained as prophet, seer and revelator, of the church for church matters) is central. Distinctive tenets include: belief in a pre-mortal and post-mortal life; sacred ordinances for deceased ancestors; moral and health codes; individual progression; the eternal nature of the **family**; family history and genealogy. In 1978 the priesthood was extended to all worthy male members of the church. Women are not ordained to the priesthood, and the church has drawn criticism from some Mormons and many non-Mormons concerning public stances against the Equal Rights Amendment, anti-**abortion** legislation and full-time employment for mothers of young **children**. However, Mormon women are active participants in congregations, auxiliary organizations and temple worship.

Further reading

Ludlow, D.J. (1992) *Encyclopedia of Mormonism*, New York: MacMillan.

Mauss, A.L. (1994) *The Angel and the Beehive: The Mormon Struggle With Assimilation*, Illinois: University of Illinois Press.

STACILEE FORD

morning television

Even before **cable** made 24-hour **television** a national reality, network programming adapted to and changed daily cycles. **Prime time** denoted highly competitive evening hours, while daytime offered a melange of **soap operas**, **game shows** and occasionally **children**'s programming, targeting a female householder, and **late-night television** became the province of talk and movies. Within this clock, early morning weekday television became the moment to capture viewers with useful information and ephemera that provide backgrounds for breakfast and departures. Morning television, then, has produced a curious combination of **news**, weather, financial information, sports and chat that has become one of the established features of contemporary television, local and national, and an area of growth (12.8 million viewers) even against cable competition in the late twentieth and early twenty-first centuries.

NBC's *Today* show, running since 1952, is the most successful model. Perhaps preceded by local farm reports, children's programming, or news, it takes over the screen from 07:00 till 10:00. Although current watchers may not remember that the first host, Dave Garroway, was paired with a chimp (1953–77), both the team formula and the established rhythm of repetitious information and coffee-cup chat survive. Successive hosts/partners, including Barbara Walters, Hugh Downs, Jane Pauley, Bryant Gumbel, Debra Norville, Katie Couric and Matt Lauer, have updated the formula, with comic relief supplied by weathermen like Willard Scott (1980–). The show opened its glass-enclosed studios to New York (a 1950s strategy revived in 1994) and has gone on location around the world. Authors, sports people and politicians have used it as a forum, and have been caught by questions not necessarily expected in "infotainment." Other network pairings have competed on ABC (*Good Morning, America*) and CBS (*CBS This Morning*); in 1999 they snare only half the market and 75 percent of *Today's* advertisement revenues.

Later morning television provides a transition to daytime as local shows and syndicated talk continue the coffee and conversation format. Daytime **talk shows** have stirred a great deal of public debate with their focus on controversial, lurid topics of sex and violence. In 1999 networks also began exploring this space. Public television generally provides an early morning alternative in children's programming (*Sesame Street*, PBS, 1969–).

Weekend differences are clearly marked as well. Saturday morning, with school out, is the terrain of kids (sometimes mimicking the infotainment format of the 1990s). Sunday, meanwhile, has been a graveyard of public service, press interviews and reflective television (Charles Kurault's essays or the political forum of *Meet the Press*, NBC, 1947), while "real" Americans are at church or play.

Further reading

Stark, S. (1997) *Glued to the Set*, New York: St. Martin's.

GARY McDONOGH

Morrison, Toni

b. 1931

Winner of the **Pulitzer Prize** for fiction in 1988 for *Beloved* (1987) and the **Nobel Prize** for Literature in 1993. Born Chloe Anthony Wofford in northern Ohio, the setting for her first novel, *The*

Bluest Eye (1970), she changed her name to Toni while an undergraduate at Howard University. After briefly teaching college, she began her first novel while a Random House senior editor. Like others that followed – *Sula* (1973), *Song of Solomon* (1977), *Tar Baby* (1981), *Beloved*, *Jazz* (1992) and *Paradise* (1998) – it charted the pains, emotions and intimacies of **race** and gender. The last three form a loose, historically based trilogy, beginning with slavery and Reconstruction, continuing with African American **migration** to 1920s **New York City**, NY, and culminating in the conflicts of an all-black township in Oklahoma in the years after the Second World War. In 1998 *Beloved* was adapted for the screen by Oprah **Winfrey**. Since 1993 Morrison has been a professor of Humanities at Princeton University.

ROBERT GREGG

mortgage *see* banks and banking; suburbs and edge cities

Moses, Robert *see* New York City and its boroughs

motels

While American **hotels** cater to various urban needs, their locations and facilities scarcely fit **automobile**-driven families exploring continental **highways**. Early travelers found lodgings in camp-sites, tourist homes and hastily constructed rooms. The name "motel," contracting motor and hotel, appeared by 1926, although tourist courts and the small-town "cottages" also competed as titles. With the wealth and highways of postwar America, many low-slung modernist L-shaped buildings with a carport by the office, a pool and easy access mushroomed nationwide. The interstate highway system eventually moved travelers towards major chains dominating intersections with signs visible for miles before arrival (hence, the isolation of the Bate's motel in Hitchcock's *Psycho*, (1960); by 1962, after decades of building, the US had over 60,000 motels. In the 1950s, public spaces and size expanded along with competition.

Motel owners established linkages through professional associations in the 1930s, followed by recommendation services and referral chains to standardize services among independent motels. Chain ownership was pioneered by the Alamo Plaza chain (founded 1929, with characteristic "Spanish-style" courts). Holiday Inn, begun along Memphis highways in 1952, became the leader in co-ownership **franchises**, with continually upgraded standards. Howard Johnson's orange-roofed lodges expanded from a franchise ice-cream **family** restaurant, while other cheaper chains offer basic standardized facilities beside the off-ramp. These predictable middle-class lodgings relegated older motels to marginal positions for poorer travelers, immigrant housing and illegal activities – prostitution or illicit sex (meanings intensified by their representations in **television** and movies).

The economic crisis among the aging owners of "mom-and-pop" motels nonetheless created a unique opportunity for immigrant entrepreneurship in the 1970s and 1980s. Ethnic entrepreneurship was not especially associated with older hotels, although Basque-run hotels of the **West** created a special niche and Taiwanese have developed new complexes in suburban **Los Angeles, CA**. Yet, by 1999, more than 50 percent of all American motels were owned by **South Asians**, generally members of a Gujarati Hindu sub-caste, either immigrants from India or displaced Indians from Uganda (portrayed in *Mississippi Masala*, 1992). These do not serve an ethnic clientele as much as they represent a fortuitous association now sustained by ethnic ownership and trade associations.

As analysts argue, though, hotels and motels are not just about travel but about cultural ideals of domesticity and family, social distinction and even style, as prepackaged rooms shaped American tastes for the **home**. They have also been stages where dramas of good and evil – cleanly lit standardized hotels versus sleazy, dangerous dives linked to prostitution, crime or immigration – are played out in media and along the road. The motor hotel, linking rooms and automobiles, has a more clearly American history, singularly transformed through contemporary **immigration**.

Further reading

Jakel, J., Sculle, K. and Rogers, J. (1996) *The Motel in America*, Baltimore: Johns Hopkins University Press.

Varadarajan, T. (1999) "A Patel Motel Cartel?," *New York Times Magazine* July 4, pp. 36–9.

GARY McDONOGH

motorcycles

Motorcycles have occupied an important place in American popular culture for more than fifty years. Whether used for sport, recreation, **police** or military purposes or simple transportation, they have come to symbolize a number of America's most cherished and controversial values. **Freedom**, **violence**, risk-taking, **masculinity** and **mobility** are all part of the motorcycle's powerful reputation and mystique. Its prominence in the songs, novels and films of the twentieth century testifies to its overwhelming contribution to America's cultural landscape.

The motorcycle was an integral part of the 1950s "bad-boy" or rebel persona. Those who rode motorcycles were on the margins of polite, **middle-class** American society. The 1954 film *The Wild One*, for example, offered Marlon **Brando** as the leader of a motorcycle gang called the "The Black Rebels" who travel from town to town, drag racing and drinking at local **bars**. When Johnny is unjustly accused of murder in a small **California** town, the conservative **community** seeks him for vigilante justice. The film was banned in several US cinemas and was not permitted in the United Kingdom for fourteen years after its release. Many feared that unruly people would riot in theaters.

In 1969's *Easy Rider*, Dennis Hopper and Peter **Fonda** put a new rebel on the seat of a motorcycle: the **hippie**. By placing his heroes on motorcycles as they traveled across America, Hopper reinterpreted the **road-movie** genre while emphasizing the notion that motorcycles were uniquely suited to the vagabond lifestyle.

Robert Pirsig's book, *Zen and the Art of Motorcycle Maintenance* (1974), is also a part of this tradition. The largely philosophical novel centers on the extended motorcycle tour of a father and his son. Pirsig's message in this American classic is that people should care for themselves (psychologically more than physically) in the same manner that a conscientious person maintains his or her motorcycle. Pirsig stresses importance of human's symbiotic relationship with technology, represented by the motorcycle.

In this vein, the motorcycle also has served as the adhesive for notorious groups. The Hell's Angels were a rough gang of motorcycle enthusiasts famous for their leather jackets, their appetite for drugs and **alcohol** and a penchant for **violence**. The Angels were an intimidating force during the 1960s (evident in their role in Tom **Wolfe**'s book about Ken Kesey and the Merry Pranksters, *The Electric Kool-Aid Acid Test*, 1968). The mere sound of their approach (the collective roar of their engines) invoked fear in the hearts of outsiders. Accordingly, the Rolling Stones hired them as security for the band's 1969 debacle of a free concert at Altamont Speedway. During the show, some spectators sustained injuries and a few died, although the Hell's Angels' role in the deaths at Altamont has been a point of contention. Many commentators trace disillusionment with 1960s counterculture to this day.

Harley-Davidson motorcycles, or "Hogs," are the objects of unparalleled cult enthusiasm. These American-made machines are almost universally considered the most beautiful and well-built motorcycles in the world. Proud owners ride them hundreds of miles to conventions where they bask in the presence of those who share their love for these machines. Still, the American monopoly on quality motorcycle manufacturing has come under fire. While BMW has almost always been known to produce well-made bikes, the Japanese have made the largest impact on motorcycle culture in the United States with faster engines and sleeker body designs. Though many consumers prefer the more performance-oriented Japanese models, Harley-Davidson enthusiasts always seem satisfied with the aesthetics and endurance possessed by their famous cycles.

Harley-Davidson memorabilia and **collectibles** and senior owners also evoke the taming of the motorcycle, in which **mass media** as well as **consumerism** have had critical roles. For example, the popular 1950s retrospective television **sitcom** *Happy Days* (ABC, 1974–84) featured Arthur Fonzarelli – Fonzie – as the motorcycle-riding auto mechanic who defined "cool." While Fonzie's reputation for toughness and daring certainly fitted the "bad-boy" image, he was a watered-down version of the motorcycle riders of the 1950s. His relationship with the thoroughly middle-class Cunningham family gave Fonzie a respectability which earlier characters had lacked.

Yet motorcycles also challenge the edges of sport and society. One of the most appealing aspects of the motorcycle in America has always been its suitability for death-defying feats of courage. America's most famous thrill-seeker, Evel Knievel, has performed his famous leaps almost exclusively on motorcycles. Moreover, motor-cross racing is one of the many maturing **X-sports** and is successful precisely because it is fast and dangerous. This is what people originally loved and feared about motorcycles. Today these machines are as popular as ever and, though with much less gender specificity, they continue to represent and reinterpret, sometimes in a more commodified mode, many of the same values that they did in the 1950s.

JAMES DAVID

Motown

A company, a sound, a polished set of star acts and a city – **Detroit, MI**. Founded by songwriter and Ford assembly-line worker Barry Gordy, Jr. in 1959, when he decided to promote his own songs and local talent on a variety of labels, including Tamla and Motown. From the "Hitsville, USA" office in Detroit, Gordy built one of the largest black entertainment companies in the country; by 1965 it earned $12 million. Gordy worked with talented songwriters like the Holland-Dozier-Holland team, who later left embittered. With 170 acts – some from local **high schools** – including superstars like Diana Ross and the **Supremes**, Marvin **Gaye**, (Little) Stevie **Wonder**, Michael **Jackson** and family, Martha and the Vandellas and others who offered catchy music and lyrics, smooth harmonies, powerful voices and elegantly

choreographed performances, Gordy changed American (and global) listening and dancing.

Gordy moved Motown to **California** in 1970 and sold it in 1988 to MCA and Boston Ventures; it was sold to Polygram in 1993 for $301 million. The Motown Historical Museum preserves the original office and studio, but Detroit is no longer the capital of **African American** – and American – music that it was when people were "Dancing in the Streets."

Further reading

Early, G. (1995) *One Nation Under a Groove*, Hopewell: Ecco.

Smith, S. (2000) *Dancing in the Streets*, Cambridge, MA: Harvard University.

GARY McDONOGH

Moynihan Report

Government Report in 1965 titled "The Negro Family: The Case for National Action." Its author, sociologist Daniel Patrick Moynihan, had served as an assistant secretary of labor in both the **Kennedy** and **Johnson** administrations (was later elected senator from New York between 1976 and 2000). Focusing on urban black communities, Moynihan made conditions that were general to all poor people seem specific to **African Americans**. This was clear in his suggestion that the black **family** was stuck within a "tangle of pathology" derived from experiences in their history of slavery and **segregation** (drawing on the work of slavery historian, Stanley Elkins, and sociologist E. Franklin **Frazier**). The critics of Moynihan's report accused him of racism, and of positing a "culture of poverty" argument that amounted to "blaming the victims" for their own condition. Moynihan's focus on the need to re-masculinize black men (if necessary with training in the armed forces), and discourage emasculating women from working, became a focus of considerable attention among black feminist scholars who noted the work's fundamental sexism.

ROBERT GREGG

Ms. magazine

Founded in 1972, at a time when "the second wave" of **feminism** was hitting its stride in America, this monthly magazine became the first nationally distributed commercial feminist publication. At the height of its popularity in the late 1970s, *Ms.* had a guaranteed circulation of 500,000. It was founded by feminist activist and writer Gloria **Steinem** and Patricia Carbine, editor-in-chief of *McCall's.* Designed to fill a perceived gap in coverage by mainstream women's **magazines** of feminist issues, it featured groundbreaking cover stories on domestic violence and **sexual harassment**, and eventually caused more traditional magazines to incorporate feminist material.

MARY-CHRISTINE SUNGAILA, ESQ.

MTV

Launched in 1981, at a time when the record industry was foundering, MTV (music **television**) injected new life into the popular music scene by hooking young people on its high-energy diet of music videos (short films set to the music of popular songs). The **cable** network's influence reached beyond music however. MTV's rise sparked the continued spread of cable television generally, and the quick-cutting, symbol-laden and visually driven style of **video**-making had an impact on directors in both television and the movies. A number of music-video directors went on to successful careers in other formats, while several prominent filmmakers took their turns as video directors.

Further reading

McGrath, T. (1996) *MTV: The Making of a Revolution,* Philadelphia: Running Press.

ROBERT ANDERSON

multiculturalism

Policy and philosophy promoting a vision of knowledge and experience that does not privilege any single group; usually directed against a Eurocentrism that defines history and value by reference to a Northern European experience in America. Multiculturalism has been especially important in the reform of universities and other educational institutions since the 1980s to embrace African American, Asian American, Latino American and other European ethnic authors, celebrations and perspectives; "culture" here is often used here indiscriminately to encompass **race**, **class** and even gender. Outside the academy, it may be linked with political coalition-building like Jesse **Jackson**'s Rainbow Coalition. Conservatives have attacked multiculturalism in the name of enduring values, **assimilation** and the threat of fragmented knowledge; their critiques have often been diluted by the impact of civil rights and new **immigration** on American society and culture itself.

GARY McDONOGH
CINDY WONG

multinationals

The traditional multinational corporation was controlled from its world headquarters (often in the US). Firm-wide policy dictated the responsibilities of its foreign subsidiaries. The subsidiaries were tightly controlled, often run by imported executives who had little flexibility in altering methods or products to conform to local cultures. "Corporate imperialism" sought new markets as an opportunity to sell existing products, not as an opportunity for development of new ideas.

The concept of "think globally, act locally" has gained credence with the increasing interrelationship technological innovation has created. Multinationals are more than just firms with operations in multiple countries. Today, foreign subsidiaries often run independently. Instead of importing Harvard MBAs, the executive ranks include locally born and educated employees who have broad power to set policies and standards. Multinationals thrive on the diversity of their employees and the markets in which they operate.

The global giants are faced with a challenge: to what extent must firms maintain control over their foreign operations? Initial forays into emerging markets produced mixed results. Cereal firms spent millions in India only to have their customers switch to generic, local alternatives as soon as they became available. Consumer product firms and automakers have had difficulty identifying **middle-class** needs. Clearly, some flexibility is needed to market products to a wide variety of cultures.

Gillette has been particularly successful without modifying its products for cultural variations. On a daily basis, 1.2 billion people use at least one Gillette product. **McDonald's** on the other hand has encountered differing tastes throughout the world, forcing it to serve vegetarian burgers in India and alcohol in other markets. Chevrolet would have had serious problems had it marketed its Nova **automobile** brand in Spanish-speaking countries, and could not sell them among **Hispanic** Americans (*No va* translated as "it doesn't go").

As the consumer markets in developed countries become saturated, multinationals are increasingly looking to emerging markets as the growth engines of the twenty-first century. **Coca Cola**, Nike, Citibank and numerous others have increased their presence in such markets. The winners in this race will be those who are able to weather the turmoil in these markets and capitalize on it. Coca-Cola (by purchasing local bottlers) and **General Electric** (by pursuing local contracts) have been aggressive in maintaining and bolstering operations during troubled times. In unveiling its list of the "World's Most Admired Companies" in October, 1998, *Fortune Magazine* highlighted the ability of firms to allow flexibility and local control as one of the most important elements of achieving global success.

The growth of multinationals creates fears of Americanization and the loss of cultural identity to the point that entire nations feel threatened. Some of these fears are well founded, although Robert Reich argues the increasing irrelevance of corporate nationality. Multinational corporations owe their allegiance to their shareholders regardless of nationality. The outdated notion of "What is good for GM (General Motors) is good for the US" masks the reality of a global economy. Reich argues that the strongest countries are those with the most skilled workers, not the largest capital base. Web-like organizations that are replacing the centralized multinationals will allow power to flow to those with the most valuable knowledge.

Further reading

Reich, R. (1992) *The Work of Nations*, New York: Vintage Books.

MARC BALCER

Mumford, Lewis
b. 1895; d. 1990

Born and educated in **New York** City, Lewis Mumford became a prominent American **intellectual** and authority on **urban planning** after the Second World War, writing multiple volumes and articles in journals like the *New Yorker* on cities and landscape. His most notable work, *The City in History* (1961), provided a bleak image of dehumanizing and dysfunctional modern **cities**. Appearing at the height of the **migration** of many Americans from cities to **suburbs**, the work rationalized increased suburbanization, even while it recognized the continued decimation of the cities caused by the migration of Americans to the suburbs.

ROBERT GREGG

Murphy, Eddie
b. 1961

African American comic and actor who has honed his edgy style in stand-up and street-smart characters on *Saturday Night Live*, which he joined at the age of nineteen. These included a **ghetto** satire of **children**'s **television** host Mr Rogers and references to black stereotypes in media (Buckwheat). Murphy's highly successful film career has included action and comic parts, often showcasing his flexibility in developing multiple characters within the movie (*Coming to America*, 1988; *Bowfinger*, 1999; *The Nutty Professor* movies, 1996 and 2000). He retains his concert career as well.

See also: actors

GARY McDONOGH

Murrow, Edward R.

b. 1908; d. 1965

One of the most respected and influential American **radio** and **television** journalists. Joining the Columbia Broadcasting System in 1935, he went to London to direct their European Bureau two years later, vividly reporting the rise of the Nazis and the Battle of Britain. Translating his CBS radio series *Hear it Now* to a new medium, he defined quality television news through his investigative magazine *See It Now* (1951–5). Here, his reputation for accuracy and objectivity were crucial when he exposed Senator Joseph **McCarthy**'s anti-communist tactics in 1954. Murrow's later *Person to Person* (CBS, 1953–61), where he interviewed **celebrities** in their homes, launched another tradition of infotainment.

GAIL HENSON

Muscular Dystrophy Association

Created by parents and muscular dystrophy sufferers in 1950 to combat neuromuscular diseases, the MDA now represents a major fundraiser in this area, as well as a significant partnership of citizens and scientists supporting research and care worldwide. It has been especially active in gene-therapy research on a number of neuromuscular syndromes. Since 1965 its public face has been particularly associated with a Labor Day weekend telethon hosted by comedian (and MDA national chairperson) Jerry **Lewis**. While the telethon raised more than $1 billion, the growing consciousness of the disabled as citizens has also led to criticism that it treats MDA sufferers paternalistically.

GARY McDONOGH

museums

Although **art museums** and **children's museums** constitute well-known genres of investiga-tion and display, Americans have created many other centers that attract local visitors and tourists. Among the most important categories are historical museums and houses, science and natural history museums, ethnic museums, "professional" or thematic museums and more offbeat idiosyncrasies celebrated in private and commercial establishments.

Historical museums, like **historical preservation**, cherish and explain the past. Many historic homes refer to past elites as owners of history – Manhattan's Tenement Museum, chronicling the struggles of European immigrants, is a rare exception. Nonetheless, social consciousness since the Civil Rights era has forced more explanation and discussion of slaves and servants who made life in the "big house" possible. Museums of **cities**, counties and **states**, as well as the **Smithsonian** as a national museum, have also sponsored diverse exhibits on the racial, gender, **class** and ethnic intersections of American history.

Historical museums may also include houses far out in the country – typical of many Southern plantation homes – or even entire rural villages which recreate snapshots of the past as open-air and working museums. Shaker settlements in Hancock, Massachusetts, and Pleasant Hill, Kentucky, for example, represent modern attempts to preserve past utopian communities, while colonial Williamsburg, Virginia, was restored with funding from John D. **Rockefeller**, Jr.

Natural history museums like **Chicago, IL**'s Field Museum or **New York** City, NY's venerable American Museum of Natural History were popular attractions in nineteenth-century cities. These, like the Smithsonian and university museums, have been centers for investigations of animals, plants and minerals. Some also have developed extensive collections for anthropological and archaeological investigation, especially in Native American research. The last was a point of controversy in the 1990s as **American Indians** demanded the return and reburial of bones and sacred artifacts.

Other science museums look forward to space, sometimes in association with planetariums or multimedia exhibits. Here, popular culture and science coincide – an exhibit on *Star Wars* was a major draw for the Smithsonian, while animated dinosaurs have drawn **children** into other science centers.

Ethnic museums may develop from collections of local ethnic societies or may represent revindications of past denials – **African American** historical museums, for example, have grown nationwide since the 1960s, while the **Bicentennial** spurred other ethnic projects. Churches, temples and seminaries may also sponsor religious/ethnic museums. These museums are as diverse as New York's Museo del Barrio or Chinese Historical Museum, or the Swedish American museum in **Philadelphia, PA**. Some are highly involved in their **neighborhoods**, while others promote a sense of elite or historical culture. Sometimes, these museums have uneasy relations with collections built by American buyers in foreign homelands that present more orientalist visions of the "other." These museums present connections between American citizens and larger historical stories, powerfully embodied in Washington's **Holocaust Museum**.

Specialized museums also portray professions or interests – firemen, **police**, military museums, the elaborate Museum of Broadcasting in Manhattan or the new **Rock 'n' Roll Hall of Fame** in **Cleveland, OH**. Naval museums, incorporating historic ships from the nineteenth century through the Second World War, have also become popular as America distances itself from the experience of **war**.

Museums can also shade over into more personal or idiosyncratic memorials. Museums celebrating **Liberace** (**Las Vegas**), Elvis **Presley** (Memphis) or **cowboy** Roy Rogers turn **celebrities** into history; other museums celebrate, for example, dolls, plastic, pretzels and locks. While such diversity speaks to individual tastes and **freedom**, some are little more than **roadside attractions**.

Many of these museums, despite their collections, face constant struggles for survival, whether in endowment, fundraising, competition for government support or competition for members and visitors. This has led to increasing commercialization in both showbiz exhibits and museum shops that offer goods with high status value. At the same time, museums must be careful of whom they offend. As heirs and guardians of American culture, museums are also caught in its debates as they shape its future.

GARY McDONOGH

music, popular

American popular music has transformed dramatically in the past half-century, so much so that now the generic term "pop music" bears only traces of its meaning at the end of the Second World War. At the most basic level, popular music has always been just that – songs that appeal to a broad listener market. In 1945, however, pop music meant "hit parade" songs, usually sung by white crooners like Bing **Crosby**, accompanied by lush instrumentation. The intent was not to assault the audience, but to provide it with soothing and occasionally danceable songs about love and romance. Such music had its roots in European classical melodies and harmonies, albeit in simplified form, and to a lesser extent in American **jazz**. Considering the breadth of the classical tradition, this was not an inelastic definition. Still, the reshaping of pop in subsequent decades allowed for a vast expansion of the term's meaning, an expansion closely aligned with the dramatic social transformations of the postwar era. Within fifteen years, Barry Gordy, the founder of the incredibly successful **Motown** Records, could convincingly say that "pop" meant popular, whether **rhythm and blues**, **rock 'n' roll**, or **country and western**.

Gordy's aesthetic populism was merely a reaction to the obvious: the explosion of regional and vernacular styles in the musical marketplace. Country and western, blues, folk, swing and jazz had existed for some time, but had been categorized as something other than "popular" – C&W, hillbilly, race music and later the more sanitized "rhythm and blues." Rock 'n' roll, the mongrel offspring of all of these styles, made the greatest inroads into the mass marketplace; indeed, it was the key style that redefined the popular, with Elvis **Presley** as its archetype. The dissemination of these styles beyond their initial audiences and their coalescence into rock 'n' roll in the 1950s was a function of deeper transformations in American society.

Most importantly, the **Civil Rights movement** opened up the marketplace – albeit only slightly – to **African American** musicians. The fights against fascism abroad and racism at home, expanding educational opportunity, internal **migration** of rural Southern blacks and **whites** to **cities** and the growth of **mass media** all played a role in America's increasing cultural egalitarianism. These roughly cut vernacular genres found audiences among American youth, beneficiaries of a broad economic boom, who possessed unprecedented disposable income and little responsibility.

Technological advances played a role as well. Music was now easier to produce and disseminate, as evidenced by both the numerous small record labels able to score major hits with blues and country and western-derived music and the successful **radio** stations that played it. People in the music business were shocked by this music's popularity, but it only occurred because the styles had become newly accessible to a potential mass audience.

The newly popular styles grafted themes idealized by youth – romantic longing, inchoate rebellion, and sex onto the raw dance music perfected by black musicians and rural white Southerners. Popular music performed by figures like Little Richard was now brasher, rougher, louder and – to put it mildly – less refined than before. By the mid-1950s, popular music was in large part youth music, although the older pop form still retained a sizable audience. American youth now set the standard, and music entrepreneurs who recognized this stood to make millions. Thus, figures like Dick Clark, who cared not one whit about the content of the rock 'n' roll, doo-wop and rhythm and blues featured on his show, latched on to the new forms. Whatever their motivations, Clark and his ilk helped redefine what "pop" meant, in the process allowing currents of American subaltern vernacular culture to flow into mainstream channels.

By the 1960s, pop music was now associated with signatures of the **baby boom** – novelty, innovation, and to a certain extent danger – rather than sentimentalism and tradition. The major change in the 1960s was that pop became, rather self-consciously, "art." Whereas pop music prior to the 1960s was perceived alternately as shallow, artificial, or sweetly naive, the new pop was aligned with its era, in which **teenage** life had become a serious affair. Now, social protest was an acceptable theme in the mass marketplace. Older forms did not disappear; body-centered dance music, saccharine "bubblegum" pop, crooners, and torch singers all retained some popularity. But the signature artists of the period – Bob **Dylan**, the Rolling Stones, Janis Joplin, the **Beatles**, Jimi **Hendrix** and Sly Stone, to name a few – had transformed from imitators of rudimentary rock and R&B into self-styled progeny of the bohemian tradition, at one with an age of radical experimentation and cultural revolution. All of them still sang simple songs about love and pleasure. Yet by the decade's end they were most famous for coupling abrasive distortion and lyrics extolling mysticism, irrationality, illicit sex, drugs and revolution. These were the themes of bohemian cognoscenti, not Frank **Sinatra**. Yet they resonated with a massive youth audience that was larger, richer and better educated than any previous generation. A sizable segment of that audience perceived themselves as radical opponents of the **Vietnam War**, as well as the culture and social system of the American establishment. For them, 1960s rock became the soundtrack of their lives.

By 1970 pop music had been fundamentally redefined. Now, it was primarily music derived from African American styles, some of it self-consciously experimental and oppositional (e.g. the Jefferson Airplane) and some of it still focused on the old themes of love and heartbreak (e.g. most of Motown). In the process of this transformation, however, a dissonance emerged, one that was irrelevant twenty-five years before. Now, many popular artists and their legions of fans saw themselves as rebels against a nebulous "system" supporting **war**, imperialism, racism and capitalism. Yet that system is what drove American popular music. Major labels at the end of the 1960s dominated the production and dissemination of this ostensibly radical content. This raised the twin specters of toothlessness and a system so resilient that it welcomed radical aesthetics as a necessity to keep pace with stylistic turnover in the broader marketplace.

As popular rebel artists, fans and critics came to the realization that they were cogs in the machinery of pop-music production, new styles emerged, this time in line with the post-1960s zeitgeist. Experimentalism, no longer a pathway to cultural revolution, became an avenue to hedonistic pleasure. **Disco** embodied this trend and, while less self-consciously revolutionary than 1960s protest music, the culture it generated was a novel one, fusing black R&B and a newly emergent gay subculture. In another development, aesthetic radicalism often degenerated into a turgid aestheticism obsessed with technical virtuosity, best exemplified by "progressive rock." Also, the raw and rough edges of blues-based music found a new carrier in the cartoonish exaggeration of heavy metal, and folk-derived pop shifted from social-protest themes to personal confessionalism. In sum, the definition of pop diversified even more, but the transformed social and political environment molded its outlines.

Perhaps the most lasting effect of post-1960s disillusionment on popular music was an ever-growing strain of irony. Sometimes paralyzing, sometimes revelatory, the irony-suffusing pop exemplified an era lacking a sense of revolutionary possibility. In much of the popular music of the post-1960s era, irony is a fundamental component, evident in the work of David Bowie, **Madonna**, David **Byrne**, Beck, and lately even U2. Certainly, some massively popular artists have mostly steered clear of it (Bruce **Springsteen**, the Clash, and Public Enemy, for instance). Also, ingenuous pop still has a large audience, as evidenced in the music of Michael **Jackson**, Debbie Gibson and Whitney Houston. Still, the fact that ironic self-consciousness is one of the key features of pop music is remarkable, given that the category once consisted primarily of earnest odes to love and heartbreak.

This is not to say that after the 1960s pop music settled into a static state, featuring only surfaces and artifice. Actually, the pop marketplace has been refueled repeatedly by unruly bursts from the host culture. The most renowned of these forms were **punk**, **rap** and new wave, all of which reintroduced a street-level urgency and raw, enthusiastic amateurism. Interestingly, even after the music industry figured out how to integrate these particular forms into their business models, the process kept reoccurring via genres such as gangsta rap, trip hop, indie rock, **grunge**, riot grrl and retro-lounge. While the process of independent innovation followed quickly by incorporation has become as predictable as the sun's morning rising, it does endow pop with an undeniable vitality.

Moreover, pop has lost whatever monolithic qualities it once had, as **niche markets** and genres flourish. Changes in the measurement of popularity have abetted this trend. *Billboard Magazine's* introduction of a new, more exacting system to gauge popularity showed that genres like metal and rap were far more popular relative to traditional pop – that is, simple love songs featuring melodic hooks and a "pleasant" sound – than once thought.

Of course, pop music has remained a profit-driven big business, where sales, not styles, are what really matter to the people who run the enterprise. In the 1980s, while new subcultural genres grew like weeds, the industry itself found a novel way to boost sales by integrating sound and image to an unprecedented degree. Almost immediately after it appeared in the early 1980s, **Music Television** became instrumental in shaping the contours of pop music. **Film** and **television** had long been important in promoting popular music, as evidenced by movies like *Blackboard Jungle* (1955). But now, an effective video was almost as important as the execution of a musical style. Pop artists and their marketers now had to consider seriously how to best marry music and image. In its early years, MTV did not acknowledge the proliferation of niche markets, particularly ones dominated by **African Americans** (in fact, many accused the institution of racism). After the massive video success of Prince and Michael Jackson in the mid-1980s, however, MTV's programming became as niche-segmented as the market itself, featuring rap, metal, top-of-the-charts, Latin and punk shows. To this day, MTV and its sister network VH1 remain crucial determinants of popularity.

At present, the market is best characterized as a hyper-segmented one, where a "pop" center does not exist except on a sales chart. Even the recent resurgence of sugary pop in the form of "boy bands" and teenage divas has not re-centered pop. Ironically, the new "pop" is a niche market in the much broader market of the popular (i.e., what sells). This new conception of popular music far better represents American culture and society than what "pop" connoted in 1945. When one thinks of pop music today, it usually is taken to encompass a dizzying array of styles. For instance, a group whose modus operandi is to shock and annoy, the goth-metal band Marilyn Manson, rightly consider themselves a pop band. The same logic applies to gangsta rappers like Ice Cube, who exaggerate the form into its most antisocial extreme. In a word, they count because they sell products in vast quantities. Moreover, at one level they are peculiarly representative of a new American culture, one that, for better or worse, has mostly dispensed with the artificial cultural hierarchies that were so pervasive in the mid-twentieth century.

Popular music, then, is now more like the actual consuming public – racially polyglot, suspicious of hierarchy, youthful, obsessed with stylistic turnover, sexually open and clearly segmented. This did not occur overnight. Rather, the process has occurred in steady increments over the last fifty years, beginning with the unprecedented popularity of African American musical styles among a mass white audience. Subsequent developments have all rested on this basic foundation.

Further reading

Chapple, S. and Garafalo, R. (1977) *Rock and Roll is Here to Pay*, Chicago: Quadrangle.

Frith, S. (1981) *Sound Effects: Youth, Leisure, and the Politics of Rock and Roll*, New York: Pantheon.

Gillett, C. (1970) *The Sound of the City*, New York: Dutton.

Gurlalnick, P. (1986) *Sweet Soul Music*, reprint edn, New York: Harper & Row.

Hoskyns, B. (1996) *Waiting for the Sun*, New York: St. Martin's.

Marcus, G. (1975) *Mystery Train: Images of America in Rock and Roll Music*, New York: Dutton.

Miller, J. (1999) *Flowers in the Dustbin: The Rise of Rock and Roll, 1947–1977*, New York: Simon & Schuster.

Rimmer, D. (1985) *Like Punk Never Happened*, London, Faber & Faber.

Savage, J. (1992) *England's Dreaming*, New York: St. Martin's.

Smith, S. (2000) *Dancing in the Street*, Cambridge, MA: Harvard University.

DAVID McBRIDE

musical, Broadway

While librettos, storylines, choreography, music and staging have seen enormous changes since the 1940s, Broadway musicals have grown in popularity and scale in the United States and abroad. Nonetheless, the annual Tony **Awards** for excellence often raise questions about the dominance of familiar works and variety reviews over new forms, audiences and sites for the future.

Following the Second World War, musicals turned from comedic, sexy, dance-oriented pieces towards more romantic, complex and lyrical works in the tradition of Jerome Kern's *Showboat* (1927). Lyricist Oscar Hammerstein II and composer Richard Rogers revitalized the genre with *Oklahoma!* (1943), *Carousel* (1945), *South Pacific* (1949), *The King and I* (1951) and *The Sound of Music* (1959) – bringing on stage such "non-musical" themes as **death**, **miscegenation**, globalization and Nazis. Another team, Frederick Loewe and Allan Jay Lerner, added *Brigadoon* (1948) and *My Fair Lady* (1956) to the canon. These golden decades also saw Cole Porter's urbane wit (*Kiss Me Kate*, 1948), the urban underworlds of *Guys and Dolls* (Frank Loesser, Abe Burrows, premiered 1950) and Leonard **Bernstein**'s gang opera *West Side Story* (1957), with Jerome Robbin's magnetic choreography.

Broadway's hegemony was reinforced by star-laden **Hollywood** films of major hits (sometimes showcasing "non-singing" **stars**). Yet despite traditional hits in the 1960s (*Camelot*, 1960, which loaned its aura to the Kennedy years; *Hello, Dolly!*, 1964; *Fiddler on the Roof*, 1964), composers and producers began to chafe at traditional formats. Shows such as *How to Succeed in Business without*

Really Trying (1961), with satiric, anti-sentimental tones, paved the way for the dark visions of Nazism and sexuality in *Cabaret* (1966). Despite challenges to character development and a "songs and scenes" layout, rock music and youthful attitudes came on stage with *Hair* (1967), *Jesus Christ Superstar* (1972) and *The Wiz* (1974), which also marked the increasing recognition of blacks on center stage.

While classic musicals became staples of local theaters and school productions across the US, Broadway musicals in the 1970s and 1980s moved towards more eclectic productions, such as those of darkly toned composer Stephen Sondheim (*Company*, 1970; *Sweeney Todd*, 1979; *Into the Woods*, 1987) and the choreographic vitality of Michael Bennett (*A Chorus Line*, 1975) and Bob Fosse (*Chicago*, 1975). English composer Andrew Lloyd Webber, with Tim Rice, fostered an alternative "mega-musical" model with lavish, long-running lyrical productions like *Cats* (1981), *The Phantom of the Opera* (1987) and *Sunset Boulevard* (1993). **Disney**'s *Beauty and the Beast* (1994) and *The Lion King* (1998) also translated **family** animated films into long-running Broadway spectacles.

Despite continuing complaints about the prohibitive cost of production and tickets and the presence of stage "elephants," the genre still allows experimentation and renewal. This vitality may be seen in the 1996 youthful *Rent* (Tony and Pulitzer winner), in continuing exploratory revivals of older musicals and in the success of off-Broadway and regional theater productions even more than Broadway itself.

Further reading

Ganzl, K. (1997) *The Musical: A Concise History*, Boston: Northeastern University.

Mordden, E. (1976) *Better Foot Forward*, New York: Grossman.

MIREILLE GOUIRAND

musical, Hollywood

While Broadway's show-stopping tunes, dancers and **stars** might seem to determine this film genre, the **Hollywood** musical has a more complex social and cultural history. At times, it has dutifully translated **Broadway** success into lavish new productions, reaching audiences far from Manhattan. Hollywood also has widened the scope of music, dance and story, creating magic with mice, mermaids and Astaire, using music to underpin or label the action rather than move it along, and targeting new audiences.

The Hollywood musical responds to the Hollywood silent, which actually relied on accompanying sound. In addition to filming existing musicals, operettas and Vaudeville acts, Hollywood explored backstage comedies (*42nd Street*, Warner Bros, 1933), biopics (*The Great Ziegfeld*, MGM, 1936). Filmed dancing showed elegance defying physics and human limits in choreography (Busby Berkeley's directing, Fred Astaire and Ginger Rogers dancing at RKO Studio), especially when MGM polished the film. Whether audiences escaped the Depression or explored new techniques of sound and vision, 1930s musicals defined a first golden age, including **children**'s classics like Shirley Temple movies, *The Wizard of Oz* (MGM, 1939) and **Disney**'s animated *Snow White* (1937). Above all, these were consummate products of a studio system able to marshal legions of stars to sing and dance. Theme songs and associated music also developed in this era for dramatic and comedic films.

Musicals went to war in the 1940s with a relentlessly cheery and patriotic face (e.g. *Yankee Doodle Dandy*, Warner, 1942). This also set the stage for a renewed golden age, stretching to the 1960s, when mature stars and new talents meshed in bigger and bigger productions that would begin to crash in the late 1960s. Characterized by an overall "niceness," even when dealing with **race**, **class**, **gambling** or selling a soul to the devil for **baseball** glory, MGM and other studios produced a string of classics like *Singin' in the Rain* (MGM, 1952), which recast the story of musicals themselves, *An American in Paris* (MGM, 1951) and *The King and I* (Twentieth Century FOX, 1956), with stars like Gene Kelly, Julie Andrews, Leslie Caron and Rex Harrison. Musicals, in fact, captured an unprecedented five Oscars for Best Picture after 1958's *Gigi* (MGM): *West Side Story* (1961); *My Fair Lady* (Warner, 1964); *Sound of Music* (FOX, 1965) and *Oliver!* (Columbia, 1968). In 1964, in fact, musicals swept the major categories, drawing in

Julie Andrews for her performance in Disney's *Mary Poppins* (1964) as well. By the late 1960s, success gave way to larger and ponderous failures like *Paint Your Wagon* (1969) and *Mame* (1974). **Star** power also became a point of conflict as non-singing (or non-dancing) stars were dubbed into parts in ways that disconnected them from fundamental action and brought the genre to a long dry spell from the 1970s onwards, broken by stellar exceptions like the work of Barbra **Streisand** or *Cabaret* (1972).

But Hollywood musicals also looked beyond Broadway. Disney, for example, has its own tradition of animated musicals translated into Broadway after the success of *Beauty and the Beast* (1991) and *The Lion King* (1993). Recording artists and appeals to **teenage** audiences were also important from roles showcasing **Sinatra** in the 1930s and 1940s to those that followed Elvis in the 1950s, the **Beatles** in the 1960s and "soundtrack" musicals like *Saturday Night Fever* (1977) or *The Big Chill* (1983), where music moves the action but surges from the stereo or background to do so. Whitney Houston's romantic role in the diva-pic *The Bodyguard* (1992) also underscores the integration of the musical, although **African Americans** were sometimes trapped in all-black stories not so far from Broadway segregation (*Cabin in the Sky*, 1943; *Carmen Jones*, 1956; *The Wiz*, 1978). Meanwhile, the centrality of movie themes and scores (marketed with **blockbuster** movies) creates yet another domain of musical entertainment.

Further reading

Mordden, E. (1981) *The Hollywood Musical*, New York: St. Martin's.

Kobal, J. (1983) *Gotta Sing Gotta Dance*, London: Spring.

GARY McDONOGH

music and television

The music industry and **television** have had a long relationship. Along with **variety shows** and **MTV**, network shows aimed at **teenagers** such as *Shindig*, *Hullabaloo*, *American Bandstand* and the still-running *Soul Train* have showcased performers singing their latest hits as well as dancers interpreting the latest discs. For both record companies and artists, appearing on these shows insured sales and exposure. The hosts – the upbeat and ever-young white Dick Clark epitomized *American Bandstand* and the black Don Cornelius' suave and deep-voiced persona symbolized *Soul Train* – also reflected the racial divide in American youth and music (see John Water's *Hairspray*, 1988).

By the late 1960s, *The Monkees* and *The Partridge Family* also combined **sitcoms** and bands. Both shows followed the adventures of studio-created groups, and the singles that were released became the centerpiece of the show. Saturday morning cartoons geared to **children**, such as *The Archies* and *Josie and the Pussycats*, also became names for bands that record companies created, using studio musicians in a genre nicknamed bubblegum music.

Meanwhile, popular music was used on the soundtracks of many shows from *The Mod Squad* to *The Man from U.N.C.L.E.* Moreover, the theme song of television shows in the 1960s and 1970s became a crucial way to lend definition to the program. Themes from *Peter Gunn*, *Perry Mason*, *Hill Street Blues*, *Mission Impossible* and *Hawaii Five-O* became audible icons of popular culture. These instrumental pieces brought viewers back to the screen with their recognizable and infinitely catchy music (interspersed with the jingles and anthems of advertisements).

With *Dawson's Creek* and other 1990s teen-oriented shows, the music industry and television have found new overlaps. Soundtracks that feature pop tunes heard on the shows are available in record stores and advertised on the show. These compilation albums market both shows and artists. The role of the soundtrack – and particularly montaged scenes without dialog with the latest "hit" playing – has become key as music videos and teen dramas converge.

EDWARD MILLER

Muskie, Edmund Sixtus

b. 1915; d. 1996

Liberal **Democratic** member of **Congress** (1946–51), **governor** (1955–9) and first elected Democratic senator from Maine (1959–80).

Muskie ran unsuccessfully for vice-president with Hubert **Humphrey** on the 1968 Democratic ticket. He lost his bid for the presidential nomination in 1972, in part because of perceptions that he cried when **newspapers** attacked his **family**. Lincolnesque in profile, Muskie was concerned by both social and environmental issues. He left the Senate in 1980 to serve briefly as Jimmy **Carter**'s **Secretary of State**.

GARY McDONOGH

Muslims *see* Islam

mutual funds *see* banks and banking; stocks and bonds

Muzak, Inc.

Corporation that pioneered the use of background music to encourage efficiency in the workplace (and later to create a soothing atmosphere in stores). In the early 1920s, General Squier merged "music" with his favorite "high-tech" company, Kodak, to name his new company, which first supplied music for elevators. This music, characterized by re-recordings of popular hits at soothing volumes, using strings in muted tones, barely noticeable at one moment and omnipresent at another, came to be known as muzak. Ironically Muzak's articulation of background music has influenced avant-garde rock artist Brian Eno and Ambient music.

EDWARD MILLER

N

NAACP

Established in 1911 by **white** and **African American** civil-rights activists, the National Association for the Advancement of Colored People led the assault on **segregation** in the **South**. *The Crisis* (founded 1911), edited by W.E.B. **Du Bois**, was for many years the most widely read journal among **African Americans**. The legal defense fund, led by Charles Hamilton Houston, a Howard University Law School professor, began the effort to overturn the 1896 **Supreme Court** decision of *Plessy v. Ferguson*, which had established the practice of "separate but equal." Houston's protégé, Thurgood **Marshall**, won the landmark victory against segregation, the 1954 ***Brown v. Board of Education*** decision, which asserted that separate is "inherently unequal."

Often viewed as biased towards elite and northern blacks, the work of E.D. Nixon, a union organizer and local leader in the NAACP, and Rosa **Parks**, secretary of an NAACP chapter, in bringing about the Montgomery bus boycott highlights the strong grassroots element of the organization.

ROBERT GREGG

Nabokov, Vladimir

b. 1899; d. 1977

Nabokov combined formidable literary talent, an incisive intellect and a cosmopolitan familiarity with Western culture to produce some of the most influential fiction of the twentieth century. Born in Russia, he left the country with the rest of his family following the Bolshevik triumph and for the next several decades lived a peripatetic existence, living for periods in England, France and Germany. He arrived in the United States in 1940 and spent the next twenty years there, much of it at Cornell University as a Professor of Literature, where one of his students was a young Thomas **Pynchon**. While in America, Nabokov wrote what many consider to be his greatest work, *Lolita* (1955). A fictional account of a cultured, self-absorbed professor who falls in love with and then seduces his twelve-year-old step-daughter, the book's frank treatment of controversial sexual material caused something of a scandal when it first appeared in the 1950s, and still makes some critics and readers uneasy. Initially, the author could not find an American publisher for it. *Lolita* was finally published by a French press, Olympia.

Encountering Nabokov's assured, flowing prose is somewhat akin to watching a skilled artist use a scalpel to sketch a scene into soft rock. His writing features a rare conjunction of lyrical gifts and a disciplined commitment to economy of style. In both his fictional writing and his critical essays he displayed a strong aversion to didactic or moralistic messages. While bracing, he can seem almost too hard and unsentimental at points. It is somehow appropriate that the other great love of his life, besides literature, was the collecting of butterflies.

Further reading

Rampton, D. (1993) *Vladimir Nabokov*, New York: St. Martin's Press.

MARK BREWIN

Nader, Ralph

b. 1934

Citizen advocate against corporate America. Nader came to national attention with *Unsafe at Any Speed* (1965) which blamed **automobile** casualties on design rather than drivers and spurred federal safety legislation. Later campaigns by this austere **Ivy League** lawyer and his "Nader's Raiders" have focused on food safety, water pollution, environmental poisons and other issues of corporate negligence. Public Citizen (founded 1971) has inspired nationwide PIRGs (public-interest research groups), while the Center for the Study of Responsive Law maintains an active schedule of **lobbying** and information. Nader appeared on the presidential ballot for the Green Party in 1996 and 2000. Yet his chief work remains creating and informing the citizen **consumer**, thereby reforming the nation.

GARY McDONOGH

NAFTA (North American Free Trade Agreement) *see* trade and trade agreements; Mexico, relations with

NASCAR

The National Association for Stock Car Auto Racing was founded in 1948 in Daytona, **Florida**, to promote the products of the major automakers, first Ford and Chevrolet, and later Pontiac/General Motors. NASCAR quickly expanded from Florida through the **Midwest** to **California** in the early 1950s, the nature of the sport changing dramatically as speeds increased from an average of just over 100 mph in 1957 to current speeds of 200 mph. In addition, dirty driving (spinning other cars on the track or bumping them from behind) has become common, increasing the popularity of the sport, and making crashes frequent occurrences. Dale Earnhardt, one of the leading drivers in the 1990s, has been notorious for his expertise in dirty driving.

The Winston Cup is the most important prize given to the driver who has the best record in the season's races. While some very popular drivers have surfaced in recent years, none has triumphed like Richard Petty in the 1970s, when he won the Winston Cup on seven occasions.

NASCAR has generally been dominated by white males from the Southern states, like Virginia and the Carolinas. Its fan-base is both national and large, especially with the Daytona 500 being shown annually by the television **networks** (NASCAR is one of the few sports that always profits the networks), but it too is largely white (**African Americans** have seldom participated, Wendell Scott being the exception in 1963).

ROBERT GREGG

Nashville and Memphis, Tennessee

Nashville, the state capital, and Memphis, on the Mississippi River, show deep roots in the **South** in transition to a **Sunbelt** future. Metropolitan Nashville, home of Vanderbilt University and the Hollywood of **country music** (Grand Ol' Opry, Opryland), grew nearly 18 percent in the 1990s to 1,156,225. Memphis, identified with **Elvis Presley** and **blues**, reached 1,093,427. Memphis remains perhaps more deeply divided by issues of **race** and **class**. In addition to Graceland, it also houses the **motel**/memorial where Martin Luther **King**, Jr. was assassinated. Both cities have sought major-league teams and other indicators of national recognition while trying not to sacrifice local cultures.

GARY McDONOGH

National Aeronautics and Space Administration (NASA)

NASA was created by the US **Congress** in 1958 to provide a coordinated governmental effort into flight within and outside the Earth's atmosphere. Answering President **Kennedy**'s call to put a man on the Moon by the end of the 1960s, NASA achieved that goal when Apollo 11 astronauts Neil Armstrong and Buzz Aldrin walked on the Moon on July 20, 1969. NASA continues manned and unmanned **space** exploration, operates the Hubble Space Telescope and coordinates the construction of the International Space Station. Good **Hollywood** films on NASA include *The Right Stuff* (1983) and *Apollo 13* (1996).

MELINDA SCHWENK

National Audubon Society (NAS)

The NAS traces its roots to the 1880s, when it began as an organization to promote the protection and appreciation of birds. Although the NAS began expanding its activities into broader environmental concerns during the 1970s and 1980s, it remains identified primarily with the naturalist and bird artist John James Audubon. Hence, NAS is considered a non-threatening wildlife advocate, supported by weekend birders and moderate environmentalists who enjoy taking walks through NAS sanctuaries. Though nationally known, its controversial stances are few and far between.

BRAD ROGERS

National Collegiate Athletic Association (NCAA)

Founded in 1906, the National Collegiate Athletic Association spent its first years as a weak organization in the shadow of the American Athletics Union (AAU), which controlled most of amateur athletics and dominated the American Olympic Committee. By the 1950s, however, this changed; college athletics became increasingly commercial and **colleges and universities** turned to the NCAA both to secure revenues from **television** and to control the labor market (to stop bidding wars between colleges for players and to keep students in line). As in other areas of American sport, college sports became centrally administered, the main intention being the pursuit of profit for the owners (the colleges) largely at the expense of the students. While the NCAA has managed to keep up the rhetoric of serving the interests of the "student athlete," it is difficult to see how this has happened over the years, and the recent initiative of star players making their way to the majors without pursuing a college degree suggests that many of them agree.

Prior to the Second World War, colleges had allowed the NCAA to supervise tournaments, but the policing of the sports was left to themselves. These self-imposed restraints were found to be inadequate, so in 1940 a new constitution was accepted allowing for the expulsion of colleges by a two-thirds vote of member schools. The NCAA did not use this new power, however, at a time when the pressure to field winning teams was becoming intense and when violations of NCAA rules were common. A "sanity code" was adopted in 1948 permitting allocation of jobs and scholarships to athletes, but these were based solely on financial need. This was found to be unworkable, however, and from 1952 full scholarships were based only on athletic ability.

In 1951 a college **basketball** scandal was unearthed, considered the biggest scandal ever in American sport. The New York District Attorney's office accused thirty-three players from seven colleges of "point shaving" – keeping the margin of points between teams within a range called for by gamblers in return for cash payments. In 1953 the NCAA reported that Michigan State, the nation's top college **football** team, operated a slush fund from which football players were paid handsomely. These revelations increased the demand for a stronger NCAA, which would actually suspend or expel recalcitrant colleges.

Television further enhanced the NCAA's authority. First, colleges needed the NCAA to negotiate with **networks** to ensure that television did not take away the large crowds commonly attending football games. Later, the colleges wanted the NCAA to negotiate lucrative financial packages with the networks, a process successfully capped in 1994 by CBS' agreement to pay $1.745 billion to cover basketball's Final Four until 2002.

Since the 1950s, the NCAA has enforced a detailed code of regulations written and voted on by members of colleges and universities. It has assisted members of schools in complying with these regulations, administered more than seventy annual championships for both men and women, produced collegiate rules of play for twelve sports and compiled and distributed statistics in football and basketball, as well as publishing a weekly newspaper. It has divided colleges into different divisions, setting rules for student athletes in each of those divisions, and, in quite intrusive ways, has governed all college-level sport.

In effect, the NCAA has governed over the establishment of farm systems for the major leagues, especially the NBA and NFL. Apprentice athletes bring millions of dollars to their colleges without receiving any payment beyond scholarships, instead playing for the opportunity to be selected as one of the yearly draft picks (achieved by only a small percentage). The Heisman Trophy winner, the best player in college football, is assured of being a first-round draft pick and of receiving a very handsome salary from the team that selects him; so are the best ten to fifteen basketball players. With stakes so high and the demands on the body so extreme in some college sports, as *The Program* (1993) showed, many student athletes engage in widespread use of **steroids** and accomplish little academically. With scholarships tied to sports eligibility, these apprentices tend not to graduate from their colleges, and those who do not make the majors end up with little to show for their labor on behalf of their colleges.

In January 1983, the NCAA adopted Proposition 48 to counteract this problem, placing the blame for the failure of the student athlete on the athletes themselves and their lack of preparation for college rather than on the practices of college sports programs. The proposition required incoming student athletes attending a Division I school to have a minimum 2.0 high-school grade-point average in a core curriculum of eleven courses and a minimum score of 700 (later raised to 820 out of a possible 1,600) on the Scholastic Aptitude Test (SAT) in order to compete as a freshman. In its first year in effect, 1986, the proposition prevented almost 700 incoming freshmen from participating in their respective sports.

This proposition has been widely criticized, especially by Georgetown coach, John Thompson, and former Celtics great Bill Russell, who believe that it cuts off opportunities to **African Americans** in particular. Harry Edwards has noted the racial bias of SATs, but he (supported early on by Arthur **Ashe**) has backed the proposition, seeing it as a first step to rectify a problem that has seen large numbers of black athletes fail in college. The fact that only 31 percent of **African American** male athletes admitted to college in 1977 had graduated six years later, and that at Memphis State University no black basketball player earned a degree between 1973 and 1985, required some response.

One of the responses of players who could not meet the new requirements was spending a year at a junior college before transferring to a Division I school. Increasingly, though, potential athletes have recognized the limited benefits they will receive from attending colleges. This tendency came to a head in the controversial basketball draft of 1996. Of the fifty-eight men registered for the draft that year, thirty-six were underclassmen (not graduated from college). Allen Iverson decided to leave Georgetown after only two years, while Kobe Bryant and Jermaine O'Neal (the latter not meeting the Proposition 48 minimum requirements) opted to skip college altogether. A few players had followed this path before (Moses Malone, Daryl Dawkins and Shawn Kemp being the most successful), but players were generally discouraged from taking this route into the NBA, many commentators and officials arguing that they needed more maturity (though the threat to the quality of the NCAA basketball product is also a factor). The success of Iverson at the Philadelphia 76'ers and Bryant at the LA Lakers represents a considerable threat to the long-term viability of the NCAA farm system.

Further reading

Rader, B. (1999) *American Sports*, Upper Saddle River: Prentice Hall.

ROBERT GREGG

National Endowment for the Arts (NEA) *see* foundations

National Endowment for the Humanities (NEH) *see* foundations

National Film Registry

The National Film Preservation Act of 1988 was passed in recognition of the monumental quality of American films in their original or restored versions amid problems from emerging techniques to alter films (colorization) and evidence of the decay of film stocks and archives preserving older silent films and experimental stocks. The Act established the National Film Preservation Board which manages the National Film Registry. Twenty-five "culturally, historically or aesthetically significant" films are chosen each year to be included in the registry. It now encompasses 250 films that define a diverse American canon across genres, eras and styles. In 1996 the National Film Preservation Foundation was founded to further the work of preserving orphan films (films that have no owners). The updated list may be viewed at http://lcweb.loc.gov/film/titles.html.

CINDY WONG

National Guard *see* army; Vietnam War; Kent State shootings

National Institute of Mental Health (NIMH)

The world's premier mental-health research orga-nization, NIMH seeks to improve the treatment, diagnosis and prevention of mental disorders that affect millions of adults, **children** and adolescents. It also serves as an informational and educational clearing-house, communicating information about the brain, mental health and related research to the public, scientists, news media and healthcare providers. NIMH is part of the National Institutes of Health (NIH), the American government's principal biomedical and behavioral-research agency, which in turn falls under the jurisdiction of the US Department of Health and Human Services.

NIMH supports both internal and external research on mental disorders, neuroscience and behavior. It funds external research through grants or contracts awarded both nationally and inter-nationally to scientists from universities or research facilities. Scientists in the field initiate most of these studies, examining issues such as schizophrenia, **depression**, anxiety and eating disorders, **Alz-heimer's disease**, **AIDS** and the delivery, financing, quality and costs of mental-health services. NIMH also identifies gaps in research and solicits applications from scientists to conduct needed studies.

NIMH's own large internal research program supports basic and clinical studies in areas that include **genetics**, psycho-immunology and brain imaging. Its internal program trains scientists from around the world, helping to meet research shortages in basic brain research, clinical studies on mental and behavioral disorders, as well as the organizational and financial aspects of mental-health services. NIMH also actively works to increase hiring of women and minority researchers and clinicians.

COURTNEY BENNETT

National League *see* baseball

National Organization for Women (NOW)

The world's largest feminist organization; the nation's foremost women's advocacy group. Founded in 1966 by twenty-eight women, includ-ing Betty **Friedan** and **African American** feminist and Episcopalian minister Pauli Murray, it was originally conceived as a corollary to the National Association for the Advancement of Colored People (NAACP). NOW's statement of purpose was "to take action to bring women into full participation in the mainstream of American society." NOW's five specific priorities became the passing of an **Equal Rights Amendment** to the US Constitution, opposing racism, advocating for **abortion** and reproductive rights, supporting **lesbian and gay** rights and ending **violence** against women.

MARY-CHRISTINE SUNGAILA, ESQ.

National Public Radio (NPR)

The Corporation for Public Broadcasting established National Public Radio in 1970. It provides quality news and cultural programming to local public-**radio** stations. Its first program (April 19, 1971) featured the United States Senate's deliberations on the **Vietnam War**. That same year, *All Things Considered* had its debut, but its morning counterpart *Morning Edition* waited until 1979 to appear. Financial troubles have plagued NPR, despite the popularity of the **jazz**, plays, concerts and **classical music** featured in its programming. With financial restructuring, the majority of NPR's income comes from member station fees and dues and only 4 percent from government sources.

GAIL HENSON

National Rifle Association (NRA)

Organized in 1871 to promote training and marksmanship, the NRA has become a vocal **lobbyist** for the **Bill of Rights** 2nd Amendment right to bear arms. Its journals (*American Rifleman, American Hunter, American Guardian*), public spokesmen like Charlton **Heston** and members defend **guns** as a means of self-defense as well as for recreational **hunting**. Due to the rise in violent crime involving guns in recent decades, however, they also find themselves engaged in a highly passionate and polarized debate in which the NRA is viewed as a right wing/conservative group, while those who support gun control are often considered left wing or liberal. The latter may believe the 2nd Amendment anachronistic or challenge NRA interpretations. As a result of widely publicized mass shootings as well as liberal efforts, gun control has gained currency in American politics. To combat even this limited trend, the NRA lobbies politicians (typically **Republicans**) for their support against gun-control legislation. It is, by all accounts, the largest obstacle to the gun-control cause.

JAMES DAVID

Nation of Islam/Black Muslims

Founded by Wallace D. Fard in 1930s **Detroit, MI**, the Nation of Islam came to national prominence under Elijah Muhammad, who moved the organization's national headquarters to **Chicago, IL**. Aiming at lower-class **African Americans**, Muhammad preached that whites were the devils and stressed both the need for self-help and a black capitalism for the whole community. The Nation was also socially conservative and very restrictive with regard to the rights of women.

Muhammad's national spokesman, **Malcolm X**, helped the organization grow rapidly during the 1950s, establishing numerous temples around the country, and heading Temple No. 11 in Boston and later Temple No. 7 in Harlem. The organization came to the national attention through a CBS documentary, "The Hate that Hate Produced," which focused on the Nation's separatism and what the documentary described as the organization's penchant for paramilitary methods of self-defense. Malcolm X broke with the Nation of Islam in March 1964, questioning many of Muhammad's practices, and formed his own Islamic organization along with the Organization for African Unity. He was assassinated a year later.

Following Elijah Muhammad's death in 1975, his fifth son, Wallace Dean Muhammad, was chosen to succeed him. The new leader began to move the organization towards more orthodox Sunni Islam, leading to a split with Louis **Farrakhan**, Malcolm X's successor as national spokesman. In 1978, Farrakhan recreated the old Nation of Islam, retaining ideas of black nationalism, self-development and cultural conservatism.

Under Farrakhan, the Nation has been more actively political in this regard, following Malcolm X. It supported Rev. Jesse **Jackson**'s presidential campaigns (causing Jackson difficulties over anti-Semitism) and was linked to hostile foreign regimes like Libya. The Nation also provided the inspiration for 1996's Million Man March.

ROBERT GREGG

National Science Foundation *see* foundations

Native American *see* American Indians

NATO

The North Atlantic Treaty Organization, bringing the US and Western Europe into an alliance against the Soviet Union, was established by President **Truman** in 1949. Designed to bolster European postwar recovery in the hope that military security would reinforce aid given in the Marshall Plan, the organization also increased American visibility and influence in the region. A product of the growing antagonism between the US and the Soviet Union, and European fears of the latter, the establishment of NATO further escalated **Cold War** animosities and led the Soviets to create the Warsaw Pact.

The end of the Cold War has transformed NATO. Pushed by **Secretary of State** Madeleine **Albright**, NATO has incorporated a number of former Warsaw Pact nations (Poland, Hungary and the Czech Republic). It has also altered its relationship with Russia, though Russia still views NATO, backed by the US, as encroaching on its allies and Russian internal affairs. Thus far, NATO has opted to keep the Russians out of the organization, but has endeavored to coordinate policy with its erstwhile foe. Lastly, NATO has begun to expand its mission from containment of a particular nation to that of regional policing. In the Balkans, it took the lead in pushing for negotiations between warring groups and in the 1999 military intervention against the Serbs in Kosovo.

During the **Clinton** administration, a rift between the US and its NATO partners grew. An increasingly consolidated European Community has tried to limit American leadership, particularly as Americans express their reluctance to commit troops to conflicts that have little strategic importance to the US. In addition, the existence of large US military bases across Europe no longer seems warranted; some have been returned to the host nations. A growing impatience towards the American soldiers and their families near such bases is now evident, especially with scuffles between locals and American soldiers and their families.

ROBERT GREGG

natural disasters/catastrophes

Two contradictory trends affected the impact of natural disasters on the United States in the second half of the twentieth century. On the one hand, thanks to advances in science and technology, the ability to predict and prepare for natural disasters has greatly increased. On the other hand, more and more Americans have moved to areas that are prone to natural disaster and, largely for that reason, natural disasters cause more damage than ever.

Hurricanes illustrate both trends. Weather satellites, combined with new research insights, have greatly increased the ability to track hurricanes and determine their intensity, although they may still take unpredictable paths. The National Hurricane Center, established by the federal government in 1974 to bring additional focus to its ongoing hurricane forecasting activities, constantly monitors the storms. In addition, advances in communication have made it far easier to alert people about approaching storms and to evacuate communities.

But more Americans than ever have moved to the portions of the Atlantic and Gulf coasts of the US where hurricanes are most likely to strike. **Florida** counties along the Atlantic Coast saw their populations double to 5.6 million between 1960 and 1980. That was one reason that Hurricane Andrew, which struck south Florida in 1992, was the most expensive storm on record, causing $26 billion in damage and twenty-six deaths.

Population density has exacerbated the ecological impact of storms as well. Scientists believe that developed barrier islands, for example, take longer to recover from storms than do pristine ones because human structures hinder the natural processes – such as the shifting of sands – that help the islands cope with the winds, waves and rains that accompany hurricanes. In addition, human activities can add pollution in the wake of hurricanes. The impact of Hurricane Floyd, which hit North Carolina in 1999, was increased because its rains caused holding tanks for pig manure from massive hog farming operations to overflow, dumping wastes into sensitive estuaries.

Many experts believe the federal government has unintentionally encouraged Americans to move to the most sensitive areas, particularly since 1968 when it began offering flood insurance. In addition, federal disaster aid often helps people rebuild homes and businesses in areas that are susceptible to future damage. "Acts of God" (as many insurance policies refer to natural disasters) seem to be followed inevitably by acts of **Congress** appropriating emergency funds in response. Since the 1974 passage of the Stafford Act, which set up a system of presidential emergency declarations, the federal government has spent between $200,000 (1975) and $5 million (1994) on emergency appropriations to the Disaster Relief Fund for all types of natural disasters (tornadoes, floods, hurricanes, earthquakes, etc.).

Earthquakes, which are more likely to affect the West Coast of the US – although virtually every state contains some earthquake-prone region – are similar. While scientists have made little headway in predicting precisely when an earthquake may strike, they have made great strides in understanding where earthquakes are most likely, and engineers have become adept at designing structures that can withstand most temblors. Since 1977 the federal interagency National Earthquake Hazards Reduction Program has worked to improve earthquake science, engineering and preparedness.

Building codes, which are set by state and local governments, have become stricter since the 1960s to try to limit the damage from earthquakes. Yet little has been done to encourage owners of buildings that were constructed before the new codes were in place to "retrofit" their property. Privately sold earthquake insurance has contributed to the problem. On the West Coast, too, population trends have increased the risks. **Los Angeles, CA**, for example, grew by about 1 million people between 1960 and 1990, when its population reached 3.5 million.

The nation may face more weather-related catastrophes in coming years if, as many scientists believe, human activities, such as burning fossil fuels, are gradually changing the Earth's climate. The warmer climate that is expected to result would also be more volatile with a greater occurrence of severe storms.

Further reading

Mileti, D. (1999) *Disasters by Design*, Washington, DC: Joseph Henry Press.
Platt, R. (1999) *Disaster and Democracy*, Washington, DC: Island Press.

DAVID GOLDSTON

nature

Nature has been a fundamental feature of American culture since the European "discovery" of a new-world Eden. This embrace of wilderness or the "great outdoors" permeates the elevation of the pastoral ideal over the city, the celebration of the **frontier** and the centrality of this concept in art, **architecture**, literature and **mass media**. Yet, like other constructs of contemporary American culture, nature as a place, a set of dynamic forces and a congerie of salient features – green space, animals, even disease – has also been shaped by issues of control and independence, consumption and representation.

Nature, as a symbol of American independence, for example, has been owned and shaped for decades: American historical narratives continually stress this conquest of the wilderness in the inevitable advance of manifest destiny (at the expense of **American Indians**, often identified with nature in popular representation). State and national **parks**, **forests** and reserves preserve some space, especially in the **West**, as public domains. Yet others have appropriated nature through giant **ranches** and estates as well as smaller **suburban** landscapes. Within both public and private domains, questions of use also confront independence: whether logging or mineral extraction, for example, supersedes public appreciation or whether private owners have unlimited use of water, beachfront, land or other resources. These debates also have raised issues of access – not only via **automobiles**, **highways**, **tourism** and **hotels** in **national parks** – but also over rights to drive **sports utility vehicles**, **motorcycles**, snowmobiles or mountain bikes into pristine areas in order to be one with nature, albeit en masse. Similar issues have erupted concerning ownership, display and scientific use of animals, whether in the wild, on **ranches**, in **zoos** or as **pets**, confronting those who espouse animal rights.

Nature has also become a theme in consumption, both directly – in these issues of access and ownership – and indirectly. Sales of vehicles, clothing and gear make nature a major industry; chains like **Eddie Bauer**, L.L. Bean and Timberland specialize in rugged clothing that may never see the wilderness. Nature may imply simplicity and anti-technology in **food**, **fashion**, or housing, yet it has also become associated with high-tech items and designs for climbing, hiking, cooking, sleeping and computing in the outdoors.

Such consumption also varies with the **life cycle** and with class access to resources as well as ethnic differences. Hence, summer camps and **family** vacations give way to more rugged sports and eco-**tourism** for many. **Home** sites and **retirement** communities in the **Sunbelt** that sell sun, water and landscape to older citizens as passive consumers differentiate citizens in rights to wilderness as do consumption issues.

Nature is also fundamental to American self-representation. Genres like the **western** (in **literature**, **film** and **television**), the **Southern**, **road movies**, **horror**, **science fiction** and **disaster movies** draw on various features of land, climate and animal life within their plots. American art and **architecture**, from the American Light of the Hudson River School or the parks of Frederick Law Olmsted in the nineteenth century to the paintings of Georgia **O'Keefe**, the **California** homes of Richard Neutra or fashions like **Southwestern** style, have all incorporated domination and reconstruction of nature into American character. Emblematic figures like the **cowboy** permeate **advertising** as well. Yet the paradox of nature outside of and more powerful than mankind, but also tamed and owned by America and Americans, continues to trouble environmental policy and planning for the future.

Further reading

Cronon, W. (ed.) (1996) *Uncommon Ground*, New York: W.W. Norton.

Davis, M. (1998) *The Ecology of Fear*, New York: Metropolitan.
Miller, C. and Rothman, H. (1997) *Out of the Woods*, Pittsburgh: University of Pittsburgh.

GARY McDONOGH

navy, US (USN)

Founded in 1775, the US navy has played a significant role in US foreign policy during both war and peacetime. The mission of the USN is to maintain, train and equip combat-ready naval forces capable of winning wars, deterring aggression and maintaining freedom of the seas. The USN employs over 360,000 active duty personnel and almost 200,000 reservists. These officers and enlisted personnel are stationed at bases throughout the US and the world, while operating over 300 ships and 4,000 aircraft.

The USN, like the army and air force, is controlled by the **president** through the Department of Defense, to whom the Secretary of the Navy reports. These appointed civilian positions oversee the military career positions of the Chief of Naval Operations and the Commandant of the Marine Corps. During times of war, the US **Coast Guard** may also fall under the command of the Secretary of the Navy if directed to do so.

Individuals working in the navy are subject to the Uniform Code of Military Justice. This body of law replaces the **Constitution** as the governing authority of conduct, crimes and punishment. This is one of the more significant areas that differentiates an individual "in the military" versus a "civilian."

In addition to full-time work with benefits that include medical coverage and retirement provisions, many enter the navy for educational opportunities. The USN offers many programs that provide on-the-job skill training and college-level classes. The US Naval Academy in Annapolis, Maryland, and the Naval War College in Newport, Rhode Island, offer undergraduate and graduate degree programs for active-duty personnel. People also join for opportunities for travel, the chance to fill the call of patriotic duty and the rewards of belonging to part of an extended tradition. It is not uncommon to find **families** that have had several generations that have either served or completed careers in this branch of the armed forces.

The navy has figured prominently in **mass-media** representations of military both as patriotic propagandists and in lighter pieces emphasizing travel and port activities. In addition to innumerable **war films**, serious modern naval works of stage and screen include *The Caine Mutiny* (1954) and *Mr Roberts* (1955).

LAURA L. COOGAN

Naylor, Gloria

b. 1950

Born in **New York** City, NY of Southern migrant parents, Gloria Naylor grew up within the **community** of Jehovah's Witnesses. Influenced by Toni **Morrison**, Naylor wrote her first novel, *The Women of Brewster Place* in 1981, focusing on the lives of women converging in a **ghetto** community. The novel was critically acclaimed and commercially successful (developed into a **television** movie by Oprah **Winfrey**). *Linden Hills* (1985) focused on a **suburban** black community and revealed sensitivity to **African American** class issues. Naylor's three other novels, *Mama Day* (1988), *Bailey's Cafe* (1992) and *The Men of Brewster Place* (1998) have not matched the success of her first novel.

ROBERT GREGG

NBA (National Basketball Association) *see* basketball

neighborhoods

Like **community**, a fundamentally positive term in American society, but nevertheless nebulous and contradictory. Historically, neighborhoods reflect the physical development and divisions of settlements through work, ethnicity and **class**. They may be united by public and private institutions – **parks**, schools, **libraries**, **markets**, churches, restaurants, **bars** and clubs – and also by patterns of face-to-face interaction and support. This *ideal*

has been challenged by changes in urban districts, since the Second World War which no longer represent class or **ethnic enclaves**. Migration, **miscegenation**, decline or even **gentrification** may be perceived as sources of destruction; nostalgic images of "the old neighborhood" clash with fears of "dangerous neighborhoods" torn by drugs and crime. On a more intimate scale, an ideal of good neighbors, in **cities** and small towns, opposes the massification and anonymity of **suburbs** and large-scale housing. At the same time, neighbors are expected to respect space and **privacy**, making the neighborhood a locus of feuds as well as solidarity.

Few formal structures of neighborhood government or identity specify boundaries and citizenship, although ad-hoc organizations spring into play to oppose policies, like **urban renewal** or **busing**, or to deal with perceived neighborhood eyesores and social problems. Older cities may have ward-level political leaders who channel local concerns into larger political units; "walking the neighborhoods" is important for city council and mayoral candidates as well as those seeking national office. Some neighborhoods maintain town watches for crime or celebrate community through street festivals and potlucks. Neighborhood **newspapers** also promote community through local events and consumption – stores, **yard sales**, etc. In the 1990s, neighborhoods have also been championed as sites of renewal for urban action after the perceived failure of government development strategies – as exemplified in **Boston**'s Dudley Street project and community-development corporations (Medoff and Sklar, 1994). Business improvement districts, which tax local citizens and merchants to provide special additional services in garbage removal and security, represent a more commercial interpretation, found in areas like **Times Square**.

Yet, patterns of exclusion, difference and competition within cities pit the interests of one group against another even if expressed in apparently neutral geographic terms. Media may cover "incidents in Crown Heights" (**New York** City) or problems in South Central **Los Angeles, CA**, but place itself is less important than the restrictions and divisions that turn neighborhoods into confinement or fortresses. Indeed, geographies of fiction and news often rely on vague neighborhood labels that obscure the complexities of interaction, context and change that make such localities dynamic urban units.

Neighborhoods, nonetheless, provide **mass-media** settings imbued with meanings – Bedford-Stuyvesant as a black neighborhood for Spike **Lee**, or the class and ethnic readings of an earlier Queens in Norman **Lear**'s *All in the Family*. Neighbors may be depicted as nosy and gossiping, intruding on individual privacy or, conversely, unwilling to talk about or know about what is going on (familiar plot devices in both **sitcoms** and crime shows). Positive values of neighborhood are underscored in **advertising**, where one insurance company presents itself as "like a good neighbor" – a title also used to label US policy towards Latin America in the **Roosevelt** Era.

Further reading

Brower, S. (1996) *Good Neighborhoods*, Westport: Praeger.

Medoff, P. and Sklar, H. (1994) *Streets of Hope*, Boston: South End.

GARY McDONOGH

neo-Dada

America witnessed a return of Dadaist practice in the work of Robert **Rauschenberg** and Jasper **Johns**. A liminal moment in the history of postwar American art, neo-Dada was at once a response to the presumed emotive possibilities of **abstract expressionism**, a challenge to the rigors of high modernist criticism, and a resurrection of early European **modernism**.

Despite the close collaboration of Rauschenberg and Johns during the 1950s, their work remained markedly distinct. Where Rauschenberg's early "combines" looked back most emphatically to German Dada and the collaged work of Kurt Schwitters, Johns' iconic flags, targets, maps and numbers resurrected the French Dadaist tradition of Marcel Duchamp. Further, where Rauschenberg's early work asserted a deeply personal iconography amidst its array of art historical and pop cultural references, Johns' early work insisted upon the resolute impersonality of the pictorial sign.

In the ensuing decades, Rauschenberg evacuated the personal from his surfaces, withdrawing from the photographic and allusive invocations of the self and foregoing the painterly gesture for the impersonality of the mechanically transferred, silkscreen image. From the 1960s onwards, Rauschenberg's work functions as an expansive visual archive of contemporary popular and political culture. Johns' work, in contrast, has maintained its sustained painterly engagement in the contested status of the pictorial sign, even as it has adopted the pictorial strategies of repetition, tracing and appropriation. Reversing the trajectory of Rauschenberg's work, Johns' work has moved, albeit obliquely, towards a more self-revelatory iconography of indexical trace and shadowy figural presence.

LISA SALTZMAN

neo-Expressionism

If neo-Expressionism is the term most often used to characterize the re-emergence of figuration in postwar German and Italian painting, in the American context, the term refers more broadly to a generation of artists who returned to the easel in the 1970s and 1980s. Unburdened by the legacy of fascism which haunted the canvases of their European counterparts, the American neo-Expressionists plumbed their artistic pasts and image-driven presents for the subjects and styles of their pictures.

Quite varied in their pictorial strategies and thematic preoccupations, the American neo-Expressionists' work ranges from Julian Schnabel's self-aggrandizing velvet and tarpaulin-based homages to art historical traditions, to David Salle's coolly ironic painterly pastiches of a media-saturated world, to Eric Fischl's psychoanalytic representations of the dark side of suburban life.

In their refusal to acknowledge the presumptive death of modernist painting, signaled not only by the demise of Greenbergian high modernist criticism but by the strategies and assumptions of pop art, performance, **minimalism**, conceptualism and **video**, the neo-Expressionists assumed the position of cultural melancholics, repeating and resurrecting the figurative impulse of historical expressionism when its power was long since extinguished. For all the anachronisms of their painterly predilections, American neo-Expressionism was ultimately far closer to the appropriative strategies and nostalgic impulses evinced in the photographically based practices of its deconstructive compatriots than to the European traditions invoked in its naming and stylistic affinities.

LISA SALTZMAN

networks, television

A television network is a central organization that distributes its programming to local stations. Usually a network sends its programs via satellite or **cable**, and programs are aired at the same time nationwide, through what is called the network's program feed. The four major broadcasting networks are American Broadcasting Company (ABC), National Broadcasting Company (NBC), Columbia Broadcasting System (CBS) and FOX. All are **advertising** driven as opposed to the **Public Broadcasting System**, which is listener, corporate/foundation and government-funded.

Of the four major commercial networks, three were originally **radio** networks. ABC emerged after the **FCC** broke up the NBC monopoly. NBC, owned by David Sarnoff and CBS, run by William Paley, moved onto **television** in 1948. With them, came the **Nielsen Ratings** which monitored the viewing habits of the American people.

The three main networks were in fact four when the FCC started to issue television licenses – until 1956 the Dumont Network also existed. Later, in 1986, ABC, NBC and CBS were joined by the FOX Network. Owned by Rupert Murdoch's News Corporation, FOX now has stations in most of the 211 markets around the country. The Big Four in recent years have been joined by two smaller networks, the Warner Brothers Network (the WB, owned by **Time Warner**) and the United Paramount Network (UPN, owned by Viacom, which owns Nickelodeon and **MTV**). Stations that

are part of the WB or UPN networks are considered independents by many in the industry because only a few hours of broadcasting time originate from the network.

Stations that use network programming generally fall within three categories. First are those called network O&Os, owned and operated by the network. Stations not owned by the network that transmit their signal are called network affiliates; stations can also be part of station groups, which means a chain of stations are owned by an entity other than the network – for example Gannett (newspaper chain) owns a station group.

While networks are vertically integrated (they produce and sell all formats of shows and often own stations), three of the Big Four also form part of larger media conglomerates that are horizontally integrated. ABC is owned by **Disney**, CBS is owned by Westinghouse/GE and FOX is owned by the News Corporation. Although NBC is owned by NBC Enterprises rather than a conglomerate, it has entered into joint ventures with Microsoft in order to gain a foothold in cable with the news station MSNBC.

Since Ted **Turner**'s foray into cable, viewership has gone down for network broadcasting. Cable has seen the success of networks owned by Viacom (MTV, Nickelodeon, VH1), USA Broadcasting (Scifi Channel, USA Network), Time Warner (HBO, Showtime, CNN), TCI (Discovery Channel, Court TV) and Cablevision (American Movie Classics, Bravo, Independent Film Channel). The Big Four, in order to maintain dominance, have launched synergistic cable stations such as ESPN, owned by FOX and TCI, or NBC/Microsoft's MSNBC. Until the opening up of the new format of digital television, viewers can expect to see more joint ventures into the limited marketplace.

Further reading

Chiasson, L., Jr. (1999) *Three Centuries of American Media*, Eaglewood: Morton.

Turow, J. (1999) *Media Today*, Boston: Houghton Mifflin.

EDWARD MILLER

New Age

Umbrella term covering various mystical, quasi-mystical and pseudo-mystical aspects of modern American culture. The term dates back to the 1980s, although the ideas it covers are often older. Some New Age concepts originated in 1960s and 1970s **hippie** or psychedelic culture, including the emphasis on self-development and expansion and on multiple forms of spirituality. However, New Age differs from psychedelic culture in several ways. New Age tends to have a more holistic emphasis, stressing the notion of people within their environment; for example, many New Agers were strongly influenced by the Gaia hypothesis (which portrays the world as a single living organism). Still, there is little or no homogeneity among the various groups within New Age culture, which range from pagans and covens of witches to health faddists and enthusiasts for cyber-culture. Some New Age groups are darkly anti-technological, others have large web-sites. Some focus on single issues of importance, others have wider agendas.

A few general themes nonetheless appear. The personal health craze which began in the 1970s overlaps with many elements of New Age culture, and many New Agers place great stress on physical and mental health and fitness, seeing the two as overlapping. Fashions in **food**, **physical fitness** and design range from the whole earth foods movement to feng shui and crystal healing. This also relates to their emphasis on holism and green philosophy. New Agers have been involved in a number of radical environmental movements.

The interest in alternative forms of spirituality is also inherited from the 1960s. A strong emphasis on Indian spirituality including yoga and tantrism continues, but the focus on Middle Eastern and Sufi philosophy has been dropped and replaced by an interest in Eastern mysticism. Most evident, though, is the growth of "indigenous" spiritual movements like wicca (see **witchcraft**). An interest in Norse and Celtic paganism is also growing, and a number of "churches" have been founded. These new spiritual groups reject what they see as a dark-light polarism in Judaeo-Christianity in favor of a more "balanced" view of the world.

Critics of the New Age movement argue that it is a jumble of fads and poorly understood mystical faiths with no real philosophical core. This criticism is in many ways justified; however, the holistic focus and emphasis on personal development are to some extent a reaction to the increasing secular materialism and technological determinism of the modern world. Interestingly, and this again separates the New Age from hippie culture, most New Age groups do not reject technology and material values. Instead, they seek to subvert these things and build them into their own neo-materialist philosophy which situates materialism within a wider world view. Things, in the New Age view, are also artifacts, resonant with a variety of values.

MORGEN WITZEL

Newark, NJ

Newark grew in the nineteenth century as an industrial city in the shadow of **New York** City, and, like other **cities**, was heavily reliant on growing immigrant communities for its labor. Beginning in the 1920s, large industrial firms left the city, creating slums like the "Hill District," considered one of the worst **ghettos** in America. A brief boom during and after the Second World War encouraged southern black migrants to settle in Newark, but, by the end of the 1950s, with the **white flight** to the **suburbs**, the city began to decline rapidly. By the mid-1960s the city had a disaffected black majority population, policed by a largely white **police** force. The black residents were victims of considerable police brutality, which resulted in the 1967 **race riot**, during which twenty-one **African Americans** died and 1,600 were injured. During this period, the city was also noted for the black nationalist cultural initiatives of Amiri **Baraka**. Since the mid-1980s, and the election of Mayor Sharpe James, the city claims to be undergoing a renaissance, with a new **museum**, **performing arts** center and bustling regional airport, though it still retains much of its negative reputation.

ROBERT GREGG

New Deal *see* Roosevelt, Franklin Delano; Attorney-General; Eisenhower, Dwight David; freedom; newspapers; backlash; Supreme Court; welfare/welfare reform

New England

When Captain John Smith voyaged to the region in 1614 he mapped the coast and named the area in his *A Description of New England*. Eventually, New England came to include the six states that form the northeastern corner of the United States: Connecticut, Rhode Island, Massachusetts, Vermont, New Hampshire and Maine. Its people, unified to a large extent by a shared geography, climate and history, are known for their conservative dress and mannerisms and their taciturn behavior – one of the most clearly defined of American regional identities.

Carved by glaciers during the Ice Age, New England is in the paths of three major **weather** systems moving from Canada, the **Great Lakes** and up the eastern seaboard. Its weather, therefore, is extreme, variable and somewhat unpredictable.

When Europeans explored and traded with the **American Indians** the latter were decimated by diseases from abroad, leaving much of the coast unpopulated. Settlements of English Puritans in the 1620s spread rapidly as thousands of families cultivated the fertile coastal area. By the late 1700s they had destroyed or absorbed almost all of the local tribes.

The English settlements established the pattern for the area's culture. Like much of rural New England today, a typical village consisted of several families with the same religion. Most people fished, farmed or harvested timber for a living and gathered weekly at the meeting house for religious service, town business and militia drills on the town green. They held an annual town meeting to discuss and vote on each item in the budget and elect officers. These meetings remain an important tradition today.

Throughout the nineteenth century, farming continued and **cities** grew. Waves of European immigrants filled the factory and day-laborer jobs, and were joined by southern **African Americans** after Reconstruction failed. Second- and third-

generation **white** New Englanders moved into management and other white-collar professions.

Twentieth-century New England experienced major social, demographic and economic changes. Farming declined and then never recovered from the 1930s Depression. General manufacturing, **fishing** and **forestry** also lost ground while new businesses, such as high-tech manufacturing, service and **tourism**, gained rapidly in the last half of the century.

Economic growth in the 1950s and 1960s brought **urban-renewal** projects to replace poor downtown **neighborhoods** with parks and businesses, and moved lower-income families to government-subsidized **public housing**. When manufacturing jobs headed south for lower labor costs, local factory closings created acute unemployment in most cities in the 1960s and 1970s, increasing **inner-city** decay, crime, family abuse, racial problems and **white flight** to the **suburbs**.

As the economy improved, interest rates lowered and unemployment rates declined at the end of the twentieth century. Some of the new urban **middle class** gentrified formerly decaying neighborhoods, and many New England cities conducted beautification programs to invigorate their centers.

Better incomes for other work and high prices for land lured most farm families to sell; by the end of the century few of New England's farms were active. Rural New England became mostly bedroom towns and new woodlands, evidenced by former farmers' stone walls lacing the forests. Suburbia grew from cities onto the farmland. Housing developments, shopping centers, **malls**, chain convenience stores and retail strips became part of the landscape.

Tourism throughout New England is substantial. Avid outdoor sports enthusiasts and other tourists find their way to New England's picturesque towns, mountains, pastoral vistas of rolling hills and farmlands, forests with brilliant autumn colors, coastlines of sandy beaches, estuaries lined with cattails and marsh grasses, and miles of craggy granite. The states' many glacially formed lakes and coast attract millions escaping summer's heat.

A deeply rooted maritime history imbues the coast with mystique and romance. Small coastal villages and towns, first established as fishing communities, later became summer havens for the wealthy and artists, and then vacation destinations for the **middle class** and tourists. While able to absorb many summer dwellers, some villages changed their character when tourist businesses took control. Nonetheless, many coastal communities from western Connecticut to eastern Maine retain their maritime culture.

The significance of local history is evident in the landmarks and historic sites that abound throughout the region. A renewed interest in many Americans' genealogy has helped maintain historic buildings and archival information through local and national historic preservation groups. It has also helped local Native Americans re-establish themselves after centuries of almost invisible existence.

The presence of many educational institutions of higher learning in New England is an important force in its culture and economy. **Boston, MA**, "The Hub" of New England, has the highest concentration of college students in the world. It attracts some of the best intellects who have stayed in the region to create new technology and service industries. Originally they concentrated on the Route 128 beltway around Boston (Silicon Alley), but then spread to the fringes of New England in the 1980s and 1990s with advanced telecommunications.

New Englanders' politics are hard to define. Conservative in much of their thinking, they are liberal about human and individual rights. While many New Englanders voted **Republican** in the twentieth century, regional politics also include many registered independent voters, women in high offices and the **Democratic Party**'s powerful **Kennedy** dynasty. The New Hampshire primary, first presidential contest, brings national attention to these political currents every four years.

The extreme climate and geography of New England, which hardened the early settlers and their ensuing generations, helped define the "Yankee Character." Although the image has eased over time due to the influences of **mass media**, **mobility** and the gradual introduction of other cultures into New England's populace, practicality, self-reliance, a strong work ethic and a stoic acceptance of life's difficulties have continued to be facets of this traditional people.

Further reading

Howe, G.W. *et al.* (1989) *New England as a Region*, Orono: New England Cooperative Extension Service.

Kay, J.H. and Chase-Harrell, P. (1986) *Preserving New England*, New York: Pantheon B.

Verrill, A.H. (1936) *Along New England Shores*, New York: Putnam.

(Also, there are more than fifty periodicals focused on New England.)

KATHLEEN GALLIGAN
WARREN RIESS

New Frontier *see* Kennedy, John F.

new journalism

Thomas **Wolfe**, one of its most famous practitioners, popularized the phrase in the 1960s, referring to a new style of non-fiction writing, the product of growing dissatisfaction with traditional reporting and a spirit of experimentation taking hold of American literature more generally. New Journalists began to develop their own innovations, for example a more personalized writing style, to produce their stories. The movement's opponents charged that these journalists were either promoting news-as-propaganda or skirting dangerously close to confusing fact and fiction. These criticisms sharpened with the discovery that 1981 **Pultizer**-prize winner Janet Cooke, using something like the New Journalism writing style in a series of stories on an eleven-year-old drug pusher, had in fact concocted the story. Although many of the techniques used by New Journalists persist in American journalism and in much modern American fiction or literary non-fiction, the term itself has become less popular.

MARK BREWIN

Newman, Paul

b. 1925

With actor-wife Joanne Woodward (1930–; m.

1958), Newman has carved out a distinguished role in American film and **theater**, where his own physical presence has been nuanced by humor and intelligence. Among Newman's best roles are those of complex, troubled outsiders (*Cat on a Hot Tin Roof*, 1958; *Hud*, 1963; *Cool Hand Luke*, 1967, etc.). Newman also directed Woodward in the Oscar-nominated *Rachel, Rachel* (1968). The couple have also become known as liberal activists, supporting causes with proceeds of the "Newman's Own" line of foods since the 1980s.

GARY McDONOGH

New Orleans, LA

Founded in 1718 near the mouth of the Mississippi River, New Orleans long has been a major **Southern** economic center with a unique cultural heritage. French and Spanish colonizers, alongside African American slave and free populations, created a distinctive **Creole** legacy, which survives in the **architecture** of the French Quarter (*Vieux Carré*), pervasive **Roman Catholicism**, Mardi Gras – America's only established carnival – and renowned foodways based on rice, seafood and spices. Additional cultural influences have come from **Cajuns** and immigrants from Ireland, Italy, Germany and the **Bible belt**.

New Orleans is not merely an artifact of the past, however it may be read as such by millions of tourists each year. Today, the city of 464,840 (metropolitan area, 1.3 million) remains a vital economic center. Its many cultural and educational centers include Tulane and the black Catholic Xavier University. Professional sports teams include the Saints (**football**) and Jazz (**basketball**), while black New Orleans is especially famous for both **blues** and Dixieland **jazz**.

The city's personalities have evoked vivid fictional and cinematic portrayals from *Jezebel* (1939) to *The Big Easy* (1986). Many of these narratives deal with **race** and **class** relations, which improved slowly in the late twentieth century. Beyond **waterfront** development and charming residential districts, in fact, crime, poverty, racism and corruption have been consistent urban issues, influencing more recent debates over casino **gambling** and **urban renewal**. Today, New Orleans thus faces the continual challenges of fostering citizenship and maintaining authenticity, while selling itself as a major global destination.

GARY McDONOGH

news, radio

By the 1940s, Americans were receiving much of their news from **radio**. Despite a 1934 agreement between the print and radio media that radio news would be limited (and that those reciting the news on the radio were to be called commentators and not reporters), radio became key for transmitting the news. The Hindenberg disaster and the encroaching war in Europe and Asia became radiophonic experiences. The obvious advantage of radio over print was immediacy, while a secondary advantage lay in the dramatics of the voice. Commentators could transmit news as it was occurring live to the audience, bringing the event into the **home** as eyewitnesses who spoke with an audible connection to it. With the Second World War, broadcast journalism was catapulted into a crucial position, and radio dramas were often interrupted by news of the war. It was this ability to interrupt programming that made network executives realize there was enough news to fill up a station's entire day.

Today there are radio stations that broadcast news 24 hours a day. The format is fast-changing with a fast-talking DJ. It is repetitive, with round-ups and headlines – a talking newspaper, as station executives called the format when it began in the 1960s. The news may vary slightly from hour to hour, but the structure of each hour is the same, which again is like the lay-out and pagination of a newspaper. These talking **newspapers** have become a mainstay among radio stations on the AM dial, operating in most major cities. The Westinghouse network was one of the forerunners of this format, which continues to be successful four decades later, perhaps because America's ability to produce news has continued to accelerate.

EDWARD MILLER

news, television

Discussions of the information society at the end of the century resonate with the prestige and immediacy of news from the earliest days of television to the present. Adding pictures and gradually building in on-site coverage and commentary by distinguished correspondents, **television** news also celebrated its independence from government control and the limits of print. Over decades, news became the flagship of **network** prestige – anchormen like Walter Cronkite mediated the memories of a generation dealing with the **Kennedy** assassinations, the Moon landing and Vietnam. Yet critics have assailed network news for confusing journalism and entertainment, like the O.J. **Simpson** trial and **Clinton** sex scandal, adapting to corporate needs and ratings rather than investigation or truth – a charge argued in movies like *Network* (1976), *Broadcast News* (1987) and *Mad City* (1999). Indeed, even the visual elements of television may work against complex non-visual news (like coverage of the **Supreme Court**). Meanwhile, network news is losing viewership and money. In 1997 only 42 percent of the viewing public watched network TV evening news, down from 60 percent in 1993. The majority of viewers, moreover, are sixty-five and older.

We must be careful, however, to relate news to multiple changing contexts. In the early days of television, seasoned **white** male journalists delivered "truth," although later critics may forget that even serious commentators were also involved with **celebrity** interviews, product endorsements and **game shows**. While Edward R. **Murrow**'s *Harvest of Shame* (1959), documenting the plight of migrant farm workers, is taken as a milestone of television news, for example, Murrow also visited **stars**' homes in his weekly *Person to Person* (CBS, 1953–61). And in the years before television reported the medical impact of **tobacco**, cigarettes were props and endorsements for thoughtful commentators. Nonetheless, generations including John Cameron Swayze, Walter Cronkite, Chet Huntley and David Brinkley, Eric Sevareid and others established a mantle for the authoritative anchor subsequently inherited by long-term network anchors Peter Jennings, Tom Brokaw and Dan Rather.

The introduction of women as anchors – pioneered by feature interviewer Barbara Walters – and the presence of blacks and other minorities as reporters and anchors respond to perceptions of audiences and issues rather than intrinsic shifts in perspectives or news. Dramatic visual images of **civil rights** that galvanized America were conveyed by white reporters and camera men; declines in **affirmative action** or issues of the Third World have been ignored by culturally diverse networks in the 1990s.

It is clear that news coverage does have an impact on how Americans understand and react to events. Hence, television news coverage on politics has sparked constant debates. Early TV news offered American politics, gavel to gavel. The immediacy of political conventions and the **Watergate** hearings drew millions to the tube, and TV news was credited with providing a relatively transparent representation of the US political process. Other Sunday-morning panels also have allowed politicians and newsmakers to discuss serious issues with journalists as hosts and interrogators. Yet, facing telegenic political contests (Kennedy versus **Nixon**, Clinton versus **Dole**), one must ask if media are channel or cause. Moreover, with the rise of the political consultants, who are adept in creating media events for the candidates or politicians, TV viewers learn to view politicians as media-generated icons, while images and soundbites avoid more substantive issues. Television news has been accused of only reporting the horse-race aspects of elections, concentrating on opinion polls and personalities.

In the 1980s and 1990s, network news has expanded into **prime time** as magazine format shows. These feature network personalities and stories of corporate corruption, personal tragedy, medical triumphs (and tragedies), **celebrity** gossip and natural disasters and have become almost nightly staples. The most senior and popular of this format, *Sixty Minutes*, has remained among the top ten shows for years since its beginning in 1968. Local news **magazines** have tended to concentrate on nostalgic history, minority populations and special events. Another extension of the morning/evening schedule was the introduction of ABC's

Nightline (1980–), which grew from coverage of the Iran hostage crisis into a monographic report after local news. PBS news has always been considered as quality and liberal news; however, researchers have pointed out that the guest list in the famous McNeil/Lehrer *News Hour* (PBS) often favors white males.

Cable, however, provides the most telling shift in American news. CNN, with its axis in **Atlanta, GA**, rose to national and international prominence through coverage of the Gulf War via 24-hour news. C-SPAN, as a public service offered by **cable** providers, offers complete, relatively neutral coverage of events, including sessions of **Congress**. Other cable news services have added talk, call-ins and gossip; many, like MSNBC, suggest **Internet** connections for immediate updates, while CNBC promotes finance and business information.

With TV a mature medium, producers, journalists, politicians, as well as the audience all understand how to manipulate or simply use the medium to their advantages. While many in the audience still believe that the evening TV news is authoritative, more are skeptical. The news media, including the print press, and electronic media were attacked by the American public for their handling of the Clinton scandal. In the end, Clinton was not convicted, no matter how big the story was.

Local TV newscasts have faced other difficulties despite strong revenues. While some early newscasts for metropolitan centers drew on extensive station resources and journalistic pools trained in radio and newspapers, others have relied on photogenic announcers and wire services to create their news. Over decades, additions like local color features, movie reviews, medical news and product testing have blurred the dimensions of "serious" news, while sensational crime and weather stories in far-away places in the country will appear on local news if the footage is good. Basic services including news, weather and sports also have been smothered with local boosterism and "happy-talk" formula that wraps every story in banter among the anchors.

Local news stations nonetheless remain linked to network affiliates and practices – acting as frontline and feeders for breaking stories, honing anchors and other personalities and following up on major stories. As they have expanded to 1- or 2-hour broadcasts in the afternoon, some even cover national and global stories before the national reports. National news, in turn, has picked up the features and, in news magazines, the chattier format of the local desk.

Further reading

Campbell, R. (1991) *60 Minutes and the News: A Mythology for Middle America*, Urbana: University of Illinois.

Herman, E.S. and Chomsky, N. (1988) *Manufacturing Consent*, New York: Pantheon.

Iyengar, S. and Reeves, R. (eds) (1998) *Do the Media Govern?*, Thousand Oaks: Sage.

Slotnick, E. and Segal, J. (1998) *Television News and the Supreme Court*, New York: Cambridge University Press.

GARY McDONOGH
CINDY WONG

newspapers

Newspapers have been entwined with American politics, culture and technology. Evolving from publications devoted to political advocacy and commerce to those emphasizing news and dependent on **advertising**, newspapers began reaching a mass audience as the United States became an industrial and urban nation in the mid- to late nineteenth century. These changes coincided with the invention of the telegraph in 1848 and the rise in literacy, allowing for news to be disseminated rapidly and consumed by greater numbers of people, particularly a growing **middle class**.

By the late nineteenth century, newspapers generally took the form they have today. The *New York Times*, owned by Adolph Ochs, contrasted sharply with the *New York World*, owned by Joseph Pulitzer, and William Randolph Hearst's *New York Journal*. While the *Times* fashioned itself as the paper of historical record, focusing on world and national events, the *World* and the *Journal* sought to entertain their audiences, with news about crimes, scandals, high society and the city in which their readers lived. Many of these distinctions still hold true, with the *New York Daily News* and the *New York*

Post, along with other urban **tabloids**, carrying on the tradition of the now-defunct *World* and *Journal*.

Other fixtures of today's newspapers developed in the 1920s. After the rise of **public relations** and propaganda, particularly during the First World War, journalists became skeptical of the reality presented to them by the government and other organizations. In response, newspapers became more interpretive, explaining the significance of events and trends to their readers. This coincided with the rise of specialized reporting, in which journalists became knowledgeable in the subject or government agency they were covering, decreasing their dependence on government officials. This period was also marked by the rise of syndicated political **columnists**, most notably Walter Lippmann, who brought even more subjectivity to newspapers.

These changes paralleled the growth in the federal government, which increased in size and function during the New Deal – a series of federal government programs designed to combat the Depression – in the 1930s. This complexity further encouraged the development of interpretive journalism as reporters sought to simplify the increasingly complex workings of government for their readers.

After the Second World War, two developments significantly altered the role of newspapers. The first was the United States' transformation into a world power and the onset of the **Cold War**. Subject to news management and deception by government officials in the 1950s, the trust between journalists and political leaders began to unravel by the 1960s as the **Vietnam War** intensified. This distrust reached new heights in the early 1970s. In 1972 the *New York Times* and the *Washington Post* published the **"Pentagon Papers"** – a secret bureaucratic history of the Vietnam War – over the objections of President Richard **Nixon**. In addition, newspapers, particularly the *Washington Post*, brought to light the Nixon administration's **Watergate** crimes. These events highlighted newspapers' shift to investigative journalism.

The other major development that altered newspapers' future was **television**, which reached most American homes by the late 1950s. In addition to providing entertainment to millions of Americans, television served as an alternative news source. The **networks'** evening news programs contributed to a sharp decline in the number of afternoon publications, leaving many cities with only a morning daily newspaper by the 1990s. However, alternative weekly newspapers, such as the *Boston Phoenix*, **African American** newspapers, such as the *Chicago Defender*, and immigrant newspapers continue to offer city dwellers other sources of print news. More significantly, television could provide news instantaneously and with pictures, meaning information in newspapers was often "old." The public came to trust television journalists more than their newspaper counterparts, a trend that held into the late 1990s.

In response to television's prominence, newspapers began emphasizing features as well as local – as opposed to national and international – news. Many newspapers, including the *New York Times*, began developing special sections devoted to topics such as **home** improvement and science, content similar to that of *Time* and *Newsweek* **magazines**. In addition, because it was more difficult for newspapers to break news on a regular basis, their stories became more analytical, explaining the significance of news events rather than simply reporting them.

The newspaper industry responded in other ways. In 1980 the Gannett Company launched a national newspaper, *USA Today*, which was intended to appeal to a news audience largely reliant on television. With shorter stories, plentiful graphics and color pages, *USA Today* shared many characteristics with television news. Even its curbside vending machines resembled television sets. In 1997 it trailed only the *Wall Street Journal*, a newspaper devoted to business news, in US daily circulation.

In the 1990s other changes affected American newspapers. Newspaper chains, such as Gannett and Knight Ridder, began owning a higher proportion of newspapers throughout the country. By 1998 newspaper chains owned 80 percent of US daily newspapers, a 17 percent increase from 1986, marking a dramatic concentration of newspaper ownership.

Yet another change, the rise of the **Internet**, posed both a threat to and an opportunity for newspapers. By 1998, 20 percent of Americans got their news from the Internet at least once a week, though not necessarily from newspapers' World Wide Web-sites, potentially reducing newspapers' overall readership. However, the Internet gave newspapers the opportunity previously afforded only television and **radio**: to publish breaking news immediately.

Newspapers have been represented in a variety of films throughout the twentieth century. *Citizen Kane* (1941), directed by Orson **Welles**, was a thinly veiled movie on the life of William Randolph Hearst. The investigative work of the *Washington Post*, which helped uncover the Watergate scandal, was documented in the movie *All the President's Men* (1976). *The Paper*, released in 1994, chronicled one day at a fictional **New York** City tabloid, focusing on the ethical aspects of news gathering.

Further reading

Cook, P., Gomery, D. and Lichty, L. (eds) (1992) *The Future of News*, Washington, DC: The Woodrow Wilson Center.

Halberstam, D. (1979) *The Powers That Be*, New York: Alfred A. Knopf.

Schudson, M. (1978) *Discovering the News*, New York: Basic Books.

JAMES DEVITT

newspapers, alternative

While competition among local English-language newspapers has almost disappeared from American cities, small-scale weekly **tabloids** often provide different viewpoints and extensive investigative coverage of local events. New York's *Village Voice*, originally a **community** newspaper responding to **Greenwich Village**'s artistic and liberal residents, is probably the dean of this press; others emerged in response to the **Vietnam War** and other divisive social issues. Some proved short-lived, based on outrage more than systematic coverage, but others became important political and economic interlocutors. In the 1990s, many were consolidated in national corporations scarcely distinguishable from the mainstream press.

GARY McDONOGH
CINDY WONG

New Urbanism

A dynamic architectural and planning movement, taking strength since the 1980s, that fights sprawl through designs that favor pedestrian interaction, mixtures of diverse residential and commercial uses, elegant public spaces, environmental sensitivity and the "neo-traditional" ambience of American small towns. Championed by Andres Duany and Elizabeth Plater-Zyberk of **Miami, FL**, the primary completed projects are the 1982 Seaside, Florida (seen in the 1998 *Truman Show*) and Kentlands, Maryland – both relatively elite suburban developments. New Urbanism, nonetheless, has been championed subsequently as a formula to rebuild **community** in **inner cities** as well, although its costs and assumptions about design shaping behavior have been called into question.

Further reading

Katz, P. (1994) *The New Urbanism*, New York: McGraw-Hill.

GARY McDONOGH

New York and its boroughs

It is no longer the largest city in the world, and no longer the single dominant city in the United States. But when Americans speak generically of "the city," the platonic ideal they usually have in mind is *The* City, namely New York City. So deeply has New York come to settle in American minds that a casual scribble of a city on paper, or a rendering of "a city" in a **children**'s book (Virginia Lee Burton's *Little House* (1942), for example) is often an abstract rendering of the skyline that was built in New York in the twentieth century.

With remarkable persistence, New York remains The City. Although the postwar world, especially in the 1960s and 1970s, brought a dramatic decline in New York's economic fortunes, a flight of people and capital to the suburbs, and cultural influence to **California** and the **Sunbelt**, New York has remained and reinvented its cultural importance as the century closed. New York has been the city of creative destruction, constantly destroying and rebuilding itself with abandon. Indeed, building and rebuilding have always been at the heart of New York's economic life. But New York has also been the city of creative destruction in a metaphorical way: it has been the place where individuals, ideas, art forms and cultural practices are created and destroyed, remade and reworked. O. Henry may have defined New York's essence most succinctly when he wrote, "It'll be a great place if they ever finish it."

The capital of capitalism

The "Fountain of Abundance," also known as the Pulitzer Fountain, sits on Fifth Avenue in front of the Plaza, the most luxurious of **hotels**. It is an apt symbol for New York. If the city itself has not always produced abundance for the United States, it has almost always been the basin into which the nation's wealth has flowed – even if it is not then disbursed equally. New York before the war was one of the great manufacturing centers, but, starting at the turn of the century, it became the command center of American capitalism. After the Second World War, manufacturing was slowly but steadily destroyed – some say it was an assassination by city and state leaders, and not natural death – with its central industries of textiles, clothing and shipping. Yet, New York remained the capital city of the financial industry and the home of corporate headquarters. Cities dependent on a single industry have fallen furthest in the era of **deindustrialization**. New York, with its anchor of **Wall Street** and its corporate offices, as well as its long tradition as the city where **information** is processed and distributed, has managed to propel itself into leadership of the service and information economies. The resulting city of glass towers and **coffee** bars in Manhattan, on the one hand, and stagnant poverty in the outer boroughs, on the other hand, encapsulates American wealth and poverty as well as any urban landscape.

City of immigrants

For many, Ellis Island enshrines the turn of the nineteenth century mass migration of Central and Eastern European immigrants to the United States, many to New York itself. Celebration of that monument (restored in 1990) has obscured the fact that New York was long before that era and long since a city of immigrants. In the post-Second World War era, and especially after the 1965 **immigration** laws, New York has seen a flood of immigrants from Asia and from Central and South America – far more than arrived to the city in that mythic "heyday" of immigration. Vast communities of **Puerto Ricans**, Haitians and others from the **Caribbean** islands, **South Asians**, Vietnamese, Koreans and Taiwanese are all centered increasingly in Brooklyn and Queens. These groups have revitalized whole **neighborhoods** and continued to make New York the home, as E.B. White so deftly put it, of those who were "born somewhere else and came to New York in quest of something." New York was the "city of final destination," the ultimate city of migrants in a nation of immigrants (1949: 121).

Urban decline and revitalization

The most politically visible street in postwar America may be Charlotte Street in the borough of the Bronx. A desolate, decaying street of tenements overlooking the Cross Bronx Expressway (urban renewer Robert Moses' greatest political technological masterpiece, and greatest social tragedy) was visited by presidents **Carter**, **Reagan**, **Bush** and **Clinton** as a symbol of urban decay. Once a vision of paradise for immigrants fleeing the squalid Lower East Side of Manhattan, the Bronx became in the 1970s predominantly **African American** and **Hispanic**. **Whites** fleeing to the **suburbs** and its cheap land and housing, away from a borough increasingly African American, burned their property to avoid city property **taxes**. Where once fresh air dominated Bronx life, now fire seemed to gain the upper hand. The ashes that were left symbolized the intractable problems of older cities and the continued, unsolved problem of racialized poverty. The flight of industry, people, wealth and taxes led New York, in the 1970s, into financial collapse. That the nation's largest city had to remain in receivership, and under tight fiscal constraints for years after, showed the extent of urban decline and served as a sobering reminder of America's rapid loss of global economic dominance.

If Charlotte Street and the Bronx were the ultimate symbols of urban decline, their revitalization in the 1980s – fitful and as yet incomplete – has symbolized the resurgence of old American cities. New York, the true phoenix city, constantly remaking itself, has also pioneered the revitalization of cities that took hold in the 1980s. Jane Jacobs, observing the complex order of urban street life from the second floor of her Hudson Street apartment in **Greenwich Village** in the late 1950s and early 1960s, issued the clarion call in her *Death and Life of Great American Cities* (1961) to reclaim America's older urban areas in the face of a mass suburban migration.

Her argument was directed against a philosophy of urban planning that was premised on remaking the city's social and moral life by violently remaking its physical landscape. New York, in the postwar era, pioneered urban renewal on a scale unimaginable (although dreamed of) in other cities. Robert Moses, one of the most powerful unelected officials ever to shape New York, remade the city's physical infrastructure and fundamentally shaped its social infrastructure as well. Demolishing slums, laying **highways** around and through boroughs, dividing neighborhoods in half, and black from white, Moses made the modern urban landscape.

The urban revitalization that has taken place in Manhattan, the Bronx, Brooklyn and Queens has not affected the restlessness of Staten Island, nor the larger trend of suburbanization. Beginning a trend that would take place in cities around the country in 1993 Staten Island, the borough furthest from Manhattan, physically and psychologically, voted to seek secession from the consolidated city union created in 1898. Although the state did not approve Staten Island's initiative – announced with cannon blasts across New York harbor – the borough's action illustrated a desire of suburban areas of cities to remove themselves from the perceived costs of being attached to a large metropolis.

Crucible of culture

If Jane Jacobs compelled planners, architects and policy-makers to reconsider the physical structure of healthy cities, she inexplicably ignored all that was happening around her in the late 1950s and early 1960s: a vibrant flowering of avant-garde art, music and ideas in Greenwich Village which would transform American culture forever.

New York and popular culture are inseparable, that much is certain. Is it sheer density of people (New York has been the largest city in the nation for a century)? Is it that New York has mastered the fine art of centralizing capital for the creation of culture and the organization, production and distribution of information of all types, artistic and otherwise? Is it simply the historical momentum of cultural "agglomeration economies," as an economist might argue? That is, once New York became the heart of cultural innovation, it drew further innovators, because proximity equals efficiency.

Whatever the case, virtually every movement in art, literature, music, **film** and **dance** has been either invented, reinvented, promoted, exploited, or popularized in New York City. High and low cultures, and the gray areas that separate the two, all were born or found their home in New York. New forms of **jazz** flourished in New York in the 1940s and 1950s, with bebop, cool jazz, hard bop and free jazz all coming out of the city's jazz clubs. Martha **Graham**, Jerome Robbins and George Balanchine made New York the center of dance innovation with younger artists, such as José Limon, Merce **Cunningham**, Paul Taylor and Alvin **Ailey**, finding that only in this city could they pull together their range of backgrounds and interests. **Broadway** defined musicals and other theater. Central developments of modern art were pioneered, or at the very least exhibited and criticized, in the city's studios and **museums** (the Museum of Modern Art, the Whitney and Guggenheim Museums). **Photography** as a fine art was pioneered by Alfred Stieglitz, and the mid-century movement of "street photography" (which might as well have been called New York photography) found its inspiration in the linear public spaces of the city.

Los Angeles, CA would draw not only the Brooklyn Dodgers **baseball** team (whose flight in 1957 tolled a symbolic death-knell for Brooklyn, once the third-largest city in the United States), but also cultural capital. Even though New York's dominance of the literary and **publishing** industry has rarely waned, **Hollywood** would by mid-century be the heart of the film and **television** world. Nonetheless, New York would eventually, in the 1980s and afterwards, lure back film-makers and television producers in great numbers. Some, of course, had never left – like Woody **Allen**. The city became the home to documentary and independent film-makers, and once again the subject of innumerable films and television programs. Turn on the television in the late twentieth/early twenty-first century and one would as likely as not be transported to New York (albeit usually via a Hollywood stage set) to laugh (*Seinfeld*, *Mad About You*, *Friends*, *Caroline in the City*, *The Cosby Show*) or cry (*NYPD Blue*, *Law and Order*, *Brooklyn South*). If one went to a movie in the 1980s and 1990s (the city's urban malaise of the 1970s left it off the silver screen for years), one would see Manhattan's skyline being celebrated (famously in Woody Allen's *Manhattan*, 1979), or destroyed (as in *Godzilla*, 1998). No other city has remained so central as the subject and setting for moving-image culture.

New York's role as the ultimate "crucible of culture" is not only in its role in promoting art and music, dance and literature, but also in serving as the setting for the remarkable but also often-tragic interaction of diverse cultures. Archie Bunker, of television's *All in the Family*, was portrayed as the typical Queens resident. But, if Archie worried about his black neighbors being too close, he would find, in the early twenty-first century, much more that was troubling. Queens, the usually ignored borough, has quietly become the future: as of the 1990 census, it was the most diverse district in America, if not the world, with over a hundred languages spoken in the public schools, and 36 percent of its population foreign born. In a further hopeful statistic about American diversity, Queens became the first district in the US where African Americans have a higher median income than whites.

But Queens and neighboring Brooklyn also provided the settings for some of the worst modern racial clashes. From Howard Beach and Bensonhurst – where young black men were murdered in white neighborhoods – to Crown Heights – where blacks and **Jews** violently clashed in the early 1990s – African Americans and white ethnic groups have clashed in wars of turf. These undermined any notion of the peaceful "gorgeous mosaic" hoped for in 1989 by David **Dinkins**, New York's first African American mayor. These "outer boroughs" became home to fundamentalist religious groups who, not willing to take to Utah as did the **Mormons** a century and a half earlier, went instead to Queens and Brooklyn.

New York remains to many Americans a place apart, an island thankfully on the edge of the continent. When Newt **Gingrich**, Speaker of the House of Representatives for much of the 1990s, sought to highlight America's moral decline, he pointed simply to New York. Ironically, however, New York has always exported the future to America – from zoning to urban renewal, the **sitcom** to the information economy and the **gated community**. To Americans beyond the city's boundaries, New York City remains a touchstone, the symbol of the "best and worst of everything," the barometer of the nation's health and sickness, poverty and wealth. Americans are married, if not always happily then always intensely and profoundly, to New York.

Further reading

Jackson, K. (ed.) (1995) *The Encyclopedia of New York City*, New Haven: Yale University.

Jacobs, J. (1961) *Death and Life of Great American Cities*, New York: Vintage Books

Mollenkopf, J. (1991) *Dual City: Restructuring New York*, New York: Russell Sage.

White, E.B. (1949) *Here is New York*, New York: Warner Books.

MAX PAGE

New York Times *see* newspapers

niche marketing

Consumer research and flexible media have allowed manufacturers and service-delivery firms to target mass marketing towards especially receptive groups, generally divided in terms of age, gender, **class** and **race**.

Age remains the most noticeable division, as producers seek to appeal to demographics known for high disposable income, for example **teenagers** for movies, music and clothes, adults for **automobiles** and household goods, or older ages for retirement, travel, insurance and pharmaceuticals. Families also constitute an **advertising** target for mini-vans and vacations in **Disneyworld**. These strategies, however, entail both advertising and placement – CBS draws an older audience, for example, while *Reader's Digest* reaches the same group.

This identification of buyers implies divisions of class as well: advertisements in the elite *New Yorker* or *Forbes* differ from those in **tabloid** newspapers. Similarly, information on **television** and movie appeal allow for both commercial sponsorship and product placement that associates brand names with lifestyles. Catalog delivery in elite postal zones provides a constant measure of status differences in consumption.

Niches are also defined by gender, evident in ads that posit women as domestic decision-makers (i.e. **food**, laundry and appliances, etc.). By contrast, advertisements for **trucks**, **alcohol** and **cigars** evoke masculine images of ruggedness, independence or sophistication. Gay marketing is relatively recent, but gay periodicals have begun to package their clients in terms of both sexuality and disposable income, as well as offering "gay voyeur" ads open to multiple interpretations.

Race has proven more controversial: while television shows and **magazines** allow **African American** companies to target black consumers, neighborhood groups have also decried billboards and advertisements pushing cigarettes and alcohol within **inner-city neighborhoods**, spurring grassroots opposition in cities **Baltimore**. Ethnic marketing has not been so clearly defined within American assimilationism, although **catalogs** and travel agencies evoke nostalgic identification for Irish, Germans, Italians, etc. New immigrants who constitute distinct language or transnational communities, however, are reached through **mass media** like Spanish **newspapers**, **cable** stations and mail solicitations like those that offer special phone rates for calls to Hong Kong or Taiwan.

Niche marketing is perceived as a threat not only because of its general divisiveness, but because of the way it links mass media products to ever narrower segments of the population. Hence, "**family**" films or teen flicks replace movies of interest to diverse populations. Electronic printing and **Internet** sales, however, have permitted websites that adapt to individual shopping patterns or catalogs tailored to previous purchases – mass marketing for individuals.

CINDY WONG

Nicholson, Jack

b. 1937

Part bohemian beatnik and part establishment, three-time Academy Award winner Jack Nicholson (*One Flew Over the Cuckoo's Nest*, 1975; *Terms of Endearment*, 1983; *As Good as it Gets*, 1997) has brilliantly painted the landscape of the American male of the 1960s, 1970s, 1980s and 1990s. His expressiveness and intelligence as an actor are undeniable. Nicholson first played lead at twenty, but his break came in the counterculture cult flick *Easy Rider* (1969). He has since worked with directing legends such as Stanley Kubrick, Antonioni, Polanski and Milas Forman. Refusing to give in to **Hollywood**'s casting conventions, Nicholson picked roles as disparate as dapper detective, mental patient, pothead anti-hero and devil – once with a capital D. His smile is phenomenal: its dazzling transformation from affectionate to demonic in *The Shining* (1980) renders the movie a horror classic.

See also: actors

MARIAELENA BARETSAGHI

Nicklaus, Jack

b. 1940

The winner of more professional major championships (eighteen) than any other player in the history of **golf**, the "Golden Bear" is considered by many to be the greatest golfer of all time. Twice the winner of the US Amateur Championship before he left his home state of Ohio to turn professional, Nicklaus enjoyed enormous success during the 1960s and 1970s, during a time when his prominence and that of fellow golfer Arnold

Palmer inspired a rise in the popularity of golf as a spectator sport. Possessed of the twin abilities to drive for show and putt for dough, Nicklaus is perhaps most famous for his astounding record of six victories at the fabled Masters tournament over a twenty-three-year span.

ROBERT ANDERSON

Nielsen Ratings

The major television rating system in the US, used by advertisers and broadcasters to determine the value of **advertising** time, based on how many people and what demographics say they watch particular shows. The company was founded in 1923 by Arthur C. Nielsen, Sr; in 1936 the "Audimeter" was introduced to track radio listening. It has continued to adapt: the Nielsen Hispanic Television Index appeared in 1991 to track Spanish-language **television**; Net Ratings were introduced in the 1990s.

The Nielsen broadcast sample includes 5,000 US households. Many critics complain that ratings are inaccurate because of the lack of representation of older people and ethnic minorities and reliance on faulty measures of attention. In 2000, Nielsen admitted it undercounted Spanish speakers in **New York** City, NY by 300,000 households. However, even knowing the ratings' weaknesses, the industry still needs an agreed-upon measure to commodify broadcast audience. This, in turn, leads to further fragmentation of the viewing public as stratified commodities.

CINDY WONG

Nixon, Richard M.

b. 1913; d. 1994

United States president, 1969–74, Richard Nixon began his political career as a conservative McCarthyite member of Congress from **California** who pursued Alger Hiss. He twice served as **Eisenhower**'s vice-president and then narrowly lost the presidential election to John F. **Kennedy** in 1960. Following an embarrassing defeat in the

California gubernatorial election of 1962, he seemed finished. But the resilient and resourceful Nixon bounced back to win the 1968 **Republican Party** nomination, fending off his more conservative and liberal adversaries (Ronald **Reagan** and **Rockefeller**, respectively), stealing a page from the racist demagogue George **Wallace** in fashioning what he later called "The Great Silent Majority of Americans," and squeezing out a surprisingly close victory over a Hubert **Humphrey** battered and bruised by the events of 1968 (the **Vietnam War**, urban riots, **campus** disorder, the chaos of the **Chicago** Democratic Convention).

Nixon built a **Southern** strategy which thrived on the resentments experienced by many white Southerners and white, ethnic workers in the North. He slowed the pace of school integration, attacked "forced **busing**," tried unsuccessfully to appoint segregationists to a **Supreme Court** which would support **abortion** rights in **Roe v. Wade** (1973) and, ingeniously, supported **affirmative action** as a wedge issue to divide trade unions from minorities.

Nixon's domestic programs were remarkably liberal, in part because of the **Democratic** congressional majorities he confronted. Under his watch, **Congress** passed significant legislation regarding the **environment**, senior citizens, Social Security, worker safety; important proposals regarding healthcare and a guaranteed national income (Family Assistance Plan) were considered before faltering. Nixon appropriated Keynesian measures to address mounting economic problems exacerbated by the OPEC oil boycott of 1973.

Foreign policy, however, was Nixon's preferred domain. He campaigned with a "secret plan" to end the war in Indochina. His efforts included: a contradictory mixture of great power and diplomacy (efforts to woo both the Soviets and the Chinese to impose a settlement on the Vietnamese); a madman approach which tried, unsuccessfully, to bluff the Vietnamese into concessions by threatening to use nuclear weapons; Vietnamization, which sought to sustain domestic support through cutting US forces and, therefore, casualties and relying on air power; and, finally, a more hawkish agenda which included the secret bombing of Cambodia, complicity in the overthrow of Sihanouk, the invasion of Cambodia in 1970 and

Laos in 1971, the mining of Haiphong harbor and the Christmas bombings of 1972. Finally, he and his "odd couple" aide, Henry **Kissinger**, fashioned a peace agreement which provided a "decent interval" before, in 1975, the Vietnamese communists crushed their Saigon adversaries and reunified Vietnam.

Nixon's greatest accomplishment was his recognition of **China** and his efforts to achieve deténte with the Soviets. These were countered by his Vietnam failures and his support for right-wing dictatorships, for example Marcos, the Shah, South African apartheid and his complicity in the military coup which overthrew the democratically elected Socialist Salvador Allende of Chile in 1973.

Finally, the **Watergate** scandal revealed Nixon's least attractive qualities – his paranoia, his bigotry, his resentments. The investigations uncovered illegal campaign funding, abuses of power and conspiracy to cover up crimes. Nixon's taping system provided the "smoking gun" which finally forced him to resign in disgrace in August 1974.

Further reading

Ambrose, S. (1987) *Nixon*, New York: Simon & Schuster.

Hersh, S. (1983) *The Price of Power*, New York: Summit Books.

Schell, J. (1975) *The Time of Illusion*, New York: Vintage.

Wills, G. (1970) *Nixon Agonistes*, Boston: Houghton Mifflin.

PAUL LYONS

Nobel Prize

While the Nobel prizes were established by Alfred Nobel's will in 1896 to honor outstanding invention, literary work or "work for fraternity among nations," like the Olympics, they have also taken on implications of national competition and prestige in a century of laureates. While the United States has dominated in sciences since the Second World War, the Nobel prizes as a whole offer an interesting representation of global recognition of American prowess and position; in the last prize established – economics – the US has averaged one laureate per year since the **award**'s creation in 1969. Within the United States, moreover, the laureates also participate in institutional competition among elite colleges: for example, the economics prize has consistently recognized professors at the **University of Chicago**, Harvard, MIT and Yale. Moreover, laureates have sometimes banded together to exercise their authority: forty-four laureates sought a speedy end to Vietnam in 1970, while seventy laureates at work in **California** in 1974 protested the inroads of scientific creationism in schools.

Prior to the Second World War, nonetheless, acknowledgement of Americans and American-based researchers proved scant. United States citizens won their earliest recognition as peace laureates, recognizing efforts of mediation and global organization by US presidents (Theodore **Roosevelt**, 1906; Woodrow Wilson, 1919) and **Secretaries of State** (Elihu Root, 1912; Frank Kellogg, 1929). As America became a global power stage, officials were honored less frequently, although the Nobel committee recognized three further Secretaries of State: Cordell Hull (1945) for work in the UN; George **Marshall** (1953) for plans to rebuild postwar Europe (1953); and Henry **Kissinger** (1973) for negotiation of Vietnam peace agreements – an award some Americans found distasteful. Instead, the modern Nobel Peace Prize has recognized American women and minorities who have stood outside the construction of foreign policy, including the **African Americans** Ralph **Bunche** (1950) and Martin Luther **King**, Jr. (1964), peace activists Jane Addams (1931) and Emily Balch (1946); and Jody Williams (1998), who has organized a global campaign against landmines. Other Peace **awards** recognized chemistry laureate/activist Linus **Pauling** (1962) and immigrant Elie **Wiesel** (1986) for his documentation of the Holocaust.

In literature, American recognition came more slowly. Novelist Sinclair Lewis became the first American laureate in 1930, followed by playwright Eugene O'Neill (1936) and novelist Pearl **Buck** (1938). After the war, émigré T.S. Elliot received the prize in 1948, followed by Southern novelist William Faulkner (1949). Thereafter, prizes have shifted from archtypically **white** male American authors – Ernest **Hemingway** (1954), John

Steinbeck (1962) and Saul **Bellow** (1976) – to more diverse voices, including Yiddish writer Isaac Bashevis Singer (1978), émigré poet Joseph **Brodsky** (1987) and African American novelist Toni **Morrison** (1993).

In sciences and medicine, as Harriet Zuckerman notes in her *Scientific Elite* (1977), the evolution of American recognition has been more dramatic. Prior to the Second World War, more than 25 percent of all laureates were German; Americans received no prizes in medicine and physiology until 1933. Between 1945 and 1976, however, more than half of all laureates were American-based, although this included a sizeable immigrant population as well as American-born researchers. Since Zuckerman's study, the intensity of investment in sciences has tended to substantiate continuing American domination of scientific categories: more than half of all chemistry awards in the 1990s, for example, went to scholars working in the US, although their origins ranged from Mexico to Egypt to Hungary; physics shows a similar pattern. In addition, many of those considered highly eligible have American affiliations each year.

This research hegemony is also contested among schools who publicize laureates among their faculty, alumni and passing researchers. Thus, Harvard, MIT, Yale, the University of Chicago, California Institute of Technology, the Rockefeller University and the **California** State system reaffirm their superiority as research institutions (and their possibility of producing further laureates). Yet, laureates have also been associated with **CUNY**, Washington University and the University of Houston.

This recognition can also be read in terms of changing interests as well as investments and power. In this sense, a more regular pace of Americans in literature or peace prizes represents America participating in global systems as partner and interlocutor, while scientific awards represent an American agenda and the wealth of the American century.

Further reading

Zuckerman, H. (1977) *Scientific Elite*, New York: The Free Press.

GARY McDONOGH

North, Oliver, Lt Col.

b. 1943

United States army officer and central figure in the **Iran-Contra affair**. In nationally televised hearings before **Congress** in 1987, North admitted to selling arms to **Iran** in exchange for help in securing the release of US hostages in the Middle East. He also diverted arms sales' profits to anti-communist rebels in Nicaragua. North defended his actions in the name of **patriotism**, both capitalizing on and fueling the country's jingoistic mood at the time. North was convicted on federal charges for his activities, but the verdicts were later overturned. In 1994 he made a failed bid for the US Senate in Virginia.

SARAH SMITH

Northeast

Unlike other regions of the United States, the unity of this highly industrial and urban area is defined as much by its power as viewed from other vantages as by a cohesive regional experience. Encompassing the Anglo-colonial foundations of American society, the "East" or "East Coast" has been a variable referent, generally encompassing Maine, New Hampshire, Vermont, Massachusetts, Rhode Island, Connecticut, **New York**, New Jersey and Pennsylvania. Yet it may be used to refer to domination (North versus **South** in the nineteenth century), modernity (industrial and post-industrial development) and decay (in opposition to the rising **West**). This cultural geography also coincides with the **Sunbelt**/rustbelt division of the US in the late twentieth/early twenty-first century, although the rustbelt also includes older, upper **Midwest** states like Ohio, Michigan, Indiana and Illinois. "East Coast," a broader term, encompasses Southern shores as well, but omits the **Great Lakes**. To make it more confusing, locals tend to orient themselves in terms of culture formations like **New England** (encompassing the first six states above) or the **Mid-Atlantic** area (parts of the last three, plus Maryland, Delaware and the District of Columbia).

From a functional standpoint, the Northeast can be defined by the **Boston-Washington** megalopolis that includes the economic (New York City) and political (Washington, DC) capitals of the nation, with important subsidiary centers in Boston, **Philadelphia** and **Baltimore** – all connected by active train and **highway** routes. Moreover, this area has been a cultural stronghold for centuries due to the historical primacy of Anglo-European settlement and culture, as well as the institutions of higher education, medicine, history and culture established there. The intensely urban character of the Northeast, which nonetheless encompasses extensive rural and small-town life, has also been renewed over the centuries by waves of **immigration**. Initially, these were dominated by Catholics and **Jews** from Europe, but, subsequently, the region has seen both increasing globalization and a strong presence of **African American** internal **migration** as well as **Hispanics** from **Puerto Rico** and **Latin America**. Immigration and industrialization have contributed to political social orientations towards a **Democratic**/labor coalition in national regimes that have dominated politics there since Franklin **Roosevelt**. Both deindustrialization and the development of sprawling **suburbs** around the major metropoles have complicated this orientation, especially since the **Reagan** revolution.

While one might still note strong divisions of accent, cuisine and heritage among eastern centers, modern transportation and continual exchanges among cities and institutions continually recreate an eastern/northeastern society. This may be described in prejudicial terms (eastern **intellectual** snobbery, eastern (mass) media establishment) or as divisions within a continental nation – e.g. "Right Coast" versus the hip and conservative "Left Coast" of the West/Pacific Rim.

Further reading

Garreau, J. (1991) *Nine Nations of North America*, Boston: Houghton Mifflin.
Gottman, J. (1961) *Megalopolis*, New York: Twentieth Century.

GARY McDONOGH

Notre Dame *see* colleges and universities; Roman Catholics

novel

For that nineteenth-century Anglo-American practitioner, Henry James, the novel was a loose and baggy monster. This genre, literally the *new* inheritor of the romance tradition and the cultural consequence of, among other things, the rise of a **middle class**, has such an extraordinary breadth of forms and formats that definition necessarily gives way to description. Customary designations of the novel may involve length, linguistic tradition, regional or national identification, established historical epoch or period, experimental correlation with developments in other disciplines or spheres, or close association with cultural movements – often those considered radical, in the mathematical sense of that word. Many of these categories of description have particular application to the American novel as one constituent element of a national literary tradition that Marius Bewley labeled "*The Eccentric Design: Form in the Classic American Novel*" (1959, italics added).

One of the earliest written prototypes of the American novel was a New Republic-era experiment by the nation's pioneering professional novelist, Charles Brockden Brown. In *Wieland; or, The Transformation* (1798), Brown introduced themes which have resonated for two centuries: a reading of the then "untamed," unfamiliar American landscape as Gothic wilderness; the preoccupation with madness, guilt and the nightmarish; a fascination with murder and suffering as acts of divine retribution; and an inexplicable alliance with the preternatural. From that 1798 narrative, one can easily trace a trajectory from Edgar Allen Poe's *Narrative of Arthur Gordon Pym* (1838) and Nathaniel Hawthorne's *House of the Seven Gables* (1851) to Flannery O'Connor's *Wise Blood* (1952).

Much of American literature has been a Bildungsroman, or novel of education, both in the literal journeys of individual characters and the nation's own symbolic **coming of age**. A very significant component of that journey from innocence to experience has been the encounter with multiple landscapes of ever-changing national borders. In his five novels known as the *Leather-Stocking Tales* (1823–41), James Fenimore Cooper narrated the exploits of Natty Bumpo and the Native chief, Chingachgook, in the confines of the allegedly "civilized" world and the philosophical textbook of the **frontier**. Such concerns would return a generation later in the works of American transcendentalists such as Emerson and Thoreau, while the journey to experience underpins Mark Twain's picaresque *Adventures of Huckleberry Finn* (1884), considered by many the pre-eminent American novel. For some, the frontier/wilderness was a mythic space in which one's mettle was tested and one's character honed by the struggle for survival. For Herman Melville, that frontier was an ocean expanse where Captain Ahab in *Moby Dick* (1851) battled for dominion against Job's Leviathan. For Tomas Rivera, however, the natural world was the concrete terrain in which the **migrant** workers of . . . *y no se lo trago la tierra/And the Earth Did Not Devour Him* (1971) interwove their achronological and elusive impressions with the recurrent cycles of the farmworker's growing seasons. For John Steinbeck, writing about the forced emigrations of Midwestern farmers in the Depression era (*The Grapes of Wrath*, 1939), nature was an equal partner in an archetypal story about survival against the odds.

In an entirely different landscape – the sophisticated world of the European salon – Henry James described the search for an American identity and a home. James, himself an American **expatriate**, painstakingly chronicled that same quest in such novels as *The American* (1877) and *The Portrait of a Lady* (1881). Incisive critiques of American manners also found elegantly nuanced expression in the novels of Edith Wharton, particularly in *The Age of Innocence* (1920).

Whether sketching out sumptuously appointed drawing rooms or virgin prairies, American writers often discovered a wilderness of interior exile. The oeuvres of Ernest **Hemingway** and F. Scott Fitzgerald contributed significant portraits to such a gallery. Nella Larsen and James Weldon Johnson captured the loneliness of racial identity confusion in *Passing* (1929) and *Autobiography of an Ex-Colored Man* (1912). In *The Surrounded* (1936) and *House Made of Dawn* (1968), D'Arcy McNickle and N. Scott Momaday described painful attempts to reconcile twinned Native and American cultures which often seemed and functioned as antagonistic or foreign to each other. Gish Jen's *Typical American* (1991) used **humor** to talk about the problematic cost of **Asian American** forms of apparently successful identity negotiation, while Bharati Mukherjee's fiction asked uncompromising questions about becoming American. The complex choreography of sexual identity also offered a "queered" reading of the American consciousness in such works as Djuna Barnes' *Nightwood* (1936) and James **Baldwin**'s *Giovanni's Room* (1956).

Narratives by voluntary as well as involuntary immigrants simultaneously explored the border crossings from **birth** to physical as well as legal and social adulthood in a new order. Anzia Yezierska's *Bread Givers* (1925) pursued the psychological clash between a father's old vistas and a daughter's new world ideals in a narrative about Yiddish cultural transplantation. A consistent and sardonic critique of the nation's repressive infantilization of boys demanding recognition of their full adult status appeared in Richard Wright's *Native Son* (1940) and Ralph **Ellison**'s *Invisible Man* (1952). Intermingling both the pain *and* the beauty of life in the American crucible, the sighted legatees of Ellison pierced the veil intended to disregard the humanity of the other in such lyrical prose poems as Sandra **Cisneros**'s *The House on Mango Street* (1984). Sometimes this demythologizing project involved a compelling, incisive and gender-foregrounded interrogation of the constraints on women's imaginative, fiscal, intellectual and psycho-sexual independence that surfaced in Kate Chopin's *The Awakening* (1899) and Theodore Dreiser's *Sister Carrie* (1900). Novelists such as Toni **Morrison**, Amy **Tan**, Gloria **Naylor** and Maxine Hong **Kingston** created new dynastic trinities of grandmothers, mothers and daughters in *Sula* (1974) and *Song of Solomon* (1977), *The Joy Luck Club* (1989), *Mama Day* (1988) and *The Woman Warrior* (1976).

American narrative experimentalists – Zora Neale Hurston, Jean Toomer, William S. **Burroughs**, William Faulkner, Gertrude Stein, Donald **Barthelme**, Toni Cade **Bambara**, Kurt **Vonnegut**, Ismael Reed, Leslie Marmon **Silko**, Norman **Mailer**, Thomas **Pynchon**, Don **DeLillo**, Toni Morrison and others – often made use of the conflation of genres or the construction of fabulation to confront simultaneously the future, the inherited and the invented past. Hence, Louise **Erdrich**'s trilogy traces almost a century of recollections about family stories; for those whose histories have been erased, distorted or discounted, fiction-as-historiography has become a compelling genre all of its own. Rememory and the haunting of buried secrets permeate such texts which make whitewater of streams-of-consciousness. Other writers like Frances Ellen Watkins Harper, Harriet Beecher Stowe and Upton Sinclair used fiction as a site of testimony where one could make a public and prophetic record of that which demanded documentation.

From the preoccupation with the sighting of whales to the haunting power of wraiths and the remembered, American novels have served as a moveable feast.

LINDA-SUSAN BEARD

nuclear age

America formally ushered in the "nuclear age" on August 6, 1945 when it dropped an atomic bomb on Hiroshima, **Japan**, to end the Second World War. Nuclear weaponry had been the American military's long-sought goal during the war as the government devoted over 2 billion dollars to the top secret "Manhattan Project," based in Los Alamos, New Mexico. At the bomb's first test, J. Robert Oppenheimer, the controversial scientific director of the project, called upon Hindu writings and famously commented: "Now I am become death; destroyer of worlds." This ominous sense of doom pervaded America's and ultimately the world's relationship to the new technology. Initially produced within a climate of warfare, nuclear energy never lost the trappings of awe and fear that surrounded its birth despite years of attempts to reshape public perceptions.

Initially, America held sole rights to the nuclear age and took advantage of its short-lived techno-logical superiority to establish itself as an unchallenged international military power. When the Soviet Union successfully tested their own nuclear weapon in 1949, the arms race between what were now two superpowers began in earnest. Over the next forty years, America and the Soviet Union devoted an extraordinary amount of financial and political capital to building more, as well as more advanced, nuclear-weapons systems. In America, this arms race and the war games that detailed how such weapons might be used became the stuff of popular culture, with phrases like "first strike capability" and "MAD: Mutually Assured Destruc-tion" – concepts that originated on the desks of military planners – entering the common vocabu-lary.

For many years, Americans maintained an absorbing political focus on nuclear weaponry. Generals and the public genuinely debated whether to use nuclear bombs in both the **Korean War** and in Vietnam. In the 1960 election John **Kennedy** falsely accused the **Eisenhower** ad-ministration of permitting a "missile gap" to arise which benefited the Soviets. As president, Kennedy himself engaged in nuclear brinkmanship with the Soviet Union over **Cuba**. In 1964 Lyndon **Johnson** implied in a famous **television** com-mercial that, if elected, **Republican** opponent Barry Goldwater would cause a nuclear war. The **bomb-shelter** craze that swept the country in the late 1950s/early 1960s reflected this public obses-sion, as did the regular "nuclear attack" drills held in schools which urged children to "duck and cover" should a bomb fall in the vicinity.

Although continuing to accelerate nuclear arms development and production, American political leaders simultaneously called for other countries – particularly the Soviet Union and the People's Republic of **China** – to slow down and limit their nuclear arsenals. To that end, Kennedy, for example, proposed a nuclear test-ban treaty in 1963. During his first term, Richard **Nixon** focused on a policy of détente with the Soviet Union – an attempt to cool down **Cold-War** tensions – and negotiated the SALT (Strategic Arms Limitation Treaty) I accord. President **Reagan** reversed this course in the 1980s by denouncing the SALT II agreement negotiated under the **Carter** administration (although never ratified by the Senate) and extensively funding research into a new, highly speculative missile defense system set in the Earth's orbit, known popularly as the "Star Wars" initiative.

Subsequent presidential administrations de-funded this project, but the proliferation of nuclear weapons around the world and the absence of genuine multilateral arms-limitation agreements reflects the long-term impact of the fact that America abandoned nuclear disarmament (outside of the Russia–US arena) as an important policy goal.

Yet, nuclear weapons are but one aspect of America's tormented relationship with the nuclear age. American policy-makers attempted to trans-form the public relationship with nuclear power from one of terror to one of affection. Public utilities saw the possibilities of a cheap energy source and began a campaign to convince Amer-icans to welcome nuclear power plants. Initially, the public relations efforts had some success and plants began to dot the American landscape in the 1950s and 1960s. Yet, just as grassroots "Ban the Bomb" movements had helped reshape disarma-ment goals in the 1960s, so too did resistance to nuclear energy on environmental and safety grounds begin to take hold in the 1970s. Protestors challenging the image of a safe, benign nuclear-energy capability received the proof they needed in 1979 when a nuclear power plant at Three Mile Island in western Pennsylvania experienced a serious nuclear accident and exposed millions to the risk of radiation poisoning. This was enough to convince many that their communities should remain "nuclear free" as a growing political movement in the 1980s argued. Movies like *China Syndrome* (1979) and *Silkwood* (1983) reflected this growing opposition to nuclear energy.

In fact, the effects of the nuclear age have been a standard in American popular culture. Not surpris-ingly, the 1950s proved to be the high-water mark for cinematic representations of nuclear disaster. Countless B-movies showed the impact of radiation on the natural world. Although exposure to radiation usually produced massive and deadly growth (giant ants in *Them* and a giant woman in *The Attack of the 50 Foot Woman*), sometimes it led to diminution (*The Incredible Shrinking Man*). These now pleasurably "campy" films provide ample evidence of an American culture trying to come to terms with a new and frightening technology.

Although the collapse of the Soviet Union after 1989 has freed some Americans from their long-standing anxiety over an imminent nuclear holo-caust, others have pointed to the unchecked proliferation of nuclear weaponry by many smaller countries as an even greater source of concern. The longstanding American security policy of "Mutually Assured Destruction" – which argued that the United States and the Soviet Union could not risk a war because no one would be left at the end – is of no interest to many nations who currently have nuclear-weapons capability. Their conflicts are more local and the attraction of nuclear weaponry more tactically engaging. In the eyes of many, the real "nuclear age" has only now just begun.

SHARON ULLMAN

nurses

Often portrayed in **mass media** as subservient female helpers to the male physician, American nurses fought in the last half of the twentieth century to be recognized as skilled care-givers whose roles include assessment and diagnosis of health situations as well as the care-giving process itself, which may establish intimate and crucial bonds with patients. In the early twenty-first century, nursing remains predominantly female (roughly 95 percent) and **white** (90 percent), although male and minority participation are growing.

Demands for recognition have been accompa-nied by increasing professionalization as hospital two-year apprentice-based programs have been replaced generally by two- and four-year programs in **colleges and universities**. The nurse-practitioner, who may operate in basic healthcare settings where physicians are not readily available, represents another strengthening of nurses' roles since the 1960s. Meanwhile, medical service workers have taken over roles not related to healthcare expertise (office management, mainte-nance services, etc.).

The 2.6 million registered nurses in the US have a strong lobbying and professional association in the American Nurses Association, which has sought to situate nurses within ongoing healthcare reforms and public consciousness. Recognition of nurses in military settings like Vietnam has also increased. Nonetheless, while **medical shows** and movies in the 1990s developed images of stronger nurse characters, with more gender and racial diversity, these shows often make nursing roles secondary, caught in romantic as well as medical subplots.

GARY McDONOGH

O

Oates, Joyce Carol

b. 1938

Novelist. Oates combines strong naturalistic prose with elements of American Gothic. Her works have also managed to combine literary quality with appeal to a wide audience. Author of many novels, among her best-known works are the trilogy consisting of *Garden of Earthly Delights* (1967), *Expensive People* (1968) and *them* (1969), which won the National Book Award. Others include *Because it is Bitter and Because it is my Heart* (1990) and *Will you always love me?* (1996).

GARY McDONOGH

obesity *see* body; diet; food

O'Connor, Sandra Day

b. 1930

First woman to serve as associate justice of the US **Supreme Court**. She was nominated by President **Reagan** and sworn in as a justice on the nation's highest court in 1981. Her influence on the court was most deeply felt in the area of 1st Amendment jurisprudence (she developed the court's controlling standard for interpreting the establishment clause). She became one of the court's leaders in declaring the unconstitutionality of government discrimination based on **race**, regardless of its goal. In 1991 she largely ended

the court's **abortion** debate by ruling: "the essential holding of *Roe v. Wade* still stands."

MARY-CHRISTINE SUNGAILA, ESQ.

off-Broadway *see* theater

oil and gas

The United States has been addicted to cheap gas, influencing both domestic and international policy. It has been one of the world's largest producers of oil (after the former Soviet Union and Saudi Arabia) and natural gas, based on its holding of 3–4 percent of world supplies of each. This has created intense localized development, especially in **Texas**, Louisiana, Oklahoma and the West as well as **Alaska**, coupled with federal strategies to expand and protect these resources. Petroleum also means major US corporations such as Texaco, Sunoco, Exxon (Standard Oil), Hess and transnational conglomerates like Shell and BP. It has fueled a postwar American lifestyle of extremely high energy consumption.

Even when US production peaked at 9.64 million barrels per day in 1970, the consumption of gasoline via **automobiles** and other energy uses since the Second World War had made the US an oil-dependent nation (with imports outstripping domestic production by the century's end). Given cheap fuel from abroad, domestic drilling also decreased dramatically. Global economics and politics, therefore, have been shaped by negotiations of an external supply of oil as a strategic resource. While oil companies once maintained their control through a neo-colonial relationship, the emergence of OPEC in the 1960s posed an alternative control on global supplies.

Crisis loomed in 1970 as world supplies tightened and OPEC began to raise prices. In 1973 Arab states shut off exports to the US in protest of American support of Israel in the Yom Kippur War. Spiraling prices and generalized inflation, lines and rationing at gas pumps challenged American hegemony, although the government favored increasing production rather than attacking demands due to sprawl, consumption, etc. **Iran**'s embargo in 1979 again raised this specter, although development of Alaskan fields and increased production worldwide has allowed Americans to think and drive as if any crisis has evaporated. Both controversial offshore drilling and the multi-billion dollar commitment of the Trans-Alaska pipeline reflect public interest in oil development even at the expense of the **environment**, which is already contaminated by automotive wastes. Critics also have accused the US of coddling dictatorial regimes (Nigeria) or even going to war in the Gulf to protect strategic supplies and allies.

Within this framework, petroleum companies have become highly visible signs of American life through the frequent gas stations of city streets and **highways**, as well as massive impact on cities like Dallas, Houston, New Orleans and Denver. Research support and corporate sponsorship of programming like PBS' **Masterpiece Theater** (Mobil) or sporting events have been used to assuage concerns about profits and environmental impacts. The names associated with the history of oil production – **Rockefeller**, Pew, etc. – also appear in monuments, **foundations** and other institutions of American life. Yet **oil spills**, smog and petrochemical wastes spur continuing opposition to the unchecked role of petroleum products and producers in American life.

Natural gas is sometimes touted as an alternative possibility, especially for home and production uses, and has led to major investment in delivery pipelines around the country. This resource, too, is concentrated in western states giving them special clout in energy planning and use, while deregulation has opened new competition among energy commodities and suppliers.

Further reading

Bromley, S. (1991) *American Hegemony and World Oil*, State College PA: Pennsylvania State University Press.

Nye, D. (1998) *Consuming Power*, Cambridge, MA: MIT.

Yergin, D. (1991) *The Prize*, New York: Simon & Schuster.

GARY McDONOGH

oil crisis *see* automobiles; highways; oil and gas

oil spills

Oil spills can occur on land or in rivers and lakes, but the most serious spills tend to involve tankers that travel the open seas. Spills represent a serious environmental risk as they threaten a wide range of marine species that can die when they or the food they need become coated with oil. The largest oil spill in US history occurred when the tanker Exxon Valdez ran aground in Prince William Sound in **Alaska** in 1989, dumping about 260,000 barrels of oil, which eventually affected about 1,100 miles of Alaskan coastline. In response to the spill, **Congress** passed the Oil Pollution Act of 1990, which enabled the federal government to issue new rules to prevent spills (such as ensuring that tanker captains and crew are fully qualified and not operating under the influence of drugs or **alcohol**, and limiting where tankers can operate) and which established the liability and financial responsibilities of any entity involved in an oil spill. Advances continue to be made in the technology to clean up oil spills, including the use of bacteria that can break down the oil into less harmful substances.

DAVID GOLDSTON

O'Keefe, Georgia

b. 1887; d. 1986

Pioneering American female artist, her bold over-sized flowers and abstract still-life representations of the **West** have made her one of the most popular figures of American abstract art. Born in Wisconsin, O'Keefe moved to **New York**, where she married (1924–46) photographer and gallery-owner Alfred Steiglitz. After his death, O'Keefe settled in New Mexico, where she vividly inter-preted **Southwestern** landscapes, **nature** and skies. Her colorful and intriguing images, incorpo-rated into major **museum** collections, have also shaped American style and design.

GARY McDONOGH

Oklahoma City bombing

The April 19, 1995 **truck** bombing of Oklahoma City's Alfred P. Murrah Federal was the deadliest act of domestic terrorism in American history. One hundred and sixty-eight people, including nineteen **children**, were killed and hundreds more injured by an ammonium-nitrate and fuel-oil (ANFO) bomb hidden in a rental truck parked outside the building's entrance. The attack precipitated the largest manhunt in US history. Two US army **veterans**, Timothy McVeigh and Terry Nichols, were put on trial by federal authorities for their role in the attack. In June 1997 McVeigh, the actual bomber, was convicted and sentenced to **death** in the federal district court in Denver. Terry Nichols was sentenced to life in **prison** for his role in the bombing. The attack was motivated by intense hostility towards the federal government, generated by the fiery end to the Branch Davidian/**Waco** stand-off on April 19, 1993.

BRIAN LEVIN

old age

Since 1945, new medical techniques have extended active life for many Americans, while the propor-tion of older people in the population has increased

and earlier systems of elder care have eroded. These changes have given older Americans new choices and powers, but a continuing cultural privileging of youth still marginalizes and endan-gers the aging.

The 1950s and 1960s saw efforts to develop ethical and affordable ways of housing and caring for seniors outside of families. With **Social Secur-ity** providing reliable **retirement** income, elders began moving away from established family **homes** into new **Sunbelt** apartment, retirement commu-nities, some of which actively discouraged younger families from locating nearby. Even without relocat-ing, many elders still had fewer **family** members to care for them. Family size was shrinking, either by design as safe, reliable birth control became available, or, especially among poorer or newer Americans, through the exigencies of **mobility**, **immigration** and high mortality. Moreover, more frequent **divorce** and remarriage could multiply the size of the kin group, making young families responsible for more elders than ever before.

Elders have increasingly used new political and cultural powers based on their numbers in the population to claim care from the whole society. Since the 1970s, activist organizations, like the **American Association of Retired Persons (AARP)**, the American Society on Aging, and the Gray Panthers, eventually supported by the large and aging postwar **baby-boom** generation, have lob-bied successfully for Social Security benefits, medi-cal rights and legal protections for older Americans.

Wide-spread anxiety, including feminist con-cern, about intrusive and expensive **healthcare**, the disproportion of poor women among the elderly, unethical nursing-home practices and indignities surrounding **death** in hospitals have spurred movements for public regulation of care facilities, greater physical independence for elders and respect for age itself, and hospice and home-care programs for the terminally ill. The 1990s especially saw a revitalized Right-to-Die move-ment, dramatized by the assisted-suicide campaign of Dr Jack Kevorkian.

Wealth and family background strongly shape the expectations of aging. Affluent, especially **white**, elders seek "independence," and plan their finances, activities and choice of retirement home so as to avoid "burdening" their children. Their wealth and leisure time has supported new consumer **markets** in special safety equipment, exercise plans and machines, medical innovations and **plastic surgery**. By contrast, less affluent seniors, including many non-whites, more often seek to avoid sundering **community** ties, and tend to rely on their children, neighbors and church community to assist and protect them. This preference varies less with wealth among non-white seniors than among whites; Asians in particular are shocked by the isolation of the elderly.

Neither has offered a perfect solution. While independent seniors can suffer from isolation or emptiness, seniors who stay rooted in their communities also sometimes endure neglect, danger, or financial loss in securing needed care. The new opportunities for American seniors have not erased the society's persistent discomfort and impatience with the late stages of human life.

Further reading

Cole, T. (1992) *The Journey of Life*, New York: Cambridge.

Friedan, B. (1993) *The Fountain of Age*, New York: Simon & Schuster.

http://www.ncoa.org (National Council on Aging)

http://www.asaging.org (American Society on Aging)

SHARON ANN HOLT

"oldies"

Vaguely nostalgic melange of rock from the 1950s, 1960s, 1970s and, sometimes, 1980s, evoking feel-good memories of **teenage** life and possibilities for **baby boomers**, removed from any context of political, economic and socio-cultural change. Popular as a **radio** format, these "greatest hits" also set the ambience for movies like *The Big Chill* (1983), while fading into everyday backgrounds of offices, cars and elevator **muzak**. Oldies seem to be creating a pseudo-nostalgia for the children of boomers as well, exemplified in the renewed popularity of the 1978 *Grease* with new generations in its twentieth-anniversary release.

GARY McDONOGH

Olympians

In the US, the **Olympics** have been the most obvious site for the intersection of sports and nationalism. Until recently, therefore, the major compensation that could be derived from being an Olympian, given the strictures associated with maintaining status as an amateur, came from the visibility afforded those who represented their country, preferably with distinction. When most Americans played **football** and **baseball**, games which had only a limited international dimension, sporting outlets for nationalist and patriotic fervor were confined to the Olympics. Television commentators were acutely aware of this and their coverage of the Olympics focused fundamentally on highlighting American successes. Moreover, nationalist intensity associated with the Olympics was exacerbated by **Cold-War** rivalries. Americans as the leader of the "Free World" competed with East Germany and the Soviet Union, the communist powerhouses.

African American **track** stars, boxers and college **basketball** players were able, at least in small measure, to reap the benefits of favorable attitudes deriving from their gold-medal winning performances. Many of the athletes also celebrated their "Americanness," often taking victory laps or in some way wrapping themselves in the American flag. Other black athletes, especially at the 1968 Mexico and 1972 Munich Olympics, used the platform to make statements of protest against racial policies in the United States.

Many of the memorable moments in Olympic sports, then, have been those that could be framed in reference to nationalism. The Soviet Union's disputed victory at the 1972 Munich Olympics against a highly favored American basketball team (the game being decided on a very controversial last-second play) was cause for dismay. Eight years later, at the winter games in Lake Placid, New York, during the Iran hostage crisis, the success of the US **hockey** team's college players against the Soviet "machine" gave rise to widespread euphoria. In gymnastics, the five-medal performance of Mary Lou Retton at the 1984 Los Angeles games (clad in new flag-motif leotards) made her the darling of games tainted by a Soviet boycott.

This identification between nationalism and the Olympics has diminished somewhat in recent years. In part this is due to the end of Cold-War rivalries, but it is also a result of the growing professionalism of the Olympics. The athletes no longer need to maintain amateur status and so no longer pin all their hopes on their Olympic performances. Moreover, some of the competitiveness has been undermined by the inclusion of professionals in recent games. Instead of a team of American basketball players drawn from the **NCAA**, the US now fields "dream teams" that pull in stars exclusively from the NBA. The winner of the gold medal is now a foregone conclusion and many of the games in which the United States plays end up being humiliating for the other team. In other Olympic sports, nationalist sentiment is on the rise. This is particularly so for women's **soccer**, where Americans dominate but maintain strong rivalries with countries like Brazil and China, and patriotic feelings feed on the other major arena of sporting nationalism – soccer's world cups.

ROBERT GREGG

Olympic Games

The first modern Olympics (Athens, 1896) were envisioned by their founder, Baron Pierre de Coubertin, as a way to transcend international divisions of politics and commerce through the celebration of amateur sport, based loosely on the games of Ancient Greece. Despite these ideals, however, the modern Olympics have, from the outset, been beset by shifting political rivalries and economic circumstances. For Americans as hosts and participants, the Olympics crystallized the major global issues and struggles of the twentieth century.

For their first three decades, the modern Olympics were linked to expositions, **world's fairs** and other large-scale organized spectacles that emphasized the march of humankind's progress, as well as the qualitative differences between nations. Indeed, the second and third Olympics took place in coordination with the 1900 Paris Universal Exhibition and the 1904 **St. Louis, MO** World's Fair respectively. Like these exposi-

tions, the Olympics celebrated the divide between the so-called civilized societies of Europe and North America, which fielded teams, and the subject peoples of the colonial world, which did not. (Loosely organized "popular" Olympics tried to overcome this division as well as that which separated elite sports from more inclusive pastimes).

By contemporary standards, the first few Olympics were relatively modest, although each Olympiad saw the inclusion of new sporting events and new national teams. While winter sports were included since the 1900 Games, in 1920, separate Winter Olympic Games were inaugurated. These events have been held in the US three times: in Lake Placid (**New York**) in 1932 and 1980 and in Squaw Valley (**California**) in 1960. The scandal-ridden 2002 games are scheduled for **Salt Lake City, UT**. Americans have not gained as many medals as in the winter games, nor do the winter games promote **tourism** and imagery in the same way as summer games. Nonetheless, interest has been created around political events symbolized by the US men's hockey team's 1980 gold medal or by the dramas of Nancy Kerrigan and Tonya Harding in 1994. Still, the Summer Olympics remain larger, more inclusive and more prestigious than the Winter Games.

The 1932 **Los Angeles** Olympics were the first to link the Games to local economic development, as well as civic pride on the part of the host-city and nation. They were also marked by an unprecedented amount of international **mass media** coverage that served to heighten the political importance of the Games. The Berlin Olympics of 1936 were particularly noteworthy in this regard, as the Nazi regime envisioned a vehicle for promoting the image not only of a resurgent Germany, but also of Aryan superiority. These latter dreams were effectively dashed, however, by the stellar performance of Jesse Owens and other **African American** athletes on the US team.

The Second World War led to the cancellation of both the 1940 Olympics (Tokyo) and the 1944 Olympics (London, hosted in 1948). Following the entry of the first team from the Soviet Union in 1952, the Games became a surrogate arena for the **Cold War** between the "Free West," led by the

United States, and the communist bloc, led by the Soviet Union.

In the 1960s, the changing scale and nature of the Games challenged some basic Olympic principles. Extensive state subsidies provided to athletes from Soviet-bloc nations were seen to undermine the basic principles of amateurism. Meanwhile, the advent of **television** coverage in 1960 intensified prospects for commercialization. For much of the next two decades, the International Olympic Committee (IOC), under the leadership of Avery **Brundage**, fought a successful rearguard action against both professionalism and commercialization.

Still, the scale and international visibility of the Olympic Games intensified their importance as symbolic arenas. Awarding of an Olympics bestowed international recognition on former pariah nations (Tokyo, Japan 1964; Munich, Germany 1972; and perhaps Barcelona, Spain 1992) and on developing nations such as Mexico (1968) and South Korea (1988). The Mexico City Games of 1968, however, became noteworthy for the military's brutal repression of student protestors. Meanwhile, at their medal ceremony, American sprinters Tommy Smith and John Carlos raised gloved fists in the **Black Power** salute, for which they were suspended from the US Olympic team and kicked out of the Olympic Village.

Global politics intensified thereafter. The 1972 Munich Games were marred by the murder of members of the Israeli Olympic team by Palestinian guerrillas. Many African nations boycotted the 1976 Montreal Games to protest New Zealand's participation (their rugby team had played a tournament in South Africa). In 1980 the United States boycotted the Moscow Games in protest of the Soviet Union's invasion of Afghanistan, which in turn provoked a Soviet-bloc boycott of the 1984 Los Angeles Games.

While the increasingly manifest politicization of the Games tarnished the luster of the Olympic movement, their growing scale also placed extreme financial burdens on the host-city and nation, notably Montreal's more than $1 billion debt in 1976. Thus, Los Angeles was the only city to bid on the 1984 Games.

The Los Angeles Olympics proved noteworthy for not only the triumph of US teams in the absence of the Soviet bloc, but also for the manner in which they were staged. Prior to 1984, public entities mounted the Olympics. The Los Angeles Games were the first to use only private funds. Organizers minimized costs, eschewing new construction in favor of temporary venues and rehabilitated facilities from the 1932 Games. Raising capital through corporate sponsorships and unprecedentedly expensive television rights, the Los Angeles Olympic Organizing Committee generated a profit in excess of $200 million. The potential profit to be realized from the Olympics undermined the IOC's historic resistance to commercialism; ensuing Olympiads have been marked by ever-increasing commercialism.

Both the Seoul Olympics of 1988 and the Barcelona Games of 1992 were accompanied by massive, state-financed urban redevelopment projects in their host cities. The Atlanta Olympics of 1996, however, manifested a return to extreme entrepreneurialism. Unlike Los Angeles, however, Atlanta organizers planned for significant new construction of Olympic venues, funded by private sources including the sale of television rights, commercial sponsorships, tickets and merchandise. Lacking a publicly subsidized safety net, Atlanta's preparations were often on precarious financial footing. Atlanta's problems with fundraising, along with criticisms of management and over-commercialization, made the IOC declare it would never again award the Olympics to a city without a significant public-sector financial commitment.

With the end of the Cold War in the early 1990s, that particular political dimension of the Olympics faded into history, although American media coverage continues to stress national triumphs (and American stories of **family**, individual dedication and **community** support). In many ways, the commercialism of the Barcelona and Atlanta Olympics already celebrated the triumph of capitalism over socialism. Beginning in the 1980s, the IOC also began to retreat from its insistence on amateurism and allowed professional athletes to compete – critical to American dominance in basketball, for example. Hence by the end of the twentieth century, the spirit of Olympism was radically revised to embrace both professionalism and commercialism, creating a vast hypermediated spectacle exemplifying the global economy.

Further reading

Dyreson, M. (1998) *Making the American Team*, Urbana: University of Illinois.

Rutheiser, C. (1996) *Imagineering Atlanta*, London: Verso.

Young, D. (1996) *The Modern Olympics*, Baltimore: Johns Hopkins.

CHARLES RUTHEISER

Onassis, Jacqueline Bouvier Kennedy

b. 1929; d. 1994

Multi-faceted American icon. Daughter of East Coast Catholic aristocracy, "Jackie" brought style and elegance to her marriage with John **Kennedy**, helping his political career and transforming the taste of the White House – and America – as **First Lady**. After JFK's **assassination** in 1963, her sorrow and grace as the martyred widow and mother of the next generation of Kennedys endeared her even more to an American public who would be shocked by her marriage (1968–75) to Greek billionaire Aristotle Onassis. In her later years, she maintained a private life in **New York** City while working as an editor for Doubleday; nonetheless, in all phases of her life she was a magnet for publicity whose photographs are emblems of the American century.

GARY McDONOGH

O'Neill, Thomas "Tip"

b. 1912; d. 1994

Massachusetts member of Congress and **Speaker of the House**. Elected to **Congress** in 1952, O'Neill made famous the phrase, "All politics is local," a credo which contends that local, rather than national, concerns drive politics. He became one of the first House leaders to oppose US involvement in the **Vietnam War**. Speaker of the

House from 1977 until his retirement in 1986, O'Neill was the longest continually serving Speaker since Congress first met in 1789. In 1979, during O'Neill's tenure as Speaker, the House began live telecasts of its floor debates.

JAMES DEVITT

opera

Opera is the most opulent and expensive of the performing arts and has historically been the province of social elites in America. In the first decades following the Second World War, opera continued to appeal to wealthy artistic patrons in the large urban centers, but, by the century's end, it achieved a level of popularity and broad-based appeal few could have predicted in the early 1960s.

At mid-century, opera in America was dominated by a handful of companies: first and foremost of which was the Metropolitan Opera Company of **New York** City (the Met), followed by the San Francisco Opera Company (CA) and the New York City Opera. Other companies of note in the early postwar era included the Lyric Opera of Chicago, IL, the Houston, Grand Opera (TX) and the Greater Miami Opera (FL). The repertoire of these companies was conservative, emphasizing the Italian, German and French canon, though new works by American composers were occasionally commissioned. Predictably, the American contributions to the operatic repertoire during this period mimicked the canon in tone, if not always in subject. Samuel **Barber**, perhaps the most favored of American composers of his generation, received prestigious Met performances, including *Vanessa* (1957) and *Antony and Cleopatra* (1958). The latter, a Met commission, had a lavish production directed by Franco Zefferelli, but was a critical and popular failure. However, composers who sought to emphasize American themes achieved somewhat greater success. Aaron **Copland**'s *The Tender Land* (1954), Carlisle Floyd's *Susannah* (1956) and Douglas Moore's *The Ballad of Baby Doe* (1966) received numerous productions by major American companies, yet none found a secure place in the repertoire of European companies.

If the principal opera companies of America proved inhospitable to new and experimental currents in music, there were alternative venues. Two professional companies that regularly featured modernist repertoire were the **Santa Fe** Opera Company (New Mexico) and the **Boston** Opera Company (Massachusetts). The latter, under the direction of Sarah Caldwell, performed such demanding works as Luigi Nono's *Intolleranza* (1961), Bernd Alois Zimmermann's *Die Soldaten* (1965) and Roger Session's monumental *Montezuma* (American premiere, 1976). The opera programs at universities and conservatories such as the Juilliard School and Indiana University also provided alternative support for composers and helped to build audiences, furthering the careers of composers such as Dominick Argento and John Eaton.

The turning point in contemporary American opera can perhaps be traced to the New York premiere of *Einstein on the Beach* by Philip **Glass** (1976). Created in collaboration with director Robert **Wilson**, the work broke new ground in several ways. First, in keeping with Wilson's emphasis on **theater** as spectacle, the work was not based on a conventional narrative. Instead, it took the form of a pageant in which loose references to Einstein were clearly subordinated to abstract structures of music and **dance**. Second, the work was the first full-length opera composed using **minimalist** procedures: the music substituted extensive repetition and subtle variation for tonal hierarchy, and thus reinforced the opera's lack of narrative structure. Third, the score called for electronic instruments, especially synthesizers, and largely eschewed solo vocal writing in favor of a chorus. (Ironically, this performance was not sponsored by the Met; the House had been rented for the occasion.) *Einstein on the Beach* enjoyed international success, and was followed by *Satyagraha* (1980), *Akhnaten* (1983) and *The Civil Wars: A Tree is Best Measured when it is Down* (1985). Glass' stature as an operatic composer was confirmed by a Met commission on the 500th anniversary of Columbus' voyage to the New World (*The Voyage*, 1992).

Glass was not the only composer associated with minimalism who achieved success in opera. John Adams achieved international acclaim for *Nixon in China* (1987) and *The Death of Klinghoffer* (1991),

proving that the art form of opera could not only accommodate a radically new musical style, but also could address contemporary political issues at the same time. By attracting a new, younger audience to opera, Glass and Adams created a more positive climate in American opera houses for young American composers. In recent years, new operas have achieved surprising popularity. Among the most significant are Anthony Davis' *X: The Life and Times of Malcom X* (1986), John Corigliano's *The Ghosts of Versailles* (1991), Tobias Picker's *Emmeline* (1996) and Tan Dun's *Marco Polo* (1996). Dun's work is especially notable for seamlessly blending contemporary Western vocabulary with music of Dun's native China.

The renewed popularity of opera in America has been stimulated by other factors besides the additions of new works. First, the repertoire has been expanded by the revival of Baroque operas (most notably works of Monteverdi and Handel) at most major houses. Second, the use of supertitles (the display of running translation above the proscenium), has made opera accessible to a much larger audience. Finally, the artistic quality of regional opera companies has improved dramatically, thus spreading the operatic experience far beyond traditional centers on the American coasts. Among the most important of these companies are the Seattle Opera (Washington), the Minnesota Opera Company and the Sarasota Opera Association (Florida).

Further reading

Dizikes, J. (1993) *Opera in America: A Cultural History*, New Haven: Yale University.

Kornick, R. (1991) *Recent American Opera: A Production Guide*, New York: Columbia University.

Parker, R. (ed.) (1994) *Oxford History of Opera*, New York: Oxford.

Richmond, E. (1992) *Opera Companies and American Opera: A Directory*, New York: American Music Center.

STEPHEN MILES

orchestras *see* classical music

organization man

Termed coined by William Whyte, in a 1956 book of that name, which suggested that business culture and the attempt to make people work for the profit of the corporation affected people's social lives. Americans, Whyte argued, acted like cogs in a machine, conforming to group values at the office and **home**. This lifestyle was represented in many movies of the 1950s and early 1960s (e.g. *The Apartment*, 1960, in which Jack Lemmon lends his apartment to his bosses for their sexual liaisons), though Whyte believed the organization man's natural habitat was the **suburb**. The sameness and impotence associated with the organization man is captured nicely in the character of Mr Arnold in *The Wonder Years* (ABC, 1988–93). The organization man also resented his wife for pushing him to succeed in this corporate world, resentment described in Philip **Roth**'s *My Life as a Man* (1974). The beats resisted the siren call of the corporation, and juvenile delinquents, like James **Dean**'s *Rebel Without a Cause* (1955), resented their fathers for their emasculation.

ROBERT GREGG

organized crime

The havoc wreaked by organized crime in the United States is usually thought to be intramural. Gangland killings and the occasional internecine war seem remote from the ordinary concerns of the public. This may account for the enormous entertainment value Americans have found in the machinations of the **Italian American** Mafia (also called *La Cosa Nostra* – "our thing") and other crime syndicates. Francis Ford **Coppola**'s screen adaptations of Mario **Puzo**'s stories of **family** life in the mob, beginning with *The Godfather* in 1971 became cultural icons. Not only did the first two films in Coppola's trilogy sweep the Academy Awards in 1971 and 1974, but they contributed to constructing the myth and image of organized crime in the United States.

Tapes of telephone conversations and private conversations collected by informants wearing "wires" revealed the extent to which **Hollywood** shaped the self-concepts of mobsters like John Gotti, who was known in the **New York** media both as the Teflon Don (though he was eventually brought down by the testimony of his associate, Sammy "the Bull" Gravano) and the Dapper Don (*Newsday* sent a **fashion** reporter to the last of Gotti's three major trials). For instance, the use of "godfather" to refer to the leader of a Mafia family was invented by Puzo, and adopted by real-life Mafia leaders, formerly known as "capo" (head or chief). The paramount Mafia leader would be known as the *capo di tutti capi*, the chief of all chiefs.

But the entertainment value of the Mafia and other interstate criminal syndicates, like the **Los Angeles** based **gangs** Crips and Bloods, is balanced by the heavy economic and social costs of organized crime. The image of a brutal, but righteous mob leader, like the fictional Don Vito Corleone protecting his family and friends, began disappearing after the Second World War, when the old "mustache Petes" were swept aside by capos and consiglieres using modern business techniques backed by **violence**. The old code of silence in the Mafia, "omerta," was broken first by Joe Valachi in 1963 before the McClellan Committee in the United States Senate and a number of times since. Mafia underlings looking for a good deal from prosecutors found little reason to protect what was no longer a **family**, but a murderous corporate enterprise.

By 1975 the National Conference on Organized Crime estimated that the annual cost to the American economy of organized criminal activity was in excess of $50 billion. Some 1990s estimates were double the 1975 figure. Even much higher dollar estimates do not encompass the huge losses caused by mob commerce in illegal drugs, including designer drugs like methamphetamine ("crystal meth"), or mob support of prostitution, illegal **gambling** and loan sharking.

As the mob has diversified into a variety of illegal businesses by providing cash and protection for illegal entrepreneurs, it continues infiltrating legitimate businesses as well. Intergenerational control of materials and solid-waste hauling – later including the illegal disposal of toxic wastes – several construction trades and related **unions** and construction companies themselves have been carefully documented in New York City and other metropolitan areas. The New York State Organized Crime Task Force found mob control so pervasive in New York City's construction industry in the 1980s that not a single yard of concrete was poured in the city without the mob taking a cut of the profit. The result, as in so many other mob-influenced businesses, was an extortionate price for concrete, often twice as high as it was in other places.

The reaction to the ascendancy of organized crime in legitimate and illegal businesses was a new federal law, the Racketeer Influence and Corrupt Organizations Act (RICO). Long recommended by legal scholars and prosecutors, **Congress** passed RICO in 1970 as part of the Organized Crime Control Act. A number of **states** followed RICO with similar statutes that allowed them to reach conduct that was not covered by the extremely broad definition of interstate commercial impact that was required to trigger federal penalties.

Law-makers had learned what everyone else in American society had absorbed from the entertainment and publishing industries: organized crime had become an integral part of the American economy. It was providing goods that people wanted and protecting illicit businesses that had huge **markets**. It would take extraordinary measures to unravel mob involvement in American life. RICO was such a measure. By defining a criminal enterprise as any individual or organization responsible for a "pattern of racketeering activity," and then defining that pattern as two or more acts of racketeering within ten years, RICO enabled federal prosecutors like Rudolph Giuliani to attack the Mafia head on. Since the passage of RICO, the leadership of all five Mafia families based in New York has been indicted, convicted and jailed, including the Teflon Don.

The reaction to the pervasive influence of the Mafia has produced such a broad law that a number of conventionally respectable enterprises may now be labeled criminal enterprises. Prosecutors in **Florida** have used RICO against **tobacco** companies, and its civil provisions have been upheld in suits against anti-**abortion** protesters who block access to clinics.

While RICO has been effective against organized crime, mob influence has expanded as a variety of ethnic groups break the hold of the old

Italian American families. Recent cases involved criminal syndicates among Mexican, Vietnamese, Colombian and Chinese immigrant groups in the United States.

See also: immigration

Further reading

Huston, P. (1995) *Tongs, Gangs, and Triads: Chinese Crime Groups in North America*, Boulder: Paladin Press.

Jacobs, J.B. (1994) *Busting the Mob: United States v. Cosa Nostra*, New York: New York University Press.

National Conference on Organized Crime (1975) *Report of the National Conference on Organized Crime*, Washington, DC: US Government Printing Office.

Peterson, V. (1983) *The Mob*, Ottowa: Green-Hill Press.

FRANK ANECHIARICO

Orthodox religions *see* Arab Americans; Armenian Americans; Greek Americans; Greek Orthodox

outing

According to Larry Gross in *Contested Closets* (1993), "outing" actually coincides with the nineteenth-century introduction of the homosexual and, thus, the homosexual closet. Since then, impulses to make public that which is private (especially sexuality) are confounded by paradoxical impulses to protect those very same issues. Journalism complicates this: where is the line in issues of public and private when discussing a public figure?

Reporting on a public figure's private sexual affairs has always stirred a controversial, yet prurient, response. Throw in gay and lesbian life and either the strong arm of the closet protects the figure from scandal or, unlike his or her heterosexual counterpart, the figure's reputation is ruined. This imbalance prompted journalist/activist Michelangelo Signorile to query the favored newsworthiness and biased protection of heterosexual affairs. Although others had "outed" previously, Signorile articulated "outing" as a complicated political gesture, making it a political tool and an art form in the gay magazine *Outweek* (1989–91). Signorile contends that "outing critiques and corrects the double standard in journalism on reporting on homosexuals and heterosexuals." Furthermore, "in cases where a closeted politician is voting anti-gay in order to protect his closet, outing displays the political hypocrisy" (interview, 11/22/98).

DAVID GERSTNER

outsourcing

Movement of operations out of the main plant/ production process to subsidiary companies and contractors who offer flexible workforces and cheaper and more efficient delivery (especially when outsourcing becomes global). A profit-making strategy within the corporate world since the 1970s, both smaller and larger corporations farm out communications, computer/systems management and even planning rather than doing them in-house. Governments have used outsourcing to meet new service needs since the 1960s, including mundane tasks like waste collection and towing, as well as administrative functions like printing and even social services including ambulances or drug treatment. Its human costs in career and corporate community underscore the transformation of the US economy towards services and consumption.

GARY McDONOGH

Owens, Jesse *see* Olympians; track and field

P

Pacific Northwest

While **state** and local boundaries are clearly defined and embodied in law, those of the **region** called the Pacific Northwest are not. Cohesion derives from the region's early geographic isolation and resulting history. In this article, "Pacific Northwest" refers to Washington, Oregon and Idaho (Schwantes), although the term is sometimes used also to include British Columbia, western Montana and/or northern **California**.

This variegated, 250,000 square mile, parallelogram-shaped region spans 480 miles north to south and 680 miles east to west. It is bounded by the Pacific Ocean to the west, the Canadian border to the north, the Klamath (Siskiyou) Mountains and Great Basin desert to the south, and the **Rocky Mountains** to the east. Its vegetative diversity reflects its climatic diversity, with three major vegetation provinces – **forest**, shrub-steppe and alpine. Unifying the region is the Columbia River, with its many tributaries, transportation and communication networks, trade and commerce patterns and a special sense of place derived from its history and geography.

What gives Pacific Northwesterners a different sense of place from others? The environment. The region's spectacular landscape offers a plethora of contrasts, from breathtaking views of jagged mountains to alpine meadows; from the glistening waters of the coast to the vast, dry, sagebrush interior; from wide sandy beaches to rugged headlands; from lush forested valleys to bare rock faces; and from placid estuaries to turbulent mountain streams.

The region's geography provides the basis for understanding its history and economy. The Pacific Northwest remained isolated from the main centers of economic and political power through the early part of the twentieth century. Because of its separateness and the fact that it supplied the country with raw materials such as furs, logs, lumber, agricultural products, seafood and metals it came to be thought of as a colonial hinterland.

The region was home to two contrasting **American Indian** cultures. The coastal and plateau peoples located in a rich natural environment produced a stable economy and sedentary culture. In contrast, the desert peoples adapted to its dry climate and scarcity of food with a semi-nomadic lifestyle.

The region's environment is an outcome not merely of geologic history, but also of values about **nature** deeply embedded in the local psyche. Pacific Northwest literature is replete with images of human interaction with the natural **environment**. It is often suggested that the environment itself determined who settled here – that the rugged mountains and gigantic forests attracted strong-willed, self-reliant people.

In all three states of the Pacific Northwest, **tourism** is one of the top three revenue generators. The area's many recreational resources not only benefit the regional economy, but are also an important contributor to Pacific Northwesterners' high quality of life. The terrain seduces world-class mountain climbers, skiiers and other outdoor enthusiasts. Hikers escape to the untrammeled wilderness areas, combers and surfers to the beaches, **fishing** enthusiasts to the streams, lakes and **rivers** and hunters to the wildlife of the forests and shrub steppes.

Bucking one of the strongest traditions of the American **West** – an individual's right to develop his or her own land – the Pacific Northwest led the country in several areas of environmental protection through growth management, as well as forest and salmon protection legislation. This was not, however, achieved without controversy – the battle lines were clearly visible from bumper stickers declaring: "I Like Spotted Owls – Fried" versus "Save an Owl, Educate a Logger."

The 1990 census showed the Pacific Northwest outpacing the national rate of population growth, with newcomers arriving from all over the United States as well as from overseas. Washington has five times the population of Idaho, while Oregon's population lies between the two. The average population density was thirty-five people per square mile in 1990, significantly lower than the national average of seventy. The Pacific Northwest's population has always been overwhelmingly Caucasian, but now includes rapidly growing Spanish-speaking, Asian and **African American** populations.

Over time, the Pacific Northwest's attitudes towards its minority populations have shifted dramatically, but differently in each state. Idaho's image is often associated with that of the white supremacists. Contrast the late nineteenth-century banner seen in Seattle proclaiming "The Chinese must go!" with the 1996 election of Washington Governor Gary Locke, the first **Chinese American** governor in US history. While discriminatory signs once excluded blacks from public places in Washington State, **African Americans** have recently been elected as County Executive (Ron Sims) and Seattle **mayor** (Norm Rice).

Although the Second World War expanded the region's economy to include manufacturing (due to Puget Sound-based Boeing's defense contracts), forestry, **mining**, fishing and agricultural industries continued to be important. In Washington's Puget Sound region in particular, the economy has taken wild rollercoaster rides as Boeing's defense and commercial contracts have alternately expanded and shriveled.

Following a dramatic downturn in manufacturing in the early 1970s, the region made a concerted effort to diversify its economy. This resulted in marked expansions in international trade, service and high-technology industries – most notably Microsoft, which catapulted the region onto the world's radar screen. The Pacific Northwest continues to dominate the high-tech industry worldwide, while spawning numerous spin-off businesses here at home.

Images of Northwest scenery in TV series such as *Twin Peaks* (ABC, 1990–1) and *Northern Exposure* (CBS, 1990–5), and Gus Van Sant's *My Own Private Idaho* (1991) have introduced millions around the globe to this region.

"Northwest cuisine" not only reflects variations in the area's landscape and ethnic populations, but captures its adventurous spirit through four sub-regional cuisines. Coastal waters cuisine dares us with dishes such as matsutake mushrooms in seaweed broth and creamy sea-urchin bisque. Farmland cuisine tempts us with Walla Walla onion frittata and Fraser Valley pheasant. Cities cuisine features microbrew steamers and cappuccino cheesecake. Finally, mountains and forests cuisine includes tasty delicacies like morels on toast and vegetable pâté with watercress and fiddlehead ferns. With Northwest wines and microbrews winning international awards, a locally made beverage is a must to accompany the region's culinary delights.

Further reading

Egan, T. (1990) *The Good Rain*, New York: Vintage Books.

Jackson, P. and Kimerling, A. (eds) (1993) *Atlas of the Pacific Northwest*, Corvallis: Oregon State University.

Schwantes, C. (1996) *The Pacific Northwest*, Lincoln: University of Nebraska.

BERYL FERNANDES

Pacific Rim

The West Coast has not only received the bulk of **Asian American** migration, but also has established increasingly strong commercial ties in the postwar era with sometimes burgeoning Asian states. The "Pacific Rim" incorporates **Califor-**

nia, Oregon, Washington (the **Pacific North-west**), **Alaska** and **Hawai'i** into a broader global vision of business and culture for the twenty-first century. The title is also applied to fusion cuisine and design styles mixing Asian elements with a jazzy California style as well as local ingredients. By contrast, "Atlantic culture and society" is generally confined to academic studies of the interchanges constituted by colonialism and slavery and their aftermath (although **NATO** – the *North Atlantic* Treaty Organization – evokes other historic ties). Meanwhile, **Texas** may be called the "third coast" while **Miami** is sometimes recognized as the capital of the **Caribbean**. All of these terms project ideological expectations that may not affect the consciousness of local, non-immigrant populations.

GARY McDONOGH
CINDY WONG

Paglia, Camille

b. 1947

Cultural analyst, writer and professor known for her flamboyant style and provocative theories concerning American culture and sexuality. Her books include *Sexual Personae* (1990), *Sex, Art, and American Culture* (1992) and *Vamps and Tramps* (1994). She is generally considered a conservative anti-feminist, though she describes herself as a "radical 1960s libertarian" and is a vocal critic of what has been termed "**political correctness**." Her supporters argue that she is a courageous independent thinker, while her critics claim that she is concerned primarily with self-promotion and that her work has been harmful to liberal causes.

NICOLE MARIE KEATING

Panama/Panama Canal

American involvement in Panama has been long and checkered since Theodore Roosevelt, unwilling to pay the Columbian government's price for access across the isthmus, fomented a nationalist uprising among Panamanians. Roosevelt backed Panama's independence and then forced the new government to cede the canal zone to the US for a price well below what Panamanians thought reasonable. Finished in 1914, the canal became a source of tension throughout the century as Panamanians protested the US' despotic control of the region and other infringements on their sovereignty, including military intervention. By the 1970s, President Jimmy **Carter**, hoping to stabilize the canal zone, felt it prudent, even against significant **Republican** opposition, to sign a treaty returning the canal to Panamanians in 2000.

Strains have not only been related to the canal, but also to Panamanian policies and leadership. In the 1980s, President Manuel Noriega acquired dictatorial powers, partly because of his work with the **CIA** and his close alliance with the United States. He also amassed a fortune through involvement in the US drug trade. Yet, his continued rule in Panama became unacceptable for American authorities when he refused to help them fight against the Sandinistas in Nicaragua. Invoking the drug trade, in 1989, President **Bush** sent an invasion force of 27,000 into Panama to capture and replace Noriega. Brought to **Florida** and not allowed to reveal all his connections with the American intelligence community during his trial, Noriega was jailed, although the drug trade was largely unhampered.

ROBERT GREGG

paperbacks *see* publishing; romance novels

parades

Whether celebrating ethnic heritages, sporting events, political candidates or controversial causes, parades reclaim urban thoroughfares as public spaces for expressions of group identity. Often, these carry memorial/patriotic associations – the bands, flags, military troops and heroes of 4th of July reverberate through media and political imagery. Others – the spectacles inaugurating Christmas shopping or celebrating **bowl games** – convey commercial messages through elaborate floats and televisual coverage. **Disney**, as well, promotes nightly events to sanctify its imagery of small-town America. Yet parades challenge as well as affirm; the legacy of **civil-rights** marches underpins contemporary Gay Pride parades and new ethnic celebrations demanding space in the American landscape.

GARY McDONOGH

Parent Teacher's Associations (PTAs)

Founded a century ago, these school-based groups bring parents into closer contact with their children's **education**, support extra school activities and lobby for educational issues. In the 1950s and 1960s, they stressed classroom life and fundraising events like bake sales. The National Association of Colored Parents merged with the older association in 1970, focusing concern with desegregation. As tax reforms and social problems like **violence** have challenged both educational budgets and quality, these associations have taken on more important supplementary roles, although involvement varies according to **class** and gender, with women being predominant.

GARY McDONOGH

parks, national and state

The concept of a protected natural area under national ownership originated in the United States in 1870 with the establishment of Yellowstone National Park. Protecting areas of outstanding scenic beauty quickly grew into a cherished aspect of national policy. The National Park Service, created in 1916 to administer the national park system, has responsibility over more than 350 separate areas totaling about 81 million acres (32.5 million hectares), visited by nearly 290 million people annually. Besides famous and majestic national parks, the system also includes and preserves monuments, recreation areas, seashores, lake shores, parkways, forts, bridges and scenic trails as well as historic parks, sites and battlefields. State parks and municipal parks and playgrounds are equally diverse and sizable. **New York** City's

urban park system alone contains some 10,530 hectares.

As **highways** spanned the United States and **automobile** ownership was democratized, national parks changed from wildernesses or playgrounds for the wealthy to accessible and affordable vacation destinations for average Americans and foreign visitors. Crowds make cursory seasonal visits, peering at scenic vistas from car windshields: tours of the parks of the **Southwest** and **West** constitute **family** pilgrimages rivaling journeys to **Disneyland** and Disneyworld. Extended families use them as gathering places for reunions. Caravans and retired elderly people cruise between campgrounds redesigned for large recreational vehicles.

National and large state parks, as multiple-use enclaves, have become pivotal battlegrounds for the innate tensions between conservation and use. Dependent for their very existence on **tourism** and stimulated by public interest in **nature** and recreation, parks, paradoxically, are involved in a constant struggle to preserve natural beauty and wildlife by attempting to control use. Those interested in **environmentalism**, backpacking and preserving a more pristine wilderness become pitted against others who prefer to open parks to more recreational and year-round pursuits such as boating, **fishing**, **hunting**, rock climbing, recreational vehicles and mountain bikes. In the West, parks have also become controversial sites of animal management, fire control, grazing, **forestry** and subsurface rights.

Chronically under-funded by **Congress**, the Park Service must mediate these competing national impulses. Parks serve as classrooms providing educational programs on naturalistic, historical and environmental issues. Environmentalists seek presentations that encourage preservation and heighten awareness of pollution. Historians and minority groups want greater accuracy and socially inclusive historical explanations. Pressure to commercialize and privatize park facilities, meanwhile, is unrelenting. Corporate financial sponsorship of programs and capital improvements, which many view as intrusive, self-serving public relations, is a constant temptation. **Lobbyists** push pork-barrel projects and commercial development under the guise of improving parks. While Americans view national parks with reverence, they also regard recreational activities as a civic right. Hence, utilization policies must balance political pressure for special and narrow uses with simultaneous protection of a heritage for the future.

Further reading

Fisher, R. (1984) *Our Threatened Inheritance*, Washington, DC: National Geographic.

MacNeice, J. (1990) *A Guide to National Monuments and Historic Sites*, New York: Prentice Hall.

JAMES KRAUS

Parks, Rosa

Widely known as the woman who, tired after a long day's work, refused to give up her seat when ordered to do so by a Montgomery, Alabama bus driver. In fact, prior to her defiance on December 1, 1954, Parks was a local secretary for the **NAACP** and had heard Rev. Martin Luther **King**, Jr.'s sermons saying that **segregation** needed to be challenged. She was not the first African American to challenge segregated **buses**, but E.D. Nixon, head of the local NAACP, believed she could withstand the threats and pressures and so organized a boycott of Montgomery's buses. The Montgomery Improvement Association formed quickly, with King appointed as the leader, and within a year the bus company was forced to desegregate. Rosa Parks was later awarded the Presidential Medal of Honor by Bill **Clinton**.

ROBERT GREGG

parks and playgrounds, municipal

The types and locations of municipal parks are as varied as those of the people who use them. They include ecological reserves, green spaces, beaches, cement slabs, sports fields and reclaimed factories, ranging in size from a tiny plaza to many acres. Central Park in **New York** City is perhaps the most famous with its acres of **lawns**, lakes and

forest in the middle of Manhattan. These green parks serve as a relief from busy **cities**; an escape to the country without going there. Others, like Gas Works Park in **Seattle, WA**, have converted abandoned industrial sites into urban recreational facilities. On a smaller scale, vest-pocket parks are small green spaces squeezed onto empty lots or between two buildings. Outside cities, metropolitan parks tend to be larger, as they have not had to compete with real-estate interests for land.

Children's playgrounds are common in all areas, existing by themselves or within larger parks. Standard playground equipment includes swings, jungle gyms, merry-go-rounds, see-saws, slides and sandboxes. Safety is a major concern.

Parks' conditions range from well-maintained lawns and facilities to dismal scenes of broken equipment and struggling plants. Funding has been problematic for many municipalities as limited budgets rank other services above public parks. Many parks, especially those of historic significance, have private **community** activist groups, who work to make up for shortcomings in municipal funding and maintenance. Safety is another concern as people tend to feel that parks are dangerous after dark, and providing adequate lighting and supervision is expensive and difficult for many cities.

Parks generally serve two main purposes: maintaining open space and providing a place for **children** and adults to play, exercise and spend active time outdoors. They are commonly used as spaces for concerts, festivals, political rallies and other community events. Factors affecting the public's use of parks include available leisure time, transportation, education and income levels. Quantity of leisure time has had the most impact on recreational activity – as work weeks have become shorter and people have more flexible schedules, many cities have seen a rise in park use.

Parks have changed according to the needs and attitudes of the general public in the century since cities first began to sponsor them. The first public parks were either for children's active play or adults' passive promenades. In the second half of the twentieth century many parks included **basketball** and **tennis** courts and **baseball** diamonds as a desire for more active recreation spread among all age groups. Parks face new challenges as recreational preferences continue to change – **skateboarding** and **in-line skating** are rough on park equipment. Some municipalities have built skating parks, the latest evolution in public recreation, ramps and jumps specially built for new high-impact, high-energy activities.

Further reading

Cranz, G. (1982) *The Politics of Park Design; a History of Urban Parks in America*, Cambridge, MA: MIT.

Eriksen, A. (1985) *Playground Design: Outdoor Environments for Learning and Development*, New York: Van Nostrand Reinhold.

BIANCA T. SIEGL

parochial schools

The **Roman Catholic** parochial school system in the United States, the largest **private school** system in the country and in the world, educates elementary through secondary students in schools affiliated with Catholic parishes. The system of parochial schools developed in the nineteenth century as a result of concerns within Catholic circles about the dominant Protestant sensibility. Catholics viewed the public schools not as secular, but as non-denominational Protestant, and sometimes audaciously anti-Catholic, especially where nativist attitudes were strong. The Catholic Church believed that attendance in public schools would lead to a decline in Catholic identity among the immigrant Catholic communities.

At the midpoint of the twentieth century, the official position of the Catholic hierarchy was that all education for Catholics should be religious in orientation and controlled by the Church, a position held by the majority of Catholics as well. The number of schools in the parochial school system doubled between 1940 and 1960, when it reached its peak in population and percentage of Catholics. The predominance of parochial schools in the Catholic **community** sustained a culture of Catholicism that imbued much of the activity of the community. From May Queen processions to beginning the school day with Mass, such socializing resulted in various attitudes among Catholics and perceptions of the Catholic community. The schools were known for their strict discipline, for children wearing **uniforms**, and for the religious sisters who tended to run the schools. While there were abuses of discipline resulting in many true and apocryphal stories about students surviving Catholic schools, the schools were effective in inculcating Catholic values in the students and making it more likely that they would remain Catholic in their later years.

Towards the end of the twentieth century, as Catholics, as a group, have become more acculturated into mainstream society, parochial schools have shifted their focus. While the majority of schools used to be urban, the majority of Catholics have now moved into the **suburbs**. Thus, schools have been built in the suburbs for the moving population and the numbers of **inner-city** schools have declined. The remaining inner-city parochial schools educate increasing numbers of non-Catholics and minorities, following the Catholic Church's concern for the poor in the inner cities, especially for **African American**, **Latino** and new immigrant populations. For inner-city families, parochial schools offer a low-cost and high-reward alternative to the decaying **public-school** structure. While urban parochial schools spend less per student than the local public school, they demonstrate higher rates of learning.

In recent years, parochial schools have become the touchstone for traditionalist religious forces. Foes of the secular public-school system promote parochial schools' values, and supporters of parochial schools often align themselves with the burgeoning force for tax-supported vouchers.

Further reading

Bryk, A.S., Lee, V.E. (contributor) and Holland, P.B. (1993) *Catholic Schools and the Common Good*, Cambridge, MA: Harvard University Press.

Greeley, A., McCready, W.C. and McCourt, K. (1976) *Catholic Schools in a Declining Church*, Kansas City: Sheed and Ward.

ERIC A. ZIMMER

parties and elections

The American election system is one of the oldest in the world. It has undergone many changes, but the basic system has remained much the same since it was written into the Constitution. The electorate has been slowly expanded through a series of constitutional amendments; additional impediments to voting, such as poll **taxes** and literacy tests, have been eliminated; and local and state laws governing the operation of parties have changed over the years. Demands for campaign-finance reform will no doubt change the system further, yet it remains highly unlikely that the system's most essential features will be changed.

Basic structure of elections

Candidates may run for three different types of office at the national level: membership in the Senate, membership in the House of Representatives and the **presidency**. In elections to most offices, the winner is the candidate who receives a plurality of votes; a majority is not required to win an election. Elections for national office take place on the first Tuesday in November of every even year (1992, 1994, 1996, etc.). Elections for membership in the Senate take place every six years on a statewide level. Each state has two senators and the elections are staggered so that both Senate seats will not be contested during the same election. Elections for membership in the House of Representatives take place every two years. Each state gets one member in the House of Representatives for every 500,000 citizens. States are broken down into districts containing 500,000 citizens and campaigns are run at this level.

Presidential elections take place every four years. The winner of the presidential election is not decided merely by calculating which candidate received the most votes nationwide; instead, a somewhat complicated system called the electoral college is used. Under this system, each state is granted one electoral vote for each representative and senator from that state. If a presidential candidate receives a plurality of votes in a given state, then he or she receives all of the electoral votes from that state. The candidate with the majority of electoral votes wins.

With the exception of most of the general guidelines mentioned above, which are written into the US Constitution, many of the laws governing the operation of elections are written and enforced at the state level. Laws governing the nomination of candidates for office, ballot access and the division of the state into congressional districts are created by the state. Even the decision to divide states into districts was originally a decision made by the state; in theory, states could elect representatives to the House using proportional representation, or any other method they chose.

It is worth noting that elections for local and state office are often not run the same way as elections for national office. Sweeping election reform at the end of the nineteenth century eliminated partisanship from approximately three-quarters of local elections. In these elections, candidates must run for office without party backing.

Ballot access laws and nomination procedures

Ballot access laws are set by the states. Generally speaking, parties that have received a certain percentage of the votes in the last election are guaranteed a place on the ballot in the next election. The **Republican** and **Democratic Parties**, then, are always assured of a space on the ballot. For those candidates and parties that cannot maintain the required percentage, getting on the ballot is often an arduous process. Generally, thousands of signatures must be collected and submitted to the state months before the election actually begins. To gain status as an official political party, a group usually needs consistently to win a certain percentage of the votes in a statewide election. This means that parties officially exist only at the state level. Individual states declare that a group is a party; the nation as a whole has no way of officially recognizing the existence of a political party.

Those parties assured of a place on the ballot choose who will run as their candidate either through primaries or caucuses, or some combination thereof; state law dictates which technique is to be used. Primaries usually take place a couple of months prior to the general election. In a primary, members of the party's rank and file vote for the candidate they want to represent them. Generally, only those citizens who are registered as members of a given political party are allowed to vote in that party's primaries. The power to nominate rests with the rank and file of the political parties, not with the party's leadership, as it does in many European countries.

Conventions

Primaries lead to summer conventions in which nominations are fought (or, more recently, nominees are enthroned), party platforms hammered out and party identity celebrated in **mass media**, urban festivals and more private parties. These have also become sites of confrontation with those outside the party, as in **Chicago, IL** 1968, or the party elite, as in Atlantic City, 1964.

Campaign finance

Unlike many European countries, the United States has a very limited system of public finance for national elections; some money is granted to presidential candidates, but only if those candidates receive a rather large percentage of the national vote. Campaigns are financed, then, almost completely by private sources. Corporations, labor unions and interest groups all are major contributors to campaigns. Fundraising is primarily the responsibility of individual candidates, not the political party. Politicians spend a great deal of time soliciting funds and attending functions in order to raise money for increasingly costly campaigns. Presidential campaigns can begin nearly a year before the actual election, and potential candidates must spend years raising funds to get the millions necessary for running the television campaign advertisements that are deemed necessary to win.

Campaign finance has become a big issue in American politics. There is a general feeling among voters that too much is spent on campaigns and that candidates are being "bought" through campaign contributions from corporations and large interest groups. Some attempt has been made to limit the amount that can be donated to campaigns; however, much of the legislation that has managed to be passed has been struck down by the **Supreme Court** for violating the freedom of speech clause in the 1st Amendment of the US

Constitution, and techniques have been devised for getting around what remains of the legislation. The issue has become particularly salient again as allegations have risen that President **Clinton** and Vice-President Al **Gore** illegally raised funds from foreign investors and officials (particularly Chinese government officials) during the 1996 election.

Political parties in America

The Republican and Democratic Parties have dominated the political scene in America since 1856, when the Republicans replaced the Whigs as one of the two major parties. Though the parties have shifted their ideological stances over the years, they have remained more or less stable since the 1930s. Since this period, the Democratic Party has taken on the role of the liberal party, the closest major party equivalent to the labor parties of Europe. The party has traditionally aligned itself with labor unions and the working class. It has generally supported the expansion of **civil rights** and a woman's right to choose an **abortion**, as well as the traditional provisions of the welfare state. The Republican Party, on the other hand, supports the expansion of the free market economy and the dismantling of the welfare state. It has generally opposed a woman's right to an abortion and has worked to promote traditional religion through government.

Though generalizations like these do hold, there is little consistency across the country when it comes to the beliefs that parties or their candidates hold. Because election laws are made and enforced on a state level and many elections take place at this level, parties are organized at the state level. Although a national convention occurs every four years (just before the presidential election) and each of the major parties has a national committee, most of the strength rests with the state parties. It is often said that the United States has fifty different party systems. Because parties are organized primarily at the state level, the ideological stances of parties can be highly regional. The best example of this is the Southern Democrats. Despite fairly conservative tendencies among voters, the **South** has remained a Democratic stronghold since the Civil War, when Abraham Lincoln, a Republican president, declared war on the seceding South. These tendencies were later confirmed when a Republican president was responsible for enforcing integration of schools and other public places. Southern Democrats are generally more conservative than the Democratic Party as a whole.

Even within a state or region, it is sometimes difficult to find much ideological consistency. Without the power to choose who will run for office, and with little control over campaign funds, parties possess little control over candidates. Individual candidates decide which issues they want to support in a campaign and the direction in which they will vote when they eventually make it to **Congress**. A political party may agree on some sort of national agenda, but candidates are not bound to that agenda. A number of prominent Republicans, for instance, support a woman's right to an abortion. An already elected politician may also switch partisan affiliation in the middle of his or her term in office. Political parties do not possess the kind of ideological unity that is seen in many countries in which parties possess more control over the nomination and funding processes, and where parties are organized at a national level.

This focus on individual candidates makes it important that the candidate be able to create a name for himself or herself independent of the party. Political campaigns rely heavily on television advertisements, which are both expensive and convey little information about the candidate involved; however, television can create name recognition for a candidate more quickly than other media. Many scholars worry that citizens have come to rely too heavily on campaign advertisements when making political decisions.

The persistence of the two-party system in America

It is notable that, despite Americans' dissatisfaction with the current political system and parties, no third party has consistently managed to gain electoral office. The US has been dominated by two political parties since shortly after its creation; furthermore, it has been dominated by the same two political parties for nearly a century and a half. While smaller political parties and independent candidates made some breakthroughs in the twentieth century, they all sunk into obscurity shortly after their campaigns. Two of the most

recent and remarkable breakthroughs of this kind were George **Wallace**'s campaign for president in 1968 and Ross **Perot**'s run for the presidency in 1992. In both cases, the candidates gained a fairly large percentage of the national vote without capturing a single electoral vote. While third-party or independent candidates sometimes manage to get elected to local or state positions, these victories are usually fairly isolated.

What prevents third parties from gaining office? This has been debated for some time, but the answer probably lies in American electoral institutions. As mentioned earlier, ballot access laws make it difficult for parties that are not well established to get their candidates on the ballot. Running a presidential campaign would require adhering to fifty sets of varying electoral rules. Once on the ballot, the increasing cost of campaigning makes it difficult for candidates from smaller parties to keep up with their major party competitors; established politicians from established parties are far more able to raise the large amount of cash necessary. Finally, an electoral system which rewards only those candidates who get the plurality of votes in their districts almost insures that a third-party candidate will not gain office.

Further reading

Aldrich, J. (1995) *Why Parties?*, Chicago: University of Chicago Press.

Beck, P. (1997) *Party Politics in America*, New York: Longman Press.

Jacobson, G. (1992) *The Politics of Congressional Elections*, New York: HarperCollins.

Key, V.O. (1964) *Politics, Parties and Pressure Groups*, New York: Crowell.

Polsby, N. and Wildavsky, A. (1996) *Presidential Elections*, Chatham: Chatham House Publishers.

Sorauf, F. (1992) *Inside Campaign Finance*, New Haven: Yale University Press.

EMILY CLOUGH

Parton, Dolly

b. 1946

Born in poverty in rural Tennessee, Dolly Parton

started her singing career at ten. With her trademark big blonde hair, her often-made-fun-of big bosom and her clear high voice, she reached the top of the country charts as a singer-songwriter with songs like "Here You Go Again" and "Jolene." She received good reviews when she moved into acting with *9 to 5* (1980), also a crossover hit song for her, and the later *Steel Magnolias* (1989). In her home state, a theme park named Dollywood (founded 1986) keeps her legend alive.

EDWARD MILLER

party machines

Before the turn of the century, strong political **parties** were a prominent feature of American **cities**. These party machines, as they were called, recruited citizens, especially new immigrants, to vote for their party. These organizations were not particularly ideological; instead, they recruited through an elaborate system of patronage run by "bosses." Those who supported the party were rewarded with jobs or other services. Party machines were largely eliminated at the turn of the century by the Progressive movement, a group consisting largely of upper middle-class reformers determined to clean up city politics.

EMILY CLOUGH

patriotism

A nation of immigrants might be expected to manifest considerable fragmentation and widespread expression of ethnic or regional loyalties, rather than vociferous declarations of love of country; however, this has not been so. Social elites in the United States have often "incorporated" notions of "Americanness" to establish their own legitimacy and have used their understanding of patriotism to attempt to either reshape or restrict **immigration**. For **African Americans** and other immigrants, then, patriotism has been both a vehicle aiding advancement or an obstacle placed in their way. In times of war (including the **Cold War**), members of many ethnic groups along with

African Americans showed their loyalty to the United States through service in the armed forces. Groups might also use patriotism to distinguish themselves from others who do not belong to the dominant white culture. Yet patriotism can also promote more inclusive social change. Thus, a **Civil Rights movement** is patriotic because it strives to help Americans reach their "highest ideals."

In recent years, debates swirling around issues of patriotism have both intensified and become confused. The lack of clear-cut **enemies** after the Cold War and increased globalization have confused obvious identification with the nation. Instabilities resulting from such developments, however, have led to the use of patriotism to justify nativist backlashes against immigrants, demands for protection and opposition to NAFTA (particularly from the AFL-CIO) and increased hostility towards the World Trade Organization. US involvement in wars from the **Reagan** administration to the present has also intensified patriotic fervor, spilling over into the demand (particularly from **Republican** politicians and especially loud during the **Gulf War**) for a constitutional amendment to ban the burning of the American flag.

ROBERT GREGG

Pauling, Linus

b. 1901; d. 1994

Scientist, activist and the only figure to have won two unshared **Nobel prizes**. Pauling's scientific work originally focused on the nature of chemical bonds and their impacts on complex formations like proteins for which he received the Nobel Laureate in Chemistry (1954). He also worked against the spread of atomic weapons, organizing a 1958 petition to the UN signed by 11,000 scientists. This work led to the Nobel Peace prize in 1962. In his later years, he became absorbed by the possibilities of Vitamin C in fighting **cancer** and extending human life, an enthusiasm other scientists did not share.

GARY McDONOGH

PBS/Public Broadcasting System

In November 1967 the Public Broadcasting Act was signed into law by President Lyndon **Johnson**. This Act established the Corporation for Public Broadcasting (CPB) as an independent, non-governmental body formed to serve as the umbrella organization for public broadcasting in the United States. Over thirty years, PBS has produced hits and changed broadcasting, while being charged with both elitism and middlebrow, safe tastes.

After the Second World War, the FCC had ensured that a certain number of stations would be reserved for educational broadcasting, but securing the money to run these was difficult. Initially, stations were usually affiliated to universities and other large institutions. In the 1960s, 125 educational **television** stations reached 6 million viewers. Notable stations included WQED in **San Francisco, CA**, which had begun in 1950; in 1955 it came up with an innovative form of fundraising – the on-air auction. This became a mainstay of both its programming and fundraising schedules and is used by other local public stations that remain reliant upon donations, especially after recent government cutbacks.

With the 1967 Act, a place on the broadcast spectrum for educational non-commercial television was secured. Within the decade, the number of public stations doubled and 30 million homes would enjoy access to public broadcasting. Today, 99 percent of Americans have access to public broadcasting. The CPB was authorized to develop educational broadcasting and finance facilities to link the independent public television stations, but was restricted from owning stations, systems, or networks. The CPB established the Public Broadcasting Service (PBS) in 1969 to manage the interconnection of independent public and educational broadcasting facilities. PBS is owned by its member stations; each member station is accountable to its local community. Programming originates from a local station and is shared by member stations. For example, *Electric Company*, the award-winning **children**'s show, was produced by the **Boston** station WGBH, but shown nationwide. The related production company, Children Television Workshop, produced *Sesame Street* for New York. Each station within the umbrella is free to produce and buy its own programming, but increasingly

stations' programming mimics that of other stations, so that PBS resembles a commercial network.

Commercial networks never registered any protest to PBS; they quickly realized that PBS was appealing to a different segment of the market. PBS showed dynamic fare such as *Eyes on the Prize*, a groundbreaking documentary on the **Civil Rights movement**, and *An American Family*, an innovative show that followed the life of a California middle-class white family. It also became the venue for many Ken Burns documentaries – from **baseball** to **radio**. Shows like *Nature* and *Nova* made it popular with educators just as *Sesame Street* and *Mr Roger's Neighborhood* made it a must-see with kids. English shows were imported via the programs *Mystery* and **Masterpiece Theatre**, while **opera** and ballets were telecast live as ways to appeal to the high-brow population. At the same time, some more daring programming was also produced, such as *Alive from Off-Center*, which showed work from avant-garde artists and performers. Both, however, redefined public as elite rather than popular (or even local). Although commercial advertisements are not broadcast on PBS, stations and programs are allowed to announce the corporations and foundations who have underwritten particular shows. This has increased as government cutbacks (spurred on by the right wing) have eroded the financial structure. Corporations are able to portray themselves through PBS as interested in the arts, concerned about the environment and involved in the technological future without having to resort to anything as gauche as a traditional advertisement. Some fear that this corporate patronage has hindered the stations' ability to develop programming free from **censorship** and to produce innovative shows as the system did in its first few years.

EDWARD MILLER

Peace Corps

Proposed by John **Kennedy** on the campaign trail in 1960. The idea of American volunteers scattering around the world to promote democracy and development came to epitomize the sometimes contradictory youthful commitment and liberal initiatives within a **Cold-War** framework. Organized by Sargent Shriver and Bill Moyers in 1961, the Peace Corps recruited 70,000 volunteers over the next decade. It sent them out after training rather weak in language and skills and strong on theory and physical and psychological training. Once abroad, these Americans found themselves less pioneers and saviors than uneasy participants in negotiations about the future that called into question their own values and identities – especially among minorities and women cast into unfamiliar settings. The Peace-Corps process became cooperative and open rather than developmental; in this way it may have helped shift American awareness of the non-European world towards a more complex global consciousness as Fritz Fischer argues in *Making Them Like Us* (1998). In later decades, the Peace Corps improved training and selection for useful skills, while operating on a smaller scale, especially under hostile **Republican** regimes. Its alumni found places in the **Carter** administration and in academic and policy circles.

Further reading

Fischer, F. (1998) *Making Them Like Us*, Washington, DC: Smithsonian.

GARY McDONOGH

Peale, Norman Vincent

b. 1898; d. 1993

Methodist minister and apostle of self-improvement, Peale gained wide exposure as pastor of **New York** City's Marble Collegiate Reformed Church, as well as through his radio and television appearances. His *Power of Positive Thinking* (1952) was the forerunner of many **self-help** texts of the 1980s and 1990s.

GARY McDONOGH

Peckinpah, Sam

b. 1925; d. 1984

Film and television **director**, writer and producer.

Most famous for his revisionist **western** films of the 1960s and 1970s, Peckinpah was also a pioneer of the adult western **television** dramas of the 1950s and 1960s, when he wrote such programs as *Gunsmoke* and directed and produced the critically acclaimed series *The Westerner* (1960). In his film masterpiece, *The Wild Bunch* (1969), his experiments with editing, slow motion, dialogue and the choreographic depiction of violence and death have been copied and emulated by a generation of action and western film-makers, most notably Walter Hill.

EDWARD MILLER

Pei, I. (Ieoh) M. (Ming)

b. 1917

Architect born in Canton, **China**, becoming a US citizen in 1954. His global works are characterized by both rational modern style and serene elegance in the interplay of planes of glass and stone/concrete. Among his best-known works are **Boston**'s John Hancock Tower (1972), the East Wing of the National Gallery of Art in **Washington, DC** and the Bank of China in Hong Kong which reunites his modernist vision with Chinese symbolism. He won the Pritzker Prize in 1983.

GARY McDONOGH

PEN/Faulkner Award

Founded by writers in 1980 to honor their peers, the PEN/Faulkner Award has become the largest juried award for fiction in the United States. Its name recognizes both **Nobel** laureate William Faulkner, who used his prize-money to create an award for young writers, and its affiliation with the international writers' organization PEN (Poets, Playwrights, Editors, Essayists and Novelists). Every year the award judges, themselves fiction writers, select five books. The top book earns a $15,000 award, while the rest receive $5,000 each. Funded by donations, in 1987 the PEN/Faulkner

Foundation established an endowment for future awards.

COURTNEY BENNETT

pension *see* retirement; strikes; Social Security; stocks and bonds; unions

Pentagon

The National Security Act of 1947, establishing the **president**'s overriding responsibility for both defense and foreign policy, created the Secretary of Defense, the **Central Intelligence Agency** and the National Security Council, centralizing the armed forces in the Pentagon. The Act aimed to end the rivalry among the military services by combining them under one power, which, theoretically at least, would be able to subordinate parochial interests and economize by ending duplication. Over time, the massive five-sided building in Northern Virginia, with miles of corridors and offices, has become symbolic of the strengths and weaknesses of American military force and planning.

With the president constitutionally enthroned as commander-in-chief, civilian control of the armed forces was secure. But the growth of forces during the Second World War, the prospect of conflicts arising with the Soviet Union and a perceived need to balance political concerns with military strategy led **Truman** to bolster his position with the establishment of a Cabinet-level Secretary of Defense to oversee all the military.

Korea firmly established the Pentagon within the American political system. While still dominated by military men, the Pentagon began to move towards civilian politics, embodied in the conflict between Secretary of Defense George **Marshall** (supported by Truman) and General **MacArthur** in Korea, which led to the latter's dismissal. By the time President **Eisenhower** retired from office, a system, which he termed the "military-industrial complex," was firmly entrenched. While this term suggested a threat to a democratic society, it also denoted a system in which the three elements (economic, political and military) of C. Wright Mills' *Power Elite* (1956) collaborated in a loose balance.

A more sinister Pentagon emerged in the 1960s under President **Kennedy** and Robert McNamara, his Secretary of Defense. Kennedy had made the "missile gap" central to his political campaign against **Nixon** in 1960 and so, following his victory, he emphasized military build-up, unrestrained by economic and political advisability. In addition, McNamara brought to the Department of Defense his experience as the CEO of Ford. Hence, he promoted approaches that had seemed to be working in the Big Three Automakers and other corporations (many of which produced goods for the Pentagon). These would soon be shown to be woefully inadequate for a changing political and economic landscape.

McNamara instituted industrial management in the federal government with the Secretary of Defense in control of a huge network of enterprises. As in multi-division firms, a Central Management Office was established to administer the "military-industrial empire." Now the federal government began to direct production of over $44 billion in goods and services aimed for military use, instead of merely contracting out projects. In other words, the federal government did not merely regulate; it actually took over the business.

Moreover, what workers at the Pentagon called "missile-gap madness" legitimized almost any expenditure to complete a project. Cost overruns, malfunctioning parts and basic tools and supplies bought at exorbitant rates became common. The C-5A transport plane came in with a $2 billion cost overrun. Forty percent of Minuteman II missiles were found to be defective after test failures had been covered up. Finally, an electronics unit for the F-III fighter (McNamara's pet project), budgeted at $750,000 per plane, ended up costing $4.1 million per plane. McNamara had encouraged centralization partly to cut back on waste, but he created the exact opposite.

Civilian control under Kennedy and Johnson also established the number-crunching mentality of McNamara and his technocrats. This mindset even influenced the way engagements were carried out, especially Vietnam. Rather than achieving strategic objectives, securing particular pieces of land or gaining other tactical advantages, American soldiers were trained to fight wars of attrition. In the language of the industrial world, this meant producing maximum bodies among the enemy at a minimum of cost in bodies for Americans. This gave rise, as Philip Caputo recounted in *Rumor of War* (1977), to the infamous "body counts." Monthly goals were set, a ratio calculated that would secure victory (believed to be twelve Vietnamese for every one American) and operations were even designed to ascertain numbers of dead on each side. That this was the period of lowest morale in the history of the American armed forces is not surprising.

Moreover, since the Pentagon was being run as a business, **public relations** were needed. What Senator J. William **Fulbright**, Chairperson of the Committee on Foreign Relations, called the Pentagon Propaganda Machine was an extremely elaborate **advertising** agency selling what the Pentagon was doing to the public. Disaster came not so much on the battle field as in the war of images waged on **television**. The Pentagon's campaign was shown to be seriously flawed when slogans like "The Light at the End of the Tunnel" were followed by setbacks like the **Tet Offensive**, or when General Westmoreland's roseate news briefings were disturbed by nearby shelling.

The war resulted in the "**Vietnam Syndrome**," or the belief that American governments would be reluctant to undertake military engagements in the future. This was not simply due to lack of public support or the media overstepping their bounds. The McNamara-designed Pentagon proved unable to reach even its own distorted objectives, let alone other strategic objectives a president might set. President **Carter**'s 1980 disaster attempting to rescue the American hostages in Teheran looked worse against the crisp efficiency of the Israelis flying into Entebbe (1976) to rescue their hostages. **Hollywood** decided to make movies of the Israelis, not the Americans!

Reagan attempted to refashion the Pentagon, partly by "throwing money at the problem" in another military build-up. His Secretary of Defense, Caspar Weinberger, believing that the problem lay in the extent of civilian control at the Pentagon itself, attempted to diminish this element. In the eyes of many, however, this left a vacuum in place. The armed forces merely continued to think in terms of old foes, like the Soviet Union, rather than reorienting themselves towards new conflicts worldwide. Engagements in **Grenada** under Reagan, and then **Panama** under Bush, re-established a sense of the American armed forces as a viable fighting force. Newer, sophisticated weapons and machines seemed vastly superior to what the Soviets had available, while Soviet forces became mired in their own "Vietnam" in Afghanistan. The long-held belief that the Red Army had western Europe at its mercy was shown to be entirely erroneous.

Towards the end of Reagan's administration, changes began to occur at the Pentagon. Frank Carlucci replaced Weinberger as Secretary of Defense and General Colin **Powell**, a relative military visionary, was appointed to head the National Security Council. Carlucci suggested a more conciliatory approach towards the Soviet Union, which was beginning to collapse, while Powell began to plan for what he saw as the likely conflicts of the future, particularly those focusing on resources like **oil**.

This culminated in the **Gulf War** in 1991, one of the first military engagements for which American military strategists were actually prepared in advance. In the process, Powell and General Norman Schwarzkopf re-established the superiority of US armed forces. It was not merely the fact that the Americans defeated Saddam Hussein's forces, it was the manner in which they did so, leaving an army of tanks utterly devastated.

Under President Bill **Clinton** the Pentagon has once again been subordinated to political considerations. While there were at first hopes of reorienting the economy in the aftermath of the **Cold War**, the perceived need to intervene abroad militarily has kept the military budget growing, and defense contractors, albeit less in the heavy-industry sector and more in high technologies, have remained producing. In addition, such military intervention, like Clinton's, has been undertaken with one eye on public reaction, evidenced by the **polls**. **Somalia** was a necessary humanitarian intervention until a few American lives were lost; the Rwandan genocide had to be overlooked because of the disaster in Somalia. Similarly, intervention in Kosovo was necessary because of the failure to act in Rwanda. All the while, actions against Iraq seemed to occur based on a schedule set by the **Independent Counsel** Starr, rather than global strategic considerations.

But such politicization is almost inevitable in a world where the old Cold-War certainties no longer remain. Indeed, Powell's visionary approach to shaping the Pentagon was not simply to prepare for a new kind of war against a new enemy in the Middle East; it was rather to prepare for all kinds of wars against many potential enemies. As such, the message has not been to diminish civilian control, since this is required of a democracy; rather it is that McNamara's approach, where everything is subordinated to the bottom line of efficiency, or a Clinton approach, where there is no bottom line (as in the debate over gays in the military), are no longer acceptable in a world where allegiances are shifting, people are migrating across boundaries and new kinds of globalization are taking place.

Further reading

Fitz, A.E. (1972) *Waste in the Pentagon*, New York: Norton.

Fulbright, J.W. (1970) *Pentagon Propaganda Machine*, New York: Liveright.

Luttwak, E. (1984) *Pentagon and the Art of War*, New York: Simon & Schuster.

Melman, S. (1970) *Pentagon Capitalism*, New York: McGraw-Hill.

ROBERT GREGG

"Pentagon Papers"

Commissioned in 1967 by US Secretary of Defense Robert S. McNamara, the "Pentagon Papers" comprise a 3,000-page history of the US in Indochina from the Second World War through May 1968. They document sabotage and terrorism against North Vietnam beginning in 1954 and the coup that overthrew South Vietnamese President Ngo Dinh Diem in 1963. The *New York Times* published articles based upon the Papers in 1971. The indictment of Daniel Ellsberg, a former government employee, for espionage, theft and conspiracy followed, though all charges were later dropped. The "Pentagon Papers" confirmed the

suspicions of many Americans who opposed the **Vietnam War** that US involvement owed a good deal to government secrecy. In tandem with **Watergate**, the Papers eroded faith in government credibility.

ROBERT GREGG

Pentecostalism

Rather than designating a single denomination, modern American Pentecostalism generally refers to Christian traditions that emphasize supernatural signs or "gifts of the Holy Spirit" – embodied in healing, speaking in tongues and ecstatic possession, or other proofs of divine favor – over ritual and hierarchy. While emotional fervor has often characterized ongoing reform in American Christianity (e.g. the Great Awakening and evangelical traditions), a revival in **Los Angeles, CA**'s Azusa Street Mission in 1906 is taken to mark the birth of modern Pentecostalism. Over subsequent decades, this stress on visible signs of personal salvation and emotional fervor spread among the disfranchised in cities and rural areas, although congregations frequently divided over interpretations of the authenticity of these very signs. While many Pentecostals became associated with the Assemblies of God, Church of God and the Pentecostal Holiness Church, splinter groups built around charismatic leaders were also a constant feature of twentieth-century Pentecostalism – and a focus of attack by outsiders and media. Films, in fact, have almost invariably concentrated on corrupted leaders and fraudulent miracles (*Elmer Gantry*, 1960; the autobiographical *Marjoe*, 1973; *Leap of Faith*, 1992). **Documentaries** as well have shown a fascination with exotic concrete signs of the supernatural – especially snake-handling, a test of faith actually confined to a small minority within Pentecostalism.

Pentecostalism experienced its own revival after the Second World War, embodied in builders like Oral Roberts, whose preaching and healing funded a university communication complex. Both tent revivals and the emergent power of television spread this coat-and-tie Pentecostalism, although competition among leaders and intersections of religious and social agendas fragmented religious experience and organization, and led to a decline in the late 1950s, even as both Pentecostalism and **Christian media** continued to evolve. In the 1990s, the major Pentecostal denominations had American memberships of over 10 million. They have also been active in missionary work among new immigrants as well as global evangelization that has established strong visible Pentecostal communities in Latin America, Asia, Africa and Europe (especially the former Soviet Union).

As with earlier general revivals, the appeal of Pentecostalism has also influenced mainstream churches, where various forms of spiritual renewal have intersected, sometimes uneasily, with more traditional rituals and orders since the 1960s. While Catholic Charismatic Renewal, for example, revitalized liturgical music, responses and even sociability in many parishes and **college** chapels, emphasis on the authority of individual spiritual redemption could also cause conflict with the authority of priests and the traditions of the larger community. In many of these denominations, however, Pentecostal elements have been reintegrated into both ritual and community structures.

Further reading

Anderson, R. (1979) *Visions of the Disinherited*, New York: Oxford.
Harrell, D. (1975) *All Things are Possible*, Bloomington: Indiana University.
Synan, V. (1997) *The Holiness-Pentecostal Tradition*, Grand Rapids, MI: William B. Eerdmans.

GARY McDONOGH

Pepsi *see* soda

performance art

Performance art is surprisingly difficult to define. It requires that an artist perform an action over time (even if very brief), either in a public or a private place, with or without an audience present, which may or may not be documented photographically or by other means. Performance art thus lacks the stylistic continuity of such avant-garde artistic movements as **abstract expressionism** or **pop art**. Nevertheless, performance in one form or another has appeared in relation to every post-1945 avant-garde movement (critic Harold Rosenberg even referred to the abstract expressionist's canvas as an arena). It has included participatory multimedia events such as Allan Kaprow's "happenings" of the late 1950s and Carolee Schneeman's erotic rituals of the 1960s. Extreme events include Chris Burden having himself shot in the arm and Vito Acconci masturbating while hidden under a gallery floor, in the early 1970s, and Karen Finley's impassioned feminist theatrical monologues of the 1980s. There are also more familiar events, such as versions of dance or stand-up comedy, which have been incorporated into art contexts.

In the American art world, performance art was most influential in the late 1960s and early 1970s. Some performance artists were concerned with the reintroduction of ritual into aesthetic experience; some used performance to bring art and activism together. Others developed from **minimalism** an interest in experience as embodied, and from both minimalism and conceptual art a concern with the production of meaning as a participatory process. In this regard, performance art appeared as a critical response to formalist, modernist orthodoxy, which required that art seek autonomy from social reality. The strongest work from the period, by feminist artists and others including Acconci and Burden, brought into question normative assumptions about relations between public and private realms of behavior. At the same time, these boundaries were being tested by the counterculture, the **women's liberation** movement, the continuation of the **civil rights** struggle and protests against the **Vietnam War**.

Further reading

Banes, S. (1993) *Greenwich Village 1963*, Durham: Duke University.
Hart, L. and Phelan, P. (eds) (1993) *Acting Out: Feminist Performances*, Ann Arbor: University of Michigan.
Henri, A. (1974) *Total Art*, New York: Oxford University.

O'Dell, K. (1998) *Contract with the Skin*, Minneapolis: University of Minnesota.

Sayre, H. (1989) *The Object of Performance*, Chicago: University of Chicago.

Schimmel, P. (1998) *Out of Actions*, New York: Thames and Hudson.

FRAZER WARD

performing arts centers

Major urban monuments of the late twentieth century reflecting public support for the arts and strategies for competitive urban development. Earlier nineteenth- and twentieth-century centers for **theater**, **opera**, symphony and ballet often depended on individual philanthropy and the power of collective elite representation evoked by "opening night" at **New York**'s Metropolitan Opera. By the 1950s, the Met's move to Lincoln Center resulted in slum clearance and neighborhood revitalization funded by city and federal revenues. Both smaller (**Louisville**'s Kentucky Center for the Performing Arts) and larger cities (**Washington**'s Kennedy Center and **Philadelphia**'s $240 million new center) have used these monuments to promote urban prestige and downtown development, alongside other features of the commoditized metropolis, including stadiums, festival marketplaces and historical theme parks.

GARY McDONOGH

Perot, H. Ross

b. 1930

Successful **Texas** businessperson, political party organizer and author, Perot came into the national spotlight in 1992 when he ran for president as a third-party candidate. Using his own money to launch his campaign, Perot focused on the economy by airing half-hour infomercials during the campaign. Perot captured 19 percent of the 1992 vote, the highest percentage captured by a third-party candidate since Theodore Roosevelt in 1912. Concerned with grassroots political involvement, Perot helped establish the Reform Party and became its presidential nominee in 1996, winning 9 percent of the popular vote.

KATE M. KENSKI

pets

In the 1990s, American households include 60 million cats and an almost equal number of dogs, and myriad birds, fish, lizards, spiders, pigs, wolves and others that constitute an important symbiosis of person and animal. Domestic animals have long been part of American life, although today's pampered companions might be surprised to know that they were once expected to work. Contemporary pets, however, also create a $20 billion industry in breeding, supplies and care.

This is coupled, unfortunately, with overpopulation. Strays and the constant demands on the American Society for the Prevention of Cruelty to Animals underscore a careless surplus of domestic animals, whether feral dog packs or unwanted kittens. These, like problematic exotics such as overgrown Vietnamese pot-bellied pigs and declawed tigers, point to the cultural definition of the pet as a cute, relatively undemanding amusement for **children** and lonely people to adopt.

Pets are treated as members of the **family** or even surrogates for family and friends. The idealization of **suburban** domesticity created a special niche for Spot the Dog, embedded in television and film even though cats passed dogs in popularity in the 1980s. Yet, the convergence of surrogacy and affluence sets apart American pets. Foods grade them by age and demands (including diets and organic foods), accessories allow owners to spend $5,000 on a dog bed and medical services rival those provided for humans (pet insurance is a relatively late invention). Veterinarians, adapting their history in a farming nation, perform not only everyday tasks, but also offer kidney transplants for cats and tumor removal for fish. Bereavement counseling and pet cemeteries create a life cycle that eerily appropriates that of humans. Some civic groups, nonetheless, have stressed the importance of animals as service providers (e.g. guide dogs) and as companions for the elderly and sick when the human family has failed.

Evidently, pets are also display animals, where breeding and care echo social differentiation. These are celebrated in registered pedigrees, whether proffered as proof of value or tested in dog and cat shows – New York's Westminster Kennel Club show receives national exposure. Meanwhile, as Vicki Hearne underscores in her insightful study of a "problem" bull terrier, *Bandit* (1991), this breed (identified as "pit bulls") is identified with lower classes and race antagonisms through its role as a fighter. And the "mutt" – a mixture of breed and heritage – is often used as a symbol of the American melting-pot. Poodles, Afghan hounds, Siamese cats, cockatiels and koi carp have all transmuted economic surplus into pet status. As commodities, they are also subject to changing mores – guard dogs have risen in value in the security-conscious 1990s, while cats become ever more exquisitely bred and even reptiles and ferrets have their "own" **magazines**.

While animals in American television and film straddle the line between **nature** and culture, American pets cross the line of animal and human in both emotions and expenses, creating dilemmas for social critics, environmentalists and owners alike.

Further reading

Hearne, V. (1991) *Bandit*, New York: Aaron Ascher.

GARY McDONOGH

pharmaceuticals

American pharmaceutical companies have proven successful in a postwar global marketplace, competing in the 1990s with ever-growing **multinationals** like the Glaxo Welcome/Smith-Kline Beecham merger. Large research investments, generally well-controlled testing and aggressive marketing have made American products household names throughout the world. At the same time, continuing price increases have made these companies domestic targets for healthcare reform. They have also raised ethical and political questions when necessary medications are not available to the poor in the US, much less for epidemics like **AIDS** in the Third World.

Drugs are big business – American companies like E.I. Lilly, Schering Plough, Merck, and Pfizer-Warner Lambert are among the largest international producers. These companies took to the airwaves in a new way in the late 1990s, with the FCC's relaxation of a longstanding ban on ads for prescription drugs. Now, $1.3 billion goes annually to sell Claritin, **Viagra** (with former presidential candidate Bob **Dole** as spokesman), Zyban, Rogaine and other prescription drugs in addition to Tylenol, Tums and other "over-the-counter" (non-prescription) drugs. In addition, manufacturers also seek to influence opinion leaders among physicians and hospitals. Over forty new prescription drugs enter the market annually, coming from $24 billion in research.

Yet pharmaceutical development also responds to existing markets. Hence, in 1999, 25 percent of new developments were linked to senses and the nervous system, while miniscule research moneys focused on tropical diseases not generally found in the US. Merck, to give one example, gains more than 30 percent of its sales from drugs whose syndromes can be related to America's problematic foodways – including cardiac issues, hypertension and high cholesterol. Since these companies are heavily involved in the funding of university research, their interests may influence entire areas of study. This disparity in potential consumption creates the specter of so-called orphan diseases, dramatized in *Lorenzo's Oil* (1992). Early money for AIDS research also was raised outside of corporate channels.

Consumer resistance to the power of big pharmaceuticals emerges in complaints, through negotiations via insurance and through a turn to generics that do not carry patented prices (although the drug industry fights to modify and repatent drugs so as to avoid generic competition). One might also see resistance in holistic/alternative health. Yet it is hard to fight an industry that may provide life to a loved one or even oneself.

Drug marketing in the US is controlled through the Food and Drug Administration, which gained fame for its rigor – especially with regards to the thalidomide crisis of the 1960s. Since 1992 the FDA has developed a fast track, demanded by AIDS patients and others looking for rapid drug approval; this twelve-month process demands that pharmaceutical companies pay $200,000 per drug. Monitoring afterwards also remains important – four drugs have been recalled in the last decade, including the diet combination Phen-Fen.

GARY McDONOGH

CINDY WONG

Philadelphia, Pennsylvania

A favorite destination for visitors since its founding in 1682, modern Philadelphia – America's fifth-largest urban center – forms the hub of a regional intersection embracing southeastern Pennsylvania, southern New Jersey and northern Delaware, encompassing some 5 million people (about 1.5 million of whom live in the city itself). Situated on the Delaware and Schuylkill rivers, the "City of Brotherly Love" was the seat of a colony which its founder, British **Quaker** gentleman William Penn, envisioned as a model "holy experiment" in democratic government. The Declaration of Independence and the American Constitution were crafted here; the area where these documents were written continues to be a major tourist attraction. Modern Philadelphia, nonetheless, struggles with rustbelt dilemmas of disappearing industry, divided and sometimes decaying **neighborhoods**, **race** and **class** divisions, crime, poverty, **homelessness** and drugs.

The city quickly became cosmopolitan. By 1800 there were numerous neighborhoods and institutions to support its great diversity: Swedes, Dutch, Germans, British, **African Americans**, **American Indians**, Catholics, **Jews** and a variety of **Protestants** formed churches, community organizations and commercial enterprises suited to their specific needs. By 1750 a college, **theater** and lending library were among the city's many attractions; by 1825 **museums**, historical societies and scientific organizations, as well as **insurance** and banking institutions provided the foundation for technological and intellectual leadership. Shipbuilding, dating from the city's beginning, was joined in the nineteenth century by factories to build railroad cars and **automobile** parts and fuel refineries. By the mid-twentieth century, textiles,

steel, beer, **cigars** and heavy machinery were among the goods exported from the thriving port to national and international destinations. The 1950s, however, saw the steady decline in maritime trade, as distribution by **truck** and air made it attractive for factories to relocate to where warmer weather and non-**union** labor reduced production costs.

Since 1950, aggressive urban planning has revived the economy somewhat and the population decline of the 1970s has slowed. The city, whose bonds hit junk status in 1990, has revitalized Center City under Mayor Ed Rendell, while the Delaware River **waterfront** has been developed for recreation. The region also seeks to become a center of international investing and biotechnical development. Scores of **colleges and universities** (including Temple and the University of Pennsylvania), six **medical schools**, more than four dozen public **library** branches, hundreds of **public schools** and **private schools** – **education** has been a hotly debated issue in local politics – have helped to provide a base for the area's uncertain and uneven transition from an industrial base to the information age.

Philadelphia is also noted for diverse contributions to American culture – from the television classic *American Bandstand*, to the "76-ers" **basketball** team or **baseball**'s Phillies, to the world-renowned orchestra, **museums** and numerous musicians, artists, scientists and entrepreneurs. Its media image, however, is complex, as evidenced in differences between movies portraying upper-class romance (*The Philadelphia Story*, 1940; *Young Philadelphians*, 1959), the urbane **AIDS** issues of *Philadelphia* (1993) and the nightmarish future of *Twelve Monkeys* (1995).

Frequently described as "the city of homes," or the "city of neighborhoods," Philadelphia is notable for its architecturally human scale, having few tall buildings outside the city center. Instead, many neighborhoods of modestly priced brick or stone row houses cluster near the Fairmount Park system, which covers 10 percent of the city – the largest contiguous city park in the world. This neighborhood network is serviced by an intricate public transportation system, including trolleys, subways and regional railroads like the Main Line linking it with suburbs.

Philadelphia politics have always been complex, with ethnicity, race and class often leading to tension and rioting around elections, through the nineteenth and early twentieth centuries. Perhaps a low point was reached in 1985 when a black mayor, Wilson Goode, bombed the headquarters of the radical group MOVE, burning nearby African American homes as well. Nonetheless, the city has been a leader in social-service development, from early hospitals, orphanages and social-work schools to women's banks, community colleges and AIDS support networks. In the 1990s, the diverse population, which is approximately 50 percent white and 40 percent African American, has built neighborhoods representative of virtually every country in the world. Despite the blemishes and challenges common to aging cities, the city remains vigorous.

Philadelphia has been the subject of classic historical and sociological studies from W.E.B. **Du Bois**' *The Philadelphia Negro* (1899) to many present-day studies.

Further reading

Warner, S. (1987) *The Private City*, Philadephia: University of Pennsylvania.

Adams, C. *et al.* (1991) *Philadelphia: Neighborhoods, Division and Conflict in a Post-Industrial City*, Philadephia: Temple University.

EMMA LAPSANSKY

philosophy

Philosophy in American academia went through two phases after the Second World War. The first was influenced and shaped by the ideas of the Vienna Circle and a small collection of thinkers from Oxford and Cambridge and lasted from the 1940s to the mid-1960s. Although there were notable exceptions, this approach, loosely known as analytic philosophy, dominated academic philosophy and largely displaced previously influential systems such as Neo-Hegelianism, transcendentalism and pragmatism. Analytic philosophers focused on areas that had achieved prominence in the first part of the century: symbolic logic, philosophy of science, philosophy of mind and language analysis. There was a marked skepticism about ethics and political theory, and an increasing disconnection between academic philosophers and mainstream society.

The second phase, which had no single dominant system, arose partly because of dissatisfaction with the analytic movement, both from analytical philosophers themselves and from those who felt that it did not adequately address a number of important social issues. From within the movement, writers like W.V.O. Quine ("Two Dogmas of Empiricism"), Edmund Gettier ("Is Justified True Belief Knowledge?") and Thomas Kuhn (*The Structure of Scientific Revolutions*, 1962) all challenged fundamental tenets of the analytic approach. Kuhn's work, moreover, had profound impact outside **colleges and universities**, introducing the notion of a paradigm into popular culture.

Concurrently, the **Civil Rights movement**, the **women's movement**, debate over Vietnam, environmental activism and advances in medical technology were only a few of the social forces that an increasing number of philosophers felt were being inadequately addressed. The desire to grapple with these, coupled with the publication of John Rawls' influential *A Theory of Justice* (1971), led to a resurgence of interest in social political philosophy and ethics. Ethics, in turn, further branched into a series of sub-specialties: medical ethics, business ethics, environmental ethics, **engineering** ethics and legal ethics – each of which gave rise to its own association, conferences and journals. Far from being disengaged from everyday concerns, many of these applied ethicists became consultants to governments, hospitals and businesses, and developed influential **think tanks** and centers throughout the country (e.g. the Hastings Center).

In addition to these reactions against the analytic approach, at least three other trends emerged: contemporary continental philosophy, **feminism** and pragmatism. The first came about in the 1960s as the work of existentialists like Jean Paul Sartre, Simone De Beauvoir and Albert Camus reignited interest in non-Anglo European philosophy. This continued into the 1970s and

1980s with the growing popularity of deconstructionism, and other variations of **postmodernism** by authors like Michel Foucault and Jacques Derrida. As the number of women in the field grew, feminism became increasingly influential, although academic philosophy remained heavily dominated by white males. Feminist texts, articles and conferences on everything from science and logic to business and politics became increasingly common. Finally, pragmatism, due in large part to the work of Richard Rorty (*Philosophy and the Mirror of Nature*), was revived and ceased being exclusively the province of historians.

Further reading

Baynes, K., Bohman, J. and McCarthy, T. (1987) *After Philosophy*, Cambridge, MA: MIT Press.

RODGER JACKSON

Phoenix, AZ

State capital and **Sunbelt** success story. The largest metropole of the **Southwest**, Phoenix literally bloomed from the desert after the Second World War – so much so that new landscapes have forced pollen and allergies on those who once escaped there for their health. The urban population increased twelvefold from 1950 to 1999 (1,198,064 census estimate) – 20 percent in the 1990s alone.

The area has been especially popular for retirees – the **retirement** complex, Sun City, developed nearby – and those escaping perceived urban crises in the East and **California**. Politically, it was the home of conservative thinker and 1964 presidential candidate Barry **Goldwater**. Later, sports (**basketball**'s Suns), cultural facilities and resorts have expanded in the city and nearby Scottsdale and Tempe. Yet, in the 1990s, growth confronted the conservative, casual city with critical issues of sprawl, automobile dependency and maintenance of open spaces, recreation and agriculture.

GARY McDONOGH
CINDY WONG

photography

Contemporary photography can be traced to the 1930s and 1940s with a burgeoning **documentary** style exemplified by Dorothea Lange and Walker Evans' Great Depression photographs of rural Americans. The work of Ansel **Adams** too, though not strictly documentary, allowed Americans to view their country through a new lens that saw detail and beauty in the American landscape and photography itself.

The American cityscape was also important. In **New York**, photographers like Helen Levitt documented **neighborhood** life, Berenice Abbot photographed the city view-by-view and Margaret Bourke-White chose to focus on the art-deco **architecture** of the city. Crime photographers like Weegee (Arthur Fellig) exposed a more lurid side of the city. Robert Capa, meanwhile, became known as a photographer of the human faces of war until he himself was killed by a landmine in Vietnam in 1954.

Beginning in the 1940s, the combination of photographic and textual material was popularized with *Life* magazine and photo-essayists like W. Eugene Smith, the photo agency Magnum Photos, fashion photographers like Irving Penn and the publication of many author/photographer collaborations, such as James Agee's and Walker Evans' *Let Us Now Praise Famous Men* (1941). In the 1990s, this combination of image and text has been adopted by photographers Carrie Mae Weems, Duane Michals and Martha Rosler to create vastly differing political and personal statements.

In the 1950s, **beat-generation** photographers saw a country poised on the edge of the civil-rights struggles and the social upheaval of the 1960s. In reaction, photographer Robert Frank published *The Americans* (1969), a series of images that subverted the comfortable, politically promoted vision of the USA. While Frank's work attracted criticism, his contemporaries, Roy De Carava and Lee Friedlander, further developed this photographic commentary on the social landscape. In the 1960s, photographer Diane Arbus continued this work with an eye for the peculiar. She and others, like William Eggleston and Garry Winogrand, photographed with irony and cultural criticism.

Moving into the 1970s and 1980s, a highly staged and newly controversial photography emerged. Richard Avedon brought celebrity and fashion into the equation. Robert **Mapplethorpe**'s male nudes attracted acclaim and criticism. His critics, including several congresspersons, lambasted the work for being "pornographic," and questioned the **National Endowment for the Arts**' funding policies. Not quite as politically controversial, Cindy Sherman's work takes a feminist look at roles and disguises. Sherman's *Untitled Film Stills* (1990) cast her as the main character in imagined filmstrips.

In the 1990s, Nan Goldin and Sally Mann departed from the staged image, returning to photography's documentary aspect. Goldin's color images of her friends, many of them showgirls and drag queens, contrast with Mann's black-and-white images of her nude **children**. Both Goldin and Mann explore issues of gender and sexuality, while expressing an understanding of the construction of familial and community relationships.

There are many important image-makers who cannot be included in this narrow overview, and the medium of photography, incorporating video, digital, installation and photo-collage work is in a state of continuous redefinition.

Further reading

Szarkowski, J. (1989) *Photography Until Now*, New York: Museum of Modern Art.

Rosenblum, N. (1994) *A History of Women Photographers*, New York: Abbeville.

GABRIELLE BENDINER-VIANI

physical fitness

An issue of federal concern since the early 1960s when concerns about the obesity and poor health of many Americans prompted President **Kennedy** to create the President's Council on Physical Fitness. Numerous publications highlighting the relationship between exercise and the prevention of heart disease bolstered commitment to the "work hard, play hard" ethic. **Running** and other forms

of workout became popular in the 1970s, especially with the success of Jane **Fonda**'s exercise video, which prompted many other celebrities (Victoria Principal, Arnold Schwarzenegger) to develop their own profitable exercise regimens. By the late 1980s, videos had been produced to tone and sculpt every part and muscle on the **body** (abs and buns of steel) and **cable** providers had developed full-time exercise channels. Building on their own tradition of muscular Christianity, **YMCA**s increasingly became preoccupied with acquiring exercise equipment, competing with the new health spas cropping up in every **mall**, and trying to draw those who wanted partial reimbursement on their health insurance. By the 1990s the new gym culture had become prominent in depictions of single social life from afternoon **soaps** to commercials, and President **Clinton**, a burger-eating **Kennedy** Democrat, appointed his own President's Council on Physical Fitness, headed by Florence Griffith Joyner.

ROBERT GREGG

physicians *see* American Medical Association; medicine; medical shows, television

physics

Simply: physics is the study of the physical universe. From the puzzling quantum world of the very small to the majestic motion of galaxies; from the wonderland world of the very fast to the almost motionless world of the very cold; from our everyday world to the beginning of time – all of the beauty, mystery and unexpected delights of the physical universe are the realm of physicists. More fully, physics is many things – a database of knowledge, a collection of paradigms and mathematical theories, a community of researchers, teachers and students and a vital and dynamic social institution affecting all parts of the American and world communities. But, primarily, physics is a way of inquiring into the physical universe. From experience, physicists expect that all of the operation of the physical universe can be explained by a few general principles and that these principles can be expressed mathematically. Most people appreciate the beauty of a rainbow, but physicists appreciate the physical beauty and more. They understand the principles of reflection and refraction and recognize other phenomena described by the same principles. Physicists also grasp and relish the **mathematics** which describe these phenomena. The general population has a very Aristotelian worldview. These ideas of motion, energy and light are based on casual observations and "common-sense" interpretations of these observations. But the operation of the physical universe is subtle and needs a more critical investigation. The worldview of physicists and the general public began to diverge after the work of Galileo Galilei and Isaac Newton, and are now (due to the theories of quantum mechanics and relativity) radically different.

Many people retain an Aristotelian worldview even after a course in physics. This has led to a widespread attempt at physics education reform. The standard texts used in American **colleges and universities** are now being challenged by texts which are more aware of the need to alter explicitly the worldview of students. The primary organization overseeing the teaching of physics in K-16 grades and at the graduate levels is the American Association of Physics Teachers. The content of physics represents a formidable collection of observations, theories and applications. Authoritative summaries of twentieth-century physics have been put together by the American Physical Society, the primary physics research organization in the USA.

The application of quantum mechanics to the structure of matter has revolutionized technology, leading to the transistor, integrated chips, lasers, nuclear power, etc. Major theories, which withstood many tests in the latter half of the twentieth century, include the standard model of particle physics, general relativity and the Big Bang. New theories, which began in the second half of the century and are still being developed and tested, include chaos, nonlinear systems and superstrings. Since the Second World War, the American physics community has pursued the Big Science approach to research, and to the education and training of physicists. Yet the collapse of Big Science led to a surplus of physicists on the world market in the early 1990s and caused the physics community to re-examine its goals, education system and research sociology.

JUAN BURCIAGA

"pill," the *see* contraception

Pittsburgh, PA

At the intersection of the Allegheny, Monongahela and Ohio rivers, Pittsburgh set production records in the Second World War as a grimy steel town. With later shifts in its heavy manufacturing economy, Pittsburgh planned the first urban-redevelopment authority in the US; the Pittsburgh Renaissance became the most extensive peacetime reconstruction of an American historical urban center. The revitalized city has changed both civic identity and its economic foundations, stressing medicine and biotechnology, research and development, education, banking and **computer** services, sports (**baseball**'s Pirates and football's Steelers) and the arts, gaining renown as a highly habitable city of just over 300,000.

MIREILLE GOUIRAND

pizza

Circular bread crust with tomato, cheese and other toppings adapted from Italian sources (New Haven, Connecticut claims priority) has become a ubiquitous American meal. Strong regional variations have emerged – especially **Chicago, IL** deep dish versus **Northeastern** thin crust – while status and quality are marked by mass preparation as opposed to hand-crafted pizza at home or in restaurants. Yet as a mass food item – available frozen, in mixes and by competing delivery services – it has become a staple for children, parties and even school lunches, while being re-exported through franchises like Dominos and Pizza Hut. Neal Stephenson's cyberpunk *Snow Crash* (1992), in fact, makes pizza delivery emblematic of a future American dystopia.

GARY McDONOGH

plastic

For many **baby boomers**, the word "plastic" immediately evokes the 1968 movie *The Graduate* when avuncular advice to young Benjamin Braddock – "Just one word: plastics" – conveys the materialism and falseness of **suburbia**. Although plastics already had shaped American life for decades, Braddock would have grown up in a world in which Formica, vinyl, Styrofoam and fiberglass were considered not only replacements but also improvements. Yet, as Jeffrey Meickle shows in his *American Plastic: A Cultural History* (1995) this triumph would end, even while plastic remains the stuff on which America is built.

"Plastic" refers not to a single chemical family/ process, but to the malleability of these synthetic compounds – facilitating curving styles in 1950s and 1960s decor and becoming a metaphor for shifting identities. John Hyatt derived the first plastic, celluloid, from pulped cotton in 1869. Unmelting Bakelite, identified with art deco, was synthesized by Leo Backland in 1907. Other plastics became commercially available through US corporations like Du Pont and Goodrich by the 1930s; some, like nylon, "went to war" were diverted to military goods in the Second World War.

The peacetime demand for nylons was only part of the plastic wave that shaped not only new suburbs, but also **Disney**'s house of the future in Tomorrowland. Plastic goods with bright colors, original lines, flexible shaping and "easy" care – for a home without servants – became ubiquitous. They were also cheap and disposable, whether diapers or fast-food packaging. They democratized luxury in household goods, fiberglass boats and vinyl siding.

Yet, 1960s reactions against consumerist abundance meant that baby boomers also identified plastics with the banality of suburbia and postwar growth even as they profited from it. Many championed returns to natural materials: cotton

Indian prints rather than plastic seat covers, or ceramic rather than melmac dinnerware. The difficulties of the "natural" – care for silk, linen, leather – fitted the opulence of the 1980s when a "Teflon" president, against whom charges never stuck, occupied the White House. Plastics became negative metaphors for older generations, lower classes and falseness.

Plastic also became an environmental enemy. Campaigns have focused on the sheer bulk of enduring plastic waste as diapers filled up landfills or the rings around beverage six-packs were cited in the death of aquatic life. At times, figures have been overstated and focus on product rather than process (ignoring, for example, the energy required in sanitizing cloth diapers). Nonetheless, fast-food servers and merchants have offered paper as an alternative.

As Meickle notes, this conveys cultural schizophrenia. Information technology comes sheathed in plastic – no one expects a teak **computer** – reinforcing an identification of plastic with the future. Plastic infrastructures – pipes, joints, shoe soles, linings and enhancements – also underpin natural facades. Indeed, vintage plastics – Bakelite radios, nostalgic toys, etc. – became collectible "authentic synthetics" in the 1990s. Plastics define the American century, then, not only in material conditions, but also in cultural interpretations (and concealments) of everyday life.

Further reading

Meickle, J. (1995) *American Plastic: A Cultural History,* New Brunswick: Rutgers.

GARY McDONOGH

plastic surgery

Although medical alteration of the body tackles congenital problems and the results of accidents and **violence**, molding the body towards beauty stereotypes underpins plastic surgery's gender and age configuration. Moreover, since most surgery is elective (uninsured), the field is associated with the wealth of both practitioners and clients. Yet, Americans undergo nearly 1 million such operations annually; females constitute 89 percent of all clients. While breast implants have been associated with severe hazards, they remain popular alongside face lifts; **baby-boom** males focus on abdomens and chests. Most plastic surgeons also are male, evoking a Pygmalion syndrome within the profession and its depictions.

GARY McDONOGH
CINDY WONG

Plath, Sylvia

b. 1932; d. 1963

American meteor: Plath won a *Mademoiselle* short-fiction prize, graduated from Smith, studied at Cambridge, married late Poet Laureate Ted Hughes and published vital, smart, musical poems (*The Colossus*) and an autobiographical novel about a brilliant, unstable young female writer, *The Bell Jar* (1971). American martyr: separated (with two children), furiously productive (two to three poems a day at the end), fiercely despondent, Plath committed **suicide** at thirty-one. Hughes edited the angry, posthumous *Ariel* (1965) and critics cite conflict of interest. In America, her tragedy supersedes her work; readers will eventually acknowledge that the poems suffice.

DANIEL BOSCH

Playboy

Magazine created in the late 1950s, promoting a sophisticated urban bachelor lifestyle. Others suggested that its then near-nude centerfold endorsed prurient sensibilities that downgraded women. In the 1960s, Playboy clubs emerged, with waitresses clad in revealing bunny costumes; while feminist Gloria **Steinem** chronicled her life as a bunny, some bunnies themselves argued that the job provided money and opportunities before the clubs languished in the 1980s. *Playboy*'s editor, Hugh Hefner, has attempted to personify the magazine's ideals as an outspoken philosopher endorsing both pleasure and consumerism, while Playboy interviews with major figures have produced political

news, justifying many a man who claimed to read *Playboy* "only for the articles."

EDWARD MILLER

Pledge of Allegiance

(Hand over heart, standing) "I pledge allegiance (pause) to the flag (pause) of the United States of America (pause) and to the Republic (pause) for which it stands; one nation (pause) under God (pause), indivisible (pause), with liberty and justice for all." This statement, repeated daily in schools, assemblies and the swearing in of new US citizens, evokes both verbal rhythms and behaviors in many Americans. Written by Francis Bellamy for the magazine *Youth's Companion* (1892), it restates fundamental ideological values of citizenship. Yet, as an apothegmatic credo, it has both chartered radical social change ("liberty and justice for all") and evoked protests in classrooms, especially in the Vietnam era and with regards to separation of church and state.

GARY McDONOGH

poetry

The last gasps of the American revolutionary spirit were choked out in the Civil War, when the most conservative form of liberal government ever invented unhinged its jaws and swallowed its antithetical self, the **South**, whole, only to have to regurgitate some of its bones, of course, every twenty years or so since 1865. The lesson is that no revolution, no matter how revolting, can avoid the voracious maw of a stable Democratic republic that will assimilate, digest and even grow fat on anything.

The political is the poetical. America is so huge that any revolution will find its audience here and none can possibly disturb it. Our pilgrim Protestantism is our special handicap: American poets believe in a personal poetics the way Luther believed in a personal God; alas, we usually skip any dreary reading of the scriptures on our way to revelation. (American poets start reading poetry only after they have started writing "poems.")

American poets don't even really like poetry (cf. Marianne Moore); it's a subject to avoid, like politics or **religion**.

We cannot agree on what makes poems good. We cannot agree on what defines the craft. We may praise our diversity publicly, but when we do so we deny our divisiveness. We bond, when we do, through our dislikes, and we will not be led, or defined, by anything but our personal constituencies. "Don't Tread On Me" and "Live Free or Die!" were the slogans on American revolutionary-era snake flags; those snakes were severed.

The unity in American poetry can be heard in our relatively democratic, demotic voices. Yet even a plain-speaking American poet is apt to dislike two or more of the following "schools" for one or more reasons: beat poetry (too loose structure, anti-establishment rhetoric, often bisexual or **homosexual** as if that were interesting); formalist poetry (uptight structure for its own sake, dead white pseudo-establishment rhetoric, often homosexual); L=A=N=G=U=A=G=E poetry (nonce or non-traditional structure, arhetorical – the last thing it wants to do is convince anyone of anything, asexual); slam poetry (dramatic structure, anti-establishment rhetoric enhanced by screaming, pan-sexual); world poetry (sounds like translation, employs traditional European rhetorics, often bi- or homosexual as if that didn't matter); and the poetry of personal growth (loose structure, earnest anti-establishment rhetoric, pan-sexual – all in fear of casting judgment). Some poets do cross over: in the Haight-Ashbury, for instance, it used to be cool to hate Ashbery; no more.

Gil Scott-Heron didn't know how right he was when he forecast that "the revolution will not be televised." He didn't know he was pointing to the impossibility of revolution in a country where everything is televisual. (Seeing **Los Angeles, CA** burn puts out fires in **Atlanta**; Mark Strand on the **Internet** encourages a beatnik in **Seattle**.) American poetry of the future will certainly be polyglot (the dominance of English will recede), published in cyberspace (less and less print) and defined by performances (preserved on CD and DVD) instead of text. Everything will be possible and nothing will matter to us all.

DANIEL BOSCH

Poitier, Sidney

b. 1924

Actor born in **Miami, FL** of **Caribbean** (Bahamian) descent. Poitier became one of the first black **actors** to reach movie stardom in the 1960s. In many roles, unfortunately, from preacher to teacher to policeman, he often seemed to gain equality only by incredible superiority. Nominated for an Oscar for *The Defiant Ones* (1958), he won Best Actor for *Lilies of the Field* (1973), the only **African American** man so honored for thirty years. Primarily a **director** in the 1970s, his career revived in the 1990s; he received an AFI achievement award in 1992.

GARY McDONOGH

police

After education, public safety is the most expensive service provided by local government in the United States. Much of the growth in the size and political power of American police agencies since the Second World War has been fueled by public anxiety about major social and demographic changes. The migration of **African Americans** from the rural **South** to northern **cities**, the explosion of **teenage** culture in the 1960s, the mainstream use of illegal drugs and the sharp increase in violent crime perpetrated by young offenders have all been raised as justifications for expanding the size and power of local police agencies.

In response to public demands for action President Lyndon **Johnson** signed the 1968 Omnibus Crime Control and Safe Streets Act, which made the federal government a factor in local crime control for the first time. The Act expanded the ability of law-enforcement officials at all levels to detect criminal behavior by broadening the legal use of wiretaps and by funding special units for the enforcement of drug laws. The new Law Enforcement Assistance Administration (LEAA) in the United States Department of Justice provided funds for equipment and personnel in police departments in nearly every jurisdiction in the country). The establishment of SWAT (Special

Weapons and Tactics) squads in even the smallest, rural police departments was often funded by the LEAA.

At the same time, federal and local officials became concerned about the image of the police. As an adjunct of the political machines that dominated city and state governments earlier in the century (and continued to dominate **Chicago, IL**, **Newark, NJ** and Albany, NY, into the 1970s), the police were viewed by many citizens as either "town clowns" in smaller jurisdictions or corrupt enforcers of the *status quo* in larger cities. Most of the **race riots** of the 1960s were reactions to encounters between **white** police officers and African American residents. The recruitment, training and demographic composition of police departments became a major issue in the planning and budgeting for law enforcement.

The idea of police professionalism runs through the modern history of American policing. In order to improve the image of the police and justify the rapid increase in public-safety budgets, states reviewed and updated training curricula. The **Federal Bureau of Investigation** Academy also began training local police officers, and a number of departments introduced educational requirements, not only for new officers, but for promotion as well.

The idea that a college education was either necessary or desirable for the cop on the beat was hotly debated as the police infiltrated public consciousness through the media. Long a staple of news, police dramas have become the mainstay of prime-time television programming (see **crime, television**). Beginning with *Dragnet* (NBC, 1952–9; 1967–70), a celebration of the new, business-like orientation to policing taken by the Los Angeles Police Department, the depiction of attractive, articulate law-enforcement figures became popular with the public, although it was inevitably satirized in the later *Police Academy* movies (1984–9). But Steven Bochco's television productions from the late 1970s to the 1990s conveyed growing ambivalence about a powerful public agency with increasingly little contact with the public. *Hill Street Blues* (NBC, 1981–7) explored an urban environment saturated with crime confronted by a group of quirky, fallible police officers who were often thrown off balance by the chaos on

the street. The more benign *Barney Miller* (ABC, 1975–82), a comedy set in New York's **Greenwich Village**, told much the same story: the police as the last line of defense in a society slipping out of control.

During the same period that the entertainment industry was exploring the quandary of modern policing, prosecutors around the country were building a body of law on the limits of police conduct under federal civil-rights guarantees and state statutes. Police brutality was increasingly challenged in minority communities where it had always been present as well as in gay communities in several cities. The 1969 **Stonewall Riot** was touched off by a routine raid by the New York City Police on a gay bar on Christopher Street in Manhattan.

Suits by federal prosecutors against local police departments in several cities, in particular **Philadelphia, PA** and **Houston, Texas**, lead to a study by the United States Civil Rights Commission entitled *Who is Guarding the Guardians?* (1981). The recommendations of the commission summarized the conflict over police professionalization, finding that even in departments with high levels of education and intensive training, a separate, defensive police culture had evolved that saw citizens and particularly citizens from groups not well represented in the department as the enemy.

Elizabeth Reuss-Ianni found that patrol officers in the New York Police Department were caught between what they considered a hostile and dangerous external environment and a professionalized, but remote administrative culture in the upper-ranks of the department. The "two cultures of policing" cut street cops loose to do whatever was necessary to keep order: a strategy that further alienated the public in many jurisdictions, but which insulated the top brass from legal responsibility when inevitable misconduct suits were filed.

The Knapp Commission investigations into corruption in the New York Police Department in the 1970s reinforced the reform impulse built by public attention to brutality and police handling of civil disorder, and led to a series of experiments in the structure and function of American policing in the 1980s and 1990s. Team policing and walking beats, patrol strategies that had been jettisoned during professionalization, were revived by reform commissioners like Patrick Murphy in New York City. Films like *Serpico* (1973) and *Prince of the City* (1981) followed in the wake of corruption revelations in New York and elsewhere.

The acquittal by a **suburban** jury of the Los Angeles police officers involved in the taped and televised beating of motorist Rodney **King** touched off riots in **Los Angeles, CA** that caused another round of self-examination among police administrators and scholars. Reforms in the 1990s centered around "community policing," an attempt to reconnect the police and the public through the broader involvement of police officers – sometimes called community patrol officers – in a variety of neighborhood activities.

Further reading

Knapp Commission (1973) *The Knapp Commission Report on Police Corruption*, New York: Braziller.

Reuss-Janni, E. (1983) *Two Cultures of Policing: Street Cops and Management CODs*, New Brunswick: Transaction Books.

Skolnick, J.H. (1993) *Above the Law: Police and the Excessive Use of Force*, New York: The Free Press.

FRANK ANECHIARICO

polio (-myelitis)

Also known as "infantile paralysis," this viral inflammation that left healthy children and adults unable to use their limbs became a source of terror for American parents and children, especially between 1945 and 1954 when it seemed as terrifying to the American dream as nuclear destruction or lurking **communism**. Thanks to a massive fundraising effort and targeted research, polio was conquered by vaccination, reducing its incidence dramatically and creating a new sense of power that would be recalled with **cancer** and **AIDS**. Nonetheless, post-polio syndrome has haunted survivors in the late twentieth century.

Although polio reached epidemic proportions in Sweden in 1885, the virus probably was experienced as a mild infantile condition until improved sanitation made that prophylactic exposure (via contact with fecal matter) improbable. A more virulent inflammation of the spine and its con-

sequences became regular threats in US outbreaks by 1916, although casualties never equaled the influenza pandemic. Polio outbreaks were met with sometimes hysterical responses – closing churches, schools and theaters as well as deserting pools and beaches to avoid the "summer plague." In 1921 it struck rising politician Franklin Delano **Roosevelt**, whose later resolute (and false) heartiness changed the image of the disease. Meanwhile, the National Infantile Paralysis Foundation raised money to support his center at Hot Springs, Arkansas, and more extensive research. In January 1938, with the help of **radio**/movie **star** Eddie Cantor and others, this foundation launched the March of Dimes, soliciting coins from radio listeners, children and adults, to total $1.8 million. By 1945 the NIPF raised $20 million, using maudlin appeals like its famous poster children.

The disease also took on new dimensions with overseas exposure for servicemen and the growth of new **baby boom** families and care. Cases rose from 10,000 annually in 1940 to 20,000 by the end of the decade. Cases peaked at 58,000 in 1952. This lead to real panic in summer months as well as isolation and stigmatization for those with even a mild case. Treatment, while improved over time, was still limited. Perhaps the most frightening image is that of the iron lung – encasing a body in a metal cylinder, causing utter dependency; immobilization was also practiced long after an Australian nurse, Sister Kenny, showed the efficacy of warm compresses and exercise.

Jonas **Salk**, among others, began looking for an effective vaccine in the mid-1940s, overcoming technical difficulties in producing dead virus vaccine and lack of support in the scientific community to achieve field tests in 1954, followed by widespread vaccination throughout schools. Dr Albert Sabin introduced an oral vaccine in 1958 and it soon replaced the Salk vaccine, effectively eliminating polio in the US for most populations.

In the 1980s, however, problems of new symptoms emerged. Whether recurrence of polio in an attenuated form or simply long-term muscle and nerve fatigue, post-polio syndrome has proven a haunting legacy of disease and triumph. Ironically, at this same time, public debate erupted over the lack of depictions of FDR in his wheelchair in his newly constructed Washington memorial.

Further reading

Gould, T. (1995) *A Summer Plague*, New Haven: Yale.

Smith, J. (1990) *Patenting the Sun*, New York: William Morrow.

GARY MCDONOGH
CINDY WONG

Polish Americans

Immigrants from Poland have developed a strong ethnic **community**, which they commonly refer to as Polonia, serving both the interests of the immigrants and endeavoring to contribute to the emergence of an independent Poland.

The first Poles to arrive in the United States in large numbers were the political exiles from the 1848 revolutions. In the 1880s they were joined by many economic emigrants from occupied Poland pulled by the lure of jobs in America's burgeoning cities. These immigrants concentrated in major industrial centers, primarily in the **Midwest** (**Buffalo, NY**, **Chicago, IL**, **Detroit, MI**, **Milwaukee, WI**, **Cleveland, OH** and **Pittsburgh, PA**) and the **Northeast** (**New York** City, NY, **Philadelphia, PA**, and **Boston**). Polonia emerged in these cities around the **Roman Catholic** Churches and the flourishing **newspapers**. Polish **Jews** tended to be identified by **religion**, replicating divisions in their homeland. Poles were also strongly committed to labor and socialist movements (stemming from their revolutionary activity earlier in the century), and New York's Polish Socialist Alliance in America published *Rabotnik Polski* (Polish Worker).

As was the case for many other ethnic groups, legislation in the 1920s virtually cut off fresh immigrants just as the independent nation emerged. But, the Polish community started to grow once again in the 1940s. With the Nazi invasion of Poland in 1939 many **refugees** (mainly Catholic) ended up coming to the United States. This trend accelerated after the Second World War, when the **Truman** administration used the Displaced Persons Act of 1948 to allow Poles fleeing Soviet occupation to enter the US. Between 1945 and 1954 as many as 178,000 Poles

arrived in the country, and 75,000 more followed prior to the easing of immigration restrictions in 1965.

Many of these new arrivals were either **intellectuals** or professionals. Having grown up in an independent Poland and wishing to protect Polish culture, they often came into conflict with the blue-collar leaders of Polonia. Such friction occurred at a time also when many second- and third-generation Polish Americans were beginning to leave the areas of Polish concentration and move to the **suburbs**. A simultaneous revival of cultural practices and communal organizations in the city occurred within the residual community that remained behind, so that when the 1960s rejection of suburban lifestyles and the celebration of ethnicity occurred, the Polish American culture was still vibrant. This strong sense of ethnic identity was drawn on by novelists like W.S. Kimiczak in *The 1,000 Hour Day* (1966) and the better-known, albeit controversial, Jerzy Kosinski.

By 1969, census estimates placed the Polish American community at about 4 million people, though many Poles felt that this was a significant under count and that the number was above 6 million. With its size and its concentration in particular metropolitan areas, the community wielded considerable political influence. Since the **Roosevelt** era, Poles had been aligned with the **Democratic Party**, especially in local elections (emphasizing the Democrats' appeal to working-class and Catholic immigrants). After the war, Poles tended to change their national vote according to American foreign policy and the handling of the Soviet Union. Truman lost Polish American voters to Dwight **Eisenhower**, who made various promises about winning back territory from the USSR. John F. **Kennedy**, as the first Catholic president and a hawk in foreign policy, was able to recapture them; while the failure of the Polish candidate Edmund **Muskie** to win the Democratic nomination in 1972 persuaded many Polish Americans to vote for **Nixon** (an irony since it was later shown that Nixon's dirty tricks had helped to destroy Muskie's candidacy). But Polish Americans also fit within the Nixon image of the "Silent Majority," working-class ethnics on whom the **Republicans** hoped to build their new post-**civil-rights** constituency. And, while nine out of ten Poles had voted for **Roosevelt**, during the **Reagan** years only about half were voting Democratic.

Besides Muskie, a senator for Maine, several other Polish Americans have been prominent in politics. John Dingell has been the Chairperson of the Energy and Commerce Committee; Leon Jaworski, led the **Watergate** investigation; and Zbigniew Brzezinski, a **Cold War** immigrant, was Jimmy **Carter**'s hawkish National Security advisor. The success of such individuals has gone a long way to counteracting the negative stereotypes associated with Polish Americans. "Polish jokes" have been a staple in comedy houses and the **networks**' **sitcoms**, long after Irish and black jokes have been considered in bad taste. In "All in the Family" (CBS, 1971–9), for example, Archie Bunker mercilessly ridiculed his son-in-law, Michael Stivik, allowing the show to expose many of the issues associated with stereotyping and, since Michael was clearly much smarter than Archie, to contest them as well.

Since the end of the Cold War and the collapse of the Soviet bloc, **immigration** from Poland has continued at variable rates. Return migration and support for the new state have also been more common, especially with the revival of the Polish economy.

Further reading

Bukowczyk, J.J. (1996) *Polish Americans and Their History,* Pittsburgh: University of Pittsburgh Press.

Lopata, H.Z. (1993) *Polish Americans,* New Brunswick: Transaction Publishers.

Pula, J.S. (1995) *Polish Americans: An Ethnic Community,* New York: Twayne Publications.

Thomas, W.I., Znaniecki, F. and Zaretsky, E. (eds) (1995) *The Polish Peasant in Europe and America,* Urbana: University of Illinois Press.

ROBERT GREGG

Political Action Committees (PACs)

PACs are political organizations that collect money, either from their members or the general public,

and redistribute it to political candidates or **parties** that support their interests. Although some form of political action committee probably existed as early as the late 1940s (the Committee on Political Education is considered one such early example), PACs were only formally authorized with the passage of the Federal Election Campaign Act of 1974. There are two types of PACs: segregated fund PACs, which are allowed to collect money only from their members, and nonconnected PACs, which raise their money from the voting public. PACs in modern American politics represent a wide variety of interests, ranging from environmental groups to conservative religious churches to pro-choice advocates.

PACs increase democratic participation in that they allow their members and contributors to effect political decision-making, at least indirectly, but their influence on the democratic process has become extremely controversial. For one thing, like political **lobbyists** more generally, they are often suspected of subverting the public good for sectarian ends. Thus PACs representing occupational groups such as teachers or **lawyers** find themselves accused of directing legislation to the advantage of their members' interests but to the detriment of the public good. Moreover, as their influence has grown, and more particularly as their monetary contributions have skyrocketed, they have helped increase the importance of fundraising generally. As a result, professional politicians must now spend much of their time and energy raising money to help finance their campaigns, at least if they wish to be elected or to stay in office. This obviously reduces the amount of time and attention they can devote to the actual business of the legislature. It also raises the question of to whom, exactly, the politician is beholden: the general public, or the special-interest PACs that provide the bulk of the campaign's financial support?

A related issue arose in the 1990s with the advent of so-called "soft money." In an effort to reduce the importance played by money in politics, particularly in campaign advertising, some legislatures attempted to place restrictions on the amount that a candidate could spend in a campaign. However, as long as they advertised not directly for a particular candidate but for some issue or set of issues, special-interest groups such as

PACs could spend unlimited amounts of money. These so-called "soft-money" expenditures seemed to allow campaigns to subvert the intent of the restrictions with highly charged and often partisan ads. In the 1996 federal congressional campaigns, for example, the AFL-CIO spent millions of dollars attacking **Republican** candidates. Moreover, whereas candidates must account to the Federal Election commission for all of the money that they spend within their campaigns, PACs are not always under such requirements.

As with political lobbying more generally, however, there are constitutional issues relating to freedom of speech and of assembly that have hampered most attempts to curtail the influence of soft money, and of PACs more generally. As a result, many potential candidates for public office in modern American politics are judged on their viability, that is whether and how well they can raise PAC and other special-interest money. This has only contributed to a growing cynicism about the ability of some private groups and individuals to "buy" politicians in order to determine public policy.

See also: parties and elections

Further reading

Plano, J.C. and Greenberg, M. (1997) *The American Political Dictionary*, Fort Worth: Harcourt Brace.
Safire, W.F. (1978) *Safire's Political Dictionary*, New York: Ballantine Books.

MARK BREWIN

political consultants

While American politicians have always relied on advisors, the visibility of political consultants increased in the late 1960s, particularly as **television** became a crucial part of American politics. In *The Selling of the President* (1968), Joe McGinniss chronicled how Richard **Nixon**'s campaign staff promoted the Republican presidential candidate like a consumer product to appeal to voters.

By the late 1980s, political consultants became nearly as prominent as the candidates for whom they worked. Roger Ailes and Lee Atwater were successful in transforming the image of Republican nominee and **Vice-President** George Bush, helping him win the 1988 presidential election.

James Carville and others were credited with overcoming the controversies surrounding **Democratic** presidential candidate and Arkansas Governor Bill **Clinton** to win the 1992 presidential election. Their efforts were portrayed in the **documentary** film, *The War Room* (1993). Carville and his wife, **Republican Party** consultant Mary Matalin, co-authored a book, *All's Fair* (1994), a memoir of their role in the campaign.

Consultants have also produced election controversies. After Republican nominee Christine Todd Whitman won the New Jersey gubernatorial election, Whitman's strategist, Ed Rollins, said he paid **African American** clergymen to discourage black voters, likely supporters of incumbent Jim Florio, from going to the polls. Rollins later retracted his claim.

Hollywood has featured political consultants in movies of fictional campaigns. *The Candidate* (1972) and *Bob Roberts* (1992) were accounts of Senate contestants who lacked experience but whose appearance and charisma, combined with consultants' packaging, charmed the electorate.

JAMES DEVITT

political correctness

Seemingly innocent phrase used by conservatives and others to denigrate multicultural efforts and sensitivities. The phrase evokes insincerity and empty rules, rather than new, complex worlds of knowledge, behavior and communication that a recognition of diversity and equality entails. Certainly, **colleges** (a frequent target for those who decry p.c. thinking) and other cultural institutions have created missteps as they try to regulate speech or interpersonal relations or interpret activities through a rigid template of **race**, **class** and gender. Nonetheless, attempts to deconstruct cultural patterns based on **white** male dominance prove both difficult and threatening towards those conservatives who throw this term (like "**family values**") around rather freely.

GARY McDONOGH
CINDY WONG

political science

The study of political relations between and within countries, political science covers topics as diverse as congressional committees in America, the development of cultural and political identities in Zambia and the arms race between Pakistan and India. In the American academy, the discipline is usually divided into four sub-disciplines: American politics, which covers such topics as the study of American political institutions, the political actions of the American public and the study of policy formation within the US; comparative politics, involving the study of the internal politics of other nations with the goal of understanding how political institutions develop or operate in different settings; international relations, the study of the relations between countries, may focus on international institutions like the United Nations, or on the study of less formal networks of communication; and political theory, which encompasses the study of more broadly theoretical approaches to politics and, in developing concepts for interpreting leadership and democracy, often has a more normative orientation than the work of the discipline as a whole.

American political science began to emerge as an academic discipline in the late nineteenth century. The creation of the discipline was tied in with the Progressive movement, a movement determined to end the practices of corrupt party politics and **party machines**, especially in **cities**. The discipline's orientation towards reform lasted until the 1940s, when an increasing drive towards professionalization and establishment of political science as a "science" led to a decreased concern with political reform and greater attempts to consider politics in an objective, and hence uninvolved, manner. Political scientists of the day considered questions of democratic legitimacy answered; interest groups insured that citizens' wishes would be heard. The political upheavals of the 1960s brought on a re-evaluation of this neutrality within the discipline; however, many of these scholars still accepted that political science should be removed from politics. Political science remains a discipline that is generally not reform-oriented.

Recently there has been some concern over whether the discipline has become too fragmented. As training has become increasingly focused on achieving mastery of one or maybe two subfields, and language becomes more specialized, it has become less likely that scholars will even be aware of work done outside their subfield. The use of sophisticated mathematical models excludes from dialogue those without advanced mathematical training. While this lack of communication between scholars from different subfields is of increasing concern, it is unclear whether anything can or will be done.

Further reading

Seidelman, R. (1985) *Disenchanted Realists*, Albany: State University of New York Press.

EMILY CLOUGH

Pollock, Jackson

b. 1912; d. 1956

Renowned **abstract expressionist** painter. He departed wildly from pre-war painting conventions, and yet was perhaps as well known for his chaotic, impassioned life. His acclaim and artistic style – dripping and staining paint, using hard brushes and sticks in broad sweeps atop large canvases laid on the floor – as a way to unravel a purer form of expression and emotionality helped to move the center of the art world from Paris to **New York**. In 1945 he married the painter Lee Krasner and his tumultuous career took off for a number of years, in part due to the support of critic Clement Greenberg. His work fell out of favor with the ascension of **pop art**, but recent art shows have restored Pollock's enduring importance.

See also: modernism; abstract expressionism

EDWARD MILLER

polls

As currently understood, "polls" refer to techniques that combine some form of questionnaire with advanced statistical techniques to produce measurements of public opinion. Although informal straw polls were already used to give rough measures of political support in the latter part of the nineteenth century, they did not gain widespread use until the twentieth century. Political writers such as Walter Lippmann, and social scientists such as Floyd Allport, dissatisfied with subjective descriptions of public opinion, began to look for more rigorous methods of measuring what the public thought of an issue. Social scientists and journalists began to look upon polls, which could be standardized and which also allowed for a more or less accurate measure of public opinion, as a way to solve the need for objectivity in discussions of public opinion. Despite some notable failures – including an infamous poll run by the *Literary Digest* for the 1936 presidential election, which seriously misread the level of support for the incumbent Franklin D. **Roosevelt** – the poll became a near-ubiquitous element in public discourse. Although the Gallup organization is still probably the most famous polling group, numerous other firms have developed reputations for their expertise. The Nielsen company's polls on television viewing patterns, for example, provided perhaps the single most important measurement for most of the American **advertising** industry in the second half of the twentieth century.

At the same time, the increasing use of the polling data has provoked criticism. Critics of modern political journalism argue that news reporters rely too much on "poll-driven" stories, especially during elections. Political news thus is reduced to stories about which candidate is ahead in the polls, and the strategies used either to get the lead or retain it; discussion of actual policy proposals is pushed aside. Others argue that as a measure of *public* opinion, polls are essentially misguided, since what they are measuring is in fact an aggregate of various *private* opinions. More critical theorists point out that polls offer only a limited number of responses to questions, effectively ignoring – and thereby marginalizing – opinions that are too radical or that cannot be standardized. Even social scientists who use polls extensively admit that they present measurement problems, especially the under-reporting of socially

deviant behavior and the over-reporting of socially-sanctioned actions.

These criticisms have provoked changes to polling procedures in recent years. Although polls are still essential to election-year coverage, many news organizations have become more circumspect in their use of polls to drive political news. Among social scientists there is a move to supplement polling with the use of focus groups and interviews, or through the development of "deliberative polls," in which the polling questionnaire is supplemented by in-depth interviews and interaction between members of the subject population. It remains an open question, however, whether polls as such "measure" or in fact "create" public opinion.

Further reading

Herbst, S. (1993) *Numbered Voices*, Chicago: University of Chicago Press.

Merkle, D.M. (1996) "The National Issues Convention Deliberative Poll," *Public Opinion Quarterly* 60(4): 588–619.

Peters, J.D. (1995) "Historical Tensions in the Concept of Public Opinion," in Glasser, T. and Salmon, C. (eds) *Public Opinion and the Communication of Consent*, New York: The Guilford Press.

Sudman, S. and Bradburn, N. (1982) *Asking Questions*, San Francisco: Jossey-Bass.

MARK BREWIN

pool *see* bars

pop art

Augured in the 1950s in the work of **neo-Dadaists** Robert **Rauschenberg** and Jasper Johns, the American incarnation of pop art, as it emerged in the 1960s, was a movement immersed in the visual languages, vernacular iconography and means of production of popular culture. Although the term was first applied to a group of British artists in the 1950s, even their work was largely based on the images of an American **mass media**.

Characterized by Andy **Warhol**'s silkscreened icons of American commodities and **celebrity** culture, Roy Lichtenstein's billboard-sized homages to the graphic style and pathos of the comic strip and Claes Oldenberg's monumental sculptures of household appliances and fixtures, pop art elevated the quotidian objects and concerns of postwar American culture into the rarified realm of high art, forever changing the meaning of that once-sanctified term.

Beyond its playful repetition of certain Dadaist strategies of quotation and appropriation and its reiteration of the Duchampian challenge to modernist autonomy and the institutions of art, pop art also evidenced a return to the thwarted political aspirations of Berlin Dada. Manifested most powerfully in James Rosenquist's pictorial assaults on American militarism or Edward and Nancy Kienholz's mixed-media indictments of the moral bankruptcy of American society, even Warhol's pictures ultimately oscillate between their veneer of bland complicity with and idolatrous celebration of contemporary popular culture and a more acute language of cultural critique.

Further reading

Madoff, S.H. (ed.) (1997) *pop art: A Critical History*, Berkeley: University of California Press.

LISA SALTZMAN

popcorn

Variant on a **American Indian** staple, popcorn (with butter and salt) has become intertwined with American fun – state **fairs**, the **circus**, sports and movies as well as family spectatorship. The latter includes **holiday** traditions like making caramel popcorn balls for Halloween (disappearing with concerns for the security of homemade goods) and stringing popcorn to decorate Christmas trees. Microwave popcorn has also been added as a snack in video chains and offices. Popcorn has been touted as a low-calorie, high-fiber food; reports on movie-theater popcorn's fat and cholesterol in the 1990s, however, forced a change in preparation if not eating.

GARY McDONOGH
CINDY WONG

popular culture

Popular culture is difficult to define, partly because both terms – "popular" and "culture" – have meant different things at different points in history, depending on the theoretical or disciplinary framework employed. In the simplest terms, popular culture is culture that is widely favored by many people – the culture "of the people." But this definition leaves unanswered the question of what culture is and what, if anything, differentiates popular culture from other conceptual categories such as folk culture, mass culture, or **working-class** culture. In making distinctions, social, economic and aesthetic criteria are not easily disentangled. For example, "culture" can refer to: (1) a general process of intellectual, spiritual and aesthetic development ("the development of Western culture"); (2) the expressive activities of communities and societies, as in sports, **holidays**, festivals, ceremonies; or (3) particular intellectual and artistic practices, as in literature, painting, **dance** and song (Storey 1993). "Popular" can mean not only "of the people," or that which is well-liked by a large number of individuals, but also "common," accessible to the average person, and even "inferior" (Shiach 1989).

As Storey has pointed out, it is often easier to understand popular culture in contrast to what it is not. Perhaps most obviously, popular culture is not elite or "high" culture, which is, by definition, unpopular and exclusive. Nor is popular culture synonymous with folk culture or working-class culture. The former generally refers to culture that is local, non-commercial and expressive of a particular group or community identity (quilting, folk tales, or **folk music**); the latter, to texts and practices associated with a working-class sensibility and enjoyed primarily by members of the working class (nickelodeons, burlesque, bingo or **bowling**, as well as organizational strategies). Of course, all three types can, and often do, overlap. Yet there is no direct one-to-one relationship between a **class** or **community** and a particular cultural form. To paraphrase Stuart Hall (1981), "class" and "popular" are deeply related, but they are not absolutely interchangeable. Moreover, it is important to bear in mind when distinguishing popular from elite culture that these categories are not fixed or static, so that what was once considered "low" may now be "high," and vice versa. For example, Shakespeare was once the most popular playwright in America, but his works were gradually "rescued" from the marketplace and enshrined in official institutions controlled by wealthy patrons; as a consequence, Shakespeare became high culture, the purview of the social and intellectual elite (Levine 1988). Likewise, as Storey notes, the seaside holiday began as an aristocratic practice and within a hundred years had become a popular one, while **film noir** started as a despised popular cinema and is now the preserve of academics and film critics. Thus it is not the specific contents of the categories "high" and "low" that matter, since these change over time, but the fact that a distinction exists, one that tends to sustain cultural hierarchy.

Nor is popular culture simply mass culture, although the overlap is perhaps greatest here. Indeed, in highly industrialized contemporary societies like the US, there is very little that we might call the culture "of the people" that is not derived from commercial culture and that is not dependent upon commercial consumption for its expression. Consequently, American popular culture is increasingly tied to mass culture, and, by implication, to mass production and mass consumption. This association more than anything reinforces popular culture as high culture's opposite: low, vulgar and base; lacking in creativity, originality and tradition.

So what distinguishes popular culture from mass culture? The difference lies less in the specific content than in the relationship between content and consumer. According to Storey, Fiske (1989) and other scholars, mass culture consists of the texts, objects and relations of the culture industries; popular culture is what people make of those texts, objects and relations. For example, the culture industry produces many **television** programs, but how people understand them and what role television plays in everyday life is not self-evident or necessarily "given" in the programs themselves. Thus mass culture is the objective repertoire from which people create subjective, popular meanings – albeit meanings inevitably circumscribed in key ways by the repertoire itself. This meaning-making not only acknowledges an active dimension to

consumption, it requires us to consider popular culture in a more local, personal and political sense. As Hall insists, the making of popular culture involves an ongoing negotiation or struggle between people's needs and desires (what he calls the forces of resistance) and the needs of the culture industries (what he calls the power bloc, or the forces of incorporation). Of course, this is hardly an equal struggle, for the power bloc by definition has disproportionate clout in establishing the terms and limits of the cultural terrain in the first place. Popular culture is contradictory in nature: both constraining and enabling; limiting how we think about the world and offering opportunities for creative social and personal expression within those limits.

Popular culture is therefore not a fixed set of objects and practices, nor a fixed conceptual category, but something constituted both through the act of consumption and through the act of theoretical engagement. Scholars have focused on different aspects of popular culture, some turning to texts (**romance**, television, film, pop music, etc.), others examining lived culture such as holidays, hobbies, or fandoms. Different scholars have employed distinct theoretical approaches, most of them "structuralist theories" that generally claim that forms of popular culture – **food**, clothing, sports, **games**, rituals, entertainment – help reveal the underlying rules, structures and values of a society. For example, Marxists emphasize the relation between popular culture and the capitalist mode of production, suggesting that popular culture reproduces class inequality by generating enormous profits for those who control the culture industries while inculcating in consumers the values and ideology necessary to justify this – and other – unjust social arrangements. Psychoanalytic approaches tend to see popular culture as symptomatic expressions of society's "collective unconscious," as articulating indirectly through the symbolic language of entertainment our collective fears, anxieties, fantasies and desires. Ethnographic approaches investigate how forms of popular culture are produced and consumed in everyday life, what it means to people, how they contribute (or not) to the formation of individual, group and community identities. What all approaches have in common is the assumption that objects and practices taken to be part of popular culture are "readable," that they "speak" to us and that they tell us important (though not necessarily positive) things about the society in which we live.

Further reading

Fiske, J. (1989) *Understanding Popular Culture*, Boston: Unwin Hyman.

Hall, S. (1981) "Notes on Deconstructing the Popular," in Samuel, R. (ed.) *People's History and Socialist Theory*, London: Routledge & Kegan Paul.

Levine, L. (1988) *Highbrow Lowbrow*, Cambridge, MA: Harvard.

Mukerji, C. and Schudson, M. (eds) (1991) *Rethinking Popular Culture*, Berkeley: University of California.

Shiach, M. (1989) *Discourse on Popular Culture*, Stanford: Stanford University Press.

Storey, J. (1993) *An Introductory Guide to Cultural Theory and Popular Culture*, Athens, GA: University of Georgia.

LAURA GRINDSTAFF

pornography

Literally, "pornography" means "the writing of whores." The term is generally taken to mean "sexually explicit words and images whose sole purpose is sexual arousal." However, in the last quarter of the twentieth century in America, pornography was at the center of a cultural, religious and political struggle. As such, pornography has been defined variously, depending on the group discussing it.

Pornography (if we understand it as sexually explicit words and images), comes in many forms in America. Justice Department figures from 1994 indicate that pornography is a $10 billion per year industry. This business includes: pornographic **magazines**; movies and **videos** (both professionally and amateur-produced, which became widely available for home rental with the advent of the **VCR**); and the ever-growing number of **Internet** sites devoted to pornographic images.

Pornographic magazines featuring nude and/or sexually explicit photographs became a recognizable feature of the American culture when Hugh Hefner began publishing *Playboy* magazine in 1953. *Playboy*, with its nude but not sexually explicit photographs of young women, was the groundbreaking pornographic magazine and today is still America's premiere magazine offering "entertainment for men" (*Playboy's* description of its role). Other major magazines in this genre include *Penthouse* and *Hustler*, as well as *Playgirl*, which features nude photos of men.

Pornography, in the myriad forms in which it has made its way into American culture, has elicited not only sexual response from those who purchase and view it, but political and religious interest as well. In 1973 the President's Commission on Obscenity and Pornography, based on the fact that no scientific data have conclusively demonstrated a link between criminal activity and exposure to obscene material, suggested legalization of sexually oriented expression between consenting adults. However, just months later, the United States **Supreme Court**, in the case of *Miller* v. *California*, wrote that any sexually oriented work could be banned unless it had "serious literary, artistic, political or scientific value." Although the Supreme Court ruling spoke of obscenity, not pornography, the two terms have frequently been linked by anti-pornography activists, and *Miller* v. *California* has been used in many cases as a pretext to demand **censorship** of sexually explicit material.

Since obscenity has come to be equated in many cases with pornography, the term "pornography" has come to be used since 1973 to describe whatever sexually oriented expression a certain group dislikes or whatever sexual representation a dominant class or group wishes to keep out of the hands of other, less dominant, classes or groups. For this reason, pornography has acquired a social and political significance in America today that goes far beyond the pages of a pornographic magazine or a scene in a pornographic movie.

The most vehement opposition to pornography in America has come from the political right wing (particularly the Religious Right and the Christian Coalition) and from the pro-censorship/anti-pornography feminist movement, the latter led by Catharine MacKinnon and Andrea Dworkin. MacKinnon and Dworkin define pornography as "sexually explicit subordination of women through pictures and/or words" (Dworkin, 1985: 8). Beginning in the early 1990s, supporters of MacKinnon and Dworkin have unsuccessfully attempted to introduce legislation in several US cities, which would ban pornographic materials that they deem degrading or dehumanizing to women.

While attempts to censor pornography continue to be launched by political conservatives and radical feminists alike, pornography as a form of expression continues to be protected under the 1st Amendment. However, the question of child pornography and what constitutes it is something of a gray area. In 1982 and 1990, the Supreme Court upheld two state statutes prohibiting showing **children** engaging in sexual activity or in a state of nudity. The issue of child pornography became a real focal point for anti-pornography activists in the early 1990s. In one of the most visible battles, a series of print advertisements for Calvin Klein underwear was attacked by anti-pornography activists because the models, who were clad only in underwear, and not engaged in any sexual activity, appeared to be adolescents and thus below the legal age of consent. No charges were filed against Calvin Klein, but, in a similar, high-profile case in 1990, the **FBI** investigated photographer Jock Sturges. The investigation was begun after Sturges' nude photographs of adolescents aroused the suspicions of a photography laboratory employee. (At no point did the FBI claim the photos depicted sexual activity of any kind, and, in 1991, a federal grand jury failed to indict Sturges.)

Thus, at the beginning of the twenty-first century, with *Playboy* entering its second half-century, the battle continues to be fought between those defending Americans' right to look at dirty pictures and those who wish to protect those same Americans from sexually explicit images they find disturbing, demeaning or dangerous.

Further reading

Dworkin, A. (1985) "Against the Male Flood: Censorship, Pornography, and Equality," *Harvard Women's Law Journal*.

Kendrick, W. (1987) *The Secret Museum*, New York: Viking.

MacKinnon, C. (1993) *Only Words*, Cambridge, MA: Harvard University.

Strossen, N. (1995) *Defending Pornography*, New York: Anchor Books.

SUSAN SCOTTO

Portland and Salem, OR

Portland and Salem lie approximately 47 miles apart in Oregon (**Pacific Northwest**). Salem is the state capital. Portland, the largest city in the state, has become known as a progressive center for its planning controls on urban sprawl and has also attracted high-tech investment in computers and media. It also hosts the Portland Trailblazers (**basketball**). Despite growth limits, this dual metropolis continues to grow rapidly, with a projected metropolitan population in 2020 of 2.8 million (a 38 percent increase from 1995), challenging the natural landscapes and lifestyles that have fostered its attractiveness for many.

KATE M. KENSKI

Portuguese Americans

Over 500,000 migrants from Portugal to the US span the complexities of Portuguese history and society. The earliest were Sephardic **Jews** fleeing from Brazil to New Amsterdam (New York) (1624). Later, migrants from the islands of the Azores and Cape Verdes became attached to **New England** coastal fishing towns and the codfish industry. Humberto Medeiros, a Portuguese American, later became Catholic Cardinal Archbishop of **Boston**. Bishop C.R. "Daddy" Grace, a Cape Verdean, became a charismatic black religious leader from the 1930s until his death in 1960. Portugal has also proven one of the most active European nations in post-1965 **immigration**.

GARY McDONOGH

postmodernism

Postmodernism is a loose term for a variety of movements that arose within the art world and the university as separate responses to two different understandings of the term "modern": modernity and **modernism**. Modernity is the term used by philosophers and historians to designate a historical period ranging from the Renaissance and extending to the early part of the twentieth century. It was marked by: a belief in the power of reason, as opposed to faith, for securing progress; the separation of science, morality and art into their own autonomous spheres; and the search for a unifying foundational theory or principle that would capture the universal aspects of existence. Modernism is a term primarily employed within the art world. The American modern movement ran from the 1870s to the late 1950s, and included the paintings of Jackson **Pollock**, the buildings of Frank Lloyd **Wright**, the **poetry** of Walt Whitman and the choreography of Martha **Graham**. The movement centered around images of **nature** and machinery, explorations of the myths and stories of American history, ambivalent feelings about urban versus rural spaces and a desire to break with European dominance. Despite the different senses of the term "modern," American postmodernists in both the university and the art world shared a number of common features. Leading postmodernist thinkers and artists resisted attempts to classify or label their work as being postmodern or as being part of any type of organized movement. In part this arose because of a skepticism about the possibility of any transcendent, trans-historical, or transcultural truths that could provide a basis for a unified all-encompassing theory. As a result there rapidly developed a highly diverse set of theories in the university (e.g. neo-pragmatism, deconstructionism, neo-Marxism, critical legal studies) and in the art world (e.g. **pop art**, cyberpunk, avant pop, **minimalism**). Although they were all lumped under the general rubric "postmodernism," they had significant methodological and theoretical differences about how to replace their predecessors. Both the intellectual and artistic versions of postmodernism began to emerge in the late 1950s and early 1960s, both were influenced by European movements (the artists were influenced by the British pop artists, while the intellectuals were influenced by the French post-structuralists) and both quickly spread from their original source (painting and literary theory) to other fields.

Furthermore, both tended to collapse or blur traditional boundaries: sometimes between genres, as in the music of John Zorn and Terry Riley or the journalism of Hunter Thompson, Truman Capote and Tom **Wolfe**; between academic disciplines as with Camila **Paglia** and Stanley Fish; or between media, as in the performance art of Laurie Anderson or the **theater** pieces of Robert **Wilson**. Both strains of postmodernism were fascinated with **popular culture** and its role in society, and both challenged the notion of any significant difference between high and low art or between avant-garde and commercial artists.

RODGER JACKSON

potluck

Informal meal arrangement among friends or colleagues in which each contributes a dish, generally within prescribed American **food** categories like appetizer, main dish or casserole, salad, dessert, etc. The host/hostess provides the basic materials and setting – in one variation, however, participants move from house to house, course by course. As larger collective events, potlucks can be used to promote social relations in schools, workplaces or churches as well as to raise money for **community** events. While emphasizing solidarity, they also permit competition in quality and display among participants. To "just take potluck" – essentially, whatever is left – suggests drawbacks of the arrangement.

GARY McDONOGH

poverty *see* "underclass"; War on Poverty; homelessness

Powell, Adam Clayton, Jr.

b. 1908; d. 1972

Civil rights leader and clergyman, elected to the House of Representatives for eleven terms. In the late 1930s, while assisting his father in his pastorate at the Abyssinian Baptist Church in **Harlem**, Powell began to organize anti-discrimination demonstrations and campaigns for jobs in **New York** City. In 1941 he was elected to the New York city council, and four years later was elected to **Congress** as a representative for Harlem. While in Congress he spoke in support of the **sit-ins**, sponsored civil-rights legislation as well as bills comprising part of Lyndon **Johnson**'s "War on Poverty."

ROBERT GREGG

Powell, Colin

b. 1937

Awarded the Purple Heart, Bronze Star and other accolades for his service in Vietnam, Powell entered the national spotlight as Chairperson of the Joint Chiefs of Staff in 1991 under President **Bush** for his role in the **Gulf War**. The first **African American** and youngest person to serve in that position, Powell retired in 1993. Considered a top contender in the 1996 presidential election, Powell declined to run. His 1995 autobiography *My American Journey* was a bestseller. Dedicated to helping young people, he became the Chairperson of America's Promise: The Alliance for Youth.

KATE M. KENSKI

POW/MIAs (Prisoners of War/ Missing in Action)

Part of the lingering nightmare of Vietnam in American consciousness has been the silence and uncertainty about those who were imprisoned and those who did not return. While every global war has resulted in these missing friends and loved ones (hence, the Tomb of the Unknown Soldier), a general sense of a lack of resolution kept alive beliefs of Americans left behind in Southeast Asia decades after formal withdrawal, and made this a major political issue in 1990s campaigns. This was exacerbated by **mass media** portrayals like *Rambo II* (1985) and continual rumors of secret POW camps. Government investigations and technological cooperation with the Vietnamese government, anxious for increased recognition

and investment, have generally alleviated the intense anxiety and distrust this issue once aroused. Pete Peterson, the first American ambassador to a united Vietnam, is himself a former POW; his office has worked actively with the Vietnamese government to find and repatriate the remains of roughly five servicemen every other month.

GARY McDONOGH

Presbyterians

Presbyterians constitute approximately 2 percent of the American population. The Presbyterian denomination of the Protestant Church traces its roots to the sixteenth century when John Calvin in Geneva and John Knox in Scotland shaped its basic theology and governance. The Westminster Confession of Faith, the creed of Presbyterianism for more than 300 years, was drafted in the mid-seventeenth century in England.

Scottish immigrants who espoused the Presbyterian way came to the Americas in the seventeenth century. They started churches in the Middle Colonies, and in 1706 the first presbytery was organized. A presbytery is a representative body formed of lay leaders, or elders, and pastors. Collectively they govern the church in a given area. Throughout the rest of the century and into the next, Presbyterians played significant roles in the Evangelical Awakening in Colonial America, in the Revolutionary War and in the beginning of the world missionary movement that grew out of the second Evangelical Awakening at the turn of the nineteenth century.

The 1967 Confession of Faith and the 1990 Brief Statement of Faith affirm the continuity of the Reformed Confessional tradition and are found in the *Book of Confessions*.

Presbyterians have historically taken their faith so seriously that disagreements over theology or the application of faith in society have led to church splits in each of the last three centuries. Equally, Presbyterians have been committed so strongly to the basic unity of the church universal that they have worked for reunification within the Presbyterian family, on the one hand, and they have been at the forefront of such ecumenical movements as the

World Council of Churches and the World Alliance of Reformed Churches, on the other.

Currently there are nine Presbyterian denominations in the United States with an aggregate membership of 3.2 million. The largest body is the Presbyterian Church (USA), with slightly less than 2.6 million members. It was formed in 1983 as a merger of the United Presbyterian Church (USA) and the Presbyterian Church (US), two bodies that had been separate since the American Civil War.

Other significant Presbyterian denominations include the Cumberland Presbyterian Church and the mostly **African American** Cumberland Presbyterian Church in America. The former, with about 90,000 members, arose in the early 1800s out of disagreements over the doctrines of election and reprobation as taught in the Westminster Confession of Faith. The latter, with about 15,000 members, was established by African Americans to give themselves a place for leadership in Presbyterian churches.

The Presbyterian Church in America, founded in 1973 as a split-off movement from the Presbyterian Church (US), was joined in 1982 by the Reformed Presbyterian Church, Evangelical Synod. The church's membership today is approximately 300,000. The Evangelical Presbyterian Church formed out of churches dissatisfied with the United Presbyterian Church (USA) in 1978. Its membership is about 60,000.

While most Presbyterians in the United States are **white**, increasing numbers of Korean immigrants are changing the face of the various Presbyterian denominations. Having received the gospel from (mostly Presbyterian) missionaries, Koreans are doing mission work of their own in the United States. The Presbyterian Church (USA), for example, has over 300 **Korean American** congregations, and a separate Korean Presbyterian Church in America has several hundred congregations.

Further reading

Ellwood, R. and Partin, H.B. (1988) *Religious and Spiritual Groups in Modern America*, Englewood Cliffs: Prentice Hall.

Gallup, G., Jr. and Castelli, J. (1989) *The People's Religion*, New York: MacMillan Publishing Company.

Lindner, E.W. (ed.) (1998) *Yearbook of American & Canadian Churches 1998*, Nashville: Abingdon Press.

Melton, J.G. (1997) *Encyclopedia of American Religions*, Gale: Detroit.

GAIL RITCHIE HENSON
JEFFERSON I. RITCHIE

presidency

The president of the United States is one of the most powerful political figures in the nation and the world. As the leader of the United States, he or she is expected to create and implement new legislation and involve the United States in the affairs of other countries. Yet little power is invested in the office of the president itself. A president cannot enact legislation on his or her own (though he or she can sometimes affect how it is implemented). The president's official power is limited to the very bare outlines of the Constitution; furthermore, the informal power that usually comes of being head of a **party** is unavailable to him or her because **Congress** is often controlled by members of another party and, even if the presidency and Congress are held by the same party, discipline in American political parties is weak. The president, then, must rely on other sources of power in carrying out the tasks he or she is expected to handle.

The official powers of the president are enumerated in Article II of the US Constitution. They include the power to pardon criminals, the power to make treaties (with the approval of two-thirds of the Senate) and the office of Commander in Chief of the armed forces. The president is also responsible for reporting to Congress on the state of the union and making recommendations to Congress. The president's legislative power is limited to the ability to veto legislation approved by Congress.

It is clear that the president's role extends beyond the completion of the duties enumerated in the Constitution. The president has become a prominent and powerful political figure. Domestically, he or she presents a budget to Congress every year, creates and introduces legislation to Congress and tries to direct the economic affairs of the nation; yet the official powers of the president have not changed since the Constitution was created more than 200 years ago. There is a great deal of debate over how it is that the president manages to acquire this power. There are those who argue that the president's power is highly personal; powerful presidents have the ability to persuade Congress to go along with what they want. Others claim that presidents can get Congress to implement particular policies by increasing public support for those policies, increasing fears that members of Congress will not be re-elected if they do not vote for policies the public wants. Still others argue that the amount of power a president wields is determined by the president's place in time; personal qualities and actions have little to do with what a president can accomplish. There are also those that believe that a president's power depends entirely on whether Congress and the president are of the same party.

Efforts have been made in recent years to increase the president's legislative power. The creation of a line-item veto, which would allow the president to veto certain parts of a bill without vetoing it in its entirety, was heavily debated in the early 1990s. Congress passed legislation giving the president the power of line-item veto over budget bills; this legislation came into effect on January 1, 1997. However, a year later the **Supreme Court** declared the line-item veto unconstitutional.

In foreign affairs, the president has considerably more constitutional power. The president's position as Commander in Chief of the armed forces has allowed him to take actions that were not endorsed by Congress, frequently using this power to involve the country in military conflicts. The **Gulf of Tonkin Resolution**, passed in August of 1964 at the request of President **Johnson**, granted the president the power to use military force to "repel any armed attack against the forces of the United States and to prevent further aggression." This allowed presidents Johnson and **Nixon** to begin and continue the **Vietnam War** without any declaration of **war**. This large grant of power was limited by Congress when they passed the War Powers Resolution of 1973; however, many pre-

sidents have refused to abide by the resolution. For instance, the initial deployment of troops into Iraq by President **Bush** was not endorsed by Congress (although Congress later voted to support these actions and allow the president to take any others he felt necessary), and Bush continued to insist that he did not need congressional approval at all.

The only way to remove a president from office is through the process of **impeachment**. A president can be impeached if he commits bribery, treason, or "high crimes and misdemeanors." While the definitions of bribery and treason are clear, the definition of "high crimes and misdemeanors" is not; it is under this category of crimes that claims of impeachable offenses are usually made. The impeachment procedure has two stages: in the first, the House of Representatives votes on articles of impeachment. If the House decides that formal charges are relevant and significant, an official trial is held in the Senate. Two presidents have been impeached: in 1868 Andrew Johnson narrowly escaped being stripped of his office by one vote in the Senate; in 1999 Bill **Clinton** was saved by a party-line vote also falling short of the necessary two-thirds majority. But, in 1974, a House committee recommended that members of the House of Representatives vote "yes" on articles of impeachment for Richard **Nixon**, leading the president to resign before the issue was voted on.

Further reading

Kernell, S. (1986) *Going Public*, Washington, DC: Congressional Quarterly Press.

Nelson, M. (ed.) (1995) *The Presidency and the Political System*, Washington, DC: Congressional Quarterly Press.

Neustadt, R. (1990) *Presidential Power and the Modern President*, New York: The Free Press.

Skowronek, S. (1993) *The Politics Presidents Make*, Cambridge, MA: Harvard University Press.

EMILY CLOUGH

Presley, Elvis
b. 1935; d. 1977

A legend whose life and career can hardly be

captured or even hinted at in so brief a space as this, Elvis Presley was one of the biggest **stars** of the twentieth century. Recording for Sam Phillips' Sun Records in Memphis, TN in 1954–5, Presley released a series of singles with a country side backed with a **blues** side. His cover of Arthur Crudup's "That's All Right (Mama)" (1954) signaled the arrival of an explosive and unique new performer. Combining the impassioned singing of the Pentecostal churches with the country and blues music he heard on the **radio**, Presley defined the mixture of black and white Southern sounds which was rockabilly.

In November 1955, now under the management of Tom Parker, Presley's contract was sold to RCA for the then exorbitant sum of $35,000. Presley continued to record startling and hugely successful **rock 'n' roll** songs, but increasingly his debt to Dean Martin was highlighted. He recorded more pop-oriented songs, with lush productions, and embarked on a **film** career. By the time he emerged from a two-year stint in the army in 1960, he had largely abandoned rock for pop. For most of the 1960s, Presley eschewed performing, instead filming two or three movies a year and recording the generally mediocre soundtracks. A stunning 1968 **television** special proved that Elvis could still rock. "Suspicious Minds" (1969) and "In the Ghetto" (1969) were both popular and critical successes. Presley spent much of the 1970s performing in **Las Vegas**, taking drugs and getting fat at his Graceland mansion in Memphis.

DEWAR MACLEOD

primaries *see* parties and elections; conventions

prime time

Most competitive and renumerative network viewing hours between 20:00 and 23:00. Here, **networks** place their most popular shows (and evening line-ups) in order to attract desired demographics and sponsor revenues; this is the home of television **sitcoms**, dramas (**westerns**, **crime**, **lawyers**, doctors, **soaps**) and, increasingly, in the late twentieth and early twenty-first

centuries, of **news** magazines and "reality" shows. Manipulation of prime time is especially notable during the three yearly sweeps months when audience data are more systematically collected and compared. The impact of **cable** has altered the stakes and viewership of prime time, yet it still constitutes an exclusive battlefield for programmers, **producers** and **actors**.

GARY McDONOGH
CINDY WONG

Princeton University *see* Ivy League

prisons

The stern edifices and high security control of penal enclosure seem, in many ways, antithetical to the promises of any American dream of freedom, opportunity and even new beginnings. Yet, a staggering investment of more than $36 billion annually in the construction of prisons and the care of prisoners and the sheer human "storage" of nearly 2 million men and women in jail suggests prisons nonetheless have become central features of early twenty-first century American culture. Indeed, rates of imprisonment in the US are higher than any country except Russia and far exceed rates that preceded the Second World War. This has stimulated intense debates over the nature of crime and control (including **capital punishment** and its efficacy or juvenile justice and **gangs**), divisions of **race** and **class** that are reified by this system and the meaning and rights of prisoners within American life. At the same time, prisons have also become businesses, whether as private investments, outsourced by governments or as vital components of the economies of depressed localities competing for new construction and jobs.

American prisons have emerged from a variety of jurisdictions and philosophies. Philadelphia's Eastern State Penitentiary, for example, incorporated Quaker reflection and individual solitude into a panoptic model. Other prisons represented the needs of small towns and burgeoning industrial states as well as military and federal security. Some names became legendary in history as well as mass media – Sing Sing, Leavenworth, Alcatraz, **Attica**.

Such mass imprisonment has not been shown to have a clear causal relationship with reduced crime. Yet, prisons also reflect attitudes about crime, especially given demographic and ideological shifts in American **cities** and society since the 1960s. Rules imposed for the drug wars – "three strikes and you're out" – have resulted in mandatory sentences for the accumulation of minor offenses that have clogged prisons. Critics have argued that minor possession and sales offenses focused on crack have also fallen especially hard on minority populations. **African American** males in major cities face high probabilities of arrest and imprisonment that scar generations – between 1986 and 1995, the number of African Americans convicted of drug offenses rose 811 percent. Here, we must also worry that prisons reproduce crime – 60 percent of those released will be back in three years.

Prisoners have also constituted an awkward category in American society – deprived of rights for voting, gun ownership, etc. even after release, depending on state laws. Federal decisions in the 1970s increased rights of education, legal counsel and activities for prisoners and forced reform of outmoded, overcrowded and unsanitary jails. **Supreme Court** decisions at the end of the twentieth century allowed states to curtail these rights. Moreover, as prisons become private corporations, efficiency and cost-effectiveness replace rights.

Many in America realize that prisons do not work to curtail crime, which has declined in conjunction with economic growth. Yet, as a decentered system embodying competing political, social and cultural interests, it is not clear if prisons can be readily changed to participate in rather than reject the American dream.

Further reading

Parenti, C. (1999) *Lockdown America*, London: Verso.
Rosenblatt, E. (1996) *Criminal Injustice*, Boston: South End Press.

GARY McDONOGH

privacy

The right to control information, access and visibility is perceived as an important cultural value in the United States, closely linked to **individualism** and **freedom**. While debated in relation to public actions and rights to knowledge claimed by governments and social institutions like schools, issues of privacy also permeate the **family** where individual social spaces (separate **bedrooms** and control of **information** by children without informing parents) are also important to family dynamics. Privacy also shapes interpersonal relations in terms of topics commonly discussed and avoided – one may be warned not to bring up money or **religion** in social gatherings, while business interviews face strict limits on information that may not be asked (marital status, criminal history not directly relevant to the position, religion, etc.). Questions of privacy in the information age have become especially important with regards to the data gathered by bureaucracies and corporations and how these data are shared and used.

Rights to privacy have been worked out in complex ways throughout American history. Provisions of the **Bill of Rights** testify to the rights to protect the home from quartering troops (3rd Amendment), unreasonable search and seizure (4th Amendment) and rights to protect the individual from testifying against him or herself (5th Amendment). Provisions dealing with freedom and gun ownership also establish private rights, while dealing with the extension of private beliefs and action into public forums. In the twentieth century, **Supreme Court** decisions extended federal rights to the states. The right to privacy has also been evoked in court cases that have protected birth control, **abortion** (*Roe v. Wade*, 1973) and euthanasia; it has been argued less successfully in areas such as **pornography** and sexuality (especially when rights of **children** are called into play). These issues are also continually debated in issues ranging from **police** rights to use materials "in plain sight" to control of garbage.

Nonetheless, many Americans feel that their privacy has been threatened in the late twentieth and early twenty-first centuries by records gathered and kept by schools, governments (Internal Revenue as well as **FBI**), medical providers and corporations. Storage and access to such records through **computers** and the **Internet**, as well as the permeability of electronic communication have increased tension. Corporate mergers also raise questions of data flows within multipurpose businesses. There is often a strong ambivalence, too, in these areas as surveillance technologies have become accepted to control crime, yet are challenged when they extend into private spaces (changing rooms, **bathrooms**) or even control of activity in public spaces (private choices to participate in public events).

Specific laws have been enacted to safeguard medical records and credit materials, but violations of these expectations are constantly revealed by media. The turmoil of legal cases involving the **Clinton** White House has also heightened questions about the private lives of public persons, as well as the ability of the powerful to have access to records that are presumed to be confidential. One striking index of public sensitivity to these issues has been the reluctance of many to complete questions of the 2000 census, including Republican politicians speaking out against this legally established duty.

Mass media have heightened sensitivity to the manipulation of private data as well. Often, this is the stuff of crime novels, programs and movies, although these issues may be equally apparent in medical dramas. The impact of the potential manipulation of private information also underscores dystopic visions like *The Net* (1995).

Further reading

Henderson, H. (1990) *Privacy in the Information Age*, New York, Facts on File.

GARY McDONOGH
CINDY WONG

private schools

Public education has been a primary institution for the creation of American citizenship since government-supported schools became widespread in the mid-nineteenth century. Despite concerns about content and efficacy, it has coalesced as a comprehensive network with interlocking local, state and federal control. It also represents a major commitment in tax support of both the people and multiple governments. Private schools at the primary and secondary levels, by contrast, offer choices, which may involve exclusivity based on **religion**, **race**, gender or **class**. In the early twenty-first century, choices also reflect concerns with **public schools**, their educational methods and contents, or violence and social issues that lead parents to seek alternatives.

The Roman Catholic **parochial school** system is the largest private system nationwide (religious orders also run private schools). Jewish day schools, at least elementary, are also widely available, while groups like the **Amish** have fought to maintain educational autonomy. Episcopalians and Quakers also run longstanding private schools less exclusively denominational in tone. Religious private schools also include Christian academies that emerged with **white flight**. Many private schools, however, have no formal religious affiliation.

Private schools have also been associated with class divisions, especially with regard to elite "prep" schools. **New England** academies like Phillips Academy in Andover, Massachusetts (founded 1778), Phillips Exeter (founded 1781), Lawrenceville, Groton, Deerfield and Choate-Rosemary Hall offer strong curricula and teachers, distinguished active alumni, historical buildings and campus landscapes, extensive facilities and well-trodden paths to the **Ivy League**, although few rival the $400 million endowments of Phillips Andover and Phillips Exeter. This entails selectivity in academic excellence and cost, since tuition may run from $15,000 to $20,000 annually before board (although schools provide financial aid). This model has been depicted in literature like Owen Johnson's *Lawrenceville Stories*, and figures in Hollywood portrayals of private schools, such as *Dead Poet's Society* (1989).

Other metropolitan areas offer a competitive, varied hierarchy of selective private schools – competition for placement in **New York** City can start almost from birth – as well as variation in costs and financial aid. In general, private schools claim to offer a superior education in facilities, teachers and selection of students. Some also offer innovative programs, including Montessori formats, more libertarian "free schools," foreign residential opportunities and seminar settings. Private schools may offer single-gender education, although many have become co-educational since the 1970s.

Debates over public and private schooling are often debates about finance, control and the nature of the public sphere. Some argue that the competition of private schools regulates and energizes public education. Here, choosing private schools criticizes the failures, moral and educational, of the public system. School vouchers, for example, that allow parents to take money from the public system to subsidize their choice of private education have been especially controversial. Proponents of public schools, meanwhile, characterize private schools as privileged and their supporters as opponents of the idea of a heterogeneous public educational space in which different races, classes and levels of ability meet. Regulations about contents, practices and standards for measuring student success remain areas where government and private schools intersect. These debates continue to rage in legislatures, school boards and **mass media** as well as the classroom.

Further reading

(1999) *Handbook of Private Schools*, Boston: Porter Sargent.

Gaffney, E. (ed.) (1981) *Private Schools and the Public Good*, South Bend: Notre Dame.

Randall, V. (1994) *Private Schools and Public Power*, New York: Teacher's College.

GARY McDONOGH
CINDY WONG

Procter & Gamble

Personal goods multinational founded in 1837 in Cincinnati, Ohio for the manufacture of candles and soap. Intensive **advertising** has made its products household staples, from Ivory Soap (1879) moving through Crisco shortening (1923), detergents (Tide, 1946), toothpaste (Crest, 1955), Pampers disposable diapers (1961) and other products that have kept **baby boomers** clean, healthy, sweet-smelling and good-looking. Indeed, P & G is famous for creating brands competing against its own products – producing not only Tide but Cheer, Dash, Bold, Era and Oxydol as well as many subtypes of each to keep the consumer constantly involved. P & G also pioneered sponsorship of **radio** cooking shows and **soap operas**, which cemented its loyal fan/consumer base. Consumers now reach 5 billion worldwide, with P & G operations in seventy countries and profits of $3.7 billion on $37 billion in sales in 1998. Despite its wholesome image, P & G has been attacked for the environmental impact of its products and the need for cleanliness it sells. Its star and moon logo, inherited from its candle-making days, was also briefly and erroneously identified as a Satanic symbol.

GARY McDONOGH

producers, film and television

Under the studio system, producers were generally employees who "ran" the movie, although some created a more personal set of choices and films. Since the end of the studio era, executive producers have played an ever-more important role in envisioning and assembling the production of film or **television**, especially its financing. Together with the directors, they overlook the budgeting of production and post-production of the project while line-producers oversee shoots. Independent film producers are often brokers between the filmmakers and the distributors. The Producers Guild of America emerged in 1966 from the Screen Producers Guild (founded 1950) and the Television Producers Guild. In 2000 it has more than 1,500 members worldwide.

Certain producers have emerged as more distinctive figures in New **Hollywood**, especially **blockbuster** film-makers like Steven **Spielberg**, George **Lucas** and James Cameron. Others, like James Schamus and Ted Hope (*Ice Storm*, 1997; *Happiness*, 1998) or Oliver **Stone**, who also writes and directs, are associated primarily with independent films. Male and female **actors** also appear as producers in film and television series.

The image of producers in media is often negative, as in Robert Altman's *The Player* (1992). Dustin Hoffman satirized government and media as a film producer asked to produce a "war" in the satirical *Wag the Dog* (1997).

Yet money is a real issue for films. While in many European countries, the government promotes some form of national cinema and television, in the US, government funding hardly exists for feature films. Producers must assemble a complex package of backing from studios and financial sources. Cable **networks** like HBO and Showtime have become major producers in the 1990s.

CINDY WONG

Promise Keepers *see* masculinity

Protestants, evangelical *see* individual denominations: Methodists; Southern Baptists; Bible belt

Protestants, mainline *see* individual denominations: Episcopalians; Methodists

Prozac

Introduced onto the market by pharmaceutical giant Eli Lilly in 1988, Prozac (Fluoxetine) is taken to combat **depression** experienced by as many as 17 million Americans. The first of many such antidepressants (selective serotonin re-uptake inhibitors, or SSRIs), Prozac is now the brand name that is generally used to refer to current medical responses to chemically induced depression, though doctors often choose to prescribe Zoloft instead. Many doctors believe that depression may be caused by a chemical imbalance of serotonin, which a daily capsule of fluoxetine can correct with few side-effects, though the drug's safety has been brought into question recently. Often considered the wonder drug of the early 1990s, Prozac has received widespread attention, from medical practice to **humor**.

ROBERT GREGG

Pryor, Richard

b. 1940

Film actor and comedian known for his crude **humor** and hilarious characterizations of **African American** life. A great influence on comedians such as Eddie **Murphy**, Pryor provided the counterpoint to Bill **Cosby**'s more genteel and genial wit. In addition to movies of his live comedy routines, he also starred in *Lady Sings the Blues* (1972) with Diana Ross, Mel Brook's *Blazing Saddles* (1973), *Stir Crazy* (1980) with Gene Wilder, and the third *Superman* movie. He injured himself badly in an accident involving cocaine, which later became a source for some of his routines. More recently, he has been stricken with multiple sclerosis.

See also: actors

ROBERT GREGG

psychology and psychiatry

The study of mind and behavior represents links with the life sciences, the social sciences, the humanities and therapeutic domains, including both the medical specialization of psychiatry and practices of clinical and humanistic psychology. With more than fifty subfields recognized by the American Psychological Assocation for its roughly 100,000 members, psychologists may be characterized by their research methods, their focal interests or the areas in which these interests are applied; they may also combine academic research and teaching with counseling and other roles. More than 250,000 psychologists are employed nationwide. Psychology is also deeply connected to research and theory in other disciplines, including **anthropology**, **biology**, **education**, information theory, **linguistics**, medicine, neurobiology and **sociology**. Psychoanalytic interpretations also have currency in the humanities including film studies.

In addition, psychology permeates popular discourse both in reference to specific terms from the field (including psychoanalytic jargon) and a more general concern with emotions, motivations and individual and social problems in which "psychologistic" explanations have become commonplace. This role is reinforced by the psychologist in mass culture as commentator on events and problems in radio **talk shows**, as news **columnist** or **television** analyst and as lead character (*Spellbound*, 1945; *High Anxiety*, 1977; *Color of Night*, 1994; *The Bob Newhart Show*, CBS, 1972–8). The highly popular 1990s **sitcom** *Frasier* (NBC, 1993–), for example, contrasts a radio psychiatrist as advisor with his own emotional and social problems.

American pscyhology has a strong experimental tradition dating back to the nineteenth century, encompassing modern work in sensory studies, physiological psychology, comparative studies (with animals) and cognitive studies. Cognitive sciences have become linked with innovations in computers and communications. Other formative figures in American psychology include more philosophical functionalists like William James and John Dewey. J.B. Watson was the father of behaviorism, which focused on stimulus-response models.

Psychoanalysis was bolstered in the US by refugees fleeing the Nazis, including Karen Horney, Alfred Adler and others who developed diverse discussions of the Freudian legacy. Psychoanalysis was seized upon by Hollywood as both practice and subject of countless, albeit often comic, expositions. Questions raised about Freud and the limits of his observations and interpretations in the late twentieth century divided the psychoanalytic community in painful, sometimes public ways.

The Second World War and the **Cold War** became a watershed, as Herman (1995) argues, in bringing clinical and therapeutic aspects to the fore in both professional and public discourses as experts in the field skyrocketed (the APA soared from 2,739 members in 1940 to 30,839 in 1970). Their work in universities and private practice included studies of personality, adjustment and social psychology, tackling questions like gender and sexuality, prejudice and individuality, contributing to a broader reformulation of these issues in American life. These studies are also linked to applied psychological investigations and treatments in clinical practice, counseling, education and industry. Abnormal psychology deals specifically with questions of different knowledge of and action in the world. Developmental psychology has also become an important field.

American Psychologist, the journal of the APA, is a central journal in the field; the APA also publishes other specialized journals and maintains databases and news releases available at its website (http://www.apa.org/psychnet). *Psychology Today*, a more popular journal, also has provided information on research and issues in the field for thirty years.

Further reading

Gilgen, A. (1982) *American Psychology Since World War II*, Westport: Greenwood Press.

Herman, E. (1995) *The Romance of American Psychology*, Berkeley: University of California.

GARY McDONOGH

public art

American art in public spaces, not surprisingly, has been dominated by memorials of war and politics – generals, presidents or obelisks and sorrowful figures recalling the fallen. **Washington, DC**, for example, takes on trappings of a mausoleum in the monumental neo-classical structures on and around the mall commemorating Washington, Lincoln and Jefferson, as well as statues of state heroes huddled in the Capitol. Additional space on the mall has been found for recognition of Franklin Delano **Roosevelt** and a controversial **Vietnam memorial** by Maya Lin. At a local scale, public art dominates busy crossroads and provides aesthetic/historical touches to squares, **parks**, **cemeteries** and **gardens**.

While generally planned as monuments to shared history, beliefs and sentiments, public art can also prove divisive. Civil-War monuments to the Confederate dead in the **South** have become controversial since the **civil-rights** era. A proposal to add a statue of **tennis** great Arthur **Ashe** to Richmond's all-white Monument Avenue brought protests from both conservative whites and the Ashe family. Political memorials in urban statuary or renamings also rekindle controversies and enmities. Overall, an inherited bias towards white males in memorialization (and choice of artists) also reifies divisions of rights to history that have been challenged since the 1960s.

The presence and meaning of public art in the early twenty-first century is also linked to special programs for public support of the arts, primarily for art initiatives established by cities and states nationwide (ranging from 0.5 to 2 percent) since the 1970s. The National Endowment for the Arts also has sponsored public-arts programs. These initiatives have forced and cajoled government projects as well as private developers to set aside moneys to pose new works in new public spaces, whether administrative offices, entrance plazas, hospitals or airports. Again, this has not been without controversy – Richard Serra's abstract curve *Tilted Arc*, in front of the Federal Plaza in New York, was removed in 1989 after complaints about its impact on the space.

Public art also has become associated with urban regeneration and revitalization. But some have argued that while its presence may be public, even the possibilities of interpretation of postmodern forms create stratification in appreciation and responses to the work. Surveillance and campaigns against vandalism also betray multiple visions of monuments and spaces around them within complex urban fabrics. Arts in "controlled" public spaces, moreover, point out that **malls** and other public forums have private owners and rules of access and use. Urban murals, while widespread in programs for **neighborhood** beautification, also have been decried as markers of urban decay that simultaneously mask and call attention to abandonment. If art is the mirror of the soul, public art reflects both visions and divisions of American community.

Further reading

Miles, M. (1997) *Art Space and the City*, New York and London: Routledge.

GARY McDONOGH

public health

Public health is a set of techniques by which communities can uniquely complement individual efforts to maintain health. Although much of public health practice is carried out by local health departments at the municipal, county and state level, lately large employers, some managed-care groups (HMOs) and some civic organizations have begun to perform public-health functions. Historically, public-health efforts were focused primarily on efforts to control contagious diseases. The basic operations still persist as governments maintain standards for environmental safety and sanitation. Regional health departments maintain disease-reporting systems to permit early control of communicable disease outbreaks. Part of communicable disease control has also involved subsidizing personal health services such as immunization, treatment and preventive counseling for potentially contagious community members who are uninsured or not inclined to overcome other social obstacles to care that remain despite insurance. Access to care remains a large problem for the American healthcare system. Many local health departments find that the traditional public health functions can be overwhelmed by the demand for personal health services.

The causes of **death** and disease have changed in the last hundred years. In 1895 the principal causes of death were tuberculosis and pneumonia. In 1995 the primary causes of death were heart disease, stroke and **cancer**, while injuries remain the leading cause of premature death. Perhaps more fundamentally the cultural construction of disease has shifted as epidemiological investigations repeatedly implicate personal and social behaviors as modifiable risk factors for disease. The frontier of public health threats now includes **violence**, unintentional injury, substance use, **tobacco**, unsafe sex, dietary fat and community disempowerment. These factors move the locus of action away from the biomedical concerns of clinical medicine, and require interventional skills quite unlike those historically stressed by **medical schools**. The medical community drifts piecemeal towards developing behavioral skills that do not resemble the technical aspects of clinical intervention in which it excels. Conflict between medical culture and public-health culture has been slow to resolve.

Because public-health techniques now include social marketing, media techniques and **information** campaigns, employers and insurers with a natural interest in the health of their populations have begun to engage in public-health practice. Public and private sectors will continue to show a greater confluence of interest and practice in public health.

A natural dilemma arises for public health as it addresses behavioral determinants of disease. There is conflict between eliminating risky behavior (abstinence) and making risky behavior safer (protection). Public-health workers tend to think in practical terms and often consider both goals compatible means to the end of disease reduction. To its chagrin, the public-health community has frequently found the puritan strains of American culture vigorous enough to squelch or temper the battle cry, "Don't indulge! But...if you do, do it safely."

Further reading

Institute of Medicine (1988) *The Future of Public Health*, Washington, DC: National Academy Press.
Winslow, C.E.A. (1923) *The Evolution and Significance of the Modern Public Health Campaign*, New Haven: Yale University Press.

DAVID BISHAI

public housing

US public housing was never the major source of housing for the poor that it was in many European societies. Even at its height in the postwar period, fewer than 5 percent of Americans lived in federally funded subsidized housing projects. The very term popularly used to refer to such housing – "the projects" – carries associations of ghettoization and social pathology, and is often used to stand for the presumed failures of liberalism as manifested in federal anti-poverty programs.

Nonetheless, in the 1930s, public housing was conceived with high hopes that it would be a stepping stone to independent private home-ownership for the majority of its tenants. The story of its failure is also the story of urban social policy more broadly, which was utilized in the service of protecting private investment and was shaped in concert with the market interests of **real-estate**

agents and developers. Moreover, most federal housing policies tended to favor programs that encouraged private home-ownership, like low-interest guaranteed mortgages.

The first public housing projects, located in cities such as **Atlanta, GA**, **New York** City, NY and **Chicago, IL** were low-rise constructions from which the poorest and those believed to be socially "deviant," like single mothers, were initially barred. In the post-Second World War era, with an increase in land values in inner cities and a massive northern **migration** of blacks, public housing design moved towards the construction of high-rise "superblocks." These seemed cost-efficient and politically expedient for the maintenance of racially segregated **neighborhoods**. Even then, however, the design of high-rise public housing was accompanied by a spirit of utopian optimism, influenced by such modernist architects and urban planners as Le Corbusier, who believed that high-rise buildings, designed by professional planners and managed by a state conceptualized as benign and rational, were the prototypical homes of the future. Such futuristic ideals quickly soured in developments like Robert Taylor Homes in south Chicago which, from the beginning, were poorly maintained and lacked such amenities as communal facilities and safe play spaces for children. They were used by city governments as places where the poorest **African Americans** could be "contained," isolated from **white** working-class and **middle-class** neighborhoods. Unlike the earliest years of public housing, any pretense of screening tenants fell by the wayside and it quickly became the housing of last resort now sheltering mostly single mothers and their children living on benefits.

The Pruitt-Igoe housing project in **St. Louis, MO** came to represent the failure of modernist high-rise public housing. Built in the mid-1950s, it was demolished a mere twenty years later after being deemed an ungovernable tangle of pathology. In his ethnographic study of life in Pruitt-Igoe, sociologist Lee Rainwater referred to it as "a federally built and supported slum."

In 1965 HUD (Department of Housing and Urban Development) was established as part of President Johnson's **War on Poverty** and took over public housing. Federal housing programs moved away from supporting new construction to emphasizing subsidized rents for the poor in buildings managed by private landlords (for example, Section 8 certificates). In 1989, when Jack Kemp was appointed HUD secretary by then-President George **Bush**, many city housing authorities had fallen into receivership or had come close to bankruptcy, overwhelmed by inadequate funding from the federal government for maintenance and repair of their aging public-housing projects. Kemp encouraged the expansion of Tenant (or Resident) Management Organizations, the oldest of which dated back to the mid-1970s, to take over the operation of their projects from government agencies deemed incompetent and overly bureaucratic. While a few Tenant Management Organizations became nationally known for the improvements they were able to make in their communities and for their charismatic leaders, this model proved very difficult to put into practice on a large scale. Few of these organizations were actually able to become completely independent of their local housing authorities. In the late 1990s, several of even the most famous tenant-management projects, including Bromley-Heath in **Boston** and Cochran Gardens in St. Louis, were removed from tenant control and returned to being managed by their local housing authorities amidst charges of financial improprieties and claims that the tenant-management board failed to enforce new strict HUD regulations regarding tenant conduct.

In 1993, HOPE VI was adopted by HUD for the rehabilitation of public housing. HOPE VI provides some federal funding for capital improvements and encourages city housing authorities to renovate their developments using a combination of public and private sources. Properties rehabilitated under the HOPE VI program are also required to maintain a balance of low-income, working-class and even middle-class tenants. Although several housing developments are currently undergoing substantive remodeling, it is unclear what the future of these mixed-income communities will be.

Further reading

Naparstek, A., Dooley, D., Smith, R. and The Urban Institute/Aspen Systems Corporation (1997) *Community Building in Public Housing: Ties that Bind People and Their Communities*, Washington, DC: Civic Practices Network.
Rainwater, L. (1971) *Behind Ghetto Walls*, Chicago: Atherton-Aldine.
Varady, D., Preiser, W.F.E. and Russell, F. (eds) (1998) *New Directions in Urban Public Housing*, Rutgers: Center for Urban Policy Research.

SUSAN BRIN HYATT

public intellectuals *see* intellectuals/culture wars

Public Radio International (PRI)

Public Radio International, founded in 1983 as American Public Radio, acquires, develops, funds and distributes programming from a variety of station-based, independent and international producers. It was founded to provide more diversity in programming sources. Together with **NPR** and the Corporation for Public Broadcasting, it began AMERICA ONE, a 24-hour English language audio channel headquartered in Munich. PRI features programming in four general areas: **news** and information; **comedy** and variety; **classical music** and contemporary music. Programming includes *St. Paul Sunday Morning*, *A Prairie Home Companion*, *Whad'Ya Know?* and *The World*, a collaborative 1-hour weekday with the BBC.

GAIL HENSON

public relations

Public-relations professionals do not simply help their clients to communicate with the public, they also create news – many of the news stories that one reads and watches come from materials provided by PR firms. For example, women's smoking stopped being a taboo when Edward Bernays, hired by American Tobacco Company, asked his women friends to smoke during an Easter parade on New York's Fifth Avenue (1929). This image of women smoking in public appeared in **newspapers**, and Bernays, a nephew of Freud, used psychology to build the image of an emancipated woman as one who smoked. Public relations is not simply a press-wing for different big corporations, governments and non-profit organizations; its professionals exert the power of persuasion by gauging cultural trends and representing them to the public in a way that is beneficial to its clients, thus affecting social policies and the cultural landscape.

PR professionals are recruited not only from young people who have specialized degrees, but are also former journalists and retired politicians who know the system of the press, the government and their relationship with the public. These firms specialize in issue and crisis management. Hence, when Cyanide-tainted Tylenol was found in 1982, resulting in seven deaths, its manufacturer, Johnson & Johnson spent millions to rebuild its image; by promoting itself as a socially responsible company, PR helped it successfully overcome this crisis.

In contemporary America, more than $10 billion is spent on public relations annually. With fewer journalists and the price of investigative news reporting high, news divisions are relying on PR news releases to fill up their pages and airtime. There are more people working for PR than for news; they provide sophisticated press packages and video clips that may be published without changes.

Government policies are affected when corporations hire public-relations firms to found so-called grassroots citizen campaigns to lobby Washington and other local and state governments. National Smokers Alliance, a group that champions smokers' rights, was created by a PR firm with money from Phillip Morris. The government itself has also relied on PR, from the setting-up of the office of War Information during the Second World War to spin-doctors hired by different administrations. Not only American government, but foreign governments, like Kuwait, during the **Gulf War**, and Colombia, also hire big American PR firms to build their image. Other non-profit organizations also hire PR firms (for example, the US Conference of Catholic Bishops, to promote an anti-**abortion** message).

The image of the PR professional remains rather unsavory in media, especially when associated in the1990s with political lies and manipulation (*Wag the Dog*, 1998; *Primary Colors*, 1999; television's *Spin City*, ABC, 1996–).

Further reading

Hazen, D. and Winokur, J. (1997) *We the Media*, New York: The New Press.

CINDY WONG

public schools

The public system of education in the United States is a government-controlled, age-graded, hierarchically structured, free and often compulsory system composed of groups of schools administered by full-time experts and staffed primarily by state-certified teachers. During the first three-quarters of the nineteenth century, industrialization, urbanization, the development of a **working class**, the shift in the definitions and role of the **family** and the **state**'s assumption of responsibility for certain aspects of social **welfare** all contributed to the establishment and standardization of state systems of education designed to achieve specific public policies and, ostensibly, to give all **children** access to educational opportunity and thus to social and economic advancement.

Within each state, public schools are generally organized into districts, originally intended to allow for local control within state systems of education, but which also lead to inequity of educational opportunity because a district is only as wealthy as the home-owners within it (see **financial aid**). Each school district is governed by a local **school board**, composed of **community** and business people, as well as an administrative hierarchy. These governing bodies choose leaders, collect school **taxes**, select curricular materials and hire teachers – all within parameters dictated by the state.

The administrative hierarchy of public schools includes, at the top, superintendents, whose primary role is to supervise classroom instruction and assure curricular uniformity and continuity across the elementary schools (kindergarten through 5th or 6th grade, for children ages five to twelve), middle schools (6th or 7th grades through 8th grade, ages twelve to fourteen) and **high schools** (9th to 12th grades, ages fourteen to eighteen) which compose a district. Next in the hierarchy, principals are responsible for administering school policy within their individual elementary, middle or secondary schools. School-board members, superintendents and principals – the three most powerful contingents in public-school systems – tend to be **white**, professional males. Teachers, however, tend to be primarily female, particularly at the elementary level.

Teachers in public schools must adhere to strict, district- and state-mandated policies and curricular guides. Throughout the history of public schooling there have been debates about curricula – what students study in school (which texts written from whose perspectives and including whom) and what they and teachers may and may not talk about (e.g. **abortion**, **religion** and other controversial issues may be defined but not discussed) – and pedagogical approaches, which range from conservative, highly structured and highly standardized models to critical, constructivist pedagogies which draw on and attempt to develop the active, creative capacities and diversities of learners. (See **education and society** for an extended discussion of these last two points.)

Questions of who has access to quality education have also been central to conceptualizations and reforms of public education. Segregation in public schools in the United States has often correlated with the maintenance of a cheap labor force. Immigrants in the late nineteenth and early twentieth centuries – first Japanese, Chinese and Korean immigrants, who worked for low wages on railroads, in factories and on farms, then **African Americans** in the **South**, who worked for industrialization and the maintenance of **agriculture**, and then Mexican farm workers in the early twentieth century – were segregated in public schools and received an inferior education to that of their European American counterparts. There were numerous "separate-but-equal" rulings in the courts regarding **segregation** in the public schools, and it was not until 1954 that the US **Supreme Court** ruled, in *Brown* **v.** *Board of Education of Topeka*, Kansas, that separate schools were inherently unequal and that school desegregation was necessary. This decision legitimated education and public schooling as an appropriate arena for societal issues and conflicts; the classroom became the context of social issues, with teachers *in loco parentis*, and the state with its agenda for its ward. While institutional segregation

has been challenged by law, unofficial segregation remains in the form of attendance patterns across schools (most students are assigned to neighborhood schools) and tracking within schools, which critics suggest often reinforces racial and socioeconomic inequities.

Just after the Second World War, the National Education Association and the American Federation of Teachers – the two largest teachers' **unions** in the United States – made several unsuccessful attempts to elicit more federal aid for schools. But it was only after the launching of Sputnik in 1957, when schools were criticized for failing to produce enough scientists and engineers, that the federal government stepped in to try to assuage the distrust in educators, and it did so with the National Defense Education Act of 1958. This Act provided money for specific educational categories, including science, **mathematics**, foreign languages and counseling and testing programs (see **standardized testing**). Its passage signified that the federal government would not simply supply monies to states, but would attempt to influence the curriculum taught in schools.

The appropriation of curricular choices from educators continued as a theme, as state departments of education as well as local governing bodies of schools became increasingly composed of politicians and business people – neither educators nor representatives of the majority of the population whom schools serve. After the Sputnik-inspired focus on math, science and foreign languages in the late 1950s, the 1960s and 1970s saw first a swing towards more progressive and alternative forms of education (see **education: values and beliefs**) and then a back-to-basics movement in the schools, with an emphasis on reading, writing and arithmetic.

The 1980s and 1990s ushered in a proliferation of options within the American public-school system. Among these are **charter schools**, which are public schools operating under a contract or charter granted by a school district, university, state education board, or some other public authority, depending on the state. Organized by teachers, business people and/or other interested parties, charter schools are generally non-selective, tuition-free, non-sectarian and based on choice. There are also vouchers and other school-choice plans that aim to offer parents and students the opportunity to select and receive public monies for where children attend school, regardless of geographical or financial status.

None of the reforms to public schools, however, has changed the reality of inequitable resources, support and access among the school children of the United States. Even in its new diversified forms, the public-school system seems to continue to reinforce social inequity, sorting students by **race**, **ethnicity**, social **class**, gender and special interest through curricular choices, pedagogical approaches, counseling and standardized testing – the gate-keeping mechanisms which regulate educational access and advancement.

Further reading

Spring, J. (1994) *The American School: 1642–1993*, 3rd edn, New York: McGraw-Hill, Inc.

Katz, M.B. (1987) *Reconstructing American Education*, Cambridge, MA: Harvard University Press.

ALISON COOK-SATHER

publishing

While traditionally seen as a "gentleman's" profession marked by small, intimate production, intellectual values and high culture (except for some commercial presses), late twentieth century book publishing in America told, once again, the story of corporate mergers within a realm defined by public discourse. The once-artisanal imagery of a pre-industrial field has given way to intensive marketing, corporate control, rapid evaluations of success and failure and balance sheets based on subsidiary rights rather than volumes sold or read. Book publishers like Simon & Schuster and The Free Press are part of Viacom, Bantam Doubleday Dell was absorbed by Bertelsmann AG of Germany, HarperCollins forms part of the News Corporation and Random House, Knopf, Pantheon, Crown and Ballantine are all under Advance Publication. While the bestsellers published by big houses dominate the marketplace, there are, nonetheless, some independent publishing houses and numerous university presses –

publishing can still be done on a relatively cheap scale. To understand American publishing culture one has to recognize its product as well as its economic structure.

Reading was one of the most popular leisure activities in the first half of the twentieth century, and led to the establishment of distinguished publishers like Random House (1925) and Alfred Knopf (1915) beside older houses like Houghton Mifflin. **New York** City, NY dominated publication, although **Philadelphia**, **Boston** and other cities were active centers. This was also an era of important editors who found and guided many of America's great writers. While sales were important, Random House also supported Modern Library editions that made world and American classics accessible for generations. Bookstores, meanwhile, were elite retreats and nurturing local establishments.

After the Second World War, both the expanding markets fostered by the **GI Bill** and new families of the **baby boom** increased the market for textbooks and other sales. This was also the era in which paperbacks – and paperback publishers – provided America with even cheaper reading. By the 1960s, publishers expanded by going public (selling stock in private companies) and merging, a pattern that would intensify thereafter. The danger was overproduction, although the number of publishers allowed both avant-garde and saccharine bestsellers to find their way to market. Yet mergers soon combined paperback and hardback houses, as well as other media companies, changing publishing inexorably into a business driven by deals rather than culture.

But what of the product? Major fiction and social issues/non-fiction attract people's attention and prestigious book reviews in the *New York Times* and other serious news publications. Yet, specialized lists and interests that distinguish houses and editors compete with the need for mass sales and links to movies or other media. Publishers need the regular summer blockbuster by Danielle Steele, Tom Clancy or Elmore Leonard, or sleepers like *Midnight in the Garden of Good and Evil*, which stayed on the *New York Time*'s bestsellers list for years. Prizes like the **Pulitzer Prize** or the American Book Award confer prestige, but do not necessarily provide the profits that a romance, a successful children's series or an instant celebrity book will rake in.

In fact, the business produces many types of books. The education book market, for example, now accounts for more than 20 percent of all book sales (over $20 billion annually) in America, dominated by Harcourt General and McGraw-Hill. This also vests power with state officials who may decide on textbooks for large markets like **Texas** schools.

With increasing affluence, there are many non-fiction "lifestyle" books published on **hunting**, **tennis**, **cooking** and home decorating. In a culture that claims everyone can succeed, more books are published on self-improvement – how to get thin, to have self-esteem, to get rich. Graphic novels, upscale **comic** books, try to appeal to people who do not read much. Audio books cater to older people and to commuters who spend a great deal of time in their cars. **Children** and **teenagers** also create a lucrative market through direct sales, and schools and **libraries**.

Book publishing then has met an extremely diversified market, but, more and more, books are published only because there is a perceived market, not because of literary and social values. This is especially true in terms of relations with other media, where books have established an ever-closer relationship with movies and, to a lesser extent, **television**. Bestsellers by authors such as Robin Cook, Michael Crichton, Tom Clancy, Stephen **King** and John **Grisham** seem to go immediately from novels into movies. In turn, novelization publishes books based on successful movies. Celebrity biographies and product linkages (e.g. *Star Trek* guides) also increase mutual sales. Mergers have intensified these connections – with their diversified holdings, conglomerates want to sell not only the book, but the toy, the **game**, the T-shirt and the music that go along with the book.

The situation is uniquely American in that publishing must compete with other **mass media** to become lucrative. While Gallimard makes an annual 3 percent profit, and is considered healthy, American publishing houses have a profit target of 12–15 percent. The big conglomerates envision their publishing arms to be as remunerative as **cable** television and film. Newhouse bought Random House for $60 million; ten years later it

is worth $1 billion. Hence, publishers bet on high advances for famous writers for perceived huge returns, while foreclosing development of unknowns or risky topics.

With publishing concentrating more and more on celebrities, the overheads of publishing houses have also increased. Instead of paying editors the same salaries as university professors, book publishers emulate the lifestyle of their colleagues in **Hollywood**. More importantly, more and more money is spent on promotion and marketing; agents shove aside editors. Sales conferences at Random House can cost up to $1 million. Publishers then see themselves unable to publish a book that will sell less than 20,000 copies to cover an average overhead of $100,000.

Large companies, like News Corporation, are also major players in American politics. The infamous $4.5 million advance proposed to Newt Gingrich by Rupert Murdoch raised many eyebrows, since the return of such a book could never offset the original payment. Furthermore, as Andre Schiffrin, director of the independent New Press, points out, "Harper, Random House, and Simon & Schuster were once bastions of New Deal liberalism. Yet the current output of US publishing is markedly to the right" (Hazen and Winokur 1997: 83). The publishing industries in the 1990s were comfortable saying that their decisions had to be made under market pressure.

Nonetheless, in a market economy where goods need to be sold and deposed regularly, books have limited shelf-lives. If they do not sell, they go back to the warehouse and will be recycled as remainders, unloaded at much cheaper prices (instead of being carried as taxable resources). This is also a related issue of the proliferation of giant chain bookstores. Barnes and Noble had 25 percent market share in the first quarter of 1996. Other big stores like Borders and the online booksellers Amazon.com all concentrate their sales on glossy bestsellers. Publishers also provide "co-op" **advertising** money to help sell their books, either through bookstore advertising or in-store advertisement placements. Independent book stores are increasingly squeezed out, as played out uncritically in *You've Got Mail* (1999) where Tom **Hanks**, a corporate type, bought up Meg Ryan's small children's bookstore.

Though the picture is bleak for independent book publishers, book stores and readers who sort these books, independent houses like Grove Press, New Directions, Beacon Press, Workman Publishing, New Left Books and the New Press have promoted more innovative publications and alternative agendas. Grove Press, for example, fought censorship in the 1950s, while New Directions fostered attention for authors as diverse as Borges and Djuna Barnes. University presses are still the major sources for scholarly publications that normally do not expect much profit. They are subsidized by universities that traditionally have seen these arms as ground for furthering intellectual debates, even though they too are getting more aware of the bottom line.

Publishing, then, has gone from being an intellectual pursuit with commercial interests to conglomerate businesses in which books are commodities. While American publishers produce tens of thousands of titles, **freedom** of **information** and democracy of thought are constrained by the structure of the market, which nonetheless allows cracks of free or alternative expression to surface and, at times, succeed. The prospect of electronic publishing and distribution may radically change this in the next few decades. Yet, the patterns rehearsed here are already familiar from other media, and may predict some of the forms that an electronic economy of culture will take.

Further reading

Coser, L., Kadushin, C. and Powell, W. (1982) *Books*, New York: Basic Books.

Hazen, D. and Winokur, J. (1997) *We the Media*, New York: The New Press.

Whiteside, T. (1981) *The Blockbuster Complex*, Middletown: Wesleyan.

CINDY WONG

Puerto Ricans

Approximately 3 million Puerto Ricans live in the continental United States, with a large concentration of 2 million in **New York** City. **Migration** from **Puerto Rico** to New York began with merchants in the seventeenth and eighteenth centuries. In the second half of the nineteenth century, most were political exiles. At the close of the century, many **cigar** makers, educated and politicized through workplace readings, settled in Lower Manhattan.

Since Spain ceded Puerto Rico to the US in 1898, the United States has served as the Puerto Rican escape valve to combat unemployment, economic hardship and overpopulation, despite mainland living conditions that sometimes were worse than those left behind. Once Puerto Ricans were granted citizenship in 1917, almost 11,000 moved to New York, creating a large enclave in East **Harlem**, where previous Puerto Rican immigrants had settled. In this **community**, later known as El Barrio, they preserved their culture and language through community groups and Spanish-language **newspapers** and books.

The most extensive migration occurred after the Second World War as thousands saw their way of life disappear as industrialization, the decimation of **agriculture** and population growth rapidly created severe unemployment. In the 1950s, airlines introduced lower fares and opportunities for unskilled, semi-skilled and agricultural labor expanded on the mainland. An estimated 470,000 predominantly **working-class** and rural Puerto Ricans emigrated, including more women than previously. During the 1950s and 1960s, most migrants settled in New York City and New Jersey, but others populated **Chicago, IL**, **Philadelphia, PA** and **Cleveland, OH**.

Although American citizens, Puerto Ricans were largely poor immigrants. They occupied substandard housing, faced unscrupulous landlords and lacked familiarity with US cities and cold weather. They faced discrimination because of their **race** and ethnicity, **language** (and accents) and **religion**. Other problems of **inner-city** poverty – crime, **gangs**, drugs and, more recently, high rates of **AIDS**/HIV – also afflicted them.

Religious and civic associations formed a collective fight against racism and discrimination, and gave the immigrants a political voice and a sense of dignity. They fought being viewed as the stereotypical **Latino** portrayed in Leonard **Bernstein**'s **musical**/film *West Side Story* (1957, film 1961). The Puerto Rican Travelling Theater, founded in 1967, presents plays in English and

Spanish. The Museo del Barrio, founded in 1969, emphasizes contemporary Puerto Rican and Latin American artists.

In the 1970s, the pattern of migration began to shift. Many low-skilled workers returned as mainland manufacturing declined and jobs moved overseas. Others, who never intended to stay permanently, returned after years of work to buy their dream house. Yet, after the 1980s, many highly skilled university graduates and professionals reversed this flow, leaving the island to settle in the states.

The generation of Puerto Ricans born in the (continental) United States follows a different path. Taking advantage of educational opportunities, fluent in English, versed in American culture and seeking employment in the **civil-rights** era, they leave the barrio and have made inroads in the professions, the visual and **performing arts**, **mass media**, education and politics.

Further reading

Rodriguez, C. (1989) *Puerto Ricans Born in the U.S.A.*, Boulder: Westview Press.
Sánchez Korrol, V. (1994) *From Colonia to Community: The History of Puerto Ricans in New York City*, Berkeley: University of California.

CARMEN C. ESTEVES

Puerto Rico

One of the largest **Caribbean** islands between **Florida** and South America, Puerto Rico is still only 100 miles long and 33 miles wide, with a total area of 3,515 square miles. It contains extraordinary beaches, one of the world's largest river cave systems and the United States **park** systems' only tropical rainforest. Its tropical climate makes it a favorite vacation destination.

Sponsored by the Spanish Crown, Columbus reached the shores of this beautiful, mountainous island on his second voyage in 1493. The approximately 30,000 Arawak (Taino) who inhabited the island continued their way of life until 1508, when the island began to be settled by the Spanish and they were enslaved to work in mines and later in **agriculture**. By 1550 the **American** **Indian** population had been decimated by European diseases and maltreatment, as well as by flight and failed rebellions. Slaves from West Africa replaced the native population, their numbers increasing sharply in the first half of the nineteenth century as Puerto Rico moved to large-scale sugar production.

Today's population of almost 4 million reflects this historical background in its racial and cultural characteristics in an extremely densely populated and predominantly urban environment. Racially, the population consists of the progeny of **white** and **African American** families, but it is a largely mulatto mixture of whites, blacks and Arawaks. Some coastal towns are inhabited by a majority of blacks, attesting to a past of plantation slavery in these areas. Puerto Rico's Spanish **language** and the dominance of Catholicism are derivatives of Spain.

Puerto Rico has never been a free and independent nation. After three centuries of absolute and often oppressive Spanish rule, Spain ceded it to the United States in 1898, after its military occupation in the Spanish American War. For more than one hundred years, this relationship with the US has been defined through a web of often tense and ambivalent political, economic, social and cultural ties. In 1917, as the US prepared to enter the First World War, for example, Puerto Ricans were granted citizenship and the right to elect their entire legislature. Nevertheless, the appointed governor maintained the power to veto legislation and to select judicial and executive officers, and **Congress** could annul legislation.

It was not until 1948 that Puerto Ricans elected their own governor. The result was a mandate for Muñoz Marín, the architect of the island's economic development program, Operation Bootstrap, and a proponent of turning Puerto Rico into an *Estado Libre Asociado* – an associated free state. On July 25, 1952, the Commonwealth of Puerto Rico was created with its own constitution. Education, health, justice and welfare are under Puerto Rican control. The United States retains control over **trade**, defense, **immigration**, the postal system, the currency and international relations.

For decades, the organization of political parties focused on the options for the political status of the island: independence, statehood or continuation of semi-autonomous Commonwealth status. When the Popular Democratic Party was formed in 1938, its program focused on improving the stagnant economy and poor living conditions. As it launched Operation Bootstrap, it was forced to take a pro-Commonwealth position to attract corporations that were hesitant to invest resources in an independent Puerto Rico.

The economy of the island has evolved from agricultural to industrial since the 1940s. In 1955, for the first time, manufacturing contributed more to the economy than agriculture. The transition displaced workers and families from rural areas, where two-thirds of the population lived in 1940, to towns and urban centers where two-thirds of Puerto Ricans live now, including the capital, San Juan (437,745 in 1990), Bayamon, Ponce, Carolina and Caguas. Manufacturing provides about 40 percent of the gross domestic product, with more than one hundred pharmaceutical companies, the main industry, accounting for one-quarter of that total.

Operation Bootstrap emphasized industry, **tourism** and the production of rum. Local tax exemptions were provided for industrial and tourism development, and promotional campaigns were initiated in the United States to attract investors and visitors. Congress also sanctioned federal corporate tax exemptions on profits earned on the island. These stimulated growth, but budget cuts pressured Congress to phase them out over ten years, beginning in 1996, exacerbating Puerto Rico's high unemployment rate.

In politics, Puerto Ricans hold US passports and vote in state and national elections when residing in the (continental) United States. They do not vote for the president or have voting representatives in Congress when living on the island.

Throughout the twentieth century, Puerto Ricans have struggled to maintain their identity under the process of acculturation that started in 1898. Although, officially, Puerto Rico has two **languages**, Spanish and English, Puerto Ricans have always considered Spanish to be their mother tongue. It reflects the diversity of Puerto Rico's heritage – many towns have maintained their pre-

Columbian names and many other pre-Columbian and African words are part of everyday speech. The intrusion of English was first felt through imported consumer products; adults asked for Singers, not sewing machines. English also became a mandated subject in **public schools**. It became the second language of millions of largely **working-class** Puerto Ricans in the continental United States, who maintain a migratory circle between the island and mainland cities.

Music and **food** are bastions of cultural resistance. **Salsa** is heard from home and car radios. American **fast food** is found throughout the island, but traditional food remains the staple in most households and restaurants. Rice and small pink or kidney beans, whole roast suckling pig, prepared for the **holidays** and large family reunions, and fresh ham, seasoned with *adobo*, a thick paste of garlic, olive oil, vinegar, peppercorns, salt and oregano, remain favorites of the Puerto Rican table. Love of the homeland, culture and strong **family** ties also prove evident in the joyful cheers that spontaneously erupt among planeloads of returning Puerto Ricans as they land on their island.

Further reading

Melendez, E. and Melendez, E. (eds) (1993) *Colonial Dilemma: Critical Perspectives on Contemporary Puerto Rico*, Boston: South End.

Morales Carrion, A. (ed.) (1983) *Puerto Rico*, New York: W.W. Norton.

CARMEN C. ESTEVES

Pulitzer Prize

Awarded annually by Columbia University since 1917, the Pulitzer Prize recognizes achievements in American journalism, letters, **drama** and music. The journalism category has fourteen separate awards, while the letters category offers awards for fiction, **history**, **poetry**, biography or autobiography, and general non-fiction. A Pulitzer-Prize board makes recommendations for the prizes, which include a gold medal for public service in journalism and $5,000 awards for the other categories. Hungarian-born immigrant Joseph

Pulitzer, publisher and owner of the *St. Louis-Dispatch* and the *New York World*, endowed both the Pulitzer Prizes and the Columbia University's Graduate School of Journalism.

COURTNEY BENNETT

punk rock

Descended from the sonic experimentation of the Stooges and the Velvet Underground and the glam performance of the New York Dolls, punk rock developed in **New York** City, NY at the CBGB club on the Bowery in 1974. The sound was alternately loud and fast, abrasive, discordant and melodic as practiced by such performers as the Ramones, the Patti Smith Group, and the Heartbreakers. Both retro-populist and avant-garde experimental, punk was defined more by attitude than musical style, as expressed in such song titles as "I Don't Care," "Blank Generation," and "I Wanna Be Sedated." In 1976 punk traveled across the Atlantic Ocean, becoming an international media sensation when British groups like the Sex Pistols and the Clash topped the charts with their scandalous calls for anarchy and violence. In London and New York punk caught the spirit of the decline of the West in the 1970s.

Punk rock spread in the following years and, by the end of the 1970s, vibrant local scenes had developed in **Los Angeles, CA**, **San Francisco, CA**, **Austin, TX**, Athens, GA, Vancouver, British Colombia (**Canada**) and countless other towns across North America. By 1980 a mutant offspring called hardcore had developed, most vibrantly in the **suburban** communities of Southern **California**. Bands such as Black Flag, the Middle Class and the Adolescents carried on the spirit of punk protest through such songs as "No Values," "Love is Just a Tool," and "Kids of the Black Hole." The hardcore punk scenes were especially noted for their violence, both between various punks and between punks and police.

DEWAR MACLEOD

puritanism

Puritanism began as a religious reform movement within the Church of England and spread to the northern English colonies in the early and middle seventeenth century. In recent years the term has often been used simply as a pejorative to designate anyone who is prudish, unemotional or intolerant. However, strains of Puritanism persisted even in the last half of the twentieth century.

Early American puritans hoped to establish a city of God that would fuse the political and religious community into a theocracy. Although less prevalent in the 1950s and 1960s, this changed in the 1970s with the development of organizations such as the **Moral Majority** and the Christian Coalition. These groups pursued avowedly Christian agendas and became influential in politics, especially at the level of congressional and senatorial primaries. A second element in Puritanism was the castigation of sensual pleasures. While the 1960s marked a substantial change in social conventions, it continued to be the case that prostitution was only legal in certain parts of Nevada, recreational drug use was severely punished and references to sex on **radio** and **television** were highly constricted. A less famous aspect of Puritanism was its emphasis on public sermons as a means of excoriating the sins of the **community**. These often strayed from traditional Biblical topics and became detailed critiques of the political system and the personal responsibility of those within it. This use of the sermon was employed by both ends of the political spectrum, from Martin Luther **King**, Jr. challenging **segregation** to conservative television evangelists attacking the moral decay of the country and its leaders.

RODGER JACKSON

Puzo, Mario

b. 1920; d. 1999

Novelist, seen by many critics as responsible for

killing **Italian American** literature with the publication of *The Godfather* (1969). **New York**-born and educated, Puzo published two critically acclaimed, but largely unread novels (*The Fortunate Pilgrim* 1965; *The Dark Arena*, 1970), before deciding to write his first pulp novel. *The Godfather* mixed narratives from Italian American **immigration** history with invented traditions about the Mafia (e.g. their use of the term "godfather"), many of which were then picked up by members of the mob (especially after the success of the **Hollywood** movie trilogy, for which Puzo's screenplays earned two Oscars). Following the Godfather series, mob family chronicles became the staple for Italian American novels.

ROBERT GREGG

Pynchon, Thomas
b. 1937

Certainly one of the most important of America's postwar novelists. In works such as *V* (1963), *Gravity's Rainbow* (1973) and *Mason and Dixon* (1997), Pynchon combined pyrotechnic verbal skills and a near-encyclopedic knowledge of both learned and popular culture to produce a distinctive fictional universe, rife with paranoiac visions and textual puzzles. Along with J.D. **Salinger**, Pynchon was also one of literary America's most famous recluses, so successfully excluding the trappings of public **celebrity** that his whereabouts became a topic of rumor and speculation. This mysterious and shadowy existence, along with his unique fictional vision, found a ready fit to an age much given over to elaborate conspiracies about the powers-that-be.

MARK BREWIN

Q

Quakers

The Religious Society of Friends of the Truth (Quakers) was introduced into the United States by groups of religious mystics arriving from England in the mid-1700s. Centered in New Jersey, North Carolina, Pennsylvania and Virginia, Quakers became known for several aspects of their theology: commitment to non-violence; wide-ranging public service (e.g. hospitals, orphanages, anti-slavery advocacy and service to the poor); an emphasis on strict religious integrity in daily life (e.g. economic transactions); worship service which lacked paid or "hireling" ministers, but instead was "unprogrammed," based upon silent waiting for Divine inspiration; and social insularity that sought to protect their communities from corruption by "the world's people." Often, these communities were marked by idiosyncratic language and dress.

The third-largest American denomination in 1750, their proportion had declined to ninth-largest by 1820. Nevertheless, during the next century, Quakers spread across the United States, holding leadership roles – both as individuals and congregations – in various reform movements (notably **African American**, Native American and women's rights and **prison** reform) and sending vigorous missionary envoys to establish schools and hospitals in Africa, the Middle East and Asia. As Quakers moved west from the US east coast, worship styles changed also, and in many locations Quakerism now includes paid profes-sional ministers and "programmed" services that include a prepared sermon and music. In 1990 there were about 300,000 Quakers in the world, of whom about one-third were in the United States. Most modern Friends have abandoned specialized communities, language and dress. However, Quakers remain active in a wide range of social reform, educational and quasi-political organizations, which promote the peace and justice testimonies that are central to their theology.

EMMA LAPSANSKY

Queens *see* New York City and its boroughs

queer

"Queer" emerged as a politically charged term around the time that **AIDS** politics gathered urgent momentum. With the advent of such groups as **ACT UP** (AIDS Coalition to Unleash Power, 1987) and Queer Nation (1990), issues of **homophobia** and **gender and sexuality** were soon recognized as key political concerns. While **Stonewall** (1969) served as the historical marker for gay and lesbian politics and identity, many younger activists saw this version of identity as too assimilated in- and abject to heterosexual culture. Strategies for AIDS activism, on the other hand, demanded a radical term that announced the fact that the disease was particularly affecting those whose sexual desire was very different from the heterosexual norm. "Queer" fit the bill.

From the streets to the radical possibilities of the ivory tower the notion of queer found its way into departments of English Literature, **Film** Studies and even **Architecture**. In 1990 Judith Butler's *Gender Trouble: Feminism and the Subversion of Identity* and Eve Kosofsky Sedgwick's *Epistemology of the Closet* (1990) arguably set the stage for queer theory. Scholars such as these and Michael Warner rethought the essentializing propositions of identity politics that most often attended traditional gay, lesbian and feminist politics. Merging especially the works of Michel Foucault, Louis Althusser and Jacques Derrida, American queer theorists queered poststructural itself. After all, Althusser and Derrida make strange bedfellows.

The vitality and importance of the term "queer" (although often perceived as recapitulating a historically pejorative adjective) is its suggestive refusal of cultural conditions that insist on an identity as such. The dilemma "queers" once again face, as does any radical social movement, is the solidification of meaning for this once radical word.

Under the aegis of capitalism, it is no surprise that "Queer Theory" has become a cottage industry.

See also: gender and sexuality

DAVID GERSTNER

quinceaños

Lavish, traditional **coming-of-age** celebration or a young woman's fifteenth birthday, practiced in Hispanic countries and **Latino** diaspora communities. Quinceaños parties in **upper-class** families are similar to debutante balls. They take place in private clubs or fancy hotels, and groups of wealthy women dressed in elegant designer gowns are formally presented to society. **Middle-class** celebrations are usually less ostentatious and often take place in family **homes**. The inclusion of a Catholic Mass as part of the festivities is losing popularity. For some assimilated families it has been replaced by a sweet-sixteen party.

CARMEN C. ESTEVES

R

race and ethnicity

The fundamental discourse of division in American culture for the last three centuries has been that of race, specifically, the division of "black" and "**white**." In many ways, in fact, this framework has eclipsed fundamental issues of **class** and confused issues of gender and citizenship, especially in everyday discussion. Other groups – Native Americans, **Asian Americans**, **Hispanics**, **Irish Americans**, **Jews**, etc. – have "fit" into American society in terms of this division as well. Hence, terms like "ethnicity" or stereotypes of new immigrants cannot be discussed without some understanding of the history and construction of race.

Race, in turn, has fundamentally referred to the social construction of **biology**. Often, this has meant phenotype – what someone looks like, based on skin color and a few associated categories – inscribed on the **body**. Genealogy was imputed via an unbalanced cultural model; "one drop" of **African American** blood determined race in many states. This also precluded the construction of intermediate groups (mestizo) found in Latin American societies; "half-breed" was an insult, not a category. In practical terms, "looking" black or Indian or Chinese was the social determinant of racial categorization. While the category "mulatto" might be recognized (or even sanctioned in **New Orleans**), legally these people were defined as black – hence, the longstanding category of the "tragic mulatto" and issues of "passing" (blacks living as white) which haunt literature and film.

These categories had further implications for policy and thought in the early Republic, where the Constitution defined slaves as the equivalent of three-fifths of a human being. Scientists also argued polygenetic versus monogenetic models of racial origin which again made non-white races less than human. Even in areas like **medicine**, **education** and the census, pseudo-biological racial assumptions underpinned unequal treatment (as sociological assumptions later would do).

The "clear-cut" categories of race were confounded by European **immigration** in the nineteenth century, which produced "white" populations that differed in **language**, culture, class and strategy from the dominant Northern European populations. Hence, the notion of ethnicity developed out of the category of race, mingling "visible" features with other distinctions of race, **religion** and perceived behaviors. In the nineteenth century, for example, the Irish would have been classified as a race separated from the English, the Scottish or the Germans; through much of the twentieth century the Irish were considered an ethnic group, part of a so-called white race. This transformation is part and parcel of the story of **assimilation**, made possible in effect by the reality that the Irish may have been considered different from mainstream **WASP**s, but they were not as different as African Americans, the Chinese, or Native Americans were deemed to be. For the Irish themselves, and for other Southern and Eastern Europeans who faced hostility from native-born Americans, considerable mileage could be gained from the process of "whitening," and by propagation of notions of ethnicity. At the same time, the idea of an "Irish" race allowed the Irish to distinguish themselves from their British colonizers and even to organize "racial" (political) action in Ireland without appearing disloyal to their new nation.

In the 1920s, immigration quotas reified certain categories of origin (older ethnics) as legitimate populations, while proscribing others as racially inferior. Here, the limitations on Asian immigration imposed between 1882 and 1943 are particularly striking. At the same time, the Great Migration of African Americans from the **South** to Northern **cities** reaffirmed the presence, meanings and tensions of the fundamental racial divide.

Race and ethnicity became major questions in politics and the social sciences from the turn of the century onward. Laws in the North and South sought to define race in terms of rights, location and boundaries in such areas as **marriage**. **Anthropology**, under the leadership of Franz Boas, developed a strong commitment to refuting race as a biological category which has continued to the present; Boas and his followers also worked with American ethnics, although this would be developed even more by **sociology** and anthropology in subsequent years (for example, the University of Chicago school of sociology). Many **foundations** were active in supporting this research and its propagation; African Americans like W.E.B. **Du Bois** also challenged the preconceptions of race on both intellectual and political grounds.

Political, demographic and cultural changes since the Second World War have further complicated concepts and usage of race and ethnicity. Continued migration of African Americans to **Northeastern** and **Western** cities, places populated by large numbers of descendants of immigrants, encouraged a competitive racism in which divisions among European immigrant groups became increasingly blurred at the expense of increasingly ghettoized and segregated black (and Asian or Hispanic) communities. That is, contact and even marriage across religious or "ethnic" lines – e.g. Irish Catholic and German Protestant – became more socially acceptable, even while laws of **miscegenation** forbade marriages between "white" and "other" in many states.

The massive **migration** out of cities into the **suburbs** after the war, encouraged by the **GI Bill** and **highway** construction, further accentuated the racial divisions between white suburbs and black de-industrialized **inner cities**. In addition, political changes occurred from the emancipation of slaves in 1865 all the way through the **Civil Rights movement**, which both provided a strong racial caste to political discourse and then assaulted that discourse in ways that would contribute to status anxiety of more marginal white populations.

Within such a context the 1960s became a key period in the creation of what Steinberg has called the "ethnic myth." In the countercultural assault on corporate America, many of the icons and mechanisms of assimilation came under attack, from the bland suburban tract to the WASP-dominated college **campus** and military-industrial complex. Expression of European ethnic heritages and sometimes the "invention of traditions" became common at this time, further exaggerated once expressions of black cultural identity (connected with **Black Power**) became seen as politically potent weapons. Ironically, what started out as a radical critique of mainstream American society soon turned into a white-ethnic **backlash** against civil-rights advances, the **War on Poverty** and **affirmative action**.

Boundaries between race and ethnicity, however, started to erode as the end of the century approached. This is particularly the case since post-1965 immigrants arriving in the United States have not fitted easily within the black–white model established in political discourse. Asian Americans have never fitted within the system, while Hispanics and immigrants from the **Caribbean** and Africa have brought their own concepts of race with them that often incorporate (or conceal) racial distinctions and mixtures within the ethnic group. Further, whereas in the nineteenth century native-born Americans and European immigrants often came together at the expense of African Americans, in some of the recent reactions to immigration African Americans and other native-born Americans have moved closer together in their opposition to the newly arriving immigrants. In both cases, we must be aware of ethnicity as a potential strategy to divide class interests, as well as of the efforts of those divided by race and ethnicity to come together in common causes. Sometimes, in fact, division and cohesion are closely interwoven, as in the long history of Black–Jewish relations in the US.

Categories have also become neutralized in public (multicultural) discourse, where "ethnicity" is sometimes used as a "softer" word than race to imply that all divisions are epistemologically equal. "Ethnic studies" has become a major academic field in research and teaching by both challenging and blurring categories of difference (see **literature, race and ethnicity**). Moreover, demographics continue to complicate simple categories of ascription or self-identification, as questions of the 2000 census already have revealed. With the elimination of laws against miscegenation since the 1960s, as well as the presence of new racial/ethnic groups, "multi-ethnic," "bi-racial" or "hyphenated" families and citizens, while not the norm, have a greater presence in everyday life. Others have also identified American as their ethnic, racial or heritage category.

"Race" and "ethnicity" are used in more confusing and sometimes sinister ways in popular culture. "Black" music, "black" audiences/consumers and "Hispanic television" are all assumptions made in marketing and **mass media**. Asian Americans have both gained and suffered from assumptions underpinning their categorization as the "model minority," while Native Americans have had to learn to reassert a complex of biological, linguistic, historical and cultural features to claim tribal identities.

"Ethnic" can refer to established American **neighborhoods**, **food** and nostalgia, or lead to the creation of "vaguely ethnic" characters in mass media, marked by clues of food, accent or religion. Here, ethnicity sometimes stands in for other categories like class. Ethnic is also used to refer to continual global borrowing – "ethnic chic" may take items from Russia, Mayans, Nepal and Zulus, while "world music" mixes rhythms, instruments and heritages. Race, by contrast, tends to be strongly marked in the same situations – no television character is "sort of black" or "maybe Asian," although light-skinned African Americans often have been highlighted as models and actors (and white female actors like Katharine **Hepburn** portrayed Chinese women on screen). Again, in reading these characters, it is important to see where "race" is an issue and where these characters are also used as vehicles for the discussion (or concealment) of issues of class, gender and "otherness."

Further reading

Churchill, W. (1998) *Fantasies of the Master Race*, San Francisco: City Lights.
Fine, M. (ed.) (1997) *Off White*, New York: Routledge.
Harris, M. (1968) *The Rise of Anthropological Theory*, New York: Crowell.
Ignatiev, N. (1995) *How the Irish Became White*, New York: Routledge.
McCarthy, C. (1998) *The Uses of Culture*, New York: Routledge.
Roediger, D. (1999) *The Wages of Whiteness*, London: Verso.
Steinberg, S. (1989) *The Ethnic Myth*, Boston: Beacon.

GARY McDONOGH
ROBERT GREGG
CINDY WONG

race riots

Race riots at the beginning of the twentieth century were generally **white** rampages through black **neighborhoods**, shooting and burning. By the 1960s, they had become uprisings within the black communities themselves.

Some historians argue that the increased black militancy led to disenchantment among whites, to the white backlash and the demise of the **Democratic Party**'s consensus on civil rights and eradicating racial discrimination. Others have argued that black militancy increased because the kind of commitment made to real changes seemed so minimal, and that militancy brought about change where none had been occurring.

Throughout the **civil-rights** era, while political changes were occurring in the **South**, things worsened for Northern urban **African Americans**. As blacks entered the **cities**, whites and businesses left for the **suburbs**, leaving impoverished segregated neighborhoods with few employment opportunities.

Between 1964 and 1968, a large number of cities witnessed major rioting. The first riot occurred in **Harlem, NY** after a policeman shot a black criminal suspect. In August riots broke out in **Newark, NJ**, **Philadelphia, PA** and **Chicago, IL**. But the riot that had the most symbolic impact broke out in Watts (**Los Angeles**) in 1965, also sparked following a case of police brutality. Thirty-four African Americans died in this riot in a section of the city where 60 percent of the adult population was on welfare relief. Coming five days after President **Johnson** passed the **Voting Rights Act**, the riot seemed to highlight the limited effectiveness of the Civil Rights movement.

The worst summer of rioting happened in 1967. Twenty-two cities witnessed riots that July and August. Forty-three people were killed in **Detroit, MI** (site of the infamous **Algiers Motel incident**), nearly all of them black, and at least a quarter of the city was burned, with $50 million worth of property destroyed. Federal paratroopers, some just back from the **Vietnam War**, were sent in to restore order.

The riots provoked a response from the federal government, most notably the **Kerner Commission**, which reported in March of 1968, and urged more development of **inner cities**, which President Johnson incorporated into his **War on Poverty**. Within a few days of the report's release, on May 4, Martin Luther **King**, Jr. was assassinated, leading to further rioting.

Apart from obvious conditions of deprivation that have been smoldering in the inner cities for decades, a major reason for this rioting has been **police** brutality. In this regard, the more recent events in 1992, in South Central Los Angeles, were typical. Rodney **King**, stopped for a traffic violation, was beaten senseless by white policemen from the notorious LAPD, and the incident was captured in graphic detail on video. When the policemen were acquitted of any wrong doing, the city erupted in a day of looting, burning and interracial **violence** that spread across the country. The riots were followed by tours from presidential candidates and by promises, still largely unfulfilled, of funding for redevelopment.

ROBERT GREGG

racial profiling

Use of phenotypical characteristics to determine **police** intervention, loosely based on potential associations with likely criminal behavior. The overwhelming tendency of **state** troopers in New Jersey and other areas to stop **African American** motorists in disproportionate numbers for questioning in the 1990s led to nationwide reform of this systematic discrimination. Such abuse has given rise to the ironic label DWB (Driving While Black) to protest such stops.

GARY McDONOGH

radio

American radio has played a prominent role in both utilitarian applications and in the transmission of American **news** and **popular culture**. The proliferation of programming options and technological development since its early days is staggering.

From those early days, radio has served for utilitarian purposes of ship-to-shore communication and military uses, as well as entertaining the nation with **game shows**, children's story hours, mysteries, **soap operas**, **science fiction**, **operas**, news and sports. The golden age of radio is generally considered to be the period between the mid-1930s and 1950. Radio provided "free" entertainment during the Great Depression of the 1930s, and brought the war into the living rooms of the American public.

As **television** asserted its emerging role in the late 1940s and early 1950s, radio had to re-define itself. As programming once only heard on radio moved into the new medium, the FM band emerged, public broadcasting developed, and new opportunities for programming arose.

FM stations account for 75 percent of radio listeners today and about 60 percent of **advertising** dollars. Stations live or die by the ratings they receive from the Arbitron company, which produces a "book" on each major market for advertisers. The advertisers see the demographic breakdown of each station's listeners, and purchase the time and format most likely to reach their target audience.

The most popular formats for radio programming in the late 1990s are (in order of decreasing popularity) country, adult contemporary, news/talk/business/sports, **religion**, **rock** and **oldies**. More than half of US radio stations play country music, particularly in the Deep **South** and **West**. Its standing as the number one program format attests to its grassroots popularity.

Adult contemporary integrates soft rock with what used to be considered "middle of the road" or "chicken rock" from the 1950s. **Talk radio/** news/business/sports provides local stations, especially AM stations, a niche for attracting listeners and revenues. While satellite delivers pre-packaged talk programming, such as Rush Limbaugh and G. Gordon Liddy, a community's individual personalities can host talk and interview programs that meet the interests and needs of a station's hometown.

Public radio provides programming that might not be commercially viable and also that is educational, to some extent. **National Public Radio** and **Public Radio International** disburse government and private funds to noncommercial radio stations. Their content includes *All Things Considered*, *Morning Edition* and *Prairie Home Companion*.

Important legislation regarding radio includes the Radio Act of 1927, the Federal Communications Act of 1934, which replaced it, and the Telecommunications Act of 1996. The 1934 Act provides the legislative foundation governing broadcast and radio transmission in the United States. The Telecommunications Act of 1996 has affected ownership restrictions and technological requirements, among other issues related to radio.

Further reading

Agee, W.K., Ault, P.H. and Emery, E. (1994) *Introduction to Mass Communications*, New York: HarperCollins.
Broadcasting & Cable Yearbook 1997, New Providence: R.R. Bowker.
DeFleur, M. and Dennis, E. (1996) *Understanding Mass Communication*, Boston: Houghton Mifflin.

GAIL HENSON

radio chains

Radio chains or groups represent an increasing portion of American radio ownership. Group ownership affects a market's programming, **advertising** revenues, technological capabilities and hiring, both with positive and negative effects on a market. The FCC rules limit the number of radio and **television** stations a group can own in any one market in order to prevent a market monopoly. Major players in the mid-1990s were CBS, Evergeen, American Radio Systems, ABC (**Disney**), Chancellor (the Hicks-Muse companies), Jacor and Clear Channel Communication.

Further reading

Broadcasting & Cable Yearbook 1997, vol. 1, New Providence: R.R. Bowker.
National Association of Broadcasters (1998) *Wall Street Journal Almanac 1998*, edited by Ronald J. Alsop, New York: Ballantine Books.

GAIL HENSON

railroads *see* trains

ranching

Ranching is the grazing of livestock over grasslands where animals may roam or feed; cattle ranching is the dominant range industry in the US. Ranching is associated with the sparsely populated **West** and Midwestern Plains states. Old World cultural stock practices were adapted to diverse environments to create Texan, Californian and Midwestern ranching practices. Modern ranches in these regions continue to accommodate constantly changing politics, technologies and markets.

Westward expansion introduced ranching as a frontier pursuit on the western fringe of settlement, displacing the native buffalo with beef cattle. The range cattle industry grew when post-Civil War cattle drives moved huge herds of untended cattle from **Texas** to railheads and markets. English breeds of cattle were introduced to the East and **Midwest**, and industrialization and eastern urbanization led to increased market demand for corn-fed beef. Refrigerated transport facilities, industrialized meatpacking plants, and large feedyards enabled stockmen to respond to increased beef demand. While ranching was less affected by government intervention than farming, governmental influence in agricultural policy encouraged the larger, specialized, high-output land tract over the smaller, diversified family farm.

Native ranchers, those with work experience and background in livestock, share their trade with many outside investors though the economic gain is limited. The attraction for many outside capital investors continues to be an American fascination with the prestige and mythology surrounding the Romantic West, the American **cowboy**, and land ownership. Ranching encapsulates deeply American values embracing **individualism**, independence, **freedom**, and open space. The cowboy ranch-hand's dress continues to influence fashion and marketing trends. Suburban sprawl and "ranchettes," small tracts primarily used for hobby ranching or status leisure retreats, actually threaten ranching cultures as land prices are driven above cattle business profits.

Corporatization of agriculture brought change to agribusiness in the 1970s. Vertical integration in animal production, confined growing from birth to finish, is not conducive to cattle-growing as it has been for swine and poultry production. Therefore, the rancher continues to supply cows grown on range grasses to the huge feeder and packer facilities. Industrial scales of efficiency presently inhibit specialized beef production such as highly marbled, organic, grass-fed or hormone-free beef, though there is increasing consumer interest. Cattle producers are forming cooperatives to purchase interests in these facilities to increase their control over beef marketing and pricing.

Land-use controversies are of growing concern to ranchers as development encroaches on agricultural land and outside interests affect formerly local politics. Private landowners are affected by rural zoning and environmental and wildlife legislation. Volatile disputes surrounding some ranchers who maintain grazing contracts with the federal government have brought widespread attention to public domain land use. As cattle grazing produces beef utilizing large land tracts while inhibiting many forms of development, controversies will likely increase.

Further reading

Jordan, T. (1993) *North American Cattle-Ranching Frontiers*, Albuquerque: University of New Mexico.

PAULA ADAMS

Randolph, A. Philip

b. 1889; d. 1979

Born in **Florida**, Randolph migrated to **New York** City in 1911, where he attended City College, becoming a socialist. In 1917 he established the radical **Harlem, NY** journal, *The Messenger*, and made his name as a writer and orator. Recruited by the Brotherhood of Sleeping Car Porters, the **union** of the Pullman Company's **African American** porters, he fought from 1925 to 1937 to gain recognition for the Brotherhood from both the American Federation of Labor and from Pullman. Following his success, Randolph, abandoning socialism, became a national spokesperson for **civil rights**. He organized a March on Washington in 1940, which he called off after President **Roosevelt** agreed to end discrimination within the government and in industries with federal contracts. He later helped persuade **Truman** to issue an executive order barring discrimination in the military. Later, he issued the call for the March on Washington for jobs and freedom in 1963, bringing together over 250,000 marchers to back President **Kennedy**'s civil-rights legislation.

ROBERT GREGG

rap/hip hop

Once derided as a flash in the pan, rap emerged as the dominant popular musical style at the end of the twentieth century. Many people call it rap, but the later coinage "hip hop" better catches its essence – the beat. Possibly the most amazing thing about rap is the ability of new practitioners constantly to refashion and revitalize the genre by incorporating new musical influences and inspirations. While the basics have remained – a stripped-down funk beat with talky vocals – rap has fused with **rock**, **jazz**, reggae and every other contemporary **popular music** form.

Rap developed in the 1970s on the streets of **New York** City, where DJ Kool Herc, DJ Hollywood and others set up turntables, sound systems and speakers on a corner and blasted out a sound collage, starting with a big, fat, booming bass, overlaying samples and scratches, topped off by a call-and-response chant. Indebted to the Last Poets, Gil Scott-Heron, Jamaican reggae toasters and James **Brown**, as well as deeper rooted **African American** rhythmic and lyrical traditions, rap brought black popular culture back to the street.

Since the first recorded rap song, the Sugarhill Gang's "Rapper's Delight" (1979), which many critics dismissed as a novelty, rap has continued to rejuvenate itself just when it seemed to have reached a dead end. When the boastful rappings of early MCs like Kurtis Blow began to sound tired, Grandmaster Flash and the Furious Five brought a social conscience with their astounding 1982 single, "The Message." Run DMC added hard rock guitar for 1984's "Rock Box" and the crossover hit "Walk This Way," a 1986 remake of an Aerosmith tune. The Beastie Boys began to fuse punk, metal and rap beginning in the mid-1980s. Their *License to Ill* (1986) was the first no. 1 hip-hop album and the bestselling rap album of the 1980s.

At the same time "gangsta rap" was emerging on the West Coast. NWA (Niggaz With Attitude) and Ice-T rapped and rocked hard, spewing incendiary lyrics, mostly about hurting and killing people, particularly women and cops. Their first-person narratives about the harsh and violent realities of **ghetto** life shot them to the top of the hip-hop charts and excited much social comment and media-driven controversy. In New York, Boogie Down Productions and Public Enemy took a more directly political stance. Led by Queen Latifah, female rappers began to combat the rampant misogyny of much gangsta rap, with women emerging as more than novelties for the first time on the hip-hop scene.

By the 1990s, rap was part of mainstream American culture, from the streets of the ghettos to sitcom theme songs and advertising jingles. Still, hip-hop culture continued to assemble and deconstruct new forms of popular and unpopular music.

Further reading

Kelley, R.D.G. (1994) "Kickin' Reality, Kickin' Ballistics: 'Gangsta Rap' and Postindustrial Los Angeles," *Race Rebels*, New York: The Free Press.
Rose, T. (1994) *Black Noise: Rap Music and Black Culture in Contemporary America*, Middletown: Wesleyan.

DEWAR MACLEOD

ratings, movies

Ratings provide a form of self-**censorship** that the media industries apply after pressure from the public and the government. The Hollywood Production Code of the 1930s was negotiated to handle issues from sex and violence to **religion** for mainstream cinema. With the break up of studio control and cultural changes of the 1960s, the Motion Picture Association of America switched from self-control to consumer advising, instituting a four-part system that tended to exclude children on the basis of **language**, sexual content and occasionally onscreen brutality, but also left open the negotiation of parental control and responsibility. While the G rating (associated with **Disney** or family films) was suitable for all, other categories sought parental guidance and parental responsibility to attend with a child (R, and, after 1984, PG-13 as well). The X rating (eagerly extended in pornographic film advertising to double and triple X) proved most troubling, leading eventually to an NC-17 rating that sought to distinguish big-budget films with sexual content from pornography. Still, the NC-17 rating greatly diminishes the number of screens available for a movie. Hence, in Kubrick's *Eyes Wide Shut* (1999), digitally inserted figures blocked key actions from American audiences to obtain an R.

This rating was flagged of course as an immediate temptation for adolescents, especially as video rentals imposed controls on parents rather than theaters. Nonetheless, it remains a model for similar systems to rate television, records and computer products, where sex and language still dominate issues of **violence**, although the latter has become more critical in music and computer **games**. Other rating systems have been devised that look at overall morality (Catholic Legion of Decency), as well as critical evaluations (by stars, thumbs, age appropriateness and even grades) that classify films for a continually competitive marketplace.

GARY McDONOGH
CINDY WONG

Rauschenberg, Robert

b. 1925

A native of **Texas**, Rauschenberg taught at Black Mountain College and later collaborated with John **Cage** and the Merce **Cunningham** Dance Company. One of several influential artists who reacted against the particular seriousness and introspection of **abstract expressionism** of the 1940s and 1950s, Rauschenberg experimented with popular imagery and found objects, incorporating them into more whimsical pieces. Rather than ignoring the city environment, he incorporated the junk and technology of industrial society into large collages and constructions out of corrugated cardboard that utilized their labels and binding tapes. His work influenced **pop art**, **minimalism** and collage work, and continues to influence experimentalists today.

EDWARD MILLER

Rayburn, Sam

b. 1882; d. 1961

Democratic congressional leader and **Speaker of the House** from 1940 to 1961. Elected to the House from rural **Texas** in 1913, Rayburn built up formidable connections with **Roosevelt** and the New Deal. As Speaker in a Congress where long-term **Southern** representatives held key posts, Rayburn continued to promote Democratic programs in labor, defense, agriculture and even **civil rights**. Lyndon **Johnson** was his protégé. A

House Office Building memorializes his decades as broker and leader.

GARY McDONOGH

Reader's Digest

Magazine founded in 1922 by George and Lila Acheson Wallace, offering a steady diet of condensed reprints, life stories, news features, self-improvement advice and jokes. *Reader's Digest* now reaches over 16 million households and appears in multiple languages in the US and abroad. Nonetheless, it is often satirized for its "good," conservative values, which let it become associated with doctors' offices, the elderly and "middle America." *Reader's Digest*'s condensed books, in particular, seemed to some to devalue reading and literature in favor of ease.

GARY McDONOGH

Reagan, Ronald

b. 1911

US **president** from 1981 to 1989. A second-tier **Hollywood** leading man, Ronald Reagan shifted from New Deal Democrat to anti-communist conservative while serving as president of the Screen Actors Guild during the **McCarthy** era. His first taste of political success came in 1964 when he made the most financially successful campaign commercial for Barry **Goldwater**. After the electoral debacle, Reagan replaced Goldwater as the voice of the **Republican Party** right wing.

In 1966 he was elected governor of **California**, running against Berkeley student radicals, **civil-rights** militants and anti-Vietnam protesters. Over the next decade, Reagan used his base in California to build what became known as the New **Right**, a coalition of free-market libertarians, traditionalists and ideological anti-communists, augmented by evangelical Christians, neo-conservative **intellectuals** and those voters, called Reagan **Democrats**, increasingly estranged from liberalism, which seemed less patriotic, more culturally deviant and more inclusive.

In the late 1970s, with stagflation and hostages dominating the news, Reagan defeated Jimmy **Carter** for the presidency. Reagan's victory seemed to mark a conservative ascendancy – the Reagan Revolution – with international parallels, for example Margaret Thatcher in Britain. Reagan, supported by conservative Democrats, pushed through a 25 percent **tax** cut, significant cuts in social welfare spending, a host of de-regulatory measures and enormous increases in the military budget. He also introduced a new anti-union use of "replacement" workers, or scabs, in breaking the **air-traffic controllers' strike** of 1981.

In foreign policy, he countered calls for a nuclear freeze with his **Strategic Defense Initiative**, or Star Wars, which sought a costly, hi-tech missile defense system. Reagan also funded a variety of efforts to combat left-wing governments in Nicaragua, **Grenada** and Afghanistan, and radical movements in El Salvador and Angola. Yet, he would later astonish his hawkish advisors by exploring radical reductions in nuclear missiles with Mikhail Gorbachev in 1986.

In 1984, with the economy reviving, Reagan romped over Walter **Mondale**, carrying forty-nine states. But, soon after, the **Iran-Contra** scandal broke, revealing that his administration had exchanged missiles for the promise of help with hostages from Iran and, in addition, had used profits from the sales to illegally fund the anti-Sandinista Contras in Nicaragua. But with no "smoking gun," Reagan himself escaped indictment.

Reagan's legacy is part of the ongoing ideological war – his supporters claim that he restored US economic prosperity and won the **Cold War**. Critics note that Reaganomics: fueled massive federal deficits and a burdensome national debt; violated conservative fiscal commitments to balanced budgets in support of dubious "supply-side" notions; ravaged the social welfare safety net; turned the clock back to the nineteenth century with his **Supreme Court** appointments; and encouraged religious dogmatism, racial intolerance and an "era of greed."

Further reading

Wills, G. (1987) *Reagan's America*, Garden City: Doubleday.

Cannon, L. (1991) *President Reagan*, New York: Simon & Schuster.

LaFeber, W. (1993) *Inevitable Revolutions*, New York: W.W. Norton.

Stockman, D. (1986) *The Triumph of Politics*, New York: Harper & Row.

PAUL LYONS

real estate

FIRE – finance, insurance, real estate named were the watchwords of urban development in late twentieth century America as the spaces of the city themselves became central commodities and motors of growth. Real estate as a focus of speculation for both individuals and corporations underpins both prosperity and debt.

For most individuals, housing is their primary investment and often, via the mortgage, their primary debt. Federal programs for buyers and developers as well as deductions on mortgage interest for income **taxes** have made this a central financial operation of the **middle class** (see **public housing**). At the same time, given American mobility, the home is an investment – middle-class homes should accrue value, whether pioneers of **gentrification** or **suburban** enclaves. Threats of loss of value, in turn, have spurred **white flight**.

Yet real estate also represents a major national and international market in which large developers negotiate with cities, states and federal governments for breaks that will presumably be offset by jobs or other revenue increases, and newspapers cover trends and projects in detail. As an investment, in fact, real estate has also attracted money from pension funds, healthcare corporations and other economic sectors. Red-hot markets, in turn, have posed problems for other land uses, whether environmental controls, preservation, planning or even basic questions of the location of schools and services.

Perhaps it is indicative of the centrality of real estate to urban and exurban planning – and American discourses of profit and success – that Donald Trump, known primarily for real-estate development in New York (and Atlantic City casinos) has been discussed as a potential pre-sidential candidate for the Reform Party.

See also: banks and banking

GARY McDONOGH

CINDY WONG

reality-based television

Genre concerned with signaling the authority of "realism" and "authenticity," where programs usually shoot on location using shaky video-camera filming and actual participants. This relatively new but popular genre originated in the 1980s with shows such as *America's Most Wanted* (FOX, 1988–), *Cops* (FOX, 1989–), *Unsolved Mysteries* (NBC, 1988–95) and *America's Funniest Home Videos* (ABC, 1990–). Many other imitators followed, especially on FOX. MTV's *Real World* (1992–) and the latest *Survivors* (2000) on CBS are new games where real people are placed in different situations in order to be simply on TV or to win million-dollar prizes.

A prototypical plot of *Cops*, for example, features actual **police** driving through inner cities and apprehending suspects. Frenetically paced edited video footage captures officers on high-speed chases. Celebrating the collective agency of the fraternal order, the stories reveal the officers' extraordinary power to establish law and order. *America's Most Wanted* is hosted by a civilian advocate for missing children. The program profiles missing children as well as fugitives using recent photographs and re-enactments of alleged crimes. Home viewers respond to the program's toll-free telephone number with relevant informa-tion that has led to hundreds of successful resolutions.

These narratives first establish a vision of normalcy and calm that is swiftly overthrown by chaos. Disorder displaces order and the world turns upside-down. While each show relies on different tropes (funny, disturbing or shocking), the dissolve of order propels the narrative.

While the programs have relatively similar production styles, techniques and economies, they have basic ideological distinctions. Programs such as *Cops* and *Emergency Call* portray official agents of the state or other powerful public institutions as social protectors. Each of these programs focuses on the cold-nerved and often violent heroics of professionals, and the means by which they restore order: firefighters pull children from burning houses; medical technicians revive accident victims; etc. In contrast, programs such as *AMW* and *America's Funniest Home Videos* focus on the authority of average people, the absence of paternalistic social control and on the private side of individual lives. Frequently, these programs demand audience participation and include a casually dressed civilian host who reinforces the legitimacy of civilian morality and agency.

Reality-based programs have proliferated in part because of relatively inexpensive production costs. Consumer appetites for the format have also been substantial. Focus and survey research have found that viewers value the format as entertaining and informative "reality." The public also tolerates the **violence** presented on these "reality" programs more than violence in fictional accounts. However, these programs have been criticized for insidious blending of exciting vérité and carefully con-structed narratives. The law-and-order variety have been further critiqued for their stereotypical portrayals of criminality that associate deviance with the dark-skinned figures populating urban terrain, ignoring larger social and economic problems and white-collar crime.

JESSICA FISHMAN

reapportionment and redistricting

The US census was established largely for the purpose of determining the reapportionment of legislative districts. As population shifts around the country, congressional seats are taken from **cities** of declining population and added to those where population has grown.

The gathering of data has become cause for significant political debate with regard to the 2000 census. **Democrats** feel that previous censuses have grossly undercounted urban populations and so have unfairly taken seats away from areas where the electorate has tended to vote for them. As a result, they wish to institute sampling techniques to compensate for any potential undercount. **Republicans**, whether or not they agree that an undercount has occurred, are happy with traditional census-gathering techniques.

Further debates have occurred over the establishment of districts to allow for or limit minority representation. A state in the **South** with a large **African American** population may nevertheless elect few black **Congress** members due to the way districts are drawn. In 1982 efforts were made to change this when the **Voting Rights Act** was amended to require certain jurisdictions to take steps to give minority voters an opportunity to elect candidates of their choice. However, first attempts to accomplish this by making constituencies out of dispersed populations have been declared unconstitutional "racial gerrymanders" by the **Supreme Court**.

ROBERT GREGG

recording industry

Since Thomas Edison first spoke the words "Mary had a little lamb" into his phonograph in 1877, the recording industry has been driven by a mixture of technological innovations and the pursuit of profit – each feeding off the other.

While Edison failed originally to see the popular entertainment uses of his phonograph (preferring the device as an office dictation machine), by the 1920s he was locked into battle with Columbia and Victor Records for talent and audience. In the 1920s, also, **radio** broadcasting of live and recorded music spread across the nation. Publishing rights to songs began to be licensed through ASCAP in 1914 and BMI in 1939.

A dazzling succession of technological breakthroughs, especially the introduction of electrical recording, allowed for a greater warmth and personality in recorded music, spawning modern **popular music**. Now, performers like Bing **Crosby** seemed to be singing directly to each individual listener.

While the Great Depression marked a low point for the recording industry (with record sales plummeting from a height of 100 million discs in 1927 to only 6 million in 1932), the onset of the Second World War brought two major changes to the business. On the technological side, wartime research in electronics led to improvements in sound quality through magnetic tape recording, the "unbreakable" long-playing ($33\frac{1}{3}$ rpm) and 45 rpm discs and "high-fidelity" playback equipment; after the war the invention of transistors by Bell Labs in 1948 revolutionized the radio. The other key to the transformation of the recording industry was the expansion of the consumer base with the **baby boom**. **Teenagers** in the 1950s spent an estimated 10 billion dollars anually, much of that on records and radios.

The technological and market growth helped transform the nature of the music industry as well. Since the 1920s, the business had been largely controlled by a few dominant corporate media conglomerations. While that is the case to this day, cheaper recording costs and an expanded marketplace allowed more independent record labels to flourish. Especially with the advent of **rock 'n' roll** as a mass-market phenomenon in the 1950s, smaller labels like Chess, Sun and Atlantic were able to achieve a degree of success in introducing popular music that the major labels ignored to varied audiences. While the majors caught on to the new musical genres and new markets (RCA, for example, bought out Elvis **Presley**'s contract from Sun in 1955 for the then astronomical sum of $35,000), independents have continued to fill the niches ignored by the majors.

Technological improvements continued to transform recorded music, from multi-track recording and Dolby noise reduction to the advent of digital recording in 1978 (though audiophiles might quarrel over whether digitization is an improvement). The compact disc and DAT in the 1980s and MP3 technology in the 1990s transformed recorded music into patterns of sound waves encoded as a sequence of numbers. The promise is of superior sound quality, but the real revolutionary possibility rests with the new methods of distribution. While the recording industry is still controlled by a handful of multinational corporations (which seemingly change ownership weekly), the transmission of recorded sound over the **Internet** threatens to break their dominance.

Further reading

Eliot, M. (1989) *Rockonomics: The Money Behind the Music*, New York: Franklin Watts.

Chapple, S. and Garafalo, R. (1977) *Rock and Roll is Here to Pay*, Chicago: Nelson Hall.

DEWAR MACLEOD

recycling

Along with the popularization of environmental concerns in the 1970s and 1980s came a growing critique of the highly consumerist, resource-intensive American lifestyle. In the wake of **Earth Day** 1990, recycling came to be seen as the perfect solution to these concerns, allowing each American to participate in a perceived ameliorative effort without actually making a substantial sacrifice in consumption. For many, advocating recycling is synonymous with environmental awareness, while purchasing recycled products (paper and plastic goods abound) is seen as a kind of consumer activism. By social convention, all businesses and academic institutions are expected to recycle.

BRAD ROGERS

Redford, Robert

b. 1937

Blond, blue-eyed handsome romantic hero whose roles have embodied some of the most characteristic images of American **masculinity**, while sometimes adding tragic or ironic reverberations. In a string of movies that made him one of the country's most popular **actors** from the 1970s onwards, Redford has been the outlaw (*Butch Cassidy and the Sundance Kid*, 1969, and others), the operator (*The Sting*, 1973), the athlete (*The Natural*, 1984), the crusading journalist (*All the President's Men*, 1976) and, always, the romantic lover (*The Way We Were*, 1973; *Out of Africa*, 1984; *Up Close and Personal*, 1996). As he has matured, Redford has also become involved in production and direction, winning a directing Oscar for *Ordinary People* (1980). That same year, he founded the Sundance Institute near his Utah resort and ranch, which has grown

to be a major site for the training and exposition of independent film-makers through the Sundance **Film Festival**.

GARY McDONOGH

rednecks

Derogatory term typically meaning ignorant, **white** and **Southern**. Although derived from reference to rural, laboring whites whose necks turned red in the sun, the term is now used for any lower-class white population taken to be racist and reactionary, including others in the interior US and Australia. "Redneck," along with "hillbilly," "cracker," "trailer-park trash" and "white trash," glosses a racial and class position taken to be synonymous with anti-government and racist sentiments combined with **Bible belt** religion. These are the last "socially approved" racist epithets.

Further reading

Goad, J. (1997) *Redneck Manifesto*, New York: Simon & Schuster.

JANICE NEWBERRY

referenda

Direct action on political issues through popular vote, either by legislative or statutory demand or as a result of citizen petition. Control on legislative activity through referenda has been especially strong in Western **states** and in **cities**; there are no equivalent federal redresses. Referenda commonly cover major bond, taxation and expenditure issues as well as structural changes in government. Divisive issues like statewide **gambling** may also be put to a popular vote. As citizen actions, however, they have embraced topics as diverse as controls on re-election, immigrant rights, property **taxes** and the use of medical **marijuana**.

GARY McDONOGH

Reform Party *see* parties and elections; Perot, H. Ross

refugees

Beyond those who immigrate via legal and illegal channels each year, 70,000–80,000 people also enter the United States as designated "victims" of political and other repressive conditions worldwide. Some of these people have established flourishing communities in the US, while others struggle to gain the support granted to those identified with **Cold War** struggles.

In the aftermath of the Second World War, US government policy favored refugees from "enemy" nations (and failures of US foreign policy – hence 38,000 Hungarians were accepted after the failed uprising of 1956). Later, thousands arrived after **Castro**'s emergence in **Cuba** and plans to reunify families, as well as massive boatlifts and escapes from the island. Other large populations of refugees followed the **Vietnam War**, including those evacuated for political reasons and subsequent waves of **boat people** who survived ocean travails and refugee camps to find American sponsorship. Many of these refugees were initially dispersed as church and civic groups across the country supported them. In time, new and specialized enclaves emerged – 100,000 Hmong resettled in the Minnesota area, while other **Southeast Asians** clustered in **Los Angeles** and suburban **Washington, DC**.

Refugee policy has shifted only slowly from its anti-communist visage to wider political and human-rights issues, including right-wing regimes in Central America and those oppressed by conditions of poverty exacerbated by globalization. Nonetheless, families from Bosnia and Kosovo or leaders of the Tiananmen incidents in China have been lionized in **mass media** and popular support, while those fleeing female circumcision in Africa or other human-rights issues have faced more obstacles. Also, many, especially those from Latin America, contest the marginal status they are given as illegal immigrants rather than escapees from terror abetted by American intervention in their homelands.

See also: Cuban Americans; immigration; Polish Americans; Vietnamese Americans

Further reading

Hein, J. (1995) *From Vietnam, Laos, and Cambodia*, New York: Twayne.

GARY McDONOGH
CINDY WONG

Regents of the University of California v. Bakke

In this 1978 case, the **Supreme Court** invalidated a fixed affirmative-action quota system used at the medical school of the University of **California** at Davis. The suit was brought by Allan Bakke, a **white** applicant rejected while non-white applicants with lower test scores and grades were admitted. The Court held that the school's set-aside procedure, guaranteeing admission places to people from various minority groups, contravened federal anti-discrimination law. The five-to-four decision still permitted **race** to be used as a remedy for past discrimination when it is one of many factors for admission.

See also: affirmative action

BRIAN LEVIN

regions and regionalism

The major geographical divisions of the United States – North, **South**, **Midwest** and **West** – reflect different attitudes, dialects, literature, **folklore**, **food**, history, perspectives, climate and lifestyle that have fostered extensive literary and historical study of each. Still, many scholars argue that the term is too imprecise to be meaningful. Subregions such as Northwest, **Southwest**, **New England**, **Rocky Mountains** and **Great Lakes** are perhaps more specific markers of culture, social ties and identity. Additionally, differences between inhabitants of a particular region may be greater than similarities. Los Angelenos may have more in common with New Yorkers than they do with residents of Taos, New Mexico, although both

California and New Mexico are considered part of the West. In spite of these complications, regional identities have been and continue to be a significant aspect of American heritages.

Stereotypes of "genteel Southerners," "**rednecks**," "reserved New Englanders" and "rugged Westerners" remain as plentiful in contemporary median culture as they were in the nineteenth century when regionalism was first identified. The labels may be adopted by residents, imposed and reproduced in film, television and popular culture, or both. Throughout history, regional identity has often been constructed in relationship to national identity and has cut across racial, **gender** and **class** differences. In the nineteenth century, for example, many white Southerners sublimated class, gender and regional consciousness in order to declare their loyalty to the Confederacy. Obviously, blacks relate differently to this heritage.

A strong interest in the study of regionalism permeates scholarship. Regionalism in American literature emerged in the nineteenth century and was manifest in the "local color" movement of the 1880s. In the twentieth century, notions of regionalism were influenced by anthropological, historical and sociological perspectives in works by William Faulkner, Willa Cather and Robert Penn Warren. Toni **Morrison**, Alice **Walker**, Louise **Erdrich** and Wallace Stegner invoke region more critically in their discussion of **race**, class, gender and multiple, changing identities in the late twentieth century.

Historians have "discovered" region in a cyclical fashion throughout the past two hundred years. Recently, studies in the "New Western History," building on earlier work in Southern history, have rekindled the regionalist impulse. Scholars attribute this to heightened localism related to **environmentalism**, preservation of historical monuments, journals and publications, and commemorative occasions. A resurgence in studies of local communities, **family** history and autobiography contributes as well. Scholars also argue that the resurgence of regionalism is linked to a late twentieth-century disillusionment with national identity. This turning inward towards region is seen as related to larger sociological and political shifts to a more conservative, locally based sense of self amidst great mobility and change.

Further reading

Ayers, E., Nelson Limerick, P., Nissenbaum, S. and Onuf, P. (1996) *All Over the Map: Rethinking American Regions*, Baltimore: The Johns Hopkins University (introduces contemporary debates, while individual regions and subregions have entries).

Garreau, J. (1991) *The Nine Nations of North America*, Boston: Houghton Mifflin (underpinned by intriguing proposals).

STACILEE FORD

Rehnquist Court

William Hubbs Rehnquist (1924–) was appointed an associate justice of the **Supreme Court** by President **Nixon** in 1972, largely because of his impeccable conservative record. He used his years in the Court before he was elevated to chief justice by President **Reagan** in 1986 to demonstrate his conservative views, extraordinary intellect and collegiality. Throughout his tenure at the Court he has maintained his commitment to supporting state sovereignty over federal power, interpreting state authority to regulate individuals expansively, constraining the power of the federal courts to review state criminal-law convictions, curtailing the constitutional protections granted criminal defendants by the **Warren Court**, limiting **affirmative action** and eliminating the **privacy** right of women to choose **abortion**.

Rehnquist's judicial philosophy took hold on the Court in the 1980s, when a conservative majority emerged following Reagan and **Bush** appointments. Rather than exercising judicial restraint, as many conservative justices profess, the Rehnquist Court has practiced a conservative-oriented **judicial activism** that has successfully continued the process, begun in the Court under Warren Burger, of limiting the impact of precedents from the more liberal era of the Warren Court while not explicitly overruling most of them. The Rehnquist Court welcomes cases brought by groups seeking to promote conservative agendas, such as the Washington Legal Foundation, while those pursuing progressive causes are increasingly relegated to state courts where they often find more receptive judicial audiences.

Further reading

Davis, S. (1989) *Justice Rehnquist and the Constitution*, Princeton: Princeton University Press.

JAMES KRAUS

religion

Americans have long been committed to the ideal of religious diversity. Though several of the early European settlements in their beginnings experimented with theocracy – Massachusetts with Congregationalism, Pennsylvania with **Quakerism**, Maryland and Louisiana with **Roman Catholicism** – by the end of the seventeenth century the energy for religious uniformity had all but drained away. Many European settlers (e.g. the **Puritans** and Quakers), who had relocated across an ocean specifically to escape theological conformity, were already in a mindset of religious rebellion, and the atmosphere of theological independence inspired new communities (e.g. Rhode Island and Delaware) to break away from original settlements, partly in pursuit of this ideal of consummate religious freedom. White settlers who drifted off to Native American settlements, or who dabbled in the religious beliefs and practices introduced by Africans, also contributed to the widely diverse mixture of religious cultures that had taken root by the time the American Revolution set the United States off on its own course, defined by a 1791 constitutional amendment requiring that the government "make no law respecting an establishment of religion, or prohibiting the free exercise thereof."

The first century of American religion

In the decades following the Revolution, the development of religious institutions increasingly followed – and created – social cleavages, along lines of culture, **class**, region and **ethnicity**. Though various versions of Christianity were – and remain – the dominant religion in the United States, important Jewish communities developed, and a few Americans, particularly those of North

African origin, worshipped in the Islamic tradition as well. Hence, early on, the United States became unique in its conscious and constitutionalized commitment to segregate church from state, to de-politicize religion, to de-religionize politics and to provide "tolerance" for a wide range of religious expression. Yet, of the diverse traditions which settlers brought to America, almost all have been shaped by just the opposite commitment – by a powerful and prescriptive relationship between religion and the everyday lives of the populace. From Catholic, Anglican, **Greek Orthodox**, Jewish and, recently, **Buddhist** and **Hindu** cultures, and numerous smaller groupings, the United States became a merging-point, and a flashpoint, for divergent religious traditions. Religious values therefore remain a persistent, if somewhat ambivalent and subterranean, part of American life in informal as well as formal intersections with politics, education, economics and life choices. As one observer phrased it, "freedom *of* religion is not freedom *from* religion."

Over the course of the century following the Revolution, American religions became fragmented as local cultural norms intertwined with religious values and as Americans raised on Puritan traditions worried that religion was dying out in the United States. Early nineteenth-century attempts to reinvigorate what some saw as fading religious energies resulted in what became known as the Second Great Awakening, accompanied by "camp meetings" or "revival meetings" in rural areas, by a phenomenal growth in evangelical and vigorously participatory Protestant religious services and by an increasing alignment between religious affiliations and social, political and/or regional positions. For example, the **Southern** Baptist denomination, separated from its Northern counterpart by its predominantly rural population and its vigorous support of slavery, became the backbone of American slave society. By contrast, Unitarianism and Quakerism came to be distinguished by their small numbers, their concentration in the Northern states and the Ohio Valley and by their devotion to the abolitionist cause. Over time, other denominations became associated with particular political and/or social causes. Northern Baptists were strong in the temperance movement, Catholics sent missionaries among Native Americans, African Methodist Episcopal (AME) churches supported black schools, Jewish synagogues underwrote urban-settlement houses for new immigrants and Northern Methodists encouraged the **Young Men's Christian Association** movement to encourage young men to remain strong in Christian faith. **Episcopalianism**, with its strong roots in the Anglican church, maintained tradition for the dwindling number of Americans of British ancestry.

Religious practice in modern America

American national rituals are almost always nominally religious, broadened in recent years from a vaguely "Christian" tradition to an equally ill-defined "Judaeo-Christian" tradition. Politicians almost always profess a belief in a "higher power," but are careful not to sound too fundamentalist, too metaphysical, or too extreme. Political officials are installed with a prayer and a Bible as part of the ceremonies, but in the most democratic of institutions – the school – prayer is prohibited lest it appear that there is official proselytizing of any particular religious practice.

Instead of a shared religion, the United States is greatly influenced by what some observers have called "civil religion" – a widespread acceptance of a unifying set of values that bind Americans to a shared code of behavior. While trying to maintain a posture of separation between church and state, Americans have attempted to balance that posture with using amorphous religious rhetoric to legitimize certain standards of ethics and behavior. One observer describes this balancing act as "an effort to find a faith sufficiently encompassing and inspiring to envelop all of 'God's New Israel' under one snugly religious quilt." Certainly a largely patriarchal Protestant and Puritan set of values has shaped the American religious mainstream, informing everything from **marriage**, child-rearing and social relationships to politics and marketplace ethics. But Native American influences can be seen in some of the religious-political framework of the Constitution, and Jews, **African Americans** and women have successfully invoked religious rhetoric to highlight social injustice.

The American openness to religious diversity has had mixed results. There has been plenty of opportunity for new denominations to flourish, such as the AME Church, which was born in **Philadelphia** in the 1790s, but there has also been plenty of opportunity for conflict and dissension. Despite the fact that unconventional forms of religious behavior have brought angry and sometimes violent responses, Americans have, to date, not been dislodged from the conviction that freedom of worship is important, even when this conviction has sparked violence. In the 1830s, Illinois residents attacked **Mormon** settlers over their practice of polyandry and drove them from the state; in the 1980s the **Branch Davidian** group, which preached that David Koresh was the modern incarnation of Jesus Christ, became involved in a shooting match with federal government officials. Yet the Mormons, who eventually found a home – and legal protection for their practices – in Utah, are now hosts to one of the most respected genealogy centers and religious choirs. The Branch Davidians have largely disbanded, but similar groups prepared to launch violent resistance in pursuit of extreme forms of religious freedom continue to flourish. One such group, the World Church of the Creator, which advocates deportation of non-whites, was brought to public attention when a former member, Benjamin Smith, went on a shooting spree in the suburbs surrounding **Chicago, IL**.

Since the Second World War, as Americans have grown increasingly sensitive to curbing any form of intolerance, the widespread recognition of rituals such as Jewish Chanukah, African American Kwanzaa and Muslim Ramadan has challenged everything from traditional bank **holidays** to national foodways to school curricula. As one observer phrased it: "the growing diversity of religious and ethnic populations in the United States [has] drawn our attention to the need to accommodate pluralism everywhere." Such postwar tolerance, however, has not staunched Americans' anxiety that excessive commitment to particular religious beliefs will lead to behaviors and loyalties that are at odds with mainstream American civil norms (e.g. Catholic loyalties to the Pope, Quaker commitments to pacifism, Muslim adherence to abstinence from alcohol, Christian Science resistance to modern medicine, shamanic invocations of other-worldly spirits, Wicca celebrations of feminist religions, etc.). The delicate boundary between religious freedom and civil authority continues to occasion dozens of legal confrontations each year. As immigration restrictions have been relaxed, Buddhist, Hindu and various smaller groupings of Old-World religions also have taken a significant place in the modern religious landscape, and these, too, sometimes are accompanied by rites and traditions that are disturbing to their neighbors.

In twenty-first century America it seems likely that the tightrope comprising civil religious impulses, commitment to religious freedom, increasing diversity among the population and tensions between conflicting religious requirements and rites will continue a dynamic relationship that defines Americans' religious experience.

Further reading

Williams, P. (1990) *America's Religions: Traditions and Cultures*, London: Macmillan.

EMMA LAPSANSKY

Reno, Janet

b. 1938

US **Attorney-General** (1993–). Nominated by President **Clinton**, Reno was the first woman ever appointed to the highest-ranking law-enforcement post in the nation. She has received mixed reviews from both sides of the political aisle. Some critics have accused her of being too deferential to both Clinton and **Republican** law-makers, while others say she has been too zealous in appointing special prosecutors to investigate the Clinton administration. Reno's handling of armed stand-offs between government agents and religious and political extremists in the earlier part of her tenure, namely the 1993 **Waco** siege, also received criticism.

SARAH SMITH

Republican Party

The more conservative of the two major political **parties**, the Republican Party is generally identi-

fied with small government and laissez-faire economics. Republicans usually support tax cuts, reduction or elimination of **welfare** for the poor and privatization of many government programs, such as **Social Security**. They also take positions on a variety of social, as well as fiscal, issues, usually opposing **abortion**, gun control, and extending to protection against prejudice for gays and lesbians and advocating the adoption of prayer in **public schools**.

The Republican Party has not always been considered the more conservative of the two parties. Formed in 1854 around a diverse group of opponents of slavery, it elected Abraham Lincoln to the presidency in 1860. Its reputation as the more conservative party in America was cemented during the 1930s, when the party's failure to deal with the severe economic depression led to the election of Franklin D. **Roosevelt**, a Democrat, and consequently to the creation of the American welfare state.

Lincoln's opposition to slavery and his actions to keep the **South** from seceding from the nation have meant that until recently Republicans have not enjoyed much support in this region of the country, even though Southern voters are considered rather conservative. This has changed in the aftermath of the **Civil Rights movement**, with which the **Democratic Party** was identified. In addition, the emergence since the late 1980s of the **Christian Right** and the Christian Coalition as serious political forces has been a major factor in the party's ability to attract Southern voters; the involvement of these groups has also moved the Republican Party to a more conservative position ideologically. The Christian Right has focused its energy on supporting socially conservative causes, such as opposition to abortion and support for school prayer.

The involvement of these new organizations and the party's new attractiveness to Southern voters helped the Republicans gain control of the House and Senate in 1994, the first time in forty years they had controlled both branches of **Congress**. This election brought a number of new, more conservative Republicans to the House. The House Freshman of 1994 were known for their energy, inexperience and their strong attachment to **Speaker of the House** Newt **Gingrich**, whom they felt was responsible for their collective victory.

This has created some tension within the party as older, less socially conservative Republicans have responded to the influx of new blood.

There has been a considerable debate about the Republicans' ability to retain their newfound dominance. The Republicans' new source of strength in the South looks as though it may endure, but outside this region and in presidential races the party has faced difficulties attracting less socially conservative voters.

Further reading

Balz, D. and Brownstein, R. (1996) *Storming the Gates*, New York: Little, Brown & Co.

Rutland, R. (1996) *The Republicans*, Columbia: University of Missouri Press.

EMILY CLOUGH

restrictive covenants

Privately negotiated written agreements, which are binding on succeeding property owners, imposing limitations on the use and ownership of real property. Pre-dating governmental zoning and land-use controls, they created privately enforceable rights involving such benign matters as offensive businesses and design aesthetics. Racially restrictive covenants, limiting property ownership to Caucasians, were widespread, including their use in the original **Levittown**. In *Shelley v. Kraemer* (1948) the **Supreme Court** held the enforcement of racially restrictive covenants by state courts unconstitutional. The Fair Housing Act of 1968 further prohibited racial discrimination in the sale, rental and advertisement of housing.

JAMES KRAUS

retirement

The term "retirement" typically refers to the partial or full separation of a person from occupational life. Most often, advancing years are the impetus for retirement, however there is no universal retirement age. Separation from the workforce prior to the age of sixty-two or sixty-five (the ages at which reduced and full **Social Security** benefits may be collected respectively) is often referred to as early retirement, however this is not an official designation. The timing of retirement may be changed by variations in employer-sponsored pension-program policies, although mandatory retirement policies are no longer legal for almost all occupations. Some individuals may choose to retire from the workplace whereas others may be compelled to step down. There are numerous factors that may contribute to the decision to retire. Separation from the workplace may be desirable for the well aged who yearn for the freedom to pursue personal interests or merely to enjoy the release from occupational structures and demands. Others may base their decision on factors relating to adequacy of pension, health benefits and overall financial security. Some find that declining physical or mental capacity or the expectation that they fill a larger role within the family necessitates withdrawal from employment.

Regardless of whether retirement is a choice or necessity, the event is typically momentous and signifies, for better or worse, disengagement from decades of remunerated productivity. For many, identity is closely linked with one's title, field and employer, and is depreciated by the act of retirement. When retirement results in reduced income, perceived status may be altered simultaneously. Successful retirement, therefore, is in part related to the ability to acquire new and meaningful roles such as volunteer, participant in social and recreational activities, care-giver or activist, particularly in American culture which values remaining productive or at least busy. Personal maladjustment, marital strain and stress related to a new budget do occur, but only in the minority of retirees at any given time.

The concept of retirement in the United States has evolved over the years and its significance has been altered concurrently. In pre-industrial times, it was expected that people would continue to work until no longer able to do so. With the advent of automation, productivity increased reducing the number of workers needed for national economic output. Retirement came to be seen as a way to limit the number of workforce participants and those seeking employment and to provide support for those less able to work, such as the old and disabled. The association between retirement and **old age** and incapacity further promoted negative attitudes. The establishment of Social Security in 1935 ushered in a new understanding of retirement. Workers were "rewarded" for their years of productivity and additionally given the opportunity to defer income for their later years. Although the evolution of attitudes took many years, retirement ultimately came to be seen as a right reserved for those who have served an adequate amount of time in the workforce. Today, the vast majority of workers intend to retire, although the timing varies greatly.

LENARD W. KAYE

reunions

Assemblies viewed with nostalgia and trepidation, as continuous media presentations underscore. Many reunions are generational, marking rites of passage in education or military service. The 25th reunion establishes a milestone for adult change with regard to **high school** and **college**, and provides a retrospective framing for many **films** and **television** shows. Other reunions deal with localities, assembling former residents of changing areas to recall "the old **neighborhood**." **Family** reunions unite space and time, whether small-scale events associated with **holidays**, more emotional coming together at **marriage** and funerals or massive assemblies that may cross race and class lines in search of history and unity. These may be associated with famous figures (descendants of Thomas Jefferson), but more often mark tradition and separation in black and white families.

GARY McDONOGH

revivals (evangelical religious gatherings associated with tents and charismatic preaching as well as pentecostal events) *see* religion

rhythm and blues (R&B)

African Americans developed rhythm and blues in the early 1940s as a hybrid of country blues and big-band swing. In the coming decades R&B evolved in one direction into **rock 'n' roll**, and in another direction into **soul**.

While "**race**" records sold well in the 1920s (Mamie Smith recorded the first **blues** record in 1920), their sales plummeted during the Great Depression. The major labels lost interest in black-oriented music, but after the Second World War small, independent labels began to take advantage of the lower cost of recording technology and the untapped market. At the same time, black music began to change as big bands were forced to pare down for lack of work and rural blues artists moved to cities. Possibly the best way to describe R&B in the early era is as a hybrid of the blues with big-band swing – a typical R&B song of the period mixing swinging horn riffs with a rolling boogie rhythm – what Louis Jordan called the Jump Blues. By the 1950s *Billboard*'s Jerry Wexler had renamed "race" music "rhythm and blues."

In Southern **California**, artists like Lowell Fulson, T-Bone Walker and Johnny Otis played to packed houses at the Barrel House in the Watts section of **Los Angeles**, while their music reached larger audiences through local labels like Aladdin, Excelsior and Specialty. In **New York**, the Erteguns started Atlantic Records, and the Chess brothers opened Aristocrat and then Chess Records (recording the transplanted Delta blues of Muddy **Waters** and Howlin' Wolf). New Orleans R&B took its boogie rhythm from the piano, with honking saxes laid over the top. Producer Dave Bartholomew was responsible for many classic early R&B sessions, including those by Fats Domino and Little Richard.

Always a melange, R&B became difficult to distinguish from rock 'n' roll by the mid-1950s, and in many ways there was no difference – the term "rock 'n' roll" gaining prevalence only when white performers and audiences took over. Still, while Fats Domino, Little Richard and Chuck Berry may have moved seamlessly into rock 'n' roll, other important black artists of the 1950s continued in a distinctly R&B vein – Big Mama Thornton, Screamin' Jay Hawkins and Ike Turner only occasionally crossed over.

R&B also developed into what came to be called soul music in the 1960s with the additional influence of the church. Artists such as Ray

Charles, Jackie Wilson and James **Brown** effected a transformation in black music from R&B to soul when they began to add the emotional expressiveness of gospel music. R&B survives today as a general category of black music, though without any formal accuracy. The influence of R&B, however, can be felt in nearly all **popular music** forms, from rock 'n' roll to disco to **rap**.

DEWAR MACLEOD

Right, the

When one refers to the Right, or right wing, in the United States, one begins with a tradition which cuts across currents associated with Jeffersonian and Jacksonian democracy. One must initially note that confusions between conservatives and reactionaries muddy the waters. A conservative tradition, resting on aspects of **Puritanism**, a more sober view of human nature and behavior, the elitism of the Federalists and, in part, the Whigs, and, importantly, the **Southern** traditionalism associated with John C. Calhoun, must be distinguished from reactionary and characteristically xenophobic movements and moments, ranging from the Alien and Sedition Acts of the 1790s to the anti-Catholic Know-Nothings to the anti-Reconstruction **Ku Klux Klan**.

In the twentieth century, the Right stood against the emergence of the welfare state most identified with the New Deal and against the secular trends towards moral relativism, which have engendered what many call "the culture wars." As such, the Right, in the 1930s through the Liberty League and neo-fascist voices like Father Charles Coughlin, and in the early Cold-War years in the form of **McCarthyism**, was, for the most part, a reactive force, able to scare and sometimes slow, but never able to halt the tides of modernization and modernity.

During the 1950s, the contemporary Right began to take form under the leadership of William F. Buckley, Jr. and his *National Review*, which produced a "fusion" of **Cold War** anti-communism, economic free-market laissez-faire and cultural traditionalism. When liberalism faltered during the 1960s, battered by failures in Vietnam, racial

and generational tensions and the beginnings of economic stagnation, the Right responded with impressive success. The **Goldwater** campaign of 1964, despite its defeat, formed the cadre and organizational base for the **Reagan** Revolution of the 1980s. George **Wallace** pointed the way with his "law-and-order" attacks on liberals, black militants, **hippies**, student activists and feminists. Richard **Nixon** modified Wallace's appeal to his Southern strategy of 1968 and proceeded to mobilize successfully his "Silent Majority" hardhats in the name of patriotism, traditional moral values and racial **backlash**.

The Right flourished because the challenges posed by the 1960s and early 1970s were so profound and, therefore, frightening (e.g. racial, gender and sexual-choice equalities, a more permissive approach to sexuality, language, dress, environmental constraints and challenges to "my country right or wrong"). During the 1970s, the Right was augmented by the rise of a religious Right under the leadership initially of Jerry Falwell and his Moral Majority and by the emergence of the neo-conservatives, mostly ex-liberals chastened by what they saw as the excesses of the 1960s. With the deepening economic stagflation of the late 1970s, combined with foreign-policy crises, such as hostages in Iran and Soviets in Afghanistan, the Right marched into power under the sunny Ronald Reagan.

The end of the Cold War has fragmented the Right, as has the relative success of Bill **Clinton**'s New **Democratic** strategy of co-opting conservative issues like **crime** and **welfare**. The Right, since the high point of the 1994 **Gingrich** congressional victory, has suffered from the mistrust between economic conservatives, mostly focused on pro-business, anti-tax policies, and its cultural conservatives, intent on rolling back what they perceive as secular humanism and cultural relativism.

Further reading

Brennan, M. (1995) *Turning Right in the Sixties*, Chapel Hill: University of North Carolina Press.
Judis, J. (1988) *William F. Buckley, Jr.*, New York: Simon & Schuster.

Nash, G. (1976) *The Conservative Intellectual Movement in America*, New York: Basic.

Siegel, F. (1984) *Troubled Journey*, New York: Hill and Wang.

PAUL LYONS

Ringgold, Faith

b. 1930

Painter, quilt-maker and storyteller. Ringgold has been particular notable in transforming memories of and observations on the **African American** family, social life and political economic context into vivid painted and stitched quilts intertwining multiple, complex stories. These take black folk traditions into **museums** and, at the same time, open them to new audiences as in her classic **children**'s story, *Tar Beach* (1991) (part of her "Woman on the Bridge" series in New York's Guggenheim collection). Raised in **Harlem**, Ringgold has become a global teacher and artist.

GARY McDONOGH
CINDY WONG

rivers

Early settlers in America clung to rivers to find safe ports, sustain settlements and then open up the continental heartland. Rivers have provided lifelines for **trade** and **agriculture** and power for industry. With **deindustrialization**, they have opened vast opportunities for recreation in postindustrial **cities** and **suburbs**. Villages, cities and regions are bound to the identities of their waterways. Rivers also demarcate state and international boundaries, like the wandering Rio Grande between the **Southwest** and Mexico.

Early **Northeast** colonies depended on multiple exploitations of rivers – the Charles in **Boston**, the Hudson and the East River in **New York** City, the Delaware and Schuylkill in **Philadelphia, PA** and the Savannah in **Savannah, GA**. Some rivers are connected to fertile watersheds, while others became impassable as the land rose inland,

producing fall-line divisions in the societies of the **South**.

Further inland, twenty-two states are united by the Mississippi-Missouri system, roughly 4,000 miles (6,400 km) in length. Tributaries like the Ohio and the Red River linked cities and markets from **Pittsburgh, PA** to **St. Louis** to **New Orleans**. The "mighty" Mississippi also influenced art, literature and other media, from Mark Twain to the **musical** *Showboat* or Pare Lorentz's 1938 **documentary** *The River*.

In the dry **West**, the 1,400 mile (2,240 km) Colorado, which carved the Grand Canyon, also sustained many Native American groups. Yet this river has been tamed for both energy and the population demands of **Sunbelt** cities like **Phoenix, AZ** and **Los Angeles, CA**. The Colorado now operates under a contentious seven-state compact representing those who claim its water and hydroelectric power. Meanwhile, the Los Angeles River has been reduced to concrete channels. The Columbia in Washington and the Sacramento in Northern California also represent important Western watersheds.

The relationship of human and river has been transformed throughout the growth of industrial America. Dams on the Niagara, above its majestic falls, and Hoover Dam on the Colorado have powered regions; other dams have been used to control the devastating floods of the Mississippi-Missouri system or to recreate the upper South through the **Tennessee Valley Authority**. Industrial pollution also killed off the aquatic life before stricter pollution controls began to revitalize rivers as centers for boating, **fishing** and even swimming. Hence, rivers have become landscapes for post-industrial development from the Charles to Savannah. This has also led to movements to remove century-old dams and to reconstitute nature.

Human versus the river – running the rapids in Georgia in *Deliverance* (1972) or fighting the floods of the Missouri in *The River* (1984) – has become an American emblem of strength and endurance, while Robert Redford's *A River Runs Through It* (1992) nostalgically explores family and love through fly-fishing in Montana. Rivers figure in generations of popular songs ("Sewanee," "Ol' Man River," Ike and Tina Turner's "Proud

Mary"), reflective journals about **nature** and Sunday family outings. Reflecting the bright lights of Manhattan, the red walls of the Grand Canyon, or the ivory tranquillity of **Washington, DC**, rivers frame the image of American lives as well.

See also: waterfronts

GARY McDONOGH

road movies

Characteristically American genre synthesizing the road (the **automobile** or **motorcycle**) and a person's individual quest for meaning and improvement. The road movie has a long heritage in American literary quests (*Huckleberry Finn*, *Travels With Charley*, *On the Road*). It also has been adapted into other national cinemas in France, Australia, Germany and Finland, while remaining deeply American.

While the postwar road movie shows special affinities with the **western**, we must recognize other important filmic roots. These include the moving albeit comic quests of Chaplin, Keaton and Preston Sturges' *Sullivan's Travels* (1941). Frank Capra also used road elements effectively in the comic *It Happened One Night* (1934) and in a more somber vein in *Meet John Doe* (1941). The presence of comic and tragic elements continues to challenge the boundaries of any genre classification.

In the postwar period, certain key movies demarcate complex changes in spectatorship and meaning generation by generation. In the 1950s, for example, the road movie allows the rebellion of **Brando** in the *Wild One* (1954). The 1960s extended this rebellion in the nihilistic crime spree of *Bonnie and Clyde* (1967) or *Easy Rider* (1969), whose motorcycle pilgrimage and violent denouement underscored the tensions of the decade.

After a spate of comedies (e.g. *Smokey and the Bandit*, 1977) and interesting foreign perspectives like Wim Wender's *Paris, Texas* (1984), more reflexive road movies returned with David Lynch's *Wild at Heart* (1989). In the 1990s, this new take allowed the genre to rethink **masculinity**, whether through the female liberty underpinning *Thelma and Louise* (1991) or the gay/hustler explorations of *My Own Private Idaho* (1991).

Further reading

Sergeant, J. and Watson, S. (1999) *Lost Highways: An Illustrated History of Road Movies*, New York: Creation Books.
Cohan, S. and Hark, I. (1997) *The Road Movie Book*, London: Routledge.

GARY McDONOGH
CINDY WONG

roadside attractions

Alligator farms, tigers at **truck** stops, **homes** of historical personages and monuments of kitsch, from giant animals to theme villages, grew up with and along American **highways** to service and amuse its mobile families. Offering respite for children and drivers, with souvenirs, **fast food** and **motel** rooms, they also reflect generations and class in road development. Those huddled along slow, two-lane roads seem quaint and crude beside the sophisticated advertising of regional tourist boards, highway **hotels** and major **theme parks** dominating interstate landscapes. Countless guides exist to both serious and tacky stops somewhere between democracy and chaos.

GARY McDONOGH

Robeson, Paul

b. 1898; d. 1976

Landmark **African American** athlete, singer, actor and activist, Robeson also epitomized the complexity of black elites in the late twentieth century. A preacher's son, he emerged as a scholar-athlete at Rutgers, and combined acting with his work at Columbia Law School. Becoming famous on stage and screen, he also became involved with leftist and Africanist causes from the 1930s onwards. This led to red-baiting in the 1940s and 1950s, including suspension of his passport (Robeson sued and won). In the 1960s, he became honored as an international leftist and paterfamilias of the **Civil Rights movement**.

GARY McDONOGH

Robinson, Jackie

b. 1919; d. 1972

An outstanding **college** athlete at UCLA, Jackie Robinson served in the Second World War and received an honorable discharge after being court martialed for refusing to conform to **segregation** in his army base. Later, he played professional **baseball** with the Kansas City Monarchs of the Negro Leagues until recognized by Branch Rickey of the Brooklyn Dodgers for his "great experiment" of desegregating major-league baseball. Signed by the Dodgers organization in 1945, Robinson played for the minor-league Montreal Royals. Joining the Dodgers in 1947, he became the first **African American** to play major-league baseball, enduring opponents' racist comments and runners' attempts to spike him with their cleats. Nevertheless, he went on to a **Hall of Fame** career with the Dodgers and became a spokesperson for **civil rights**. The burden of the "great experiment," however, took its toll – he aged rapidly and died only fifteen years after retiring from baseball.

ROBERT GREGG

Rockefellers

As proverbial measures of wealth in American society, the Rockefeller family have cut a broad swath through American business, politics and philanthropy for more than a century. The family's wealth emerged with John D. Rockefeller, Sr (1839–1937), stern founder of Standard Oil (1870) who came to monopolize oil refining and marketing, becoming the enemy of unions and antitrust legislation. Nonetheless, Rockefeller established a health research institute (1901) that grew into the graduate science Rockefeller University and the massive **foundation** that bears the family name (1913). He donated over $500 million to education, medicine and religious projects. His son, John D. Rockefeller, Jr. (1874–1960), in addition to his business interests, distributed another $1 billion between 1917 and 1960, often to advance a Christian America. He also built Rockefeller Center (1930–9), an art-deco **New**

York City, NY landmark, patronized historic preservation of colonial Williamsburg and provided the land for the UN headquarters in Manhattan.

The family's third generation turned to politics and public service, including the liberal Republican leader Nelson (1912–73). Nelson Rockefeller was governor of New York from 1953 to 1973, but his hesitation as well as liberal politics (and an unprecedented **divorce**) cost him the presidential nomination repeatedly. He was appointed vice-president in 1974 when Gerald **Ford** succeeded Richard **Nixon**. John D. Rockefeller III focused on philanthropy, Winthrop (1912–73) became **Republican** governor of Arkansas (1967–71) and David became president of Chase Manhattan Bank.

The fourth generation of Rockefellers includes the liberal Democrat John D. Rockefeller IV, who went to West Virginia as a VISTA volunteer but stayed to become governor (1976–84) and senator (1985–). Other Rockefeller cousins have become scientists, artists and philanthropists while dealing with the legacy of their name and position. Unlike the more flamboyant and newer **Kennedy** family, the Rockefellers have established an institutional structure in philanthropy, public service and education that belies the **celebrity** of the wealthy while underscoring the discreet continuity of American **upper classes**.

Further reading

Collier, P. and Horowitz, D. (1976) *The Rockefellers: An American Dynasty*, New York: Holt, Rinehart and Winston.

GARY McDONOGH

rock 'n' roll

The search for the origins of rock 'n' roll leads into the thickets of American history, including tangles of **race** relations, population movements, **class** politics and **regionalisms**. This much is clear: rock 'n' roll developed from the mixing of **African Americans** and **white** rural folk musics in American **cities** after the Second World War. Who deserves credit – and blame – remains disputed. The single indisputable fact about the roots of rock 'n' roll is the influence of African American musical forms, from Africa through Southern churches to the **blues** to electrified **rhythm and blues**. Throw in the cross-pollination of white folk and **country musics**, and **jazz**, especially its swing and jump-blues variations.

Dating the origins of rock 'n' roll is no less difficult. Were Charlie Christian and T-Bone Walker playing rock 'n' roll guitar in 1940? Was "Rocket '88" (1951) the first rock 'n' roll record? Roy Brown's "Good Rockin' Tonight" (1947)? Listen to 1940s recordings by Lionel Hampton or Hank Williams and you will hear at least hints of rock 'n' roll, if not the real deal.

Part of the confusion comes from the fact that from the start (whenever that was) rock 'n' roll already varied, especially by region, although with wartime and postwar mass migration and mass media, no region remained self-contained for long. This cross-fertilization, in fact, defined rock 'n' roll. While Elvis **Presley** revered the bluesman Arthur "Big Boy" Crudup, Howlin' Wolf listened to country yodeler Jimmie Rodgers.

Rather than focusing on rock 'n' roll solely as a musical form, it is more productive to see it as a social phenomenon created when white **teenagers** in **cities** and expanding **suburbs** began to listen to black music in large numbers. The signal moment for this development came when disc jockey Alan Freed titled his Cleveland radio show the *Moondog Rock 'n' Roll House Party* (1952). Thereafter, racially mixed bands and audiences gathered – not without controversy – in northern cities for gala performances.

Rock 'n' roll, more than any other single cultural phenomenon, defined the new $10 billion a year teen market amid postwar affluence.

Rock 'n' roll is also a business. Most early rock 'n' roll was recorded and distributed by small independent labels like Sun in Memphis and Chess in **Chicago**. Soon major record labels, seeing the profits to be made, began to buy up artists' contracts. Most famously, in 1956, RCA paid a then-staggering $35,000 to bring Elvis **Presley** into their fold. Thereafter, Elvis was the King of rock 'n' roll; his controversial performance on *The Ed Sullivan Show* (where cameras only recorded his

movement above the waist) signaled, as the song goes, "Rock 'n' roll is here to stay."

Within the business, racial exploitation and **segregation** abounded. Alan Freed's name appeared on the songwriting credits for Chuck Berry's "Maybelline," assuring radio play and Freed's share in the profits. Even more egregious were the lame, tame versions recorded by white "artists," most notoriously Pat Boone's insipid cover of Little Richard's "Tutti Frutti." The arrival of England's **Beatles** on American shores in 1964 rescued rock 'n' roll from the oblivion into which white crooners and corporate executives had been steering it. Paying explicit homage to rock's African American pioneers, the Beatles placed rock 'n' roll back on the American creative and social landscapes. **Woodstock** (1969) signaled that rock 'n' roll was central to a generation, an entertainment industry and, indeed, American life. Since then the fusion of musical forms which created rock 'n' roll has proceeded apace, as every possible transmogrification creative artists could come up with has continued constantly to revitalize rock 'n' roll, often when it seems most stagnant, and even when the purpose of rock 'n' roll seems increasingly to be no more than selling beer and cars.

Further reading

DeCurtis, A. *et al.* (1992) *The Rolling Stone Illustrated History of Rock & Roll*, New York: Random House.
Palmer, R. (1995) *Rock & Roll: An Unruly History*, New York: Harmony.

DEWAR MACLEOD

Rockwell, Norman

b. 1874; d. 1978

Painter and illustrator. Rockwell's mythic vision of America drew on and created images of a small-town world of insightful and emotional interactions, but he could also extend this vision to encompass the human meanings of events as varied as homecomings and school integration. His work came into American homes through mass-circulation **magazines** like *Saturday Evening Post* and *Ladies' Home Journal*, for which he frequently created covers, leading many to dismiss it as popular kitsch. Recent critics have nonetheless re-evaluated both the works and their iconic meanings.

GARY McDONOGH

Rocky Mountain states

Eight states – Arizona, Colorado, Idaho, Montana, Nevada, New Mexico, Utah and Wyoming – encompass a territory larger than Western Europe (864,000 square miles), shaped by the dramatic Rocky Mountains. This region encompasses the continental divide, separating tributaries flowing to the Pacific from those that eventually feed into the Gulf. It also holds Utah's Great Salt Lake. Yet, despite mighty **rivers** like the Snake and Colorado, water is a precious, contested commodity amid wide deserts and deep-hewn canyons.

Known for vast open spaces, this region encompasses many **national parks** and extensive lands dedicated to grazing for **ranches** as well as herds of elk, bison and deer. In addition to agricultural resources, these states also have exploited subsurface riches, including, coal, oil, natural gas, copper and uranium. Rights to these resources have often pitted environmentalists and federal regulators against citizens; responses have included the **Wise Use movement** as well as anti-regulation politics creating conservative Republican majorities in many areas.

Culturally and historically, these states epitomize complex features associated with the West, including its Native Americans (thirty tribes and 38 million acres of reservation land) and the heritage of Spanish conquest. They have also sheltered later groups as diverse as the **Mormons** and Basque sheep herders. Finally, these states are strongly identified with **cowboys** and images of **freedom**, independence and relations to **nature** that have spurred interests by migrants escaping rustbelt cities, as well as more extreme **survivalists** and anti-government militias. These images often eclipse historical labor struggles and quests for civil rights by Native Americans and **Hispanics**.

The Rockies have undergone intensive postwar development, spurred by **agriculture**, energy,

tourism and federal intervention, including **highways** as well as high-tech development. This has promoted the rapid growth of important capitals like **Denver**, **Las Vegas** and **Salt Lake City** and an ever-stronger presence of these states in Congress and national politics. Vacation centers from Jackson Hole and the Grand Tetons, Aspen and other elite ski resorts to **Santa Fe** and **Southwestern** destinations have also appropriated the beauty and solitude of the "natural" landscape. While resorts promote outdoor activities, both winter and summer, professional teams in **basketball**, **baseball** and **football** have also found receptive homes in major metropolitan areas, alongside universities, the arts and other cultural development.

The rugged, natural and heroic images of the Rockies permeate media, from commercials for Coors beer (based in Colorado) to the romanticization of Montana in films like Robert **Redford**'s *A River Runs Through It* (1992). Redford has also turned his Sundance Institute and annual festival in Utah into a center for **independent film**. In the 1990s, narratives conveyed both nostalgia and change, as a fiercely independent region faced rapid growth and celebrity status. These disruptions have evoked local questions and the specter of **violence** and **hate crimes** against the backdrop of America's heartland.

Further reading

Findlay, J. (1992) *Magic Lands*, Berkeley: University of California.

Sprague, M. (1967) *The Mountain States*, New York: Time.

GARY McDONOGH

rodeos

Rodeos probably emerged from friendly competitions of work skills among **cowboys**. Although amateur and even junior competitions (through 4-H) highlight fairs throughout the **West**, rodeos constitute a professional sport, controlled by the Rodeo Cowboys Association. Regular events pit individual riders, rather than teams, against ranch animals – riding bareback bulls, steer-wrestling (from horseback), calf-roping (from horseback) and bronco-riding. Between these dangerous events, clowns and displays of roping skill create a lively rhythm. In addition to their **individualism**, rodeos are also highly masculine; although women competed as early as the 1920s, their participation in modern rodeos is generally confined to barrel-racing (a precision-speed competition). Rodeos, as a symbol of the West and a sport, can be found in small towns, Angola State **Prison** (Louisiana) and Manhattan's Madison Square Garden. They figure in **westerns** to indicate both festive elements and the dangers of cowboy life.

GARY McDONOGH

Rodriguez, Richard

b. 1944

Vocal critic of **affirmative action** and **bilingual education** in the 1970s and 1980s. Known for elegant, poetic prose, his autobiographical essays are widely used in college composition classes. His **coming of age**, Americanization apologia in *Hunger of Memory* (1982) solidified his status as cultural traitor for **Chicanos/as** and **Left** critics, but was praised by conservatives and mainstream critics for its courageous and painful reflections on Mexican cultural and Spanish **language** loss. In *Days of Obligation* (1992) and other essays Rodriguez intensifies his ironic complications of various cultural identities with his own **queer** sexual identification and sensibility.

RANDY A. RODRIGUEZ

Roe v. *Wade*

Controversial 1973 decision of the US **Supreme Court** announcing women's constitutional right to an **abortion** based on the 14th Amendment's right to **privacy**. Adopting a much-criticized trimester analysis, the court struck down **Texas'** at criminal abortion legislation (and, by inference, those of other states) outlawing all abortions except those necessary to save the mother's life. The

decision denounced as unconstitutional laws that restricted a woman's right to an abortion during the first trimester of pregnancy, but permitted states limited regulatory rights in the second trimester and allowed complete proscription of abortions in the third trimester, after the fetus reached viability.

MARY-CHRISTINE SUNGAILA, ESQ.

Roman Catholics

The Roman Catholic Church, the largest Christian denomination in the world, is also the largest single church in the United States, with approximately one-quarter of the population as members. Adherents tend to be more numerous in the **Northeast**, the **Great Lakes/Midwest** and the **Southwest/California**, with fewer members in the **South** and in the Plains states, though shifting economic growth has altered this pattern somewhat. Additionally, large influxes of Catholic **Hispanics** have emigrated from Mexico and areas of Central and South America into the Southwest and other areas of the country, with the total population of adherents in the United States growing over the last decades.

Early Catholic immigrants in the US faced religious persecution from the Protestant and nativist populations, though, with time, Catholic numbers afforded them a measure of security against prejudice. They built schools and initiated strong mutual support systems, including **parochial schools** and religious colleges. As they worked towards **assimilation** into US culture, tensions with Rome arose over the extent of interaction the Church might have with this rapidly modernizing culture. The Papal condemnation of this assimilation in 1890 suppressed attempts at change for nearly seventy years. Ultimately, however, the ghetto mentality of the Church in the US was fractured by the election of John XXIII as Pope in 1958 and his calling of the Second Vatican Council (1962–5), a watershed in the life of the Roman Catholic Church.

The Second Vatican Council had a dramatic effect on the lives of the faithful in the United States. Among the changes instigated by the council, three stand out. The first is the emphasis on the importance of the laity in the Church. As an increasingly affluent and educated group of believers, Catholic laity in America desired a larger role in influencing Church governance and in determining how their donations might be spent.

The second is the change in the language of the liturgy from Latin to English. Previously, many congregants were unable to follow the Latin Tridentine liturgy and would often be occupied in practices such as praying the Rosary during the Mass. With the use of English, and with the priest now facing the people rather than with his back to them, the laity were expected to participate actively in the Mass. This change resulted in the expectation of many of the laity that they might take larger roles in the liturgy. These expectations have been fulfilled to some extent, with lay people assisting in the proclamation of the scripture and in the distribution of communion during the Mass as well as, in many parishes, acting in advisory capacities in the decision-making of the parish.

A third result of the council is the affirmation of the goodness in other faith traditions, Christian and otherwise. In the time before the council, the Church taught that salvation was available only through the Catholic Church and emphasized this point through the discipline of the parish setting with its close-knit communities. Other Christians and people of other faiths could not receive the salvation of Jesus Christ, according to Church teaching. In relation to other Christians, the council stated that the ideal for Christianity was the restoration of Christian unity rather than the return of non-Catholic Christians to the Roman Catholic Church. In relation to people of other faiths, the Council also effectively conceded the possibility of revelation outside the Christian faith, a concession unique among Christian denominations. Thus, the RCC no longer considers itself the unique path to salvation, only the pre-eminent one. This position is a remarkable turnaround for the Church and one that has led to continued tension and confusion among some of the faithful as it has called into question the centrality of the Church for community and for the faith of the laity.

In reaction to these changes in the self-understanding of the Church, groups espousing the older teachings of the Church have arisen since the council. Some groups have lobbied for the return to the Latin Tridentine Mass, others have emphasized more traditional pieties, such as the Rosary and novenas, and others have emphasized a more rigorous following of the magisterium, or teaching authority of the Church. This authority is often equated with the pronouncements of the headquarters of the Church, the Roman Curia, though traditionally it has also rested in the work of theologians.

Other movements in the Church include an increased emphasis on the social teaching of the Church, especially in regard to the rights of the poor and homeless, to the **environment**, to nuclear armaments and to the economy. The United States bishops have released pastoral letters addressing these issues and suggesting an appropriate, faith-based response to them. These teachings have not been without controversy, as socially and politically conservative Catholics have taken issue with most of them and publicly attacked the bishops' position. At the same time, Pope John Paul II, with his socially progressive and theologically conservative agenda, has appointed increasing percentages of theologically conservative but socially progressive bishops in US dioceses.

Developing from the Second Vatican Council and its emphasis on personal moral decision-making, the heightened role of the laity has called into question the central role of the clergy and of religious men and women. Far fewer men enter seminaries and religious orders than prior to the Council, while most women's orders have only a fraction of previous numbers. Those seminaries that do attract larger numbers of candidates often espouse a more traditional religious sensibility. Where priests, brothers and sisters once worked, now lay people do much the same work of teaching and administering parishes. Other issues with which the Church has struggled are charges of sexual abuse by the clergy, the role of women and the possibility of married priests.

Further reading

Bokenkotter, T.S. (1990) *A Concise History of the Catholic Church*, New York: Image Books.

McBrien, R. (1994) *Catholicism*, San Francisco: Harper.

Morris, C.R. (1997) *American Catholic*, New York: Times Books – Random House.

Greeley, A. (1990) *The Catholic Myth*, New York: Charles Scribner's Sons.

ERIC A. ZIMMER

romance novels

These bestselling, serially produced novels of love and happiness target female readers who may devour dozens per month, purchased in drugstores and supermarket check-out lines as well as bookstores. While often scorned for formulaic plots and patriarchal ideologies, they inspire intense reader loyalty, while working out fundamental questions of **gender and sexuality**. This has led to re-evaluations of the genre in cultural studies and feminist readings like Janice Radway's (1992) *Reading the Romance.*

The romance has its roots in fictions of love and fantasy that have been staples of American book and magazine **publishing** as well as **Hollywood.** The romance also derives its accessibility from paperback production and mass marketing (even **libraries** buy paperback romances to keep up with reader demand). Romances have also created alternative modes of circulation and discussion through clubs and book trading and stores that buy and sell used copies in bulk.

While similar genres cater to readers in other cultures, this has become a major phenomenon in American publishing for imprints like Harlequin, Avon, Fawcett and Pinnacle who create multiple lines to facilitate **niche marketing**; they have also moved into **cable** television. **BET** and others have produced series for African Americans; Hispanic and Asian consumers draw on materials produced outside the US as well.

Among the different romance series available are those that promote varying degrees of sexual intimacy, from chastity to explicit involvement. Others use special historical settings (Victorian America, the **West**, Regency England) or exotic locales. Still other series deal with family issues like engagement, pregnancy, **divorce** and paternal responsibility. Some may also intersect with Gothic horror and mysteries. In general, however, all offer a satisfying solution to travails and setbacks, generally enshrining heterosexual **marriage** and **family** as ideals.

Among authors especially associated with the romance are Nora Roberts, Elizabeth Lowell, Catherine Coulter and Kathleen Eagle (names are invariably **WASP**ish albeit sometimes pseudonymous). Others slide over into wider mass marketing, like Danielle **Steele**. Elements of the romance as literature have also been explored in more innovative works by Joyce Carol **Oates**, among others.

Mass-market romances are also known for their distinctive cover art, usually showing a couple in an embrace in which the young, lovely yet vulnerable heroine perhaps struggles to escape the strong arms and piercing gaze of the dark, mysterious hero. The model Fabio, in fact, constructed his **celebrity** from his appearance on bodice-ripper covers.

Further reading

Radway, J. (1992) *Reading the Romance*, Chapel Hill: University of North Carolina.

GARY McDONOGH
CINDY WONG

Romanian Americans

Romanian **immigration** to the US began in the 1880s. Following independence from the Ottoman empire, the government of King Carol I ruled with a heavy hand, and worsening economic conditions meant that work was scarce. Most of the immigrants to America were landless young males, though some families went as well. Many Romanian Jews also fled to escape persecution, settling into the larger Jewish community in **New York** City, NY; other Romanians moved west to centers like **Chicago, IL** and **Detroit, MI**, in search of work. Romanian refugees also came to America during the **Cold War**, and others fled following the collapse of the Ceaucescu regime in 1991. The most famous Romanian American is probably the Olympian gymnast Nadia Comeneci, who emigrated in the early 1990s.

MORGEN WITZEL

Roosevelt, (Anna) Eleanor

b. 1884; d. 1962

Patrician by birth and **marriage**, Roosevelt became loved – and hated – on her own for her stands on **race** and human rights. Niece of President Theodore Roosevelt, she began a tumultuous marriage with her cousin Franklin **Roosevelt** in 1905. Increasingly active after his bout with **polio**, Roosevelt became (and continued to be, even after his death) a leading figure in the New Deal and liberal Democratic politics. Her commitment to integration had been made more public by her dramatic resignation from the Daughters of the American Revolution when that group barred Marian Anderson from Constitution Hall. In 1946 she founded the Americans for Democratic Action to support liberal voices within the **Democratic Party**, while from 1945 to 1953 she served as US delegate to the United Nations, chairing the drafting of the Universal Declaration of Human Rights. In 1961 President John F. **Kennedy** re-appointed her to the UN as well as to his Commission on the Status of Women; decades later, Hillary **Clinton** has identified her as a vital presence in the redefinition of the role of **First Lady**.

GARY McDONOGH

Roosevelt, Franklin Delano

President from 1933 until his death in 1945, Roosevelt was the architect of the New Deal and the leader who guided the United States to victory over **Japan** and Germany in the Second World War. His legacy remained great through much of the second half of the twentieth century.

Elected to the presidency in 1932, Roosevelt and the **Democratic Party** benefited from Herbert Hoover's failure to respond to the plight of many Americans suffering the economic consequences of the Great Depression. In fact, Roosevelt's own response to the Depression was neither radical nor systematic. Many of his policy initiatives were ones that Hoover had tried unsuccessfully to implement. Roosevelt was not an ideologue committed to the idea of a welfare state. Instead, he was a pragmatist

who moved with the times and carried out different policies as conditions warranted. Unlike Hoover, he realized that Americans wanted action, if only to give the appearance that something was being done. As he said during the 1932 campaign, "the country demands bold, persistent experimentation."

In March 1933, therefore, when inaugurated, Roosevelt immediately set about establishing what he called a New Deal for the American people, including a plethora of acts establishing different bodies to administer the economy (e.g. the National Recovery, Social Security, Agricultural, and Works Progress Administrations). While both liberals and conservatives at the time proclaimed its revolutionary character, more revisionist views have recognized there was very little that was systematic about the New Deal. It included many ad hoc initiatives to deal with particular problems, some of which cancelled out or undermined others. Marked by the pragmatic and reactive politics of which Roosevelt was the master, the reforms were essentially conservative in nature, endeavoring to re-establish stability for corporate capitalism in the United States.

This lack of an ideological justification for welfare was both a strength and a weakness in the reforms. The New Deal actually failed to accomplish its major goal (re-establishing economic health for the country), but this was achieved by wartime prosperity. However, its apparent success and Roosevelt's obvious popularity gave some of the programs a longevity that they might not have had, had they been more ideologically grounded. Consequently, following the Second World War, presidents from **Truman** to **Carter** remained committed to the New Deal. By the same token, when the prosperity of the postwar years was threatened during the 1970s, there was no ideological commitment to welfare that might safeguard it from the onslaught of a **Reagan**, who argued that it was a millstone weighing down American capitalism.

As the president who guided the United States through the Second World War, Roosevelt was able to enshrine Wilsonian internationalism at the heart of American foreign policy. However, while he was able to secure American support for the United Nations, his internationalism was also more pragmatic than ideological. Bringing together a wartime coalition to defeat Hitler, he was unable to guide this alliance towards a new relationship with the Soviet Union that could survive their postwar competition. Consequently, his repudiation of isolationism fed into a greater commitment to engagement abroad to counteract the Soviets rather than to a philosophical commitment to internationalism.

Further reading

Fraser, S. and Gerstle, G. (eds) (1989) *The Rise and Fall of the New Deal Order*, Princeton: Princeton University Press.

ROBERT GREGG

Roth, Philip

b. 1933

Jewish American novelist, whose novels have focused primarily on the experiences of being a person who has grown up **middle class**, male and Jewish in the early 1950s. His first publication was the novella and short stories *Goodbye, Columbus* (1959). Ten years later he published his most notorious work, *Portnoy's Complaint* (1969), which found the central character seeking relief from insecurity through masturbation and sex with *shiksas*. The series of Zuckerman novels followed (*My Life as a Man*, *The Ghost Writer*, *Zuckerman Unbound*, *The Anatomy Lesson* and *The Counterlife*).

ROBERT GREGG

rowing

Central to many **colleges and universities**' sports programs since the nineteenth century, especially the **Ivy League** universities, crew is an expensive sport (racing shells cost as much as $20,000) and is generally available only to wealthier Americans at university or Olympic levels. Rowers along **rivers** like **Boston**'s Charles and **Philadelphia**'s Schuylkill (immortalized in Thomas Eakin's paintings) thus have drawn ire from residents of surrounding communities. Hence,

Philadelphia administrators have occasionally suggested that the city's boathouses (used for equipment and social activities) should provide camps or other low-cost facilities to disadvantaged kids.

Visibility of women in the sport grew dramatically after the passage of **Title IX**. Since colleges already had the necessary equipment, rowing easily served to move towards funding parity. By 1997, 96 **NCAA** schools had women's varsity rowing teams. Reaching parity was made easier still in 1997 when the NCAA made women's rowing a sanctioned sport, while men's rowing remained a varsity or club sport. Consequently, in many schools women rowers outnumber men.

This has had increasing impact on gender conventions beyond the crews. Bodybuilding sports, before Title IX at least, generally had been considered unfeminine. Now these constitute the backbone of many women's sporting programs.

ROBERT GREGG

running

The "loneliness of the long-distance runner" is a phenomenon of the past. A sport earlier in the century associated in many people's minds with alienation and escape has become in the new century a pastime marked by conformity and **fashion**. By 1998 an estimated 32 million Americans engaged in running, and, instead of finding deserted paths to run down, they did so down busy thoroughfares and on health-club treadmills dressed in the trendiest sports outfits. In George Sheehan's *Running and Being* (1978) the sport found its answer to existentialism; in Jimmy **Carter** it found its own president.

The running craze took off in the 1970s, following the publication of works like Kenneth Cooper's *Aerobics* (1968), which highlighted the relationship between exercise and the prevention of heart disease. During the 1970s several runners brought attention to the sport. Frank Shorter won the gold medal at the 1972 **Olympics**, while Bill Rodgers was a four-time **Boston** and **New York** marathon winner between 1975 and 1980. In 1977 Jim Fixx published his bestselling *Complete Book of Running*, though his death from a heart attack seven years later led many to question the sport's curative qualities.

The sport also attracted women in great numbers, whether for purposes of competition, training, overall **physical fitness**, or losing weight. The Olympics originally had no track and field for women. In 1928 women were allowed to compete only in races shorter than 800 meters. By the late 1960s many women wanted to begin competing in road races. A showdown occurred in 1967 at the Boston Marathon, where Katherine Switzer, using just her first initial and last name to register, received a number and finished the race. Within two years women could officially enter into both the Boston and New York marathons, and, in 1970, fifty-five women finished in the New York Marathon. Longer races were gradually added to the Olympic Games after 1972. Currently 32 percent of finishers in road races are women, about 50 percent in 5K races, and about 28 percent in marathons. Joan Benoit was the winner of the first women's marathon at the 1984 Olympics bringing the same attention to women's running that Shorter had brought to the sport in the 1970s.

ROBERT GREGG

Russell, Richard

b. 1897; d. 1971

Richard Russell, a long-serving US senator from Georgia and a conservative **Democrat**, was Chairperson of the Senate Armed Services Committee from 1951 to 1952 and from 1955 to 1968, where he oversaw government defense and intelligence operations. A mentor to Senator, then President, Lyndon **Johnson**, Russell was a confirmed segregationist and resisted Johnson's efforts to pass the comprehensive **Civil Rights Act** of 1964. Johnson forcefully persuaded Russell to serve on the **Warren Commission**, but Russell refused to sign the Commission's report until a clause was added that a conspiracy to assassinate President John **Kennedy** was still a possibility.

MELINDA SCHWENK

Russia

Since 1917, relations between Russia (or the Soviet Union) and the United States have been marked by extraordinary hostility, occasionally tempered by periods of cooperation.

The US refused to recognize the new Bolshevik government when it assumed power in 1917, and even contributed several thousand troops to an international military force intended to dislodge the new regime from power from 1918 to 1920. These actions left a legacy of hostility on the part of the Soviets who treated the invasion as proof of the determination of capitalist countries to subvert the Soviet Republic. The United States withheld diplomatic recognition of the USSR until 1933.

Relations between the two countries remained tense until the United States entered the Second World War, at which time they became allied against the Axis powers. In the US, sympathy and affection for "Mother Russia" and "Uncle Joe" Stalin developed. From the Soviet perspective, however, American unwillingness to open a second front in continental Europe until 1944, after the Red Army had been combating Nazi armies for three years at the cost of nearly 20 million Soviet lives, left the impression that the US was willing to let Soviet citizens fight Hitler alone in order to spare American casualties. Resentment helped to fuel Soviet suspicion of American postwar intentions at the outset of the **Cold War**.

Any lingering benevolent wartime feelings between the two countries evaporated during the Cold War, which periodically flared into "hot" wars, on the Korean peninsula and in Vietnam, and nearly over the **Cuban missile crisis** (1962) and the Berlin Crisis (1958–62). American suspicion of an expansionist, aggressive and Marxist Soviet Union exporting revolution and instability to capitalist nations friendly to the United States was a foundation of American foreign and domestic policy until the late 1980s.

The 1970s were largely a period of détente, a warming of relations highlighted by increased cultural and student exchanges and **tourism**. In light of an essential parity of nuclear weapons arsenals, arms-control treaties limited, but by no means stopped, the arms race. Nevertheless, much of the American media continued to depict the

Soviet Union as a ruthless and cunning enemy, as did most of **Congress**, which in 1979 refused to ratify the SALT II arms-control treaty negotiated by President **Carter**.

The first half of the **Reagan** presidency (1981–9) brought renewed rhetorical battles and a reheated Cold War. Reagan coined the term "Evil Empire" to describe the Soviet Union, and effectively ended the 1970s détente. American spending on the development of new missile systems (and anti-missile systems) increased dramatically, and the Soviets attempted, unsuccessfully, to match American capabilities.

Only the unexpected ascension of the reformer Mikhail Gorbachev to the post of General Secretary of the Communist Party in 1985 created the conditions for a new thaw in Soviet–American relations. Gorbachev, with his commitment to reducing Soviet expenditures on defense, which were severely damaging an already weakening Soviet economy, to increased "openness" (glasnost) in the press, and his rhetoric of liberalizing the socialist system, eventually became enormously popular among **Washington** elites and the American public, softening anti-Soviet attitudes. His efforts to introduce "socialism with a human face" to the USSR met with an extraordinary enthusiasm in the US, not matched in his own country. His refusal to crush with force the Eastern European revolutions in 1989–91 also met with approval and raised him – and the Soviet Union – in the eyes of many Americans.

Gorbachev's downfall, made inevitable with the failed right-wing putsch of August 1991, and the subsequent dissolution of the Communist Party by Russian President Boris Yeltsin, marked the end of Soviet–American relations.

After the collapse of the Soviet Union, Russian–American relations temporarily improved but have since cooled significantly. Many Russians blamed American economists for imposing upon Russia "shock-therapy" measures. These measures, including the privatization of state-owned property, the end to price subsidies and foreign investment, have been blamed for the sharp decline in living standards for the majority of Russians, while a small minority have quickly accumulated enormous wealth. More recently, America's support for the expansion of the **NATO** military alliance into

the countries of the former Eastern bloc, followed by the 1999 war with Serbia, provoked the worst American–Russian relations since the end of the Cold War. Many Russian leaders and citizens have accused America and its European allies of "aggression" in an attempt to isolate and humiliate Russia during this period of internal turmoil and economic collapse.

Further reading

Boyle, P.G. (1993) *American-Soviet Relations*, London: Routledge.

Crockett, R. (1995) *The Fifty Years War: The United States and the Soviet Union in World Politics*, London: Routledge.

Gaddis, J.L. (1987) *The Long Peace*, New York: Oxford University Press.

The Cold War International History Project website: http://cwihp.si.edu/.

JAMES HEINZEN

Russian Americans

Immigrants came to the United States from **Russia** and the Soviet Union in several waves during the late nineteenth and twentieth centuries. Evading the Russian draft, 5,000 pacifist sectarians emigrated to **California** between 1904 and 1912. A much larger surge of approximately 90,000, composed mainly of poor Jewish agriculturalists, fleeing pogroms and famine in Tsarist Russia, fled between 1890 and 1910 and particularly after the Russian Revolution of 1905. They settled mostly in large northeastern **cities** and in nearby industrial settlements. Many Russians were involved in socialist political parties before 1920, and the Red scare particularly targeted the Russian American community in search of revolutionaries. Thousands of arrests ensued. The stereotyping of Russians as communists, anarchists, or otherwise un-American blossomed in this period.

Another large **immigration** flowed out of Soviet Russia in the years following the Bolshevik Revolution of November 1917 and subsequent Civil War (1918–21). These people were mostly deeply anti-Soviet former members of the nobility, merchants, academics and members of the professions. The majority settled in European capitals such as Prague, Berlin and Paris, but approximately 20,000 continued on to the United States. Many of them ended up in American universities, establishing some of the first courses in Russian language, literature, culture and history in the United States.

Post-Second World War **refugees** comprised the second post-revolutionary wave. A mish-mash of national and social groups, they settled in many cities, often after lengthy stays in displaced-persons camps in Europe and South America. After a period of pride among Russian Americans during the Second World War alliance between the US and the Soviet Union, the **McCarthyism** of the late 1940s and 1950s again encouraged many Russians to keep a low profile.

The third wave of immigrants from the Soviet Union mainly comprised Jews who were allowed to join family members in Israel and the United States. About 300,000 Jews left the USSR between 1970 and 1989, most of them going to Israel. Jewish immigration was subject to the vicissitudes of **Cold War** antagonisms and was interrupted periodically. After the Soviet invasion of Afghanistan in 1979, for example, Jewish immigration was temporarily suspended. In 1977, approximately 500,000 first-generation Russian immigrants and their descendants were living in the United States, though that figure has since jumped higher.

The latest wave of immigration is ongoing and very large, beginning after the collapse of the Soviet communist government in 1991 and intensifying with the subsequent economic and political instability in Russia. Tens of thousands of people of all ethnicities have left the territory of the former Soviet Union and settled in the United States. They have settled primarily in Southern **California**, **Baltimore, MD**, **Philadelphia, PA**, **New York** City, NY and **Boston, MA**. Many were highly educated in the USSR and have applied their skills in several areas of American life, including academics, **engineering**, music and **theater**, and the **computer** industry.

Russians face stereotyping by a **mass media** fascinated with notions of immigrant illegality. A new villain has appeared in films and **television** – the leather-jacketed and ruthless Russian Mafioso, involved in gun-running, prostitution and illegal **gambling**. Extensive reports of pervasive **organized crime** in post-Soviet Russia have reinforced this stereotype.

Further reading

(1980) *Harvard Encyclopedia of American Ethnic Groups*, ed. S. Thernstrom, Cambridge: Belknap Press.

Kovach, H. and Vrga, D.J. (1971) "The Russian Minority in America," in Feinstein, O. (ed.) *Ethnic Groups in the City*, Lexington: Heath Lexington Books.

Handelmann, S. (1994) *Comrade Criminal*, New Haven: Yale University Press.

JAMES HEINZEN

Rustin, Bayard

b. 1910; d.1987

Tactician and organizer behind many of the successes of the **Civil Rights movement**. In the 1940s, Rustin helped organize **CORE** and laid the groundwork for the **freedom rides**. Testing the **Supreme Court** decision outlawing interstate travel on a "journey of reconciliation," he was arrested in North Carolina and spent thirty days on a chain gang. In the 1950s, Rustin assisted Martin Luther **King**, Jr. during the Montgomery Bus Boycott, bringing to the movement his experience of using non-violent action learned from his **Quakerism** and work with Gandhi. Also, Rustin organized the 1963 March on Washington, but lost his leadership role as the movement turned away from non-violence towards **Black Power**. Nevertheless he continued his civil-rights work, leading a campaign against *de facto* school **segregation** in **New York** City, and supported other causes, including gay rights, aid to **refugees**, rights for workers and opposition to apartheid in South Africa.

ROBERT GREGG

S

Saarinen, Eero

b. 1910; d. 1961

Finnish-born architect, son of Eliel Saarinen. His poetic buildings grace and transform monumental spaces from the soaring TWA terminal at JFK airport in **New York** City, NY and Dulles airport near **Washington, DC** (both 1962) to the lofty poetry of the Jefferson National Purchase Arch in **St. Louis, MO** (1962–4). He also created American embassies abroad and contributed to college **campus** architecture at Yale and the Massachusetts Institute of Technology.

GARY McDONOGH

Sagan, Carl

b. 1934; d. 1996

Planetary astronomer and public **intellectual**. Professor at Harvard and Cornell, Sagan won the **Pulitzer Prize** in 1978 for *The Dragons of Eden*, which explored human intelligence. While he became a host on the **PBS** series *Nova*, he also became a science "star" with his *Cosmos* series (PBS, 1980–1), whose vivid explanations of the universe attracted a global audience as well as frequent satires of his hyperbolic delivery. Sagan was also active in establishing exobiological studies and working with those interested in the search for extra-terrestrial intelligent life.

See also: Space; UFOs/extraterrestrials

GARY McDONOGH

Said, Edward W.

b. 1925

Palestinian-born **intellectual** known for both his groundbreaking research in comparative literature and his incisive political commentary, especially on issues relating to Palestinians. Author of *Orientalism* (1978), which radically altered the study of literature and colonialism, and *Culture and Imperialism* (1993), Columbia professor Said is one of the most prominent intellectuals in the United States today. A member of the Palestine National Council, he has been an outspoken critic of American foreign policy in the **Middle East**.

ROBERT GREGG

sailing

Sport with regional popularity (the coasts and the **Great Lakes**, especially) among white middle-class Americans. Recreational sailing took off in the middle of the nineteenth century as commercial sailing lost ground to steam in shipping. Competition has focused on the America's Cup, first raced in 1851, the main purpose of which was showcasing the New York Yacht Club's (NYYC) ability to build vessels technologically superior to those of all other contenders. This stress on technology has increased in recent years, with the adoption of supercomputers to help determine aerodynamic designs and predict better wave-resistant materials.

The NYYC successfully defended the Cup twenty-four times over a 134-year period, the longest winning streak in sports history. However, the streak ended in 1983, when the Australians introduced a "winged keel" on their boat and defeated Dennis Conner and the NYYC's *Liberty*. Conner returned four years later at the helm of the *Stars and Stripes* to win the Cup for the San Diego Yacht Club, but has since lost the Cup to New Zealand.

In 1995 the first all-women team competed in the America Cup. A key aspect in competitive sailing is "grinding" the huge winches that control the sail. Male grinders normally stand six feet tall, weigh around 200 pounds and can bench press between 250 and 300 pounds. Women grinders, able to bench press between 150 and 180 pounds, are at a disadvantage. The success of *The Mighty Mary* caused both surprise and consternation among the men, Conner dismissing the women crew as "a bunch of lesbians." The sponsor, Bil Koch, eventually put a man at the helm.

For the 2000 America Cup the San Francisco Yacht Club sponsored *America True*, featuring a co-ed crew managed and captained by Dawn Riley, the first woman CEO in the Cup.

ROBERT GREGG

Saipan

American trust territory in the Marianas (Western Pacific), controlled under UN aegis from the Second World War until 1986. It provoked a US scandal in the 1990s because of sweatshop production conditions in factories "legally" entitled to use made-in-America labels. A class-action lawsuit, settled in 1999, resulted in a settlement for 50,000 guest workers.

GARY McDONOGH
CINDY WONG

Salinger, J. D.

b. 1919

Full name, Jerome David, Salinger is a reclusive American author, best known for *Catcher in the Rye* (1951), whose hero, Holden Caulfield, became a prototype for teenage rebellion and rejection of "phony" adults. The book has long been a lightning rod for fights over **censorship** in **public schools**, but still enjoys wide popularity among **teenagers**. Salinger also wrote other chronicles of the fictional Glass family, including *Franny and Zooey* (1961) and *Seymour: An Introduction* (1963). His self-imposed solitude was shattered in the 1990s by revelations of his former companion, Joyce Maynard.

GARY McDONOGH

Salk, Jonas

b. 1914; d. 1996

Doctor/medical researcher who led the team that discovered the first viable **polio** vaccine. Son of **Russian Jewish** immigrants, Salk became a public hero despite reserve within the wider scientific and medical community. His vaccine, based on dead virus, received wide use after 1954 until it was replaced by Albert Sabin's oral, live-virus vaccine. As a public **celebrity**, Salk founded the Salk Institute for Biological Studies in **San Diego**, which he envisioned as a center for research and philosophy. In the 1990s, he also became interested in a similar **AIDS** vaccine.

GARY McDONOGH

salsa

Salsa's origins are fluid, but scholars say the term started circulating in the 1960s to describe the new Latin musical styles **New York** City musicians created by fusing a "broad range of musical genres, instrumental combinations, and cultural influences." *Latin Beat* magazine says musicians used to call out "salsa!" (hot sauce) during really hot jams. While most consider Cuban *son montuno* as salsa's primary inspiration, New York salsa musicians also incorporated other elements such as Afro-Cuban percussion instruments, be-bop, Dominican *merengue*, *bata* drums from the ritual music of Cuban *santeria* and stylistic features from Puerto Rican *bomba* and *plena* music.

COURTNEY BENNETT

Salt Lake City, UT

Capital of Utah and headquarters for the Church of the Latter Day Saints. **Mormons** founded the city as a well-ordered grid between the mountains and the Great Salt Lake in 1847. While its population and cultural institutions have grown more diverse over time, the geography of Mormonism still dominates the city, from the institutions of Temple Square to the commercial enterprises centered around the Zion Cooperative Mercantile Institution (founded 1868). The relatively small city (under 200,000) also acts as a center for regional agriculture, wholesale and services, as well as a center for education (University of Utah), culture and recreation (Utah Jazz **basketball** team and mountain sports nearby). The setting and regional opportunities have contributed to rapid service-sector employment growth and population expansion. The metropolitan area grew 18 percent between 1990 and 1998 to reach 1,267,745 inhabitants with development of 1,000 acres per month, increasing **highways**, sprawl and congestion.

The Winter Olympics of 2002, a rare hosting by an urban center, appeared to be the capstone for this development. The city's reputation for conservative integrity, however, was marred by influence-peddling scandals surrounding its bid and questions about financial support for its development.

GARY McDONOGH
CINDY WONG

Samuelson, Paul

b. 1915

Massachusetts Institute of Technology professor and **Nobel Prize** winner whose introductory textbook, *Economics* (1995), influenced a generation of college students' understanding of the field. His use of **mathematics** to formalize the study of economics led to major contributions at the frontiers of the social science, while his clear writings on economic subjects to a popular audience made his a household name. Though generally advocating a more liberal role for the government in national economic affairs than other economists, his research led him to conclude that governments should restrain themselves from interfering with international **trade**.

A. JOSEPH BORRELL

San Antonio, TX

Situated in South Central **Texas**, San Antonio combines a long Mexican heritage and later immigrants with rapid recent development that has made it one of America's ten largest **cities**, passing **Dallas** by 2000. Hence, the "Fiesta City" illustrates multiple fractures of border and global relations.

Mission churches shaped San Antonio's eighteenth-century foundation, the best known of which is the Alamo, site of an iconic battle in the American Texans war against Mexico, now a shrine in the center city. A large Mexican American population nonetheless still shapes the city, its festivals and even recent **architecture** like Legorreta's vivid public **library**. Author Sandra **Cisneros**, however, has fought authorities to paint her house in colors she feels true to a Mexican spirit.

Other settlers included Germans and Anglo-Americans. Military development, livestock and service industries have all spurred growth, bringing problems of ethnic and class antagonism, **gangs** and **gated communities**. The city gained national attention in 1999 through its NBA championship **basketball** team, the Spurs. Yet the heart of a livable downtown remains the charming Paseo del Rio, a WPA project that offers walkways, restaurants and other amenities along the bends of the San Antonio River.

GARY McDONOGH
CINDY WONG

Sandburg, Carl

b. 1878; d. 1974

Poet of Swedish American heritage who celebrated the **Midwest** as an American heartland. Popular for his lyrical images of modern America and the common person, his critical reputation was more uneven. His poems were interwoven with his rural upbringing, life on the road and his years working with newspapers in **Chicago, IL**. He also won a **Pulitzer Prize** for his monumental biography of Abraham Lincoln (1926, 1939).

GARY McDONOGH

San Diego, CA/Tijuana, Mexico

Founded as a mission in 1749, San Diego's first growth came with its conflictive integration into transportation and production networks of **California** and the **Southwest** in the nineteenth century. Since the Second World War, **Sunbelt** metropolitan growth has boomed not only along the Bay, but also in northern, coastal and inland **suburbs** (La Jolla, Escondido, Imperial Beach) stretching south along highways towards Mexico. By 1990 San Diego became the sixth-largest city in the US (2000 estimates 1,208,998). Its Mediterranean climate and ambiance and attractions like the **zoo** and Sea World Aquarium bring in tourists, while military facilities and service-sector development have sustained economic growth. The **University of California**, San Diego and **baseball**'s Padres enrich the metropolitan area.

Tijuana, a contiguous Mexican boom-city has provided labor, consumers, leisure and "vice" for the US, especially since the 1920s. US–Mexico border issues today focus on industrial development, environment and **immigration**. While Tijuana remains famous for **gambling** and **alcohol**, illegal/cheap pharmaceuticals are big business and coastal resorts are growing. As in other border areas, the dialectic of development shapes both cities.

See also: Mexico, relations with

Further reading

Herzog, L. (1990) *Where North Meets South*, Austin: University of Texas.

GARY McDONOGH
CINDY WONG

San Francisco, CA

California is a state of mind as much as a geographical area, and San Francisco is a city of dreams as much as it is the actual city by the bay, where seekers can go west no further. San Francisco became a boomtown in 1848 with the discovery of gold in California, and since that time has been characterized by ethnic diversity, economic opportunity and certain relish for the oddball and madcap. From the reign of the daft but beloved self-proclaimed Emperor Norton I at the turn of the nineteenth century to the preoccupation of residents with Mayor Willie Brown's dapper fedoras at the turn of the millennium, San Francisco has had a sense of humor, style and civic pride.

Originally inhabited by the Costanoan Indians, the first European outposts were built on the hilly peninsula in 1776, and four flags have flown since then: Spanish, Mexican, the Republic of California and the United States. It is known for sea-scoured air and fog, as well as the looming specter of earthquakes that have devastated the city. The city itself has 750,000 inhabitants in 47 square miles, but is also the heart of the San Francisco Bay Area, the fourth-largest metropolitan area in the US, which is at the forefront of high-technology research and development in many fields, as well as home to the **University of California-Berkeley** and **Silicon Valley**.

Like every large city, San Francisco boasts myriad **museums**, theaters, art galleries, shops, music venues, restaurants and historic districts. In fact, the city is a tapestry, a symphony of vistas and fragrances and atmospheres. Some of these have become global images of the city and its landscape: giggling young women promenading past mural-painted walls in the Mission; the breathtaking island views from plush offices in the skyscrapers of the financial district; the aged voices practicing

Chinese opera in a cellar in a Chinatown alley and the **Italian Americans** of North Beach; the tourists walking Fisherman's Wharf, enjoying the food and the views; the view from wind-tossed Baker Beach, with the trees and hills behind and the spectacularly foreshortened view of the Golden Gate Bridge ahead; and the picture-postcard views of the "painted ladies," the lovingly detailed Victorian houses. These have been repeated in many media depictions of the city as well, whether *Vertigo* (1958), *Bullitt* (1968) or *The Rock* (1996), incorporating the famed Alcatraz **prison**.

San Francisco has also been a city marked by diversity of peoples, cultures, classes and sexuality: extravagantly dressed transvestites strutting Polk Street, cheerily greeting shop owners and immigrant neighbors; the preoccupied business people giving orders over cellular phones as they dash down Market Street; the **salsa** dancers on a sunny afternoon at the Ramp; or the elegant women examining the latest paintings displayed in the echoing marble halls of the Palace of Legion of Honor. There are the gay men of the Castro, jostling and joking on the streets and in the restaurants; the spiritual seekers walking the labyrinth inside Grace Cathedral; the artfully tended homes of the very rich in the spectacular Seaside neighborhood, perched on the cliffs above the sea; and the bookstores and **coffee** houses tucked into every corner of the city. It also hosts championship sports teams in **football** (the 49-ers), **baseball** (Giants) and **basketball** (Warriors).

Diversity shapes politics as well. There are the neo-hippies and neo-punks of the Haight Ashbury and the political rallies by activist groups of every stripe. San Francisco has been a home for gay activism embodied in the rise and assassination of Harvey **Milk** as a San Francisco politician. The potential for fragmentation has honed strong politicians on the national scene, including mayors Dianne Feinstein and Willie Brown. Yet the refurbished Beaux Arts City Hall, sporting gold trim and earthquake retrofitting, contrasts with the **homeless** encampments on the lawns of the Civic Center.

San Francisco is a city of tremendous energy and diversity, a city at the geographical edge of the continent and perhaps at the cutting edge of much of what is most heartening about American culture.

JULIE PRITCHARD WRIGHT

Sanger, Margaret

b. 1879; d. 1966

Pioneer in birth control. Trained as a nurse, Sanger opened the world's first birth-control clinic (in Brooklyn) in 1915; she also helped organize the Planned Parenthood movement. She fought in the courts for the right to disseminate **information** on birth control through the mail and films; her writings on the subject faced global bans. Later, she proved instrumental in supporting the development of an effective oral contraceptive (FDA approved in 1960).

GARY McDONOGH

Santa Fe, New Mexico

This state capital, founded in 1610, embodies the sometimes conflicting heritages of Native American peoples, Spanish colonialism, American railroad expansion and automotive tourism that have created the **Southwest**. Although small (55,859) in the mid-1990s, Santa Fe has been a tourist center for decades, altering its cityscape to meet these expectations. In addition to cultural facilities from **opera** and **colleges** to **museums** and Indian handicrafts, it is also a gateway to outdoor recreation and artistic retreat, identified with nearby Taos. Santa Fe has also been taken as an emblem of Southwestern style in **architecture**, design and **food**.

GARY McDONOGH
CINDY WONG

Santana, Carlos

b. 1947

Mexican-born guitarist, considered one of the founding fathers of "world music," who blends guitar-based **rock 'n' roll** associated with the "British invasion" with **blues** music and Afro-Cuban rhythms. Also developing influences from **jazz** saxophonist John Coltrane, he developed rhythms and themes of a more eastern origin, which he explored in collaborations with guitarist John McLaughlin.

Santana burst onto the music scene, first in 1966 in San Francisco and then internationally at the **Woodstock Festival** of 1969. He followed up the Woodstock triumph with the double-platinum *Santana* (1967) and quadruple-platinum *Santana Abraxas* (1968). During his career he has produced many different kinds of albums from rock to experimental jazz with changing back-up bands. His 1999 album, *Supernatural*, gained widespread acclaim and a record-tying eight Grammy Awards.

ROBERT GREGG

Santería

Cuban **Santería** (the way of the saints) is a complex religion which combines the rituals and beliefs of the Yoruba people from Nigeria with corresponding **Roman Catholic** saints, which slaves were forced to worship. An initiate in Santería leads a rigorously disciplined life dedicated to the cult of a particular oricha (deity) for life. The eclectic pantheon of divinities must be frequently gratified and appeased through festive ceremonies that include veneration, offerings and drumming. The ritual offering of slaughtered animals has created conflicts between practitioners and the American Society for the Prevention of Cruelty to Animals.

CARMEN C. ESTEVES

Sarandon, Susan

b. 1946

Beginning with her breakthrough role as Janet in the 1975 cult classic *Rocky Horror Picture Show*, Sarandon's characters have had a powerful influence on both popular culture and substantive social debate. Her portrayal of a hardened, but hopeful

Southern woman in the 1991 film *Thelma and Louise* reflected women's awareness of both their power and vulnerability in modern society. Sarandon's Oscar-winning role as a nun in *Dead Man Walking* (1996) articulated new complexities in the moral debate over **capital punishment**. Sarandon's unusual looks also defied traditional concepts of beauty and sex appeal. Her long-term relationship with Tim Robbins is also part of her political and public persona.

SARAH SMITH

SATs (Scholastic Aptitude Tests) *see* standardized testing; universities and colleges

Savannah, GA

This port and tourist center of 137,000 inhabitants often epitomizes the **South** in popular media (e.g. John Berendt's 1994 bestseller *Midnight in the Garden of Good and Evil*). Founded in 1733 by James Oglethorpe with a unique **urban plan** based around a succession of squares, its antebellum center survived the Civil War to be restored since the 1950s as a gentrified historical district. The city's majority **African American** population also has created educational (Savannah State College) and religious legacies (First African/First Bryan Baptist Church are among the earliest independent congregations in the US). The city hosted **Olympic** yachting events (1996).

GARY McDONOGH

savings and loans *see* banks and banking

Sayles, John

b. 1950

As a film-maker, John Sayles has often been drawn to historical subjects, which he uses to illustrate injustice (racial, ethnic, gender and **class**), as well as the sheer complexity of social interaction in modern America. *Matewan* (1987) chronicles the 1920 coal miners' strike in West Virginia, while

Eight Men Out (1988) investigates **baseball**'s Black Sox scandal of 1919. More recently, *Lone Star* (1996) confronted the weight of history itself, delving into the past and present life of a small town in southern **Texas**. Though rarely commercial successes, Sayles' films display a rare willingness to address difficult issues of identity and social justice.

SUSAN SCHULTEN

scab labor *see* strikes

Scandinavian Americans

Although Swedes participated in the colonial settlement of the **Mid-Atlantic**, most Scandinavian immigrants arrived in the US between 1880 and 1920, including some 300,000 from Denmark, 750,000 Norwegians and 1.25 million Swedes. While smaller than some other groups, these numbers were extremely large for the populations involved – one-fifth of all Swedes lived in the US at the turn of the nineteenth century. Subsequent **immigration**, however, has been primarily professionals and sojourning business people; in the 1970s, emigration to Sweden (a haven for Vietnam protestors) exceeded immigration to the US.

While Danes scattered throughout the northern United States, Norwegians and Swedes often chose rural homesteads in the upper **Midwest** – especially Minnesota, Wisconsin, Illinois and South Dakota. Nonetheless, in 1900, **Chicago, IL** was the second-largest Swedish city in the world after Stockholm. Lutheran churches, ethnic press and society and a liberal populist political orientation united these communities, although all were highly assimilated by the 1930s. By this time Swedish Americans became American heroes (aviator Charles Lindbergh) and interpreters (poet Carl **Sandburg**).

As older institutions and language faded, some pan-Scandinavian associations solidified through Lutheran church mergers, social clubs and parades attuned to the new ethnicity of the 1960s and 1970s. In the 1980s, radio essayist Garrison **Keillor** also popularized a nostalgic yet tender vision of "bachelor Norwegian" farmers and Scandinavian American rural life in his fictional Lake Woebegon.

Further reading

Ljungmark, L. (1979) *Swedish Exodus*, Carbondale: Southern Illinois.
Lovoll, O. (1998) *The Promise Fulfilled*, Minneapolis: University of Minnesota.

GARY McDONOGH

Schlafly, Phyllis

b. 1924

Republican activist who came to prominence with her *A Choice Not an Echo* (1964), which stridently decried American kingmakers while promoting the conservative candidacy and platform of Barry **Goldwater**. Since 1972 she has guided the Eagle Forum, a grassroots organization claiming 80,000 members, committed to lower **taxes** and limitations on government at **home** and abroad, as well as conservative and Christian values in the classroom and family and an antifeminist agenda. Schlafly herself has become a radio commentator, **Internet** spokesperson, columnist and newsletter author, as well as organizer and witness at congressional hearings.

GARY McDONOGH

school boards

School boards govern the nation's public and **private schools**. While each **state** has its own board of education for **public schools**, most educational decisions are handled at the local level by appointed or elected boards of education. School boards make policies and decisions concerning educational standards, bond issues, teacher salaries, accreditation issues, equity issues and compliance with federal, state and local regulations. They may also make decisions regarding textbook selection, **censorship**, expulsion and personnel decisions. The National School Boards Association's mission statement asserts that "local school boards are the nation's pre-eminent expression of grass roots democracy and that this form of governance of the public schools is fundamental to the continued success of public education." In the late twentieth century, urban school boards often found themselves caught in conflicts with city governments and with demands of programs and parental aspirations exceeding revenues.

Further reading

National School Boards Association (1998) "Beliefs and Policies", June 7: http://www.nsba.org.

GAIL HENSON

school prayer

Upholding the constitutional separation of church and state, the US **Supreme Court** in 1963 interpreted the 1st Amendment and the **Bill of Rights** to mean that children should not be subject in **public schools** to involuntary participation in the prayers of others. Those who advocate instituting school prayer, often heard on **Christian media** and among those on the **Christian Right** of the **Republican Party**, argue that the 1st Amendment should protect them from government interference in the practice of their faith. In some areas of the country (e.g. the **Bible belt**), communities continued after 1963 to sanction prayer in the schools, leading to cases like that in Pontotoc County, Mississippi, when new-comers objected and took the school board to court. Focus has shifted to the word "voluntary" and supporters of prayer in schools have been pushing for the introduction of a moment of silence during which students may pray. Opponents, led by the **American Civil Liberties Union**, question how voluntary this may be and whether it would not still be oppressive to **atheists**, **Buddhists**, **Hindus**, **Jews** and Muslims, among others, who might feel obliged to conform to Christian-imposed ritual.

ROBERT GREGG

school vouchers *see* private schools

Schwartz, Delmore

b. 1913; d. 1966

Intellectual poet of alienation and short-story writer. Schwartz had many issues to work out about both his family and his place in society; his later work is marked by a descent into madness. His major works include *In Dreams Begin Responsibilities* (1938), *The World is a Wedding* (1948), *Summer Knowledge* (1959) and the verse-play *Shenandoah* (1941).

GARY McDONOGH

science fiction, film

Since early cinema, the power to present marvelous effects and visions of societies in future time and distant space has made film a choice medium for science fiction. While these possibilities often have been realized as serializations of war/adventure dramas with rockets and exotic creatures (like the 1930s *Buck Rogers*), science-fiction cinema also has envisioned society and its possibilities through prisms of horror, philosophy and fantasy – the power of *Blade Runner* (1982) or *Alien Nation* (1988). At the end of the century, computers and related technologies have revitalized epic science-fiction film-making at the same time that they have become the subjects of ominous speculation (*The Matrix*, 1999).

Postwar science fiction reflects many images and concerns of the **Cold War**. It shows a continuing fascination with new technology and its impacts – whether in George Pal's *Destination Moon* (1950) or the more ominous *Forbidden Planet* (1956). Yet technology also had an edge, disrupting the natural order in the creation of monstrous ants (*Them!*, 1954), spiders, shrews and even women (*Attack of the 50 Foot Woman*, 1958). Especially chilling were situations in which technological advances combined with extra-terrestrial control, whether aimed at world conquest (*The Thing*, 1951, remade 1982; *Invaders from Mars*, 1953; *Invasion of the Body Snatchers*, 1956) or world peace (*The Day the Earth Stood Still*, 1951). These films evoke concerns with the speed and motives of scientific changes, especially nuclear energy, and the scientist, who often ends fighting some heroic heterosexual couple who restore order.

Science fiction remained a genre to meditate on the present and future throughout the 1960s, as evidenced in Stanley Kubrick's very different visions of the future in the anti-nuclear war *Dr Strangelove* (1964), the spaceship meditations of *2001: A Space Odyssey* (1968) and the alternative society of *Clockwork Orange* (1971). Indeed, moral dimensions of science-fiction arguments rather than science itself also pervade more popular series like those that envisioned humans replaced and enslaved by apes (*Planet of the Apes*, 1968 and sequels). These movies also drew on important authors like Arthur C. Clarke and Anthony Burgess. Ray Bradbury's *Fahrenheit 451* was also transformed into a movie by French director François Truffaut.

Science fiction began to experience a rebirth in the late 1970s through George **Lucas** and Steven **Spielberg**, who produced blockbuster combinations of visionary plots, human engagements with the limits of their possibilities on Earth, and off it, and fantastic special effects. *Close Encounters of the Third Kind* (Spielberg, 1977), *Star Wars* and sequels (Lucas, beginning 1977) and *E.T.* (Spielberg, 1982) changed the ways in which movie-goers saw the future, and underpinned a renaissance of science-fiction movies for the decades that followed.

Despite technological inventiveness and exotic characters, however, many science-fiction movies replicate stereotypic themes of gender, **race** and American idealism, and coincide with well-established genres and scenarios of **Hollywood**. There remains a strong, sometimes xenophobic relationship with **horror films**, suggesting that what's out there *will* hurt us. Masculine heroism, teamwork and democratic ideals also underpin the action of *Total Recall* (1990) and the **Star Trek** series. Hence, dreams, fears and memories meet on the sci-fi screen for spectators in the US and the world.

Further reading

Biskind, P. (1983) *Seeing is Believing*, New York: Pantheon.

Kuhn, A. (1990) *Alien Zone*, London: Verso.

Khn, A. (1999) *Alien Zone II*, London: Verso.

GARY McDONOGH
CINDY WONG

science fiction, literature

The literature of change. After its European origins with the Industrial Revolution, American science fiction has flourished since Edgar Rice Burroughs' *A Princess of Mars* (1912). An American imagination was fired by the ideas of new **frontiers** and new possibilities, as well as social, economic and religious freedoms unimaginable in worlds left behind. Science fiction, in many ways, is a literature of hope and the human potential to rise above circumstances and adapt to change.

American science fiction began to grow in depth and breadth with the first science-fiction magazine, *Amazing Stories*, edited by Hugo Gernsback (1926), followed in 1938 by *Astounding Science Fiction*, edited by John W. Campbell, Jr., who fostered science fiction's golden age. Writers explored themes still pondered today, including robots, **computers**, cheap energy, overpopulation, world government, alternative social structures, particle transference, genetic engineering, alien encounters, faster-than-light travel, interplanetary travel, communication and settlement, galactic empires, telepathy, immortality, time travel, alternative histories and utopias/dystopias. In the 1940s and 1950s, Robert A. Heinlein, (*Methuselah's Children*, 1941), Isaac **Asimov** (*Foundation*, 1942), Arthur C. Clarke (*Childhood's End*, 1953) and others published stories of "hard" science fiction, using scientific or military knowledge to detail backgrounds for high-technology futures. Science fiction was seen largely as escapist literature, until Hiroshima taught the world that the unimaginable was here already. After the war, science fiction competed with science fact in **space** and technology. Other important writers include Ray Bradbury (*Fahrenheit 451*, 1951), Frank Herbert (*Dune*, 1966) and Theodore Sturgeon (*More Than Human*, 1953).

In the 1960s and 1970s, interest turned towards cognitive speculations. The New Wave brought in some darker stories (Philip K. Dick, *Do Androids Dream of Electric Sheep?*, 1968), more human-oriented stories (Ursula LeGuin, *Left Hand of Darkness*, 1970) and experimental writing styles (Harlan Ellison, *Repent Harlequin, Said the Ticktockman*, 1965). A broader science fiction included more non-Americans, writers of color (Octavia Butler, *Mind of My Mind*, 1977) and authors of alternative sexualities (Samuel Delany, *Dhalgren*, 1975). Women (Kate Wilhelm, *Margaret and I*, 1971; Anne McCaffrey, *Dragonflight*, 1967; feminist Joanna Russ, *The Female Man*, 1975) found themselves slightly more welcome in science fiction, although Alice Sheldon wrote for decades as James Tiptree, Jr. Science fiction also expanded full-scale into **television** and **film**, as well as cartoons and comic books. Radio, film and other genres were established earlier, but blossomed with new technologies and audiences.

In the 1980s and 1990s, science fiction has matured. The quality of the writing increased and the genre speaks to a much wider audience. William Gibson (*Neuromancer*, 1984) ushered in the age of cyberpunk, while other notable writers include Margaret Atwood (*The Handmaid's Tale*, 1985), David Brin (*The Postman*, 1985), Orson Scott Card (*Enders Game*, 1986), Pat Murphy (*The Falling Woman*, 1988), C.J. Cherryh (*Cyteen*, 1989), Michael Crichton (*Jurassic Park*, 1991), Vernor Vinge (*A Fire Upon the Deep*, 1994), Kim Stanley Robinson (*Blue Mars*, 1997) and Connie Willis (*To Say Nothing of the Dog*, 1999). Often impressionistic, these novels have texture and grace, and they create credible cultural paradigms – these worlds were built to last!

Shorter-length stories common in science fiction reflect the tradition of **magazine** publication (hence many anthologies by author or theme as well). In the 1980s, the glossy science-fiction magazine *Omni* had a good run. Currently, the field is dominated by *Asimov's Science Fiction*, *Analog Science Fiction and Fact* (a descendant of *Astounding*), *The Magazine of Fantasy and Science Fiction*, and *Science Fiction Age*. Fantasy is a closely related genre, yet, while fantasy is characterized by mythic tradition and the supernatural, science fiction writes about the theoretically possible. In fact, science fiction has not only pre-dated scientific and social developments but has also influenced them.

Science fiction also inspires many related associations. The writings of science-fiction writer L. Ron Hubbard form the foundation of the high-profile Church of Scientology. Science fiction also creates long-term relationships between the fan and finely nuanced worlds that grow with each installment. Hundreds of science-fiction conventions featuring various authors or themes are held all over the world. The yearly Hugo and Nebula Awards are also key events.

Science fiction provides an arena in which to imagine some of the possibilities, good and bad, that technological change might bring America and the world. Perhaps through this it is possible to make more intelligent decisions about the small planet on which we live . . . for now.

JULIE PRITCHARD WRIGHT

science fiction, television

Although television presented a postwar door to the future, even its visionary series have faced difficulties balancing family audiences (fewer monsters), small screens (diminished special effects) and continuing characters. Hence, science-fiction television has tended to borrow plots from other genres – especially **westerns** and war movies – and sometimes recycled sets and props as well (evident in *Star Trek* or *Time Tunnel* and even later shipboard ensembles like *Battlestar Galactica*). **Space** and technological wizardry, nonetheless, have underpinned children's programs, including the 1950s *Space Patrol* and *Tom Corbett, Space Cadet* and the animated **sitcom** *The Jetsons* (ABC, 1962–3). Beyond science fiction, moreover, **TV crime** adapted sci-fi technology and formula morality to anachronistic settings and international intrigue (*The Wild Wild West*). Meanwhile, a submarine framed high-tech melodrama in *Voyage to the Bottom of the Sea* (ABC, 1964–8), and robots and monsters enlivened a **family** *Lost in Space* (CBS, 1965–8). *Night Stalker* (ABC, 1972) even brought newsroom humor to revisit classic monsters. Nevertheless, a few series really tested the medium and its mass audiences.

The Outer Limits (ABC, 1963–5) and Rod Serling's eerily masterful *Twilight Zone* (CBS 1958–65, 1985–7, syndicated 1987–8) both became classic not only on the basis of their disquieting imaginations, but also through careful direction and vivid acting. Each set itself apart from television itself in famous introductory sequences – the first warned the viewer not to try to control the set, which had been taken over by unknown forces, while *Twilight Zone* offered a surrealist montage with Serling's clipped voiceover. Both the entire series and individual episodes have become classics.

The 1980s and 1990s proved dry decades for science fiction, unlike movies, although a new sci-fi **cable** network presents movies and older series. *Alien Nation*, however, extended the premise of a refugee alien population in the United States beyond the 1988 movie's themes of race and drugs to encompass family, culture and sexuality. The closing of the millennium, moreover, coincided with the *X-Files* (FOX, 1993–), where aliens and unexplained phenomena converge with paranoia about the government itself. In 1999 Matt Groening, creator of *The Simpsons*, launched *Futurama*, vaulting a New York teenager into the year 3000.

Sci-fi TV betrays roots of American media and culture. Only after decades did *Star Trek's* universes produce female and black *leadership*, although it offered a wider range of characters than many mainstream shows. Family, nation, consumption and morality, moreover, seem continuous, however futuristic worlds lament twentieth-century **war**, pollution, racism and poverty). Perhaps the primary divide between shows like *Star Trek* and the alternative *Twilight Zone*, *Outer Limits* and *X-files*, however, is the divergence between the future as a continuation of the American way and those shows that underscore an unease with the way things are and might be.

GARY McDONOGH

scientific creationism

Explanation of the origin of the Earth on the basis of Biblical interpretations. In an extreme form, adapting fundamentalist interpretations that life was created by divine action 10,000 years ago; a moderate vision notes that the complexity of life systems shows evidence of a supreme intelligence. The debate between **religion** and science formed the heart of the famous 1920s Scopes trial in Tennessee; many thought this a dead issue in the postwar era. Yet creationism remained a prominent issue in local Christian activism in the **South** and **Midwest**. While the **Supreme Court** ruled that this could not be forced on school curricula, partisans have also attacked evolution as an

"unproven theory." In 1999, for example, the Kansas School Board ruled, over protests from teachers and scientists, that macro-evolution and the big bang theory could no longer be included in state science curricula.

GARY McDONOGH

Scientology *see* cults

Scotch-Irish Americans

Descendants of the 2 million Protestant, mostly Presbyterian, emigrants from Ulster, the northern province of Ireland, who arrived in the US from the seventeenth to the twentieth century. "Scotch Irish," a North American term, was increasingly used to distinguish them from the Catholic **Irish Americans** who emigrated to America after the Great Famines of the late 1840s. One in eight Americans traces ancestry to the Scotch Irish. While found everywhere in the US, most live today in Pennsylvania, the Virginias and the Carolinas. They have excelled in American **education**, **publishing**, commerce, finance, the military, **religion** and politics. No fewer than ten presidents of the US were of Scotch-Irish descent.

THOMAS M. WILSON

Scottish *see* Scotch-Irish Americans

scouts

Scouting programs are service and recreation organizations that nurture character development, respect, self-esteem and **patriotism** in young people. Both the Boy Scouts of America (BSA), organized in 1909, and the Girl Scouts of the United States (initially American Girl Guides), organized in 1912, replicated English programs created by Boer War hero Lord Robert Baden-Powell. An amalgamation of Christianity, Kipling's *Just So Stories*, military culture and Native American **folklore**, scouting developed in tandem with other youth and social-reform movements.

Membership figures soared during the first half of the twentieth century when scouts were involved in wartime projects. During the Second World War scouts sold war bonds, distributed defense housing surveys, kept victory gardens and worked with the Red Cross. Since the 1960s both groups have tried to keep pace with societal changes while preserving founding ideals. Seen as exemplars of **white middle-class** American values, both organizations have worked to adapt their programs to different geographical areas and time periods. Both have been celebrated and lampooned in media representations of scouts and scout leaders.

Recent controversies concerning references to God in the BSA oath, accusations of homophobia in both organizations and ongoing debates about single-gender groups are the subject of discussion in the media. However, both groups boast healthy membership numbers (5 million Boy Scouts and 3.5 million Girl Scouts as of 1990) and have launched national campaigns against child and drug abuse, **crime** and illiteracy in addition to more conventional scouting activities such as hiking, **camping** and environmental conservation.

STACILEE FORD

screenwriters

Ambivalent category of **Hollywood** creators, whose role took shape with the feature film (especially sound). Over the years, Hollywood has hired top writers from William Faulkner to Ben Hecht to John Irving to adapt their own and other works. It also has produced notable talents within the industry. Yet, the role of the screenwriter competes unsuccessfully in public acclaim and auteur theory with that of the **director** (which some screenwriters have also become). Moreover, Hollywood productions may also call on multiple writers and script doctors, especially in expensive and problematic projects, undercutting the vision of a single author.

GARY McDONOGH
CINDY WONG

Seattle, WA

Entering Seattle one is immediately struck by an all-pervasive vibrancy and sense of youthful optimism. Construction activity, whether related to fixing potholes, the elegant Symphony Hall, sports stadiums, or the Jimi **Hendrix** museum, suggests a city on the move. Before long, however, traffic, among the worst in the country, is sure to ensnarl you. While stuck in traffic look east and stunning views of the snow-capped Cascade Mountains or sailboat-studded Lake Washington present themselves. Look west and the jagged peaks of the Olympic Mountains and Lake Union stare back. A glance south and majestic Mount Rainier mesmerizes. Winding one's way through Seattle's intentionally individual **neighborhoods** – staid, trendy, or funky – one is sure to spot an expresso stand.

Named after Chief Seattle of the Duwamish tribe, Seattle's beginnings as a white settlement date back to 1851. From log cabins at Alki Beach it grew as a sawmill town on a series of hills between Puget Sound and Lake Washington, soon becoming an important seaport, which it still is today. Despite its rainy reputation, Seattle's 32 inch annual rainfall, less than that of many US cities, explains its picturesque, verdant landscapes.

The city's population is just over half a million, with a sprawling metropolis of some 2 million. The residents generally pride themselves on being politically progressive, culturally tolerant, environmentally sensitive and global in outlook. In 1989 Seattle's overwhelmingly white majority elected an **African American** mayor.

The city's changing image emerges in comparing the 1937 movie *Stage Door*, in which Lucille **Ball** complains: "Am I supposed to apologize for being born in Seattle?", to *Sleepless in Seattle* (1993) and *Frasier* (NBC, 1993–), in which single **yuppies** give the city an image envied by millions around the world.

Seattle's rich cultural amenities reflect the eclectic, experimental tastes of its population, which encompass classical Western ballet, **Asian American** theater, African American **poetry**, Native American dance, Mexican American music, gay choirs, fringe **theater** and **grunge** music made internationally famous by several local celebrities, including Seattle bands Nirvana and Pearl Jam. While forward-looking, its active citizenry has fought vigorously to preserve historical landmarks such as the Pike Place Market, Pioneer Square, the Space Needle and the Chittenden Locks.

Seattle's postwar, Boeing-based economy was deliberately diversified to prevent the previously devastating boom-bust cycles. The economy now includes global giants like Microsoft, numerous spin-off high-technology companies, outdoor recreation stores like REI and **Eddie Bauer**, Starbucks **coffee**, Nordstrom **department stores** and biotechnology companies like Immunex.

An offshoot of the enormous success of these home-grown businesses is the emergence of uncharacteristically young millionaires and billionaires like Bill **Gates** and Paul Allen, and an unprecedented wave of philanthropy and civic-minded activism that will undoubtedly leave a lasting imprint on the city.

Further reading

Dorpat, P. (1994) *Seattle Now and Then*, Seattle: Tartu.

Sale, R. (1976) *Seattle Past to Present*, Seattle: University of Washington.

Seattle-King County Tourism Bureau (1996) *Multi-Ethnic Guide to Seattle and King County*, Seattle: Seattle-King County Tourism Bureau.

BERYL FERNANDES

Secretary of State

The Secretary of State is the **Cabinet** member responsible for US foreign policy. As such, the office is one of the most important posts in the United States government. The Secretary of State is one of the senior members of the Cabinet, along with the Secretaries of Defense and the Treasury. The Secretary is nominated by the president along with other Cabinet members, usually at the start of an incoming administration; the appointment must be confirmed by both houses of **Congress**. Should a Secretary of State resign or be replaced in mid-term, the same nomination and confirmation process is observed.

The Secretary of State was one of the four posts in George Washington's original Cabinet. Early Secretaries of State were powerful political figures; Thomas Jefferson and James Madison, both Secretaries of State, went on to become presidents. More recently, Secretaries of State have tended to be less overtly political, and have been picked by presidents on the basis of their loyalty to the latter.

To most people overseas, the Secretary of State is, after the president, the most visible figure in the US administration, and much of American prestige abroad depends on the character and effectiveness of the incumbent. Among the most high-profile Secretaries of State in recent years is the controversial Henry **Kissinger**, who served in Richard **Nixon**'s administration. Kissinger negotiated with the Vietnamese foreign minister, Li Duc Tho, in Paris to bring about the end of the **Vietnam War**, and was later jointly awarded the Nobel Peace Prize. The award caused outcry both within the US and abroad as Kissinger was widely seen as one of the architects of US war policy, including the bombing of Cambodia. Kissinger was also largely responsible for the US rapprochement with **China** in the early 1970s.

Another controversial Secretary of State was the former general Alexander Haig, appointed by President **Reagan** in 1980. In the confusion following the assassination attempt of 1981, Haig famously declared, "I'm in charge at the White House," thus appearing to usurp the authority of the **vice-president**, to whom control ordinarily passes when the president is incapacitated. Haig was dismissed soon after.

Haig's successor, George Schultz, had a demanding role as Secretary of State during the last years of the **Cold War** and then the thawing of relations with the Eastern bloc. However, he was able to exercise little or no influence over the warring parties in the Middle East. Schultz was often at odds with other members of the administration, and was hampered by the fact that Reagan ran what amounted to a parallel foreign policy through the National Security Council and his own private office, employing officials such as Lieutenant-Colonel Oliver **North**.

James Baker, Secretary of State under George **Bush**, was widely hailed as a success – his tenure included the revolutions in Eastern Europe of 1989–90 and the beginnings of a peace process in the Middle East. Warren Christopher held the post during Bill **Clinton**'s first term of office; perceived as a compromise candidate, his influence was limited. He was replaced in the second term by Madeleine **Albright**, former US ambassador to the United Nations, the first woman ever to hold the post.

MORGEN WITZEL

segregation

Segregation, which kept blacks and whites separate in their social relations, developed in the aftermath of Reconstruction as a system of race control and oppression. Its constitutionality was questioned and then affirmed in the infamous *Plessy* v. *Ferguson* decision of 1896, in which the **Supreme Court** made "separate but equal" legal – blacks and whites could be segregated, so long as separate facilities were provided. Until the 1950s, therefore, segregation on streetcars and railroad carriages, and at movie theaters grew throughout the **South** despite intermittent protests. Under the regime commonly referred to as "Jim Crow" in the South, separate **public schools**, washrooms, water fountains and park benches were established for blacks and whites, while churches, clubs and neighborhoods echoed this division.

In the North *de facto* segregation also existed, with blacks commonly required to sit in balconies at neighborhood movie theaters in cities like **Chicago, IL**, or excluded from downtown hotels and restaurants. **Restrictive covenants** kept blacks out of white **neighborhoods**, while **unions** and employers also enforced divisions of **race** and **class**.

Challenges to segregation came early nonetheless. Even *Plessy* v. *Ferguson* was itself a challenge, while individuals like Ida B. Wells endeavored to fight discrimination through the legal system. In a climate of pervasive **lynching**, however, such challenges faced a veritable reign of terror. However, the establishment of the **NAACP** in

1911, and its strong legal department, brought more systematic challenges in the courts. By the 1930s and 1940s, the NAACP had numerous incremental successes, generally challenging instances of segregation where southern states were clearly not providing equal facilities for blacks (e.g. *Gaines* v. *University of Missouri*, 1938).

The 1940s also witnessed two other important milestones in changing American apartheid. One was President **Truman**'s 1948 decision (urged by A. Philip **Randolph**) to desegregate the armed forces. The other was Branch Rickey's 1945 signing of Jackie **Robinson** for the Brooklyn Dodgers, beginning the desegregation of **baseball**. Both, in turn, profoundly influenced the South. Desegregating army bases increased pressure to integrate areas surrounding US army bases. Similarly, northern teams with black players put pressure on the towns hosting their spring training to change.

By the mid-1950s, other challenges to segregation emerged through the Supreme Court and black consumer power. The NAACP made a full-frontal assault on segregation, persuading the Supreme Court to declare in **Brown v. Board of Education of Topeka** (1954) that segregation was "inherently unequal." Other decisions attacked segregation on interstate travel. But such decisions were meaningless unless they were enforced. It fell to **African Americans** to test the decisions and make federal and local authorities enforce them. In 1957, at **Little Rock**, Arkansas, black school children enrolled at Central High School, pushing President **Eisenhower** to send in troops and federalize the national guard to protect them. In 1960 **CORE** and **SNCC** volunteers embarked on **freedom rides** on interstate buses through the South, forcing **Attorney-General** Robert **Kennedy** to intervene.

Meanwhile, attempts were made to pressure businesses and communities. In 1956, in Montgomery, AL, E.D. Nixon, the regional representative of the NAACP, orchestrated a bus boycott following the arrest of Rosa **Parks**. The rise of Martin Luther **King**, Jr. during this boycott and its successful conclusion led to the creation of **SCLC** and further attempts to dismantle segregation. Students, first in North Carolina and then throughout the South, developed the strategy of

sit-ins employed at the lunch-counters in stores like Krell's and Woolworth's.

The **Civil Rights movement** successfully destroyed the southern system of segregation. It was not as effective at breaking down less concrete racial barriers in the North, or creating equal and integrated societies. Further, integration was not without its own negative side effects. While some commentators have overly romanticized the segregated communities that existed around schools, colleges and baseball leagues, it is nevertheless true that the black **middle class** of these segregated communities was greatly disrupted by desegregation. Though members of the segregated elite parlayed their talents into successful positions in previously all-white schools and sporting leagues, the effect also severed the black middle class from the rest of the black community in ways not seen by immigrants who had "escaped" earlier ghettos.

Further reading

Chafe, W.H. (1980) *Civilities and Civil Rights*, New York: Oxford.

Gregg, R. (1993) *Sparks from the Anvil of Oppression*, Philadelphia: Temple University Press.

Kluger, R. (1976) *Simple Justice*, New York: Knopf.

ROBERT GREGG

Seinfeld

NBC **situation comedy** (1989–98). Dubbed the "show about nothing" for its obsessive focus on everyday minutiae of New York life, it won consistent top ratings and multiple **awards**, becoming the most successful 1990s TV **comedy**. Star Jerry Seinfeld (1954–) combined his actual stand-up **comic** activities with his urban character, working alongside a talented ensemble cast to show four friends somewhat adrift in the city. Many critics have remarked that despite the show's undeniable humor, its main characters (all thirty-somethings and white) are essentially selfish and immature – themes the show itself brought home in its final episode.

NICOLE MARIE KEATING

selective service *see* draft

self-help/self-esteem

American **individualism** stresses individual responsibility for actions and advancement, whether getting a job and getting off **welfare**, learning **math** or surviving illness. Government programs and cultural changes have sought to even the playing field through compensatory support, regulation of opportunities and specific interventions associated with civil rights or later rights movements. Yet, for many, the responsibility for success rests with the person as autonomous agent who must learn to correct him- or herself and develop survival skills. This has created a massive market for those who offer self-help, from religious institutions to **physical fitness** movements to Martha **Stewart**.

Many self-help strategies aim at concrete "improvement," whether in vocabulary, appearance (weight, hair, etc.) or social skills. Dale Carnegie's early *How to Win Friends and Influence People* (15 million copies sold since 1936) grew out of public speaking classes. Self-improvements also pervade *Reader's Digest* and women and men's **magazines** (which may concentrate on appearance or relationships), as well as popular financial journals. Other strategies focus on making individuals feel better about themselves and problem situations (self-esteem). Self-help programs may be packaged through organizations, like **Alcoholics Anonymous**, through books and videos and through self-help "gurus" who market their programs via mass media.

One cannot help relating these forms to the longer spiritual traditions of revival and conversion that have shaped American evangelical **religion** since colonial days. By the twentieth century, these great awakenings had become Pentecostal meetings and tent revivals and then radio and television programs promising salvation in return for commitment and belief. Indeed, **Christian media** met self-help in Rev. Norman Vincent Peale's *Power of Positive Thinking* (1952). In the 1960s, psychologically based groups like Esalen Institute were accused of neo-religious dimensions as well. Cultish overtones are not distant from the fervent witness of self-help infomercials and rallies. Advice columnists, magazines and etiquette books also have offered continuing guidance on self-improvement and manipulation of images, whether to early immigrants or to upwardly mobile suburbanites after the Second World War. These betray American status anxiety when about the hidden issues of **class** – self-improvement can be extremely other-directed in terms of standards or competition for resources.

Since the 1980s, self-help/self-esteem has represented a major industry, starting in the classroom and continuing through adulthood, while identifying widespread areas of change and uncertainty. Many books are directed towards women and women's assertions – cf. John Gray's bestseller *Men are From Mars, Women are from Venus* (1993) – as well as love and romance; others deal also with image and health. Writing tends to mix vaguely Christian platitudes with pep talks and psychologistic data. Wit and nostalgia are also selling points in series like Canfield and Hansen's *Chicken Soup for the Soul/Child*, etc., which became a television feature, or Robert Fulghum's works. Still other works, like Stephen Covey's *Seven Habits of Highly Effective People* (1989), deal with organizational and workplace issues. Some prove much more blunt in their promises, like Gray's *How to Get What You Want and Want What You Have* (1992). Series and authors as celebrities are linked, in turn, to counseling, rallies and conventions.

Catchy titles, while effective in marketing, also make these works easy targets for satire; *Saturday Night Live* has continually taunted "feel-good" stylemakers, while the **sitcom** *Frasier* has raised many questions about "pop" psychology. Yet mass media also promise better lives, thus creating anxiety and appealing to self-help solutions. In fact, **stars** also become caught up in crossover promotions of couples therapy (John Tesh), psychic friends (Dionne Warwick) and other self-help strategies. Hence, the outlines of the American dream and nightmares of failure become blurred and disquieting.

See also: advice columnists

GARY McDONOGH

Senate *see* Congress

Serling, Rod *see* science fiction, television

service sector

The service sector has provided a cushion to millions of Americans who have lost manufacturing jobs since the 1970s. The service sector includes firms whose final outputs are intangible. The value of a service depends primarily on the skills or knowledge used in its creation, not in any physical good provided to consumers. In most cases, workers facilitate the process by dealing directly with customers in selling or providing services.

When Americans think of the service sector, they often think of young, low-paid, part-time, unskilled workers. Visions of **McDonald's** employees flipping hamburgers or **GAP** salespeople hawking the latest **fashion** trends dominate contemporary thought. In reality, **lawyers**, doctors, entertainers and athletes are all employees of the service sector. The residual nature of the sector's definition groups individuals who have little in common. The Bureau of Labor Statistics classifies wholesale and retail trade, finance, entertainment and recreation, professional services, public administration and many other categories as service industries.

Regardless, the stereotypical unskilled worker is the most vulnerable in the service economy. The growth of "McJobs" has struck fear in the minds of young Americans embarking on uncertain careers. Businesses have commoditized work, treating employees as interchangeable and accepting the accompanying high turnover and low commitment. Part-time employment is widespread in the United States. While convenient for young workers and working parents, the growth limitations and lack of benefits inherent in unskilled service professions (sometimes called "dead-end jobs") are worrisome.

The ephemeral nature of service goods creates a fear that the US economy relies on non-productive activities for economic growth. Nonetheless, the prosperity of the post-Second World War period created consumer markets for a vast array of services. Specialization led Americans to rely on others for dry cleaning, food preparation and professional advice.

Service industries now represent over three-quarters of the American labor force. Manufacturing employment has fallen 10 percent to 19.7 million between 1979 and 1996, while employment in the services has risen 44 percent to 83.8 million. The Walmart department store chain is the fourth-largest US corporation, employing 720,000 primarily in low-skilled retail sales positions. Many such jobs are located in remote **suburban** settings, creating difficulties for struggling **inner cities** and their inhabitants.

As Jeremy Rifkin argues in *The End of Work* (1998), however, the rash of downsizings and consolidation in the service industry has yet to reach its peak. While services will always require human assistance (if only to program computers), innovation in voice-recognition technology threatens phone operators, **Internet** commerce threatens salespeople and just-in-time inventory threatens warehousing jobs. As jobs are eliminated through automation, the social safety net of extended families, government **welfare** and low employment may not be as guaranteed as it appeared in the past.

Further reading

Herzenberg, S., Alic, J. and Wial, H. (1998) *New Rules for a New Economy*, Ithaca: ILR Press.

Rifkin, J. (1998) *The End of Work*. New York: Putnam.

MARC BALCER

Seven Sisters

Prestigious women's **colleges** in the **Northeast**, often paired socially with the older and richer male **Ivy League** schools. The group includes Radcliffe, Wellesley, Smith and Mt Holyoke in Massachusetts, Vassar (Poughkeepskie, New York), Barnard (**New York** City) and Bryn Mawr (outside **Philadelphia, PA**). Women's **education** and environment in these **private schools** have ranged from a high academic focus including graduate programs (Bryn Mawr) to the urban partnerships of Radcliffe/ Harvard and Barnard/Columbia to the rural vistas

of Mt Holyoke. In the 1960s, Ivy League co-education put pressure on both admissions and mission. Vassar went co-ed, after unsuccessful merger talks with Yale, while others entered wider consortia; Radcliffe merged with Harvard in 1999. These colleges have become focal points in rethinking women's education and civic roles in subsequent decades – both Barbara **Bush** and Hillary **Clinton** attended Wellesley.

GARY McDONOGH

Sexton, Anne

b. 1928; d. 1974

Poet. Her deeply troubled life was shadowed by bouts of mental illness, addiction and preoccupations with death and suicide. These added power and terror to her often-confessional **poetry** in works like *To Bedlam and Part Way Back* (1960) and *The Death Notebooks* (1974), published in the year that she committed suicide.

GARY McDONOGH

sexual harassment

A form of unlawful sex discrimination at work primarily perpetrated by men against women. First recognized by the US **Supreme Court** in 1986. Defined as unwelcome sexual advances, requests for sexual favors and verbal or physical conduct of a sexual nature. Two forms of harassment are recognized: quid pro quo, where submission to sexual demands is an explicit or implicit employment condition; and hostile work environment, where harassment unreasonably interferes with work performance and creates an intimidating, hostile or offensive working environment. Same-sex harassment (including that of men) was eventually recognized as a valid legal claim as well.

MARY-CHRISTINE SUNGAILA, ESQ.

sharecroppers

Southern tenant farmers who rented land and supplies from landlords in return for substantial portions of their crops. This could be half in the case of a farmer who had no mules or tools; in addition, exorbitantly priced living expenses added to annual debts creating a cycle of poverty for families. At their peak in the 1930s, such arrangements encompassed 65 percent of cotton-belt farmers, identifying the **South** as an economically blighted zone. Increased mechanization after the Second World War slowly eliminated this neo-feudal agricultural relationship while forcing many rural Southerners to migrate to **cities** and even to move outside the South.

GARY McDONOGH

Shepard, Sam

b. 1943

Playwright and actor. Shepard has written more than forty plays, generally produced off-**Broadway**. These often explore **family** dynamics as well as the intersection of representation and reality in the **West**. He won a **Pulitzer Prize** for *Buried Child* (1979). At the same time, Shepard has developed an active career both behind and in front of the movie camera, adapting his work as the screenplay for Wim Wender's *Paris, Texas*, 1984, and bringing a lank, laconic presence to many **Hollywood** roles. He was nominated for an Academy Award for his depiction of Chuck Yaeger in *The Right Stuff* (1983).

GARY McDONOGH

shopping centers *see* malls

Sierra Club

Founded by John Muir as an outing group in the 1890s, the Sierra Club was one of the first private organizations to advocate environmental protection. During the 1960s, club president David Brower led the group to national prominence by fighting the construction of dams within the Dinosaur National Monument and the Grand Canyon National **Park**. Though still prospering, the Sierra Club has not played the same unquestioned leadership role in recent decades. Nonetheless, many Americans who wish to contribute to an environmental cause will become Sierra Club members because of its broad political agenda and widespread name recognition.

BRAD ROGERS

silent majority *see* backlash; Nixon, Richard M.

Silicon Valley

Growing from the 1950s **Stanford** University Industrial Park, a university project to facilitate corporate and academic ties in research and development, "Silicon" Valley became the model for high-tech entrepreneurship and lifestyle in computers and related industries. This aura of constantly shifting boundaries of information and processing, instant billionaires and soaring real-estate prices belied problems. These include the need for unskilled and low-paid workers in computer assembly (often third-world women), the lack of public culture and service centers and the fragility of technology rapidly exported to offshore assembly areas. Nonetheless, this techno-**suburb** has provided both a model and a nickname for other research/production complexes like Massachusett's Route 128 and New York's Silicon Alley (as well as global avatars).

GARY McDONOGH

Silko, Leslie Marmon

b. 1948

Poet and novelist of mixed Native American, Mexican and Euro-American parentage, raised on the Pueblo Indian reservation. Her novels have explored the oral traditions of the Laguna peoples, before the arrival of whites or in deep cultural conflict with them. In *Ceremony* (1977), *Storyteller* (1981), *Almanac of the Dead* (1991) and other works, she defines and champions alternative voices of American storytelling.

GARY McDONOGH

Simon, Paul

b. 1941

Enduring, popular songwriter/performer since the early 1960s. Simon combined with Queens, **New York** schoolmate, Art Garfunkel, as Simon and Garfunkel, gaining recognition with the 1965 hit "The Sound of Silence." The duo's songs struck a chord with alienated adolescents from middle-class **suburbs**, an association intensified by their soundtrack for *The Graduate* (1967). Yet after even greater success with "Bridge Over Troubled Water" (1970), the two singers separated. Simon continued briefly as a successful solo performer with "There goes Rhymin' Simon" (1973) and "Still Crazy after all these Years" (1975). Later, South African influences revitalized his career in "Graceland" (1986), for which he won his second Grammy. Initially criticized for breaking the boycott of South Africa, after the end of Apartheid, Simon came to be hailed as one of the founders of "World Music."

ROBERT GREGG

Simpson, Orenthal James ("O.J.")

b. 1947

Winner of the Heisman Trophy in 1968 while at the University of Southern California, O.J. Simpson signed for the Buffalo Bills where he broke single-season and single-game rushing records. Retiring in 1979, he went on to a career in **television**, movies and **advertising**, and was inducted into the **football** Hall of Fame in 1985. He acted in the *Naked Gun* series (1988, 1991, 1993), joined the commentary team for *Monday Night Football* and teamed up with Arnold Palmer to represent Hertz in his best-known commercials.

In 1994 he was the center of the sensational **Los Angeles, CA** murder case of his former wife,

Nicole Brown Simpson, and her friend. After a protracted trial, covered live and featured in **talk shows** and check-out counter **magazines**, Simpson was acquitted on all charges. But a wrongful death suit followed in 1997 in civil court, finding him liable to the sum of $33.5 million.

ROBERT GREGG

Simpson-Mazzoli Act *see* immigration

Simpsons, The

Offbeat cartoonist Matt Groening created this animated half-hour program **television** series that gained widespread popularity in the late 1980s and early 1990s as the premier offering of the then upstart FOX television network. While loathed by some parents for its portrayal of a **family** headed by a boorish, unintelligent father named Homer and plagued by an irreverent, rambunctious boy named Bart, the show was enormously popular with young people (not surprisingly) and critics (more surprisingly). Just below the surface the show offered a social critique built on a myriad of references to politics and popular culture. In its first two seasons, the show sparked a merchandising craze, largely through the sale of T-shirts portraying Bart uttering one of several catchphrases.

ROBERT ANDERSON

Sinatra, Frank

b. 1915; d. 1998

Frank Sinatra came to prominence in the 1940s as a crooner of mood music and went on to become perhaps the most famous and beloved singer in the history of American popular music, despite his alleged connections with the mob. Through a series of incarnations, from teen idol to movie star to living legend status as "the Chairman of the Board," the one constant in Sinatra's career was his incomparable vocal talent, which spanned through five decades of almost uninterrupted popularity. Some of his most famous songs, though penned by others –

"My Way," "I've Got You Under My Skin," "It Was A Very Good Year" – have become forever linked with a man who seemed more to inhabit songs than merely sing them.

ROBERT ANDERSON

sitcoms (situation comedies)

If **television** is "eye candy," a situation comedy (sitcom) is its tastiest morsel. Sitcoms allow viewers to develop long-term relationships with a stable cast of characters, whose conflicts, flaws and problems are depicted as endearing, amusing and almost always resolvable in twenty-two minutes or less. The program's "situation" remains virtually unchanged throughout the run of the show and typically revolves around the characters' **home** or work or a combination of the two.

Arising from the venerable traditions of farce, vaudeville and **radio** serials, sitcoms meet television's need for new and inexpensive material. Primary sets are built once and used for years. Actors are signed to long-term contracts so that a "hit" show is not threatened by a key player's departure. Four to ten writers, who become familiar with the situations, character and tone of the show, craft the season's scripts. By the 1970s, **networks** and **producers** learned that sitcoms with a hundred or more shows "in the can" could be sold for re-broadcast to distributors for lucrative **syndication** fees.

Sitcoms generally portray the white **middle class**. In the 1950s and 1960s, popular sitcoms featured silly adults (*I Love Lucy*, CBS, 1951–61; *Gilligan's Island*, CBS, 1964–7), **family** life (*Leave it to Beaver*, CBS, ABC, 1957–63; *Ozzie and Harriet*, ABC, 1952–66; *Donna Reed*, ABC, 1958–66), supernatural powers in suburbia (*I Dream of Jeannie*, NBC, 1965–70; *Bewitched*, ABC, 1964–72; *My Favorite Martian*, CBS, 1963–6) and a sanitized Second World War (*McHale's Navy*, ABC, 1962–6; *Hogan's Heroes*, CBS, 1965–71). Sitcom plots often had broadly physical humor, or played out the small triumphs and misunderstandings of everyday life for their humor. Through **comedy**, people's foibles are humanized; sitcoms reassure audiences because no problem or person upsets the show's

status quo. The best early sitcom, *The Dick Van Dyke Show* (CBS, 1961–6), successfully combined work and home situations and offered an appealing portrayal of marriage.

In the early 1970s sitcoms like *The Mary Tyler Moore Show* (CBS, 1970–7), *All in the Family* (CBS, 1971–92) and *M*A*S*H* (CBS, 1972–83) addressed more serious subjects. Thus, *M*A*S*H*'s creator Larry Gelbart changed sitcom's conventions by incorporating both a major and minor plot in many shows. *M*A*S*H* plunged viewers, long weary of Vietnam on television, into existential musings over life and **death** in the **Korean War**. In its prosaic setting of working-class Queens, New York, *All in the Family* explored previously taboo subjects, including homosexuality, sexism and racism. A program that introduced the workplace as a surrogate **family**, *The Mary Tyler Moore Show*, inaugurated television's first successful professional woman. Starting in the late 1980s, three of the longest running sitcoms presented dichotomous class issues – *The Cosby Show* (NBC, 1984–92) offered an engaging portrait of an upper-middle-class **African American** family, whereas *Married . . . With Children* (FOX, 1987–97) and *Roseanne* (ABC, 1988–97) portrayed the trials and tribulations of crass working-class white families. Successful sitcoms, such as *Seinfeld* (NBC, 1990–8), *Frasier* (NBC, 1992–) and *Friends* (NBC, 1994–), evidence Americans' teleliteracy by including large casts and intricate plots. Liberated from the constraints of the soundstage, cartoons like *The Simpsons* (FOX, 1989–) and *South Park* (Comedy Central, 1996–) twist and expand upon sitcom conventions. Sitcom has emerged as an acronym for Single Income Two Children Oppressive Mortgage, connecting once again family and representation.

Further reading

Jones, G. (1993) *Honey I'm Home! Sitcoms: Selling the American Dream*, New York: St Martin's.

MELINDA SCHWENK

sit-ins

Four students from North Carolina A&T College, a **black college** in Greensboro, asked to be served at the Woolworths' lunch-counter in early February

1960. Remaining in place after they were refused service, they began the sit-in movement. News of the sit-ins spread rapidly and within two weeks Fisk students, led by James Lawson, had instituted their own sit-in at Nashville's Kress store. The sit-ins were then copied in cities throughout the **South**, and soon sympathy sit-ins were being undertaken in Kress and Woolworths' stores in northern cities **Boston**, **Chicago, IL** and **New York**, receiving the vocal support of northern black leaders Adam Clayton **Powell**. The fact that these stores belonged to national chains contributed to the success of the southern protests against **segregation**.

The sit-ins were first seen as an extension of the work of the **SCLC**, but, in fact, the Greensboro sit-ins were done independently of both the SCLC and the **Congress of Racial Equality** and never received the support of Martin Luther **King**, Jr. **CORE**, however, quickly attempted to lead the new sit-in movement, and the SCLC attempted to harness the energy of the student movement by establishing the **Student Non-violent Coordinating Committee (SNCC)** later in the year.

The willingness of **African Americans** to withstand beatings and terror during the sit-ins opened the eyes of **white** southerners to the depth of black discontent. This discontent was not fully acknowledged by the SCLC with its stress on non-violence, and students became increasingly radicalized, shifting towards an emphasis on **Black Power**.

ROBERT GREGG

skateboarding

Now a staple in ESPN's **X-Games**, skateboarding took off as a fad in the 1960s. As portrayed in the movie *Back to the Future* (1985), it started with children tinkering with go-carts and roller skates, yet quickly migrated from playgrounds to downtown as skateboarders sought the best surfaces for their fast-developing techniques and tricks. The sport's novelty, its athletes' penchant for practicing in places where "suits" carried out their business and the inheritance of some **surfing** etiquette gave skateboarding an anti-authoritarian aspect. This lessened with growing commercialization and the establishment of custom **parks** designed to keep the skateboarders away from "public" space. New urethane wheels and fiberglass for the boards, introduced in the 1970s, increased costs, but also made boards more able to ride over bumpy terrains like uneven sidewalks. But the main thrills remain in the skating parks, where the boarders have developed tricks ranging from aerials and grinders to rock and rolls.

ROBERT GREGG

skiing and snowboarding

Americans have seldom challenged Alpine skiers' dominance in skiing. Skiing is a very expensive sport that Americans have taken to as a recreation, but very few have been brought up in the kind of skiing environment necessary to compete. Even Americans living in the **Rocky Mountain** region treat skiing as a vacation sport, compared to Alpine communities that depend on skiing for transportation and communication. Victories, like the Picabo Street in the 1998 Nagano **Olympics**, are rare exceptions.

Snowboarding, by contrast, has been developed and dominated largely by Americans. The first snowboard was built in Sherman Poppen's garage in 1967. Many early designs borrowed from **surfing** and, until 1985, metal edges were included on all snowboards. By 1993 there were over fifty different snowboard manufacturers.

Generally cheaper than skiing, snowboarding was first viewed as low-class and countercultural, and many American resorts banned it. Gradually, the Snowboarding Outreach Society began to gain acceptance for the sport and for the competitive racing begun in 1981. After Stratton Mountain in Vermont offered the first snowboarding instruction in 1986, the sport gained respect and widespread popularity.

Women also established themselves as athletes in the sport competing against men. The emphasis on jumps and spins as opposed to speed has given women equal chances.

The sport has become increasingly professionalized in the 1990s, sponsored by manufacturers and covered since 1993 on ESPN. With its emphasis on daredevil antics, snowboarding has also been a mainstay of **X-games**.

ROBERT GREGG

slackers

Term popularized by Richard Linklater's 1991 film about "twenty-somethings" in **Austin, TX**, the term underscores the diminished expectations of **Generation X**. This is evident in underdeveloped careers and questions about family and society, yet is coupled with an ability to consume media and other commodities. Many have questioned this broad generalization as well as its localization of issues in a group of people rather than their social, economic and cultural context.

Further reading

Daly, S. and Wice, N. (1995) *Alt.culture*, New York: Harper.

GARY McDONOGH
CINDY WONG

slang *see* language

Slavic Americans

The largest wave of **immigration** into the United States from Eastern Europe took place between 1880 and 1914, when some 7 million people from this region arrived in America. Apart from about 1.8 million **Jews**, mostly of **Russian** origin, who had been forced out by persecutions, nearly all these peoples were of Slavic stock. Poles were the largest single group, consisting of about 1.1 million people, but there were also substantial numbers of Russians, Hungarians, Lithuanians, Ukrainians, Belorussians, Latvians, Czechs, Slovaks, Slovenes, Serbs, Croats and Romanians.

Some of these immigrants, like the Russian Doukhobors, came searching for religious freedom, while others, especially from the lands of the Austro-Hungarian empire, were avoiding conscription into the army. Most, however, were attracted to America by economic opportunities. Rising populations, collapsing agricultural prices and changes in land tenure meant that many peasant families could no longer subsist. America had acquired the reputation of a "promised land," where work could be found and there was a chance of advancement. Many of the immigrants were in fact recruited by agents in their home countries; others took passage to America trusting that the rumors of plentiful work would turn out to be true. Many of the immigrants were single young males looking for work rather than land.

Most of the immigrants did find work, especially in the rapidly growing industrial centers of the **Midwest**. The large Polish community in **Chicago, IL**, for example, dates from around this time. However, wages were low and the immigrants suffered much discrimination. Some stuck it out and put down roots; others moved west to establish homesteads in the Great Plains. Many returned. In the decade before the First World War, immigration records show that around half of all Hungarian, Croat, Slovak and Slovene immigrants returned to Europe soon after their arrival.

The collapse of the Austro-Hungarian and Russian empires at the end of the First World War brought more Slavic immigrants, though in smaller numbers, and there were more after the Second World War. Refugees from behind the Iron Curtain continued to arrive in small numbers; for example, the events of 1956 brought several thousand Hungarians to the USA, while the first suppression of the Solidarity movement in 1982 resulted in around 8,000 Poles fleeing to America.

In many ways, the Slavic immigrants have been model members of the "melting-pot" society. The initial immigrants tried to integrate quickly into American society and culture, sometimes even changing their names to Anglicized forms. Unlike German and Jewish immigrants, who retained political affiliations and set up strong inter-community organizations, the Slavs did not become highly political. During the **Cold War**, the **Republican Party** in particular canvassed for votes among immigrants who had families behind the Iron Curtain, but the Slavs never developed the political voice of, for example, Jewish Americans or **Irish Americans**. In the 1970s, however, following the success of the **Black Power** movement, some groups of Slavic descent such as Polish Americans and Ukrainian Americans did establish cultural associations with the aim of reawakening pride in their own culture and counteracting racism from WASP segments of society.

MORGEN WITZEL

small-town ideals

Post-war growth overwhelmed small towns but never erased their symbolic appeal. Small towns began losing residents in the 1920s, but postwar educational opportunities lured still more, and younger, townspeople away. Sprawling suburban developments also transformed independent towns into mere bedroom communities for nearby **cities**, as new **highways** enabled routine commuting from residential neighborhoods created virtually overnight. Suburban tracts offered privacy and autonomy hitherto unattainable outside cities, while the relocation policies of corporate employers discouraged ambitious employees from forming any sentimental attachments to place. This postwar culture of education, **mobility**, growth and anonymity sapped the civic energy, inter-generational connection and **community** feeling of small-town life.

Pre-war townspeople purchased a wide range of personal services from familiar merchants, shopkeepers and mechanics, many of whom began to close up in the 1960s and 1970s. New interstate highways bypassed thousands of towns, stranding "**mom-and-pop stores**" that had traded with motorists traveling the local roads. New mass-market retailers offered large inventories of cheaper goods to local shoppers and tourists alike. Unable to compete, local stores closed, diminishing the uniqueness that was each town's pride and treasured inheritance.

Small-town services, neighborliness and civic unity had always involved uneven quality, intrusiveness and unchallenged prejudice. But by the 1970s and 1980s, new suburban communities, with names like "Hometown," "Pleasant Valley" and "Littleton," traded on rosy nostalgia for small-town life. Developers of "new towns" featuring artificial centers with the same retailers that lined the interstates advertised a perfect mix of town-style

community and suburban prestige, themes also seen in **New Urbanism**.

Surviving small towns began in the 1990s to assert their own version of the past, reaching out for tourist dollars by rediscovering local **history** and refurbishing fine old buildings. Nineteenth-century town boosters had eagerly exaggerated local get-up-and-go and promised that their growing town would be a new Colossus within the year. In the 1980s, town leaders, seeking new corporate and light industrial employers, sold their communities as quiet, traffic-free, family friendly and homogenous.

The poorest towns, lacking political strength, acquired the most problematic new economic resources. In the 1970s and 1980s, **Appalachian** towns, along with southern **African American**, southwestern **Hispanic** and Native American reservation towns, began spending local economic development funds to build facilities for imported hazardous waste. In the 1990s, as mandatory sentencing swelled the **prison** population, job-starved towns also reached out for new federal prison-building contracts.

Visible reverse **migration** from cities to towns began in the 1980s, notably among African American families. Parents who had left southern towns for northern cities before 1940 saw their adult children return to look after elders or family land, or simply to escape what had not, after all, been a promised land up north.

Old towns, dead towns, ersatz towns and new towns cover the late-twentieth-century landscape. Though nothing has restored the pre-war American town, small-town life remains a compelling ideal.

Further reading

David, P. (1982) *Hometown*, New York: Simon & Schuster.
Stack, C. (1996) *Call to Home*, New York: Basic.
http://www.bestsmalltowns.org.

SHARON ANN HOLT

Smithsonian Institution

Founded in 1846 and named for British scientist James Smithson, who had donated $508,318 to increase and diffuse knowledge in America. The largest museum complex in the world, most of its buildings cluster around the Washington mall. The Smithsonian includes sixteen **museums** in New York and the District of Columbia, as well as four field stations; the National Art Gallery is affiliated, with a separate board. Its collections encompass American art, space, natural history, American history, Asian art, African art, science and technology, sculpture and associated themes of popular culture. The Smithsonian runs an **African American** history museum in Anacostia (Washington), the National **Zoo** and the Cooper Hewitt Design Museum in New York. The newest hall, to open in 2000, will be devoted to Native Americans, incorporating New York's Museum of the American Indian.

All these museums are free to the public. The Smithsonian assembles important travelling exhibits as well, since less than 1 percent of the total collection can actually be exhibited at any time. It also has extensive educational outreach facilities (accessible at its web-site: http://www.si.gov). The Institution also constitutes an important center for advanced research, scholarship and publication through both its press and *Smithsonian* **magazine**. An independent agency, its board includes the vice-president, chief justice of the **Supreme Court**, Congress members and citizens.

The Smithsonian, as America's museum, often challenges the boundaries of what constitutes history and how it should be presented. It has added television memorabilia alongside the gowns of the First Ladies and taken American diversity into the mall in its Folklife Festivals. It was also caught in a bitter controversy in the late 1990s over how to present the reasoning behind and impacts of atomic devastation in **Japan** – the "*Enola Gay*" controversy – which remind us how complex the past can be for a contested present.

GARY McDONOGH

soap operas, daytime

In spring 1999, the daytime serial *All My Children* ended thirty years of family and community intrigue and relationships, presented every Monday through Friday. It was soon replaced by the younger and steamier *Passion*. Demographics and settings may change, but the idea scarcely varies. Soaps provide dramas of emotion and conversation over coffee and cocktails rather than politics or work. Women are central, as peacemakers and bitches, although men have a variety of roles from paterfamilias to villain to stud. The sheer endurance of soap operas means that they have invited generations of fans to enter webs of romance, affairs, cat-fights, consumption, **weddings**, births (not in that order) and murders among the men and women of Pine Valley, Glen Cove and other "typical" American places.

Soaps easily made the transition to **television** from long-running **radio** serials (taking their name from detergent sponsors). These **family**-centered dramas related to the viewers of new media, especially the housewife whom writers and advertisers have taken as the long-term viewer. Feminist scholars have examined how the form of soap operas fits into a woman's daily routine. Soap operas do not always demand continuous concentration; hence, the ideal woman viewer can come in and out, watching the show while doing other chores. Multiple plot lines take away the clear beginning and end in a strict narrative, allowing the viewers to start watching the show at any point.

Soaps are also cheap to produce – writers create up to 5 hours of programs every week, taped by three studio cameras, with the actions rolling along without cuts (different scenes are put together in post-production). These are grueling scripts for actors, although soaps have provided both security and a sure proving ground for many **stars**.

Over decades, soap operas have added serial **divorce** and infidelity, company battles, crime, sex and nudity which may have shocked their fans. *Dark Shadows* (ABC, 1966–71) cast the soap into Gothic shadows. **African American** characters arrived in the 1980s (although black viewers have learned to watch the scandals of whites in many media). Teens and young hunks were increasingly promising in the 1990s.

Audiences have also varied. Educated professionals and college students videotape their soaps daily, although daytime soaps do not have the same public appeal to straight males. Celebrities, however, have turned fanship into participation;

Elizabeth **Taylor** and Carol Burnett have made cameo appearances in their favorite shows.

Soaps, as prominent television artifacts, have been skewered in other series (the ironic evening comedies *Soap* (ABC, 1977–81) and *Mary Hartman, Mary Hartman* (1976–77, syndicated) even as **networks** vied to create glamorous **prime-time soaps**. *Tootsie* (1982) and *Soapdish* (1991) also imputed other layers of human complication to dramas on screen.

Cable television has brought *telenovelas* and other long-running dramas from around the world to American screens (and PBS has come close with some more sophisticated British imports). Yet these scarcely rival decades in which *Days of Our Lives, All My Children, The Bold and the Beautiful* and others have become everyday worlds as well as stories.

Further reading

Modlewski, T. (1979) "The Search for Tomorrow in Today's Soap Operas," *Film Quarterly* 33(1): 12–21.

GARY McDONOGH

CINDY WONG

soap operas, prime-time

Melodrama has long been a staple of American entertainment; hence long-running, involved tales of **family**, relationships, conflict and passion have dominated daytime fare on **radio** and **television** for decades. Television's first soap opera, *Faraway Hill* (Dumont Network, 1946), nonetheless, was broadcast on Wednesday night, 21:00–21:30. A dramatization of Grace Metalious' popular novel *Peyton Place* later briefly renewed the night-time soap (ABC, 1964–9). After the success of various **miniseries**, however, competitive **prime-time** serial dramas regained prominence in the 1980s, generally coinciding with the social and economic shifts of the **Reagan** era, including growing **class** polarization and the rise of the **Sunbelt**.

Dallas (CBS, 1978–91), the pioneer, followed the affairs of three generations of the plutocrat Ewing family of the South Fork ranch. It synthesized glamour, sexuality, politics and **oil**, and gained worldwide popularity (whose readings Ian Ang has studied in *Watching Dallas*, 1985). Seasonal cliffhanger endings included "Who shot J.R.?" (referring to an attempt on villain J.R. Ewing, played by Larry Hagman); 41 million households tuned in for the answer, among the most-watched shows in history. Plot twists became more contrived as characters shifted in later seasons.

Dynasty (ABC, 1981–9) also mixed money, power and oil in the couplings and cat-fights of two wealthy **Denver** families. Blake Carrington, played by a former TV **sitcom** father, John Forsythe, was husband to naive, honest Krystle (Linda Evans) and patriarch to a troubled company and kindred, including one of television's first gay male characters. Blake's nemesis/ex-wife, Alexis Carrington, became closely associated with the persona of actor/author Joan Collins. The series offered loyal fans marketing tie-ins like perfume and short-lived spin-offs (*The Colbys*, ABC, 1985–7), but it also sparked parodic parties and camp humor. Again, its images of power and sin sold well abroad, confirming dreams and stereotypes of the US.

Other related series, with lustful couples, scheming older villains (often reviving **Hollywood** stars' careers) and money included *Falcon Crest* (CBS, 1981–90, with former Reagan wife Jane Wyman as the matriarch of a **California** winery) and *Knots Landing* (CBS, 1979–93), set among middle-class California suburbanites. All disappeared into **syndication** by the mid-1990s, eclipsed by police and **medical shows** which sometimes claimed to be higher-brow entertainment, yet incorporated similar melodramatic personal stories.

Stories of the beautiful and comfortable later re-emerged to prime-time popularity, sometimes finding different fans on emergent **networks** like FOX. *Melrose Place* (FOX, 1992–), with *Dynasty* alumna Heather Locklear, proved popular among **Generation X** viewers. *Beverly Hills 90210* (FOX, 1990–), an Aaron **Spelling** serial, tracked both its stars and audience from **Hollywood** high-school chic through college affairs. Perhaps as a response to changing times, these seem to focus more on sexuality and betrayal than on the glamorization of sheer wealth that underpinned *Dynasty* and *Dallas*. Nonetheless like daytime soaps – and real-life dramas portrayed by news media in the same melodramatic and cliffhanger styles, from O.J. **Simpson** to the **Clinton** White House – these continue to be staples of the American dream.

Further reading

Ang, I. (1985) *Watching Dallas*, London: Methuen.
Bianculli, D. (1996) *Dictionary of Teleliteracy*, New York: Continuum.

GARY McDONOGH

soccer

One of the fastest growing sports in the United States, both in terms of participation and spectatorship, largely owing to its appeal among women and girls who have been shut out of other professional team sports. Such appeal was manifest at the 1999 Women's World Cup Final, played between the United States and China at the Rose Bowl in front of 90,000 plus spectators – the largest-ever audience for a women's sporting event. The images of Briana Scurry making the crucial penalty save, and Brandi Chastain pulling off her shirt after slotting home the final penalty, will be remembered in the minds of many American girls for as long as English boys remember events at Wembley in 1966.

Soccer in the United States developed slowly due to the strength of American **football** in colleges and the strength of **baseball** among working-class Americans. Immigrants from countries associated with Association Football – Germany, Italy and Ireland, for example – left their homelands before soccer was firmly established and so readily adopted a game that was being promoted as the "American game."

Soccer's popularity increased at the end of the 1960s with coverage of the 1966 World Cup because of a continued identification among many Americans with England. In 1967 the North American Soccer League was established, using the formula of attracting big names from European and South American soccer. Only the New York Cosmos thrived under this system, signing Pele, George Best and Franz Beckenbauer, and the league suffered due to the lack of talent and the limited availability of native-born players with whom crowds could identify. By the end of the 1970s the league was all but moribund.

The situation in the 1990s has been very different. Soccer now has very strong roots in communities around the country. It ranks as the fastest-growing team sport in terms of levels of participation, dwarfing **little-league baseball**, with between 4 and 6 million children participating in organized leagues. Soccer has also established very strong roots in colleges, particularly among women players, whose sporting facilities have improved in response to **Title IX**.

The international soccer federation (FIFA) tried to enter the lucrative American market for many years, but this remained difficult until the emergence of **cable** television, as the major networks catered to exceedingly profitable football, **basketball** and baseball leagues. The rise of ESPN, the cable sports channel, provided a new outlet for small sporting markets and growing markets like that for soccer.

The World Cup in 1994, held in the United States, set attendance records for the competition and helped cement the position of soccer in the United States. Large crowds witnessed a respectable American national team led by Alexi Lalas, Eric Wynalda and John Harkin, stars from the fledgling major-league soccer. This league has avoided the pitfalls of the NASL, and, by limiting each team to four foreign players, has given the league a more American flavor and ensured considerable corporate sponsorship.

Continued success for soccer in the United States is likely to depend on the blending of two traditions, similar to that occurring earlier in the rise of basketball. One is the **suburban** sporting tradition, undergoing a shift as parents turn away from basketball, associated with the inner city, and football, seen by many as being too violent for their children. The strength of soccer in suburban communities is seen in the political significance attached to the "soccer mom" as a constituency in recent political elections.

The other tradition is that of the new immigrants coming into the country. New arrivals following the easing of **immigration** quotas in the 1960s have left places where soccer is firmly established as the leading spectator sport. Instead of identifying with baseball, which has been losing its hold as the American game, many of these immigrants enter communities where ethnic soccer teams and leagues are commonplace.

And the success of the game has been amply demonstrated by the Women's World Cup of 1999, which, building on the USA's leading position in the women's game, has produced record-breaking crowds and widespread attention from bastions of male dominance. The Gatorade commercial pitting Mia Hamm, the superstar of the women's game, against Micheal Jordan highlights the newfound commercial appeal of the game and its players.

Further reading

Gardner, P. (1999) *Soccer Talk*, Chicago: Masters Press.

Longman, J. (2000) *The Girls of Summer*, New York: Harper Collins.

ROBERT GREGG

socialists *see* communism; Left, the

Social Security

The Social Security Act of 1935, part of President Franklin **Roosevelt**'s New Deal program, was drafted in response to a need to address financial insecurity in **old age**. While it did provide public assistance for the aged poor, it more notably legislated a national social-insurance system to provide pensions for retirees. Although not made explicit at the time, it is commonly believed that the legislation was also intended to address the problem of unemployment by removing a significant number of persons from the jobless statistics. While improving income security for older Americans, it simultaneously and unintentionally set the stage for a form of age discrimination by insinuating that older adults do not have a place in the labor force, a sentiment still held by some today. Maximum payments in 1999 are set at $1,373 dollars for fully vested individuals, although benefits vary widely in terms of amount of contribution, time of withdrawal and additional income.

The Old-Age Assistance component of the Social Security Act, Title I, is funded through general **tax** revenues, and guarantees public assistance to poor elders regardless of employment history. In contrast, Title II, which mandates universal pensions for retired workers, is financed through a payroll tax shared equally by employee and employer. When first enacted in 1935 only workers in commerce and industry were covered, representing approximately 60 percent of the labor force (Myers 1987). It wasn't until the 1950s that subsequent legislation broadened the scope of the program to include most of those previously excluded, such as farm workers and the self-employed.

Social Security pension benefits were originally and deliberately portrayed as having been earned by the elderly through premium-like payments into the system during their working years. However, it has become increasingly understood that the Social Security system is a tax on today's generation of workers to support those who are currently retired – not an insurance program. There are, in reality, no reserves of accrued premiums – a deliberate feature of the program. Thus, there exists an arrangement whereby elderly recipients are, in a sense, at the mercy of the current workforce and their continued commitment to supporting the program as it now stands. Many fear that the sense of obligation to perpetuate the system will diminish, which will usher in momentous modifications to its structure and potentially undermine its solvency.

A further threat to the Social Security system is the changing demographic profile of the American people. As an aging society, the United States is experiencing an increase in the elderly dependency ratio, the number of dependents over sixty-five per hundred persons aged eighteen to sixty-five. This figure for the year 2030 is projected to be twice what it was in 1960 (Pifer and Bronte 1986), reflecting an increasing pool of Social Security beneficiaries dependent upon a significantly smaller cohort of labor-force participants. Given a design founded on resource redistribution, not insurance, this connotes high and increasing costs for maintaining the elderly. The potential for strained relations among generations is apparent.

There is significant debate over the future of the Social Security program. Many still subscribe to the belief that the structure will collapse due to inadequate funding to perpetuate the system, despite significant legislated improvements in

1983. Public confidence has declined drastically in light of such commentary. In reality, the ability of the nation to keep the system solvent is not in question and there is, in fact, a substantial surplus of funds at present. The question is, therefore, not *whether* the United States can guarantee the continued existence of the Social Security system but *how*. Those who have subjected the program to critical scrutiny answer that question with solutions ranging from minor tweaking to a significant overhaul (Dentzer 1999). Regardless, the critical issues to be addressed include the formula used to collect the necessary funding, the amount of benefits to be distributed to individuals, the criteria under which benefits are distributed and the source of financing.

Future retirees across the generations are deeply concerned about the ongoing successful management of the Social Security program and fear that they may receive no benefits in exchange for their years of contributions. Today's politicians recognize the alarm among the populace and are crafting various proposals to "fix" the system. Some are acting out of a sincere concern for their constituents while others, perhaps, merely see the universal fear as an opportunity for political gain. The politicization of the issue has been both beneficial, by drawing needed attention to the matter, and harmful, by generating undue panic over the continued solvency of Social Security.

Debates, both political and scholarly, over the matter of adjusting benefit levels based upon the relative economic status of beneficiaries have contributed to the polarization of the American public. At the heart of the matter is the question of whether means-testing is a useful method of improving the financial health of the Social Security system or simply a path towards the further division of the American populace along class lines. Those in support of the latter position argue that better ways of modifying the program exist (Scharlach and Kaye 1997).

Further reading

Atchley, R.C. (1997) *Social Forces and Aging*, 8th edn, Belmont: Wadsworth.

Dentzer, S. (1999) "The Stakes," *Modern Maturity*, pp. 44–55.

Myers, R.J. (1987) "Social Security," in Maddox, G. L. (ed.) *The Encyclopedia of Aging*, New York: Springer Publishing Company.

National Academy on Aging (1997) "Facts on Social Security: The Old Age and Survivors Trust Fund, 1997," *Gerontology News* (24)6: 7–8.

Pifer, A. and Bronte, L. (1986) *Our Aging Society: Paradox and Promise*, New York: W.W. Norton & Company.

Scharlach, A.E. and Kaye, L.W. (eds) (1997) *Controversial Issues in Aging*, Boston: Allyn and Bacon.

Schulz, J.H. (1995) *The Economics of Aging*, 6th edn, Westport, CN: Auburn House.

LENARD W. KAYE

sociology

Sociology, as a field of study, focuses on the interactions of individuals, groups and organizations within a social structure. The discipline of sociology has always been shaped by the political and social climate of the times and can be traced back to the works of Karl Marx (1818–83), Emile Durkheim (1858–1917), Max Weber (1864–1920) and W.E.B. **Du Bois** (1868–1963), whose political and social philosophies on labor, capital, **religion**, culture, morality and modern life continue to influence the field of sociology as well as other disciplines.

During the early twentieth century, the **University of Chicago** was known to be the hub of American sociology. While at Harvard University, around the mid-century, Talcott Parsons (1902–79), considered the founder of American sociological theory, worked on general theories of social action, helping make that institution a center of sociological research. Likewise, Robert Merton's work at Columbia University helped to forge sociology into an intellectual science with its own terminology of concepts and standards of application, making Columbia the other recognized center for sociology.

Up until the mid-twentieth century, the field of sociology was dedicated mostly to structural analysis. Social changes occurring in the 1950s inspired the emergence of new sociological concepts. With the

Civil Rights movement and other social movements, the political and social climates of the United States were altering quickly, and sociologists responded by focusing their research less on structural analysis and more on political and moral concerns prevalent during the late 1950s and 1960s. Younger sociologists began to put into practice those theories they had learned by researching less advantaged groups in society, like women, **African Americans** and **Latinos**. As sociologists embarked on this new direction, their influence increased with summons coming from the White House, Senate and Congress to advise on the plethora of social problems facing the country.

In the 1990s, most **colleges and universities** housed a sociology department, but the prestige of these departments had diminished significantly from the heyday of the 1950s and 1960s. Partly this was a result of the **backlash** against many of the policies and programs that they had recommended to politicians, many of them associated with President Lyndon **Johnson**'s "Great Society." Backing away from public policy, sociologists have in a way synthesized the earlier impulses, studying individuals and the social structures within which they operate. Areas of research vary from **feminism** to **education** to ethnic identity to the HIV/ **AIDS** epidemic. With a broader, more complex field of study most sociologists still utilize the classic theories to understand the intricacy of contemporary problems.

Further reading

Lemert, C. (1997) *Social Things: An Introduction to the Sociological Life*, Lanham: Rowman and Littlefield Publishers, Inc.
Lemert, C. (ed.) (1993) *Social Theory: The Multicultural & Classic Readings*, Boulder: Westview Press.

LORELEI ATALIE VARGAS

soda

Names vary regionally ("pop" in **New England**, "soft drinks" or "cola" in the **South**), as do local favorites. Yet, Coca-Cola, Pepsi and related non-alcoholic carbonated beverages have built global empires, as emblematic of contemporary America as tea in Japan or wine in France. Over a century, strong cultural associations have been forged between these drinks and child and **teenage** sociability (1950s soda jerks and soda fountains or 1990s **fast-food** packages). Meanwhile, darker associations have been drawn between aggressively marketed sodas and poor nutrition or tooth decay, while teen folklore has identified coke and aspirin as a contraceptive (or whispered about drugs hidden in innocent beverages).

Atlanta pharmacist John Pemberton created "Coke" in 1886, a "temperance" version of his previous Bordeaux-coca combination. Mixing fruit flavors, spices, *coca* and *kola*, Pemberton added carbonated water in 1887 before selling out to pharmacist Asa Candler. Candler expanded sales through regionalized syrup production and local bottling franchises. In the 1920s, the Woodruff dynasty took Coke worldwide, including to the frontlines of the Second World War. Advertising and placement in fast food, foreign policy and children's sight made Coke an American staple, reinforced with catchy jingles like "I'd like to teach the world to sing." The company diversified into diet drinks and other markets, but faced a major misstep in 1985, with a change in its highly secretive formula. The **Atlanta**-based company recovered with 1992 **Olympic** sponsorship, Coke memorabilia, stressing American nostalgia, and insistent placement through advertising and monopolistic sales arrangements.

Pepsi, created by a North Carolina pharmacist in the 1890s, grew slowly until after the Second World War, when markets expanded through advertising pitched towards a younger "Pepsi Generation." By the 1970s, it pulled even in-store sales and skirmished over both fast-food placements and international diplomacy (**Nixon** took Pepsi to China). Like Coke, Pepsi seeks monopolistic placements, whether in schools or on airlines.

Pepsi and Coke diversification encompasses lemon-lime sodas, fruit drinks and related products. Competitors have included Dr Pepper (with snappy youth-oriented ad campaigns) and Royal Crown Colas, fruit flavors (orange, grape and peach Nehi), creme soda and root/birch beer and chocolate sodas. Asian and Latino stores supply coconut, vegetable and sugarcane beverages, while 1990s competition for non-alcoholic markets has been heightened by bottled, flavored iced teas and sparkling waters, often with European cachet (albeit conglomerate ownership).

Further reading

Pendergast, C. (1993) *For God, Country and Coca-Cola*, New York: Charles Scribner's Sons.

GARY McDONOGH

softball

Baseball game adapted for women by educators who believed that the women's game should differ from the men's in terms of the size of the ball, the pitching (which, though underarm, can be a fast-pitch game at the top levels) and the vigor with which it was played. Only the first two strictures remained as the game spread rapidly in the industries that employed women during the Second World War (as many as 40,000 teams existing around the country in 1944). Following the war, softball remained largely unsupported in **colleges and universities** until the passage of **Title IX** in 1972, but by the 1990s an estimated 40 million men and women were playing softball in the US. Among men the game is normally given recreational status, but for girls and women it has become a major school and college sport, especially noted for being a new source of scholarships for women athletes at the larger universities.

Efforts to internationalize the game occurred throughout the 1970s, with a simultaneous attempt to have softball accepted as an **Olympic** sport. Softball was introduced at the **Atlanta** games of 1996 as a full Olympic sport. Led by shortstop Dot Richardson, the American team defeated seven other nations in a round-robin tournament, securing the gold medal.

Further reading

Walsh, L. (1978) *Contemporary Softball*, Chicago: Contemporary Books.

ROBERT GREGG

SoHo

This lower Manhattan area is located SOuth of HOuston Street and was in the early 1900s an area of cast-iron factory buildings. In the 1960s and 1970s, after many factory closures, the artists rediscovered the area, using low-rent factories as lofts. An art scene grew up in SoHo and property values increased. In the 1990s, SoHo boasts institutions like the SoHo Guggenheim as well as luxury shops and residences. Although some long-time residents remain, SoHo has become more about the sale and display of art than its production. The stump-compound name of SoHo has also been extended to NoHo (North) and mimicked elsewhere – hence SoBe for South Beach, in **Miami, FL**.

GABRIELLE BENDINER-VIANI

Somalia

Continuing drought brought widespread famine to the Horn of Africa during the early 1990s, leading the United Nations to send humanitarian aid. By December 1992, however, warring Somali factions were diverting UN sanctioned food-relief shipments to black markets, so President **Bush** dispatched 30,000 American troops to Somalia to protect food deliveries.

The deployment of troops became controversial as tensions arose between UN and US officials in Somalia, while Somali factions began to fight back. It became clearer that American officials did not know enough about the region and its peoples to make the mission work smoothly. These problems were exacerbated when President **Clinton** expanded the American military's mandate to restoring order and state building. When eighteen marines were killed fighting the forces of Somali warlord Mohammed Farah Aidid and television cameras recorded a mob dragging an American body down the street, public support for the mission deteriorated. Clinton withdrew all troops in 1994, and remained wary of using American force in **Africa**, something that would have dire consequences when genocide began in Rwanda.

ROBERT GREGG

Sontag, Susan

b. 1933

Susan Sontag is an American essayist, novelist, and film-maker known for her insightful analyses of contemporary culture. Born in **New York** City, her diverse accomplishments include a prolific literary career, a performance in Woody **Allen**'s *Zelig* (1983) and an uncompromising dedication to humanitarian concerns. She has written many highly original essay collections, short stories and novels, and has also written and directed films. Her essay collections include *Against Interpretation* (1966), *About Photography* (1977), *Illness as Metaphor* (1978) and *Under the Sign of Saturn* (1980). Her novels include *The Volcano Lover: A Romance* (1992).

NICOLE MARIE KEATING

soul

Soul music became the voice of black America in the 1960s, but that voice was hardly a singular one. Mixing the sacred sounds of gospel with the profane of the **blues** – and a dash of lush, pop production – soul brought black music to new heights of expressiveness. Lyrically, soul veered from complex, adult romance to optimistic anthems of black pride, a reflection of the social changes and **civil rights** activism taking place in the United States.

Ray Charles, Sam **Cooke**, Jackie Wilson and James **Brown** pioneered the form in the late 1950s with their mixtures of gospel and **R&B**. In the 1960s, major soul music scenes centered around labels, producers and studios in **Detroit, MI** (Motown), Memphis (Stax/Volt), **Philadelphia, PA** (Gamble & Huff) and Alabama (Muscle Shoals). Throughout the decade, artists such as Smokey Robinson, the **Supremes**, Ben E. King, the Temptations and Curtis Mayfield brought the sounds of sweet soul music to listeners – black and white – across mainstream America. The demand for "Respect" in the Otis Redding song, as performed by Aretha **Franklin** in 1967, stands as much as anything for the spirit of soul.

The soul era is generally considered to have died out when the **Civil Rights** era ended, signified most dramatically by the assassination of Martin Luther **King**, Jr. in 1968. Musically, soul lived on, though it spawned the new variations of funk (Sly Stone, James Brown, Parliament/Funkadelic) and disco (the Trammps, Donna Summer) and the singular sounds of Stevie **Wonder**.

DEWAR MACLEOD

South

This region includes the former slave-holding states of the Confederacy during the Civil War – Alabama, Arkansas, Florida, Georgia, Louisiana, Mississippi, North and South Carolina, Tennessee, Texas and Virginia. Nearby "border" states of Missouri, Kentucky, Maryland and West Virginia also share many traits and connections. The South's defining historical features include social polarization around **race** and **class**, intense political campaigns defending these interests, a stratified rural agricultural base and torturous cultural debates over these features, in the South and in confrontation with the rest of the nation. The South remains paradoxical in the very salience of its positive and negative images – friendly, yet embittered, or genteel but ignorant and provincial. Such stereotypes permeated coverage of the 1996 Atlanta **Olympics** as they had in the **civil rights** campaigns, which fundamentally changed the Solid South.

Change is a fundamental feature of modern Southern contradictions. In the 1930s, this area, and its black and white population, was labeled the number one economic problem in America, even while romanticized in movies like *Gone With the Wind* (1939), which continued to shape visions of Southern history worldwide. Abandoned by many African Americans as a hell of slavery and **segregation**, its whites expressed both guilt and defiance in dealing with the rest of the nation. After the Second World War, the South was segregated, fundamentalist, rural, **Democrat** and poor, yet it also held an aura of mystery, aristocratic culture and verdant passions. By the 1990s, the South was generally and visibly integrated, marked by **Sunbelt** development, diverse and **Republican** –

without totally belying or erasing its earlier lives and reputation.

Economic development had already begun to change the South in the 1930s and 1940s, with the work of the WPA and the **Tennessee Valley Authority**, controlling flooding and generating power throughout the upper South. Other stimuli to growth came from manufacturers moving production to non-**union** and cheap-wage states, a pattern still present in exploitative industries like poultry and clothing. Military development also generated continuing investment in the South, whose Congress members and citizens stayed committed to the armed forces even in periods of American doubt like the **Vietnam War**. The South remains covered by military bases and suppliers to this day. Agriculture, forced into modernization by the exodus of cheap, controllable labor, continued as an economic base. While King Cotton never recovered its pre-eminence after turn of the nineteenth century boll weevil infestations, **tobacco**, sugar, fruits and vegetables, meats and fish have all contributed to state and local economies.

In the 1950s, however, the issues were less economic than social and political, as disfranchised blacks across the South demanded equal rights of participation within their societies. Segregation, for decades, had denied citizens the vote, job opportunities, schools and even access to stores, restaurants and bathrooms on the basis of race. Bloody campaigns to gain these rights tore across rural areas, small towns and the cities of the South. Figures such as Rosa **Parks**, Martin Luther **King**, Jr. and Lillian Smith emerged as consciences not only for the region but for the nation which had accommodated to the oppression of so many citizens. Meanwhile, segregationist politicians like George **Wallace**, Lester Maddox and Strom **Thurmond** charted a course which broke the South from the New Deal Democrats towards a conservative union with Republicans which became evident in Barry **Goldwater**'s 1964 triumphs there against Lyndon **Johnson**, a Texan identified with civil rights.

Slow resolutions of decades of injustice came with development as well as constitutional revindication. In the 1970s, as protest tore across America's industrial cities, a new South beckoned with investment opportunities and images of leisure in a lush climate (aided by widespread **air-conditioning**). **Florida**, already a **tourism** center, boomed into the fourth-largest state in the country with retirees and coastal development; all Southern states except Arkansas and Tennessee have coasts which saw massive development into the 1990s. Yet the gaps between plutocratic Palm Beach and Florida's inland agricultural towns like Belle Glade still speak of both human and environmental exploitation. **Texas**, whose trajectory also differs from the rest of the South, burgeoned with **oil** and gas in boom-and-bust metropoles like **Houston** and **Dallas**, while facing deep divisions between **Latino** populations, old and new, and Anglo settlers and immigrants. Meanwhile, the **Appalachian** Mountains and Mississippi Delta remained mired in poverty as mines closed and small farms failed to compete – even when new resort developments would later spring up nearby.

By the 1980s, new capitals had emerged. **Atlanta** took command of air, government offices and ultimately media with Ted **Turner**. **Charlotte, NC**, however, challenged Atlanta's control of finance through the aggressive national mergers of many North Carolina banks, while **Miami** and **Houston** evoked a more global South with ties to **Latin America** and the **Caribbean**. **Nashville**, in music, Orlando, with **Disneyworld** development, and **New Orleans**, in everything, also blend old and new South, where tourists come to experience, buy and even resettle in areas scorned only decades before.

Development has not erased divisions, as blacks continue to fight for equal funding and access as well as political representation across the South. Conservative national politicians and judges may often seem to be more of an enemy than local leaders. Meanwhile, the area that produced almost all modern Democratic presidents – Johnson (who balanced Massachusett's young, liberal **JFK**), **Carter** (Georgia) and both **Clinton** (Arkansas) and his VP **Gore** (Tennessee) – has increasingly voted Republican in Congress and the statehouse. In 1996 the Democratic president and vice-president and the Republican Speaker of the House Newt **Gingrich**, of Georgia, and Senate Majority Leader Trent Lott, of Mississippi, were all

Southerners, yet polarized by party and, to some extent, ideology. The 2000 elections has seen Southerners heading the tickets for both parties. Ironically, inroads by blacks, women and other minorities have been more notable in urban politics and local elections.

Other cultural features of the South are also in flux. The isolation of underdevelopment has given way to national and international migrations. **Yuppies** and "twenty-somethings" are as much a feature of the North Carolina research triangle as the Houston **suburbs**. In cities, new Asian and **Caribbean** communities have also appeared, often in the suburbs.

The religious panorama of the South, identified with **Bible belt** preachers in both white and black evangelical traditions, was always more complex, including elite **Episcopalians** and urban Catholics and **Jews**. **Buddhism**, **Islam** and **Santería** have complicated this vision, but 1990s Southern spiritualities also encompass large, secular populations for whom the gods and guilt of the South no longer have the same meanings.

Education has also changed. Centuries of segregated education gave way to **white-flight** academies and *de facto* divisions, which the South now shares with public education nationwide. Although the College of William and Mary, in Virginia, is one of the country's oldest schools, Southern universities were once more known for sports and gentlemanly finishing than academics. While the Southeastern Conference remains a powerhouse in **football** and **basketball** – highly integrated sports – other schools like Duke, University of North Carolina, Vanderbilt, Tulane, Georgia Tech and Emory have increased national prestige as well.

The culture of the South, through all of these changes, has also demanded reflection – the drive, as a Faulkner character put it, to "tell about the South." Authors including Faulkner, Eudora Welty, Maya **Angelou**, Reynolds Price, James Agee, Alice **Walker**, Tennessee **Williams** and Ralph McGill have found inspiration and dilemmas in their region. John **Grisham** and Anne Rice have dominated popular fiction, exploring the darkness of the South as well as its changes. Southern musical traditions – **blues**, **Cajun**, **country-western**, gospel, **jazz**, ragtime and tejana – have infused American culture in voices from Mahalia Jackson to Elvis **Presley**.

In movies and television, however, images produced outside the South have changed much more slowly. The "guilty" South has haunted classic movies like *To Kill a Mockingbird* (1962), *Cool Hand Luke* (1967) and *Driving Miss Daisy* (1989). Alternate visions of tortured struggle (*Wise Blood*, 1979, based on Flannery O'Connor's religious novel; or the labor panorama of *Harlan County, USA*, 1976) and complicated corruption (Robert Altman's *Nashville*, 1975) exist alongside creative communities of minorities and women (Julie **Dash**'s exquisite *Daughters of the Dust*, 1989; Hollywood's *The Color Purple*, 1985). Television has changed even more slowly, finally abandoning the bucolic comedy of the *Andy Griffith Show* for sophisticated and sardonic women in *Designing Women*.

Facing the twenty-first century, the South and its inhabitants still constitute one of the most strongly marked regions of the United States. Yet, rapid changes in the area in the last five decades and its complexity today also mark the South as quintessentially American. The South shares the same dilemmas, development and population in a manner scarcely imaginable before the Second World War. Images and realities, division and identity are continually reshaped against a history perhaps more distant yet hardly escaped.

Further reading

Reagan, C. and Ferris, W. (1989) *Encyclopedia of Southern Culture*, Chapel Hill NC: University of North Carolina Press.

GARY McDONOGH

South Asians

People of South-Asian origin living in the United States have emigrated mostly from India, Pakistan, Bangladesh, Sri Lanka, Nepal and Bhutan. Some scholars of South Asia also include Burma and Tibet in this group, while others see them as being part of East and Southeast Asia. **Immigration** to the United States from South Asia can be divided into two main phases. The early phase, from the mid-nineteenth century to the early 1920s, was marked by the arrival in **California** of immigrant farmers and laborers from the state of Punjab in India. Initially absorbed into the economy as cheap labor, these Punjabi farmers made significant contributions to the development of large-scale agribusiness in California. This was the period during which the immigration laws in the US discriminated against Asian immigration. Many of the Punjabi men, who had arrived single in America, married Mexican women leading to the creation of that awkward category of people called "Mexican Hindus." Members of the Punjabi-Mexican second generation imbibed both cultures, but defined themselves consciously as Americans.

The second phase of South-Asian immigration to the US was ushered in by changes in the Immigration and Naturalization Act in 1965. Large numbers of Indians started entering the country, as, for the first time, a person's right to enter the United States did not depend on race. The new Act allowed people with skills to immigrate and, subsequently, professionals from various countries took advantage of the legal welcome. By 1995 there were approximately 1 million Asian Indians, constituting the largest group among South Asians in the United States. The post-1965 immigrants came from different parts of South Asia, but still predominantly from India and, particularly, from the states of Gujarat, Punjab and the four Southern states of Andhra Pradesh, Karnataka, Tamil Nadu and Kerala. Those with professional educational training took advantage of opportunities in medicine, **engineering**, business management and computer science, and established themselves as the group with the highest annual income in the US; many others set up successful businesses in **New York** City, NY, **Chicago, IL** and **California**. Besides nostalgia and memory, strong socio-economic and cultural investments link the new immigrants with their countries of origin. In the new economic regime of liberalization in South Asia, national governments, eager for investments from South Asians abroad, are seeking to create a favorable atmosphere by speaking of transnational communities and unified diasporic entities. Satellite television, **video** and the **Internet** have accelerated the pace of cultural exchanges between the parent country and the diaspora.

South-Asian Americans, as one of the more economically successful groups in the United States, have turned their attention and resources to establishing several religious and cultural centers of distinctively South Asian origin. **Hindu** temples, Islamic community centers, Sikh gurudwaras, ethnic churches and electronic communication links have enabled the establishment and maintenance of thriving diasporic communities. While participation in the political life of the US has been limited to fundraising and small-town politics, many South-Asian organizations in the US are known to sponsor actively a range of political activities in South Asia. Right-wing Hindu political formations in India as well as Islamic fundamentalist organizations in Pakistan enjoy considerable support from their respective diasporic communities.

Presently, the South-Asian community in America is engaged in a fascinating intergenerational negotiation about identity and other cultural values. While an unambiguous "Indian" or "Sri Lankan" identity was crucial for their parents' self-definitions, the second generation of South Asians seems comfortably to embrace hyphenated identities, calling themselves American with an "Indian" or "Sri Lankan" background or origin. Among children of Indian origin, for example, "Indianness" is not foregrounded in their self-perceptions, and there seem to be divergent understandings of what it means. Many respect their heritage and even don't hesitate to flaunt it in the new multicultural marketplace of ethnic America. Racial identity is as much a reality to them as it has been for their parents, although, unlike their parents' hesitant approach to matters of race, the second generation South-Asian Americans engage with **race** much more explicitly and confidently. Race, ethnicity, **class**, **religion**, **language**, gender and sexuality are some of the components of their identities that shape their perceptions of who they are and how they like to be perceived by others.

Further reading

Leonard, K.I. (1997) *The South Asian Americans*, Westport: Greenwood Press.

Rayaprol, A. (1997) *Negotiating Identities*, New Delhi: Oxford University Press.

APARNA RAYAPROL

Southeast Asians

War and political strife have been the reasons Southeast Asians find themselves in the United States. With the declaration of war between Spain and the United States in 1898 Americans entered into the affairs of Southeast Asians in the Philippines. Americans moved there and **Filipinos** later followed colonial relationships and education to the US. The **Vietnam War** brought several "hill tribes," particularly the Hmong, from Laos and Vietnam to the United States for resettlement because of their involvement with US counter-insurgency campaigns (sponsored by the CIA and US military) against the North Vietnamese. After the end of US involvement in the war, many south Vietnamese "escaped" Vietnam by boat (known as "boat people") for **refugee** camps located throughout Southeast Asia, later to be resettled in the United States. Political upheavals in Cambodia and along its borders with Vietnam, Laos and Thailand have also fostered Southeast Asian **immigration** to the US.

Southeast Asian groups living in the US, then, are for the most part refugee populations. In the racial politics that continue to shape the US social structure, Southeast Asians (except for established Filipinos) have little political power or representation apart from "**Asian American**" status and politics. Compared with other Asian groups, like the Chinese and Japanese "model minorities," they are still closer to the margins of the US social and economic system, working in low-paying or informal jobs and sometimes relying on welfare.

See also: Vietnamese Americans

Further reading

Haines, D.W. (ed.) (1989) *Refugees as Immigrants: Cambodians, Laotians, and Vietnamese in America*, Totowa: Rowman & Littlefield.

Hein, J. (1995) *From Vietnam, Laos, and Cambodia: A Refugee Experience in the United States*, New York: Twayne Publishers; London: Prentice Hall International.

STEVE FERZACCA

Southern Baptists

The Southern Baptist Convention represents a general organization of the 15.8 million members of 40,887 churches. Southern Baptist beliefs include freedom of religion, the priesthood of all believers and the individual soul's competency before God, and belief in Jesus Christ whose will is revealed in the Bible as the sole authority for faith and practice, as noted in the 1925 Statement of Baptist Faith and Message, adopted in 1963 by the Southern Baptist Convention. The 1998 convention adopted an amendment to the 1963 statement, regarding the structure of the **family**, **marriage** and the role of women, defining marriage as the monogamous relationship between a man and a woman, and asserting that the husband is head of the family and the woman should "graciously submit" to him.

Southern Baptists have played an increasing and often controversial role in American political life, allying themselves most closely with the **Republican Party** and conservative issues. In 1997 they voted to boycott all **Disney** products because they said that Disney policies did not promote a pro-family image and supported gay and lesbian lifestyles and agendas.

Southern Baptists enjoy independence congregationally. They do not adhere to one confession of faith or creed, noting that "any group of Baptists, large or small, have the inherent right to draw up for themselves and publish to the world a confession of their faith whenever they think it advisable to do so" (1925 statement). The 1925 confession, adopted in 1963, is not binding on congregations, but rather constitutes a guide for interpretation with no authority over conscience.

The Southern Baptist Convention traces its roots to 1845 in Augusta, Georgia during increasing tensions among people in the North and **South**. Debates concerned slavery, the denominational authority to discipline church members, the rights of Southerners to receive missionary appointments and the neglect of the South in missionary appointments. Prompted by decisions to decline to appoint several slaveholders as missionaries, 293 Baptist leaders from the South representing 356,000 Baptists convened to determine the best means of promoting the foreign-mission cause and other interests of the Baptist denomination in the South.

On May 10, 1845, the Southern Baptist Convention was organized, a constitution adopted, a structure developed, the mission and purpose written, the Foreign Mission Board and the Home Mission Board established and very soon after this the first missionaries were appointed.

Southern Baptists have emphasized mission and evangelism since their beginnings. Currently 4,000 foreign missionaries serve in 133 foreign countries; 4,857 home missionaries serve in the United States. The Executive Committee of the Southern Baptist Convention assists its churches and agencies in a variety of ways. It serves as the fiscal agent for the Convention, represents the Convention in legal matters, provides promotion and publicity for the Cooperative Program through the Baptist Press, presents a budget for the Convention and its agencies, authorizes the work of the Southern Baptist Foundation and provides advice.

Further reading

Smith, J. (ed.) (1995) *The HarperCollins Dictionary of Religion*, San Francisco: American Academy of Religion and HarperCollins.

"Southern Baptist Convention," "Southern Baptist Beliefs," "The Executive Committee," June 8, 1998: http://www.sbcnet.org.

GAIL HENSON

Southern Christian Leadership Conference (SCLC)

SCLC was founded in 1957, emerging out of the Montgomery Improvement Association, which had successfully orchestrated the bus boycott. Led by Martin Luther **King**, Jr. as president, until his death in 1968, and by Ralph **Abernathy**, SCLC

advocated non-violent resistance to **segregation** and racial oppression. In 1960 it helped establish a student organization, the **Student Non-violent Coordinating Committee** (SNCC), which would challenge the parent organization's philosophy of non-violence and embrace **Black Power**. Until the mid-1960s the influence of SCLC was felt in all the cities of the **South**; but it was unable to have similar success in northern cities like **Chicago**.

ROBERT GREGG

Southwest

The Southwest region includes New Mexico, Arizona, southern Utah, southern Nevada, and the adjoining parts of Colorado, **Texas** and **California**, mingling Native Americans, **Hispanics** and waves of European American **immigration**. Although the Southwest, more than many other US regions, connotes a coherent regional style in architecture, food and other aesthetics, the meanings of the Southwest have varied over time. From an early association with the "primitive" **West** of "wild Indians," to the tranquil vacation destination of the 1950s, to its current association with the border and **retirement** communities, the Southwest remains a touchstone for what is essentially American.

The romance of the early Southwest attracted nineteenth-century collectors of antiquities and pot-hunters alike, whose influence remains clear today in the development of Native American crafts industries. The status of Native Americans as subjects of a colonizing state was clear in the early ethnological and archaeological explorations among the pueblo dwellers funded by the Bureau of Indian Affairs and the concessions given to **mining** companies such as Peabody Coal, despite the fact that the reservations of the Navajos, Hopis and Zunis are sovereign territories. Early visitors also established discourses of the region, talking about both Native Americans and the colors and forms of deserts and mountains.

In the postwar years, the desert Southwest grew as a destination for American families on vacation, lured by the Grand Canyon and the last reminders of the **frontier**, evident in abandoned mines, ghost towns and places like Tombstone, Arizona. **Roadside attractions** like the Cadillac Ranch in Amarillo (Texas) and trading posts, natural phenomena like the Petrified Forest and historical sites such as Los Alamos (New Mexico), **Santa Fe**, the alleged **UFO** landing site at Rosewell (New Mexico), Native American reservations and missions from **San Antonio** (Texas) to the California coast all pulled in tourists. Like the **road movie**, the family driving vacation along western **highways**, including Route 66, has produced enduring images of the neon-lit motor courts and the station wagon as symbols of American freedom, **family values** and leisure.

The monumental landscape of the Southwest also figured significantly in the romantic imagination of North Americans in literature and film. The red rocks of Monument Valley, evident in John **Ford westerns** such as *The Seekers* (1956) and *Cheyenne Autumn* (1964), suggested not only the desolation and wildness that was the American West, but the epic proportion of human struggles there. This evocation of the West as a lonely place in which to hide, where freedom and danger were mixed, remains a theme in more recent films such as *Butch Cassidy and the Sundance Kid* (1969) and *Thelma and Louise* (1991); the quest also underpinned television's 1960s series *Route 66*. The landscapes and intersecting peoples of the desert Southwest also have inspired popular authors such as Barbara Kingsolver, Tony Hillerman and Leslie Marmon **Silko**.

As the industrial Northeast declined, the Southwest grew into the **Sunbelt**, attracting an influx of rich **white** North Americans to planned retirement communities like Sun City and poor South and Central Americans to its transient-based service economy. Early predictions of a massive movement of people from the Rustbelt to the burgeoning Southwest have not been entirely borne out, although **Phoenix**, the largest city in the region, proved popular as a vacation and conference site. Beginning in the 1960s and 1970s, the Southwest also became a mecca for those seeking an alternative lifestyle. Inspired by writers such as Carlos **Castañeda**, young whites moved to Tucson and northern New Mexico. The **New Age** movement is the heir to this earlier migration;

mystical places like Sedona, Arizona continue to draw those interested in harmonic convergences and holistic healing.

The contemporary Southwest is also organized by the border, which produced a mixed population including white retirees, ranchers, entrepreneurs, transient white laborers, Mexican cross-border workers, Native Americans, a **Chicano** underclass and a Mexican American middle class, among others. Pockets of Hispanics, descendants of the original Spanish land grantees, can also be found. **African Americans** remain under-represented. This hybridity is clear in the development of the distinctive Southwestern **architecture**, cuisine and culture: Southwest style.

The architecture of the Southwest, for example, spans Navajo hogans and Hopi pueblos, retirement cities and condo complexes. The architectural style that characterizes the region, often referred to as Santa Fe style, is based on traditional single-story adobe houses with saguaro cactus rib-ceilings. Modern home construction now produces pink, orange and pastel versions of these houses all over the Southwest. The frequent inclusion of ornamental ladders reminiscent of those found in pueblos indicates increasing commodification, while the saguaro cactus is now an iconic design element. Art and architecture have become kitsch in the Southwest, where Navajo turquoise jewelry vies with painted wooden coyotes wearing kerchiefs and howling at the moon. The artistic richness of Georgia **O'Keefe** is now overlaid with the prolific paintings of Amado Peña, known for his prints of Native American and **Latina** women depicted with pottery and/or children. Native American crafts have also been subjected to the mass marketing and production which have degraded local artisanal values while simultaneously producing a Southwestern "look" across the US.

Food in the Southwest shows the influence of cross-border traffic and a longstanding hybrid cuisine of Native American and Latino traditions. Tex-Mex refers to the spicy blending of border foods that has led to chili with beans and meat, the use of guacamole and sour cream and the success of Taco Bell as a franchise. Navajo tacos, made with Navajo fry bread rather than tortillas, also show the creative mixing of ingredients and cooking styles found in the Southwest. What is generically referred to as "Mexican food" includes many variations, from Tex-Mex to the Sonoroan home-style cooking with its *carne asada* and *salsa verde*. The national ubiquity of salsa attests to the widespread appeal of the hybrid cooking coming out of the Southwest.

The turbulence produced by the border is clear not only in aesthetic hybridity, but in regional politics. The Southwest often has been characterized by the conservative, libertarian politics of white politicians like Barry **Goldwater**, who exemplified the western individualist's rejection of federal government intervention. Yet, issues of ethnicity, historical memory, bilingualism and illegal **immigration** (captured in John Sayles' *Lone Star*, 1995) have worked to consolidate a more liberal, Latino political consciousness. A radical political tradition associated with the Tucson-based Earth First! was inspired by the radical environmentalism of Edward **Abbey** in his *Desert Solitaire* (1968). Environmental politics also focus on water – the Southwest has been particularly shaped by disputes over saline water in the Colorado River system, treaty obligations to **Mexico** and large-scale water projects like the Hoover Dam and Lake Powell. The relevance of these border politics to the rest of the country is clear in the controversy surrounding **NAFTA**.

Further reading

Findlay, J. (1992) *Magic Lands*, Berkeley: University of California.

Hill, J. (1993) "Hasta la vista, baby: Anglo Spanish in the American Southwest," *Critique of Anthropology* 13 (2):145–76.

JANICE NEWBERRY

Soviet Union *see* Russia

Space

The US exploration of space emerged in large part because of the pressures of national defense during the **Cold War** with the Soviet Union. The civilian side of the space effort began as a result of the International Geophysical Year (IGY), a scientific endeavor conducted around the world in 1957 and 1958, one component of which involved the launching of an orbiting scientific satellite. The Soviet Union launched *Sputnik* on October 4, 1957, ushering in the space age in a very deliberate and identifiable manner.

A full-scale crisis resulted in the United States as a result of *Sputnik 1*. It had a "Pearl Harbor" effect on American public opinion, creating an illusion of a technological gap, and provided the impetus for increased spending on aerospace endeavors, technical and scientific educational programs, and the chartering of new federal agencies to manage air and space research and development.

Sputnik led directly to several critical efforts aimed at "catching up" to the Soviet Union's space achievements. Among these:

- A full-scale review of both the civil and military programs of the United States (scientific satellite efforts and ballistic missile development).
- The establishment of a Presidential Science Advisor in the White House who had responsibility for overseeing the activities of the federal government in science and technology.
- The creation of the Advanced Research Projects Agency in the Department of Defense, and the consolidation of several space activities under centralized management.
- The establishment of the National Aeronautics and Space Administration to manage civil space operations.
- The passage of the National Defense Education Act to provide federal funding for education in the scientific and technical disciplines.

Even though the space frontier opened as a result of the Cold War crisis, the seeds of acceptance had been a part of American popular culture for several years. For example, in 1952 the designer of the German V-2 and an émigré to the US, Wernher von Braun, burst onto the public stage with a series of articles in *Collier's* magazine about the possibilities of space flight. Three special issues about space flight from the popular magazine appeared in the next two years, each expertly illustrated with striking images by some of the best illustrators of the era.

The first issue of *Collier's* devoted to space appeared on March 22, 1952. In it readers were asked "What Are We Waiting For?" and were urged to support an aggressive space program. An editorial suggested that space flight was possible, not just science fiction, and that it was inevitable that humanity would venture outward. It framed the exploration of space in the context of the Cold War rivalry with the Soviet Union and concluded that "*Collier's* believes that the time has come for Washington to give priority of attention to the matter of space superiority. The rearmament gap between the East and West has been steadily closing. And nothing, in our opinion, should be left undone that might guarantee the peace of the world. It's as simple as that."

Following close on the heels of the *Collier's* series, Walt **Disney** Productions contacted von Braun to ask his assistance in the production of three shows for Disney's weekly television series. The first of these, *Man in Space*, premiered on Disney's show on March 9, 1955, with an estimated audience of 42 million. The second show, *Man and the Moon*, also aired in 1955 and sported the powerful image of a wheel-like space station as a launching point for a mission to the Moon. The final show, *Mars and Beyond*, premiered on December 4, 1957, after the launching of *Sputnik 1*. Von Braun appeared in all three films to explain his concepts for human space flight, while Disney's characteristic animation illustrated the basic principles and ideas with wit and humor.

Because of this, during the decade following the Second World War, a sea change in American perceptions took place on the viability of space travel as a near-term reality. This can be seen in a December 1949 Gallup poll where only 15 percent of Americans believed humans would reach the Moon within fifty years, while 15 percent had no opinion and a whopping 70 percent believed that it would not happen within that time. In October 1957, at the same time as the launching of *Sputnik 1*, only 25 percent believed that it would take longer than twenty-five years for humans to reach the Moon, while 41 percent believed firmly that it would happen within twenty-five years and 34 percent were not sure. An important shift in perceptions had indeed taken place, and it was largely the result of well-known advances in rocket technology coupled with the efforts of such popularizers as Wernher von Braun about the possibility of space flight.

During the first years of the space age, the United States emphasized its civil space program consisting of several major components:

- Human space-flight initiatives – Mercury's single astronaut program (flights during 1961–3) to ascertain if a human could survive in space; Project Gemini (flights during 1965–6) with two astronauts to practice for space operations; Project Apollo (flights during 1968–72) to explore the Moon; and sustained operations in Earth orbit with the space shuttle (1981–).
- Robotic missions to the Moon (*Ranger, Surveyor* and *Lunar Orbiter*), Venus (*Pioneer Venus*), Mars (*Mariner 4, Viking, Pathfinder,* and *Mars Global Surveyor*) and the outer planets (*Pioneer, Voyager, Galileo* and *Cassini*).
- Orbiting space observatories (*Orbiting Solar Observatory, Hubble Space Telescope* and *Chandra*) to view the galaxy from space without the clutter of Earth's atmosphere.
- Remote-sensing Earth-satellites for **information** gathering (landsat satellites for environmental monitoring and a host of others).
- Applications satellites such as communications (*Echo 1, Tinos* and *Telstar*) and weather monitoring instruments.
- An orbital workshop for astronauts (*Skylab*).
- A space station for a permanent presence in space.

The capstone of this effort was, of course, the human expedition to the Moon, Project Apollo. A unique confluence of political necessity, personal commitment and activism, scientific and technological ability, economic prosperity and public mood made possible the May 25, 1961 announcement by President John F. **Kennedy** to carry out a lunar landing program before the end of the decade as a means of demonstrating the United States' technological virtuosity.

The first Apollo mission of public significance was the flight of *Apollo 8*. On December 21, 1968, it took off atop a *Saturn V* booster from the Kennedy Space Center, **Florida**. It orbited the Moon on December 24–5, and then fired the boosters for a return flight. That flight was such an enormously significant accomplishment because it came at a time when American society was in crisis over Vietnam, race relations, urban problems and a host of other difficulties. If only for a few moments, the nation united as one to focus on this epochal event.

The first lunar landing came during the flight of *Apollo 11*, which lifted off on July 16, 1969 and landed on the Moon on July 20, 1969. Astronauts Neil A. Armstrong and Buzz Aldrin soon set foot on the surface, Armstrong telling millions who saw and heard him on Earth that it was "one small step for [a] man – one giant leap for mankind." The next day they launched back to the *Apollo* capsule orbiting overhead and began the return trip to Earth, splashing down in the Pacific on July 24.

Five more landing missions followed at approximately six-month intervals through December 1972, each of them increasing the time spent on the Moon. The scientific experiments placed on the Moon and the lunar soil samples returned have provided grist for scientists' investigations ever since. The scientific return was significant, but the program did not answer conclusively the age-old questions of lunar origins and evolution. Three of the latter *Apollo* missions used a lunar rover vehicle to travel in the vicinity of the landing site, but none of them equaled the excitement of *Apollo 11*.

Project Apollo in general, and the flight of *Apollo 11* in particular, should be viewed as a watershed in the nation's history. It was an endeavor that demonstrated both the technological and economic virtuosity of the United States and established national pre-eminence over rival nations – the primary goal of the program when first envisioned by the Kennedy administration in 1961. It had been an enormous undertaking, costing $25.4 billion with only the building of the **Panama** Canal rivaling the Apollo program's size as the largest non-military technological endeavor ever undertaken by the United States and only the Manhattan Project being comparable in a wartime setting.

After Apollo the human space-flight program went into a holding pattern as nearly a decade passed before the first flight of the space shuttle. On April 12, 1981, the *Columbia* took off for a test mission. By January 1986, there had been twenty-four shuttle flights, but the system had not delivered on all of its promises in making possible inexpensive, routine and reliable operations in space.

Criticisms of the shuttle reached crescendo proportions following the tragic loss of *Challenger* during a launch on January 28, 1986. Although it was not the entire reason, the pressure to get the shuttle schedule more in line with earlier projections throughout 1985 prompted NASA workers to accept operational procedures that fostered shortcuts and increased the opportunity for disaster. The accident, traumatic for the American people even under the best of situations, was made that much worse because *Challenger's* crew-members represented a cross-section of the American population in terms of race, gender, geography, background and religion. The explosion became one of the most significant events of the 1980s, as billions around the world saw the accident on television and empathized with any one or more of the crew-members killed.

With the *Challenger* accident, the space shuttle program went into a two-year hiatus while NASA worked to redesign the system. The space shuttle finally returned to flight without further incident on September 29, 1988. By the end of 1999 NASA had launched a total of ninety-three shuttle missions, all but one without incident. Through all of these activities, a good deal of realism about what the space shuttle could and could not do emerged as the century ended.

In the late 1980s, a new generation of planetary exploration began. Numerous projects came to fruition during the period. For example, the highly successful *Magellan* mission to Venus by 1993 had provided significant scientific data about the planet. Another such project was the troubled *Galileo* mission to Jupiter, which even before reaching its destination had become a source of great concern for both NASA and public officials because not all of its systems were working properly, but it did return useful scientific data.

Finally, planetary exploration received new impetus beginning on July 4, 1997, when *Mars Pathfinder* successfully landed on Mars, the first return to the red planet since *Viking* in 1976. Its small, 23-pound robotic rover, named *Sojourner*, departed the main lander and began to record weather patterns, atmospheric opacity and the chemical composition of rocks washed down into the Ares Vallis floodplain, an ancient outflow channel in Mars' northern hemisphere. This vehicle completed its projected milestone thirty-day mission on August 3, 1997, capturing far more data on the atmosphere, weather and geology of Mars than scientists had expected. In all, the *Pathfinder* mission returned more than 1.2 gigabits (1.2 billion bits) of data and over 10,000 tantalizing pictures of the Martian landscape.

At the end of the twentieth century, the effort to develop an international space station, inaugurated in the 1980s with the launch of the first components in 1998, promises a future permanent presence in space and the possibility of renewed exploration of the Moon and the nearby planets in the twenty-first century. A truly international effort, fourteen other nations have contributed to the project, ranging from **Canada**, the nations of western Europe, **Japan** and **Russia**. Once in orbit, this space station is intended to enhance human understanding of the rigors of space flight as no other research facility has been able to do.

Since its inception in 1958, space exploration has transformed the lives of all Americans, whether it be in applications made possible by global satellite communications or by research and development that has found its way into commercial products or by other altogether unknowable means. Perhaps most important, space exploration has taught us to view the Earth, the cosmos and ourselves in a new way. Because of space flight, humanity has seen its home from afar – a tiny, lovely and fragile "blue marble" hanging in the blackness of space. Writer Archibald MacLeish summed up the feelings of many people when he wrote in the 1960s that "To see the Earth as it truly is, small and blue and beautiful in that eternal silence where it floats, is to see ourselves as riders on the Earth together, brothers on that bright loveliness in the eternal cold – brothers who know now that they are truly brothers."

Further reading

Burrows, W.E. (1998) *This New Ocean: The Story of the First Space Age*, New York: Random House.

Chaiken, A. (1994) *A Man on the Moon: The Voyages of the Apollo Astronauts*, New York: Viking.

Heppenheimer, T.A. (1997) *Countdown: The History of Space Exploration*, New York: John Wiley & Sons.

Launius, R.D. (1994) *NASA: A History of the US Civil Space Program*, Malabar: Kneger Publishing Co.

Launius, R.D. (1998) *Frontiers of Space Exploration*, Westport: Greenwood Press.

McCurdy, H.E. (1997) *Spaceflight and the Myth of Presidential Leadership*, Urbana: University of Illinois Press.

McCurdy, H.E. (1997) *Space and the American Imagination*, Washington, DC: Smithsonian Institution Press.

McDougall, W.A. (1985) *The Heavens and the Earth: A Political History of the Space Age*, New York: Basic Books.

ROGER D. LAUNIUS

Spam

Canned, processed pork luncheon meat created by Hormel in 1937. It holds an ambivalent place in American cuisine – rejected by some because of associations with institutional **food**, others have championed it as comfortable nostalgia. The official web-site (http://www.spam.com) offers a history of the US from a spamish perspective, as well as a fan club and gift items. The word has also come to be used for unwanted e-mail.

CINDY WONG

Speaker of the House

Second in line to the **presidency** after the **vice-president**, the Speaker is chosen by the majority party in the House of Representatives. All the people who have held this position have wielded considerable power, but particularly so if they have belonged to the party not currently occupying the presidency. When this is not the case, then the Speaker has generally been overshadowed, having the purpose mainly to ensure that the president's legislative program is passed through the House. In such a case, the Speaker is judged merely according to success in this endeavor.

Sam Rayburn provided the exception to this rule. Rayburn, a Texas **Democrat**, was Speaker during the **Kennedy** administration and, along with most Southern Democrats, opposed much of the northerner's "New Frontier" agenda. When fellow Texan, Lyndon **Johnson** became president following the Kennedy **assassination**, however, Rayburn's role was reduced to that of an assistant to Johnson in the passage of his "Great Society" legislation.

William "Tip" O'Neill, as Speaker during the **Reagan** administration, was highly visible as Democrats negotiated with the presidency over which elements of "Reagonomics" and the rollback of the welfare state to pass through **Congress**. This power and visibility were curtailed considerably, however, by Reagan's 1984 landslide re-election victory over Mondale.

Newt **Gingrich** succeeded in giving the position of Speaker perhaps the greatest visibility it has received. Only two years after the election of **Clinton** on a platform of "change," Gingrich trumped him in the 1994 elections by demanding more change still. Announcing his "Contract with America," Gingrich pushed for tax cuts and an end to big government. The **Republican Party**'s astounding victory, giving the Grand Old Party control of both Houses, placed Gingrich in the unusual position of dictating policy to a presidency that had lost control of its legislative agenda.

Gingrich's ability to inspire great hostility among those who were not in his faction of the Party made his ascendancy relatively short-lived. Miscalculations leading to the 1995 shut-down of government over the budget, which greatly reduced Gingrich's popularity and increased Clinton's, began to provide room for congressional Democrats and moderate Republicans to begin to oppose the Speaker. When ethics violations were unearthed that appeared to far outweigh the magnitude of those that had caused the downfall of Democrat Jim Wright (and for which Gingrich would be fined $300,000), the Speaker's claims to being a new style of politician were destroyed. An attempted Republican coup in 1998 failed, but following the surprise setbacks in the November elections of that year Gingrich resigned.

Another power struggle ensued within the Grand Old Party which saw the rise and fall of Bob Livingstone, who was forced to step down because of claims of marital infidelity (which didn't look good for the Party endeavoring to impeach the president for acts arising out of extra-marital liaisons). Into the vacuum left by Livingstone moved ex-House Deputy Majority Whip J. Dennis

Hastert, whose main appeal was that, in contrast to Gingrich, he was offensive to none.

ROBERT GREGG

speed limits

As in other nations, variable speed limits "zone" roads and highways according to local norms and contexts, from 15 mph in active school zones to accelerated speeds for limited access expressways (which, in some western states, had no limits). The energy crisis in 1974 allowed the federal government to fix 55 mph as a national maximum, raised to 65 mph in some areas in 1987. Yet, both individual drivers and advocates of **states**' rights chafed under these limits, which soon became justified on the basis of safety as much as energy (given the growing popularity of large fuel-eating **automobiles**). Speed connotes **freedom**, whether in **advertising**, driving or western states' attempts to get around these laws. In 1995 federal rules were repealed, allowing most states to adjust some highways to 70 or 75mph.

GARY McDONOGH

speed traps

Areas of especially vigorous enforcement of **highway** speed limits, often involving marked cars or abrupt changes of posted velocities. While argued as legitimate controls on speeding, these traps, which may endure for decades, are viewed by motorists as harassment or money-makers for local sheriffs. They also figure prominently in **road movies**.

GARY McDONOGH

Spelling, Aaron

b. 1928

Aaron Spelling has produced almost one hundred different TV series and movies, many in **syndication**. In four decades, he has created some of the most popular – if not critically acclaimed – 1-hour television shows, often appealing to the ever-sought-after eighteen to forty age group. He is best known for *Mod Squad, Dynasty, Melrose Place, The Love Boat, Charlie's Angels* and *Beverly Hills, 90210*. He is also known for casting virtually unknown (but beautiful) **actors** and placing them in projects with a clear formula and target audience. Spelling was born in **Dallas, TX** and started out as a teleplay writer. After working with partners, he formed his own production company in 1986 and started Spelling Entertainment, which has diversified concerns, including merchandising and film production.

EDWARD MILLER

Spielberg, Steven

b. 1946

The most financially successful Hollywood **director/producer**, with **blockbusters** *E.T. the Extra-Terrestrial* (1982), *Jurassic Park* (1993; 1997) and *Indiana Jones* (1981; 1984; 1989). Spielberg has also achieved critical success by attacking such subjects as slavery, the Holocaust and the Second World War. His visually striking films, *Schindler's List* (1993) and *Saving Private Ryan* (1998), will likely represent the Second World War era for future audiences, a fact which troubles some **documentary** filmmakers and historians. Spielberg's film *Jaws* (1975) is also credited with being the first "Summer Event" movie. In 1997, with David Geffen and Jeffrey Katzenberg, Spielberg created the film studio Dreamworks, SKG.

See also: Hollywood

MELINDA SCHWENK

Spock, Benjamin

b. 1903; d. 1998

Pediatrician to the **baby boomers**. Spock's *Common Sense Book of Baby and Child Care* (first published in 1946 but undergoing multiple revisions and new editions thereafter) revolutionized childcare for postwar America. He promoted warmth,

creativity and respect for the child's individuality rather than discipline and distance (although later physicians and parents have challenged his ideas, ranging from guidance to nutrition). In the 1960s, Spock also became a leader in the anti-**Vietnam War** movement so many of his "children" had embraced; in 1972 he became the presidential candidate of the People's Party.

GARY McDONOGH

sports and gender

Radical changes have occurred in women's sports in the United States, especially in the last two decades, having a lasting impact on many aspects of American culture and society. While women have not achieved parity – especially in professional salaries – it is no longer a man's game.

Victorian notions that women were physiologically inferior and that sports would diminish a woman's **femininity** began to give way to new notions about sport and gender after the First World War. Two new perspectives towards sports emerged: one stressing equal rights and access to a system already in place; the other, promoted initially by female educators in the 1920s and picked up later by radical feminists, advocated alternative sports (based on the notion that women were indeed different from men). While proponents of the equal-rights view believed that facilities should be equal for both sexes, and that women would begin to catch up with men once the effects of their socialization were overcome, female educators tended to be more critical of the commercialism and excessive competitiveness associated with organized sports and wanted games that complemented what they considered "female" characteristics.

The passage of **Title IX** as part of the Educational Amendment of 1972 led to the triumph of the equal-rights approach to sports. In order for **colleges and universities** to receive federal funding, it became necessary for them to provide equal funding for men and women. A redistribution of funding occurred to establish facilities and teams for women in places where there had been none before. Discrimination is still evident, with men's college football programs eating up vast resources and women still receiving in 1996 only one-third of all scholarship money. Overall, male athletes receive $179 million dollars more per year than female athletes. The change has nevertheless been a momentous and irreversible one.

Moving together in terms of **body** types, sports considered anathema among women before – body-building and **wrestling**, for example – are now engaged in with great enthusiasm. Others have been transformed as women have begun to incorporate men's approaches to particular games, or have become more physically capable of performing the same feats. **Basketball** has seen a radical transformation partly as a result of the success of the equal-rights approach to sport. In the 1940s the game most commonly played was "girl's-rules" basketball, akin to the game called netball in Britain. On the grounds that many women could not tax their hearts the same way as men without doing themselves permanent physical damage, educators developed the game in which women were confined to particular zones and were not allowed to dribble more than a few paces before passing. This allowed for the emergence of a more passing-oriented game with less physical contact than men's basketball. By the 1960s this game was already losing ground, and by the 1980s the game had all but disappeared except in a few elite colleges. One irony of this transformation is that women who had taken on coaching positions in the women's game found themselves displaced by men who were more familiar with men's basketball. This was also an effect of Title IX generally since better-funded women's teams meant that coaching such teams became more attractive to men. The visibility of some very successful women coaches, however, has challenged this gender imbalance.

The notion of gender difference has survived, however. There has been no rush among women to establish American **football** teams; this is not expected any time soon. Even in basketball there is the assumption that women's height disadvantage requires that their game be one based less on dunking the ball through the hoop and more on shooting (with lower field-goal percentages, since the basket is further away).

In another major sport, **softball**, the move towards the men's game hasn't occurred. Perhaps because this game has been played on an informal basis by both sexes in parks and colleges across the country, it has retained legitimacy apart from traditional **baseball**. Moreover, the proficiency of women in throwing fastballs, spitballs and curve balls underarm has been such that the game has an appeal that is different from, but complementary to, that of men's baseball. Moreover, baseball officialdom has been very slow to recognize the need to attract women as individuals and athletes to the sports arena; instead, it has tended to rely on the notion that it is a "**family**" game, the whole family turning out to watch the son perform. While women may have been content with such a role in the past, the fact that little-league baseball is losing out to rising sports like **soccer** suggests that this is no longer the case. The one short-lived attempt to establish a women's baseball league, memorialized in *A League of their Own* (1992), was made possible by the exigencies of the World War. Nonetheless, it spurred many women to continue to demand opportunities for themselves and their daughters in the years following the war.

The accentuation of difference is especially noticeable in the commercial world of **advertising**. Sporting-goods producers, like other capitalists in the marketplace, have realized that catering to different consumers is the key to selling more goods. While **automobile** manufacturers before them built cars to appeal to particular segments of the market, thereby expanding the number of consumers overall, sporting-goods producers like Nike and Reebok have realized that they should be marketing their products to different groups based upon gender difference. Whether or not actual differences do exist (and the high level of demand for such women's products suggest that many women feel they do), completely different product lines exist in all goods from clothing to equipment not just in terms of color but also in terms of design. The effect of stressing that women have different feet and need different kinds of shoes, for example, serves both to bring about product diversification and the suggestion to women who haven't **run** before that they perhaps might have done so had they not been discouraged by the male bias inherent throughout sport. This gendering of sports products also means that women role models like Chris Evert (**tennis**), Mia Hamm (soccer) and Linda Swoopes (basketball) can be used to promote the goods to impressionable youngsters less impressed by Andre Agassi, Alexi Lalas and Michael Jordan, respectively.

Sex appeal has also been an important element of sports promotion. While women athletes' body types have transformed significantly in the years since the passage of Title IX, with the increased level of training, so has the growing divergence in notions of attractive female forms (identified by men and, perhaps more significantly, women themselves). Women's sports have made women's bodies the objects of the spectator's gaze, and some women have used this to their advantage. The soccer team for the Women's World Cup of 1999 posed in T-shirts for a photo given to the David Letterman Show. The establishment of the Women's National Basketball Association was also accompanied by hype that the players had more sex appeal than their counterparts in the NBA. Such appeal, though, is no longer always accompanied by gestures to heterosexuality in the face of media and public scrutiny. While the old assumption that the woman athlete may be gay (something that haunted both Billie Jean **King** and Martina Navratilova, who later confirmed on the *Phil Donahue Show* that she was) is not dead, it is muted nonetheless. Concern with female sexuality has also deflected discussion of homophilic and homophobic behaviors in male sports, as well as rare cases of "out" athletes like Greg **Louganis** (though the growing support for the Gay Games suggests gay athletes may be more common in future). Many of these issues relating to women athletes were raised in the movie *Personal Best* (1982).

Sexual difference has also been used in other ways. Women figure skaters and gymnasts, for example, although many of them are capable of outperforming men in terms of their ability to execute jumps and spins, will not do away with their different styles of costume and performing and methods of adjudication since the present system has demonstrated its audience appeal.

Two events in recent years have served well to highlight the transformation that has occurred in sports. First the Atlanta **Olympics** of 1996, which for the first time saw an equal number of women

athletes as men performing. At the event, more interest was shown in the women's teams than the men's in sports like softball (as compared to baseball), basketball (in which the winner of the men's event was a foregone conclusion) and soccer. The success of these games led to the emergence of two professional women's basketball leagues (one of which was dismantled within three years). Similarly, great attention was given to the American women's soccer team, which also captured the gold medal, leading to considerable anticipation for the second event of note, the Women's World Cup held in the United States in 1999. The largest crowds ever to witness women's team events in the United States greeted every game in which the American team played (the US eventually defeating China in the final). This can only increase the interest among girls and women in this sport, perhaps reaching new, untapped groups like **African Americans** who will have seen the numerous feature stories on Briana Scurry.

The combination of these two events symbolizes the success of the equal-rights approach thus far. Whether women are able to avoid some of the pitfalls of commercial sports more generally, and whether they should try to do so, are questions that remain unanswered. The final verbal exchange of *Pat and Mike*, a 1952 movie about a male promoter and a female athlete, suggests that the athlete will "own" the promoter. This remains to be seen.

Further reading

Cahn, S.K. (1994) *Coming on Strong: Gender and Sexuality in Twentieth-Century Sport*, New Jersey: The Free Press.

Dyer, K.F. (1982) *Challenging the Men*, New York: University of Queensland Press.

Twin, S.L. (ed.) (1979) *Out of the Bleachers*, New York: Feminist Press.

(1996) "Women Muscle In," *The New York Times Magazine* special issue, June 23.

ROBERT GREGG

sports and media

Television has been the central medium in sports since the end of the 1950s. It has established

football as the most lucrative of all sports, helped refashion **basketball** in the 1980s and has been the financial backbone for almost all the major sports. With the emergence of **cable** channels like **ESPN**, the number of sports benefiting from **television** coverage has increased, and the bidding wars for major-league sports have become still more intense. By 1996 sports consumed about 40 hours of every week on the four major **networks**, in addition to the 24-hours-a-day sports broadcasting on several cable channels. Building on this nexus of sport and television, **newspapers**, talk **radio**, **magazines** and catalogs have raised sports to the level of virtual obsession.

The establishment of sports television as a major commercial and cultural force in the United States is usually dated to December 28, 1958, when a national NBC audience watched the Baltimore Colts come back to tie the New York Giants in the championship game of the NFL, and then, under the leadership of Johnny Unitas, win in sudden-death overtime. Played in **New York** City (and so watched by key figures in **advertising** and broadcasting), the game brought millions of new fans to the game of football.

Pete Rozelle, commissioner of football in the 1960s and 1970s, built on this newfound strength. Negotiating with the networks on behalf of the league he managed to secure large contracts (most notably the CBS bid of $14.1 million in 1964), revenues from which were divided evenly among the teams, securing the financial health of even teams in smaller markets. **Congress** complied, passing the Sports Antitrust Broadcast Act, permitting professional leagues to pool revenues and to sell their television rights as a single entity.

The power of television was further demonstrated in 1970 during a mid-season game between the New York Jets and the Oakland Raiders. With the Giants leading, 32–29 and with 65 seconds playing time remaining, NBC cut away from the game to show a children's special, *Heidi*. Meanwhile, in the game, the Raiders scored two touchdowns and won 43–32. Ten thousand enraged football fans called NBC in New York, blowing a fuse on its switchboard. Since then, no network game has been pre-empted, and even sponsors of CBS' *60 Minutes*,

which follows football on Sunday, do not mind being delayed by overtime games.

Roone Arledge added Monday Night Football to the ABC prime-time schedule in 1970. With Howard Cossell, the most controversial sports commentator of his day, Don Meredith and former star Frank Gifford, the show was an instant success. Even after the addition of the tongue-tied O.J. **Simpson**, the dumping of Cossell and other personnel changes, the show has remained strong, cementing a national audience for otherwise local fixtures (though the hiring of comedian Dennis Miller as a commentator for the 2000 season suggests a less confident outlook at ABC).

The relationship between football and television has been a symbiotic one. The networks were seen as crucial in the establishment of football; now football is seen by television executives as fundamental to their network's financial health. Thus, Rupert Murdoch established FOX as a network to contend with in 1993 by bidding $1.6 billion to win the right to televise NFL games for four years ($500 million more than CBS had paid for the preceding four years), in addition stealing away CBS' best commentary team, John Madden and Pat Somerall. Although CBS had lost money on its previous contract, it came back with an astonishing bid of $4 billion over eight years to wrest control of AFC games from NBC. Owing to such network contracts (the total of which amount to $18 billion), the value of the average football franchise has now reached over $200 million.

Other sports have also been successful in using television, though, unlike in football, focusing on players has often been crucial. Basketball was in the financial doldrums until the mid-1980s when CBS made a deliberate move to concentrate all its efforts on games featuring marquee players on major teams, such as Magic Johnson and Kareem Abdul-Jabbar for the Los Angeles Lakers, Larry Bird for the Boston Celtics and Julius Erving for the Philadelphia 76ers. This plan paid off with the ascendancy of the Chicago Bulls' Michael **Jordan**, considered the best player ever to play the game. The downside has been witnessed in Jordan's second retirement, followed by declining basketball TV ratings as the sport waits for its next crop of stars to emerge.

Golf similarly has benefited from the sudden arrival of Tiger **Woods**. Prior to Woods' emergence, networks expected major **golf** championships to be watched in approximately 20 million homes. In 1997, when Woods captured the Masters, about 30 million homes tuned in. The $100 million investment the networks made in professional golf began to produce a much better return.

The impact of TV has been seen in the way the games themselves are performed. Almost every team sport now has additional timeouts to allow for commercials (**soccer** has found it more difficult to gain large television revenues because it doesn't have such commercial breaks). The result is longer games. One hour of football or basketball takes 3 hours to play. In addition, television officials believe that to draw viewers they must avoid having ties, so most sports now institute sudden-death overtimes.

Often the success of a sport is determined not by the number of people who participate in the game, but by the number who will watch on television. Tennis "arrived" with Billie Jean **King**'s 1973 "battle of the sexes" against Bobby Riggs; the success of women's **soccer** was acknowledged when the 1999 World Cup pulled down a better rating than that year's NBA playoff. This has been frustrating for enthusiasts of new sports, especially since the major sports of football, **baseball** and basketball have been able (largely through exemptions to antitrust legislation) to establish virtual monopolistic control over the networks. With the arrival of cable and the overall threat to the existence of the networks, this vaunted position for the major leagues is no longer guaranteed. All kinds of games are now seen on television, not merely those shown on ABC's *Wide World of Sports*.

Journalists at newspapers have tended to be boosters for their **cities** and the teams they cover. A surface indignation about racism, sexism, commercialism and other excesses in different sports (like the failure of players to be good "role models") is often undermined by the clamor for good performances from their cities' teams. Some change may be expected as more women journalists and commentators are read in print and seen on television, from the pre-game shows to the commentary boxes. Issues have arisen, however, as a result of revelations concerning the parentage of Alexandra Stevenson, a rising **tennis** star whose mother, the sports journalist Samantha Stevenson, contested restrictions placed on women journalists' access to sportsmen at the end of the 1970s. The fact that her interviews with Julius Erving led to the conception of their daughter has resulted in some women journalists feeling let down, and some sports officials maintaining that their opposition to such contacts had been justified.

The long-time standard in sports journalism has been *Sports Illustrated*, but each sport has its own magazines, some independent, others run by national and regional sports federations. In addition to such magazines, each sports enthusiast can expect the arrival in the mail of a plethora of **catalogs** promoting sporting goods. This saturation has carried over into **talk radio** and television sports news programs, during which the performance of local teams, their coaches and owners are dissected. Such programming is now so common that a **sitcom**, *Sports Night* (ABC), has been loosely based on them.

Further reading

Davies, R.O. (1994) *America's Obsession*, Fort Worth: Harcourt Brace.

ROBERT GREGG

sports and race

Most professional sports have fostered continued institutional racism, although overt **segregation** generally ended after the Second World War. However, with former players who are **African American** beginning to achieve management and ownership positions on teams, there are signs of change occurring. Black advancement has paved the way for **Latinos** and Asians, but issues of **immigration** and stereotyping also affect their levels of participation.

During the first half of the twentieth century nearly all sports were segregated, **boxing** being the most important exception. In this sport, Jack Johnson won the world heavyweight title, receiving considerable vilification from white Americans for doing so and beginning the search for the "great white hope" in that sport, which continued when the sport became dominated by African Americans. Joe Louis was greeted with more favor from **whites**, in part because he represented the nation against Hitler's champion, and whites began to classify black boxers as either "good" or "bad" Negroes. The former includes Louis and Joe Frazier, and the latter men such as Muhammad **Ali** (who both converted to **Islam** and refused to fight in the **Vietnam War**) and Mike Tyson. The stereotyping implicit in these characterizations provides just one example of the way forms of discrimination continued even when a sport appeared to be integrated.

The other two sports that opened doors to blacks relatively early were **track and field** and **basketball**. In the former, the importance of the **Olympic Games** and of **colleges and universities** which counted a few African Americans among their students meant that a few great athletes could make their mark and bring about a demand for other black athletes. Jesse Owens winning four gold medals at the 1936 Berlin Olympics made a lasting impression on track and field. Once colleges and universities were forced to integrate more fully in the 1950s and 1960s, they quickly began to encourage more black athletes to join their sports programs.

In the case of basketball, also, some black athletes played for white varsity teams outside the segregated **South**, but only rarely did they start for the team or gain pivotal roles on the court. The major change occurred with the success of the Harlem Renaissance, a team made up primarily of West Indian immigrants and **Philadelphia, PA** players. The Rens' victories over the (then **New York**) Celtics during the 1930s heralded the beginning of integrated basketball, though Southern universities still resisted for decades.

But the great landmark in the fight against segregation occurred in baseball with the signing of Jackie **Robinson** to the Brooklyn Dodgers organization. Baseball, at the time the "American game," had excluded blacks from the 1890s, and had bitterly resisted integration during the 1920s and 1930s, even when it was clear that many of the best players in the country were playing in the Negro Leagues. Jackie Robinson played his first

game in a Dodgers' uniform in 1947 and was so successful that he was followed by other leading players from the Negro Leagues, which subsequently disbanded. A number of teams like the Philadelphia Phillies and **Boston** Red Sox resisted the pressure to hire black players and often taunted those African Americans playing for opposing teams. But by the early 1960s integration was well established throughout the National League. Baseball also opened up to Latino players from **Puerto Rico**, **Cuba**, the Dominican Republic and, in the 1990s, to a few Japanese ballplayers.

However, a shift in racism occurred very rapidly from segregation to structural inequalities and racial stereotyping. In many sports like **golf** and **tennis**, for example, a certain degree of wealth was required before a person could reach the highest level of the game. For many years after integration was firmly established this limited the number of black players reaching the highest levels. In many cases, country clubs would practice forms of discrimination, especially against **Jews** and blacks, leading to players being excluded from membership and competitions. African Americans like Charlie Sifford in golf, and Arthur **Ashe** or Althea Gibson in tennis, were the exceptions helping to pave the way for current players like Tiger **Woods** and the Williams sisters. Michael Chang has been the one **Asian American** star. His career has been followed perhaps more closely in Asia than America.

Other kinds of stereotyping have been very common. In many sports certain positions are considered "thinking" positions – guards in basketball, quarterbacks in **football**, pitchers in baseball, for example – and these have tended to be associated with whites. This has led to obvious structural inequalities with the more elite, visible positions dominated by white players. For many years, it was impossible for a black college quarterback to get onto an NFL team except as a wide receiver or running back. This has begun to change with the success of quarterbacks like Doug Williams, Randall Cunningham and Warren Moon, but the changes have been slow in coming, and teams have often showed such players less loyalty than their white counterparts.

Moreover, the assumption that black players rely on athleticism rather than intelligence has meant that relatively few have been able to break into coaching after their playing careers have ended. When Al Campanis commented on ABC's *Nightline* commemoration of Jackie Robinson that blacks were good athletes but would not be good managers, he stated what was the unspoken rule in baseball at the time. The storm of protest following this broadcast actually began the shift away from this practice. Changes have occurred as African Americans begin to gain visibility in all positions and as coaches. But even successful coaches, like Dennis Green at the Minnesota Vikings (in football), feel that they receive more criticism from their fans and management than they would if they were white. The high turnover of African American coaches suggests that they are correct.

There are also racial assumptions regarding the way different games are played. Commentators and journalists will often assume that African Americans bring "street" traditions and natural athleticism to games, and that they need coaching and discipline from white coaches to shape their games and make them most effective. CBS football analyst, Jimmy "the Greek" Snyder, even suggested that this was a result of anatomical differences between the races. The assumption that blacks are natural while whites disciplined means that a bad streak of performances for a white player will lead to calls for patience and nurturing, while a bad streak for a black player will lead to a belief that the player has lost his or her gift, followed by demands that the player be traded. Moreover, such racial stereotypes give white coaches undue license to treat their players in demeaning ways in the name of discipline, without reprimand from management or college authorities. This has led to friction on occasion – all-star basketball player, Latrell Sprewell, assaulted his coach after such treatment. Meanwhile, black coaches, on the rare occasions when they are appointed, have sometimes been unfairly criticized for identifying too much with their players.

Certain sports remain dominated by whites. Some remain so because of the legacy of past racial stereotypes – like the assumption that blacks do not make good swimmers. Others derive from regional and **class** differences. Seldom have their been any black ice-**hockey** players, even though the market

has now extended to the whole country. Dominique Dawes has been a pioneer for African Americans in women's gymnastics. Soccer, a game largely associated with the **suburbs** and immigrants, may see boosted interest among African Americans following the success of Briana Scurry in the Women's World Cup of 1999. Asian Americans, stereotyped as non-athletes, have a low profile, except in women's **figure skating**.

Basketball remains the team sport most associated with blacks, but white players are at a premium. Teams in certain markets will often endeavor to encourage a white player of limited abilities to come to their team in the hope that the largely white crowds will identify with the player. Such players will also generally receive disproportionately large salaries. However, the success of players like Magic Johnson, Julius Erving and, above all, Michael Jordan has diminished this tendency. It remains to be seen whether these players have the same success after the game in coaching and ownership (Johnson's move into agency and Erving's association with the Orlando Magic suggest that there is some movement at this level).

Further reading

Edwards, H. (1973) *Sociology of Sport*, Illinois: Dorsey Press.

Hoberman, J. (1997) *Darwin's Athletes*, New York: Houghton Mifflin.

Lapchick, R.E. (1984) *Broken Promises: Racism in American Sports*, New York: St. Martin's/Marek.

ROBERT GREGG

sports cars

The combination of America's love affair with the **automobile**, vast **highways** and ideals of **individualism** seem to make the nation a natural habitat for automobiles defined by the speed, handling, design and power that they give the driver. Indeed, the Corvette dominates American imagery of the fast, sleek, two-seater convertible and has been projected as an American image abroad, even if never a sales success. Yet, American production of sports cars has been overshadowed continually by European models sold in the US, which also out-raced American sports cars worldwide. Issues of class and cultural capital also permeate a world where speed and handling may also be addressed through a Maserati or modification of standard cars into "**hot rods**." From origins to the contemporary period, sports cars are defined socially and by media as toys for boys – "babe magnets."

Prior to the Second World War, sports cars in America tended to be designed and produced by small companies targeting **niche markets**, their fame often exceeding their sales. The most prominent early entrant was Stutz, who introduced the Bearcat in 1913, yet, despite subsequent advances, closed in 1935. The Depression also destroyed the Cord, Auburn and Duesenberg, whose Model J was a very high performance luxury model. By this time, France, Italy, Britain and Germany also had created legendary sports cars whose dominance would continue after the war.

Amid postwar affluence, suburbanization and the impact of European models, the Big Three automakers experimented with the sports car in the form of the Corvette (Chevrolet/GM) and the Thunderbird (Ford). The unmistakable new 1955 Thunderbird two-seater was changed in 1958 into a four-passenger personal luxury car. Ford later re-entered the "sporty" market with the Mustang (1964–). The corvette, with a fiberglass body on a Chevy chassis, hit the road in 1953. Despite design changes after 1957, it has defined the American sports car. Kaiser, Nash and Studebaker also introduced sports cars in the 1950s. Artisanal alternatives over the years have included the Bricklin, Cobra and Delorean, while family cars have gained sporty power and features. Yet, the markets of the 1950s and 1960s always included a range of European cars, from the MG and Porsche to the Jaguar and Ferrari alongside larger American "performance" cars.

American sports cars, nonetheless, lost popularity until disposable income in the 1990s made toys for the rich more popular again. European cars and Japanese manufacturers have effectively claimed the market, despite Corvette's continuing production. Sports cars are also only one option within a range of automotive expressions of money,

power and self that includes **sports utility vehicles**, "sporty and powerful" touring cars, luxury cars, family vans, pick-up **trucks**, etc.

Further reading

Boyne, W. (1990) *Power Behind the Wheel*, New York: Stewart, Tabori and Chang.

GARY McDONOGH

sports stadiums

Icons of "major-league cities." Historical ball-fields for **baseball** and **football** – Fenway Park in **Boston, MA**, Comiskey Park in **Chicago, IL**, Candlestick Park in **San Francisco, CA** – provided centers and landmarks for metropoles imitated by later monumental public constructions like **Houston**'s enclosed Astrodome (**Texas**). As neighborhoods and audiences changed and owners sought to cash in on lucrative boxes, these stadiums have also become battlegrounds for urban planning. While **Cleveland, OH** and **Baltimore, MD** have used them to stimulate revitalization of waterfront areas, others question the public expenditures and corporate perks, including naming, that hold cities hostage to franchise-owners against the promise of sometimes ambivalent returns in jobs, revenues and image.

Further reading

Cagan, J. and Demause, N. (1998) *Field of Schemes*, Monroe, ME: Common Courage.
http://www.fieldofschemes.com website.

GARY McDONOGH

sports utility vehicles (SUV)

Off-road vehicles adapted to unpaved excursions emerged in **California** in the 1970s; their impact on wilderness areas was soon decried nationwide. In the 1990s, however, **nature** and freedom have been repackaged in massive, luxurious cars far distant from the functional dune buggies or jeeps of the past. Sports utility vehicles, which are **trucks**, have been attacked for gas guzzling, dangerous designs in collisions and sheer bulk that strains urban roadways and the environment. Yet they connote status and security in a hot market dominated by American **automakers** building ever-more elaborate vehicles that will never ford a stream or climb a mountain, despite their ads. In 2000, Ford acknowledged that SUVs cause serious safety and environmental problems.

GARY McDONOGH

CINDY WONG

Springsteen, Bruce

b. 1949

Coming of age in the late 1960s, Bruce Springsteen reflects the musical and social influences of the time, combining social critique of the folk tradition with the exuberance of **rock 'n' roll**. Though his live performances have always earned him a devoted audience, his popularity exploded in the mid-1980s when he released "Born in the USA." The album's title song, a searing critique of a nation embattled by the **Vietnam War** and economic decline, was misinterpreted by many (including President **Reagan**) as a nationalistic anthem. Springsteen has raised money for political organizations such as the Christic Institute and the anti-nuclear movement. A 2000 song, "41 Bullets," criticizes **police** brutality in **New York** City, NY.

SUSAN SCHULTEN

standardized testing

Inspired by the efforts of French psychologist Alfred Binet, who in 1904 designed a measure to determine students at risk of failure in school so that those students could receive remedial attention, there emerged what came to be known as intelligence tests which yielded a number defined as a person's intelligence quotient or IQ. This and related tests were developed using the population of enlisted men during the First World War, and this group of **white**, **middle-class** males came to be the "norm" to which all other individuals and groups were compared.

Mental measurement and scientifically grounded assessment tools were part of a general movement at the beginning of the twentieth century to develop a "science of education," which reflected the obsession of schools and culture with the efficiency of production at that time. As schools became like factories, and under pressure from a tax-paying public (whose money supports public education), school administrators needed clean, fast, relatively inexpensive and accurate ways of measuring their schools' products. The Educational Testing Service, founded in 1947 with the support of the Carnegie Foundation, emerged as (and has remained) the primary regulator of students' access to learning at all levels and to professional opportunities beyond school through their production and control of standardized tests. These include the SATS (Scholastic Aptitude Tests), LCATS (law), MCATS (medicine) and GREs (graduate school).

Standardized tests are mass-produced, primarily multiple-choice, criterion-referenced tests administered to students individually and *en masse* under highly regulated (timed, directed, monitored) conditions as early as preschool and regularly (as often as several times a year) subsequently. These tests are intended to measure students' aptitude and achievement, and they are used to compare and sort individuals and groups of students within and across classes, grade levels and schools.

In recent years, there has been substantial debate about the efficacy and fairness of standardized tests. Advocates argue that what American **education** lacks is rigor, high standards of excellence and effective measures for holding schools and students accountable. Because they judge all students according to the same criteria, standardized tests appear to offer "scientific" data upon which to make educational decisions, and thus they are thought by some to be objective and fair.

Critics argue that the tests are biased in terms of **race**, **class**, **gender** and other forms of diversity and that they offer an unfair advantage to those students whose **home** and **community** experiences most closely parallel the middle class, Anglo-American values generally emphasized in **public schools** which were established as the norm over eighty years ago through the first IQ tests.

Furthermore, critics argue that standardized tests reinforce meritocratic competitiveness, fear of failure, curricular influence and manipulation by those who create the tests, over-emphasis on results and a trivialization of knowledge in their emphasis of facts (as opposed to critical thinking).

The basic disagreement is that proponents of standardized tests argue that the scores reflect students' intelligence and potential, and critics argue that the tests reflect the biases of those who design them and serve to reinforce the inequities inherent in the status quo.

ALISON COOK-SATHER

Stanford University

Founded in 1885 by railroad magnate and political leader Leland Stanford and his wife in memory of their son, Leland Jr., who died as a teenager. Located 35 miles south of **San Francisco, CA**, at the northern tip of "**Silicon Valley**," whose hi-tech business and research facilities the University spawned. Stanford emerged after the Second World War as one of America's premier institutions. Its undergraduate and graduate schools consistently rank within the top five and it boasts numerous **Nobel Prize** winners on its faculty. Students and alumni have included President Herbert Hoover, **Olympic** gold medalist Summer Sanders, Astronaut Sally Ride, computer magnates William Hewlett and David Packard, **Supreme Court** justices William H. **Rehnquist** and Sandra Day **O'Connor** and **Secretary of State** Warren Christopher.

BRIAN LEVIN

Stanislavski, Konstantin *see* actors

stars and sex symbols

Stars and sex symbols are a crucial part of popular culture and the pleasure the audience takes in watching **film** and **television**, but they are also crucial to the economics of the entertainment industry as well. The tradition of the star precedes twentieth-century **mass media** (nineteenth-century **theater** and **opera** promoters advanced the careers of certain performers in order to boost sales of tickets). Yet, postwar American entertainment worlds have increasingly fixated upon the **body** of the sex symbol in order to encourage public consumption.

Perhaps because of the importance of the **Hollywood** studio system, sex symbols in the 1940s and 1950s emerged from film. In the 1950s, women who moved from this realm onto the pages of **magazines**, **newspapers** and posters, and into the popular imaginations of men, seemed to reflect the growing economy of the country. These women, such as Marilyn **Monroe** and Jayne Mansfield, were buxom, breathy, blonde and, at first glance, seemed to exist for the sexual and visual pleasure of men. Sex symbols stood in contradistinction to the more appropriate standards of domesticated **femininity** that were being portrayed in television in the 1950s. These women stood outside traditional **marriage** and were more interested in seeking out fun than in keeping a good, clean home.

Similarly, the male sex symbols that emerged out of the crumbling studio system, James **Dean**, Marlon **Brando**, Paul **Newman** and Montgomery **Clift**, unlike the efficient corporate model of **masculinity**, were intense brooders who refused to fit into suburbanized America.

Richard Dyer, who writes on the meanings of **celebrity** and film in *Stars* (1979) and elsewhere, argues that for famous **actors**, films are a vehicle for the display of the star's persona. The performance of this persona requires repetition of key elements of narrative, visual style and iconography. Thus when Marilyn Monroe became a star, her roles, the way she looked and the ways in which she became styled and shot in film and publicity outlets became similar, solidifying a persona. Although a sex symbol is unattainable and an object of fantasy, he or she must also seem knowable and familiar to the masses.

After the Hollywood studio lost power, agents and **public relations** have taken over the management of stars. Along with this change, stars have tended to emerge from different sectors of the entertainment industry. For example, one of the most popular sex symbols of the 1980s and 1990s,

Madonna, started out as a pop singer. Her career benefited from **MTV**, where her **videos** featured her dancing and knowing sexual come-ons. Although she has never successfully maintained a film career, she has always managed her persona well – with the help of agents, publicists, magazine editors and gossip columnists eager for copy. The contemporary sex symbol is also a corporate entity who, like Madonna, has moved into book publishing, as well as the music and film industry. Much of what Madonna's work has centered upon is her experience of her own body and her popular philosophizing on the importance of sex.

The body of the sex symbol in the 1990s changed dramatically. Whereas in the 1950s the female body featured an hour-glass figure and the male body was wiry, the 1990s sex-symbol body for both was lean, muscular and sculpted, reflecting the importance of working out and also marking the entrance of the **fashion** model as a mass-marketed sex symbol. White models Cindy Crawford, Kate Moss and Christy Turlington have moved from the runway into superstardom with forays into television, video and film. Black models such as Naomi Campbell and Tyra Banks have become the first minority stars that have been marketed as sex symbols to both black and white audiences. A black male model, Tyson, sporting the clothing of **WASP**-aspiring Ralph Lauren, has established himself as a sex symbol, as have black actors Denzel Washington and Wesley Snipes. In 1999 **Latino** singer Ricky Martin broke into the mainstream of sex symbolism, recognized as much for his gyrating hips just as Elvis punctuated the meanings of his songs with his pelvic thrusts.

Even as America's sex symbols diversify, one rule remains in place: when the star sings and speaks of love, his or her body must make the audience think of sex. As a result the movement and posture of the star, as well as the publicity machinery that supports him or her, is always crucial for keeping sales up.

EDWARD MILLER

Star Trek and "Trekkies"

NBC **science-fiction** television series (1966–9), created by Gene Roddenberry. Originally pitched as a **space**-faring **western**, *Star Trek* was notable for its cerebral engagement with questions of identity in addition to more traditional action, and for the humanitarian, even utopian, project behind its multicultural crew of pioneers. Its appeal lay more in the dynamic between its regular characters – the impetuous Kirk frequently clashing with the cool, logical Mr Spock – than in the crew's interaction with alien cultures. While **white** males still dominated the *Enterprise*, the series broke new ground with the first "interracial kiss" broadcast on American television. Technically a ratings failure, the series was cancelled after three years but retained immense fan loyalty through protest campaigns, conventions and fanzines. It has been kept alive through **syndication**, a series of feature films, bestselling **novels** and further television spin-offs from the original premise, including *Star Trek: The Next Generation*, *Voyager* and *Deep Space Nine*.

The degree of affection and involvement displayed by Star Trek fans has led them to be stereotyped as social rejects and obsessives; indeed, the very term "Trekkies" has become pejorative ("Trekkers" is often preferred). Jenkins (1992) has suggested the complexity at work in these fan-groups, whose interpretations frequently highlight the series' egalitarian portrayal of gender and **ethnicity**. Some, like the "Gaylaxian" organization, are still lobbying for their own **queer** readings to be incorporated in the current program.

Further reading

Jenkins, H. (1992) *Textual Poachers*, London: Routledge.

WILL BROOKER

states and government

Each of the fifty states of the United States has its own government. These governments are very similar to the national government in form, each having its own executive (headed by a **governor**), its own legislature and its own **judiciary**. State government responsibilities are quite broad, and include fields as diverse as **environment**, roads and vehicle licensing, public safety and corrections, business regulation and licensing. States are responsible for policing, **education** and **public health**, although in these areas the federal government also has much responsibility. Some powers are shared concurrently, but in other cases there is no clear division, and there are frequent disputes between the states and **Washington, DC** over jurisdiction.

State legislatures are bicameral, with houses of representatives and senates mirroring the national structure; Nebraska is unique in being unicameral. Legislators, like governors, are usually elected on a four-year term. In many states the legislatures are dominated by representatives from rural areas, who are often more conservative (and **Republican**) than their urban counterparts and have little interest in or affinity with issues affecting the **cities**. The larger cities in turn tend to seek to guard their own privileges and are reluctant to recognize the authority of the state government – **New York** City and **Los Angeles, CA**, for example, are virtually independent of state control as far as day-to-day administration goes.

State judiciaries consist of several types of trial courts and appellate courts, headed by a state supreme court. The decisions of the latter can usually be referred to the federal **Supreme Court** in Washington. In most states judges are elected; terms of four years are most common, but some terms are for as little as two years, and in Rhode Island and Massachusetts judges are elected for life.

States themselves are divided into various subordinate levels of government, including counties, cities, towns and townships. These are responsible for exercising various powers devolved to them by the state government, such as education, fire and police services, waste disposal and so on.

As noted previously, conflicts between state governments and the federal government are common. Most of these concern the infringement of the jurisdiction of one party by officials of the other. Many federal agencies (the **FBI**, the Bureau of Alcohol, Tobacco and Firearms, and so on) have wide-ranging powers which allow them to usurp jurisdiction from state authorities. This is often strongly resented by the latter, so also is the fact that cases concerning jurisdiction are always heard by federal courts.

Perhaps the most famous and bitter conflict in recent years was that which took place in the 1960s over the desegregation of schools. In forcing the Southern states to accept mixed-race schools, federal **Attorney-General** Robert **Kennedy** used the courts and even mobilized some elements of the armed forces to push federal policy through (see **Civil Rights movement**). All the protests of the state governments were ineffectual in the face of a determined effort to enforce federal policy.

MORGEN WITZEL

state university systems

Unlike many other nations, the United States has not promoted universities under direct federal control – apart from military academies – although federal funding and intervention in research, **affirmative action** and regulation of individual rights have shaped tertiary education in the postwar era. Instead, public education has evolved through systems organized and substantively funded by **states** and their citizens. These systems include major research universities such as the **University of California**-Berkeley, University of Michigan, UCLA, Penn State, University of Indiana, University of Illinois and others in systems whose enrollments in undergraduate, graduate, professional and related programs may surpass 100,000 students. These institutions also become interwoven with local development and identity in politics, medicine and sports. Yet these great universities also participate in systems that incorporate formerly limited regional colleges and teacher's colleges, divisions inherited from segregation, **community colleges** and extension programs. In all, state institutions have spread college and advanced education beyond the elite served by **private schools**, at minimal costs – tuition at public four-year colleges in 1998 averaged $3,000, about one-quarter the cost of private institutions. Nonetheless, state universities face important questions of quality, funding, politics and social meanings far beyond the **campus**.

The earliest state schools emerged in the South – University of Georgia (1789), University of North Carolina (1789) and Thomas Jefferson's University of Virginia (1923). Northern states, instead, debated public control over finance and curriculum in the private institutions that became the **Ivy League**, leading to a court battle confirming the private charter of Dartmouth College. State foundations were helped by federal allocations of land as endowment through the 1862 Morrill Act that funded agricultural and mechanical universities. Some states founded separate schools (Texas A&M), while others expanded state universities. Over time, states also founded and took over regional institutions serving specific areas – Eastern Michigan versus Western Michigan – or specific functions like teacher training (normal schools) and rural outreach. Consolidated state systems, in turn, grew in the postwar period with junior and community colleges that extended public education, albeit in a highly stratified manner.

There remains great variety between systems and within them. California has highly elaborated relationships among **colleges and universities**, while SUNY has sought to unify and improve New York colleges into universities since 1948 while increasingly funding another public-complex system in **CUNY** (City University of New York). Some systems focus on a single university (New Hampshire, Vermont), while others have multiple universities and feeder schools (Kentucky, **Texas**, **Florida**, etc.). In the South, the role of historically **African American** colleges within desegregated state systems has often proved problematic.

State systems, as they extend education to more citizens, often face fights over resources within the state to be allocated to each unit and within programs or cities that may compete for recognition. The mass culture of such institutions also has entailed constant challenges of sports versus academics, and demands for mass (practical) and vocational education versus research. While desegregation has made these systems of diversity, they have faced 1990s challenges over the use of race and class to foster admissions that reflect state populations. Student behavior, including excessive **alcohol**, problems of sex and relationships and social unrest, has also arisen as student organizations have competed with other university ideals – whether **fraternities and sororities** or the radical political associations in the 1960s who took over campus offices. Here political traditions

clearly differentiate a leftist Berkeley from more social campuses, and the problems of college towns dominate myriad students and academic employers.

Fights over programs also go beyond the campus. While most state universities have been buffered from direct political influence by independent Boards of Trustees, these may be targeted by governors in terms of influential appointments. Moreover, political issues of diversity, salary and productivity, and ideology can spill over into the state legislature and funding process.

Costs are also an issue. The early commitment of public tertiary education often involved free tuition for qualifying students (within the state). This has given way to fees substantially lower and sometimes more flexible than private schools, but not necessarily negligible. Out-of-state tuition, in fact, may equal that of private schools, although research universities may offer generous stipends to foreign students as well as a cross-section of American scholars. Still, containment of costs in salaries, construction and other areas is as real for these systems as for most private universities.

Nonetheless, state universities still embody the triumph of American democratic education as a limited right. They are also constant scenarios for media depictions of **coming-of-age** events – a somewhat more adult extension of high-school dramas of romance, sports and mayhem.

Further reading

Campbell, J. (1995) *Reclaiming a Lost Heritage*, Ames: University of Iowa.

GARY McDONOGH

Steele, Danielle

b. 1947

Alternatively termed a "teflon novelist," and the companion to "Sunday afternoons with a box of bonbons," Danielle Steele remains unarguably a **publishing** sensation. Her **romance** novels, featuring often glamorous heroines grappling with the demands of work, love and **family** and moving through melodrama towards emotional catharsis, have soared to the top of the bestseller list over twenty-five times and sold 85 million copies in over forty-two countries. Steele's readers run the gamut of age and income; 40 percent are male. Born to privilege (the Lowenbrau beer family), Steele found writing – poems, reviews and ad copy as well – a comfort from loneliness after a **divorce**, and quietude from the limelight. Her reign also encompasses the television **miniseries**, including ABC's *Crossings*, *Wanderlust* and *Thurston Place*.

MARIAELENA BARTESAGHI

Steinem, Gloria

b. 1934

Author, editor, feminist activist and cofounder of **Ms**. magazine. Deemed by some historians to be as important to the second wave of American **feminism** as Susan B. Anthony was to the first. Steinem began her career as a journalist. As a feminist, she organized protests, recruited supporters, raised money, founded new feminist pressure groups and made speeches on behalf of the **women's movement**. She published numerous books, including: *Outrageous Acts and Everyday Rebellions* (1983), a collection of articles previously printed in *Ms.*; a feminist interpretation of Marilyn **Monroe**'s life; and *Revolution from Within* (1992), a guide to enhancing self-esteem.

MARY-CHRISTINE SUNGAILA, ESQ.

steroids

Anabolic steroids, artificial synthetic derivatives of the male sex hormone testosterone, promote the growth of muscle tissue, increase overall body strength and improve athletes' recovery time to facilitate intense training regimens, while adversely affecting the liver and both the cardiovascular and reproductive systems. Limitations in testing equipment account for the failure to detect the drug at major sporting events, along with competitors' efforts to evade detection, timing their dosages to avoid testing positive, or substituting urine samples by various clandestine methods (many of which

were graphically depicted in the movie *The Program*, 1993, about a university **football** program). The requirement in American football that players bulk up has made this a sport in which the use of **body**-building drugs is endemic.

ROBERT GREGG

Stevenson, Adlai Ewing

b. 1900; d. 1965

Urbane intellectual and liberal **Democratic** candidate for the **presidency**. After an **Ivy League** education and foreign service career, Stevenson became governor of his home state of Illinois in 1948. Drafted as presidential candidate against the popular military hero Dwight **Eisenhower**, he was trounced in 1952 and 1956. When the Democrats regained the White House in 1960, Stevenson became Ambassador to the **United Nations** under Presidents **Kennedy** and **Johnson**, although he was sometimes troubled by their policies. His erudite speeches, sense of politics as pedagogy and dry wit seem impossibly distant from the popularity contests and spin control of later politics.

GARY McDONOGH

Stewart, James

b.1908; d. 1997

Actor. A quintessentially nice guy, whether in Frank **Capra** classics like *It's a Wonderful Life* (1939) or **Hitchcock**'s *Vertigo* (1958), where he epitomized ambivalent virtue within moral dilemmas beyond his control. Stewart's Midwestern drawl and gawky presence nonetheless became the stuff of a Second World War pilot and a leading man for over four decades, until the 1970s. He won an Oscar for *Philadelphia Story* (1940) and for lifetime achievement (1985), as well as tributes by the American Film Institute and the Kennedy Center, and the Medal of Freedom (1985). The **Los Angeles, CA** airport is named after him.

GARY McDONOGH

Stewart, Martha

b. 1941

Doyenne of style for 1990s **baby boomers**. Stewart, a former caterer, offers multimedia guides to elegant home life – planting, ornamenting, arranging, color-coordinating and adding extra touches that show leisure time as well as taste. Her **magazine**, *Martha Stewart Living*, soared from 250,000 subscribers to over 5 million by mid-decade; her **television** specials delineate propriety for **holidays**, while syndicated features appear daily. Moreover, Stewart integrated sales with major corporations like the discount **department store** K-Mart and the media conglomerate **Time Warner**. Her presence has been parodied in television (and by Stewart herself in an American Express commercial), but her advice and sales appeal to middle-class affluence and insecurity.

GARY McDONOGH
CINDY WONG

St. Louis, MO

Eero **Saarinen**'s glistening Gateway Arch towers over this Mississippi River port, marking it as both a hub in transcontinental journeys westward and a crossroads on the **Midwest**'s North–South axis since its foundation by the French (1764). These routes fostered a diverse city, with German immigrants alongside Southern **African Americans** and **Midwestern** farmers. In its heyday, St. Louis became known as a center for finance, manufacturing, education (Washington University), arts (**blues** and **jazz**) and information (the **Pulitzer** family's *Post-Dispatch*). Its sports teams have included the historic Cardinals (**baseball**), the Blues (**hockey**) and the Rams (**football**).

Yet, choked by burgeoning suburbs and **deindustrialization**, St. Louis' population declined 50 percent between 1970 and 1990, reaching 339,316 in 1998 Census Bureau estimates. The city, and the more depressed and predominantly African American East St. Louis, Illinois, have come to embody issues of dualization in postindustrial American urbanism.

GARY McDONOGH
CINDY WONG

stocks and bonds

Stocks and bonds are the primary instruments for financing large corporations in the United States. In contrast to many European companies which depend primarily on bank loans for capital, American corporations rely heavily on public issuance of debt (bonds) and equity (stocks).

Bonds are IOUs of a company or government body. They typically pay a fixed (sometimes floating) rate of interest for a stated period of time. They may be backed by specific revenues or the credit quality of the entity. At maturity, the initial investment, or principal, is due to the investor. Stocks, on the other hand, represent a share of ownership in a company. Stockholders are entitled to a portion of any distributions and proceeds from a liquidation. Bonds are generally safer than stocks because interest on bonds must be paid before stockholders may receive any distributions. If a firm goes bankrupt, bondholders are paid before stockholders.

With added risk goes reward and thus stockholders stand to benefit more from success of the issuing company. A successful bond investment will provide little more than the stated interest and return of principal, while a stock investment's return is only limited by the growth prospects of the company. Historically, stocks have produced after-inflation returns of 7.2 percent, while bonds have earned just 3.7 percent (Henwood 1997: 326).

Although stocks and bonds initially serve to finance an enterprise, there is an active secondary market for these financial instruments. The NYSE (New York Stock Exchange) and NASDAQ (National Association of Securities Dealers Automated Quotation) dominate the market for stock trading, while a network of institutional dealers dominate bond-market trading. The NYSE is an example of an organized exchange. In this environment, orders are transmitted to a central floor where brokers negotiate prices for their customers using an auction process. The NYSE dominates trading in the largest American companies. However, its conservative nature caused it to miss much of the explosive growth of computerized trading. The NASDAQ market is an example of an over-the-counter (OTC) trading environment. Here, brokers still represent customers, but trades are negotiated by phone or computer. The NASDAQ market includes technology firms such as Intel and Microsoft, as well as thousands of smaller firms that do not meet NYSE requirements.

The concept of "making a market" also defines exchanges. On the NYSE, "specialists" are charged with keeping an orderly market by providing liquidity, but most activity is between two customers. In the over-the-counter market, "market makers" hold themselves out as willing to buy *and* sell a security at almost any time. Thus, transactions take place between a customer and a market maker. The latter earns a spread – the difference between the price at which he or she will sell and that at which he or she will buy. While there are numerous regional exchanges, the NYSE and NASDAQ dominate US trading.

In the US, bonds are traded over-the-counter. Trading is led by financial institutions specializing in government debt. The yield on the thirty-year US Treasury Bond or "Long Bond" is a benchmark upon which numerous other rates such as savings-account and loan rates are set. Annual trading volume exceeds $100 trillion per year (Henwood 1997: 25), but is primarily the domain of institutions using the market to manage their interest-rate exposure.

Investments in stocks and bonds were traditionally dominated by large institutions which managed pension plans, endowments and foundations. An acclaimed book, *Where Are the Customers' Yachts?* (Schwed 1940), highlighted the fact that individuals faced an uphill battle in achieving investment success. The investing industry has seen broad changes since 1980. Greater **tax** incentives for investing, the growth of deep-discount ("do-it-yourself") stockbrokers and the advent of the 401k retirement savings plan spurred heightened interest in investing and fueled the great bull

market of the 1980s and 1990s. By 1983, 19 percent of households owned stock and over one-third owned mutual funds. This explosive growth has come on the heels of a decades-long bull market, meaning most new investors have never weathered a downturn in financial fortunes.

The tremendous growth of mutual funds has contributed to the democratization of investment. A mutual fund is an investment company that pools money in order to invest in a diversified portfolio of securities. This arrangement allows for professional management, economies of scale and exposure to a wide variety of investments, reducing overall risk (diversification). From its infancy in the 1970s, US mutual-fund assets have mushroomed from less than $100 billion to $4.5 trillion in 1997. Mutual funds hold 19 percent of all US stocks and a similar percentage of US bonds. They have become the primary vehicle for individual investment through the growth of defined-contribution (401k) plans.

Further investment democratization is coming in the form of **Internet** access to trading markets and greater individual control over pension assets (perhaps negatively affecting mutual funds). Brokerage commissions have plummeted as full-service stockbrokers are threatened by deep-discount brokerages that offer limited investment advice, but rock-bottom commissions. Do-it-yourselfers have embraced Internet trading as an inexpensive way to gain exposure to surging equity markets (some firms even offer commission-free trades).

At the same time, traditionally defined benefit pensions managed by corporations are being replaced with defined-contribution plans that put the investment decision-making in individuals' hands. While these developments have meant increasing control by investors over their savings, experts are concerned with the individual's ability to remain calm during extended market downturns, the likes of which investors haven't seen since the early 1970s.

Further reading

Graham, B. (1973) *The Intelligent Investor*, New York: HarperCollins.

Henwood, D. (1997) *Wall Street*, New York: Verso.
Malkiel, B.G. (1990) *A Random Walk Down Wall Street*, New York: W.W. Norton & Company.

MARC BALCER

Stone, Oliver

b. 1946

Controversial and powerful **director**, writer and **producer** whose movies since the mid-1980s have probed some of the most sensitive issues of contemporary American domestic and global politics. Stone's work confronts history, often through profound male struggles with temptation and conspiracy, amid complex atmospheres charged with violence. His initial films, *Salvador* (1985) and the Oscar-Winning *Platoon* (1985), scored the moral dilemmas of involvement in **Latin America** and Vietnam, where Stone returned with the powerful transformations of *Born on the Fourth of July* (1989) and *Heaven and Earth* (1989). Equally controversial revisions of domestic issues emerged from the greed of *Wall Street* (1987), the shadowy powers of *JFK* (1991) and *Nixon* (1995) and the violence of *Natural Born Killers* (1994).

GARY McDONOGH
CINDY WONG

Stonewall Riot

On the evening of June 27, 1969 a routine police raid on a homosexual bar, the Stonewall Inn, in **New York** City, NY's **Greenwich Village** turned into what the New York Mattachine Society newsletter called "The Hairpin Drop Heard Round the World." The gay liberationist movement, officially organized by the Gay Liberation Front (GLF), now had an historical marker for its birthplace. According to John D'Emilio, "[w]ord of the Stonewall riot and GLF spread rapidly among the networks of young radicals scattered across the country, and within a year gay liberation groups had sprung into existence on college campuses and in cities around the world" (1983: 233).

Further reading

D'Emilio, J. (1983) *Sexual Politics, Sexual Communities*, Chicago: University of Chicago Press.

DAVID GERSTNER

Strasberg, Lee *see* actors

Strategic Defense Initiative (SDI)

Nicknamed "Star Wars" by its critics, SDI was first presented by President **Reagan** in 1983 as a system to defend against a nuclear missile attack. Influenced by Edward Teller, a scientist involved in the development of the hydrogen bomb and a model for the war-crazed advisor in *Dr Strangelove* (1964), Reagan announced the missile system on national television without full discussion with his military advisors. Development of such a defense system was unrealistic, though the multi-billion dollar expenditures that were forthcoming from **Congress** produced some scientific advances. The goal was impractical because the defense system was intended to keep intercontinental ballistic missiles (ICBMs) from striking the United States by intercepting them once they left the Earth's atmosphere. Since the Soviet Union was developing new cruise missiles, which remained in the atmosphere, the system could never be a foolproof defense.

Recent developments have renewed the popularity of SDI: the much exaggerated success of the Patriot Missile during the **Gulf War**, which suggested that anti-missile systems might work (though striking a nuclear missile within the Earth's atmosphere might be as disastrous as letting it strike its target); and the growing fear that the end of the **Cold War** may have made the world's nuclear arsenals less secure. The fact that a terrorist organization, which might be a possible source of a nuclear incident, would be unlikely to attach a nuclear device to an ICBM has not been factored into the budgetary equation. Hence, it emerged anew as an initiative of the Clinton administration and an issue in the 2000 election.

ROBERT GREGG

street vendors

Small-scale, non-corporate entrepreneurs in kiosks, mobile carts or specialized vehicles who sell **food**, periodicals, cigarettes and other sundries in urban areas. They add color and life to plazas where office-workers and other citizens pause to eat or drink outdoors (a more accepted activity than in many European public settings). Certain specialties – hot dogs, knishes and chestnuts in **New York**, City pretzels in **Philadelphia, PA**, or ethnic specialties in other neighborhoods – also demarcate territory and identity. Other vendors specializing in books, art, jewelry and illegal reproductions of designer clothes represent more problematic agents of street life – some, for example, appear only at night when police surveillance is lax. Here, regulation of access to public space through licensing, limited locations and taxation have raised questions about rights of free speech in the 1990s, as cities balance vitality against middle-class **consumers** and established stores. This has been an especially acid debate under Mayor Giuliani in New York, but other controversies about changing street life have emerged on the Washington, DC mall and with regard to food trucks serving collegiate campus life. In the end, these debates are not only about commerce but also about public space and citizenship.

GARY McDONOGH
CINDY WONG

Streisand, Barbra

b. 1942

Streisand's appearance in **Broadway**'s "I Can Get it For You Wholesale" (1960) showcased her to New York City audiences as a singer of intensity and a comedian who utilized her Jewish upbringing for her persona. After a short-lived **television** show in the 1960s, she went on to a major career as an actor, beginning with *Funny Girl* (1968). Streisand is now also a **director** and **producer** (*Yentl*, 1983; *The Mirror Has Two Faces*, 1996), but has maintained her presence as a singer of ballads with a distinctive interpretation, never shying away from the sentiment of the song. This quality has made her not only a favorite among New Yorkers, but has also helped her keep her devoted gay following.

EDWARD MILLER

stress

Stress, often described as America's number one health problem, has become so prevalent in American culture that many health professionals argue that we are currently in the throes of a "stress epidemic." Despite this increasing awareness, definitions of stress are sometimes ambiguous. The term is simultaneously used to describe the external stimulation that causes strain on the system, the resulting internal damage and the rate of this damage. There are also different types of stress, including acute stress (short term), episodic acute stress (frequent acute stress) and chronic stress (long term). Symptoms of high stress include emotional distress (anger, irritability, anxiety and **depression**), insomnia, substance abuse, headaches, muscular problems, stomach and bowel problems, high blood pressure, heart palpitations, chest pain, shortness of breath, sweaty palms, cold hands or feet and dizziness. Over the long term, stress has been associated (directly or indirectly) with a number of serious conditions including cardiovascular disease, **cancer**, accidental injuries and **suicide**. Stress also aggravates many pre-existing health problems.

Researchers have attempted to pinpoint exact causes of stress, but this has proven difficult since all individuals have varied levels of tolerance. A stressful event that exhausts one person may actually invigorate another. American culture has often been associated with high-stress lifestyles due to efforts to attain the "American dream," but researchers argue that this dream may quickly turn into a nightmare if high-stress warning signals (including those mentioned above) are not addressed. One measure used to determine stress levels is the Holmes-Rahe scale. In the 1950s, psychiatrist Thomas Holmes and psychologist Richard Rahe tried to determine causes of stress by asking 5,000 people to rate the amount of stress associated with various "life-change events." The top five most stressful events in the scale include **death** of a spouse, **divorce**, marital separation, imprisonment and death of a close **family** member. Other researchers have argued that the everyday hassles of life (such as rushing to meet deadlines, waiting in traffic, excessive paperwork, etc.) actually contribute more to illness than major life changes. The truth is probably somewhere in between. In either case, it is important to note the "ripple effect": very often, one highly stressful event – such as the end of a significant relationship – may gradually spiral out of control and lead to problems in many areas of life.

As a result of the increasing awareness of the problems associated with stress, more Americans are becoming interested in various forms of stress management. Researchers have discovered that many techniques used to promote relaxation have consistently high success rates. Meditation in particular has been strongly correlated with a reduction in stress-related disorders. Muscle relaxation, music therapy, biofeedback, rhythmic breathing, proper nutrition and regular exercise are all highly effective methods of managing stress. A strong, trustworthy support system and the commitment to maintaining a balanced lifestyle are also crucial elements of any stress-management program.

Further reading

Foxman, P. (1996) *Dancing with Fear: Overcoming Anxiety in a World of Stress and Uncertainty,* Northvale: Jason Aronson.

NICOLE MARIE KEATING

strikes

There are several categories of strikes. In the United States, the most prevalent is the wage and working-conditions strike. Here, **labor unions** negotiate for better wages and an improved quality of life. Strikes related to disagreements over contract terms are less common. Occasionally, workers strike to force an employer to recognize a union that will represent its employees. Closely related to the strike is the lockout, an employer-imposed closing used to bring economic pressure on disenchanted workers.

The industrial and political characteristics of the United States provide fertile ground for labor strife. Favorable laws guarantee the right to strike for most non-public employees, although there are restrictions against strikes that may significantly affect the life of the nation. While firms may hire replacement workers or scab labor, this is commonly a last resort because it results in strained relations between replaced workers and the employer. Other types of labor disturbances, such as slowdowns, sitdowns and sympathy strikes, are generally illegal.

While strikes by public employees are forbidden, they have become increasingly common. A milestone in this area was the 1970 strike by US postal workers. The strike was resolved to the benefit of the workers. In the early 1980s, however, President Ronald **Reagan** squashed a national **air-traffic controllers' strike**, permanently banning strikers from work in the traffic-control industry.

By nature, strikes by skilled workers are most effective. This is because replacements are not easily found. Thus, the primary successes of the labor movement have been realized among professional unions such as teachers' unions. These strikes are usually settled quickly with strikers demands at least partially met. Interestingly, all of the four major professional sports have seen lockouts or strikes in the past two decades. The strikes normally oppose efforts by team owners to restrict player salary escalation by imposing caps or taxes. These strikes have had a significant impact on attendance and fan interest, but salary growth has not slowed.

The most prominent trend in industrial labor strife is the opposition to part-time and subcontracted labor. US labor laws require that most full-time, permanent employees be covered by extensive benefit packages, including **healthcare**, pension and disability insurance. To control rising labor costs, many firms have sought to outsource tasks or hire temporary workers. A 1997 strike by UPS package deliverers, 1998 strikes by transit workers in **Philadelphia, PA** and **automobile** strikes across the country have brought these issues to the forefront.

Large work stoppages have declined from pre-1980 levels. According to the Bureau of Labor Statistics, the US averaged over 300 stoppages involving more than 1,000 employees per year from 1947–79. Since 1980, the average has declined to just fifty-eight such work stoppages per year.

The term "strike" has additional applications. Hunger strikes and student strikes have been undertaken to oppose political undertakings such as the **Vietnam War** or investment in South Africa under Apartheid, as well as socio-economic conditions such as the plight of the **inner cities**.

Further reading

Zieger, R. (1994) *American Workers, American Unions*, Baltimore: Johns Hopkins University.

MARC BALCER

Student Non-violent Coordinating Committee (SNCC)

Civil-rights organization formed in 1960, following the success of the **sit-ins**. Ella Baker, executive director of **SCLC**, convened a group of student activists at Shaw University in Raleigh, NC. Encouraging them to maintain their independence of SCLC, Baker helped establish one of the most radical organizations created by the **Civil Rights movement**. At first including **white** and black members, the organization remained largely committed to the **King** vision of non-violence, supporting the **freedom rides** and carrying out registration drives. With the election of Stokely **Carmichael** as chairperson to replace John L. Lewis, the organization became increasingly radical. Carmichael adopted **Black Power** as his slogan, leading many white members to leave the organization. Following the election of H. Rap **Brown**, SNCC was renamed the Student National Coordinating Committee, shedding its last connections with the civil-rights movement. Under Brown's leadership the organization became virtually defunct.

ROBERT GREGG

Students for a Democratic Society (SDS)

In 1962, forty American college students gathered in Michigan to discuss some of the gravest problems facing the nation, and in this meeting Students for a Democratic Society was born. SDS confronted the nation's presence abroad, especially in Vietnam, challenged racial discrimination at home and asked serious questions about the nation's commitment to participatory democracy. Among its most significant contributions was leading the free-speech movement. Significantly, members of SDS and the "New **Left**" were raised in an era of relative affluence; having experienced neither depression nor war, they were in many ways liberated to focus on issues both on **college** campuses and in the larger society.

SUSAN SCHULTEN

suburbs and edge cities

Neither urban nor rural, yet idealized as the prototypical habitat of the American **middle class**, suburbs stand betwixt and between in both a spatial and social sense. In the course of the twentieth century, technological and socio-economic developments have transformed the function and meaning of **cities** and suburbs, as well as their relations. As the twentieth century closed, suburban areas were home to more than one-half of all Americans and much of the nation's commerce and industry – what was once peripheral was now central. The "edge cities" that cluster around the juncture of interstate **highways** and orbital beltways are the new multi-functional cores of the sprawling, poly-nucleated metropolitan regions that dominate American society.

Beginning in the 1830s, transportation innovations facilitated the development of residential enclaves for urban elites on the rural fringes of **Boston**, **New York**, **Philadelphia, PA**, **Chicago, IL** and other American cities. Steam ferries, horse cars and railroads allowed the wealthy to live in carefully landscaped, quasi-pastoral settings and to commute to work in congested urban centers. Between 1890 and 1929, electric streetcars and the

automobile accentuated residential deconcentration and put suburban homes within the reach of an emergent middle class. Cities frequently responded to the growth of their unincorporated suburban frontiers by annexing them.

During the roaring 1920s, US suburbs grew at a faster rate than the cities they surrounded and, for the first time, proved successful in resisting annexation. Unlike the dense, vertical industrial metropoles of the nineteenth century, cities that experienced their initial significant growth in the 1920s, such as Los Angeles and Atlanta, were characterized by a low-rise, low-density landscape more suburban than urban. Although the Great Depression and the Second World War ended this suburban boom, decentralizing tendencies would return strongly after 1945.

The postwar period marked a quantitative and qualitative shift in the scale, intensity and meaning of suburbanization. Twenty years of Depression and war created a tremendous unmet demand for new housing, the vast majority of which was built on undeveloped land outside city boundaries. The direction of growth was not merely the case of the private sector responding to consumer preferences, but was shaped and partially subsidized by public policy. Government agencies, such as the Federal Housing Authority (FHA) and the **Veterans** Administration (VA), subsidized mortgages for the construction of new homes in suburban areas, while denying funds for repair or new construction in many other urban **neighborhoods**. In subsidizing the risk borne by lenders, the FHA and the VA allowed for long-term, low-cost mortgages that made home-ownership cheaper than renting for families of even relatively modest means.

Fueled by abundant capital, home builders operating on vast economies of scale used assembly-line techniques to mass produce millions of standardized, low-cost homes in hitherto rural areas adjacent to major cities. One of the earliest and best known of these developers was the Levitt Brothers of New York, whose trio of "**Levittowns**" in Long Island, Pennsylvania, and New Jersey became a synonym for suburbia during the 1950s and early 1960s. The Levitts' approach to home building was echoed by developers in virtually every metropolitan region in the country. American urbanism was completely transformed:

between 1950 and 1980, three-quarters of the nation's largest cities experienced a net loss of inhabitants, while suburban areas more than doubled. By the early 1970s, more Americans lived in the suburbs than in either cities or rural areas.

The pale of suburban settlement

While popular with the American home-buying public, from the 1950s onwards, suburbia often proved an object of criticism and scorn in scholarly texts, popular fiction and Hollywood film (*Mr Blanding Builds his Dream House*, 1948). Although subsequent social-science research (e.g. Gans 1976) revealed a multiplicity of suburban forms, many suburbs imposed an authoritarian conformity of belief, behavior and identity on their residents. Although most new communities lacked the **restrictive covenants** of earlier suburbs that banned the sale of homes to members of particular ethnic and racial groups, discrimination against persons of color was widely practiced in the suburban real-estate industry. During the 1950s and 1960s, suburbs (and their representations in film and television) were overwhelmingly **white** domains. The idealized racial character of the suburban realm was reinforced in the 1960s as school desegregation, riots and fear of crime prompted working-class and middle-class white ethnics to flee to the suburbs in record numbers. Thanks to **white flight** and **blockbusting**, by the 1970s, most large American cities had majority minority populations, and the term "urban" acquired a distinctly racial connotation, more often referring to someone or something that was not white.

Federal support for suburbanization was not limited to mortgages. As early as 1916, the US Government provided financial support for the improvement of major roads linking the country's major cities. However, local and state governments paid most of the cost. In 1956 the Interstate Highway Act committed the federal government to paying 90 percent of the cost for more than 40,000 miles of multi-laned, high-speed expressways over the following three decades. This system and related roads not only linked major American cities and their existing suburbs, but also opened up rural land, dozens of miles from city centers, for speculative development.

As the suburbs grew, downtown **department stores** and other urban retail establishments followed their customers and, in the process, helped create the built environments and social institutions of a new "**drive-in** culture" (Jackson 1985). One of the earliest of the new institutional environments was the shopping strip, a corridor of disparate retail establishments that opportunistically developed along the main roads outside the older business districts of suburban communities. A second environment was the shopping **mall**, which debuted in the late 1950s. The shopping strip and shopping mall devastated the business districts of large city and small town alike, creating a new geography of retailing dominated by large national chains.

Industrial production also suburbanized during the postwar period. Suburban governments lured inner-city factories to new industrial parks with generous packages of financial incentives, while fleets of cargo **trucks** freed many industries from locational dependence on the nation's railroads. Frequently, industrial relocation assumed an inter-regional as well as an urban-to-suburban character. During the Second World War, new defense plants tended to be located in suburban areas of the industrial Northeast and Midwest, as well as the hitherto non-industrialized South and West. This pattern continued after 1945 as the **Cold War** fueled the expansion of aerospace and electronics industries in what was soon to be referred to as the **Sunbelt**. By the 1970s, suburban locales throughout the country had become significant employment centers in their own right, in many cases more significant than the cities they surrounded, and had ceased to be mere bedroom communities.

Office space was the last traditional urban function to migrate to the suburbs, which offered lower costs, easier commutes and more bucolic settings compared with the expensive and congested central business districts of most American cities. The first suburban corporate campus was built outside New York City in 1954, but the move to the office park by the highway did not begin in earnest until the early 1970s. During the 1970s and 1980s, more office space was built in suburban locales than existed in central cities; **Silicon Valley** embodied a new suburban economic center. By 1990 many central business districts across the nation had experienced significant disinvestment and struggled to reinvent a new role for themselves in the metropolitan economy. The new economic geography of the American metropolis was evident in the change in commuter patterns. In the early 1990s, more than twice as many Americans commuted from suburb to suburb than from suburb to city.

The migration of people, jobs and capital to the metropolitan peripheries has produced a new, unprecedented human settlement, variously called the non-place urban realm, the galactic metropolis and the horizontal, new, or post-urban city. Such sprawl celebrates the very scale of American land. The new centers of this post-urban world include the clusters of office parks, shopping **malls**, **hotels** and residential developments called "edge cities" (Garreau 1991). Most major metropolitan areas have several of these multi-functional cores, clustered around the intersections of major highways with the perimeter or orbital beltways that encircle the center city. Originally envisioned as bypasses for through traffic, perimeter beltways have instead become the "**Main Street**" of the new American metropolis. With more jobs than bedrooms, edge cities have also spawned their own residential suburbs, sometimes referred to as the exurbs. Yet, while edge cities possess many of the economic functions of earlier urban centers, they lack many of the city's social, cultural and political characteristics. Edge cities do not constitute legal-administrative units, nor do they possess central public spaces or distinctive identities. With their replacement of locality by the homogenizing forms of a globalizing market culture, edge cities seem a-geographic (Sorkin 1992), literally both Anyplace and No place, USA. Still, the social realities of contemporary suburbia are much more diverse than its increasingly generic built environments. By the late 1970s, the so-called new **African American** middle class had begun their own suburban exodus, as had middle-class **Hispanics**, **Asian Americans** and other formerly characteristically urban minorities. Ethno-racial diversity, however, has not necessarily translated into integration. Three decades of federal civil-rights legislation has done little to lessen discrimination in mortgage-lending practices and ameliorate residential **segregation** in most US metropolitan areas. While some integration has occurred in housing, contemporary American suburbia reiterates an earlier urban ecology of territorial separation by **race** and **class**.

Just as suburbs are no longer prototypically white, nor are they middle class. Poverty is no longer the monopoly of central cities, it, too, has suburbanized. The suburbanization of poverty has been particularly acute in those older suburbs whose employment centers have deteriorated and/or where the original inhabitants have migrated to the exurbs. Older suburbs (e.g. Newark, New Jersey) have also attracted the new wave of Latin American, Asian, African and European immigrants and refugees that have entered the US since 1965. In Sunbelt metropolitan areas, new immigrants grab the apartment complexes and strip shopping centers of the suburban fringe. Meanwhile, the wealthy have responded to the perceived threats of the other by literally walling off their enclaves behind a perimeter of security devices in **gated communities**.

In the twentieth century the excesses of suburban sprawl began to generate critical responses. Architects and planners of the Congress of **New Urbanism** have advanced the notion of building communities that are both more socially integrated and ecologically sustainable. Environmental legislation will necessitate either cleaner burning fuels or transportation alternatives to the automobile. The latter may well encourage higher density patterns of residence and work. A number of metropolitan regions, such as **Portland**, **Minneapolis** and **Denver** have also embarked on efforts to coordinate regional planning and limit sprawl through the use of growth boundaries. On a national level, however, the political influence of major developers combined with popular opposition to increased government regulation raises serious questions as to whether efforts to plan and coordinate sustainable metropolitan growth will ever be implemented.

Further reading

Gans, H.J. (1967) *The Levittowners*, New York: Pantheon Books.

Garreau, J. (1991) *Edge Cities*, New York: Doubleday (assesses later changes).

Jackson, K.T. (1985) *Crabgrass Frontier*, New York: Oxford University (a classic assessment of the history and meaning of suburbia).

Sorkin, M. (1992) *Variations on a Theme Park*, New York: Hill and Wang (provides architectural and social criticism of new urban and suburban forms).

CHARLES RUTHEISER

suicide

The ninth leading cause of **death** for all Americans, and the second leading cause of death for **teenagers** (ages fifteen to nineteen). Clues as to reasons for taking one's life may be written in notes for those left behind to decipher. Causes range from revenge against parents to acute **depression**, to drug and **alcohol** abuse and at times – as mass suicides of cult followers have shown – the belief in a better afterworld. Romantic notions coexist with socio-psychological interpretations, and the Centers for Disease Control have declared suicide a "serious public health problem." Copycat behavior of teens following rockstar suicides, the Supreme Court's intervention in doctor-assisted suicides and the condemnation of the Catholic Church make suicide an act of contested and uncomfortable signification in cultural consciousness.

MARIAELENA BARTESAGHI

Sunbelt/Rustbelt

Since the 1970s, the Sunbelt has agglomerated – and represented – disparate centers of population and economic growth, generally in the Southern tiers of the US from **Florida** to **California**. Some of these areas were underdeveloped before the Second World War; hence the term also refers to a major shift in communities and power in the US. In contrast, older, declining industrial centers have been labeled the "Rustbelt." Although cities like **Los Angeles, CA** and **Miami, FL** long have been models of recreation, leisure and dreams, the

Sunbelt as a new boom region has encompassed both cities and suburbs, including new financial and government nodes – **Atlanta, GA**, Charlotte (North Carolina) and **Houston, TX**. **Retirement** and **tourism** centers also have blossomed, including **Phoenix, AZ** and Orlando/**Disneyworld** (Florida), whose population grew by 50 percent between 1980 and 1990. By analogy, some stretch "Sunbelt" to include other areas of new growth since the 1970s, including **Denver, CO** and **Hawai'i**. Rustbelt is used less as a term, since it does little for boosterism or growth, but taints cities such as **Buffalo, NY**, **Cleveland, OH** and **Philadelphia, PA**.

The Sunbelt nonetheless encompasses uneven growth patterns as well as changes over time. Southern California and South Florida, its early centers, already have faced problems of sprawl and racial and ethnic divisions exacerbated during recessions. Smaller cities like **Santa Fe, NM** and **Nashville, TN** have challenged other Sunbelt metropoles with their more relaxed lifestyles, while all areas face increasing growth and the insistent franchising of both **malls** and downtowns. Throughout the Sunbelt, meanwhile, long-settled populations have complained about intruders. Some – **African Americans** in the **South** and **Latinos** and Native Americans in the **Southwest** and **West** – have fought their exclusion from new growth. New immigrants from outside the US have also created new diversity, exemplified by Asian strip malls forming part of suburban highway sprawl from Atlanta to Los Angeles.

After decades of growth, Sunbelt states have gained a large voice in politics (especially among **Republicans**), manifest in the mass presidential primaries of "Super Tuesday" (the first Tuesday in March), when eight Southern states vote together. They are centers for industry, **services** (including **tourism**) and, increasingly, for culture, whether in research centers, new arts and **museum** complexes, or sports. The Sunbelt also sets national styles, exemplified in fads for Southwest designs. Yet it faces competition from other regions that tempt mobile Americans with economic opportunity and an enhanced "quality of life," whether the "Ecotopia" of the **Pacific Northwest**, revivals of **New England** towns or the diversity of older industrial cities. At the same time, the explosion of Sunbelt urban and rural areas also has created gaps in **education**, **healthcare** and social services, while new and old citizens search for civic identities that will build bridges from bucolic pasts into rapidly changing futures.

Further reading

Miller, R. and Pozzetta, G. (eds) (1988) *Shades of the Sunbelt: Urbanization and Ethnicity in the Modern South*, Westport: Greenwood.

Rutheiser, C. (1996) *Imagineering Atlanta*, London: Verso.

GARY McDONOGH

Sunday School

Sunday School, also known as Christian Education, Church School or Sabbath School, provides religious education, primarily for **children** and young people. Sunday Schools have been important in North America, primarily in Protestant churches, to provide religious instruction because the historic separation of church and state prohibits religious education in **public schools**. Lay volunteers teach most Sunday School classes, receiving varying degrees of training, and following denominational Christian education policy, curriculum and social and theological emphases.

Further reading

Coalter, J.M., Mulder, J.M. and Weeks, L. (1996) *Vital Signs. The Promise of Mainstream Protestantism*, Grand Rapids: William Eerdman.

National Council of the Churches of Christ in the USA (1998) *Handbook of American and Canadian Churches, 1998*, 66th edn, E.W. Lindner (ed.), Nashville: Abingdon Press.

GAIL HENSON

Superbowl (Sunday)

Created in 1967 following the merger between the National and fledgling American Football Leagues, in which the champions of the leagues would play each other. The NFL commissioner, Pete Rozelle, attached Roman numerals to the games to further associate the game with a gladiatorial contest. The first contests were easy victories for the NFL team and not great spectacles (as few Superbowls end up being), but the 1969 game in which Joe Namath's AFL New York Jets defeated the favored Baltimore Colts stimulated the public's interest in this event.

Condensing a season into a single contest has made this game more significant than **baseball**'s World Series and the NBA's Championship Series, which are spread over a week or more's play. The fact that more than 50 percent of American people watch the game, meeting for parties and **gambling** furiously (adding to the statistical rise in domestic **violence** on this Sunday), has meant that broadcasters and advertisers have had a bonanza. The NFL charges the **networks** more than $20 million for the game and this money is recouped by charging upwards of $1.2 million for each 30-second commercial.

ROBERT GREGG

Superfund

Superfund is the name commonly used for the federal program to clean up hazardous waste sites, which is administered by the **Environmental Protection Agency** (EPA). The program was created by the Comprehensive Environmental Response, Compensation and Liability Act of 1980 (CERCLA), which has been copied by many states, which have their own "Superfund" programs. The program is called "Superfund" because CERCLA created a special government fund to help pay for the clean-up of abandoned hazardous waste sites.

The passage of the Superfund law reflected growing public concern with hazardous waste sites, an issue that had been largely overlooked in the burst of environmental legislation that Congress had passed in the early 1970s. Public interest in the issue was brought to a head by the case of **Love Canal**, a **neighborhood** in Niagara Falls, New York, from which the state had evacuated 237 families in 1978. The neighborhood had been built alongside a former industrial waste site, which began leaching the chemicals that had been dumped into it for decades, damaging the health of the residents who had never been informed of the hazard.

Under the Superfund law, the EPA determines whether a hazardous waste site qualifies for the clean-up program by assessing the threat the site poses to human health and the environment. Every state has had at least one site on the Superfund list, with New Jersey having the largest number of sites. Once a site is listed, EPA (or other federal agencies, if the site is owned by the government) develops a plan to clean up the site.

The Superfund law has been pathbreaking in a number of respects. First, it holds companies (and municipalities) financially responsible for cleaning up hazardous waste sites even if dumping the wastes was legal at the time they were brought to the site. The Superfund law imposes "strict liability," meaning that if you had disposed of any wastes at a hazardous site, you are considered liable, even if you did nothing considered legally negligent. And liability is "retroactive," applying to wastes that were dumped before the law was passed.

The second unusual feature of the law concerns the Superfund itself, which is based on the principle of "polluter pays." The fund was established to pay for a site clean-up if the waste had been dumped by a company that no longer existed, or if it was impossible to determine who was responsible. The Superfund was financed by new **taxes** on the chemical and petroleum industries and other industries most likely to have dumped hazardous wastes. In 1995, the year the taxing authority under the law expired, the Superfund taxes brought in about $1.5 billion. **Congress** has generally appropriated about $250 million a year out of general tax revenues to cover some of the program's administrative costs.

The Superfund program has succeeded at cleaning up sites, but at a slower rate than originally expected. As of September 1998, EPA had listed 1,370 sites, but clean-up was complete at only 176 of them.

The Superfund program has become increasingly controversial as debates have developed over how to make the program more efficient and less costly. Industry has sought to change the liability scheme in the law, which has produced an enormous amount of litigation as each entity that dumped wastes at a site tries to limit its own liability. Industry and some municipalities have also sought to change the standard for cleaning up a site so that more wastes can be contained – preventing them from leaching into drinking water, for example – rather than being removed or treated.

Further reading

Brown, M. (1980) *Laying Waste*, New York: Pantheon.
Harr, J. (1996) *A Civil Action*, New York: Vintage.

DAVID GOLDSTON

superheroes

Television in the 1950s gave us the image of a muscle-bound superman standing in front of the American flag, committed to "truth, justice and the American way." In the late Depression, these comic-book superheroes reinvented and replaced strong men of earlier American **folklore**. Superman, Batman and Wonderwoman shared not only extraordinary strengths and talents but also compelling traits like mysterious origins and disrupted families, a secret identity concealed by an ordinary position within a complex city (usually resembling **New York City, NY**), a patriotic devotion to country and justice that overrode the "letter of the law," and powerful demonic antagonists who mingled science and magic in bizarre plots. After going to war, these superheroes spread into television and cinema; after the mid-1950s, surviving early figures were joined by ever-wider legions who slowly incorporated more minorities and real-life social problems – drugs, racism, sexuality – into this mythic world. While television's *Batman* became camp in the 1970s, elaborate **Hollywood** productions of *Superman* and *Batman* in the 1980s and 1990s, which also grapple with the heroes' humanity, have adapted these figures to changing social mores. The success of 2000's *X-Men* shows that superheroes still have American – and global – appeal.

Further reading

Reynolds, R. (1992) *Super Heroes: A Modern Mythology*, Jackson: University of Mississippi.

GARY McDONOGH

Supreme Court

The paramount court in the federal **judiciary** and the final arbiter of constitutional matters emanating from the parallel systems of **state** courts. Soon after its inception in 1789, under the leadership of Chief Justice John Marshall, the Court legitimized its own constitutional authority through a series of decisions which still constitute the foundation of its power. In *Marbuty* v. *Madison* (1803) the Court enunciated and justified its power of judicial review and held a congressional statute unconstitutional. *Fletcher* v. *Peck* (1810) concluded that the federal courts could test the constitutionality of state laws. *Martin* v. *Hunter's Lessee* (1816) recognized the Court's power to review the constitutionality of decisions made by state courts and the supremacy of such Supreme-Court decisions. Finally, in *McCuiloch* v. *Maryland* (1819), the Court validated **Congress**' use of enumerated and implied legislative powers and the supremacy of the exercise of such national authority over conflicting state actions. As a result of these decisions the Court established its role as the constitutional monitor of actions by other branches of the national government and the delineator of federalism, determining the balance and interrelationship between national power and that of state governments.

Using the mechanism of deciding specific cases, the Supreme Court interprets the Constitution and shapes public policy. Most of its decisions do not engage the general public. But it still reaches enough politically charged rulings with broad impact to result in an institution tinged with controversy. Recurring contentious themes have involved federalism, the limits of legislative economic and social regulation, construing **civil rights** and liberties, protecting the expression of unpopular political viewpoints and preserving the rights of racial and religious minorities and of criminal defendants.

The Court supported the institution of slavery in a decision that eroded public confidence in its judicial integrity. *Dred Scott* v. *Sandford* (1857) ruled that slave-owners' property rights enabled them to retain ownership of slaves taken into free states, upholding a Missouri law over Congress' attempt to prohibit the spread of slavery into territories.

After the beginning of the twentieth century, the Court, using constitutional theories stressing freedom to contract and narrow the scope of the federal power to regulate interstate commerce, curtailed economic and social legislation passed by Congress and the states to ameliorate child labor, harsh working conditions and **union** organizing. This approach generally prevailed into the Great Depression of the 1930s which Congress attempted to alleviate with emergency social and economic programs. In a dramatic shift, after President Franklin D. **Roosevelt**'s failed threat to "pack" the Court with sympathetic justices, the Court suddenly changed course and granted constitutional leeway to federal and state corrective New Deal programs.

The post-Second World War constitutional era is marked by continued latitude for legislative control of economic matters and a switch to a focus on questions of individual rights. Its rulings ushered in the **Civil Rights movement**. It struck down racially **restrictive covenants** in real property transactions, outlawed racially segregated **public schools** in *Brown* v. *Board of Education* (1954) and desegregated other public places. The **Warren Court**, attaining the high-water mark of progressive constitutional **judicial activism**, struggled with questions involving prayer in the public schools, taxpayer funding of religious schools, revolutionizing the rights of criminal defendants, gender discrimination, reapportionment, the death penalty and, in *Roe* v. *Wade* (1973), recognizing a privacy right for women to choose an **abortion**.

The Court has been able to maintain its credibility even though eventually it becomes immersed in all society's political and moral controversies. It is the most highly respected and trusted by the general public of all government bodies. It accomplishes this despite a limited power to enforce its judgments and the secretive nature of its internal functioning. Oral arguments, usually interrupted by piercing questions from the justices,

are open to the public, as is access to the records of cases and printed briefs – written arguments – but Court proceedings are never televised. The entire process of considering and selecting cases for full review, discussing and voting on cases after oral argument and circulating drafts of opinions takes place in a strictly closed environment. The Court lacks tools to carry out directly many of its most significant rulings, especially those with broad impact. It commands no **army** or **police** to force a resistant executive branch or state officials to implement its orders. It cannot levy taxes and appropriate money to fund change as legislatures can. It must rely on government officials to effectuate and assure compliance, prodded by the public, which acquiesces in the Court's rulings and respects the rule of law.

The Court also preserves its credibility by using self-protective devices to avoid extremely contentious cases. It has almost total discretion in choosing cases. For example, for years it refused to accept any case that directly questioned the constitutionality of the **Vietnam War**; yet it acted quickly to rule that the government could not restrain the press from publishing the **"Pentagon Papers"**, which were critical of the war. Despite about 7,500 requests for review each term, the Court accepts about 90 for argument.

Many constitutional terms, such as "due process" and "speech," are couched in vague, value-laden language. This provides justices with flexibility to reinterpret subjective constitutional language and enables successor Courts to overrule prior decisions and adjust constitutional doctrine to meet current social and economic needs. The practice of writing detailed, dissenting opinions allows justices to voice opposition to the majority, spurs legal debate and encourages optimism in discontented groups that, as society's views or the composition of the Court changes, minority positions will prevail. The Court's direction remains constantly intertwined in the current of history, but at times, courageously, it moves to the forefront and shapes history.

Further reading

Schwartz, B. (1993) *A History of the Supreme Court*, New York: Oxford University Press.

Shnayerson, R. (1986) *The Supreme Court of the United States*, New York: Harry N. Abrams, Inc.

Woodward, B. and Arnstrong, S. (1979) *The Brethren, Inside the Supreme Court*, New York: Simon & Schuster.

JAMES KRAUS

Supremes, the

Undisputed queens of the girl-group scene and one of Motown's leading acts, with their sweet harmonies, choreographed dances and chic visual styles. Originally formed as the Primettes in Detroit in 1959, they signed to Motown in 1960 with original members Diana Ross, Mary Wilson, Florence Ballard (replaced by Cindy Birdsong in 1967) and Barbara Martin (who left in 1961). Beginning with "Where Did Our Love Go" and ending with "Someday We'll Be Together," the Supremes launched twelve number-one singles between 1964 and 1969. After their split-up, Diana Ross went on to fame as a solo artist and film actor. A purported reunion with Ross and substitutes failed to attract audiences in 2000.

EDWARD MILLER

surfing

The "hot dog" style of surfing based on a traditional Hawai'ian practice began on the west coast of the United States in the mid-1950s, made possible by the development of new boards manufactured from light synthetic materials. Surfing quickly became a cult, popularized by the teen movie, like the series and later television sitcom, *Gidget* (1959), the Frankie Avalon and Annette Funicello movies *Beach Party* (1963), *Bikini Beach* (1964) and *Beach Blanket Bingo* (1965), the documentary *The Endless Summer* (1966), as well as the music of the **Beach Boys**.

Californians introduced their Malibu boards to Australia and a few years later, in 1962, an Australian won the first unofficial world championship. This began a long rivalry between Australia, **California** and **Hawai'i** for dominance in surfing.

In conjunction with this emerging rivalry, surfing became a big business. Gerry Lopez, a leading surfer in his own right, began to sell boards through a shop outlet in Honolulu. Then he established the Bolt Corporation with partners in California, and set up a franchise arrangement that gave manufacturing rights to companies in all the major surfing countries. In conjunction with business growth came technological developments, such as the introduction of V-bottoms on boards, which improved the surfer's ability to surf waves for longer.

The possibility that surfing will become an **Olympic** sport in the future has increased with the opening of indoor surfing pools in **Japan** and Arizona.

ROBERT GREGG

Surgeon General

Chief of the Public Health Service of the US (under the Department of Health and Human Services). Statements on **tobacco** (now printed as a warning on all cigarette boxes), **physical fitness**, **diet**, **AIDS** and other issues have made this a moral and political position, turning Surgeon Generals like C. Everett Koop into public figures. The consequences of politicization were also apparent in the forced resignation of **Clinton** appointee Jocelyn Elders (1933–), the first woman and **African American** to hold the post. Her views on **guns**, legalizing drugs, sexuality and sex education proved too controversial for the staid vision of a healthy America.

GARY McDONOGH

survivalists

American apocalyptics who express their rejection of issues or changes by choosing to withdraw from American society and await its destruction, armed with tools of both living and conquest. While such groups were exacerbated by Y2K anxieties, their choice of life in a wilderness, individual values over collectivity and a highly personal (small collective) vision of the American dream has clear antecedents in both Utopian and reformist groups. The dilemma in the late twentieth century, in fact, was where one went and what one did to survive.

GARY McDONOGH

Susann, Jacqueline

b. 1918; d. 1974

Potboiler author of scandalous novels set in the entertainment industry. *Valley of the Dolls* shocked the 1960s with descriptions of sex and loose lifestyles, while the film version of the novel (1967) became a camp classic. Ms Susann also wrote *Every Night, Josephine, The Love Machine* (another roman à clef set in network **television**), *Once Is Not Enough, Delores* (a thinly veiled portrait of "the other Jackie") and *Yargo* (an attempt at science fiction). A biography by Barbara Seaman shows that her own life was replete with bisexuality and pills. In 2000 Bette Midler depicted Ms Susann in *Isn't She Great.*

EDWARD MILLER

sweatshops

The 1995 bust of an El Monte, **California** factory where seventy-five Thai immigrants worked 18-hour days behind barbed wire producing designer clothes for $1.60 per hour underscored the dark side of American **fashion** and **consumerism**. While this case led to new California laws banning such labor conditions and practices, and compensations ranging from $10,000 to $80,000 for the workers, demands for 8 billion items of clothes per year in America have fostered sweatshop conditions in the US and abroad. In the US, they are especially associated with **ethnic enclaves** or manufacturers in the US–Mexico **borderlands**. More corporations have been accused of underpaid and dangerous labor conditions overseas – in the US-controlled territory of **Saipan** (hence, "Made in America") or Vietnam, Indonesia, **China**, **Latin America** and **Africa**. Major

designers and distributors like Nike, DKNY, Guess and others have been implicated; **celebrity** television host Kathie Lee Gifford broke down in tears on air after accusations that her clothing line was produced by child labor. **College** students and labor activists in the 1990s increasingly organized boycotts of these products and lobbied institutions, government and manufacturers for changes – although ethics, here, must struggle against constant demand.

GARY McDONOGH

swimming

The most popular recreation for Americans. Upper middle-class Americans build pools in their yards or belong to expensive country clubs; **middle-class** Americans will belong to **YMCA**s or other health clubs and/or go to public community pools that are also frequented, especially in the cities, by members of the lower classes. Swimming is also an important aspect of vacationing at lakes and ponds, as well as at the shore.

Competitive swimming was popular in nineteenth-century Britain, mainly involving a gentlemanly breaststroke. In 1844, two American Indians demonstrated a stroke akin to what would become crawl at a London pool, but observers considered it "un-European." The stroke was then introduced to **California** by an Australian who had learned the stroke in the South Sea Islands, and it quickly became established as the major Olympic speed race. The sport's growing popularity was very much connected with the career of Johnny Weissmuller, who won eight gold medals at the 1924 and 1928 Olympic Games before going on to star in eighteen **Hollywood** movies as Tarzan.

More recently, several Americans have dominated the sport: Donna deVarona, the "Queen of Swimming" in the early 1960s; Mark Spitz, winner of seven gold medals, and Shirley Babashoff, winner of eight medals altogether at the 1972 Olympics; Tracy Caulkins, generally considered one of the greatest all-round swimmers of all time and awarded the title "Swimmer of the Decade" by *USA Today* in 1990; Matt Biondi, winner of gold medals at three Olympiads (1984–92); and Greg

Louganis, acknowledged as the greatest diver of all time.

Recently, news reports have suggested that boys have been giving up the sport in large numbers as they reach puberty, partly because they find the newer streamlined swimming trunks too revealing. With so many sports options available at school and home, young boys are selecting those that they think will project the best image. As a result, swim teams have become increasingly populated by girl athletes, some programs becoming 70 percent female. The likelihood of any more Spitzs or Louganis emerging in the United States is slim, but the chances that an American woman may produce similar feats may be increasing with the growing numbers of athletic scholarships at colleges going to women (following **Title IX**), and in the aftermath of the collapse of support for the military-style training programs of the former Soviet Union and East Germany.

Synchronized swimming, largely associated with women athletes, has experienced tremendous growth in the 1980s and 1990s. Its origins in the 1933 **World's Fair** of **Chicago, IL**, synchronized swimming was popularized during the 1940s in Hollywood's "water ballets" or "aqua musicals," identified with "America's mermaid," Esther Williams (e.g. *Bathing Beauty*, 1944; *Million Dollar Mermaid*, 1952). It continued to develop in the Midwestern collegiate programs as an alternative to speed swimming, though with the appeal of its stunts and physically demanding routines it was not exclusively associated with women.

First adopted as a non-medal sport at the 1952 Helsinki Olympics, synchronized swimming was finally introduced as a medal sport at the 1996 **Atlanta** games (though some medal events have been dropped since), as Americans wanted to showcase American talent and to meet the demand for more women participants in the Olympics.

Since pools were already in place for the other swimming events, synchronized swimming was considered a low-cost, high-entertainment addition to the program.

In the process, synchronized swimming has disrupted gender associations in sports, in ways similar to figure skating. While the sport plays on notions of femininity, witnessed also in the feminizing of cheerleading, it also demands great athleticism, and so is further breaking down the gendered linkages of male with "athletic" and female with "grace"

See also: sports and gender

ROBERT GREGG

syndication

Syndication refers to the non-network distribution of shows. There are two main ways to license programs to individual outlets. The first way is with programs that are new and created especially for syndication, such as *The Oprah Winfrey Show*, *Wheel of Fortune* and *Xena: Warrior Princess*; games and talk shows are popular products. In off-network syndication, the distributor takes a program that has already been shown (for at least three seasons) and rents episodes to local stations or to cable **networks**. *Nick at Nite*, for example, has used this form – reruns of baby boomer **sitcoms** – to gain an adult audience. Syndication also has impact on international markets and the exporting of American products – during the 1990s when American television was dominated by sitcoms that did not sell well abroad, syndicated shows such as *Baywatch* found bidders overseas.

EDWARD MILLER

T

tabloids

"Tabloids" generally refers to any paper produced in the tabloid format, that is, relatively smaller than conventional "broadsheets" and without physically separate sections. For urban commuters, these features make the "tab" easier to read than the broadsheet. So too do a number of other characteristics associated with most – not all – North American tabloids: short news items, large print and a simplified writing style. Tabloids' colorful headlines often feature puns, slang, or hyperbole, for example, describing a murder in a **New York** strip club as "Headless Body Found in Topless Bar." A tendency to cultivate a broad audience often results in sensationalist or salacious stories. Tabs generally eschew abstract discussions of state policy or political analysis, favoring instead news about **crime**, **celebrity**, sports, or the bizarre. The most notorious tabloids, weekly national "supermarket tabloids," invariably trumpet tales of celebrity romance, dubious "scientific" breakthroughs, or alien abductions in their pages. Not surprisingly, these journals often face charges of illegitimate news gathering or even outright fabrication.

In the 1980s and 1990s, worried media critics charged that the success of tabloids had begun to infect the culture, leading to growing "tabloidization" within journalism and a gradual erosion of news ethics. This was precipitating, or at least evidence of, a decline in the nation's public culture more generally. Similar debates have taken place in the past – with the advent of both the penny press and the yellow press – as established news organs find their niches threatened by more popular, more explicitly commercial sources.

Further reading

Fox, W.J. (1997) *Junk news*, Cambridge, MA: Joan Shorenstein Center, JFK School of Government.
Schudson, M. (1978) *Discovering the News*, New York: Basic Books.

MARK BREWIN

Taft-Hartley Act *see* unions

Talking Heads *see* Byrne, David

talk radio

Talk **radio** is a programming format that encompasses a wide range of topics, such as health, finance, religion, politics, community issues and sports. Listener call-in and interview shows enjoy considerable popularity. The personality of the host is the key ingredient to talk radio's popularity.

There has been an explosion in talk radio since the 1980s due to the need by AM radio for programming and technological advances made possible by satellite transmission, drastically reducing costs of traditional telephone lines. Early talk radio was primarily overnight programming, such as with *Larry King Live* and *Talk Net* in the 1980s. Later successes include Howard Stern, conservative anti-gay activist, the controversial conservative Rush Limbaugh, psychologist Dr Laura Schlesinger and former Watergate conspirator G. Gordon Liddy. In 1997, 588 radio stations reported a talk format and 1,008 reported a news/talk format.

Further reading

(1997) *Broadcasting & Cable Yearbook*, vol. 1, New Providence: R. R. Bowker.

GAIL HENSON

talk shows, television

The talk show as a broad generic category is one of the oldest and more durable electronic media forms, with roots dating back to the early days of radio in the US. Quite simply, talk shows are performative conversations featuring a host and some combination of experts, **celebrities** and/or "average citizens." They cover a wide array of subjects including news, politics, current events, sports, **religion**, hobbies, the arts, gossip, tips for home-makers, **self-help** therapy, as well as advice. As Rose (1985) notes, although it appears to be the loosest and most casual of genres, the talk show is carefully and purposefully crafted, based on the concept of "controlled spontaneity" and adhering to a predictable progression of situations and segments.

According to Wayne Munson (1993), talk shows of various sorts constituted between 15 and 25 percent of the total schedule during radio's golden age, and their popularity has increased steadily over time. While the earliest programs consisted mainly of monologues by hosts and experts or celebrity guests, radio quickly embraced the concept of audience participation and by the early 1960s call-in "talk radio" had gained a permanent foothold in the schedule. Initially focused on current affairs and targeting an older male audience, in the 1970s talk radio fragmented to include several discrete subgenres that attracted women and younger listeners: talk/service and psychological advice; sports talk; the news/talk "gripe" show (sometimes known as "hot talk," exemplified first by *The Joe Pyne Show* and then later by *Rush Limbaugh*); and "non-controversial" talk such as

The Larry King Show, which combines issue and celebrity interviews with call-ins.

On television, the talk show was traditionally devoted to either light entertainment, with comedy, skits, music and celebrity guests, or to more serious discussion of news and public affairs among experts. In the early 1950s, the National Broadcasting Corporation (NBC) developed the long-running **late-night** celebrity talk/variety *Tonight Show*, the news/talk *Today Show* and an afternoon program geared towards home-makers called *The Home Show*. More serious interview programs like *Mike Wallace Interviews* and Edward R. **Murrow**'s *Person to Person* also appeared on network **prime time** during the 1950s, early forerunners of a long line of male-oriented political talk shows such as *Face the Nation*, *Firing Line* and *Crossfire*.

The late 1960s and early 1970s saw the emergence of daytime (and early evening) variety chat shows, often known by the name of their host, including Mike Douglas, Merv Griffin, Dinah Shore, and girl talk, popular among **middle-class** female audiences. This remains a volatile field for stars in the 1990s where failures (Whoopi **Goldberg**, Chevy Chase) are constantly replaced by new hosts and packages like Rosie O'Donnell or Roseanne.

The late 1960s also witnessed the debut of *The Phil Donahue Show*, the first of what would become a popular daytime format featuring a participatory studio audience and "ordinary people" as panelists (along with experts and the occasional celebrity). For almost two decades, *Donahue* was the only nationally syndicated program of its kind on the air. Eventually, however, concommitant with the rise of "reality-based" programming more generally, Donahue was joined by Sally Jessy Raphael, Oprah **Winfrey**, Geraldo Rivera and Montel Williams. By the mid-1990s there were more than a dozen different daytime talk shows available in syndication from which local broadcasters might choose.

Most talk shows highlight "ordinary people" talking about their personal experiences. Some shows are more serious and restrained, focusing on issues with a social or policy dimension such as sexual harassment, teen pregnancy, or gang violence; others are more sensational or **tabloid**, centered on interpersonal conflict and confrontation (love triangles, cheating spouses, or **family** feuds). Among the most controversial tabloid talk shows are those of Jerry Springer, whose guests and audience members routinely argue, shout and even come to physical blows, and Jenny Jones, whose on-stage confrontations have had serious real-life consequences, including murder.

See also: talk radio; late-night television

Further reading

Munson, W. (1993) *All Talk*, Philadelphia: Temple University.

Rose, B. (1985) "The Talk Show," in Brian Rose (ed.), *TV Genres*, Westport: Greenwood.

Shattuc, J. (1997) *The Talking Cure*, New York: Routledge.

LAURA GRINDSTAFF

Tan, Amy

b. 1924

Chinese American novelist and child of immigrants, whose stories are interwoven into her fiction. Tan has focused on relations of new and old mediated through complex and painful relations of mother and daughter. Her first novel, *The Joy Luck Club* (1989), won the National Book Award and became a breakthrough movie depiction of **Asian American** women beyond **Hollywood** stereotypes (1994). Later works include *The Kitchen God's Wife* (1991) and *The Hundred Secret Senses* (1996); she has also produced children's books and become involved in a literary band.

CINDY WONG

Tarantino, Quentin

b. 1963

Charismatic and creative independent **director/** actor/**screenwriter/producer** whose films show wide knowledge of popular genres and global cinema even as he has transformed them. Emerging from his experience as a video clerk alternating with acting, Tarantino's eclectic sensibilities

became apparent in *Reservoir Dogs* (1992), before gaining global accolades with *Pulp Fiction* (1993). He continues to be both the creator and subject of **mass media** attention; meanwhile, his *Jackie Brown* (1997) revitalized **blaxploitation** films across racial lines.

See also: independent films/video

CINDY WONG

tattoos *see* body piercing and tattoos

taxes

"In this world, nothing can be said to be certain, except death and taxes." So wrote Benjamin Franklin, American statesman, in 1789. To this day, the rhetoric regarding taxes often overshadows the reality of an immensely complex system of federal, state and local taxation. Taxes, the nearly inevitable result of civilized society, support numerous purposes. They raise revenue for government expenditures, redistribute wealth, and provide economic stability. Taxes play a predominant role in American political dialogue through their creation, implementation and impact. Strong disagreement exists over the role that taxes, and the governments that levy them, should play in the US.

As a percentage of national income, personal income taxes are 12.3 percent. The percentages for social insurance taxes, sales/excise taxes, corporate taxes and property taxes, are 10.4 percent, 4.9 percent, 3.6 percent and 3.3 percent respectively. At the federal level 67.4 percent of taxes are collected, with the remainder going to state and local authorities. Social-insurance taxes finance **retirement** and health benefits. Benefits are distributed in proportion to the taxes paid during one's working years. Financial difficulties confronting the system aside, it is essentially a forced savings plan. Sales and property taxes are collected at the **state** (or local) level as an alternative to income taxes. In 1994 such taxes accounted for over half of state and local revenues. Delaware, the "Home of Tax-Free Shopping," is one of five states without a sales tax. These states compensate with higher income taxes, use taxes or reduced services. Just 9 percent of US businesses are subject to corporate income tax, normally at a rate of 35 percent. The effective rate is significantly lower due to numerous credits, deductions and depreciation allowances.

When Americans speak of taxes, however, they typically refer to personal income taxes. First imposed during the Civil War, income tax became permanent in 1913, after ratification of the 16th Amendment to the Constitution. Income tax was an appealing alternative to tariffs, excise taxes and property taxes that were regressive in nature. The first income tax was aimed at the very rich. Fewer than one percent of citizens filed returns. Personal income taxation played a small role until just before the Second World War, when exemptions were reduced and tax rates increased to finance wartime production. By this time, one-third of the population was responsible for some tax.

The progressive spirit of the tax code burdens the wealthy with additional responsibilities to pay for the services that contributed to their wealth. Marginal tax rates provided for low rates at low-income levels. As income increases, tax rates increase as well, with each additional dollar of income taxed at one's highest rate. The post-Second World War period saw the top marginal rate slide from a growth-impeding 94 percent in 1944–5 to 70 percent through the 1970s. Tax reform focusing on the Laffer Curve and supply-side economics, which argued that low tax rates increase tax revenues by increasing total economic output, led to a top rate of 28 percent by 1988.

While progressive in spirit, loopholes have developed over the life of the tax code to the point that wealthy families deduct significant portions of income. Charitable exclusions, exclusions for government-bond interest and generation-skipping trusts are common tax-avoidance techniques. Middle-class taxpayers, often the most vocal tax-reform advocates, benefit from the largest deduction of all – the ability to exclude mortgage interest paid from taxes.

Income taxes are collected by the Internal Revenue Service (IRS). Tax returns are filed annually but paid primarily from paycheck withholding. As the deadline, April 15 approaches, media depictions of Americans rushing to complete complicated paperwork and figure out how to afford the bill grow abundant. The IRS uses the fear of audits (fewer than 2 percent of returns are audited), information reporting from employers and tax withholding to enforce tax laws. Even so, $150 billion in revenue is lost to non-compliance. The IRS has developed a reputation for poor service and predatory collection practices, which it addressed in the 1990s with customer-service initiatives.

Americans tend to share a general antipathy for taxes. There are two primary explanations for anti-tax sentiment. The attitude of "everybody wants everything and nobody wants to pay for it" provides an explanation for tax hatred without theoretical basis. On the other hand, general opposition to the size, motivation and goals of government provide a strong base of support for tax reform.

There are numerous advocacy groups that support tax cuts and reforms. The Tax Foundation annually calculates a "Tax Freedom Day." In 1998, "Tax Freedom Day" was May 10, meaning that Americans spent 35.4 percent of the year earning money to pay various taxes. In general, taxes have risen with "Tax Freedom Day" occurring on February 12 (1930), April 15 (1960) and May 1 (1990). Tax is also a strong feature of Republican political rhetoric.

The implication from the above is that Americans pay too much in taxes. In fact, the US has lower taxes than the majority of economically developed countries. A 1993 study indicates that US taxes are equal to 29.7 percent of GDP. Only Japan had a lower rate, with the United Kingdom (33.6), Germany (39.0) and Sweden (49.9) shouldering significantly higher burdens (Slemrod and Bakija 1996: 20). While personal and corporate income taxes are similar across countries, the US has far lower sales and value-added taxes than other nations.

Further reading

Graetz, M. (1997) *The Decline (and Fall?) of the Income Tax*, New York: W.W. Norton.

Slemrod, J. and Bakija, J. (1996) *Taxing Ourselves: A*

Citizen's Guide to the Great Debate Over Tax Reform, Cambridge, MA: MIT Press.

MARC BALCER

Taylor, Elizabeth

b. 1932

Academy Award-winning film actor. Although British-born, Taylor at the peak of her celebrated career was the definitive American movie goddess. Her lavish lifestyle and her unabashed appetite for romance fed the dreams of stargazers and sustained the gossip pages in the 1950s and 1960s. Taylor's numerous, high-profile **marriages** – three to actor Richard Burton – were both a reinforcement and a rebellion against women's dependence on men. After her acting career waned, Taylor became a tireless campaigner in the fight against **AIDS**. Her association with the cause was crucial to raising public awareness about the deadly epidemic.

See also: Academy Awards; actors

SARAH SMITH

Teamsters Union

The most notorious **union** in the United States, the Teamsters have been at the center of controversies regarding the power of organized labor. In the years after the Second World War, the Teamsters became the nation's largest labor organization. At the same time, the union's leaders attracted attention because of their associations with organized crime. This notoriety helped justify new efforts to halt union-organizing campaigns.

Founded in 1899 as a national union for men working on horse-drawn wagons, the organization began to evolve dramatically in the 1930s. Ambitious new leaders, such as Dave Beck and Jimmy **Hoffa**, pioneered new organizing techniques that harnessed the strategic power of the interstate truckers. Eager for new members these leaders ignored traditional craft and jurisdictional distinctions to organize a wide range of workers. The union grew to be the nation's largest and its

membership became increasingly diverse. Actively organizing among the unskilled workforce of the country, especially in the **South**, the Teamsters became an interracial organization. By the early 1960s, it included some 200,000 **African American** members, about 20 percent of all the blacks belonging to organized labor. Women workers joined in large numbers as well, especially as the union began aggressively to organize warehouse and cannery operations. Seeking to attract and hold such members, the Teamsters' leadership promised them equal wages and fair treatment. At the local level, however, where white male members adhered to the dominant prejudices of the day, discrimination frequently occurred.

Known for its aggressive and ambitious organizing, the union also became famous for its alleged links with **organized crime**. Hoffa, president of the Teamsters from 1957 to 1971, openly proclaimed his friendship with a number of well-known gangsters, although he insisted that those associations did not influence his leadership. Most people assumed that Hoffa's disappearance in 1975 followed a dispute with the Mafia that led to his abduction and murder. In Hoffa's wake, the next four successors to the union's presidency all reputedly had connections with organized crime. In one case, Jackie Presser (president 1983–8) served as an undercover **FBI** informant, while at the same time campaigning to gain the assistance of the Mafia in achieving the union's presidency.

Beginning in the 1950s, critics of organized labor focused attention on the Teamsters in order to raise questions about the power of organized labor. The combination of the union's aggressive organizing activities and the allegations of organized-crime influence made it an inviting target. A sensational investigation conducted by the Senate's McClellan Committee (1957–9) linked together the power of the Teamsters, the misconduct of some of its officers and the dangers of organized crime to justify new legal restrictions on all union activity. The resulting legislation, the Landrum-Griffin Act (1959), was known as the "law to get Jimmy Hoffa." In fact, Hoffa's notoriety offered organized labor's opponents the chance to create a law that further hampered union organizing efforts across the board.

Further reading

James, R.C. and James, E.D. (1965) *Hoffa and the Teamsters*, Princeton: D. Van Nostrand.

Leiter, R.D. (1957) *The Teamsters Union*, New York: Bookman Associates.

DAVID WITWER

teenagers

Those between thirteen and twenty-something represent both the "downfall" of American society and serve as its trend-setters and hopes. Teens have also become icons of modernity and symbols in a culture deeply oriented towards youth in the postwar era. Nonetheless, social dependency on the ability of teenagers to replicate the social roles of adults produces a type of anxiety that consistently revolves around the activities of youth (Cohen, 1972).

The teenage years are viewed as the definitive time of identity formation. This becomes the focus of school and extra-curricular activities like sports, as well as **family** anxiety. While religious rites, social celebrations (coming out, **commencement**) and civic landmarks – especially acquisition of a driver's license at sixteen – mark increasing adulthood, it remains partial. Even as many teenagers work in addition to school and family obligations, they are often treated as potential victims. Hence, laws censor adult information and shield them from vice (**alcohol** and **tobacco** sales are legally discouraged). Teens are also viewed as vulnerable to problematic peer relations – whether status groups or **gangs**. These prohibitions, in turn, become foci of rebellion.

Hence, the activities of American teenagers have become the focus of countless social-science studies that tend to focus largely on the notion of deviance. These studies were concentrated during the 1960s, which remains an iconic decade of teen rebellion, from Vietnam to **Woodstock**. Drug use, teenage **suicide** and sex remain consistent trends among analysts (Gaines 1990) and policy-makers. Moreover, both underscore the special stress on those who are marked as different in race, class, **gender** or ability from the larger society. Teenagers can be cruel, yet this is often only a refraction of cultural values and socio-economic opportunity. Hence, the socially constructed category of adolescence becomes a series of trials, tribulations and experimentation that one will survive, it is hoped, to become an adult.

Yet teenagers, individually and *en masse*, have also become important agents in their own right. Since the Second World War, teenagers have become a major consumer force with a large amount of disposable income. An entire cultural industry has been created in the United States to appeal to this age group in the form of clothing stores, music trends and entertainment, incorporating a rapid obsolescence despite the endurance of sex, jeans and rock 'n' roll as primary motifs. In the 1990s, the survival of many corporate entities depended on teenage consumer power.

While often viewed as frivolous, teenagers have also been at the center of important social changes in society. Teenagers have been involved in landmark political events and moments of social upheaval, including social demonstrations in the 1960s, especially the antiwar and civil-rights movement. With the draft beginning at eighteen, and the voting age being lowered to eighteen nationwide in the 1970s, this has made them real as well as potential actors in major issues, even if politicians speak of them still in terms of tutelage (on issues such as abortion).

Representations of teenagers in popular culture often reflect their position as consumers in **fashion**, music and **mass media**. Again, this historically focused on the notion of deviance and rebellion, with some interesting changes. Films such as *Blackboard Jungle* (1955), *Rebel Without a Cause* (1955) and *West Side Story* (1961) portrayed rebellious teenagers of the 1950s, coupled with subtexts of **class**, **race** and social hierarchies. The tension between teens on the beach or at the **drive-in** and those in the gang or the "hood" continues to shape teen flicks. Teenage anxiety permeated films such as *The Breakfast Club* and *Sixteen Candles* in the 1980s, while also reflecting on dysfunctional families. In the 1990s, the sobering *Kids* (1995) and *Basketball Diaries* (1995) have treated drug use and sex, while being criticized as causes, rather than effects of youth violence. Representations of teenagers in television have generally dealt with less political teenage dilemmas or have focused on family interrelations in shows such as *Happy Days* (1974–84) or *Beverly Hills 90210* (1990–9), although news media often play up stories of gangs and victimization.

Further reading

Cohen, S. (1972) *Folk Devils and Moral Panics*, Oxford: Basil Blackwell.

Gaines, D. (1990) *Teenage Wasteland: Suburbia's Dead End Kids*, New York: Pantheon.

MATTHEW DURINGTON

teen fiction

While American youths spend more time watching television than they spend in school, adolescents do read. Adolescents like to read what everyone else is reading and they like good-looking book covers and prefer paperbacks to hardbacks. The genres of adolescent fiction are as varied as are those of children's and adult literature, including historical fiction and adventure tales, **coming-of-age** stories, contemporary horror tales and social-issue stories that treat such topics as **AIDS**, **divorce**, disability and **immigration**. Some books are clearly tailored to an adolescent market, especially for younger readers, while others are introduced through education and peer groups in high school and college, by which time they will generally be reading "adult" books.

Adolescent fiction also addresses struggles adolescents face, such as coming of age, **religion**, **divorce** (Voight, *A Solitary Blue*), **suicide** (McRae, *Going to the Dogs*), loneliness (Bethancourt, *The Me Inside of Me*), eating disorders (Levenkron, *The Best Little Girl in the World*), **death** (Paulson, *Hatchet*), disease and disabilities (Mahy, *Memory*; Adler, *Eddie's Blue-Winged Dragon*), emotional problems (Riley, *Crazy Quilt*), abuse (Barbara Kingsolver, *The Bean Trees*), alcoholism (Paulson, *The Crossing*) and sexuality (Dizeno, *Why Me? The Story of Jenny*). Discussions and concerns with racism and ethnicity often lead adolescents to classics such as Ralph **Ellison**'s *Invisible Man*, Toni **Morrison**'s *The Bluest Eye*, Alice **Walker**'s *Color Purple*, Maxine Hong **Kingston**'s *Woman Warrior*, or Sandra **Cisneros**' *The House on Mango Street*.

Historical fiction includes popular prehistory series such as Jean Auel's *The Clan of the Cave Bear*, which captivates readers with adventure, survival and discovery themes. Katherine Paterson has contributed other significant titles to adolescent historical fiction, including *The Sign of the Chrysanthemum*, set in twelfth-century Japan. Adolescents also enjoy **westerns**, including the series by Louis L'Amour and Janet Dailey's *Calder* series, and read fiction set in the Second World War, Vietnam and the civil-rights eras. Paterson and Walter Dan Myers are familiar names to adolescent readers; Second World War themes are found in Paterson's *Jacob Have I Loved*. Sook Nyul Choi's *Year of Impossible Goodbyes* treats a North Korean family fleeing the communists, while *Echoes of the White Giraffe* follows this family's life in a **refugee** camp. Myers' *Fallen Angels*, Marsha Qualey's *Come in from the Cold* and Bobbi Ann **Mason**'s *In Country* all deal with Vietnam.

Adolescents are drawn to **romances**, from the Christian historical romances of Bacher (Heartland Heritage series) and Thoene (Shilo Legacy Series) to more traditional female-oriented novels. Meanwhile, science fiction and fantasy permit adolescent readers to explore new and old worlds in creative, divergent ways, whether through adventures with dragons or travels in space with aliens. Alternative worlds such as those found in Madeline L'Engle's *A Wrinkle in Time* series and Roger Zelazny's *A Dark Traveling* pique adolescent imagination. So does humorous science fiction by Gilden and Adams, while Michael Crichton's *Jurassic Park* attracts older adolescents as well as adults. Other popular fantasy genres of later adolescent reading include cyberpunk, aliens, utopias and dystopias. Graphic novels (Speigelman's *Maus*, *Maus II*) and **comics** are also widespread, especially among males.

As comics may suggest, teens also have a great capacity for horror, mystery and **crime fiction** – and for following similar series of **horror films**. Popular crime and mystery writers include Stephen **King**, Mary Higgins Clark and Sue Grafton, who all have strong adult markets. Christian mystery writing for adolescents includes the *Jennie McCrady Mysteries*. The cinematic ties and high adventure novels of Tom Clancy and Robin Cook's thrillers are also compelling, while teen novels of adventure and survival include works by Jean George and Gary Paulsen.

Further reading

American Library Association "Outstanding Books for the College Bound: Fiction": http://www.a-la.org/yalsa/booklists/obcb/fiction.html

Gillespie, J. (ed.) (1991) *Best Books for Junior High Readers, 12–15*, New Providence: R.R. Bowker.

Herald, D. (1997) *Teen Genreflecting*, Englewood: Libraries Unlimited.

GAIL HENSON

telecommunications

Telecommunications refers to communication that involves and surmounts distance. In addition to telephony, the term includes electronic communication via media such as **radio**, telegraph, **television**, **computer** (coupled with a modem connecting it to the **Internet**), facsimile machines and newer forms of telephony such as cellular or digital telephones.

Information that is telecommunicated can be cast out in the form of voice, symbols, pictures, digital data, or some combination of these. A telecommunications system includes a transmitter, a receiver and a channel of communication – air, water, cable, satellite, telephone wire, broadband technologies. As the economy becomes increasingly post-industrial, in the so-called information economy, the speed and efficiency of transfer of messages becomes a crucial objective in the running of institutions and the profitability of electronic exchange. Telecommunications is thus a huge business nationally and globally, with geopolitical ramifications.

Although the telephone is not the sole instrument for telecommunications, it has become the predominant form. It is the cornerstone of modern two-way communication. The telephone is accessorized by the answering machine or voice-mail systems so that increasingly it is more difficult to speak with another live person on the phone, while at the same time it is rare to get a busy signal or unanswered phone. Alternate forms of message exchange, such as electronic mail or e-mail, that use telephone lines but send written text from a computer have become increasingly popular for both business and non-business purposes.

With the dawn of new technologies, the familiar telephone is undergoing a monumental transformation, in which it is becoming an intelligent, multimedia center. As newer forms of telecommuting emerge, the phone becomes a companion: the modem is a medium between computers and telephone lines transforming digital data into analog information; video conferencing too requires the use of the telephone. No doubt, in its new, advanced form, the telephone will facilitate interactions between and among people, machines, content, financial transactions, shopping, entertainment and games. Thus, it is essential that the telephone and other networked terminals like the fax machine, cellular phone, and personal and business computers are easy for the user and profitable for manufacturer, wholesaler and retailer. With the advance of computer technology, increasingly, people's activities on the computer and telephone can be traced, raising concerns on issues of **privacy** and big-brother surveillance.

With the Communications Act of 1934 and the legislation that set up the **FCC**, telecommunications was established as a regulated and official industry, although the telephone and the telegraph had long been part of the American technological landscape. One objective of this Act was to create an affordable, universal telephone service for the American people. As a result, **AT&T** was chosen to monopolize the industry (RCA/NBS continued its dominance of radio). Under the protection of the federal government, it became the dominant telephone company ("Ma Bell") and still exerts a tremendous influence even after the government broke up the monopoly in 1984 (creating "Baby Bells"). The trend was reversed in the 1990s, when AT&T bought big cable operators, like Media One, and multi-national mergers of telecommunication firms were common. Investors in the twenty-first century bet that telecommunications will assert its role in the exchange of information and commerce.

Further reading

Crowley, D. and Heyer, P. (eds) (1999) *Communication in History*, New York: Longman.

Fischer, C. (1992) *America Calling*, Berkeley: University of California.

Marvin, C. (1988) *When Old Technologies Were New*, New York: Oxford.

EDWARD MILLER

telephones *see* telecommunications

televangelism *see* Christian media

television

The technology for television was developed in the 1920s. Nonetheless, it was not until after the Second World War that television became popular in America. Since then, television has been attacked as a detriment to its watchers' lives and hailed as an educational tool that opens up people to the world beyond their everyday experiences. Both charges are true.

Despite differences in the media, American television was modeled after its counterpart in radio. It took on a similar industrial set-up – around a few major **networks** and local franchises – and early programming relied on staples like **soap operas** and **talk shows**. Similar governmental regulations – under the jurisdiction of the **FCC** – were also adopted. That means that, like most **mass media** in America, commercial television dominates, with public broadcasting playing a minor role.

Television's expansion came at a time when Americans were emerging as a superpower. With the soldiers coming home, the rise of **suburbia** and the new abundance of material goods, TV became a new symbol for American wealth. The number of television receivers rose from 10 million in 1951 to 50 million in 1959. Local stations became points of metropolitan identity (while **radio** could be very localized, entire states like New Jersey could be left without a commercial station).

Television was initially viewed by Hollywood as serious competition; cinema attendance fell in the 1950s. Yet, the two media differ in their relationships with space and audiences. The box in the house keeps its audience in, while the screen in the movie theater takes people out of their homes. The success of TV in the 1950s was partly embodied by the strong nuclear **family** suburban living arrangement. However, over decades, closer relationships grew between television and film industries; they benefit from each other by sharing their resources from production to distribution. The arrival of color TV in the 1960s underscored this symbiosis. American TV is also global – syndicated shows are sold worldwide, creating a dominance not unlike Hollywood's.

American television relies on **advertising** revenue even as it presents itself as providing services to the public (publicly funded television, **PBS**, was a late innovation in the 1960s, targeting high culture and underserved populations). Commercial television must sell its programs to the audience, then sell its audience to the advertisers. Hence, broadcasters developed the **Nielsen rating** system to measure viewership at home. Though inaccurate, these ratings can determine the life and death of TV programs. These ratings have also promoted a culture where the group who has the highest spending power becomes the group that TV pleases. Broadcasters can also claim that they are making shows that the public demands, while avoiding those with small audiences.

American television is about show business and **news**. Following closely the successes of radio, major TV genres include **game shows**, talk shows, **sitcoms**, various dramas, soap operas, **variety shows** and sports events. News can exemplify how this evolved over time. Television news not only provides information, local and national, but also sells a prestige product. Television changed the delivery of news. As in radio, it is instantaneous, but it is also visual. Edward R. **Murrow** became the father and hero of broadcast journalism, with his famous 1954 exposé of Senator Joseph McCarthy on *See It Now*. While people debate television's role in the explosive events of the 1960s, from the civil-rights movement to the Vietnam War, TV news was well respected for its independence and authority. However, the **television news** department, like other TV production departments, also relies on audience ratings. In the 1990s, with TV stations increasingly owned by even larger media conglomerates, TV news needed to be more sensational. It is generally believed that this new news is exploitative, spending hours on crime, celebrities' deaths and fluff features, rather than any investigative journalism.

Political and critical debates about TV arise because it is seen to be a great force of socialization. Television enters people's **bedrooms**, and it connects people from children to old age to worlds beyond their immediate environment. Despite its independence from government control, TV content, because it needs to appeal to the widest possible audience, tends to be middle-of-the-road American fare, whether in dramas or in news. Radicals point out a lack of diversity, while the ultra-conservatives find TV to have a liberal bias with its slight engagement with issues of homosexuality or its attacks on isolated corporate misdeeds. Yet television, especially with **cable** diversification, is about audiences rather than ideas or even difference.

In the 1980s, the introduction of cable TV challenged the dominance of the three national networks. New broadcast networks – FOX, Warner Brothers, UPN and Pax – added further competition to the traditional three. Increasingly, the mass audience became more of a targeted, niche audience where the industry seeks the most disposable income. CBS' *Murder She Wrote* (CBS, 1984–97) for example, had impressive ratings, but since its demographics were mainly older, the show was cancelled. In the 1990s, shows geared towards a young audience dominated. At the same time, one of the top shows, *Seinfeld*, never attracted a minority audience. Both **NAACP** and La Raza have challenged major networks to include minority characters in their sitcom line-ups at the end of the century, while worrying that other networks have become new ghettos.

Television has also been agglomerated into ever larger corporations. Of the three surviving early networks, NBC is owned by GE, CBS by Viacom and ABC by Disney.

New technological developments like Web/interactive TV and HDTV will probably not so much change television as offer more sophisticated delivery systems. Television will still be contained in the home. The multiple-TV home, **VCRs** and the ability for the new technologies to allow more self-selection may encourage more individualized

home entertainment. Yet, the development of HDTV would not only mean sharper pictures for the consumers, it would also effectively eliminate the development of small networks because of the prohibitive investment involved.

Further reading

Bianculli, D. (1996) *Dictionary of Teleliteracy*, New York: Continuum.

Stark, S. (1997) *Glued to the Set*, New York: The Free Press.

CINDY WONG

television and minorities

Protests by **NAACP**, La Raza and other activists in 1999 highlighted the absence of minority characters on new **network** shows, leading NBC, ABC, FOX and CBS to scramble to retrofit, offering and forcing them into negotiations about ethnicity and casting as well as longer-term commitments to employment behind the camera. At the same time, other networks like UPN were accused of pandering to young **African American** demographics with irresponsible **teen** shows. The dearth of **Asian Americans** on any network beyond roles as newscasters or passing characters was hardly discussed. Meanwhile, **cable** opportunities like **BET** and the growth and changes of Spanish-language stations like Telemundo and Univision complicate any simple conclusions about race and television even before one considers the limited minority presence in the upper echelons of the broadcast industries as **producers**, **directors** and writers. If television both reflects and shapes America, it is important to understand how it has dealt with – and continues to deal with – critical divides like race and ethnicity.

In the golden age of television and its aftermath, "whiteness" functioned as a norm against which some black racial stereotypes emerged in crossover shows from radio like the popular albeit racist *Amos 'n Andy* or the roles given black women as maternal servants in shows like *Beulah*. The *Nat King Cole Show* (1957) was the first African American show on prime-time network TV, but disappeared after one season. Asians took on such safe domestic roles in generations of cooks on *Bonanza, Bachelor Father* and *Dynasty*, while **Hispanics** added local color to **westerns**. There was hardly any presence of Native Americans outside westerns, or people of **Arab** and **South Asian** origin.

Julia (1968–71), which cast Diahann Caroll as an attractive, educated black professional single mother, seemed to be a breakthrough in fighting stereotypes, although some critics argued that the character and plots were so anodyne as to make race irrelevant. The lack of black men was also problematic, although the spy series *I Spy* (NBC, 1965–8) had brought Bill **Cosby** as Alexander Scott onto screen as a Rhode's scholar and arch commentator on companion Kelly Robinson (Robert Culp).

In fact, the presence of African American stars seemed to grow thereafter. *The Jeffersons* (1975–85), whose upwardly mobile title characters spun off from Norman **Lear**'s *All in the Family*, provided comic yet edgy commentary on problems like intermarriage, class and exclusion in American society, played out by African American characters with evident flaws. *Good Times*, a spin-off of another Lear series, played out even grittier issues in a working-class family in public housing. Capping off this golden age of minority television, in a sense, were such **miniseries** as *Roots* (1977, 1979). In 1982 Cosby began his decades of involvement with the *Cosby Show* and other productions, while *Miami Vice* (1984–9) confused categories of ethnicity and virtue.

At the same time, African Americans and others began to be integrated into the faces of television, including news, sports coverage and ensemble television – long-running hospital, crime and sci-fi dramas (***Star Trek*** and its heirs) invariably had at least one African American star amid other minor minority characters. Critics have argued that the additions of minority characters only serve as tokens of diversity, although at times of national convulsion like the Los Angeles riots, these became pivotal perspective characters.

Yet, if urban television implied local color, it was also clear that other shows had lengthy careers in segregated worlds – whether the sometimes leftist humor of *Murphy Brown* or the sophisticated urbanity of *Frazier*, where the whole cast is white. These were balanced by (almost) all-black shows

that soon found a special home on UPN. The division, however, was one of audience as well as plot, as black and white viewers consistently chose different shows as their favorites – ***Seinfeld***, for example, did not appeal to black audiences. When *City of Angels* brought the predominantly black inner-city medical drama to prime-time network in 2000 it thus challenged not only network history, but consumption of media within a segregated society. Moreover, it asked whether the integrated model of dramas and soaps or the separate but equal presentations of UPN and the networks more accurately reflected the state and desires of race and ethnic relations in America at the end of the century.

GARY McDONOGH
CINDY WONG

Tennessee Valley Authority (TVA)

Federal development project in the Upper **South**. Constructing sixteen dams between 1933 and 1945, the Tennessee Valley Authority brought jobs and training, flood control and electricity to marginal rural areas in seven states. By the postwar period, TVA converted the extensive valley into a balanced industrial, military and agricultural core for the future **Sunbelt**. Since the 1960s, the agency has been criticized for its environmental record, including pollution and reliance on strip-mined coal, and its disastrous interests in nuclear power in the 1970s and 1980s. These are signs, perhaps, that the region has outgrown its engine of change.

GARY McDONOGH

tennis

Once largely the preserve of **white** upper-class men and women, tennis has become popularized in the years following the Second World War, influenced by patterns of suburbanization, **immigration** and technological change.

At the beginning of the 1940s, tennis was still dominated by its country club and amateur image.

Leading players like "Big" Bill Tilden, from an elite **Philadelphia, PA** family, Donald Budge, Jack Kramer and Helen Wills Moody epitomized the "old-stock" immigrant backgrounds of most players. By the early 1950s, many players were being drawn into the professional tournaments dominated by Kramer and Pancho Gonzalez, leaving the Grand Slam tournaments like Wimbledon and Forest Hills dominated by Australian amateurs.

The film *Pat and Mike* (1952) highlighted some of the changes occurring in American society that would influence the development of tennis. Pat, a women's college physical-education teacher, played by Katharine Hepburn, is snatched up by a sports promoter, Mike (Spencer Tracy), who turns her into a professional sportsperson. The film evokes the transformation occurring from amateurism to commercialism, the increasing marketability of women athletes and the increasing access to tennis available for many Americans at this time that would dramatically increase the popularity of the sport.

Suburbanization accounted for much of this transformation. The **migration** out of the **cities** following the world war brought middle-class Americans into close proximity with tennis facilities, which were incorporated into the planning of many of the suburban developments and **public school** building projects. Elite lawn tennis clubs remained, but their influence declined as more communities played on hard court surfaces.

From the 1960s onwards, therefore, shifts in tennis demography began to occur. More tennis players began to emerge from "ethnic" groups, such as Jimmy Connors and John McEnroe (Irish), Vitas Gerulaitus (Greek) – Stan Smith being the obvious exception to this rule. They no longer graduated only from elite **Ivy League** universities, but instead were gaining their college playing experience from the large land-grant **state universities**. They were not merely growing up in **Northeastern** elite urban communities, but were instead coming from the new **Sunbelt** states, particularly **Florida**, where the climate allowed for more professional tennis tournaments and intensive camps, like that of Nick Bollitieri which produced such leading players as Andre Agassi and Aaron Krickstein.

Tennis was slow to have a significant impact on African Americans. Excluded from the United States Lawn Tennis Association, **African Americans** created their own American Tennis Association. Two products of this development were Althea Gibson, the first African American to compete and win at Wimbledon in 1957, and Arthur **Ashe**. But the exclusion of African Americans from much of the process of suburbanization occurring at this time meant that these two players were not followed by others until changing demographic patterns (and Ashe's efforts to bring tennis to **inner-city** communities) began to alter these things. In recent years the success of the Williams sisters, Venus and Serena, has increased the visibility of the game among African Americans, including their triumphs at the 1999 US Open and 2000 Wimbledon.

The game has made a lasting impression on gender relations. The leading American women's player of the early 1970s, Billy Jean **King**, helped transform the game both through her court performances and her campaigns off the court for reform away from the amateur elitism of the game and for greater gender equity. King was instrumental in bringing World Team Tennis to fruition, encouraging promoters and sponsors, like Texan Lamar Hunt, to pump money into the game, and in challenging the stereotypes regarding women. She also defeated Bobby Riggs in the "Battle of the Sexes" in 1973 at the **Houston** Astrodome before a worldwide television audience of nearly 50 million and the largest audience ever for a tennis match. King's straight-sets victory silenced Riggs' claims of sexual superiority and brought further attention to the women's game (which now draws more fans than, but still not equal prize-money to, the men's game).

The late 1970s was notable mostly for the emergence of the naturalized American Martina Navratilova. Czech-born Navratilova developed a game more akin to the men (serve and volley), forcing American baseline players like Chris Evert and Tracey Austin either to improve the power and accuracy of their baseline shots or increase the range of their games. As a result the men's and women's games are now closer to each other in style and power than was the case prior to Navratilova's ascendancy.

The introduction of new rackets in the 1980s

and 1990s has radically altered both the women's and men's games. Gone are the old wooden rackets, which produced power in proportion to their weight. The new graphite composite rackets are light and powerful, and allow for much greater spin with a flick of the wrist. In part this accounts for the lessening appeal of the men's game (dominated by Pete Sampras' power game) as compared with the women's. The injection of power into the women's game has broadened its appeal; it is fast killing the men's as the importance of the serve has increased.

Further reading

Collins, B. (1997) *The Tennis Encyclopedia*, Detroit: Visible Ink Press.

ROBERT GREGG

Tet Offensive

In late 1967, General William Westmoreland, Commander of the American forces in Vietnam, claimed that the war effort was nearing its successful end. Yet, on January 30, 1968, the North Vietnamese unleashed a massive surprise assault on major urban centers in Southern Vietnam, while American military attention had been focused further north at Khe Sanh. Striking thirty-six of forty-four provincial capitals in South Vietnam, including the American embassy, the Tet Offensive was intended to create a general uprising across the south. Though the offensive failed, the effect on American morale was devastating. **Television** brought the chaos of the **war** into American **homes**, and the offensive galvanized national antiwar sentiment.

SUSAN SCHULTEN

Texas

Citizens of Texas often say Texas is not a state, but a state of mind. Perhaps no other state has been represented more in popular culture than Texas – yet stereotypes of the **oil** baron, **cowboy**, super-patriot and cheerleader distill (and conceal) com-plex, dynamic histories. As an economic power-house and the birthplace of two postwar presidents (**Eisenhower** and **Johnson**) and home of a third presidential family (**Bush**), the myths and changes of Texas influence all of America.

The 28th state in the Union and largest of the continental states, Texas was annexed on Decem-ber 29, 1845. Americans had settled there after 1821 in territory ruled by Mexico. Tensions between colonizers and the state eventually meant war, including the famous 1836 Battle of the Alamo (**San Antonio**), where **frontier** heroes Davy Crockett, Jim Bowie and William Travis died. Films and books have kept this memory alive, although, as Holly Brear suggests in *Inherit the Alamo* (1995), this shrine also divides Mexican American and Anglo-American consciousness. Prior to an-nexation, Texas was the only state in the union that had been an independent nation (1836–45).

The nickname "Lone Star State" also suggests a conception shared by Texas citizens and others in the United States and abroad. Texas, called the "Third Coast," is characterized by vast spaces, **freedom**, opportunity and more nationalistic sentiment than in the United States itself. This independent ethos is supported by history and through economic success and population growth that have made Texas the third-largest state in the country. Oil and gas lead the way in the twentieth century; the international success of the prime-time soap opera *Dallas* made Texas oil-millionaires global stereotypes. Metropoles like **Dallas** and **Houston**, and burgeoning San Antonio, El Paso and **Austin, TX** have incorporated more eco-nomic diversity, including agriculture and livestock, shipping, retail, military development, electronics, communications and **tourism**.

Growth complicates a potentially conflictive cultural landscape. While sharing a long border with Mexico, the large Mexican American popula-tion was repressed for generations. **African Americans** reflect the state's slave heritage as well as its attraction for blacks who sought opportunities as cowboys or oil workers. Both have gained more prominence since the civil-rights era, although many argue that they have been left out of postwar wealth and power. Other older immigrant groups include Germans and Czechs, while new immigration from Vietnam, **China** and

Latin America continues to change the state's **Sunbelt** agglomerations.

Many outside Texas would reduce its culture to mythic characters and spaces. Yet Texas also has a large and well-funded state university system, which has made cities like Austin cosmopolitan enclaves, in addition to elite private schools like Rice (Houston). Its wealthy cities and citizens have built museums and concert halls and contributed to modern architecture. Sports are also part of Texas culture: **football**'s Dallas Cowboys ("America's Team"), the basketball champion San Antonio Spurs and the Houston Astrodome represent this prominent role. Yet the small-town independence of Texas may be better captured in **college** and **high-school** football, chronicled in Bissinger's *Friday Night Lights* (1990).

Money, population and dynamism made Texas an electoral prize even before the Second World War, when the state was solidly Democrat. While Johnson kept it in Kennedy's camp, Texas has subsequently become a powerhouse of conservative Republicans in Congress as well as the middle-of-the road Bush family. Governor George Bush, Jr.'s ability to raise $36 million in the first quarter of his campaign shows both local power and national attention that make Texas a major region and actor in the American future.

The University of Texas Press produces excellent works on state history and culture.

Further reading

Bissinger, B. (1990) *Friday Night Lights*, Reading: Addison-Wesley.

Brear, H. (1995) *Inherit the Alamo*, Austin: University of Texas.

Ivins, M. (1991) *Molly Ivins Can't Say That, Can She?*, New York: Random House (gives a sardonic political and cultural commentaries).

Limon, J. (1994) *Dancing with the Devil*, Madison: University of Wisconsin.

MATTHEW DURINGTON

thalidomide

A drug responsible for devastating birth defects in the early 1960s may make a comeback almost forty years later to help treat leprosy and **AIDS**. Thalidomide, manufactured by Chemie Grüenthal, was sold from 1958–62 in approximately forty-six countries as a sedative or anti-nausea drug for pregnant women. Thalidomide severely deformed thousands of babies whose mothers took it in their first trimester of pregnancy. Never sold in the US because Federal Drug Administration (FDA) scientist Frances Kelsey single-handedly blocked its approval, it was internationally banned by 1962. The tragedy led to laws requiring rigorous testing procedures for American pharmaceutical products.

COURTNEY BENNETT

theater

During the latter half of the twentieth century, following the advent and rise of first film and then television, live theater in the United States scrambled to find a niche in American culture. Because producing live theater is extremely labor-intensive, mounting professional productions necessitates selling tickets at a prohibitive price for many Americans. Despite vigorous efforts on the part of many producing organizations to diversify their audiences, theater audiences remain largely white and affluent.

Contemporary American theater falls into several categories. It varies according to location, size, the physical configuration of the performance space and the financial structure of the producing organization, among others. All of these factors must be taken into account when theaters decide what kinds of plays to produce. While theater struggles to maintain its role in American culture, an audience member can still view some type of live theater in virtually every community in the country. Performances occur in a variety of buildings and spaces, from converted warehouses to state-of-the-art **Broadway** houses. (Broadway refers to both the location of theater within a several-block radius of the intersection of Broadway and 42nd Street in midtown Manhattan, as well as to the financial structure of the producing organization.) An audience member can have an intimate performance experience in a ninety-nine seat black box theater, or be part of a thousand-plus throng at a Broadway **musical**.

Throughout the twentieth century, **New York** City has remained the center of live theater in the United States, boasting a full range of theater spaces and showcasing works from minimalist **performance art** to Broadway extravaganzas. Tourists from across the country and abroad flock to New York's Broadway musicals, but the more seasoned or adventurous theater-goer can find a wide range of performance styles in what are called the off-Broadway and off-off-Broadway theaters. In counterpoint to the highly commercial aspect of Broadway theater, New York's avant-garde venues boast some of the most innovative and experimental performances in the country, showcasing works from across the cultural spectrum, including the voices of **African American**, **Latino**, **Asian American** and gay and lesbian playwrights and performers.

In the early 1960s, led by such pioneers as Tyrone Guthrie, founder of the Guthrie Theater, in **Minneapolis**, the United States saw a renaissance of regional theaters. These medium- to large-sized theaters became established in communities with an affluent population large enough to fill the theater's seats, as well as a large enough "giving" community to subsidize productions with personal, corporate, foundation and public donations. Consequently, cities such as **Seattle**, **Chicago, IL** and Minneapolis/St. Paul have become dynamic theater centers in their own right. In the wake of the arrival of well-established regional theaters, a host of smaller theaters have sprung up offering an eclectic range of styles. For example, St. Paul is the home of Penumbra Theater. Founded in 1976, it is one of the country's oldest and most well-established theaters dedicated to presenting theater from an African American perspective.

While successful professional theaters have usually been established in large urban areas, some American Shakespeare Festivals are a noted exception. Ashland, a small town in central Oregon, hosts the Oregon Shakespeare Festival. With three separate stages, the festival is in operation from mid-February through October playing to a steady stream of tourists from across the country. The town has become primarily a support industry for the festival. In addition, professional dinner theaters and amateur community theaters, some old and well-established, others nearly as ephemeral as the 2 hours traffic on their stages, can be found throughout the country.

Live theater in the United States is financed under one of two systems, either for-profit or not-for-profit. Broadway productions are for-profit endeavors with investors. Their contracts with such labor unions as Actors Equity Association (AEA), representing actors, dancers and stage managers, and the International Association of Theatrical Stage Employees (IATSE), representing stage hands, requires that they pay union members top wages. To fill the large Broadway houses, producers also employ highly paid **star** performers for leading roles and spend lavishly on spectacular sets, lighting, costumes and special effects. The fact that Broadway productions are so costly to mount and also require a return of profit to the investors dictates the repertoire. Broadway relies on appealing to a broad-based, largely tourist audience to fill the seats and turn a profit for investors. Some off-Broadway theaters (defined by the smaller size of their houses and the nature of their labor contracts rather than by their specific location within New York City), dinner theaters (which exist across the nation and range in size from intimate dining rooms to multi-stage complexes serving up mostly musicals and romantic comedies, along with cuisine for the patrons) and a smattering of other theater companies are also for-profit. But the majority of producing organizations in the country are organized under the not-for-profit model.

Not-for-profit organizations generally rely on contributions to supplement revenue from ticket sales. Live theater in America has never enjoyed the kind of widespread governmental support found in many other nations. Indeed, even the pittance allocated to performing arts through the **National Endowment for the Arts (NEA)** and through various state or local government funding agencies has been, since the late 1980s, under continuous attack from political conservatives and the **Christian Right**. Already minimal public funding has actually declined. However, in the United States not-for-profit organizations may register under a provision of the tax code allowing them to solicit tax-deductible contributions from corporations and individuals. Contributors receive no return on their investments, but are able to deduct their contributions from their taxable profits or income. Many not-for-profits, such as **San Diego**'s Old Globe Theater and Chicago's Goodman Theater, are thus heavily endowed with donated funds. Others constantly struggle to keep their financial heads above water. But, even though pundits in every decade in the latter half of the twentieth century wrote the obituary of theater in America, a portion of the population continues to find the immediate and engaging experience of live performance irresistible.

PAMELA R. HENDRICK

theme parks

Sites of mass entertainment, incorporating rides (rollercoasters, carousels, etc.), games, shows, curiosities, animals and **junk food**, which became staples of American urban leisure in the late nineteenth century, exemplified by **New York City**, NY's Coney Island or trolley parks like **Philadelphia, PA**'s Willow Grove. Suburbanization and urban conflicts (including desegregation) pushed many of these local amusement parks into hard times as they were eclipsed by new regional/national destinations like **Disneyland**. The late twentieth century mega-park represents corporate investment in a multi-day family vacation destination whose tab may run to hundreds of dollars. Contemporary options include chains (Six Flags, King's Island), cross-corporate developments (Hershey Park, with links to **chocolate**, or the Busch Gardens chain linked to brewers) and media synergies like Disney, Universal Studios and Sesame Place. Their success has also changed entertainment development in **zoos** and aquaria, urban centers and **tourism** outside the US. "Theme parking" is also an accusation leveled against many recent urban development schemes as well as the creation of new private public spaces (such as **malls**).

Further reading

Sorkin, M. (ed.) (1992) *Variations on a Theme Park*, New York: Random House.

GARY McDONOGH
CINDY WONG

think tanks

Think tanks have grown in number and flourished as research and educational organizations as US society has become more complex. The educational components of the think tank address two main audiences: the general public and the public policy-making community, which includes federal government appointees and agencies, associations, **lobbyists** and **Congress**. The research looks at, among other areas, government regulation, **healthcare** and **welfare reform**, **education**, **taxes**, foreign policy, **mass media**, race and legal issues. Think tanks have weak to very strong political affiliations. One ideologically well-defined think tank is the Heritage Foundation, which assisted the **Reagan** administration in clearing people for political appointments. The primary think tank "products" are reports, books and magazines. Think tanks also hold conferences for public policy-makers and the press, often televised by the satellite **cable** company C-Span.

Think tanks may wish to limit their ideological affiliations to enhance the credibility of their research. Founded in 1916, the Brookings Institution maintains its political independence through its large endowment. Some think tanks' research agendas are more strongly tied to the ideological objectives of their donors, including the government, corporations and philanthropic foundations. In its descriptive materials the American Enterprise Institute defines its ideological position as one that will work to preserve and strengthen "the foundations of **freedom** – limited government, private enterprise, vital cultural and political institutions, and a strong foreign policy and national defense." One would not expect to find AEI research that contradicted this statement of purpose. Whereas AEI addresses many areas of public policy, the Carnegie Endowment for International Peace studies only foreign policy. The Center for Strategic and International Studies also focuses on international affairs. CSIS' research is nonpartisan, but the overall goal of the organization is to improve the strategic planning and implementation of business, media and government operations in the international arena.

Some think tanks, like the libertarian Cato Institute, focus their efforts on reaching the general public with their ideas so that a grassroots change in American polity will take place. Unlike most think tanks, the Cato Institute accepts no government funding. In the 1950s and 1960s, the federal government set up dummy think tanks and funded established think tanks to conduct covert operations. The Rand Corporation was pre-eminently a **Cold War** think tank dedicated to studying national security issues. Although it has since diversified, Rand still receives most of its funding from government contracts.

Think-tank scholars, most of whom hold advanced degrees, come from many professions but have all achieved recognition in their areas of expertise before being hired. Think tanks also hire scholars who will help entice donors to fund programs. During a Democratic presidential administration, more conservative scholars may find homes at Heritage, AEI or the Hoover Institution. When political fortunes change, these scholars frequently receive political appointments in the new administration. News organizations turn to think-tank scholars with established areas of expertise. When scholars appear repeatedly on news shows, they may be nicknamed "talking heads," but the media exposure can enhance scholars' standing in the policy community.

MELINDA SCHWENK

Thomas, Clarence

b. 1948

Conservative African American jurist. His 1991 nomination to the **Supreme Court** by President George Bush to replace liberal activist Thurgood **Marshall** provoked even more controversy when a former associate, law professor Anita Hill, accused him of sexual harassment. The ensuing televised hearings riveted and divided America around issues of race and gender – while Thomas' supporters evoked the specter of a "high-tech lynching," others were repelled not only by the charges but by the interrogations of a white, male Senate panel. Thomas was narrowly confirmed, and has taken a conservative albeit low-key stance in the Court. Issues and reflections surrounding

these hearings are reviewed in Toni **Morrison**'s *Race-ing Justice, En-Gendering Power* (1992).

GARY McDONOGH
CINDY WONG

Three Stooges

Slapstick team of vaudeville and movies (in the 1950s) popular among those amused by hitting, eye gouging and similar antics. The original members were Moe Howard (1897–1975), Shemp Howard (1900–75) and Larry Fine (1911–75), although various replacements also appeared. Through television reruns and cult status, their fan base remains dedicated to this day.

GARY McDONOGH

Thurber, James

b. 1894; d. 1961

Poet, cartoonist, playwright and essayist, Thurber's wry humor explored alternative relations of gender in which men sought less to dominate than to escape from gender battles, work and modernity. A frequent contributor to the *New Yorker*, Thurber's best-known works include *Is Sex Necessary?* (with E.B. White, 1929), "The Secret Life of Walter Mitty" (1942) and the *Thurber Carnival* (1945), as well as children's books and a memoir, *The Years with Ross* (1959). Films and a television series have been based on his works.

GARY McDONOGH

Thurmond, Strom

b. 1902

Perennial senator from South Carolina. Thurmond was elected as a Democratic **governor** in 1946, but veered away from Truman's **civil rights** agenda to head the splinter **Dixiecrat** presidential ticket in 1948. Winning a write-in ballot for the Senate in 1954, Thurmond has held onto his seat and beliefs for decades, although he switched to the

Republicans in 1964, a watershed year for the transformation of the Democratic South into a conservative **Republican** enclave. Despite increasing black voter registration and Sunbelt development, Thurmond represents a power broker for his state in addition to his hawkish, moralistic roles in the Senate. As of 1996, he became the oldest person ever to serve in the Senate.

GARY McDONOGH

Till, Emmet

b. 1941; d, 1955

Fourteen-year-old **African American** Chicagoan who visited his uncle in Mississippi for the summer of 1955. Unfamiliar with the racial code of the **South**, he spoke casually to a married **white** woman in a store, and received retribution at the hands of the woman's husband and his half-brother. Unlike countless **lynchings** that either went unrecorded or never resulted in a case against the lynchers, the Till case went to court owing to the bravery of his uncle who was willing to identify the assailants. While the two defendants were acquitted by an all-white jury, the national attention the case received and the outrage the verdict unleashed helped to mobilize many **African Americans** and northern white liberals who joined the **Civil Rights movement**.

ROBERT GREGG

Times Square

On New Year's Eve, **New York** City, NY's Times Square becomes the focus of thousands gathered in the cold and of a televisual nation that marks the countdown as an illuminated ball descends atop the former Times Building. Times Square, at the heart of New York's **theater** district, with a giant subway exchange below and a variegated neon canopy above, has become a global emblem of the city. The "crossroads of **Broadway**" has also sheltered talent agencies, souvenir stands, adult entertainment and prostitution, a seediness that

preoccupied city administrators and tourists in the 1970s. Subsequent clean-up campaigns include a Times Square Business Improvement District (that taxes local merchants to provide extra cleaning and security) and promotion of national franchises and high-rise development. The new, clean Times Square represents both the Americanization of Manhattan and the dual city where public space is appropriated by urban elites.

GARY McDONOGH
CINDY WONG

Time Warner

Time Inc. began in 1922 with its namesake magazine; in the same year Warner Bros, a film company, opened its first studio. These two companies merged in 1989 forming the world's largest and most diversified entertainment conglomerate that exerts an amazing amount of control in the film, publishing, television and recording industries. In 1995 Time Warner bought TBS, becoming the most important force in **cable** broadcasting. Today, Time Inc. is still the premier magazine publisher with twenty-four publications – *Time*, *Sports Illustrated*, *People* and many others; the book division includes Warner Books, Little, Brown and Co., as well as Book of the Month Club. The Warner Music Group is the most diversified music entertainment company; Warner Bros' film entertainment unit produces TV shows such as *Friends* and *ER* (both NBC, 1994–), as well as operating the WB network. This conglomerate also includes HBO, Cinemax and Time Warner Cable, the second-largest owner and operator of cable systems.

EDWARD MILLLER

tipping

A tip of 15–20 percent added on to pre-**tax** bills for restaurants, **hotels**, beauty salons, taxis and other services hardly seems an extraordinary surcharge in a global economy. Yet, for many workers, tips represent a primary source of income, eclipsing any hourly wage (which may be lowered to reflect tips or erased by government deductions from a presumed higher income). Hence, tipping is not only a reward or recognition for service but a necessity. For those in elite establishments, this may mean a substantial and rapid cash income, but it may also uncomfortably underscore dependence and difference in **service-sector** interactions.

GARY McDONOGH

CINDY WONG

Title IX

The most far-reaching of federal educational laws, Title IX of the Education Amendments of 1972 prohibits discrimination on the basis of sex in any program or activity at a private or public educational institution receiving federal funds. Title IX regulations forbid sex discrimination in financial assistance, discriminatory course assignments and sexual harassment. They also mandate equal athletic opportunities for both sexes.

See also: sports and gender

MARY-CHRISTINE SUNGAILA, ESQ.

tobacco industry

America's tobacco industry has a long, profitable history. Virginia colonist John Rolfe (Pocahantas' husband) produced the first commercial crop in 1612. In 1890 James Buchanan Duke founded the American Tobacco Company (ATC). A 1902 merger with Britain's Imperial Tobacco Company created the British-American Tobacco Company (BAT). In 1911 the US Supreme Court dissolved Duke's monopoly into several smaller companies, including R.J. Reynolds (RJR), Liggett & Myers (L&M), American Tobacco (AT) and Weyman-Burton. The other major tobacco manufacturers, Lorillard, Philip Morris (PM) and Brown & Williamson (B&W), formed in the 1930s.

Cigarette sales grew steadily until the early 1950s when stories about health risks to smokers proliferated. In 1964 the US **Surgeon General**'s report *Smoking and Health* concluded that smoking was a health hazard. In 1965 the US **Congress**

began requiring the Surgeon General's warning on all cigarette packages. The year 1971 brought a ban on broadcast tobacco-product **advertising**. By 1990 all interstate **buses** and domestic airline flights banned smoking.

The tobacco industry reacted to these changes by diversifying and expanding internationally. PM, manufacturer of Marlboro and Virginia Slims, led both trends. Its major domestic purchases included Miller beer, General Foods and Kraft. RJR, manufacturer of Camel, went into foil products, **oil** and **food** operations. In 1986, the company became RJR-Nabisco. AT, maker of Pall Mall and Lucky Strike, diversified into liquor and golf brands, changing its name to American Brands in 1969. American Brands left the tobacco business after B&W bought Gallaher, its cigarette division, and changed its name again to Fortune Brands in 1997. Still controlled by parent company BAT, B&W, maker of Kool, diversified relatively late. Its acquisitions included the elite retail **department store** Saks Fifth Avenue. Lorillard, maker of Newport, was purchased in 1968 by the Loews Corporation, which also owns insurance company CNA Financial Corporation. L&M, maker of Chesterfield and Lark, successfully diversified into **pet**-food products and **alcohol**, becoming the Liggett Group in 1964. In 1980 Grand Metropolitan Limited took over L&M, reducing its presence in the tobacco industry. These changes reduced the original "Big Six" cigarette manufacturers to the "Big Four." Meanwhile, chewing tobacco manufacturer United States Tobacco (formerly Weyman-Burton), producer of Copenhagen and Skoal, branched into wine, **cigars** and entertainment programming.

The tobacco industry faced increasing legal pressure in the 1990s. In 1994, led by Mississippi, the states began suing the tobacco industry to recoup tobacco-related Medicaid costs. In October 1996, Congress passed the FDA (Food and Drug Administration) rule to regulate tobacco, especially sales and marketing aimed at minors. Liggett also broke ranks with the industry in 1996, eventually settling with five states over Medicaid suits and releasing internal documents. In 1997 the industry negotiated a national tobacco settlement with the state Attorneys General, prompting Congress to consider legislation to regulate the industry. Further suits and strategies continue to challenge the industry in the US, including a $145 billion judgement in Florida (2000) against these manufacturers.

Further reading

Finger, W. (ed.) (1981) *The Tobacco Industry in Transition*, Raleigh NC: North Carolina Center for Public Policy.

White, L. (1988) *Merchants of Death*, New York: Beech Tree.

COURTNEY BENNETT

tourism

"See the USA in your Chevrolet!" Mass tourism in the postwar era has been mediated by the hegemony of the **automobile** that had emerged earlier in the century and by cheap mass transport via train, bus and aviation. Together, these opportunities for an affluent society to spend leisure time away from the home have transformed an American infrastructure of services as well as the imagery and even identity of places within a burgeoning national and international tourist economy.

Tourism at the end of the century is the second-largest retail operation in the US, employing 7 million people in addition to indirect profits and jobs. Domestic travel expenditures in the US topped $350 billion in 1995; American travelers also spent $57 billion abroad, while foreign travelers spent $68 billion in the US. Some view it as the postmodern successor to industrial capitalism. Certainly, with growing **deindustrialization**, tourism is avidly promoted as an economic solution by federal, **state** and local offices through information centers, **advertising** and professional outreach. Tourism and service courses are offered in **colleges**, while places seek to transform themselves in terms of salient images (historical landmarks, **museums**, consumption, slogans), as well as services (convention centers, **hotels**, restaurants, **airports**, etc.).

The most common tourist destinations in the US as states are **California** (25.7 percent), Florida (25 percent), New York (21 percent) and **Hawai'i** (14 percent) – showing the impact of both **Disneyland/Disneyworld** as the number-one single attraction and the more general development of resort culture. Among cities, **New York** City, NY remains the most popular destination, followed by **Los Angeles**, **Miami** and **San Francisco**, though **African Americans** are drawn to **Philadelphia, PA**, home of the Liberty Bell, Mother Bethel and important underground railroad sites. **Santa Fe** and **New Orleans** have developed especially distinctive images that foster regular visits, while events from the **Superbowl** or **Olympics** to horse races, business conventions and **celebrity** fads all influence choices of destinations. The tourism industry includes magazines, newspaper features, advertisements and **Internet** sites that shape the choices and the tourist experience; offers from transportation and lodging providers compete nationally and globally.

Tourism and travel may embody many individual and collective goals – an expression of leisure, pursuit of knowledge, consumption, status, family bonding or simple escape – or some meshing of all these. Moreover, "tourism" may be combined with business or other pursuits. Goals, in turn, mean different destinations and travel. The station wagon crammed with tents, children and pets for **camping** differs from a rented villa in Florence or Maui, a honeymoon in Niagara Falls or eco-trekking in Nepal. Budget, time, social relations and cultural capital shape the tourist venture as does acceptance – African Americans in the postwar period experienced difficulties in finding lodging and even bathrooms in the South; interstate travel was an early target of civil-rights activism.

Differing goals and foundations also influence how tourism will be recalled later through photography (slides in the 1950s and 1960s giving way to video), social narrative and souvenirs. The latter range from kitsch reproductions of the Statue of Liberty or gaudy "Mexican" hats to works of art, high fashion and web-site chronicles.

Tourism also demands adjustments among hosts, depending on attractions and specializations. Services must converge with historic or natural landscapes, collections of particular patrimonies or cultural diversity and even quaintness and isolation in defining an attraction. This leads to a paradox of success that Rothman calls "devil's bargains," when tourism alters the life and authenticity of the visited place and people. Hence the Hawai'ian hula becomes a female "show" rather than a male religious event; Amish farms are replaced by motels and malls for those who want to see a simple life in comfort; and **national parks** are clogged with cars and pollution.

Not all American tourism stays in America. While in the past, trips to Europe or Latin America represented elite privilege or bohemian escape, in the 1990s, more than 50 million Americans travel abroad annually, with Canada (13 million) and Mexico (18 million) primary destinations; roughly 8 million go to Europe. In the postwar period of American economic dominance, mass tourism created the image of an "Ugly American" abroad – crass, untutored and unresponsive to places and cultures. Mass tourism has grown to serve multiple niches from academic travelers to special packages based on race and ethnic heritage, age, sexuality, or environmental and political issues.

More than 40 million foreign tourists also arrive in the US annually, with Canada the largest single source (14 million), 8.7 million from Europe and 6.6 million from Asia. Many of these visitors see the US through the prism of Disneyworld or other packaged attractions. Yet their experiences of poverty, divisions and antagonisms in the US also challenge American representations of success abroad.

Tourism and tourists tend to figure in mass media as subjects of ridicule, although travel writing itself has been a long-established and evocative genre in American literature (Mark Twain, Henry James, John Steinbeck, etc.). While **road movies** may evoke an American quest, tourism as a theme often focused movies on differences, confusions and adjustments. Neil Simon's *The Out-of-Towners* (originally filmed 1970) chronicles the mishaps of travel to New York City that are refracted in films as distinctive as *Brother from Another Planet* (1984) or *Home Alone 2* (1992). More sinister images are evoked by dislocation and vulnerability in the sci-fi resort of *Westworld* (1973) or the vulnerability of Sandra Bullock as a woman whose identity is stolen in *The Net* (1995). Tourism abroad is even more torn between the ludicrous (*If It's Tuesday, This Must be Belgium*, 1969; *National Lampoon* films or many sitcom travel episodes), the

romantic (many films set in Paris, including *Funny Face*, 1957 and *French Kiss*, 1995) or more personal crises and quests (*Havana*, 1990; *Beyond Rangoon*, 1998; *Men with Guns*, 1998). Among depictions of American tourists abroad by non-Americans, one might note Hitchcock's *The Man Who Knew Too Much* (1956) or Jacques Tati's remarkable *Playtime* (1967).

Further reading

Jakle, J. (1985) *The Tourist*, Lincoln: University of Nebraska.

Rothman, H. (1998) *Devil's Bargains: Tourism in the Twentieth Century American West*, Lawrence: University of Kansas.

Wilson, C. (1997) *The Myth of Santa Fe*, Albuquerque: University of New Mexico.

GARY McDONOGH
CINDY WONG

toys

American **children** and toys, in many ways, scarcely differ from their consociates worldwide except in affluence – more toys and more expensive ones. Dolls, wagons, costumes, **bicycles** and **war** toys have been gendered dreams for generations, even as historically American toys – **cowboy** outfits and guns or the postwar **Barbie** – have spread around the globe. **Class** and **race** have changed perceptions of these "standard toys," as Toni Morrison sadly underscored in her novel *The Bluest Eye*, yet children have scarcely been more equal in other nations. Nonetheless, several important characteristics may set American toys and play apart from other nations.

Affluence and ownership are still important characteristics. For postwar children, as cinema and television reinforce imagery, Christmas and birthdays became intensive and competitive celebrations of goods including multiple and expensive toys. Electronic games, elaborate outdoor toys and innumerable small toys create a bounty that children are taught to own. Even if they share with friends, lines of property (and position) are drawn early on by who owns what, or by who fails to get coveted toys (a parental competition satirized in media). Obviously, this leaves out some children from the experience of a general cultural ideal – while cities, schools and institutions push drives to collect "toys for tots," the return to school or neighborhood gatherings after Christmas remain difficult.

American toys also differ in quality, price and even style. **Yuppie** parents may favor educational toys or classic (sometimes expensive) basics in wood and cloth. Some ask for dolls that reflect their own features and lifestyles – **African American** toys represent a special subgenre even within Barbie lines. Toys are also highly gendered in advertising and consumption, and graded for age divisions that encompass an adult market as well as metaphoric extensions (sports cars or electronics, for example, may be referred to as toys for adults).

The sheer numbers of toys and the created desire that drives sales also underscores a long-standing synergy of media and commodities. Captain Midnight Decoder Rings, Howdy Doody puppets, Brady Bunch lunch-boxes, Carebears and generations of *Star Trek* toys all speak to the power of television and film to sell to younger audiences (and their beleaguered parents). While children's television codes have attacked direct manipulative marketing, media giants like **Disney** have had generations of spin-off toys that sell movies, television, fantasy vacations and "happiness." Indeed, Disney's *Toy Story* and its sequel represent both reflections on toys and a continuing bonus in sales – old and new toys are agents in the narrative, markers of memory and commodities in stores. In another synergy, **McDonald's** represents one of the world's largest toy manufacturers, in independent productions and linked to media.

While these are now global phenomena, many have been honed on generations of postwar children who, as **baby boomers**, bring both nostalgia and criticism to new generations of sales. This also creates secondary markets for toys as **collectibles** that influence not only family relics but new purchases, as exemplified in the Beanie Baby craze, where value is besmirched by any signs of actual play.

Hence, intense marketing and production also shape American toys. While hand-crafted toys or designer lines appeal to wealthier consumers, Toys 'r' Us – now global – has a strong monopoly on general sales in concert with major manufacturers like Mattel. In the 1980s and 1990s, toy marketing has been driven by "the toy" of the year, from Cabbage Patch Kids to Furby, where constructed scarcities drive prices to extremes as demonstrations of Christmas love. This **consumerism** also made toys a vanguard for development of e-commerce.

GARY McDONOGH

track and field

American athletes in track-and-field sports have been able to maintain their dominance as a result of the emphasis **colleges and universities** place on the sport. Backed by the **NCAA** and an elaborate system of sports scholarships, colleges and universities have been able to offer opportunities to athletes to compensate for the sport's amateur status (a status that no longer remains). The significance of the college-based system on the lives of athletes has been explored in numerous movies from *Personal Best* (1982) to *Without Limits* (1998). The pressure to succeed created by this system has given rise to the widespread use of performance-enhancing drugs.

The widespread attention given to track and field derived in large part from its association with the **Olympic** movement, which provided a forum for the expression of nationalist sentiments. As such, the efforts of athletes competing against countries with which the United States is in competition (economically and ideologically) have often taken on considerable significance. During the Cold War, therefore, considerable attention would be paid to Americans competing against athletes from the Soviet Union and East Germany. Owing to the prominence of **African American** athletes in many track-and-field events, the possibilities of harnessing patriotic fervor to racial advancement were commonly acknowledged. Jesse Owens' success at the 1936 Berlin Olympics, winning four gold medals in front of a furious Hitler (who would have been more furious still had the Americans included their Jewish sprinters on their relay team), was just one example of this. Owens (1913–80) became a nationally recognized and celebrated athlete and, along with Joe Louis, helped pave the way for Jackie **Robinson**'s desegregation of baseball.

Wilma Rudolph (1940–84), the first American to win three gold medals in the 1960 Rome Olympics (100m, 200m and 400m relay), continued this tradition. Her achievement, a triumph also over childhood **polio**, made her one of the most celebrated female athletes of all time. Her celebrity also helped to begin the process of breaking down gender barriers in previously all-male track-and-field events prior to the passage of **Title IX**.

The identification between athletes and their country, opening up opportunities to black athletes that might otherwise have been closed, remained in place at least until the end of the **Cold War**. President **Carter**'s boycott of the 1980 Moscow Olympics, in the aftermath of the Soviet invasion of Afghanistan, was considered by many a major blow to African American athletes, not merely on the grounds of their pursuit of gold medals. But African American track-and-field athletes also used this spotlight to make comments about racial conditions in the United States. Tommie Smith and John Carlos at the 1968 Mexico Olympics raised their fists in the **Black Power** salute during the medal ceremony to make the point that while they were representing their country, that country discriminated against them (both were suspended from the US team).

The 1968 Olympics also witnessed major track-and-field landmarks: Bob Beamon won the gold medal in the long jump with a world record (29ft, 2½in), shattering the old mark by nearly 2 feet (unlike most records, this one remained unbroken until 1991 when Mike Powell jumped 2 inches further); and Dick Fosbury fundamentally altered the high jump with his "Fosbury Flop."

Two other track-and-field stars deserve mention. Florence Griffith Joyner (1959–98), known as "FloJo," was a triple gold medalist at the 1988 Seoul Olympics. She was recognized around the world for both her colorful and asymmetrical running outfits and her long, painted fingernails. Smashing the world records for the 100- and 200-meter runs in Seoul and also winning a gold medal in the 4×100 relay, she later served as co-chairperson of President Clinton's Council on **Physical Fitness**, before suffering a heart attack

and dying in 1998. As with Rudolph before her, Griffith Joyner's performances challenged assumptions about the relationship between **sport and gender**.

Carl Lewis (1961–) dominated track-and-field events throughout much of the 1980s and early 1990s. Unable to run in Moscow because of the boycott, Lewis amassed a record in sprints and long jump equaled by no other athlete. Widely regarded as the greatest track-and-field athlete of all time, he matched Jesse Owen's record in 1984, won three medals in 1988 (two gold and one silver) and another two gold medals in 1992. At the 1991 World Championships in Tokyo he also set the world record for the 100m (9.86 seconds).

See also: Olympians; running; steroids

ROBERT GREGG

trade and trade agreements

For much of American history, trade policy has meant protection of domestic resources and fledgling industries through tariffs and controls on importation. In the postwar period, however, a stronger America has lowered its own trade barriers substantially while using trade as a carrot and stick, reducing barriers globally in order to open markets internationally to US goods, agricultural, industrial and intellectual, and to affirm special relationships ("most favored nation status"). Economists, on the whole, tend to favor free trade, foreseeing greater efficiency and long-run benefits.

Global trade increased more than fourteen-fold from 1950 to 1998, contributing to improved standards of living/consumption for many in the US and abroad. This growth also has resulted in a large persistent American trade deficit since the 1970s and diverse reactions from the American people to arrangements made by both the government and multinational negotiators under the GATT (General Agreement on Tariffs and Trade, first signed in 1947) and the WTO (World Trade Organization) that has replaced it since 1994/5.

America's undamaged industrial and agricultural infrastructure allowed it to capture a preeminent place in global marketing in the postwar period, which was eventually undercut by its own development practices and investments that created cheaper, more efficient manufacturing abroad. Hence, former enemies Japan and Germany have become major sources of the trade deficit along with neighbors **Mexico** and **Canada** (under NAFTA, the North American Free Trade Agreement) and new Asian industrial nations. By contrast, the US ran a surplus with Europe until 1991, and maintains this relationship with Britain and the Netherlands. Trade balances may be affected by limits and subsidies (in the case of the European Union and Japan) or by weaknesses in local currency and markets that undercut buying power (Canada, Mexico, Asia). Trade wars may be raged through such apparently unlikely products as bananas (with Europe) or film (with Japan). Relations with **China** have created especially thorny issues.

Such imbalances in manufacture and trade cost jobs in the United States, even when they involve offshore investments of American corporations and **multinationals**, leading unions to charge that profits and consumption are being traded for workers' lives. Issues of environmental conditions of the non-US workplace, child labor, respect for intellectual property, morality and political regimes and related topics have also been brought by critics to debates over trade as moral policy.

Many of these issues were galvanized in the debate surrounding NAFTA (1994), which 1992 third-party candidate Ross Perot characterized by a "giant sucking sound" of jobs going to Mexico, but which nonetheless gained approval with solid bipartisan presidential and congressional support. To some extent, NAFTA built on years of special relations among the three North American states, including many measures for development of the Mexican American **borderlands**. Critics both before and after passage have challenged its impact on employment and wages, both in the US and an increasingly polarized Mexico, as well as failures to protect the environment and human rights equally under the agreement.

Frustration with the impacts of such agreement spilled out into days of civil action at the WTO meetings in **Seattle, WA** in 1999. Unions, environmentalists, anarchists and other citizens from the US and abroad joined in to protest both

policies and domination of trade by this international group. Thus, trade became a popular as well as political issue in a new way for the nation and the world.

Further reading

Coffey, P. *et al.* (1999) *NAFTA*, Boston: Kluwer.

GARY McDONOGH

trains

Train stations tell the stories of railroads since the Second World War. Once, they were the temples of nineteenth-century American civic progress. Transcontinental railroads (built by immigrant Irish, Chinese and Mexicans as well as **African Americans**) united peoples and goods, and stations became marble and gilt gateways for **cities**. Cities and companies competed; even small towns vied for connections and identity within national mass transportation. The demolition of **New York** City, NY's Pennsylvania Station in 1963, a rallying point for **historic preservation**, and the conversion of other once-proud stations to museums (**Savannah, GA**), malls (**Cincinnati, OH**) and abandonment shows railroads' loss of position to **automobiles**, **trucks** and airplanes. Despite 1990s plans for a new "old" Penn Station in New York – in the shell of a central post office now more effectively connected to trucks and air – outside the Northeast and some Pacific Rim routes, new generations of Americans experience domestic railroads as nostalgic rides in amusement parks or along special, scenic routes. Even in media, railroads belong to **westerns**, **film noir** and Disneyworld rather than contemporary life.

American railroads emerged in a constant interaction of government interests and private speculation. By the turn of the nineteenth century, the Interstate Commerce Commission had taken control over the worst excesses of cut-throat capitalism and corruption. Trains were taken over temporarily by the government in the First World War and remained strong and central economically through the Second World War. They were also embedded in popular culture as film backdrops, settings for arrivals and departures for **war**, college and new lives, and the tracks on which presidential campaigns and hoboes rode.

By the 1950s, diesel engines were replacing steam and panoramic cars added new dimensions to western runs. Yet, the Interstate **Highway** system slowly ate into freight and passenger revenues. Trucks were more flexible in cargo, while pipelines and barges also cut into cargo profits. Expanding airlines later captured passengers and rapid delivery. Meanwhile, railroads, with a century of contracts and regulations, found themselves unable to trim budgets or staff while taxed to pay for new airports. By 1965 railroads carried only 18 percent of total intercity passenger service and only 44 percent of freight. Most ran deficits and sought to consolidate via mergers; the giant Penn Central declared bankruptcy in 1970.

Here, government intervention was called upon to save public service. Amtrak was created in 1971, providing government support to maintain a multicompany national passenger service. A similar freight plan, Conrail, built on the Penn Central and other bankrupt northeastern lines in 1976. Corporate mergers consolidated other regional freight service as railroads steadily cut workers and lines, increasing efficiency and ultimately stabilizing freight handling. President Carter promoted deregulation in 1980, allowing railroads to change rates and compete with other transport. In 1995 rail freight doubled its 1944 peak, although only holding 37 percent of the market. Conrail was sold to the public in 1984, although Amtrak continued to struggle, despite its rapid reserved Metroliner service in the Northeast and vacation packages. Clinton eliminated the ICC in 1995.

Politicians and entrepreneurs have nonetheless sought to keep passenger travel alive and connecting their regions. In the late 1990s, the Northeast prepared for new high-speed trains. Auto-trains connected northern vacationers and Florida, while West Coast lines and regional connector systems grew. Another rapid line is proposed for Florida, to connect Tampa, Orlando, Jacksonville and Miami. Still, these generally demand government subsidies, which raise questions among citizens and representatives for whom rail service is no longer a daily concern. Problems with wastes and safety have also been raised with regards to passenger and freight

lines – a 1999 television movie, for example, featured a run-away train carrying nuclear waste.

Commuter rails are more limited and secure, with government subsidies, especially on the East Coast. Yet, cars and highways carry the future for most Americans. At the same time, railroads may provide warnings for subsequent developments in mass transportation and **mass media**, where negotiations of government responsibility over public goods and private profits continue.

Further reading

Stover, J. (1997) *American Railroads*, Chicago: University of Chicago.
Yenne, B. (1989) *All Aboard*, New York: Barnes & Noble.

GARY McDONOGH

transexuals

Conventionally defined as individuals who have undergone a sex change operation in order to become a member of the opposite sex. Yet, this definition is imposed upon transexuals from the largely hostile American mainstream; many transexuals themselves disagree with it.

First, there are many degrees of transexuality which some transexuals feel are obscured by the conventional definition. Certain individuals who identify themselves as transexual do not desire medical intervention. Others have undergone some medical procedures, such as hormone treatments, yet do not wish to undergo surgical procedures. Finally, some have undergone an entire sex-change operation.

Second, the conventional definition assumes that a transexual changes *from* one sex *to* another. This idea is based on a sex dichotomy which only concedes of two possibilities: male and female. Some scientists, such as Anne Fausto-Sterling of Brown University, have argued that there are more than two sexes.

Mainstream American culture generally considers transexuality to be indicative of abnormal or poorly adjusted individuals. Owing to their deviant status, transexuals continually face the threat of brutality from those who hate and fear them. Also, the medical establishment requires transexuals to undergo psychological testing before treatment is given. It is considered in the best interests of transexuals to be thoroughly screened before they are allowed to obtain the medical help that they desire. Unfortunately, this process is often experienced as difficult and demeaning by transexual people themselves.

Further reading

Wilchins, R. (1997) *Read My Lips: Sexual Subversion and the End of Gender*, Ithaca: Firebrand.

ELIZABETH A. GALEWSKI

transgendered *see* bisexuality; gay and lesbian life and politics; gender and sexuality

transvestites

Transvestites challenge the established norm for gender behavior. While the most visible transvestites are the male drag queens, whether politicized or in show business, others have adopted cross-dressing as a more private behavior. Adoption of clothing, hair and facial preparation and other attributes appropriate to another sex has deep roots in American folklore and history.

For women, this allowed more freedom to take on roles of power and independence in wars and immigration (as fictionalized by Barbra **Streisand** in *Yentl*, 1983). As women's clothing has become casual and functional, cross-dressing is more complex. Few women who dress in men's clothes would call themselves transvestites.

Males have also taken on female clothing for ritualized occasions, including mock weddings and mock **cheerleading** in the **South**, rites of initiation for male fraternities and vaudeville humor, whether Milton Berle in early television or New York Mayor Rudolph Giuliani on *Saturday Night Live*. Like many others perceived to be engaged in alternative sexuality, transvestites tended to keep their interests private until liberation movements in the 1960s opened a wider discussion and range of public behavior. Transvestite males, in particular, are often taken to be gay

although their use of women's clothing may be based on other aesthetic or tactile features.

The most flamboyant modern exposure of transvestite life has been the "drag show," with male and female celebrity impersonators, following lip-synched song and dance routines and attracting diverse audiences. Drag shows, as urbane entertainment, have also broken through in Hollywood and Broadway with comedies like *Victor/Victoria* (1982) or *To Wong Fu Thanks for Everything, Julie Newmar* (1995), and the celebrity status accorded to RuPaul. Director Ed Woods, who treated transvestisim as a clinical condition in his own terrible (now cult) films, was treated as a sympathetic closet transvestite in Tim Burton's 1994 bio-pic. Dennis Rodman, the NBA star, has made cross-dressing a more confrontational issue of **masculinity** and choice in his public demeanor.

This is an area fraught with multiple and contradictory meanings as well as reactions.

Further reading

Feinberg, L. (1998) *Trans Liberation*, Boston: Beacon.
Newton, E. (1972) *Mother Camp: Female Impersonators in America*, Englewood Cliffs: Prentice-Hall.
Wheelwright, J. (1989) *Amazons and Military Maids*, London: Pandora.

GARY McDONOGH
CINDY WONG

trucks and trucking

The **highways** that reshaped America moved goods as well as passengers. Experimentation with car bases followed the initial mass production of autos, but trucks gained special impetus with First World War mobilization. Trucks were produced by the Big Three automakers as well as specialists like Mack Trucks. In the 1930s they extended their reach through urban and rural areas, forcing government regulations (although the situation remained chaotic through the Second World War). As the Interstate Highway System expanded, trucks became a major force in national transportation, challenging **trains** with their flexibility and connections. Smaller trucks adapted to the urban landscape – from deliveries to ice-cream vendors whose music evokes summer days and cold popsicles – or rural work, where pick-ups have replaced horses. Over decades, moreover, trucks and truckers have changed American geography with truck stops and motels and have created an American folklore of the freedom of the road in songs, language (on CB radios) and activities of the **Teamsters Union** that represents many drivers.

Trucks may be owned by companies (private carriers) or leased from for-hire carriers. Roughly 100,000 independent truckers own and operate their own vehicles, although often within permanent lease arrangements. The 1973 **oil** crisis and later deregulation, in fact, increased some aspects of dependency and lessened government protection. These truckers, nonetheless, sometimes depicted as modern **cowboys**, have captivated American media in representations of **class**, independence and generally male stereotypes (in the female **road movie** *Thelma and Louise* (1991), blowing up a man's truck declares independence). *Convoy* (1978) and *Over the Top* (1987) offer more standard visions of men grappling with social challenges. Trucker music – "Six Days on the Road and I'm Gonna See my Baby Tonight" – has also defined road folklore, alongside "urban legends" of vanishing hitchhikers and media representations of killer trucks.

Another characteristic adaptation to life on the road is the truck stop, which offers fuel, food, relaxation, showers, even occasional religious services. Like gas stations, truck stops have sometimes been templates to play with modernist design, but more often they are functional service and food clusters near major highways. Nearby **motels** may offer lodging, but many large trucks are designed with living and sleeping quarters for long hauls.

This is not to say that trucks are without enemies. Concerns over congestion and safety in urban areas as well as highway dangers are often spurred by media reports on speeding, fatigue and accidents. Damage to roadways through overloads and environmental deterioration are also concerns of a truck-reliant society.

Most of these concerns are aimed at multiple-axle, large vehicles. Other trucks in common commercial use include vans and pick-ups. In fact, in the 1990s, small pick-up trucks have moved beyond the workplace to become mass recreational vehicles.

Further reading

Childs, W. (1985) *Trucking and the Public Interest*, Knoxville: University of Tennessee.

Agar, M. (1986) *Independence Declared*, Washington, DC: Smithsonian.

GARY McDONOGH

Truman, Harry S.

b. 1884; d. 1972

Elected **vice-president** in 1944 when Franklin D. **Roosevelt** won a fourth consecutive presidential term, Truman became president when Roosevelt died in April 1945. Within months he had made pivotal foreign-policy decisions: at the Potsdam Conference he and Allied leaders agreed to prosecute German leaders for war crimes committed during the Second World War; and, in August, he approved the dropping of atomic bombs on Japanese cities Hiroshima and Nagasaki, bringing an end to the Second World War.

Early in the **Cold War**, his administration adopted the Truman Doctrine, which developed into the policy of "containment" to halt Soviet expansion. One aspect of the Doctrine was the Marshall Plan, an economic recovery program for European nations, and the North Atlantic Treaty Organization (**NATO**), a military alliance designed to protect Western Europe from Soviet aggression.

Truman began the 1948 presidential campaign as an underdog to Republican nominee Thomas Dewey. However, he defeated Dewey, proving wrong experts and a premature headline in the *Chicago Tribune*: "Dewey Defeats Truman."

In June 1950, communist North Korea invaded South Korea, prompting Truman to send United States forces to the region to protect South Korea. Led by General Douglas **MacArthur**, United Nations' (UN) troops brought most of South Korea under UN control by October.

Truman is most often remembered for developing a civil-rights agenda, issuing executive orders banning discrimination in the civil service and in the armed forces, and for his phrase, "The buck stops here," meaning ultimate responsibility rests with the president.

Further reading

McCullough, D. (1992) *Truman*, New York: Simon & Schuster.

JAMES DEVITT

Trump, Donald

b. 1946

Real-estate financier. In the 1980s, Trump built an estimated $2 billion fortune through investments in luxury properties in and around **New York** City. Combining bold business tactics and a high public profile, Trump established himself as a financial and political power, as well as a social **celebrity**. The early 1990s recession pushed him to the brink of bankruptcy, but Trump rebounded after ceding control of much of his **real-estate** empire to creditors. He maintains his association with such prestigious New York City holdings as the Trump Plaza Hotel and several casinos in **Atlantic City**.

SARAH SMITH

Tupperware

Earl Tupper's refined plastics, used in Second World War gas masks, created a classic American brand among postwar families who relied on its airtight storage containers for food storage between shopping trips. Unsuccessful in stores, by the late 1940s, Tupperware developed direct distributors and Tupperware parties, which mingled cooking and entertaining demonstrations, **games**, snacks, sociability and sales for female buyers. The company sells more than $1 billion annually in household, educational and related goods; 85 percent of sales occur outside the US. After fifty years of parties, it has experimented with mall kiosks, corporate-controlled online sales, commer-

cials and **Disney** tie-ins to reach working parents and new consumers.

GARY McDONOGH

turkey

The symbolic weight of this bird crashes onto American dinner tables every Thanksgiving. Although a New World species, the Pilgrims probably knew it in England before any mythic dinners of peace with Indians. Still, custom patterns a "traditional" Thanksgiving menu replete with stuffing, cranberries, potatoes and pies. Regional and ethnic variations in stuffing (cornbread versus white bread or oysters) and cooking abound, as do cynical responses in popular media to dry meat and endless leftovers. Benjamin Franklin proposed the turkey as a national bird instead of the eagle, but it is also renowned for stupidity, especially as a domestic fowl. While marketed for other large meals and as a healthy alternative to other kinds of meat, turkey remains bound to the holiday as a cultural symbol.

GARY McDONOGH

Turner, Ted

b. 1938

Ted Turner (R.E. Turner III) is largely credited for the popularization of **cable** TV with TBS, one of the first stations to reach a nationwide audience in 1975. This station carried only the minimal amount of **news** required by the **FCC** and showed mostly reruns. Another one of his groundbreaking stations, CNN, was initiated in 1981, and has had an incredible influence both in news broadcasting and in reporting mostly national events to international audiences from its Atlanta base. An outspoken and controversial figure, he is married to actor Jane Fonda; he has challenged other wealthy men to give more with his planned $10 billion gift to the UN. In 1995 TBS was sold to **Time Warner**, Inc. and Turner rose to the position of vice-chair within the huge conglomerate. He also became the largest single land-owner in the US in 2000 with 1.7 million acres.

EDWARD MILLER

TV Guide

Brainchild of *Philadelphia Inquirer* publisher Walter Annenberg, *TV Guide* was created in 1953 as the ephemeral bible of the television generation. It was sold to Rupert Murdoch in 1988. Its multiple local program guides, meshed with national features on **stars**, programming and even investigative work, have allowed it to vie with *Reader's Digest* as the most popular American **magazine** (13 million plus circulation). Still, like **television**, it remains absent from scholarly settings like **libraries**, even though the magazine may figure as a **collectible** in its own right. Annenberg, ambassador to Britain under **Reagan**, used his media wealth to fund communication studies and civic and educational projects.

GARY McDONOGH

Tyson, Mike *see* boxing

U

UFOs/extraterrestrials

Among the most discussed immigrants of the postwar period are those many believe have never actually arrived – aliens from other worlds. For many, these stories are the stuff of science fiction – where an alien threat has remained big box office from *The Thing* (1952; 1982) and *War of the Worlds* (Orson **Welles**' radio version 1938; film 1953) through *Close Encounters of the Third Kind* (1977) and *E.T.* (1982) to *Independence Day* (1997) and *Men in Black* (1998). American scientists, military and government agencies have generally concurred in rejecting any such possibilities. Yet, other Americans assemble sightings, photographs, personal testimonies, reinterpretations of historical texts and material evidence to prove alien contact, covered up by a vast government conspiracy (as in television's *The X-Files*). Indeed, whether to treat such evidence as incitement to further research or signs of mass hysteria continues to divide analysts.

Despite many earlier science-fiction accounts of extra-terrestrial life and alien arrivals, clear changes arrived in the **Cold War** era. Pilot Kenneth Arnold's report of a formation of incredibly fast blue-white objects over Washington's Cascade mountains on June 24, 1947 is generally taken as inaugurating the modern UFO era (Unidentified Flying Objects; more popularly, "flying saucers"). This incident was followed on July 2 by reports of a UFO crash in Roswell, New Mexico, later dismissed by the government as a weather balloon; skepticism here makes Roswell critical for later ufologists. Thousands of reports followed, forcing an air force investigation, Project Blue Book, from 1948 to 1969. By 1953, the CIA-sponsored Robertson Panel concluded that UFOs did not exist, but that stories about them threatened national security; after August 1953, reports became classified. Yet, in a few months, Donald Keyhoe's bestselling *Flying Saucers from Outer Space* (1953) restated these claims and debate has never disappeared since. Intense sightings in 1957 and 1973, for example, showed the liveliness of saucers and watchers.

Various genres of UFO narratives complicate evaluations of evidence. Reports (and photographs) of bright lights and unusual movements have tended to be explained as other airborne objects or reflections or weather phenomena, without convincing skeptical audiences. Contact has been more problematic. The type case for alien abduction was Betty and Barney Hill's hypnosis-induced narrative of a 1961 abduction. Examination of abduction narratives as factual evidence by professors David Jacobs (Temple) and John Mack (Harvard **Medical School**) has created subsequent firestorms in academic communities (see *Secret Life*, 1992). T. Matheson, by contrast, in *Alien Abductions* (1998) reads these stories as the emergence of a new mythology. Others have related such narratives to anxieties of changing roles of Americans and whites in a global economy.

Analysis of UFOs diverges from a scientific search for extra-terrestrial intelligence (SETI), spurred on in the 1970s by Carl **Sagan** and distinguished researchers. Whether or not Earth has been visited, this project assumes, others may still be there. Space flights have included materials to establish contact with such beings.

It is tempting to read extra-terrestrial beings as symbols of race, class and change (developed by the film *Alien Nation*, 1988, which depicted massive extra-terrestrial arrivals through analogies with African Americans and recent refugees). Yet, other Americans read them as truth, personal experiences or symbols of conspiracy, a theme of vocal debate on the Internet.

Further reading

Curran, D. (1985) *In Advance of the Landing*, New York: Abbeville.

Keyhoe, D. (1953) *Flying Saucers from Outer Space*, New York: Henry Holt.

Jacobs, D.M. (1992) *Secret Life*, New York: Simon & Schuster.

Matheson, T. (1998) *Alien Abductions*, Amherst: Prometheus.

GARY McDONOGH

ugly American *see* American images abroad; tourism

Ukrainian Americans

Exact numbers of Ukrainian immigrants in the US are difficult to determine as **immigration** authorities often used labels such as "Carpatho-**Russian**" or "Galician" to describe Ukrainians. The official number is about 250,000, but the real number may be double this. Many Ukrainians fled to the US during the Russian Civil War (1918–21). Unlike some other **Slavic Americans**, the Ukrainians have maintained a fairly strong ethnic identity; many people are proud to identify themselves as being of Ukrainian descent, even if it is mixed with that of other groups. A number of cultural and political organizations have been formed: the Ukrainian Congress Committee of America represents Ukrainian political interests; and the Washington Group (established in 1984) informs the public about issues of concern to Ukrainian Americans.

MORGEN WITZEL

unabomber

Between 1978 and 1995, sixteen mail-bomb attacks were attributed to "the unabomber," so-called because the victims were often associated with universities. Theodore Kaczynski was arrested at his home – a hand-built cabin in the Montana Rockies – after his brother recognized the style of an anti-technology manifesto which the unabomber had written, and which the **FBI** had persuaded newspapers to publish. Although his ability to elude police for almost two decades made him a minor folk hero, his most lasting effects on daily life were the identification practices instituted at post offices during his time at large.

DAVID J. PHILLIPS

"underclass"

A term introduced by *Time* magazine in 1977 which describes what some saw as a new class of poor people, not cursed simply with a lack of money, but with a whole host of social pathologies, from single parenthood, to drug addiction, to high rates of participation in crime, and low willingness to pursue legitimate work. The members of the "underclass" had allegedly fallen out of society's traditional structures of work and family. They would, it was argued and feared, reproduce a class of dependent poor. The term is best written in quotation marks as it reveals as much about a cultural moment in the history of attitudes towards the poor and a community's obligation to them as it does an actual group of people.

New, troublesome phenomena facing the United States and its cities gave rise to a series of books and endless articles about a "new" poverty. It is no accident, for example, that the term came out of an era of declining economic fortunes for the United States, as well as a wrenching transformation of cities and the larger economy which left many **cities** destitute in ways they had not seen before. With a rapidly declining industrial base, consequent growth of suburban area, a retrenchment of "Great Society" welfare and urban development goals, many urban areas had been left devoid of an industrial base. Most gravely affected were "newer" immigrants, **African Americans** and **Hispanics**, in major urban areas. Poverty among these groups in urban centers did worsen as economic opportunities fled once-flourishing neighborhoods, ever more so as industry and new service-sector jobs moved out to **suburbs** and exurbs. A new American apartheid, as Douglas S. Massey and Nancy A. Denton called it, was taking over, not through southern segregation law, but by northern economic change and political decisions. The impact of economic desolation – "when work disappears" in William J. Wilson's phrase – was a breakdown in a whole host of social structures and mores that maintain a community.

So, there were indeed new, troubling aspects of poverty in the 1970s and 1980s. But behind an apparently descriptive term of new problems, lay a century or more of attitudes and policies towards the poor and a more recent intense battle over poverty, economic change and government's role in social **welfare**. With the apparent failure of the "Great Society," many conservative commentators looked for answers not in lack of opportunities or income but in a "culture of poverty." This was in many ways old wine in new bottles – the notion of the "undeserving" and irredeemable poor from the nineteenth century recast for the late twentieth century. The term has been largely rejected by liberal scholars of American cities and social policy as at the very least useless – it offers no new insight into the new problems of poverty – and, at the worst, disastrous for the effort – once a real goal, now a starry-eyed dream – of eradicating poverty. For, by focusing on the behaviors of the poor and the "dysfunctional" life of poor, usually minority, communities, it turns attention away from structural changes in the economy which have created new, and in some ways, unprecedented problems of inequality.

Further reading

Katz, M. (ed.) (1993) *The Underclass Debate*, Princeton: Princeton University.
Wilson, W.J. (1987) *The Truly Disadvantaged*, Chicago: University of Chicago.

MAX PAGE

uniforms, school

Used in many private schools, school uniforms are becoming increasingly popular in **public schools** across the country. Supported by President Bill **Clinton** in his 1996 State of the Union address, school uniforms are used in several school districts in twenty-one states. Although some claim that uniforms make schools safer by eliminating gang markings through clothing and leveling the appearance of material wealth, some individuals have challenged school-uniform policies, claiming that they infringe upon students' 1st Amendment **freedom** of expression rights.

Further reading

Sanders, S. (1998) "Making the Grade; Children's School Uniforms," *Children's Business* 13(1): 56.

KATE M. KENSKI

unions

As in other countries, the union movement grew in the United States in tandem with industrialization, artisans and craft laborers combining to protect their positions in the labor market from capitalists' attempts both to de-skill certain occupations and to replace native-born workers with cheaper immigrant laborers. Despite scattered local organizations prior to the Civil War, attempts at national organization like the National Labor Union (1866–72), and even the resort to terrorist methods by the Irish Molly Maguires in the mid-1870s (inspiring the exceptional 1970 movie of that name), unionization remained stymied throughout much of the nineteenth century. Capitalists used private force (e.g. the Pinkertons) and the power of the state to crush **strikes** like that in 1892 at Andrew Carnegie's Homestead Mill (near **Pittsburgh, PA**). In doing so, they were bolstered by Supreme Court decisions that interpreted the 14th Amendment so as to protect corporation rights rather than those of workers. Moreover, union organization and action were also complicated by the concealed issues of **class** and mobility in the United States that shaped the history and consciousness of the **working** and **middle classes**.

Nevertheless, Samuel Gompers managed to establish the American Federation of Labor during the 1890s by stressing "pure and simple unionism," concentrating on organizing only skilled laborers and eschewing political action (unlike unions outside the US, thereby remaining apart from labor and socialist parties). Consequently, Gompers endeavored to isolate the more politically oriented unionists connected to organizations like the Knights of Labor and, later, the Industrial Workers of the World (the Wobblies). In the process, the union movement became associated with attempts to exclude Chinese in the **West** and generally remained antagonistic to **African Americans** in the **Northeast**. Further, made up primarily of craft organizations, the AFL remained relatively weak in the face of the consolidation of corporate capitalism. By the turn of the nineteenth century, more than 2 million workers belonged to unions.

Advances during the First World War, with Gompers and other labor leaders being brought into the War Industries Board, were followed by an assault on unionism in 1919 and attempts by businesses to establish their own labor organizations, captured nicely in John **Sayles**' *Matewan* (1987). The 1920s, therefore, saw a union movement at a low ebb, though the immigration restrictions of 1924 can be seen as partly a concession to labor. African Americans began to push for their own unions, A. Philip **Randolph** forcing both the Pullman Company to recognize the Brotherhood of Sleeping Car Porters and labor leaders to accept the Brotherhood as a member organization within the AFL.

Union fortunes shifted dramatically in the 1930s, the Depression provoking growing labor unrest. President Franklin D. **Roosevelt** endeavored to appeal for labor support and instituted some protections for unions in the Wagner Act of 1935, which established the National Labor Relations Board. In addition, the labor movement became more inclusive, a new breakaway organization known as the Congress of Industrial Organizations forming under the leadership of John L. Lewis of the United Mine Workers (UMW). Formed around industries rather than crafts, these unions were able to take on the major **automobile** and steel companies and win – **state** and federal authorities for the first time not

supporting the companies with military assistance. With union membership expanding to 14 million by 1945, organized labor was able to establish itself as an accepted part of the **Democratic Party** coalition, though it never achieved the position attained by unions in the British Labour Party.

The radicalism of the New Deal spread from the industrial Northeast, and, after the Second World War, attempted to organize black and white laborers in the **South**, as part of Operation Dixie. The success of this movement was curtailed by the period of **McCarthyism**, which saw the purge from the Congress of Industrial Organizations (CIO) of labor radicals accused of being communists, and by the Taft-Hartley Act of 1947, which overturned many of the gains of the previous decade (including outlawing the closed shop and secondary picketing). Operation Dixie faltered and the laborers in the South divided once again along racial lines, leading African Americans to move down the path towards the more respectable **Civil Rights movement** as opposed to labor activism.

With the more radical unionists purged, the American Federation of Labor (AFL) and CIO were in a position to combine under Geroge **Meany**'s leadership (1955–79). The AFL-CIO remained distinctly conservative in orientation through the early 1970s, concentrating on securing better wages and working conditions, making only half-hearted attempts to organize the so-called "unorganizable" – women, African Americans and the newest immigrants (often **Latinos**; see **Chavez, Cesar**). It remained detached from the civil-rights and anti-Vietnam War movements of the 1960s. It was also associated in many people's minds with corruption, particularly the splinter Teamsters under Jimmy **Hoffa**, the Longshoremen, whose corruption was highlighted in *On the Waterfront* (1954), and the United Mine Workers, whose internal corruption was a background for the vivid strike documentary *Harlan County, USA* (1977).

The 1970s witnessed a concerted effort by the AFL-CIO both to reform and to expand the trade-union movement. The latter impulse was nicely captured on screen in *Norma Rae* (1979), based on the efforts of a Southern woman textile worker and a Northeastern Jewish labor organizer to organize a mill whose owners had successfully resisted unionization for decades. Any momentum in this direction was halted by the election of **Reagan** to the presidency (partly due to the support of working-class Democrats) and the ensuing efforts of the **Republican Party** to once again weaken the labor movement. This assault on unionism was most evident in the **air-traffic controllers' strike** of 1981, during which Reagan laid off 11,000 PATCO workers, replacing them with strike breakers.

During the 1980s and 1990s, particular unions remained strong, especially those serving the more skilled, professional "middle-class" workers, such as teachers and airline pilots, as well as those in public-sector organizing. Nonetheless, the overall movement as a whole has continued to decline and now fewer than 20 percent of all workers belong to unions. The Democratic Party has retained the support of the union movement, especially the leadership, although workers still have rallied to Republican issues. Yet, the decline in union membership, the movement of many industries abroad (to countries where the union movement is weaker still) and the loss of majority status for Democrats in Congress has diminished the union movement's political influence dramatically. This was witnessed in the passage of **NAFTA** in spite of vociferous opposition from trade unionists, as well as the concessions on salary and other issues that have become a constant part of contract negotiations. This malaise permeates a more recent documentary on a union city, Michael Moore's *Roger and Me* (1989).

The future of the union movement in the US and its ability to reverse the decline in its fortunes over the last twenty years will be determined by its ability to adjust to the rapidly changing economic environment. The continuing influx of immigrant labor, increasingly rapid changes in the workplace (with larger proportions of Americans now working outside factories and employed in the service sector), the movement of capital to offshore sites, as well as the growing influence of trade organizations like the World Trade Organization, present problems and opportunities for a trade-union movement that has seen reverses before only to re-emerge as a major force in American politics and society.

See also: mining

Further reading

Bell, T. (1991) *Out of this Furnace*, Pittsburgh: University of Pittsburgh Press.

Docherty, J. (1996) *Historical Dictionary of Organized Labor*, Lanham: Scarecrow Press.

Fraser, S. and Gerstle, G. (1989) *The Rise and Fall of the New Deal Order*, Princeton: Princeton University Press.

Montgomery, D. (1979) *Workers Control in America*, New York: Cambridge University Press.

ROBERT GREGG

unions, public sector

Labor organizations of employees who work for government agencies have grown and proliferated since World War II. After 1970, as the private economy shifted its orientation from industrial to white-collar and **service sector** employment, and non-union and foreign competition erupted, traditional union membership plummeted, while public employment and public sector unions grew rapidly. By the end of the 1980s, less than 17 percent of American workers were organized, yet in some **cities**, 90 percent of public workers were represented by unions. Some are conventional unions, while others are professional organizations that have evolved from civil service associations or police fraternal organizations. They have substantial **African American** and **Latino** membership, many of whom are employed as teachers in **public schools** and **nurses** in public health.

Although the right to organize for federal and almost all state and local employees is protected by law, public sector unions and employees are often precluded from striking by federal and state laws. Punishments include fines levied against unions and individual strikers, dismissal of strikers and imprisonment of union leaders. Restrictions on public employee strikes have been justified under legal theories that emphasize state sovereignty and the governmental duty to protect the general welfare, public health and safety, and by the essential nature of transit, health, sanitation, fire fighting and police services. Demands continue for selective limitations on strikes, since employees performing similar functions in private industry may strike and many public employees, for example, librarians, and workers in state and national parks are not essential to health and safety.

Unlike in some European countries, there is little tolerance in America for strikes, especially by public employees. President Ronald **Reagan**'s 1981 discharge of striking government-employed **air-traffic controllers** crystallized a resurgence of anti-unionism. Because of sanctions and the lack of public support, tactics of temporary slowdowns, sickouts and the threat of strikes have generally replaced actual strikes. Strike threats ensure enormous **mass media** coverage and are usually effective in imposing pressure to bargain effectively and to reach contract settlements before deadlines.

Public sector unions have learned that they can succeed by exercising political power and applying their resources to influence public opinion. Most were strong supporters of the **Civil Rights movement**. **Martin Luther King, Jr**. was assassinated while in Memphis to support a sanitation workers' strike. More recently, teachers unions have led the opposition to school vouchers. Generally favoring liberal **Democratic Party** positions, they use **lobbyists**, research publications, political contributions, members as campaign workers, and members voting power to influence elections and the decisions of politicians who control the appropriations and budgets on which public employee salaries and benefits depend. Adversaries, in turn, brand them as special interest groups seeking narrow gains incompatible with the welfare of the public their members serve.

Further reading

Aronowitz, S. (1998) *From the Ashes of the Old: American Labor and American's Future*, Boston: Houghton Mifflin.
Galenson, W. (1996) *The American Labor Movement, 1955–1995*, Westport: Greenwood.

JAMES KRAUS

Unitarian Universalist Association

Religious community formed by the 1961 merger of the Universalists (founded 1793) and Unitarians (founded 1825). Eschewing creeds and keeping a remarkably open mind on any religious questions (sometimes to the confusion of outsiders), UU churches and their 215,000 members have also been deeply associated with liberal social and cultural movements.

GARY McDONOGH

United Nations

Although founded in the US as a successor to the League of Nations (which the US had not joined) and headquartered beside **New York** City, NY's East River, the UN has often faced problems and divisions within the US. Conservatives like the **John Birch Society** and others on the **Right** have rejected any implications of global sovereignty while interventionist **presidents** have chafed under its restrictions and censure on military actions or debates over **China** and the **Middle East**. The US has also become a notable delinquent in dues, representing both rejection and criticism of the UN.

GARY McDONOGH

Updike, John

b. 1932

Updike is one of an increasingly rare number of American twentieth-century writers who manages to combine some degree of popular success with serious critical attention. Although also an accomplished essayist and a poet, his fame primarily derives from his work as a novelist. One of his most successful fictional creations was former high-school basketball star and small-town businessman Harry "Rabbit" Angstrom, the hero of four different novels. Congenitally unfaithful and proudly unreflective, difficult to truly dislike in his essential innocence, Rabbit often seemed to personify Updike's notion of America in the last decades of the twentieth century. While sometimes criticized for too narrow a focus, at his best Updike uses his considerable lyrical gifts to fashion a complex anthropological picture of a large segment of America – **suburban**, **white**, upper **middle class** and Protestant – coming to grips with the possibility of its decline.

MARK BREWIN

upper class

From the early Republic, America has touted itself as a land without kings or nobles, however patrician the Founding Fathers might be in education, holdings and connections. Throughout American history, the idea of dominant groups able to reproduce its control of wealth and power over generations has been a cause for alarm. Muckraking studies by Gustavus Myers and Ferdinand Lundberg and populist rhetoric decried any attempt to publicly condone the existence of an American upper class. Yet, the ability to rise to wealth is central to the American dream, whether embodied in Benjamin Franklin, John D. **Rockefeller**, Oprah **Winfrey**, Bill **Gates** or Vito Corleone. The tension between social mobility and social reproduction produces a convoluted discourse of perhaps nowhere more tortured than in describing an American upper class.

In fact, euphemisms underscore this ambivalence. Since the Second World War, for example, it has been easy to talk about "elites" in a way that conveys a synergy of expertise, intelligence or even style rather than a substrate of mere wealth; or scholars divide "political," "economic," "social" and "intellectual" elites as if these were parallel categories. Popular American sociology has also focused on status – and the markers of status that permeate consumerism in the late twentieth/early twenty-first century, when Gucci can be bought at outlet malls – rather than a Marxist analysis of power, which often has held sway among academics.

Such elites are also divided by race and ethnicity. Jewish, Catholic and **African Amer-ican** elites – whether defined by political power, cultural presence or wealth – have established separate institutions, family associations and even vacation spots. While there are some indications of coalescence in government, corporations and other institutions, these families also underscore the general WASPish cast of American elites. Gender, too, has played a role – women's positions have tended to be defined socially rather than politically or economically; not as founders or managers of wealth and power, but instead as mediators like Eleanor **Roosevelt** in relation to Franklin **Roosevelt**.

In the end, though, whether looking at tax reforms, **Ivy League** alumni publications or presidential politics, America has an upper class that Americans are ashamed to talk about. One way of avoiding this is through a belief in circulation of wealth – "Old Money" slowly disappears over time, "shirt sleeves to shirt sleeves in three generations." While Puritan Boston seems distant, however, one notes that institutions like Harvard and family lines and foundations have continued over centuries. New money becomes old – Dupont, Rockefeller, Ford and Mellon – through shared political economic interests and shared social and cultural institutions. **Education**, **marriage**, patronage and **foundations** all mingle economic and cultural capital – one need only think of universities bearing names like Johns Hopkins (Quaker merchant), Vanderbilt (shipping), or Duke (tobacco).

This does not deny new resources, industries and opportunities – trade, oil and tobacco have given way over time to finance, computers and media. Hence, names like Gates, Annenberg, **Turner**, **Spielberg**, **Trump** and Eisner, among others, control resources, fame and increasing attributes of older upper classes, including roles of civic patronage, foundations and public service. Relations of power, money and celebrity in politics also underscore meshings of elites. Indeed, can upper classes be defined in national terms, given multinational corporate interests and cultural ties? Can Rupert Murdoch belong to the American upper class? His descendants? Issues from taxation to battles over government control of resources like media and computers to definitions of "approved" places, pedigrees and behaviors continue to bridge from old to new. Indeed, they suggest interesting questions that should be addressed to subsequent generations of new wealth and the reconstitution of upper classes.

Further reading

Fussell, P. (1983) *Class*, New York: Summit.

Mills, C.W. (1956) *The Power Elite*, New York: Oxford University Press.

GARY McDONOGH

urban planning

The term "urban planning" can be said to refer to a wide range of city-oriented activities: what planners do; what planners say they do; what citizens do to plan their cities; the process by which comprehensive plans are produced; and what planning schools teach. These activities can be quite different, yet all are facets of the ongoing creation of American cities.

Planning involves an understanding of the concept of "city," as well the underlying social and governmental processes that shape a city. Its practice entails establishing goals and objectives, developing and evaluating alternatives for attaining those goals and selecting an appropriate course of action. This process is viewed by some as primarily "rational," based in the scientific method, by others as primarily political, and by others still as a combination of the two. Differences in these viewpoints are reflected in professional practice. Some planners emphasize professional expertise while others emphasize organizing, interaction and consensus building. American planning has evolved from a focus on development of the physical plan (City Beautiful) in the first half of the twentieth century to an emphasis on analytical modes in the 1960s and 1970s. Communicative and collaborative modes dominated the 1980s and 1990s.

The focus of modern urban planning up to the 1960s was the "comprehensive plan," of which the centerpiece was the "image" or "form" of the city. Plans were created by governmental entities to address rapid growth by implementing changes in physical, social and economic patterns. Viewed by some as a mechanism of control over development, planning was viewed by others as a process for balancing competing private and public interests, or addressing pressing problems such as inner-city decay, transportation, pollution and housing.

Pre-1960s planning was typically a government-controlled, centralized process that was later found to be inadequate for dealing with issues like transportation that transcended urban boundaries, for achieving public support, or adapting to the rapidly changing and uncertain conditions of the cities. Although the last two decades of city planning emphasized procedural activities and planner–stakeholder interactions, some suggest that a renewed interest in urban design has sparked a revival in the image of the city and the plan.

Today, public participation is mandated by law in most planning activities. This entails bringing more and new players into the planning process, transferring power from government representatives to citizens and re-defining planning in ways that often defy the bounds of a traditional academic discipline or profession. These idiosyncrasies notwithstanding, planning can be said to distinguish itself from other disciplines by including some or all of these themes: (1) improvement of human environments; (2) forging interconnections among various sectors; (3) consideration of the future; (4) consideration of equity issues; (5) public participation; and (6) linking knowledge and action (Myers 1997).

See also: cities; urban renewal

Further reading

Hoch, C. (1994) *What Planners Do: Power, Politics and Persuasion*, Chicago: Planners Press.

Myers, D. (1997) "Anchor Points for Planning's Identification," *Journal of Planning Education and Research* 16: 223–4.

Neuman, M. (1998) "Planning, Governing, and the Image of the City," *Journal of Planning Education and Research* 18: 61–71.

BERYL FERNANDES

urban renewal

Refers, on one level, to a specific series of federal acts and programs enabling radical replanning of the physical fabric of American cities. In a broader cultural sense, urban renewal stands for a political movement and cultural attitude towards the redevelopment of old, dense **cities** and their new, predominantly **African American** inhabitants after the Second World War. It was one of the more cataclysmic eruptions of a longstanding American fear and hatred of the big city. Urban renewal was the planning end of modern **architecture** that despised the nineteenth-century city – its crowds and historic buildings, its dirt and disease – and sought to replace it with a new, logical and planned system of urban living.

The "origin" of urban renewal is often tied to the passing of the 1949 Housing Act, which authorized the radical demolition of whole areas of central cities to make way for **highways** and new housing. In fact, fifty years previously, the City Beautiful movement, Progressive Era slum clearance and urban park reforms had created precedents. Federal and **state** powers were harnessed to demolish aging and crowded housing stock, creating a cleaner and more efficient place for business (which widely endorsed the remaking of downtowns), and making the city more amenable to the increasingly dominant automobile. Urban renewal was also put to a distinct social purpose: establishing *de facto* walls, in the form of highways and public buildings, between growing African American districts and white **neighborhoods** and downtowns. Despite its messianic overtones,

urban renewal was also a code word for "Negro removal."

Urban renewal's destructive impact on cities quickly led to a counter-movement, most articulately presented in two seminal works. Jane Jacobs' *Death and Life of Great American Cities* (1961) celebrated the very old, complex neighborhoods which urban-renewal planners sought to eradicate. Against the aerial view of cities, which urban renewal presupposed, Jacobs looked at the view from the street and found something remarkable: the "blighted" (the favorite term of urban renewal) neighborhoods were in fact good places in which to live. Robert Caro, in his massive *The Powerbroker: Robert Moses and the Fall of New York* (1974), portrayed urban renewal, as embodied in Robert Moses, the primary builder of every public work in postwar New York City and region, as anti-democratic, destructive of good communities and racist. The demolition of the massive Pruitt-Igoe housing complex in **St. Louis, MO** in 1973, only eighteen years after it was built along orthodox urban-renewal models, has become a convenient date to mark the end of the movement.

MAX PAGE

USA Today *see* newspapers

USSR *see* Russia; Cold War

V

vacation Bible camps

Summer child-education programs, generally under the aegis of Protestant and fundamentalist churches. They occupy the space of secular camps and daycare, but focus on religious training, including memorization of the Bible, plays, prayer and games. They are often associated with the Southern evangelical tradition, although they have been adapted to wider circumstances, including the pressing need for summer care in working families.

GARY McDONOGH

Valens, Richie

b. 1941; d. 1959

Born Richard Valenzuela in the San Fernando Valley, Valens died before he could realize his full potential as a **rock 'n' roller** before his eighteenth birthday. His first single, "Come On, Let's Go," recorded when he was 17, was a western regional hit in 1958. Later that year the ballad "Donna" reached number two on the charts. Valens' fame would rest ultimately on the flipside, the traditional Latin party song "La Bamba." Valens died in a plane crash on his first major US tour with Buddy Holly and J.P. Richardson (the Big Bopper).

DEWAR MACLEOD

variety shows, television

Combinations of multiple acts – singing, dancing, comedy and drama – strung together by a genial host like Milton Berle linked early television to Vaudeville and radio. In subsequent decades, variety shows have gone through cycles of popularity and innovation as well as decline in the 1990s.

Ed Sullivan, who moved from Broadway columnist to famously wooden host, created the classic variety show (*Toast of the Town*, CBS 1948–55; *The Ed Sullivan Show*, 1956–71). While known for bizarre juxtapositions – "Next Week, the Beatles and the Pietà" – Sullivan also showcased Elvis **Presley**, **Broadway**, Vaudevillians and emergent black performers between acrobats and hand puppets. Other classic early shows include the *Ernie Kovacs Show* (various networks), *Your Show of Shows* (NBC, 1954–7) and the long-running *Tonight Show* (see **late-night television**).

Subsequent shows have tended to use comedy or music as a skeleton for skits and spotlight appearances. While white male-dominated, variety shows' eclecticism has created mass media entrée for African American performers, including hosts Nat King Cole, Sammy Davis, Jr. and Flip Wilson, who had their own shows from the 1950s through the 1970s. Strong women like female comedian Carol Burnett (CBS, 1967–78) also have made their mark.

Other shows marketed **Las Vegas, NV** (Dean

Martin), **rock** (Hullabaloo), **Nashville** (Hee-Haw) and puppets (the ***Muppet*** shows). Variety shows nonetheless rarely looked beyond Americans and occasional British celebrities (until the arrival of cable chains like Univision). Meanwhile, linkages of television to other fields have fostered guest spotlights to promote film, music and celebrity sports.

Given television's orientation towards mass audiences, variety-show comedy is often tame, involving take-offs on television or movies or suggestive soundbites like those of the rapid-fire Rowan and Martin *Laugh-in* (NBC, 1968–73). Political humor did appear in the 1960s with the short-lived satirical review *That Was the Week that Was* (NBC, 1964–5). Later, the controversial *Smother's Brothers Comedy Hour* (CBS, 1965–7) brought countercultural performers on screen while attacking the **Vietnam War** and other sensitive issues before CBS pulled the plug. Sexual **humor** was more controlled but safe, although Flip Wilson (NBC, 1970–4) challenged categories of gender and propriety. Other variety shows, in fact, promoted the merging of politics and entertainment – Richard **Nixon** appeared on *Laugh-In*, while Bill **Clinton** campaigned on late-night shows. Sonny Bono, who moved from music to variety shows with wife Cher, later became a mayor and a member of **Congress**.

In the 1990s, variety shows seem to have played out their popularity, except for late-night viewers. *Saturday Night Live*, begun in the 1970s, offers a hip sensibility in ensemble television that has produced star comics for the baby boomers and **Generation X**, with hot musicians and guest hosts ranging from Joe Namath to Jesse **Jackson**. Despite this network decline, **MTV**, **cable** television networks like E! and even **talk shows** have picked up some of the elements that made variety shows a showcase, nursery and sales department for American entertainment.

GARY McDONOGH

V-chip

A technical device that supposedly allows parents to control their **children**'s TV-watching activities by screening out undesirable programs. The 1996 Telecommunication Act mandated that all TVs manufactured after January 1, 2000 need to be equipped with the V-chip (V stands for either violence or veto). This goes hand-in-hand with the requirement that broadcasters (not cable operators) establish a rating system for objectionable programming. This allows the conservatives to claim victory over the decaying media culture, and put the burden of TV censorship into the hands of the parents, i.e. the public/consumer, not the producers.

CINDY WONG

Venturi, Robert

b. 1925

Architect, theorist and forerunner of **postmodernism**. Venturi broke the spell of **modernism** with his controversial book *Complexity and Contradiction in Architecture* (1966) and later *Learning from Las Vegas* (1972). Winner of the Rome Prize in Architecture (1954), Venturi looked to history and the vernacular in his designs, as exemplified in his Vanna Venturi House (1963). He also designed the Sainsbury Wing of the National Gallery, London (1986), and the **Seattle** Art Museum (1991). Venturi, based in **Philadelphia** in partnership with architect and wife Denise Scott Brown, has expanded his designs with a series of furniture.

ISABEL KRIEGEL

veterans

Like other nations that have engaged in the bloody wars of the twentieth century, the United States honors those who have risked their lives for their country. Official **holidays** of remembrance for those who saw combat in the armed forces include Veteran's Day, November 11, commemorating the armistice ending of World War I, and Memorial Day, in May. Meanwhile, politicians of the post-Second World War era, especially, have used their status as veterans to help catapult them into positions of importance in **Congress** or the **presidency** (e.g. **Eisenhower**, **Kennedy** and

Bush). John McCain's surprise performance in the 2000 **Republican** primaries owed a great deal to the candidate's experiences as a **navy** pilot and **POW** in Vietnam, which gave him a degree of gravitas not shared by his younger and non-veteran opponent.

In a country reluctant to provide social **welfare** benefits to its citizens, the reverence paid to veterans is shown by the support available to them since the Civil War. Indeed, one of the largest departments in the federal government, given Cabinet status by **Reagan** in 1988, is Veterans Affairs (VA), which coordinates a range of benefits from provision of housing and education loans, healthcare and funeral assistance (including burial in specially designated cemeteries). Eligibility for veterans' benefits requires ninety days of active service in combat or two years of enlistment, and discharge or release from active duty under conditions that are not in any way dishonorable. Those in the Reserve or National Guard currently (Congress must extend eligibility past 2003) need to complete a total of six years to receive the same benefits.

These benefits were dramatically increased by President **Roosevelt** in the **GI Bill** of 1944, intended to counteract the problem of readjustment many veterans returning from the First World War had faced (including great class turmoil). The GI Bill helped fundamentally to alter American society. When the Department of Veterans Affairs was established in 1930, there were 4.7 million veterans alive, and the department ran fifty-four hospitals around the country with as many as 31,600 employees. By 1993 the number of employees at the VA had grown to over 266,000; only the Department of Defense is a larger federal agency.

That the readjustment act reflected reverence for veterans, needs some qualification. Indeed, the emergence of the VA occurred at a time when many veterans were facing considerable hostility. Those who came back from fighting "to make the world safe for democracy," and complained that the war had not done so, faced the vigilantism of the American Legion, with its 100 percent Americanism campaigns. Further, while the Second World War was "The Good War" and most veterans were welcomed home (although **Wyler**'s *Best Years of Our Lives*, 1946, challenges this), the

Korean conflict became a protracted "police action" and many veterans returning from the "Forgotten War" felt that their struggles were neglected. The greatest hostility met those who fought in Vietnam, as the popularity of the war waned and as atrocities came to light. Vietnam veterans often felt reviled. In addition, fighting in conditions for which they often were not prepared, sensing the futility in the way the **Pentagon** prosecuted the war, they often suffered acute difficulties overcoming the trauma of their frontline experiences. Media depictions of the crazed or addicted Vietnam vet became ubiquitous during the 1980s. Meanwhile, the *Rambo* movies suggested that the Vets themselves would have been able to take care of the Vietcong and/or rescue MIAs (missing in action) and POWs (prisioners of war), if the government had let them.

African Americans and other minorities (including female veterans, for whom the VA hospitals were unprepared) often were not revered alongside white veterans, whether or not the war was popular. A frequent cause of the lynching of African Americans in the **South** was the treatment meted out to the returning soldier. Nor did African Americans generally reap the benefits from the GI Bill, since they could not buy newly constructed **suburban** houses. The prominence of African American soldiers in the armed forces in **Grenada**, **Panama** and the Gulf, however, has begun to change this experience.

See also: Gulf War Syndrome

ROBERT GREGG

Viagra

The pharmaceutical company Pfizer hit the big time with Viagra (sildenafil citrate), finding what it proclaimed to be the cure for erectile dysfunction, a problem which may affect as many as 30 million Americans. The drug, administered in tablet form, essentially increases blood flow to the penis enabling a man to have an erection. By 2000, the drug had been prescribed to over 5 million men in the United States, and its use had spread worldwide. Part of its fame resulted from its stint as a staple for late-night comedy and also from former presidential candidate Robert **Dole**'s declaration that he benefited from the drug.

ROBERT GREGG

vice-presidency

In the last fifty years, and especially during the most recent presidential administrations, the office of the vice-president has grown from a position of relative powerlessness to one of some importance. The vice-president's official responsibilities are few: should the president die or be deemed unable to fill his or her position, the vice-president takes on the role of president; the vice-president is also the official head of the Senate and has the power to cast a tie-breaking vote. In recent times, however, presidents have begun to allow their vice-presidents to become more involved in the policy process and have allowed them greater access to White House resources.

The vice-president now meets often with the president, has an office in the White House and a staff of his or her own. Although these are privileges granted by the president and could be removed at any time, the likelihood that this will happen decreases as the practices become more institutionalized. It has been suggested that the fact that these privileges were retained during the tenure of Dan Quayle (George **Bush**'s vice-president), who was widely regarded as a poor choice for the job, indicates their likely permanence.

The manner and method of choosing the vice-president have also changed over the years. For almost the whole first half of the twentieth century, vice-presidential candidates were chosen by party bosses. This changed in 1940 when Franklin **Roosevelt** insisted on choosing his own running-mate. This practice has remained in place allowing presidents to choose vice-presidents with whom they are compatible. Before this time, it was not unusual for vice-presidents to disagree openly with presidents under whom they were serving; it is almost unheard of today. The greater compatibility between vice-president and president has also facilitated the expansion of the vice-president's powers and responsibilities.

Many vice-presidents have gone on to run successfully for the presidency. Holding the office of vice-president can aid a politician by providing national name recognition and executive experience; however, there are also drawbacks. Because vice-presidents are expected to support the president, it can be difficult for them to create their own political identity in the eyes of the public. It was widely believed that George Bush suffered from this problem. Although **Reagan** was very popular, Bush was often regarded as unable to form opinions independent of the president. Matters became even more complex as questions arose regarding Bush's role in the **Iran-Contra affair**. Al **Gore**, who has longstanding presidential ambitions, has faced a similar dilemma in dealing with the scandals surrounding Bill **Clinton**; he had to support the president while distancing himself from Clinton's actions. This balance is difficult to maintain and can make it especially difficult for former vice-presidents to run for president.

Further reading

Pika, J. (1998) "The Vice Presidency: New Opportunities, Old Constraints," in M. Nelson (ed.) *The Presidency and the Political System*, Washington, DC: Congressional Quarterly Press, pp. 527–64.

EMILY CLOUGH

Vidal, Gore (Eugene Luther)

b. 1925

Patrician chronicler, playwright and critic of the American century. Vidal has skewered politics, sexuality and religion in novels and essays, identifying himself with the historical establishment through family ties, yet standing outside it through his wit, homosexuality and preferences for Europe. *The City and the Pillar* (1948) shocked readers with its discussion of homosexuality, while in *Myra Breckinridge* (1968) the sexual/media satire is broad. *Messiah* (1954) tackles American religion. Historical novels, including *Burr* (1973), *Lincoln* (1984), *Hollywood* (1990) and *The Smithsonian Institution* (1998) recast American history. Vidal, who twice ran for

Congress, has published extensively as a liberal political critic and essayist on American sexuality (*Gore Vidal, Sexually Speaking*, 1999).

GARY McDONOGH

video

The portable consumer video cameras that came out in the late 1970s extended the range of the portable 16mm camera that had allowed cinéma vérité to flourish. Unlike film cameras, video cameras first used analog, and then digital, technologies to capture sound and image, dramatically lowering the price of footage and potentially democratizing production as well as distribution of moving images. On the other hand, the moving-image industries also incorporated new video delivery systems to reach an even larger audience, through **video cassette recorders**, **cable** and satellite.

The availability of cheap video technology in the 1970s allowed average lay people to produce moving images. Many more families have home videos now, even though their content differs little from previous 8mm home movies, except for accessibility. While most associated video in America with the VHS cassette, other formats have been used by professionals or independents. Hence, there was euphoria when the U-Matic was introduced with good quality BetaSP tape. More "prosumer" models followed, including 8mm, high-8 and super VHS; all are analog videotapes.

The digital age arrived in the mid-1990s, further improving the quality of the image and sound of the taped event. The camera became cheaper, smaller, even more portable. With digital technology, nonlinear editing becomes more accessible as well.

On the industrial side, digital technology has helped made *Titanic* a success, as well as creating other works from *Toy Story* to the *Matrix*. More and more films are now edited first in video rather than film.

With the development of the **Internet**, video technology has found a new channel for distribution and exhibition. It can be both broadcast, reaching whoever hits the site, or narrowcast,

where only the target audience will be reached. Technology is developing quickly so that the quality of cyber-video constantly improves both in resolution and the time needed to transmit images.

We cannot fully understand the implication of these new technologies for the production and transmission of moving images and sound without placing them in the basic cultural and economic landscape of the US. When new, better quality, cheaper, more accessible technologies arrive, different people in society will find diverse uses for them, be it portable video or digital nonlinear editing systems. Lay people shoot home videos, activists make community/advocacy works, artists create avant-garde works and George **Lucas** makes Hollywood **blockbusters**. In the US, while all these possibilities coexist, the commercial broadcasting and entertainment systems inevitably devise ways to make the most profitable use of the medium.

Hence, home video stays at home, while consumer camera sales go up. Activists can use video to create community and have their messages heard, but are confined to limited constituents. Artists will find small grants and museums open to their new pursuits. **Hollywood** will have the best machine to produce the most expensive images, mesmerizing the audience with the mystique of technologies. The Internet sites that get the most hits mean bigger companies and the richest Internet companies will have the largest capacities for the transmission of video data in cyberspace. The marketplace is not only an economic phenomenon, but also a cultural one. Technologies are intertwined with the market, channeling money, talent and other resources, and benefiting the owners of the means of such production and distribution.

CINDY WONG

video cassette recorder (VCR)

After the VCR was introduced to the American mass market in the mid-1970s, the home entertainment options for many Americans were greatly expanded. In combination with the emergence of **cable** television and satellite, the VCR initially seemed to pose a substantial threat to the dominance of **network** television and movie theaters. The VCR not only enables viewers to rent movies that they can watch comfortably in their own homes, it also allows them to record programs from television, allowing greater flexibility in terms of viewing schedules. Renting videos is less expensive than the cost of a ticket (or multiple tickets) at a movie theater. Hence, the VCR has also transformed the film industry – film producers now make the most of their profits from **video** rentals (even in cases when films are quite successful at the box office). By the mid-1990s, over 86 percent of American households owned a VCR.

The VCR is not the last word on home entertainment, however. Films are also available on laser-discs and DVDs (digital video discs or digital versatile discs). These technologies promise to transform once again the home viewing experience. Laser-discs have been available in the United States since the late 1970s, but they never became popular. They are cumbersome and can only contain approximately 1 hour of material per side. Laserdiscs also have analog video components (like videotapes) so they suffer from some generational degradation. DVDs, on the other hand (available since 1996), hold more promise. They are digital, and therefore suffer very little generational degradation, and are comparable in quality to studio masters. They are also much smaller than laser-discs, and can contain up to 4 hours of material (8 hours if both sides are used). Both laser-discs and DVDs have features that videotapes do not have (such as scan and search functions), but only DVD is capable of interactivity. While all these new technologies allow consumers to have control over the time and space of the consumption of media goods, the goods are still primarily produced by **Hollywood**, allowing the New Hollywood to demand ever-increasing market share in the US and abroad.

Further reading

Nmungwun, A. (1989) *Video Recording Technology*, Hillsdale: Lawrence Erlbaum Associates.

Taylor, J. (1998) *DVD Demystified*, New York: McGraw-Hill.

NICOLE MARIE KEATING

Vietnamese Americans

After the fall of Saigon in 1975, many Vietnamese fled their homeland. Over 900,000 **refugees** arrived in the US from Southeast Asia between 1975 and 1989, most of them from Vietnam, although many had passed through refugee camps and horrifying voyages as boat people. When they first arrived, most Vietnamese refugees were received warmly by different religious and social agencies, although this often isolated them from their country people. More than 30 percent settled in **California**, with other substantial numbers in **Texas**, Washington, New York, Minnesota and Massachusetts. Because of their recent arrival, Vietnamese Americans have the largest (90 percent) foreign-born population in the country.

Many Vietnamese Americans are ethnic minorities in Vietnam, including the Cham, the Khmer, the Montagnards and the Chinese. While the first three groups did not already have significant presence in America, the Chinese Vietnamese could immerse themselves in the established Chinese American communities. With the influx of this population, many Chinatown businesses are now owned by Vietnamese Chinese immigrants.

Despite the cultural impact of Vietnamese Americans, such as Maya Lin, who designed the once-controversial **Vietnam War Memorial** on the Washington mall, and film-maker Trin T. Min-Ha, who explored Vietnamese and American women's identities in her *Surname Viet, Given Name Nam* (1989), others have struggled to make sense of the rapid and painful adjustments of their displacement. **Gang** activity, portrayed in the 1994 film *Bui Dai* and in less sympathetic media, is one image of difficulties within the generally "model immigrant" **Asian American** community.

The shadow of the **Vietnam War** also hangs over relations between the US and the changing homeland of Vietnamese Americans, as well as disputes occurring between Vietnamese Americans from historically different regions that became the North and the South. In 1999, for example, when an Orange County (California) Vietnamese videostore-owner put up a picture of Ho Chi Minh in the store, widespread demonstrations and boycotts followed.

Further reading

Kibria, N. (1993) *Family Tightrope: The Changing Lives of Vietnamese Americans*, Princeton: Princeton University.

Rutledge, P. (1992) *The Vietnamese Experience in America*, Bloomington: Indiana University.

CINDY WONG

Vietnam memorials

After the fall of Saigon in May 1975, most Americans wanted to forget the **Vietnam War** and the servicemen who had fought there for sixteen years. Inspired by the film *The Deerhunter* (1978), Jan Scruggs formed the Vietnam Veterans Memorial Fund, which sponsored a design search for a memorial for this difficult war. Maya Lin, an **architecture** student at Yale, submitted the winning design: a black granite V-shaped wall nestled in the ground below the Lincoln Memorial in Washington, DC, which both bears the names of over 58,000 American dead and reflects the faces of those who look at "the Wall." Although some **veterans** and administration officials considered the memorial insufficiently heroic, after its 1982 consecration "the Wall" quickly became a place of remembrance and catharsis for civilians and veterans, with people leaving gifts and letters for lost comrades and family members.

MELINDA SCHWENK

Vietnam Syndrome

The US catastrophe in Vietnam gave rise to the popular belief in the 1970s that presidents would hesitate to commit American troops abroad again, fearing the indignation of electorates if they became embroiled in wars and once body bags returned with American GIs. This syndrome, if it ever contributed to military inaction, was certainly short-lived. Within five years of the end of the Vietnam War, American troops were being sent into action in **Grenada**, and all presidents after Carter would commit troops abroad.

A more realistic syndrome reflects an inducement to throw caution to the wind in international affairs. George **Bush** endeavored to counter the "wimp factor" by using force on several occasions, while Bill **Clinton**, who had the charge of being a draft dodger made against him during the 1992 election, proved more willing to commit American forces than any other president. After trouncing Saddam Hussein in 1991, Bush announced that Americans had "kicked the Vietnam syndrome once and for all." But the syndrome (as with much of the war itself) concerns credibility, something that cannot be kicked.

ROBERT GREGG

Vietnam War

The Vietnam War was a pivotal turning point in American history. If the Second World War marked the apogee of American power in "America's Century," Vietnam emphasized the limits of that power. America had long believed itself an exceptional nation, the world's exemplar of democracy, freedom, individualism, Christianity and all-round moral superiority. More than any other event, the Vietnam War presented a monumental challenge to those beliefs and provoked a marked erosion of America's sense of innocence and infallibility.

Background

Vietnam has fought for survival through much of its existence. For several millennia the main danger came from **China**. In the nineteenth century, a weak and divided Vietnam faced a new threat, European imperialism, and was easily conquered by France. Vietnam's history of resistance to China made it an intractable colony, however. A young exile who would become known as Ho Chi Minh became the acknowledged leader of an active Vietnamese independence movement after pleading that cause at the Versailles Conference in 1919.

When diplomatic efforts to gain support for Vietnamese independence failed, Ho Chi Minh turned to the Soviet Union, became a communist and started developing an organization, known as the Vietminh, to overthrow the French by force.

When **Japan** seized Vietnam during the Second World War the Vietminh had a new enemy and cooperated with the OSS (predecessor to the **CIA**) in fighting the Japanese. When the war ended, Ho Chi Minh issued a declaration of independence and hoped for American support in preserving Vietnam's independence under his control.

Those hopes were dashed. The US was preoccupied with other matters. France reoccupied Vietnam, and the Vietminh launched a bloody, ten-year war to drive the French from their country. That effort seemed successful when, after increasing opposition at home to "*le guerre sale*" ("the dirty war") and a disastrous defeat at Dienbienphu in 1954, France withdrew from Vietnam.

Once again, Ho Chi Minh's dream proved elusive. As the **Cold War** heated up, the US increasingly viewed Ho as an agent of global **communism**. After the outbreak of the **Korean War**, Harry **Truman** and Dwight D. **Eisenhower** heavily subsidized the French war. When France withdrew, the US took up the mantle. The Geneva Agreement negotiating France's withdrawal provided for a temporary division of Vietnam as a prelude to nationwide elections and unification. The Vietminh controlled the northern half of the country. The remnant French government in the southern half was led by Ngo Dinh Diem. With US support, Diem cancelled the elections and began the creation of a separate South Vietnam.

Diem's government was unpopular, repressive and dictatorial. An internal opposition movement, the National Liberation Front (NLF, informally known as the Vietcong), developed with covert support from North Vietnam. Eisenhower and John F. **Kennedy** sent more than 16,000 military "advisors," some of whom regularly acted in combat capacities. But despite economic and military aid, Diem continued to lose control of the country. By the early 1960s Vietnam was in crisis. Kennedy made a series of statements that indicated both his reluctance to get more deeply involved in Vietnam and an even greater unwillingness to see South Vietnam fall to communism. Hoping that Diem was the crux of the problem, the US promoted a military coup in November 1963 that overthrew and murdered Diem and his widely despised brother Nhu. (They committed "accidental suicide" in one report.) Three weeks later

Kennedy himself was assassinated. The problem of Vietnam fell into the unfortunate lap of Lyndon **Johnson**.

America's war

Johnson was forced to make decisions that Kennedy had put off. A series of military governments were even less competent and popular than Diem had been. Johnson could abandon South Vietnam and let the communists win, or dramatically increase American involvement. With private *angst* and public bravado, following the advice of former Kennedy advisors, including Robert MacNamara, Dean Rusk and Maxwell Taylor, Johnson chose the latter course.

American action took two primary forms: bombing of opposition forces in the South and of North Vietnam itself; and the introduction of combat troops. A minor naval confrontation in the Tonkin Gulf in August 1964 was exaggerated and fabricated into an international incident, allowing Johnson to obtain, with almost no opposition, congressional authority for military action in lieu of a declaration of war. (When the extent of the deception later became known, the **Gulf of Tonkin** incident became the most famous example of the "credibility gap" – government lying over Vietnam.) Johnson initiated bombing raids against North Vietnam. Combat troops were introduced in March 1965 to protect US air bases and personnel. But, when bombing proved ineffective, William Westmoreland, the new military commander in Vietnam, persuaded Johnson that South Vietnam could only survive with a larger commitment of American soldiers.

Over the next three years Vietnam became increasingly America's war. The bombing campaign turned into the largest in world history, surpassing by several times Allied bombing of Germany and Japan in the Second World War. By 1967 Westmoreland was directing more than 500,000 American troops. Using "search-and-destroy" tactics, the US measured success in terms of "body count," fighting a war of attrition whose object was to kill more enemy than could be infiltrated from the North or recruited in the South. The result was a steady escalation of death and destruction. Perhaps half-a-million enemy troops were killed, along with another half-million civilians. Four to five million South Vietnamese became homeless **refugees**. But the ultimate goals of defeating the enemy and leaving a strong, independent South Vietnam were never reached. The Vietcong and NVA (North Vietnamese army) developed guerrilla warfare tactics to counter US firepower. In the first large-scale confrontation between US and NVA troops, in the Ia Drang Valley in 1965, the NVA killed 240 men of the elite First Air cavalry. Infiltration of troops and supplies down the Ho Chi Minh trail continued unabated, while peasants blamed the destruction of their society on the US and South Vietnamese government, making Vietcong recruitment easier and weakening the government the US was supposed to be supporting.

Tet Offensive and 1968

By 1968 the war was a stalemate. The US had prevented the collapse of South Vietnam, but at a cost of nearly fifty US soldiers killed each day. The price for North Vietnam and the Vietcong was much higher, with no end in sight. The **Tet Offensive** of 1968 was a dramatic effort to break the stalemate. After a diversionary attack on the mountain base of Khe Sanh, the Vietcong broke an informal ceasefire during Vietnam's New Year celebrations with a widespread series of assaults. Despite catching the US unprepared, by almost all accounts the Tet Offensive was a military failure. The departure from hit-and-run guerrilla tactics led to the exposure and destruction of much of the carefully built up Vietcong infrastructure.

Ironically, while the Tet Offensive may have been a military victory for the US, it was a political and public-relations disaster. For three years American officials had confidently foreseen a "light at the end of the tunnel," that the war would soon be over. The Tet Offensive shattered that illusion. During Tet the Vietcong overran the US embassy, a large section of Saigon and all of Hue, the second-largest city of South Vietnam. Tet also provided dramatic, graphic media symbols of the war's futility and brutality: the summary execution in front of television cameras of a Vietcong suspect by a high-ranking South Vietnamese official and a statement by an anonymous American military

official that "it was necessary to destroy the town – Ben Tre – in order to save it." During the edgy aftermath of Tet, Charlie Company under Lieutenant William **Calley** murdered almost 400 innocent, unarmed civilians in the village of My Lai, probably the most gruesome atrocity incident in American military history. After Tet, Walter Cronkite went to Vietnam and came back believing the war was unwinnable. Johnson's most respected advisors, the Wise Men, defected. In the face of a growing antiwar movement and challenges from within his own party, a dejected Johnson announced on March 31 that he was withdrawing from the presidential race.

Nixon and Vietnam

In the wake of Tet, Robert Kennedy's assassination, and widely publicized rioting at the Democratic National Convention in **Chicago, IL**, Richard **Nixon** was elected to the presidency. Vietnam became Nixon's war. He and his chief foreign-policy advisor Henry **Kissinger** had few pretensions to "winning" in Vietnam. Public opposition was growing rapidly, expanding from a small contingent of college students associated with **Students for a Democratic Society (SDS)**. More powerful were congressional opponents, led by Senate Foreign Relations Committee Chairperson William **Fulbright**. A damaging secret history of the war, the **"Pentagon Papers"**, was leaked to the *New York Times*. Military morale was tenuous: drug use was rampant, as were reports of fragging, the killing of unpopular officers by their own men.

Nixon needed peace, but "peace with honor," which meant not obviously losing the war. His solution was "Vietnamization," turning the fighting and dying back to the South Vietnamese, while supporting them with ever-increasing bombing. The war went on for four more years. Almost 30,000 more Americans died, and perhaps another million Vietnamese. But Nixon's plan was politically astute. American troops came home, casualties declined, the draft was ended. The antiwar movement reached a crescendo after Nixon's April 1970 invasion of Cambodia and the National Guard's killing of four students at **Kent State**, then fizzled out.

Nixon was re-elected by a landslide in 1972. Secret negotiations to end the war progressed slowly but inexorably. After mining and blockading North Vietnam's ports, and a final, brutal Christmas bombing campaign, the US and North Vietnam reached an agreement for US withdrawal in early 1973. But the peace agreement turned out to be only a temporary ceasefire. Both sides violated the agreement almost before the ink was dry. Judging that the US would have no stomach for resuming the war in the aftermath of **Watergate** and Nixon's resignation, the NVA/Vietcong renewed the war. In the spring of 1975 South Vietnamese resistance collapsed. Saigon fell in April. Vietnam was reunited, though Ho Chi Minh was no longer alive to see his dream come true. He had died in 1969. But peace had come to Vietnam.

Legacies

The Vietnam War is slowly fading from prominence. But it created deep, long-lasting scars that still plague the country. The war was refought in numerous movies and several television series. The US maintained a diplomatic and economic blockade of Vietnam for more than thirty years after the war ended. The issue of POW/MIAs possibly left behind in Vietnam was wrenchingly emotional, as was the legacy of **Agent Orange** and post-traumatic stress syndrome (PTSS). In Clinton's 1992 presidential campaign, his past as an antiwar "draft dodger" was an issue. Government secrecy and illegal surveillance of antiwar activists by the CIA and **FBI** contributed to the Watergate scandal and **Iran-Contra affair**, and helped promote a pervasive cynicism and distrust of America's government.

Even the legacy of representation of the war reveals these conflicts. Apart from some clichéd patriotic efforts like John **Wayne**'s *Green Berets* (1968), **Hollywood** did not generally depict what **television news** carried live into the home everyday. A series of powerful later movies, however, including *The Deer Hunter* (1978), *Coming Home* (1978) and *Apocalypse Now* (1979) opened up a critical discussion of the war and its pain, followed in the late 1980s by a plethora of compelling films, including Oliver **Stone**'s *Platoon* (1986) and Stanley Kubrick's *Full Metal Jacket* (1987), *Born on the Fourth*

of July (1989) and even a more tender comic perspective in *Good Morning, Vietnam* (1987). This filmic heritage and other representations, including the television series *China Beach* (ABC, 1988–91), have become part of memory, interpretation and healing. Later explorations have even found positions combining experiences of Vietnamese and Americans, like Trinh T. Min-Ha's *Surname Viet, Given Name Nam* (1989) or the 1999 documentary *We Regret to Inform*.

Americans still disagree on the basic meaning of the war. Was it a tragic but unintentional blunder, the result of corrupt and evil politicians and policies, or a "noble cause," a just war that could and should have been won if the politicians and protestors had not lacked the will to win? The black granite "Wall," the **Vietnam memorial** in **Washington, DC**, with the names of more than 58,000 Americans who died in Vietnam, has been a source of healing and unity, but Vietnam still deeply divides Americans. It was surely one of the most important, complex and controversial events in shaping contemporary American culture.

Further reading

Herring, G. (1996) *America's Longest War*, New York: McGraw-Hill.

Karnow, S. (1983) *Vietnam: A History*, New York: Viking.

Olson, J. (ed.) (1987) *Dictionary of the Vietnam War*, Westport: Greenwood.

Wells, T. (1994) *The War Within*, New York: Henry Holt.

Olson, J. and Roberts, R. (1991) *Where the Domino Fell*, New York: St Martins.

KENT BLASER

violence

Discussions of violence often distinguish between two different dimensions: personal crimes and group violence. The first includes such activities as murder, molestation, robbery, rape and assault, while the latter refers to riots, **gang** warfare, conflicts between labor movements and the **police**, **lynchings**, terrorism and political uprisings. Although this is a plausible method of classification, there are violent acts not easily placed into one category or another; for example the Kennedy **assassination** (1963) or the mass suicide at Jonestown. Moreover, there is frequently a complex interplay between these two dimensions that increases the difficulty of making clear-cut divisions.

The overall rate of personal crime reached a century low period in the mid-1950s and then began a relatively steady climb, peaking in the 1980s and then beginning a steady downward trend for most of the 1990s. Despite the fluctuations throughout this period a number of patterns emerge. Assaults and killings were typically done by young men against other men of similar age and race with whom they were acquainted; rapes and fatal incidents of domestic violence were overwhelmingly committed by men against women; assaults, most homicides and suicides involved the use of a gun; and both offenders and victims of violent crime have been disproportionately black.

The United States had roughly similar crime rates when compared with the other Western nations, but significantly higher levels of lethal violence. There was no shortage of theories as to why it was so or how to resolve it. Several researchers argued that as long as there were significant levels of poverty, income inequality and racial **segregation**, the United States would continue to have high levels of violence. Some argued that strengthening positive cultural institutions, such as **marriage** and the two-parent **family**, and attacking negative social practices, such as drug use among the young, would decrease the propensity for individuals to engage in violent crime. Others contended that more effective crime-fighting techniques such as community-based policing, along with sentencing reform, and an increase in **prisons** would discourage the relatively small subset of the population responsible for most violent crimes. Perhaps the most frequently cited difference between the United States and the other Western nations was the powerful role **guns** play in American culture. While almost all researchers agreed that guns constituted one of the critical contributing causes in explaining the country's uniquely high levels of violence, there was only intermittent and minimal political action regarding the topic.

Group violence in post-Second World War America followed a slightly different pattern. Labor violence which had been a significant issue in the 1930s generally vanished, although there were some notable exceptions (e.g. the national strike of independent truckers in 1974). Far and away the most intense and widespread source of group conflict centered on the issue of **race**. The **Civil Rights movement**, which began to make inroads in the 1950s, was constantly met with verbal harassment, beatings, cross burnings, lynchings, bombings and assassinations. Leaders of the movement capitalized on these reactions by deliberately going into dangerous areas of the **South** where their presence would frequently lead to savage reactions by the local **police** and citizens. The media images of peaceful protesters being attacked by fire hoses and police dogs helped galvanize the country and its political leaders to support them in their goal of racial desegregation.

As the gains of the civil-rights movement only partially translated into improvements for **African Americans**, there began in the mid-1960s a series of riots in almost every major northern city with a sizeable black population. These riots resulted in millions of dollars of damage, the destruction of entire **neighborhoods** and the deaths of nearly 250 people, most of whom were shot by police or National Guardsmen. By the early 1970s this trend slowed down, but throughout the 1980s and 1990s there were major riots in **Miami, FL** (1982, 1984, 1987), **Philadelphia, PA** (1985) and **Los Angeles, CA** (1965, 1992). Most of these riots involved African Americans or **Latinos**, and were sparked by incidents involving police and the arrest of a minority suspect.

Political debates about the causes of violence and about how best to prevent it played a significant role in several elections, one obvious example being the 1968 campaign in which both Richard **Nixon** and George **Wallace** cast themselves as law and order candidates. Throughout the 1980s a general consensus developed among policy-makers, although not necessarily among social scientists, that more aggressive measures were required to cope with the increasing levels of violence. As a result there was a boom in prison construction, hundreds of laws were added to federal and **state** criminal codes, increasing penalties and decreasing the discretionary power of the **judiciary**, the **FBI** was given increased authority to wiretap and infiltrate suspicious groups and there was a substantial increase in the use of the death penalty.

One prominent and ongoing feature of the debate about violence in America has been the role of the media. The quantity and graphic nature of violent images in most forms of media, especially those targeted at younger consumers, increased dramatically from the 1950s into the 1990s. The release of John Carpenter's *Halloween* (1978) introduced a whole new genre of violent horror movies known as "slasher" films (e.g. *Nightmare on Elm Street*; *Friday the 13th*; *Scream*) in which several characters per film were brutally slaughtered in explicit detail. Many of the bestsellers of the 1980s and 1990s were by authors who frequently employed violent imagery in their work such as Stephen **King**, Clive Barker, and R.L. Stein. **Supreme Court** decisions in the late 1960s that struck down many **censorship** laws thereby increased availability of **pornography**, which then subsequently increased the amount of sexually violent material. Although television presented less graphic images than movies, it was frequently cited as a major cause of violence in society both because of the high number of violent crimes presented in news and entertainment shows and because of its enormous audience (see **violence and media**).

However, social-science researchers were unable effectively to demonstrate causal connections between violence in the media and actual incidents of violence. There were several studies associating extensive exposure of young males to violent television images with an increased probability of aggressive behavior, but even here there have been a number of challenges as to the strength of the evidence to support this claim. Some researchers concluded that the most significant effect of violence in the media was the perception it created of criminals in American society and how this perception translated into increasingly violent and severe criminal-justice policies.

Further reading

Gurr, T.R. (ed.) (1989) *Violence in America*, Newbury Park: Sage.

Zimring, F. and Hawkins, G. (1997) *Crime is Not the Problem*, New York: Oxford.

RODGER JACKSON

violence and media

Since early this century, debate has raged among American academics, parents, media producers, network officials, the **FCC**, the PTA and mental-health organizations about the effects of viewing violent images. Most discussion and research on violent imagery has limited itself to studying **television** (although video games, movies and music are increasingly targeted). Television differs from other media in its pervasiveness – in the average American home it is on 6 hours daily. In addition, the audience includes many **children** (who are presumed to be more vulnerable to its effects than adults). The mimetic quality of the television is also thought to present realistic portrayals that can serve as powerful socializing agents.

The **Kefauver** congressional hearings of the 1950s investigating juvenile delinquency implicated violent TV images as a potential cause. TV violence was not to banned, but **networks** were pressured to be more accountable in their program development. Networks intended that the family viewing hours from 19:00–21:00 would air less violent programming. The prolonged focus on media violence legitimized it as a public-policy matter with increased budget funding and calls for further research.

During the 1960s, the National Commission on the Causes and Prevention of Crime and the **Surgeon General** published reports addressing possible connections between violence in media and real life. Since then, researchers have formulated a number of competing arguments as to the existence and nature of violent media effects. Among them are claims that violent media: desensitize the viewer; stimulate or arouse the viewer; disinhibit the viewer so that violent inclinations are more readily expressed; or provoke a catharsis that alleviates aggressive impulses. For instance, studies investigating the stimulation and arousal theory have sought to determine if exposure to aggressive stimuli will increase the level of physiological and emotional arousal which, in turn, will increase the probability of aggressive behavior. Proponents of the imitation theory suggest that people may learn aggressive behavior by observing aggression in media portrayals. Proponents of cultivation theory suggest that fear and paranoia lead to violence and, more generally, that TV cumulatively and progressively shapes the perception of the audience by instilling a particular view of the world – not by directly influencing behavior.

Numerous studies, however, have produced inconsistent research findings, leaving it unclear as to what effects, if any, there are from viewing violent media images. The competing findings reflect different definitions of violence and other methodological choices, as well as the concerns of investigators. Researchers have conducted lab experiments that manipulate the subjects' exposure to violence. Some field experiments have tried to measure more real-life settings. Researchers have also relied on surveys to measure real-life exposure to violent media images. Each of these methodological approaches contains certain weaknesses and strengths and can provide, at best, only a partial answer. Yet the debate continues among politicians and educators amid lurid newspaper coverage and occasional abashed concessions from television and movies before summer blockbusters roll around again.

JESSICA FISHMAN

Virgin Islands

The United States purchased more than fifty islands from Denmark for $25 million in 1917. Today, these constitute the territory of the US Virgin Islands (as distinct from British holdings), whose 101,800 citizens are US citizens, although they do not vote in presidential elections. The three main islands – St. Thomas, St. Croix and St. John – offer safe American centers for **Caribbean** resort life, which is the backbone of the local economy. Despite this successful modern incorporation, tensions of race have become apparent in both local development (and the role of the

predominantly Afro-Caribbean population) and in treatment of Caribbean migrants.

GARY McDONOGH
CINDY WONG

Visa *see* credit and credit cards

VISTA (Volunteers in Service to America) *see* War on Poverty

visual arts

Prior to the Second World War, Paris remained the most important center of modern art, while American art labored under a sense of relative cultural impoverishment. By the mid-1950s, however, with the emergence on the international scene of **abstract expressionism**, a specifically American form of avant-garde painting (also known as the New York School), dominance moved from Paris to **New York** City, NY. The central individual figure in this shift was the painter Jackson **Pollock**, whose canvases covered in "all-over" compositions of dense skeins and swirls of dripped and thrown paint remain the most familiar icons of abstract expressionism. His stylized machismo and early death in a car accident provided a powerful image of the American artist as a hard-drinking, hard-living individualist driven by existential angst.

The abstract expressionists and a subsequent generation of American abstract artists were championed by the critic Clement Greenberg, whose essay "Modernist Painting" (1961) became the most influential account of a version of modernism that seemed largely devoid of social content – its criticality lay in the degree of autonomy it could achieve through the rigor of its reflection upon the essential qualities of a specific medium.

Pollock himself had been associated with the Works Progress Administration's New Deal public art projects, and with leftist Mexican muralists like David Siqueiros, as well as the conservative American regionalist painter, Thomas Hart Benton. But both Pollock's rugged individualism and

Greenberg's formalism were able to be used, in the political context of the **Cold War**, to promote the dynamism of American liberalism and to generate cultural capital to match America's military and industrial dominance. Hence the interest of the CIA in such exhibitions as the survey of modern art in the United States that toured Europe in 1955–6 (see Guilbaut 1985).

The case of abstract expressionism and the ideological service into which it was pressed set the tone for the role of the visual arts in American culture after 1945. The visual arts have frequently provided stakes in contests, ostensibly to do with questions of artistic form or social engagement, which were as much political as aesthetic.

The political content of American visual arts has not always been explicit. Younger American artists in the mid-1950s, among them Robert **Rauschenberg** and Jasper **Johns** (see neo-Dada), and later in the 1960s Andy **Warhol**, unburdened themselves of the portentousness of abstract expressionist heroism. They opened their work up to the contingency of the everyday, contesting the separation of high and mass cultures. In the mid-1960s, the minimalists' simple, geometrical objects deflected viewers' attention away from themselves towards the immediate physical conditions of aesthetic perception. This facilitated subsequent investigations of the institutional production of aesthetic value, in opposition to traditional, ideologically weighty notions of universal or transcendent values.

In other instances, however, it has been very clear what was at stake in battles over the value of particular forms of representation. Artists provided imagery in support of the Civil-Rights movement and anti-**Vietnam War** protests. The **Feminist Art** movement of the 1970s, including artists such as Judy Chicago and Miriam Schapiro, directly challenged assumptions about who could make art, and what constituted appropriate subject matter. This introduced such taboo or undervalued aspects of women's experience as menstruation and domestic labor. They were especially critical of the ways in which women were commonly represented, both in art and mass culture, and concerned with asserting a right to self-representation. Some artists staged confrontational performances in public to dramatize and criticize

conventional representations of women, while others, such as Mary Kelly, made theoretically sophisticated work examining the psychological mechanisms of patriarchal domination.

Ronald **Reagan**'s **presidency** saw the elaboration of various forms of critical visual arts practice, grounded in developments of the 1960s and 1970s. Individually, or in collaboration with activist organizations like **ACT UP** (AIDS Coalition To Unleash Power), artists attempted to turn mass-media techniques to different, politically oppositional purposes. But the 1980s also saw a resurgence of traditional styles of painting (**neo-expressionism**), and the art market boomed along with the stock market, as if to re-emphasize art's historical relation to privilege.

The stock market fell and the boom subsided. In the late 1980s, a body of work emerged that was grounded in "identity politics," that is, in the specific experiences of artists who saw themselves as members of ethnic and other minorities. This pointed to a history of limited access to the institutions of art, but it had the unintended consequence of specifying and fixing identities in categories.

The election of **Republican** George **Bush**, after two terms of Reagan, encouraged Democratic politicians to begin to move towards centrist positions on economic issues. This would eventually contribute to the election of **Democratic** President Bill **Clinton**. Meanwhile, riding an ideological tide propelled by a conservative Christian minority, and claiming to be disgusted by artistic representations of anti-normative identities, Republican leaders including Senator Jesse **Helms** seized upon "traditional values" and "morality" issues for political leverage. One highly visible result of this was the "culture war" of the late 1980s and early 1990s (though it might be observed that few Democratic politicians defended culture very strongly). Sexually explicit art by openly gay artists such as Robert **Mapplethorpe** and David Wojnarowicz, which had appeared in institutions or exhibitions supported in part by federal funds, became a political football as conservatives attacked the funding organization, the **National Endowment for the Arts**. They succeeded in cutting the NEA budget dramatically, and in changing its procedures for making awards.

Federal support for the arts in America was already relatively very low among developed nations (American artists and institutions rely relatively heavily on **foundations**, the philanthropical support of corporations and the wealthy). So, in the light of the electoral success of congressional Republicans in the mid-1990s, perhaps what was most significant about the "culture wars" was that they demonstrated again the relationship in the American context between the desire to control representation (who represents whom and what, and how), and the desire to control, influence or maintain social values. In the 1990s, when American arts institutions must compete globally for tourist revenues and are confronted by increasingly diverse local audiences, such contests seem bound to become increasingly complex.

Further reading

Bolton, R. (ed.) (1992) *Culture Wars*, New York: New Press.

Broude, N. and Garrard, M. (eds) (1994) *The Power of Feminist Art*, New York: Abrams.

Foster, H. *The Return of the Real*, Cambridge, MA: MIT.

Gibson, A. (1997) *Abstract Expressionism*, New Haven: Yale.

Greenberg, C. (1986–93) *Collected Essays and Criticism*, vols 1–4, edited by John O'Brian, Chicago: University of Chicago.

Guilbaut, S. (1985) *How New York Stole the Idea of Modern Art*, Chicago: University of Chicago.

Krauss, R. (1986) *The Originality of the Avant-Garde and Other Modernist Myths*, Cambridge, MA: MIT.

Wallis, B. (ed.) (1984) *Art After Modernism*, New York: New Museum of Contemporary Art.

FRAZER WARD

volleyball

Invented in 1895 at the Holyoke, Massachusetts **YMCA** by William G. Morgan, the expansion of volleyball traces global interests in the twentieth century. Taken up in the Philippines and Cuba when these were colonies, volleyball was played by soldiers on the western front after the United States joined the First World War. It expanded through-

out Asia and into Latin America, often through the YMCAs, between the wars; during the Second World War further expansion occurred from the South Pacific to Western Europe.

At the Tokyo games in 1964, volleyball was accepted as an **Olympic** sport, with the Soviet Union winning among the men and the Japanese winning among the women. Since then Latin American teams like Brazil have grown in stature, while the end of the **Cold War** led to a decline in East European teams and a rise in American fortunes.

For many Americans, volleyball means the beach. This game is played informally at all resorts around the country, but recently has become a major televised sport, with its base in **California**. In the early 1920s, courts were put up at Santa Monica, and volleyball quickly became a popular recreational sport, sometimes associated with European nudist camps. By the 1950s, tournaments were held regularly at five beaches in California, and the sport became linked to **surfing** and **teenage** culture. Since 1974, when Winston cigarettes sponsored a tournament in San Diego, beach volleyball has been a commercial sport. In 1986 professional beach volleyball made its network debut on ABC's *Wide World of Sports* and, at the Atlanta Games in 1996, beach volleyball became an Olympic sport. It is still dominated largely by Californians, like Karch Kiraly and Kent Steffes among the men, and Karolyn Kirby and Liz Masakayan among the women.

ROBERT GREGG

Vonnegut, Kurt, Jr.
b. 1922

Writer whose continual mixture of broad American incisive satire and apocalyptic warning has made him a guru to generations of youths since the 1960s. Vonnegut's novels mingle techniques and voices from memoir, **science fiction** and journalistic essays in books that range from imaginative universes to dialogues with the reader about the problems of a changing world. *Slaughterhouse-5* (1969), which revolves around his own experiences of the bombing of Dresden in the Second World

War, exemplifies this mixture. Vonnegut has also considered themes as diverse as religion, the end of the world (*Cat's Cradle*, 1963) and politics (*Slapstick*, 1976).

GARY McDONOGH

Voting Rights Act of 1965

Act passed by **Congress**, at President **Johnson**'s behest, following the attack by state troopers and white extremists on Martin Luther **King**, Jr. and **civil rights** marchers in Selma, Alabama. King had been demonstrating the disparity between eligible black voters and the number registered in the counties around Selma.

The Act made all testing for literacy, character, or constitutional awareness illegal, allowing only age, residence and citizenship for determining eligibility to vote. Reinstating powers for the federal government that had not been seen in the **South** since Reconstruction, the **Attorney-General** was empowered, where necessary, to appoint federal examiners to register voters.

ROBERT GREGG

Voudou

A religion with origins in West Africa, practiced in the Americas due to the large-scale displacement of Africans during the slave trade. Voudou thus combines elements of **Roman Catholicism** and native West Indian practices with traditional African rituals. It is characterized by worship of the spirit world of ancestors, and ritual practices include prayers, ecstatic trances, drumming, dancing, feasts and "fits of possession." A priest or priestess acts as a medium, works charms and curses, and recalls zombies, otherwise known as the "living dead."

Despite both social and legal repression, Voudou has continued to thrive, particularly in among **Haitian American immigrants**

NICOLE MARIE KEATING

Waco (Branch Davidians)

The Branch Davidians are an offshoot fringe group of the Seventh Day Adventist denomination founded in 1935. On February 28, 1993 the Branch Davidians, led by their Patriarch, David Koresh (aka Vernon Howell), were involved in a deadly shootout with federal agents at the groups' fortified compound near Waco, **Texas**, attempting to execute a warrant for weapons violations. A fifty-one-day siege with federal authorities ensued until the **FBI** attempted to drive members out by ramming the compound with tear gas equipped armored vehicles. In response the Davidians apparently shot some of their own members and set their own structure on fire killing seventy-eight people including many children. Waco soon became a rallying of an emerging political movement distrustful of government known as the "Militia" or "Patriot" movement. In 1999 revelations about the failure of federal authorities to disclose various details about the siege reignited debate on the topic. Nonetheless, a Texas jury cleared the federal government of responsibility in 2000.

BRIAN LEVIN

Walker, Alice

b. 1944

Novelist and poet, born a sharecroppers' daughter in Eaton, Georgia. After dismissal from Spelman College for participating in **civil rights** demon-strations, she transferred to Sarah Lawrence, but went south to Mississippi to participate in the 1966 registration drive. She taught at Tougaloo and Wellesley while publishing short stories (*Love and Trouble*, 1973). Influenced by Zora Neale Hurston and Flannery O'Connor, Walker focused on the experiences of **African Americans** in the segregated **South**. In 1982 she published *The Color Purple* (which Steven **Spielberg** filmed in 1985). Her work also explores the interaction between race and gender – the plight of her women characters shaped not merely by racism but by oppressive relationships with men. Since 1985, she has published *The Temple of My Familiar* (1989), *Possessing the Secret of Joy* (1992) and *By The Light of My Father's Smile* (1998).

ROBERT GREGG

Wallace, George

b. 1919; d. 1998

Fiery segregationist politician. Losing the Alabama governorship to a racist contender in 1958, Wallace became a vehement segregationist who would be elected in 1962, 1970, 1974 and 1982, with his wife Lurleen becoming an interregnum governor in 1966. Wallace began his first term promising "Segregation now! Segregation tomorrow! Segregation forever!" He tried to bar blacks from the University of Alabama and faced Martin Luther **King**, Jr. in the **state** capital. Wallace unsuccessfully attempted to parlay his fame into the Democratic presidential nomination in 1964;

as candidate of the American Independent Party in 1968 he received 10 million votes (13.5 percent of the popular total), underscoring growing racial concerns outside the **South**. In 1972 he re-emerged as a **Democratic** "regional" law and order contender, again showing strength in the **Northeast** and **Midwest** as well as the South; this campaign was cut short by an **assassination** attempt that left him paralyzed. Thereafter, he stayed with his Alabama power base, gradually developing a more inclusive development platform that even attracted black votes before his 1987 retirement.

GARY McDONOGH

Wallace, Michele

b. 1953

African American feminist scholar first noted for *Black Macho and the Myth of the Superwoman*, her 1979 study of the effects of sexism and racism on **African American** women. Much criticized within the black community, the work dissected the racial stereotypes associated with black **masculinity** and **femininity** that trap black women in roles that simultaneously require them to be assertive and successful, and blame them for being emasculating. In *Invisibility Blues* (1990), Wallace continues her work on the intersection of race and gender in African American visual and popular culture.

ROBERT GREGG

Waller, Robert James

b. 1939

Writer, photographer, musician and former business-school professor. His novel *The Bridges of Madison County* was a slow, phenomenal bestseller and 1995 hit film starring Clint **Eastwood** and Meryl Streep. The tale of two midlife characters involves a four-day love affair that changes the life of an Iowa farmer's wife. The enduring popularity of a simple love story took the publishing world by stealth turning to storm. Waller also authored *A*

Slow Waltz in Cedar Bend (1993), *Old Songs in a New Cafe* (1995), *Border Music* (1995) and *Puerto Vallarta Squeeze* (1995); his recording *The Ballads of Madison County* was released by Atlantic Records.

EDWARD MILLER

Wall Street

Wall Street is the modern American "Street of Dreams," built on the remains of a seventeenth-century fort wall. It is the financial capital of the United States, spanning a seven-block stretch of downtown Manhattan, **New York** City, NY. The district surrounding Wall Street is home to numerous investment banks (Goldman Sachs, JP Morgan), securities firms (Smith Barney, Merrill Lynch) and insurance companies (Metlife). Additionally, the New York Stock Exchange and other major exchanges are located here. Wall Street embodies highs and lows of American life, economic prosperity and tickertape parades or Depression, recession and corporate greed (in the movie *Wall Street*, 1987).

MARC BALCER

Wall Street Journal *see* newspapers; Wall Street

Walters, Barbara *see* news, television

Walton, Sam

b. 1918; d. 1992

A successful Arkansas five-and-ten entrepreneur, Walton opened his first discount Walmart in 1962, building it into the largest retailer in the US. Slashing costs through lower profit margins, computerized inventory control and high volume with limited service, his "big-box" stores mushroomed in malls and small towns. While the latter came to see Walmarts as threats to local economic life, the company continually advertises "Americanness," community involvement and support for workers. By the mid-1980s, Walton became the richest man in America; his 1992 autobiography is *Sam Walton: Made in America*.

GARY McDONOGH

war

The United States Constitution grants the power to declare war to **Congress** (Article 1: Section 8; clause 11) and given this definition, the United States has not been to war since the Second World War. However, employing an alternative definition (such as that of von Clausewitz) in which war is described as an act of violence by a state intended to compel its opponents to fulfill its will, the United States has been in an almost constant state of warfare since 1945. That both accurately apply to the United States characterizes the nation's equivocal approach to war in the last half of the twentieth century.

One aspect of the country's ambivalence was the proliferation of conflicts that stopped short of being full-fledged wars. The overarching framework for the first forty years of the US after the Second World War was the "**Cold War**," a term used to designate the prolonged struggle with the Soviet Union and to a lesser degree the People's Republic of **China**. Although this "war" shaped and structured American politics, economics, social institutions and, especially, military policy, the US and the Soviet Union never sent troops against each other and the US and Chinese only fought against each other in the **Korean War**. There were also a series of "covert" or "surrogate" wars, such as those against the governments of Guatemala and **Iran** in the 1950s, Cuba in the 1960s and Nicaragua in the 1980s. These were armed conflicts sanctioned by the US and often conducted by US intelligence agencies (**CIA**). Although not publicly involved, US personnel performed **assassinations**, mined harbors, engaged in psychological operations, as well as supplying arms, training, logistical support and intelligence to groups engaged in overt hostilities against US **enemies**. A second feature was the increasing power of the presidents to unilaterally decide whether to engage in a conflict and how exactly that conflict would be conducted. Harry **Tru-**

man's decision to lead the country to war in Korea under UN auspices, rather than seek a formal declaration from Congress, provided a blueprint that both George **Bush** in the **Gulf War** (1990) and Bill **Clinton** in Bosnia (1996) and Kosovo (1999) followed. In each case the president chose when to start and when to conclude hostilities and left Congress to cast largely symbolic votes whether to support or denounce the policy. Although the **Vietnam War** was not a UN operation, both Lyndon **Johnson** and Richard **Nixon** also followed Truman's example of ignoring Congress, arguing that the Constitution gave the president war-making powers in his role as commander in chief. There was an attempt to undercut this tactic by passage of the War Powers Act (1973), which held that the president could send troops into battle for sixty days, but then had to seek congressional approval. However, this proved largely ineffectual.

A third effect, related to the second, was the use of euphemisms, like "police action" in Korea (1950–3) and Vietnam (1962–74), "peacekeeping mission" in the Dominican Republic (1965) and Bosnia (1991–3) and "rescue operations" in **Grenada** (1984) to describe events that were, for all intents and purposes, wars. These often grew out of the Cold War and were situations where the two superpowers would actively involve themselves on opposing sides of a regional conflict, but did not wish to take the final step of declaring war. On the other hand, the government began to increasingly characterize non-military social-policy initiatives in explicitly military terms. From the 1960s to the 1980s there were a number of "wars" declared by the government on such things as poverty, drugs, **crime**, **AIDS** and **cancer**.

A fourth feature of this ambivalence was the way it contributed to the rise of what **Eisenhower** called the military-industrial complex; a relationship that grew to include the cooperation of the government, scientific community, higher education and organized labor. According to the congressional Budget Office, the **Pentagon** budget for military spending, if measured in real terms, continued to remain at the same level of the height of the Cold War of the early 1960s. As a result, 10 percent of all US business was derived from military-related production. The argument given in support of such enormous expenditures was that it was only through continued strength and readiness that the US could avoid the horrors of the wars of the first half of the century.

The ambivalence about war was also reflected in other ways in post-Second World War popular culture. While the Civil War, the Spanish American War, and both world wars produced a number of highly popular songs that promoted the cause, this was virtually non-existent for any of the conflicts after 1945. Only Vietnam produced any significant number of songs, directed mostly against the war, and none of them achieved the status of "The Battle Hymn of the Republic" or "Over There." Representations of war on television were relatively scarce with only two successful series using war as their backdrop, *Combat* (1962–7) and *M*A*S*H* (1972–83). There was an interesting contrast in the film industry between the popularity of **science-fiction** war films versus those about real wars. The most successful reality-based war films tended to present complex and highly critical views of war, while the science-fiction films were marked by a stark contrast between good and evil and glorified war while ignoring its costs. However, despite the large number of movies explicitly about real wars made since the Second World War, only a handful gained any widespread popularity: *The Bridge on the River Kwai* (1957); *M*A*S*H* (1970); *Platoon* (1986); and *Saving Private Ryan* (1998). When adjusted for inflation only *The Best Years of Our Lives* (1946), about the aftermath of war, is in the top sixty most successful films. This is in stark contrast to the immense popularity of fantasy war films such as the *Star Wars Anthology* (1977; 1980; 1983; 1999) and *Independence Day* (1996), which are among the thirty-two most popular films of all time.

See also: war movies; Latin America

RODGER JACKSON

Warhol, Andy

b. 1928; d. 1987

Ensconced during the 1960s in the subcultural scene of his **New York** studio, "The Factory," Andy Warhol transposed and transcended the defining ethos of his industrial **Pittsburgh** origins.

In his silkscreen icons of American consumer culture and its **celebrities**, from Campbell's Soup and Coca-Cola to Marilyn **Monroe** and Jacqueline Kennedy **Onassis**, Warhol turned mass culture into high art. As such, his work was the **pop art** avatar of **postmodernism**, fundamentally blurring and destabilizing the boundary between "avant-garde and kitsch" that had been so rigorously maintained in high modernist criticism and practice.

LISA SALTZMAN

war movies

One of the most influential, profitable and popular genres in American cinema. Although influenced by films and film-makers in the silent and early talking picture eras, war films as a **Hollywood** genre came of age during and after the Second World War. From the 1940s to the 1990s these Second World War films, and related movies about Korea and Vietnam, both reflected and effected changes in American cinema and society.

Initial Second World War movies mobilized the American people for the war effort, usually through patriotic tales of bravery and defiance in defeat (*Wake Island*, 1942), martyrdom (*The Purple Heart*, 1944), resistance to fascism (*The North Star*, 1943), family sacrifice (*The Sullivans*, 1944), women in war (*So Proudly We Hail*, 1943) and the home front (*Mrs Miniver*, 1942). Because many of these films were either subsidized or supported by various government agencies, there was little cinematic criticism of the armed services and of war policy and strategy.

Propaganda gave way to realism and social commentary in many postwar films, which explored the plight of returning **veterans** (*The Best Years of Our Lives*, 1946), the toll on those who fought and commanded (*Twelve O'Clock High*, 1949), racism (*Home of the Brave*, 1949) and the conditions of physical and mental misery which faced the common soldier (*Battleground*, 1949).

Mixed messages of **patriotism**, sacrifice and uncertainty about the necessity of war continued through the Korean and **Cold War** eras of the 1950s and 1960s, up to the early years of the

Vietnam War. Yet, such films did little to advance the structure of the genre, established in the 1940s. Since that decade a number of common themes in plot, dialogue and direction have resulted in distinct subgenres of war movies. "Platoon" films portray a cross-section of American society who find themselves thrown together to face unknown and savage perils (*Bataan*, 1943; *Platoon*, 1986). The emotional and physical difficulties in ordering men to their deaths shape "Commander" movies (*The Dawn Patrol*, 1938; *Command Decision*, 1948). Those who wait and serve the war effort in non-combatant roles are the focus of "Home Front" films (*Since You Went Away*, 1944; *Coming Home*, 1978). "Epics" provide semi-documentary ac-counts of campaigns, battles, or heroes' accom-plishments (*The Longest Day*, 1962; *A Bridge Too Far*, 1977). While antiwar sentiments are part of every war movie, some, like Kubrick's *Paths of Glory* (1957) clearly convey pacifist messages. Some of the best of these have been black comedies that satirized war and the politicians and generals who started and continued them (*M*A*S*H*, 1970; *Catch-22*, 1970).

The evolution of war movies can be seen in the works of two directors, Lewis Milestone (*All Quiet on the Western Front*, 1930; *A Walk in the Sun*, 1946; *The Halls of Montezuma*, 1950; *Pork Chop Hill*, 1959) and Sam Fuller (*The Steel Helmet*, 1951; *Fixed Bayonets*, 1951; *The Big Red One*, 1980). Their influential films encompass a number of the subgenres and have been benchmarks in the changing images of American war and society. Since 1998, new attention has been paid to war movies due to the critical and popular success of Steven **Spielberg**'s *Saving Private Ryan*.

Further reading

Dick, B.F. (1985) *The Star-Spangled Screen*, Lexington: The University Press of Kentucky.

THOMAS M. WILSON

War on Drugs *see* drug policy; Reagan, Ronald

War on Poverty

In 1962 Michael Harrington published *The Other America*, arguing that one-fifth of Americans lived in substandard housing, suffered from malnutrition and received inadequate medical care. Harring-ton's shocking revelations influenced many in America, including Lyndon **Johnson**, a man of humble beginnings with whom the problem of poverty resonated deeply. The sudden death of President John **Kennedy** in 1963 moved many in the government, first among them the new President Johnson, to fulfill the goals Kennedy had targeted, one of which was the creation of a War on Poverty.

The War on Poverty had its roots in the New Deal of the 1930s. In terms of enlarging the powers of the federal government, the two reform move-ments were equally ambitious. But unlike the 1930s, the early 1960s was an era of unprecedented prosperity in America, which emboldened Johnson and others all the more to believe that poverty could be erased from the American landscape.

At the same time, many researchers began to talk about a "culture of poverty" in America, arguing that poverty tended to strike certain groups more than others, and to be handed down through generations. That is, nonwhites, the elderly, those with less education, and female-headed households were much more likely to be affected by poverty, and to pass down this condition to future generations. How to break this cycle was a much more difficult question.

The ambitions of the War on Poverty included Medicare, a national health-insurance program initially created in 1964 for the elderly and then expanded to include recipients of **welfare**. In addition, the Elementary and Secondary Educa-tion Act of 1965 gave aid to underfunded **public schools**, while the Higher Education Act of the same year allocated funds for needy **college and university** students. Johnson's administration also created the Department of Housing and Urban Development.

But the War on Poverty involved individuals at the grassroots level as well as the highest levels of the government. In this regard, Johnson's vision was premised on the belief that the poor needed to be involved in the programs that were to affect them if those programs were to succeed. In this spirit, the Johnson administration created the Office of Economic Opportunity in 1964. First headed by R. Sargent Shriver, John Kennedy's brother-in-law, the OEO administered a budget of $800 million to a variety of programs geared to community development and job training.

Some of the more notable programs of the War on Poverty included: legal services for the poor; Volunteers in Service to America (VISTA), a form of domestic Peace Corps, training the young as teachers to be sent to underprivileged school districts; the Job Corps, which attempted to train those who had dropped out of formal education; and Project Head Start, initiated to provide preschool education for poor children. Some of these programs, such as Head Start and Food Stamps, are still current, but for the most part the War on Poverty had a minimal impact. Many have argued that the programs fell victim to the **Vietnam War**'s voracious appetite for funding, while others have charged that the entire enterprise was little more than a superficial attempt to mend a system with deep structural problems.

Further reading

Matusow, A. (1984) *The Unraveling of America*, New York: Harper & Row.
Patterson, J. (2000) *America's Struggle Against Poverty, 1900–1994*, Cambridge, MA: Harvard University Press.

SUSAN SCHULTEN

Warren, Earl (Court)

b. 1891; d. 1974

Earl Warren emerged from a working-class family to become Alameda County district attorney, Attorney-General of California, three-term governor of California and chief justice of the Supreme Court. Appointed in 1953 by President **Eisenhower**, Warren served until 1969. He transformed the Court from one sharply divided between

justices favoring judicial restraint and practitioners of **judicial activism** into a more unified body that moved from a focus on economic issues to confront many of the most significant issues in the Court's history. The **Warren Court** had a willingness to overturn legislative enactments, especially those from the state level, employing a methodology rooted in social justice, morality and fairness rather than strict doctrinal constitutional analysis. Most notable are: **Brown v. Board of Education** (1954), unanimously holding racial segregation unconstitutional and triggering the **Civil Rights movement**; *Baker* v. *Carr* (1962), requiring reapportionment of congressional voting districts; **Roe v. Wade** (1973), recognizing a privacy right for women to choose **abortion**; and decisions expanding the rights of criminal defendants. Warren's enduring legacy is the modern era of the Supreme Court in which groups concerned with **women's liberation**, **environmentalism**, gay and lesbian politics, criminal justice, poverty and **immigration** could utilize the Supreme Court and other levels of the judicial system, rather than the legislative process, as instruments for social change and protection of the disadvantaged.

Further reading

Schwartz, B. (1983) *Super Chief: Earl Warren and His Supreme Court*, New York: New York University.

JAMES KRAUS

Warren Commission

Named after its chairperson, Earl **Warren**, chief justice of the US **Supreme Court**, the Warren Commission probed the **assassination** of John F. **Kennedy** from December 1963 until its report in September 1964. The Commission concluded Lee Harvey Oswald, angered by Kennedy's anti-**Castro** policies, acted alone. While the report was extensive, debates linger as to its exhaustiveness, fueling conspiracy theories (see Oliver **Stone**'s *JFK*, 1991). Left unexplained were several sightings of a second gunman on the "grassy knoll" and Jack Ruby's rationale for killing Oswald in the Dallas **police** headquarters. Assistant Counsel

Arlen Specter, later senator from Pennsylvania, explained the amazing trajectory of a single bullet, later called derisively the "magic-bullet" theory.

ROBERT GREGG

Washington, DC

Washington, DC, the capital of the United States, has become increasingly central to American culture in the postwar period as the federal government has grown in size and power. Once almost universally described as a "sleepy Southern" town, Washington, DC was often viewed dismissively well into the 1960s. President John F. **Kennedy**, for example, quipped that the city was the worst of all worlds, a city of "Northern charm and Southern efficiency."

But, by the 1990s, Washington, DC boomed: the population of its metropolitan area had quadrupled to more than 4 million since the 1950s (although the city itself had been losing population since 1950). It had incontestably become one of the nation's leading media centers (especially for political journalism and commentary) and became a headquarters for corporate associations (which increasingly needed to lobby the government). Its monuments and **museums**, such as those of the **Smithsonian Institution**, had become cultural icons and meccas for domestic and international tourists. Its universities had gained in stature and prominence (in part because of access to the media) and its arts community expanded: the Kennedy Center strove – largely unsuccessfully – to be a national center for the performing arts. The city and suburban population became more diverse as an expanding government attracted workers from more parts of the nation and as refugees – Vietnamese, Central American, Ethiopian – and immigrants began to move to the area. Even its economic base became more diverse as biotechnology firms formed near the National Institutes of Health in the Maryland suburbs and as the Internet spawned high-technology industry in its Virginia suburbs.

By the 1990s, Washington, DC and its inhabitants were more likely to be resented than dismissed – a resentment often expressed through the contemptuous phrase "inside the Beltway." The phrase, popularized by Reagan conservatives in the early 1980s, suggests that Washingtonians – particularly politicians, federal employees and lobbyists – are cut off from the "real world" and have no sense of the problems faced by, and the values cherished by, the rest of the nation. (The Beltway is the interstate highway loop, I-495, which, since the 1960s, has circled the city. The metropolitan population is indeed statistically wealthier and better educated than the national average.)

But official Washington, DC has been only part of the city's public face and private existence. The city's tortured history of race relations has also been part of its reputation and its contribution to postwar culture. The population of Washington, DC proper had long been overwhelmingly minority, and African Americans accounted for about two-thirds of the city's population in 1990. While Washington, DC had begun officially desegregating in the 1950s – before other Southern cities – its residential and social patterns as well as its politics continued to be racially polarized through the 1990s. Washington, DC was a center of local black civil-rights activism throughout the 1960s, as well as host to such central civil-rights events as the 1963 March on Washington.

Racial tensions boiled over in 1968 when two days of rioting followed the assassination of Martin Luther **King**, Jr. As many as 20,000 Washingtonians participated in the riots, which led President Lyndon **Johnson** to call out federal troops, who occupied the city for a week. The riots killed twelve people, caused about $15 million in damage, led many businesses and residents to quit the city and left blocks of the city in ruins, some of which were still evident at the end of the 1990s.

Race relations hit another low in 1990 when Washington Mayor Marion Barry was arrested by the **Federal Bureau of Investigation** in a drug bust. While Barry was a controversial figure even in the black community, many of his supporters viewed the bust as a concerted attack against a black with political power. Barry's arrest brought increased national attention to the city's drug problem, which had led the city to have the highest murder rate per capita in the country in the late 1980s.

Barry's arrest also set back the cause of "home rule." For most of its history, Washington, DC had been governed by **Congress**, increasing racial tensions as white members of Congress oversaw a largely black populace. Washington, DC was unable to cast electoral votes until the ratification of the 23rd Amendment to the Constitution in 1961. In 1974 Congress granted limited "home rule," allowing Washingtonians to elect a mayor. Barry's arrest killed any immediate chances that "home-rule" powers would be expanded.

Racial conflict – the aspect of local Washington, DC most apparent to the nation as a whole – was only part of the story of black Washington, DC though. While Washington, DC had long had a thriving black middle class, black prosperity expanded after the 1960s as desegregation and affirmative action enabled blacks to benefit from the expanding number of government and private jobs. However, the black middle class often moved out of the city, especially to Maryland's once rural Prince Georges County, which became a predominantly black suburb.

Further reading

Abbott, C. (1999) *Political Terrain*, Chapel Hill: University of North Carolina.

Jaffee, H. and Sherwood, T. (1994) *Dream City*, New York: Simon & Schuster.

DAVID GOLDSTON

Washington, Denzel

b. 1954

Television and movie actor of the 1980s and 1990s. Washington's first movie role, *Carbon Copy* (1981), was followed by a stint as the resident Dr Chandler on NBC's doctor show *St Elsewhere* (1982–8). A part in the Civil War movie *Glory* (1989) earned him an Academy Award for Best Supporting Actor. His performance in this movie led to roles in other big-budget productions, including *The Pelican Brief* (1993), *Philadelphia* (1993) and *Courage Under Fire* (1996). His portrayals of *Malcolm X* (1992), directed by Spike **Lee** (with whom he has worked in two other films), and the South African Steve Biko, in

Cry Freedom (1987), received critical acclaim. Washington also starred in *Devil in a Blue Dress* (1995), the inaugural movie of his production company, Mundy Lane Entertainment, and *Hurricane* (1999) for which he was nominated for Best Actor. He continues to mix box office hits with serious films.

See also: actors

ROBERT GREGG

Washington press corps

Beginning in the 1960s, the relationship between the American press and elected officials in **Washington, DC** changed from informal gatherings to ceremonious, and often contentious, events. The shift was symbolized by President Richard **Nixon**'s converting the White House swimming pool into a press briefing room in 1969. **Television**, particularly 24-hour **news** stations, helped create this new environment. The medium contributed to the rise of political commentators and made news from Washington available continuously and instantaneously. A mistrust between the press and Washington officials – largely the result of the Vietnam War and Watergate – became part of this atmosphere.

JAMES DEVITT

WASP (White Anglo-Saxon Protestant) *see* upper class; white

waterfronts

Many American cities took shape around ports that provided outlets for trade and later facilitated the growth of industry, as produce and heavy goods were shipped around the world from factories in **Philadelphia, PA**, **Buffalo, NY**, **Chicago, IL** and **San Francisco, CA**. In the late twentieth century, these same cities – and others – rebuilt their waterfronts as new urban recreational and commercial centers.

With the end of the Second World War mobilization, waterfront landscapes became a grimy jumble of warehouses, factories, ships and piers that provided the dark and dangerous ambience of many film noir classics. Indeed, the gritty construction and labor conflicts of these ports remained a hallmark of urban success, epitomized in the classic labor movie *On the Waterfront* (1954). **Deindustrialization**, coupled with a shift to container transport that demanded different, centralized facilities articulated by trucking and train, changed this narrative radically by the 1960s. Rust and abandonment eventually claimed many waterfronts, while pollution choked **rivers** and harbors.

By the 1970s and 1980s, large stretches of centrally located post-industrial land and the recreational and aesthetic potential of reclaimed water began to experience large-scale revitalization across the US. Some projects made use of the functions and buildings of the older port areas. Fishing facilities in smaller ports (and occasional larger ones, like San Francisco) added color and culinary interest. **Markets** were transformed into festival marketplaces in **Boston** (Fanieul Hall), **New York** (South Street Seaport embracing Fulton Fish Market) and **Baltimore, MD**'s Inner Harbor, juxtaposing local historical themes with placeless tourist franchises and a smorgasbord of restaurants. A smaller city, **Savannah, GA**, refashioned cotton warehouses into shops and services, while Monterey, California, preserved the literary landmark of Cannery Row. Elsewhere, ample pier buildings have been turned into restaurants, dance clubs and recreational zones. Through these facilities, many cities also covet the fame and markets of tourist cruises.

Other developments have reclaimed industrial space for public **parks** and plazas. Aquaria, maritime museums and sports stadiums (**Pittsburgh, PA**, **Cleveland, OH**, Baltimore) have also emphasized the waterfront as a focal attraction for tourists and local residents alike. In some further cases, reuse of government/military facilities provides opportunities for new **urban planning** – Governor's Island in New York City or Alcatraz and the Presidio in San Francisco. Even older recreational complexes that would be anathema to current environmental planning have taken on period charm in the attractions of the **Atlantic City, NJ** boardwalk (with new casinos) or the amusements of the Santa Monica (Los Angeles) pier (which has figured prominently in movies and television, e.g. *Falling Down*, 1993).

Residential development also has transformed older industrial buildings while adding high-rise condominia and luxury hotels that combine convenience and views. The most successful cases create new cities within cities, in which yuppies support urban stores and services that become attractions for outsiders – the hallmark of Boston, Baltimore and San Francisco, among others. Waterfronts also provide strong images of the city for mass media – via both active urban life and dramatically framed skylines. As competition for tourists and investments eclipses past rivalries for shipping itself, other cities have achieved only partial success – an uneasy collage of malls and attractions amid crumbling toxic skeletons of the industrial city. Even in successful redevelopments, disconnection from nearby inner-city populations and the socio-economic difficulties of deindustrialization beyond the port remain problems.

Further reading

Breen, A. and Rigby, D. (1994) *Waterfronts*, New York: McGraw Hill.

The National Research Council (1980) *Urban Waterfront Lands*, Washington, DC: National Academy of Sciences.

GARY MCDONOGH
CINDY WONG

Watergate

On June 17, 1972 **Washington, DC** police arrested five burglars at the headquarters of the **Democratic** National Committee at the Watergate apartment complex. These men, employees of the Committee to Re-Elect the President (CREEP), had broken in to tap phones and photograph documents. Their arrest was the first of many revelations of misconduct within the **Nixon** administration, culminating in one of the most serious abuses of presidential power in the nation's history.

Though the Nixon administration denied any White House involvement in the burglary, and dismissed it as a bungled attempt engineered by overzealous minions, the **FBI** eventually traced the burglary to sources within the administration. A few weeks later the *Washington Post* revealed that Attorney-General John Mitchell had managed secret funds to undermine Nixon's political enemies by gathering damaging information, planting spies, forging letters, stealing campaign plans and feeding false information to the media.

The trial of the Watergate burglars and planners began in January of 1973, with Judge John Sirica presiding. Five pleaded guilty, and two were convicted, upon which one of the burglars sent a letter to Sirica confirming that the White House had in fact been involved with the original break in. When Sirica called for further investigation, Watergate became a national story.

The Senate also began investigating Nixon's campaign practices, creating a Special Committee on Presidential Campaign Activities. The committee's televised hearings began in May 1973, and for six months the nation watched a parade of witnesses uncover the crimes and plots of the administration, including burglary, bugging, perjury, dirty tricks, tampering with judicial proceedings, political surveillance, shredding evidence, blackmail and granting executive clemency to those who stay silent. All of these were hatched in the Nixon White House, and the circle of corruption came ever closer to the president himself.

In October of 1973, Vice-President Spiro **Agnew** resigned after being found guilty of cheating on his **taxes** and accepting bribes as both governor of Maryland and vice-president. As Nixon's approval ratings continued to sink, the House Judiciary Committee began to gather evidence of presidential wrongdoing, a first step towards **impeachment**. In March 1974, Judge Sirica's grand jury indicted Nixon aides Haldeman, Ehrlichman, Mitchell and four others for conspiracy to obstruct justice. White House Counsel John Dean pleaded guilty to the conspiracy charge, and cooperated with the grand jury. The grand jury's sealed report named Nixon as an unindicted co-conspirator, and in May 1974 the Senate Judiciary Committee began formal impeachment hearings.

Crucial to the committee's investigations was the discovery that Nixon had recorded all conversations in the Oval Office, but it took the **Supreme Court** to force Nixon to submit these tapes. These provided the smoking gun that proved Nixon had ordered the cover-up of the Watergate burglary just six days after it had occurred, meaning that he had been lying to the public ever since. Faced with this evidence, Nixon resigned on August 8, 1974. One month later he was given a full pardon by President Ford.

Further reading

Bernstein, C. and Woodward, R. (1974) *All the President's Men*, New York: Simon & Schuster.
Schell, J. (1975) *The Time of Illusion*, New York: Knopf.

SUSAN SCHULTEN

Waters, John

b. 1946

Director. **Baltimore**-born independent auteur/ cult **director** who sarcastically celebrates and skewers his city, the **middle class** and **suburbia** gone bad. After his initial experience of pornographic film, his *Mondo Trasho* (1970) and *Pink Flamingos* (1972), showcasing the 300-pound transvestite Divine, offered visual offenses that rivaled Bunuel and Dali. This partnership and vision continued in *Female Trouble* (1975) and *Polyester* (1981). Waters has become more mainstream in his later work, although maintaining a wry vision of race relations (*Hairspray*, 1988), American domesticity (*Serial Mom*, 1994) and urban aesthetics (*Pecker*, 1998). See Waters' autobiographical *Shock Value* (1995).

GARY McDONOGH
CINDY WONG

Waters, Muddy (McKinley Morganfield)

b. 1915; d. 1983

Electric bluesman, born on a sharecropping farm

in Mississippi, who garnered his nickname from playing as a child in a local creek. Waters was discovered in 1940 by folk-song archivists Alan Lomax and John Work. In 1943 Waters moved to **Chicago, IL** where he took up electric guitar and his countrified urban blues became a staple of the South Side club circuit and, in the 1950s, the Chess label. Touring constantly and appearing at every major **blues**, **jazz** and folk festival, Waters was a key influence on the British bands of the 1960s blues revival.

DEWAR MACLEOD

Watts *see* Los Angeles, CA; race riots

Wayne, John (Marion Michael Morrison)

b. 1907; d. 1979

John "Duke" Wayne embodied a conservative, Cold War, patriotic heroism during his forty-year reign as one of Hollywood's most popular stars. In the mythical **westerns** and Hollywood wars he inhabited, Wayne cut a forthright, paternal, but occasionally violent, figure. Director John **Ford** made Wayne a star in *Stage Coach* (1939), and both Ford and Howard **Hawks** used Wayne to good advantage in several films, including Hawks' *Red River* (1948). During the Vietnam War, Wayne co-directed and starred in the pro-war *The Green Berets* (1968). Ironically, Wayne assiduously avoided seeing action during the Second World War and Korea.

MELINDA SCHWENK

weather

"Everybody talks about the weather, but no one does anything about it," according to Mark Twain. But weather provides more than chatter – the experience and interpretation of the American climate has deeply shaped national growth and culture.

By Twain's day, the United States already spanned a continent. Hence, storm systems swept across the Plains to the East Coast, while droughts and floods affected not only local **agriculture**, but also national business and population. Better forecasting today makes it possible to envision these systems on a national scale. At the same time, weather reports remain extremely local, geared to activities like vacations, school closings, celebrations and commuting.

The US also has unique weather phenomena that have shaped its sense of the power of **nature**. Three-quarters of all tornadoes occur here; the Eastern and Gulf Coasts, like **Hawai'i**, lie in major hurricane routes. "Blizzard" is an American word as well, capturing the strength of Arctic snows blanketing the Midwest. The Great Depression's Dustbowl, Midwestern floods, fire seasons in **California** and **Florida** and other dramatic phenomena also influence markets, families and the national experience.

Moreover, variations in perceptions of weather, from the sultry **South** to **Southwestern** deserts to the rainy **Pacific Northwest**, shape regional meaning and identity. These pervade images of rugged **New Englanders** or in Tennessee William's steamy evocations of the South. Although urbanites may seem more immune to natural phenomena than farmers, **Chicago, IL** is still the Windy City, while a climatic inversion of sunny **Los Angeles** set a futuristic stage in *Blade Runner* (1980).

Does anyone do anything about it? Knowledge of the weather and attempts to control its effects were envisioned as a national research project by President Thomas Jefferson, whose legacy was developed by both the **Smithsonian Institution** and military research. New technology like the telegraph allowed simultaneous measurements and early reports of climactic changes. Since the Second World War, radar, satellites and **computers** have all changed manipulation of weather data and the reliability of predictions, centralized and distributed through the National Weather Service.

Technology has also changed the ways in which Americans learn about weather, as newspaper forecasts have given way to the immediacy of radio and television. Five minutes for weather is a staple of local news. In television's early days, weather reports became notorious for their lack of journalistic or scientific prowess – whether relying on attractive "weather girls" or "characters" with make-up and props. Subsequently, more accurate prediction has coincided with computer imaging of storm movements, while reports on snows, floods, tornadoes and hurricanes have become staples of news as well; the impact of the El Niño current off **California** received frequent coverage. The Weather Channel, begun in 1982, reaches 90 percent of cable users with 24-hour reports. Weather reports may also underpin environmental concerns, whether local issues of farming/gardening, pollution, water supplies or more general concerns of global warming.

Further reading

Laskin, D. (1996) *Braving the Elements*, New York: Doubleday (provides a wonderful introduction to American weather and history.)

GARY McDONOGH

Weather Underground

"You don't need a weatherman to know which way the wind blows," a line from Bob **Dylan**, inspired a radical, Maoist off-shoot of **Students for a Democratic Society** at the end of the 1960s. Led by SDS activists Bernardine Dohrn and Mark Rudd, the Weathermen were to the student movement what **Black Power** represented to **SNCC**, radicalizing and then rejecting major aspects of **civil rights** and New **Left** ideology. Stock phrases like "kill the pig" and "kicking ass" captured some disaffected with the Vietnam War and "corporate capitalism," though they remained relatively few. The Weathermen eventually turned to urban guerilla methods and, as efforts at robbery and kidnapping made them fugitives, tended to separate themselves in clandestine organizations, akin to **cults**. In the 1980s and 1990s, several former Weathermen who had created new identities were arrested or turned themselves in to the police, recalling the more radical 1960s counterculture to the public mind.

ROBERT GREGG

weddings

Weddings in the United States constitute a $33 billion unregulated industry annually, where the average wedding budget for the late 1990s was estimated at $20,000. Approximately 2.5 million couples marry annually in the United States, after emotional, social and legal negotiations between the couple and among families (providing the grist for constant television and movie narratives). Despite commitment, cost and preparation, it is also estimated that four out of ten **marriages** will fail.

Parents generally do not arrange marriages, unless their religious tradition strongly encourages it. Most states require both parties to be eighteen, unless they have parental consent. In fact, brides and grooms have been getting older since the Second World War, the average age being 24.5 years for brides and 26.9 years for grooms. Engagements are lasting longer, too, averaging fourteen months.

Weddings may be civil and religious; these rules may also conflict. Bigamy and polygamy, for example, are not permitted in the United States, despite religious traditions that permit those practices (**Islam**, **Mormons**). Some religions require a waiting period, counseling or conversion prior to a wedding. Clergy conduct religious ceremonies (sometimes multiply in inter-faith marriages), and judges or other recognized officials conduct civil ceremonies. In other cases, the time it may take to make it to a drive-in chapel may suffice – **Las Vegas** is famous for this industry. Small civil ceremonies have reflected economic constraints and a desire for privacy.

The wedding event itself may be rich in family or religious traditions or a unique experience reflecting the personalities or lifestyles of the couple; often, a classic American "large wedding" influences even rebellions against formalities. Different ethnic and cultural traditions are also influenced by perceptions of this American model in synthetic ceremonies and receptions.

The mother of the bride used to have the most responsibilities for planning the wedding, for which the father paid. Today's bridal couples often take responsibility for their own weddings. As they are older, they have established tastes, careers and a wider circle of friends. The best man and maid of honor tend to be peers, either close friends or relatives; friends and family are also incorporated as bridesmaids, ushers and junior attendants. Numbers and elaboration of dress depend on the size and cost of the wedding.

June used to be the traditional month for weddings, following **commencements**. Today, more marry in the fall or during winter holidays. Brides still prefer white or ivory bridal gowns, costing between $500 and $2,500, but more radical or practical choices may be adapted to the ceremony.

Couples may register for household products at discount stores and hardware stores in addition to the traditional china, crystal and silver selections. Cash gifts are favored by many. These may be applied to the honeymoon, a traditional vacation after the wedding, or to setting up a new household.

Weddings have been affected by combined families, mixed traditions and changing gender roles. Children and former families may be dealt with in the planning and ceremony; multiple in-laws and step-families often demand careful juggling. In 1999 the Vermont Supreme Court outlawed discriminatory practices that precluded same-sex marriages, while some other sates, cities and groups have worked to recognize commitment ceremonies. This remains a hotly contested point among social and religious groups and for the changing nature of marriage in the twenty-first century.

Further reading:

Mann, L. (1988) "The Bride of the '90s," *Chicago Tribune* May 24: 1.

Nussbaum, D. (1998) "If Sentiment Fails, Cold Cash Will do," *New York Times*, May 24: 12.

GAIL HENSON

welfare/welfare reform

The American income maintenance system is in reality a patchwork of programs aimed at different populations and financed and administered by federal, state and local governments. Further, it is divided into "insurance-like" programs, for which eligibility is based on a history of wage earning, and "welfare" programs, for which eligibility is based on "means-testing," the determination of need according to levels of income and wealth. "Welfare reform" denotes sweeping policy changes in the means-tested programs, mainly in terms of initial eligibility and continuing assistance.

Until passage of the **Social Security** Act in 1935, welfare was a state and local matter. The Social Security Act, and many subsequent amendments, made federal and state governments partners in the administration and financing of welfare benefits for families and the elderly, blind and disabled. Federal rule-making, buttressed by US **Supreme Court** decisions, attempted to ensure a rough equity on a national basis. In 1974 benefits for the elderly, blind and disabled were consolidated in one federally administered and financed program. The states continued to share administration and financing of the program for families. After 1988, and gaining momentum with the **Republican** ascendancy in **Congress** after 1994, administrative control of the family aid program began to shift towards the states, but remained tethered to overarching federal rules. The most dramatic change of this sort was accomplished by the Personal Responsibility and Work Opportunity Reconciliation Act of 1997 (PRWO).

The PRWO eliminated the entitlement to benefits in the family program. Previously, any eligible family had a legal right to benefits, regardless of budgetary considerations. Now, states receive "block grants," fixed sums of federal dollars calculated by formula. When these funds are exhausted, aid may be denied to eligible families by states unwilling to spend their own funds. The PRWO also limits federal benefits to five years in a lifetime for most family aid recipients and allows states to adopt shorter terms. Further, it mandates the states to enroll increasingly large proportions of adult family aid recipients in work or training programs. Failure to meet scheduled goals results in the loss of a percentage of block grant funds.

Historically, welfare programs incorporated a suspicion of poverty, and welfare programs were overlaid with "morals testing." Until the 1970s, putatively dissipated or licentious poor folk frequently were denied aid, restricted to institutional care, or had their benefits carefully supervised. The PRWO reinvigorated this tradition by imposing on recipients of family aid "behavioral requirements" for initial eligibility and continuing assistance. (The PRWO also allows the states to impose others.) The most significant of these make ineligible or impose penalties on those who commit drug felonies or use illicit drugs, fail to have their children immunized or attend school regularly, or refuse work or training opportunities. In a similar spirit, though by different legislation, substance abuse was eliminated as an eligible impairment in both the insurance-like and welfare versions of the federal disability program.

In sum, in its present cast, welfare reform is intended to limit federal financial liability, force welfare parents into the labor market and discipline the behavior of poor people. Its results remain to be seen.

Further reading

Handler, J.F. (1995) *The Poverty of Welfare Reform*, New Haven: Yale University Press.

JIM BAUMOHL

Welk, Lawrence

b. 1903; d. 1992

Lawrence Welk, known for his "champagne" music complete with large bubbles dancing about the set, began with his traveling orchestra hosting dance parties in ballrooms of the Midwest. After twenty-six years of these shows, often broadcasted on radio, he moved to local television in 1951 and national television in 1955, where he ran until 1972 (and then moved into **syndication**). Often thought of as a favorite of the blue-haired set, this upbeat show featured an orchestra that was able to shift from waltz to polka to a fox trot in rapid succession, keeping at-home dancers on their toes. Welk had on offbeat, unlikely charm, which kept him as a favorite in front of cameras.

EDWARD MILLER

Welles, Orson

b. 1915; d. 1985

One of America's most revered film-makers, Orson Welles was already an accomplished **director** and actor before he made his first movie at age twenty-four. Welles initially received wide acclaim for his stage direction, and notoriety for his 1938 radio adaptation of *War of the Worlds*. Told through a series of simulated news bulletins, it sparked nationwide panic. Welles achieved his greatest success with his first movie *Citizen Kane* (1941), hailed by some as the greatest motion picture ever made. Unfortunately, although Welles continued to enjoy periodic success in films as both director and actor, the remainder of his life consisted of losing battles for the right to control his subsequent films, and ultimately to make films at all.

ROBERT ANDERSON

West

Comprehending the American West is a Herculean task. This essay will take the West to include the tier of Great Plains states from Texas to the Dakotas and everything westward, including **Alaska** and **Hawai'i**. This categorization easily makes the West the largest of America's regions, comprising nineteen states and well over half the nation's territory. This enormous and diverse area is in some views not a region at all, but a conglomeration of very different regions: the desert **Southwest**; the Pacific Northwest; the Great Plains; and the mountain interior. But the West offers unity as well as diversity.

What are the unifying characteristics of this vast region? Aridity is one widespread feature of a generally difficult, inhospitable climate. Most of the West is also relatively empty; the landscape is imposing, both in its grandeur and its harshness. The West is home to America's oldest, largest and best-known **national parks**, and is the center of the nation's **tourism** and recreation industries. The federal government owns and controls a large portion of Western land.

It is the most multicultural part of the country, with the largest concentrations of **Hispanic**, Asian and Native Americans. Virtually all of America's Indian reservations are located in the West. Surprisingly, it is also the most urban region, with the highest percentage of its people living in cities.

A large part of what makes the West cohere is its history. For most Americans the West is defined primarily by its **frontier** heritage. The West is the land of explorers and fur trading "mountain men," gold rushes and Indian conflicts, **cowboys**, overland trails and hardy pioneers. This "West of the imagination" became the focal point for an immense popular-culture industry, incessantly portrayed in art and music, a vast literature and above all in movies and on television.

The contemporary West, then, combines mythological popular-culture nostalgia and modern reality. Nonetheless, change has come to the West in a particularly dramatic way in the past half century. For most of its history, the West was in a subaltern position – politically, economically and culturally dominated by the East. The Second World War was its watershed. With the growing importance of Asia and the **Pacific Rim**, the West became a central, and often even pace-setting region.

The growth, maturity and influence of the West in contemporary American culture can be traced in many areas. Politically, the New Right, the main development in American politics since the decline of New Deal liberalism, is a Western phenomenon. Barry **Goldwater**, who began the movement, is from Arizona; Ronald **Reagan**, from **California**, was its culmination. Richard **Nixon**, a pivotal figure of recent American politics, was another Californian. Prior to the Second World War no American president had been from the West. Since the Second World War, only **Kennedy**, **Carter** and **Clinton** have not had western affiliations (and Kennedy ran with Lyndon **Johnson**).

The tilting of American political power westward was propelled by population shifts. The West has been the most rapidly growing region in America for decades. California surpassed New York as the nation's most populous state in the 1960s. **Texas** will soon rank second. **Los Angeles** recently overtook Chicago as the nation's second-largest city, and **San Diego**, **San Antonio** and **Phoenix** continue to push upwards.

Economically, since the Second World War, the West has left behind its colonial status as a plundered province. Three Pacific wars – the Second World War, Korea and Vietnam – promoted westward shifts in military spending and the defense industry. A highly symbiotic relationship exists between the West, the military and America's emergence as a global superpower, as San Diego and **Seattle** attest.

Moreover, America's military might was closely tied to "big science." Again the West played a prominent role: from Berkeley to Los Alamos and Alamagordo to **Silicon Valley**, it has been a twentieth-century laboratory. In addition, the West is America's main energy producer. During energy shortages in the 1970s and 1980s, energy-oriented cities like **Denver** and **Houston** boomed.

The West is now arguably the nation's cultural leader. Even in the 1920s and 1930s, **Hollywood** was a major shaper and exporter of American culture, and California was already pioneering lifestyles that would become standard nationwide after the Second World War. **Disneyland** is an American and global cultural icon, as is **Las Vegas**. The counterculture of the 1960s originated in the **San Francisco** Bay area, and influential American rock music, from the **Beach Boys** to the Doors to acid rock, came from California. In the 1990s, Seattle has been the home of alternative rock and **grunge** lifestyles. From the popularity of sun tanning and outdoor barbequing to the television programs *Dallas* and *Baywatch*, from Pacific Northwest or "cowboy chic" influences in fashion to California, Tex-Mex and Southwest cuisine, the West has set the standards for American popular culture in recent decades.

At the same time, America's growing **environmentalism** also has Western roots. Environmental symbols, including the wolf, the buffalo, the grizzly bear, the redwood and the spotted owl, are mostly Western. America's leading environmental advocates have come from the West and crucial environmental battles have taken place there.

The West has been one of the most dynamic regions of the country in the past half century. Its vitality is reflected in a lively and widely varied Western regionalism. Examples include the flourishing of Western literature, especially Hispanic, Native and **Asian American** variations; the New West **History**; a resurgent popularity of **country and western** music; influential Southwestern and postmodern architecture and interior design; and Western art and photography. All of these factors make the West arguably the most intriguing and important of the nation's regions. Americans have always been fascinated with the historic West. Now the contemporary West is at the center of attention too.

Further reading

Johnson, M. (1996) *The New Westers: The West in Contemporary American Culture*, Lawrence: University of Kansas.

Nash, G. (1973) *The American West in the Twentieth Century*, Englewood Cliffs: Prentice Hall.

White, R. (1991) *It's Your Misfortune and None of My Own*, Norman: University of Oklahoma.

KENT BLASER

West, Cornel

b. 1953

Considered by Henry Louis Gates, Jr., who brought him to Harvard University's Afro-American Studies program in 1994, the pre-eminent **African American** intellectual of our time. Author of the bestselling *Race Matters* (1993), and collaborator with bell **hooks**, West has blended religious homilies with loose-fitting Marxist analysis. His criticism of the black **middle class** for being "decadent" resembles that of E. Franklin **Frazier**, and his discussion of the "psychic pain" inflicted upon the urban poor fits with current views that the **"underclass"** is dysfunctional. He has criticized hip-hop culture for being nihilistic, in contrast to **intellectuals** like Robin D.G. Kelley and some of the practitioners themselves, who have emphasized its deep politicization.

ROBERT GREGG

westerns, film

Westerns, perhaps the most important, recognized and popular genre of **Hollywood** movies worldwide, are as old as narrative film itself. Many scholars consider *The Great Train Robbery* (1903) to be the first important narrative film, which coincidentally established cinematic themes that would define westerns to this day: outlaws and lawmen, a train robbery, a chase on horseback and a shoot-out, all within a wilderness setting. These motifs, which along with those of **cowboys**, cattle, Native Americans, cavalry, settlers and covered wagons had been established in American culture since the nineteenth century through the popularity of dime-store novels, wild-west shows and the writings of authors such as James Fennimore Cooper and Bret Hart, sustained the genre through to the era of the Second World War, when more mature and complex themes surfaced.

The era of the classic western feature film was ushered in with *Stagecoach* (1939), by veteran director John **Ford**, regarded by many critics and fans as the premier western film-maker in American cinema. Ford's westerns had an epic quality that, along with an attention to characterization and dialogue, marked most western films throughout the 1940s and 1950s. This was the period of the epic western, filmed on location, which dealt with the broad sweep of American myth and history, yet found time to confront the social problems and psychological torments which were the root causes of the conflicts between such groups as ranchers and homesteaders (*Shane*, 1953), whites and Indians (*The Searchers*, 1956), lawmen and badmen (*High Noon*, 1952) and cattlemen and society (*Red River*, 1948). Many of these films transcended the confines of the western genre to deal with issues relevant to contemporary America, but did so in ways which did not confront the mythical roots of the western itself.

The 1960s brought the anti-hero to westerns in films where protagonists, doomed in a West that could not survive a civilizing America, turned to violence as mercenaries (*The Magnificent Seven*, 1960), outlaws (*Butch Cassidy and the Sundance Kid*, 1969), or sociopathic killers (*The Wild Bunch*, 1969). These "end of the **frontier**" themes paralleled growing American alienation in the 1960s and 1970s, which led western film-makers and authors to question the accuracy of western history and the role of the West in the origins of American culture. As a result, views of Native Americans, long portrayed as the stereotyped "other" in the

Manifest Destiny sagas of the epic western, were revised in such films as *Little Big Man* (1970) and *Dances With Wolves* (1990). This grittier approach to the people and events of the filmic West, both Old and New, has been mirrored in the novels of Elmore Leonard, Larry McMurtry and Thomas McGuane.

Many great directors of western films such as Ford, Howard Hawks and Anthony Mann won critical acclaim and fame in other movie genres. Some, like Sam **Peckinpah** and Budd Boetticher, seemed most at home in the West. This was also true of actors, like John **Wayne**, whose career was inextricably linked to his celluloid image as a Westerner, and Clint **Eastwood**, famed over the last four decades for his western film acting and directing.

Further reading

Buscombe, E. (ed.) (1988) *The BFI Companion to the Western*, London: The British Film Institute.
Kitses, J. (1969) *Horizons West*, Bloomington: Indiana University Press.

THOMAS M. WILSON

westerns, literature

The western occupies a permanent place in American literature, as it does in other media. The **individualism** of the American culture seems nowhere better captured than in stories of the **cowboy** – the ultimate American hero – and in rugged individualists who populated the landscape of the **West**. The western appeals to the need for **freedom**, wide open spaces and frontiers, self-sufficiency, triumphing over adversaries and survival against the elements. Westerners' corrals, groups of collectors, writers and historians all write about the history, way of life and heroes of the West, past and present.

Westerns are nonetheless interpretations and ideologies. Stereotyped plots, overly romantic dialogue and misuse of dialect characterize one popular form of western. As Diana Herald writes in *Genreflecting*: "the stereotypic western can be recognized on the first page: a lone rider is crossing a valley or desert and a shot knocks off his hat or hits a rock, startling his horse, and a range war

begins" (1995: 18). Other themes and types of westerns include plots about wagon trains moving west, mule trains and stage lines, mining and lost mines, captivities, cattle **ranching** and cattle drives, range wars, boys becoming men, romance, picaresque heroes and parodies of cowboys. **Texas** and **Mexico** and **American Indian** territories provide settings and issues. Characters include mountain men, buffalo runners, black cowboys, Mormons, marshals, strong women, doctors, preachers and celebrity characters.

Popular series have been written by Louis L'Amour and Hank Mitchem, among many others, providing a seeming masculine counterpart to female-oriented **romances**. Contemporary westerns, such as those by Barbara Kingsolver, Edward Abbey and William Eastlake, set in the twentieth century keep the themes of the cowboy, wide open spaces, wild adventures and Indian-Anglo relations, although they may add on more environmental sensitivity or an Indian viewpoint (e.g. Tony Hillerman's **Southwestern** mysteries). Larry McMurtry and Cormac McCarthy have also added new literary dimensions to classic scenarios.

Other contemporary trends include "adult" westerns of heroic, sexual adventures that started with **Playboy** Press in 1975. The western, as a genre, has been the subject of numerous parodies as well. Even these underscore its place in the myth-making of all America.

See also: westerns, television; television; westerns, film

Further reading

Herald, D. (1995) *Genreflecting. A Guide to Reading Interests in Genre Fiction*, 4th edn, Englewood: Libraries Unlimited.
Perkins, G., Perkins, B. and Leininger, P. (1991) *Benet's Reader's Encyclopedia of American Literature*, New York: HarperCollins.

GAIL HENSON

westerns, television

From 1955 to 1975, *Gunsmoke*, the longest running prime-time ensemble drama in **television** history, told stories of a sheriff, his sidekicks, Miss Kitty in the saloon and other drifters through a Western city. In the heyday of the TV western, literature and prior films spurred a plethora of **cowboys**, rugged landscapes and moral issues of the **frontier** for viewers every week. These series both launched stars – Clint Eastwood, Steve McQueen, James Garner – and showcased cinematic legends like Barbara Stanwyck, confronting a male world in *The Big Valley* (ABC, 1965–9). While no major shows followed *Gunsmoke*, the impact of the western nonetheless lingers.

The Brauers (1975) have categorized the television western by three phases. The first horse phase included cowboys and chases with heroes like *Roy Rogers* (NBC, 1951–7), the Lone Ranger (ABC, 1949–57) and the Cisco Kid (syndicated, 1950–6). This family entertainment (including Saturday morning fare) offered comical sidekicks and idealistic cowboys. Rogers merged public and private life with Dale Evans, while the Lone Ranger introduced a terse Indian companion, Tonto, and *Sky King* (ABC, 1953–4) substituted a plane for a horse.

The second, adult evolution of the western followed the gun (e.g. *Gunsmoke*, CBS, 1955–75), with increased violence and retribution. The sheriff or some honest man versus criminals and occasional Indians recapitulated themes of freedom, justice and gunplay found in movies such as *High Noon* (1952). Moral ambiguities and irony crept in with the gambling Maverick family (ABC, 1957–62) as well as Bat Masterson (NBC, 1959–61) and his cronies. *The Wild, Wild West* (CBS, 1965–9) paired the western formula with James Bond-like espionage, humor, vamps and toys.

The consummate example of property was the vast Ponderosa ranch, owned by Ben Cartwright and his boys in *Bonanza* (NBC, 1959–1973), another top show. But this was echoed by both Stanwyck and Lee J. Cobb in *The Virginian*.

In all these melodramas of "Americanness," strong, independent and virtuous men overcame obstacles for weak and evil men as well as forces of nature – floods, stampedes, blizzards – that tempered their character. Indians were not so badly defined as in earlier Hollywood westerns, but were rarely central to action or perspective. Hispanics also had a slight presence in the

nebulous West; Asians were drawn between *Bonanza's* faithful cook, Hop Sing, and David Carradine's later half-Chinese Caine, wandering the West dispensing justice and wisdom in *Kung Fu*. Females tended to be love interests, domestic or flirtatious, until a stronger female/family perspective emerged with *Little House on the Prairie* (NBC, 1974–83). In the 1990s, however, the only long-running western, *Dr Quinn Medicine Woman*, cast a female star in a professional role.

While the Hollywood western was rekindled in the 1990s by films that introduced dark lines into heroes amidst epic grandeur, no such rebirth hit television. Yet westerns retain an impact in other ways. *Star Trek* (NBC, 1966–9) is heavily indebted to this schema on "the final frontier." Moreover, prime-time soaps like *Dallas*, *Dynasty* and *Falcon Crest*, all set in the West (the latter including a faithful Chinese servant), recalled the freewheeling property and even guns of older days, although in boardrooms rather than saloons and corrals.

Further reading

Brauer, D. and Brauer, R. (1975) *The Horse, The Gun and the Piece of Property*, Bowing Green, OH: Bowing Green University.

Stark, S. (1996) *Glued to the Set*, New York: St. Martin's.

GARY McDONOGH

whiskey *see* alcohol

white

The color white represents base on the color scale. This symbolic meaning has often been presupposed when white, or whiteness, represents racial identity. When white represents racial identity it often represents normalcy, naturalness or homogeneity. It is this type of affiliation that often leads white identity to be unexamined by cultural or social studies. Yet, this lack of critical engagement solidifies a conundrum where various racial identities are constantly discussed, but whiteness is left simply to exist. Thus, white becomes a substitute for power and stands atop a supposed racial hierarchy that represents a natural order. A critical understanding of white identity is found when various histories, affiliations and representations are critiqued for their attachment to whiteness over time (see Frankenberg 1997).

White identity has historical roots in a worldview generated in Enlightenment Europe and a Victorian ideal of beauty and civility. The historical attachment of white identity to normalcy and power can be found in many scientific and social proclamations of the eighteenth and nineteenth centuries (see Gould 1991). These historical accounts often skewed scientific methodology and fact to assert that white identity had a natural position atop a racial order, especially in the United States. This coincided with slavery, colonialism and an influx of **immigration** that brought various others into contact with a white Anglo-Saxon Protestant social order that was dominant at the time. Therefore, the attempts to assert white identity as a natural occurrence became a defense mechanism and fed a Eurocentric worldview. White has also been affiliated with national and ethnic identity. The idea and conception of national identity, especially in England and the United States, has been synonymous with whiteness historically. This has had a number of consequences for cultural representations of the United States where model citizenship becomes synonymous with being white and, usually, male.

The affiliation of white identity to **class** status is prevalent as well. The notion of white privilege has come to symbolize this affiliation due to the fact that people socially defined as white often possess greater opportunity and rapid class mobility. The relationship of whiteness to class status is often found in the built environment. The **segregation** of public facilities, social services and **neighborhoods** as "white only" throughout the United States in the beginning of the twentieth century demarcated white identity. Upper-middle-class neighborhoods became a code word for white neighborhoods in a process known as "**white flight**" after the Second World War. This movement to the **suburbs** essentially "whitened" an entire generation of people previously considered to be ethnic others, but now possessing new racial identities because of their class mobility. Solidification of this new white identity was found in television shows of the time like

Leave it to Beaver. This entire process was dependent on the consistent racial segregation of **African Americans** and other people socially constructed as "others" in the United States.

Further reading

Gould, S. (1991) *The Mismeasure of Man*, London: Cambridge University Press.
Frankenberg, R. (ed.) (1997) *Displacing Whiteness: Essays in Social and Cultural Criticism*. Durham: Duke University Press.

MATTHEW DURINGTON

White, Edmund

b. 1940

American writer, essayist and gay activist whose works depict the evolution of gay life in the United States, particularly the complex issues of the **AIDS** epidemic. White worked as an editor for *The Saturday Review* and *Horizon*. He co-founded the Violet Quill, a group of gay writers, in the mid-1970s. His most notable works include two largely autobiographical novels and an anthology, *Gay Short Fiction* (1991). His most recent works include a biography of Jean Genet, whose exploration of homosexuality through plays and novels long has interested White. White has lived and worked in France since 1983.

JIM WATKINS

white collar *see* class; middle class

white-collar crime

White-collar crime refers to offenses such as **tax** evasion, misuse of public funds, embezzlement, fraud and abuse of power. Its perpetrators are most often members of the social elite who have positions of influence in business and government. The term "white-collar crime" was first popularized in 1940 by criminologist Edwin H. Sutherland. However, the phenomenon first became prominent in the American consciousness in the early 1970s, when President Richard M. **Nixon** was forced to resign amid allegations that he had abused his presidential power to cover up his involvement in the **Watergate** scandal.

The legal system has traditionally been lenient in its punishment of white-collar criminals, while penalties for crimes like burglary, drug dealing and murder have grown increasingly stringent since the Second World War. This trend has reinforced class divisions between white-collar and traditional criminals, who often come from poor backgrounds.

Authorities have grown more vigilant in their prosecution of white-collar offenders since a wave of highly publicized cases in the 1980s and early 1990s. Successful **Wall Street** traders Ivan Boesky and Michael **Milken** paid millions of dollars in fines and served substantial prison terms during this period for their involvement in illegal insider trading on the stock market. White-collar crime also played a role in the financial collapse of the savings and loan industry. Banking executive Charles H. Keating, Jr., whose institution was one of about 700 that went bankrupt, was prosecuted and jailed for defrauding his customers by persuading them to make high-risk investments in his bank's parent company. Several US senators who had received large contributions from Keating were reprimanded for ethics violations after a Senate investigation found that they had lobbied federal regulators on Keating's behalf. The federal government's ultimate decision to help rescue the savings and loan industry with $130 million in federal funds (as of the end of 1996) angered many taxpayers. They accused the government of protecting the interests of wealthy business people at the expense of average citizens.

The federal government focused increasing attention in the 1990s on its own victimization by white-collar criminals. Growing numbers of businesses and individuals have faced prosecution for defrauding government agencies. Financial abuses have been especially prevalent in the federal Medicare and Medicaid entitlement programs.

All forms of white-collar crime expanded in scope in the 1990s as perpetrators began to use the **Internet** and the World Wide Web as tools for corporate espionage and other illegal business practices.

SARAH SMITH

white flight

In the 1960s, as blacks and **Latinos** slowly integrated school and housing in American **cities**, many **white** middle-class families abandoned changing neighborhoods for newer, segregated **suburbs**. This created a fundamental shift in demography, wealth and power as cities lost income and property while governed by new majorities of color in Detroit, Washington, Philadelphia, Los Angeles, etc. Middle-class blacks sought new suburban options, while poor and older whites, often in **ethnic enclaves**, built uneasy defenses. **Gentrification** later returned younger, wealthier whites to a **dual city**, but zones between the downtown and suburbs have been scarred by decades of neglect.

GARY McDONOGH
CINDY WONG

Whitewater scandal

In 1978 Arkansas Attorney-General Bill **Clinton** and Hillary Rodham Clinton joined a partnership with James and Susan McDougal to buy and develop riverfront land as vacation homes: the Whitewater Development Corporation. The plan failed and the Clintons reported a loss of more than $40,000. McDougal also owned Madison Guaranty Savings and Loan Association, which, like many such institutions, went under in the 1980s partly as a result of fraudulent loans, and Hillary was the lawyer for Madison Guaranty. In addition, many opposed to the Clintons believed they had paid McDougal hush money.

Following the chronicling of the Whitewater case in *The New York Times* in 1992, the **Republican**-led **Congress** called for a special prosecutor. In August 1994 Kenneth W. Starr was appointed **independent counsel** (replacing the more moderate Robert Fiske) and he quickly expanded the hearings to encompass the firing of White House travel office clerks (Travelgate), the suicide of the Clinton's friend/advisor Vince Foster (Filegate), and then the Paula Jones **sexual harassment** case against Clinton and the Monica Lewinsky affair. Besides mushrooming into the

1999 **impeachment** case against Clinton, the Starr grand jury investigations achieved few indictments. The McDougals both spent time in prison (James died of heart failure a few months before his scheduled release, while Susan defied the court and was imprisoned for contempt). Clinton's successor as governor of Arkansas, Jim Guy Tucker, also spent eighteen months in home detention for his involvement in Madison Guaranty.

ROBERT GREGG

Wideman, John Edgar

b. 1941

Novelist educated at the University of Pennsylvania; in 1963, only the second **African American** to receive a Rhodes Scholarship. Wideman returned to the **Ivy League** university to teach English and to write. His first novel, *A Glance Away* (1967), was followed by a succession of fictional works leading to *Sent for You Yesterday* (1983), which won the PEN/Faulkner Award of 1984. Wideman's next work, the non-fictional *Brothers and Keepers* (1984), focused on the divergent paths he and his brother, who was imprisoned for armed robbery, had taken. Subsequent novels have blended fiction and historical events: *Fever* (1989) described yellow fever in eighteenth-century Philadelphia, while *Philadelphia Fire* (1990) touched on the aftermath of the 1984 police bombing of the MOVE cult in West Philadelphia.

ROBERT GREGG

Wiesel, Elie

b. 1928

Émigré Jewish author, activist and historical consciousness. Born in Romania, both his parents were killed in Auschwitz. His works, fiction, memoirs and non-fiction, have poignantly explored the Holocaust and the Jewish experience. Wiesel became an American citizen in 1963 and chaired the President's Commission on the Holocaust. He received the Congressional Medal of Honor in 1985 and the **Nobel** Peace Prize in 1986 for his work in promoting human rights. The next year he established the Elie Wiesel Foundation for Humanity.

CINDY WONG

Wilder, Billy

b. 1906

Director and screenwriter. Nazis forced Wilder to abandon his native Austria in 1933. In the US, he became a remarkably insightful auteur into American relationships. His career as **director** and collaborative screenwriter included classics in noir (*Double Indemnity*, 1944), gender farce (*Some Like it Hot*, 1959) and savage depictions of media frenzies (*The Big Carnival*, 1951). In *Lost Weekend* (Oscar, 1945), Wilder also won Oscars for directing and shared screenwriting, a feat repeated with the *The Apartment* (1961). He shared another screenwriting Oscar for his *Sunset Boulevard* (1950), a haunting portrait of lost **Hollywood**.

GARY McDONOGH

wilderness *see* environmentalism; frontier; nature; parks, national and state

Williams, Hank

b. 1923; d. 1953

Hank Williams became a legendary **country music** star. Born in Montgomery, Alabama, he began a meteoric career after a spectacular Grand Old Opry debut in 1949. Fame and fortune complicated Williams' troubled personal life. He died at age thirty, of a combination of alcohol and drugs, in the back seat of his famous pink Cadillac during an overnight road trip. An inspiration for numerous singer/writers, including Elvis **Presley**, Williams left behind some of the best-known and loved songs in all of country music, including "Your Cheatin' Heart," "I'm So Lonesome I Could Cry" and "Lovesick Blues."

KENT BLASER

Williams, Tennessee (Thomas)

b. 1911; d. 1988

Powerful playwright whose works explored and exploded myths of the **South**. His highly personal and poetic dramas are imbued with sensuality, guilt, decay, illusion and the power of love. Works such as *The Glass Menagerie* (1945), the **Pulitzer Prize**-winning *A Streetcar named Desire* (1947) and *Cat on a Hot Tin Roof* (1954) have become staples of global as well as American **theater** (see Almodovar's *All About My Mother*, 1999). These, and other plays, have also been made into powerful movie and television presentations, bringing Williams' images and speeches into a wider public realm of reference. Williams' life and work have also been influential in defining gay expression in contemporary America.

GARY McDONOGH
CINDY WONG

Wilson, August

b. 1945

Pittsburgh-born **African American** playwright and winner of the **Pulitzer Prize** for Drama in 1987 and 1990. Wilson's plays often stem from impressions formed growing up during the 1950s and 1960s in the city's black community, known as "The Hill." In *Ma Rainey's Black Bottom* (1985), *Two Trains Running* (1993) and *The Piano Lesson* (1990), Wilson builds dramas on the words and dreams of **working-class** African Americans. Recently, Wilson has become embroiled in debate over the representation of African Americans in theater. His manifesto for black artists in the American theater argues that it is the responsibility of theaters to endeavor to understand the culture of non-Europeans, rather than that of non-white artists to transform and compromise their work for white audiences.

ROBERT GREGG

Wilson, Edmund

b. 1895; d. 1972

Poet, novelist, journalist and cultural and political essayist, Wilson was one of the most prodigious writers of the twentieth century. After attending Princeton University and serving in the First World War, he became a theater critic, a book editor for *The New Republic* and cultural critic for *The New Yorker*. During the Depression, he made his name publishing essays such as those found in *The American Jitters*, which, influenced by post-Second World War anti-**communism**, he edited and republished as *The American Earthquake*. His widely acclaimed history of European revolutions, *To the Finland Station* (1940), highlighted a shift among many American leftists away from socialism to a more pragmatic liberalism, and shaped much of the discussion of Marxism among American intellectuals for about thirty years.

ROBERT GREGG

Wilson, Pete

b. 1933

Elected **governor** of **California** in 1990 and re-elected in 1994, Wilson supported tough **welfare reform** and anti-crime measures. He gained national attention in 1994 with his backing of Proposition 187, a California referendum approved by the state's voters that prohibited illegal immigrants from receiving public education and other social services. Wilson also opposed **affirmative action**. He supported a successful 1996 California initiative, Proposition 209, that banned racial and gender preferences in state and local public programs, including college admissions. Wilson was mayor of **San Diego** from 1971 until 1983, when he became a United States senator.

JAMES DEVITT

Wilson, Robert

b. 1941

Trained in painting and architecture, Robert Wilson has become a pre-eminent theater artist whose visionary stagings of standard and original work has transformed both scenography and directorial technique. He is best known for the groundbreaking *Einstein on the Beach*, a collaboration with composer Philip Glass and choreographer Lucinda Childs, first performed in 1976. This nonlinear, abstract 4–5 hour musing on the scientist was stark, abstract and pictorial: Wilson used graphical, architectural and multiple performing arts. Resoundingly multimedia, Wilson has staged operas in Europe and has collaborated with artists such as Susan Sontag, Allen Ginsburg and Red Grooms. He has worked again with Glass on *Monsters of Grace* (1998), based on the works of the fourteenth century Sufi poet Rumi.

EDWARD MILLER

wine *see* alcohol

Winfrey, Oprah

b. 1954

Through her **talk show**, syndicated since 1986, and her active production company, Winfrey has become one of the most influential and wealthy **African Americans** in history with a power to make media as well as appear in them. Her gender, aggressive yet intimate style as an interviewer and her ability to shape middle-class tastes through her program and book club, while surviving tabloid reports on her loves and diet, make this more remarkable. Although nominated for an Oscar for *The Color Purple* (1985) her later acting career proved less striking; *Beloved* (1998) was a confusing failure for Toni **Morrison**'s novel.

GARY McDONOGH

Wise Use movement

An ideological consortium that opposes federal authority over rural public lands. Most adherents reside in the far **West**, where the federal government exercises substantial ownership and control of public land. Wise Use proponents are an offshoot of the larger Patriot anti-government movement. Specifically, their activists support the return of federal land to individuals and local governments and an end to most environmental and rural zoning regulations.

BRIAN LEVIN

witchcraft (Wicca)

In late twentieth-century America this referred primarily to a postwar religious movement, also known as Wicca, or The Craft. *Wicca* is said to derive from Anglo-Saxon *wicce* meaning "wise" or alternatively "to bend," although its actual provenance is unknown. Modern witches worship both male and female deities, often represented by the Horned God and the Triple Goddess (Maiden, Mother and Crone). Major holidays occur at regular points in the year: February 2 (Imbolc); Spring Equinox; May 1 (Beltane); Summer Solstice; August 2 (Lammas or Lughnasa); October 31 (Samhain); and Winter Solstice. In addition, many witches also celebrate the new and full moons. Modern witchcraft is a nature religion in the sense that all nature is considered to be sacred.

Wicca developed in Great Britain in the 1950s, and its earliest practitioners claimed its beliefs and rituals were the survivals of pre-Christian agricultural religions of Northern and Western Europe. While in Britain, Wicca has developed as a predominantly nativist movement maintaining an emphasis on its British cultural roots, in the US its growth since the 1970s has been strongly influenced by left-wing social movements, environmentalism and feminism. In the 1970s the traditional image of the witch as a marginalized yet wise and powerful figure was "reclaimed" by feminists. Furthermore, a religion which emphasized a female deity and had women in positions of power was naturally attractive to feminists. This combination of religion and politics gave rise to a feminist witchcraft, which by the 1980s and 1990s was becoming incorporated into the wider "Goddess Movement."

As modern witchcraft becomes more high profile in the United States, more witches are working to ensure that their practices and beliefs are accepted as valid religious expression. Organizations such as the Witches Anti Discrimination League have been founded to ensure that witches receive full freedom of religious expression under United States Law. Salem, Massachusetts, where the infamous witch trials of 1692 took place during which twenty people were executed, is now home to a thriving community of modern witches.

AMY HALE

Wolfe, Tom

b. 1931

Wolfe came into prominence in the 1960s as a young, particularly passionate exponent of the "**New Journalism**." In 1972 Wolfe wrote a now-famous piece for *New York* magazine propounding New Journalistic principles and declaring the traditional novel dead. Ironically, Wolfe would later write a bestselling novel on yuppie New York, *Bonfire of the Vanities* (1987). Often writing in a coolly detached voice, Wolfe's singular genius has been to capture the spirit of a time or place in a single work (*The Electric Kool-Aid Acid Test*, 1968) or even a phrase, such as the term "radical chic" to describe the romance between well-heeled liberals and militant revolutionaries in the late 1960s and early 1970s. A number of Wolfe's books have become **Hollywood** movies, including *Bonfire* and *The Right Stuff* (1994), exploring the first generation of American astronauts.

MARK BREWIN

women and film-making

Hollywood has long lavished attention on female **stars** and sex goddesses. Marketing strategies have simultaneously targeted the female consumer by

narrative, genre or other intertextual appeals. This entry explores instead the women behind the camera. Here, women achieved some early success in fields such as editing and also took on stereotypically "feminine" tasks (interior design, costume, etc.) as well as clerical roles. Women in various guises have also been deeply involved in writing scripts, although often in subordinate roles. A 1980 survey by the Directors Guild of America, however, listed only fourteen features directed by women out of 7,332. The picture has changed somewhat in subsequent years with directors like Barbra **Streisand**, Penny Marshall, Susan Seidelman, Jodie **Foster**, Julie Dash, Kathryn Bigelow, Martha Coolidge, Nora Ephron, Amy Heckerling and Sondra Locke. Besides women **directors** for feature films, women have been independent directors, producers and animators. Yet, this remains a male-dominated world where even the enrollment in film schools has stood at a 2:1 ratio for a long time. Hence, since 1972, the American Film Institute has set up Directing Workshop for Women, whose alumni include Maya **Angelou** and Randa Haines, a token gesture to increase the representation of women in directing.

While women's films through the history of Hollywood have sometimes presented women with their own agencies and contradictions, the history of women directors suggests common threads and diverse contributions – and how this relates to images on screens and beyond them.

In the formative year of movies, when movies were smaller businesses, women were actually important players. Alice Guy Blache (1875–1968) ran Solax Studio in Fort Lee, New Jersey. Lois Weber (1882–1939), a top-salaried director of the silent era, made social-realist films, with subjects ranging from prostitution to capital punishment. With the transition to sound, Dorothy Arzner (1900–79) was the only woman working in the male-dominated Hollywood mainstream. She made seventeen films between 1927 and 1943. Her heroines were strong working women, and female relationships and bonding were recurring themes in her movies. Ida Lupino, first an actor in noir films in the 1940s, formed her own company, and directed six films for it between 1949 and 1954. The route from actor to director has proven a common path.

Breaking into the all-male Hollywood proved even harder for women of color trying to break into feature film-making. In 1989 Martinican Euzhan Palcy became the first black woman to direct a Hollywood film – *A Dry White Season*. Christine Choy, an Asian American film-maker, is known for her political documentaries. Julie **Dash**'s *Daughters of the Dust* was a critical success, but it had taken her years to complete – and fund – this period piece about a Gullah family in South Carolina.

While Hollywood poses a great barrier to women directors, women directors have accomplished a great deal as independent and avant-garde film-makers. Maya Deren (1917–61) was the first to receive a Guggenheim grant to engage in motion picture. She saw her films as poetry, not prose. Yvonne Rainer has made films that challenge the notion of the female gaze in Hollywood films. Toni Cade **Bambara** combined literature with film and community activism. Lesbian film-makers have also combined activist explorations with a growing screen presence.

Yet the AFI's 100 Years...100 Movies list released and voted on in 1998 does not include a single feature movie directed by a woman. These movies were chosen from a list of 400, including only five films directed by women, all produced between 1986 and 1993. While *Prince of Tides* was nominated for Best Picture at the 1991 Oscars, the Best Director nomination eluded even Barbra **Streisand**. Hence, the struggle and recognition accorded to women behind the camera comments on the gains and limits of gender and equality in the late twentieth century.

Further reading

Acker, A. (1991) *Reel Women*, New York: Continuum.

CINDY WONG

women in politics

Women have influenced and participated in American politics as voters, symbols, activists, campaigners and elected officials. Since the Second World War, women have broadened the definition of political work, though they did not begin winning numerous electoral contests until the 1980s.

The non-partisan League of Women Voters, founded after the ratification of the 19th Amendment, has long advocated good government and informed voter participation. In 1960 the League began sponsoring its popular televised election-year presidential debates.

Direct activism in the 1950s, 1960s and 1970s around international peace, human rights, civil rights, education, labor unions, anti-nuclear issues and general environmental protection brought formative political experience to women, including Fannie Lou **Hamer**, Jessie Lopez De La Cruz and Jane Fonda, who would otherwise have been excluded from politics. Increasing participation in waged labor politicized many middle-class women by making systematic wage disparities, open sex discrimination in job placement and training, and choices in family life and reproduction into political issues. These economic changes and the reinvigorated **feminism** of the 1960s and 1970s helped bring female experiences to the center of political debates and produced some successful electoral campaigns by women.

A small early group of elected leaders, including US representatives Bella Abzug and Shirley **Chisholm** and senators Margaret Chase Smith and Nancy Kassebaum, grew substantially after 1980. EMILY's List, an organized fundraising group created in 1985 to elect pro-choice Democratic female candidates, has helped especially to bring high-level financing to women's campaigns. Between 1975 and 1995, women went from 4 to 10 percent of the US Congress and from 8 to 21 percent of state legislators.

Beginning with Eleanor **Roosevelt**, who bridged suffrage and feminism in her own life, **First Ladies** have been lightning rods for cultural debates and have helped to shape the image of political womanhood. Some worked on timely national issues, for example Lady Bird Johnson's tireless efforts at highway beautification and Nancy Reagan's championing of her husband's "War on Drugs." Pat Nixon's very low, and loyal, public profile in the 1970s enhanced the **Republican** Party's appeal to what her husband called the "Silent Majority" of social conservatives. Nixon's successors, Betty **Ford** and Rosalyn Carter, acted more independently and were admired for it. Ford encouraged many to seek help with addiction problems by publicly admitting her own. Carter's controversial role as her husband's advisor set the stage for the even more controversial 1990s White House career of Hillary Rodham Clinton. Between **Democrats** Carter and Clinton, Nancy Reagan and Barbara Bush tried to re-establish a more formal role for the First Lady, echoing the growing conservatism of the Republican political platform.

American women, from famous First Ladies to individual activists, have helped define modern politics as well as influence it, galvanizing voters as well as representing them.

Further reading

Chisholm, S. (1990) *Unbought and Unbossed*, Boston: Houghton Mifflin.

Jetter, A., Orleck, A. and Taylor, D. (1997) *The Politics of Motherhood*, Hanover: Dartmouth University Press.

Kunin, M. (1994) *Living a Political Life*, New York: Knopf.

Schneir, M. (ed.) (1994) *Feminism in Our Time*, New York: Vintage.

SHARON ANN HOLT

women's liberation

Betty **Friedan** inspired this political and cultural movement for women's rights by writing *The Feminine Mystique* in 1963. Supporters, calling themselves "feminists," borrowed ideas from the **Civil Rights movement** and also pioneered techniques like consciousness-raising to persuade women that personal experiences had political significance. While independent, feminist-inspired activity erupted in many arenas of American life, the organized movement itself struggled with a bias towards white, middle-class women. The defeat of the **Equal Rights Amendment** somewhat obscured the movement's success in passing sports-equity legislation, legalizing **abortion**, increasing educational and professional opportunities for women and weakening **fashion** hegemony.

SHARON ANN HOLT

Wonder, Stevie

b. 1950

Born Steveland Morris and blind since birth, Stevie Wonder became one of the biggest artists on the **Motown** label until he terminated this contract in 1971. By the mid-1970s he was the bestselling American singer/songwriter, with successes like *Talking Book* (1972), *Innervisions* (1973) and *Songs in the Key of Life* (1976). Mastering many instruments at an early age, he led the way in embracing the new electronic synthesizers and recording techniques, and often played all the instruments on his records. His songs have combined different musical traditions – gospel, **blues**, reggae and **rap** – with strong social commitment, as in the songs "Living for the City" (1973), about a migrant new to New York City caught up in a drug deal, and "Happy Birthday" (1980), advocating the nationwide adoption of the Martin Luther **King** holiday.

ROBERT GREGG

Woods, Tiger

b. 1975

Already believed by many to be the greatest player to have played **golf**, regularly breaking records for lowest scores on the world's courses, and at the age of twenty-four becoming the youngest player to win a career Grand Slam – 1997 Masters, 1999 PGA tournament, 2000 US Open, the 2000 British Open (two years earlier than Jack **Nicklaus** achieved this feat). He has brought record numbers of viewers to televised golf, and, as the son of an **African American** father and a Thai mother, has opened up the sport to previously excluded or uninterested minorities. Now largely competing against himself, he sets new goals to achieve: tournaments without making a bogey; the first Grand Slam in a single year; and Nicklaus' achievement of eighteen major career victories.

ROBERT GREGG

Woodstock

Rock and art festival in 1969 in Bethel, New York, that became a symbol of **baby-boom** dreams. For three days in August, an unexpected crush of 500,000 plus participants adapted to freedom, music, drugs and a lack of sanitation. In addition to performances by Jimi **Hendrix**, Janis Joplin, the Who, the Grateful Dead, **Santana**, the Band, Jefferson Airplane and others, the celebration itself became myth, aided by the film and soundtrack *Woodstock* (1969). Nonetheless, this was a commercially organized concert, charging $18 for three-day admissions, paying performers and controlling film rights. Nonetheless, the experience of being there created an alternative vision of *Woodstock Nation* (1969). This myth also opposed the Rolling Stone's Altamount concert that year, at which Hells' Angels, hired as bodyguards, beat a fan to death (recorded in David and Albert Maysle's *Gimme Shelter*, 1970).

Attempts to recreate this event/ambiance have proven less successful. Woodstock 1994, the twenty-fifth anniversary, became highly commercialized, with sponsorship from Polygram and Pepsi and pay-per-view retransmission; musician Neil Young dubbed it "Greedstock." Although Woodstock 1999 gathered strong contemporary bands and 1969 veterans, it, too, was marred by costs and commercialism ($150 entrance tickets). Fires and destruction at closing and a disturbing misogyny, marked by reports of multiple rapes, made it seem even further from the original or its myth. Whether the result of the high expectations set by the first or increasingly exploitative concerts and festivals in the interim, it seems one cannot go back to Yasgur's farm.

Further reading

Hoffman, A. (1969) *Woodstock Nation*, New York: Vintage.

Makower, J. (1989) *Woodstock: The Oral History*, New York: Doubleday.

GARY McDONOGH

working class

If the **middle class** represents "the American dream," the situation, goals and meanings of working-class life and identity are immediately thrown into question in the United States. Since the Second World War, one notes a continual decline in the presence, organization and impact of the working class as a result of both intergenerational changes in working-class families and external pressures from government and business. Indeed, the American working class at the end of the century tended to be represented in negative or nostalgic terms. Moreover, difference in work itself in the postwar period complicated any definitions that might convey an identification of working-class and factory life. Are service workers working class, whether flipping burgers at **McDonald's** or typing in an office? Truckers? Farmers? Artists and **intellectuals** who speak for a **class**?

Hence, it is impossible to talk about American working-class culture or organization in a sense comparable to traditions of Europe or Latin America. In fact, even while the situation of workers has become endangered by deindustrialization, lack of welfare safety nets, offshore production and imports, their response has tended to be conservative and patriotic. Nonetheless, the **Left** has seen this class as a potential locus for organization whose success might be epitomized in activities protesting **trade agreements** like the WTO in Seattle (1999).

Since the emergence of American industrialization, certain features have worked against the cohesion of working-class consciousness and action. One of these was the ideology of individual worth and mobility that the United States has held dear. Even if workers were trapped in a routine, they were taught that their children might find more security and gain, through education, home-ownership, connections and hard work – the working class was a point of origin, not an end. Here, class and gender also coincided as the mother became especially charged with guiding children upward (or, in the case of the 1930s tearjerker *Stella Dallas*, not holding them back).

This was also tied to the politics of **immigration** and ethnicity. As immigrants found work in factories, they began to assimilate and identified mobility with citizenship. This meant that in the postwar period, Americanism could be identified with moving to the **suburbs** out of the old neighborhood (a battleground with new races or ethnicities trying to enter the workplace), replacing the blue-collar work shirt with a white shirt and tie, and getting a college education. Again, a generational perspective was important, as the GI Bill, 1950s prosperity and limits on new immigration promoted a generalized sense of mobility. Moreover, **race** clearly divided this class.

Some were left behind – especially where class intersected with race. **African Americans** moved into the Northeastern and Midwestern industrial workforce with the Great Migration, but found their opportunities for advancement constrained. Even in the Second World War and civil-rights era, they were often "last hired, first fired." For many blacks, a solid upper-working-class job – post office or steady employment – has been read instead as a marker of middle-class identity. Single mothers, white and black, also constitute a large proportion of the "working poor."

Yet the dynamics of the disappearance of the working class do not rest with the working class. Business and government have long been uneasy about working-class organizations, especially if they betray any leftist or revolutionary consciousness (often imputed to "foreignness" or "anti-American sentiments"). Businesses have fought **unions** for a century, often with government assistance. Meanwhile, both elites have often co-opted workers into a sense of an American mission – to fight the Depression, win wars (where the working classes, black and white, are more likely to be soldiers), or rally against **communism**. Perhaps the most successful manipulation of this was the **Reagan** Revolution of 1980, where a conservative, elite Republican establishment rallied workers against the perceived threats of welfare moms, illegal immigrants and the Evil Empire rather than around issues of security, safer and more just societies or healthcare and environmental stewardship.

The imagery of the working class in the US problematizes consciousness and culture. Working-class culture is often defined, even in academic tomes, in terms of deficits or substitutes for institutions that reaffirm the middle class –

neighborhoods, bars and churches for clubs and civic associations, etc. Clothes, accent, behavior and even body type tend to be treated as inferior versions of a middle-class norm (uneasily aping upper-class representations). Hence Paul Fussell writes sarcastically in *Class* that "If you can gauge people's proximity to prole status by the color and polyester content of their garments, legibility of their dress is another sign.... When proles assemble to enjoy leisure, they seldom appear in clothing without words on it" (1992: 56).

Mass media representations also affirm this generally negative overview, sometimes interlaced with nostalgia for a simple life now lost. Many actors use working class roles – smudged and unglamorous – in a manner analogous to portrayals of the disabled – to show their skills in being what they actively are not. Barbara Stanwyck in *Stella Dallas* (1937), Jane Fonda and Robert De Niro in *Stanley and Iris* (1989) and Sharon Stone in *The Mighty* (1999) all demarcate a tradition of the working class as other for Hollywood. Works like John Sayle's *Matewan* (1987) or some works of Barry Levinson and John Waters, among others, present more independent exceptions. Television has done little more, although there were appeals to ethnic working-class neighborhoods in the golden age and a clear exaltation of working-class domesticity in *The Honeymooners* (CBS, 1955–71). The *Roseanne* (ABC, 1988–97) show, starring female comedian Roseanne Barr, also confronted issues of job insecurity and family budget, domestic tension, teenage behavior and other issues with humor and integrity. Documentaries, including *Salt of the Earth*, Barbara Kopple's *Harlan County USA* (1976) and *American Dream* (1990) and grassroots/activist videos have confronted these issues more politically.

While this may seem to present a bleak portrait of the working class and its future, one should not overlook possibilities of organization and action in coalition that continue to crop up in cities, environmental causes and even international politics. These are especially important where divisions of race, ethnicity and gender are overcome. Even intergenerational differences may pose compelling questions about the dream and its costs for children and grandchildren of working-class families.

Further reading

Fussell, P. (1992) *Class*, New York: Simon & Schuster.

Kelley, R. (1997) *Yo' mama's disfunktional!*, Boston: Beacon Press.

(1985) *Labor in America: a Historical Bibliography*, Santa Barbara: ABC-Clio.

(1949–) *Labor in Postwar America* (periodical).

Roediger, D. (1999) *The Wages of Whiteness*, London: Verso.

Terkel, S. (1974) *Working*, New York: Pantheon.

GARY McDONOGH

world's fairs

International celebrations hosted by American cities (and American participation abroad) has highlighted the growing strength of the nation and significant visions for the future. **Chicago, IL**'s World's Columbian Exposition (1893) shifted American urbanism towards the planned City Beautiful, while the 1939 New York World's Fair (controlled by Robert **Moses**) foreshadowed technological shifts to follow the Second World War. Later, while **Seattle** (1962) focused on science and the 1964–5 New York World's Fair introduced exciting futuristic visions and Disney audio-animatronics, other fairs have been seen as economic and urbanistic failures (Knoxville, Tennessee, 1982; **New Orleans, LA**, 1984); enthusiasm shifted towards the Olympic media stage. American participation abroad has produced notable buildings but it, too, has lacked enthusiastic government and corporate support, especially in Brussels (1958) when exhibits treated America's social problems. Subsequent exhibits abroad have stressed space and technology as well as innovative design like Buckminster **Fuller**'s geodesic dome for Montreal (1968).

GARY McDONOGH

Wounded Knee

In 1973 the American Indian Movement (AIM) occupied the town of Wounded Knee, South Dakota, the site of the massacre of Sioux Indians in 1890. The **American Indian** activists wanted to draw attention to the impoverished social conditions on Native American reservations. In response, FBI agents (fresh from their battles with Black Panthers) stormed the town killing an activist. These events were portrayed in the docudrama *Incident at Oglala – The Leonard Peltier Story* (1992). The conflict marked a new, more militant phase in the resistance to oppression among American Indians.

ROBERT GREGG

wrestling

Two very different stories are encompassed in the term "wrestling" – the **college** and professional games. College wrestling has been strong since the nineteenth century and featured in the revived **Olympic Games** held in Greece in 1896. There are now believed to be around 750,000 participants in the sport nationwide, with a large number concentrated in Pennsylvania and Ohio, the heartland of the sport.

The amateur sport has come under threat from a number of directions, however. First, the impact of **Title IX** has been felt most heavily in minor sports like wrestling without female opportunity. Unwilling to cut into funding for football programs to make money available for women's sports, colleges tended to cut back on wrestling. Of the 788 schools with programs in 1982, only 247 have programs in 1997.

This has had an impact on the number of scholarships available to wrestlers and has served to increase the intensity of the competition in wrestling. There is a long history of wrestlers trying to lose weight to remain in a lower weight class, but since 1997 there have been at least three deaths at colleges resulting from starvation and dehydration. One wrestler, for example, who normally weighed over 235 pounds attempted to wrestle at 190 pounds. Managing to bring his weight down to 195 pounds, he died of heart failure. Deaths have also occurred due to muscle-building dietary supplements like creatine. These events have caused the **NCAA** to place new restrictions on the way wrestlers shed pounds, ending the use of rubber exercise suits and diuretics. Amateur wrestling was also tainted by its association with John Du Pont, a multimillionaire who had never fulfilled his own wrestling ambitions. After funding the American Olympic team for many years and providing housing on his grounds, Du Pont shot and killed Dave Schultz, the leading American freestyle wrestler, in 1996.

Professional wrestling was transformed after the Second World War with the new medium of **television** and the establishment of the National Wrestling Alliance (NWA) in 1948 by Midwestern promoters. Instead of merely presenting athletic bouts, as previously, these promoters staged athletic **soap operas** with themes of good against evil and of American wrestlers fighting off foreign enemies – Japanese, Middle-Eastern, or Soviet. Although these events required great physical prowess and considerable training, the choreography involved fundamentally altered the nature of wrestling as a sport.

The 1980s saw a further explosion of wrestling on cable television. Ted Turner bought out the NWA in 1988 and established World Championship Wrestling (WCW), which became a mainstay of TNT, TBS and USA networks. The World Wrestling Federation (WWF) emerged as the other dominant wrestling federation picked up by a variety of television channels. In addition, many local professional organizations appeared in the late 1990s that promoted the same style of wrestling but in which the wrestlers, with great fan enthusiasm, suffered actual injuries.

Wrestling, with its combination of acting and athleticism, has become central to American popular culture. Commercials and movies frequently feature wrestlers like "Hollywood" (so-called by his detractors) Hulk Hogan, "Stone Cold" Steve Austin and Dwayne "The Rock" Johnson. Sony PlayStations and other television consoles feature games that many children can play, from which they can learn moves and holds that they try out with their friends, occasionally with catastrophic results. The death of a young boy, clothes-lined by his elder brother, has fueled the controversy about the impact of television violence on the young.

The election of former wrestler Jesse Ventura, as **governor** of Minnesota on a reform ticket, has illustrated the cultural significance of professional wrestling, helping to determine the outcome of a contest in the sport of name-recognition – politics.

ROBERT GREGG

Wright, Frank Lloyd

b. 1869; d. 1959

Wright's buildings reinforce American ideals of democracy, individual **freedom** and **family**. His inexpensive **middle-class** Usonian (United States-onian) homes and low, extended Prairie houses have led to the development of a uniquely American, **suburban** housing type. Consistent placement of the fireplace at the heart of a house was both a metaphorical and physical organizing principle. He utilized natural imagery and materials while accepting modern machinery, demonstrated in the Fallingwater house, Larkin Building and the Guggenheim Museum. His promotion of the American natural and social landscape in architecture still influences design decades after his death.

BIANCA T. SIEGL

Wright, Richard

b. 1908; d. 1960

After a difficult childhood described in his autobiography, *Black Boy* (1945), Wright moved from Tennessee to **Chicago, IL** in 1927 hoping to become a writer. In the Depression he belonged to the Communist Party; in 1935, he also joined the Federal Writers Project of the Works Progress Administration. By 1937 he moved away from the **Communist** Party and Chicago, resettling in **Harlem, NY**. In 1938 Wright published *Uncle Tom's Children*. Two years later, *Native Son*, comparable in impact to **Ellison**'s *Invisible Man*, cemented Wright's international reputation, especially in Europe. His study of Kwame Nkrumah (*Black Power*, 1954) contributed to his influence among Pan-Africanists and provided a term for American black militants when the **Civil Rights movement** began to falter.

ROBERT GREGG

WTO (World Trade Organization) *see* trade and trade agreements; Left, the

Wyler, William

b. 1902; d. 1981

Wyler's reputation as a **Hollywood** film **director** veers from that of a meticulous and creative craftsperson to a plodding dullard who had little eye for visual storytelling. Wyler did his best work when he worked for producer Samuel Goldwyn, who supported his efforts with studio artisans like cinematographer Gregg Toland. He drifted visually and thematically in the 1960s when the studio system had broken down. Three Wyler films won Best Director and Best Film Oscars: *Mrs Miniver* (1942), *The Best Years of Our Lives* (1946) and *Ben-Hur* (1959).

MELINDA SCHWENK

Wynette, Tammy

b. 1942; d. 1998

Born Virginia Wynette Pugh in Mississippi and raised by grandparents who picked cotton, Tammy became the First Lady of **country music** (although the "real" **First Lady**, Hillary Rodham Clinton, said in 1992 she was no "Stand by Your Man" woman). Ms Wynette left her hairdressing career behind and moved to Nashville in 1966 to record; her resonant voice came to epitomize the female country voice in the 1970s, singing of love and loss. After her fifth husband, she released her most famous song "Stand by Your Man" (1969), although her comeback hit with the English pop act KLF, "Justified and Ancient" (1992), sold more records internationally. She also performed duets with Smokey Robinson, Aaron Neville and Elton John.

EDWARD MILLER

X

Xerox

The Haloid company (founded 1906) acquired Chester Carlson's patents for a xerographic process in 1947, introducing its first copier two years later. Plain-paper copying followed in 1959. The Xerox corporation (renamed 1961) not only dominated copy machines, but entered American speech as a synonym for copying (despite warnings about trademark use). By the 1980s, copiers became staples in workplaces, educational facilities, churches and even homes. As copiers have been integrated into **computer** technology, often combined with fax machines, scanners and printers, and companies like Sharp compete for the market, Xerox has recast itself as "the document company."

JAMES DAVID

X-Files *see* science fiction, television; UFOs/ extraterrestrials

X-games/X-treme sports

First held in Providence, Rhode Island, in October 1993, Extreme Games were promoted by the sports cable company ESPN to highlight rising sports (many of them noted for their danger) that networks had previously neglected. Featuring such sports as street luge, **skateboarding**, skiboarding, bungy jumping, downhill **in-line skating**, sky-surfing, wakeboarding and **bicycle** stunts, they emphasize daredevil acts rather than races against time. Planned as biannual events, the first games were so successful (watched by over 220 million domestic viewers and carried in over 150 countries) that organizers decided to hold the games every year. The US Post Office offered a 1999 stamp series honoring them.

Further reading

Tomlinson, J. (1996) *The Ultimate Encyclopedia of Extreme Sports*, New York: United Media.

ROBERT GREGG

Y

Yale University *see* Ivy League

yard sales/flea markets/ consignments

Decades of accumulation in many American households have outstripped social channels of disposal – giving away, handing down and throwing away. **Life cycles** – growing up, moving out, divorce, or the move to retirement housing – also convert clothes, **toys**, appliances, furniture and memories into surplus. Yard sales (also known as tag or rummage sales) offer one outlet with a limited commercial reward. Throughout America every weekend, signs sprout in yards and on telephone poles; ads appear in supermarkets and flyers. Families and neighbors tackle both separation and market evaluation of life experience – how much is a trophy, crib or wedding dress worth to strangers? Can we really get rid of this? On Saturday, **suburban** lawns, **garages** and patios explode with tables and mounds of goods. Consumers, sometimes connoisseurs of these "opportunities," still move within similar social and geographic spaces: commodity recycling becomes a chain disposal system as once-cherished items converted to cash eventually end up in someone else's trash – or their sale. At the end of the day, moreover, goods that remain may still be given to charities or hauled away as rubbish.

Flea markets, by contrast, bring together multiple sales, including both one-time sellers and professionals offering used goods and newer arts and crafts. These may become highly professional and stratified events, and act as alternative commercial spaces in marginal neighborhoods like **Los Angeles**' Watts section, or in appealing to particular ethnic niches. At times, the flea market name only implies potential bargains in a commercial mall. Antique flea markets, for example, emphasize the quest for a bargain rather than informal pricing, ownership or inventory.

Thrift and consignment shops offer other more regular store outlets, usually associated with charitable organizations. Consignment shops offer space and take commission on sales of items that may well include expensive furs, jewelry, clothes and furniture. Thrift shops sell goods already donated to charities, encompassing a wider range of rehabilitated materials and bringing together bargain-seekers and those who must rely on used goods for their everyday lives. Inner-city thrift stores may become critical resources for poor **neighborhoods**, while shops associated with elite neighborhoods or associations (symphonies, suburban hospitals) often establish reputations which may lead to inclusion in regional directories or other media reports. Goods, even when discarded, reaffirm boundaries of **class**, **space** and knowledge for both donor and those who acquire them.

See also: consumerism

GARY McDONOGH
CINDY WONG

YMCA and YWCA

The Young Men's and Young Women's Christian Associations started in the late nineteenth century, linked to the urban-settlement house movement. Aiding in the process of assimilating immigrants and **African Americans** and teaching uplift, the Ys propagated a form of muscular Christianity. Hence, **basketball** was invented at the YMCA in Springfield, Massachusetts, to keep urban youth off the streets in winter. Jewish communities followed suit creating Hebrew Associations, often nicknamed the Jewish Ys.

With rapid suburbanization following the Second World War, the YMCAs lost their settlement-house character. Many relocated to the **suburbs**, downplayed their Christian emphasis and became swimming and exercise clubs for the **middle class**. Membership dwindled until the last two decades of the twentieth century, when the growing exercise fad and the growing demand for childcare from two-income families led to a resurgence in growth.

The YWCAs (a separate organization), however, kept their missionary impulse and remained in the cities, providing housing and support for urban women. Because of this they have suffered financially, and in many cities are being forced to close down.

ROBERT GREGG

Young, Andrew

b. 1932

A Georgia clergy member when the **Civil Rights movement** began to spread around the **South**. Young became active in crusades from Birmingham, Alabama, to St. Augustine, **Florida**. Increasingly prominent in **SCLC**, he was elected vice-president of the organization under Ralph **Abernathy**. He left to pursue a political career, becoming the first **African American** elected to the Georgia House of Representatives since 1870. In 1977 Jimmy **Carter** appointed him US ambassador to the United Nations; he was forced to resign two years later after it became known that he had met secretly with members of the Palestinian Liberation Organization. From 1982 to 1990 he was a highly regarded **mayor** of Atlanta.

ROBERT GREGG

yuppies

*Y*oung *u*pwardly-mobile *p*rofessionals became both models and targets as **baby boomers** met the affluence of the Reagan years. The epithet makes ironic reference to preppies (a middle-class button-down style associated with but not exclusive to prep schools), whom yuppies assimilated, and **hippies**, whom yuppies, in some cases, had been in earlier incarnations. This ambiguous class term has been defined by patterns of consumption rather than wealth, power, or ethnicity; often, its connotations seem too negative for self-attribution. Other related terms – *b*uppies (black), *g*uppies (gay), *ch*uppies (Chinese) – reveal questions of diversity and spreading wealth.

GARY McDONOGH

Z

Zappa, Frank

b. 1940; d.1993

Social satirist, culture critic, cynic, parodic transgressor, musical innovator, pre-postmodern American composer, monster guitarist and rock 'n' roller. With the debut of "Freak Out" (1966), Frank Zappa and his Mothers of Invention took on American popular culture with a repugnance and a taste for the bizarre. His work captured the absurdities of flower power, plastic people, **rock 'n' roll** ("Does this Kind of Life Look Interesting to You?"), sexual desire, body envies ("Penis Dimensions") and youth culture, but also cynically critiqued the commodification of life in general. Early in his career he asked his audience to drop out of high school in favor of a library education. He proposed that ugly was beautiful, and that his music had no commercial potential. Some of his finest moments came in September 1985 when he appeared before the Senate Committee on Contents of Music and the Lyrics of Records. He wrote, recorded and performed doo-wop songs, rock anthems, **jazz** interludes and orchestral scores, and made films and **videos**, bucking the music business all along the way.

STEVE FERZACCA

zoos and aquaria

Collections of animals, fish and natural curiosities open to the public have consistently intersected with and reinforced the societies that created them. America's more than 160 credited zoos and aquaria receive more than 100 million visitors annually. They also speak to changing values of US society.

Victorian zoos, emerging around private menageries and urban modernization, became showplaces for architecture and landscapes as well as animals, exemplified in the **Philadelphia, PA** zoo's elaborate buildings or Frederick Law Olmsted's planning for **Boston, MA**'s Franklin Zoo and Manhattan's marvelous pocket menagerie in Central Park. The last was redone by Robert **Moses** in the 1930s, a period in which other zoos were expanded under Works Progress Administration (WPA) patronage.

In the 1960s, zoos were criticized for their cramped cages and unnatural displays. These attacks, as well as scientific evolution, shifted the impetus of many zoos from collection towards conservation, where US zoos became world leaders. Placards discussing breeding programs, genetic engineering and habitat preservation have complemented open exhibits and complex habitats. At the same time, zoos use "blockbuster" attractions like Philadelphia's white lions or the **Washington, DC** National Zoo's giant pandas, fruit of Nixon's rapprochement with China.

America's other great contemporary zoos, defined by size, programs and resources, include the **San Diego** Zoo, **Chicago, IL**'s Lincoln Park, New York City's Wildlife Conservation Society (including the Bronx Zoo) and the National Zoo in Washington, part of the **Smithsonian Institution**. Nearly half of all zoos are municipal projects, although they must also rely on foundation assistance and wider civic memberships. None-theless, such zoos represent regional and global tourist attractions – the **St. Louis, MO** Zoo gained wide media exposure through television's *Wild Kingdom*, featuring its director, Marlin Perkins, while **Miami, FL**'s Metrozoo merited a Frederick Wiseman **documentary**.

Large-scale public zoos also have been sha-dowed by smaller private and commercial collec-tions, ranging from a few animals imprisoned beside a highway to larger exhibits like South Carolina's Brookgreen Gardens, created by Archer Huntington and his wife in 1931 on their estate. As America sprawled along newly paved interstates, larger enterprises – safari parks, reptile-lands and **Disney**'s Wild Kingdom – followed. Zoos and acquaria have also become features of (and taken as characteristics of) amusement parks.

Aquaria, less attractive than zoos, began with Washington's National Aquarium, located in the Department of Commerce building. Other early aquaria opened in Battery Park, Manhattan (1895, moved to Coney Island in 1957) and Belle Isle (**Detroit, MI**, 1904). Many declined after the Second World War, but 1980s **waterfront** devel-opment spurred renewed interest in **Baltimore, MD**, **New Orleans, LA** and other cities. These scientific collections also have competed with private commercial venues like the Sea World chain, which specializes in marine circus acts.

The Victorian zoo highlighted exoticism and hierarchy in humans' domination of fierce **nature** and other humans. The modern American zoo, by contrast, has become a center of ecological concern and pedagogy as much as display – yet this, too, reflects the changing cultural meanings of both nature and its viewers.

Further reading

Davis, S. (1997) *Spectacular Nature*, Berkeley: Uni-versity of California.

Sedwick, J. (1988) *The Peaceable Kingdom: A Year in the Life of America's Oldest Zoo*, New York: William Morrow.

GARY McDONOGH

Index

Page numbers in **bold** indicate references to the main entry. Please refer to the thematic list for individual entries on major topics (actors, cities, labor, etc.).